KU-606-824

The Irish Legal System

Third Edition

by

Raymond Byrne
BCL, LLM (NUI), Barrister-at-law
Lecturer in Law, Dublin City University

and

J Paul McCutcheon
BCL, LLM (NUI)
Senior Lecturer in Law, University of Limerick

with Foreword to the First Edition
by

Mr Justice Niall McCarthy
Judge of the Supreme Court of Ireland
1982-1992

Butterworths

Ireland	Butterworth (Ireland) Ltd, 26 Upper Ormond Quay, DUBLIN 7
United Kingdom	Butterworths a Division of Reed Elsevier (UK) Ltd, Halsbury House, 35 Chancery Lane, LONDON WC2A 1EL and 4 Hill Street, EDINBURGH EH2 3JZ
Australia	Butterworths, a Division of Reed International Books Australia Pty Ltd, Chatswood, NEW SOUTH WALES
Canada	Butterworths Canada Ltd, Markham, ONTARIO
India	Butterworths India, NEW DELHI
Malaysia	Malayan Law Journal Sdn Bhd, KUALA LUMPUR
New Zealand	Butterworths of New Zealand Ltd, WELLINGTON
Singapore	Butterworths Asia, SINGAPORE
South Africa	Butterworths Legal Publishers (Pty) Ltd, DURBAN
USA	Lexis Law Publishing, Charlottesville, VIRGINIA

© Butterworths Ireland Ltd 1996

All rights reserved. No part of this publication may be reproduced or transmitted in any form or by any means, including photocopying and recording, without the written permission of the copyright holder, application for which should be addressed to the publisher. Such written permission must also be obtained before any part of this publication is stored in a retrieval system of any nature.

A CIP Catalogue record for this book is available from the British Library.

First Edition 1986
Second Edition 1989
Third Edition 1996

Reprinted 1996
Reprinted 1997
Reprinted 1999

ISBN 1 85475 8152

ISBN 1-85475-815-2

9 781854 758156

Printed and bound in Great Britain by Anthony Rowe, Chippenham, Wiltshire
Visit us at our website: http//www.butterworthsireland.com

BRAINSE CABRACH
CABRA BRANCH
TEL: 8691414

Foreword to the First Edition

Mr Justice Niall McCarthy

Judge of the Supreme Court of Ireland

1982 - 1992

Shakespeare had a word for it - indeed, as was his practice, he had several words for it. In Henry VI Pt 2 one of the rabblement said - "The first thing we do, let's kill all the lawyers."[1]

This cry derived in part, at least, from ignorance. It is in the nature of man to fear what he does not understand. In Ireland, ignorance of the law is compounded by a suspicion and fear that springs from our history. The law, as it touched upon the average Irishman of a hundred years ago, was an instrument of oppression in the enforcement of either the criminal law or of taxation. The average Irishman seldom sought its help because the law was of little use to him; it was administered by the propertied classes for the propertied classes, it was the visible instrument of British rule through its buildings, local symbols of imperial might, and through its Judges and practitioners, garbed in ancient forms of dress and speaking an arcane language. Although the revolutionaries of 1916 proclaimed a republic and the author of the Constitution of 1937 often vouchsafed the State to be such, as it was proclaimed in 1948,[2] the structures, formal approach, and, most regrettably, attitudes of lawyers in Ireland remain English orientated. In a sense, this is not the fault of the lawyers of this generation because they inherited it from the last and the generation before that; but it is the fault of this generation because of a failure to examine and analyse the law, rather than take refuge in an unthinking and uncritical citation of precedent. Forensic forelock touching is as much a part of the cultural cringe that has beset our country as the mimicry of English accents and manners, but it may be more damaging in its long term effects. Whilst no lawyer of the last sixty years can escape his share of blame, some have sought at least to inform the public as to some of the intricacies of the legal system but none to the extent that this work seeks to do. Although one is mildly conscious of it at the Bar, it is really since I have sat on the Bench that I have become so aware of the degree to which the citation of precedent is made a substitute for reasoned argument and analysis of principle. Messrs Byrne and McCutcheon in this book, make a valiant effort to examine the doctrine of precedent recognising

1. Henry VI Pt 2 - Act IV - Scene II - line 86.
2. Republic of Ireland Act 1948.

the vital distinction that it is the reason for the decision that is important, rather than the decision itself; that if the reason be good, it matters not in what Court such reason were used; if the reasoning be defective, then the leather binding of the Law Reports does not give it authenticity or merit. A recent exposure of defective reasoning is to be found in the robust language of Professor Glanville Williams in his article "The Lords and Impossible Attempts, or *quis custodiet ipsos custodes*?"[3]

In the memoirs of Lord Shandon, of which the type-script is in the King's Inns Library, that worthy did not spare even the great Chief Baron on this score. "There can be no question" he said "that his judgments were held in deserved respect, but his mind was of the type which I dislike though it was one which our legal system necessarily encourages with its slavish adherence to mere precedent. Palles not only had an immense knowledge of case law but his industry was colossal and one might always rely upon Palles's disinterring some forgotten authority which everyone else had failed to discover. Such men remind me of the contrapuntal musicians who by the application of purely empirical rules occasionally produce the most magnificent harmony. So it was with the Chief Baron. His method was always the same, that of piling up analogy on analogy but often to produce a most logical and coherent result. In the same way he worshipped technicality as if it were a fetish and even when he was fully conscious that the result at which he arrived was imminently unsatisfactory he was unable to burst the bonds of precedent and technicality. He was ably abetted - indeed often inspired in the matter of technicality by his Co-adjutor, Baron Fitzgerald who would subdivide the split hair that his Chief had divided."[4] Strong words indeed, but it is still at times refreshing to be referred to the earlier cases in which Judges appeared to be able to enunciate both principle and decision in a few pages whilst now, armed with the dictating machine gun, we sometimes get lost in a sea of words.

When the Supreme Court decided *Brogan v Bennett*[5] in June 1952, the report indicates that judgment was delivered on the day of hearing. The unfortunate Christopher Brogan had believed a pamphlet entitled "TB CONQUERED by Mr J H Bennett, Lamagh, Newtownforbes, of Kelly & Bennett, Divining Specialists, Longford. Tel: Longford 53", and requested some relatives to get in touch with Mr Bennett who undertook to cure Christopher Brogan and make him fit for work within three months, charging fees of £100 for a rich person and £20 for a poor person, into which category the unfortunate Christopher Brogan fell; as a result, he left

3. (1986) Cambridge Law Journal 33.
4. Memoirs of Lord Shandon - type-script - p 183.
5. [1955] IR 119.

Longford tuberculosis hospital and returned home where he took a medicine "prescribed" by Bennett for approximately five weeks and then died. His parents sued for damages for negligence and called evidence from the relatives who had interviewed Bennett, who "produced a bullet on the end of a string, and said he was going to X-ray the patient. He then caused the pendulum to oscillate and pronounced the case to be a fairly bad one. He purported to diagnose the exact percentage of impairment of all the main organs of the patient, and claimed that by means of his pendulum he could diagnose the ailments of a person at the other end of the world." When Kingsmill Moore J, sitting as a Judge of the High Court on Circuit, stated a case for the Supreme Court as to whether he could legally hold that the death of Christopher Brogan was caused by the wrongful acts, neglect, or default of the defendant within the meaning of those words as used in the Fatal Accidents Act 1846,[6] the Supreme Court unanimously, and without hesitation, answered - Yes. With enviable brevity, James Murnaghan J said at page 127:

> "There are various kinds of skill which can be exercised. If a person professes to use skill for reward he is liable for negligence in not using that skill ... The defendant made elaborate claims of power and success. It was not unreasonable for the deceased to believe what he was told and it seems clear that he did believe it and that the defendant failed to fulfil the representations which he made, and he is therefore liable."

Is this much different from what it took the House of Lords innumerable pages to express in *Hedley Byrne and Company Limited v Heller and Partners Limited*?[7] You may search, however. the textbooks and find no reference to *Brogan v Bennett.* Every law student knows what happened to Mrs Donoghue to the extent, even, of the variety of spellings of her names[8] or whether or not there ever was a snail in the bottle although the way had been identified in *Heaven v Pender*[9] almost fifty years before.

This excursus on grinding a private axe is a feature of the writing of Forewords to legal textbooks. Partly it derives from a sense of frustration with the ignorance of the general public about the legal structures of the State. The man in the Cabra bus or, indeed, on the DART has little interest in the law except when it impinges on him directly - obviously in the

---

6. The relevant statute would now be the Civil Liability Act 1961.
7. [1964] AC 465.
8. *Donoghue v Stevenson* [1932] AC 562. [The case is sometimes incorrectly cited, using Mrs Stevenson's maiden name, as either *Donoghue (M'Alister) v Stevenson* or *M'Alister v. Stevenson.* See Lord Macmillan, 'The Citation of Scottish Cases' (1933) 49 LQR 1 - eds]
9. (1883) 11 QBD 503.

enforcement of the criminal law and of taxation. His knowledge of the Constitution is mostly one of "rights" and seldom one of "duties". He is not to blame; he is taught nothing of these structures when he is at school or at any level of education unless he takes up the study of the law as an object in itself or as ancillary to some other discipline. The requirement of knowledge of the law in all its aspects is so great that, indeed, those who qualify to practise are often themselves ill equipped to examine and explain the underlying theory - the underlying principle. In this book the authors have set out to pierce that great curtain of ignorance; this book is directed towards the general public as well as to the student and practitioner; it is a book that requires concentration and study; it deserves both; although one may not agree with all of the authors' sentiments, it is right to pay tribute to their energy, research and initiative and, particularly, to their clarity of expression. The law is often the victim rather than the victor in the battle of words. If this book does, as I believe it can, create a more informed body of citizens who will recognise and accept that the law is a two-way traffic, their efforts will have been justly rewarded. If their readers can come to recognise that the Constitution is not merely a document to be quoted and misquoted when the electorate is much exercised about personal or family rights, but is also the fundamental law of the State governing our relationships with each other and with the State itself, their achievement will have been great.

Niall McCarthy,
July 9 1986.

Preface

In the seven years which have elapsed since the publication of the previous edition of this work a number of significant developments have occurred and the pace of developments has been particularly swift in 1995 and 1996. It is fair to say that many features of the legal system have been subjected to a greater measure of scrutiny than was the case in past decades. By the same token the administration of justice has continued to occupy a central position in the public process. At the most dramatic level this is reflected in the considerable public attention which was devoted to events such as the decision in *Attorney General v X*, the fees generated by those members of the legal profession who participated in the Tribunal of Inquiry into the Beef Industry and the mechanisms for appointment to the Bench. While these events may have contribued significantly to the politics of the early 1990s, they should not be allowed to deflect attention from the less news-worthy but highly significant changes which occurred during the same period and which we have attempted to describe in this expanded edition.

In Chapter 1, we discuss the nature of the Irish legal system, introduce the principal sources and divisions of law and outline some of the intellectual influences which have been brought to bear on its development. In Chapter 2, we outline its history from medieval times to the establishment of the two jurisdictions on the island of Ireland in the early 1920s. This historical legacy continues to resonate today at the end of the 20th century.

In Chapter 3, we discuss the influential recommendations of the 1990 Report of the Fair Trade Commission on the Legal Profession. These produced significant reforms within both branches of the legal profession, solicitors and Bar, as well as in the court system. While the Report also led to the establishment of an Advisory Committee on Legal Education and Training (ACLET), this has had little success in resolving important issues concerning access to and training for the legal profession. For those beginning their legal studies in Autumn 1996 and considering becoming a solicitor, the recent *Bloomer* and *Abrahamson* cases have removed the former exemption from the Law Society's FE-1 Examination in respect of a law degree obtained from a university in the Republic of Ireland. Such is the uncertainty surrounding the issue at the time of writing that it remains to be seen whether any alternative arrangement will be put in place in the future.

In Chapters 4 to 7, we discuss the effects of the important jurisdictional, structural and procedural changes to the court system effected by, for example, the Courts Act 1991 and the Courts and Court Officers Act 1995. The range of matters dealt with in the 1995 Act is enormous: the establishment of a Judicial Appointments Advisory Board; the first appointment of solicitors to the Circuit Court; the introduction of compulsory judicial training for new appointees to be funded by the Department of Justice (together with the associated establishment of a Judicial Studies Institute, albeit formally outside the terms of the 1995 Act); a significant increase in the number of the judicary; the conferral of additional powers on court officers; procedural changes in civil matters to facilitate greater efficiency, including greater pre-trial exchange of medical reports in personal injuries claims; the proposed transfer of the functions of the Court of Criminal Appeal to the Supreme Court; an increase of three in the number of Supreme Court judges and conferral on the Court of the power to sit in divisions. The background of the enormous growth since the 1960s in the volume of court business, both civil and criminal, and the consequent delays in handling this contributed to the key recommendation in the First Report of the Denham Working Group on a Courts Commission in 1996 that an independent Courts Service be established. The acceptance of this recommendation by the government, at least in principle, will affect the day to day working of the courts well into the 21st Century. This development also coincides with the tentative emergence of the judiciary into the media age, with television cameras being permitted into the Supreme Court for the first time in 1995 to witness legal argument in a 'live' case and the willingness of sitting judges to run the gauntlet of robust media criticism on views of public controversy. As with much else, many of these developments reflect, but do not mirror exactly, events in the United Kingdom.

In Chapter 8, we discuss the impact on the administration of justice of the role of the government and the functions of the Ombudsman and similar offices. We refer to the emergence of Alternative Dispute Resolution (ADR), though the continued importance of well-established arrangements such as arbitration are discussed. Important quasi-judicial bodies such as the Coroners Court and other adjudicative bodies are also discussed. In Chapter 9, we discuss recent developments in access to law, in particular the enactment of the Civil Legal Aid Act 1995, which provides for the establishment on a statutory footing of a civil legal aid scheme. In Chapter 10, we discuss the remedies and enforcement mechanisms available in civil and criminal matters. Chapter 11 outlines the principal mechanisms by which law reform is effected in the State.

In Chapters 12 to 17, we describe the ways in which the courts have continued to reflect upon sources of law and the accompanying questions of legal methodology. Common law and statute law continue to be important sources of law and, not surprisingly, an appreciation of precedent and statutory interpretation remain vital to an understanding of the legal system. The fundamental rule of *stare decisis* is still adhered to in the process of adjudication, thus providing a central discipline to judicial law-making, and is outlined in Chapter 12. Nonetheless, as the judiciary acknowledge themselves, while the essential principles underlying *stare decisis* may be easily stated, they can be difficult to apply in practice. Chapter 13 deals with the phenomenon of legislation and includes consideration of the legislative process and origins of legislation, including the ever-growing volume of delegated legislation. Chapter 14 is devoted to the interpretation of legislation. In the seven years since the previous edition, the volume of litigation involving questions of statutory interpretation has increased strikingly, reflecting the increasing role of the State as a regulator (as outlined in Chapters 8 and 11) and a correspondingly greater importance of legislation as a source of law. Fundamental principles of interpretation have remained largely unaltered but the courts have availed of the opportunity to restate the applicable rules and have provided an up-to-date body of authority.

In Chapter 15, we discuss the impact of the growing body of judicially-created principles of constitutional law. Many constitutional cases have attracted considerable public attention, which is inevitable given the subject matter of the more important of these. Perhaps the most important development has been the emergence of the harmonious approach of interpretation and the apparent demotion of the natural law school of constitutional interpretation. While acknowledging the importance of these developments, we also attempt to indicate the limits to constitutional judicial review by comparison with the great power of the institutions with political power, the Government and Oireachtas. We have been able to note only briefly the important recommendations in the 1996 Report of the Review Group on the Constitution, which is to be considered by an Oireachtas Committee established to consider whether further wide-ranging reform of the Constitution is required.

In Chapter 16 we discuss the increasing effect on domestic law of European Community law. The supremacy of Comunity law and its applicability within the domestic legal system has long been accepted and is now beyond question. More and more substantive areas of domestic law are being shaped by obligations deriving from Community law; indeed, as we acknowledge, hardly any area of domestic law has *not* been affected. Interpretive principles developed at Community level have also been highly influential in the development of the teleological approach to statutory interepretation and the harmonious approach to constitutional interpretation. Moreover, the implementation of Community obligations by means of delegated legislation which has been used to effect changes to primary legislation (given a *nihil obstat* if not an *imprimatur* by the Supreme Court in *Meagher v Minister for Agriculture and Food*) has had a profound effect on the state of the statute book. In Chapter 17, we discuss the less direct, though very important, impact of international law in Ireland, in particular membership of the Council of Europe.

In the course of preparing this edition, we have benefited from the assistance of a number of people. It is with gratitude we acknowledge the contributions of Joachim Barnett, Sheila Boughton, Deirdre Ruddy, Denis Cusack, Phil Drury, Kieran Mooney, Peter Kavanagh, Gillian Moorhead, Donal Motherway, Clara O'Callaghan, Sheila O'Keeffe, Martin Phillipson, David Tomkin and Brian Tucker. We are especially grateful to the staff of Butterworths (Irl) Ltd, in particular Gerard Coakley and Louise Leavy, whose support and patience considerably lightened our task. And Marian Sullivan ensured that the manuscripts submitted to her were transformed into a polished text, and we are very grateful for that.

We also owe a debt of gratitude to the family of the late Mr Justice Niall McCarthy, who kindly agreed to allow us reproduce his Foreword to the first edition of this text. Mr Justice McCarthy and his wife Barbara died in a motoring accident in Spain in 1992; an obituary to the couple in the 1992 volume of the Dublin University Law Journal identified the effect of their deaths on the legal and wider community. We are very glad to acknowledge Mr Justice McCarthy's many kindnesses to us by including his views in this third edition.

With the indulgence of the publishers we have attempted to describe the legal system on the basis of materials available to us at the end of July 1996, but the usual disclaimer for any errors and omissions applies.

Raymond Byrne and J Paul McCutcheon,

August 1996.

Contents

Foreword to the First Edition v
Preface ix
Contents xiii
Table of Statutes xvii
Table of Constitutional Articles liii
Table of Cases lix

Chapter 1 Introduction to the Irish Legal System

Introduction 1
Law and Laws 2
The Irish Legal System as a Common Law System 4
Sources of Law 5

Chapter 2 Development of the Irish Legal System

Introduction 19
Pre-Norman Ireland and the Brehon law 19
The Arrival of English Law in Ireland 20
The Institutions of State in the 19th century United Kingdom 28
The establishment of Northern Ireland and the Irish Free State 40
Ireland and Northern Ireland 44

Chapter 3 The Legal Profession

Introduction 47
Solicitors 50
Barristers 58
The Law Officers 67
Legal Education Generally 72
Other Professionals 76

Chapter 4 The Court System, the Judiciary and Court Administration

Introduction 79
The Administration of Justice in Courts 81
The Need to Establish a Post-1937 Court System 94
The Court System in Ireland: Judicial Composition and Structure 95

Appointment and Qualifications 108
Judicial Independence 122
Vacating of Judicial Office and Retirement 133
Court Officers and Administration 136
Management of the Court System: The Need for Major Reform 140

Chapter 5 The First Instance Jurisdiction of the Courts

Introduction 147
The Original Jurisdiction of the Courts in Civil Cases 155
The Original Jurisdiction of the Courts in Criminal Cases 173

Chapter 6 Civil and Criminal Court Procedure

Introduction 185
Civil and Criminal Procedure Compared and Contrasted 185
Civil Procedure 191
Criminal Procedure 207
Court Procedure and Rules of Evidence 215
Judge and Jury 221

Chapter 7 The Appellate Jurisdiction of the Courts

Introduction 227
Appellate Jurisdiction in Civil Cases 231
Appellate Jurisdiction in Criminal Cases 238
Appellate Jurisdiction of Courts from Adjudicative Bodies 250
Appellate Jurisdiction of the Court of Justice of EC 250

Chapter 8 The Government, Administrative Law and Adjudicative Bodies

Introduction 255
The Organisation of the Government 259
Adjudicative Bodies and the Judicial Power 264

Chapter 9 Access to Law

Introduction 283
The Constitutional Setting: Access to the Courts 283
Provision of State-Funded Legal Aid 287
State-Assisted Criminal Legal Aid 288

State-Assisted Civil Legal Aid 291
Court Fees 299
Legal costs 299

Chapter 10 Remedies and Enforcement

Introduction 301
Remedies in Civil Matters 301
Procedure for Enforcement of Court Orders 306
Enforcement in Criminal Matters 308
Contempt of Court 311
Judicial Review 312

Chapter 11 Law Reform

Introduction 315
Judicial Decisions and Law Reform 315
Legislative and Constitutional Reform 316

Chapter 12 Precedent

Introduction 319
Stare Decisis in the Irish Courts 324
The Ratio Decidendi and Obiter Dictum 354
Precedent in Action: An Example 376

Chapter 13 Legislation

Introduction 411
Legislative Process 418
Legislative Product 435
Delegated Legislation 449

Chapter 14 Interpretation of Legislation

Introduction 475
The Principal Approaches 486
Aids To Interpretation 508
External Sources 532

Chapter 15 The Constitution and its Interpretation

Introduction 545
The 1922 Constitution 545
The 1937 Constitution 552
Fundamental rights and constitutional judicial review 577
Principles of constitutional interpretation 606
Report of Constitution Review Group 652

Chapter 16 European Community Law and the European Union

Introduction 655
Origins of the European Communities 657
The Three European Communities 658
Development of the European Community and Union 666
European Community Law and the European Union 669
The Nature of European Community law 672
Institutions of the European Community and European Union 689
The Form of European Community and Union laws 703
Implementation of European Community law in Ireland 712

Chapter 17 International Law

Introduction 719
Membership of International Organisations 719

Index 733

Table of Statutes

Acts and Bills of Oireachtas of Irish Free State and Ireland

Abattoirs Act 1988
  s 16 .... 8.52
Adaptation of Enactments Act 1922 .... 13.52
Adoption Act 1988 .... 5.68
Adoption (No 2) Bill 1996 .... 17.11
Age of Majority Act 1985
  s 2(2)(a) 14.22
Air Pollution Act 1987 .... 16.153
Altamont (Amendment of Deed of Trust) Act 1993 .... 13.23, 13.26
Animal Remedies Act 1993 .... 13.79, 16.81
  s 22 .... 6.62
    (2) 6.08
Anti-Discrimination (Pay) Act 1974 .... 14.35-14.36, 14.48, 16.157
  s 2 .... 14.36
    3 .... 14.36
Arbitration Act 1954 .... 3.85, 8.32-8.36
  s 35 .... 8.35
Arbitration Act 1980 .... 3.85, 8.32-8.36
  s 5 .... 8.33
Bank of Ireland Act 1929 .... 13.23
Bank of Ireland Act 1935 .... 13.23
Bankruptcy Act 1988 .... 5.59
Building Societies Act 1976
  s 80 .... 14.30
  Pt IV 14.30
Building Societies (Amendment) Act 1983 .... 11.02, 13.32, 14.31
Capital Gains Tax Act 1975 .... 14.09
  s 12 .... 14.09
    33(5) 14.09

Central Bank Act 1942 .... 17.21
Central Bank Act 1989 .... 13.79, 17.21
Child Abduction and Enforcement of Custody Orders 1991 .... 9.33, 14.92
s 1(2) 14.79
Child Care Act 1991
s 25 .... 9.08
26 .... 9.08
City of Dublin (Extension of Boundaries) Order 1953 .... 13.23
Civil Legal Aid Act 1995 .... 9.25-9.29, 9.38
s 4 .... 9.25
5 .... 9.25
9 .... 9.25
10 .... 9.26
11 .... 9.26
24 .... 9.29
25 .... 9.28
(3) 9.31
26 .... 9.31
(2) 9.31
(4) 9.28
27 .... 9.28, 9.34
28 .... 9.28
(2) 9.33
(3) 9.33
(5) 9.33
(8) 9.34
(9) 9.32-9.35
(c) 9.35
(10) 9.35
29 .... 9.29-9.33
30 .... 9.26
33-36 .... 9.38
Civil Liability Act 1961
s 34 .... 12.67

59 .... 15.43
60 .... 13.72
(1) 13.43
(7) 13.43
Civil Service Commissioners Act 1956 .... 8.13
Civil Service Regulation Act 1956 .... 8.13
Committees of the Houses of the Oireachtas (Compellability, Privleges and Immunity of Witnesses) Bill 1995 .... 8.55
Companies Act 1963 .... 5.59, 12.85, 16.152
s 99 .... 14.30
205(7) 4.20
Companies Act 1990 .... 5.59, 8.47, 14.63, 16.152, 17.20
Companies (Amendment) Act 1977 .... 16.152
Companies (Amendment) Act 1983 .... 16.152
Companies (Amendment) Act 1990
s 33 .... 14.62
Competition Act 1991 .... 3.05, 14.85, 16.156
Competition Act 1996 .... 3.05, 16.156
Comptroller and Auditor General Act 1923 .... 15.23
Comptroller and Auditor General Act 1993 .... 15.23
Conditions of Employment Act 1936
s 6 .... 15.43
Constitution of the Irish Free State (Saorstát Éireann) Act 1922 ..2.56, 4.03
.... 15.03
s 1 .... 15.14
2 .... 15.14-15.15
Constitution (Amendment No 16) Act 1929 .... 15.09, 15.13
Constitution (Amendment No 17) Act 1929 .... 15.09
Constitution (Amendment No 22) Act 1933 .... 15.09
Constitution (Amendment No 24) Act 1936 .... 15.09
Constitution (Amendment No 27) Act 1936 .... 15.09
s 1 .... 15.43
Constitution (Removal of Oath) Act 1933 .... 15.08, 15.14

Consumer Credit Act 1995 ....5.12, 5.34, 5.45, 13.79
s 13 .... 5.73
Consumer Information Act 1978 .... 5.12
Convalescent Home Stillorgan (Charter Amendment) Act 1958 .... 13.23
Cork Harbour Act 1933 .... 13.23
Coroners Act 1962 ....8.37-8.39
s 30 .... 8.38
40 ....8.37-8.39
Corporation Tax Act 1976 .... 14.81
s 54 .... 14.38
Court Officers Act 1926 ....4.117, 4.119-4.123
Court of Justice Act 1936
s 34 .... 4.51
35 .... 4.51
Courts Act 1964
s 6 .... 5.82
Courts Act 1971 .... 3.22
s 2 .... 5.18
6 .... 4.52
7 .... 5.18
13 .... 4.54
Courts Act 1977
s 2 .... 4.53
Courts Act 1981 .... 5.52, 6.39
s 2 .... 5.40
5 .... 5.43
6 .... 5.18
17 .... 5.29
18(1)(a) 4.41
22 .... 4.118, 10.08
31 .... 5.82, 15.109
Courts Act 1988 .... 3.47, 5.10, 6.99
s 1 .... 4.50
5 .... 5.24

Courts Act 1991 .... 5.34, 6.30, 6.53
s 2.......... 5.40, 5.45-5.48, 5.54
4.......... 5.18, 5.30-5.37
(c).......... 5.31
8.......... 5.33
9.......... 5.34, 5.45
10 .... 5.36, 5.46
11 .... 5.33
14 .... 5.29
15 .... 5.29
16 .... 5.19
21 .... 4.40, 4.54, 4.91
(1)(a) 4.54
Courts Act 1996
s 1.......... 4.40, 4.52
Courts (Establishment and Constitution) Act 1961 ..... 4.04, 4.35-4.37, 4.64
.... 5.01, 12.12, 12.15, 12.17, 12.32
s 1(1).......... 4.41
(2) 4.41
(3) 4.41
(4) 4.41
2(1).......... 4.49
(2) 4.49
(3) 4.49
(4) 4.49
(5) 4.49
3(1).......... 7.36
(2) 7.36
4(1).......... 4.52
(2) 4.52
5(1).......... 4.54
(2)(b) 4.54
6.......... 4.108
22-4 .... 4.53
25 .... 4.53
48 .... 5.71
3rd Sch 4.53

Courts (No 2) Act 1986 .... 5.42, 10.19
s 4 .... 5.32
Courts (No 2) Act 1988 .... 4.110
Courts (No 3) Act 1986 .... 4.14-4.15, 6.64, 11.02
s 3 .... 6.08
Courts (Supplemental Provisions) Act 1961 ...... 4.04, 4.35-4.37, 4.64-4.67
.... 4.70, 4.86, 4.87, 4.102
.... 5.01, 7.02, 14.79
s 4(1) 4.41
(2) 4.49
5(2) 4.66
7(1) 4.41
(3) 4.42, 12.20
(4) 4.42
(5) 4.41-4.43
8 .... 5.53, 5.60
(1) 4.49
9(1) 5.61
(4) 5.61
10(1)(a) 5.69
(b) 5.69
(3) 4.49
11(1) 5.84
(2)(b) 4.50
12 .... 7.36-7.36
16 .... 4.52
17(2) 4.66
18 .... 4.109
20(1) 4.53
21 .... 4.52
22 .... 5.39-5.48, 7.20
(1)(b) 5.40
23 .... 7.20
24 .... 5.42
25 .... 5.81-5.83
(2) 5.85
28 .... 4.54
29(2) 4.65

30(1) 4.110
32(1) 4.55
33 ....5.30-5.33
35(2) 4.55
36 ....4.55
39-42 ....4.55
45(1) 4.20
46 ....4.104, 4.112
48 ....4.39, 4.54, 4.91, 4.109, 7.20
51 ....7.14, 7.30
52 ....7.13-7.17, 7.30
(2) 7.17, 7.31
54....................10.25
55(2) 4.123
(3)....................4.123
3rd Sch 5.18, 5.39, 5.45-5.48
4th Sch 5.39
6th Sch 4.55
8th Sch 4.117, 4.119
Courts (Supplemental Provisions) (Amendment) Act 1991 ....4.05, 4.112
Courts (Supplemental Provisions) (Amendment) (No 2) Act 1968 .....4.104
Courts and Court Officers Act 1995 ....3.07, 3.23, 4.05, 4.43-4.44
....................4.59, 4.77, 4.109, 4.118, 5.01, 5.10
....................6.56, 6.85, 6.94, 7.36, 7.38, 7.54
....................13.16, 13.28, 15.102, 16.120
s 4....................2.70, 4.03-4.04, 7.35, 7.38
6....................4.40
(1) 4.41
(2) 4.41
7....................4.41-4.43, 12.20
8....................4.41
9....................4.40
(1) 4.49
(2) 4.49
10 ....4.40, 4.52
11 ....4.40, 4.54-4.55
12 ....4.81
13 ....4.80-4.84
(3) 4.83

14 .... 4.84
16 .... 4.85, 4.88
(7) 4.86
(8) 4.86
17 .... 4.86
18(3) 4.82
19 .... 4.86
20 .... 4.86
21 .... 4.84
22 .... 4.84
23 .... 4.81
24 .... 4.10, 4.118
25(1) 4.118
(2) 4.118
27 .... 5.29
28 .... 4.67
30 .... 4.67
32 .... 5.82
33 .... 4.39, 4.52
34 .... 4.123
36 .... 4.53
38 .... 4.55
39 .... 4.55
44 .... 7.50
46 .... 5.29
47 .... 4.111
(1) 4.109
(2) 4.109
(3) 4.109
48 .... 4.88
49 .... 3.52, 5.11, 5.58
50 .... 4.118
(1) 4.118
53 .... 5.44
1st Sch 4.41
2nd Sch 4.123

Courts of Justice Act 1924 .... 2.63-2.73, 4.03-4.05, 4.30
.... 4.35, 4.64, 4.71, 4.111, 5.01
.... 5.17, 5.53, 6.28, 6.100, 7.02, 15.10-15.13
s 1(iii) 8.11

2(1) 8.11
3 .... 5.84
4 .... 4.40, 4.49-4.49
5 .... 4.40-4.41
6 .... 4.41, 4.49
7 .... 4.41
8 .... 7.34-7.36
9 .... 4.39
10 .... 4.59
11 .... 4.108
12 .... 4.109
13 .... 4.103
15 .... 4.112
16 .... 4.66
17 .... 4.49
18 .... 4.41
19(1) 5.61
(2) 5.69
(3) 5.69
24 .... 4.50, 5.60
25 .... 5.29
29 .... 7.36, 7.38, 14.70, 15.102
30 .... 7.36
31 .... 7.36, 7.41
32 .... 7.41
34 .... 7.43
37 .... 4.40, 4.52
38 .... 4.39, 4.61
39 .... 4.91
40 .... 4.109
41 .... 4.103, 4.112
44 .... 4.53
45 .... 4.108
46 .... 4.52
47 .... 4.52
48 .... 5.18, 5.39
(i) 5.40
49 .... 5.81
50 .... 5.42

51 .... 5.39
63 .... 7.36, 7.41
67 .... 4.54-4.54
68 .... 4.40
69 .... 4.65
70 .... 4.108
71 .... 4.55
72 .... 4.110
74 .... 4.103
75 .... 4.112
76 .... 4.54
77 .... 5.18-5.18, 5.30, 5.71
(A) 5.31, 5.32
(a)(i) 5.33
(ii) 5.37
(iii) 5.31-5.33
(v) 5.31-5.33
79 .... 4.56
80 .... 5.77
83 .... 7.13-7.14, 7.30
84 .... 7.13, 7.20
94 .... 4.50, 4.52, 12.76-12.77
95 .... 6.111
99 .... 4.90
Sch Pt II 8.11

Courts of Justice Act 1926
s 4 .... 5.84

Courts of Justice Act 1928
s 5 .... 7.43
18 .... 7.29

Courts of Justice Act 1936
s 4 .... 4.41
5 .... 4.49
9(1) 5.61
14 .... 4.52
(1) 4.66
31 .... 7.20
37 .... 7.20

38(1) 7.20
(3) 7.20-7.21
51 .... 4.54
(1) 4.65
57 .... 7.13
58 .... 7.29

Courts of Justice Act 1946
s 9 .... 4.49

Courts of Justice Act 1947 .... 4.103
s 9 .... 4.52
(3) 4.39
10 .... 4.53
14 .... 4.52
15 .... 4.109
16 .... 7.21, 7.35

Courts of Justice Act 1953 .... 4.103
s
11 .... 4.49
16 .... 4.53
18 .... 4.52
21 .... 4.55

Courts of Justice (District Courts) Act 1946
s 4(2) 5.77
20 .... 4.91
Sch Pt II 5.77

Courts of Justice (District Courts) Act 1949
s 2 .... 4.110

Criminal Damage Act 1991 .... 4.22, 5.13, 5.91
s 8 .... 13.51

Criminal Evidence Act 1992 .... 5.13
s 27 .... 6.82

Criminal Justice Act 1951 .... 5.75-5.76, 6.71, 10.23
s 8 .... 14.73

Criminal Justice Act 1960 .... 5.14
s 2 .... 10.23

Criminal Justice Act 1964 .... 9.14

Criminal Justice Act 1984 ....5.13, 6.61, 6.66, 6.85, 15.107
s 5 .... 9.18
21 .... 6.94
22 .... 6.94
25 .... 6.111
Criminal Justice Act 1990 .... 6.59, 9.14
Criminal Justice Act 1993 .... 5.13, 5.85
s 2 .... 7.44
6 .... 6.04
Criminal Justice Act 1994 .... 5.13, 10.30
Criminal Justice (Administration) Act 1924 .... 6.74
s 9 .... 3.61
Criminal Justice (Community Service) Act 1983 .... 5.13, 10.26
Criminal Justice (Drug Trafficking) Act 1996 ....5.13-5.14, 6.66
Criminal Justice (Forensic Evidence) Act 1990 .... 5.13
Criminal Justice (Legal Aid) Act 1962 ....7.42, 9.14-9.16
....9.21, 9.31, 9.39, 15.63
Criminal Justice (Public Order) Act 1994 ....5.13, 6.13, 15.56
s 1(3) 13.41
17 ....5.76, 6.60
(3) 6.60
19 .... 5.76
20-22 .... 13.32
Criminal Justice Bill 1996 .... 6.61
Criminal Law Amendment Act 1935 .... 15.88
s 17 ....15.106, 15.127
(1) 15.128
(3) 15.128
(4) 15.128
Criminal Law (Incest Proceedings) Act 1995
s 6 .... 4.22
Criminal Law (Jurisdiction) Act 1976 ....5.68, 5.75, 6.71
s 5 ....6.59, 13.51
23 .... 6.75

Criminal Law (Rape) Act 1981
s 2(1) 14.94
6 .... 4.22
Criminal Law (Rape)(Amendment) Act 1990 .... 5.13, 9.31
s 10 .... 5.85
11 .... 4.22
Criminal Law (Sexual Offences) Act 1993 .... 1.21, 5.13, 13.32, 15.88
.... 15.130, 17.11, 17.17

Criminal Procedure Act 1967 .... 5.75, 6.70
s 6 .... 6.72
7 .... 6.72
8 .... 6.72
12 .... 6.72
13(2)(b) 7.36
17 .... 4.22
34 .... 7.49
Criminal Procedure Act 1993 .... 5.13, 7.43, 7.47
s 2(1)(b) 7.47
3 .... 7.43
7 .... 7.48
11 .... 7.50
Criminal Procedure (Amendment) Act 1973
s 1 .... 7.36
Daniel McGrath Foundation Act 1945 .... 13.23
Data Protection Act 1988 .... 17.12
Decimal Currency Act 1970
s 9(1) 13.52
Defence Act 1954 .... 5.87, 15.21
Dentists Act 1985 .... 8.57
s 38-40 .... 4.14
Diseases of Animals Act 1966 .... 13.44
Domestic Violence Act 1996 .... 5.11
Dublin United Tramways (Lucan Electric Railway) Act 1927 .... 13.23
Dundalk Harbour and Port Act 1925 .... 13.23

Dáil Éireann (Privilege and Immunity) Act 1994 .... 4.75
Dáil Éireann Courts (Winding-Up) Act 1923 .... 2.63
Eighth Amendment of the Constitution Act 1983 .... 15.72
Electoral Act 1923 .... 14.90
Electoral Act 1959 .... 15.84
Electoral Act 1963 .... 15.84
Electoral Act 1992 .... 15.72
s 132 .... 5.62
Electoral (Amendment) Act 1961 .... 5.68

Electricity Supply Act 1927
s 27 .... 8.36
Electricity Supply (Amendment) Act 1985 .... 8.36
Eleventh Amendment of the Constitution Act 1992............................ 15.72
Emergency Powers Act 1976 .... 5.68, 15.84
Enforcement of Court Orders Act 1926 .... 10.19
Enforcement of Court Orders Act 1940 .... 10.19
Enforcement of Judgments (European Communities) Act 1988 .... 10.21
Enforcement of Judgments (European Communities) Act 1993 .... 10.21
Environmental Protection Agency Act 1992 ....6.62, 8.47, 8.63, 16.153
Erasmus Smith Schools Act 1938 .... 13.23
Ethics in Public Office Act 1995
s 37 .... 5.73
European Communities Act 1972 ....8.53, 13.54, 16.70
....16.131, 16.147, 16.153
s 1 .... 16.71
2 ....14.36, 16.73-16.74
3 ....5.74, 13.67, 13.79, 15.86, 16.74-16.81
....16.86, 16.148, 16.151-16.152
(2) 16.82
4 .... 13.78-13.78, 16.74-16.75
European Communities (Amendment) Act 1973 .... 13.78, 16.74
European Communities (Amendment) Act 1986 .... 16.63

European Communities (Amendment) Act 1993 .... 16.48
s 5(1) 16.81
(4) 16.81
European Communities (Amendment) Act 1994 .... 16.71
European Communities (Amendment) Act 1995 .... 16.74
s 1 .... 13.78
European Communities (Confirmation of Regulations) Act 1973 .... 13.78
.... 16.74

Executive Authority (External Relations) Act 1936 .... 15.09, 15.41
s 3 .... 15.43
Executive Functions (Consequential Provisions) Act 1937
s 2 .... 3.45
Executive Powers (Consequential Provisions) Act 1937 .... 15.46
Extradition Act 1965 .... 5.79
s
11 .... 14.90
47(5) 7.13
50 .... 14.46, 14.83, 14.90
Pt II 13.32, 14.90
III 14.90
Extradition (Amendment) Act 1987 .... 3.58, 4.78
Factories Act 1955 .... 14.58, 15.43
Family Home Protection Act 1976 .... 14.32, 14.37
s 1(1) 14.28
3(1) 14.28
(2) 14.28
(3) 14.28
(4) 14.28
4(1) 14.28
(2) 14.28
(3) 14.28
9 .... 5.33
10(5) 5.33
54 .... 14.38
Pt IV 14.38

Family Law (Maintenance of Spouses and Children) Act 1976
s 23 .... 5.33
Family Law Reform Act 1989 .... 5.44
Family Law Act 1995 .... 5.11, 10.20
Family Law (Divorce) Bill 1996 .... 5.11
Fifth Amendment of the Constitution Act 1972 .... 15.72, 15.139
Fifteenth Amendment of the Constitution Act 1996 .... 1.21, 15.72, 15.112
Finance Act 1971
s 22 .... 14.42
Finance Act 1975 .... 14.81
s 31 .... 14.40
Finance Act 1976 .... 13.70
s 46 .... 13.71
Finance Act 1980 .... 15.66
s 41(2) 14.38
42 .... 14.41
(2) 14.39
Finance Act 1982
s 26 .... 14.38
Sch 2 .... 14.38
Finance Act 1984 .... 15.85
Finance Act 1989
s 86 .... 14.10
Firearms Act 1925 .... 5.91
Fire Services Act 1981 .... 8.47
s 4 .... 8.48
20 .... 8.48
Firearms Act 1990 .... 5.91
First Amendment of the Constitution Act 1939 .... 15.69
Fisheries (Consolidation) Act 1959 .... 13.56
s
310 .... 7.29, 12.59
Fourth Amendment of the Constitution Act 1972 .... 15.72
Fourteenth Amendment of the Constitution Act 1992 .... 15.72
Galway Harbour Act 1935 .... 13.23

Geneva Conventions Act 1962 .... 13.32
Genocide Act 1973 .... 10.30, 13.32
Greyhound Industry Act 1958
s 13 .... 13.60
25 .... 13.60
48 .... 13.60
Guardianship of Infants Act 1964
s 3 .... 14.47
Harbours Act 1946
s 53(1) 14.57
Harbours Act 1953
s 53(1) 14.68
Health Act 1947 .... 8.47
Health Act 1970
s 2 .... 13.72
52 .... 13.72
56 .... 13.72
72 .... 13.67, 13.72
Health (Family Planning) Act 1979 .... 1.21, 15.88
Health (Family Planning) Act 1993 .... 1.21
Health (Family Planning) (Amendment) Act 1985 .... 15.88
Health (Family Planning) (Amendment) Act 1992 .... 15.88
Health (Family Planning) (Amendment) Act 1993 .... 15.88
Health (Fluoridation of Water Supplies) Act 1960 .... 15.50, 15.54
Health (Mental Services) Act 1981 .... 13.45
Hire-Purchase Act 1946 .... 5.34, 5.45
Hire-Purchase (Amendment) Act 1960
s 19 .... 5.34, 5.45
Hire-Purchase Act 1980 .... 5.34, 5.45
Holidays (Employees) Act 1961 .... 13.72, 14.90
Hotel Proprietors Act 1963
s 10(1) 5.45
(2) 5.34
Housing Act 1966 .... 14.81
Housing Act 1988 .... 15.56

Housing (Private Rented Dwellings) Act 1982 .... 15.85
Imposition of Duties Act 1957
s 1 .... 13.70-13.71
2 .... 13.70
Income Tax Act 1967 .... 3.86, 8.60, 13.56, 14.24
s 156 .... 8.60
192-196 .... 15.65, 15.85
428(6) 14.65
428-430 .... 8.60
Indemnity Act 1923 .... 15.06-15.10
Industrial Relations Act 1946 .... 13.76
s 17 .... 8.43
Pt IV 8.45
Industrial Relations Act 1990
s 42 .... 13.04
48 .... 13.60
Industrial and Provident Societies (Amendment) Act 1978
s 14(8) 14.68
Institute of Chartered Accountants in Ireland (Charter Amendment) Act 1966 .... 13.23
Insurance (No 2) Act 1983 .... 13.10, 13.32
Interpretation Act 1923 .... 14.22
Interpretation Act 1937 .... 14.22-14.23
s 6(2) 13.46
(3) 13.46
7(1) 13.38
11
(a) 14.22
(b) 14.22
(c) 14.22
(g) 13.47
15 .... 13.59
21(1)(e) 14.75
Interpretation (Amendment) Act 1993 .... 14.22-14.23
Irish Aviation Authority Act 1993 .... 8.47

Judicial Separation and Family Law Reform Act 1989 .... 5.11, 5.43, 13.19, 13.28, 15.90

s 5-8 .... 8.30

9 .... 5.44

29 .... 14.61

31(2) 5.44

32 .... 5.44

33 .... 3.51, 5.44, 5.58

45 .... 3.51

Juries Act 1927 .... 6.100, 15.61, 15.83

Juries Act 1976 .... 8.37, 11.02, 15.61

s 6 .... 6.100

7 .... 6.101

8 .... 6.101

9 .... 6.101

(8) 6.101

11 .... 6.102

12 .... 6.102

15 .... 6.102

17 .... 6.104

18 .... 6.104

19 .... 6.104

20 .... 6.103

21 .... 6.103

34 .... 6.102

1st Sch

Pt I 6.101

Pt II 6.101

Jurisdiction of Courts and Enforcement of Judgments (European Communities) Act 1988 .... 4.118

Jurisdiction of Courts and Enforcement of Judgments (European Communities) Act 1993 .... 4.118

Labourers Act 1936 .... 14.81

Landlord and Tenant Act 1931 .... 14.81

Landlord and Tenant (Amendment) Act 1980

s 3 .... 5.48

Landlord and Tenant (Amendment) Act 1994 .... 13.19, 13.28

Larceny Act 1990 .... 13.32
s 14(3) 14.79
33 .... 14.75
Law Reform (Personal Injuries) Act 1958
s 1 .... 12.67
Law Reform Commission Act 1975 .... 11.09
s 14(1)(a)(i) 4.41
(b)(i) 4.49
Liability for Defective Products Act 1991 .... 13.79
Licensing Acts 1833 to 1994 .... 5.42
Limerick Harbour Act 1926 .... 13.23
Limerick Harbour Tramways Act 1931 .... 13.23
Livestock Marts Act 1967 .... 15.77
Local Government (Irl) Act 1898
s 16 .... 13.60
Local Government (Petitions and Disqualifications) Act 1974
s 2 .... 5.50
Local Government (Planning and Development) Act 1963 .... 8.36, 14.28
.... 14.81
s 82 .... 8.56
Local Government (Planning and Development) Act 1976 .... 8.56
s 17 .... 14.76
24(2) 14.76
Local Government (Planning and Development) Act 1992 .... 8.56
Local Government (Water Pollution) Act 1977 .... 5.36, 5.46
s 10 .... 5.36, 5.46
Local Government (Water Pollution) Act 1990 .... 5.36, 5.46
Local Government and Public Health Provisional Order Confirmation Act 1953 .... 13.23
Maintenance Act 1994 .... 9.33
Malicious Injuries Act 1981 .... 5.49, 8.40
s 5 .... 14.74
6 .... 14.74
Malicious Injuries (Amendment) Act 1986 .... 5.49, 8.40, 8.41

Malicious Injuries (Amendment) Bill 1996 .... 8.40
Medical Practitioners Act 1978 .... 8.57
s 27(2)(d) 14.76
Medical Practitioners (Amendment) Act 1993 .... 6.92
Mental Treatment Act 1945
s 260 .... 9.03

Merchant Shipping Act 1992
s 1(3) 14.79
Merchant Shipping Acts 1894-1983 .... 14.79
Methodist Church in Ireland Act 1928 .... 13.23
Minimum Notice and Terms of Employment Act 1973 .... 14.81
Ministers and Secretaries Act 1924 .... 8.11
s 6 .... 3.54-3.59
Ministers and Secretaries (Amendment) Act 1977 .... 8.12
Misuse of Drugs Act 1977 .... 5.74, 6.66, 13.38, 13.42, 13.46
s 5 .... 13.06
15(1) 13.06
41(2) 13.41, 13.42
43(2) 13.41, 13.42
Misuse of Drugs Act 1984 .... 5.74, 6.66
National Standards Authority of Ireland Act 1996 .... 8.47
Ninth Amendment of the Constitution Act 1984 .... 15.72
Nurses Act 1985 .... 8.57
Occupiers' Liability Act 1995 .... 12.67
s 4(2) 13.07
Offences against the State Act 1939 .... 5.89-5.90, 6.66
s 6 .... 5.85
7 .... 5.85
8 .... 5.85
30 .... 12.58, 14.58, 14.68
35(6) 5.88
36 .... 5.91
39 .... 5.95
44 .... 7.36, 7.41

46 .... 5.92
Pt V 5.88, 5.94
Offences against the State (Amendment) Act 1940 .... 5.68, 17.17
Offences against the State (Amendment) Act 1985 .... 13.10, 13.32
Oireachtas (Allowances to Members) and Ministerial, Parliamentary and Judicial Offices (Amendment) Act 1977 .... 4.104
Oireachtas (Allowances to Members) and Ministerial, Parliamentary and Judicial Offices (Amendment) Act 1983 .... 4.104
Oireachtas (Laying of Documents) Act 1966 .... 13.77
Ombudsman Act 1980 .... 8.25, 8.28
s 4 .... 8.25
5 .... 8.26
6(3) 8.26
Ombudsman Act 1984 .... 8.25, 8.28
Package Holidays and Travel Trade Act 1995 .... 13.79
Patents Act 1964 .... 14.90
Patents Act 1992 .... 8.50, 16.67
s 96(7) 8.51
Pier and Harbour Provisional Order Confirmation Act 1932 .... 13.23
Pigs and Bacon Act 1937 .... 13.66
Plebiscite (Draft Constitution) Act 1937 .... 15.17
Postal and Telecommunications Act 1983
s 90 .... 13.62
Poë Name and Arms (Compton Domvile Estates) Act 1936 ... 13.23, 13.40
Prevention of Electoral Abuses Act 1923
s 50 .... 14.71
Prices Act 1958 .... 13.73
s 22A 13.73
(1) 13.74
Prices Act 1972 .... 13.73
Prosecution of Offences Act 1974 .... 6.68
s 2 .... 3.61-3.62
(5) 3.62
3(1) 3.61

4 .... 3.53
5(1) 3.63
7 .... 3.64
Protection of Animals (Amendment) Act 1965 .... 13.28
Public Safety Act 1927 .... 15.11
Radio and Television Act 1988 .... 4.41
Redundancy Payments Act 1967 .... 14.81
Referendum Act 1994 .... 15.91
Regulation of Information (Services Outside the State for the Termination of Pregnancies) Act 1995 .... 5.68, 15.89, 15.134
Rent Restrictions Act 1946 .... 14.47, 15.85
Rent Restrictions Act 1960 .... 15.85
Republic of Ireland Act 1948 .... 2.71, 15.34
s 2 .... 15.41
3 .... 15.41
Restrictive Practices Act 1972
s 12 .... 3.05
Road Traffic Act 1933
s 170 .... 15.43
Road Traffic Act 1961 .... 5.74
s 3(4) 13.04
49 .... 6.64, 14.11
116 .... 15.43
Road Traffic Act 1968 .... 14.90
s 44(2) 14.87
Pt III 14.11
Pt V 14.11
Road Traffic Act 1994 .... 5.10
Road Traffic Act 1995 .... 5.10, 5.74
Road Traffic (Amendment) Act 1978
s 23 .... 14.11
Pt III 14.11
Royal College of Physicians of Ireland (Charter and Letters Patent Amendment) Act 1979 .... 13.23
Royal College of Surgeons in Ireland (Charter Amendment) Act 1965 13.23

Safety in Industry Act 1955 .... 6.39-6.43
Safety in Industry Act 1980 .... 6.39-6.43
Safety, Health and Welfare at Work Act 1989 .... 5.10, 6.43, 8.47-8.48
.... 8.63, 13.32, 13.61, 14.58, 16.153
s 12 .... 6.39
36 .... 10.29
37 .... 10.29
39 .... 10.29
51(3) 6.08
52 .... 7.29
Sale of Goods and Supply of Services Act 1980 .... 5.12, 13.03
.... 13.07, 13.79
Second Amendment of the Constitution Act 1941 .... 15.70
Seventh Amendment of the Constitution Act 1979 .... 15.72
Sixth Amendment of the Constitution Act 1979 .... 4.16, 15.72
Sligo Lighting and Electric Power Act 1924 .... 13.23
Social Welfare Act 1952
s 75 .... 13.68-13.69
Social Welfare Act 1979
s 7 .... 13.69
Social Welfare Act 1984 .... 16.143
Social Welfare (Consolidation) Act 1981 .... 13.56
Social Welfare (Consolidation) Act 1993 .... 8.62, 13.56
Solicitors Act 1954 .... 3.10, 3.16, 9.26, 13.60
s 14 .... 5.69
26 .... 3.12
40 .... 3.14, 3.75
41 .... 3.13
58 .... 3.19, 3.84
71 .... 3.24
Pt IV 3.79
Solicitors (Amendment) Act 1960 .... 3.10, 3.16, 4.14, 13.32
Solicitors (Amendment) Act 1994 .... 3.07, 3.16-3.19, 8.28
s 4 .... 3.10
42 .... 3.12
49 .... 3.75
50 .... 3.13

68(2) 3.25
69 .... 3.24
70 .... 3.18
80 .... 3.83
Solicitors (Amendment) Bill 1994 .... 3.19
Status of Children Act 1987 .... 10.16
Pt IV 5.33
Statute Law Revision Act 1983 .... 13.56
Statute Law Revision (Pre-Union Irish Statutes) Act 1962
s 2.......... 14.92
Statute of Limitations 1957 .... 6.07, 6.23, 12.76
s 11(2)(b) 15.77
Statute of Limitations (Amendment) Act 1991 .... 6.07, 6.23, 13.32
Statutory Instruments Act 1947 .... 13.62
s 1(1) 13.61
2(1)(b) 13.62
Succession Act 1965 .... 13.46, 13.56
s 2.......... 13.42
90.......... 13.47, 14.83
124.......... 13.47
Tenth Amendment of the Constitution Act 1987 .... 15.72
Third Amendment of the Constitution Act 1972 .... 15.72
Thirteenth Amendment of the Constitution Act 1992.......... 15.72
Tourist Traffic Act 1939 .... 13.73
Tourist Traffic Act 1970 .... 13.73
Trade Marks Act 1996 .... 8.50
s 79(3) 8.51
Trade Union Act 1975
s 2.......... 14.47
3.......... 14.47
4.......... 14.47
Transport Act 1936 .... 8.63
Treason Act 1939
s 2.......... 5.85

3 .... 5.85
Tribunals of Inquiry (Evidence) (Amendment) Act 1979 .... 4.13
.... 8.63-8.64, 13.32
Unfair Dismissals Act 1977 .... 8.46
Unfair Dismissals Act 1994 .... 8.46
Valuation Act 1988 .... 8.59
s 5 .... 8.59
Value Added Tax Act 1972 .... 14.81

United Kingdom

Act of Settlement 1701 .... 4.91
Act of Union 1800 .... 2.18-2.23, 2.27, 2.43, 3.79
s 1 .... 2.18
Acquisition of Land (Assessment of Compensation) Act 1919 .... 8.36
Administration of Justice Act 1969 .... 2.75
Administration of Justice Act 1985 .... 3.84
Ballot Act 1872 .... 14.90
Bankers' Books Evidence Acts 1879 .... 14.64
Bill of Rights 1689 .... 2.16
Building Societies Act 1962 .... 14.30
Catholic Emancipation Act 1829 .... 2.41
Children Act 1908
s 23 .... 14.77
37 .... 13.04
s 98 .... 9.08
Companies (Consolidation) Act 1908
s 18(1) 12.75
Conspiracy and Protection of Property Act 1875
s 7 .... 5.91
Contempt of Court Act 1981 .... 10.31, 17.23
Coroners (Irl) Act 1846 .... 8.37
Courts and Legal Services Act 1990 .... 3.09, 3.84
Criminal Appeal Act 1968 .... 7.48
Criminal Justice Act 1925 .... 4.23

Criminal Justice (Scotland) Act 1980 .... 15.129
Criminal Law (Irl) Act 1828 .... 13.39
Criminal Law Act 1967 .... 6.61
Criminal Law Amendment Act 1885 .... 15.129
Crown Cases Act 1848 .... 7.34
Crown Proceedings Act 1947 .... 15.43, 15.45
s 40 .... 15.44
Crown Proceedings (Armed Forces) Act 1987 .... 15.45
Customs Consolidation Act 1876
s 42 .... 15.128
186 .... 15.128
Employment Act 1980 .... 14.90
European Communities Act 1972 .... 13.54
Excise Act 1835
s 7 .... 14.69
Excise Management Act 1827
s 27 .... 14.73
Explosive Substances Act 1883 .... 5.91
Government of Ireland Act 1914 .... 2.43-2.44, 15.03
Government of Ireland Act 1920 .... 2.45-2.46
.... 2.54-2.60 2.67-2.72
.... 15.03, 15.37. 15.39
Grand Jury (Irl) Act 1836
s 135 .... 14.81
Health and Safety at Work Act 1974 .... 2.72
Income Tax Act 1918 .... 14.24
Infanticide Act 1949 .... 13.52
s 1(4) 13.51-13.53
Interpretation Act 1889 .... 14.22
Irish Appeals Act 1783 .... 2.18
Irish Free State (Agreement) Act 1922 .... 2.62, 15.03, 15.12
Irish Free State (Consequential Provisions) Act 1922 .... 15.03
Irish Free State (Constitution) Act 1922 .... 2.56, 15.03
Irish Land Act 1903 .... 2.42

Irish Land Act 1909 .... 2.42
Judicature Act 1873 .... 8.03
Judicature (Northern Ireland) Act 1978 .... 2.74
Land Law (Irl) Act 1881 .... 2.42
Land Law (Irl) Act 1896 .... 2.42
Larceny Act 1861 .... 5.75, 6.71
Larceny Act 1916 .... 5.74, 6.71, 14.79
s 3 .... 14.75
23 .... 6.59, 13.51
A 6.75
29 .... 5.76
33 .... 14.75
Lunacy Regulation (Irl) Act 1871 .... 5.61
Malicious Injuries (Irl) Act 1853
s 1 .... 14.81
Malicious Damage Act 1861 .... 5.91
Merchant Shipping Act 1894 .... 8.63
s 638 .... 14.54
Pt II 14.54
Municipal Corporations Act 1840
s 125-127 .... 13.60
Northern Ireland Constitution Act 1973 .... 2.72
Offences against the Person Act 1861 .... 5.74
s 38 .... 5.76
47 .... 6.59
58 .... 15.130
59 .... 15.130
60 .... 13.51, 15.88, 15.129, 15.130
61 .... 15.88, 15.129, 15.130, 17.17
62 .... 17.17
Petty Sessions (Irl) Act 1851 .... 2.52, 4.05, 5.01, 6.64, 16.79, 16.80
s 10 .... 4.15, 6.08, 16.78
(4) 16.84
29 .... 12.11
Poyning's Act 1494 .... 2.11, 2.18

Prevention of Crimes Act 1871
s 15 .... 15.57
Probation of Offenders Act 1907 .... 10.24
s 1 .... 10.25
Punishment of Incest Act 1908
s 5 .... 4.22
Purchase of Land (Irl) Act 1885 .... 2.42
Purchase of Land (Irl) Act 1891 .... 2.42
Rape Act 1976 .... 14.94
Rateable Property (Irl) Amendment Act 1860
s 7 .... 14.39
Roman Catholic Relief Act 1793 .... 2.18
Roman Catholic Relief Act 1829 .... 2.41
Settled Land Act 1882
s 63(1) 14.03
Sexual Offences Act 1967 .... 15.129
Solicitors (Irl) Act 1898 .... 3.10
Statute of Westminster 1931 .... 15.12-15.15
Summary Jurisdiction Act 1857 .... 2.52, 4.05, 5.01
s 2 .... 7.14-7.17, 7.30
Supreme Court of Judicature Act 1873 .... 2.28-2.31
.... 2.40, 2.74
Supreme Court of Judicature (Irl) Act 1877 .... 2.28-2.31
.... 2.40, 2.46, 2.53
.... 2.58-2.60, 2.73, 8.03
Supreme Court Act 1981 .... 2.74
Telegraph Act 1863 .... 14.52
Towns Improvement (Irl) Act 1854
s 1 .... 14.24
Tribunals of Inquiry (Evidence) Act 1921 .... 4.13, 8.63-8.64, 13.32
Vagrancy Act 1824
s 4 .... 15.56-15.60, 15.78
Valuation (Irl) Act 1852 .... 15.85
Westminster Parliament of the Courts Act 1971 .... 2.74

Wills Act 1837
s 15 ..... 12.79
Yelverton's Act 1781 ..... 2.17

European Community

Single European Act 1986 ..... 15.72, 15.79, 15.86, 16.01, 16.21
..... 16.36-16.46, 16.63-16.72, 16.88
..... 16.100-16.104, 16.110, 16.123, 16.139
Treaty Establishing the European Community (Treaty of Rome) 1957 16.02
Art 2 ..... 16.19, 16.40
3 ..... 16.22
b 16.24
4 ..... 16.89
7 ..... 16.20
a 16.21
9-17 ..... 16.26
12 ..... 16.54, 16.127
18-29 ..... 16.26
30-37 ..... 16.26
38-47 ..... 16.26
48-66 ..... 16.26
67-73 ..... 16.26
74-84 ..... 16.26
85 ..... 16.148, 16.156
85-92 ..... 16.26
86 ..... 16.148, 16.156
92-94 ..... 16.55
100 ..... 16.26
118-119 ..... 16.26
119 ..... 16.128, 16.157
137 ..... 16.106
137-188 ..... 16.26
168a 16.123
188a 16.125
189c 16.139
145 ..... 16.101
146 ..... 16.99, 16.103
148 ..... 16.104

157 .... 16.93
164 .... 16.52, 16.112
165 .... 16.119
166 .... 16.121
167 .... 16.119
169 .... 16.91, 16.114, 16.118, 16.140
170 .... 16.114
171 .... 16.114
173 .... 16.115
174 .... 16.115
175 .... 16.115
177 .... 16.54, 16.73, 16.116-16.117, 16.124, 16.143
188c 16.125
189 .... 16.26, 16.80, 16.84, 16.129, 16.136, 16.144-16.149
193 .... 16.97
199-209 .... 16.26
210 .... 16.26
236 .... 16.105
240 .... 16.26
Treaty on European Union 1992 .... 16.01
Article
A 16.41
N 16.105

Council of Europe

Convention for the Protection of Human Rights and Fundamental Freedoms 1950 .... 17.06-17.09, 17.16, 17.18
Art
1
1st protocol 17.07
4th protocol 17.07
6th protocol 17.07
7th protocol 17.07
2 .... 17.07
1st protocol 17.07
4th protocol 17.07
7th protocol 17.07
3 .... 17.07
1st protocol 17.07
4th protocol 17.07

7th protocol 17.07
4 .... 17.07
4th protocol 17.07
7th protocol 17.07
5 .... 17.07, 17.17
7th protocol 17.07
6 .... 17.07
7 .... 17.07
8 .... 17.07, 17.17
9 .... 17.07
10 .... 1707, 17.23
(2) 17.23
11 .... 17.07
12 .... 17.07
13 .... 17.07
Convention for the Protection of Individuals With Regard to the Automatic Processing of Data 1982 .... 17.12
European Convention on Social Security 1972 .... 17.12
European Convention on the Legal Status of Migrant Workers 1977 . 17.12
European Social Charter 1961 .... 17.12

Australia

Commonwealth of Australia Constitution Act 1900
s
9 .... 15.43
Judiciary Act 1903
Pt
9 .... 15.43

Canada

Petition of Right Act 15.43

New Zealand

Crown Proceedings Act 1950 .... 15.43

South Africa

Crown Liability Act 1910 ....15.43

United States

Federal Torts Act 1945 ....15.43

Statutory Instruments

Ireland

Courts (No 2) Act 1986 (Commencement) Order 1988 (SI 176/1988) 5.32

Criminal Justice Act 1984 (Treatment of Persons in Custody in Garda Síochána Stations) Regulations 1987 (SI 119/1987) 6.66

District Court Rules 1948 (SR & O 431/1947) 5.31, 6.01, 6.24, 6.53

r 3 .... 4.62

16 .... 4.124

District Court (Small Claims Procedure) Rules 1991 (SI 310/1991) 5.35

District Court (Small Claims Procedure) Rules 1993 (SI 356/1993) 5.35

District Court (Small Claims Procedure) Rules 1995 (SI 377/1995) 5.35

Employment Regulation Order (Hotels Joint Labour Committee) 1978 .... 13.76

European Communities (Control of Oestrogenic, Androgenic, Gestagenic and Thyrostatic Substances) Regulations 1988 (SI 218/1988) 16.76

European Communities (Control of Veterinary Medicinal Products and their Residues) Regulations 1990 (SI 171/1990) 16.76

European Communities (Freedom to Provide Services) (Lawyers) Regulations 1979 (SI 58/1979) 3.81

European Communities (General System for the Recognition of Higher Education Diplomas) Regulations 1991 (SI 1/1991) 3.80

European Communities (Milk Levy) Regulations 1985 (SI 416/1985) 14.32

European Communities (Misleading Advertisements) Regulations 1988 (SI 134/1988) 5.12

European Communities (Prohibition of Trade with the Federal Republic of Yugoslavia (Serbia and Montenegro)) Regulations 1993 (SI 144/1993) 14.33

European Communities (Review Procedures for the Award of Public Supply, Public Works and Public Services Contracts) Regulations 1994 (SI 309/94) 8.58

European Communities (Rules on Competition) Regulations 1993 (SI 124/1993) 16.148

European Communities (Second General System for the Recognition of Professional Education and Training) Regulations 1996

(SI 135/1996) 3.80

European Communities (Unfair Terms in Consumer Contracts) Regulations 1995 (SI 27/1995) 5.12, 13.03, 13.40, 13.79, 16.138

Garda Síochána (Discipline) Regulations 1989 ....8.57

Health Services Regulations 1971 (SI 105/1971)

art 6..13.72

Industrial Relations Act 1990 Code of Practice on Dispute Procedures (Declaration) Order 1992 (SI 1/1992) 13.04

Limerick Harbour Order 1932 ....13.23

Local Government (Planning and Development) Regulations 1977 (SI 65/1977)

art 36 ....14.76

Local Government (Planning and Development) Regulations 1994 (SI 86/1994) 8.56

Misuse of Drugs Act 1977 (Commencement) Order 1979 (SI 28/1979) 13.42

Offences against the State (Scheduled Offences) Order 1972 (SI 282/1972) 5.91

Rules of the Circuit Court 1950 (SI 179/1950) 4.05, 5.40, 6.01, 6.52

Order 2 ....4.124

3 r2 ....4.61

58 r 1 ....14.65

Rules of the Superior Courts 1986 (SI 15/1986) 4.05, 4.41, 6.01
.... 6.24, 6.33, 6.37, 6.42
....6.49-6.50, 13.61, 15.35

Order 49 r1 ....4.50

84..10.35

118...4.124

119 r1 ....4.59

App A 6.31

Safety in Industry (Abrasive Wheels) Regulations 1982 ....6.39

Safety, Health and Welfare at Work (General Application) Regulations 1993 ....6.43

Pt IV 6.39

Safety, Health and Welfare at Work (Signs) Regulations 1995
(SI 132/1995) 13.61

Social Welfare (Insurance Appeals) Regulations 1952 (SI 376/1952) 14.65

Social Welfare (Overlapping Benefits) (Amendment) Regulations 1979
(SI 118/1979)
art 4 .... 13.69
38 .... 13.69

Social Welfare (Overlapping Benefits) Regulations 1953 (SI 14/1953) ......
13.69

Solicitors Acts 1954 and 1960 (Apprenticeship and Education)
Regulations 1991 (SI 9/1991)
Reg 15 .... 3.14
Reg 30 .... 3.14

Solicitors Acts 1954 and 1960 (Apprenticeship and
Education) (Amendment) (No 2) Regulations 1992 (SI 360/1992) . 3.14

Succession Act 1965 (Commencement) Order 1966 (SI 168/1966) ... 13.43

United Kingdom

Health and Safety at Work (Northern Ireland) Order 1978
(SI 1039/1978) 2.72

Provisional Government (Transfer of Functions) Order 1922 .... 2.62

Table of Constitutional Articles

1922

Article

2A ... 15.09, 15.13, 15.69
6 ... 15.06, 15.10
7 ... 15.06
8 ... 15.06
9 ... 15.06
14 ... 15.08
34.1 ... 4.10
43 ... 15.06
50 ... 15.08, 15.14, 15.68
62 ... 15.23
63 ... 15.23
64 ... 4.03, 4.21
70 ... 15.06
72 ... 15.13
73 ... 4.03, 12.12, 15.07, 15.27-15.29

1937

Article

1 ... 15.36, 15.43
2 ... 15.19, 15.37-15.40, 15.42, 15.79, 15.87, 15.111, 15.139
3 ... 15.19, 15.37-15.40, 15.42, 15.79, 15.87, 15.111, 15.139
4 ... 2.71, 15.41-15.41, 15.43
5 ... 15.41-15.43, 15.43, 15.129, 16.66
6 ... 4.09, 15.43, 15.128, 16.60
6.1 ... 15.428 15.35
8.1 ... 15.30
8.2 ... 15.30
8.3 ... 15.33
10 ... 15.43
12 ... 4.41-4.42, 15.21
12.1 ... 15.21
12.3.1° ... 5.64
13 ... 15.21, 15.43, 15.43
13.1.1° ... 8.08
13.4 ... 15.21

13.5 .... 15.21
13.9 .... 4.63, 8.07, 15.21
15 .... 15.43, 16.79, 17.17
15.2 .... 1.11, 13.68, 16.60-16.62
15.2.1° 8.08, 12.66, 13.01, 13.58, 13.65, 15.27
15.4 .... 15.27
15.5 .... 1.34, 14.60, 14.62, 15.48
15.6 .... 14.46
15.8 .... 15.48
15.10 .... 13.13
16 .... 15.72-15.72, 15.129
16.1.2° 15.48
16.1.4° 15.48, 15.84
16.2 .... 15.84
16.2.3° 15.48
18 .... 15.72
21 .... 13.09
22.1.1° 13.09
23 .... 13.09, 13.12
23.1.1° 13.09
24 .... 5.65, 13.09-13.10
24.1 .... 13.09
24.2 .... 15.70
25.2.1°. 13.10
25.2.2° 13.10
25.3° 13.10
25.4 .... 15.70
25.4.1° 13.41
25.4.2° 13.10
25.4.3° 15.31-15.34
25.4.4° 13.37, 15.34
25.4.5° 13.10
25.4.6° 15.34
25.5.1° 15.31
25.5.2° 15.31
25.5.4° 15.32
26 .... 4.37, 4.41-4.42, 5.65-5.68, 12.11
.... 13.11, 15.21, 15.28, 15.62, 15.70
.... 15.77, 15.78, 15.84, 15.109, 17.17
26.1.3° 5.67
26.2.1° 5.66

26.2.2° 5.66
26.3.1° 5.67
26.3.3° 5.67
27 .... 13.12, 15.43
28 .... 8.06, 15.43, 16.61
28.1 .... 8.05, 8.14
28.2 .... 8.05
28.3.3° 15.69-15.70, 15.84
28.4.1° 8.08
28.4.2° 8.05
28.4.3° 8.06
28.5 .... 8.05
28.6 .... 8.05
28.8 .... 13.13
28.10 .... 8.08
28.12 .... 8.11
29 .... 15.43, 16.01, 16.61-16.63, 17.17
29.2 .... 15.39
29.3 .... 1.16, 16.62, 17.19
29.4 .... 8.06, 15.72-15.72, 16.62, 16.67, 16.70, 16.79, 17.01
29.4.1° 15.41, 16.61
29.4.2° 15.41, 16.61
29.4.3° 1.13, 16.63-16.67, 16.82, 16.100
29.4.4° 16.82
29.4.5° 16.68-16.73, 16.79-16.82, 16.87, 16.147
29.4.6° 16.67
29.6 .... 1.16, 14.49, 16.62, 17.01, 17.17
30 .... 3.54-3.59, 15.22
30.3 .... 3.61
31 .... 15.21
33 .... 15.23
34 .... 4.04-4.06, 4.24, 4.41, 4.49
.... 4.52-4.54, 4.63, 4.109, 7.36
.... 7.54, 8.20, 8.37, 8.43, 8.55
.... 8.64, 12.32, 15.27, 15.43, 15.70
.... 15.83, 15.109, 15.140, 16.60, 17.25
34.1 .... 4.07-4.24, 4.34, 4.91, 9.02, 12.17, 15.48
34.2 .... 4.25
34.3 .... 4.26
34.3.1° 4.26, 5.51, 5.84, 7.13, 7.29, 15.109
34.3.2° 4.26, 5.41, 5.56-5.58, 15.28

34.3.3° 5.68, 12.11, 13.11
34.3.4° 4.30, 5.30, 5.38, 7.02, 7.13, 7.29, 7.36, 12.59
34.4 .... 4.26, 12.12
34.4.1° 4.26, 5.52-5.54, 7.24
34.4.3° 4.26, 7.02, 7.17, 7.24, 7.26, 7.31, 7.50, 15.28, 15.101
34.4.4° 4.26, 7.24, 15.28
34.5 .... 4.7934.5.1° 4.90
34.5.1° 4.92
35.1 .... 4.63
35.2 .... 4.90, 4.100, 4.106
35.3 .... 4.90
35.4 .... 4.92
35.4.1° 4.91
35.5 .... 4.100-4.103, 4.112
36 .... 4.32, 4.40, 4.54, 8.11
36.iii 4.64
37 .... 4.06-4.10, 4.118, 11.02, 15.43, 15.72, 15.109
37.1 .... 4.08-4.11, 4.16-4.18, 4.24, 4.33
37.2 .... 4.16
38 .... 4.04-4.06, 4.24, 4.33, 6.58, 13.69, 15.102, 15.109
38.1 .... 4.110, 7.29, 9.15, 10.34, 12.59, 15.48, 15.59, 15.83
38.2 .... 5.04, 5.70-5.72, 5.87
38.3 .... 5.86-5.91
38.3.2° 5.88
38.4 .... 5.87, 5.95
38.5 .... 5.80-5.84, 5.87, 6.100, 12.59, 12.61, 15.48
39 .... 5.85, 14.46
40 .... 15.48, 15.103, 15.128, 15.129, 17.22
40.1 .... 13.67, 15.48, 15.59-15.61, 15.83, 15.107, 15.117
40.2 .... 15.48
40.3 .... 6.04, 9.02, 15.50, 15.52-15.54
.... 15.77, 15.84, 15.88, 15.94, 15.103
.... 15.117, 15.125-15.128, 15.129
.... 15.135, 15.140, 16.57
40.3.1° 15.103, 15.134, 15.138
40.3.2° 15.103, 15.137
40.3.3° 4.95, 15.72-15.72, 15.89, 15.125, 15.130-15.133
40.4 .... 15.48, 15.59, 15.83
40.4.2° 9.02, 9.05-9.09, 9.17, 10.36, 15.70, 17.17
40.4.4° 4.50
40.5 .... 15.48

40.6 .... 15.48
40.6.1°iii 1.32, 14.47
41 .... 14.47, 15.19, 15.48, 15.66, 15.72
.... 15.85, 15.88-15.90, 15.111
.... 15.124-15.128, 15.129, 15.139
41.1 .... 15.112-15.115
41.2 .... 15.112
41.3 .... 15.112
41.3.1° 15.112
41.3.2° 15.112
42 .... 15.48, 15.128
42.1 .... 14.47
43 .... 15.48, 15.85, 15.124, 15.128
44 .... 15.19, 15.48, 15.72, 15.128
45 .... 15.43, 15.129
46 .... 15.26, 15.43, 15.134
46.2 .... 13.10
46.5 .... 13.10
47 .... 15.43
49 .... 15.43
50 .... 12.12, 12.35, 15.07, 15.29, 15.64, 15.128, 17.17
50.1 .... 15.27
51 .... 15.68
58 .... 4.34-4.37
62 .... 15.17
73 .... 2.64, 13.52

Table of Cases

A

AD v Ireland [1994] 1 IR 369 .... 6.04
Aamand v Smithwick [1995] 1 ILRM 61 .... 14.58, 14.84
Abrahamson & Ors v Law Society of Ireland (HC) unrep, 23 July 1996 .... 3.14, 15.67
Addie (Robert) & Sons (Collieries) Ltd v Dumbreck [1929] AC 358 .. 12.13
Adoption (No 2) Bill 1987, Re [1989] IR 656 .... 5.68, 15.54
Aer Lingus Teo v Labour Court [1990] ILRM 485 .... 8.43
Airey v Ireland (1979) 2 EHRR 305 .... 9.21-9.24, 17.11, 17.18
Amministrazione della Finanze dello Stato v Simmentha [1978] 1 ECR 629 .... 14.36
Anisminic Ltd v Foreign Compensation Tribunal [1969] 2 AC 147 .... 12.54
Anns v London Borough of Merton [1978] AC 728 .... 12.75
Ashville Investments Ltd v Elmer Contractors Ltd [1989] QB 488 ..... 12.52
Attorney General (Fahy) v Bruen [1936] IR 750 .... 7.17, 7.31, 8.36
Attorney General (Society for the Protection of Unborn Children Ltd) v Open Door Counselling Ltd [1988] IR 593 3.59, 15.130
Attorney General v Coyne & Wallace (1967) 101 ILTR 17 ...... 15.33-15.35
Attorney General v Deignan [1946] IR 542 .... 15.128
Attorney General v Edison Telephone Co (1886) 6 QBD 244 .... 14.52
Attorney General v Hamilton (No 1) [1993] 2 IR 250 .... 3.59, 12.55
Attorney General v Leaf Ltd [1982] ILRM 441 .... 14.69
Attorney General v McBride [1928] IR 451 .... 15.11
Attorney General v Paperlink Ltd [1984] ILRM 343 .... 15.54
Attorney General v Ryan's Car Hire Ltd [1965] IR 642 .... 12.12, 12.14 .... 12.17, 12.32-12.33, 12.35
Attorney General v Simpson [1959] IR 105 .... 12.33
Attorney General v Smith [1927] IR 564 .... 7.43
Attorney General v Times Newspapers Ltd [1974] AC 273 .... 17.23
Attorney General v X [1992] 1 IR 1 .... 1.21, 3.59, 4.95, 12.54, 15.89 .... 15.109, 15.125, 15.131-15.133, 15.137

B

B v B [1975] IR 54 .... 7.24
Bailey v Bullock [1950] 2 All ER 1167 .... 12.77
Baker v The Queen [1975] AC 774 .... 12.52
Bakht v The Medical Council [1990] 1 IR 515 .... 7.26, 14.76
Bankers' Case (1700) 14 St Tr 1 .... 15.43

Barrington v Lee [1972] 1 QB 326 .... 12.81
Battle v Irish Art Promotion Centre Ltd [1968] IR 252 .... 9.09
Batty v Metropolitan Realisations Ltd [1978] QB 554 .... 12.76
Bean v Wade (1885) 2 TLR 157 .... 12.77
Beecham Group Ltd v Bristol Myers Co (HC) unrep, 13 March 1981 14.90
Berns v Bethell [1982] Ch 294 .... 12.52
Best v Wellcome Foundation Ltd [1993] 3 IR 421 .... 7.11, 9.08
Blake v Attorney General [1982] IR 117 .... 15.62, 15.85
Blanco Case (1873) 15.43
Bloomer & Ors v Law Society of Ireland [1995] 3 IR 14 (HC); (SC) unrep, 6 February 1996 .... 3.14
Blottner v Bestuur van de Niewe Algemene Bedrijfsvereniging [1977] ECR 1141 .... 14.48
Bonham's (Dr) Case (1610) 8 Co Rep 114(a) 14.60
Boorman v Brown (1842) 3 QB 511; (1844) 11 Cl & Fin 1 .... 12.77
Bosphorus Hava v Minister for Transport [1994] 2 ILRM 551 .... 14.33
Bourke v Attorney General [1972] IR 36 .... 14.84, 14.90
Bourne v Norwich Crematorium Ltd [1967] 2 All ER 576 .... 14.71
Boylan v Dublin Corporation [1949] IR 60 .... 12.33, 12.35
Boyle v Allen [1979] ILRM 281 .... 5.50
Brady v Donegal County Council [1989] ILRM 282 .... 9.02
Brasserie du Pêcheur SA v Federal Republic of Germany/Reg v Secretary of State for Transport, ex p Factortame Ltd [1996] 2 WLR 506 .... 16.143
Brennan v Attorney General [1983] ILRM 449 (HC); [1984] ILRM 355 (SC) 15.85
Brennan v Minister for Justice [1995] 1 IR 612 .... 4.13, 10.23
Brosnan v Leeside Nurseries Ltd [1994] 2 ILRM 459 .... 14.39
Browne v Attorney General [1991] 2 IR 58 .... 15.85
Browne v Bank of Ireland Finance Ltd [1991] 1 IR 431 .... 7.07
Buchanan & Co v Babco Ltd [1977] QB 208; [1978] AC 141 .... 14.32
.... 14.33
Buckley & Ors (Sinn Fein) v The Attorney General [1950] IR 67 .... 15.128
Burke v Minister for Labour [1979] IR 354 .... 8.45, 13.76
Burt v Claude Cousins & Co [1971] 2 QB 426 .... 12.81
Butterly v Mayor of Drogheda [1907] 2 IR 134 .... 12.67
Byrne v Ireland [1972] IR 241 ....9.02, 15.41-15.43, 15.44-15.45
.... 15.59-15.64, 15.76, 15.86, 15.93

C

Cahill v Governor of Military Detention Barracks, Curragh Camp [1980] ILRM 191 .... 9.09

Cahill v Sutton [1980] IR 269 .... 15.62, 15.77, 15.85, 15.127
Campus Oil Ltd v Minister for Industry and Energy [1983] IR 82 .... 7.58
Campus Oil Ltd v Minister for Industry and Energy (No 2)
[1983] IR 88 .... 10.13
Canada Southern Ry Co v International Bridge Co
(1883) 3 App Cas 723 .... 14.79
Candler v Crane, Christmas & Co [1951] 2 KB 164 .... 12.54, 12.75
Carroll v Clare County Council [1975] IR 230 .... 12.09
Carron v McMahon [1990] 1 IR 239 .... 12.09, 12.19
Cassell & Co Ltd v Broome [1972] AC 1027 .... 12.09
Cassidy v Minister for Industry and Commerce [1978] IR 297 .... 13.73
.... 13.74
Chemical Bank v McCormack [1983] ILRM 350 .... 14.64
Chestvale Properties Ltd v Glackin [1993] 3 IR 35 .... 14.63
Chief Adjudication Officer v Foster [1993] 2 WLR 292 .... 14.94
Chisholm v Georgia 2 Dall 419 (1793) 15.43
City of London v Wood (1701) 12 Mod Rep 669 .... 14.60
Cityview Press Ltd v An Chomhairle Oiliúna [1980] IR 381 .... 13.67
.... 13.72, 15.84, 16.79, 16.85
Clancy v Irish Rugby Football Union [1995] 1 ILRM 193 .... 8.57
Clancy, Re [1943] IR 23 .... 12.24
Clark v Kirby-Smith [1964] Ch 506 .... 12.77
Cleary v Booth [1893] 1 QB 465 .... 13.04
Close v Steel Company of Wales [1962] AC 367 .... 12.12
Coakley (Denis) & Co Ltd v Commissioner of Valuation
[1991] 1 IR 402 (HC); [1996] 2 ILRM 90 (SC) 14.39
Coleman v Clarke [1991] ILRM 841 .... 7.11
Collier v Hicks (1831) 2 B & Ad 663 .... 9.09
Commissioners of Public Works v Kavanagh [1950] IR 142 .... 15.43
Comyn v Attorney General [1950] IR 142 .... 15.43
Conroy v Attorney General [1965] IR 411 .... 5.73
Conroy v Minister for Defence [1934] IR 342 .... 15.43
Considine v Shannon Regional Fisheries Board [1994] 1 ILRM 499
.... 7.29, 12.44, 12.53, 12.59
Cook v Swinfen [1967] 1 WLR 457 .... 12.77
Cooke v Walsh [1984] IR 710 .... 13.67, 13.72
Cork County Council v Whillock [1993] 1 IR 231 .... 14.24, 14.50
Corley v Gill [1975] IR 313 .... 7.21, 12.16
Corry v Lucas (1869) IR 3 CL 208 .... 12.73
Costa v ENEL [1964] ECR 585 .... 16.55-16.57, 16.63, 16.68
.... 16.113, 16.117, 16.131, 16.140

Cotter & McDermott v Minister for Social Welfare [1991] ECR I-1155 .... 16.143
Cowan v Freaghaile [1991] 1 IR 389 .... 4.49
Cox (RD) Ltd v Owners of MV Fritz Raabe (SC) unrep, 1 August 1974 .... 4.29
Criminal Law (Jurisdiction) Bill 1975, Re [1977] IR 129 .... 5.68, 5.96 .... 14.64, 15.19, 15.39
Croke v Smith & Ors (HC) unrep, 31 July 1995 .... 14.49
Cronin (Inspector of Taxes) v Strand Dairy Ltd (HC) unrep, 18 December 1985 .... 14.38, 14.41
Cronin v Cork & County Properties Ltd [1986] IR 559 .... 14.80
Cronin v Lunham Brothers Ltd [1986] ILRM 415 .... 14.66
Cronin v Youghal Carpets (Yarns) Ltd [1985] IR 312 .... 14.80-14.81
Crotty v An Taoiseach [1987] IR 713; [1987] ILRM 400 .... 4.50, 4.98 .... 15.79, 15.86, 16.36, 16.62 .... 16.63, 16.100, 17.19
Cumann Luthchleas Gael v Windle [1994] 1 IR 525 .... 6.63, 6.67

D

D v C [1984] ILRM 173 .... 12.65
D, in re [1987] IR 449 .... 5.61
Dalton v Minister for Finance [1989] IR 269 .... 7.24
Daniels v Heskin [1954] IR 73 .... 12.83, 12.85
Davies v Lock (1844) 3 LT (OS) 125 .... 12.77
Day v Savadge (1614) Hob 85 .... 14.60
Deane v Voluntary Health Insurance Board [1992] 2 IR 319 .... 14.85
de Burca v Attorney General [1976] IR 38 .... 1.23, 6.100, 11.02, 15.61 .... 15.83, 15.107
Deighan v Ireland [1995] 2 IR 56 .... 4.107
Delap v an tAire Dlí agus Cirt (HC), unrep, 13 June 1990 .... 15.35
Derry v Peek (1889) 14 App Cas 337 .... 12.75
Desmond v Brophy [1985] IR 449 .... 12.43, 12.81
Desmond v Glackin (No 2) [1993] 3 IR 67 .... 14.49, 15.75, 15.110 .... 17.20-17.23
DG, an Infant, in re 7.07
Dillane v Ireland [1980] ILRM 167 .... 9.39
Dillon v Minister for Posts and Telegraphs (SC) unrep, 3 June 1981 .. 14.71 .... 14.74
Dillon-Leetch v Calleary (No 2) (SC) unrep, 31 July 1974 .... 5.62
Dolan v Corn Exchange [1975] IR 315 .... 7.20-7.21

Donnelly v Timber Factors Ltd [1991] 1 IR 553 .....4.92
Donoghue v Stevenson [1932] AC 562 .....1.22, 12.13, 12.71-12.73
.....12.74-12.75, 12.79-12.80
Donovan v Landy's Ltd [1963] IR 441 .....12.13
Dowling v Ireland [1991] 2 IR 379 .....14.45, 14.48
Doyle v An Taoiseach [1986] ILRM 693 .....7.58, 14.60, 16.69
Doyle v Hearne [1987] IR 601 .....7.20-7.21, 12.16, 12.20
DPP v Byrne [1994] 2 ILRM 91 .....6.09
DPP v Doyle [1994] 2 IR 286 .....6.64
DPP v Flanagan [1979] IR 265 .....14.17
DPP v Grey [1986] IR 317 .....14.73
DPP v McCreesh [1992] 2 IR 239 .....14.56
DPP v Ottewell [1970] AC 642 .....14.24
DPP v Wexford Farmers' Club [1994] 1 IR 546 .....14.22
Dublin Corporation v Dublin Cinemas Ltd [1963] IR 103 .....14.69
Dublin County Council v Eighty Five Developments Ltd (No 1)
[1993] 2 IR 378 .....14.80
Dublin County Council v Grealy [1990] 1 IR 77 .....14.61
Dublin Wellwoman Centre Ltd v Ireland [1995] 1 ILRM 408 .....4.92
Dudgeon v United Kingdom (1981) 4 EHRR 149 .....15.129, 17.17
Duff & Ors v Minister for Agriculture (No 2) (HC) unrep,
10 July 1992 .....15.67
Duffy v Dublin Corporation [1974] IR 33 .....14.73
Duffy v News Group Newspapers Ltd [1992] 2 IR 369 .....4.41
Duggan v Dublin Corporation [1991] ILRM 330 .....14.74
Dunne (Brendan) Ltd v FitzPatrick [1958] IR 29 .....12.53
Dunne v National Maternity Hospital [1989] IR 91 ... 4.98, 7.26, 9.08, 9.11
Dunne v O'Neill [1974] IR 180 .....12.26
Dutton v Bognor Regis UDC [1972] 1 QB 373 .....1.22
Dwyer decd (1908) 46 ILTR 147 .....12.24

E

E v E [1982] ILRM 497 .....17.18-17.19
East Donegal Co-Operative Livestock Mart Ltd v Attorney General
[1970] IR 317 .....13.67-13.68, 14.44, 15.77, 15.78
Eccles v Ireland [1985] IR 545 .....5.96
Educational Company of Ireland Ltd v Fitzpatrick (No 2)
[1961] IR 323 .....12.35
Eisenstadt v Baird 405 US 438 (1972) 15.128
Electoral (Amendment) Bill 1961, Re [1961] IR 169 .....5.68
Electoral (Amendment) Bill 1983, Re [1984] IR 268 .....5.68

Electricity Supply Board v Gormley [1985] IR 129 .... 8.36
Ellis v Goulton [1893] 1 QB 350 .... 12.81
Elwyn (Cottons) Ltd v Master of the High Court [1989] IR 14 .... 12.47
Emergency Powers Bill 1976, Re [1977] IR 159 .... 5.68, 14.58, 15.84
Emmott v Minister for Social Welfare [1991] ECR I-4269 .... 16.143
Esso Petroleum v Mardon [1976] QB 801 .... 12.77
European Chemical Industries Ltd v Bell [1981] ILRM 345 .... 10.14
Exham v Beamish [1939] IR 336 .... 12.33, 12.35, 12.74

F

F (F) v CF [1987] ILRM 1 .... 14.92, 14.94
F (T) v Ireland [1995] 1 IR 321 .... 15.90
F (U) (orse UC) v JC [1991] 2 IR 330 .... 12.34, 12.65, 12.68
Fallon v Gannon [1988] ILRM 193 .... 12.82
Farrell v Alexander [1975] 3 WLR 642 .... 14.24
Feeney v Pollexfen & Co Ltd [1931] 589 .... 12.67
Finlay v Murtagh [1979] IR 249 .... 12.34, 12.76, 12.77
.... 12.78, 12.79, 12.85
Finucane v McMahon [1990] 1 IR 165; [1990] ILRM 505 .... 12.18
.... 14.47, 14.83
Flynn & Village Crafts v Irish Nationwide Building Society Ltd
(HC) unrep, 31 July 1995 .... 14.93
Flynn v Denieffe [1989] IR 722 .... 14.96
Flynn v Power [1985] ILRM 36 .... 8.46
Foley v Independent Newspapers (Irl) Ltd [1994] 2 ILRM 61 .... 3.43
Fothergill v Monarch Airlines Ltd [1980] 3 WLR 209;
[1981] AC 251 .... 12.42, 14.90
Frailey v Charlton [1920] 1 KB 147 .... 15.128
Francovich v Italian Republic [1991] ECR I-5357 .... 16.83, 16.118
.... 16.141-16.142, 16.157
Franklin v Gramaphone Ltd [1948] 1 KB 542 .... 14.58
Frescati Estates Ltd v Walker [1975] IR 177 .... 14.28, 14.57
Furniss v Dawson [1984] AC 474 .... 14.09

G

G v An Bord Uchtála [1980] IR 32 .... 4.16, 12.06, 15.54
.... 15.130, 15.137
G v Director of Public Prosecutions [1994] 1 IR 374 .... 6.69
G (O) v An Bórd Uchtála [1991] 1 IR 491 .... 7.07
Gaffney v Gaffney [1975] IR 133 .... 12.35
Garvey v Ireland [1981] IR 75 .... 6.22

Gavin v Criminal Injuries Compensation Tribunal (HC) unrep, 9 February 1996 .... 8.41
Geoghegan v Institute of Chartered Accountants in Ireland [1995] 3 IR 86 .... 8.57, 15.46
Glavin v Governor of Mountjoy Prison [1991] 2 IR 421 .... 4.69
Gleeson v Feehan [1993] 2 IR 113 .... 12.43
Goodman International v Hamilton J [1992] 2 IR 542 .... 4.13, 8.64
Gorris v Scott (1874) LR 9 Ex 125 .... 14.20
Gough v Kinsella (1971) 105 ILTR 116 .... 14.81
Green v McLoughlin [1991] 1 IR 309 (HC); (SC) unrep, 26 January 1995 .... 8.39
Greene v Minister for Agriculture [1990] 2 IR 17 .... 14.32
Gregory v Windle [1994] 3 IR 613 .... 2.51
Grey v Pearson (1857) HL Cas 61 .... 14.17
Grimes v Owners of SS Bangor Bay [1948] IR 350 .... 4.30
Griswold v Connecticut 381 US 479 (1965) 15.128, 15.128
Groom v Crocker [1939] 1 KB 194 .... 12.77

H

H (J), in re [1985] IR 375 .... 14.47
H v Director of Public Prosecutions [1994] 2 ILRM 285 .... 6.69
H v H [1978] IR 138 .... 14.08, 14.15, 14.74
Hadmor Productions Ltd v Hamilton [1981] 3 WLR 139 .... 14.90
Hall v Meyrick [1957] 2 QB 455 .... 12.77
Hamilton v Hamilton [1982] IR 466 .... 12.20, 14.60, 14.61
Hanafin v Minister for the Environment (HC) unrep, 1 March 1996; [1996] 2 ILRM 141 (SC) 4.50, 5.11, 5.62, 15.91
Hanrahan v Merck, Sharpe & Dohme Ltd [1988] ILRM 629 .... 4.98, 7.09
Harrington v Hoggart (1830) 1 B & Ad 577 .... 12.81
Harrison v National Coal Board [1951] 1 All ER 1102 .... 14.58
Harvey v Facey [1893] AC 552 .... 14.26
Harvey v Minister for Social Welfare [1990] 2 IR 232 .... 13.68
Haughey, in re [1971] IR 217 .... 8.55, 15.54
Hay v O'Grady [1992] 1 IR 210 .... 7.07
Hedley Byrne & Co Ltd v Heller & Partners Ltd [1964] AC 465 .... 12.54
.... 12.75, 12.77, 12.79, 12.80
Hefferon Kearns Ltd, Re (No 1) [1993] 3 IR 177 .... 14.60, 14.62
Herrington v British Railways Board [1972] AC 877 .... 12.13
Hetherington, Re [1990] Ch 1 .... 12.52
Heydon's case (1584) 3 Co Rep 7a 14.19
Heywood v Wellers [1976] QB 446 .... 12.77

Hoey v Minister for Justice [1994] 3 IR 329 .... 4.98
Holohan v Donohoe [1986] IR 45 .... 7.26
Home Office v Dorset Yacht Co Ltd [1970] AC 1004 .... 12.75
Housing (Private Rented Dwellings) Bill 1981, Re [1983] IR 181 .... 5.68
Howard v Commissioners of Public Works [1994] 1 IR 101 .... 14.08
.... 14.94
Howell v Young (1826) 5 B & C 259 .... 12.77
Hynes Ltd v Independent Newspapers Ltd [1980] IR 204 .... 12.43
Hynes-O'Sullivan v O'Driscoll [1989] ILRM 349 .... 12.15, 12.68

I

Iarnród Éireann v Ireland (SC) unrep, 16 July 1996 .... 15.79
Iarnrod Eireann v Ireland [1995] 2 ILRM 161 .... 12.43
Inspector of Taxes v Arida Ltd [1992] 2 IR 155 .... 14.65
Inspector of Taxes v Kiernan [1981] IR 117 .... 14.09, 14.24, 14.38, 14.42
.... 14.59, 14.70, 14.80, 14.96
Internationale Handelsgesellschaft v Einfuhr-und Vorratsstelle
für Getreide und Futtermittel [1970] ECR 1125 .... 16.56, 16.63
.... 16.68, 16.113, 16.117, 16.131
Ireland v United Kingdom (1978) 2 EHRR 25 .... 17.11
Irish Agricultural Machinery Ltd v Ó Culacháin [1990] 1 IR 535
.... 14.40-14.42, 14.81
Irish Commercial Society Ltd v Plunkett [1986] IR 258 .... 14.68
Irish Creamery Milk Suppliers Association Ltd v Ireland
(1979) 3 JISEL 66 .... 7.58
Irish Leathers Ltd v Minister for Labour [1986] IR 177 .... 14.81
Irish Nationwide Building Society Ltd v Revenue Commissioners
(HC) unrep, 2 October 1990 .... 14.69
Irish Press Plc v Ingersoll Publications Ltd [1994] 1 IR 176 .... 4.21
Irish Refining plc v Commissioner of Valuation [1990] 1 IR 568 .... 14.77
Irish Shell Ltd v Elm Motors Ltd [1984] IR 511 .... 12.06, 12.33-12.35
Irish Trust Bank Ltd v Central Bank of Ireland [1976-7] ILRM 50 ..... 12.26

J

J (a Minor), Re [1991] Fam 33 .... 15.137
J (P) v J (J) [1992] ILRM 273 .... 14.08
Jarvis v Moy, Davies, Smith, Vanderell & Co [1936] 1 KB 399 .... 12.76
.... 12.77
Johnson & Kelly v Horace [1993] ILRM 594 .... 12.43
Jordan v O'Brien [1960] IR 363 .... 14.47

K

K (N) v K [1985] IR 733 .... 15.112
Kavanagh v Government of Ireland [1996] 1 ILRM 133 .... 5.96
Kawananakoa v Polyblank 205 US 349 (1907) 15.43
Keane v An Bord Pleanála (HC) unrep, 4 October 1995; (SC) unrep, 18 July 1996 .... 14.53, 14.96
Keane v Electricity Supply Board [1981] IR 44 .... 1.22, 12.75
Kearns v Manresa Estates Ltd (HC) unrep, 25 July 1975 .... 12.25
Keegan v de Burca [1973] IR 22 .... 10.33
Keegan v Ireland (HC) unrep, 26 May 1994 .... 17.11
Keenan Brothers Ltd, in re [1985] IR 401 .... 12.42
Kehoe v CJ Louth & Son [1992] ILRM 282 .... 12.82
Kelly (Dermot C) & anor v Finbarr J Crowley [1985] IR 212 .... 12.84
Kelly & Deighan, in re [1984] ILRM 424. .... 4.107
Kelly v Haughey Boland & Co [1989] ILRM 373 .... 12.78
Kelly v Ireland [1986] ILRM 318 .... 7.47
Kellystown Co v Hogan [1985] ILRM 200 .... 14.59
Kennedy v Ireland [1987] IR 587 .... 10.07, 15.54
Kenny v Quinn [1981] ILRM 385 .... 14.69
Kiberd v Mr Justice Hamilton [1992] 2 IR 257 .... 8.64
Kielthy v Ascon Ltd [1970] IR 122 .... 14.69
Kiely v Minister for Social Welfare 14.65
King v Attorney General [1981] IR 233 .... 15.56-15.60, 15.78, 15.126
Kirby v Burke & Holloway [1944] IR 207 .... 12.43, 12.73
Kirkwood Hackett v Tierney [1952] IR 185 .... 12.15
Kirwan v Minister for Justice (HC) unrep, 29 July 1993 .... 9.17
Klench v Secretaire d'État à l'Agriculture et à la Viticulture [1986] ECR 3477 .... 14.48
Knetch v United States 364 US 361 (1960) 14.09
Kruse v Johnson [1898] 2 QB 91 .... 13.61

L

Larkins v National Union of Mineworkers [1985] IR 671 .... 10.17
Lawless v Ireland (1961) 1 EHRR 25 .... 17.11, 17.17
Lawlor v Minister for Agriculture [1990] 1 IR 356 .... 14.32, 14.33
Leemac Overseas Investment Ltd v Harvey [1973] IR 160 .... 12.81
Liston v Munster & Leinster Bank [1940] IR 77 .... 12.76, 12.77
Listowel Urban District Council v McDonagh [1968] IR 312 .... 13.75
Liversidge v Anderson [1942] AC 206 .... 12.54
Logan v O'Donnell [1925] 2 IR 211 .... 12.67

London Street Tramways Co v London County Council
[1898] AC 375 .... 12.08, 12.12
London Transport Executive v Betts (Valuation Officer)
[1959] AC 213 .... 12.12
Lonergan v Morrisey (1947) 81 ILTR 130 .... 14.22
Lotus case (1927) PCIJ Ser A No 10 .... 14.64
Luke v The Inland Revenue Commissioners [1963] AC 557 .... 14.30
Lynham v Butler (No 2) [1933] IR 74 .... 4.10

M

M (orse G) v M [1986] ILRM 515 .... 12.68
M v An Bord Uchtála [1977] IR 287 .... 4.16, 11.02
M v M [1979] ILRM 160 .... 7.07
M(C) v M(T) (No 2) [1991] ILRM 268 .... 15.54
Macauley v Minister for Posts and Telegraphs [1966] IR 345 .... 9.02, 15.54
MacCurtain, Re [1941] IR 43 .... 5.96
MacGabhann v Incorporated Law Society of Ireland
[1989] ILRM 854 .... 3.11
MacGarbhith v Attorney General [1991] 2 IR 412 .... 9.04, 9.37
Madigan v Attorney General [1986] ILRM 136 .... 15.85
Magee v Culligan [1992] 1 IR 223 .... 4.54, 4.91, 14.60
Maher v Attorney General [1973] IR 140 .... 12.68, 14.87, 14.90
.... 15.75, 15.129
Mannix (GJ) Ltd, Re [1984] 1 NZLR 309 .... 9.09
Mapp v Gilhooley [1991] 2 IR 253 .... 6.82
Marbury v Madison, 1 Cranch 137 (1803) 15.93
Mareva Compania Naviera SA v International Bulkcarriers SA
[1975] 2 Lloyd's Rep 509 .... 10.11
Mason v Levy [1952] IR 40 .... 14.22
Matrimonial Home Bill 1993, Re [1994] 1 IR 305 .... 5.68
McC (M) v J McC [1994] 1 IR 293 .... 12.37
McCabe v Lisney & Son Ltd [1981] ILRM 289 .... 8.46
McCann (Charles) Ltd v Ó Culacháin [1986] IR 196 .... 11.02, 14.29, 14.38
.... 14.41-14.42, 14.59
McCarthy, Re [1990] ILRM 84 .... 5.69
McCausland v Ministry of Commerce [1956] NI 36 .... 14.38
McCord v ESB [1980] ILRM 153 .... 13.03, 13.64
McDaid v Sheehy [1991] 1 IR 1 .... 13.70
McDermott & Cotter v Minister for Social Welfare
[1987] ECR 1453 .... 16.143
McDonald v Bord na gCon (No 2) [1965] IR 217 .... 4.12-4.13

McDonnell v Byrne Engineering Co Ltd The Irish Times, 4 October 1978 .... 12.09
McGee v Attorney General [1974] IR 284 .... 1.22, 12.54, 15.53 .... 15.88, 15.106, 15.128-15.131
McGimpsey v Ireland [1988] IR 567 (HC); [1990] 1 IR 110 (SC) .... 15.39 .... 15.79, 15.87
McGlinchey v Governor of Portlaoise Prison [1988] IR 671 .... 5.96, 15.39
McGlinchey v Ireland [1990] 2 IR 215 .... 9.05
McGlynn v Clark [1945] IR 495 .... 12.67
McGonagle v McGonagle [1951] IR 123 .... 14.72
McGrath v Kiely [1965] IR 497 .... 12.76, 12.77
McGrath v McDermott [1988] IR 258 .... 14.09, 14.15
McGurrin v The Campion Publications Ltd (HC) unrep, 15 December 1993 .... 14.96
McIlwraith v Fawsitt [1990] 1 IR 343 .... 4.106
McKenna v An Taoiseach [1995] 2 IR 10 .... 15.90
McKenzie v McKenzie [1971] P 33 .... 9.09
McKerring v Minister for Agriculture [1989] ILRM 82 .... 8.54
McKinley v Minister for Defence [1992] 2 IR 333 .... 15.64
McLoughlin v Minister for the Public Service [1985] IR 631 .... 14.87
McMahon v Attorney General [1972] IR 69 .... 14.90, 15.84
McMenamin v Ireland [1994] 2 ILRM 368 .... 4.112
McMullen v Farrell [1993] 1 IR 123 .... 12.82
McNally v Ó Maoldomhnaigh [1990] 2 IR 513 .... 14.42
McNamara v Electricity Supply Board [1975] IR 1 .... 12.13, 12.16 .... 12.68, 12.75
Meagher v Minister for Agriculture and Food [1994] 1 IR 329; [1994] 1 ILRM 1 .... 6.08, 12.54, 13.67, 13.79 .... 15.86, 16.68, 16.76, 16.82, 16.85, 16.142
Melling v Ó Mathghamhna [1962] IR 1 .... 5.73
Mellowhide Products Ltd v Barry Agencies Ltd [1983] ILRM 152 .... 4.118
Metropolitan Properties Ltd v O'Brien [1995] 2 ILRM 383 .... 12.43
MF v Legal Aid Board [1993] ILRM 797 .... 9.33
Midland Bank v Hett, Stubbs & Kemp [1979] Ch 384 .. 12.76, 12.77, 12.79
Midland Silicones Ltd v Scruttons Ltd [1962] AC 466 .... 12.12
Millar v Taylor (1769) 4 Burr 2303 .... 14.90
Minister for Finance & Attorney General v O'Brien [1949] IR 91 .... 12.33, 12.35
Minister for Industry and Commerce v Hales [1967] IR 50 .... 13.72, 14.18 .... 14.29, 14.56, 14.82, 14.87, 14.90

Minister for Industry and Commerce v Hammond Lane Metal Co Ltd
[1947] Ir Jur Rep 59 .... 14.27
Minister for Industry and Commerce v Pim Brothers Ltd
[1966] IR 154 .... 14.26
Minister for Justice v Wang Zhu Jie [1993] 1 IR 426 ....7.17, 7.24, 7.31
Miranda v Arizona 384 US 436 (1966)... 9.18
Mixnam's Properties Ltd v Chertsey Urban District Council
[1964] 1 QB 214 .... 13.74
Mogul of Ireland Ltd v Tipperary (North Riding) County Council
[1976] IR 260 ....12.14-12.17, 12.32, 14.81
Montagu v Earl of Sandwich (1886) 32 Ch D 525 .... 12.26
Montgomery Decd, Re (1953) 89 ILTR 62 .... 12.25
Moore v Attorney General [1930] IR 471 .... 3.59
Moore v Attorney General [1934] IR 44 .... 2.16
Moore v Attorney General [1935] IR 472 .... 15.12
Morelle Ltd v Wakeling [1955] 2 QB 379 .... 12.61
Morrissey, Re [1944] IR 361 .... 12.24
Mullen v Quinnsworth Ltd (No 2) [1991] ILRM 439 .... 7.11
Murphy v Attorney General [1982] IR 241 ....4.15-4.17, 12.41, 15.60
....15.65-15.67, 15.85
Murphy v Bayliss (SC) unrep, 22 July 1976 .... 7.13
Murphy v Bord Telecom Éireann [1989] ILRM 53 .... 14.35, 14.48
.... 16.128, 16.157
Murphy v Dublin Corporation [1976] IR 143 .... 14.81
Murphy v Greene [1990] 2 IR 566 ....9.03-9.06
Murphy v Minister for Defence [1991] 2 IR 161 .... 7.24
Murphy v Stewart [1973] IR 97 .... 15.54
Murray v Ireland [1985] IR 532 (HC); [1991] ILRM 465 (SC) 15.54

N

National Union of Journalists v Sisk [1992] ILRM 96 .... 14.47
Nestor v Murphy [1979] IR 326 ....10.15, 11.02, 14.28, 14.30
....14.32-14.33, 14.36-14.37
Nocton v Lord Ashburton [1914] AC 932 .... 12.75, 12.77
Nolan, Re [1939] IR 388 .... 12.24
Norris v Attorney General [1984] IR 36 ....1.22, 4.47, 7.07, 12.54, 15.55
....15.62, 15.88, 15.128, 15.130, 17.17, 17.18
Norris v Ireland (1988) 13 EHRR 186 ...13.32, 15.88, 15.130, 17.11, 17.17
Northern Bank Finance Corporation Ltd v Charlton
[1979] IR 149 ....7.07, 12.76, 15.129

O

Ó Culacháin v Hunter Advertising Ltd [1990] 2 IR 431 ....14.39, 14.42
Ó Domhnaill v Merrick [1984] IR 151 .... 6.09, 12.50, 14.49
Ó Laighléis, in re [1960] IR 93 .... 12.17, 14.49, 17.17
.... 17.18-17.20, 17.23
Ó Laochdha v Johnson & Johnson (Ireland) Ltd [1991] 2 IR 287
....14.41, 14.42
Ó Monacháin v An Taoiseach [1986] ILRM 660 ....4.55
O'B v Patwell [1994] 2 ILRM 465 ....12.10
O'Brien v Bord na Móna [1983] IR 277 ....4.13
O'Brien v Brown 92 SCT 2718 ....4.17
O'Brien v Ireland [1991] 2 IR 387 ....14.32
O'Byrne v Minister for Finance [1959] IR 1 ....4.100
O'Callaghan v Attorney General [1993] 2 IR 17 ....6.105, 6.111
....15.83, 15.107
O'Connor, in re [1930] IR 623 ....4.113
O'Donovan v Attorney General [1961] IR 114 ....4.17, 15.84
O'Donovan v Cork County Council [1967] IR 173 .... 12.83-12.85
O'Dwyer v Cafolla Ltd (1950) 84 ILTR 44 ....14.69
O'H v O'H [1990] 2 IR 558 ....14.61
O'Leary v Wood Ltd [1964] IR 269 ....12.13
O'Neill v Ryan & Ryanair Ltd (No 3) [1992] 1 IR 166 ....4.21
O'Reilly & Judge v Director of Public Prosecutions
[1984] ILRM 224 ....5.93
O'Reilly v Cassidy [1955] 1 ILRM 306 ....4.92
O'Reilly v Limerick Corporation [1989] ILRM 181 .... 1.23, 4.17, 15.97
O'Shaughnessy v Attorney General (HC) unrep, 16 February 1971
....9.21-9.23
O'Sullivan v Leitrim County Council [1953] IR 71 ....14.69
Offences against the State (Amendment) Bill 1940, Re
[1940] IR 470 ....5.68, 12.17, 17.17
Oliver, Re 333 US 257 ....4.19
Ostime v Australian Mutual Provident Society [1960] AC 459 ....12.12

P

Park Hall School Ltd v Overend [1987] IR 1 ....12.82
PC, in re [1939] IR 305 ....15.43
Peilow v ffrench O'Carroll (1971) 105 ILTR 21 ....4.42
People (Attorney General) v Conmey [1975] IR 341 .... 7.24, 7.50, 12.61
People (Attorney General) v Coughlan (1968) 1 Frewen 325 ....12.10
People (Attorney General) v Dermody [1956] IR 307 ....12.10

People (Attorney General) v Doyle (1964) 101 ILTR 136 .... 12.09, 12.61
People (Attorney General) v Kennedy [1946] IR 517 .... 14.70, 15.102
People (Attorney General) v McGlynn [1967] IR 232 .... 14.17
People (Attorney General) v Mills (1955) 1 Frewen 153 .... 12.10
People (Attorney General) v Moore [1964] Ir Jur Rep 6 .... 12.29, 12.31
People (Attorney General) v O'Brien [1965] IR 142 .... 12.61, 15.83
People (Attorney General) v O'Brien [1966] IR 501 .... 15.83
People (Attorney General) v O'Dwyer [1972] IR 416 .... 12.42
People (Attorney General) v O'Neill [1964] Ir Jur Rep 1 .... 12.29
People (DPP) v Farrell [1978] IR 13 .... 14.58, 14.68
People (DPP) v Gilligan [1992] ILRM 769 .... 14.75
People (DPP) v Kenny [1990] 2 IR 110 .... 12.55, 12.61
People (DPP) v Lynch [1982] IR 64 .... 12.43, 12.61
People (DPP) v Rock [1994] 1 ILRM 66 .... 7.49, 12.10
People (DPP) v Shaw [1982] IR 1 .... 12.47, 12.61
People (DPP) v T (1988) 3 Frewen 141 .... 14.72
People (DPP) v Walsh [1980] IR 294 .... 12.55
People v Bell [1969] IR 24 .... 5.84, 9.39
People v Doran (1987) 3 Frewen 125 .... 6.109
People v Doyle (1943) 77 ILTR 108 .... 5.96
People v Earls [1969] IR 414 .... 7.45
People v Healy [1990] 2 IR 73 .... 9.18, 12.61
People v Kelly [1982] IR 90 .... 7.36, 14.72
People v Kelly (No 2) [1983] IR 1 .... 7.36, 14.22
People v Marley [1985] ILRM 17 .... 9.07
People v McDonagh (SC) unrep, 11 July 1996 .... 14.94
People v MacEoin [1978] IR 27 .... 4.92
People v McGlynn [1967] IR 232 .... 7.35
People v Murray [1977] IR 360 .... 7.36
People v O'Callaghan [1966] IR 501 .... 6.73
People v O'Shea [1982] IR 384 .... 7.29, 7.50, 12.58, 12.59
.... 15.101-15.104, 15.108
People v O'Shea (No 2) [1983] ILRM 592 .... 12.58
People v Pringle [1995] 2 IR 547 .... 7.47
People v Quilligan & O'Reilly [1986] IR 495 .... 5.89, 7.50, 12.58, 14.94
People v Quilligan & O'Reilly (No 2) [1989] IR 46 .... 7.50, 12.58-12.59
People v Quilligan & O'Reilly (No 3) [1993] 2 IR 305 .... 6.66, 7.50
People v Singer (1961) 1 Frewen 214 .... 9.07
People v Tiernan [1988] IR 250 .... 6.78
People v WM [1995] 1 IR 226 .... 4.22
People v Z [1994] 2 IR 476 .... 4.21
Pepper v Hart [1993] 1 All ER 42; (1993) 56 MLR 695 .... 14.88, 14.94

Phillips (Inspector of Taxes) v Bourne [1947] KB 533 ....14.80
Photo Production Ltd v Securicor Ltd [1978] 1 WLR 856 ....12.76
Pigs Marketing Board v Donnelly [1939] IR 413 ....13.65
Piller (Anton) KG v Manufacturing Processes Ltd [1976] Ch 55 ....10.11
Pine Valley Developments v Minister for the Environment
[1987] IR 2 ....13.44
Poe v Ullman 367 US 497 (1961) 15.128
Point Exhibition Co Ltd v Revenue Commissioners
[1993] 2 IR 551 ....14.69
Post Office v Estuary Radio Ltd [1968] 2 QB 740 ....14.90
Powerscourt Estates v Gallagher [1984] ILRM 123 ....10.11
Prendergast (WJ) & Son Ltd v Carlow County Council
[1990] ILRM 749 ....5.49, 7.24
Priestly v Fowler (1837) 3 M & W 1 ....12.67
Pringle v Ireland [1994] 1 ILRM 467 ....7.47

Q

Quinn v Wren [1985] IR 322; [1985] ILRM 411 ....14.46
Quinn, Application of [1974] IR 19 ....14.69
Quinn's Supermarket Ltd v Attorney General [1972] IR 1 ....15.138
Quirke v Folio Homes Ltd [1988] ILRM 496 ....1.23

R

R Ltd, in re [1989] IR 126 ....4.21
R v R [1984] IR 296 .... 5.43, 5.52, 5.58
R (Cooney) v Clinton [1935] IR 245 ....15.06-15.10
R (Kelly) v Maguire [1923] 2 IR 58 ....2.63
R (Moore) v O'Hanrahan [1927] IR 406 ....2.16
R (O'Brien) v Military Governor, North Dublin Union
[1924] 1 IR 32 ....15.10
R v Bakewell (1857) 7 E & B 848 ....13.01
R v Gibson (1887) 18 QBD 537 ....6.90
R v Norman [1924] 2 KB 315 ....12.29
R v O'Connell (1845) 7 Ir Law Rep 261 ....3.37
R v Peters (1886) 16 QBD 636 ....14.96
R v Pilkington (1971)..12.81
R v Stanley [1920] 2 KB 235 ....12.29
R v Taylor [1950] 2 KB 368 ....12.12, 12.30
R v Warwickshire County Council, ex parte Johnson
[1993] 1 All ER 299...14.94
Rafferty v Crowley [1984] ILRM 350 .... 11.02, 13.32, 14.30
.... 14.31, 14.37, 15.62

Rahill v Brady [1971] IR 69 .... 14.14, 14.96
Ramsey (WT) Ltd v IRC [1982] AC 300 .... 14.09
Rayner v Paskell & Another (1971) 12.81
Regulation of Information (Services Outside the State for the Termination of Pregnancies) Bill 1995, Re [1995] 1 IR 1 .... 1.22, 4.23, 5.68, 15.89 .... 15.109, 15.134-6
Reilly v Gill (1951) 85 ILTR 165 .... 12.15
Revenue Commissioners v Doorley [1933] IR 750 .... 14.09, 14.59
Rexi Irish Mink Ltd v Dublin County Council [1972] IR 123, at 130 .. 12.60
Rice v Begley [1920] 1 IR 243 .... 13.47
Robertson v Fleming (1861) 4 Macq 167 .... 12.79
Robinson v National Bank of Ireland 1916 SC (HL) 150 .... 12.75
Roche v Peilow [1985] IR 232 .... 12.84, 12.85
Roe v Blood Transfusion Service Board [1996] 1 ILRM 555 .... 4.22
Roe v Wade, 410 US 113 (1972) 15.130
Rohan Construction Ltd v Insurance Corporation of Ireland plc [1988] ILRM 373 .... 12.78
Rondel v Worsley [1969] 1 AC 191 .... 12.82
Rooney v Minister for Agriculture and Food [1991] 2 IR 539 .... 13.44
Ross v Caunters [1980] Ch 297 .... 12.79
Rowe v Law [1978] IR 55 .... 13.47, 14.83
Russell v Fanning [1988] IR 505 .... 12.09, 12.18, 14.47, 15.39
Ryan v Attorney General [1965] IR 294 .... 15.45, 15.50-15.54, 15.77 .... 15.84, 15.103, 15.126-15.30
Ryan v Director of Public Prosecutions [1989] IR 399 .... 6.73
Ryan v Ireland [1989] IR 177 .... 15.45

S

S v Landy & Ors (Legal Aid Board) (HC) unrep, 10 February 1993 ..... 9.24
Saif Ali v Sydney Mitchell & Co [1980] AC 198 .... 12.82
Salomon v Commissioners of Customs and Excise [1967] 2 QB 306 .... 14.90
Savage v Director of Public Prosecutions [1982] ILRM 385 .... 5.93
School Attendance Bill 1942, Re [1943] IR 334 .... 5.68
Securities Trust Ltd v Hugh Moore & Alexander Ltd [1964] IR 417 .... 12.75
Shannon Realties v St Michel (Ville de) [1924] AC 185 .... 14.17
Shannon Regional Fisheries Board v An Bord Pleanála [1994] 3 IR 449 .... 14.05, 14.96
Shelly v Mahon [1990] 1 IR 36 .... 4.69, 4.110

Shipping (CW) Co Ltd v Limerick Harbour Commissioners [1989] ILRM 416 ....14.57, 14.68
Short v Dublin County Council [1982] ILRM 117 ....14.73
Simmons v Pennington & Son [1955] 1 WLR 183 ....12.84
Sirros v Moore [1975] QB 118 ....4.106
Society for the Protection of Unborn Children Ltd v Coogan [1989] IR 734 ....15.79, 15.130
Solicitors Act 1954, Re [1960] IR 239 .... 3.16, 4.13, 13.32
Solomons, Re [1949] IR 3 ....12.24
Somers v Erskine [1943] IR 348 .... 12.34, 12.76, 12.77
Sorrell v Finch [1977] AC 728 ....12.81
Sports Arena Ltd v O'Reilly [1987] IR 185 ....7.14, 7.30
State (Aer Lingus Teo) v Labour Court [1987] ILRM 373 ....8.43
State (Boyle) v Neylon [1986] IR 551 ....4.30, 5.82
State (Browne) v Feran [1967] IR 147 ....15.43
State (C) v Frawley [1976] IR 365 ....15.54
State (Clarke) v Roche [1986] IR 619 .... 4.13, 6.64, 11.02
State (Costello) v Bofin [1980] ILRM 233 ....8.39
State (Creedon) v Criminal Injuries Compensation Tribunal [1989] ILRM 104 ....8.41
State (D & D) v Groarke [1990] 1 IR 305 ....14.77
State (Dowling) v Kingston (No 2) [1937] IR 699 ....12.11
State (DPP) v Walsh [1981] IR 412 .... 4.107, 10.34, 14.49, 17.23
State (Duggan) v Tapley [1952] IR 62 ....12.11
State (Elm Developments) v An Bord Pleanála [1981] ILRM 108 ....14.76
State (Ennis) v Farrell [1966] IR 107 ....6.63, 6.67
State (Foley) v Carroll [1980] IR 150 ....12.10
State (Harkin) v O'Malley [1978] IR 269 ....12.09, 12.61
State (Harrington) v Wallace [1988] IR 290 ....13.61
State (Hayes) v Criminal Injuries Compensation Tribunal [1982] ILRM 210 ....8.41
State (Healy) v Donoghue [1976] IR 325 ....9.15, 9.18-9.23, 15.54, 15.63
State (Hunt) v Donovan [1975] IR 39 ....7.36
State (Kennedy) v Little [1931] IR 39 ....15.07
State (Kershaw) v Eastern Health Board [1985] ILRM 235 ....8.62
State (Killian) v Minister for Justice [1954] IR 207 ....4.34, 12.32
State (King) v Minister for Justice [1984] IR 169 ....4.98
State (Lynch) v Cooney [1982] IR 337 .... 4.37, 12.17, 12.32, 12.61
State (M) v Attorney General [1979] IR 73 ....15.54
State (McCarthy) v Lennon [1936] IR 485 ....15.07
State (McCormack) v Curran [1987] ILRM 225 ....5.93

State (McKeown) v Scully [1986] IR 524 .... 8.39
State (Minister for Lands and Fisheries) v Judge Sealy [1939] IR 21 .... 14.65
State (Murphy) v Johnson [1983] IR 235 .... 14.11
State (Murray) v McRann [1979] IR 133 .... 4.50
State (O'Connell) v Fawsitt [1986] IR 362 .... 6.09
State (O'Connor) v Ó Caomhanaigh [1963] IR 112 .... 14.51
State (O'Flaherty) v Ó Floinn [1954] IR 295 .... 4.05
State (Quinn) v Ryan [1965] IR 110 .... 4.37, 12.11, 12.12 .... 12.32, 12.35, 12.52
State (Raftis) v Leonard [1960] IR 381 .... 12.61
State (Rollinson) v Kelly [1984] IR 248 .... 14.11
State (Royle) v Kelly [1974] IR 259 .... 9.16
State (Ryan) v Lennon [1935] IR 170 .... 15.13-15.15, 15.128
State (Sheehan) v The Government of Ireland [1987] IR 550 .... 13.43-13.44 .... 13.72, 14.80
State (Sheerin) v Kennedy [1966] IR 379 .... 12.54
State (Smith) v Governor of Mountjoy Gaol (1964) 102 ILTR 93 .... 9.05
State (Smullen) v Duffy [1980] ILRM 46 .... 8.57
State (Turley) v Ó Floinn [1968] IR 245 .... 7.14
State (Walshe) v Murphy [1981] IR 275 .... 4.50, 4.64-4.68, 10.38
State (Williams) v Kelly [1970] IR 259 .... 4.42
Statens Control v Larsen [1978] ECR 1543 .... 14.48
Stuart (Carl) Ltd v Biotrace Ltd [1993] ILRM 633 .... 14.96
Stubbings v Webb [1993] 2 WLR 120 .... 14.94
Subramaniam v Public Prosecutor [1956] 1 WLR 965 .... 6.90
Sussex Peerage Case (1844) 11 Cl & Fin 85 .... 14.13

T

Tate v Minister for Social Welfare [1995] 1 IR 419 .... 15.67 .... 16.143, 16.157
Taylor v Ryan (HC) unrep, 10 March 1983 .... 12.84
Texaco (Ireland) Ltd v Murphy [1991] 2 IR 449 .... 14.25, 14.59
Tileston v Ullman 129 Conn 84 .... 15.128
Tilson, in re [1951] IR 1 .... 15.43
Times Newspapers Ltd v United Kingdom (1979) 2 EHRR 245 .... 17.23
Tormey v Ireland [1985] IR 289 .... 4.41, 5.52, 5.82, 7.13 .... 7.29, 15.109
Tradax Ltd v Irish Grain Board Ltd [1984] IR 1 .... 3.79
Transactus Investments Ltd v Dublin Corporation [1985] IR 501 .... 8.48
Travers v Ryan [1985] ILRM 343 .... 9.08
Tromso Sparebank v Beirne (No 2) [1989] ILRM 257 .... 6.50, 12.36
Truloc Ltd v McMenamin [1994] 1 ILRM 151 .... 14.22

Trustees of Kinsale Yacht Club v Commissioner of Valuation [1994] 1 ILRM 457 .... 14.08, 14.59, 14.96
Tuck & Sons v Preister (1887) 19 QBD 629 .... 14.24

U

Union of India v Jasso AIR 1962 Punj 315 (FB) 15.43
United Bars Ltd & Ors, in re (HC) unrep, 3 June 1988 .... 12.36
United States Tobacco International Inc v Minister for Health [1990] 1 IR 394 .... 14.71
United States v Lee 106 US 196 (1882) 15.43
Unwin v Hanson [1891] 2 QB 115 .... 14.24

V

Van Gend en Loos v Nederlandse Belastingenadministratie [1963] ECR 1 .... 16.53-16.57, 16.63, 16.68 .... 16.113, 16.117, 16.127-16.131, 16.140
Vere (de) decd, Re [1961] IR 224 .... 12.25
Von Colson & Kamann v Land Nordrhein-Westfalen [1984] ECR 1891 .... 14.48

W

Wadda v Ireland [1994] ILRM 126 .... 14.92
Waldron v Junior Army & Navy Stores [1910] 2 IR 318 .... 12.65
Wall v Hegarty & Callanan [1980] ILRM 124 .... 10.04, 11.02, 12.47 .... 12.79, 12.80
Walsh v Minister for Local Government [1929] IR 377 .... 12.61
Walsh v President of the Circuit Court & DPP [1989] ILRM 325 .... 12.27
Warburton v Loveland (1828) 1 Hud & B 623 .... 14.17
Ward of Court, Re [1995] 2 ILRM 401 .... 1.22, 5.61, 15.89 .... 15.136-15.138
Ward v Kinahan Electrical Ltd [1984] IR 292 .... 5.29
Wavin Pipes Ltd v Hepworth Iron Co Ltd [1982] 8 FSR 32 .... 12.23 .... 14.90, 14.92
Webb v Ireland [1988] IR 353 .... 15.46
Weekes v Revenue Commissioners [1989] ILRM 165 .... 8.61, 14.29
Welch v Bowmaker (Ireland) Ltd [1980] IR 251 .... 14.72
Woods (Applications of) [1970] IR 154 .... 9.09
Worth Library, in re [1995] 2 IR 301 .... 3.59
Wunder v Hospitals Trust (1940) Ltd (HC), unrep, 1 April 1966 .... 9.06

Y

Young v Bristol Aeroplane Co Ltd [1944] KB 718 .... 12.23

Chapter 1

Introduction to the Irish Legal System

[1] INTRODUCTION

[1.01] Popular perceptions of the law are derived from a variety of sources. From childhood thoughts which often perceive law in terms of policing (with the police often being referred to as 'the law') to a diverse range of cultural sources, which include literature, cinema and television, certain images of the law are conveyed. Be it the nostalgic warmth of *Rumpole of the Bailey* or the corporate glamour of *LA Law* pictures of the law and lawyers are portrayed. While these might be distorted and do not reflect the reality as recognised by lawyers they do contain grains of truth. Cumulatively they point to the law as being a process or a system which possesses an authority and mechanisms of enforcement. Later chapters will deal with the history of the Irish legal system, its institutions and, crucially, the sources of law in which particular legal rules are located. At this stage it is sufficient to observe that those rules are found in various sources of law which are the product of different legal institutions such as the courts and the legislature.

[1.02] Our study is primarily functional in that it concentrates on the relationship between legal institutions and sources of law. We concentrate on the processes of law-making and adjudicating which are central to the legal system and which are the reality of a lawyer's professional life. However, a more abstract examination would focus on what has been called the 'ideational'[1] source of law, that is the theoretical or conceptual source of the law. Such a source is essentially meta-legal and involves the notion of some underlying belief or theory which confers validity on the legal system and the laws which it produces. This might involve belief in a deity ('the will of God'), nature, human reason, a particular political philosophy or the consent of the people. This is to enter into the domain where legal theory interacts with politics and philosophy. While our focus is, in the main, institutional this broader dimension is important in two respects. The first is that it emphasises that law does not exist in isolation from a wider community of ideas and beliefs and that law-making in one way or another draws on them. Second, and more specifically, the Constitution of Ireland

1. See generally Goodrich, *Reading the Law* (Basil Blackwell, 1986) pp 4-13.

1937, which is the source of that important body of law known as constitutional law, spans both the institutional and ideational. As an element of the legal system the Constitution is one of its institutions yet it is drafted in terms which are comparatively vague and aspirational, leaving it for the interpreter to ascertain its meaning in the light of its underlying values. This theme will be considered in greater depth in the chapter on the Constitution.[2]

[1.03] The law is one part of a set of processes - social, political, economic and cultural - which shape and direct the development of society. Like other mechanisms the law seeks to govern human behaviour either by prohibiting identified forms of conduct or by attaching particular consequences to specified forms of behaviour. We are all familiar with the prohibitions on unlawful killing, injuring or depriving of property which are central to the criminal law. Equally most of us are aware of the obligation to make recompense, by means of compensation, to those who are harmed by our conduct, which is the focus of the civil, or private, law. But these prohibitions and obligations are shared with other normative systems such as morality, religion or etiquette. Moreover, the latter with their implicit threats of damnation, divine retribution or social ostracism might be more effective in ensuring that people obey the various commands. However, what is distinctive about law is that it possesses a binding or obligatory quality which is enforceable, either by means of punishment or a re-adjustment of rights and liabilities. It is this quality, which we might call the force of law, which sets it apart from the others.

[2] Law and Laws

[1.04] The English language lacks the terminology to reflect the distinction made in Latin between *ius* and *lex*, in French between *droit* and *loi* and in German between *Recht* and *Gesetz*. The term 'law' is used to mean both the general body or system of law and individual rules of law.[3] The distinction was summarised by one commentator thus:[4]

> "We commonly speak of both law and laws…and these terms, though not used with precision point to two different aspects under which legal science may be approached. The laws of a country are thought of as

2. See generally paras **[15.98]-[15.138]**.
3. See also Allott, *The Limits of Law* (Butterworths, 1980) where 'law' is used in three senses, each of which is represented by a different typeface. There 'law' is used to mean (i) the general concept of legal institutions, as opposed to any occurrence of them (ii) a particular legal system and (iii) a particular rule in a legal system.
4. Geldart, *Introduction to English Law* 10th ed (Oxford University Press, 1991) p 1 (emphasis in original).

> separate, distinct, individual rules; the law of a country, however much we may analyse it into separate rules, is something more that the mere sum of such rules. It is rather a whole, a system which orders our conduct; in which the separate rules have their place and their relation to each other and to the whole; which is never completely exhausted by any analysis, however far the analysis may be pushed, and however much the analysis may be necessary to our understanding of the whole. Thus each rule which we call *a* law is part of the whole we call *the* law. Lawyers generally speak of *law*; laymen more often of *laws*."

This quotation encapsulates the focus of this work. As explained above our concern is with the functioning of the legal system rather than particular individual rules. Indeed to the extent that we encounter individual rules of law it is principally to illustrate some particular feature of the legal system. It is important to realise that a complete understanding of legal rules ('the laws') is necessarily based on an understanding of the legal system ('the law'). The latter explains the origin of the rules, their relationship with one another and their place in the overall system. But while the law is composed of laws it also embraces something more; the whole is greater than the sum of its parts. The manner in which laws are created and developed, their interpretation and application are part of the law and it is that which is our central concern.

[1.05] One of the principal elements of a study of a legal system is that it identifies the sources from which rules are derived. Those which are most readily identifiable are laws which have a distinct and separate origin, in other words laws which are specifically created. These laws bear the general title *legislation*, a term which denotes their origin as enacted laws. In the main, legislation consists of Acts of the Oireachtas (sometimes called *statute law*) and *delegated*, or *secondary, legislation*. Legislation accounts for large sections of the law as might be expected in an era where the State assumes the principal regulatory role in society. However, other laws have not been created in this manner but have emerged from or developed out of the legal system. By and large the origin of these laws lies in judicial decisions which have been delivered over the past centuries and which have incrementally grown to produce an identifiable body of law which is called the *common law*. Through the practice of *precedent*, by which a court is required to follow an earlier similar decision, judicial decisions enjoy the force of law. The common law shaped and defined the principal legal categories or subjects into which laws are placed - criminal law, contract law, law of torts, land law and the like. The essential principles and concepts which underlie these areas of the law were developed by the courts as common law rules and despite the more recent enactment of legislative rules the common law remains a significant component of the legal system. This is reflected in the fact that the Irish legal system is called a common law system.

[3] THE IRISH LEGAL SYSTEM AS A COMMON LAW SYSTEM

[1.06] The Irish legal system belongs to a family of legal systems known as common law systems. The original common law system was that which was established in England by the Normans after the invasion of 1066. Being the first country colonised by the Normans after England, Ireland has been described a providing the common law's first adventure.[5] Indeed, much of the history of the common law in Ireland is a direct mirror image of that which occurred in England. Subsequently the common law was introduced into each country which was colonised by the English or British and, with some exceptions, it is the system which is found in those countries which formerly made up the British empire.[6] Thus 49 states of the United States of America (the exception is Louisiana which was colonised by the French), the provinces of Canada (with the exception of Quebec which was a French colony), Australia, New Zealand, India, Nigeria and Kenya possess common law systems. In general, common law systems operate in the anglophone world. The other major family of systems consists of civil law systems which operate in continental European countries and their former colonies.

[1.07] The description common law system indicates both the English origin of a system and its central feature, which is that it possesses an identifiable body of law called the common law. As noted in the preceding paragraph this is the body of law which grew out of centuries of judicial decisions and which has established the major categories into which legal rules are placed. The growth of this body of law has been gradual and has occurred over the nine centuries since its initial establishment in England by the Normans. Historically the common law accounted for the vast bulk of the law and it remains as an important source of law. Decisions reached by the courts several centuries ago still enjoy the force of law and will do so until they are altered by some other legal rule. Common law is sometimes, inaccurately, referred to as case law, which reflects its significant feature, namely that it is made by judges, not legislators. It might be noted that the incremental development of the common law was essentially pragmatic. Since it depended on cases being initiated in the courts by aggrieved parties the law responded to actual rather than anticipated problems. In contrast, the law in a civil law system is contained in comprehensive codes which are enacted by

---

5. Johnston, 'The First Adventure of the Common Law' (1920) 36 LQR 9.
6. Scotland, South Africa and Sri Lanka resisted the wholesale incorporation of the common law and have mixed systems.

legislators and which attempt to provide for every legal contingency. Case law, in French called *la jurisprudence*, has a lesser significance and lacks the quality of enjoying the force of law.

[1.08] The term common law bears a third meaning. It refers to a body of law which was developed in the common law courts. In this sense it may be contrasted with *equity* which is a body of law which was developed in and administered by the Court of Chancery. At its inception the common law, through a rigorous adherence to precedent, was inflexible and, in particular, was incapable of reacting to provide a remedy for individual cases of injustice. As a result aggrieved litigants who felt that they suffered an injustice at the hands of the common law courts petitioned the King for relief. In time, as the number of petitions increased, the task of deciding these petitions was assigned to the Lord Chancellor, the King's chief minister. The Lord Chancellor, who often was a cleric and came from a canon law background, determined these petitions on the basis of their individual merits in the Court of Chancery. The essence of equity was that unlike the common law it was flexible, remedial and designed to meet the needs of individual justice. Eventually equity grew into a coherent body of law and by the beginning of the 19th century it had become as rigid as the common law which it was designed to supplement. Equity now exists as a distinct body of rules which is applied in conjunction with common law rules.

[4] Sources of Law

[1.09] Sources of law are the legal origins of rules. They are understood in an institutional sense rather than a broader political or socio-legal sense. That is not to say that the latter is unimportant or that it is not an area worthy of study in it own right. However, from a lawyer's perspective a crucial feature of a legal system is that it identifies the origins of different rules and establishes their relations to one another. A lawyer must know where to find particular rules which apply to the problem with which he or she is presented.[7] Of equal importance the lawyer must know where different rules fit into an overall scheme and, where conflict arises, which is to prevail. Thus the legal system sets out various sources of law within a hierarchical framework, so that some sources will prevail over others in the event of conflict. In the Irish legal system we can identify four principal, or primary, sources of law.

7. See O'Malley, *The Round Hall Guide to Sources of Law* (Round Hall Press, 1993).

Common law[8]

[1.10] This source of law originally was the core of the laws enforced by the system. It consists of the hundreds of thousands of decisions which have been delivered by the courts over the centuries and which, by virtue of the demands of the doctrine of precedent, enjoy binding force of law. The accumulation of these decisions over time allowed the common law to grow into a coherent body of law. To this day significant areas of the law are governed by common law rules unaffected by rules derived from other sources.

Legislation[9]

[1.11] This source consists of law enacted by an agency which is conferred with law-making power. Unlike the common law it is specifically created and its origin is clearly identifiable in a particular exercise of law-making. Legislation was the mechanism by which common law rules were altered. In the past this was based on the doctrine of parliamentary supremacy, but now rests on the provision of the Constitution of Ireland 1937 which designates the Oireachtas as the sole law-making body in the State.[10] Statute law (Acts of the Oireachtas) is enacted by the Oireachtas, the National Parliament. Secondary legislation is enacted by bodies or individuals which are conferred with that power by statute.

The Constitution[11]

[1.12] The Constitution was enacted by the People in a referendum which was held in 1937. The adoption of a written constitution containing fundamental principles and guarantees of individual rights marked a break from the 'British' tradition. The British Constitution is essentially unwritten and flexible and English law lacks a concept of fundamental rights which are judicially enforceable. The Constitution is the basic law of the State and it takes precedence over other, inferior, sources of law. Indeed, rules which derive from those sources depend on the Constitution for their validity. A common law or legislative rule which conflicts with a provision of the Constitution is invalid and, consequently, has no legal effect. The Constitution establishes the State and its institutions and articulates in broad terms the fundamental principles on which the governance of the State is based. The Constitution may be amended only by popular referendum and in

8. See generally paras **[12.01]-[12.84]**.
9. See generally paras **[13.01]-[13.80]**.
10. Article 15.2.
11. See generally paras **[15.17]-[15.140]**.

this respect it is rigid. Nevertheless, its provisions are amenable to interpretation which function is entrusted to the courts who, given the manner in which it is drafted, enjoy a considerable discretion in this regard. Once the courts have determined the interpretation of a provision it may only be overturned either by a later judicial decision or by a referendum. In practice the latter rarely happens with the result that the courts enjoy extensive power in determining the meaning of the Constitution. Since the courts under the guise of constitutional interpretation have considered the validity of a wide range of laws which have a bearing on social and economic matters the significance of the courts' role extends beyond the legal domain into the political. Decisions of the courts on matters of constitutional law have affected the formulation of economic and social policy. The growth of constitutional law and, the accompanying role of the courts in the governance of the State, is probably the most significant legal development since 1922.

European Community law[12]

[1.13] From the perspective of international organisations a distinctive feature of the European Communities is that they possess their own legal system complete with a body of law which is applicable and enforceable in each member state. The legal system is presided over by the Court of Justice of the European Communities which sits in Luxembourg. Community law enjoys supremacy over conflicting national law (including national constitutional provisions) both as a matter of Community law and national law. From the Community law stance supremacy is established in the Treaties which established the Communities and which require member states to accede to Community supremacy. It followed that entry to the European Communities entailed yielding to Community law and to this extent national sovereignty was curtailed. In Ireland the Constitution was amended by the insertion of a provision which reflected this arrangement.[13] Within its sphere of competence, which is set out in the various Community Treaties, European Community law enjoys unquestioned supremacy. In practice this has affected, in the main, the laws governing economic and social matters and significant areas of national law which lie beyond the Communities' remit have remained unaffected.

12. See generally paras **[16.01]**-**[16.157]**.

13. Article 29.4.3°. The effect of this was to authorise membership of the Communities. Subsequent amendments were adopted to facilitate more recent developments in the Communities' structure and competences.

[1.14] Aside from the formal sources of law which are outlined in the preceding paragraphs other influences (or secondary sources) should be noted. These do not enjoy the force of law *per se* but might prove to be significant either because they are incorporated into law by a law-making act or influence the interpretation of a law by an adjudicative body. These include:

Custom

[1.15] With the establishment of the common law in both England and Ireland the customary law which preceded it was progressively eliminated. In Ireland the common law competed with the native Irish customary law, the Brehon law, for a number of centuries before the latter was finally expunged in the early 17th century. However, custom still has a residual role and the common law has recognised and tolerated the existence of customs which are local or particular in nature. In this context a custom is a habitual practice which by virtue of continuous practice and general acquiescence acquires the legal force. This is based on the assumed consent of those who are materially affected by the custom. The custom operates in circumstances which might otherwise be governed by a general common law rule. Two conditions must be satisfied before a custom may enjoy the force of law. One is that it is certain, reasonable and continuous. The other is that it exists in a particular locality in respect of some particular matter and other matters are governed by the ordinary common law. The law does not recognise general customs which extend throughout the State. They have either been eliminated or incorporated into, and become part of, the common law itself.

International law[14]

[1.16] International law is the body of law which governs states in their relationships with one another. It consists of a variety of sources including customary international law, treaties and international decisions of judicial bodies. In international law terms the Irish legal system is dualist, that is to become part of domestic law an international measure must be specifically incorporated. This is reflected in the provision of the Constitution which requires an Act of the Oireachtas to incorporate treaties into domestic law.[15] Nevertheless, international law might prove to be influential. Article 29.3 of the Constitution provides that the State acccepts the generally recognised principles of international law in its relations with other states, a provision which might be invoked in domestic legal proceedings. The courts also adopt a presumption of compatibility with international law when

14. See generally paras **[17.01]-[17.26]**.
15. Article 29.6.

interpreting legislation,[16] which indirectly might ensure that international legal obligations are matched by domestic provisions. An important international legal instrument is the European Convention on Human Rights which the State has ratified. The Convention, which should not be confused with European Community law, establishes a regime for the protection of the rights of the individual in signatory states and complaints are adjudicated by the European Court of Human Rights which sits in Strasbourg. The State is expected as a matter of international law to give effect to the Court's rulings but, of course, this is not enforceable in domestic law. However, the Convention might be invoked by an Irish court when it interprets a domestic legal rule.

Canon law

[1.17] Canon law is the law of the Christian Church. Originally it consisted of an unsystematic series of canons, but it became codified by the late medieval period. In general canon law exists separately from the secular law of the State and does not enjoy the force of law. However, in some circumstances legal rules, especially in the area of marriage law, have been shaped by their canon law equivalents.

Commentaries and scholarly writing

[1.18] In some instances a formal legal rule might be lacking and recourse is had to the writings of recognised commentators and scholars. From the medieval period onwards the works of pre-eminent writers, such as Coke,[17] Hale[18] and Blackstone,[19] were relied on and treated as being authoritative. In fact, their writings were accorded a status which approached that of judicial decisions. In the 20th century the growth of the academic branch of the legal community has been accompanied by a commensurate volume of legal writing, consisting of textbooks, encyclopediae, articles in scholarly journals and the like. Again these writings might be relied on but unlike those of the medieval jurists they are only 'persuasive' with courts being free to 'adopt' their conclusions as they consider appropriate.

Intellectual influences

[1.19] We have already noted that this text does not examine in detail the more general political context within which legal principles and rules are made. Nonetheless, it is important to note that they are not made in an

16. See para **[14.49]**.
17. *Institutes*.
18. *Pleas of the Crown*.
19. *Commentaries on the Laws of England*.

intellectual vacuum. Legislators and judges alike are influenced by intellectual and philosophical concepts in the formulation of principles and rules. Law students must examine these concepts as part of their study of legal theory or jurisprudence, the science of law. Many theories of law have been put forward over the centuries, and these form the basis for courses on legal theory or jurisprudence. Central to many of these is whether legal principles and rules ought to be based on certain core moral principles or whether morality should play little or no role in the formulation of legal rules.

[1.20] We have already noted that, prior to 1922, the legal principles and rules of the Irish legal system were determined in England. Throughout the 19th century, many important reforms in the legal system were influenced by the writings of the political philosopher Jeremy Bentham, who developed the concept of utilitarianism.[20] He argued that political and legal change should be based on the principle of utility, that is, seeking to achieve an increase in the overall benefits (or 'pleasures') of society.[21] Bentham's views, and those of other utilitarians, and liberals such as John Stuart Mill, remain influential in the development of legal principles and rules in England and Ireland in the 20th century. The close association between the utility principle and efficiency or cost-effectiveness formed the basis for another theory called the Economic Analysis of Law, which was developed in the 1970s by the American lawyer Richard Posner, then a Professor of Law and later a senior judge in the United States federal court system. Utilitarianism and the Economic Analysis of Law have a wide application; they are of particular relevance to the legal regulation of business, exemplified in the mixed economies of many States, including Ireland, and expressed in many aspects of European Community law. They may also be of relevance in the reolution of liability in road traffic accidents.[22] The concept of cost-effectiveness and of value for money in the provision of State services has also been deployed in the context of recent proposals for reform of the Irish court system.[23]

[1.21] The content of legal rules and principles in England was also influenced by the Christian tradition, whose theological principles have been developed by the theory of natural law.[24] Christian and religious teaching was highly influential in the formulation of legislation in the Irish Free State and in Ireland between the 1920s and 1960s and the views of the Roman

20. See para **[2.21]**.
21. See further paras **[15.118]-[15.119]**.
22. See Carolan, 'Economic Analysis and the Law: An Introduction' (1995) 13 ILT 162.
23. See *First Report of the Working Group on a Courts Commission: Management and Financing of the Courts* (Pn 2960, 1996), discussed at para **[4.130]**.
24. See paras **[15.113]-[15.125]**.

Catholic hierarchy in particular weighed heavily with legislators.[25] Indeed, the Constitution of Ireland 1937 referred to the 'special position' of the Roman Catholic church 'as the guardian of the Faith professed by the great majority of the citizens'.[26] This provision was removed from the Constitution in 1972.[27] In recent years, the influence of the Roman Catholic church has been less marked. This can be seen, for example, in the enactment of legislation removing virtually all restrictions on the use of contraceptives, including condoms and femidoms,[28] the interpretation of the Constitution as permitting termination of pregnancy, at least in limited circumstances,[29] the decriminalisation of consensual sexual relations between homosexual men[30] and the narrow approval in a 1995 constitutional referendum of the removal of a ban on divorce.[31]

[1.22] In certain areas of law, the combined influence of Christian thought and of utilitarianism can be seen. Thus, the neighbour principle developed in the English case *Donoghue v Stevenson*[32] owes its origins, at least in part, to the biblical parable of the Good Samaritan. However, the later development of the neighbour principle, both in Britain and Ireland, seems to owe more to utilitarian concepts than to Christianity.[33] Natural law and utilitarianism have also been referred to in a number of decisions of the Supreme Court concerning constitutional judicial review.[34] In 1995, the Supreme Court rejected the concept that the natural law theory took priority over the text of the 1937 Constitution[35] but also accepted that, since the Constitution reflects

---

25. This influence is traced in textbooks on Irish history, such as Lee, *Ireland 1912 - 1985* (Cambridge UP, 1990).
26. On its origins, see Keogh, 'The Constitutional Revolution: An Analysis of the Making of the Constitution', in Litton (ed), *The Constitution of Ireland 1937-1987* (Institute of Public Administration, 1987).
27. See para **[15.72]**.
28. Health (Family Planning) Acts 1979 to 1993: see para **[15.88]**.
29. *Attorney General v X* [1992] 1 IR 1: see paras **[15.131]-[15.133]**.
30. Criminal Law (Sexual Offences) Act 1993: see paras **[15.130]** and **[17.18]**.
31. Fifteenth Amendment of the Constitution Act 1996: see paras **[15.90]-[15.91]**.
32. [1932] AC 562: see para **[12.71]**.
33. Eg the judgment of Lord Denning MR (the highly influential former Master of the Rolls, judicial head of the civil division of the English Court of Appeal: see para **[2.37]**) in *Dutton v Bognor Regis UDC* [1972] 1 QB 373 and the decision of the Irish Supreme Court in *Keane v Electricity Supply Board* [1981] IR 44. See further Carolan, *op cit*, and paras **[12.70]-[12.85]**.
34. *McGee v Attorney General* [1974] IR 284 (para **[15.128]**) and *Norris v Attorney General* [1984] IR 36 (para **[15.129]**).
35. *In re the Regulation of Information (Services Outside the State for the Termination of Pregnancies) Bill 1995* [1995] 1 IR 1: para **[15.134]**.

religious and spiritual values, these remain important in the development of legal principles.[36]

[1.23] Other influential political theories have also featured in decisions of the courts. Thus, the distinction between communitarian and distributive justice, developed by the Greek philosopher Aristotle, was used to describe the division between the role of the judiciary, who determine whether the rights of citizens have been breached by the State, and the executive and legislature, who have political responsibility for the distribution of State resources.[37] The growing concern for gender equality and gender studies have also been influential in constitutional litigation and in the wider area of law reform.[38] Finally, we should note that while at least one judge found 'much appeal' in the maxim of Karl Marx, 'From each according to his ability, to each according to his need', it was rejected as an appropriate aid to statutory interpretation.[39]

Divisions of the law

[1.24] The various sources of law do not exist as a homogenous whole but are broken down into various components or divisions (see Figure 1.01). These divisions have emerged over time with some being recognised since the early years of the common law. The first distinction to be drawn is that between *substantive law* and *procedural*, or *adjectival*, *law*. Substantive law embraces the different legal subjects that confer rights or impose obligations and liabilities. Procedural law is that which implements substantive law and consists of the law of civil and criminal procedure and the law of evidence.

[1.25] Substantive law may be further divided into *public law* and *private law*. The distinction between the two is not wholly clear-cut,[40] but broadly speaking public law is that which pertains to the State, its agencies or which affects the public interest. Public law embraces:

Constitutional law, which is the body of law which has grown out of the Constitution and it affects the State in its most fundamental respects. It is

---

36. *In re a Ward of Court* [1995] 2 ILRM 401: para **[15.136]**.

37. *O'Reilly v Limerick Corporation* [1989] ILRM 181: see para **[15.97]**.

38. *de Burca v Attorney General* [1976] IR 38 (see para **[15.83]**). See also Connelly (ed), *Gender and the Law in Ireland* (Oak Tree Press, 1993), which focuses on the growing impact of women in the legal profession and the impact of gender equality studies in the formulation of laws.

39. *Quirke v Folio Homes Ltd* [1988] ILRM 496, at 500 *per* McCarthy J, quoting Marx, *Critique of the Gotha Programme*.

40. See Harlow, '"Public" and "Private" Law: Definition without Distinction' (1980) 43 MLR 1.

concerned with the powers and functioning of the State and with the rights of the individual which are guaranteed by the Constitution.

Administrative law is the body of law which governs the administration of the State and the operation of public authorities. It could be considered to be a cousin of constitutional law but while the latter is concerned largely with issues of principle administrative law is concerned with matters of detail.[41] The range of bodies which are subject to administrative law is broad and includes the executive, individual Ministers, semi-state bodies, the Gardaí, the Defence Forces, prison governors and statutory bodies.

Criminal law defines conduct which is prohibited and provides punishment for breach of its prohibitions. In general, the investigation and prosecution of offences is a public matter and is undertaken by public agencies such as the Gardaí and the Director of Public Prosecutions.

[1.26] Private law is, in the main, concerned with individual relationships in which there is no significant public interest. It should be noted that public bodies are also subject to private law when they act in the same capacity as private bodies. It is more difficult to divide private law into individual subjects. It is convenient to employ two overlapping classifications. The first consists of the 'traditional' legal subjects that form the 'core' of private law:

Contract law is that body of law which governs voluntary relationships between two or more parties.[42] It identifies the agreements which the law considers to be binding, provides for their interpretation and enforcement.

The *law of torts* is concerned with private wrongs which usually result in injury to another. It includes a variety of wrongs such as assault, battery, false imprisonment, defamation and negligence. There is an obvious overlap with the criminal law, but the purpose of the law of torts is to provide compensation for the injured party by the wrongdoer, rather than with punishment of the wrongdoer.

Property law is the body of law which governs the ownership of property. It may be further divided into *real property* (in the main land and interests in land) and *personal property* (both tangibles and intangibles).

[1.27] The second subdivision of private law is to focus on the areas of activity or social life around which distinctive and identifiable bodies of law

41. See Hogan & Morgan, *Administrative Law in Ireland* 2nd ed (Sweet & Maxwell, 1991) p 3 and paras **[8.01]**-**[8.02]**.

42. See Friel, *The Law of Contract* (Round Hall Press, 1995) p 1.

have grown or been identified. Each of these bodies contains relevant elements of contract law, the law of torts and property law. These subjects, whose titles are self-explanatory, include *family law*, *company law*, *labour law*, *commercial law*, *intellectual property* and the like.

Figure 1.01 sets out the foregoing divisions and classifications.

.

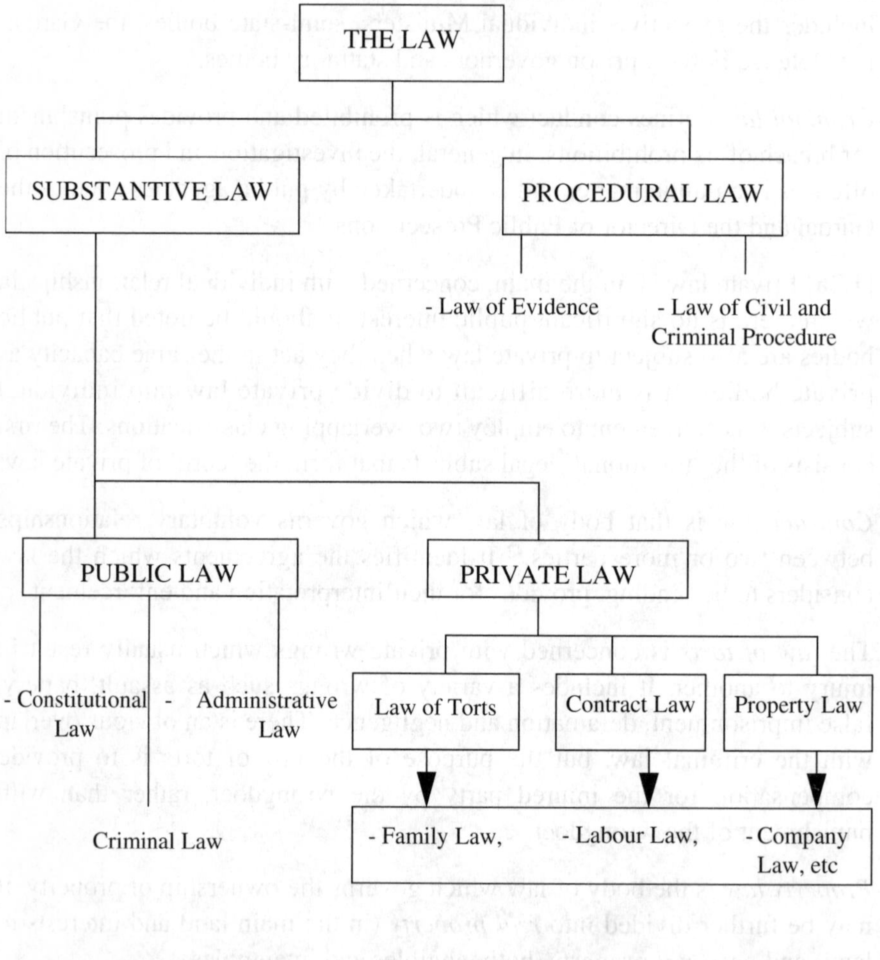

Figure 1.01

[1.28] It should be realised that the various subjects into which the law is divided overlap to a degree and that a legal problem might invoke several different bodies of law. For instance, an unlawful attack would result in criminal proceedings for assault or battery initiated by the Gardaí or the Director of Public Prosecutions; but the same event might also be the subject of civil proceedings for the torts of assault and/or battery initiated by the victim. Moreover, a civil or private law dispute might embrace several different subjects. A client who suffers loss due to the negligent conduct of his or her solicitor would have a claim for both breach of contract and the tort of negligence.

Common expressions

[1.29] It will be obvious, at this stage, that vital terms such as common law and civil law are used in different senses which should be distinguished. It might be helpful if the various meanings which such terms bear were set out.

(i) Common law A general description of the Irish legal system and others of English origin	*Civil law* A general description of the legal systems of continental European countries
(ii) Common law Law developed by the courts; 'case law'	*Legislation* Law enacted by parliament ('statute law') or a delegated body ('delegated legislation')
(iii) Common law Law developed by the common law courts; a subset of common law sense (ii)	*Equity* Law developed in the Court of Chancery to supplement that developed in the common law courts
(iv) Civil law The secular law of the State; applicable to all	*Canon law* Church law; operates within the confines of that body
(v) Civil law Private law; one of the principal divisions of substantive law	*Public law* Law involving the public interest; one of the principal divisions of substantive law

Legal personality

[1.30] In respect of those who are subject to its commands the law recognises different forms of legal personality. A legal person is an individual or entity to which, for the purposes of the law, the character of being a 'person' is attributed. It is obvious that human beings possess this capacity and they are known as *natural persons*. In addition, however, the law recognises artificial entities which possesses legal personality. The most common such entity is a *corporation* which may be created by one of a number of devices. In the past corporations were created by royal charter, but this device is now redundant; examples of such corporations include universities, the Royal College of Surgeons and certain trading companies.[43] A second device is the creation of particular corporations by legislation; this is most commonly the case with 'semi-state' bodies such as An Post, Bord Telecom Éireann and the Electricity Supply Board. The third device, which is the most frequently employed nowadays, is the voluntary creation of a corporation by a number of individuals in the manner prescribed by the companies legislation which is applicable at the time. In each case the corporation is a separate legal entity from its members, and it continues in existence regardless of the fates of its individual members. Such corporations are sometimes known as *corporations aggregate*, a term which distinguishes them from *corporations sole*. The latter are essentially offices which are occupied by individuals, such as the President and Government Ministers of State, and are typically designated as such by legislation. The office is legally distinct from the holder and survives changes in its occupation - the legal incidents attach to the office rather than the individual. Thus, proceedings which are commenced against, say, the Minister for Health will continue despite a new individual being appointed to that office.

[1.31] Like natural persons corporations are, in general, subject to the law. They are capable of acting in their own capacity as 'persons'- of owning property, entering into contracts, suing and being sued. On the other hand, there are certain transactions, such as marrying and making wills, which are unique to human persons and cannot be conducted by a corporation. But with that caveat in mind it can be said that corporations are subject to the general body of private law in much the same manner as natural persons. In respect of public law the matter is less straight-forward. Corporations in general, unlike their individual members, do not enjoy the guarantees of constitutional rights. Moreover, the extent to which a corporation is subject to the criminal law is uncertain. It is only with some difficulty that a corporation can be punished, as unlike a human being it is said to have 'no soul to damn, no body to kick.'[44] In other words the physical sanctions which were traditionally associated with the criminal law could not be enforced against an artificial person. Likewise, an artificial person lacks a conscience or moral sense which might be said to be affected by the condemnation which is implicit in criminal punishment. Moreover, the 'acts' of an artificial person lack the element of culpability which underlies most criminal offences.

43. In many cases the royal charters have been supplanted by legislation.

44. See Coffee, '"No Soul to Damn, no Body to kick": an Unscandalised Inquiry into the Problem of Corporate Punishment' (1981) 79 Mich L Rev 386.

[1.32] The right to form associations is guaranteed by the Constitution[45] but where such associations are not incorporated the legal position is different from that of corporations. Unincorporated associations do not, in general, possess legal personality and are not considered to be distinct from their members. The property of the association is jointly held by each of the members, rather than the association itself. Acts performed and transactions entered into on behalf of the group are considered to be the joint (all the members) and several (any particular member) responsibility of the members. In theory any individual member could be held liable for all the acts of the association in his or her own right. In some circumstances special legal provision has been made for certain categories of association, such as partnerships, charities and trade unions, each of which is governed by its own body of law.

The rule of law

[1.33] Underpinning the legal systems in most liberal democracies is the notion of the rule of law, sometimes referred to as the principle of legality. The values implicit in the rule of law transcend and permeate the various sources of law. Thus a particular principle might take legal effect as a common law rule, a section of an Act of the Oireachtas and a constitutional provision. Central to the rule of law is the idea of limited governmental power. The government of society functions according to legal rules which have been established in advance. Moreover, the separation of powers ensures a distribution of governmental power amongst different organs of state, the legislature, the executive and the judiciary. The relationship between the different organs is one of checks and balances, with no one organ enjoying supremacy at the expense of the others. The details of this governmental structure vary from one State to another but the crucial feature common to all democratic societies is the notion of limited power. This may be contrasted with systems where power is concentrated in the hand of one individual, such as a despot or dictator, or one entity, such as a political party or the bureaucracy.

[1.34] The rule of law requires that rights and obligations are prescribed in legal form and may be altered only in the matter permitted by law. Moreover, an individual is entitled to fair notice of the laws which govern his or her conduct. Several propositions flow from this. One is that laws must be enacted in advance and retrospective laws, that is laws which apply to past events, are to be avoided. It is clear that it is fundamentally unfair to punish a person for an act which was lawful at the time it was performed but

45. Article 40.6.1°.iii.

is later declared to be unlawful. The hostility to retrospective laws, encapsulated in the Latin maxims *nullum crimen sine lege* and *nullum poena sine lege*,[46] is amplified in Article 15.5 of the Constitution which provides that '[t]he Oireachtas shall not declare acts to be infringements of the law which were not so at the date of their commission.' Moreover, the courts adopt a presumption against retrospection when interpreting legislation.[47] Fair notice also requires that the law be announced to those who are to be bound by it. It would be pointless to enact laws in advance if that exercise is not accompanied by measures to bring them to the attention of the public. This is an issue of accessibility and provision is made for the formal promulgation of legislation[48] while judicial decisions are formally announced by their being delivered in court. However, a question of availability is also involved. It is necessary that laws are published in a manner which facilitates their being traced and located with comparative ease. Hence legislation is published by the Stationery Office[49] while law reports are published containing the most important judicial decisions.[50] A further question is that of intelligibility. Laws should be understandable and should not be formulated in opaque and unintelligible terms. Laws which are unduly vague fail in this regard and are potentially unconstitutional - in general laws should be formulated in precise terms which are clear and which do not admit of any ambiguity. However, there is a tension between the demands of intelligibility and precision. The drafting of laws with the desired precision is apt to lead to the use of lawyers' language, or legalese, and to render them less understandable by the general public. Whether this dilemma has been satisfactorily managed remains to be seen.[51] With these observations in mind we may now proceed with our examination of the Irish legal system.

---

46. Respectively, no crime without law and no punishment without law.
47. See paras **[14.60]-[14.63]**.
48. See paras **[13.10]** and **[13.62]**.
49. See paras **[13.48]-[13.50]**.
50. See para **[12.07]**.
51. See paras **[13.54]** and **[13.57]**.

Chapter 2

Development of the Irish Legal System

[1] INTRODUCTION

[2.01] In this chapter we trace the historical development of the Irish legal system to the beginning of the 20th century when the Irish Free State was established. This development runs parallel with the political history of England and Ireland, from the Anglo-Norman invasion of the 12th century to the creation of two separate jurisdictions on the island of Ireland in 1921 and 1922.

[2] PRE-NORMAN IRELAND AND THE BREHON LAW

[2.02] Prior to the arrival of the Anglo-Normans in the 12th century, Ireland was governed largely by a system of tribal 'royal' families or provincial chiefs. In the aftermath of the arrival of Christianity in the 5th century, Ireland may have been an 'island of saints and scholars', from which much learning made its way to mainland Europe, but it was also subject to considerable inter-tribal rivalry. Nonetheless, a quite sophisticated indigenous system of law, Brehon law, had also been developed. This was a system of law based primarily on custom. The system was administered by judicial figures known as Brehons, the equivalent of travelling justices, and are thought to have been successors to the pre-Christian Celtic druids. Many of the key elements of the Brehon system of law are to be found in the Irish law tracts, which were written in the 7th and 8th centuries. These ancient sources of law have been the subject of scholarly research, beginning towards the end of the 19th century, when interest in Celtic civilisation was revived by German scholars such as Thurneysen. This research has continued into the 20th century, when a great deal of annotation of the ancient Irish law tracts was completed by Professor Daniel A Binchy, culminating in the publication of a multi-volume annotation of the extant ancient law tracts.[1] The study of the Brehon law continues to the present, and a number of accessible summaries of the main principles of Brehon law have been published.[2] However, Brehon law has, in practice, been eclipsed by the

1. Professor Binchy's *Corpus Iuris Hibernici* (Institute for Advanced Studies, 1979) is a six volume annotation of the surviving ancient Irish law tracts.
2. See Kelly, *A Guide to Early Irish Law* (Institute for Advanced Studies, 1988).

dominance of the English common law system and is largely of interest to celtic scholars and social and legal historians.

[3] The Arrival of English Law in Ireland

[2.03] In theory at least, English law (or at least Anglo-Norman law) arrived in Ireland with the Anglo-Norman invasion of Wexford in 1169, led by 'Strongbow', Richard FitzGilbert, Earl of Pembroke.[3] In 1171, King Henry II followed Strongbow, to some extent to reassert his royal authority. He landed at Waterford and held a Council. This was an important symbolic act because the King's Council, or *Curia Regis*, was the crucial decision-making body or group of advisers for the feudal Anglo-Norman kings. It is worth remembering that, at that time, the king enjoyed virtually absolute power, but the Council was the principal mechanism for acting in the king's absence, for example during the Crusades or some other foreign adventure. In its early manifestation, the Council comprised two departments, the Exchequer, headed by the Treasurer, and the Chancery, headed by the Chancellor, the chief adviser to the king. As we will see, the Council later 'expanded' to produce a court system, a Parliament and an executive or government, eventually reducing the English monarch to a symbolic Head of State. However, when Henry II landed at Waterford, the king was the indisputable holder of ultimate power and authority. The Waterford Council declared that 'the laws of England were by all freely received and confirmed.' However, this 12th century communiqué hardly reflected local realities and it was not until the end of the 17th century that it could be said that English law prevailed in the greater part of Ireland. While the landings of Strongbow and Henry II may have had immense symbolic significance, they did not have the immediate effect of transplanting English law to Ireland. There were, as yet, no printing presses or photocopying facilities, still less a CD-ROM version of the laws of England to download onto laptop computers.

The development of the common law

[2.04] As Ireland was the first recipient of the Anglo-Norman common law system, the development of the English system of law after the Norman invasion of 1066 must be referred to briefly.

[2.05] After 1066, the conquering kings began the process of extending control over the whole territory. The obvious strength of the conquering

3. See Hand, *English Law in Ireland, 1290-1324* (Cambridge UP, 1967) and McEldowney and O'Higgins (eds), *The Common Law Tradition: Essays in Irish Legal History* (Irish Academic Press, 1990).

army was one method of subjugating the native English. However, as time passed, the need for more mundane law and order was clear and a Norman system of courts, manned by the king's justices and with his authority, was established in Westminster, which was also to become the location of the English Parliaments. These courts and the later Parliaments originated as off-shoots of the royal power, or royal prerogative, originally exercised in the King's Council, the *Curia Regis*. As well as hearing cases brought to London, the king's justices travelled throughout the kingdom twice a year on what were called the Assizes.[4] The primary function of these twice-yearly forays were, of course, to reinforce the king's rule. Since the king was the ultimate source of all law at this stage in history, there being no elected Parliament to approve laws, it followed that the king's judges had immense power and authority to apply his law throughout the kingdom. This historical development of the role of judges explains the continuing importance of judges within the common law system today.

Historical separation of Common Law and Civil Law systems

[2.06] It is clear from English history, therefore, that the judges were the first to apply rules of law within the kingdom. As centuries passed and the English system developed, the judges retained a central role in the actual development of new legal rules. In effect, the judges came to have delegated to them the king's role in setting out the basic rules of law which were to be applied in the kingdom. As we have observed,[5] these rules came to be known collectively as the common law of England, and any system of law which is based to a large extent on the development of rules by judges is known as a common law system. By way of contrast, the system of law which developed on the mainland of Europe was and is based on Codes of Law which contain rules applicable to all types of dispute. This system, called a Civil Law system, is based on the ancient Roman and Greek legal systems whose legal texts were rediscovered by Continental scholars during the Middle Ages.[6] By this time, however, the English system had developed its own approach. The minimal amount of 'knowledge transfer' between mainland Europe and England at this critical developmental stage thus resulted in quite different systems of law. Many of these differences, notably

4. The practice of twice-yearly forays into the hinterland survives in the statutory arrangements for the High Court on Circuit: see para **[4.51]**.
5. See para **[1.06]**.
6. For historical reasons, Scotland also developed a Civil Law system. It was only after the English and Scottish kingdoms were united after the defeat of James II in 1691 that England began to exercise full law-making powers for Scotland. Despite this, however, many elements of the Scottish legal system remain quite distinct from those in the rest of Britain.

the absence of comprehensive Codes of Law in common law systems, persist to the present day.

The historical development of equity in the courts of chancery

[2.07] We have already referred to the separate historical development of the courts of common law and the chancery courts, the courts of equity.[7] In terms of the political structure of the medieval English kingdom, we have seen that the royal power was largely exercised through the King's Council, the *Curia Regis*. The head of the administrative or secretarial department of the *Curia*, called the Chancery Department, was the Lord Chancellor who came to play an important role in the court system. In order to initiate a claim in the king's common law courts, a person was required to file in the Chancery Department a document called a writ, in effect a summons issued in the king's name ordering the other party in the case to appear in court. The Lord Chancellor's Chancery Department was, in effect, a clearing house for the writs and it vetted whether the writ filed by a litigant came within one of the established forms of writ. If it did not, the common law courts would simply refuse to hear the matter. If this was the case, an appeal would lie to the king. At some time, the king delegated the function of hearing such appeals to the Chancellor, with full authority to decide the case according to 'the justice and equity' of the matter. The idea behind this was that the Chancellor could make a decision which was not bound by what was regarded as the rigidity of the common law system.

[2.08] Ultimately, the Chancellor's Department began to deal with so many of these 'appeals' from the common law courts that it developed into a separate court of law, which became known as the Court of Chancery, where rules of equity were applied. The decisions of the Chancellor's Court were once described as being so free of common law rigidity that decisions as to the equity of a case were said to vary according to the length of the Chancellor's foot. This phrase has been handed down the centuries as a mark of disapproval of arbitrary judicial decisions. By the 17th and 18th centuries, however, the rules of the equity courts had become well established, and there were very few areas which had not been covered by previous cases which had come to Chancery.

Parliaments and statute law as a source of law

[2.09] While the concept of Parliament as a law-making institution emerged much later than the development of the judicial law-giving function, it had become well-established in the medieval period as a method of curbing the

7. See para **[1.08]**.

absolute authority of the Crown and as an alternative source of legal rules, called statute law or legislation. However, the judges were very slow to acknowledge that statute law could take priority over the common law rules which had been in existence for many centuries previously. The acceptance by the judges of the superiority of statute law did not fully emerge until the reign of the Tudors in the 16th century. Ultimately, however, the judges accepted that Parliament had full authority to overturn the common law, and that remains the position that exists in England today. Parliament, not the monarch, is the supreme and only source of laws, and the function of the judges is to interpret those laws. In British constitutional theory at least, the Westminster Parliament is unfettered and could enact, rather like Herod of biblical fame, that all blue-eyed babies be put to death.

Judges as law makers

[2.10] However, this is not to say that judges in English courts have no 'law-making' function. It is true that at one time nobody would object to the statement that 'judges do not make law; they merely declare what the common law is.' However, it is usually accepted nowadays that since common law rules are regularly applied to new settings, this involves something close to 'law-making'. Where legislation has not yet been enacted to deal with a particular area of law, the judges therefore continue to be the sole sources of the law to be applied in such situations. And in spite of the increased amount of legislation in recent years a substantial amount of law remains as laid down by the common law.[8] However, even where legislation has been enacted to deal with a particular area, the judges have an important role in interpreting that law where a dispute arises as to its meaning.[9] In Ireland, the role of the judges is further enhanced by the Constitution of Ireland as they are empowered to declare invalid any law passed by the National Parliament, the Oireachtas, as well as to modify any common law rule to meet constitutional requirements.[10]

The initial reception of English law into Ireland to 1494

[2.11] The Anglo-Norman invasion of Ireland resulted, at least initially, in the extension of English law to most of the eastern portion of the island of Ireland in what we have already seen was described as 'the first adventure of the common law'.[11] The practical application of English rule arose, as with the Norman conquest of England in the previous century, from a

8. See further Ch 12.
9. See further Ch 14.
10. See further Ch 15.
11. See para **[1.06]**.

combination of military and civilian authority: the granting by Henry II of feudal land rights to Strongbow over most of the eastern province of Leinster and the appointment in 1172 of Hugh de Lacy as the first justiciar of Ireland (the chief governor or representative of the King). The first recorded judicial appointment of an Anglo-Norman judge in Ireland occurred in 1221[12]. From that time until the 20th century, concerted efforts were made to ensure that persons versed in English law were appointed to apply its principles in Ireland. However, the influence of English law went into decline between 1300 and the end of the 15th century, during which time the original Norman invaders became 'more Irish than the Irish themselves' through inter-marriage with the native Irish noble families. Attempts were made to curb this decline by legislation which attempted to confirm the supremacy of English laws and the supremacy of the English Parliament over any Irish Parliament.[13] In the 1480s, matters came to a head when a claim was made by certain Anglo-Norman merchants in Waterford that English legislation restricting trade did not apply to them. Although the courts initially decided in their favour, the final decision was that the English Parliament had full authority to legislate for Ireland.[14] Nonetheless, it was felt better to have the matter clarified and Henry VII dispatched Edward Poyning as his lord deputy (the successor to the position of justiciar) to Ireland for this purpose. At a Parliament held in Drogheda in 1494, the Act usually referred to as Poyning's Law sought to put a brake on any Irish Parliament by providing that, henceforth:

> no Parliament be holden hereafter in the said land [Ireland], but at such season as the King's lieutenant and counsail [the Privy Council] there first do certifie the King ... all such acts as them seemeth should pass ... and if any Parliament be holden in that land hereafter, contrary to the form and provision aforesaid, it be deemed void and of none effect in law.[15]

[2.12] While the language may be a little archaic, Poyning's Law clearly established that, from 1495, any Parliament assembled in Ireland required the prior approval of the King's Lieutenant in Ireland and of the King's

12. See Ball, *The Judges in Ireland, 1221 to 1921* (Round Hall Press Reprint, 1993), a two volume work chronicling all known appointments to the Irish Bench prior to the establishment of the two jurisdictions in 1921 and 1922.
13. See Richardson and Sayles, *The Irish Parliament in the Middle Ages* (Philadelphia, 1952).
14. *Case of the Merchants of Waterford* (1483-4) YB Ric III f12; YB 1 Hen VII f2. 'YB' refers to the Yearbooks, the first form of law reports: see para **[12.07]**. On the background to the case, see Johnston, 'The English Legislature and the Irish Courts' (1924) 40 LQR 91.
15. 10 Hen VII, c 4 (Irl), entitled 'An Act that no Parliament be holden in this Land until the Acts be certified in England'. The text of Poyning's Law is contained in *The Irish Statutes 1310-1800*, Revised Edition (1885) (Reprint, Round Hall Press, 1995), p 761.

Privy Council in London. This supremacy was underpinned by another Act passed at Poyning's Parliament in Drogheda, which provided:

> That all estatutes, late made within the ... realm of England, concerning or belonging to the common and publique weal of the same, shall henceforth be deemed good and effectuall in the law, and over that be acceptyd, used, and executed within this land of Ireland in all points at all times requisite according to the tenor and effect of the same; and over that by authority aforesaid, that they and every of them be authorized, proved and confirmed in this said land of Ireland. And if any estatute or estatutes have been made within this said land, hereafter to the contrary, they and every of them by authority aforesaid be adnulled, revoked, voyd, and of none effect in the law.[16]

[2.13] The clear intention of the two Acts passed in 1494 was to affirm for Ireland the supremacy of English laws, but in subsequent centuries the Irish Parliaments of the Middle Ages sought to assert their independence from the English Parliament and occasionally purported to overstep the bounds set for them in 1494. In addition, some confusion (real or apparent) was expressed as to the precise meaning of the catch-all phrase 'concerning or belonging to the common and publique weal' contained in the second Act passed at Poyning's Parliament.[17]

[2.14] Moreover, whatever the formal terms of these Acts of 1494, the political reality was that English law in Ireland applied only so far as a military presence in support of the civil authorities assured this to be so. In 1494, English law was being applied primarily in the eastern part of the island extending in an arc from Dublin known as 'The Pale' where the English settlers (and, to some extent, the native Irish)[18] were entitled to the benefit of the king's law. Outside the Pale, Brehon Law continued to be applied, particularly in the western and northern parts of the country.

16. 10 Hen VII, c 22 (Irl), entitled 'An Act confirming all the Statutes made in England'. See *The Irish Statutes 1310-1800*, *op cit*, p 3. A note to the text states that the Drogheda Parliament was the first to use the English language for its Acts. Prior to this, most official texts were in Latin, and Latin remained the most common language for such official texts for some time thereafter.

17. For an illuminating description of the difficulties associated with the scope of this Act passed at Poyning's Parliament, see Osborough's introductory essay to the 1995 Reprint of *The Irish Statutes 1310-1800*, *op cit*.

18. Within the Pale, the native Irish appeared to have the status of feudal villeins, and were known as *betaghs*. It was not until 1612 (11, 12, & 13, Jac I, c 5) that the Irish Parliament enacted that all natives of Ireland were 'taken into his Majestie's gracious protection, and doe now live under one law as dutiful subjects of our Sovereigne Lord and Monarch.'

The Tudor Settlements or Plantations

[2.15] The extension of English law outside the Pale to the greater part of Ireland only began in earnest under the Tudor monarchs. In the mid-16th century, Henry VIII proceeded with a large-scale 'surrender and re-grant' of land held by the native Irish noble families, bringing them within the English feudal landholding system. In addition, his break with the Church of Rome resulted in the extension of the dissolution of the monasteries to Ireland and the redistribution of church land. In the reign of Elizabeth I, a failed rebellion by the Irish noble families in Ulster led to the 'Flight of the Earls' in 1607 and the consequent settlement or 'Plantation' of Ulster, under which much of the land in Ulster formerly in the ownership of the departed Earls was granted to Scottish and English settlers. The events of the early 17th century continue to have an enormous political influence over 300 years later in the political debates on the future of the people who share the island of Ireland. The Flight of the Earls also removed from Ireland the remaining source of patronage for the Brehons, the jurists of the Brehon law system.

[2.16] The early 17th century also saw the courts in Ireland firmly accepting the dominance of the English laws of succession and, in turn, rejecting the Brehon systems of succession known as *tanistry* and *gavelkind*.[19] These decisions, linked to the further military conquest of Ireland in later years and centuries, signalled the death knell of the Brehon law as an influential body of law except in minor areas of law.[20] The middle of the 17th century saw the further conquest of Ireland by Oliver Cromwell's Commonwealth army between 1649 and 1652 and the resettlement of many of the Irish landowners in the western part of Ireland (made famous for Irish nationalists by the cry 'to Hell or to Connaught'). After the Restoration of the English monarchy under Charles II, the end of the 17th century saw the victory in 1691 at the Battle of the Boyne of the Protestant William III (William of Orange or 'King Billy') over the Roman Catholic James II and his Jacobite supporters, leading to the reassertion of a distinctly Protestant form of English rule in England and Ireland. While the accession of William III to the English throne was accompanied by his acceptance of limits on royal power in the Bill of Rights 1689,[21] the rights contained therein were

19. *Case of Gavelkind* (1605) Dav 49 and *Case of Tanistry* (1607) Dav 28, both cases reported in a series of law reports collated by the then Attorney General for Ireland, Sir John Davies, later Chief Justice of the English Queen's Bench. See Prawlish, *Sir John Davies and the Conquest of Ireland* (Cambridge UP, 1985).

20. During the brief operation of the revolutionary Dáil Éireann courts between 1919 and 1922, Brehon law was cited as a persuasive authority on a variety of matters: see further para **[2.61]**. Since that time, Brehon law has been consulted in relation to certain fishery rights in *R (Moore) v O'Hanrahan* [1927] IR 406 and *Moore v Attorney General* [1934] IR 44.

21. 1 Will III & Mary II, sess 2, c 2. The Bill of Rights remains a key element of the English Constitution to the present day.

confined to those of the Protestant faith. Those in England and (more numerously) in Ireland who chose the 'Papish' Roman Catholic faith were excluded from full participation in the civil life of the kingdom through a series of legislative measures in the 18th century known collectively as the Penal Laws.

Grattan's Parliament and the Act of Union

[2.17] Despite the occasional assertion of independence from the Irish Parliaments of the Middle Ages, the 18th century saw an extension and clarification of the earlier Acts passed during Poyning's Parliament, when the Irish Parliament passed Yelverton's Act 1781. This provided that all English statutes:

> for the settling and assuring [of] forfeited estates ... concerning commerce ... and ... the seamen of England and Ireland, ... the stile or calendar ... and ... the taking any oath or oaths ... or relate to the continuance of any office, civil or military or of any commission, or of any writ, process, or proceeding at law or in equity ... shall be accepted, used, and executed in this kingdom ...[22]

[2.18] Ironically, just two years later, under the Irish Appeals Act 1783,[23] the Westminster Parliament repealed Poyning's Act and renounced its claim to legislate for Ireland. For a brief time, between 1783 and 1800, the Irish Parliament in Dublin, known as Grattan's Parliament, enacted some legislation ameliorating the Penal Laws for the Roman Catholic population, including conferral of a limited right to vote and admission to practice at the Bar.[24] This period also saw a growth in prosperity in Ireland and the creation of the great Georgian streets of Dublin, most of which have survived into the late 20th century. However, the exclusive legislative powers of the Irish Parliament were short lived and, moreover, against the background of the American and French revolutions of the time, there was an unsuccessful but influential rebellion in parts of Ireland in 1798 against the existing regime. Shortly after this, and before another unsuccessful revolt in 1803, the Act of Union of 1800[25] completely disbanded the Dublin Parliament and established the Westminster Parliament as the sole legislative assembly for what was, until the establishment of the Irish Free State in 1922,[26] the United Kingdom of Great Britain and Ireland. Article 8 of the 1800 Act also 'carried

22. 21 & 22 Geo III, c 48 (Irl), entitled 'An Act for extending certain of the Provisions' of Poyning's Act 1494. See *The Irish Statutes 1310-1800*, *op cit*, p 580.
23. 23 Geo 3, c 28.
24. Roman Catholic Relief Act 1793, 33 Geo 3, c 21 (Irl). On the exclusion of Roman Catholics from the legal profession, see Dr Colum Kenny's article, (1987) 5 Ir Hist Stud 337.
25. The Union was effected by identical Acts passed in London and Dublin: 39 & 40 Geo 3, c 67 and 40 Geo 3, c 38 (Irl) For the Irish Act, see *The Irish Statutes 1310-1800*, *op cit*, p 723.
26. Section 1 of the Act of Union had provided that the Union, which took effect on 1 January 1801, should be 'for ever'.

over' the prior laws and court system into the new United Kingdom by providing that:

> all laws in force at the time of the union, and all courts of civil and ecclesiastical jurisdiction within the respective kingdoms, shall remain as now by law established within the same, subject only to such alterations and regulations from time to time as circumstances may appear to the parliament of the united kingdom to require ...

[2.19] By establishing the Westminister as the principal legislative body for Ireland (as well as the rest of the United Kingdom), the 1800 Act brought all major institutions of State, legislative, executive and judicial, firmly back within the control of the London administration.

[4] The Institutions of State in the 19th century United Kingdom

Separation of powers

[2.20] It is appropriate at this stage to mention that during the 19th century, the essential elements of the system of government familiar today began to take shape. The United Kingdom had not faced the revolutionary change that occurred in the United States of America or France in the late 18th century, though it was directly affected by both in the sense of losing a valuable colony and in suppressing an attempted counterpart of both in Ireland in 1798. However, a substantial reform and radical movement made itself felt in other less dramatic ways in the early decades of the 19th century. There was no Declaration of the Rights of Man or the overthrow of an *ancien régime*, but there was real, if gradual, change in the relationship between the three branches of government, legislative, executive and judicial which reflected the sudden separation of the powers of revolutionary America and France.

[2.21] Many important political philosophers, such as Jeremy Bentham and John Stuart Mill, as well as writers such as Charles Dickens, had an enormous influence in effecting significant law reform and modernisation of State institutions in the wake of the onset of the industrial revolution that marked the 19th century. Economic development and law reform went hand in hand.

Legislature

[2.22] The legislative branch of government, embodied in Parliament, had, of course, long before established its law making or legislative function, taking over the powers exercised by the medieval King's Council, the *Curia*

Regis. A critical element of its 'coming of age' in law-making functions was the acceptance by the monarch of its right to raise taxes. The early medieval Parliaments of barons and earls grew into the House of Lords. Later, the House of Commons emerged to become the second half of what was now a bicameral Parliament. By the mid-19th century, while legislative proposals continued to require royal assent in order to become Acts of Parliament, this assent was, in reality, given as a matter of course once a Bill had been passed by both Houses of Parliament. Another aspect of the legislative power was the long fought battle by the 'Commons' to wrest real legislative control from the House of Lords. Without minimising its protracted nature, it was clear that, by the beginning of the 19th century the House of Lords was beginning to lose real power. However, it was not until 1911 that legislation was enacted to secure the primacy of the House of Commons, leaving the House of Lords with an advisory and delaying power only. Indeed, prior to 1911 a number of 'Home Rule' Bills[27] had failed to be enacted because of a negative vote in the House of Lords, even after they had been passed in the House of Commons.

Executive

[2.23] As to executive power, such as the power to declare war, to enter into international treaties and to administer the great Departments and Ministries of State, this had also been taken gradually from the king's immediate control. Thus, real executive power had in effect been transferred to the Crown's Ministers. These were selected by the Houses of Parliament from their members, but increasingly as the 19th century progressed many of the more powerful Ministers were Members of the House of Commons, another indication of the shift in power between the two Houses. These Ministers were presided over by a Prime Minister and increasingly they acted collectively through a Cabinet. Arising from the Act of Union of 1800, the Crown's principal representative in Ireland was now the Chief Secretary for Ireland, a member of the Cabinet in London. However, since the headquarters of the executive in Ireland was in Dublin Castle, it was the Under-Secretary of State, who resided more or less permanently in Dublin who retained real control along with the Crown's official representative in Dublin, the Lord Lieutenant or Viceroy.

[2.24] These basic components of a 'constitutional monarchy' were based on a combination of various laws (such as the Act of Union 1800) and unwritten convention (such as the precise role of the Prime Minister), rather than a single text called the Constitution, as was the case in the United States

27. See para **[2.43]**.

of America. They also became more firmly entrenched as the 19th century progressed and the shift of power away from the monarch accelerated with the move towards a, more or less, popularly elected House of Commons.

Judiciary

[2.25] The third great institution of State, the judiciary, also became the subject of considerable reform in the 19th century.[28] We will refer later to the three principal common law courts that were to emerge from the *Curia Regis*.[29] In addition, the medieval role of the Lord Chancellor in the administration of justice as head of the Chancery Department of the *Curia Regis* was transformed into overall head of the judiciary and, hence, the court system. The Lord Chancellor was the presiding judge in the Judicial Committee of the House of Lords, the final court of appeal in the Kingdom. It might seem surprising that one of the Houses of Parliament was, and remains today, the final court of appeal in the kingdom, but this can be explained by the fact that it was really another off-shoot of the King's Council which ultimately held all power. However, a practical difficulty for the House of Lords as a court of law was that, well into the 19th century, any member of the House was entitled, at least in theory, to sit in judgment in an appeal to the House of Lords acting in its judicial capacity. However, as with the development of the other branches of government, legislation was enacted to ensure that the Judicial Committee comprised full-time judges only, the 'Law Lords', who were appointed to the House of Lords for this particular purpose. As a matter of convention, the Law Lords rarely participate in the legislative work of the House of Lords, though they may contribute to debates on Bills connected with the courts or the administration of justice generally.

[2.26] As indicated, the Lord Chancellor presides over the Judicial Committee of the House of Lords, and though this is less common in the late 20th century he still occasionally sits as a judge with the other Law Lords. However, the Lord Chancellor also wore, and continues to wear, two other hats which appear anomalous in the context of the supposed separation of powers. The Lord Chancellor was, and remains today, the effective Chairman of the House of Lords acting in its legislative capacity as a House of Parliament. He also was, and remains today, a member of the British Cabinet, with a ministerial portfolio covering the regulation of the legal profession, the court system and connected issues such as legal aid.

28. See para **[2.30]**.

29. See paras **[2.33]**-**[2.36]**.

[2.27] In the context of the appointment of the judiciary in Ireland, we have already mentioned that the Anglo-Norman monarchy had begun in 1221 to appoint lawyers versed in English law to the Irish bench. Before and after the Act of Union of 1800, the London government continued to maintain close control over judicial appointments to the Irish courts, even if by this stage Irish lawyers, including Roman Catholics, began to be appointed later in the 19th century.

Amalgamation of the common law and chancery courts

[2.28] Turning to the reform of the court system in the 19th century, it could be said that at the beginning of that century, the common law courts dealt primarily with what today would be regarded as commercial law matters such as contracts between businesses and claims for damages. The chancery courts dealt with many issues relating to land, wills and similar areas of law. But the boundaries between the two were never entirely clear-cut. The two systems had become so complex to operate that many years could be spent simply litigating in which of the two systems a particular claim should be brought. Novels such as Charles Dickens' *Bleak House*, with its savage criticism of the interminable litigation in the fictional wardship case *Jarndyce v Jarndyce*, played an important part in highlighting these anomalies in the system, and throughout the 19th century procedural reforms were introduced to ameliorate the worst anomalies. This culminated in the enactment at Westminster for the courts of England and Wales of the Supreme Court of Judicature Act 1873,[30] the equivalent for Ireland being passed four years later, the Supreme Court of Judicature (Ireland) Act 1877.[31]

[2.29] The effect of the 1873 and 1877 Acts was that the administration of common law and equity was fused into one unified court system. Once a case was begun in the new court system the court could apply either the rules of equity or of common law.[32]

The Supreme Court of Judicature Acts 1873 and 1877: Superior Courts

[2.30] As already indicated, the 1873 and 1877 Acts established a unified Court called the Supreme Court of Judicature, comprising the High Court of Justice, with original jurisdiction as well as power to hear appeals from courts of local jurisdiction, and the Court of Appeal, which was conferred with appellate jurisdiction. The Judicial Committee of the House of Lords,

30. 36 & 37 Vict c 66.
31. 40 & 41 Vict c 57.
32. See Keane, *Equity and the Law of Trusts in the Republic of Ireland* (Butterworths, 1988) and Delany, *Equity and the Law of Trusts in Ireland* (Round Hall Sweet & Maxwell, 1996).

presided over by the Lord Chancellor, retained its status as the ultimate court of appeal for Ireland. This essential framework remains the basis for the court system in the United Kingdom to the present day. Indeed, in Ireland, a similar structure continues to apply, subject to the modification that appeals from the High Court lie to the Supreme Court and there is no further domestic appellate court.

[2.31] Under the 1877 Act, the High Court of Justice of Ireland sat in Dublin, and this Court, housed in the Four Courts building, was the principal court for the island of Ireland. As well as fusing the courts of common law and equity into a unified court, the 1873 and 1877 Acts also provided that the High Court of Justice was to be divided in turn into a number of divisions, which amalgamated and rationalised the many different courts which had developed in England from medieval times.

The Superior Courts

[2.32] The High Court of Justice established by the 1873 and 1877 Acts was the successor to the courts established in medieval times backed with the power and authority of the king. Because these courts acted on behalf of the king, and could trace their ancestry back to the King's Council, the *Curia Regis*, they were regarded as having certain inherent powers, simply by virtue of their being the royal courts. These included the power of the King's Bench Division to issue the prerogative writs[33] and that their power extended over the whole kingdom. These courts came to be known as the superior courts of justice, by contrast with the inferior and local courts established over the centuries and whose powers were limited in some form or another, whether in terms of the type of case they were empowered to deal with or the geographical limits of their powers. We will return to the inferior and local courts below.[34]

[2.33] The four principal superior courts which had developed from the Middle Ages, and which had given the title to the Four Courts building, were as follows.

1. The Court of Exchequer

[2.34] This court emerged from the Exchequer Department of the King's Council, the *Curia Regis*, presided over by the Treasurer, the other great adviser to the king along with the Lord Chancellor. Originally, the Court of Exchequer dealt mainly with disputes by subjects concerning whether moneys were owed to the king's Treasury. It was presided over by a Chief

---

33. See paras **[2.36]** and **[10.35]**.
34. See para **[2.48]**.

Baron, the other judges being referred to as *puisne*[35] barons, that is, inferior or 'ordinary' judges. Eventually, this court extended its jurisdiction by developing one of the 'fictions' of the law. The court was prepared to hear a civil case in which one party claimed that a debt owed to him by the other party would be used to discharge a debt owed to the Crown. As indicated, this device was ultimately used purely *pro forma* in order to ensure that the case would be heard by the Court of Exchequer. In the 19th century, the Irish Court of Exchequer also comprised a Lord Chief Baron and *puisne* barons, the last Chief Baron also being the longest-serving, Christopher Palles.[36]

2. The Court of Common Pleas

[2.35] This court was established to deal with 'common' disputes, that is disputes between private individuals or commoners, concerning what would be described today as civil claims, that is, as opposed to criminal matters. The Court comprised a Chief Justice of the Common Pleas and other *puisne* judges. By the 19th century, the Irish Court of Common Pleas comprised the Lord Chief Justice of the Common Pleas and a number of *puisne* judges.

3. The Court of King's, or Queen's,[37] Bench

[2.36] This court was the third common law court to emerge from the *Curia Regis* and therefore, in historical terms, remains more closely associated with the royal power and thus was regarded as being more important and influential. It dealt with criminal and civil matters, thus overlapping with the Court of Common Pleas. It also acted on behalf of the king's interest by exercising a supervisory jurisdiction over the inferior courts established over the years, through the mechanism of the prerogative writs.[38] The Court of King's Bench comprised the Chief Justice of the King's Bench and other *puisne* judges. By the 19th century, in Ireland the King's Bench comprised the Lord Chief Justice of Ireland and a number of *puisne* judges.

4. The Court of Chancery

[2.37] We have already noted that the Court of Chancery had developed from the Lord Chancellor's jurisdiction in equity. By the late 1860s, the Irish Court of Chancery comprised the Lord Chancellor of Ireland,[39] the Vice-Chancellor and the Master of the Rolls in Ireland.[40]

---

35. Pronounced 'puny'.
36. See further para **[4.94]**.
37. The title King's Bench or Queen's bench varies, depending on whether the monarch is a King or Queen.
38. See para **[10.35]**.
39. See O'Flanagan, *Lives of the Lord Chancellors of Ireland*, 2 vols (Longman Green, 1810).
40. The Master of the Rolls had originally been keeper of the State Papers but later became a judicial office holder. The position remains in place in England, where the Master of the Rolls is the judicial head of the civil division of the Court of Appeal.

5. House of Lords

[2.38] Finally, although outside the realms of the four courts listed, it is convenient to reiterate here that the House of Lords, acting in its judicial capacity, was (and remains today) the final court of appeal for the kingdom.[41]

6. Other superior courts

[2.39] In addition to these courts, there had developed over the centuries the following:

- the High Court of Admiralty, which dealt with maritime claims;
- the Landed Estates Court, which dealt with certain land matters;
- the Court of Bankruptcy and Insolvency;
- the Court of Probate, which dealt with cases arising from wills;
- the Court of Matrimonial Causes and Matters; and
- the Court for Crown Cases Reserved, which operated to some extent as a court for appeals in criminal matters before the right to appeal in such cases was established.

[2.40] This is not a comprehensive list, but it provides some indication of the complexity which had developed in the system up to the mid-19th century. After the 1873 and 1877 Acts, some further rationalisation of the pre-1873 court system was effected between 1897 and 1907, resulting in the High Court Divisions being reduced to two: the King's Bench Division and the Chancery Division (with two Judicial Commissioners of the Irish Land Commission also being High Court judges).

19th century land reform

[2.41] Returning to the impact of English law on Ireland in the early 19th century, further significant relaxation of the Penal Laws was effected, symbolised by the passing of the Roman Catholic Relief Act 1829,[42] more commonly known by its supporters as the Catholic Emancipation Act and generally associated with the Irish barrister and Member of Parliament Daniel O'Connell. Among other reforms effected by the 1829 Act was the removal of the ban on Roman Catholics being elevated to the Bench. In 1836, the first Irish Roman Catholic was appointed to a senior judicial position.[43] However, O'Connell's wider campaign to repeal the Act of Union was not successful.

---

41. See para **[2.75]**.
42. 10 Geo 4, c 7.
43. Michael O'Loghlen, 'O'Connell's legal understudy' was appointed a Baron of the Court of Exchequer in 1836 and Master of the Rolls in 1837: see Ball, *The Judges in Ireland, 1221 to 1921* (Round Hall Press Reprint, 1993), Vol II, p 274.

[2.42] While the relaxation of the Penal Laws was welcomed by what might be described as the Roman Catholic establishment, an even greater political movement surrounded the plight of tenant farmers in Ireland in the 19th century, whose difficulties were exacerbated by the calamity of the Great Famine of 1845 to 1847. Agitation for agrarian law reform became the focus of mass political action, exemplified by the Land League, founded in 1879 by Michael Davitt with Charles Stuart Parnell, the leader of the Irish Parliamentary Party at Westminster, as its President. Arising from the Land League's aggressive campaigning, considerable reform was effected through parliamentary methods by the Land Law (Ireland) Act 1881,[44] which established the Irish Land Commission and gave legal effect to the Ulster tenant right and campaign slogan of 'fair rent, free sale and fixity of tenure.' Later Acts passed between 1885 and 1909 also enabled tenant farmers to buy out their tenancies and purchase the freehold title to their land, with the landlords being paid a land purchase bond rather than cash.[45]

The Home Rule Movement

[2.43] Despite the significant land reforms,[46] the land agitation movement spilled over into the call by Irish nationalists for the repeal of the Act of Union of 1800 and, initially at any rate, the granting of limited Home Rule to Ireland. At Westminster, the Home Rule campaigns of the Irish Parliamentary Party received some support from Liberal Prime Minister Gladstone but met with opposition from Conservatives and Ulster Unionists. By the early years of the 20th century, Unionist opposition to Home Rule (mainly concentrated in the province of Ulster and reflecting the Tudor Plantation or Settlement) solidified under the leadership of one of the leading barristers of the day, Sir Edward Carson. In 1914, the Irish Parliamentary Party, by now led by John Redmond, had secured the passing of the Government of Ireland Act 1914, the first Home Rule Act to be enacted. This provided for limited legislative powers for a Parliament of

---

44. 44 & 45 Vict, c 49.

45. These included the Purchase of Land (Ireland) Act 1885, 48 & 49 Vict, c 73, the Purchase of Land (Ireland) Act 1891, 54 & 55 Vict, c 48, the Land Law (Ireland) Act 1896, 59 & 60 Vict, c 47 (the latter two Acts known as the 'Balfour Acts'), the Irish Land Act 1903, 3 Edw 7, c 37 ('Wyndham's Act') and the Irish Land Act 1909, 9 Edw 7, c 42 ('Birrell's Act'). The successors to the original Irish Land Commission and the associated land bond purchase scheme continued in operation in Northern Ireland until 1937, while its equivalent in the Republic of Ireland was only wound down in the late 1980s: see the discussion of the Irish Land Commission (Dissolution) Act 1992 by Humphreys, *Irish Current Law Statutes Annotated* (Sweet & Maxwell).

46. The land purchase scheme, which extended to the entire island of Ireland, resulted in a much greater proportion of freehold farmers than is the case in England and Wales today, where 'absentee landlords' and tenant farmers remain common.

Ireland, subject to continuing overall control from Westminster, as well as an executive drawn from the Irish Parliament which would replace the executive headed by the Chief Secretary for Ireland and chosen from London. However, the 1914 Act was suspended for the duration of World War I and, in any event, was to be amended to take account of Ulster Unionist opposition.

[2.44] Moreover, from a nationalist perspective, two further events made the 1914 Act irrelevant. Easter 1916 saw a highly influential nationalist rebellion or Rising in many parts of Ireland. While the Rising was a military failure and initially unpopular with the general populace, its crude suppression, including the execution of many of its leaders by the British authorities resulted in a significant swing to militant nationalism, represented by the Sinn Féin Party, and away from the Irish Parliamentary Party. In the 1918 general election to the Westminster Parliament, Sinn Féin (many of whose candidates were still in prison or else in hiding for their participation in the 1916 Rising) almost completely supplanted the Irish Parliamentary Party. Rather than taking their seats in Westminster, Sinn Féin called a meeting in January 1919 of what, from the nationalist perspective, was the meeting of the first National Parliament, Dáil Éireann. From the British perspective, of course, this was a seditious assembly. However, the first Dáil adopted a declaration of independence and passed decrees establishing a Constitution, a Provisional Government and court system.[47] At about the same time, a nationalist guerrilla-style armed campaign, commonly called the War of Independence by nationalists, began against British rule. Attempts to suppress the nationalist rebellion ultimately failed and, by 1921, it was accepted by the British government that continued British rule was impossible in most parts of Ireland.

Government of Ireland Act 1920

[2.45] Prior to this, however, the Westminster Parliament passed the final Home Rule Act, the Government of Ireland Act 1920.[48] This amounted to a consolidated version of the 1914 Act, and it envisaged the establishment of two political units, Southern Ireland and Northern Ireland, with Dublin and Belfast as capitals. Significantly, Northern Ireland was to comprise six counties of Ulster, namely, Antrim, Armagh, Down, Fermanagh, Londonderry and Tyrone, with Southern Ireland to comprise the remaining 26 counties. Each was to have a Parliament, as well as an executive chosen from the Members of the Parliaments, and a court system comprising a High

47. On the Dáil Éireann courts, see para **[2.60]**.

48. 10 & 11 Geo 5, c 67.

Court and Court of Appeal, with a further layer added which envisaged a High Court of Appeal for Ireland to hear appeals from the Court of Appeal of Northern Ireland and the Court of Appeal of Southern Ireland. As with the 1914 Act, both Parliaments would ultimately be subject to the Parliament at Westminster and the Crown would continue to be represented by the Lord Lieutenant. The 1920 Act also held out the unlikely prospect of 'Irish union', provided the two Parliaments voted for this.

[2.46] In paving the way for the separate court systems that would be required for the two jurisdictions that ultimately emerged in 1922, the Government of Ireland Act 1920 followed the model of the 1877 Act, with a Supreme Court of Judicature comprising a High Court of Justice and Court of Appeal. While the 1920 Act initially maintained, at least on paper,[49] a single court system for the island of Ireland for the period up to 1922, the 1920 Act also envisaged that this would be split in two, with a separate High Court and Court of Appeal for both jurisdictions.

[2.47] By 1921, immediately before the two new jurisdictions, the Irish Free State and Northern Ireland, came into effect, the Supreme Court of Judicature in Ireland comprised a Court of Appeal of six judges and a High Court of Justice of 12 judges, the High Court being divided into a King's Bench Division of eight judges, a Chancery Division with four judges and two other High Court judges, the Judicial Commissioners of the Irish Land Commission. It should be clear from the number of judges of the King's Bench Division (as well as the continued existence of a Chancery Division) that the vast bulk of civil and criminal business previously conducted by the pre-1877 courts had been absorbed into the King's Bench Division. It remains the case in England and Northern Ireland that the Queen's Bench Division deals with the vast majority of civil and criminal business of the High Court.

The inferior courts prior to 1922

[2.48] Before proceeding to discuss the arrangements made in 1921 and 1922 for the two jurisdictions established in Ireland, we discuss the nature and development of a number of inferior and local courts which dealt with those less significant civil and criminal matters not dealt with in the High Court of Justice. By the 19th century these inferior courts included the following.

49. See para **[2.60]**.

1. The Assize Courts

[2.49] We have already observed that the Assizes or sessions had developed early in the Norman legal system. They involved holding hearings of criminal and civil cases outside London where these had not already been heard at the sessions held by the courts at Westminster. This was an early indication of 'consumer-oriented' administration of justice, since the Assizes, or *Nisi Prius* hearings,[50] were clearly intended to avoid the inconvenience for those involved of having to come to London. The judges of the Assize Courts were, in effect, travelling judges of what ultimately became the High Court of Justice. This finds a modern echo in the twice-yearly sittings of the High Court on Circuit.[51]

2. Quarter Sessions and Petty Sessions: Justices of the Peace

[2.50] Quite early in the development of the English legal system, judges who ultimately became known as Justices of the Peace (JPs) had emerged to hear less serious criminal matters than those heard at Assizes, and these Justices sat about four times a year in what were known as Quarter Sessions. Over the centuries, the jurisdiction of the Justices of the Peace was extended by statute, but the more serious criminal offences, such as murder and offences connected with rebellion, were 'reserved' for the Assizes.

[2.51] In addition to dealing with minor criminal matters, the Justices were also required to conduct preliminary hearings for the Assize Courts. These were held outside the Quarter Sessions dates, and were known as Petty Sessions. If the Justice of the Peace found that there was sufficient or *prima facie* evidence to justify a trial, a document known as a 'bill of indictment' would be referred to a Grand Jury, whose function was to decide if the bill was correct in form and whether there was in fact *prima facie* evidence. If they considered that there was, the bill of indictment became an indictment, triable by Petty Jury (which, in spite of its title, was the final decision-making body in the case) at the Assize hearing. Another important function conferred by statute on the Justice of the Peace was the power to require any person 'not of good fame' to agree to keep the peace and to be of good behaviour.[52] This power to 'bind to the peace' remains in place in the late 20th century.[53]

---

50. The Second Statute of Westminster of 1285 had provided that all civil matters were to be dealt with at Westminster '[u]nless the itinerant justices shall have come before into those parts.' As the Statute was enacted in Latin, the reference to the travelling justices not having heard the case would have involved the words '*nisi prius*' and so the Assize or hearings of the 'itinerant justices' came to be known as the *Nisi Prius* hearings.

51. See para **[4.51]**.

52. The jurisdiction was first conferred in 1361 by the statute 34 Edw III, c 1.

53. See para **[10.24]**.

[2.52] In Ireland in particular, arising from the sporadic outbreaks of rebellion and other less localised disturbances, the power to bind to the peace was used extensively as an instrument of control and amounted to an informal type of internment. For those who opposed the political connection with England, particularly in the 19th century, binding to the peace was a symbol of repression by an 'alien power.' This was compounded by the fact that the Justices were, in general, part-time appointees and not necessarily qualified lawyers, raising the suspicion that they were prone to make decisions favoured by the political establishment rather than capable of independent decision-making. The Dublin administration responded at least to some extent to the criticisms of the JP system with the appointment of paid Resident Magistrates (RMs) to deal with petty sessions matters outside Dublin.[54] Although this might be described today as being 'too little, too late' against the overall political background, this had at least one lasting effect. The 'petty sessions' courts in the legal system discussed here, the District Courts, are presided over by full time judges who must be former practising lawyers.[55] Thus, what was the bitter experience of the 19th century for Irish nationalists has been remembered to that extent. Indeed, while the District Court system derives its validity from the Constitution of Ireland 1937, we should also note that certain procedural aspects of the District Court's jurisdiction are to be found in pre-1922 legislation that remains in place.[56] In the English and Northern Ireland legal systems, the modern day equivalent of Petty Sessions, the Magistrates Courts, continue to be presided over by part-time lay magistrates, but they are guided in matters of law by legally qualified Magistrate Court clerks.

3. County Courts

[2.53] The County Courts dealt with minor civil cases that would otherwise have overburdened the Assize hearings. The 1877 Act provided for the appointment of County Court judges, who also held the position of Chairman of Quarter Sessions. The document used to initiate a claim in the County Court was the civil bill, an initiating document unique to Ireland and not shared by the equivalent County Courts in England. The civil bill still forms the basis for many claims initiated in the Circuit Court today, the successor to the County Courts in this legal system.[57] In Northern Ireland and

54. The Sommerville and Ross *Irish RM* short stories of the early 20th century cast a comical eye on this aspect of the legal system.
55. See para **[2.65]**.
56. These include the Petty Sessions (Ireland) Act 1851 and the Summary Jurisdiction Act 1857.
57. See para **[6.52]**.

England, the County Courts remain in place, but only in Northern Ireland are claims initiated by the civil bill procedure.

[5] THE ESTABLISHMENT OF NORTHERN IRELAND AND THE IRISH FREE STATE

[2.54] The Government of Ireland Act 1920 was completely unacceptable to Irish nationalists, represented by Sinn Féin, who continued to press for a 32 county independent State. However, Ulster Unionists assented to the provisions of the 1920 Act. In May 1921, elections were held for the Parliaments of Northern Ireland and Southern Ireland. Although Sinn Féin had rejected the 1920 Act, the party used the electoral arrangements to renew their mandate to what was the Second Dáil Éireann. In Northern Ireland, Unionists won 40 of the 52 seats in the Northern Ireland House of Commons, while (in a largely uncontested election) Sinn Féin won 124 of the 128 seats in what to nationalists was the Second Dáil Éireann or, in terms of the 1920 Act, the House of Commons of Southern Ireland. The Parliament of Northern Ireland was opened in June 1921.

[2.55] As already noted, a Truce between the British and the Irish nationalists was agreed in July 1921 and the British recognised the Sinn Féin regime as the 'provisional government' of Southern Ireland and, in effect, transferred a large measure of control over to what the nationalists regarded as the cabinet of Dáil Éireann. Ultimately, after difficult negotiations, Articles of Agreement for an Anglo-Irish Treaty were signed by British and Irish plenipotentiaries in December 1921. While this provided for the establishment of the Irish Free State, and that this might comprise the entire island of Ireland, the Irish negotiators were forced to accept a number of concessions, including an oath of loyalty to the Crown and what amounted to an 'opt-out' for those elected to the Parliament of Northern Ireland. This opt-out was duly taken up in December 1921. After a bitter debate in Dáil Éireann, which resulted in a split within Sinn Féin followed by a Civil War until 1923, the Articles of Agreement (or 'The Treaty') were approved in January 1922. This paved the way for the creation of the Irish Free State.

[2.56] Under the post-1922 regime, therefore, Northern Ireland remained part of what became the United Kingdom of Great Britain and Northern Ireland, while the Irish Free State became a member of the British Commonwealth. The Westminster Parliament passed the Irish Free State (Constitution) Act 1922,[58] and this also repealed the Government of Ireland Act 1920 in so far as it applied to Southern Ireland. The equivalent Act in the

58. 13 Geo 5, sess 2, c 1.

Irish Free State was the Constitution of the Irish Free State (Saorstát Éireann) Act 1922, which enacted into law the Constitution of the Irish Free State, in turn largely based on the 1921 Articles of Agreement. While the outcome differed in a number of respects from that envisaged in the 1920 Act, it remained the case that two separate jurisdictions emerged in Ireland after 1922. For the first time in the history of the island, therefore, a formal division into two separate jurisdictions was effected in 1922, and this remains in place to the present day.[59]

The court systems in the two jurisdictions in 1922

[2.57] As indicated, the emergence of the separate jurisdictions on the island in 1922 resulted in the split of the unitary Supreme Court of Judicature of Ireland into two separate court systems.

[2.58] The Northern Ireland legal system retained the nomenclature of the 1877 and 1920 Acts, with the Supreme Court of Judicature for Northern Ireland comprising a High Court and Court of Appeal, the High Court being divided into the King's Bench and Chancery Divisions (with one Judicial Commissioner of the Irish Land Commission as an additional judge). As with the 1877 and 1920 Acts, a final appeal lay to the House of Lords. This underlined that Northern Ireland remained within the (somewhat smaller) United Kingdom.

[2.59] In the Irish Free State, the nomenclature provided for in the Constitution of the Irish Free State broke with the 1877 and 1920 Acts, though the essential components remained. The superior courts[60] to be established by the 1922 Constitution were to comprise a High Court of Justice and a Supreme Court of Justice, the latter being the equivalent of the Court of Appeal of Southern Ireland envisaged by the 1920 Act. However, by contrast with the 1877 and 1920 Acts, a final appeal lay to the Judicial Committee of the Privy Council. This recognised that the Irish Free State had now stepped outside the United Kingdom, albeit tentatively, into the emerging British Commonwealth of Nations.[61]

---

59. On the general impact of the division in terms of legal systems, see Boyle & Greer, *The Legal Systems, North and South* (1983), a study prepared for the New Ireland Forum. See also Dickson, *The Legal System of Northern Ireland*, 3rd ed (SLS Publications, 1991) and Dawson & Ors (eds), *One Hundred and Fifty Years of Irish Law* (SLS Publications/Round Hall Sweet & Maxwell, 1996).

60. See para. **[2.32]**.

61. This appeal mechanism, which required the permission of the Privy Council itself, was not often used and was in fact abolished by an amendment of the Free State Constitution in 1933: see para **[15.09]**. The Privy Council remains the final court of appeal from British Commonwealth states, though increasing numbers opted out of this arrangement as the 20th century progressed.

The revolutionary Dáil courts

[2.60] The transition from the pre-1922 to the post-1922 system was relatively straightforward for Northern Ireland, but was not as simple for the Irish Free State as the above might indicate. As we have already outlined, from 1919 to 1921 there was widespread insurrection and insurgency against British rule in many parts of Ireland. This had two consequences for the existing court system. It was virtually impossible to operate the court system created by the 1877 and 1920 Acts, whether in Dublin or the provinces. In addition, the parliamentary assembly of the Irish nationalists, Dáil Éireann, had passed decrees in 1920 establishing courts of Dáil Éireann. These comprised the following:

1. *Parish Courts*, which were to meet weekly to deal with minor civil and criminal matters.
2. *District Courts*, which were to meet monthly to deal with more serious civil and criminal matters and to hear appeals from the Parish Courts.
3. A *Circuit Court*, organised on the basis of four Circuits, and with unlimited civil and criminal jurisdiction, to hold three sessions per year, each Circuit to be presided over by a Circuit judge.
4. A *Supreme Court*, to sit in Dublin, composed of at least three judges, to operate both as a court of first instance and an appellate court.

[2.61] These Dáil Éireann courts were to apply the law as it stood at January 1919, when the first Dáil Éireann sat, as amended by any subsequent Dáil decrees. English law textbooks were not to be cited, but the Brehon laws, referred to as 'the early Irish codes' could be used as persuasive precedents as could decisions of civil law European courts and the principles of (ancient) Roman law. These courts lacked validity from the point of view of the governing law and were suppressed by the British authorities in so far as this was possible. This was largely achieved in the Dublin area, but in the provinces the Parish and District Courts operated quite extensively between 1920 and 1922, thus providing a brief revival of the Brehon laws in Ireland in the 20th century.

[2.62] In the wake of the signing of 'The Treaty', in June 1922 the British formally handed over control of the court system provided for in the Government of Ireland Act 1920 to what English law regarded as the 'provisional government' of the Irish Free State.[62] It was ultimately decided,

62. This was done by means of the Provisional Government (Transfer of Functions) Order 1922, an Order in Council (see para **[2.72]**) made under the Irish Free State (Agreement) Act 1922, an Act passed at Westminster to give effect to the December 1921 Articles of Agreement.

by two decrees of the cabinet in July and October 1922, to abolish the Dáil Éireann courts and to 'resurrect' the courts of the 1920 Act.

[2.63] After the establishment of the Irish Free State, the Dáil Éireann Courts (Winding-Up) Act 1923 conferred some validity in law on the decisions of the Dáil Éireann courts, but this was subject to the overriding powers of a judicial commissioner appointed under the 1923 Act with authority to make final determinations arising out of any decision of the revolutionary courts. In effect, the abolition of the Dáil courts and the taking over of the 1920 Act court system represented a 'retreat from revolution'[63] and the courts established under the Constitution of the Irish Free State held that the decisions of the Dáil courts were void and of no legal effect.[64]

1923 Judiciary Committee and Courts of Justice Act 1924

[2.64] In January 1923, the newly installed Executive Council (the Cabinet) of the Irish Free State appointed a Judiciary Committee to recommend the shape of the court system to be established under the 1922 Constitution. The terms of reference of the Committee appeared to give its members *carte blanche*, because it was authorised to make recommendations 'untrammelled by any regard to any of the existing systems of judicature' and the pre-1922 regime was described disparagingly as 'a standing monument of alien government'. However, it must be borne in mind that the Committee was, in fact, limited by the essential outline contained in Article 73 of the Constitution of the Irish Free State, which envisaged a High Court of Justice and Supreme Court of Justice, together with 'courts of local and limited jurisdiction.'[65] In the Report of the Judiciary Committee, published in May 1923, the court system recommended for the Irish Free State was as follows.

1. District Court

[2.65] The District Court was to replace the functions performed at Petty Sessions by the Justice of the Peace. The new Justices of the District Court would be full-time judges with legal experience. The Court would have jurisdiction in minor civil and criminal matters.

2. Circuit Court

[2.66] The Circuit Court would also have a criminal and civil jurisdiction. On the civil side, it would replace the County Courts, while its criminal

---

63. For a discussion of the Dáil Éireann courts, see Kotsonouris, *Retreat from Revolution* (Irish Academic Press, 1994).

64. See *R (Kelly) v Maguire* [1923] 2 IR 58.

65. See further para **[4.03]**.

jurisdiction would mirror that of the Assizes in that it would try serious criminal matters, subject to certain 'reserved' offences. It would also hear appeals from the District Court in civil and criminal matters.

3. High Court

[2.67] As already noted, the Constitution of the Irish Free State 1922 required the establishment of a High Court. The Judiciary Committee recommended that it assume the functions exercised by the High Court of Justice of Southern Ireland under the Government of Ireland Act 1920. It would thus have a virtually unlimited civil jurisdiction (subject only to the matters to be dealt with in the District and Circuit Courts) and in criminal matters would deal with the most serious 'reserved' offences, such as murder. The High Court would be presided over by a President of the High Court.

4. Court of Criminal Appeal

[2.68] The Judiciary Committee also recommended the establishment of a Court of Criminal Appeal along the lines of the court of the same name established in England in 1907. This would hear appeals from the Circuit Court and High Court in serious criminal matters, and a further appeal to the Supreme Court would be possible in cases involving points of law of exceptional public importance.

5. Supreme Court

[2.69] As with the High Court, the Report was bound to recommend that a final court of appeal entitled the Supreme Court be established. Its functions were to be virtually identical to those of the Court of Appeal of Southern Ireland under the 1920 Act. The Supreme Court would be presided over by the Chief Justice of Ireland, the most senior member of the judiciary in the State.

[2.70] The recommendations of the Committee were enacted in the Courts of Justice Act 1924. As we will see, while the Constitution of Ireland 1937 required the establishment of a 'new' court system in 1961, the arrangements put in place by the 1924 Act were repeated at that time,[66] and this layout of the system continues to the present day.[67]

[6] Ireland and Northern Ireland

[2.71] The 26 county Irish Free State remained in place until 1937 when it was succeeded by the establishment of the entity known as Ireland through

66. See para **[4.04]**.

67. However, the Courts and Court Officers Act 1995, s 4, envisages the abolition of the Court of Criminal Appeal and the transfer of its functions to the Supreme Court. See further para.**[7.35]**.

the passing by referendum of the Constitution of Ireland, *Bunreacht na hÉireann*, in 1937. Ireland formally remained a member of the British Commonwealth until 1949 when the Republic of Ireland Act 1948, passed by the Oireachtas, the National Parliament of Ireland, came into effect. The 1948 Act also provided that Ireland may be described as the 'Republic of Ireland', but since Article 4 of the Constitution of 1937 provides that the name of the State in the English language is Ireland, the official description preferred by successive Governments since 1937 is 'Ireland'.[68] While we will see that the passing of the 1937 Constitution has had important implications for the development of law in Ireland, the court system currently in place reflects the arrangements made in 1922.

[2.72] In Northern Ireland, the Parliament envisaged by the Government of Ireland Act 1920 remained in operation, for the most part at Stormont, near Belfast, until 1972 when it was prorogued (disbanded) by the Westminster Parliament arising from the violence that emerged in the late 1960s. Between 1972 and the present, the Westminster Parliament has been the sole legislative body for Northern Ireland and the arrangements for the governance of Northern Ireland by means of this 'direct rule' are currently contained primarily in the Northern Ireland Constitution Act 1973, passed at Westminster. Some Acts passed at Westminster, such as the 1973 Act, apply directly to Northern Ireland. However, much of what would have, until 1972, been enacted by the Stormont Parliament of Northern Ireland has, since 1972, been enacted by means of Orders in Council made at Westminster. These are a form of secondary or delegated legislation,[69] but for all intents and purposes are Northern Ireland Acts of Parliament.[70]

Relevance of pre-1922 High Court Divisions to post-1924 court system

[2.73] To some extent, the High Court Divisions in operation prior to 1922 are of historical interest only for the jurisdiction discussed in this text, because since the passing of the Courts of Justice Act 1924 which established the essential elements of the present court system,[71] there have been no formal divisions of the High Court, and any judge of the High Court may be assigned to hear any case. In practice, however, the business of the

---

68. Given the variety of legislative and constitutional provisions touching on the subject, it is perhaps not surprising that Ireland is variously referred to as 'Southern Ireland', 'the Irish Free State', 'Éire' and 'the Republic of Ireland': see further para **[15.41]**.

69. See para **[13.58]**.

70. Eg, the equivalent for Northern Ireland of the British Health and Safety at Work Act 1974 (1974, c 37) is the Health and Safety at Work (Northern Ireland) Order 1978 (SI 1039/1978), which is also given a parallel Northern Ireland 'Act' Number (1978, NI 9) to indicate that it is the equivalent of an Act.

71. See para **[4.04]**.

High Court is administered in accordance with an informal division much along the lines established by the 1877 Act.[72] In addition, the legislation which established the court system that operates at present in the State 'carried forward' the jurisdiction of the courts that was in place prior to 1922, so that some knowledge of the essential elements of the 1877 Act is required in order to understand the present arrangements. Indeed, it may be that, in the future, formal divisions may re-emerge with the advent of increasing specialisation and the need to manage court business in a more systematic manner.[73]

Relevance of pre-1922 system to Northern Ireland and English court systems

[2.74] The regime established by the 1873 and 1877 Acts continues to reflect the arrangements in place in Northern Ireland and in the courts of England and Wales. As will become clear in later chapters, decisions of English courts, and to a limited degree those of Northern Ireland, continue to be referred to in Ireland.[74] The current divisions of the English and Northern Ireland High Courts are identical, comprising the Queen's Bench Division, the Chancery Division and, since the passing by the Westminster Parliament of the Courts Act 1971 and its Northern Ireland equivalent the Judicature (Northern Ireland) Act 1978, the Family Division. The 1971 and 1978 Acts also replaced the ancient system of twice-yearly Assizes with the Crown Court, now also part of the Supreme Court of Judicature in these jurisdictions. The Westminster Parliament consolidated the changes first introduced by the 1873 Act in the Supreme Court Act 1981.

[2.75] For Northern Ireland and English courts, the appeal system remains remarkably similar to that in the 1873 Act, with an appeal from the High Court to the Court of Appeal (whether that in Belfast or London) and the possibility of a further appeal to the House of Lords, leave to appeal by either the Court of Appeal or the House of Lords being required. An alternative method available since the passing the Administration of Justice Act 1969 is a direct ('leap frog') appeal from the High Court to the House of Lords where the High Court judges certifies that the case involves a point of law of exceptional public importance and where the House of Lords also grants leave to appeal.

---

72. See para **[4.50]**.
73. See para **[4.137]**.
74. See para **[12.40]**.

Chapter 3

The Legal Profession

[1] INTRODUCTION

[3.01] In this chapter we discuss the many legal professionals who contribute in different ways to the operation of the Irish legal system. Principally, we look at the practising lawyers, solicitors and barristers. We also discuss the roles of the Law Officers, the Attorney General and Director of Public Prosecutions. The role of lawyers who are appointed as judges in the different courts is discussed elsewhere.[1] We also examine here the role of universities in legal education. Finally, we outline how other professionals are involved in the legal system.

The two branches of the legal profession

[3.02] The legal profession in Ireland, as in England and Northern Ireland, is divided into two branches, solicitors and barristers, the latter usually known collectively as 'the Bar'. As with much of our law, this division was carried over from the situation which pertained prior to the creation of the two jurisdictions in Ireland in 1922.[2]

[3.03] The distinctions between the branches of the profession as they operate at present are quite significant. One essential starting point is that, in the vast majority of cases, a person with a legal problem must first consult a solicitor for legal advice. A barrister is not permitted to take instructions directly from a member of the public, except in a small number of specific instances which we mention below. Again, broadly speaking, the solicitor tends to specialise in legal work which involves the preparation of cases for court rather than for advocacy in court. The barrister is, generally speaking, regarded as specialising in the preparation of cases for court as well as advocacy in court itself.

[3.04] The solicitor is, therefore, in the front line of dealing with the public and for most people their only contact with a lawyer is a visit to the office of

1. See para **[4.63]**.
2. See Hogan, *The Legal Profession in Ireland 1789-1922* (Incorporated Law Society of Ireland 1986) and Hogan and Osborough (eds), *Brehons, Sergeants and Attorneys: Studies in the History of the Irish Legal Profession* (Irish Academic Press/Irish Legal History Society, 1990).

the family solicitor in order, for example, to deal with legal problems related to the sale of a house (conveyancing) or the drafting of a will. This is commonly referred to as non-contentious business, that is, it does not involve a court hearing or similar matter such as arbitration. The local solicitor might also appear in court in relation to some contentious business, such as a summons regarding a road traffic offence. The picture of the solicitor as dealing primarily with conveyancing, wills and minor criminal matters is a common one, and indeed generally accurate. However, it must be borne in mind that, in the case of larger firms, a high level of legal advice, particularly in the commercial area, might call for an extremely wide range of legal services, including international litigation or arbitration. But all solicitors share in common the fact that they may do business directly with the public from a high street office. The barrister, on the other hand, does not in general have an individual office or chambers and, as indicated, may generally only give legal advice to a member of the public after receiving instructions from a solicitor.

Fair Trade Commission Report 1990

[3.05] It will become clear from this and subsequent chapters that the legal profession and the court system has been the subject of considerable debate since the 1980s and that this has resulted in extensive reforms, which will affect the profession into the future. In particular, the recommendations in the Fair Trade Commission's *Report into Restrictive Practices in the Legal Profession*,[3] published in 1990, resulted in substantial changes in the organisation of the profession and the courts. In 1984, the Commission had been requested by the then Minister for Industry, Trade, Commerce and Tourism to undertake a wide-ranging inquiry into the legal profession and connected areas, particularly in connection with any practices that might be causing increased costs to consumers of legal services or causing limited employment opportunities within the professions.[4] While the Commission was thus formally limited to a consideration of restrictive practices within the profession, its 1990 Report was extremely wide in scope. The matters dealt with in the 1990 Report included the following:

- an analysis of costs connected with legal services.
- limitations on the provision of legal services.

3. Hereinafter the FTC Report. The Report runs to 334 pages.
4. The Commission's study was made under the Restrictive Practices Act 1972, s 12 by which studies into any trade or profession could be made to determine if practices in any trade or profession constitute a restrictive practice or might unreasonably restrict free and fair competition. The 1972 Act has since been replaced by the Competition Acts 1991 and 1996.

- division of the legal profession into two branches.
- education and admission to the profession.
- the solicitor's right of audience in the courts.
- direct access to barristers.
- the number of legal representatives involved in a court case.
- professional indemnity insurance.
- how legal fees are determined, including contingency fees.
- advertising by members of the legal profession.
- disciplinary procedures against members of the legal profession and liability for negligence.
- services provided by legal personnel in employment and legal executives.
- the appointment of judges, particularly restrictions on appointment of solicitors.
- the organisation of the courts, including court dress and the working hours of the courts.

[3.06] It is clear from this list that the 1990 Report covered almost all issues of importance to the future of the legal profession and indeed the court system. It would be fair to say that the consultations leading up to the 1990 Report, and the reaction to its recommendations, led to considerable debate within the legal profession on its future and a degree of tension between those who represented the profession and the Government as to what changes should follow it. Given the range and diversity of the topics dealt with, it is hardly surprising that there was no unanimity about the changes to be effected in order to achieve the thrust of the recommendations in the 1990 Report.

[3.07] Arising directly or indirectly from the 1990 Report emerged the following: the terms of the Solicitors (Amendment) Act 1994, significant changes in the manner in which the Bar organised that branch of the profession, the establishment of an Advisory Committee on Legal Education and Training, as well as much of the contents of the Courts and Court Officers Act 1995.[5]

Reform, not fusion

[3.08] A significant conclusion of the Commission was that the existing separation or division of the profession was not necessarily a restrictive

5. We discuss the impact of the 1995 Act in Chs 4 and 5.

practice which should be ended. Thus the Commission did not recommend 'fusion' into a unified profession such as is found in the United States of America, where the single entity 'attorney' exists in most States. However, substantial reform was recommended by the Commission and, by the end of 1995, many of these had been implemented in one way or another. In addition, the Commission recommended that nothing should be placed in the way of future fusion of the branches of the profession if that was desired.[6] It seems quite improbable that this will happen in the near future, as those who represent both branches would appear to indicate that, if anything, the requirements of specialisation may require the branches to be considered, in effect, as two separate professions.

[3.09] Many provisions of the 1990 Report and the subsequent action taken on foot of its recommendations mirror some reforms, though not all, which occurred in England arising from a series of reports published in the late 1980s concerning the legal profession and the administration of justice. As in this State, these reports, and the reaction to them, caused considerable tension between the British Government and the legal profession. Nonetheless, considerable reorganisation of the English legal profession and the court system was effected by the enactment of the Courts and Legal Services Act 1990.[7] While the changes effected in Britain differ in a number of respects from those in this legal system, many are similar in tone. It would be difficult to deny therefore that, in the late 1990s, many changes effected in Britain remain highly influential in this State.

[2] SOLICITORS

[3.10] While originally connected to the barrister's branch of the profession, the solicitors ultimately developed to be a distinct branch. The Incorporated Law Society of Ireland was formed in 1830 for the purpose of securing the independent existence of the solicitors as a branch of the profession and it was subsequently incorporated by Royal Charter in 1852. The Solicitors (Ireland) Act 1898 established for the first time that the Incorporated Law Society of Ireland was to have control over the education of students wishing to become solicitors as well as giving it important disciplinary powers over those who qualified as solicitors. The Society, which in 1994 was renamed the Law Society of Ireland, continues in this dual role and its activities are now regulated by statute, the Solicitors Acts 1954 to 1994.[8] The Director General of the Law Society, its chief executive officer, also

6. FTC Report, pp 71-3.

7. See Walker & Walker's *English Legal System*, 7th ed (Butterworths, 1994), Ch 10.

8. The Solicitors Act 1954, which consolidated the statutory regulation of this branch of the profession, has been amended in significant respects on two occasions: by the Solicitors (Amendment) Act 1960 and the Solicitors (Amendment) Act 1994. Section 4 of the 1994 Act removed the word 'Incorporated' from the name of the Law Society of Ireland.

acts as the principal spokesperson in the media for the solicitor's branch of the profession.

Increased numbers of solicitors

[3.11] Table 3.01 indicates the increase in the number of practising solicitors from the 1960s.[9]

Year	Number
1960	1,335
1970	1,363
1975	1,655
1980	2,139
1983	2,788
1985	3,188
1987	3,360
1989	3,422

Table 3.01

This increase, which reflected the huge growth in the popularity of law degrees in the 1970s and 1980s in particular, has continued into the 1990s. By 1995, the number of persons enrolled as solicitors with the Law Society had reached 4,000.[10] This has created enormous pressures on the arrangements for the legal education of solicitors and ensuring that those who qualify have a reasonable future. The balance between ensuring continued access to the profession and the need to assure entrants a reasonable standard of living for those who become qualified solicitors was discussed in detail in the 1990 Fair Trade Commission Report. The Commission recommended that the profession itself should not be entitled to determine the appropriate numbers to enter the profession, fearing that a 'quota' system might be against the public interest.[11] Rather, it was recommended that freedom of access, subject to proper standards of education, be the governing principle, with the market for professional services determining the number of practitioners. The Commission did, however, also recommend that, if necessary, a body might be established to

9. Source: 1990 FTC Report, p 80.

10. Source: Law Society of Ireland, 1996.

11. Suggestions that a 'quota' system had been operated by the Law Society emerged in *MacGabhann v Incorporated Law Society of Ireland* [1989] ILRM 854, but this was contested by the Law Society. A declaration was made in the case that such a quota would be *ultra vires* the powers of the Law Society under the Solicitors Acts.

determine if limits on entry were required in the future. At present, no such body has been established so that entry levels are not limited and, in effect, the market determines the numbers of practising solicitors.

Admission to the profession

[3.12] Before becoming a solicitor, most persons must serve a period of apprenticeship to an established solicitor. Prior to 1995, the minimum period for this was three years, but this was reduced to two years.[12] Obtaining a contract of apprenticeship, referred to as articles of indenture, became increasingly difficult from the mid-1980s onwards when the number of persons seeking admission to the profession increased dramatically.

[3.13] In addition to obtaining articles of indenture, most persons must also complete the courses of study organised by the Law Society at its headquarters in Blackhall Place, Dublin. A pre-condition to consideration for admission to these courses of study is that a prospective student must hold a university degree or its equivalent or be a barrister or equivalent: this is referred to as the Preliminary Examination requirement.[13] If a person meets these requirements, he or she must then complete the Society's Final Examination, which is divided into three segments, commonly referred to as FE-1, FE-2 and FE-3.

[3.14] The FE-1 Examination is the crucial examination in terms of the transition from university student to the Law Society's examinations. It comprises eight 'core subjects', Company Law, Constitutional Law, Contract Law, Criminal Law, Equity, European Community Law, the Law of Real Property (Land Law), and Tort Law (Equity and European Community Law having been added in 1994). Prior to 1995, pursuant to Reg 15 of the Solicitors Acts 1954 and 1960 (Apprenticeship and Education) Regulations 1991,[14] the Law Society had granted exemptions from FE-1 to law graduates from the universities of the Republic of Ireland provided they had successfully completed these 'core' subjects in their law degrees.[15] The exemption in Reg 15 of the 1991 Regulations was removed arising from *Bloomer and Ors v Incorporated Law Society of Ireland.* [16] The plaintiffs, law graduates of Northern Ireland universities, had sought parity with their

12. Solicitors Act 1954, s 26, as amended by Solicitors (Amendment) Act 1994, s 42.
13. Solicitors Act 1954, s 41, as amended by Solicitors (Amendment) Act 1994, s 50.
14. SI 9/1991, as amended by the Solicitors Acts 1954 and 1960 (Apprenticeship and Education) (Amendment) (No 2) Regulations 1992 (SI 360/1992). The Regulations are made under the Solicitors Act 1954, s 40, as amended.
15. Other aspects of the Law Society's arrangements had given rise to litigation in the 1980s: see *Gilmer v. Incorporated Law Society of Ireland* [1989] ILRM 590.
16. [1995] 3 IR 14 (HC); Supreme Court, unrep, 6 February 1996.

counterparts from the Republic of Ireland. It was held by Laffoy J in the High Court that the exemption in Reg 15 of the 1991 Regulations for law graduates from the universities in the Republic of Ireland was invalid because it was in conflict with the prohibition of discrimination on grounds of nationality in Article 6 of the EC Treaty.[17] In light of the High Court decision, the Law Society stated that it would henceforth require all persons to sit the FE-1 Examination rather than extend the prior exemption. However, pursuant to Reg 30 of the 1991 Regulations, which empowers it to modify any requirement of the Regulations 'in exceptional circumstances,' it decided that the plaintiffs in *Bloomer* be granted an exemption from FE-1.[18] Subsequently, in *Abrahamson and Ors v Law Society of Ireland*,[19] over 800 undergraduate law students in the Republic's universities[20] sought to restore the position prior to *Bloomer*, at least for those 'already in the system.' It was held by McCracken J in the High Court that, since Reg 15 had been declared invalid in *Bloomer*, the 800 applicants in *Abrahamson* were no longer entitled to rely on the expectation that they would be exempt from FE-1. However, he also held that the position of the 800 applicants constituted 'exceptional circumstances' under Reg 30 of the 1991 Regulations and directed the Law Society to consider granting them the exemptions they would have had if Reg 15 had been valid. The Law Society subsequently decided that all law students attending the previously exempted law degrees at the time of the decision in *Abrahamson* were exempt from FE-1. At the time of writing (July 1996), it would thus appear that students beginning their law studies in universities in the Republic from the academic year 1996-97 are no longer exempt from FE-1. It remains to be seen whether some alternative arrangement will be put in place in the future.

[3.15] The FE-2 and FE-3 Courses and Examinations are the principal courses conducted by the Law Society in Blackhall Place, Dublin. They comprise courses primarily of a practical or vocational nature rather than academic in tone. FE-2 is commonly described as the Professional Course and involves 14 weeks intensive full-time instruction followed by examination. If successfully completed, this is followed by 18 months in-

17. On European Community law, see Ch 16.

18. The effect of this was that the plaintiffs in *Bloomer* had achieved the objective of their proceedings, namely, exemption from FE-1. The plaintiffs had already appealed the High Court decision to the Supreme Court, but the Law Society's decision rendered this moot. Consequently the Supreme Court judgment in *Bloomer* was concerned primarily with the question of, though the Court's formal order confirmed the High Court decision that Reg 15 of the 1991 Regulations was invalid.

19. High Court, unrep, 15 July 1996.

20. See *The Irish Times*, 3 July 1996, p 4.

office training for the students as part of their apprenticeship. Finally, the FE-3 Course, the Advanced Course, comprises seven weeks further intensive full-time instruction, also followed by an examination. Once the FE-3 has been completed, and the indentures have expired, the person is entitled to be admitted to the roll of solicitors.

Discipline and Compensation

[3.16] After admission as a solicitor, every solicitor is subject to the disciplinary powers of the Law Society. Under the Solicitors Acts 1954 to 1994, the Disciplinary Tribunal of the Law Society may investigate an allegation of misconduct such as misappropriation of client funds, by a solicitor and it may refer the matter to the President of the High Court. The President may take a number of courses of action, including suspending the solicitor from the roll of practising solicitors. The effect of this is that the solicitor may not practice for the period of the suspension. The President of the High Court also has power to lift the suspension. Under the Solicitors Act 1954 as originally enacted, the Disciplinary Committee was empowered to suspend a solicitor, but this power was held to be unconstitutional.[21] The Solicitors (Amendment) Act 1960 accordingly transferred the disciplinary function to the President of the High Court. Short of the drastic powers of suspension, the Solicitors (Amendment) Act 1994 conferred powers on the Law Society to investigate complaints against solicitors concerning, for example, overcharging and to requires repayment to clients if the complaints are upheld. An appeal lies to the High Court concerning any decision of the Law Society and, to ensure general confidence in the system, the 1994 Act required that a number of lay persons be members of the Disciplinary Tribunal and that an independent adjudicator oversee the operation of the Law Society's investigative powers.

[3.17] Connected with this is the requirement that all solicitors make payments, usually annually, to the statutory Compensation Fund established by the 1960 Act to compensate clients of solicitors who have suffered loss arising from the wrongdoing (including fraud) of solicitors. The Compensation Fund amounts to a levy on all practising solicitors. Claims by solicitors' clients have increased dramatically since the 1970s, and the 1994 Act placed a cap of £250,000 in any particular case. Prior to the 1994 Act, no cap on an individual claim existed. To compensate for this, the 1994 Act also imposed requirements on solicitors to satisfy the Law Society that their personal professional indemnity cover is sufficient before the annual practising certificate is granted.

---

21. *In re the Solicitors Act 1954* [1960] IR 239: see para **[4.13]**.

Practice: firms and incorporated practices

[3.18] In relation to practice as a solicitor, a significant feature of this branch of the profession is that solicitors may form a partnership as a firm of solicitors. Many such firms exist, particularly in the larger towns and cities, but there are also many 'sole practitioners', that is, one person firms. Clearly, there are advantages in having a partnership and the larger firms are capable of providing a high level of expert advice to their clients. It is envisaged that provision will be made for solicitors to form incorporated practices, that is equivalent to the formation of companies, subject to certain restrictions,[22] though detailed Regulations on this matter had not been made at the time of writing (July 1996).

Non-contentious business and conveyancing

[3.19] There are no express limits as to the areas of law in which solicitors may practice. In relation to non-contentious business (that is work not connected with court proceedings or analogous work such as arbitration), the drafting of wills and conveyancing are important areas for many solicitors. Indeed, under s 58 of the Solicitors Act 1954 solicitors enjoyed what was generally described as a 'conveyancing monopoly'. Under s 58 as originally passed, a solicitor was the only professional person who could advise on the legal validity of title to land. The result was that the services of a solicitor were invariably required in relation to all land transactions, including the sale of houses. There was, of course, no legal prohibition on a purchaser checking that everything was in order in relation to the house being purchased, but in practice most purchasers would be advised to have the matter checked by a professional adviser. In any event, since the vast majority of house purchases in Ireland are made with the aid of a mortgage or other loan from a financial institution, it is generally a condition of the granting of the loan that title is checked by a professional person. The 1990 Report of the Fair Trade Commission recommended removal of the 'monopoly', following a similar move in Britain, and that financial institutions be empowered to provide such services. However, while this was initially proposed in the Solicitors (Amendment) Bill 1994, it was abandoned in the course of its passage through the Oireachtas and is thus not found in the Solicitors (Amendment) Act 1994. It is expected that solicitors will be required to show in future that fees charged for such services in the future are not excessive, and the disciplinary arrangements in place in the 1994 Act concerning overcharging, referred to above, must be seen in that light.

---

22. Solicitors (Amendment) Act 1994, s 70.

[3.20] In addition to these areas of non-contentious practice, the larger firms of solicitors are, for example, involved in the formation of private companies, the flotation of companies on the stock exchange, engaging tax advisers for clients and many other areas of commercial law.

Contentious business, the right of audience and judicial appointments

[3.21] As indicated above, many solicitors do not become engaged in advocacy, except in some cases, civil and criminal, in the lower courts. In relation to proceedings in the High Court and Supreme Court in particular, the tendency is for solicitors to instruct a barrister (counsel) to appear in court. Indeed, this also occurs quite frequently in Circuit Court and District Court cases. The solicitor's primary function in such circumstances is to prepare the papers in the case for the court hearing. This will include, in a civil case for example, writing on behalf of the client to the firm of solicitors for the other party in the case and obtaining reports from expert witnesses, such as medical consultants and engineers. The solicitor also liaises with the barrister in relation to what is required at the court hearing.

[3.22] Since the enactment of the Courts Act 1971 solicitors have, in fact, the same right to appear in any court, including the High Court and Supreme Court, as barristers. Prior to the 1971 Act this right, called the right of audience, was severely limited, but the 1971 Act provided for complete parity between the branches of the profession in Ireland in this respect.[23] Despite this, relatively few solicitors take full advantage of the right of audience, though in many instances they appear in the High Court and Supreme Court in relation to preliminary matters relating to a case and this has proved extremely convenient. Subject to a small number of exceptions, therefore, much of the advocacy and arguing of full cases in the High Court and Supreme Court remains in the hands of the Bar. The Fair Trade Commission in its 1990 Report expressed disappointment that this was the case and recommended that the Law Society should encourage their members to make fuller use of their right of audience.[24]

[3.23] A related issue is the question of the suitability of solicitors for appointment as judges. Prior to 1995, solicitors were qualified for appointment to the District Court only. However, since the enactment of the

23. The 1971 Act gave effect to the recommendations in the *13th Interim Report of the Committee on Court Practice and Procedure*, published in 1971. It is notable that, even after the radical changes effected in Britain in the wake of the Courts and Legal Services Act 1990 (see para **[3.09]**), solicitors in Britain do not enjoy the full rights of audience granted to solicitors in this jurisdiction by the 1971 Act.

24. FTC Report, pp 131-2.

Courts and Court Officers Act 1995, direct appointment of solicitors to the Circuit Court has now become a reality, with the further possibility of 'promotion' to the High Court and Supreme Court also permissible, if still in the future.[25]

Advertising

[3.24] The 1990 Fair Trade Commission Report recommended that restrictions on advertising by solicitors, in particular any restrictions on fee advertising, be removed. Section 69 of the Solicitors (Amendment) Act 1994 gave effect to this by amending s 71 of the Solicitors Act 1954, which deals with the power of the Society to make Regulations with respect to the professional practice, conduct and discipline of solicitors. The Law Society may not in general prohibit advertising by solicitors, including fee advertising, except in the case of advertising which is likely to bring the profession into disrepute, is in bad taste, reflects unfavourably on other solicitors, is false or misleading, is contrary to public policy or consists of unsolicited approaches to individuals for business.

'No foal, no fee' litigation

[3.25] In recent years, many solicitors have engaged in litigation, particularly involving personal injuries, on the basis that the client will not be charged a professional fee if the claim is unsuccessful. This is usually referred to as the 'no foal, no fee' arrangement. While such practices have been criticised by those outside the legal profession as encouraging a proliferation of litigation, they have not been prohibited by legislation. However, s 68(2) of the Solicitors (Amendment) Act 1994 prohibits a solicitor from charging a client on the basis of a percentage or proportion of any damages awarded to the client, except in cases relating to recovery of a debt or a liquidated demand. We consider this in more detail elsewhere.[26]

Chief State Solicitor and State Solicitors

[3.26] Since the State is involved in much litigation, whether criminal or civil, there is a requirement of a permanent solicitor to represent the State and to instruct barristers on the State's behalf. This is the function of the Chief State Solicitor who is a civil servant and is solicitor to the Attorney General, the Director of Public Prosecutions as well as Government Departments and State bodies. In addition to the Chief State Solicitor, solicitors in private practice are appointed to appear at local level on behalf of the State, and are referred to as State Solicitors. They are usually paid on a fee-per-case basis.

---

25. See further para **[4.67]**.
26. See para **[5.08]**.

[3] BARRISTERS

[3.27] As mentioned already, the barristers' branch of the profession is generally also known collectively as The Bar. Individually, they may be referred to as barristers or counsel.[27] The Bar is usually regarded as the senior branch of the profession, though like the solicitors' branch it has gone through many changes over the centuries, so its precise roots are difficult to trace. Again the English influence is important in this context. Originally, Inns of Court were established in London for the purpose of providing, amongst other things, for the education of those who wished to practice as advocates. A similar institution, the Honourable Society of King's Inns,[28] was established in Dublin and it remains the body which provides post-graduate legal training for those who wish to practice at the Bar, in a system parallel to the Law Society. Virtually all members of the Bar are also required to be members of the Law Library, situated in or near the Four Courts Building, Dublin. Disciplinary matters are regulated by the Council of the Bar of Ireland. Unlike the solicitors' branch, the Bar is in general not regulated by statute.

Increased numbers of barristers

[3.28] As with the solicitors' branch of the profession, there has been a substantial increase in the number of barristers in Ireland, as Table 3.02 of membership of the Law Library indicates.[29]

Year	Number
1968	217
1970	253
1975	292
1980	429
1983	481
1985	534
1987	638
1989	722

Table 3.02

27. Thus many of the extracts from judgments in this text include phrases 'Counsel for the plaintiff has submitted ... '

28. On its early history, see Kenny, *King's Inns and the Kingdom of Ireland: the Irish 'inn of court' 1541-1800* (Irish Academic Press, 1992).

29. Source: 1990 FTC Report, p 85.

Again, as with the solicitors' branch, this number has continued to rise into the 1990s. By 1996, the total membership of the Law Library stood at just under 900.[30]

Admission to the profession

[3.29] The Honourable Society of King's Inns, situated in Henrietta St. Dublin,[31] at one time operated under Royal Charter granted in 1792, but this, it appears, was later revoked. The King's Inns therefore operates at present as a voluntary society, under the control of a body known as the Benchers of the Honourable Society of King's Inns. These Benchers include a number of members of the judiciary as well as senior members of the Bar. The Benchers exercise ultimate control over the courses of education provided by the King's Inns, which lead to the award of the degree of barrister-at-law.

[3.30] Since the early 1980s, when applications for places at the King's Inns began to increase, the number of places available annually was capped at about 100. A minimum of 50% of the places are reserved for law graduates, 40% are reserved for holders of the King's Inns Diploma in Legal Studies, a two-year diploma course for which lectures are provided in the Inns' own premises, and the remaining 10% of places are allocated by the Education Committee of the King's Inns. For those seeking admission with a law degree, the 'core' subjects for King's Inns are: Constitutional Law, Contract Law, Criminal Law, Equity, the Law of Real Property (Land Law) and Tort Law. Because of the restrictions on numbers, those holding a law degree have, in recent years, been required to achieve a high second class honours degree to gain admission.

[3.31] The length of the barrister-at-law degree course at the King's Inns is currently two years. In addition to completing the course of studies prescribed, the student of King's Inns must also 'keep commons' by dining in the Hall of the Honourable Society on ten days in each of the two academic years of the barrister-at-law degree course. The tradition of dining reflects a much earlier time when no precise course of academic study was prescribed for those wishing to become a barrister. Rather, by dining with established barristers the students would become familiar with the practice of the law in a more informal academic context. When a student has successfully completed the course of studies prescribed by the King's Inns he or she is 'called to the Bar' in the Supreme Court, located in the Four Courts building Dublin, in the presence of the Chief Justice and, generally speaking, other members of the Supreme Court bench. The barrister then

30. Source: Bar Council of Ireland, 1996.

31. The Society's premises also front onto Constitution Hill in Dublin.

signs the roll of members of the Bar which is also located in the Four Courts. While at this stage, the person in question is a barrister-at-law, there are further additional requirements in place before the person may engage in paid legal work.

The Law Library

[3.32] The call to the Bar means that the person is admitted to practice as a barrister-at-law, or junior counsel. A significant feature of the Bar in Ireland is that barristers may not join together to form groups or 'chambers' of barristers as is the practice in England. Instead, most members of the Bar practice from what is called, simply, the Law Library. For over 200 years, the Law Library was housed in part of the Four Courts building in Dublin and this is where the 'old' Law Library remains. However, due to the expansion in numbers in the late 1980s, additional accommodation was provided adjacent to the Four Courts in what is now referred to as the 'new' Law Library. In the wake of the creation of the two jurisdictions in Ireland in the 1920s, a similar 'Library' arrangement was made in Northern Ireland and continues to prevail in the Royal Courts of Justice, Belfast.

[3.33] It has been a long-established requirement of the Bar that barristers be members of the Law Library in order to practice. The 1990 Report of the Fair Trade Commission regarded this as a restrictive practice and should be removed, if necessary by legislation. However, in its response to the Report, the Bar Council and the members of the Law Library voted in 1991 to retain the existing requirement in the Code of Conduct concerning membership. No legislative action had been taken in the wake of this when this text went to print (July 1996).

[3.34] Before entering the Law Library, the barrister must ensure that an established barrister of at least five years' standing has agreed to act as 'master' for the new member of the Law Library, the new member being referred to as a 'devil' (a more archaic word being 'tyro'). This, in effect, mirrors the apprenticeship for solicitors. The period of pupillage is generally 12 months. During this time, the master is expected to introduce the devil or pupil to the general practice of the Law Library, legal research, court work and to ask the devil to assist with drafting pleadings and other documents for court. The devil will assist the master in all aspects of the master's practice and will generally attend court with the master as a means of learning the role of the barrister.

[3.35] In the Law Library in Dublin, barristers are provided with accommodation and access to legal textbooks, on payment of an annual membership fee. The Four Courts building houses all the major courts in the

State, including the High Court and Supreme Court as well as some other courts. The location of the Law Library is, therefore, ideally suited to the needs of the Bar. However, not all members of the Bar practice on a permanent basis from the Four Courts. Many barristers practice primarily outside Dublin, that is 'on circuit' and practice only occasionally in the courts in Dublin. For those who practice primarily in the Cork and Southern regions, many barristers in fact have chambers in Cork city, though generally these are not shared with other members of the Bar.

Discipline and conduct

[3.36] The general conduct of the members of the Bar is controlled by a non-statutory body, the General Council of the Bar of Ireland. The Council is elected annually by the members of the Bar, and a Chairman is also elected to chair the most important business committees and also to represent the Bar in, for example, discussions with government or for interview by the media. The Bar Council issues to each member a Professional Code of Conduct which is amended from time to time by the members themselves.

[3.37] The provisions of the Code of Conduct cover such matters as the requirement that a barrister accept only so much work that he or she can give adequate attention to it within a reasonable time; the need to ensure confidentiality concerning client matters; taking of instructions from solicitors; the duty of the barrister to the courts, in particular not to mislead a court in any manner;[32] prohibitions on touting and advertising his or her services to the public; the precedence between barristers on the basis of call to the Bar and general conduct between members of the Bar; the relationship between barristers and the Law Library and Bar Council; specific rules on the duty of a barrister in criminal cases; the position of senior counsel; charging fees; and the position of overseas lawyers.

[3.38] Prior to 1991, complaints against members of the Bar, whether from the public, a solicitor, another barrister or a judge, were investigated by the Disciplinary Committee of the Bar Council. Where a barrister was found by the Disciplinary Committee to be in breach of the Code of Conduct, he or she was liable to disciplinary sanctions, including admonishments as well as suspension, and ultimately expulsion, from the Law Library. In addition, he or she could be reported to the Benchers of the King's Inns who appeared to retain the ultimate disciplinary sanction of disbarment, that is, removal of the person's name from the roll of members of the Bar.

---

32. See generally the comments of Crampton J in *R v O'Connell* (1845) 7 Ir Law Rep 261, at 313 on the duties of the barrister.

[3.39] As the Fair Trade Commission noted in its 1990 Report, 'the constitutionality of the powers of neither the Bar Council nor the King's Inns has been challenged, unlike those of the Law Society.'[33] The Commission recommended that the Bar Council alone be responsible for discipline within the Bar and that it was not appropriate that the King's Inns be involved, particularly as many of its Benchers were members of the judiciary. Although the Commission recommended that legislation might be required on foot of this recommendation, non-statutory measures have, instead, been put in place on this point. In 1991, the Bar Council adopted substantial amendments to the Bar's Code of Conduct. Since then, allegations of breach of the Code are investigated by the Professional Practices Committee of the Bar Council. This Committee includes lay members, that is persons who are not members of the Bar. The Committee has extensive powers to impose fines on members of the Bar found in breach of the Code of Conduct as well as issue admonishments and, ultimately, to suspend or exclude a member from the Law Library. Appeals from the Professional Practices Committee can be made to the Appeals Board, which is chaired by a Circuit Court judge and which also comprises a lay member.

Instructions, direct access and fees

[3.40] A barrister was, as already indicated, traditionally required to receive instructions from a solicitor and was prohibited by the Code of Conduct of the Bar from receiving instructions from other professionals or from members of the public. This prohibition on what is described as direct access was regarded as an essential *indicium* of the independence of the Bar and as essential to ensure the continued strength of the Bar as advocates. A corollary of this convention was that, once a barrister received instructions from a solicitor, he or she was obliged to accept the instructions unless it was in an area in which the barrister had no previous experience or expertise. This is known as the 'cab rank' rule.

[3.41] In the context of appearing in court, judges would also be loathe to 'hear' counsel unless a solicitor was physically present in court to instruct the barrister. This rule was applied with greater or lesser strictness by different judges but, on many occasions, matters would be adjourned where a solicitor was not present in court with counsel. Another consequence of receiving instructions through a solicitor was that the solicitor was also responsible for ensuring that the barrister's fees were paid. The convention which followed was that a barrister could not sue for fees due, though this convention had not been put to the test in recent times, but most barristers

33. FTC Report, p 281.

continue to rely on a good relationship with their instructing solicitors to ensure collection of fees.

[3.42] The practice of requiring instructions from a solicitor and prohibiting direct access was examined in detail by the Fair Trade Commission in its 1990 Report. It considered that the blanket ban on direct access was a restrictive practice and should be deleted from the Professional Code of Conduct. However, it also considered that in certain instances, particularly concerning litigation, the continued involvement of solicitors was desirable. Thus, it accepted that a barrister could, in an individual case, refuse to accept direct instructions from a client and could insist that a solicitor be engaged. As a consequence, the Commission recommended that there should no longer be any statutory or other rules requiring the physical attendance of a solicitor in court to instruct a barrister. These recommendations of the Fair Trade Commission have not been implemented in full, and the Bar continue to defend restrictions on direct access on the basis that they are fundamental to the separation of the Bar from the solicitors' branch of the profession. However, a number of amendments to the Code of Conduct were made to extend the circumstances in which direct access is permitted. These now include, direct access from certain professionals (Direct Professional Access), such as accountants.

[3.43] The level of fees charged by barristers has also been the subject of some public criticism in recent years, and in at least one instance this resulted in a successful claim for libel by a senior member of the Bar. In *Foley v Independent Newspapers (Ireland) Ltd*,[34] the plaintiff had been appointed by a Government Minister as an inspector to investigate the affairs of a State company. Shortly after his appointment, he had agreed a daily fee with the relevant State authorities. The investigation took six months to complete and the plaintiff's fee amounted to £250,000. Although this had been based on the agreed fee, the plaintiff was criticised in a newspaper article for the level of fee charged. He successfully sued the newspaper and was awarded £30,000 damages for libel. In 1996, considerable comment emerged concerning a total of £6.75m in legal fees awarded to solicitors and barristers who had been involved in a three year tribunal of inquiry into the Irish beef industry.[35] This included a fee of £923,170 awarded to the leading senior counsel, Mr Dermot Gleeson, who had, in the meantime, been appointed Attorney General.[36] However, it has been estimated that, for more day-to-day matters, fees earned are less

34. [1994] 2 ILRM 61.
35. See paras **[8.63]-[8.65]**.
36. The Irish Times, 31 July 1996, pp 1 and 5.

spectacular. In personal injuries civil actions, a brief fee of between £350 and £400 would be common in the Circuit Court, while for a High Court action a brief fee of £750 might be appropriate. Fees are lower in criminal matters, reflecting the fact that these are primarily State-funded.[37] In a trial on indictment in the Circuit Criminal Court, a fee of between £450 and £500 would be paid. For State-funded civil actions, principally in the family law area, a basic hourly fee of £44 for senior counsel and £31.50 for junior counsel was payable in 1996. While a small percentage of the Bar earn well into six figures annually, the average earnings for barristers in 1996 were estimated at about £30,000, 'not dissimilar to those in other professions.'[38]

Junior counsel and senior counsel

[3.44] A distinction exists within the Bar between junior counsel and senior counsel. The initial call to the Bar is to the ranks of junior counsel, sometimes referred to as the Outer Bar. The general rule is that a barrister will practice for a number of years as a junior counsel before considering whether to become a senior counsel. The move from junior to senior counsel is also referred to as 'taking silk', since by tradition the black gown worn by senior counsel is of silk rather than the poplin of junior counsel. Senior counsel are collectively referred to as the Inner Bar. The abbreviation 'SC' is often inserted after that of a 'senior', but 'JC' is never used to signify that a person is a member of the junior bar. The distinction between junior and senior counsel replaced the distinction between junior counsel and Queen's (or King's) Counsel that preceded the establishment of the two legal systems on the island in the 1920s. In 1990, there were 112 Senior Counsel in the Law Library, representing about 15% of the total membership of 728.[39]

[3.45] Progression from junior to senior counsel is not a simple matter of automatic 'promotion' after a specified number of years. Indeed, many eminent members of the Bar choose not to become senior counsel and remain as 'juniors' into their 70s and 80s. However, in general, most barristers consider 'taking silk' after about 15 years' practice, when they reach their late 30s or early 40s. Once a barrister decides to become a senior counsel, he or she applies to the Chief Justice and Attorney General for approval, but the actual appointment is made by the government,[40] acting on

37. See paras **[9.13] - [9.16]**.
38. The figures quoted are contained in The Irish Times, 6 August 1996, p 4.
39. FTC Report, p 85.
40. The government issues a formal letter patent to senior counsel under the Executive Functions (Consequential Provisions) Act 1937, s 2 carrying over a function formerly given to the monarch when issuing a letter patent to Queen's or King's Counsel under the pre-1922 arrangements: see para **[15.46]**.

the advice of the Attorney General who also liaises with the Chairman of the Bar Council. There are no strict rules setting out the criteria for granting an application to become a senior counsel, though as the Fair Trade Commission Report put it, '[a]pproval depends on considerations such as personal observation of the barrister's work in court, and his [or her] general reputation and standing.'[41] While approval is thus not automatic, it could be said that virtually no member of the Bar applies unless they have already made informal soundings amongst their colleagues that they are 'qualified' to be approved. The Fair Trade Commission was not attracted to some of the mystery and apparent secrecy surrounding the 'taking of silk' and recommended that the government's function in the process be terminated and that the status be a less formal matter for the profession.[42] However, no action has been taken on this recommendation.

[3.46] In general, the functions of a junior counsel include the drafting and preparation of pleadings as well as conducting some cases in court, generally in the lower courts though not exclusively so. The senior counsel's functions, on the other hand, include scrutiny of draft pleadings which have been prepared by a junior counsel (called 'settling' pleadings) as well as the conduct of some of the more difficult legal cases in the High Court and Supreme Court. While a minority of senior counsel do not engage in court work, the majority of 'SCs' or 'silks' are known for their court-room wizardry.

[3.47] A number of conventions developed over the years (many again predating the 1920s) as to the circumstances in which junior and senior counsel would be retained in a case. An important example was that, in the vast majority of cases, a senior counsel was precluded from appearing in a case unless a junior counsel was also retained. And in civil claims for personal injuries (colloquially called 'running down' cases because of the number of road traffic accidents involved) it was the convention that one junior and two senior counsel would be retained by each side. This 'two senior' rule was subject to some criticism and, since the passing of the Courts Act 1988 (which provided that High Court personal injuries cases should no longer be decided by a judge and jury, but by a judge alone and which had also indicated that the 'two senior' rule would be abolished by legislation unless abandoned 'voluntarily') the practice in many cases is to retain one junior and one senior counsel.[43]

---

41. FTC Report, p 107.
42. FTC Report, pp 122-3.
43. See further para **[5.24]**.

Advocacy and the Bar

[3.48] The general picture of barristers, and in particular senior counsel, is of great orators and in many instances the most eminent practitioners are indeed extremely persuasive advocates and speakers.[44] This may be particularly important in cases heard before juries where the barrister is expected to 'tug the jury's heartstrings.' But apart from those barristers who specialise in criminal cases and also the civil cases which tend to receive a large degree of publicity (and which form the basis for most films or television series on the law) the reality of practice at the Bar is that much time is spent on 'paperwork', in other words the preparation of pleadings in anticipation of a court hearing. Given that the vast majority of cases in which a barrister receives instructions are settled before a court hearing,[45] the true position is that advocacy plays a relatively minor part in the normal work of the practitioner. Of much greater practical importance is the ability to give advice on a legal problem and to draft documents which will begin the process of accelerating the satisfactory settlement of the legal problem presented, whether through a court hearing or otherwise.

[3.49] Ireland has, of course, produced well-known and brilliant advocates, including Daniel O'Connell and Sir Edward Carson, and it may be no coincidence that both were also well-known and successful politicians. The mixture of law and politics as a career continues to the present, a feature of most countries. Ireland has also produced its quota of anecdotal publications about life at the Bar, which tend to emphasise the moments of courtroom mirth.[46]

Mode of Dress

[3.50] A further long-standing distinction between the two branches of the legal profession relates to the mode of dress of a member of the Bar in court. Until 1996, barristers were required by statutory rules of court to wear a wig, usually made of horsehair, as well as a black gown over dark dress. The barrister's shirt, or blouse, has, generally speaking, a winged collar and, in place of a tie, the barrister wears a white band. These requirements were carried over from the rules of court which existed prior to the creation of the two jurisdictions in the 1920s. During the 1980s, the question of wearing wigs in court in particular became the subject of considerable debate.

---

44. See the views of the former Chief Justice, Mr Justice Finlay, in an address to Law Society students 'Criminal Defence Advocacy' (1981) 1 Crim Law Journal 1 and his 1986 address at Fordham University School of Law 'Advocacy: Has it a Future?' published as a Supplement to the December 1986 issue of the *Irish Law Times*.

45. See para **[6.54]-[6.56]**.

46. See Maurice Healy, *The Old Munster Circuit* (Mercier Reprint, 1981), Rex Mackey, *Windward of the Law* (WH Allen, 1965) and McArdle, *Irish Legal Anecdotes* (Gill and Macmillan, 1995).

[3.51] In its 1990 Report, the Fair Trade Commission noted that while the issue was peripheral in many ways to its main recommendations it was important to a number of persons, particularly those who represented the consumers of legal services, who felt that the wig created an element of intimidation for those unaccustomed to appearing in court. The Bar Council indicated it had no firm views on the wearing of the wig, but that it would not like to see it disappear completely. The Commission also referred to some judicial criticisms of the continued wearing of wigs,[47] and noted that it had been prohibited in family proceedings.[48] It also pointed out that the continued wearing of wigs might have an inhibiting effect on solicitors representing their clients. The Commission also considered that, since judges also wore wigs, 'this may convey the impression of an association and a community of interest between the two.' The Commission therefore considered that 'it would be a sensible move towards a more modern profession if barristers no longer wore wigs.'

[3.52] While the prohibition of the wearing of wigs had been proposed in the Courts and Court Officers Bill 1995, ultimately, s 49 of the Courts and Court Officers Act 1995 provides only that the wearing of wigs by members of the Bar 'shall not be required' and thus is a matter for their own discretion and is no longer mandatory. As this discretionary rule only became effective in December 1995, it is difficult to measure its full impact, but it would appear that, for the present, the majority of members of the Bar continue to wear wigs, those appearing 'wigless' remaining the notable exceptions. It should be noted that, for those appearing without a wig, the traditional gown, wing-collared shirt and tab remains in place. Finally, the requirements concerning mode of dress do not apply in relation to sittings of the courts during the Vacations.[49]

[4] THE LAW OFFICERS

[3.53] We turn now to discuss the two Law Officers in the State. Prior to 1922, a number of lawyers, primarily barristers, were appointed to represent the Government and to some extent the general public in matters of law and legal opinion. This tradition was carried over into the Irish Free State. The

47. The Commission referred to the paper delivered by the late Mr Justice McCarthy to the 1987 MacGill Summer School in which he had described the 'post-colonial servitude' of the Irish courts system. He described the continued wearing of wigs as 'absurd' and as 'comic' that women should wear what were originally male wigs. The Report noted that Mr Justice McCarthy also heard it had been suggested that wigs afforded a sense of protection against clients 'as if they were a form of forensic condom'.

48. Judicial Separation and Family Law Reform Act 1989, ss 33, 45.

49. On the Vacations, see para **[4.124]**.

present Law Officers in the State are the Attorney General and the Director of Public Prosecutions.[50]

The Attorney General

[3.54] Article 30 of the Constitution of Ireland provides that the Attorney General is 'the adviser of the Government in matters of law and legal opinion' and that he shall perform any additional functions conferred on him by law. Section 6 of the Ministers and Secretaries Act 1924[51] provides that the Attorney General was vested with the functions of the Attorney General for Ireland, that is the Attorney General in the pre-1922 era.

[3.55] Article 30 also provides that the Attorney General (sometimes referred to as 'the AG' or 'the Attorney') is appointed by the President of Ireland on the nomination of the Taoiseach. The Attorney General must retire from office on the resignation of the Taoiseach, thus indicating that the office has a close personal connection with the fate of the Taoiseach of the day. The position of Attorney General as principal adviser to the government and as a close confidante of the head of the executive also echoes the position of the Attorney General for Ireland in the pre-1922 era and indeed the title Attorney General was adopted by the first such legal adviser to the Government, Hugh Kennedy, who later became Chief Justice.

[3.56] The Attorney General is, by convention, a practising member of the Bar and a senior counsel.[52] The Attorney General is also what is by convention referred to as the leader of the Bar, in other words he ranks as the most senior member of the Bar. This is largely a ceremonial position. While there is no rule requiring the Attorney to cease private practice while acting as Attorney, this has in fact been the case in recent years.

---

50. The phrase 'law officers' is also used in the Prosecution of Offences Act 1974, s 4 to refer to the present offices of Attorney General and Director of Public Prosecutions. The definitive account of the history and role of the Law Officers, in particular that of the Attorney General and the Director of Public Prosecutions, is Casey, *The Irish Law Officers: Roles and Responsibilities of the Attorney General and Director of Public Prosecutions* (Round Hall Sweet & Maxwell, 1996).

51. The 1924 Act concerned the Attorney General of the Irish Free State, but it appears to be accepted that it has been 'carried forward' to apply to the Attorney General under the 1937 Constitution: see Casey, *op cit*.

52. An exception was the appointment in 1977 of John M Kelly, then Government Chief Whip, as Attorney General. Professor Kelly had practised at the junior Bar in the early 1960s but had left the Bar having been appointed Professor of Jurisprudence and Roman Law at University College Dublin. In 1969, he was elected to Dáil Éireann. Immediately prior to his appointment as Attorney General, he also 'took silk' to become a senior counsel.

[3.57] As legal adviser to the government, the Attorney General (or, more accurately, the staff of the Attorney General's office) scrutinises all draft legislation which any Government Department proposes to bring before the Oireachtas, and is in effect the head of the Office of the Parliamentary Draftsman.[53] The Attorney also advises the Government in an international context, for example in relation to the ratification of international agreements.[54]

[3.58] Prior to 1976, all serious criminal offences were prosecuted in the name of the Attorney General, but this function has, in most instances, been transferred to the Director of Public Prosecutions, whose functions we describe below. However, in an area connected with criminal law, extradition requests, the Attorney General was conferred with certain new functions by the Extradition (Amendment) Act 1987.[55]

[3.59] Section 6 of the Ministers and Secretaries Act 1924 also provides that the Attorney General, as successor to the pre-1922 Attorney General for Ireland, is to represent the public 'in the assertion of or protection of public rights'. This provision refers to the traditional right of the Attorney General in England as the representative of the 'public interest' to oppose a particular legal claim that is being litigated. Thus, a claim by a person to be entitled to private fishery rights over a river and to exclude the public might be contested by the Attorney General on behalf of the general public.[56] A development of this was that the Attorney General would 'lend' his title as a 'relator' in proceedings initiated by private citizens who might otherwise lack the necessary connection or standing concerning a particular legal point.[57] Although Article 30 of the Constitution recognises the political nature of the Attorney's role, as upholder of the general public good, the Attorney General acts independently of the Government of the day. Indeed, this aspect of his role has given rise to a number of celebrated cases in recent

53. See para **[13.33]**.

54. See para **[17.01]**.

55. In December 1994, the then Government collapsed arising indirectly from the exercise of these functions: see paras **[4.75]-[4.79]**.

56. See *Moore v Attorney General* [1930] IR 471. Similarly, the destination of an important library collection whose original home has ceased to exist: *In re the Worth Library* [1995] 2 IR 301.

57. Some of the litigation concerning abortion and the right to life of the unborn began as relator proceedings: see *Attorney General (Society for the Protection of Unborn Children Ltd) v Open Door Counselling Ltd* [1988] IR 593. In later proceedings concerning the same issue, the courts held that the 'relation' of the Attorney General was not required because of the general importance of the right to life of the unborn: *Society for the Protection of Unborn Children Ltd v Coogan* [1989] IR 734: see further para **[15.130]**.

years.[58] In the context of the Constitution of 1937, the Attorney General is always the principal defendant in cases challenging the constitutionality of legislation and in this regard his function as upholder of the public interest is to argue for the constitutionality of any challenged legislation. In some instances, the Attorney himself has argued such cases in the High Court and Supreme Court but in the majority of cases other senior counsel are chosen to appear in Court on his behalf.

[3.60] Finally, a convention which applied until 1995 was that the Attorney General had 'first refusal' on any judicial vacancy that arose in the High Court or Supreme Court. Arising from a highly-publicised debate about this convention, it no longer applies.[59]

The Director of Public Prosecutions

[3.61] We have already mentioned that, prior to 1976, all serious criminal offences were prosecuted in the name of the Attorney General. Section 9 of the Criminal Justice (Administration) Act 1924 and Article 30.3 of the Constitution of Ireland 1937 provide that all serious crimes be prosecuted in the name of the People at the suit of the Attorney General. However, Article 30.3 of the Constitution also provides that this function may be carried out 'by some other person authorised in accordance with law to act for that purpose'. The office of the Director of Public Prosecutions (commonly referred to as 'the DPP' or 'the Director') was created by s 2 of the Prosecution of Offences Act 1974 against this background. The 1974 Act came into effect in 1976 when the first Director took up his appointment. Section 3(1) of the 1974 Act provides:

> Subject to the provisions of this Act, the Director shall perform all the functions capable of being performed in relation to criminal matters ... by the Attorney General immediately before the commencement of this section ...

---

58. In *Attorney General v X* [1992] 1 IR 1 (see further para **[15.131]**, another celebrated abortion-related case, the Attorney General successfully applied to the High Court for an injunction to restrain a 14-year-old girl from leaving the State for any purpose, but in particular with a view to obtaining an abortion in England. Although the injunction was set aside on appeal to the Supreme Court (on the ground that, in the particular circumstances where the girl had been raped and threatened to commit suicide if she was forced to carry the foetus to full term and give birth to the baby, she was not prohibited by the Constitution from obtaining an abortion) the Court confirmed that the Attorney General was perfectly correct to bring the matter to the courts and that, in fact, he could not have taken any other course. To the same effect, see *Attorney General v Hamilton (No 1)* [1993] 2 IR 250.

59. See para **[4.75]-[4.79]**.

[3.62] The rationale behind the 1974 Act was that it was felt that an officer, independent of an appearance of political connections, was required to discharge these functions, similar to the situation in England where the same office had already been established. Although the Director is appointed by the Government, the office is that of a civil servant, so that the Director does not resign when a Government falls, unlike the position of the Attorney General. This ensures an important element of continuity in the prosecution of offences.[60] Section 2(5) of the 1974 Act also provides that the Director 'shall be independent in the performance of his functions'. The Director may be removed by the Government, but only on consideration of a report into the Director's health or conduct made by a committee comprising the Chief Justice, a judge of the High Court and the Attorney General.

[3.63] The Attorney General, however, retains some functions in relation to certain criminal matters having an international dimension,[61] and s 5(1) of the 1974 Act provides that the Government may by Order[62] declare that the Director's functions 'in relation to criminal matters' may be performed only by the Attorney General where the Government is 'of opinion that it is expedient in the interests of national security to do so'. However, since the 1974 Act came into force no such Order has been made.

[3.64] Section 7 of the 1974 Act provides that the Attorney and the Director must ensure that the distribution of retainers to the panel of barristers retained by them to act on their behalf is done on the basis of a 'fair and equitable' distribution. Apart from indicating that there must be a fair distribution of business between those on the Attorney's or Director's panel of barristers, s 7 also implies that much of the work of both offices is, in fact, done by barristers in private practice rather than by barristers in the paid employment of the State. In relation to criminal prosecutions in this jurisdiction, therefore, there is no equivalent of salaried officials entitled 'public prosecutors' as is the case in many states of the United States of America and in the case of the Crown Prosecution Service in England.[63]

---

60. At the time of writing (July 1996) the first Director of Public Prosecutions, Mr Eamonn Barnes, continues as the only holder of the office.

61. For example under the Genocide Act 1973 and the Fisheries (Amendment) Act 1978. See also the Attorney's functions under the Extradition (Amendment) Act 1987, referred to at para **[4.78]**.

62. A form of secondary or delegated legislation: see para **[13.58]**.

63. On the procedure in criminal matters, see para **[6.65]**.

[5] Legal Education Generally

Role of universities in legal education

[3.65] We have mentioned already that both the Law Society of Ireland and the Honourable Society of King's Inns provide courses of study leading to the admission of persons to the roll of solicitors and barristers, respectively. Admission to these 'professional courses' require the candidates in question to have a high level of knowledge of the various 'core' subjects in law specified by both bodies.

[3.66] Most solicitors and barristers who have qualified in the past 25 years hold a law degree from one of the universities in the State. This was not always the case, and until the 1960s the state of law schools in Ireland was less than satisfactory. It was only in the 1960s, for example, that the universities increased the number of full time law lecturers to a level which was capable of offering a law degree in the form in which it is recognised today. Up to that time, and continuing to the end of the 1960s, many of the lecturers were practitioners who divided their time between the universities and the courts.

[3.67] Because of the state of the law schools for much of this century, many of the senior practitioners of the law - solicitors, barristers and judges - hold general university degrees such as a BA and/or MA followed by the training provided by the Law Society or King's Inns as the case may be. Whether this was an advantage or a disadvantage at the time is a matter of debate, but it is the case that many of the important decisions given by Irish judges in the last 30 years were delivered by persons whose university education did not include a law degree.

[3.68] The result of the change to full-time staff in the universities has been significant. As indicated, many students now follow a path from law degree through to professional qualification, although there are also a number who take a general degree followed by the equivalent of the King's Inns Diploma in Legal Studies. A number of comparable courses are provided by the many other third level colleges who prepare students for the professional course entrance examination. The university law school sector has increased in size and importance since the 1970s in particular. Apart from the more professional contribution to legal education which has resulted from this, much of the increased level of publications on Irish law in recent years has been produced by the university sector.[64]

---

64. See the Appendix to O'Malley, *The Round Hall Guide to Sources of Law*, (Round Hall Press, 1993).

Fair Trade Commission Report

[3.69] Although the role of the universities has expanded in recent years, it is also the case that both the Law Society of Ireland and the Honourable Society of King's Inns have also expanded and increased their investment in legal education since the 1980s. In this respect, it may be said that they have maintained a discreet distance from the universities as to the extent to which the universities should be involved in 'professional' courses in particular. In addition, they have also maintained some distance between themselves as professional law schools in terms of the distinctiveness of the courses provided to aspiring solicitors and barristers.

[3.70] The 1990 Report of the Fair Trade Commission on the Legal Profession considered in great detail the arrangements then in place concerning legal education and the respective roles of the universities and the professional law schools. Bearing in mind that the Commission did not recommend the fusion of the two branches of the legal profession, the Report did not recommend that the educational role of the Law Society or of the King's Inns should end. Nonetheless, the Commission made some radical proposals.[65]

[3.71] On the academic side, the Commission considered that knowledge of the basic or core elements of the law was essential for a person to progress to the vocational or professional stage of legal education. While a three or four year law degree was regarded by the Commission as the best indicator of academic competence, it also accepted that a qualification similar to the King's Inns Diploma in Legal Studies should also be acceptable, particularly as this would ensure that a certain number of persons from a non-law academic background would continue to be attracted to the legal profession. The Commission also considered that such a Diploma route might also 'help widen the socio-economic background of entrants to the legal profession.' The Commission also considered that entry to the professional stage might be conditional on attaining a certain level of performance in the degree or diploma.

[3.72] As to the vocational element of legal education, the Commission recommended the establishment by the Minister for Justice 'as a matter of urgency' of an Advisory Committee on Legal Education and Training (ACLET) with a view to reviewing all aspects of legal education, including the academic university element and the vocational element. However, especially far-reaching was the Commission's recommendation that the

65. FTC Report, pp 117-120.

proposed ACLET would be responsible for 'implementing a system of common vocational training', which would in effect require some amalgamation or rationalisation of the existing arrangements in the Law Society and the King's Inns. The Commission added that this might require the foundation of an Institute of Legal Education, independent of the Law Society, King's Inns and the universities but which could make use of the Law Society's and King's Inns premises. The Institute would arrange the vocational training of prospective solicitors and barristers, with the element of instruction comprising no more than 12 months, with a further period of pupillage of perhaps a year.

[3.73] Many of the radical elements of the Commission's recommendations appear to have been influenced by the existence of such a system in Northern Ireland. The Council of Legal Education for Northern Ireland, the equivalent of the Commission's proposed ACLET, is the governing body in Northern Ireland for all aspects of legal education. It is also responsible for the Institute of Professional Legal Studies, the equivalent of the Commission's proposed Institute of Legal Education. The Institute of Professional Legal Studies, situated in Queen's University Belfast but independent of that university, organises an integrated system of vocational education for intending solicitors and barristers.

Advisory Committee on Legal Education and Training (ACLET)

[3.74] The main thrust of the recommendations in the 1990 Report of the Fair Trade Commission have not been implemented to date. However, in 1993 an Advisory Committee on Legal Education and Training was indeed established, though this was not at the behest of the Minister for Justice. Rather the Law Society, the King's Inns, the universities and other third level institutions involved in legal education came together on a voluntary basis to examine legal education, primarily though not exclusively with a view to an examination of the vocational phase of legal education. This voluntary ACLET is chaired by Mr Justice Ronan Keane, judge of the Supreme Court. At the time of writing (July 1996), no report of the deliberations of ACLET has been published. It thus remains to be seen whether any further action will be taken on this aspect of the 1990 Report.

[3.75] In the meantime, s 49 of the Solicitors (Amendment) Act 1994 amended s 40 of the Solicitors Act 1954 concerning the Law Society's educational functions. Under s 40 of the 1954 Act, as amended, the Society may provide, either on its own or in association with other institutions, educational courses for its own students and for students of other educational and training institutions. In addition, the Society is also empowered to join with other institutions in providing joint or common courses leading to a joint or common qualification. These provisions clearly have in mind some form of joint courses with the King's Inns, though not necessarily on the lines envisaged in the 1990 Report. Whether these new powers will be activated remains to be seen.

Continuing Legal Education

[3.76] While the 1990 Report of the Fair Trade Commission did not deal with the question of Continuing Legal Education (CLE), this is an area in which there has been considerable development in recent years, in common with most other professions. It has become increasingly important for professional persons, whether doctors or lawyers, to provide themselves with 'refresher' courses on an ongoing basis in the practice of their profession. While in the past it was felt that this was a matter for each individual practitioner, it is increasingly a matter of good professional conduct that a professional person take a number of continuing education modules over a given period.

[3.77] Both the Law Society and the King's Inns provide CLE as a matter of course, and it is likely that such courses will become more common and a more central part of 'in-practice education' in the future. Similar requirements have been introduced for members of the Bench, again reflecting developments in best practice internationally.[66]

Recognition of foreign qualifications

[3.78] It was the case for many years that lawyers qualified in any other jurisdiction had no right to practice as a solicitor or barrister in the State or to the more limited right of audience in the courts of the State, except where special leave was granted.

[3.79] The position of solicitors and barristers who qualified in Northern Ireland and in England was somewhat different to lawyers from other jurisdictions given the historical connections. Since the creation of the two jurisdictions on the island in the 1920s and the separation from the United Kingdom created by the Act of Union of 1800, there has been an element of continued connection between the branches of the profession in the jurisdictions, largely based on mutual or reciprocal arrangements to facilitate practice in the different jurisdictions. For the solicitor's branch, the mechanisms for recognition of qualifications from Northern Ireland and England are contained in Part IV of the Solicitors Act 1954, as amended by subsequent Acts. For the Bar, recognition is a matter for the Bar Council, but

66. See para **[4.88]**.

it remains the case that many who are called to the Bar in Dublin later seek admission to one of the Inns of Court in London or to the Bar of Northern Ireland. Indeed, some leading senior counsel have been called to the Inner Bar of Northern Ireland as Queen's Counsel.[67] As to the more limited issue of rights of audience in the courts, it is also the case that members of the Bar of Northern Ireland or of England present arguments in the courts of this jurisdiction,[68] and *vice versa*.

[3.80] As to lawyers from other jurisdictions, membership of the European Community has resulted in substantial changes to the recognition laws. The European Communities (General System for the Recognition of Higher Education Diplomas) Regulations 1991[69] and the European Communities (Second General System for the Recognition of Professional Education and Training) Regulations 1996[70] provide a framework within which the Law Society and King's Inns are the designated bodies charged with the task of recognising professional qualifications in law obtained in EC Member States. Provision is made for aptitude and proficiency tests and appeals lie to the High Court for any person aggrieved by an adverse decision.

[3.81] The European Communities (Freedom to Provide Services) (Lawyers) Regulations 1979[71] also provide for limited recognition of professional qualifications in law in respect of any EC Member State. The 1979 Regulations provide that any lawyer qualified in an EC Member State has the right of audience in the courts, though this must be exercised in conjunction with a qualified barrister or solicitor of this jurisdiction. The Regulations do not permit such a person to provide conveyancing services or to prepare the documents required to obtain title in order to administer the estate of a deceased person.

[6] Other Professionals

[3.82] As mentioned at the beginning of this chapter, persons other than solicitors and barristers are also involved in the operation of the law.

67. Media coverage of such an event has tended to focus on whether, at the granting of the letter patent for Queen's Counsel, the recipient is required to swear an oath of allegiance to the British monarch.
68. Eg *Tradax Ltd v Irish Grain Board Ltd* [1984] IR 1.
69. SI 1/1991, implementing Directive 89/48/EEC. See also Solicitors (Amendment) Act 1994, s 80.
70. SI 135/1996, implementing Directives 92/51/EEC, 94/38/EC and 95/43/EC.
71. SI 58/1979, implementing Directive 77/249/EEC.

Law clerks

[3.83] Under s 58 of the Solicitors Act 1958, activities normally associated with solicitors may be done by any person employed by a solicitor if acting under the solicitor's directions. This provision allows law clerks, a group of persons employed by many solicitors' firms, to engage in much work connected with conveyancing and certain court work, in particular appearances in the Master's Court in the High Court.[72] Many law clerks have progressed to being fully qualified solicitors and special account of their experience in the law is made in this respect in the Solicitors Acts 1954 to 1994.

Para-legals and legal executives

[3.84] In its 1990 Report on the Legal Profession, the Fair Trade Commission considered the emergence of 'para-legals' or legal executives, who have mirrored the emergence of para-medics in the field of medicine and similar persons in other professions.[73] Such para-legals or legal executives involve to some extent an additional form of law clerk. The Commission did not consider that such persons should be accorded any special statutory recognition, as this might lead to a further divisions within the legal profession and that, in any event, such persons could be accommodated under the existing 'employee' provisions of s 58 of the Solicitors Act 1954. By contrast, legal executives are a recognised additional form of legal staff in England and Wales, employed mainly in solicitors' firms but also in large companies where a large deal of conveyancing work is performed by such persons. This reflects the licensed conveyancing system introduced in England and Wales in the 1980s,[74] but which has not been followed in this jurisdiction.

Other professions

[3.85] Engineers and architects may require detailed knowledge of, for example, patent and copyright law and many textbooks are written for that audience. In addition, however, such professionals may serve as specialist arbitrators in hearings conducted under the Arbitration Acts 1954 and 1980.[75]

[3.86] Other professionals such as accountants are likely to have more detailed knowledge of the practical operation of certain areas of law than even some barristers who specialise in particular areas. Accountants are likely to be familiar with the details of the Income Tax Act 1967 and other

---

72. See para **[4.118]**.
73. FTC Report, pp 272-7.
74. Administration of Justice Act 1985. See now Courts and Legal Services Act 1990.
75. See para **[8.31]**.

revenue legislation, as well as some aspects of company law. For this reason, they will also be given a good grounding in the basic principles of law associated with those areas of legislation in their university degrees and professional courses.

[3.87] In effect, such professional persons may be in the 'front line' of the application of the law in the sense that many disputes concerning legal rules may be dealt with informally without recourse to the courts, such as the application of a particular provision in taxation legislation. Moreover, even where a dispute cannot be resolved informally, they may encourage their clients to resolve differences by means other than litigation in the courts. We refer to such alternative dispute resolution (ADR) elsewhere.[76]

76. See para **[8.30]**.

Chapter 4

The Court System, the Judiciary and Court Administration

[1] INTRODUCTION

[4.01] In this chapter we begin by examining the provisions of the 1937 Constitution that outline the essential elements of the court system. We then describe the main statutory provisions that describe in more detail the organisation of that system of courts. Following this, we discuss the role of the judiciary, who make up the most visible part of the court system, as well as the recent changes to the judicial appointments procedure. Finally, we examine the arrangements for the management of the court system and the role of the various court officers and other persons involved in the administration of the courts. Fundamental proposals for reform of the arrangements for managing the court service are also outlined.

[4.02] This chapter should be seen as introductory to subsequent chapters that describe the original jurisdiction of the courts,[1] court procedure[2] and the appellate jurisdiction of the courts.[3]

[4.03] When Saorstát Éireann, the Irish Free State, was established in 1922, Articles 64 to 73 of the 1922 Constitution of Saorstát Éireann[4] outlined the essential elements of the court system to be established in the new State. The broad outline envisaged by these Articles was filled in by the detailed provisions of the Courts of Justice Act 1924. The 1924 Act made permanent provision[5] for the establishment, as well as a description of, the jurisdiction (that is, the principal functions) of the following courts:

- the Supreme Court;
- the Court of Criminal Appeal;[6]

1. Chapter 5.
2. Chapter 6.
3. Chapter 7.
4. The 1922 Constitution was enacted as a Schedule to the Constitution of The Irish Free State (Saorstát Éireann) Act 1922, the first Act passed by the Oireachtas of Saorstát Éireann.
5. For the courts in operation prior to 1924, see paras **[2.60]-[2.63]**.
6. The Courts and Court Officers Act 1995, s 4, envisages the abolition of the Court of Criminal Appeal and the transfer of its functions to the Supreme Court. See further para**[7.35]**.

- the High Court;
- the Circuit Court ; and
- the District Court.[7]

[4.04] The 1922 Constitution was replaced in 1937 by the present Constitution of Ireland, *Bunreacht na hÉireann*, Articles 34 to 38 of which contained some new provisions concerning the court structure, but the essential elements of the existing system envisaged in 1922 remained in place. As we will see,[8] the 1937 Constitution required the establishment of a new court system, but this was not formally done until the passing of the Courts (Establishment and Constitution) Act 1961. This Act, together with the Courts (Supplemental Provisions) Act 1961,[9] provided for the establishment of, as well as a description of the jurisdiction of, the following courts:

- the Supreme Court;
- the Court of Criminal Appeal;[10]
- the High Court;
- the Circuit Court; and
- the District Court.

It should be clear from this listing that the two 1961 Acts largely involved a re-establishment of the pre-1961 court system that had been in place since the passing of the Courts of Justice Act 1924. Indeed, many provisions of the 1924 Act were carried over into the 'new' system by the Courts (Supplemental Provisions) Act 1961. In that sense, there was no complete break with the pre-1961 court system and it will become clear from this and subsequent chapters that certain provisions of the Courts of Justice Act 1924 remain the statutory basis for large elements of the courts' jurisdiction.

[4.05] Thus, the 1924 Act as well as the two 1961 Acts (all as subsequently amended) contain the essential legislative source of the jurisdiction of the

7. While the 1924 Act added the words 'of Justice' to each Court's formal name, the names as listed in the text were the usual descriptions given to the courts.
8. See para **[4.34]**.
9. The Courts (Establishment and Constitution) Act 1961 is a short Act providing for the formal establishment of the courts listed in the text. By contrast, the Courts (Supplemental Provisions) Act 1961, which was signed into law on the same date, is a lengthy Act since it describes the detailed jurisdiction of the various courts established under the Courts (Establishment and Constitution) Act 1961.
10. The Courts and Court Officers Act 1995, s 4, envisages the abolition of the Court of Criminal Appeal and the transfer of its functions to the Supreme Court. See further para **[7.35]**.

courts[11] supplemented by detailed statutory rules concerning the formal procedures to be followed in civil and criminal matters.[12] We will discuss these Acts in more detail later in this chapter.[13] For the present, we discuss the provisions of the 1937 Constitution concerning the court system.[14]

[4.06] As already indicated, Articles 34 to 37 of the 1937 Constitution (which are headed 'The Courts') provide an outline of the essential elements of the court system. Article 38 (which is included under the heading 'Trial of Offences') contains provisions regarding the jurisdiction and procedure of the courts in criminal matters. Although it can be said that the various Courts Acts fill in the detail contained in Articles 34 to 38, that detail must, like any legislation, conform with the basic framework established by the Constitution.

[2] THE ADMINISTRATION OF JUSTICE IN COURTS

[4.07] Article 34.1 of the 1937 Constitution provides:

> Justice shall be administered in courts established by law by judges appointed in the manner provided by this Constitution, and, save in such special and limited cases as may be prescribed by law, shall be administered in public.

[4.08] Article 37.1, which should be read in conjunction with Article 34.1, provides:

---

11. Delany, *The Courts Acts 1924-1991* (Round Hall Press, 1993) is an excellent resource containing the annotated text of 36 Acts of relevance to the jurisdiction of the courts, from the Courts of Justice Act 1924 through to the Courts (Supplemental Provisions) (Amendment) Act 1991. Since 1991, further significant legislative changes have been effected, notably by the Courts and Court Officers Act 1995. In addition to the Acts passed between 1924 and 1995, a number of pre-1922 Acts, such as the Petty Sessions (Ireland) Act 1851 and the Summary Jurisdiction Act 1857, contain important provisions describing the jurisdiction of the courts in Ireland. There is a strong case for the consolidation of these Acts into a single Courts Act.
12. The current rules of court for the High Court and Supreme Court are the Rules of the Superior Courts 1986 (SI 15/1986), as amended. The relevant rules for the other courts are the Rules of the Circuit Court 1950 (SI 179/1950), as amended, and the District Rules 1948 (SR&O 431/1947), as amended. The leading decision as to what constitutes 'practice and procedure', the subject matter of such rules, is *The State (O'Flaherty) v Ó Floinn* [1954] IR 295.
13. See para **[4.34]**.
14. Because of the broad similarities between the 1922 and 1937 Constitutions in this respect, we will outline the relevant provisions of the 1937 Constitution only. For a detailed discussion of the provisions of the 1922 Constitution, see Kohn, *The Constitution of the Irish Free State* (Allen & Unwin, 1932).

> Nothing in this Constitution shall operate to invalidate the exercise of limited functions and powers of a judicial nature, in matters other than criminal matters, by any person or body of persons duly authorised by law to exercise such functions and powers, notwithstanding that such person or such body of persons is not a judge or a court appointed or established as such under this Constitution.

These provisions lie at the heart of the operation of the courts and other decision-making bodies in Ireland.

[4.09] Article 34.1 provides that 'justice' cannot be administered in any place other than a court which has been established in accordance with the Constitution, presided over by a properly appointed judge, and that, in general, the courts should operate in public.[15] Article 34.1 reiterates the basic 'separation of powers' principle contained in Article 6,[16] namely that the judicial power is to be administered separately from the two other arms of government, the legislature and the executive.

[4.10] However, Article 37.1 also authorises persons other than judges or courts to exercise 'limited' functions and powers of a judicial nature, except in criminal matters. Article 37.1 was intended to deal with the existing situation that there were a number of persons and bodies already given certain powers of a judicial nature and that these could continue, provided that they were 'limited' and did not deal with 'criminal matters'. It has been suggested that Article 37.1 was inserted into the 1937 Constitution to validate the functions of bodies such as the Land Commission[17] and the Master of the High Court.[18]

[4.11] What did Article 34.1 envisage when referring to the 'administration of justice'? This is an important question, because where a person or tribunal *other than* a duly appointed judge engages in the 'administration of justice', that person or tribunal acts in violation of the Constitution, and their

---

15. The issue of the administration of justice in public is considered in paras **[4.19]-[4.23]**.
16. See para **[15.42]**.
17. On the Land Commission generally, see para **[2.42]**. The Commission's powers, though limited to land-related matters, were extensive in the sense that it was empowered to acquire land compulsorily and to sell it to smallholders in order to create economically viable land holdings. The validity of its powers were challenged in *Lynham v Butler(No 2)* [1933] IR 74, where it was held that they were administrative rather than judicial in nature, and were thus not in breach of the equivalent in the 1922 Constitution of Article 34.1. Despite the *Lynham* case, Article 37.1 was intended to put the matter beyond doubt by legitimising the Land Commission's powers, and those of other similar bodies. It has been suggested, however, that Article 37.1 created more doubt than clarity: see generally Hogan & Whyte, *Kelly's The Irish Constitution*, 3rd ed (Butterworths, 1994), p 336 *et seq* and 560 *et seq*.
18. The Courts and Court Officers Act 1995, s 24, expressly conferred on the Master limited functions and powers within the meaning of Article 37: see para **[4.118]**.

decisions are thus invalid, unless they are 'limited' in the sense envisaged by Article 37.1. Indeed, there have been many cases over the years in which the courts have been asked to rule on whether certain persons or tribunals have been exercising powers in conflict with Article 34.1, and whether such powers are 'saved' by Article 37.1. The question is also important because it determines what issues are capable of being dealt with by the courts, what are called justiciable matters, and those which are not, which can be described as non-justiciable.[19]

Characteristic features

[4.12] In *McDonald v Bord na gCon (No 2)*,[20] the following five 'characteristic features' of an administration of justice within the meaning of Article 34.1 were suggested:

> (1) a dispute or controversy as to the existence of legal rights or a violation of the law;
>
> (2) the determination or ascertainment of the rights of parties or the imposition of liabilities or the infliction of a penalty;
>
> (3) the final determination (subject to appeal) of legal rights or liabilities or the imposition of penalties;
>
> (4) the enforcement of those rights or liabilities or the imposition of a penalty by the court or by the executive power of the State which is called in by the court to enforce its judgment;
>
> (5) the making of an order by the court which as a matter of history is an order characteristic of courts in this country.

These factors have been very influential in the cases that have come before the courts, though it should be noted that they do not provide a definitive answer in all cases. In particular, the reference to whether as a matter of history the issue is one characteristically dealt with by courts has been criticised.[21]

[4.13] However, it may be useful to provide some examples of the matters dealt with by the courts through the years:

- in 1960, the Supreme Court held that, in striking a solicitor off the roll of solicitors, the Law Society of Ireland *was* exercising the judicial power and that this was not a limited power within the meaning of Article 37.1;[22]

---

19. See para **[4.17]**.
20. [1965] IR 217.
21. See Hogan & Whyte, *Kelly's The Irish Constitution*, 3rd ed (Butterworths, 1994), pp 339 *et seq*.
22. *In re the Solicitors Act 1954* [1960] IR 239.

- in 1965, the Supreme Court held that, in making an exclusion order against a greyhound trainer, Bord na gCon, the Greyhound Board, *was not* exercising the judicial power;[23]
- in 1982, the Supreme Court held that, in deciding whether to acquire land compulsorily, Bord na Móna, the Turf Development Board, *was not* exercising the judicial power;[24]
- in 1986, the Supreme Court held that, where a Clerk of the District Court was required to be satisfied that a District Court summons was valid, the Clerk *was* exercising the judicial power;[25]
- in 1992, the Supreme Court held that a tribunal of inquiry invested with the powers of the Tribunals of Inquiry (Evidence) Acts 1921 and 1979 was *not* exercising the judicial power;[26]
- in 1995, the High Court held that, in commuting (that is, reducing) fines imposed by a District Court judge in a criminal case, the Minister for Justice was *not* exercising the judicial power.[27]

In the cases of Bord na gCon and Bord na Móna, of course, the decisions of the Supreme Court indicated that they were not prohibited by Article 34.1 from exercising their powers. However, the courts have made the point that such bodies, though they might be described as exercising administrative powers, must *exercise their powers in a judicial manner.* This requires such bodies to comply with certain principles of fair procedures, such as the obligation to give advance notice to affected parties, to conduct any hearings on the basis of allowing both sides an equal hearing and to ensure that those making decisions have not been affected by any bias.[28]

[4.14] However, in the case of the powers of the Law Society of Ireland and of District Court Clerks, the consequences of the Supreme Court decisions were that alternative arrangements had to be put in place. As to the Law Society, the Solicitors (Amendment) Act 1960 provides that, while it remains the disciplinary body for solicitors, any decision to strike a person off the roll of solicitors must be made by the High Court. This approach has been repeated in similar legislation for the different professions.[29] As to the functions of District Court Clerks, the Courts (No 3) Act 1986 now provides

23. *McDonald v Bord na gCon (No 2)* [1965] IR 217.
24. *O'Brien v Bord na Móna* [1983] IR 277.
25. *The State (Clarke) v Roche* [1986] IR 619.
26. *Goodman International v Mr Justice Hamilton* [1992] 2 IR 542.
27. *Brennan v Minister for Justice* [1995] 1 IR 612.
28. These principles of fair procedures are based on the common law principles of natural justice. See generally, Hogan and Morgan, *Administrative Law in Ireland*, 2nd ed (Sweet & Maxwell, 1991).
29. Eg the Dentists Act 1985, ss 38 to 40.

that they are not required to make any judgment as to whether District Court summonses outline a criminal offence. The Clerk simply processes the summons as an administrative matter; and any decision-making in relation to it is now performed by the relevant judge of the District Court, who is obviously a judge appointed in accordance with Article 34.1 of the Constitution. Thus, even though the broad outline of the system has not changed in any substantial way, the form of the procedure has been altered.

[4.15] While the problems connected with the functions of District Court Clerks were 'solved' by the 1986 Act, some difficulties might be noted. First, the decision invalidating the pre-1986 Act system meant that many thousands of summonses, in particular those under the Road Traffic Acts and including those relating to driving with an excess of alcohol, were declared invalid. Indeed, it proved impossible to issue new, valid, summonses in these cases as the six month time limit for their issue[30] had, by then, expired. Second, what was the legal status of the hundreds of thousands of summonses issued between 1937 and 1986 in a manner that had been found, in 1986, to be in conflict with the Constitution? Of course, the Supreme Court decision in 1986 related to the particular summons being challenged in that case, but it could be argued that all previous summonses were equally invalid. While this is a complex problem, the short answer would appear to be that the courts are reluctant to make all their decisions fully retrospective and that the passage of time, and various other factors, would make the pre-1986 Act summonses immune from legal challenge.[31]

Constitutional amendment required

[4.16] There has been at least one instance where the suggestion that a particular body or tribunal was exercising powers contrary to Article 34.1 led to immediate remedial action. It was suggested, in the course of legal submissions in *M v An Bord Uchtála*,[32] that when making adoption orders An Bord Uchtála, the Adoption Board, was exercising the judicial power under Article 34.1 and that such functions might not be 'limited' within the meaning of Article 37.1. While this suggestion was not translated into a definitive decision of the Supreme Court in the case,[33] the potential spectre of all adoptions being declared invalid led to the holding of a referendum to

30. The time limit is set out in the Petty Sessions (Ireland) Act 1851, s 10. See further para **[6.08]**.
31. See the discussion of *Murphy v Attorney General* [1982] IR 241, para **[15.65]**.
32. [1977] IR 287.
33. The High Court judge in the *M* case rejected the argument and the Supreme Court did not deal with the issue on appeal. In a later decision, *G v An Bord Uchtála* [1980] IR 32, Walsh J suggested that the Adoption Board was exercising administrative powers only, but no other Supreme Court judge expressed a view on the point. See Hogan & Whyte, *Kelly's The Irish Constitution*, 3rd ed (Butterworths, 1994) p 570.

amend the Constitution in order to prevent even that possibility.[34] In this instance, the importance of ensuring that existing adoption orders were copperfastened was given a high priority, even though it seemed somewhat unlikely that courts would retrospectively invalidate those orders.

Justiciable and political controversies

[4.17] One other aspect of the 'administration of justice' is that the courts have also indicated that certain disputes are correctly the business of the courts, described as justiciable controversies, whereas others are more appropriate to the executive, described as political or non-justiciable controversies. The distinction between justiciable and political or non-justiciable controversies is based on terminology developed under the United States Constitution. For example, the United States Supreme Court held that it had no function determining a dispute concerning the seating arrangements for delegates at the Democratic Party's National Convention in 1972.[35] However, as with other aspects of Article 34.1, the precise boundary between justiciable and non-justiciable matters is difficult to draw. For example, the courts have declared invalid electoral laws where constituency boundaries have failed to comply with the provisions of the Constitution,[36] and have also declared invalid income tax laws where these have failed to comply with constitutional provisions.[37] Both these areas would generally be regarded as being very close to the executive power and to involve questions of politics and public policy, though in neither instance were the judges required to make decisions about the allocation of public resources. The courts have been more reluctant to become involved where their decisions would involve explicit decisions about how funds should be allocated and they will generally not intervene but will allow the executive or legislative arms of Government to make these difficult choices.[38]

[4.18] In sum, therefore, Articles 34.1 and 37.1 provide that certain functions are exclusively a matter for the courts but that certain limited functions may be dealt with by other persons or bodies and also provides an indication that certain matters are justiciable and others not. The precise boundary between those matters which must always be assigned to the courts and those which may be conferred on other persons or bodies remains difficult to draw with precision, but the principles adopted by the courts provide some useful indicators.

34. The Sixth Amendment to the Constitution Act 1979 inserted Article 37.2 into the Constitution, which provides that no adoption is invalid by reason only of the fact that the order was made by a body or person other than a judge or court: see para **[15.72]**.
35. *O'Brien v Brown* 92 SCt 2718 (1972).
36. *O'Donovan v Attorney General* [1961] IR 114.
37. *Murphy v Attorney General* [1982] IR 241.
38. See for example *O'Reilly v Limerick Corporation* [1989] ILRM 181 and para **[15.97]**.

Administration of justice in public, with exceptions

[4.19] Article 34.1 of the Constitution provides that the courts must, in general, sit in public, 'save in such special and limited cases as may be prescribed by law.' A sitting other than in public is usually described as being *in camera*.[39] Where a case is heard *in camera*, members of the public as well as representatives of the media are excluded from the courtroom, attendance being restricted to the judge, the jury (if applicable), the court registrar or clerk, the parties to the proceedings and their legal representatives. As with many provisions of the Constitution, Article 34.1 reflects a long-established antipathy to court proceedings being held in private. This arose from the persecution associated with the Spanish Inquisition, the English Court of Star Chamber and the French monarchy's abuse of the *lettre de cachet*.[40] Of course, Article 34.1 provides for certain legislative exceptions, but the courts have emphasised that the general rule should be public hearings.

[4.20] Section 45(1) of the Courts (Supplemental Provisions) Act 1961 provides for a number of cases in which justice may be administered otherwise than in public. These are:

- applications of an urgent nature for *habeas corpus*, bail, prohibition or injunction;
- matrimonial causes and matters (such as judicial separations or nullity cases);
- lunacy and minor matters (that is, the wardship jurisdiction of the High Court and matters concerning persons under 18 years of age); and
- proceedings involving the disclosure of a secret manufacturing process.

In addition, High Court proceedings under s 205 of the Companies Act 1963, where a company shareholder alleges oppression by the majority shareholders in the company, may be heard *in camera*. Section 205(7) of the 1963 Act provides that this may happen where the High Court is of the opinion that a public hearing 'would involve the disclosure of information the publication of which would be seriously prejudicial to the legitimate interests of the company.'

[4.21] The priority given to public hearings in Article 34.1 was underlined by the Supreme Court in *In re R Ltd*,[41] which concerned proceedings under s 205 of the Companies Act 1963 instituted by the former chief executive of

39. The phrase *in camera* indicates a court sitting 'in a box'. Some legislation refers to hearings 'in private' or 'in chambers'.
40. See the judgment of Black J in *In re Oliver*, 333 US 257, at 268-270 (1948).
41. [1989] IR 126.

the airline Ryanair Ltd.[42] The company argued that the proceedings should be held *in camera* because its share price could be affected by some of the information that might emerge in evidence in the case. However, the Supreme Court ordered that the proceedings be held in public. Walsh J made the following comment in the course of his judgment:

> "The issue before this Court touches a fundamental principle of the administration of justice in a democratic State, namely the administration of justice in public. [*He then recited Article 34.1*] The actual presence of the public is never necessary but the administration of justice in public does require that the doors of the courts must be open so that members of the general public may come and see for themselves that justice is done."[43]

[4.22] In addition to these limited instances of proceedings being held otherwise than in public, a number of other restrictions apply in the context of criminal proceedings. These include the following:

- in criminal proceedings on indictment, restrictions apply on the information that may be published concerning the defendant once proceedings have been initiated;[44]

---

42. While the official title of the case in the law reports is *In re R. Ltd*, it was widely known that the proceedings involved Ryanair Ltd. Indeed, on foot of the decision of the Supreme Court, there were a number of subsequent public hearings and judgments in this case where the full names of the parties are given: see, for example, *O'Neill v Ryan and Ryanair Ltd (No 3)* [1992] 1 IR 166. In a subsequent case on public hearings under s 205 of the Companies Act 1963, *Irish Press Plc v Ingersoll Publications Ltd* [1994] 1 IR 176, the full names of the parties were given in the judgment determining that the proceedings be in public. However, in *The People (DPP) v Z* [1994] 2 IR 476, an application for an *in camera* hearing under s 45(1) of the 1961 Act, the defendant was not named as it arose in a criminal prosecution for sexual assault on a young person and the anonymity of the defendant was preserved to protect the victim.

43. [1989] IR 126, at 134. Walsh J noted that Article 64 of the 1922 Constitution of Saorstát Éireann had provided for public hearings without any apparent provision for exemptions. He also pointed out that the general requirement that justice be administered in public was included as a right in the Sixth Amendment to the United States Constitution and was also contained in many international declarations and conventions, such as Article 10 of the United Nations Organisation's Universal Declaration of Human Rights (1948) and Article 6 of the Council of Europe's Convention on Human Rights and Fundamental Freedoms (1950).

44. Criminal Procedure Act 1967, s 17 provides that once a preliminary examination has begun, usually in the District Court, the only information that may be published are the following: (a) the fact that the person has appeared in court ('John W Doe'); (b) the name and address of the person ('of 13 Bridge Street, Dublin'); and (c) the charge brought against the person ('appeared in the District Court charged with criminal damage contrary to the Criminal Damage Act 1991'). These restrictions apply until the hearing of the trial of the offence, when the evidence given in court may be reported, provided that the case is one that is heard in public.

- in prosecutions for rape and other sexual offences, the trial judge is required to exclude the general public, but *bona fide* representatives of the media as well as the court officers and those directly involved in the case can attend the hearing; and while the verdict and sentence (if any) must be pronounced in public, the names of the defendant and the complainant may only be published by the media where the court authorises this;[45]
- similar restrictions apply in prosecutions for incest.[46]

The requirement that justice be administered in public has also been interpreted as requiring that litigants in civil proceedings use their given names, thus preventing them from suing under assumed names.[47]

[4.23] Finally, we should note that, while there is a strong leaning in the Constitution towards hearings in public, until 1995[48] the courts in Ireland and England[49] invariably prohibited photographers or television cameras from court. While 'Court TV' may be a feature of certain parts of the United States of America, it seems unlikely that such a development will emerge in Ireland in the near future.[50]

Outline of the Court System

[4.24] We have seen that Articles 34.1 and 37.1 describe certain essential features of the court system envisaged by the Constitution. In addition, the

---

45. Criminal Law (Rape) Act 1981, s 6 as amended by the Criminal Law (Rape) (Amendment) Act 1990, s 11.

46. Criminal Law (Incest Proceedings) Act 1995, s 6 replacing the Punishment of Incest Act 1908, s 5 in the wake of the decision of the High Court in *The People (DPP) v WM* [1995] 1 IR 226.

47. *Roe v Blood Transfusion Service Board* [1996] 1 ILRM 555. By contrast, in the United States, such assumed names are relatively common. The landmark decision in which the United States Supreme Court held that the right of privacy encompassed the right to terminate a pregnancy, *Roe v Wade* 410 US 113 (1972), involved the use of a pseudonym.

48. In April 1995, television video cameras from the State broadcasting service, Radio Telefís Éireann, were allowed to film the opening arguments in the Supreme Court hearing of *In re the Regulation of Information (Services Outside the State for the Termination of Pregnancies) Bill 1995* [1995] 1 IR 1. This was the first occasion in the history of the State that TV cameras had been allowed to film any court in session: see McGonagle, *A Textbook on Media Law* (Gill and Macmillan, 1996), p 197.

49. While there are no statutory restrictions in place in Ireland concerning cameras in court, permission to take pictures, whether still or video, was generally refused prior to 1995. In England, an express prohibition had been introduced in the Criminal Justice Act 1925.

50. The Law Reform Commission recommended, in its 1994 *Report on Contempt of Court*, (LRC 47-1994) that an advisory committee on this question be established by the Minister for Justice. For a discussion of this area, see McGonagle, *op cit*, pp 197-8 and Lambert, 'Cues, Cameras and Courtroom Actors: Resisting the Temptation of Courtroom Television Cameras' (1996) 14 ILT 13.

basic structure of the system is also outlined in Articles 34 to 38. A significant feature of Articles 34 to 38 is that they refer specifically to the High Court and Supreme Court. In addition, the Constitution envisaged the continuation of the existing system of other courts with 'local and limited jurisdiction' but these are not mentioned by name.

Courts of first instance and of appeal

[4.25] Article 34.2 states:

> The Courts shall comprise Courts of First Instance and a Court of Final Appeal.

Article 34.2 thus envisaged the continuation of the existing system, whereby certain courts have first instance jurisdiction, that is, are designated as the court with original jurisdiction to hear and determine cases *ab initio*. It also envisaged that there would be at least one Court of Final Appeal whose functions would not ordinarily involve hearing a case *ab initio* but would be empowered to make a definitive determination on issues of law.

The High Court and the Supreme Court

[4.26] Articles 34.3 and 34.4 describe the essential powers of functions of the High Court and Supreme Court.

Article 34.3.1° states:

> The Courts of First Instance shall include a High Court invested with full original jurisdiction in and power to determine all matters and questions whether of law or fact, civil or criminal.

Article 34.3.2° provides:

> Save as otherwise provided by this Article,[51] the jurisdiction of the High Court shall extend to the validity of any law having regard to the provisions of this Constitution, and no such question shall be raised (whether by pleading, argument or otherwise) in any court established under this or any other Article of this Constitution other than the High Court or the Supreme Court.

Article 34.4.1° states:

> The Court of Final Appeal shall be called the Supreme Court.

Articles 34.4.3° and 34.4.4° provide that:

> 3° The Supreme Court shall, with such exceptions and subject to

51. Article 34.3.3° provides that no court (thus including the High Court) shall have jurisdiction to question the validity of any law which is enacted after a reference to the Supreme Court pursuant to Article 26 of the Constitution. On Article 26 references, see paras **[5.65]-[5.68]**.

such regulations as may be prescribed by law, have appellate jurisdiction from all decision of the High Court, and shall also have appellate jurisdiction from such decisions of other courts as may be prescribed by law.

4° No law shall be enacted excepting from the jurisdiction of the Supreme Court cases which involve questions as to the validity of any law having regard to the provisions of this Constitution.'

[4.27] These provisions indicate the importance of the High Court and the Supreme Court in the court system. The High Court is conferred with 'full original jurisdiction in and power to determine all matters and questions whether of law or fact, civil or criminal'. This includes the power to decide whether any law is invalid having regard to the Constitution. And since the Supreme Court is, subject to exceptions specified by law, given appellate jurisdiction from all decisions of the High Court, the Supreme Court is also conferred with very wide powers as the Court of Final Appeal. Significantly, no law can be enacted that would delimit the Supreme Court's appellate jurisdiction from the High Court in cases concerning the constitutional validity of laws. Finally, the Constitution also envisages that the Supreme Court may also be a Court of Final Appeal from courts other than the High Court.

[4.28] The specific reference to the High Court and Supreme Court is significant in a number of ways. Thus, it would seem clear that neither the High Court nor Supreme Court could be abolished by statute law unless the relevant provisions of the Constitution were themselves deleted. This gives a permanence to the High Court and Supreme Court which other courts established by statute cannot claim.

[4.29] Another effect is that, since the High Court is conferred with 'full original jurisdiction in and power to determine all matters and questions whether of law or fact, civil or criminal', its powers, and those of the Supreme Court on appeal, are not entirely dependent on the limits of the powers conferred by statute. While, as we will see,[52] statute law confers jurisdiction on the High Court in specific instances, the 'full' jurisdiction it enjoys adds a further layer over and above this. Thus, judges of the High Court and Supreme Court will occasionally refer to the 'inherent' jurisdiction of the High Court or Supreme Court as a basis for making a decision which might not fit into an already established approach.[53] This is

---

52. See paras **[5.51]** and **[5.84]**.

53. See the discussion of *RD Cox Ltd v Owners of MV Fritz Raabe*, Supreme Court, 1 August 1974, in Hogan & Whyte, *Kelly's The Irish Constitution*, 3rd ed (Butterworths, 1994), p 410. An example in connection with the Supreme Court is *Holohan v Donohoe* [1986] IR 45, where the Supreme Court held it could, in certain instances, substitute its own award of damages in place of that given in the High Court, even though such power of substitution was not provided for by statute.

similar to the position of the King's (or Queen's) superior courts of record under the system which operated in Ireland prior to 1922.[54] The Court of Appeal and High Court that operated in the pre-1922 system did so with the authority of the monarch, and were for that reason said to possess certain 'inherent' powers arising from the royal prerogative, including powers over and above those actually conferred by statute law.[55] While such royal prerogative powers no longer apply in the post-1922 arrangements,[56] the 'full' jurisdiction conferred on the High Court and Supreme Court is similar. On the other hand, the same kind of inherent powers simply cannot be claimed by judges of the other courts that are envisaged by the Constitution.

Courts of local and limited jurisdiction

[4.30] The courts other than the High Court and Supreme Court are provided for in Article 34.3.4° as follows:

> The Courts of First Instance shall also include Courts of local and limited jurisdiction with a right of appeal as determined by law.

We have already seen that, in 1937, courts of local and limited jurisdiction - the Circuit Court and District Court - existed pursuant to the 1922 Constitution and the Courts of Justice Act 1924. Indeed, these were the successors of pre-1922 'inferior' courts, especially the County Courts and the Justices of Petty Sessions, who also had limited powers and functions.[57] Such courts have an important role in the court structure, by ensuring local and less expensive venues for people involved in litigation than would be the case were they required to initiate claims in the High Court.[58] Of course, the courts envisaged by Article 34.3.4° cannot be conferred with the 'full' jurisdiction already reserved for the High Court and Supreme Court. The use of the words 'local and limited' indicate that there should be a geographical limit on the jurisdiction of a District Court or Circuit Court judge and that the nature of the cases (whether civil or criminal) would be relatively less serious than those in the High Court.[59] In addition, whether referring to the local and limited courts prior to 1922 or those contemplated by the 1937 Constitution, judges of the High Court and Supreme Court have often referred to the District Court or Circuit Court as 'creatures of legislation', indicating that such courts only have powers to the extent that they are actually granted by statute.[60]

---

54. On the nature of a court of record, see n 77.
55. On the pre-1922 system, see para **[2.32]**.
56. On the question of prerogatives under the Constitution, see para **[15.46]**.
57. See paras **[2.48]-[2.53]**.
58. See *The State (Boyle) v Neylon* [1986] IR 551.
59. See generally *Grimes v Owners of SS Bangor Bay* [1948] IR 350.
60. On the first instance jurisdiction of the Circuit Court and District Court, see Ch 5. On their appellate jurisdiction, see Ch 7.

Judicial appointment and independence

[4.31] The Constitution provides for extensive protections for those appointed as judges, in particular those appointed as judges of the High Court and Supreme Court. We discuss the appointment and independence of judges later in the chapter.[61]

Regulation of court business by law

[4.32] Article 36 of the Constitution is an important provision concerning the extent to which the general business of the courts may be regulated by statute law. It provides:

> Subject to the foregoing provisions of this Constitution relating to the Courts, the following matters shall be regulated in accordance with law, that is to say:
>
> i. the number of judges of the Supreme Court, and of the High Court, the remuneration, age of retirement and pensions of such judges,
>
> ii. the number of the judges of all other Courts, and their terms of appointment, and
>
> iii. the constitution and organisation of the said Courts, the distribution of jurisdiction and business among the said Courts and judges, and all matters of procedure.

This provision recognises the reality that the matters referred to, such as the number of judges, their salaries and pensions as well as the distribution of business between the different courts, will be subject to change from time to time. As we shall see, the distribution of business between the courts has been the subject of much legislation since 1937, reflecting the need to respond to changing needs in society and the increased amount of civil and criminal matters coming before the courts.[62]

Criminal matters

[4.33] As we have seen already, Article 37.1 empowers persons or bodies other than courts to exercise limited functions and powers of a judicial nature, but not in relation to any criminal matters. This indicates that all criminal matters, even of a limited nature, must be dealt with in the courts. In addition, Article 38 sets out important general principles concerning the conduct of criminal trials in the courts. These include the requirement that

---

61. See paras **[4.89]-[4.93]**.
62. See paras **[5.07]-[5.16]**.

criminal trials be held 'in due course of law', that minor offences may be tried in courts of summary jurisdiction, and that, subject to certain limited exceptions, a person charged with a non-minor offence cannot be tried without a jury. These provisions are considered elsewhere.[63]

[3] The Need to Establish a Post-1937 Court System

[4.34] One further consequence of the provisions contained in Articles 34 to 38 should be mentioned at this stage. In *The State (Killian) v Minister for Justice*,[64] the Supreme Court considered an aspect of Article 34.1 of the Constitution that had received little attention until then. The Court held that, where Article 34.1 provided that 'Justice shall be administered in courts established by law', this should be read as 'Justice shall be administered in courts *to be established* by law'. The Court thus concluded that the courts in operation at that time (including the Supreme Court itself) were not those referred to in Article 34.1 of the 1937 Constitution, but rather the courts referred to in Article 58, which provided for the continuance of the court system that operated under the 1922 Constitution. In effect, the *Killian* decision was that Article 34.1 required the fresh establishment of a court system.

Courts (Establishment and Constitution) Act 1961

[4.35] The Courts (Establishment and Constitution) Act 1961 was passed to 'regularise' the position and to 'establish' the court system envisaged by Article 34.1. However, as the summary at the beginning of this chapter indicates, this short Act merely carried forward the existing court system which had been created by the Courts of Justice Act 1924 pursuant to the provisions of the 1922 Constitution. At the same time, the opportunity was taken in the Courts (Supplemental Provisions) Act 1961 to update and clarify the different jurisdictions of the courts. This latter Act, as subsequently amended, contains the detailed provisions on the current jurisdiction of the courts.

[4.36] In addition to being aware of the changes effected to the two Acts of 1961 since their initial passing, it is also necessary to reach back in time to appreciate the full picture concerning the jurisdiction of the courts. The reason for this is that both of the 1961 Acts refer back to previous legislation conferring functions on the different courts. This includes references to the various jurisdictions conferred on the pre-1961 courts by the Courts of Justice Act 1924. In addition, since the 1924 Act had 'carried over' various

---

63. See paras **[5.71]-[5.76]**.
64. [1954] IR 207.

pre-1922 jurisdictions, it is also necessary in some instances to consult pre-1922 legislation.

The 'former' courts

[4.37] Aside from the jurisdictional alterations made by the 1961 Acts, it might be asked whether the establishment of a 'new' court system had any significant effect? Arguably, it should because the courts in operation prior to the 1961 Act were 'transitory' courts under Article 58 of the Constitution. This might, for example, justify the courts created by the 1961 Act treating the decisions of the pre-1961 courts as having less force as precedents than decisions of the courts established under the 1961 Act,[65] though it would seem that this has not happened.[66] However, it has become common practice to refer to the pre-1961 courts as, for example, 'the former Supreme Court', 'the former High Court' and so forth.[67] Other, more difficult, problems do arise in this context, such as whether the Supreme Court which operated prior to the 1961 Act was entitled to hear references of Bills from the President under Article 26 of the Constitution, though this has not arisen in any decision of an Irish court.[68]

[4] The Court System in Ireland: Judicial Composition and Structure

[4.38] We shall discuss in turn the judicial composition of each court established by the Courts (Establishment and Constitution) Act 1961, beginning with the Supreme Court. The other administrative arrangements necessary to ensure the effective running of the court system will be described later in the chapter.[69]

Judicial precedence, numbers and titles

[4.39] Section 9 of the Courts of Justice Act 1924 provides that the precedence between the judges of the Supreme Court and High Court is as follows. The Chief Justice ranks first, then the President of the High Court, then the judges of the Supreme Court (in priority of appointment), then the ordinary judges of the High Court (also in priority of appointment). Section 9(3) of the Courts of Justice Act 1947 provides that the President of the Circuit Court takes precedence over all other Circuit Court judges and s 38

65. This had been suggested in argument in *The State (Quinn) v Ryan* [1965] IR 110: see para **[12.11]**.
66. See *The State (Lynch) v Cooney* [1982] IR 337, per Henchy J, para **[12.17]**.
67. *Ibid.*
68. See Hogan & Whyte, *Kelly's The Irish Constitution*, 3rd ed (Butterworths, 1994) p 398.
69. See para **[4.115]**.

of the Courts of Justice Act 1924 provides that the Circuit Court judges rank among themselves according to priority of appointment.[70] No similar ranking is provided for in connection with District Court judges. However, since the President of the District Court is an *ex officio* judge of the Circuit Court,[71] this creates some form of precedence for the holder of that office.

[4.40] In accordance with Article 36 of the Constitution,[72] the number of judges of the different courts is fixed from time to time by legislation. In general, it must be said that, over the years, the number of judges has been substantially increased to reflect the increased workload in the different courts.[73] In 1924, the maximum permissible number of permanent judges in the different courts was 50, comprising three Supreme Court judges, six High Court judges, eight Circuit Court judges and 33 District Court Justices.[74] By 1996, this had more than doubled to 107, comprising eight Supreme Court judges, 20 High Court judges, 28 Circuit Court judges and 50 District Court judges.[75]

The Supreme Court

[4.41] The Supreme Court established in 1961 pursuant to Article 34 of the Constitution[76] is a superior court of record.[77] From 1961 to 1996, the Court comprised five judges, the Chief Justice,[78] who presides over the Court, and

70. The statutory provisions on precedence were carried forward by the Courts (Supplemental Provisions) Act 1961, s 48.

71. Courts and Court Officers Act 1995, s 33.

72. See para **[4.32]**.

73. See para **[4.127]**.

74. See Courts of Justice Act 1924, ss 5, 4, 37 and 68, respectively.

75. See Courts and Court Officers Act 1995, ss 6, 9, 10 and 11, respectively, s 10 having been amended by Courts Act 1996, s 1. The Courts Act 1991, s 21 produced the change in title from 'Justice of the District Court' to 'Judge of the District Court'.

76. Courts (Establishment and Constitution) Act 1961, s 1(1) formally established the Supreme Court envisaged by Article 34 of the Constitution, replacing the Supreme Court established by the Courts of Justice Act 1924, s 5.

77. Courts (Supplemental Provisions) Act 1961, s 7(1) replacing the Courts of Justice Act 1924, s 18. The concept of a court of record is of some antiquity. Originally, it referred to a royal court, with authority to impose fines and to imprison. It also was a court whose acts and proceedings were to be enrolled 'for perpetual memorial and testimony', the rolls thus being its permanent record. The authority of the monarch has been replaced by the authority conferred by Article 34 of the Constitution, but the concept of keeping records for perpetuity remains an important indication that a court has a permanent standing. The description of the Supreme Court and, we will see later, the High Court as 'superior' courts of record also reflects pre-1922 arrangements, where the Court of Appeal and High Court were the superior courts and the County Courts and Justices comprised the inferior courts: see paras **[2.30]** and **[2.48]**. It is notable also that the rules of court for the High Court and Supreme Court are titled the Rules of the Superior Courts 1986 (SI 15/1986).

78. The title in the Irish language is An Príomh-Breitheamh.

four ordinary judges.[79] The Courts and Court Officers Act 1995 provided for an increase in the number of ordinary judges from four to seven, thus bringing the total membership of the Supreme Court to eight.[80] The additional three judges were appointed to prepare for the transfer to the Supreme Court of the functions of the Court of Criminal Appeal.[81] The President of the High Court is also an *ex officio* member of the Supreme Court.[82] The Chief Justice, as well as being the presiding judge, is responsible for the general organisation of the Court's work.[83] Each ordinary judge is formally styled or titled 'Judge of the Supreme Court'.[84] In the event of the illness of a judge of the Supreme Court or where, for any other reason,

---

79. The Supreme Court established by the Courts of Justice Act 1924, s 5 comprised three judges, the Chief Justice and two ordinary judges. This reflected the composition of the Court of Appeal of Southern Ireland which it had replaced: see para **[2.59]**. The number of judges was increased to five by the Courts of Justice Act 1936, s 4. The Courts (Establishment and Constitution) Act 1961, s 1(2) provides that the Court comprises the Chief Justice and 'not ... less than four' ordinary judges. The Courts (Supplemental Provisions) Act 1961, s 4(1) provided that the number of ordinary judges of the Court 'shall be four'. Section 4(1) was repealed by the Courts and Court Officers Act 1995, First Schedule. Articles 12 and 26 of the Constitution and the Courts (Supplemental Provisions) Act 1961, s 7(5) (as amended by the Courts and Court Officers Act 1995, s 7) require that the Court comprise at least five judges in cases having a constitutional dimension (as to which see paras **[5.64]** and **[5.66]**).

80. Courts (Establishment and Constitution) Act 1961, s 1(2) as amended by the Courts and Court Officers Act 1995, s 6(1). Note also that the Law Reform Commission Act 1975, s 14(1)(a)(i) as originally enacted, provided that, where a judge of the Supreme Court was appointed President of the Law Reform Commission, the number of ordinary judges of the Supreme Court would be five. From 1975 to 1985, Walsh J, at that time a Supreme Court judge, was the President of the Law Reform Commission and so the number of ordinary Supreme Court judges for that time was five. On the appointment of a High Court judge as President of the Law Reform Commission in 1986 (see para **[11.11]**) the Court continued to comprise six judges in all. In November 1988, Henchy J resigned to take up the position of Chairman of the Independent Radio and Television Commission, established by the Radio and Television Act 1988. After that, the Supreme Court reverted to the 'normal' position of comprising five judges. The Law Reform Commission Act 1975, s 14(1)(a)(i) was amended by the Courts and Court Officers Act 1995, s 6(2) to take account of the increase in ordinary Supreme Court judges from four to seven, so that if at some future time a Supreme Court judge is appointed President of the Law Reform Commission, the number of ordinary judges will be increased to eight.

81. See para **[7.35]**.

82. Courts (Establishment and Constitution) Act 1961, s 1(3). See also the Courts of Justice Act 1924, s 6.

83. Courts and Court Officers Act 1995, s 8 modifying the Courts Act 1981, s 18(1)(a). Section 8 of the 1995 Act appears to be the first statutory recognition that the Chief Justice is responsible for the general organisation of the Court's work, though in practice this had always been the case.

84. The title in the Irish language is Breitheamh den Chúirt Uachtarach: the Courts (Establishment and Constitution) Act 1961, s 1(2) (as amended by the Courts and Court Officers Act 1995, s 6(1)).

a sufficient number of Supreme Court judges is not available to transact the Court's business, the Chief Justice may request a High Court judge to sit as an additional judge of the Supreme Court.[85]

[4.42] In cases having what might be described as a constitutional connection, the Supreme Court sits as a five judge Court. Articles 12 and 26 of the Constitution require that when the Court performs its functions under those provisions,[86] the Court must consist of not less than five judges. In addition, the relevant legislative provisions in place between 1961 and 1995 provided that the Court also comprised five judges in cases involving the validity of any law having regard to the Constitution, but that, in any other case the Chief Justice, or in his absence the senior ordinary judge of the time being available, could direct that the Court comprise three judges only.[87]

Simultaneous sittings in divisions

[4.43] Until 1995, the Supreme Court sat either in plenary session as a five-judge Court or else as a three-judge Court, but never, for example, in two divisions of three judges simultaneously. However, the Courts and Court Officers Act 1995 provided for the first time that the Supreme Court 'may sit in two or more divisions and they may sit at the same time.'[88] The 1995 Act affirmed the existing arrangement that the Court must comprise five judges in cases involving the validity of any law having regard to the Constitution,[89] but it amended the prior legislative arrangements for three-judge courts to read that, in any other case the Chief Justice (or in his or her absence the senior available ordinary judge) may direct that the Court will comprise *a division of five or three judges only.*[90]

85. Courts (Establishment and Constitution) Act 1961, s 1(4), replacing the Courts of Justice Act 1924, s 7. See, for example, *Tormey v Ireland* [1985] IR 289 (Barrington and Carroll JJ) and *Duffy v News Group Newspapers Ltd* [1992] 2 IR 369 (Costello J).

86. See n 79.

87. See the Courts (Supplemental Provisions) Act 1961, s 7(3) and (4) and *The State(Williams) v Kelly* [1970] IR 259 and *Peilow v ffrench O'Carroll* (1971) 105 ILTR 21. In the latter case, a Supreme Court judge had died before judgment was delivered and the Chief Justice directed that a re-hearing of the matter be heard by a three-judge Court.

88. Until the change effected by the 1995 Act, the physical location of the Supreme Court was a single courtroom in the Four Courts building, Dublin which was almost exclusively set aside for the Court. With the coming into force of the 1995 Act, there was a need for the first time to provide extra courtroom accommodation for simultaneous sittings of the Court

89. As to whether it is constitutionally permissible for the Court to sit as a five-judge Court to deal with the constitutional validity of laws, to the possible exclusion of the remaining three judges provided for by the 1995 Act, see the doubts expressed in Kelleher, 'The Courts and Court Officers Act 1995 - the Main Provisions' (1996) 14 ILT 18.

90. Courts and Court Officers Act 1995, s 7 re-numbered the Courts (Supplemental Provisions) Act 1961, s 7(3) and (4) as s 7(4) and (5) (with the consequential changes concerning five-judge and three-judge court as noted in the text) and also inserted a new s 7(3) which introduced the innovation that the Court may sit in two or more divisions which may sit at the same time.

[4.44] This significant innovation allowing the Supreme Court to sit in divisions was intended to deal with two matters. First, it was aimed at relieving the increasing backlog of appeals to the Supreme Court. In February 1996, the average delay was between two and three years.[91] Second, it was introduced with a view to transferring to the Supreme Court the functions of the Court of Criminal Appeal. The combination of these two measures replaced an earlier proposal to retain the Court of Criminal Appeal and to create a Civil Court of Appeal which would have heard, for example, personal injuries appeals from the High Court, which comprised many of the appeals to the Supreme Court.[92] The eventual proposal contained in the 1995 Act, namely, to combine the functions of the existing Court of Criminal Appeal with the suggested Civil Court of Appeal and to incorporate both within the jurisdiction of the Supreme Court, resulted from consultation between the Government and the senior judiciary.[93] The result, allowing the Court to sit in divisions, may be compared with the similar position of the Court of Justice of the European Communities which regularly sits simultaneously in chambers of judges.[94]

Collegiate court

[4.45] An important feature of the Supreme Court is that it is a collegiate court, in other words it always consists of a number of judges, not just one. From this point of view it is different from most of the other courts discussed below.[95] Being a collegiate court presents two points of note which we discuss here briefly.

[4.46] First, as there is a common law convention that each judge on a collegiate court is entitled to express a view on the legal issues arising in a case, this means that in a Court with five judges, a case may be decided by the views of three of the judges sitting. This has implications for the doctrine of precedent, and we discuss this elsewhere.[96]

---

91. *First Report of the Working Group on a Courts Commission* (Pn 2690), April 1996, p 37. See further para **[4.135]**.

92. The proposal to create a Civil Court of Appeal was contained in the Courts and Court Officers Bill 1994, whose origins are discussed at para **[4.77]**. While this aspect of the 1994 Bill was not proceeded with, the bulk of its other provisions became the substance of the Courts and Court Officers Act 1995.

93. See 458 Dáil Debates c 1756. The changes effected in the 1995 Act had also been recommended in 1966 in the *7th Interim Report of the Committee on Court Practice and Procedure*.

94. See para **[16.120]**.

95. In some instances, the High Court comprises a three-judge Divisional Court, though this is the exception rather than the rule: see para **[4.50]**. The Special Criminal Court (para **[5.96]**) and Court of Criminal Appeal (para **[7.36]**) are also collegiate courts, but their decisions are announced by one member of the Court only.

96. See para **[12.54]**.

[4.47] Second, as a collegiate body, how the judges of the Supreme Court arrange their workload, and in particular to what extent they exchange views after the hearing of a case but before their decision is announced in open court, must differ from the situation that applies where a case is dealt with by a lone judge. Very little has been published about this aspect of the Court's work. What is known is that the judges of the Supreme Court meet in conference to discuss cases after they have been argued in Court. The discussions at these conferences remain confidential, but it is clear from reading judgments delivered in the Supreme Court that drafts are circulated between the judges prior to the date when they are delivered in open Court.[97]

Research assistants/clerks

[4.48] One other aspect of the Court's decision-making is worthy of note. Prior to 1994, the judges of the Supreme Court were entirely dependent on counsel to ensure that all aspects of a case had been dealt with at the hearing in court.[98] Once this had been completed, the judges were largely alone in their endeavours to research the legal issues arising. However, since 1994, the Supreme Court has had available the services of a number of legal research assistants to aid them in the difficult task of preparing their judgments.[99] It may be that, as yet, this arrangement has not developed to the level that applies for those law graduates in the United States who 'clerk' for senior members of the judiciary, or for the equivalent *référendaires* to judges of the European Court of Justice, both of whom actively assist their judges in the preparation of judgments.[100] Nonetheless, the advent of legal research assistants in the Supreme Court is a significant development.

High Court

[4.49] The High Court established in 1961 pursuant to Article 34 of the Constitution[101] is a superior court of record.[102] The Court comprises the

97. See for example the judgment of McCarthy J in *Norris v Attorney General* [1984] IR 36 where he quotes extracts from the other judgments which had just been delivered. This clearly required advance circulation of the judgments between the judges.

98. It has become increasingly more common, particularly in constitutional cases, for counsel to be requested to submit detailed written submissions of the arguments to be addressed to the Court: see Collins and O'Reilly, *Civil Proceedings and the State in Ireland* (Round Hall Press, 1990) p 163.

99. This had been recommended in the *11th Interim Report of the Committee on Court Practice and Procedure* (1970).

100. See para **[16.120]**.

101. Courts (Establishment and Constitution) Act 1961, s 2(1) formally established the High Court envisaged by Article 34 of the Constitution, replacing the Courts of Justice Act 1924, s 4.

102. Courts (Supplemental Provisions) Act 1961, s 8(1) replacing the Courts of Justice Act 1924, s 17. On the concept of a court of record, see para **[4.41]**.

President of the High Court[103] and such number of ordinary judges as may from time to time be fixed by Act of the Oireachtas.[104] The number of ordinary judges fixed in 1961 was not more than six[105] but since then this has been increased by a number of Acts[106] to be not more than 19.[107] The President of the High Court, as well as being the second most senior judge in the State,[108] is responsible for the general organisation of the High Court's work.[109] Each ordinary judge is formally styled or titled 'Judge of the High Court'.[110] The Chief Justice and the President of the Circuit Court are both *ex officio* additional judges of the High Court.[111] In the event of the illness of a judge of the High Court or where, for any other reason, a sufficient number of High Court judges is not available to transact the Court's business, the Chief Justice, at the request of the President of the High Court, may request a Supreme Court judge to sit as an additional judge of the High Court.[112]

[4.50] Unlike the position that obtained prior to 1922, there are no formal separate divisions of the High Court, though administratively certain cases are in practice referred to particular judges and proposals for reform of the court system may involve the re-introduction of specialist divisions.[113] However, each High Court judge is empowered to hear and determine any case whether civil or criminal, in equity or at common law.[114] Under s 94 of the Courts of Justice Act 1924, a litigant in a High Court civil action was

---

103. The title in the Irish language is Uachtarán na hArd-Chúirte.

104. Courts (Establishment and Constitution) Act 1961, s 2(2).

105. Courts (Supplemental Provisions) Act 1961, s 4(2). The High Court established by the Courts of Justice Act 1924, s 4 had comprised the President of the High Court and five ordinary judges and this was increased by one by the Courts of Justice Act 1953, s 11.

106. For the various increases between 1961 and 1991, see Delany, *The Courts Act 1924-1991* (Round Hall Press, 1993), p 144.

107. Courts and Court Officers Act 1995, s 9(1). Note also that the Law Reform Commission Act 1975, s 14(1)(b)(i), as amended by the Courts and Court Officers Act 1995, s 9(2), provides that, where a judge of the High Court is appointed President of the Law Reform Commission, the maximum number of ordinary judges of the High Court shall be increased to 20.

108. See para **[4.39]**.

109. Courts (Supplemental Provisions) Act 1961, s 10(3).

110. The title in the Irish language is Breitheamh den Ard-Chúirt: Courts (Establishment and Constitution) Act 1961, s 2(2).

111. Courts (Establishment and Constitution) Act 1961, s 2(3) and (4), replacing the Courts of Justice Act 1924, s 6 and the Courts of Justice Act 1946, s 9.

112. Courts (Establishment and Constitution) Act 1961, s 2(5), replacing the Courts of Justice Act 1936, s 5. For an example, see *Cowan v Freaghaile* [1991] 1 IR 389 (O'Flaherty J).

113. On the divisions prior to 1922, see para **[2.47]**. On the administrative arrangements for chancery matters, see para **[5.60]**, and on the suggested introduction of a Commercial Court in the High Court, see para **[4.137]**.

114. Courts of Justice Act 1924, s 24.

entitled to have the case determined by a judge and jury. This was extended to personal injuries actions arising from road traffic and work-related accidents. However, as a result of criticisms of the allegedly high levels of awards by juries in such cases,[115] s 1 of the Courts Act 1988 provides that personal injuries actions are now heard by a High Court judge alone.[116] Juries in High Court civil actions are thus now confined to defamation (libel and slander) and much less common actions such as false imprisonment and malicious prosecution. In effect, therefore, in many civil actions 'the High Court' means 'a judge of the High Court.' We have already seen that, where the High Court hears major criminal matters, the Constitution requires that the Court comprise a judge and jury.[117] In some instances, the President of the High Court may direct that a panel of two or more judges (usually three judges) shall sit to hear certain cases. In this situation the panel of judges is known as a Divisional High Court.[118]

[4.51] The High Court ordinarily sits in Dublin,[119] but on two occasions each year, High Court judges (as well as such Supreme Court judges as may be assigned) sit in various venues around the country to hear appeals from the Circuit Court and also to determine cases at first instance. This is known as the High Court on Circuit,[120] and their twice-yearly nature can be traced to the *Nisi Prius* hearings which originated in the Anglo-Norman period.[121]

---

115. See paras **[5.08]-[5.10]**.

116. For criticism of the removal of juries in High Court personal injuries actions, see Kerr, *Annotation to the Courts Act 1988*, Irish Current Law Statutes Annotated (Sweet & Maxwell, 1988).

117. On juries see further para **[6.99]**.

118. Article 40.4.4° of the Constitution provides that the President of the High Court may order a panel of three judges to sit in cases of inquiries into the validity of a person's detention in custody: see for example *The State (Murray) v McRann* [1979] IR 133. The Courts (Supplemental Provisions) Act 1961, s 11(2)(b) provides that the President may direct that two or more judges sit for the purposes of a criminal trial in the Central Criminal Court. It would appear, however, that no such Divisional Court has been convened for a criminal trial since 1961. Order 49, rule 1 of the Rules of the Superior Courts 1986 (SI 15/1986) also provides that the President may order that two or more judges (usually three) sit to hear any civil case. Divisional Courts were convened for *Crotty v An Taoiseach* [1987] IR 713 (see para **[16.63]**), *The State (Walshe) v Murphy* [1981] IR 275 (see para **[4.68]**) and *Hanafin v Minister for the Environment*, High Court, unrep, 7 February 1996; [1996] 2 ILRM 161 (SC) (see para **[15.91]**).

119. Virtually all sittings of the High Court take place in the Four Courts Building, Dublin, but on occasion other premises in Dublin, such as those of the Honourable Society of the King's Inns or of the Law Society of Ireland, have accommodated sittings.

120. See the Court of Justice Act 1936, ss 34 and 35.

121. See para **[2.49]**.

Circuit Court

[4.52] The Circuit Court established in 1961 pursuant to Article 34 of the Constitution[122] is a court of record.[123] The Court comprises the President of the Circuit Court[124] and such number of ordinary judges as may from time to time be fixed by Act of the Oireachtas.[125] The number of ordinary judges fixed in 1961 was not more than eight[126] but since then this has been increased by a number of Acts[127] to be not more than 27.[128] Since 1995, the President of the District Court is an *ex officio* member of the Circuit Court.[129] In addition, in the event of the temporary absence from duty for any cause of a judge of the Circuit Court or where, for any other reason, the business of the Circuit Court may fall into arrears, the Government is empowered to appoint persons to act as 'temporary' Circuit Court judges, over and above the maximum provided for at the time.[130] Each ordinary judge is formally styled or titled 'Judge of the Circuit Court'.[131] In general, a Circuit Court judge sits alone to hear cases, except in those cases where the Court hears serious criminal cases when a jury trial is required.[132]

[4.53] Whereas the High Court is, with the exception of the twice-yearly High Court Circuits, in permanent session in Dublin, the Circuit Court is organised on a regional basis, with the State currently divided into eight Circuits, namely the Cork, Dublin, Eastern, Midland, Northern, South East,

122. Courts (Establishment and Constitution) Act 1961, s 4(1) formally established the Circuit Court as a Court of First Instance envisaged by Article 34 of the Constitution.

123. Courts (Supplemental Provisions) Act 1961, s 21, replacing the Courts of Justice Act 1924, s 47. On the concept of a court of record, see para **[4.41]**.

124. The title in the Irish language is Uachtarán na Chúirte Chuarda.

125. Courts (Establishment and Constitution) Act 1961, s 4(2).

126. Courts (Supplemental Provisions) Act 1961, s 16. The Circuit Court established by the Courts of Justice Act 1924, s 37 comprised eight judges in all, the office of President being created by the Courts of Justice Act 1947, s 9 in relation to the 'former' Circuit Court and s 14 of the 1947 Act also providing for an additional ordinary judge. The Courts of Justice Act 1953, s 18 provided for another judge, bringing the total to the number that obtained in 1961.

127. For the various increases between 1961 and 1991, see Delany, *The Courts Act 1924-1991* (Round Hall Press, 1993), pp 153-4.

128. Courts and Court Officers Act 1995, s 10, as amended by s 1 of the Courts Act 1996.

129. Courts and Court Officers Act 1995, s 33.

130. Courts of Justice Act 1936, s 14, replacing the Courts of Justice Act 1924, s 46. On the constitutionality of the similar power in respect of 'temporary' District Court judges, see n 146. In recent years, this power has not been exercised.

131. The title in the Irish language is Breitheamh den Chúirt Chuarda: Courts (Establishment and Constitution) Act 1961, s 4(2).

132. See para **[5.80]**. The Courts Act 1971, s 6 abolished the right to a jury in the trial of a civil action in the Circuit Court, thus effectively rendering otiose the elements of the Courts of Justice Act 1924, s 94 in so far as they concerned civil actions in the Circuit Court.

South West and Western Circuits.[133] At least ten judges, including the President of the Circuit Court, are permanently assigned by the Government to the Dublin Circuit, at least three to the Cork Circuit and the remaining Circuits are assigned one judge each.[134] Where practicable, a person assigned as a judge to a Circuit where the Irish language is in general use should possess enough knowledge of the language to enable proceedings to be conducted without the aid of an interpreter.[135] Each Circuit outside Dublin incorporates a number of towns in which the Circuit Court judge sits on dates specified in advance on a yearly basis. The towns in which the judge for the Eastern Circuit sits, for example, are: Athy, Drogheda, Dundalk, Kells, Naas, Trim and Wicklow.[136] Subject to the important exceptions that the Government determines the number of size of Circuits and the assignment of judges to those Circuits, the President of the Circuit Court is responsible for the general organisation of the Circuit Court's work, including the allocation of dates for the sittings of the Court in the different Circuits.[137] Underlining the 'local' element of the Circuit Court, a Circuit Court judge may only exercise jurisdiction in the Circuit to which he or she is assigned.[138] This geographical limitation of the Circuit Court's jurisdiction in different areas is a feature shared with the District Court.

District Court

[4.54] The District Court established in 1961 pursuant to Article 34 of the Constitution[139] is a court of record.[140] The Court comprises the President of the District Court[141] and such number of other judges as may from time to time be fixed by Act of the Oireachtas.[142] The number of other judges fixed

133. Courts of Justice Act 1953, s 16 carried forward by the Courts (Supplemental Provisions) Act 1961, s 20(1).

134. Courts Act 1977, s 2 as amended by Courts and Court Officers Act 1995, s 36.

135. Courts of Justice Act 1924, s 44. There is a similar requirement concerning judges of the District Court: see n 151. On the Irish language generally, see paras **[15.30]-[15.35]**.

136. For a full list of the Circuits and the towns they serve, see *The Law Directory 1996* (Law Society of Ireland, 1996).

137. Courts of Justice Act 1947, s 10.

138. In civil matters, see the Courts (Establishment and Constitution) Act 1961, ss 22-4 and the Third Schedule. In criminal matters, see s 25 of the 1961 Act.

139. Courts (Establishment and Constitution) Act 1961, s 5(1) formally established the District Court as a Court of First Instance envisaged by Article 34 of the Constitution.

140. Courts Act 1971, s 13. The District Court established by the Courts of Justice Act 1924, s 67 had not bee conferred with the title of a 'court of record', though s 13 of the 1971 Act would seem to have merely given effect to the existing *de facto* position: see Delany, *The Courts Act 1924-1991* (Round Hall Press, 1993), p 240. On the concept of a court of record, see para **[4.41]**.

141. The title in the Irish language is Uachtarán na Chúirte Dúiche.

142. Courts (Establishment and Constitution) Act 1961, s 5(2).

in 1961 was not more than 34[143] but since then this has been increased by a number of Acts[144] to be not more than 50.[145] In addition, in the event of the temporary absence from duty for any cause of a judge of the District Court or where, for any other reason, the business of the District Court may fall into arrears, the Government is empowered to appoint persons to act as 'temporary' District Court judges, over and above the maximum provided for at the time.[146] Each judge is formally styled or titled 'Judge of the District Court'.[147] In all cases, whether civil or criminal, a District Court judge sits alone.

[4.55] As already indicated, the District Court is, like the Circuit Court, organised on a regional basis, with the State currently divided into 24 District Court Districts, comprising the Dublin Metropolitan District and 23 other Districts.[148] The President of the District Court must be assigned by the Government to the Dublin Metropolitan District.[149] A number of the other District Court judges are permanently assigned to the Dublin and Cork Districts and the remaining District Court Districts are assigned one judge each.[150] Where practicable, a person assigned as a judge to a District where

143. Courts (Supplemental Provisions) Act 1961, s 28. The District Court established by the Courts of Justice Act 1924, s 67 comprised not more than 33 Justices, there being no office of President of the District Court at that time.

144. For the various increases between 1961 and 1991, see Delany, *The Courts Act 1924-1991* (Round Hall Press, 1993), pp 153-4.

145. Courts and Court Officers Act 1995, s 11.

146. Courts of Justice Act 1936, s 51 replacing the Courts of Justice Act 1924, s 76. The constitutionality of this power, as carried over by the Courts (Supplemental Provisions) Act 1961, s 48 was upheld in *Magee v Culligan* [1992] 1 IR 223 on the ground that it was a valid regulation of the business of the courts under Article 36 of the Constitution: see para **[4.32]**. However, in recent years, the power has not been exercised.

147. The title in the Irish language is Breitheamh den Chúirt Dúiche: the Courts (Establishment and Constitution) Act 1961, s 5(2)(b) as amended by the Courts Act 1991, s 21(1)(a). As originally enacted, s 5(2)(b) provided that the title of each judge was 'Justice of the District Court' but s 21 of the 1991 Act amended this to 'Judge of the District Court'. This was intended primarily to ensure that judges of the District Court were seen as no less judges than their counterparts in the other courts. The older term 'Justice' reflected the pre-1922 position where the Justice of the Peace (see para **[2.52]**) might not have the legal training now required of a District Court judge. The change effected by the 1991 Act only applied to the English language title, the Irish language style remaining 'Breitheamh den Chúirt Dúiche.'

148. Courts of Justice Act 1953, s 21 carried forward by the Courts (Supplemental Provisions) Act 1961, s 32(1). These 23 Districts outside Dublin are further divided into over 200 District Court Areas. For a full list of these Districts and the Area towns they serve, see *The Law Directory 1996* (Law Society of Ireland, 1996).

149. Courts (Supplemental Provisions) Act 1961, s 35(2).

150. The arrangements for assigning District Court judges, contained primarily in the Courts (Supplemental Provisions) Act 1961, ss 39-42, and the Sixth Schedule as amended by the Courts and Court Officers Act 1995, ss 11, 38 and 39 are less prescriptive than for the Circuit Court.

the Irish language is in general use should possess enough knowledge of the language to enable proceedings to be conducted without the aid of an interpreter.[151] Subject to the important exceptions that the Government determines the number and size of District Court Districts and the assignment of judges to those Districts, the President of the District Court is responsible for the general organisation of the District Court's work, including the allocation of dates for the sittings of the Court in the different Districts.[152]

[4.56] Again, as with the Circuit Court, a judge of the District Court may only exercise jurisdiction in the District to which he or she is assigned.[153]

Mode of address and notation

[4.57] Brief mention will be made of the statutory requirements as to addressing a judge and the manner of noting a judge's name in written form. This is, to some extent, a companion to correct citation of names of cases and law reports.[154] The correct mode of address of a judge should, however, be regarded as somewhat more serious.

Judges of the High Court and Supreme Court

[4.58] We have already seen that the Supreme Court comprises the Chief Justice, the president of the Court, and seven ordinary judges, each ordinary judge being formally styled or titled Judge of the Supreme Court.[155] We have also seen that the High Court comprises the President of the High Court and

151. Courts of Justice Act 1924, s 71. There is a similar requirement concerning judges of the Circuit Court: see n 135, above. Section 71 of the 1924 Act does not require proceedings in Irish speaking areas to be held in the Irish language, but substantial efforts must be made to facilitate a person who wishes to give evidence in the Irish language: see *Ó Monacháin v An Taoiseach* [1986] ILRM 660, which appears to be the only recent decision of the courts to have been reported in the Irish language. On the Irish language generally, see paras **[15.30]-[15.35]**.

152. Courts (Supplemental Provisions) Act 1961, s 36. In addition, the President is empowered to hold meetings with the other judges of the District Court, not more than twice yearly, concerning the discharge of the Court's business, including the avoidance of undue divergences in the exercise by the judges of the Court's jurisdiction and the general level of fines and other penalties. Each judge of the District Court must attend these meetings if convened, unless unable to do so owing to illness or other unavoidable cause. There is no equivalent for such judicial conferences in relation to the other courts.

153. Courts of Justice Act 1924, s 79 as amended. For the various amendments and restrictions affecting s 79, see Delany, *The Courts Acts 1924-1991* (Round Hall Press, 1993), pp 37-9.

154. See para **[12.07]**. O'Malley, *The Round Hall Guide to the Sources of Law* (Round Hall Press, 1993) contains an invaluable guide to citations.

155. See para **[4.41]**.

not more than 19 ordinary judges, each ordinary judge being formally styled or titled Judge of the High Court.[156]

[4.59] The modes of address for the judges of the High Court and Supreme Court are prescribed separately in rules of court.[157] The current rules of court[158] specify that the judges shall be addressed in Irish or English by their respective titles and names, and that they may be referred to, in Irish, as 'An Chúirt' or, in English, as 'The Court.' In practice, when counsel appear in the High Court or Supreme Court, they generally use one of two alternative modes of address. The first is 'The Court', the mode provided for in the current rules of court, as in the following: 'If the Court pleases, might I make the following application.' The second mode of address, not found in any rules of court, is to address an individual judge as 'My Lord' or 'Your Lordship'. To some extent this form of address reflects practice in Ireland prior to 1922, and while still in common usage might be thought by some to be outdated.[159] Indeed, while the first woman High Court judge, Miss Justice Carroll, initially accepted the mode of address 'My Lord', she was later reported to have requested counsel to address her in the mode prescribed by the rules of court, namely 'judge' or 'the Court.'[160]

[4.60] When writing a High Court or Supreme Court judge's name, the following is correct: 'Mr Justice Blayney' or 'Blayney J' (note that the latter reads as 'Mr Justice Blayney' and not 'Blayney Jay'). When addressing a High Court or Supreme Court judge directly, but not in court, the correct mode of address is: 'Judge Blayney', but, perhaps confusingly, when introducing a judge the method is: 'Mr. Justice Blayney'. Thus, at a public meeting, the person who proposes a vote of thanks might say: 'I would like to thank on your behalf Mr. Justice Blayney for his presence this evening' and then turn to the judge and say to him directly 'Thank you Judge

156. See para **[4.49]**.

157. Courts of Justice Act 1924, s 10.

158. Order 119, rule 1 of the Rules of the Superior Courts 1986 (SI 15/1986).

159. But see the mode of address for judges of the Circuit Court, para **[4.61]**. In the course of the Oireachtas debate on the Courts and Court Officers Act 1995, it was proposed that the use of the form of address 'My Lord' be abolished as no longer being appropriate. While there was general acceptance of this point, it was decided to retain the discretion concerning modes of address with the Superior Courts Rules Committee, as provided in the 1924 Act: see 459 *Dáil Debates* c.1219-22. However, the Oireachtas members appeared to be under the impression that these informal modes were actually provided for in the current 1986 Rules, whereas they are a matter of long-standing convention. Whether the Rules Committee might at some stage actually prohibit the informal modes remains to be seen.

160. See The Irish Times, 9 April 1991. The report indicated that Carroll J had been influenced in this through her immersion in the work of the Commission on the Status of Women, of which she was the Chair at the time. Carroll J was also reported to have replied 'No' when Mr Rex Mackey SC had asked if he could refer to her as 'Madam'.

Blayney.' Special notations exist for the Chief Justice and President of the High Court. 'The Chief Justice, Mr Justice Hamilton' is usually noted as follows: 'Hamilton CJ', while 'the President of the High Court, Mr Justice Costello' is usually noted thus: 'Costello P'.

Judges of the Circuit Court

[4.61] We have already seen that the Circuit Court comprises the President of the Circuit Court and not more than 24 ordinary judges, each ordinary judge being formally styled or titled Judge of the Circuit Court.[161] As with the High Court and Supreme Court, the mode of address is prescribed separately in rules of court.[162] The current rules of court[163] specify that the mode of address for judges of the Circuit Court is 'A Thiarna Bhreithimh' or 'My Lord.'[164] The written notation for the President of the Circuit Court, as an *ex officio* judge of the High Court, is 'the President of the Circuit Court Mr. Justice Spain, or 'Spain J'. When addressing any other judge of the Circuit Court in direct conversation outside of Court, the correct form of address is 'Judge Buckley'. A similar notation is used is the written form.

Judges of the District Court

[4.62] We have already seen that the District Court comprises the President of the District Court and not more than 50 other judges, and that each judge is formally styled or titled Judge of the District Court.[165] The President of the District Court may be referred to thus 'the President of the District Court, Judge Smithwick'. The mode of address provided for in the current rules of court is 'Justice',[166] but this reflects the former title of the judges of the District Court and is obsolete. Both inside and outside court, therefore, the correct mode of address is 'Judge'.

[5] APPOINTMENT AND QUALIFICATIONS

[4.63] Article 35.1 of the Constitution provides:

> The judges of the Supreme Court, the High Court and all other Courts established in pursuance of Article 34 hereof shall be appointed by the President.

While the formal appointment of judges is made by the President through the presentation of seals of office to those appointed, this power is, pursuant

161. See para **[4.52]**.
162. Courts of Justice Act 1924, s 38.
163. Order 3, rule 2 of the Rules of the Circuit Court 1950 (SI 179/1950).
164. On whether such a mode of address is appropriate, see n 159.
165. See para **[4.54]**.
166. Rule 3 of the District Court Rules 1948 (SR&O 431/1947).

to Article 13.9, exercised 'only on the advice of the Government', so that, in fact the real power of appointment rests with the Government.

Formal qualifications

[4.64] The Courts of Justice Act 1924 had set out various minimum qualifications for appointment as judges and these were, in large part, repeated in the Courts (Supplemental Provisions) Act 1961 for the courts established by the Courts (Establishment and Constitution) Act 1961. Although the Constitution does not expressly deal with qualifications, it has been held that the criteria set out in the Courts (Supplemental Provisions) Act 1961 are within the contemplation of Article 36.iii, which provides that the 'constitution' of the courts shall be regulated in accordance with law.[167] As to the formal qualifications themselves, they vary according to the Court to which a person is to be appointed.

[4.65] Beginning with the District Court, s 29(2) of the Courts (Supplemental Provisions) Act 1961 provides that a person 'who is for the time being a practising barrister or solicitor of not less than ten years' standing' is qualified for appointment as a judge of the District Court.[168] A similar requirement applies to the appointment of persons as judges of the District Court on a temporary basis.[169]

[4.66] In relation to the other courts, until 1996 only members of the Bar had been qualified for appointment. Thus, s 17(2) of the 1961 Act as originally enacted provided that only a practising barrister of at least ten years' standing was qualified to be appointed as a judge of the Circuit Court, with a similar requirement applying to the appointment of persons as judges of the Circuit Court on a temporary basis.[170] And s 5(2) of the 1961 Act provided that only a person who is for the time being a practising barrister of 12 years' standing may be appointed as a judge of the High Court or Supreme Court.[171] From this it is clear that only practising barristers of the relevant years standing were qualified to be appointed to the Circuit, High or Supreme Courts. To that extent, therefore, all the important judgments which had developed the law until 1996 were written by judges who had been practising barristers prior to their appointment.

---

167. See *The State (Walshe) v Murphy* [1981] IR 275.

168. This replaced Courts of Justice Act 1924, s 69 which had required six years standing only.

169. Courts of Justice Act 1936, s 51(1): see para **[4.54]**.

170. Courts of Justice Act 1936, s 14(1): see para **[4.52]**.

171. Replicating the Courts of Justice Act 1924, s 16 though the 1924 Act provided that holders of certain pre-1924 judicial offices were qualified for appointment to the new courts: see n 184.

[4.67] For many years, solicitors had pressed for an amendment to the 1961 Act so that they could be qualified for appointment to the Circuit Court as well as the High Court and Supreme Court.[172] Ultimately, a significant change was effected in the Courts and Court Officers Act 1995. Section 30 provides that, in addition to a practising barrister of ten years' standing, a practising solicitor of ten years' standing is qualified for appointment as a judge of the Circuit Court.[173] As to appointment to the High Court and Supreme Court, s 28 provides that a judge of the Circuit Court of four years' standing is qualified for appointment as a judge of the High Court or Supreme Court. Thus, although solicitors are not qualified for 'direct' appointment to the High Court or Supreme Court, the 1995 Act opened up at least the possibility that a former solicitor, having been appointed as a judge of the Circuit Court, might become a judge of the High Court or Supreme Court. Another significant amendment effected by s 28 of the 1995 Act was that service as a judge of the Court of Justice of the European Communities, as a judge of the Court of First Instance attached thereto or as an Advocate-General of the Court of Justice are to be deemed practice at the Bar for the purposes of appointment.[174]

[4.68] The meaning of some of the relevant legislative phrases was considered by the High Court in *The State (Walshe) v Murphy.*[175] Although the Court dealt with the qualifications of a person being appointed as a judge of the District Court, we have seen that the basic qualifications are quite similar for all the courts, so that the decision is relevant to all appointments. The prosecutor in *Walshe* had been charged with offences under the Road Traffic Acts and been convicted in May 1981 by the respondent, who had been appointed a temporary judge of the District Court in April 1981. The respondent had been called to the Bar in 1962 and from that time had practised at the Bar for over 8 years until April 1971, when he took up a post as legal assistant in the Attorney General's office until 1973, and from then until his appointment as a judge in 1981 was an examiner in the Land

---

172. See the Fair Trade Commission's *Report of Study into Restrictive Practices in the Legal Profession* (1990), pp 296-9. To a large extent, the broad recommendations in the 1990 Report were implemented in the 1995 Act. On the 1990 Report generally, see para **[3.05]**.

173. The first appointments of solicitors to the Circuit Court were made in July 1996.

174. In the immediate aftermath of the passing of the 1995 Act, Barrington J, who had been a judge of the Court of First Instance, was appointed to the Supreme Court. Although Barrington J had been a judge of the High Court prior to being appointed a judge of the Court of First Instance, and before that had been an eminent member of the Bar, there was a doubt over whether the 1961 Act required a person to have been in practice and/or have been a judge of the Irish courts *immediately* prior to being appointed to the Bench. Section 28 of the 1995 Act remedied this particular difficulty, thus paving the way for Barrington J to be appointed to the Supreme Court.

175. [1981] IR 275.

Commission. The prosecutor claimed that his conviction was invalid and should be quashed on *certiorari* on a number of grounds, including the argument that the respondent was not 'a practising barrister of ten years standing' when he had been appointed a judge. The High Court agreed. As to 'ten years standing', the Court examined whether this referred to ten years between a person's call to the Bar as a barrister and appointment as a judge (in which case the respondent would have been qualified) or referred to ten years' practice as a barrister (in which case the phrase 'practising barrister' would have to be examined in more detail). The Court accepted that there was some ambiguity in the legislation in this respect, so that it should look to the presumed or apparent intention of the legislature.[176] Delivering the main judgment,[177] Finlay P stated:[178]

> "I have no doubt that the apparent intention of the legislature was to provide a minimum standard of competence and skill for the person eligible for appointment as a Justice of the District Court."

[4.69] He concluded that the Court would be failing to implement that intention if it interpreted 'ten years standing' as meaning simply the lapse of time from call to the Bar, without regard to the period during which the person practised law before appointment as a judge. The Court therefore concluded that it was necessary for a person to have practised as a barrister for ten years before appointment, though the Court did *not* interpret the legislation as requiring that 'those ten years must have immediately preceded the date of the appointment or that there must have been a continuous period of ten years.'[179]
As to the term 'practising barrister', Finlay P stated that, although not defined in the legislation, it had a generally accepted meaning:[180]

> "That meaning ... refers to a person who, having the degree of barrister-at-law and having been called to the Bar, offers himself on hazard to take work (whether as an advocate or as an adviser) from persons who, through the agency of a solicitor, seek his services in the field in which he practises."

He held that a person employed in the Attorney General's office or in the Land Commission 'could not be said to be on hazard and offering himself as a barrister to the world at large.' On this basis, the Court concluded that the

176. On interpretation in cases of ambiguity, see para **[14.42]**.
177. The Court was a three-judge Divisional Court comprising Finlay P, Gannon and Hamilton JJ. Finlay P delivered the main judgment in the case, the other two judges concurring. On Divisional Courts, see para **[4.50]**.
178. [1981] IR 275, at 289.
179. *Ibid.*
180. [1981] IR 275, at 290.

respondent had not been a 'practising barrister' on his appointment and, as already indicated, the applicant's conviction was quashed on *certiorari*.[181]

Informal aspects of the appointments process: political allegiances

[4.70] As already indicated, while the formal appointment of all judges is made by the President, the reality is that, since this power is exercised on the advice of the Government, it is the Government who control appointments. And while the Courts (Supplemental Provisions) Act 1961, as amended, indicates that only barristers or solicitors of a number of years standing will be appointed, this does not provide a full picture of the appointments procedure.

[4.71] In general, many of those appointed to judicial office have had connections, to some extent or another, either with the political party or parties whose members form the Government of the day or have become known to the Government in some other way. This, indeed, had been the case prior to 1922. During the 19th century, many of the barristers appointed to the Irish Bench had either been MPs in the Westminster Parliament or served as Attorney General or some other law officer in Ireland. This indicated the connection between political activity and judicial preferment, and it must be said that this arrangement was similar to that in the remainder of what was the then United Kingdom.[182] Of course, the situation concerning Ireland was complicated by the growing movement for Home Rule and, later, the movement for the creation of an independent State, and judicial appointments became part of this wider political picture. By the time the Irish Free State was established in 1922, many of those who had been appointed to the Bench would not have shared the political outlook of those who now determined judicial appointments. Nonetheless, the new Government did appoint some judges who had been part of the pre-1922 regime to the new court system established by the Courts of Justice Act 1924.[183]

---

181. While the Court did not consider the effect of this decision on the other convictions handed down by the respondent, it would seem that they would be equally invalid: see *Shelly v Mahon* [1990] 1 IR 36 and *Glavin v Governor of Mountjoy Prison* [1991] 2 IR 421, discussed at n 279.

182. See Delany, *The Administration of Justice in Ireland*, 4th ed (Institute of Public Administration, 1975), p 74. On the circumstances surrounding the appointment of Chief Baron Palles, see Delany, *Christopher Palles* (Allen Figgis, 1960) pp 75-85

183. Of the three judges of the new Supreme Court, (Charles) O'Connor J had been Master of the Rolls in the pre-1922 Court of Appeal. Of the six judges in the new High Court, four had been members of the pre-1922 regime: Wylie J had been a member of the pre-1922 High Court, both O'Shaughnessy and Johnson JJ had been members of the lower courts and Hanna J had been a law officer. See Delany, *The Administration of Justice in Ireland*, 4th ed (Institute of Public Administration, 1975), p 75.

[4.72] In a study conducted in 1969,[184] the system of judicial appointment established in the post-1922 era was described as follows:[185]

> "A general consensus exists that there are no promises of judgeships for party service and this same consensus holds that no appointments are made of those unqualified for the judicial posts ... This is not to say that the best person available is always named but that usually those named are of judicial calibre.
>
> However, there is the very realistic point that, with rare exceptions, a person named as judge will be one who is favourably regarded by the Government perhaps out of gratitude for past services either to the party or to the State. Even in the rare instance where an adherent of the opposition party is named this may well be of indirect advantage of the Government party in that such a "non-partisan" appointment projects an image of objectivity to the public with concern for the quality of the courts rather than considering only political and partisan factors.
>
> A judicial appointment does not "just happen". It is in a very real sense the finest and the most desirable appointment that the Government can make. It is a status appointment. The choice is not made casually... The "inner circles" of the party and of the Government always have in mind potential appointees for judicial vacancies before they actually occur... The Minister for Justice makes up a list of prospects and presents it in Cabinet meeting. The "list" may contain a single name. The Ministers may add names to this list. Persons on it may be politically active or politically neutral.
>
> Some judges have thought that their work as a counsel in 'State cases' has helped their cause, that this gave them an opportunity to get to know the Taoiseach. Other have had members of the Government as clients and the personal friendship resulting helped. Another judge pointed out that his uncle was a friend of influential persons. One judge said simply that he met the Minister for Justice through a member of parliament and proceeded to tell the Minister that he was interested in an appointment. Persons who feel that they have a chance to be appointed commonly put in an application for the post.
>
> No formal vote is taken at the Cabinet meeting; an informal agreement on

184. Bartholomew, *The Irish Judiciary* (Institute of Public Administration, 1971). This study was the result of a 1969 survey of judges and other persons in Ireland conducted by Professor Bartholomew, the then Professor of Government and International Studies at the University of Notre Dame, Indiana, during a residency in the Faculty of Law, University College, Dublin. The study, described by the author as being in part 'a mildly behavioural investigation of judges as persons' was a pioneering one in the Irish context, and has not been repeated in published form since then, though such studies are common in other States.

185. *Ibid*, at pp 32-36.

> a particular person evolves. If the Taoiseach ... has a favourite, that man[186] will get the appointment. Certainly no one has ever been named judge over the objections of the Taoiseach.[187] The person chosen is then formally consulted and his consent secured. Then the President, who has not been consulted on the appointment, is told the name of the appointee and the formal appointment is made by the President ...
>
> A former Taoiseach made the statement that "all things being equal" a person's politics is controlling in such appointments. All Irish governments have to a greater or lesser degree been politically motivated in the making of judicial appointments. The English used judges as patronage and the new government after independence named judges that agreed with its aims."

As this account notes, there was certainly a political element to judicial appointments for many years. It must, of course, be borne in mind that those appointed to judicial office were required to meet the qualification standards specified in legislation and that, on their appointment, they were required to be independent in their decisions.[188] Nonetheless, the system was criticised from time to time and, since 1995, new arrangements have been in place which establish a more transparent process for judicial appointments.[189]

Allegiances, ideology and class

[4.73] Two other aspects of the 1969 study are worthy of note. First, while it indicated that political *allegiances* in general played a part in appointments, it also noted that political *ideology*, in the sense of liberalism or conservatism, seemed to have played little part. This would appear to reflect the general lack of a 'left-right' political divide in the State. However, it is of interest that, in 1969, 43% of the judges interviewed in the study characterised themselves as liberals, with about 13% professing conservatism.[190] As to the Supreme Court, the study's author stated:

---

186. At the time the author was writing, the only woman member of the judiciary was District Justice Eileen Kennedy: see his reference to this at p 40. The first woman High Court judge, Carroll J, was appointed in 1980. The first woman Supreme Court judge, Denham J, was appointed in 1992, having been a judge of the High Court since 1991. The first woman judge of the Circuit Court, Judge McGuinness, was appointed in 1994. In 1996, she became McGuinness J on her appointment to the High Court.

187. See, however, the discussion of the nomination of the President of the High Court in 1994, discussed at para **[4.79]**.

188. See para **[4.90]**.

189. See para **[4.80]**.

190. Bartholomew, *op cit*, at p 37. The terms 'liberal' and 'conservative' were not further defined by the author.

> "On the current Supreme Court there appears to be an interesting 3-1-1 division on a "liberal", "centrist", "conservative" basis."[191]

This view that the Supreme Court of the 1960s had a broadly 'liberal' perspective would appear to be supported by academic commentators in Ireland who have addressed this point.[192] This also reflected the general development of Irish society in the 1960s, based on a departure from political isolationism that had characterised Ireland up to the 1950s.[193] It would seem that judicial appointments were also seen by those in Government as an element of the modernisation of Irish society.[194]

[4.74] The other point worthy of note concerned the background of the judges. The 1969 study made this comment:

> "None of the Irish judges has been of humble family origin. On the contrary almost two-thirds came from admittedly upper middle class social and economic backgrounds and almost all of the remainder from middle class. A number of the judges attended private preparatory schools ... A goodly number were "born to the law", that is, more came from families where the father was a lawyer than where the father had any other occupation. Overall more than half of the judges have lawyers somewhere in their family relationship ... After law the chief paternal occupation was business on the managerial level, civil service, medicine and farming ... With this family background the encouragement and finances for the necessary education for law were readily available. Also from such families may well have come the proper attitudes of civic responsibility and social consciousness that produced "men of the law".[195]

While there have been a large number of changes in society since 1969 when this survey was compiled, it is probably true to say that the members of the judiciary remain largely from the middle classes.

Appointment of President of High Court in 1994

[4.75] For many years, the question of judicial appointments would not have been a subject for debate in the wider media, but certain events in 1994

191. *Ibid.* The judges of the Supreme Court at the time were: Ó Dálaigh CJ, Walsh, Budd, Fitzgerald and McLoughlin JJ.

192. See further para **[15.81]**.

193. For a general discussion, see Lee, *Ireland 1912 to 1985* (Cambridge UP, 1990).

194. Mr Justice Brian Walsh has stated that, on his appointment to the Supreme Court in 1962, the then Taoiseach Mr Seán Lemass, had indicated that, where the opportunity arose, there was a case for the Supreme Court to engage in active development of the 'Fundamental Rights' provisions of the 1937 Constitution. See Sturgess (ed), *Judging the World* (Butterworths, 1989).

195. Bartholomew, *op cit*, at pp 41-2.

brought the issue into sharp focus and led, in part, to the establishment of a Judicial Appointments Advisory Board.[196] The background to this was as follows.[197]

[4.76] In 1994, the Government of the day (a coalition consisting of two political parties, Fianna Fáil and the Labour Party) became involved in considerable public controversy concerning the nomination of the President of the High Court. In early 1994, the then Attorney General, Mr Harold Whelehan SC expressed an interest to the then Taoiseach, Mr Albert Reynolds, in being nominated to the Presidency of the High Court if a vacancy should arise. It was known that the then Chief Justice, Finlay CJ, would reach retirement age in September 1994 and that a judicial vacancy would therefore arise. Mr Reynolds gave Mr Whelehan an informal commitment that he would support his candidacy for the High Court in the event of a vacancy arising. This would appear to have been partly influenced by the informal convention that the Attorney General had 'first refusal' on any judicial vacancy.[198]

[4.77] During the summer of 1994, there was considerable publicity in the various media to the effect that the then Tánaiste and leader of the Labour Party, Dick Spring, was not prepared to assent to the nomination of Mr Whelehan.[199] In September 1994, the then President of the High Court, Hamilton P, was nominated by the Government to fill the vacancy in the post of Chief Justice arising from the retirement of Finlay CJ, and having duly been appointed by the President as Chief Justice, this created a vacancy in the Presidency of the High Court. There were continuing disagreements over the appointment of Mr Whelehan, and an informal committee comprising four Government Ministers was established to end the continuing impasse. At a meeting between the Taoiseach and Tánaiste at

196. The shortcomings of the system by which appointment were entirely within the hands of the Government had been criticised by a number of writers since the foundation of the State: see Delany, *The Administration of Justice in Ireland*, 4th ed (Institute of Public Administration, 1975), pp 76-7. In 1990, the Fair Trade Commission, *Report of Study into Restrictive Practices in the Legal Profession*, p 299, had explicitly recommended the establishment of a Judicial Appointments Advisory Board (on the Report generally, see para **[3.05]**. While the 1990 Report was, ultimately, implemented in the 1995 Act, the events of 1994 may be regarded as the immediate catalyst.

197. This account is based largely on the *Report of the sub-Committee on Legislation and Security* (Pn 1478, 1995). This Report was published on foot of resolutions passed by Dáil Éireann and the enactment of the Select Committee on Legislation and Security of Dáil Éireann (Privilege and Immunity) Act 1994, authorising the Committee to inquire into certain events in November 1994, including those discussed in the text.

198. See para **[3.60]**.

199. Some of the newspaper coverage is included in the material in Appendix 3 of the *Report of the sub-Committee on Legislation and Security, op cit*, pp 735-45.

Baldonnel military airdrome on 9 October 1994, the elements of a Courts Bill to effect substantial reform of the court system as well as to amend the arrangements for future judicial appointments were agreed. It appeared for a time that this Baldonnel meeting had produced a compromise, with the appointment of Mr Whelehan to go ahead in return for the changes to be contained in the Courts Bill.[200]

[4.78] However, almost simultaneously, in October 1994 there were media reports, including a documentary on Ulster Television, indicating that there had been a seven month delay in the Office of the Attorney General in the processing of an application for the extradition to Northern Ireland of a Roman Catholic priest, Fr Brendan Smyth, to face charges of sexual assault on children.[201] The Government requested Mr Whelehan, as the Attorney General, to prepare a report on this delay for discussion at Cabinet. The report was circulated to Ministers before the Cabinet meeting, but it appeared that the Labour Party Ministers did not consider that it adequately explained the delay in dealing with the extradition request, and they reluctantly came to the conclusion that they could not support the nomination of Mr Whelehan as President of the High Court.[202]

[4.79] On 11 November 1994, the Cabinet formally discussed Mr Whelehan's report, and the Labour Party Ministers then withdrew from the meeting. Mr Whelehan's nomination as President of the High Court was then put to and approved by the remaining Ministers (in the absence of the Labour Party Ministers) and later that day, he was formally appointed by the President of Ireland to his position as President of the High Court, and he made his declaration as President of the High Court on 15 November 1994.[203] However, arising from subsequent developments, on 17 November 1994 Mr Whelehan resigned as President of the High Court[204] on the same day as a motion of No Confidence in the Government was passed by Dáil Éireann. While the wider political aspects of these events are outside the scope of this book,[205] it can be said that they were the genesis, at least in part, of the establishment of a Judicial Appointments Advisory Board.[206]

---

200. This became the basis for the Courts and Court Officers Bill 1994, which was presented to Dáil Éireann by the then Minister for Justice in November 1994. However, the 1994 Bill lapsed on the fall of the Government later that month. An amended version of the 1994 Bill became the Courts and Court Officers Act 1995.

201. The Attorney General had been conferred with certain functions in extradition cases by the Extradition (Amendment) Act 1987.

202. See letter from Mr Spring to Mr Reynolds in the *Report of the sub-Committee on Legislation and Security, op cit*, p 725.

203. On the declaration required by Article 34.5 of the Constitution, see para **[4.90]**.

204. Mr Whelehan subsequently recommenced his practice at the Bar: see further n 287.

205. For an informal account of the events, written by the Government Press Secretary of the day, see Duignan, *One Spin on The Merry-Go-Round* (Blackwater Press, 1995).

206. See also n 198.

Judicial Appointments Advisory Board

[4.80] Section 13 of the Courts and Court Officers Act 1995 provides for the appointment of a Judicial Appointments Advisory Board for the purposes of 'identifying persons and informing the Government of the suitability of those persons for appointment to judicial office.'

[4.81] Section 12 of the 1995 Act defines 'judicial office' as being: 'the office of ordinary judge of the Supreme Court, ordinary judge of the High Court, ordinary judge of the Circuit Court or judge of the District Court (other than the President of the High Court.' Thus, the remit of the Board excludes the offices of Chief Justice, President of the High Court, President of the Circuit Court and President of the District Court, though in relation to these offices, the Government is subject to some limitations in that it is required to 'have regard first' to the qualifications and suitability of existing judges.[207]

[4.82] The Board consists of the following ten persons:

- the Chief Justice, who chairs the Board,
- the President of the High Court,
- the President of the Circuit Court,
- the President of the District Court,
- the Attorney General,[208]
- a practising barrister nominated by the Chair of the Council of the Bar of Ireland,
- a practising solicitor nominated by the President of the Law Society of Ireland and
- not more than three persons appointed by the Minister for Justice who are engaged in or have appropriate knowledge or experience of commerce, finance or administration or persons who have experience as consumers of the services provided by the courts.[209]

[4.83] The nominated solicitor and barrister and the three members appointed by the Minister remain on the Boards for a three year term,[210] thus indicating that it has a continuing presence and is thus not empanelled only

207. Courts and Court Officers Act 1995, s 23.

208. Section 18(3) specifies that where the Attorney General wishes to be considered for appointment for judicial office, he or she shall withdraw from any deliberations of the Board concerning his or her suitability for office.

209. The first Board took office in 1996 on the appointment of the three members nominated by the Minister for Justice and advertisements later appeared in national newspapers seeking applications for consideration by the Board. The first appointments under this procedure were also made in 1996 to fill the judicial positions created by the 1995 Act.

210. Courts and Court Officers Act 1995, s 13(3) which also provides that such persons are eligible for re-appointment.

where a judicial vacancy arises. It may also be noted that the three members appointed by the Minister introduce the first formal mechanism by which non-lawyers are involved in judicial appointments. This reflects the 'lay' involvement in the Council of the Bar of Ireland and of the Law Society of Ireland.[211]

[4.84] Section 14 of the 1995 Act empowers the Board to adopt its own procedures, and in this respect it may:

- advertise for applications for judicial appointment,
- require applicants to complete application forms,
- consult persons concerning the suitability of applicants to the Board,
- invite persons, identified by the Board, to submit their names for consideration by the Board and
- arrange to interview applicants who wish to be considered for judicial appointment.

The Board thus has extensive powers to identify those persons suitable for appointment in accordance with its function under s 13 of the 1995 Act.[212]

[4.85] Section 16 of the 1995 Act specifies that a person who wishes to be considered for judicial appointment:

> shall so inform the Board in writing and shall provide the Board with such information as it may require to enable it to consider the suitability of that person for judicial office, including information relating to education, professional qualifications, experience and character.

Section 16 also specifies that, where the Minister for Justice requests, the Board must submit to the Minister the name of each person who has informed the Board of his or her wish to be considered for judicial office. In general, the Board is required to recommend at least seven names from the list it submits, but this can be a lesser number where there are multiple vacancies for which there are less than the requisite multiple of seven who the Board considers it can recommend.

[4.86] As regards who the Board can recommend, any such person must comply with the relevant qualifications set out in the Courts (Supplemental Provisions) Act 1961.[213] In addition, s 16 provides that the Board must not recommend a person unless, in the Board's opinion, the person:

---

211. See paras **[3.16]** and **[3.39]**.

212. Section 21 of the 1995 Act also provides for staffing for the Board, while s 22 is a standard provisions that the expenses incurred by the Board shall be paid out of moneys provided by the Oireachtas.

213. See paras **[4.65]-[4.67]**.

(a) has displayed in his or her practice as a barrister or solicitor, as the case may be, a degree of competence and a degree of probity appropriate to and consistent with the appointment concerned,

(b) is suitable on grounds of character and temperament,

(c) is otherwise suitable, and

(d) undertakes in writing to the Board his or her agreement, if appointed to judicial office, to take such course of training or education, or both, as may be required by the Chief Justice or the President of the court to which the person is appointed.[214]

Clearly, this involves a new and elaborate procedure for judicial appointments. However, it must be remembered that, ultimately, the Constitution requires such appointments be made by the President acting on the advice of the Government. This is recognised in s 16(6) of the 1995 Act, which provides:

> In advising the President in relation to the appointment of a person to judicial office the Government shall firstly consider for appointment those persons whose names have been recommended to the Minister pursuant to this section.

Thus, while the recommendations of the Board will undoubtedly be of considerable importance,[215] the final decision rests with the Government. In addition, we have already noted that the functions of the Board do not extend to appointments to the offices of Chief Justice, President of the High Court, President of the Circuit Court and President of the District Court.[216] One other limitation is that the Board's recommendation function does not apply where the Government proposes to 'promote' a sitting judge.[217] However, these limitations aside, the changes effected by the 1995 Act created a degree of openness in the appointments procedure[218] which did not apply until the Board's establishment.[219]

214. Section 16(7) and 19 of the 1995 Act.

215. Section 16(8) of the 1995 Act provides that appointments made under the procedure envisaged by the Act must be published in *Iris Oifigiúil*, the Official Gazette, and the notice must include a statement, if that is the case, that the name of the person was recommended by the Board to the Minister. This would appear to be an 'encouragement' to the Government to advise the appointment of recommended persons only.

216. See para **[4.81]**.

217. Section 17 of the 1995 Act.

218. Section 20 of the 1995 Act provides that the proceedings of the Board and all communications to it are confidential and shall not be disclosed except for the purposes of the Act.

219. On the procedure for judicial appointment in the United Kingdom, see Zander, *The English Legal System*, 6th ed (Butterworths, 1993).

Other informal aspects

[4.87] While the Courts (Supplemental Provisions) Act 1961 lays down minimum qualifications, and the terms of reference of the Judicial Appointments Advisory Board provide further information on the appointments process, other informal aspects of the appointments process remain to be mentioned. Thus, while the 1961 Act refers to 10 and 12 years' practice, in most instances those appointed to the Bench have considerably longer experience, and the average age of judges on appointment is in the mid 50s.[220] Another important convention is that, in most instances, only senior counsel are considered for appointment to the High Court and Supreme Court. It has also been a long-standing convention that at least one judge of the Supreme Court is not a Roman Catholic, while a number of judges in the other courts are also from other religious faiths, including the Church of Ireland, the Presbyterian Church and the Jewish Community. More recently, the convention has grown that judicial appointments reflect a gender balance in proportion to the increasing number of women at senior levels in the profession. As to progression from the High Court to the Supreme Court, there is a general tendency for judges appointed to the High Court to be considered for later appointment to the Supreme Court on the retirement of a Supreme Court judge, but no clear rules exist in this respect either and a number of appointments to the Supreme Court in the 1980s had been made directly from the ranks of senior counsel. As to the Circuit Court, many of the appointments up to 1996 were also from the ranks of the inner Bar. In addition, another convention was that Circuit Court judges were rarely 'promoted' to any of the higher courts. An exception to both of these conventions was the late McWilliam J, who was first appointed to the Circuit Court at a time when he was a junior counsel, and was appointed to the High Court in 1977. Arising from the changes effected by the Courts and Court Officers Act 1995, a more structured approach to judicial progression, based on recommendations from the Judicial Appointments Advisory Board, may become more common.[221]

---

220. There have been some notable exceptions, such as Walsh J and Denham J, who were appointed judges in their early 40s. In July 1996, a number of judges appointed to the Circuit Court were in their 30s.

221. In 1996, Circuit Court judges Moriarty and McGuinness were appointed to the High Court. The possibility of a greater degree of judicial promotion had been discussed in the Fair Trade Commission's, *Report of Study into Restrictive Practices in the Legal Profession* (1990), pp 296-9. Bartholomew, *op cit*, p 39, had suggested that a formalised system of promotions might lead some judges to 'look over their shoulder' and become more deferential towards the government of the day. However, the existence of the Judicial Appointments Advisory Board is likely to minimise this risk.

Judicial training and education

[4.88] Section 16 of the Courts and Court Officers Act 1995 introduced for the first time a mandatory requirement that candidates for judicial appointment undertake to agree to take any course of training or education as may be required by the Chief Justice or the President of the court to which the person is appointed. While such training and continuing education is not mandatory for those appointed prior to 1996, a Judicial Studies Institute, under the auspices of the Chief Justice, has been established with a view to providing continuing education for all judges.[222] This is similar to arrangements in Britain. Section 48 of the 1995 Act provides that such training and education may be funded by the Minister for Justice.

[6] JUDICIAL INDEPENDENCE

[4.89] Whatever the genesis of a person's appointment to judicial office, the Constitution underlines the independence of office once a person is appointed.

'Without fear or favour, affection or ill-will'

[4.90] First, Article 34.5.1° requires all judges to make the following declaration on their appointment:

> In the presence of Almighty God I do solemnly and sincerely promise and declare that I will duly and faithfully and to the best of my knowledge and power execute the office of Chief Justice (*or as the case may be*) without fear or favour, affection or ill-will towards any man, and that I will uphold the Constitution and the laws. May God direct and sustain me.[223]

Article 35.2 and 35.3 both underline this declaration by providing that:

2. All judges shall be independent in the exercise of their judicial functions and subject only to the Constitution and the law.
3. No judge shall be eligible to be a member of either House of the Oireachtas or to hold any other office or position of emolument.

Two practical elements in the independence of the judges of the High Court and Supreme Court are made explicit in the Constitution: the extreme difficulty of removing a judge from office and a guarantee that their salary cannot be reduced. In addition, we consider some other aspects of judicial independence not explicitly dealt with in the constitutional text.

---

222. 458 *Dáil Debates* col 1765 (28 November 1995).
223. This replaced the declaration provided for in the Courts of Justice Act 1924, s 99.

Removal for stated misbehaviour or incapacity

[4.91] On the issue of removal from office, Article 35.4.1° provides:

> A judge of the Supreme Court or the High Court shall not be removed from office except for stated misbehaviour or incapacity, and then only upon resolutions passed by Dáil Éireann and Seanad Éireann calling for his removal.

A similar form of protection, though in statutory form only, has been extended to judges of the Circuit Court[224] and District Court.[225] Like the provision in Article 34.1 concerning the administration of justice in public, these protections reflect the lessons of history and the need to ensure that the judiciary are independent of the current political climate. For the judiciary in the higher courts of Great Britain and Ireland, such provisions date back to 1701[226] and similar protections exist under many Constitutions.[227]

---

224. Courts of Justice Act 1924, s 39 which was carried forward by the Courts (Supplemental Provisions) Act 1961, s 48 provides: 'The Circuit Judges shall hold office by the same tenure as the Judges of the High Court and the Supreme Court.' This is taken to mean in particular that the dual resolution required by Article 35.4 of the Constitution applies to the removal of a Circuit Court judge: see Hogan & Whyte, *Kelly's The Irish Constitution*, 3rd ed (Butterworths, 1994), p 551.

225. Courts of Justice (District Court) Act 1946, s 20 which was carried forward by the Courts (Supplemental Provisions) Act 1961, s 48 provides (as adapted by the Courts Act 1991, s 21): 'District Judges shall hold office by the same tenure as the Judges of the Supreme Court and the High Court.' See the comments on s 39 of the 1924 Act, n 224, above. This protection greatly extended the tenure of judges of the District Court by comparison with that contained in the Courts of Justice Act 1924, s 73. It would seem that the requirement for a resolution by both Houses does not apply to a temporary judge of the District Court, as the 1946 Act excludes a temporary judge from its definition of judge: see the High Court judgment of Lynch J in *Magee v Culligan* [1992] 1 IR 223, cited in Delany, *The Courts Acts 1924-1991* (Round Hall Press, 1993), pp 112-3. A similar exclusion may not apply to temporary judges of the Circuit Court, s 39 of the 1924 Act containing no similar limitation. Finally, there are two provisions that apply to judges of the District Court only and which concern their general conduct or health. First, the Courts of Justice (District Court) Act 1946, s 21 provides that the Minister for Justice may request the Chief Justice to appoint a Supreme Court or High Court judge to investigate the condition of health or inquire into the conduct of a judge of the District Court, and to report the result of the investigation or inquiry to the Minister. No sanction is provided for in s 21 of the 1946 Act. Second, the Courts (Supplemental Provisions) Act 1961, s 10(4) provides that where the Chief Justice is of opinion that the conduct of a judge of the District Court has been such as to bring the administration of justice into disrepute, the Chief Justice may interview the judge privately and inform him or her of that opinion. Again, no further sanction is provided for.

226. The Act of Settlement 1701, which united the Scottish and English kingdoms, provided that judges of the higher courts held office for life 'subject to a power of removal by Her Majesty by both Houses of Parliament'. Similarly, in 1782, the Irish Parliament in Dublin ('Grattan's Parliament') passed 'An Act for securing the Independency of Judges, and the impartial administration of Justice', 21 & 22 Geo III, c 50. This Act provided that all commissions of judges would 'continue and remain in full force during their good behaviour... notwithstanding the demise of the King (whom God long preserve)', that all salaries would be continued while their commissions remained in force, and that removal of a judge could only be by the King 'upon the address of both houses of Parliament': see *The Irish Statutes, 1310-1800* (Round Hall Press, 1995 reprint), p 582.

227. For example, Article III of the US Constitution, Articles 64 and 65 of the French Constitution, Article 97 of the German Basic Law: see Forde, *Constitutional Law of Ireland* (Mercier Press, 1987) p 185.

[4.92] The question of removal of a judge, sometimes referred to as impeachment, has never been given serious consideration since 1937, and so the phrase 'stated misbehaviour or incapacity' has not been interpreted by the courts. It has been suggested that the word 'incapacity' suggests physical unfitness for office, in the sense that the judge in question was suffering from a physical or other disability such as a stroke or mental illness.[228] The words 'stated misbehaviour' would appear to include both misbehaviour off the bench, such as a conviction for a serious criminal offence,[229] as well as misbehaviour on the bench, such as accepting a bribe, and most commentators would accept that such eventualities are unlikely to occur.[230] It seems that the question of what amounts to misbehaviour might embrace more general matters, such as a judge's endorsement of a particular political party's views. Such a problem has not arisen. In an individual case, a judge may be required to recuse himself or herself from adjudicating on the matter where it might appear that he or she had previously expressed a view on the issue in question. A fundamental principle of natural justice or fair procedures[231] is expressed by the phrase *nemo judex in causa sua*, that a person may not be a judge in their own cause or in a matter in which they have an interest, whether financial or otherwise. Thus, in *Dublin Wellwoman Centre Ltd v Ireland*,[232] the Supreme Court held that the High Court judge Carroll J ought not adjudicate in a case concerning access to information on abortion as she had previously, as Chairwoman of the Second Commission on the Status of Women, written a letter to the Taoiseach expressing the support of the Commission for the right of access to abortion counselling and information services. Speaking for the Supreme Court, Denham J pointed out that there had been no suggestion that this letter would have resulted in any actual bias on the part of Carroll J in adjudicating the points of law at issue in the case; rather a judge should offer to recuse himself or herself where there was even an *appearance* of bias. This test of the appearance of bias rather than actual bias is consistent with the constitutional declaration in Article 34.5.1° to execute the judicial office 'without fear or favour, affection or ill-will'. The decision in *Dublin Wellwoman* indicates the high standards of impartiality thus required.

228. Hogan & Whyte, *op cit*, pp 551-2.

229. Hogan & Whyte, *op cit*, p 552 fn 20 suggest that a conviction for an offence under the Road Traffic Acts would not come within the definition of 'stated misbehaviour', but that a series of convictions for drink-related driving offences might. In 1993, it was reported that a High Court judge (Carney J) had apologised for seeking a drink in a Dublin hotel after closing hours: see The Irish Times, 9 March 1993, p 1. it could not be suggested that this behaviour came within Article 35.4 of the Constitution.

230. The most recent(!) and only instance of an impeachment since 1701 was in 1830 when Sir Jonah Barrington was dismissed for mishandling funds of wards of court. Charles Dickens' *Bleak House*, in describing the fictitious litigation of *Jarndyce v Jarndyce*, largely concerned the (mal)administration of the wardship jurisdiction in 19th century England,

231. See para **[8.22]**.

232. [1995] 1 ILRM 408.

Similarly, judges may not become actively engaged in the proceedings by excessive interruption of the legal representatives in their submissions or examination of witnesses, because that would be to breach another fundamental principle of natural justice, *audi alteram partem*, which requires that both sides be given an equal opportunity to present their case.[233] It has been held that a judge is not required to recuse himself merely on the ground that his daughter is appearing as counsel for one party.[234]

Independence, public criticism and the place of the judiciary in society

[4.93] As a corollary that judges can only be removed for stated misbehaviour, there has been an implicit convention pre-dating the 1937 Constitution, and indeed the establishment of the State in 1922, that judges do not generally become involved in any matter of public controversy. Indeed, until recent years, a judge would not give interviews to the media while he or she was a sitting judge, particularly in relation to a case in which the judge had been involved. In a sense, the view was that judges made decisions, but that any political implications of such decisions were matters for the executive and legislative branches of government and the judiciary should stand aloof.[235]

[4.94] Many writers on the law would agree that there have been a number of highly influential judges over the years who, as individuals, have had a significant impact on the development of the law.[236] These individuals would have been the subject of major autobiographies and biographies were it not

233. See *The People v MacEoin* [1978] IR 27 and *Donnelly v Timber Factors Ltd* [1991] 1 IR 553.

234. See *O'Reilly v Cassidy* [1995] 1 ILRM 306.

235. For example, see the interview with Mr Justice O'Higgins, former Chief Justice, *The Irish Times,* 7 and 8 October 1991. This was given after Mr Justice O'Higgins had retired as a judge of the Court of Justice of the European Communities.

236. Thus, of the Irish judges of the 19th century, Christopher Palles, the last Lord Chief Baron, stands out, both for the length of his judicial tenure of almost 50 years stretching from the mid-19th century virtually to the establishment of the Irish Free State and also that his judgments continue to be cited as authority in many common law jurisdictions. In the 20th century, there have been a number of judges in Ireland who have contributed greatly to the development of Irish law, in particular constitutional law. Among these were Hugh Kennedy, the first Attorney General of the Irish Free State, an important architect of the 1924 court system and the first Chief Justice. George Gavan Duffy, who had been Roger Casement's solicitor in his treason trial and a member of the delegation that had signed the 1921 Anglo-Irish Articles of Agreement, was later a distinguished President of the High Court. Later, the developments both in the interpretation of the Constitution and of Irish law in general were associated with Cearbhall Ó Dálaigh (Chief Justice, judge of the European Court of Justice and then President of Ireland), Thomas O'Higgins (Government Minister and later Chief Justice and judge of the Court of Justice), Thomas Finlay (Chief Justice), Kenny J, Kingsmill Moore J, Walsh J and Henchy J. This list is inevitably selective and also excludes those many brilliant advocates who brought to the courts innovative submissions without which the law might not have developed as it did. Among these advocates who did not go on to become members of the judiciary might be mentioned Mr Thomas Connolly SC and Mr Séan McBride SC (who had also been a Minister for External Affairs).

for the conventional reticence attaching to holders of judicial office. The result has been that judicial autobiographies are a rarity in Britain and Ireland,[237] and any biographies have largely involved judges of an earlier era.[238] In their absence, students of law have had to be content largely with collections of anecdotes.[239]

[4.95] It is, perhaps, not surprising that, in an era of media power and rapid changes in Irish society in the 1980s and 1990s, this convention should begin to break down. Thus, in 1987 the present Chief Justice, Hamilton CJ, then the President of the High Court, agreed to appear on an edition of an RTÉ television series, *Open File*, in which various influential public figures were questioned about their work. In that instance, Hamilton CJ was questioned by a two person panel, one a lecturer in law in University College Dublin and the other a well-known investigative journalist. Such a programme would have been unthinkable ten years previously. Similarly, in 1986 there was a significant level of public discussion arising from a judicial inquiry conducted into what became known as the 'Kerry Babies Case'.[240] The High Court judge who conducted that inquiry, Lynch J, responded to adverse comments on the inquiry's report which had appeared in the current affairs magazine *Magill.*[241] In former times, the judiciary's response to public criticism would be to ignore the matter, or to bring a claim for defamation against the publication, or initiate contempt of court proceedings.[242] In 1992, the public comments of O'Hanlon J, then a High Court judge, on proposed changes in Irish law on abortion were subjected to

---

237. Exceptions in Britain include Lord Denning's *My Family Story* (Butterworths, 1981). There would appear to be no autobiographies written by members of the High Court or Supreme Court since 1922. Lindsay, *Memories* (Blackwater Press, 1992) is an extended memoir by a former Government Minister and Master of the High Court. At the time of writing it is expected that memoirs of Mr Justice O'Higgins will be published in late 1996.

238. See Delany, *Christopher Palles* (Allen Figgis, 1960) and Golding, *George Gavan Duffy* (Irish Academic Press, 1982). Other important biographical collections include Ball, *The Judges in Ireland, 1221-1921*, 2 vols (Round Hall Press, 1993 reprint). An exception to the convention that only long-distant judges are recognised in biography is Mathews (ed), *Immediate Man: Cuimhní ar Chearbhall Ó Dálaigh* (Dolmen Press, 1983). In addition, *festschrifts* in honour of Irish judges of the recent past have been published. These include O'Reilly (ed), *Human Rights and Constitutional Law* (Round Hall Press, 1992) (in honour of Walsh J) and Curtin and O'Keeffe (eds), *Constitutional Adjudication in European Community and National Law* (Butterworths, 1992) (in honour of O'Higgins CJ). Durcan, *Daddy, Daddy* (Blackstaff Press, 1990) includes a series of poems on the poet's relationship with his father, a former President of the Circuit Court.

239. See para **[3.49]**.

240. *Report of the Tribunal of Inquiry into the 'Kerry Babies Case'* (Pl 3514, 1985).

241. *Magill*, March 1986.

242. On contempt of court, see para **[10.31]**.

considerable media attention and adverse comment.[243] The removal of O'Hanlon J as a judge did not arise from such comments, but it underlined the difficulties involved, even in the 'age of communication', when judges become embroiled publicly in matters on which they, and other members of the community, hold strong views.[244] In this changing situation, it is inevitable that the tone of comment on the work of the judiciary, whether from the academic and wider legal community or from the media, will become more robust, replacing what in the past would have been quite deferential and indeed reverential comment.

[4.96] Legal publishing in Ireland, in particular academic legal writing, has only emerged in any real sense since the late 1970s and early 1980s, and many textbook writers have focused on 'black letter' law, describing the essential legal rules applicable to a particular subject area. However the 1990s has also seen the emergence of studies that focus on the societal context within which law operates.[245]

[4.97] More general socio-legal studies of the British judiciary have appeared in recent years and these include Professor Griffith's *The Politics of the Judiciary*[246] and Professor Lee's *Judging Judges.*[247] Both books provide a wider analysis of the political context in which the judiciary operate than have appeared to date in Ireland. Professor Lee's book suggests, for example, that in the age of the media, the courts may need to consider agreeing to hold media briefings in relation to their more important decisions. Indeed, it would appear that some moves in this direction are

243. In *Attorney General v X* [1992] 1 IR 1 the Supreme Court had held that Article 40.3.3° appeared to authorise abortion in limited circumstances. The case generated enormous publicity and controversy. O'Hanlon J publicly stated that he disagreed with the decision of the Supreme Court and that any attempt to amend the Constitution or to legislate for abortion would be contrary to natural law and therefore prohibited: see (1993) 11 ILT 8. By the time O'Hanlon J had made his comments, the Government had committed itself to amending the Constitution and/or introducing legislation on the topic. O'Hanlon J was, at that time, also President of the Law Reform Commission (see para **[11.11]**). The Taoiseach of the day wrote to O'Hanlon J objecting to the fact that he had made these views public and also purported in this letter to terminate his appointment as President of the Law Reform Commission. In reply, Mr Justice O'Hanlon made a public statement to the effect that the purported termination had no legal effect, but he also simultaneously withdrew from the position as President of the Law Reform Commission, in effect resigning. See Hogan & Whyte, *op cit*, p 552, fn 21.

244. See further para **[15.130]-[15.135]**.

245. These include Duncan (ed), *Law and Social Policy* (Dublin University Law Journal, 1987), Whelan (ed), *Law and Liberty in Ireland* (Oak Tree Press, 1993), O'Mahony, *Crime and Punishment in Ireland* (Round Hall Press, 1993) and Quinn and Ors (eds), *Justice and Legal Theory in Ireland* (Oak Tree Press, 1995). In his Foreword to McMahon and Binchy, *A Casebook on the Irish Law of Torts* (Professional Books, 1983), Mr Justice Walsh, the then senior ordinary judge of the Supreme Court, suggested that the decision-making process of collegiate courts 'should be studied under the rubric of small group sociology.'

246. Fontana, 1985 (3rd ed).

247. Faber & Faber, 1988 (1989 paperback edition containing additional material).

likely to result if recommendations for the creation of an independent Courts Service are implemented.[248]

[4.98] As for the approach of the media in general, there has been a steady stream in recent years of best-selling books describing 'famous trials', both criminal and civil.[249] Earlier pioneering work by the journalist Nell McCafferty during the 1970s on the Dublin District Court was collected as *In the Eyes of the Law*[250] The descriptions of the people who came into contact with the law at this level of the criminal justice system reflected poorly on the overall system. The following provides a flavour of her vivid descriptions:

> "The gowns and wigs may imply majesty, though they too are faded and torn sometimes. The Dublin District Courts themselves have the trappings of sadness ... Within the court itself, no room. Three hard benches, and the unlucky ones line the walls. It gets too hot, too cold, too stuffy, too noisy, too quiet. Even the gardaí don't know how to use the microphones. The Justice is irritated. Justice is flawed. The solicitor arrives late. Justice is delayed. The lists are long and the bailsmen have to come back next day. People don't know what to do and other people are too busy to help them. Tempers flare, spirits flag, and the long hopeless grind grinds on. Around in the High Court, planning permission is debated in leisure, and the dignity befitting high finance."

The conditions described there might be thought to reflect a bad day in Dickensian times, but conditions in the courthouses of Ireland in the late 20th century have led to a number of court proceedings in which the Minister for Justice has been ordered to comply with statutory obligations concerning the maintenance of courthouses.[251]

---

248. See para **[4.139]**.

249. Collections of 'famous criminal trials' include Deale, *Beyond any Reasonable Doubt?* 2nd rev ed (Gill and Macmillan, 1990) and Reddy, *Murder Will Out: A Book of Irish Murder Cases* (Gill and Macmillan, 1990). Dunne and Kerrigan, *Round Up the Usual Suspects* (Magill, 1984) and Joyce and Murtagh, *Blind Justice* (Poolbeg, 1984) deal with the 'Sallins Train Robbery case' of the mid 1970s. The 'Arms Trial' of 1970 is discussed in McIntyre, *Through the Bridewell Gate* (Faber & Faber, 1971) and Kelly, *Orders for the Captain?* (published by the author, 1971). See also Williams, *The General* (O'Brien Press, 1994), an account of the life of an alleged 'godfather' of crime. As to civil cases, Crotty, *A Radical's Response* (Poolbeg, 1988) is an account of the background to *Crotty v An Taoiseach* [1987] IR 713 (see para **[16.63]**) written by the plaintiff. Two other books of note are Kerrigan, *Nothing But the Truth* (Tomar, 1990), an account of *Dunne v National Maternity Hospital* [1989] IR 91, and O'Callaghan, *The Red Book* (Tomar, 1992), an account of *Hanrahan v Merck, Sharpe & Dohme Ltd* [1988] ILRM 629 see para **[7.09]**.

250. Ward River Press, 1981.

251. The poor physical condition of many courthouses in the State has given rise to litigation initiated by members of the legal profession seeking orders requiring the relevant State agencies to carry out their statutory duties concerning their upkeep: see *The State (King) v Minister for Justice* [1984] IR 169 (decided in 1975) and *Hoey v Minister for Justice* [1994] 3 IR 329. See also para **[4.14]**.

[4.99] The criticism of courthouse conditions in *In the Eyes of the Law* are exceptionally mild by comparison with the more wide-ranging criticism of judicial performance to be found, for example, in the United States. Possibly the most controversial book published in this respect was Woodward and Armstrong's *The Brethren.*[252] This 'inside' account of the workings of the United States Supreme Court from 1969 to 1975 clearly required the active assistance of some of the law clerks who are assigned to assist the Supreme Court Justices. The 'colour journalism' style of the authors can be seen from the following sketch:[253]

> "Earl Warren, the Chief Justice of the United States, hailed the elevator operator as if he were campaigning, stepped in and rode to the basement of the Supreme Court Building, where the Court limousine was waiting. Warren easily guided his bulky, 6-foot-1-inch, 220-pound frame into the back seat. Though he was seventy-seven, the Chief still had great stamina and resilience."

Despite the changes that have occurred in recent years, it remains unlikely that a similar account of the work of Irish judges would appear in Ireland.[254]

Remuneration

[4.100] On judicial remuneration, Article 35.5 of the Constitution provides:

> The remuneration of a judge shall not be reduced during his continuance in office.

Again, this is an important provision ensuring that the judiciary do not feel that they are in any way 'obliged' to the Government of the day, by contrast with members of the judiciary in the distant past who might have considered that their continued remuneration was dependent on making decisions that did not offend those in authority. However, judges are liable to income tax

---

252. (Martin Secker & Warburg, 1979).

253. *Op cit*, p 9. The book was, when published, highly controversial, particularly because of its style, which concentrated on personalities and portrayed some Supreme Court Justices in a better light than others. In addition, one of the authors, Bob Woodward, was one of the *Washington Post* journalists who had 'broken' the Watergate story that led to the downfall of US President Richard Nixon in 1974. Woodward was seen by some as 'hostile' to those judges on the Court who had, prior to their appointment, been associated with the US Republican Party, some of whom had been appointed on President Nixon's nomination.

254. There are two possible explanations for this: first, journalistic concerns that an Irish version of *The Brethren* could be defamatory or in contempt of court, and second that, in a small society, many of the points that might form the content of such a book are passed by word of mouth, perpetuating the 'oral traditions' of Irish life. Of course, in terms of fiction, the performance of the judiciary and the court system has, for many generations, been subjected to public scrutiny. Banville, *The Book of Evidence* (Martin Secker & Warburg, 1992) examined aspects of the criminal mind and is said to have been based on a true story.

on their salaries. In *O'Byrne v Minister for Finance*,[255] the Supreme Court held that Article 35.5 did not preclude the deduction of income tax from the gross salary of a judge, provided that such deductions were similar to those for other persons having the same income level. In the *O'Byrne* case, the widow of Mr Justice John O'Byrne, who had been a judge of the High Court and later the Supreme Court from 1926 to 1954, claimed that subjecting a judge's salary to income tax was in conflict with Article 35.5. This claim was, however, rejected in the Supreme Court, by a 3-2 majority of the judges. The three judges in the majority stated that Article 35.5 must be read with Article 35.2 as protecting the independence of the judges from governmental interference. In this light, the Court held that to require a judge to pay income tax like other citizens could not be described as an attack on judicial independence.

[4.101] The salaries of the judges are fixed from time to time by legislation. At the beginning of the 19th century, judicial salaries were very high by the standards of the day. Thus, prior to 1832, the Lord Chancellor of Ireland enjoyed an annual salary of £10,000, when it was reduced to £8,000. The salary of the Lord Chief Justice of Ireland was fixed at £5,000 in 1877, with ordinary High Court judges receiving about £3,500.[256]

[4.102] The establishment of the Irish Free State in 1922 saw a reduction in salaries from the old regime, and it would seem that judicial salaries were pegged at about half of their English counterparts.[257]

[4.103] The following salaries were fixed in 1924:

- Chief Justice: £4,000
- Supreme Court judges (and High Court President): £3,000
- High Court judges: £2,500
- Circuit Court judges: £1,700
- District Justices: £1,000 to £1,200.[258]

There were modest increases in 1947 and 1953,[259] but in June 1957 all the judges of the High Court and Supreme Court sent a memorandum to the Government indicating that they considered that their salaries had fallen well below comparable salaries in the public sector and making

255. [1959] IR 1.
256. See Delany, *The Administration of Justice in Ireland*, 4th ed (Institute of Public Administration, 1975), p 74.
257. See File S 15010 C, National Archives of Ireland, in the files relating to what became the Courts (Supplemental Provisions) Act 1961.
258. Courts of Justice Act 1924, ss 13, 41 and 74.
259. Courts of Justice Act 1947 and Courts of Justice Act 1953.

unfavourable comparisons with their English and Northern Ireland brethren. It is also notable that the judges suggested that the imposition of income tax on their salaries was in breach of Article 35.5 of the Constitution, an issue which was, at the time, pending before the Supreme Court in the *O'Byrne* case and on which the Supreme Court ultimately held in effect against themselves, albeit by a 3-2 majority. While the Government considered that, in general, judicial salaries were appropriate some further increases were made on the re-organisation of the courts in 1961.

[4.104] Further increases were effected in the 1960s,[260] and by 1975 the following scales applied.

- Chief Justice: £14,210
- President of High Court: £12,315
- Supreme Court judges: £11,999
- High Court judges (and Circuit Court President): £10,419
- Circuit Court judges: £8,652
- President of District Court: £8,773
- District Justices: £6,757.[261]

In 1977, judicial salaries were linked to other senior office holders in the public sector.[262] By the 1980s, it was accepted that these salaries had fallen well behind what was acceptable, with the potential effect this might have on attracting people of high calibre to these positions. Recommendations of the Review Body on Higher Remuneration in the Public Sector[263] resulted in major increases taking effect in 1989 and 1990.

[4.105] By October 1990, the following salaries applied:

- Chief Justice: £72,356
- President of High Court: £64,927
- Supreme Court judges: £62,274
- High Court judges (and Circuit Court President): £57,498

---

260. Between 1961 and 1968, judicial salary changes required an Act amending the levels specified in s 46 of the 1961 Act. The Courts (Supplemental Provisions) (Amendment) (No 2) Act 1968 amended s 46 by specifying that further changes could be effected by Orders rather than an amending Act.

261. Courts (Supplemental Provisions) Act 1961 (s 46) Order 1975.

262. The arrangements for judicial salaries were brought under the general umbrella of those for Government Ministers and members of the Oireachtas by the Oireachtas (Allowances to Members) and Ministerial, Parliamentary and Judicial Offices (Amendment) Act 1977. See also the Oireachtas (Allowances to Members) and Ministerial, Parliamentary and Judicial Offices (Amendment) Act 1983.

263. The Review Body had been chaired by Mr Dermot Gleeson SC, appointed Attorney General in 1995.

- Circuit Court judges (and President of District Court): £45,825
- District Justices: £38,397.[264]

The most recent increases, which took effect in 1995, produced the following scales:

- Chief Justice: £95,920
- President of High Court: £86,109
- Supreme Court judges: £82,840
- High Court judges (and Circuit Court President): £76,300
- Circuit Court judges (and President of District Court): £56,680
- District Court judges: £46,870.[265]

Immunity from suit and contempt of court

[4.106] In addition to the provisions of the Constitution concerning judicial independence, certain common law principles have been accepted as consistent with the independence recognised in Article 35.2.[266] Thus, the common law recognised that a judge was absolutely immune from any claims arising from any acts of the judge in his or her judicial capacity, such as a claim in negligence or a claim that words spoken by a judge were defamatory.[267] In *McIlwraith v Fawsitt*,[268] the Supreme Court upheld the traditional common law rule that in judicial review proceedings, no order for costs should be made against a member of the judiciary where the decision was made *bona fide.*

[4.107] The common law courts had also developed the concept of contempt of court to protect their independence. Under the common law principles of contempt, where a judge became aware of any interference with the administration of justice, he or she could order the arrest of the alleged offender (contemnor), try the charges and impose sentence. Since contempt

264. Courts (Supplemental Provisions) Act 1961 (s 46) Order 1989 (SI 204/1989), giving effect to Report No 30 of the Review Body. The 1989 Order provided for three phased increases of 40%, 30% and 30% respectively over the period July 1989 to October 1990.

265. Courts (Supplemental Provisions) Act 1961 (Section 46) Order 1994 (SI 273/1994), giving effect to Report No 35 of the Review Body of 1992. The 1994 Order provided for a 50% increase over that contained in the 1990 Order with effect from April 1994 and a further 50% increase from May 1995. The Explanatory Note to the 1994 Order also stated that these figures would be further uprated in 1996 and 1997 to take account of the Programme for Competitiveness and Work, agreed by the social partners in 1994.

266. See Hogan & Whyte, *op cit*, pp 547-50.

267. See McMahon and Binchy, *Irish Law of Torts*, 2nd ed (Butterworths, 1990) and *Sirros v Moore* [1975] QB 118.

268. [1990] 1 IR 343.

of court has not been regulated by statute in Ireland, there is no limit to the sentence that a judge may impose.[269] Ordinarily, of course, such an offence would be initiated by the State authorities and would require a jury trial. However, in *The State (Director of Public Prosecutions) v Walsh*,[270] the then Chief Justice referred to Article 35.2 as supporting the common law power of a judge to punish a contempt in the face of the court without the need to await the institution of criminal proceedings by the executive arm of Government or to have a jury trial.[271] In a later case, *In re Kelly and Deighan*,[272] two people had been imprisoned for contempt in this way by the High Court, but the Supreme Court had held that, in the particular circumstances, it had not been necessary for the High Court judge to exercise the jurisdiction to imprison summarily. However, in *Deighan v Ireland*,[273] the High Court dismissed a claim for damages against the State by one of those who had been imprisoned in the *Kelly* and *Deighan* case, primarily on the ground that to allow such a claim would undermine the independence of the judiciary.

[7] Vacating of Judicial Office and Retirement

Vacating of judicial office

[4.108] Although no provision is made in the Constitution for the vacating of a judicial office, other than where the judge is removed or reaches retirement age, this is dealt with by statute. A vacating of office can occur either where the judge is appointed to another judicial office or where the judge resigns office 'in writing under his hand addressed to the President and transmitted to the Taoiseach.'[274] The latter form of vacating of office amounts, in effect, to a voluntary retirement.

Retirement ages

[4.109] Between 1924 and the end of 1995, the age of retirement for High Court and Supreme Court judges was 72,[275] and this retirement age continues

269. Proposals for statutory reform in this area are contained in the Law Reform Commission's 1994 *Report on Contempt of Court* (LRC-47-1994).

270. [1981] IR 412.

271. On contempt of court generally, see para **[10.31]**.

272. [1984] ILRM 424.

273. [1995] 2 IR 56.

274. Courts (Establishment and Constitution) Act 1961, s 6 replacing the Courts of Justice Act 1924, ss 11, 45 and 70.

275. Courts of Justice Act 1924, s 12 as applied by the Courts (Supplemental Provisions) Act 1961, s 48.

to apply to judges appointed prior to 1996.[276] For judges appointed to the High Court and Supreme Court since the Courts and Court Officers Act 1995 came into operation in December 1995, the retirement age is 70. For a Circuit Court judge the age of retirement is also 70 years.[277]

[4.110] For a District Court judge, the general retirement age is 65.[278] However, a judge of the District Court who is about to reach 65 may be continued in office on a year-to-year basis until the age of 70 if he or she applies for such continuation to a Committee comprising the Chief Justice, the President of the High Court and the Attorney General. In order to continue the judge in office, the Committee (after consultation with the Minister for Justice) must be satisfied that the judge 'is not suffering from any disability which would render him unfit to continue to discharge efficiently the duties of his office.'[279]

[4.111] While these retirement ages are higher than the general 65 years' retirement age for many occupations in the public sector,[280] a retirement age

276. Courts and Court Officers Act 1995, s 47(1) introduced the 70 years of age retirement for judges appointed after the Act came into effect, which was 15 December 1995. Section 47(2) provides that 72 continues to be the retirement age for judges appointed before the 1995 Act came into force and s 47(3) provides that the 72 years retirement age also applies to any person who holds judicial office before the Act came into force in any of the courts established under Article 34 of the Constitution or in the Court of Justice of the European Communities or of the Court of First Instance attached thereto.

277. Courts (Supplemental Provisions) Act 1961, s 18. Courts of Justice Act 1924, s 40 had also specified 70 as the retirement age, though between 1947 and 1961, the retirement age had been set at 72: the Courts of Justice Act 1947, s 15.

278. Courts (Supplemental Provisions) Act 1961, s 30(1). Courts of Justice Act 1924, s 72 had provided for a retirement age of 70 years for District Court judges appointed to Dublin and Cork, but a 65 age of retirement for other judges of the District Court.

279. Courts of Justice (District Court) Act 1949, s 2. In *Shelly v Mahon* [1990] 1 IR 36 and *Glavin v Governor of Mountjoy Prison* [1991] 2 IR 421, the Supreme Court held to be invalid a summary conviction and a sending forward for trial on indictment made by a judge whose continuance in office had not complied with s 2 of the 1949 Act. An error had been made concerning the judge's true age, and he had, in fact, reached 65 before he had sought continuance in office under the 1949 Act. When the error was discovered, the Courts (No 2) Act 1988 was passed with a view to validating retrospectively his decisions for the periods when he had not been validly continued in office. However, the 1988 Act also expressly provided that the validation was without prejudice to any constitutional rights of citizens. In the *Shelly* and *Glavin* decisions, the Supreme Court held that the 1988 Act could not retrospectively validate any decisions that affected the rights of persons to a trial 'in due course of law', as required by Article 38.1 of the Constitution and thus the two decisions in question were held invalid.

280. It had been suggested in the Oireachtas debate on what became s 47 of the 1995 Act that a 65 year retirement age be introduced for all judges, but this was resisted on the ground that the reduction from 72 to 70 had effectively introduced a common age of retirement for all judges (subject to the particular arrangements for judges of the District Court). It was also pointed out that, since many judges are appointed in their 50s, a retirement age of 65 would provide them with relatively little time to develop as a judge. See *Select Committee on Legislation and Security*, L5, No 11 (7 December 1995), cc 675-81.

for judges of the higher courts did not exist prior to 1924[281] and was a novelty introduced by the Courts of Justice Act 1924. In Britain, retirement ages for judges of the High Court and above were not introduced until the 1940s. In the United States, there is no retirement age for Justices of the Federal Supreme Court, who continue to hold office for life.

Pensions

[4.112] Pension provision for retired judges and judges who have otherwise vacated their office is made by legislation.[282] In 1991,[283] pension entitlements already available to other public servants were extended to the judiciary and other court officers.[284] The effect is that some level of pension is payable after five years of service.[285] In *McMenamin v Ireland*[286] certain elements of the pension provisions for District Court judges were found to be in conflict with Article 35.5 of the Constitution, largely arising from the effects of inflation since the provisions had been introduced in 1961.

Retired judge may be precluded from appearing in court

[4.113] A long-established convention is that a retired judge does not practice in a court of equal or lower jurisdiction to that in which he or she sat as a judge.[287] In *In re O'Connor*,[288] the Supreme Court held that Sir James O'Connor, who had been a Lord Justice of Appeal in the pre-1922 Irish Court of Appeal, was entitled to be admitted to the roll of solicitors, but only on the condition that he refrain from practising in the courts. The Court took the view that it would affect the administration of justice were a former judge to appear in court as an advocate in circumstances where he might be

281. Thus, the Last Chief Baron, Christopher Palles, resigned judicial office in 1916 at the age of 85. He died in 1920. Lefroy CJ had been appointed Lord Chief Justice of Ireland in 1852, when he was 76, resigning judicial office in 1866 at the age of 90. Earlier that year he had successfully resisted suggestions in a House of Commons debate that he and the then Chancellor of Ireland (Blackburne LC, a mere 83) were unable to carry out their judicial functions. He died in 1869.

282. Courts (Supplemental Provisions) Act 1961, s 46 replacing the Courts of Justice Act 1924, ss 15, 41 and 75. See generally Delany, *The Courts Acts 1924-1991* (Round Hall Press, 1993), pp 172 and 316.

283. Courts (Supplemental Provisions) (Amendment) Act 1991.

284. The court officers covered by the 1991 Act are the Master of the High Court, Taxing Masters and county registrars. On court officers generally, see para **[4.115]**.

285. The 1991 Act had a substantial retrospective content and was applied to appointments going back to the 1970s. This led to some criticism expressed as the Act was being passed. For reaction, see the comments of the former Chief Justice, O'Higgins CJ, *The Irish Times*, 24 April 1991.

286. [1994] 2 ILRM 368.

287. See the discussion in Bartholomew, *op cit*, at pp 6-7. The convention is included in the Code of Conduct of the Bar of Ireland.

288. [1930] IR 623.

required to challenge some of his decisions as a judge or, at the least, fail to support them in argument.

[4.114] This convention, as affirmed in the *O'Connor* case, continues to be applied. Thus, former High Court and Supreme Court judges would be barred from practice on their retirement in those courts, creating an effective ban on practice.[289] Former Circuit Court judges could appear in the High Court and Supreme Court as advocates,[290] while former District Court judges could appear in the Circuit Court as well as the High Court and Supreme Court, but not the District Court.[291]

[8] Court Officers and Administration

[4.115] The judiciary represent the public face of the court system and, subject to the power of juries where they sit, the judges make the final decisions in virtually all situations. However, the administration of the court system rests largely with public servants who fall under the general heading of court officers. As we discuss below, the volume of work in the different courts, both in civil and criminal matters, has greatly increased since the 1960s. This, in turn, has placed great strains on the court system that has been in place since 1924. We note elsewhere that, in response to this, additional judges have been appointed to the different courts from time to time[292] and that other procedural changes have attempted to streamline court procedure.[293]

[4.116] Despite these changes, it has been increasingly recognised that more fundamental reform was required, and in 1996 recommendations were made by a Working Group on a Courts Commission which, if implemented, would effect a fundamental shift in the overall management of the court system. Before turning to the general background to those recommendations and their potential impact, we describe the functions of the various court officers engaged in the administration of the court system.

Court Officers in the High Court and Supreme Court

[4.117] Among the officers and offices attached to the High Court and Supreme Court are the following:

- the Master of the High Court

289. In the case of Mr Harold Whelehan SC, who had been President of the High Court for a matter of days in late 1994 (see para **[4.79]**), a General Meeting of the Bar of Ireland subsequently approved a resolution that, because of the shortness of his judicial tenure, he should be permitted to appear as counsel in any court.

290. Mr Frank Roe SC, former President of the Circuit Court, resumed his practice at the Bar on his retirement in the late 1980s.

291. Former District Court Justice Mr Robert Ó hUadhaigh recommenced his practice at the Bar after his retirement in the 1980s.

292. See para **[4.40]**.

293. See para **[5.10]**.

- the Central Office
- Registrars of the High Court,
- the Taxing-Masters' Office and
- the Registrar of the Supreme Court.[294]

Master of the High Court

[4.118] Prior to the passing of the Courts and Court Officers Act 1995, the Master of the High Court was largely confined to exercising powers conferred by rules of court.[295] These functions include:

- granting orders for discovery, interrogatories and extension of time for various matters[296];
- in civil claims initiated by special summons,[297] ensuring that the legal documentation is correct (that 'the papers are in order') before it is forwarded to a High Court judge; and
- giving judgment in non-contested cases, for example where a claim for a sum in default of a loan is made by a bank and there is no defence to the claim or no real defence;
- hearing applications for the enforcement of certain orders of courts of European Community Member States.[298]

The Master continues to exercise these functions, but the Courts and Court Officers Act 1995 added significantly to the scope of the powers of the office of Master. The 1995 Act provides that:

294. See the Court Officers Act 1926 and the Eighth Schedule to the Courts (Supplemental Provisions) Act 1961 for a complete list. In addition to the offices and officers considered in the text are the following: the Probate Office (which deals with the administration of estates), the Office of the Official Assignee in Bankruptcy, the Examiner's Office (with responsibility for many chancery matters, including company law cases), the Accountant's Office (which is responsible for any moneys lodged in court) and the Office of the Wards of Court (responsible for those persons whose affairs are administered by the Court after an application to Court based on their inability to look after their own interests).

295. Court Officers Act 1926 and the Eighth Schedule to the Courts (Supplemental Provisions) Act 1961. Although the 1961 Act appeared to envisage more substantial functions being conferred on the Master, the office had, until 1995, been largely confined to powers conferred by rules of court: see Barron and Ford, *Practice and Procedure in The Master's Court* (Round Hall Press, 1994) on the Master's functions prior to the passing of the Courts and Court Officers Act 1995.

296. See paras **[6.50]** and **[6.51]**.

297. See para **[6.28]**.

298. Jurisdiction of Courts and Enforcement of Judgments (European Communities) Acts 1988 and 1993.

- the Master is empowered to exercise limited functions of a judicial nature within the scope of Article 37 of the Constitution;[299]
- the Master may exercise all the powers of a High Court judge in *ex parte* applications or applications on notice and in applications for judgment by consent or in default of appearance or defence: in effect, the Master may enter final judgment in these cases, whereas up to the passing of the 1995 Act, a decision by a High Court judge was required;[300]
- in a case for a debt or a liquidated sum where an application is made for judgment in default of defence, the Master may award interest on the sum claimed.[301]

Central Office

[4.119] The Central Office of the High Court is essentially the administrative headquarters of the High Court.[302] All High Court business, both civil and criminal, is initiated and processed through the Central Office and is then transmitted, where relevant, either to the Master of the High Court or a High Court judge. While we have already noted that there are no formal divisions of the High Court,[303] the various civil and criminal matters are, from an administrative point of view, processed by the Central Office to the appropriate judge or judges who have been appointed by the President of the High Court to deal with particular matters.

Registrars of the High Court

[4.120] A number of Central Office staff are nominated from time to time to be Registrars for the High Court.[304] In effect, a Registrar is the essential

---

299. Section 24 of the 1995 Act. The 1995 Act gave belated effect to the principal recommendations in the 16th Report of the Committee on Court Practice and Procedure (1972): see Barron and Ford, *op cit*, at pp 2-3. On Article 37 of the Constitution, see para **[4.10]**.

300. Section 25(1) of the 1995 Act. Section 25(2) also contains a list of matters excluded from the Master's jurisdiction, such as any matter of a criminal nature and certain civil matters such as judicial review proceedings or any matter relating to the custody of children.

301. Section 50(1) of the 1995 Act. The power to award interest on claims in general was conferred on High Court judges by the Courts Act 1981, s 22. In *Mellowhide Products Ltd v Barry Agencies Ltd* [1983] ILRM 152, Finlay P held that s 22 of the 1981 Act did not confer on the Master any power to award interest, though he commented that he saw no logical reason why the Master should not be given this power. Section 50 of the 1995 Act gave effect to this recommendation.

302. Court Officers Act 1926 and the Eighth Schedule to the Courts (Supplemental Provisions) Act 1961.

303. See para **[4.50]**.

304. Court Officers Act 1926 and the Eighth Schedule to the Courts (Supplemental Provisions) Act 1961.

administrative assistant to a judge and will sit in court with the judge, usually in front of the judge facing the well of the court. A Registrar's functions include the drawing up of the formal court order which represents the official record of the decision for the purposes of the parties in the case. This formal order is what is presented by one party to any other person to prove in law that a particular decision was made in the case by the Court. The judge will, of course, be required to approve the wording of an order but, in most cases, it is the Registrar who is responsible in the first place and may well liaise personally with the lawyers for the two parties to ensure that the wording of the order reflects their understanding of the decision of the judge.

Taxing-Masters' Office

[4.121] The principal function of the Taxing Master is to determine whether legal costs being sought by parties to proceedings in the High Court are appropriate. We consider the Taxing Master's functions elsewhere.[305]

Registrar of the Supreme Court

[4.122] The Registrar of the Supreme Court is specifically assigned to the Chief Justice in order to carry out the administrative functions relevant to the functions of the Chief Justice and of the Supreme Court.[306]

Court Officers in the District Court and Circuit Court

[4.123] In the Circuit Court, the system is administered through County Registrars who also have considerable administrative support teams.[307] The Courts and Court Officers Act 1995 conferred additional powers on County Registrars, comparable (but not identical) to those conferred by the 1995 Act on the Master of the High Court.[308] In the District Court, the administrative side of the court system is the responsibility of District Court clerks.[309]

Court Sittings and Vacations

[4.124] Four terms are fixed for the sitting of the High Court and Supreme Court.[310] The Michaelmas Term runs from the first Monday in October to 21 December; the Hilary Term begins on 11 January (or, if this falls on a Saturday or Sunday, the following Monday) and ends two weeks before Good Friday; the Easter term runs from the Monday after Easter week and

305. See para **[5.26]**.

306. Court Officers Act 1926 and the Eighth Schedule to the Courts (Supplemental Provisions) Act 1961.

307. Court Officers Act 1926 and the Courts (Supplemental Provisions) Act 1961, s 55(2).

308. Section 34 of and Second Schedule to the 1995 Act.

309. Court Officers Act 1926 and the Courts (Supplemental Provisions) Act 1961, s 55(3).

310. Order 118 of the Rules of the Superior Courts 1986 (SI 15/1986).

ends on the Thursday preceding Whit Sunday; and the Trinity terms begins on the Wednesday following Whitsun week and ends on 31 July. The periods outside Term time are referred to as Vacation periods and the period between 31 July and the first Monday in October is called the Long Vacation. The Supreme Court does not, in general, sit outside Term time. As for the High Court, business continues to be transacted outside Term time, though at a reduced level. As to the Long Vacation, while in the past there was relatively little court activity, nowadays a substantial amount of both administrative and judicial activity continues during this period.[311] Similar Terms operate for the Circuit Court,[312] but the District Court sits for much longer terms, generally the same as for other public institutions.[313]

[9] Management of the Court System: The Need for Major Reform

[4.125] We have already mentioned that, in 1996, recommendations were made which may have a significant impact on the manner in which the court system will be managed into the 21st century. Since the establishment of the Irish Free State in 1922, the budget and management of the courts has primarily been in the hands of the Department of Justice, with a number of other State agencies as well as local authorities being responsible for connected issues such as the upkeep and maintenance of courthouses. The court system operates in quite a different social context at the end of the 20th century than at its beginning, and we have already seen how the judges have, to some extent, responded to change.[314] At a wider level, the workload of the courts had expanded greatly, but while additional judges and administrative personnel were appointed from time to time, the overall management and administration has not changed to reflect the many additional pressures placed on the system. We will outline below the extent of the growth in court business and some of the important procedural and substantive changes made, particularly in recent years, to deal with this.

[4.126] However, in addition to these changes, the manner in which the court system itself is managed has been the subject of substantial debate. Against a background of dissatisfaction concerning the inability of the court system to cope with the demands placed on it as well as problems with the physical condition of courthouses in the State,[315] a Working Group on a

311. As to whether the courts should sit for longer periods, see the Fair Trade Commission *Report of Study of Restrictive Practices in the Legal Profession* (1990), p 299.
312. Order 2 of the Rules of the Circuit Court 1950 (SI 179/1950).
313. Rule 16 of the District Court Rules 1948 (SR&O 431/1947) provides that judges of the District Court are entitled to six weeks' holiday in the year.
314. See para **[4.95]**.
315. See fn 248.

Courts Commission was appointed by the Government in December 1995 to make recommendations on how the court service should be managed. We outline the contents of the first report of that Working Group below,[316] but we first outline the growth in the workload of the courts and the various responses to date to this phenomenon.

The growth in civil and criminal cases

[4.127] Tables 4.1 and 4.2 indicate the overall increase in a number of civil and criminal matters in the period 1965 to 1994. They do not represent all civil or criminal cases in the periods referred to, but have been chosen to indicate some general trends.[317]

Civil Cases					
Year	**1965**	**1975**	**1981**	**1986**	**1994**
High Court Plenary Summons	2,576	4,767	13,307	12,101	7,594
High Court Summary Summons	1,245	3,150	9,059	4,230	1,476
Circuit Court Ordinary Civil Bills	11.262	19,102	31,758	23,625	11,731
District Court Civil Proceedings	52,625	67,912	63,927	141,01	134,613

Table 4.01

Criminal Cases					
Year	**1965**	**1975**	**1981**	**1986**	**1994**
Circuit Court criminal hearings/trials on indictment	480	1,008	1,300	1,356	1,513
Circuit Court criminal appeals	3,149	6,854	7,725	9,707	14,663
District Court: summary and indictable charges	219,197	422,809	676,078	648,442	541,758

Table 4.02

These figures underline the enormous increase in the volume of business assigned to the courts in the 30 year period from 1965 to 1994. Even if we take these figures as representing merely the number of forms to be filed in the different courts, there has been a great increase in work generated. However; these figures also represent an increase in the volume of cases actually disposed of by the courts in those years. Of course, in some areas, it

316. See para **[4.129]**.

317. The sources for the figures for both civil and criminal matters were: *Statistical Abstract 1966*, *Statistical Abstract 1976*, *Statistical Abstract 1982-85*, *Statistical Abstract 1986*, *Statistical Abstract 1995* (all published by the Stationery Office, Dublin).

is also clear that the graph has not always been on the increase, but the general trend is upwards.

[4.128] This general increase gives rise to complex issues that affect the manner in which the business of the courts is determined. At a very simple level, if the number of civil or criminal cases increases in a given period, there may be a need to appoint more judges and administrative staff to process those cases. In addition, changes in society in recent years have been reflected in legislative changes, which in turn have increased the range and complexity of the type of cases coming before the courts. We discuss these in some detail elsewhere.[318]

Reforming the management of the court system

[4.129] Given that the court system has had to cope with enormous growth in civil and criminal litigation, with changes in the type of cases being heard and with consequent substantive and procedural changes in court practice, it is hardly surprising that the First Report of the Working Group on a Courts Commission dealt with the general management of the court system.[319] The Working Group's Report recommended the establishment of a State agency to be called the Courts Service, with a chief executive officer to be responsible for day-to-day budgetary allocation, subject to overall control by the Department of Justice. This proposal was accepted by the Government[320] and, at the time of writing, it would appear that such a Courts Service may be established in 1997. The establishment of an independent Court Service would bring the State into line with similar systems established in the United Kingdom (where separate services were established for England and Northern Ireland), Australia and New Zealand.

The need for an efficient and high quality service

[4.130] Against the background of the constitutional provisions concerning the courts, the Working Group's Report emphasised the importance of an efficient management system and the need to provide a high quality service to the public:

> "An effective court system should provide a high level and quality of service to the public with the minimum of waste and effort. The service which is provided in the court system is the means by which the public

---

318. On the changing nature of civil and criminal matters coming before the courts, see paras **[5.07]-[5.16]**.

319. *First Report of the Working Group on a Courts Commission: Management and Financing of the Courts* (Pn 2690), April 1996, hereinafter the Working Group Report. The Working Group is chaired by Denham J, a judge of the Supreme Court.

320. The Irish Times, 22 May 1996, p 8.

> obtain justice. An inefficient service impedes justice. In addition the Courts Service is of importance in commerce and the business community. Commerce is at a disadvantage if the system is inefficient or ineffective."[321]

This passage indicates a fundamental shift in the 'philosophy' of the courts system, requiring it to take account of the concepts of quality, service and competitiveness more associated heretofore with the private sector. While the Working Group's Report does not point in the direction of a privatised or 'pay-per use' justice system, there can be no doubt of a move from 'court system' to 'court service'.

The existing arrangements

[4.131] The Working Group's Report pointed that, prior to the establishment of the Irish Free State, the Lord Chancellor had overall responsibility for the courts system, but that, since 1922, the majority of his management functions had been transferred to the Minister for Justice. The Report noted that, since the Lord Chancellor had legislative, executive and judicial roles,[322] the judiciary had been represented 'at the highest level' of decision-making, whereas since 1922 they had become separated from this aspect of decision-making. Although the Report accepted the need to ensure that any new arrangements did not breach the principle of the separation of powers, it also noted that the constitutional requirement of judicial independence was impaired if there was 'an absence of adequate administrative infrastructure and resources.'[323]
The Working Group pointed out that the existing administrative structure was operated by eight separate sectors, although most had links with the Department of Justice.[324] The Report described this arrangement as 'cumbersome, unwieldy and outmoded.'

Deficiencies in the existing structure

[4.132] The Report went on to discuss in detail the deficiencies which this structure had created.[325] Thus, on the administrative side of the system, there was no clear management structure with accountability and responsibility and no adequate performance measurements were in place for the 800

321. Working Group Report, p 17.

322. On the roles of the Lord Chancellor, see para **[2.26]**.

323. Working Group Report, p 18.

324. The eight sectors referred to in the Report were: the Department of Justice; the Presidents of each Bench of judges; the Circuit Court Registrars and District Court Clerks; High Court Registrars; Supreme Court Registrars; the Office of Public Works; local authorities; and Sheriffs: Working Group Report, p 24.

325. Working Group Report, pp 35-6.

persons who staffed the different courts, so that there was minimum planning beyond day-to-day procedural matters. In addition, no strategic plan or annual reports on the work of the courts existed, there was minimum training and development of staff and there was a lack of professional management to support training and development needs. Allied to this, there was a lack of financial or statistical information on the courts in any understandable format.

[4.133] Moreover, there was no clear reporting structure with regular channels of communication between the various people involved in the system, including a lack of an organisational relationship between the Department of Justice and court staff. This poor level of communications had restricted initiatives for change and there was a fragmentation in the administrative systems between the different courts. The Report also stated that there was an apparent remoteness of the administrative system from the judiciary.

[4.134] The Report found that no structure existed to respond to the needs of court users, nor was there an information service to the public in general; that many existing courthouses were inadequate and lacked dignity; and there were substantial delays in bringing both civil and criminal matters to the different courts.

Delays in the courts

[4.135] As to delays, the Working Group provided the following examples.[326] Of the 20 cases awaiting a date for hearing in the Supreme Court in February 1996, the length of time between the High Court hearing and a Supreme Court date for hearing varied from two to eight years. In the High Court, there was an average delay in personal injuries cases of almost three years from the date of setting down and its hearing. As for criminal trials in the High Court (the Central Criminal Court) delays in returns for trial varied from between two months to almost six years. In December 1995, of 16 murder trials listed, eight had been adjourned, three adjourned with priority, two listed for trial and three had provisional trial dates fixed. Of 40 rape trials listed in December 1995, seven had dates fixed for trial, two had provisional dates fixed, two were arraigned and 29 were adjourned. The delays in High Court family law cases between readiness and hearings varied from a week to six months, but in the Circuit Court, delays in family law cases varied from three months to two years in the different Circuits. In other civil matters, delays in the Circuit Court ranged from one to three

326. *Ibid*, pp 36-9.

years. In the District Court, the delays were not as dramatic, but there were delays of up to eight months from the issuing of a summons in criminal prosecutions under the Road Traffic Acts.

Financing the court system

[4.136] The Report of the Working Group also provided the first global information on the overall financial costs of the court system as well as information on the resources required to upgrade and maintain the physical condition of courthouses. The Report estimated that the cost of the courts system, including salaries, building work, pensions, administration, legal aid, law reporting and witness expenses was about £46.77m in 1995, up from £24.73m in 1990. This cost did not include the day-to-day cost of providing and maintaining court accommodation outside Dublin, as these figures had not been available to the Working Group. The court system earned an estimated income of £10.3m in 1995, largely from fees imposed on the filing of court pleadings,[327] and this was similar to the amount raised in 1990. Because of the rise in costs between 1990 and 1995, the net cost of the court system to the State had thus risen from £13.8m in 1990 to £36.4m in 1995. This sum, rounded up by the Working Group to £40m, represented 0.28% of total Government expenditure (estimated at just over £14bn) for 1996. This compared with estimated Government spending of about £2bn each in the Departments of Education and Health. The Report noted that given the number of personnel involved (about 1,000), the State was receiving good value for is investment. However, the Report also considered that reform could produce further benefits for the State.

[4.137] Thus, while a policy of self-financing would be inappropriate having regard to the constitutional right of access to the courts,[328] the Report noted that certain reforms could increase State income from the courts. Thus, a Commercial Court managed by judges with specially trained Registrars could facilitate speedier litigation, with consequent benefits to business and commerce as well as the State through the generation of more court fees.[329]

Proposed Courts Service

[4.138] Against this background the Working Group recommend the establishment of an independent statutory State agency, to be called the Courts Service, to manage a unified court system.[330]

327. On pleadings, see para **[6.21]**.
328. See para **[9.02]**.
329. Working Group Report, p 34.
330. *Ibid*, pp 42-53.

[4.139] The functions of the Court Service would include the following: management of the courts system; preparation of a three-year plan for the courts service; preparation of its annual budget for submission to the Minister for Justice; management of the budget; publication of annual performance reports; the provision, management and maintenance of suitable court buildings, both in terms of physical suitability and matters such as improved public address systems; the provision of secretarial, research and other administrative services to the judiciary; the establishment of a communications system between staff and judges; provision of a public information system on the court service, including the introduction of a Charter for Court Users and improved communication with the various media.

[4.140] The Working Group recommended that the Courts Service comprise a Board, representing the judiciary, the legal profession and court users, together with a full-time chief executive officer. The chief executive of the Courts Service would have the rank of the Secretary of a Government Department and would have day-to-day responsibility for the management of court staff, who should operate in a unified, single stream and be redesignated as civil servants. The Courts Service would be accountable to the Oireachtas through the Minister for Justice for issues concerning finance and administration, and its funding would be audited by the Comptroller and Auditor General. It would not be accountable to the Oireachtas for judicial decisions, as this would be in breach of the separation of powers provided for in the Constitution

[4.141] The Report of the Working Group was the first fundamental assessment of the court system since the foundation of the State, and the implementation of its recommendations would involve a profound change in the entire ethos of the court system. Even the title 'Court Service' for the proposed State agency indicates a shift towards a customer or consumer-based approach, requiring the incorporation of modern business management methods into an element of the public sector steeped in tradition.

Chapter 5

The First Instance Jurisdiction of the Courts

[1] INTRODUCTION

[5.01] In Chapter 4, we described the essential elements of the court system in Ireland created by the Courts (Establishment and Constitution) Act 1961. In this chapter, we outline the present first instance, or original, jurisdiction of the courts in civil and criminal matters. In other words, this chapter outlines the basis on which one determines which court is designated by law to hear a particular civil or criminal case in the first place.[1] The most significant legislative source of jurisdiction are the many Courts Acts, beginning with the Courts of Justice Act 1924, through to the Courts (Supplemental Provisions) Act 1961 and culminating most recently in the Courts and Court Officers Act 1995.[2]

Basis of jurisdiction in civil claims

[5.02] In the case of a civil claim for damages, the question as to which court is designated by law to hear the case may be simply a matter of the amount of damages being claimed. In other civil claims, where damages are not the primary claim, the question may be resolved by reference to the subject-matter of the claim, such as whether it involves an application to wind-up a company.

[5.03] A brief outline containing select examples of the original jurisdiction of the courts in civil cases is contained in Figure 5.1.

1. In Ch 7, we describe the appellate jurisdiction of the courts.
2. Delany, *The Courts Acts 1924-1991* (Round Hall Press, 1993) is an excellent resource containing the annotated text of 36 Acts, from the Courts of Justice Act 1924 through to the Courts (Supplemental Provisions) (Amendment) Act 1991. Since 1991, further significant legislative changes have been effected, notably by the Courts and Court Officers Act 1995. In addition to the Acts passed between 1924 and 1995, a number of pre-1922 Acts, such as the Petty Sessions (Ireland) Act 1851 and the Summary Jurisdiction Act 1857, contain important provisions describing the jurisdiction of the courts in Ireland: see further para **[4.05]**, n 11.

.

Original Jurisdiction of Courts in Civil Cases

SUPREME COURT
(5 Judges)

- **Reference of Bill by President**

HIGH COURT
(High Court judge; jury in some instances)

- **Full original jurisdiction**
- **Damages claimed: £30,000 or more**
- **Constitutional cases**
- **Company winding-up**

CIRCUIT COURT
(Circuit Court judge)

- **Subject matter similar to High Court**
- **Damages claimed: £5,000 - £30,000**
- **New intoxicating liquor licence**
- **Judicial separations and nullity**

DISTRICT COURT
(District Court judge)

- **Excluded from hearing some matters**
- **Damages claimed: £5,000 or less**
- **Intoxicating liquor licence renewal**
- **Maintenance for spouses and children**

Figure 5.1

[5.04] Jurisdiction in criminal cases depends, in the first instance on whether the offence charged is classifiable as summary or indictable. Summary offences are also known as 'minor' offences, the term used in Article 38.2 of the Constitution. As we shall see,[3] that Article provides that minor offences may be tried summarily, which in practice means in the District Court. Indictable offences, to which the right to trial by jury attaches with some exceptions under Article 38.5, are tried in one of the 'higher' criminal courts. A brief outline of the courts' criminal jurisdiction is provided in Figure 5.2

3. See para **[5.71]**.

Original Jurisdiction of Courts in Criminal Cases

CENTRAL CRIMINAL COURT
(High Court)
(High Court judge and jury)

- **Murder, attempted murder, conspiracy to murder**
- **Treason**
- **Piracy**
- **Rape, rape offences**

CIRCUIT COURT
(Circuit Criminal Court)
(Circuit Court judge and jury)

- **Indictable offences other than those triable in Central Criminal Court**

SPECIAL CRIMINAL COURT
(Three judges, no jury)

- **Scheduled offences**
- **Non-scheduled offence, DPP certifies**

DISTRICT COURT
(District judge, no jury)

- **Minor/summary offences**

Figure 5.2

[5.05] In the more detailed discussion of the original jurisdiction of the courts that follows, we deal first with the jurisdiction of the courts in civil cases, beginning with at the lower end of the court system, the District Court, and ending with a discussion of the original jurisdiction of the Supreme Court. We then proceed to discuss the original jurisdiction of the courts in criminal matters.

[5.06] As it would be almost impossible to provide a comprehensive treatment of all statutes that affect the courts' jurisdiction, what follows is a description of the principal legislative provisions. It should be realised that the general framework thereby established is supplemented by many statutes that confer jurisdiction in individual instances on particular courts. We provide some examples of such legislation for illustrative purposes.

Development of the business of the courts

[5.07] The description of the courts' jurisdiction should be seen against the background of the proposals for reform of the management of the court service made in 1996 by the Working Group on a Courts Commission, which we discussed in Chapter 4.[4] In order to put the present first instance jurisdiction of the courts in context, we begin by outlining the development of the business of the courts in recent years. This has influenced both the appointment of additional judges to the courts as well as the distribution of business between the courts. In relation to civil claims, we refer to the impact of increased personal injuries claims, increased family law cases and the emergence of consumer claims. On the criminal side, we will refer to the impact of increases in criminal business generally. The examples we have chosen are not exhaustive, but are merely indicative of the trends revealed by the Working Group on a Courts Commission.

Civil claims: personal injuries actions

[5.08] There has been a substantial increase in the number of personal injuries actions in the courts in recent years,[5] many of them concerning accidents on the road, in supermarkets or at work. There would appear to be general agreement that, in recent years, people who incur personal injuries are more prepared than their counterparts of the 1960s to seek compensation for such injuries. However, there is a great deal of disagreement about what should be done to deal with this phenomenon. One side of the argument concerning this 'Compo Culture', as it is colloquially described, might include the following points. It is said that the increase in claims has been fuelled by the increase in the number of solicitors since the early 1980s who, in an increasingly competitive business environment, encourage litigation by promising a 'free first consultation' and a commitment to process personal injuries cases on a 'no foal, no fee' basis.[6] Court awards, alleged to be excessive and in any event well above European norms, are also said to lead potential litigants to believe that a financial bonanza awaits them in court. It is also alleged that the fees charged by some members of the legal profession in such cases are somewhat inflated. In addition, it is alleged that insurance companies may settle too many claims, thus further encouraging future claims. Finally, there has been some criticism of the fact that personal

4. See para **[4.129]**.

5. The *First Report of the Working Group on a Courts Commission* (Pn 2690), p 37, stated that personal injuries actions accounted for over 86% of the plenary summons actions put down for trial in the High Court in recent years. In 1994/95 period, of the 9,603 plenary summonses issued, 5,453 were set down for trial, of which 4,682 were personal injury actions. See further para **[4.129]**.

6. See para **[5.23]** for discussion of the 'no foal, no fee' arrangement.

injuries awards involve a once-off lump sum payment to a plaintiff, much of which is calculated on the basis that interest earned on the capital sum should enable the plaintiff to obtain whatever medical and other treatment and facilities he or she requires. By contrast, in the United Kingdom, it is possible to have interim or staged payments of awards rather than a once-off lump sum award.

[5.09] This picture is contested by a number of people involved in the area. Thus, it is said that many employers fail to take appropriate precautions to prevent accidents, and that there exists a 'Negligence Culture'. It is also said that, in the absence of a comprehensive civil legal aid system,[7] solicitors are obliged to engage in a 'no foal, no fee' approach to personal injuries claims. The legal profession also vehemently deny that fees charged are excessive, pointing to the high level of legal fees in other States. As to excessive court awards, they are certainly higher than those in comparable cases in the United Kingdom, though the English Law Commission has suggested that awards there may be too low. As for settling cases, insurance companies argue that they would fight in full any cases where a defence would be available, and that claims are settled where it is clear to fight the case (unsuccessfully) in court would result in further costs being incurred, causing in turn ever higher insurance premiums. On the question of staged or interim payments of awards, there has been some suggestion that this would make insurance premiums difficult to calculate, whereas the present arrangements have the benefit of certainty.

[5.10] It remains the case that this matter involves complex disputes in which agreement is difficult to find.[8] Despite this, various solutions have been attempted to deal with the problem since the late 1980s in particular. These included the abolition in 1988 of the statutory right to have High Court personal injuries actions heard by a jury as well as the introduction of restrictions on the number of counsel who might be briefed in such cases.[9] Legislation providing for procedural changes to facilitate earlier settlements as well for additional judicial appointments to clear the backlog of civil litigation has also been enacted.[10] On the preventative side of traffic-related accidents and claims, 'crackdowns' on speeding and drink driving have occurred, as well as more stringent legislative provisions and penalties for traffic offences.[11] Improvements in the standards of roads in the State has

7. On civil legal aid generally, see para **[9.19]-[9.35]**.

8. For a summary of the debate, see for example Fitzgerald, 'The Compo Culture', *Business and Finance,* 16 May 1996. On the level of settlements, see para **[6.55]**.

9. This was effected by the Courts Act 1988: see further para **[4.50]**.

10. Courts and Court Officers Act 1995.

11. Eg the Road Traffic Act 1994, which reduced the permitted blood-alcohol level for a person driving a motor vehicle and increased the penalties involved (the penalties being modified in the Road Traffic Act 1995).

also occurred. As to accidents arising in the workplace, legislation was enacted to encourage accident prevention in all places of work.[12] However, despite these initiatives, accident rates continue at a high level, and the debate on further solutions continues at the time of writing. These include the suggestion that personal injuries claims be taken out of the court system completely and should be dealt with by a statutory tribunal, in which interim or staged awards could be made. Such a system was introduced in New Zealand.[13]

Civil claims: family law

[5.11] There has also been an enormous increase in the amount of what is described as family law business conducted by the courts since the 1960s. In particular, proceedings arising from marital breakdown in the State have increased substantially, again requiring changes to reflect this reality. Thus, legislation has been enacted to update the law concerning judicial separation and to provide for a more informal court atmosphere, such as dispensing with the wearing of the traditional wigs and gowns worn by judges and barristers.[14] Other changes have been effected to update the mechanisms for protecting women, in particular, from violent spouses[15] and also to improve arrangements for ensuring that awards of maintenance can be enforced against recalcitrant spouses.[16] In 1995, a referendum to remove the constitutional prohibition on divorce was narrowly approved and, after an unsuccessful challenge to the result of the referendum,[17] legislation to give effect to this change was published in 1996.[18] As with the increase in civil claims in general, a further response was the appointment of additional judges to the different courts. Although substantial changes have thus been made to reflect the increase in family-related cases, a substantial backlog of such cases had built up in the early 1990s. Further reform to deal with this area has been recommended.[19]

Civil claims: consumer and small claims

[5.12] A feature of the second half of the 20th century has been the exponential growth of the 'consumer society'. Reflecting the growth in

12. Safety, Health and Welfare at Work Act 1989.
13. See generally, Cane, *Atiyah's Accidents, Compensation and the Law*, 4th ed (Weidenfeld and Nicolson, 1987) for an overview of this area.
14. See the Judicial Separation and Family Law Reform Act 1989. On the wearing of wigs generally by barristers, see Courts and Court Officers Act 1995, s 49 discussed at para **[3.50]**.
15. Domestic Violence Act 1996.
16. Family Law Act 1995.
17. *Hanafin v Minister for the Environment*, High Court, unrep, 1 March 1996; [1996] 2 ILRM 141 (SC).
18. Family Law (Divorce) Bill 1996.
19. See *Report of the Law Reform Commission on the Family Courts* (1996).

commercial transactions involving consumers, a substantial body of legislation has been enacted to ensure greater protection for individuals who enter into cash or credit-based agreements. This has included legislation to protect against misleading advertisements,[20] increased protection in contracts for the sale of goods and supply of services[21] as well as protective measures involving all forms of consumer credit, whether contracts involving hire-purchase, leasing, credit cards or mortgages.[22] In addition, an enforcement agency, the Office of the Director of Consumer Affairs, was established in order to ensure that such protective legislation became widely known and accepted by the market operators.[23] However, consumer groups also pointed out that, where an individual's complaint could not be resolved by direct complaint to a retailer, the court system represented an expensive and forbidding place of resort. Thus, in keeping with many other States, a less formal system for dealing with what are called small claims has been developed, operating through the District Court.[24]

Criminal cases

[5.13] We have already described how there has been an enormous increase in the criminal business of the courts, leading to increased judicial and administrative personnel.[25] There has been substantial public debate about the causes of crime and also the appropriate responses to the increase, both in terms of society and the court system. In brief terms, the response can be broken into two general categories. First, there has been a recognition of the need to update the general criminal law to reflect the type of criminality common in the late 20th century. The 1990s in particular has seen a substantial body of legislation to update the criminal law concerning such areas as drug trafficking,[26] sexual offences[27], public order[28] and even

20. Eg Consumer Information Act 1978 and the European Communities (Misleading Advertisements) Regulations 1988 (SI 134/1988).
21. Eg Sale of Goods and Supply of Services Act 1980 and the European Communities (Unfair Terms in Consumer Contracts) Regulations 1995.
22. Consumer Credit Act 1995.
23. The Office of the Director of Consumer Affairs was established by the Consumer Information Act 1978 and was given further powers under the Consumer Credit Act 1995 in particular. Non-statutory arrangements, such as the voluntary Codes of Practice operated by the Advertising Standards Authority of Ireland, also play an important role in this area: see para **[13.05]**.
24. See para **[5.35]**.
25. See para **[4.127]**.
26. Eg the Criminal Justice Act 1994 and the Criminal Justice (Drug Trafficking) Act 1996.
27. Eg the Criminal Law (Rape) (Amendment) Act 1990 and the Criminal Law (Sexual Offences) Act 1993.
28. Criminal Justice (Public Order) Act 1994.

computer hacking.[29] As to the procedures to be followed in criminal matters, legislation has been passed to facilitate detention of persons in garda custody for up to 20 hours and provide for majority verdicts in criminal trials,[30] to facilitate forensic testing of accused persons (including taking DNA samples),[31] to facilitate video-link evidence in certain cases, especially sexual offences,[32] to ensure that sentencing takes account of the impact of the crime on the victim, to provide for appeals against lenient sentences and the payment of compensation to victims of crimes,[33] to provide for alternatives to imprisonment, such as community service,[34] and also to facilitate the investigation of possible miscarriages of justice.[35] This partial list indicates the extent of legislative activity to deal with the criminal side of court business in recent years.

[5.14] However, other matters continue to be debated robustly. For example, there is much political and public debate as to whether the right to bail should be restricted to combat, for example, offenders who are said to commit crimes while awaiting trial in order to put together a 'nest egg' for their dependants.[36] Other matters include calls to build more prison spaces to accommodate the increasing number of people who are released early on temporary release,[37] and which has given rise to the suggestion that a 'revolving door' policy operates in which the sentences of the courts are not carried into effect in the manner intended. The particular problem of increased drug-related crime has led to the introduction of seven-day detention of suspects in garda custody, subject to some judicial control.[38] This, in turn, has given rise to suggestions that the criminal justice system in Ireland should move from its common law accusatorial tradition to embrace the civil law inquisitorial system employed in many other European States.[39] At a wider level, the general role of the Gardaí has also been subject of debate, particularly the changing nature of policing in an increasingly urbanised community and the use of developments such as 'Community

29. Criminal Damage Act 1991.
30. Criminal Justice Act 1984.
31. Criminal Justice (Forensic Evidence) Act 1990.
32. Criminal Evidence Act 1992.
33. Criminal Justice Act 1993.
34. Criminal Justice (Community Service) Act 1983.
35. Criminal Procedure Act 1993.
36. For a discussion, see O'Mahony, 'The Proposed Constitutional Referendum on Bail: An Unholy Grail?' (1995) 13 ILT 234. At the time of writing (July 1996) a constitutional amendment to restrict the right to bail is expected to be held in late 1996: see further para **[15.83]**.
37. The Criminal Justice Act 1960 empowers the Minister for Justice to release a convicted person on temporary release, in effect a release on licence that is almost equivalent to parole. See para **[10.23]**.
38. Criminal Justice (Drug Trafficking) Act 1996.
39. See further on this para **[6.66]**.

Watch' programmes. As with the civil side of the work of the courts, many of these matters continue to be debated and substantial disagreement exists about the appropriate way forward. At the very least, however, increased judicial numbers indicates one response to the problem.

[5.15] In summary, both in terms of the civil and criminal workload of the courts, substantial legislative changes in recent years as well as proposals in the offing have reflected the many changes in society in Ireland and this will undoubtedly continue into the future. The overall picture is of a system that has changed dramatically in recent years, even if many of the changes have been the result of piecemeal reform rather than based on an overall framework approach.

[5.16] We discuss below some of the changes effected over the years to the courts since 1924, primarily those altering the distribution of business between the courts. As already mentioned, in order to take account of the increase in volume of work, there have been substantial increases in the number of judges in the various courts. In order to take account of inflation, the limits to the monetary awards in the different civil courts have been raised a number of times, increasingly so since the 1970s. To some extent also, financial criminal penalties have also been raised to take account of the fall in the value of money since the 1970s. We can now proceed to discuss the first instance jurisdiction conferred on the different courts.

[2] The Original Jurisdiction of the Courts in Civil Cases

Changes in the monetary limits

[5.17] As we already noted, a major factor in describing the original jurisdiction of the different courts in civil matters is the different level of damages that may be awarded. The general monetary jurisdiction of the different courts has been altered from time to time since the passing of the Courts of Justice Act 1924. These changes have, in large part, reflected the need to respond to changes in the value of money arising from inflation and the consequent need to ensure an even distribution of business between the different courts.

[5.18] Thus, in 1924, the District Court was confined to a maximum award of £25 in damages,[40] while the Circuit Court was confined to an award of £300.[41] The effect of this was that any claim in excess of £300 would be dealt with in the High Court. These limits have been substantially changed since 1924. By 1971, the general jurisdiction of the District Court had been

40. Courts of Justice Act 1924, s 77.

41. Courts of Justice Act 1924, s 48.

raised to £250[42] and that of the Circuit Court to £600.[43] In 1981, the jurisdiction of the District Court was raised to £2,500[44] and that of the Circuit Court to £15,000.[45] The most recent changes, in 1991, have seen the District Court's jurisdiction raised to £5,000[46] and the Circuit Court's to £30,000.[47] Since 1991, therefore, claims in excess of £30,000 are heard in the High Court.

[5.19] All these changes were effected by Act of the Oireachtas. However, s 16 of the Courts Act 1991 provides that any further variations to the monetary jurisdiction of the courts may be made by way of Statutory Order by the Government. Section 16 of the 1991 Act specifies that any such variation may only be made 'having regard to changes in the value of money generally in the State' since any previous alteration. In addition, any Order made to be made under s 16 must be laid before each House of the Oireachtas and requires a positive resolution in both Houses before it can come into effect. Thus, although such changes are no longer liable to be made by way of an Act, a vote in both Houses in still required.

Monetary limits and the relative seriousness of a claim

[5.20] The changes in the monetary limits have an important practical consequence for litigants and practising lawyers. The intention in 1924 when the £25 limit for the District Court and the £300 limit for the Circuit Court were set was that the District Court should deal with relatively minor civil claims, that the Circuit Court would deal with relatively more serious claims and that the High Court should be confined to serious claims, in the sense that it is concerned with claims involving large sums of money or which involve complex legal issues. This is also reflected in the general content of the various procedural rules of court, in particular those governing the preparation of the formal documents or pleadings required to initiate and process a civil claim. The requirements for a District Court claim are relatively informal by comparison with those for the Circuit Court, while those for the High Court are more complex than those for either the Circuit or District Court.[48] However, the effect of inflation since the 1960s in particular has been that, if the monetary limits set in 1924 had been left unaltered the High Court would have been left to deal with virtually all civil

42. Courts Act 1971, s 7 amending Courts of Justice Act 1924, s 77.
43. Courts Act 1981, s 2 amending the Courts (Supplemental Provisions) Act 1961, the Third Schedule.
44. Courts Act 1981, s 6 amending Courts of Justice Act 1924, s 77.
45. Courts Act 1981, s 2 amending the Courts (Supplemental Provisions) Act 1961, the Third Schedule.
46. Courts Act 1991, s 4, amending the Courts of Justice Act 1924, s 77.
47. Courts Act 1991, s 2, amending the Courts (Supplemental Provisions) Act 1961, the Third Schedule.
48. See para **[6.24]**.

claims, even those involving a modest claim for £301 arising from a traffic accident where a car was scratched. Hence the changes in the monetary limits to ensure the courts deal with the kinds of cases intended for them in 1924.

Monetary limits and the award of costs

[5.21] The importance of changing monetary limits is especially obvious when the circumstances surrounding a commonplace civil action, such as a claim for damages for personal injuries, are considered. There are two points to be noted here.

[5.22] First, it is clear that, the more serious the injury, the more care will be needed to prepare the case for court. This will require more advice from, for example, medical experts as to the extent of a person's injuries as well as a prognosis on the long-term effects of the injuries. Another feature of many personal injuries case is the need to prove negligence, thus necessitating an expert view from, for example, an engineer to give a view on the state of a road or the appropriateness or otherwise of safety precautions in a place of work.

[5.23] A second connected issue is the cost of a civil action and who is required to pay for the experts and lawyers engaged in the case. In general terms, where a party (whether the plaintiff or defendant) is successful in his or her civil claim, the court will order that the losing party must pay the successful party's legal costs: this is referred to as the rule that 'costs follow the event'.[49] In general, the court order for costs should cover most of the expenses incurred by the successful party, in particular the fees charged by the solicitor and (where briefed) the barristers who appeared for that party. Traditionally, it has been practice for more lawyers to be involved in a High Court civil action than for one in the Circuit Court or the District Court.

---

49. The losing party must also pay their own costs, including the fees charged by their lawyers as well as any other professional fees. This system that 'costs follow the event' is quite different from that in the United States of America, where both parties in civil claims are, in general, required to discharge the fees incurred by their professional advisers, regardless of the outcome of their claim. Thus, a successful party in a civil claim in the United States will, in general, pay a percentage of their award to their lawyer, the precise percentage (ranging from 20% to 50% of the award) usually being agreed in advance. This system of fee paying has been widely criticised as encouraging litigation and 'ambulance chasing' by lawyers. The system has, traditionally, been regarded as unethical in the United Kingdom and Ireland, though it should be distinguished from the 'no foal, no fee' arrangement, in which the lawyer will agree to initiate a claim for a plaintiff on the basis that a fee will only be charged if the claim is successful. The 'no foal, no fee' alludes to the traditional rule of veterinary surgeons. This type of arrangement is not regarded as unethical within the legal profession, though it has been the subject of much criticism from outside the profession, where it is equated with the United States system of percentage or contingency fees. See para **[5.08]**.

[5.24] As a general rule of thumb, the parties in a High Court civil claim would each engage a solicitor who, in turn would brief one junior counsel and at least one senior counsel.[50] In a Circuit Court civil action one would expect to find each party being represented by a solicitor and, usually, junior counsel, while in a District Court action the general rule would be to find the parties represented by a solicitor alone.[51] In general also it should be said that, in a High Court civil action it is more likely that there will be a need for professional witnesses to provide evidence to the court, particularly in a personal injuries action where expert opinion evidence of negligence and expert opinion medical evidence of the extent of injuries will be required.

[5.25] It should be clear from these different arrangements that the costs of a High Court civil action will be more expensive (for the losing party) than a Circuit Court or a District Court action. The changes in the monetary jurisdictions of the different courts has, in part, reflected the change in the value of money; it would clearly be wrong for the District Court to be limited to the £25 limit set in 1924 so the changes are a clear attempt to ensure that, in the late 1990s, the civil claims dealt with in the District Court reflect the intention that the District Court deal with relatively minor civil claims, that the Circuit Court deal with relatively more serious claims and that the High Court should be confined to serious claims, in the sense that it deals with claims involving large sums of money or which involve complex legal issues.

Taxation of costs

[5.26] If there is a dispute between the parties concerning the level of fees charged in a case (in particular those charged by the lawyers and expert witnesses in a case), the losing party may require that these be reviewed by an officer attached to the courts, in the High Court by the Taxing Master, in the Circuit Court by the County Registrar. This is referred to as the taxation of costs. The question whether a particular fee charged was appropriate or indeed whether it was appropriate, for example, for a solicitor to have briefed one or more barristers will be a matter for the Taxing Master or the

50. The almost invariable practice of engaging one junior counsel and two senior counsel (the 'two senior' rule) in High Court civil actions was common until 1988, but has to some extent been discontinued since then arising from calls to restrict legal costs in High Court actions, in particular personal injuries actions. The Courts Act 1988, s 5 empowers the Minister for Justice to make rules restricting the number of counsel in respect of whom costs would be allowed by the Taxing Master, but voluntary self-regulation by the Bar in this area since 1988 has meant that no rules have been made under s 5 of the 1988 Act.

51. It should also be noted, however, that solicitors have had a legal right of audience in all the courts since 1971 and would thus be entitled to represent a party to an action in all the courts: see para **[3.22]**. What is described here is the general practice.

County Registrar to consider. For the lawyers and professional witnesses involved in a claim, it is important to know whether their fees 'will tax', that is whether the Taxing Master or County Registrar will order that the losing party must pay the fee involved.

[5.27] The Taxing Master will only 'tax' what are referred to as 'party and party' costs, which essentially involves those costs which are regarded as necessary for the conduct of the action. These are to be contrasted with what are referred to as 'solicitor and client' costs, which might be described as fees arising from the use of more lawyers or experts than were necessary for the correct conduct of the action. In any taxation of costs, the losing party in an action will argue that many items being claimed were 'solicitor and client' costs, while the successful party will attempt to argue that all items should be regarded as 'party and party' costs.

[5.28] In addition to the issue whether one or two or three counsel should have been retained, a significant point of dispute on taxation will be the size of the fee charged, in particular by barristers.[52] Many efforts have been made over the years to ensure that the costs associated with civil litigation are appropriate to the seriousness of the claim. In this respect, various provisions have been included in the Courts Acts that have altered the monetary jurisdiction of the courts that only certain costs 'will tax' and that the level of fees to be charged by lawyers and others involved in a claim are appropriate to the seriousness of the case. The most recent provisions on this aspect of court procedure deal with a number of connected issues.

[5.29] First, the powers of judges to 'remit' a case to a lower court where the case has been initiated in a higher court have been strengthened.[53] Second, there are provisions to limit the costs where the total sum actually awarded falls short of the thresholds currently laid down for the different courts,[54] for

52. Eg in a High Court civil claim, where a solicitor engaged one junior and one senior counsel. It is a traditional rule that the fee set by the senior counsel will influence that set by the junior counsel. Assume that the senior counsel sets a 'brief fee' of £1,000 and a daily fee of £550 and that the case concluded after two days, the senior counsel's fee would come to £2,000. Traditionally, the junior counsel's fee for the case would be in the region of two-thirds of that charged by senior counsel (the 'two-thirds' rule), and would therefore come to an additional £1,500. The total fees for both counsel would therefore be in the region of £3,500. The 'two-thirds' rule was criticised by the Fair Trade Commission in its 1990 Report on the Legal Profession (see generally para **[3.05]**). On fees generally, see para **[3.43]**.

53. Courts of Justice Act 1924, s 25 as amended, deals with the remittal of a case initiated in the High Court to either the Circuit Court or District Court. Its constitutionality was upheld in *Ward v Kinahan Electrical Ltd* [1984] IR 292. On the operation of s 25 of the 1924 Act, as amended, see Delany, *op cit*, pp 4-9. Courts Act 1991, s 15 introduced for the first time the power of the Circuit Court to remit a case to the District Court. On s 15 of the 1991 Act, see Delany, *op cit*, at pp 308-9.

54. See the Courts Act 1981, s 17 as amended by the Courts Act 1991, s 14.

example where in a High Court claim very much less than £30,000 was actually awarded or where less than £5,000 was awarded in a Circuit Court claim. Third, provisions have been introduced to ensure that Taxing Masters and County Registrars have sufficient powers to determine the appropriate level of fees that 'will tax'.[55] Fourth, the possibility of introducing statutory levels of fees to regulate the legal profession has been provided for.[56] All these provisions are intended to ensure or persuade lawyers and litigants that the appropriate court is chosen for the particular case in which they are involved.

The District Court

[5.30] As we have already seen,[57] the District Court is a court of local and limited jurisdiction within the meaning of Article 34.3.4° of the Constitution and, broadly, the successor to the jurisdiction exercised at Petty Sessions.[58] As a 'creature of statute' therefore, the simple rule is that the jurisdiction of the District Court is restricted to whatever has been expressly conferred on it by legislation.[59] It is not possible to provide a complete listing of all civil matters with which the District Court deals, so that what follows are the principal features of its original civil jurisdiction.

(a) General and monetary jurisdiction

[5.31] In cases of contract, breach of contract and tort (except libel, slander, seduction,[60] slander of title, malicious prosecution and false imprisonment)[61] and in proceedings brought on behalf of the State or a local authority to recover a debt due to the State or local authority the District Court is empowered to award damages not exceeding £5,000.[62] In addition, where the parties to a District Court action consent in writing, the District Court is conferred with jurisdiction in excess of this limit.[63]

---

55. Courts and Court Officers Act 1995, s 27.
56. Courts and Court Officers Act 1995, s 46. See generally, Kelleher, 'The Courts and Court Officers Act 1995 - The Main Provisions' (1996) 14 ILT 18 and para **[3.43]**.
57. See para **[4.30]**.
58. See para **[2.50]**-**[2.52]**.
59. The main jurisdiction-conferring provision is s 77 of the Courts of Justice Act 1924, carried forward by the Courts (Supplemental Provisions) Act 1961, s 33 and amended from time to time, most recently by the Courts Act 1991, s 4. For the changes effected to s 77, see Delany, *op cit*, pp 34-36.
60. Seduction here refers to a claim by an employer arising from the loss of services of an employee, for example, during the pregnancy of an unmarried woman employee.
61. The exempted categories of torts contained in brackets are 'reserved' for the Circuit Court and High Court: see para **[5.39]**.
62. Courts of Justice Act 1924, s 77(a)(i), (iii) and (v) carried forward by the Courts (Supplemental Provisions) Act 1961, s 33, and amended from time to time, most recently by the Courts Act 1991, s 4.
63. Courts Act 1991, s 4(c). At the time of writing, however, no amending District Court Rules had been made to give effect to this.

(b) Renewal of intoxicating liquor licences

[5.32] In 1924, the District Court was conferred with the jurisdiction to grant certificates of renewal to the holder of a spirit and other intoxicating liquor licence.[64] Up to 1988, the holder of an intoxicating liquor licence was required to apply each year to the District Court to obtain a certificate that they were a fit person to continue to hold a licence.[65] Since 1988,[66] a licence holder may now obtain a renewal of most liquor licences from the Revenue Commissioners without the need to produce a District Court certificate. An application to the District Court is now required only in certain instances, such as where there is an objection lodged to the licence renewal.

(c) Family proceedings

[5.33] In family law proceedings, the District Court has a limited jurisdiction. Thus, it is not given jurisdiction to grant a decree of judicial separation or nullity, such matters being reserved for the Circuit Court and High Court.[67] However, where judicial separation proceedings have already been initiated, the parties may apply to the District Court for variation of maintenance. In such circumstances, the Court is empowered to award maintenance to a spouse up to a maximum of £200 per week and to a maximum of £60 per week per child.[68] The Court also has jurisdiction concerning the disposal of household chattels, up to a value of £5,000, in proceedings under s 9 of the Family Home Protection Act 1976.[69]

(d) Commercial and consumer protection: general

[5.34] The District Court is empowered to deal with civil claims under the Hotel Proprietors Act 1963[70] and the Consumer Credit Act 1995,[71] again with limits of £5,000 as to the amount of damages that may be awarded.

64. Courts of Justice Act 1924, s 77(A).
65. The licensing session of the District Court occurred in November of each year.
66. Courts (No 2) Act 1986, s 4 which was brought into effect in 1988: Courts (No 2) Act 1986 (Commencement) Order 1988 (SI 176/1988).
67. See para **[5.44]**.
68. Family Law (Maintenance of Spouses and Children) Act 1976, s 23 as amended by the Courts Act 1991, s 11. The effect of the Status of Children Act 1987, Part IV is that the same rules as to maintenance now apply regardless of whether the parents of the child are married.
69. The jurisdiction is conferred by s 10(5) of the 1976 Act, as amended by the Courts Act 1991, s 8.
70. Hotel Proprietors Act 1963, s 10(2) as amended by the Courts Act 1991, s 9.
71. The 1995 Act replaced the Hire-Purchase Acts 1946 to 1980. The Hire-Purchase (Amendment) Act 1960, s 19 as amended by the Courts Act 1991, s 6 had conferred jurisdiction on the District Court in relation to proceedings under the Acts of 1946 to 1980.

(e) Commercial and consumer protection: small claims

[5.35] We have mentioned already[72] that, in line with other States, a procedure for dealing with small claims has been introduced and is administered principally by Clerks of the District Court. The procedure had been introduced on a pilot basis by the District Court (Small Claims Procedure) Rules 1991[73] and was extended to the entire State by the District Court (Small Claims Procedure) Rules 1993.[74] The 1993 Rules provide for an initial application to a clerk of the District Court who is empowered to attempt to reach a compromise between the parties in dispute, described as the claimant and respondent. A fee of £5 for the entire procedure is laid down in the Rules. In the event of continued dispute, the matter may be referred to a judge of the District Court for resolution. A 'small claim' is defined in Rule 4 of the 1993 Rules as one involving a claim not exceeding £600[75] and which comes within the three categories mentioned in that Rule. The first category concerns consumer contracts such as the retail purchase of goods, but not a claim arising from an alleged breach of a hire-purchase or leasing agreement. The second category is a 'minor' property damage claim in tort ('minor' not being further defined, but obviously subject to the £600 overall ceiling) provided the claimant is not a corporate body and excluding personal injuries claims. The third category is a claim by a tenant for the return of rent deposit or any sum known as 'key money'.

(f) Environmental matters

[5.36] The District Court is empowered to deal with claims for damages arising under the Local Government (Water Pollution) Acts 1977 and 1990, again limited to a maximum award of £5,000 in damages.[76]

(g) Land and equity matters

[5.37] Unlike the Circuit Court, the District Court has no jurisdiction to determine title to property or in other connected matters generally described as the equity jurisdiction. In this area, the District Court is limited to cases of ejectment for non-payment of rent or overholding in any class of tenancy, provided that the rent does not exceed £5,000 per annum.[77]

---

72. See para **[5.12]**.
73. SI 310/1991.
74. SI 356/1993.
75. The 1993 Rules had set a ceiling of £500, but this was increased to £600 by the District Court (Small Claims Procedure) Rules 1995 (SI 377/1995). It is envisaged that the ceiling will be lifted progressively to £1,000.
76. Local Government (Water Pollution) Act 1977, s 10 as amended by the Courts Act 1991, s 10.
77. Courts of Justice Act 1924, s 77(a)(ii) as amended by the Courts Act 1991, s 4.

The Circuit Court

[5.38] Like the District Court, the Circuit Court is a court of local and limited jurisdiction within the meaning of Article 34.3.4° of the Constitution[78] and is thus empowered to deal only with those matters which have been expressly assigned to it by legislation. Again, broadly speaking, it is the successor to the County Courts and Courts of Quarter Sessions.[79] As with our description of the jurisdiction of the District Court, what follows is a selection of the original civil jurisdiction of the Circuit Court.

(a) General and monetary jurisdiction

[5.39] In terms of general subject-matter, the Circuit Court is, pursuant to s 22 of the Courts (Supplemental Provisions) Act 1961, conferred with the same jurisdiction as that exercised by the High Court in over 20 different areas, which are listed in the Third Schedule to the 1961 Act.[80] The jurisdiction of the Circuit Court thus extends to all claims in contract or tort, including those which are outside the jurisdiction of the District Court, namely libel, slander, seduction, slander of title, malicious prosecution and false imprisonment.[81] It should be noted, however, that this concurrent jurisdiction of the Circuit Court is limited in two significant respects.

[5.40] In the first place, the Circuit Court is limited to an award of damages not exceeding £30,000.[82] However, it should also be noted that, as in the case of a civil claim in the District Court, the parties to a Circuit Court action can, if both of them consent, confer unlimited jurisdiction on the Court.[83]

---

78. See para **[4.30]**.
79. See para **[2.53]**.
80. For the text of the Third Schedule as amended by subsequent Acts, up to and including the Courts Act 1991, see Delany, *op cit*, pp 194-204. Section 22 of and the Third Schedule to the 1961 Act involved a complete restatement of the Circuit Court's jurisdiction, radically changing the provisions of the Courts of Justice Act 1924, s 48 as amended, which they replaced.
81. See para **[5.31]**. Section 22 of the 1961 Act and the Fourth Schedule to the Act (replacing a similar provision in the Courts of Justice Act 1924, s 51) also expressly conferred jurisdiction on the Circuit Court concerning other matters dealt with prior to 1924 by Recorders, County Court judges and Chairmen and Courts of Quarter Sessions.
82. Third Schedule of the Courts (Supplemental Provisions) Act 1961, as amended by the Courts Act 1991, s 2. This replaced the general limit of £15,000 set by the Courts Act 1981, s 2.
83. Courts (Supplemental Provisions) Act 1961, s 22(1)(b) replacing a similar though not identical provision in the Courts of Justice Act 1924, s 48(i). This consent must be in writing and in the form prescribed for this purpose by the Rules of the Circuit Court 1950. On the consent jurisdiction of the District Court see para **[5.31]**.

[5.41] In the second place, the jurisdiction of the Circuit Court is limited in the sense that, where exclusive jurisdiction is given to another Court over certain matters, the Circuit Court is necessarily precluded from hearing such cases at first instance. Thus, although s 22 of the Courts (Supplemental Provisions) Act 1961 confers extensive jurisdiction on the Circuit Court concurrently with the High Court, Article 34.3.2° of the Constitution confers exclusive jurisdiction on the High Court in cases involving the constitutional validity of any law.[84] In terms of exclusive jurisdiction conferred by legislation, we have already seen that the District Court has been conferred with the jurisdiction concerning the renewal of intoxicating liquor licences.[85]

(b) New intoxicating liquor licences

[5.42] The Circuit Court has exclusive jurisdiction to grant (or refuse) applications for new intoxicating liquor 'on-licences', within the meaning of the Licensing Acts 1833 to 1995.[86] This is not affected by the Courts (No 2) Act 1986 which, as we saw, has limited the jurisdiction of the District Court in relation to renewals of licences.

(c) Family proceedings

[5.43] The Circuit Court has a much more extensive jurisdiction in family proceedings than the District Court.[87] Section 5 of the Courts Act 1981 conferred on the Circuit Court the jurisdiction to award a decree of divorce *a mensa et thoro*, since 1989 referred to as judicial separation.[88] While the intention of the 1981 Act seemed to be to have all such cases heard in the Circuit Court, it was held in *R v R*[89] that the High Court retained a concurrent jurisdiction in relation to these areas by virtue of the inherent jurisdiction conferred on the High Court by Article 34.3.2° of the Constitution.[90] This decision resulted in some judicial separation cases being heard in the High Court, while others were assigned to the Circuit Court.

[5.44] Further substantial substantive and procedural changes were effected in this area by the Judicial Separation and Family Law Reform Act 1989, and in deference to the decision in *R v R*, s 31(2) of the 1989 Act conferred

84. See para **[5.56]**.
85. See para **[5.32]**.
86. Courts (Supplemental Provisions) Act 1961, s 24 replacing the Courts of Justice Act 1924, s 50. On licensing law generally see Cassidy, *The Licensing Acts 1833-1995* (Round Hall Sweet & Maxwell, 1996).
87. For the District Court's limited jurisdiction in this area, see para **[5.33]**.
88. See the Judicial Separation and Family Law Reform Act 1989.
89. [1984] IR 296.
90. See para **[5.52]**.

concurrent jurisdiction on the Circuit Court and High Court in judicial separation proceedings. Section 32 of the 1989 Act also provides that, when dealing with family law matters, the Circuit Court is described as the 'Circuit Family Court', and, in an attempt to make the court atmosphere more suitable to such cases, s 33 of the 1989 Act also provided that judges, barristers and solicitors involved in such cases shall not wear wigs or gowns.[91] Section 53 of the Courts and Court Officers Act 1995 conferred jurisdiction on the Court in nullity cases for the first time. We should note that while s 9 of the 1989 Act deals with the precise issue raised in *R v R*, that decision casts a constitutional shadow over the legislation conferring exclusive jurisdiction on the Circuit Court relating to landlord and tenant and malicious injuries.[92] However, these exclusive powers remain in operation unless they are successfully challenged in a constitutional action.

(d) Commercial and consumer protection

[5.45] The Circuit Court, like the District Court, is empowered to deal with civil claims under the Hotel Proprietors Act 1963[93] and the Consumer Credit Act 1995,[94] but subject to the higher limits of £30,000 as to the amount of damages that may be awarded.

(e) Environmental matters

[5.46] The Circuit Court, like the District Court is empowered to deal with claims for damages arising under the Local Government (Water Pollution) Acts 1977 and 1990, but again subject to the higher limit of £30,000 as to the amount of damages that may be awarded.[95]

(f) Land and equity suits

[5.47] As to issues involving title to land and certain actions for ejectment, the Circuit Court has jurisdiction where the rateable valuation of the land does not exceed £200.[96] In cases involving the grant of probate or the

---

91. While the Courts and Court Officers Act 1995, s 49 (see para **[3.52]**) provides that the wearing of wigs by counsel is now generally optional, s 33 of the 1989 Act is clearly more wide-ranging in the family law context.

92. See paras **[5.48]-[5.49]**.

93. Hotel Proprietors Act 1963, s 10(1) as amended by the Courts Act 1991, s 9.

94. The 1995 Act replaced the Hire-Purchase Acts 1946 to 1980. The Hire-Purchase (Amendment) Act 1960, s 19 and the Courts (Supplemental Provisions) Act 1961, the Third Schedule the latter as amended by s 2 of the 1991 Act had conferred jurisdiction on the Circuit Court in relation to proceedings under the Acts of 1946 to 1980.

95. Local Government (Water Pollution) Act 1977, s 10 as amended by the Courts Act 1991, s 10.

96. Courts (Supplemental Provisions) Act 1961, s 22 and references 8, 9, and 10 of the Third Schedule to the 1961 Act, as amended by the Courts Act 1991, s 2.

administration of an estate, the dissolution of a partnership, the specific performance of contracts, the partition or sale of land or an action concerning property claiming an injunction (all of which are commonly referred to as equity matters or equity suits), the Court has jurisdiction where either the subject-matter does not exceed £30,000 or, where relevant, the rateable valuation of any land involved is not greater than £200.[97]

(g) Landlord and tenant

[5.48] The Circuit Court has been conferred with extensive jurisdiction concerning most landlord and tenant cases,[98] This includes jurisdiction to determine claims for new leases, whether business or private and, unlike other matters, this jurisdiction applies regardless of the amount of rent payable or the value of the property in question.[99] However, where a claim is made concerning arrears of rent, the Court's jurisdiction is again limited by the requirement that either the subject-matter does not exceed £30,000 or, where relevant, the rateable valuation of any land involved is not greater than £200.[100]

(h) Malicious injuries

[5.49] Exclusive jurisdiction was conferred on the Circuit Court by the Malicious Injuries Acts 1981 and 1986. Up to 1986, the Circuit Court heard many thousands of cases each year in which owners of property sought compensation from local authorities for damage to their property if it was caused maliciously. The cost to local authorities was enormous. Under the Malicious Injuries (Amendment) Act 1986, a claim may now only be made where the damage is caused in the course of a riot or arising from the activities of an unlawful organisation or an organisation advocating the use of violence related to Northern Ireland. The 1986 Act has, therefore, led to a large decrease in the number of malicious injuries cases in the Circuit Court.[101]

---

97. Courts (Supplemental Provisions) Act 1961, s 22 and references 16, 17, 18, 22, 23 and 27 of the Third Schedule to the 1961 Act, as amended by the Courts Act 1991, s 2.

98. For the limited jurisdiction of the District Court, see para **[5.37]**.

99. Landlord and Tenant (Amendment) Act 1980, s 3. See generally Wylie, *Landlord and Tenant Law in the Republic of Ireland* (Butterworths, 1992).

100. Courts (Supplemental Provisions) Act 1961, s 22 and references 11, 12 and 13 of the Third Schedule to the 1961 Act, as amended by the Courts Act 1991, s 2.

101. For an example of post-1986 litigation, see *WJ Prendergast & Son Ltd v Carlow County Council* [1990] ILRM 749. The Malicious Injuries (Amendment) Bill 1996 proposes to repeal in full all remaining provisions of the malicious injuries code.

(i) Local government election petitions

[5.50] The Circuit Court is also the nominated court for the purposes of petitions challenging the validity of an election to a local authority.[102]

The High Court

[5.51] By virtue of Article 34.3.1° of the Constitution,[103] the High Court is vested with 'full original jurisdiction in and power to determine all matters and questions whether of law or fact, civil or criminal'. This marks the High Court as different from the District Court and Circuit Court, the courts of local and limited jurisdiction and it reflects the position of the High Court prior to 1922 as a court possessing inherent powers, and as having substantial supervisory functions in relation to the inferior courts.[104] While Article 34.3.1° appears to give the High Court full jurisdiction in all cases, this has not generally been taken quite as literally as it appears. Thus, the lower courts can be assigned functions over certain matters, as described in the preceding sections - otherwise there would be no point in having other courts, and the Constitution itself envisages such other courts. In this context, Article 34.3.1° has been interpreted as having a two-fold effect.

[5.52] First, Article 34.3.1° has the effect that the High Court retains some jurisdiction, whether by way of appeal or by its traditional supervisory role of judicial review,[105] though first instance jurisdiction in certain areas may be given to the local and limited courts. This is the effect of the decision of the Supreme Court in *Tormey v Attorney General*.[106] Second, there is some doubt as to whether a lower court can validly be given exclusive jurisdiction over an entire subject-matter. We have already noted that, in *R v R*,[107] it was held that the High Court still retained its 'full' jurisdiction under Article 34.4.1° even where the Courts Act 1981 had appeared to confer exclusive jurisdiction on the High Court in certain family law cases.

[5.53] Bearing in mind these difficulties, therefore, the jurisdiction of the High Court is as provided for in legislation, subject to whatever the Constitution, by implication, has additionally (or concurrently) been reserved to the High Court. This reality is reflected in s 8 of the Courts (Supplemental Provisions) Act 1961, which provides that the Court shall

102. Local Government (Petitions and Disqualifications) Act 1974, s 2. See *Boyle v Allen* [1979] ILRM 281.

103. See para **[4.26]**.

104. See para **[2.32]**.

105. On judicial review, see Ch 10.

106. [1985] IR 289: see para **[15.109]**.

107. [1984] IR 296. See para **[5.43]**.

have 'such original and other jurisdiction as is prescribed by the Constitution'. Section 8 of the 1961 Act goes on to specify that the High Court is invested with such jurisdiction as was vested in the former High Court under the Courts of Justice Act 1924.

What follows, therefore, is what is generally understood in practice to be the current jurisdiction of the High Court.

(a) General monetary jurisdiction

[5.54] The effect of s 2 of the Courts Act 1991 is that (subject to the unlimited consent jurisdiction of the Circuit and District Courts) the High Court is the appropriate court to hear cases involving claims for damages in excess of £30,000.[108] No legislation has set an upper ceiling on the damages which may be awarded by the High Court, and indeed any such attempt might very well conflict with Article 34.4.1° of the Constitution.

[5.55] The result of the £30,000 threshold is that serious personal injuries cases are heard in the High Court because, between the sum of money required to provide for medical treatment in the future as well as compensation for the actual pain and suffering involved, the £30,000 threshold is passed in cases where an injury has long-term effects.[109] As well as such personal injury cases, many of the more significant civil claims between business undertakings, such as those involving building or other contracts, are heard in the High Court, again as the monetary consequences of breaches in such cases are likely to exceed £30,000.[110]

(b) Constitutional cases

[5.56] As already mentioned,[111] Article 34.3.2° confers on the High Court the exclusive function of determining the constitutional validity of legislation. No other court, other than the Supreme Court on appeal from the High Court, may make such a determination.

---

108. This £30,000 'floor' is based on the maximum limit imposed by s 2 of the 1991 Act on the jurisdiction of the Circuit Court: see para **[5.40]**. Prior to the changes effected by the 1991 Act, the High Court's original jurisdiction would have extended to claims in excess of £15,000.

109. However, since the effective threshold was raised from £15,000 to £30,000 in 1991, many quite important personal injuries actions are now heard in the Circuit Court. On the background to changes in the monetary jurisdiction, see paras **[5.17]-[5.19]**.

110. Many consumer contract cases are, correspondingly, likely to be heard in the Circuit Court, such claims unlikely to exceed the £30,000 threshold.

111. See para **[4.26]**. On constitutional adjudication generally, see Ch 15.

(c) Judicial review

[5.57] As already indicated, the High Court's 'full' jurisdiction extends to the general supervision of the 'inferior' or 'local and limited' courts as well as other decision-making tribunals by means of judicial review. While this jurisdiction might not easily fall into the civil jurisdiction of the court, it is important to note its place in the Court's functions.[112]

(d) Family proceedings

[5.58] We have noted that in *R v R*,[113] it was held that the High Court retained a concurrent jurisdiction with the Circuit Court in relation to family law matters by virtue of the 'full' jurisdiction conferred on the Court by Article 34.3.2° of the Constitution[114]. As a result, some judicial separation cases are heard in the High Court, while others were assigned to the Circuit Court. As with the Circuit Court, and in an attempt to make the court atmosphere more suitable to such cases, s 33 of the Judicial Separation and Family Law Reform Act 1989 provides that High Court judges, barristers and solicitors involved in family proceedings shall not wear wigs or gowns.[115]

(e) Company and personal insolvency

[5.59] The Companies Act 1963 designated the High Court as the court with exclusive jurisdiction in connection with the winding up of companies established under the 1963 Act. Similarly, the Companies Act 1990 conferred exclusive jurisdiction on the High Court concerning the appointment of an examiner to a company. As to personal insolvency, the Bankruptcy Act 1988 continues the long-standing position of the High Court as the court which deals exclusively with bankruptcy cases, regardless of the amount involved.

(f) Equity and chancery

[5.60] Subject to the concurrent jurisdiction of the Circuit Court in claims concerning land,[116] the High Court has jurisdiction over the kind of claims concerning land and land ownership which were dealt with in the Chancery Division of the High Court prior to 1922.[117] While there are currently no divisions within the High Court,[118] in practice such chancery matters are

---

112. See para **[10.35]**.
113. [1984] IR 296, discussed at para **[5.43]**.
114. See para **[4.26]**.
115. While the Courts and Court Officers Act 1995, s 49 (see para **[3.52]**) provides that the wearing of wigs by counsel is now generally optional, s 33 of the 1989 Act is clearly more wide-ranging in the family law context.
116. See para **[4.50]**.
117. Courts of Justice Act 1924, s 24 as carried over by the Courts (Supplemental Provisions) Act 1961, s 8.

channelled in administrative terms quite separately from other cases and will be heard by judges whose expertise lies in this area. Company law cases are also dealt with by the High Court chancery judges.

(g) Wardship

[5.61] The High Court is invested with the jurisdiction concerning the judicial protection of wards of court exercised by the Lord Chancellor of Ireland and the Lord Chief Justice of Ireland prior to 1922 and by the Chief Justice between 1924 and 1936.[119] This involves conferring the status of a ward of court on a person who is not capable of managing his or her affairs, whether because he or she is a minor[120] or by reason of mental illness or a brain injury. The High Court is thus empowered to administer any property of the person in question as well as determine other important issues concerning the fate of the person.[121]

(h) Oireachtas election and referendum petitions

[5.62] The High Court is designated as the Court to which petitions may be brought challenging the validity of any election to the Oireachtas[122] or of any referendum result.[123]

---

118. See para **[4.50]**.

119. Courts (Supplemental Provisions) Act 1961, s 9(1) describes this as the jurisdiction in 'lunacy and minor matters'. This phrase derives from the Lunacy Regulation (Ireland) Act 1871, the relevant legislation for the exercise of what is also described as the *parens patriae* jurisdiction: see *In re D* [1987] IR 449. Section 9(4) of the 1961 Act provides that the words 'ward of court' or 'person of unsound mind' should be substituted for the word 'lunatic' in the 1871 Act. Courts of Justice Act 1924, s 19(1) had conferred the wardship jurisdiction on the Chief Justice, but this was transferred to the High Court by the Courts of Justice Act 1936, s 9(1). The Court may be addressed by the guardian *ad litem* who represents the interests of the ward of court generally through solicitors and counsel.

120. For example, if a person under 18 years of age is involved in a traffic accident that does not involve a brain injury, and subsequently is awarded a sum of money in civil proceedings, that person may be made a ward of court and the High Court will administer the money in question until the person reaches the age of majority. In earlier times, in so far as the wardship jurisdiction applied to young people it largely concerned those who were 'expectant heirs' whose property might become involved in excessively complex litigation in the Chancery Division of the High Court, presided over by the Lord Chancellor. The abuses of this wardship jurisdiction were pilloried in Charles Dickens' *Bleak House*.

121. In *In re a Ward of Court* [1995] 2 ILRM 401, the High Court and, on appeal, the Supreme Court made orders authorising the withdrawal of a feeding tube to a 42 year old woman, the ward of court referred to in the title of the case, who had been in a near-persistent vegetative state (near-PVS) for over 20 years. The person in question died shortly after the removal of the tube. The case became a *cause celebre* as the 'right to die' case: see para **[15.136]**.

122. Electoral Act 1992, s 132. See *Dillon-Leetch v Calleary (No 2)*, Supreme Court, unrep, 31 July 1974.

123. Referendum Act 1994, s 42. See *Hanafin v Minister for the Environment*, High Court, unrep, 1 March 1996; [1996] 2 ILRM 141 (SC).

The Supreme Court

[5.63] The Supreme Court is primarily an appellate court.[124] There are, however, two provisions of the Constitution which allow for the Court to hear matters at first instance. In addition, certain first instance jurisdiction is conferred personally on the Chief Justice.

(a) Incapacity of President

[5.64] First, Article 12.3.1° provides that the question whether the President of Ireland has become 'permanently incapacitated' must be 'established to the satisfaction of the Supreme Court consisting of not less than five judges'. This issue has not arisen for decision since 1937.

(b) Reference of Bills by President

[5.65] The other first instance function of the Supreme Court has been of more practical importance. Pursuant to Article 26 of the Constitution, the President of Ireland may, after consultation with the Council of State, refer a Bill passed by both Houses of the Oireachtas to the Supreme Court which is required to pronounce on whether the Bill, or any provision of the Bill, is repugnant to the Constitution. Article 26 provides that this reference power applies to any such Bill other than the following three types: a Money Bill, a Bill whose consideration by Seanad Éireann was abridged under Article 24 of the Constitution[125] or a Bill containing a proposal to amend the Constitution.

[5.66] For the purpose of such a reference, Article 26.2.1° provides that the Court must consist of at least five judges who must consider every question referred to it by the President. In practice, the President refers a single question: whether a Bill is repugnant to the Constitution. Article 26.2.1° also provides that the Court shall hear arguments addressed by or on behalf of the Attorney General and by counsel assigned by the Court. The Attorney General will argue for the validity of the Bill, while counsel assigned by the Court will argue that the Bill is repugnant to the Constitution. Having heard these arguments, the Court is required by Article 26.2.1° to give its decision in open court 'as soon as may be, and in any case not later than sixty days after the date of the reference.' This two month deadline requires the Court to give priority in its lists to Article 26 references. As to the decision itself, Article 26.2.2° provides that the decision of the majority of the judges shall be the decision of the Court and that the decision is to be pronounced by one judge from the majority and that no other opinion whether assenting or

124. See para **[7.02]**.
125. See para **[13.09]**.

dissenting is to be disclosed. This 'one-judgment' rule has been criticised by a number of commentators over the years.[126]

[5.67] Article 26.1.3° prohibits the President from signing a Bill referred to the Supreme Court pending the pronouncement of the Court's decision and Article 26.3.1° prohibits the President from signing into law any Bill which is held by the Court to be in any respect repugnant to the Constitution. If, however, the Court finds there is no repugnancy, Article 26.3.3° requires the President to sign the Bill into law 'as soon as may be' after the date of the Court's decision.

[5.68] At the time of writing, there had been ten references to the Court under Article 26 of the Constitution.[127] It should be remembered that, while the Article 26 reference procedure has proved useful, the vast majority of litigation concerning the Constitution has arisen where a person initiates a case in the High Court alleging that enacted legislation, or some other instrument, or even the activity of private citizens, contravenes the rights contained in the Constitution. Thus the Article 26 procedure remains, and will remain by comparison, relatively insignificant as far as the development of constitutional law is concerned. Two difficulties with the Article 26 reference procedure have been noted in this respect.[128] First, the Supreme Court has, over the years, expressed some disquiet at being required, on an

---

126. The *11th Interim Report of the Committee on Court Practice and Procedure* (1970) criticised the one judgment rule as inhibiting the development of alternative rules and recommended that Article 26.2.2° be amended accordingly. A similar recommendation was made by the Constitution Review Group (1996): see generally para **[15.139]**. See also Hogan & Whyte, *Kelly's The Irish Constitution*, 3rd ed (Butterworths, 1994) p 530.

127. The following are the Article 26 references and a brief note on their outcome. *In re the Offences against the State (Amendment) Bill 1940* [1940] IR 470: Bill not repugnant to the Constitution; signed into law as the Offences against the State (Amendment) Act 1940. *In re the School Attendance Bill 1942* [1943] IR 334: Bill repugnant to Constitution. *In re the Electoral (Amendment) Bill 1961* [1961] IR 169: Bill not repugnant to the Constitution; signed into law as the Electoral (Amendment) Act 1961. *In re the Criminal Law (Jurisdiction) Bill 1975* [1977] IR 129: Bill not repugnant to the Constitution; signed into law as the Criminal Law (Jurisdiction) Act 1976. *In re the Emergency Powers Bill 1976* [1977] IR 159: Bill not repugnant to the Constitution; signed into law as the Emergency Powers Act 1976. *In re the Housing (Private Rented Dwellings) Bill 1981* [1983] IR 181: Bill repugnant to the Constitution. *In re the Electoral (Amendment) Bill 1983* [1984] IR 268: Bill repugnant to the Constitution. *In re the Adoption (No 2) Bill 1987* [1989] IR 656: Bill not repugnant to the Constitution; signed into law as the Adoption Act 1988. *In re the Matrimonial Home Bill 1993* [1994] 1 IR 305: Bill repugnant to the Constitution. *In re the Regulation of Information (Services Outside the State for Termination of Pregnancies) Bill 1995* [1995] 1 IR 1: Bill not repugnant to the Constitution; signed into law as the Regulation of Information (Services Outside the State for Termination of Pregnancies) Act 1995: see para **[15.134]**.

128. See Casey, *Constitutional Law in Ireland*, 2nd ed (Round Hall Sweet & Maxwell, 1992). Professor Casey also notes the existence of similar consultative provisions in other Constitutions.

Article 26 reference, to consider the validity of a Bill 'in a vacuum', that is, without the benefit of a factual context within which to judge the application of the proposed legislation. Second, Article 34.3.3° of the Constitution provides that where the Court upholds the constitutionality of a Bill on an Article 26 reference, the validity of what would then become an Act on being signed by the President cannot be questioned in any court. This immunity from further constitutional challenge at any time in the future builds in a degree of inflexibility into the Article 26 procedure which has also not been regarded as appropriate.[129]

(c) Functions exercised by Chief Justice

[5.69] Certain functions exercised prior to 1922 by the Lord Chancellor of Ireland and the Lord Chief Justice of Ireland were transferred to the Chief Justice in 1924, including certain matters concerning the admission of persons to the roll of solicitors.[130] In addition, the Chief Justice has exclusive jurisdiction to appoint notaries public and commissioners to administer oaths.[131]

[3] THE ORIGINAL JURISDICTION OF THE COURTS IN CRIMINAL CASES

[5.70] As with civil matters, the distribution of criminal business between the courts has altered over the years. In general, the issue of which court deals with criminal matters revolves around whether the criminal charge brought may be classified as minor, within the meaning of Article 38.2 of the Constitution. As we have already seen,[132] minor offences may be tried by courts of summary jurisdiction, such as the District Court. By a process of elimination, therefore, other criminal matters, involving major criminal offences, can only be dealt with by the Circuit Court and the High Court (the Central Criminal Court), or the special criminal courts when they are in operation.

The District Court

[5.71] We have seen that the District Court is a court of local and limited jurisdiction.[133] In criminal matters, it can also be described as a court of summary jurisdiction.[134] Since Article 38.2 of the Constitution provides that

129. See the recommendations of the *Constitution of Review Group*, para **[15.139]**.
130. Courts of Justice Act 1924, s 19(2) since replaced by the Solicitors Act 1954, s 14 and the Courts (Supplemental Provisions) Act 1961, s 10(1)(a).
131. Courts (Supplemental Provisions) Act 1961 s 10(1)(b), replacing the Courts of Justice Act 1924, s 19(3). On the appointment of notaries public, see *In re McCarthy* [1990] ILRM 84.
132. See para **[4.33]**.
133. See para **[4.30]**.
134. Courts of Justice Act 1924, s 77 carried forward by the Courts (Establishment and Constitution) Act 1961, s 48.

minor criminal offences may be tried by courts of summary jurisdiction,[135] the District Court is empowered to hear and determine minor criminal offences, that is, what can generally be categorised as less serious criminal offences, such as assault, drink-driving, minor larcenies and criminal damage. While such offences are generally regarded as less serious than, say, murder or rape, they constitute, in terms of numbers, the largest portion of criminal cases heard in the State. In that sense, the District Court is the busiest, and therefore perhaps the most significant, criminal court in the State.[136]

(a) Minor offences in general

[5.72] Although Article 38.2 of the Constitution provides that minor offences may be tried in the District Court, it does not provide a definition of what distinguishes a minor from a non-minor offence. This has, however, been dealt with by way of decisions of the courts which have provided a framework against which to consider whether an offence, either at common law but more particularly where created by legislation, is minor and may be tried in the District Court.

[5.73] In *Melling v Ó Mathghamhna*[137] and *Conroy v Attorney General*[138] the Supreme Court indicated that two factors in particular were important:

(1) the primary consideration is the severity of the punishment authorised by law, whether imprisonment or a fine;

(2) a secondary consideration is the moral quality of the acts required to constitute the offence in question, thus indicating that certain offences such as murder, manslaughter and rape could never be regarded as minor offences.

As a result of these decisions, the general 'rule of thumb' in legislation creating criminal offences triable summarily has been to limit the maximum prison sentence permissible to 12 months. In relation to fines, a limit of £1,000 was common until 1994, but since 1995 a maximum of £1,500 has been prescribed in some instances.[139]

---

135. See para **[4.33]**.

136. See para **[4.127]**.

137. [1962] IR 1.

138. [1965] IR 411.

139. Two Acts passed in the same month in 1995 indicate the changing pattern. The Ethics in Public Office Act 1995 s 37 provides that, on summary conviction, a person who commits an offence under that Act is liable to a fine not exceeding £1,000 and/or imprisonment for a term not exceeding six months. By contrast, the Consumer Credit Act 1995, s 13 provides that, on summary conviction, a person who commits an offence under that Act is liable to a fine not exceeding £1,500 and/or imprisonment for a term not exceeding 12 months.

(b) Specific instances of minor offences

[5.74] In light of these factors, the range of offences with which the District Court deals includes the following:

- most offences under the Road Traffic Acts 1961 to 1995, including parking offences, speeding, and what is generally described as drunken driving;[140]
- possession of controlled drugs under the Misuse of Drugs Acts 1977 and 1984, where there is no evidence of intention to supply these to others;[141]
- minor larcenies under the Larceny Act 1916;[142]
- simple assaults and other similar offences contained in the Offences against the Person Act 1861;[143]
- criminal damage under the Criminal Damage Act 1991;[144]
- offences under Regulations made pursuant to s 3 of the European Communities Act 1972.[145]

(c) Indictable offences triable summarily

[5.75] The Schedule to the Criminal Justice Act 1951[146] specifies certain offences which, although they may be tried on indictment in one of the higher criminal courts, can be dealt with in the District Court. These are referred to as indictable offences triable summarily. They include certain offences under the Larceny Acts 1861 and 1916, indecent assault, and obtaining goods by false pretences.[147] For these to be tried in the District Court, two (and in some instances three) conditions must be fulfilled.

[5.76] First, the judge of the District Court must be satisfied that the offence is one fit to be tried summarily. This requires the judge to examine the factual circumstances relating to the particular alleged offence and then to

140. See Pierse, *Road Traffic Law*, 2nd ed (Butterworths, 1995) and de Blacam, *Drunken Driving and the Law*, 2nd ed (Round Hall Press, 1995).

141. See Charleton, *Controlled Drugs and the Criminal Law* (An Cló Liúir, 1986).

142. See McCutcheon, *The Larceny Act 1916* (Round Hall Press, 1988).

143. See Charleton, *Offences Against the Person* (Round Hall Press, 1992).

144. The offence of criminal damage replaced, *inter alia*, the old offence of arson, but it also introduced offences connected with computer 'hacking'.

145. See para **[16.151]**.

146. As amended by the Criminal Procedure Act 1967 and the Criminal Law (Jurisdiction) Act 1976.

147. For a full list (up to date to early 1983) of indictable offences, including those triable summarily, see Appendix H of Ryan and Magee, *The Irish Criminal Process* (Mercier, 1983).

decide whether those circumstances make the offence a minor or a non-minor offence. Second, the accused must be informed of the right to have the case tried before a jury, and the accused must not object to having the case tried in the District Court. In this context, the accused will be aware that if the case is heard in the District Court the maximum sentence which may be imposed will be no greater than 12 months' imprisonment. Generally speaking, in the offences mentioned in the 1951 Act, a maximum sentence of two years imprisonment is possible in a higher court. In some instances, a third condition, the consent of the Director of Public Prosecutions, is also required. In certain cases, this consent is only required where there is damage to property over a certain limit. An example of where the consent is required without reference to any property damage is assault with intent to resist arrest.[148] In relation to demanding money with menaces (blackmail),[149] the Director's consent to summary trial in the District Court is required where the money demanded exceeds £200.

(d) The Children's Court: persons under the age of 16

[5.77] Section 80 of the Courts of Justice Act 1924 specifies that, in relation to minor offences alleged against children, defined as persons under the age of 16, the District Court shall sit once a week, if required, in a special Court in certain cities,[150] the Court being described as 'The Children's Court'. Section 80 provides that the judge of the District Court assigned to the Court 16 shall 'deal in such manner as shall seem just with all charges against children, except charges which by reason of their gravity or other special circumstances he shall not consider fit to be so dealt with.' This allows greater flexibility for the judge than in cases involving an accused over the age of 16.

(e) Preliminary examinations

[5.78] Another important function of the District Court in criminal matters is to act as a 'clearing house' for non-minor criminal cases. In general, a serious criminal matter will be sent for trial in the other criminal courts only

148. This is an offence under the Criminal Justice (Public Order) Act 1994, s 19 replacing the Offences against the Person Act 1861, s 38.

149. This is an offence under the Criminal Justice (Public Order) Act 1994, s 17 replacing the Larceny Act 1916, s 29.

150. The cities currently specified are Cork, Limerick and Waterford. As originally enacted, s 80 also included Dublin in this requirement, but this reference was repealed by the Courts of Justice (District Courts) Act 1946, s 4(2) and Part II of the Schedule. Despite this repeal, what is commonly described as 'the Children's Court' continues to hold regular hearings in Dublin. A new courthouse for this purpose was constructed in the Smithfield are of Dublin in the 1980s and continues to be used for this purpose up to the time of writing.

after a 'preliminary examination' of the case has occurred in the District Court. We examine this procedure elsewhere.[151]

(f) Extradition applications

[5.79] Applications for the extradition of a person to face criminal charges in another jurisdiction are made at first instance to the District Court.[152] Although such applications do not involve the District Court in making a finding of guilt or innocence, and is therefore not, strictly speaking, part of its criminal jurisdiction, the standard of proof required in such cases is the criminal standard, that is beyond reasonable doubt.[153]

The Circuit Court

[5.80] The Circuit Court is empowered to hear many serious criminal offences, that is those which are tried on indictment. Since Article 38.5 of the Constitution provides that non-minor criminal offences must, in general, involve trial with a jury,[154] it follows that a significant feature of the Circuit Court as a criminal court is that it comprises a Circuit Court judge sitting with a jury.[155]

(a) General

[5.81] The Circuit Court is empowered to deal with all indictable offences which the High Court may hear, save for certain specified offences which are exclusively within the jurisdiction of the High Court. These 'reserved offences' include treason, murder, attempted murder and conspiracy to murder.[156] In addition to these exempted offences, the High Court has, since 1991, been conferred with exclusive jurisdiction in relation to other offences, notably rape and aggravated sexual assaults.[157]

(b) Restrictions on transfers of trial

[5.82] A first reading of s 25 of the 1961 Act might indicate that many serious criminal offences, such as manslaughter, robbery and other serious offences against the person and against property, would be tried in the Circuit Court. However, until 1981, the position was more complicated because, under s 6 of the Courts Act 1964, the prosecution or the accused

---

151. See para **[6.72]**.
152. Under the Extradition Act 1965, as amended.
153. See generally, Forde, *Extradition Law in Ireland*, 2nd ed (Round Hall Press, 1995).
154. See para **[4.33]**.
155. In practice, the Circuit Criminal Court when sitting as a court of first instance to deal with serious criminal offences is described as the Circuit Criminal Court, though this has no formal status.
156. Courts (Supplemental Provisions) Act 1961, s 25, replacing the generally similar the Courts of Justice Act 1924, s 49. For the full list of these 'reserved offences', see para **[5.85]**.
157. For the full list of these additional 'reserved offences', see para **[5.85]**.

could apply for a transfer of the trial to the High Court, such transfer being mandatory when requested. Many such transfer applications were granted in practice, thus generating an increased workload for the High Court. In 1981, the right of transfer in s 6 of the 1964 Act was abolished, and replaced by s 31 of the Courts Act 1981, which provided for a limited right of transfer from any Circuit Court outside Dublin to the Dublin Circuit Court. Challenges on constitutional grounds to s 31 of the 1981 Act were rejected in *Tormey v Ireland*[158] and *The State (Boyle) v Neylon.*[159] Section 31 of the 1981 Act was itself replaced by s 32 of the Court and Court Officers Act 1995, which now provides that any such transfer from a Circuit Court outside Dublin to the Dublin Circuit Court is entirely a matter for the discretion of the Circuit Court judge to whom the application is made.

[5.83] The effect is that, since 1981 to a large extent and even more so since 1995, the provisions of s 25 of the 1961 Act may now be relied on as reflecting what happens in practice, namely that the High Court generally only hears the 'reserved' offences, while the Circuit Court generally hears all other serious indictable offences, such as manslaughter, robbery and other serious offences against the person and against property.

The High Court

[5.84] As we have already noted in the context of the civil jurisdiction of the High Court, Article 34.3.1° of the Constitution invests the Court with full original jurisdiction in all matters, whether civil or criminal.[160] And since Article 38.5 of the Constitution provides that non-minor criminal offences must, in general, involve trial with a jury,[161] the High Court as a criminal court comprises a High Court judge sitting with a jury. When exercising its first instance criminal jurisdiction, the High Court is known as the Central Criminal Court.[162]

158. [1985] IR 289: see para **[15.109]**.
159. [1986] IR 551.
160. See para **[5.51]**.
161. See para **[4.33]**.
162. Courts (Supplemental Provisions) Act 1961, s 11(1), replacing the definition in the Courts of Justice Act 1924, s 3 and the jurisdiction conferred by the Courts of Justice Act 1926, s 4. This name was used in the 1923 *Report of the Judiciary Committee* (see para **[2.64]**) and was borrowed from its English counterpart which, in addition to being described as the Central Criminal Court, is also known by the place in London where it sits, the Old Bailey. However, the *6th Interim Report of the Committee on Court Practice and Procedure* (1966) recommended that the title 'Central Criminal Court' be abolished and that the Court be known simply as 'The High Court'. The then Chairman of the Committee, Walsh J, later drew attention to this point in *The People (Attorney General) v Bell* [1969] IR 24, noting that the Constitution had given the High Court one name, whether dealing with civil or criminal matters, thus casting some doubt on the validity of the designation in s 11 of the 1961 Act. No action has been taken on these views, and the High Court as a criminal court continues to be referred to as the Central Criminal Court, whether in newspaper reports or by members of the judiciary, even Walsh J when he was the senior ordinary judge of the Supreme Court: see *The People (DPP) v Shaw* [1982] IR 1, 26.

[5.85] Section 25(2) of the Courts (Supplemental Provisions) Act 1961 provides that the High Court has exclusive jurisdiction to deal with the following 'reserved offences':

- treason (an offence defined by Article 39 of the Constitution, with some further details being dealt with in the Treason Act 1939);
- an offence under ss 2 or 3 of the Treason Act 1939, namely encouragement or misprision of (concealing knowledge of) treason, respectively;
- offences under ss 6, 7 or 8 of the Offences against the State Act 1939, namely offences relating to the usurpation of the functions of government, obstruction of government and obstruction of the President, respectively;
- murder, attempted murder and conspiracy to murder; and
- piracy.[163]

In addition to these exempted offences, the High Court has, since 1961, been conferred with exclusive jurisdiction in two further categories of offences:

(1) offences under the Genocide Act 1973; and

(2) rape, aggravated sexual assault and attempted aggravated sexual assault, as defined in the Criminal Law (Rape)(Amendment) Act 1990.[164]

As already indicated, the effect of s 25(2) of the 1961 Act is that, aside from these offences, the Circuit Court has full jurisdiction to deal with indictable offences.[165]

Special Criminal Courts

[5.86] The title 'Special Criminal Courts' provides two clues as to the nature of these particular courts.[166] First, they are courts that function in relation to

163. Offences by an accessory before or after the fact are also included: s 25(2) of the 1961 Act.

164. Section 10 of the 1990 Act. The effective transfer of jurisdiction in rape and other serious sexual assault cases from the Circuit Court to the High Court, as well as the other substantive amendments in the 1990 Act were made, in part, on foot of the recommendations of the Law Reform Commission. The transfer of jurisdiction reflected in large part concern over the perceived low sentencing level for such offences in the Circuit Court. On the general background, see Fennell's Annotation to the 1990 Act, *Irish Current Law Statutes Annotated* (Sweet & Maxwell). The sentencing issue was also a major catalyst in the enactment of the Criminal Justice Act 1993: see para **[5.13]**.

165. See para **[5.81]**.

166. See generally, Hogan and Walker, *Political Violence and the Law in Ireland* (Manchester UP, 1989).

criminal trials only. As to being 'special', the courts derive their legal standing from Article 38.3 of the Constitution.

(a) Constitutional setting: non-jury court

[5.87] While Article 38.5 of the Constitution contains a general right to trial with a jury concerning criminal charges,[167] this is expressly stated to be subject to Article 38.2 (minor offences),[168] Article 38.3 (special criminal courts) and Article 38.4 (military courts).[169] This indicates that a feature of trial by special criminal courts is the absence of a jury.

[5.88] Article 38.3 states:

> 1° Special courts may be established by law for the trial of offences in cases where it may be determined in accordance with such law that the ordinary courts are inadequate to secure the effective administration of justice, and the preservation of public peace and order.
>
> 2° The constitution, powers, jurisdiction and procedure of such special courts shall be prescribed by law.

The relevant law enacted in accordance with Article 38.3 is contained in Part V of the Offences against the State Act 1939. Section 35 of the 1939 Act provides that Part V comes into force (and special criminal courts may thus be established) only where the Government makes and publishes a proclamation declaring that it 'is satisfied that the ordinary courts are inadequate to secure the effective administration of justice and the preservation of public peace and order'.[170] As can be seen, this formula is taken verbatim from Article 38.3 of the Constitution. Part V of the 1939 Act also provides for the matters referred to in Article 38.3.2° of the Constitution, namely the composition of the special criminal courts as well as providing for the detailed procedures by which they are to operate.

[5.89] Underlying the establishment of special criminal courts is a belief that the operation of the ordinary courts, and in particular the independent functioning of juries, might be undermined by the activities of subversive

167. See para **[4.33]**.

168. See para **[5.71]**.

169. The military tribunals provided for under Article 38.4.1° concern the trial of offences during a state of war or armed rebellion. As they do not deal with what might be described as 'ordinary' criminal law, their functions and powers are not considered here. Article 38.4.2° deals with trial by court-martial, which is regulated by the Defence Act 1954. See generally, Hogan & Whyte, *Kelly's The Irish Constitution*, 3rd ed (Butterworths, 1994) pp 652-6.

170. This proclamation must be published in *Iris Oifigiúil*, the Official Gazette: s 35(6) of the 1939 Act.

organisations. The background to the enactment of the 1939 Act was the issuing of 'proclamations' by the IRA to the effect that it had become the Government of the Republic and an expected increase in violent activity on their part.[171] Nevertheless, while concern over subversive crime lies behind the establishment of special criminal courts their jurisdiction is not so confined and extends to non-subversive, or 'ordinary', crime.[172]

(b) Scheduled offences and transfer of trials

[5.90] One of the important features of the 1939 Act as far as special criminal courts is concerned is that it is possible to have cases transferred from the ordinary criminal courts, that is, the District Court, the Circuit Court and the High Court. This can be effected in one of two ways.

[5.91] First, s 36 of the 1939 Act provides that certain lists of offences may be specified by the Government by statutory Order as offences which the ordinary courts are to be deemed inadequate within the terms of Article 38.3 of the Constitution. These offences are referred to as 'scheduled offences' and are transferred automatically to the special criminal courts.[173] The current list of scheduled offences is:[174]

- any offence under the Malicious Damage Act 1861 (since replaced by the Criminal Damage Act 1991);
- an offence under s 7 of the Conspiracy and Protection of Property Act 1875;
- any offence under the Explosive Substances Act 1883;
- any offence under the Firearms Acts 1925 to 1990; and
- any offence under the Offences against the State Act 1939 itself.

This list reflects the primary concern with subversive crime and it is notable that other serious offences, such as murder, rape and robbery are not scheduled.

[5.92] Second, even where an offence is not a scheduled offence, such as murder, s 46 of the 1939 Act provides that an individual trial may be transferred to a special criminal court where the Director of Public Prosecutions issues a certificate stating that in his opinion the ordinary courts are inadequate to secure the effective administration of justice and the

---

171. See 74 *Dáil Debates* cols 1283-1292.
172. *The People (DPP) v Quilligan* [1986] IR 495.
173. Such cases can, however, also be transferred back to the ordinary courts under the 1939 Act.
174. Listed in the Offences against the State (Scheduled Offences) Order 1972, SI 282/1972.

preservation of public peace and order. Once such a certificate is issued the case must be transferred by the ordinary court to a special criminal court.

[5.93] The combined effect of ss 36 and 46 of the 1939 Act is that all serious criminal offences may be transferred from the ordinary courts and tried by special criminal courts, including the offences 'reserved' to the High Court such as murder[175] or the other serious offences such as robbery that might be tried in the Circuit Court.[176] The courts have indicated that they will be extremely reluctant to invalidate such a transfer even where the accused person claims he has no connection with any terrorist type organisation.[177]

(c) Special criminal courts in operation

[5.94] Special Criminal Courts do not exist on a permanent basis but only where Part V of the Offences against the State Act 1939 is in force. Part V has been in operation on two separate occasions. The first was at the outset of World War II in 1939. The special criminal courts continued to operate until 1946, when in effect they ceased to function, though the government proclamation bringing Part V of the 1939 Act into force was not actually revoked and the special criminal courts were revived in 1961 to deal with a number of offences connected with what was termed the 'border campaign' of that time. The 1939 proclamation was revoked in 1962 and thus Part V of the 1939 Act ceased to be in force. In 1972, a new Government proclamation was issued bringing Part V of the 1939 Act into force, and a single special criminal court was established. That court has continued to operate from 1972 to the present (1996), dealing with cases primarily connected with subversive activities and other offences largely, though not exclusively, related to Northern Ireland.[178]

(d) Composition of courts

[5.95] The Special Criminal Court established in 1972 differed in a number of respects from the previous manifestations of World War II and the early 1960s. First, only one such court was established. However, the most significant difference was the composition of the Court. Section 39 of the 1939 Act provides that a person may be appointed as a member (in effect, a

175. See para **[5.85]**.

176. See para **[5.81]**.

177. See *Savage v Director of Public Prosecutions* [1982] ILRM 385, *O'Reilly and Judge v Director of Public Prosecutions* [1984] ILRM 224 and *The State (McCormack) v Curran* [1987] ILRM 225.

178. Some offences connected with 'organised' drugs activity were also transferred from the ordinary courts to the Special Criminal Court.

judge) of a special criminal court if he or she is a judge of the High Court, or the Circuit Court, or the District Court, a barrister or solicitor of not less than seven years standing or an officer of the Defence Forces not below the rank of commandant. All members of special criminal courts sitting between 1939 and 1972 were Defence Forces officers.[179]

[5.96] However, since 1972 the Special Criminal Court comprised three judges of the ordinary courts, usually one High Court judge, one Circuit Court judge and one judge of the District Court, with the High Court judge presiding. Any of these three might either be a sitting or retired judge. This change in composition from previous special criminal courts could largely be attributed to queries as to the constitutional validity of a person being tried with an ordinary criminal offence before officers of the Defence Forces. Numerous challenges to the constitutional validity of special criminal courts have been made, but all of these have been unsuccessful[180].

179. Military tribunals, operating under Article 38.4, were also in existence separately at that time.

180. Two such challenges concerned the courts established in 1939: *In re MacCurtain* [1941] IR 43 and *The People (Attorney General) v Doyle* (1943) 77 ILTR 108. As to the Court established in 1972, see *In re the Criminal Law (Jurisdiction) Bill 1975* [1977] IR 129, *Eccles v Ireland* [1985] IR 545, *McGlinchey v Governor of Portlaoise Prison* [1988] IR 671 and *Kavanagh v Government of Ireland* [1996] 1 ILRM 133.

Chapter 6

Civil and Criminal Court Procedure

[1] Introduction

[6.01] In this chapter we outline some of the basic rules of civil and criminal court procedure which are set out in statutory rules of court[1] and some conventions of practice. We will see that there are many differences between the statutory rules and conventions concerning civil procedure on the one hand and criminal procedure on the other. It is thus important to distinguish between the two. Nonetheless, there are a number of common principles which it is also important to bear in mind.

[2] Civil and Criminal Procedure Compared and Contrasted

Private law and public law

[6.02] A critical distinction between civil and criminal procedure is the nature of disputes with which they are concerned and the mechanism by which they are initiated. Civil procedure tends to involve what are described as private law disputes. Typical examples of such 'private' disputes would be personal injuries claims arising from traffic accidents or accidents in the workplace, claims for breach of contract and family proceedings, where the proceedings are initiated by one or other of the parties themselves, generally by consulting lawyers who will act as the agents of the parties in processing the claim through the court system. By contrast, criminal procedure deals with the processing of some activity regarded as a wrong against society or the public in general, hence its description as a public law matter. In general also, criminal prosecutions are initiated by a State authority, such as the Director of Public Prosecutions or the Garda Síochána. It is possible for criminal prosecutions to be initiated by private individuals,[2] but they are a

---

1. The relevant rules for the different courts are the District Court Rules 1948 (SR & O 431/1947), the Rules of the Circuit Court 1950 (SI 179/1950) and the Rules of the Superior Courts 1986 (SI 15/1986), the latter covering the High Court, the Supreme Court and the Court of Criminal Appeal. Each set of Rules has been amended substantially from time to time, largely to take account of changes to substantive law effected by Acts of the Oireachtas. On the legislative authority to make rules of court, see para **[4.05]**.
2. See paras **[6.63]** and **[6.67]**.

rarity. There are some exceptions to this neat categorisation,[3] but it provides a general picture.

Compensation and punishment

[6.03] The purpose of a civil claim is, in general,[4] to seek compensation or some other form of remedy such as an injunction or declaration.[5] In contrast, the purpose of criminal proceedings is to punish a person, for example by means of a monetary fine to be paid to the State or a sentence of imprisonment.

[6.04] The general rule is that a fine is paid by the offender to the State rather than the victim, and this has traditionally been one way to emphasise the distinction between criminal and civil proceedings; in a civil claim, any award of damages is to be paid to the 'victim/plaintiff'. This traditional distinction may be contrasted with the arrangements in place for many years in civil law legal systems in which compensation to the victim may be dealt with in tandem with criminal proceedings. This concept has now been incorporated into Irish law.[6]

[6.05] As to the sentence of imprisonment, while its primary intention is to punish the offender, other purposes of the sentence have also been referred to through the years. A simple purpose served by the sentence was to exact retribution on behalf of society: a kind of judicially authorised or sanitised revenge. In addition, at one time a cardinal principle of imprisonment was the concept that the offender would be reformed or rehabilitated into society by means of hard labour, some elements of craft training and an element of education (including religious instruction). Similarly, the element of

---

3. Judicial review proceedings, while falling into the civil law arena, are part of public law. For discussion of judicial review, see para **[10.35]**.

4. However, for discussion of aggravated or punitive damages in civil cases, see para **[10.07]**.

5. For the different remedies in civil proceedings, see paras **[10.02]** and **[10.16]**.

6. Criminal Justice Act 1993, s 6 provides that a court may order a convicted person to pay compensation to 'any person ... who has suffered [any personal] injury or loss' arising from the commission of an offence. Section 6 is, however, limited in the sense that it allows for compensation awards to the victims of offenders who are of some means, but provides no redress to victims of impecunious offenders. A non-statutory criminal injuries compensation scheme was established in 1972 and administered by the Criminal Injuries Compensation Tribunal, but its parameters were severely restricted in 1986, since when only special damages, such as medical expenses or loss of earnings, may be claimed; general damages for the pain and suffering involved cannot be claimed. In *AD v Ireland* [1994] 1 IR 369, it was held that this 1986 alteration to the 1972 Scheme was not in conflict with the right of bodily integrity of victims of crime contained in Article 40.3 of the Constitution. Thus, the victim of an impecunious offender currently remains without an effective remedy after the 1993 Act.

deterrence, both of the offender and more generally of others who might be tempted to commit criminal acts, has been an avowed basis for imprisonment. More recently, after widespread disenchantment with what were seen as the failures of the earlier models of reform and rehabilitation, minimalist and negative concepts such as 'secure custody' came into vogue, with imprisonment being seen as an end in itself, and any attempt at rehabilitation was seen as a futile exercise. In Ireland, it may be said that a mixture of all of these elements permeate current thinking on 'crime and punishment'.[7]

Notification of both sides

[6.06] An essential procedural requirement in all legal systems is that before a case may proceed to court certain documents must be drafted, then filed in Court and a copy given to the other party to the court proceedings. This basic requirement of advance notice from one side to the other applies in both civil and criminal cases, although the precise mechanisms by which this is achieved is substantially different in civil and criminal matters. As we will see below, in civil matters, the documents are usually called pleadings (of which there are many types), while in criminal matters the documents include a summons and an indictment.

Time limits

[6.07] For civil proceedings, various time limits for initiating proceedings are laid down in legislation, notably in the Statute of Limitations 1957 and 1991.[8] In the most common claims, those for personal injuries or breach of contract, the limitation periods vary from three years to six years. It is important to note that these time limits refer to the period between the occurrence of the event in question, the accident or the breach of contract, and the lodging of the initial document notifying the other party of the claim; that is 'the clock starts' at the time of the accident or breach of contract and a person has three years or six years, as the case may be, from that time to initiate the claim. It may very well be that a further two or more years elapses before the case comes to hearing, if indeed it does come to hearing.[9]

[6.08] As to criminal proceedings, a distinction should be drawn between summary prosecutions and prosecutions on indictment. Since 1851, the general rule for summary prosecutions is that proceedings must be initiated

7. See further O'Mahony, *Crime and Punishment in Ireland* (Round Hall Press, 1993).

8. The Statute of Limitations 1957 is the only Act of the Oireachtas bearing the title 'statute' in its short title, and the Statute of Limitations (Amendment) Act 1991, which amended the 1957 Statute, contains (perhaps confusingly) both forms.

9. As to the settlement of proceedings prior to a court hearing, see para **[6.54]**.

within six months of the date of the alleged offence,[10] though in recent years a period of one year has been more common[11], with some legislation allowing up to two years.[12] As for prosecutions on indictment, by tradition the common law provided for no limitation period and this convention has been maintained.

[6.09] However, in relation to civil proceedings as well as summary criminal matters and prosecutions on indictment, it is possible that delay in proceeding with a case will cause the courts to prohibit the case from proceeding to hearing for being an abuse of process. In recent years, the courts have ordered that civil and criminal cases be discontinued, where there has been unreasonable delay in proceeding and, equally if not even more importantly, where that delay causes prejudice to the other parties in the case.[13] Thus, even where the requirements of a limitation period have been met (as in civil proceedings or summary prosecutions) or where no limitation apparently exists (as with prosecutions on indictment), the courts may order that the case not proceed because of the prejudicial effects of delay. This view is based on the general principle that a fair hearing is not possible if one party has been unduly prejudiced by delay. It is important to bear in mind that it is not the mere fact of delay, but whether prejudice has resulted from any delay that would cause a case to be stopped in this way.

Civil and criminal proceedings from a single event

[6.10] While the purposes of civil and criminal proceedings are different, it is important to note that both a civil compensation claim and a criminal prosecution can arise from just one event. Take a traffic accident between two cars as an example. The Garda Síochána may be involved in bringing a criminal prosecution against the driver of one of the cars: this is the criminal side of the accident. Quite separately, a person injured in that accident might bring a civil claim for damages (compensation) against the driver of one of the cars. The criminal prosecution and the civil compensation claim will be dealt with in separate proceedings, but they originate in the one event.

There are, of course, instances where a dispute will clearly involve only a civil claim, for example, where one company claims that another company is in breach of the terms of a building contract. Nonetheless, it is important to

10. Petty Sessions (Ireland) Act 1851, s 10; Courts (No 3) Act 1986, s 3.

11. Eg Safety, Health and Welfare at Work Act 1989, s 51(3).

12. Eg Animal Remedies Act 1993, s 22(2). For justification of such longer periods, see *Meagher v Minister for Agriculture* [1994] 1 ILRM 329: see para **[16.76]**.

13. See *Ó Domhnaill v Merrick* [1984] IR 151, *The State (O'Connell) v Fawsitt* [1986] IR 362 and *Director of Public Prosecutions v Byrne* [1994] 2 ILRM 91.

bear in mind that, in many cases, one event may give rise to separate civil and criminal proceedings.

Individuals and corporate bodies

[6.11] In civil disputes, claims can be initiated by individuals against individuals, as would be the case in a traffic accident, though any insurance companies would be closely involved in the case also. Claims may also be initiated by individuals against corporate bodies, such as limited liability companies or other corporate bodies such as local authorities, or *vice versa.* Claims may also be initiated by one corporate body against another. As for criminal prosecutions, the most common instances are where an individual is prosecuted but prosecutions of corporate bodies are also common, particularly for 'regulatory' crimes such as breaches of environmental legislation.

Titles of the parties

[6.12] The titles allocated to parties in civil and criminal matters also appears to reflect the distinction between compensation and punishment. In a civil claim, the person initiating the claim is, in general, called a plaintiff (whether a company or an individual) while the party against whom the claim is brought is called the defendant. In some instances, such as family cases, the parties may be described as petitioner and respondent or, in a case of judicial review, applicant and respondent. By contrast, in a criminal matter, the parties are referred to in somewhat stronger terms as the prosecution (or prosecutor in the case of an individual) and defendant.

Describing the case and its processing

[6.13] The description of the processing of civil and criminal litigation is, in general, distinct, though some similarities of expression are also used. Civil proceedings are initiated by a plaintiff, while criminal proceedings are initiated by the prosecution (or prosecutor). The continuation of the cases may, however, be described in similar tones. The criminal case will almost always be 'prosecuted' by the prosecution; on occasion, however, lawyers may refer to 'prosecuting' a civil claim with all due speed or 'to the full extent of the law'.[14] The court hearing for both civil and criminal cases is

14. It is regularly asserted that, since trespassing is a civil matter, the sign 'Trespassers will be prosecuted' is an inappropriate notice to post on one's property. However, the sign is quite acceptable if it understood as a truncated version of 'Take notice. That any person or persons audaciously presuming to trespass on this property, will be punished with the utmost severity of private chastisement, and prosecuted with the utmost rigour of the law', as in the case of Mr Boythorn's rather elaborate sign in Charles Dickens' *Bleak House.* See also now the various offences in the Criminal Justice (Public Order) Act 1994.

usually referred to as a 'trial', though 'trial of the action' is used in connection with civil claims only.

Different courts

[6.14] We have already seen that the arrangements by which civil cases and criminal cases are allocated to the different courts is quite different.[15] Similarly, in virtually all civil claims, the case will be decided by a judge, whereas in serious criminal trials a trial by judge and jury is very common.

Outcomes described

[6.15] The different outcomes in civil and criminal matters are also described using different terminology. For example, where the plaintiff loses a personal injuries claim, it is said that the defendant is not liable, whereas if the prosecution loses a criminal case the defendant is found not guilty or is acquitted. Where the plaintiff is successful in a personal injuries claim, the defendant is found liable, whereas is a criminal prosecution is successful, the defendant is found guilty of an offence.

Burdens of proof

[6.16] One further critical distinction between civil and criminal cases is the question of the burden of proof. In general, in a civil case any particular issue as well as the overall question of liability is determined by establishing the issue or the question of liability on the balance of probabilities, while in a criminal case all issues and the question of guilt must be proved beyond reasonable doubt. In many instances, it may be that this distinction will not lead to different results but it is certainly possible.

[6.17] Take the example of the traffic accident already referred to. Let us assume that both civil and criminal proceedings resulted from the accident. In general, the criminal proceedings will come to trial in the District Court long before any civil proceedings. Again, let us suppose that the driver of one car is charged with careless driving and that the driver of the other car (appearing as a witness for the prosecution) testifies that the defendant had been driving on the wrong side of the road, but that the defendant then testifies that she had been driving on the correct side of the road. This obviously presents a clear conflict of evidence for the trial judge. In order to find the defendant guilty of careless driving, the judge must be satisfied beyond reasonable doubt that the defendant was indeed driving on the wrong side of the road. The judge might be prepared to convict in the example given, and indeed that would happen in many instances; but if the judge has

15. See Ch 5.

a reasonable doubt about the question, the benefit of that doubt must be given to the defendant. Thus, even if the judge considers that it is more likely than not that the defendant was driving on the wrong side of the road, the judge should find the defendant not guilty.

[6.18] Assuming then that the defendant in the criminal case is found not guilty and that, some time later, the same incident becomes the subject of a civil claim in the High Court.[16] On this occasion, we might suppose that the person who gave evidence for the prosecution in the criminal case is the plaintiff in the civil action. Again, the same evidence is given. On this occasion, the High Court judge, faced with precisely the same evidence, must decide whether the defendant had been negligent and thus liable to pay damages to the plaintiff. Here, the judge would be perfectly entitled to conclude that, although it is by no means certain that the defendant was on the wrong side of the road, this was, on the balance of probabilities, the more likely explanation for the accident. In this instance, the balance of probabilities test comes down to saying that one party's version of events is more likely (or more believable) than that of the other.

[6.19] Some people may object to what appear to be conflicting outcomes in the two cases. The defence put forward to this is that the consequences of a guilty verdict in the criminal case (fine and possible imprisonment) justify a high standard of proof, and that a lesser standard of proof is acceptable in civil cases where the consequences are less drastic (payment of damages to the plaintiff in circumstances where the defendant is likely to insured). Moreover, a criminal conviction amounts to a moral condemnation in a way that is not usually present in a determination of civil liability. This is certainly true in cases where the criminal penalties are relatively high but the consequences in the civil case are relatively small. We can now proceed to describe in some detail the different methods by which civil and criminal matters are processed through the legal system.

[3] Civil Procedure

[6.20] As we have already noted, it is important for both sides to be fully informed of the basic outline of the legal case being made by the other side so that there can be no complete surprises when and if the case comes to court. This is achieved by requiring both sides to furnish written documents outlining their cases to each other. In civil matters, these documents are called pleadings.

---

16. This assumes any personal injuries incurred would bring the case within the jurisdiction of the High Court.

Pleadings

[6.21] It important to note that there is a major difference between pleadings and what is sometimes called pleading on behalf of a client in court. Pleadings are formal written documents, their intention being to state the claim being made by the plaintiff or defendant. Pleading in court forms part of the great oral tradition of advocacy, although it must be said that full-blooded rhetorical pleading is not as common as film and television might lead us to believe. In fact, a barrister is much more likely to be found at a laptop (or a Dictaphone) composing the words of pleadings than regaling a court in the manner of the lawyers of popular fiction.

[6.22] The language used in pleadings might be described as arcane and severe rather than informal. Barristers will, in general use phrases that are well-established in legal practice rather than adopt a more contemporary mode of expression. The reason for such caution lies in the fact that it was once the case that even the slightest fault in the pleadings could result in a case being dismissed by a court. This can still occur on occasion[17] and the fear of such a calamitous result for a client has meant that barristers take a particularly cautious approach to the wording of pleadings. Consequently, pleadings are written in language which might appear more at home in the late 19th century but this is based on the notion that erring on the side of caution is the better course than attempting to draft pleadings which are a delight to read.

[6.23] The consequences of a failure to 'plead accurately' can be illustrated with a simple example. Take a personal injuries action in which the initial pleadings were filed in Court two years and six months after the accident to which they relate. If the barrister has failed to state a basic legal ground on which the case either stands or falls the matter may be dismissed by the court. But the defect might not be discovered until, say, a year later, that is three and a half years after the accident. It may then be impossible to

---

17. In *Garvey v Ireland* [1981] IR 75, the plaintiff had been dismissed as Commissioner of the Garda Síochána by the Government. He brought proceedings claiming that the dismissal was invalid on the ground that the Government had acted in breach of the principles of fair procedure in failing to inform him at the time of the basis on which the dismissal was being made. The Government defended the case on the basis that it was entitled to dismiss a Commissioner without disclosing the basis for a dismissal, but the Supreme Court decided in favour of the plaintiff on this point. The Government then stated that it had intended that this point be decided without prejudice to its intention to introduce evidence that indicated the plaintiff had in fact been given the basis for his dismissal and that, in the circumstances, it should be allowed to alter its pleadings to reflect that intention. However, the Supreme Court declined to allow the Government to amend its pleadings at that late stage in the case: see The Irish Times, 26 April 1979, p 13.

recommence proceedings because the relevant time limit under the Statute of Limitations 1957 and 1991 may have expired.[18] This explains why pleadings tend to be over-inclusive documents which attempt to cover every possible ground on which the plaintiff or defendant might have a cause of action.

Level of formality in the different courts

[6.24] It may also be noted here that the requirements of the rules of court differ from one court to another. The most complex rules of court so far as all aspects of procedure and pleadings are concerned are those which apply in the High Court and Supreme Court, namely the Rules of the Superior Courts 1986. The requirements for the Circuit Court, set out in the Rules of the Circuit Court 1950, are significantly less complex, while those for the District Court, contained in the District Court Rules 1948 do not set out pleadings requirements as such at all. Substantial changes are made from time to time in the rules of court in the light of new insights into problems which have come to light in litigation or where new legislation has been enacted to dealt with a particular problem.

[6.25] We will provide in what follows a brief description of the course of civil proceedings in the High Court. This should not be taken in any way as a definitive account of a typical High Court case, but is simply designed to indicate the kind of language which appears in pleadings which, as indicated above, is a staple of the practice of law and must become familiar to any practising lawyer.

High Court pleadings

[6.26] Under the Rules of the Superior Courts 1986 (which in essence update but continue in force the system of practice which had developed in the court system by the end of the 19th Century), there are three basic forms of initiating documents for the broad range of civil cases which are dealt with by the High Court. These documents are all give the title summonses. In addition the 1986 Rules provide for initiating documents called petitions, which are used in relation to family law matters and also company law matters. Yet another form of procedure is provided for in relation to seeking orders for judicial review.[19] For present purposes, we will concentrate on the summonses only.

---

18. See para **[6.07]**.
19. See para **[10.39]**.

Summary summons

[6.27] The first of the initiating documents is called the Summary Summons, which is the appropriate document used in relation to claims for what is called a liquidated sum of money. This means a sum of money which can be readily calculated. A typical case in which a summary summons may be issued is where a bank claims that, on default of a loan given by the bank, a customer owes a certain sum of money. Obviously, there may be complex calculations as to the rate of interest payable in order to calculate the precise sum owing on the date when the case comes to Court, but once the sum can be calculated by reference to rates of interest which were agreed when the loan was taken out, then the Summary Summons procedure is the appropriate initiating document in the High Court.

Special summons

[6.28] The second form of initiating document is the Special Summons, which is used primarily for legal disputes relating to land, for example, a claim by a building society that, on foot of a mortgage on which a person has defaulted the building society is entitled to possession of the property. These special summonses will be dealt with by what are, in effect, the Chancery judges of the High Court. Although as we have seen the divisions of the High Court were abolished on the passing of the Courts of Justice Act 1924, the administrative arrangements within the Court system still exist by which such cases are directed towards particular judges who deal on a regular basis with these areas of law.[20]

Plenary summons

[6.29] The third major initiating document in the High Court is the Plenary Summons. This is used in connection with all other civil cases which are not appropriate for either a summary or special summons; in effect, it is the residual 'catch all' High Court Summons. The Plenary Summons is used, for example, in relation to any claim in which it is anticipated that a full hearing requiring oral evidence under oath. It is also used where the amount of damages claimed cannot be reduced to a liquidated sum of money. Thus, the many thousand of personal injuries actions which take up much of the time of the High Court in civil matters are initiated by way of a Plenary Summons. Although an experienced barrister, whether junior or senior, may have an accurate estimation of the amount of damages (compensation) that might be recoverable, there is no definitive system for calculating in advance the precise sum of money which should be awarded in damages, so that a

20. See para **[4.50]**.

Summary Summons would not be appropriate in such a case. Other cases in which a Plenary Summons is appropriate include defamation actions. We will use the procedure by which a personal injuries action is processed to illustrate the pleadings system.

The plenary summons in action

[6.30] When a barrister receives instructions in relation to a personal injures action, it is clear that the plenary summons procedure is the appropriate path to take. The first document must be filed by the plaintiff in the action who invariably is the person who has been injured. The example we will use is of a person who has been injured in the eye by fragments of glass from an abrasive wheel (which is a rotating wheel used to grind metals and other materials such as glass) while working for a company which manufactures glass. The barrister will, as indicated, know that this injury is quite serious and, although the medical prognosis for the employee may not be fully known at the time the barrister is first instructed, it will be regarded as in most cases being sufficiently serious to warrant being brought in the High Court. In other words, the barrister will make an estimate that the level of damages which might be received by the employee would be over £30,000, the level set by the Courts Act 1991 as the 'floor' for the High Court.[21] This estimate will be made on the basis of an assumption that the employee was not at all to blame for the accident in question.

Plenary summons and indorsement of claim

[6.31] The first document in the Plenary Summons procedure is the plenary summons itself, which contains little more than the names of the parties and a brief outline of the claim being made by the plaintiff. The Plenary Summons consists of three standard form pages, the basic contents of which are set out in Appendix A to the Rules of the Superior Courts 1986. The first page of the Plenary Summons is as follows:

THE HIGH COURT

1996 No. 10,000P

Between	**Raymond Byrne**	Plaintiff
and	**McCutcheon Glass Company Limited**	Defendant

To the defendant McCutcheon Glass Company Limited
of 23 Glass Lane, in the City of Dublin.

21. See para **[5.54]**.

This plenary summons is to require that within eight days after the service thereon upon you (exclusive of the day of such service) you in person or by solicitor do enter an appearance in the Central Office, Four Courts, Dublin in the above action; and TAKE NOTICE that, in default of your so doing, the plaintiff may proceed therein, and judgment may be given in your absence.

BY ORDER, Liam Hamilton,
Chief Justice of Ireland,

the 31st day of February one thousand nine hundred and ninety six.

N.B. - This summons is to be served within twelve calendar months from the date hereof, and, if renewed within six calendar months from the date of the last renewal, including the day of such date, and not afterwards.
The defendant may appear hereto by entering an appearance either personally or by solicitor at the Central Office, Four Courts, Dublin.

[6.32] It may be noted that the Summons is, in effect, a call by order of the Chief Justice to the defendant to answer the claim by the plaintiff in the case. This form of initiating document has medieval roots, because it reflects the form of the old writs issued in the Lord Chancellor's Department, issued of course on the authority of the monarch.[22] That is, indeed, the form of summons which continues to operate in the courts of the United Kingdom to the present day.

[6.33] The number '1996 No. 10,000P' which appears at the top of the plenary summons is the official file number for the case and is extremely important administratively. It identifies the case for the court officials who receive any further pleadings which are delivered in the case as well as identifying the case should it proceed to court hearing. The plenary summons is brought to the Central Office of the High Court in the Four Courts, usually by the solicitor for the plaintiff and, if it appears to be in the correct format set out in the 1986 Rules, it will be accepted by the officials of the High Court Central Office. The plenary summons will then be given its official court number and the fact that a plenary summons has been issued will be entered in the Central Office records. These records include sufficient space to record any subsequent pleadings. Once the summons has been entered in the Central Office records, it is officially stamped, in accordance with the requirements of the 1986 Rules. It then becomes an official court document which may be served on the defendant. In fact the

22. See para **[2.07]**.

original summons is retained by the court officials, and the plaintiff's solicitor will serve on the defendant what is called a certified copy of the original summons.

[6.34] The second page of the plenary summons contains a space for a brief outline of the plaintiff's claim, called the General Indorsement of Claim. The relevant outline for our example might be as follows:

The Plaintiff's Claim is for Damages for Personal Injuries Arising from the Breach of Duty of the Defendant its servant or agents.

This may seem a relatively uninformative list of information but it is merely the first stage in what becomes later an increasingly complex and, sometimes, long drawn out process.

[6.35] In addition to the General Indorsement of Claim, this part of the summons will also include a verification that the summons was served on the defendant. In the case of a n individual, this is usually done at his or her residence, but in our example where a company is being sued as employer, service will take place at its registered place of business. Finally, the Plenary Summons also contains a space for the insertion of the place of residence of the plaintiff and where court documents in response to the summons may be served.

[6.36] The filing of the plenary summons has a great significance for the law on the limitation period for bringing claims to court. If a plenary summons is correctly issued under the three year limitation period for personal injuries actions, then this is the crucial date for the Statutes of Limitations 1957 and 1991, which do not require that the case comes to hearing before a court within 3 years; all that is required is that the plenary summons is issued within that time.[23]

[6.37] Once the plenary summons is duly issued and then served on the defendant, it is up to the defendant to respond. As the first page of the plenary summons indicates there is an obligation to enter an appearance within eight days of being served with the documents. In fact this requirement is not an absolute obligation and in many instances an appearance might not be entered for a number of weeks. If the plaintiff attempted to obtain a decision from the High Court nine days after serving a plenary summons on the defendant the Court would be most unlikely to grant such judgment without giving the defendant an opportunity of

23. See para **[6.07]**.

defending the case. In fact many of the time limits specified in the Rules of the Superior Courts 1986 for various stages of the court procedure are not adhered to, and it is usually a year or even longer before all the relevant documents are served on both sides so that the stage is reached when the case is ready for hearing.

Appearance

[6.38] As indicated, in response to the plenary summons, the defendant must enter an Appearance. The Appearance is a very brief document which is, quite simply, an instruction to the Court that an appearance should be entered for the defendant and that the defendant intends to defend the claim brought. The appearance also usually indicates the solicitor representing the defendant and the address at which further pleadings may be served, usually the solicitor's office. The claim is then back in the plaintiff's hands.

Statement of claim

[6.39] The next document to be filed by the plaintiff is, usually, the Statement of Claim which provides in much more detail the circumstances surrounding the accident which is the subject matter of the case. The Statement of Claim is in a standard format as with the Plenary Summons, but in this instance the amount which must be filled in by the plaintiff is considerably greater. The relevant part which a barrister will draft would, in our example, be something along the following lines.

THE HIGH COURT

1996 No. 10,000P

Between **Raymond Byrne** Plaintiff

and **McCutcheon Glass Company Limited** Defendant

1. The plaintiff, maintenance fitter, resides at 2 Sunnybank Terrace, in the City of Dublin.
2. The defendants are a limited liability company having their registered place of business at 23 Glass Lane, in the City of Dublin.
3. On or about the 23rd day of May 1995, the plaintiff suffered severe personal injury, loss, distress and damage while working at an abrasive wheel in the premises of the said defendants when he was struck in the eye by a fragment of glass which projected from the said abrasive wheel.
4. At the time of the said accident the plaintiff was the servant or agent of the said defendants, acting in the course of his employment.

5. The said personal injury, loss, distress and damage were caused solely by virtue of the breach of duty, including statutory duty, of the defendants, their servants or agents in or about the care, management and control of the said premises and more particularly the said abrasive wheel.

PARTICULARS OF PERSONAL INJURY

[*In this portion of the Statement of Claim the barrister would insert information as to the extent of the eye injury which would be gleaned from the medical reports obtained by the plaintiff's solicitor. This could be in the form of a number of points relating to the immediate impact of the glass fragments, the extent to which this affected the eye immediately as well as some indication as to the prognosis. In addition, the particulars might add: 'Further adverse sequelae cannot be ruled out', a phrase which allows for subsequent medical information to be taken into account in the claim.*]

PARTICULARS OF SPECIAL DAMAGE

[*In this section the plaintiff will insert those items such as medical expenses and loss of earnings to date which are available. Some aspects of these claims may, however, be left over for further detailing later in the proceedings.*]

PARTICULARS OF BREACH OF DUTY

[*In this section the barrister will include the details of the manner in which it is alleged that the employer was in breach of some obligations which are owed by an employer to an employee in respect of safety in the workplace. The particulars might be as follows:*]

The defendants, their servants or agents, were in breach of duty in that:

1. They failed to provide the plaintiff with a place of work which was reasonably safe in all the circumstances.
2. They failed to provide the plaintiff with plant and machinery which was reasonably safe in all the circumstances.
3. They failed to provide the plaintiff with a system of work which was reasonably safe in all the circumstances.
4. They failed to provide the plaintiff with co-workers who were in the all the circumstances reasonably competent.
5. They exposed the plaintiff to a danger of which they knew, or ought reasonably to have known.
6. They exposed the plaintiff to danger from the said abrasive wheel of which they knew or ought reasonably to have known.

7. They failed to provide the plaintiff with any, or any adequate, training or supervision in relation to the use of the said abrasive wheel.
8. They were in breach of statutory duty and in particular of the provisions of the Safety in Industry Act 1955 and 1980, the Safety in Industry (Abrasive Wheels) Regulations 1982, section 12 of the Safety, Health and Welfare at Work Act 1989 and Part IV of the Safety, Health and Welfare at Work (General Application) Regulations 1993.

In the premises, the plaintiff claims damages in Negligence for severe personal injury, loss, distress and damage.

And the plaintiff claims costs.

And the plaintiff claims interest pursuant to the Courts Act 1981.

[*The names of counsel for the plaintiff will appear here.*]

[6.40] It is clear from this that the language of the Statement of Claim is careful, to what might appear to be an excessive degree. The reader may see many different aspects of this, so they need not be indicated here. It is, however, the particulars of negligence on which we might focus. The reader may notice a certain degree of overlap between the eight different paragraphs of the Statement of Particulars. The point here is that the barrister will wish to ensure that this aspect of the statement of claim is particularly comprehensive, even at the expense of being over-inclusive. In this context, particularly having regard to the Statutes of Limitations 1957 and 1991, it is better to be safe than sorry.

[6.41] It may be noted also there are also references to legislation, both primary and secondary, in claiming a breach of duty. In this respect, we should note that the primary purpose of the legislation in question is to prevent accidents and ill-health in the factory context by setting down standards which, if broken, may result in a criminal prosecution. However, a barrister will be aware that these statutory provisions are also actionable, that is they may be used in support of a civil claim for personal injuries if it can be shown that the injury in question is attributable, at least in part, to a failure to observe a statutory requirement. This is known as breach of statutory duty.[24]

[6.42] In response to the statement of claim, the defendants' approach may become more complex. One possible step is for the defendants to file a

24. See McMahon and Binchy, *Irish Law of Torts*, 2nd ed (Butterworths, 1990).

pleading known, simply, as the Defence. But they may not be happy with several aspects of the plaintiff's Statement on Claim. A defendant is entitled, under the Rules of the Superior Courts 1986 to seek further information from the plaintiff in respect of the claim being made. This is called seeking further and better particulars of the claim and is an almost automatic procedure in personal injuries actions. The format of the claim for particulars is, usually, a letter to the solicitors for the plaintiff which lists the points in respect of which more detail is required. For example, the precise circumstances of the incident in which the glass fragment struck the plaintiff may be sought; the details of medical expenses, if these are not specified; and the precise provisions of the legislative provisions in respect of which the defendants are alleged to be in breach.

Defence

[6.43] Having received satisfactory replies to these queries (in the absence of which the matter may be brought by way of motion to the High Court for a judge to determine whether the replies were in fact adequate) the defendants may then file a Defence in response to the Statement of Claim. This may be along the following lines.

THE HIGH COURT

1996 No. 10,000P

Between	**Raymond Byrne**	Plaintiff
and	**McCutcheon Glass Company Limited**	Defendant

DEFENCE

1. The alleged accident the subject matter of these proceedings did not occur in the manner alleged or at all.
2. The defendant denies that the premises are a factory within the meaning of the Safety in Industry Act 1955 and 1980, as alleged or at all, or that the provisions of the Safety, Health and Welfare at Work Act 1989 or of the Safety, Health and Welfare at Work (General Application) Regulations 1993 are applicable to the alleged accident the subject matter of these proceedings, as alleged or at all.
3. The defendant denies that the plaintiff was injured in the manner alleged, or at all.
4. The defendant denies that the plaintiff suffered the alleged or any personal injury, loss, distress or damage as a result of the alleged accident or at all.

5. The defendant denies that it was by itself, its servants or agents or any of them guilty of the alleged or any negligence, breach of duty or breach of statutory duty as alleged or at all or in or about the matters alleged or at all.
6. Each and every particular of negligence and breach of duty including breach of statutory duty as alleged against the defendant its servants or agents is denied as if the same was herein set out and traversed seriatim.
7. If the plaintiff suffered the alleged or any personal injury, loss, distress or damage, which is denied, the same was not caused or contributed to as a result of any negligence or breach of duty or breach of statutory duty on the part of the defendant or any of its servants or agents.
8. The plaintiff was guilty of contributory negligence.

[*The names of counsel for the defendant will appear here*.]

[6.44] The above Defence indicates even further perhaps the somewhat stilted style of prose in which the Bar must engage, at least in written form. A cardinal rule of a Defence in civil proceedings is that each and every claim by the plaintiff must be denied. If the case goes to court, the plaintiff will then be obliged to prove each of the allegations contained in the Statement of Claim. If the defendant does not deny a particular claim made by the plaintiff, this is regarded as having been admitted by the defendant. By denying each allegation the defendant is forcing the plaintiff to prove the elements of the claim, a matter of some tactical importance. Thus, the sense of 'overkill' by the defendant in the Defence. It should be noted that the defendant retorted at the end of the Defence by claiming that the plaintiff was guilty of contributory negligence. Again, should the case proceed to hearing, the defendant will be allowed to argue that, even if as employer they were in breach of some obligation to the plaintiff then some action of the plaintiff, such as lack of due care, may at least allow the defendant to be held less than 100% responsible in terms of the amount of compensation payable.

Defence and Counterclaim

[6.45] In certain other cases also the defendant may go on the offensive to an even greater extent. For example, in a dispute over the sale of a car the plaintiff might be the seller who brings a claim for breach of contract against the buyer for non-payment. The buyer might not only put in a defence to such a claim but might also counterclaim against the seller on the basis that the car was defective causing the buyer to pay a certain sum in renting another car. If the defendant's case is believed in court, the defendant may be awarded damages in the sum of the cost of renting the other car, as well as dismissing the plaintiff's claim. This indicates that the defendant may, in a civil case, turn the tables completely.

Pleadings closed

[6.46] When the parties have served all the pleadings which they consider necessary on each other it is said that the pleadings have closed and the case is now ready to be placed in the list of cases for which dates for hearing may be assigned in order of priority. On a regular basis the list of cases which are due for hearing on a specified date or dates are published in a document called the Legal Diary, which is published on a daily basis while the High Court is sitting. Some members of the Bar and many of the larger firms of solicitors subscribe to the Legal Diary in order to keep themselves informed of forthcoming cases in which they are involved.

[6.47] As to the delay between the closing of pleadings and receiving a date for hearing, considerable public disquiet has existed since the early 1980s due to the considerable time lag involved. We discuss this phenomenon elsewhere.[25]

Reply and further pleadings

[6.48] The above example of pleadings have dealt only with the Statement of Claim and Defence in a High Court plenary summons action. It by no means provides a comprehensive view of what the pleading process may involve or the length of time spent prior to a case coming to hearing in relation to the presentation of evidence for either side. In addition to the Statement of Claim and Defence, parties may wish to serve on each other further pleadings. Thus, where in a particular case a completely new issue is raised in the Defence, the plaintiff may serve on the defendant a Reply. And in response to the Reply, the defendant may issue a Rejoinder. This could be followed by a Surrejoinder from the plaintiff, and the process could, conceivably, continue on indefinitely. However, in most cases the Reply will mark the close of pleadings.

Motions in default

[6.49] There are many other pre-trial remedies available to either side in a civil High Court action. As mentioned previously, a party may apply, for example, to Court where there has been failure to comply with some time limit specified by the Rules of the Superior Courts 1986, such as in failing to

25. See para **[4.135]**.

enter an appearance within eight days from service. But, as also indicated, the Court is unlikely to enter judgment in favour of the plaintiff without giving the defendant an opportunity of putting the other side of the case and explaining the delay. There are many occasions in the course of a case proceeding through the court system in which such applications will come before the Court. These are always brought by way of motion to the Court, and must be on notice to the other side in the case. In most cases, these motions involve one side being given a specific period of time within which to file in the Central Office the relevant documents.

Discovery of documents

[6.50] One pre-trial remedy is of particular importance. Subject to certain exceptions, either party is entitled under the Rules of the Superior Courts 1986 to obtain possession of documents within the control of the other party. This process is known as the discovery of documents. In some instances this may simply amount to the exchange of originals which were in the possession of each party, and in such a case there will be no dispute as to the scope of discovery. But over the years there have been many examples of cases in which documents obtained by discovery ('discovered' being used in a somewhat unusual manner in this context) have been the key to success in a case. As indicated, there are limits to what may be sought on discovery. For example, any communications from a legal adviser which was obtained by one party at a time when court proceedings were either contemplated or were already started are privileged from discovery. In addition, one party cannot simply come to court on a 'fishing expedition', claiming that the other side has unnamed documents which would help the applicant's case; the discovery must be in relation to either a named document such as a letter or there must be some, even limited, basis on which something concrete can be identified. Up to the time of the coming into force of the Rules of the Superior Courts 1986, discovery could only be obtained by one party from another party to the proceedings, but now discovery may be obtained from a person who is not involved in the court proceedings provided that that non-party has relevant information.[26]

Interrogatories

[6.51] There are other pre-trial remedies which are also available to either party in High Court civil proceedings, such as interrogatories, by which one party may pose formal questions for answer by another party to proceedings in order further to identify an issue in dispute. The general rule concerning

---

26. See *Tromso Sparebank v Beirne (No 2)* [1989] ILRM 257.

such interrogatories is that the question must be posed in such a way as to admit of a 'yes' or 'no' reply.

Circuit Court: Civil Bill

[6.52] The procedure in civil cases in the Circuit Court is, as indicated earlier, somewhat less complex than in the High Court, bearing in mind the fact that the Court tends to deal with cases of lower monetary value, even if they may very well be important for those involved in the case. The basic originating document in the Circuit Court is the Civil Bill, the document used in the County Courts prior to 1922.[27] The Civil Bill contains the equivalent of the High Court Statement of Claim from the plaintiff. In response, the Circuit Court Rules 1950 provide for the defendant filing a Defence, which is in similar terms to the High Court Defence. There is no further provision for pleadings in the Circuit Court.

District Court: Civil Process

[6.53] In the District Court, the originating document is called the Civil Process, and it usually contains a brief description of the claim made by the plaintiff. There is no provision in the District Court Rules 1948 for any pleadings as such, and certainly not a defence. However, in practice, many solicitors will issue what amounts to a Defence by way of formal letter to the plaintiff. The lack of any formal pleading system in the District Court reflects the fact that in 1924 when it was established it heard cases of a very trivial nature. Since the ceiling on awards was lifted to £5,000 by the Courts Act 1991, however, this lack of formality has created some problems in relation non-consumer cases which are dealt with in the District Court and some changes to the present system would appear to be appropriate.

Compromise or settlement

[6.54] The preceding pages have outlined the formal process required to initiate a civil claim in the different courts. However, it is important to note that the vast majority of cases initiated each year will not require a court hearing: many are in fact compromised or settled before they are due to be heard in the different courts. Indeed, there are countless instances of disputes in which proceedings might not have been initiated but in which a formal letter from a potential plaintiff's solicitor (the well-known 'solicitor's letter') will produce a favourable response from a potential defendant. Of the cases in which such approaches do not produce the desired result, many will be settled quite early on, largely because the initiation of proceedings is sufficient to induce an offer of settlement from the defendant. But even

27. See para **[2.53]**.

where a case has progressed though all the stages referred to above and has been set down for hearing in court, a settlement is quite common even on the day the case is due to be heard: a settlement 'at the door of the court'. In view of the negotiating skill of Irish people in general, and the wish on both parties to maximise their negotiating position, this is hardly surprising.

[6.55] There has been relatively little detailed research done on the rate of settlements in civil litigation in Ireland, but some research has been conducted by the Irish Business and Employer's Confederation (IBEC) concerning personal injuries claims initiated against employers. In a survey of over 2,000 claims notified to IBEC member companies in the period 1989 to 1992, the following were the outcomes:[28]

Outcome	No.	%
Claim withdrawn before court hearing:	115	5
Claim withdrawn during court hearing:	7	0
Out of court settlement:	926	42
Court award in favour of plaintiff:	138	6
Court dismissed plaintiff's claim:	17	1
Claims under negotiation or not settled:	993	45

Table 6.1

It may well be that the low figure for claims being dismissed has increased since the time of that IBEC survey,[29] but it remains that many cases continue to be settled rather than proceed to hearing in court.

[6.56] Many factors go into the negotiation of a settlement, and it is impossible to deal with all the issues that arise in the present context. However, we refer elsewhere to the general context within which personal injuries claims have given rise to substantial legislative changes to encourage the more efficient management of such cases, whether in terms of

28. *Employer/Public Liability Claims for Personal Injury*, Survey Report No 23/93, Research & Survey Unit, Irish Business and Employer's Confederation, November 1993, p 30.

29. It was suggested that, by 1996, more claims for personal injuries were being dismissed in the courts, particularly in connection with 'serial' claimants, that is, those plaintiffs who had initiated a number of claims in their life: see Fitzgerald, 'The Compo Culture', *Business and Finance*, 16 May 1996.

encouraging earlier settlements or facilitating speedier hearings for those which are not destined to be settled.[30]

[4] CRIMINAL PROCEDURE[31]

[6.57] Having discussed the procedures for processing civil claims, we can now proceed to outline the essential elements of criminal procedure. As already mentioned, a crucial distinction here is that most criminal prosecutions are initiated by a State agency, such as the Director of Public Prosecutions or the Garda Síochána.

Summary trial and trial on indictment

[6.58] For many centuries in Ireland, there have been two different procedural methods by which a criminal case comes to trial. The first method, used for relatively less serious criminal cases, is by way of summons, leading to a summary trial. The second method, used in relation to more serious offences, is by way of indictment, leading to a trial on indictment. We have already seen that Article 38 of the Constitution provides that, except in connection with minor offences, a person charged with a criminal offence is entitled to a trial with a jury.[32] Since trial on indictment has traditionally involved trial by jury, the effect of Article 38 is that serious criminal matters are heard in the Circuit Criminal Court or the Central Criminal Court, while minor cases are, in general, heard in the District Court by way of summary trial. We have also seen that the penalties provided for on foot of a trial on indictment are greater than on a summary prosecution, again reflecting constitutional requirements.[33]

[6.59] The distinction drawn in the Constitution between minor offences and offences requiring a jury trial is not easy to fit with the pre-existing common law categorisation of criminal offences. The basic distinction drawn at common law was between felonies, generally the more serious offences and in respect of which a member of a police force could arrest without warrant,[34] and misdemeanours, generally the less serious category and for which an arrest warrant was required. However, while this is the general rule, there are exceptions. Thus, murder is a felony at common law, but

30. See para **[5.10]** and the provisions of the Courts and Court Officers Act 1995.

31. See generally Ryan and Magee, *The Irish Criminal Process* (Mercier Press, 1983).

32. See para **[4.33]**.

33. See para **[5.73]**.

34. Originally, felonies carried the death penalty, though the number of felonies for which this was true gradually reduced in number. The death penalty was formally abolished for all offences in Ireland by the Criminal Justice Act 1990. Conviction for felony also involved forfeiture of property to the Crown, which was abolished by the Forfeiture Act 1870.

assault occasioning actual bodily harm is a misdemeanour under common law and s 47 of the Offences against the Person Act 1861 while assault with intent to rob is a felony under s 23 of the Larceny Act 1916.[35] Moreover, a number of serious offences, such as obtaining by false pretences and fraudulent conversion, are misdemeanours.

[6.60] It should be noted that, since the 1950s in particular, where new criminal offences are created by statute in Ireland, the distinction between felonies and misdemeanours has tended to be disregarded. Instead, the penalties attaching to the offence are specified by reference to whether the charge is to be brought by way of summons or indictment. For example, s 17 of the Criminal Justice (Public Order) Act 1994 creates an offences of demanding money with menaces. s 17(3) of the 1994 Act provides:

> A person guilty of an offence under this section shall be liable -
>
> (a) on summary conviction to a fine not exceeding £1,000 or to imprisonment for a term not exceeding 12 months or to both,
>
> (b) on conviction on indictment to a fine[36] or to imprisonment for a term not exceeding 14 years or to both.

[6.61] This avoidance of the felony-misdemeanour distinction mirrors the introduction in Britain in 1967[37] of the concept of an 'arrestable offence', an offence which carried a possible sentence of imprisonment of five years and for which a member of a police force could arrest without warrant. The Criminal Justice Bill 1996 proposes to introduce the concept of 'arrestable offence' into Irish law, and to abolish the outdated distinction between felonies and misdemeanours, and indeed much of recent criminal law legislation is based on the five year period. An example is the Criminal Justice Act 1984, which introduced new arrest and detention powers in respect of offences carrying a potential punishment of five years imprisonment.

Summary prosecution

[6.62] The initiation of many of the less serious crimes is, in general, a matter for a member of the Garda Síochána, such as offences under the Road Traffic Acts. Other minor offences created by legislation may be prosecuted by other regulatory authorities, for example the Environmental Protection Agency in relation to offences under environmental protection legislation[38]

35. As amended by the Criminal Law (Jurisdiction) Act 1976, s 5.

36. The effect of this is that the person would be liable to an unlimited fine.

37. Criminal Law Act 1967, c 58.

38. See generally the Environmental Protection Agency Act 1992 and Scannell, *Environmental and Planning Law in Ireland* (Round Hall Press, 1994).

or the Minister for Agriculture in connection with the use of prohibited growth promoters in animals.[39]

[6.63] However, it should also be noted that, at common law, any person is empowered to initiate and prosecute a criminal charge by means of a private prosecution. Such a person has the rather ungainly title of common informer and indeed the Garda Síochána frequently operate under this banner in the absence of specific statutory authorisation for initiating prosecutions. This common law right of private prosecution has not, it seems, been affected by the Constitution of Ireland 1937.[40]

[6.64] In relation to a summary prosecution, the procedure is relatively straightforward. A summons is issued by a person authorised by legislation, such as a District Court Clerk,[41] on application (sometimes called the complaint) by, for example, a member of the Garda Síochána who alleges that a named person has committed an offence, for example, driving a motor vehicle with an amount of alcohol in excess of that permitted under s 49 of the Road Traffic Act 1961, as amended. In such a case, the summons contains the allegation of the offence together with information as to the registration number of the vehicle, the owner of the vehicle (who, if the driver, is also the person charged) and the date and location of the alleged offence. This summons is then the basis for the charge being brought to the District Court. There may be other evidence, such as the results of the test conducted by the Medical Bureau of Road Safety on the urine or blood sample which must be provided by the driver of the vehicle under the Road Traffic Acts. The summons is, however, the basic document on which the criminal trial in the District Court will take place and, in general, no further information will be furnished by the prosecution to the defence.[42]

Prosecution on indictment

[6.65] As to trials on indictment the procedure is more complex, both in terms of how it is initiated and in how it is proceeds. The prosecution system in Ireland for trials on indictment is not unitary and is currently divided between three State agencies. In the vast majority of cases, investigations

39. Animal Remedies Act 1993, s 22.

40. See *The State (Ennis) v Farrell* [1966] IR 107; *Cumann Luthchleas Gael v Windle* [1994] 1 IR 525. See Hogan and Whyte, *Kelly: The Irish Constitution*, 3rd ed (Butterworths, 1994), pp 310-2.

41. See the Courts (No 3) Act 1986, enacted to overcome the difficulties under the Petty Sessions (Ireland) Act 1851, identified in *The State (Clarke) v Roche* [1986] IR 619.

42. In exceptional cases, the concept of fair procedures under the Constitution may require that the prosecution furnish the defence with the information on which it proposes to run the case in the District Court: see *Director of Public Prosecutions v Doyle* [1994] 2 IR 286.

into serious crime are conducted by the Garda Síochána, the files collected by them are considered by the Director of Public Prosecutions who determines whether a criminal prosecution is initiated and the Chief State Solicitor[43] then briefs counsel in private practice for the prosecution itself.[44]

[6.66] In connection with their investigative functions, the Garda Síochána have been conferred with extensive legislative powers of arrest and detention.[45] While the courts are reluctant to acknowledge that the Gardaí have an express right to question those arrested and held in custody, this has in effect been conceded, subject to certain safeguards to the right to silence.[46] The right to silence, although indirectly diluted through the effect of the various powers of arrest and detention,[47] remains a key formal feature of the common law accusatorial system, by contrast with the inquisitorial system of the Civil Law jurisdictions of Europe where investigating magistrates are entitled to require answers to questions put to those charged with offences.[48] Although a common law system such as Ireland's professes to be accusatorial rather than inquisitorial, it has been suggested that the extensive powers conferred on the Garda Síochána correspond to the powers of investigating magistrates in the Civil Law jurisdictions, and that the safeguards currently in place in Ireland are not sufficient to prevent vulnerable people from wrongly confessing to crimes.[49] It nonetheless remains that, consistent with the common law tradition, the Garda Síochána continue to investigate while the courts deliberate on guilt or innocence, but in recent years there has been some debate on whether the existing system should be substantially remodelled on Civil Law lines or whether some form of 'intermediate' system be introduced. The Criminal Justice (Drug Trafficking) Act 1996 would appear to envisage such an intermediate system, with increased powers of detention in connection with serious drugs

43. See para **[3.26]**.

44. A unitary system has existed in Britain since the 1980s in the form of the Crown Prosecution Service (CPS), and similar regimes operate in the United States of America in form of the District Attorney system.

45. Eg the Offences against the State Act 1939, the Misuse of Drugs Acts 1977 and 1984 and the Criminal Justice Act 1984.

46. See the Criminal Justice Act 1984 (Treatment of Persons in Custody in Garda Síochána Stations) Regulations 1987 (SI 119/1987). On the constitutional protections available to persons in custody, see *The People (DPP) v Quilligan and O'Reilly (No 3)* [1993] 2 IR 305.

47. It is sometimes stated by the police themselves that confessions obtained by the Garda Síochána account for about 80% of successful criminal prosecutions.

48. See generally Van den Wyngaert et al, *Criminal Procedure Systems in the European Community*, (Butterworths, 1993).

49. See, eg, Irish Council for Civil Liberties, *Interrogation Endangers the Innocent* (ICCL, 1993).

offences, subject to judicial control if the detention is intended to proceed beyond four days.

[6.67] As already indicated, in general the decision whether to prosecute is in the hands of the Director of Public Prosecutions. However, we should also bear in mind the common law right of a common informer to initiate a private prosecution. As far as trials on indictment are concerned, it would appear that a private prosecution can be brought as far as the preliminary examination in the District Court up to the return for trial by the judge of the District Court,[50] but that the matter is in the hands of the Director of Public Prosecutions thereafter.[51]

[6.68] The office of the Director of Public Prosecutions was created by the Prosecution of Offences Act 1974. Up to the 1974 Act, prosecutions on indictment were initiated by the Attorney General and, while the Attorney General retains some functions in criminal matters, the Director of Public Prosecutions now takes the lead role in this respect.[52]

[6.69] In general the Director of Public Prosecutions, like any other prosecuting authority such as the Garda Síochána, has a discretion as to whether to prosecute in an individual case. Where the Director decides not to prosecute, the courts are reluctant to interfere with that decision or order a prosecution to proceed.[53] The precise reasons behind the decisions of the Director as to whether to prosecute are not made public in relation to individual cases, but two general principles can be identified as being the basis for the decision whether to prosecute. First, is there, on the basis of the file presented to the Director by the Garda Síochána, sufficient evidence to indicate that a conviction is likely.[54] The second factor is whether the public interest lies in favour of a prosecution. These two factors will in most

50. On the preliminary examination, see para **[6.70]**.

51. See *The State (Ennis) v Farrell* [1966] IR 107 and *Cumann Luthchleas Gael v Windle* [1994] 1 IR 525.

52. See para **[3.61]** on the 1974 Act.

53. See *H v Director of Public Prosecutions* [1994] 2 ILRM 285, where the Supreme Court refused to order the Director to proceed with a prosecution for sexual offences which the applicant alleged her husband had committed against their children and which the Director had already decided not to prosecute.

54. This generally involves the simple question as to whether the evidence involved is sufficiently credible that a jury would be likely to convict, but in recent years the Director has also been required to consider whether, if there is a very long lapse between the crime and the initiation of the prosecution, the right to a speedy trial and to fair procedures can be upheld. This has occurred, for example, in the context of child sexual abuse cases which, typically, only come to light many years after the event: see, for example, *G v Director of Public Prosecutions* [1994] 1 IR 374.

instances coincide but in exceptional cases, the public interest may militate against a prosecution even where there is some evidence that a conviction is likely. The Director's decision is, in effect, final and as the law stands at present no private prosecution can proceed beyond the District Court without the Director's consent.[55]

Preliminary examination

[6.70] Once the decision is made to prosecute, the person will be brought before the District Court and formally charged. Where the accused is charged with an indictable offence, the Criminal Procedure Act 1967 provides in general for two options: one is that the judge of the District Court may in some instances be empowered to deal with the case summarily; the other is that the judge must otherwise conduct a preliminary examination of the charge.[56]

(a) Indictable offences triable summarily

[6.71] We have already see that the Schedule to the Criminal Justice Act 1951[57] specifies certain offences which, although they may be tried on indictment in one of the higher criminal courts, can be dealt with in the District Court. These are referred to as indictable offences triable summarily. The offences mentioned include certain offences under the Larceny Acts 1861 and 1916, indecent assault, and obtaining goods by false pretences.[58]

(b) Preliminary examination

[6.72] If the indictable offence cannot be dealt with summarily, the Criminal Procedure Act 1967 requires that before the case can proceed to trial, a preliminary examination by a judge of the District Court must take place.[59] The preliminary examination is the successor to the grand jury system by which depositions from all relevant witnesses would be heard by a jury (or until the 1967 Act by the judge of the District Court) and then formally

55. Arising from some criticism of decisions of the Director, specifically in connection with the non-prosecution of some child sexual abuse cases, the Director agreed that, beginning with the year 1996, an annual report on the work of the office would be made to the Oireachtas.

56. One other option is that the accused may plead guilty in the District Court to an offence which cannot be tried summarily in the District Court, in which case the judge of the District Court will send the case forward to the Circuit Criminal Court for sentencing only.

57. As amended by the Criminal Procedure Act 1967 and the Criminal Law (Jurisdiction) Act 1976.

58. For further para **[5.75]**.

59. The Criminal Procedure Act 1967, s 12, provides that the accused may waive the right to a preliminary examination.

committed to writing before the case could proceed to trial.[60] In place of this, s 6 of the 1967 Act requires that the prosecution must provide to the defence all the evidence which the prosecution intends to use at trial. This material, colloquially called the Book of Evidence, includes a statement of the charges, a list of the witnesses it is proposed to call at trial and their statements and a list of exhibits (such as photographs) and any other relevant material such as forensic evidence, including genetic fingerprinting (DNA evidence). It remains permissible under s 7 of the 1967 Act for the defence to examine any prosecution witness by way of sworn deposition, but in many instances this does not take place,[61] and most cross-examination is left to the trial itself. When the Book of Evidence has been served on the defence, the judge must decide whether a sufficient case has been presented to the Court in order to justify sending the case forward for trial. Section 8 of the 1967 Act specifies that, if so satisfied, the judge is required to send the case forward for trial. The case will then be sent forward to either the Circuit Criminal Court or the Central Criminal Court.[62]

Bail

[6.73] The accused person is, usually, entitled to bail,[63] thus being free up to the time of the trial.

Form of indictment

[6.74] The form of most indictments is specified in the Criminal Justice (Administration) Act 1924, which simplified to a great extent the procedural requirements regarding an indictment.[64] The Act also provides that defects in the indictment may be remedied at any time provided that this does not cause an injustice to the defendant.

---

60. See para **[2.51]**. The grand jury system survives in other common law jurisdictions, such as the United States of America.
61. This can be put down in most instances to a tactical decision that the defence does not wish to indicate to the prosecution any possible line of defence that may be taken at trial.
62. See para **[5.81]**.
63. See *The People (Attorney General) v O'Callaghan* [1966] IR 501; *Ryan v Director of Public Prosecutions* [1989] IR 399. The criteria on which bail is granted are politically controversial, and at the time of writing (July 1996) a constitutional referendum to restrict the scope for granting bail has been proposed by the Government.
64. See Ryan and Magee, *The Irish Criminal Process* (Mercier Press, 1983), Appendix B and also the Draft Indictments included in Charleton, *Offences Against the Person* (Round Hall Press, 1992).

[6.75] An indictment for the offence of assault with intent to rob might be in the following form:

> ***The People (at the suit of the Director of Public Prosecutions) v Raymond Byrne***
>
> Circuit Criminal Court, Dublin
>
> Raymond Byrne is charged with the following offence:
>
> [*Statement of offence*]
>
> Assault with intent to rob, contrary to s 23A of the Larceny Act 1916, as inserted by s 23 of the Criminal Law (Jurisdiction) Act 1976.
>
> [*Particulars of offence*]
>
> Raymond Byrne on the 1st day of May 1996 at Glass Lane, in the city of Dublin, robbed Paul McCutcheon of a sum of money in cash.

[6.76] The core of the indictment is the statement of the offences, or counts, which are charged. As can be seen from the example given, each count is in two parts: the statement of the offence and the particulars of the offence. The statement of the offence describes the offence in relatively straightforward language, and where the offence is one created by statute it is necessary to specify the legislation, as amended if appropriate. The particulars of the offence then set out the circumstances in which it is alleged that the defendant committed the offence, but these particulars are not always as specific as the particulars in a civil pleading. In the above example, the date and place of the assault and the allegation that there was an intent to rob may be specified as having taken place on a particular date. However, in the case of murder, the precise date may be unknown so that the particulars may state 'on a date unknown'. This is an acceptable form of particulars.

Arraignment

[6.77] It is not until an accused has been brought before the court of trial that the formal reading of the indictment is made. This is called the arraignment, and involves the calling of the person before the Court, reading the indictment and asking the accused whether he or she pleads guilty or not guilty. If the accused pleads not guilty at this stage,[65] a jury must be empanelled to hear the case.[66]

---

65. The accused may withdraw a plea of guilty entered in the District Court and plead not guilty in the trial court.

66. On the right to trial with a jury, see para **[4.33]**.

Guilty plea

[6.78] If the accused has pleaded guilty, the trial judge will impose sentence on the accused. Many factors may lead the accused to plead guilty, though in general the crucial factor may be the expectation that a lesser sentence will be imposed by the judge than would be the case if the accused pleads not guilty but is then found guilty after a full trial. In effect, a plea of guilty carries a discount on what the normal sentence might otherwise be. A person facing a possible five year sentence after a full trial might thus expect a sentence of three years' on a guilty plea. Such discounting will apply even where the offence is particularly serious, such as rape. Where the accused pleads guilty in such a case, the court will generally allow some discount on the basis that the person against whom the offence was committed has been spared the ordeal of giving evidence and having to re-live the rape itself.[67]

[6.79] The decision to plead guilty may also be linked to an informal 'plea bargain' with the prosecution, whereby the accused might decide to plead guilty to certain charges in return for the prosecution declining to proceed with others. Again, the prosecution may decide to accept a plea to save witnesses from the ordeal of testifying to save the substantial cost to the public of a long criminal trial. Clearly, there are many difficult issues that arise in connection with plea bargaining in general, whether for the accused, prosecution counsel or defence counsel. Plea bargaining is a subject that has resulted in much debate in the United States, both in academic circles and in the wider media, though it is rarely discussed in Ireland, so to that extent any debate on its use remains somewhat speculative.[68]

[5] Court Procedure and Rules of Evidence

Adversarial system

[6.80] The system of court procedure that operates in most legal systems, whether common law or civil law, is an adversarial system. This means that the judge in a case plays the role of impartial referee between two sides in the contest that takes place in the courtroom.[69] The two sides, and their lawyers, play what has been described as a 'mutually antagonistic role', but this simply means that each side presents and argues its side. This adversarial system operates in both civil claims and criminal prosecutions.

---

67. See *The People (DPP) v Tiernan* [1988] IR 250.

68. See Ryan and Magee, *op cit*, pp 283-7, for a general discussion of some of the issues involved.

69. On the constitutional obligation of impartiality, see paras **[4.90]-[4.92]**.

Evidence under oath

[6.81] The basis for many court hearings, whether civil or criminal, is that evidence to the Court is given under oath. This is, of course, the requirement in most legal systems, and its origins reflect the religious basis of much of our law. The oath originally had both a spiritual and temporal aspect, but in the context of this book the temporal aspect has more significance. Giving false evidence under oath constitutes the crime of perjury and although prosecutions and convictions for perjury are relatively rare they still constitute as much of a deterrent as any other criminal sanction.

[6.82] In criminal cases, all testimony, including testimony by young persons, must be given under oath,[70] unless there is consent by both the prosecution and the defence that the evidence need not be sworn. In civil proceedings only, there are some instances where sworn testimony is not mandatory, and a trial judge is given a discretion to determine whether unsworn evidence may be given, even if both parties do not consent.[71]

Oral and written testimony

[6.83] A feature of many court proceedings in common law systems is that testimony is given orally rather than in writing. The adversarial system has long regarded oral testimony as having a high probative value, that is as carrying great value in relation to proving a particular assertion. The reason for this lies in the fact that the oral testimony is tested in court, the judge (and where relevant the jury) will have an opportunity to see the reaction of the witness and to test the veracity of the evidence given on that basis.

[6.84] However, while the general rule is that all evidence must be sworn, this does not necessarily require that the evidence be given orally. Sworn evidence may be given in writing, in the form of an affidavit, which is a document that is sworn in solemn form by a witness before a Commissioner for Oaths. Any untrue statements contained in an affidavit are equally subject to the crime of perjury as evidence sworn orally in court.

[6.85] Despite certain legislative changes,[72] it remains the case that the common law court hearing is characterised by oral evidence and oral presentations by the lawyers involved in the proceedings, whether civil or criminal. In criminal trials, the defence lawyers are unlikely to agree in advance that certain crucial evidence is 'agreed', particularly where there is any doubt about its admissibility, for example, where it might be that a

70. See the Criminal Evidence Act 1992, s 27.
71. See *Mapp v Gilhooley* [1991] 2 IR 253.
72. Criminal Justice Act 1984; Courts and Court Officers Act 1995.

crucial witness who handled certain evidence might not be available for the trial. This is particularly so where vital forensic evidence might be at issue.

Rules of evidence

[6.86] The law of evidence has developed over many centuries in an attempt to regulate what may be used for the purpose of proving facts in court. Virtually all court cases require proof of facts, for example that a person was driving a car, that a contract was entered into, that a confession or inculpatory statement admitting to a crime was made. Evidence of a fact is whatever assertion or other matter tends to prove a fact, and the rules of evidence determine whether certain assertions or other matters are admissible as proof in a court of law. We deal here only with a limited number of the rules of evidence to illustrate some of its important features: a more extensive discussion is outside the scope of this work.[73]

[6.87] The general intention behind the rules of evidence is to ensure that any evidence given is reliable and will provide the best opportunity for a true and fair verdict, whether in a civil or criminal trial. While the general rules of evidence are identical for civil and criminal proceedings, it may be that they are applied more vigorously in criminal trials than in civil trials, but even in civil trials the rules of evidence remain important.

[6.88] The general law of evidence can be summed up by the principle that all evidence that is sufficiently relevant to an issue is admissible, while all evidence that is not sufficiently relevant should be excluded. There are two major exceptions to the relevancy principle, namely that evidence of hearsay and evidence of opinion are, in general, inadmissible. The rule against hearsay and against opinion evidence are therefore known as exclusionary rules of evidence. However, to indicate the complexity of the rules of evidence, a number of exceptions to both these exclusionary rules have been developed, so that in certain instances hearsay and opinion evidence is admissible. The most common example of admissible hearsay is the confession or inculpatory admission, and opinion evidence is regularly used in civil and criminal cases where it is given by an expert witness. Because of their importance, we will discuss briefly hearsay and opinion evidence.

Hearsay

[6.89] A common definition of hearsay is that it consists of evidence of a fact not actually perceived by a witness with his or her own senses. In general, the rule against hearsay requires that witnesses may only assert the

73. See generally Fennell, *The Law of Evidence in Ireland* (Butterworths, 1992); *Cross on Evidence*, 7th ed (Butterworths, 1990).

truth of facts or events of which they are aware and are thus prevented from asserting the truth concerning facts or events of which they have no direct knowledge. However, the rule does not always prevent the 'reporting' by a witness of what another person said: what is in general prohibited is giving the evidence of another person and asserting that the statement by the other person is true.

[6.90] An example of an inadmissible hearsay statement arose in a case where a person had been charged with unlawful wounding by throwing a stone at a person.[74] The victim of the wounding gave evidence that a woman had said to him immediately after the stone had been thrown: 'The man who threw the stone went in there', pointing to the defendant's house. The victim's repeating of this woman's statement was inadmissible hearsay because it had been introduced with a view to asserting that the woman's statement was true. By contrast, in a case where a person was charged with unlawful possession of firearms and the defendant was relying on the defence of duress,[75] it was held that he should be allowed to give evidence of threats made to him by a group of alleged terrorists. In that case, the reported threats were admissible because the purpose of referring to them was to establish that they had been made rather than that they were true. No doubt the distinction is a fine one, but what the defendant said about the reported threats is not a question of admissibility of the evidence but about the weight to be attached to it: in that case, the real question is whether the evidence (and the persons giving it) is believable.

[6.91] An effect of the hearsay rule is that, in general, a witness will not be allowed testify to the truth of something where the direct witness has not been called to prove the truth of the fact stated. This has led courts to exclude what might otherwise appear to be apparently reliable evidence. Thus, in a drink driving prosecution, blood or urine samples to establish the blood-alcohol level of the driver must be taken by a registered medical practitioner. Failure to comply with a direction from a registered medical practitioner to supply a blood or urine sample is, itself, an offence. In any subsequent prosecution for refusal to comply with a direction, the evidence of the person who demanded the sample is crucial.

[6.92] How is it proved that the person who later gives evidence in court of requesting the sample and being refused, and who asserts that he or she is a registered medical practitioner, is in fact what they claim to be? Surely the answer is: if they are on the register of medical practitioners, they are

74. *R v Gibson* (1887) 18 QBD 537.
75. *Subramaniam v Public Prosecutor* [1956] 1 WLR 965.

registered. However, a register (whether in the form of a computer printout or any other form) is hearsay in the sense that it is a record of information. If the person who entered the information originally (the registrar at the time of registration) is unavailable to testify that they entered that information, then the register would be inadmissible hearsay as it amounts to an assertion concerning the truthfulness of its contents. This particular hearsay problem has been dealt with by legislation,[76] but it illustrates the difficulty of the hearsay rule in a society where computerised records are relied on in many different contexts but where the hearsay rule may render them inadmissible in the absence of special legislation. In addition to such statutory exceptions, we have already mentioned that numerous exceptions to the hearsay rule have been developed at common law, such as the rule allowing the admissibility of confessions in criminal cases.

Opinion evidence

[6.93] Another exclusionary rule is that which prevents the admissibility of opinion evidence, to which there are a number of exceptions. The most significant exception is that 'expert' witnesses are permitted to give evidence of their opinion on certain matters within their area of expertise. In a civil claim for negligence, for example, a medical consultant may express an opinion as to whether a medical procedure was performed in accordance with current standards of medical practice. In many criminal prosecutions, the evidence of a forensic scientist as to whether the results of certain DNA fingerprinting can connect the defendant to the crime may be crucial. By contrast with the 'expert' witness, the 'ordinary' witness may not express an opinion on any evidence they give.

Legislative alterations to the rules of evidence

[6.94] In addition to the legislative amendments to overcome the extremities of the hearsay rule, in recent years legislation has been enacted to encourage certain items to be agreed in advance of court proceedings, in order to facilitate more efficient discharge of business and prevent unduly lengthy court hearings. Thus, ss 21 and 22 of the Criminal Justice Act 1984 provide for proof of certain matters by way of formal statement and formal admission. It should be noted that these statements and admissions are not sworn statements and they do not relate in any way to the admission of confessions as evidence. Similarly, the Courts and Court Officers Act 1995 provides that rules of court may be made to provide that in civil proceedings concerning personal injuries certain documents, such as medical reports,

---

76. Medical Practitioners (Amendment) Act 1993.

may be exchanged prior to court hearings rather than requiring both sides to call medical consultants in court to confirm the information contained in their reports.[77]

The sequence of witnesses

[6.95] The adversarial system requires that witnesses are called in a certain sequence to give their evidence, rather than there being a free-for-all. In a civil case, the witnesses for the plaintiff are called by the plaintiff's counsel or solicitor, as the case may be, to give evidence. After examination by the plaintiff's lawyer (which is called examination-in-chief), the witness for the plaintiff may then be cross-examined by the lawyer appearing for the defendant. A similar procedure operates in relation to the witnesses for the defendant, if any. In civil cases it is quite common for all parties to give evidence. A similar procedure of examination in chief and cross-examination applies to criminal prosecutions, with the prosecution being required to present its witnesses first. However, in a criminal trial the defendant is not obliged to go into evidence.

The accusatorial nature of criminal trials

[6.96] The procedure in criminal cases is governed to a large extent by the accusatorial nature of the common law criminal justice system. Under the accusatorial approach (as opposed to the inquisitorial system of Civil Law criminal justice systems),[78] where a person is charged with having committed a crime, this must be established by independently gathered evidence and without resorting to evidence from the defendant.

[6.97] This approach is also regarded as an important expression of the presumption of innocence, another central feature of the common law system of criminal justice. The presumption of innocence is modified somewhat by allowing the prosecution to rely on confessions or incriminating statements made by the accused person to, for example, a member of the Garda Síochána while the accused was in custody under a lawful arrest.

[6.98] Under the accusatorial system, the presumption of innocence means that the defendant is entitled to refuse to give evidence in a criminal trial and, at the end of the evidence for the prosecution, the case may go to the

---

77. Courts and Court Officers Act 1995.

78. It should be borne in mind that it is only in criminal proceedings that the Civil Law systems apply an inquisitorial approach in which judges take an active investigative role. In civil proceedings, the Civil Law courts apply the adversarial model, and in such cases the judge plays the non-interventionist role familiar to Common Law systems.

jury who must make a decision without reference in some instances to the defendant's version of events. The defendant is entitled to be acquitted by the jury if the State has failed to prove its case beyond a reasonable doubt. This means that even if the jury considers that the State has made a case which requires some explanation from the defendant, the defendant is still entitled to be found not guilty if there is a reasonable doubt in their mind. It may be noted that in a Civil Law system operating the inquisitorial system, the accused person may be asked a number of questions by an investigating judge, which the accused person is, in general, obliged to answer. While this is quite different from the position in Irish law, it would be a caricature of the Civil Law system to describe it as operating a presumption of guilt. Indeed, the extensive use of confessions evidence in the common law world has led some commentators to note that formal procedural safeguards in the Civil Law system may, in certain respects, give greater protection to the accused person's state of innocence.[79]

[6] JUDGE AND JURY[80]

[6.99] Finally, we make some comments on the function of the judge and jury in civil and criminal cases. As we have already seen,[81] juries in civil cases are quite unusual since the passing of the Courts Act 1988, only being retained in a limited number of High Court cases. In criminal cases, the jury is present in serious trials in the High Court (the Central Criminal Court) and the Circuit Court.

Representative nature of jury

[6.100] The Juries Act 1927 provided that juries were to be drawn principally from panels of property (that is, land) owners, and indeed the level of property which qualified a person for jury service varied from one are of the State to another. The effect of the 1924 Act was that it effectively excluded women from jury service, as very few women qualified under the property-owning requirement. In its 2nd Interim Report, published in 1965, the Committee on Court Practice and Procedure recommended that jury service be available to all adult citizens, including women.[82] The 1965 Report was not acted on, but in *de Burca v Attorney General*[83], the Supreme Court found that the 1924 Act in breach of the requirement of Article 38.5 of

79. See generally Van den Wyngaert, *op cit*.
80. See Devlin, *The Judge* (Oxford University Press, 1979).
81. Para **[4.50]**.
82. The minority report to the 1965 Report of the Committee contains a dissent regarding the place of married women which no longer reflects reality.
83. [1976] IR 38.

the Constitution requiring a jury trial. In particular, the Court found that the property qualifications and effective barring of women from juries deprived such juries of the representative character, that is trial by a representative cross-section of the community, which was essential to the concept of a jury contained in Article 38.5. As a result of the *de Burca* case, s 6 of the Juries Act 1976 now provides that jury members are to be drawn primarily from the electoral roll, that is persons over the age of 18 who are registered to vote in elections to Dáil Éireann. This has resulted in an increasing number of young people and women forming the juries which sit in criminal and civil cases.

Unqualified, ineligible, disqualified and excused persons

[6.101] The 1976 Act also provides that certain persons are not qualified, are ineligible or are other disqualified to sit on juries s 6 of the 1976 Act provides that persons on the electoral roll over the age of 70 are not qualified to serve on juries. Section 7 of the 1976 Act provides that certain named persons listed in Part I of the First Schedule to the Act are ineligible to serve. These include the President of Ireland, judges or former judges, coroners, the Attorney General and members of his staff, the Director of Public Prosecutions and members of his staff, barristers and solicitors practising as such, court officers, court stenographers, members of the Garda Síochána, prison officers, probation officers, persons employed in a forensic science laboratory, members of the Defence Forces, persons who because of an insufficient ability to read, deafness or other permanent infirmity are unfit to serve and any person suffering from a mental illness or disability as a result of which they are either resident in a hospital or are regularly attended for treatment by a doctor. Section 8 of the 1976 Act provides that a person is disqualified from jury service if they have at any time been sentenced to a term of imprisonment for five years or more or, within the preceding ten years, been sentenced to a term of imprisonment of three months. Section 9 of the 1976 Act authorises a County Registrar to excuse any person from jury service, provided the person meets certain criteria. Certain persons listed in Part II of the First Schedule to the Act are excusable as of right. These include members of either House of the Oireachtas, members of the Council of State, the Comptroller and Auditor General, the Clerk of Dáil Éireann, the Clerk of Seanad Éireann, a person in Holy Orders, a regular minister of any religious denomination or community, a vowed member of a religious order living in a monastery, convent of other religious community, whole-time students, ships masters, aircraft pilots and persons between the age of 65 and 70. The list also includes the following professional persons if actually practising: doctors, dentists, nurses, midwives, veterinary surgeons and pharmacists. Various other categories are excusable as of right provided that it is certified that their functions cannot reasonably be performed by another person or postponed. These include a member of the staff of either House of the Oireachtas, Heads of Government Departments and other civil servants, chief executive officers and employees of local authorities, health boards and harbour authorities, school teachers and university lecturers. In addition, s 9 of the 1976 Act also excuses as of right persons who have served on a jury within the preceding three years or who have been excused by a judge at the conclusion of a previous period of service for a period that has not ended. It also provides that the County Registrar or the trial judge may also excuse any other person if satisfied there is 'good reason' for so excusing the person. Finally, s 9(8) provides that, at the conclusion of a case 'of an exceptionally exacting nature', the trial judge may excuse the jury members from jury service 'for such period as the judge may think fit.'

Selection of jury

[6.102] Section 11 of the 1976 Act requires each County Registrar to draw up a panel of jurors for each court from the electoral roll: this is referred to as empanelling of jurors. s 12 provides that each person on the panel is then summoned to appear in court on a named date and any dates thereafter. Failure to appear on the date or dates in question is an offence, for which penalties are specified in s 34 of the Act. Section 15 provides that, on the date set for selection of a jury or juries from the panel, the method of selection is by 'balloting in open court'. This generally involves the selection of names from a box and each name is called out in court.

[6.103] Jury members may be challenged by any party in civil or criminal proceedings. Such challenges can be either 'without cause shown', that is where no reason to the objection is given, or 'for cause shown', where a reason must be advanced. Section 20 of the 1976 Act provides that, in both civil and criminal cases, seven jurors may be challenged without cause, while s 21 provides that there is no limit to the number that may be challenged for cause. It may be noted that the often lengthy pre-trial challenges to jurors in civil and criminal trials which occasionally occur in the courts of the United States of America are not a feature of jury trials in this jurisdiction or in those of Northern Ireland or England.

[6.104] The number of jury members in civil and criminal cases is not formally stated as 12, but this has been the tradition for many centuries.[84] Sections 17 to 19 of the 1976 Act prescribe the form of oath or affirmation

84. See also the provisions on majority verdicts, para **[6.111]**.

required of each jury member. In a criminal case, each jury member must swear as follows:

> I will well and truly try the issue whether the accused is (or are) guilty of the offence (or the several offences) charged in the indictment preferred against him (or her or them) and a true verdict give according to the evidence.

[6.105] In a civil claim, the oath required is as follows:

> I will well and truly try all such issues as shall be given to me to try and true verdicts give according to the evidence.

Having been sworn, a foreman is selected by the jury members. The foreman acts as an informal chairperson of the jury. It should be noted that the deliberations of the jury are confidential and judges have often emphasised the secrecy of jury deliberations, even after a trial has been completed.[85]

Judge to direct jury on legal issues

[6.106] One of the judge's principal functions in a jury trial is to ensure that no inadmissible evidence is introduced and that the lawyers do not breach any of the relevant procedural rules. In addition, the judge must direct the jury on any points of law that arise. In civil cases, it may be to explain to the jury what amounts to defamation in law, while in a criminal case it may be to explain the ingredients of murder so that they can arrive at a verdict which conforms to that rule, whether the verdict is guilty or not guilty. At the end of the case in a civil or criminal case, it is also conventional for the judge to summarise the evidence given in Court and indicate to the jury its obligation to arrive at a verdict in accordance with the evidence and not on the basis of any impression they might have obtained from any other source. In summary, therefore, the judge rules on the law while the jury gives the verdict in the case.

Judge directing verdict

[6.107] However, in some instances the role of legal arbiter also allows the judge a more significant function. For example, in a civil case, if the judge considers that there is no basis on which the jury could find for the plaintiff the judge may withdraw the case from the jury and enter judgment for the defendant. The plaintiff can, of course, appeal such a decision. Once the judge allows the case to go to the jury, he or she cannot, however, instruct them to find for the plaintiff or defendant; that is a matter for the jury.

---

85. Eg the judgment of O'Flaherty J in *O'Callaghan v Attorney General* [1993] 2 IR 17. While newspaper interviews with jury members remain a rarity in Ireland, there have been some cases where the confidentiality of the jury room has been broken in recent years.

[6.108] In a criminal trial, the equivalent rule allows the judge to withdraw a case from the jury and direct them to find the accused not guilty, where the judge has arrived at the conclusion that no jury could reasonably convict the defendant. By contrast with a civil case, the prosecution has no power to appeal such a direction to the jury to find the accused not guilty.[86] Once the judge decides to let the case go to the jury, he or she cannot direct the jury to find the accused guilty; again, that is a matter for the jury.

[6.109] Anecdotal evidence from practitioners would appear to indicate that some judges will 'sway' a jury in a particular direction, whether in civil or criminal cases. While hard evidence on this is difficult to come by, there have been some instances in which, for example, a trial judge who emphasised the strength of the prosecution case in a criminal trial was held not to have overstepped the line into the jury's domain.[87] However, more common are cases where convictions are overturned where they appear to have resulted form overly robust directions by the trial judge to the jury.

Scope of jury's decision-making

[6.110] In the Irish legal system the jury in a civil case is empowered not merely to determine the liability issue but also to determine the level or quantum of damages to be awarded to a successful plaintiff. Of course, any such verdicts are subject to appeal. Nonetheless, the allegedly widely varying levels of such awards in personal injuries cases was one of the grounds on which it was successfully argued in 1988 that jury trial in such civil cases be abolished.[88] As for criminal trials, we have already seen that the jury determine whether a person is convicted or acquitted; but it for the trial judge in a criminal trial, rather than the jury, to determine the appropriate sentence to be imposed on the convicted person. This may be contrasted with other common law systems, in which certain sentencing decisions are within the province of the jury; thus, in certain states of the United States of America, the juries determine whether the death penalty should be imposed in the particular circumstances of a capital case.

Majority verdicts

[6.111] In a civil action, s 95 of the Courts of Justice Act 1924 provides that the verdict may by reached by a majority of nine of the twelve members. In a criminal case, s 25 of the Criminal Justice Act 1984, which introduced majority verdicts in criminal cases for the first time, provides that a verdict

86. See para **[7.50]**.
87. See, eg, *The People (DPP) v Doran* (1987) 3 Frewen 125.
88. See para **[5.10]**.

may be given where ten of the members are agreed on the verdict. Special safeguards are built into the 1984 Act requiring the trial judge for example to be satisfied that the jury has considered the case for a reasonable period of time, and not less than two hours.[89]

Trial by judge alone

[6.112] In the large number of civil cases in particular where there is no jury, of course, the judge is both the legal arbiter and the person with the responsibility to arrive at the verdict. It is this function which a judge performs in delivering written judgments, and with which students must become familiar in their study of law.[90]

89. The constitutional validity of s 25 was upheld in *O'Callaghan v Attorney General* [1993] 2 IR 17.

90. See Ch 12 on the importance of precedent.

Chapter 7

The Appellate Jurisdiction of the Courts

[1] INTRODUCTION

[7.01] In Chapter 5 we described the original or first instance jurisdiction of the courts in civil and criminal matters. It is also a feature of the court system that the decisions of a court may be appealed to a higher court. As with Chapter 4, we first discuss the appellate jurisdiction of the courts in civil cases and then proceed to the appellate jurisdiction in criminal cases. We then note that an extensive appellate jurisdiction arises in connection with appeals from adjudicative bodies other than courts.[1] Finally, we also consider the arrangements under which the Court of Justice of the European Communities may hear appeals form the courts in Ireland as well as from other adjudicative bodies.[2]

Constitutional setting

[7.02] In relation to the courts of local and limited jurisdiction, Article 34.3.4° of the Constitution provides that they are to have 'a right of appeal as may be determined by law.' In relation to the High Court, Article 34.4.3° provides that the Supreme Court has appellate jurisdiction from all decisions of the High Court 'with such exceptions and subject to such regulations as may be prescribed by law'.[3] These general provisions have been greatly amplified by the Courts of Justice Act 1924 and the Courts (Supplemental Provisions) Act 1961, as amended,[4] and other legislative provisions.

Two forms of appeal

[7.03] The forms of appeal may be divided into two general types.

1. De novo *hearing*

[7.04] First, there are some instances where either party may seek to have the case, whether it is civil or criminal, reheard in full in a higher court. This is called a hearing *de novo*, and as its name signifies this form of appeal involves a complete rehearing of the case to the extent that it is as if the first

---

1. On the functions of such bodies, see Ch 8.
2. On European Community law, see Ch 16.
3. See para **[7.24]**.
4. See generally Delany, *The Courts Acts 1924-1991* (Round Hall Press, 1993).

hearing in the lower court had not taken place at all. In other words, the hearing *de novo* is conducted as if it was a first instance hearing. Such appeals are possible in connection with cases heard at first instance in the District Court or the Circuit Court. Thus, in a *de novo* hearing in the Circuit Court on appeal from the District Court, the case will be heard 'from start to finish' including any oral evidence from witnesses. The advantage of a *de novo* hearing is that it is an opportunity for a 'second bite at the cherry' in the Circuit Court. There are, however, some limits on the appellate court's powers in such instances. Thus, again in a *de novo* hearing in the Circuit Court on appeal from the District Court, while the Circuit Court may reach a decision different to that in the District Court, the Circuit Court is limited to the maximum powers conferred on the District Court, whether in civil or criminal matters.

2. Appeal on point of law

[7.05] The second form of appeal is an appeal on a point of law. This is a more limited form of appeal, and involves a resolution by the higher appeal court of some issue of law rather than a complete rehearing of the entire case. Two important and connected points should be noted concerning the functions of an appellate court when hearing an appeal on a point of law. It is clear that a complete rehearing must be different in certain respects to a hearing on a point of law. The difference is in relation to the finding of facts made by the court whose decision is under appeal. The appellate court does not hear any witnesses, but is given a transcript of the evidence as taken by the stenographer at the trial hearing. In examining the transcript the appellate court will, of course, be able to ascertain whether the findings of fact made by the trial court have some foundation in the evidence which was given. But once there is a foundation in the evidence given, the appellate court will not generally interfere with the findings of fact made in the lower court.

[7.06] The rationale for this has been explained on many occasions. This is that the trial court will have had an opportunity to see the witnesses give their evidence and to detect the nuances of human reaction to examination and cross-examination which may not be apparent from a transcript, such as a hesitation in answering a particular question. The appellate court will, therefore, leave intact what are called the primary findings of fact. There is, however, another category of findings which the appellate court does have certain control over; these are what are called secondary findings. These are the findings of the trial court which arise by way of inference from the primary findings, and they do not depend on an assessment of the witness's candour in giving evidence.

(a) Findings of primary fact

[7.07] In a case, the trial court might decide to rely on the evidence of one particular witness and not accept the evidence of another. This is, in effect, a finding of primary fact which will, in general, not be interfered with by an appellate court, even if, looking at the transcript, it feels that the evidence of the witness whose testimony was not accepted appeared plausible. If the issue is one of plausibility and there are two possible versions of what happened but the trial judge relies on one instead of another, the appellate court will not generally interfere with that decision.[5] However, there are some exceptional circumstances in which an appellate court would reverse the findings of primary fact by a trial court. This would only arise where the evidence in the trial court was so overwhelmingly in one direction that the trial judge, in relying on evidence that was in the other direction, came to conclusions that could not be upheld.[6]

(b) Findings of secondary fact

[7.08] By contrast to findings of primary fact, the trial judge may draw a particular inference from the evidence given; this is a finding of secondary fact. On an appeal, the appellate court may consider that this inference is not warranted in the circumstances and in that situation the secondary finding can be overturned and a different conclusion reached.

[7.09] This was the position in *Hanrahan v Merck Sharp & Dohme Ltd.*[7] In that case, the plaintiffs, who were dairy farmers, had sued the defendant, a pharmaceutical company, claiming that emissions from the company's factory had caused them, and their farm animals, to suffer various respiratory illnesses. The plaintiffs relied on various items of evidence to support this claim, including that of local people who testified as to noxious smells in the vicinity of the defendant's factory at the same time that they saw animals in distress. Other evidence included the opinion of a specialist in respiratory illnesses who had treated John Hanrahan, one of the plaintiffs, and who testified that, in his opinion, if there were fumes and chemicals present in the atmosphere the balance of probabilities favoured the conclusion that John Hanrahan's lung disease could be attributed to a toxic substance. In its defence, the company accepted that the plaintiffs and their animals had suffered illness but that these were not connected with factory. The company presented detailed scientific evidence of readings taken on the plaintiffs' farm which aimed to show in particular that, while there were greater concentrations of certain acid vapours in the plaintiffs' soil, any emissions were well within accepted guidelines and could not have affected the health of the plaintiffs or their farm animals.

5. See *Northern Bank Finance Corp Ltd v Charlton* [1979] IR 149, where the Supreme Court declined to overturn findings of primary fact by the High Court trial judge in that case. See also *Browne v Bank of Ireland Finance Ltd* [1991] 1 IR 431; *Hay v O'Grady* [1992] 1 IR 210.

6. See *M v M* [1979] ILRM 160 and *Norris v Attorney General* [1984] IR 36, *per* Henchy J; *In re DG, an Infant; OG v An Bórd Uchtála* [1991] 1 IR 491.

7. [1988] ILRM 629.

[7.10] The High Court judge concluded that the plaintiffs had failed to prove their case. As to the specialist's opinion, the judge noted that the plaintiffs' family doctor had not been called to give evidence for them and that this failure weakened the specialist's opinion. On the illness and abnormalities in their animals, the judge concluded that the company's scientific evidence indicated that there was no connection between the emissions and these illnesses. The plaintiffs appealed to the Supreme Court and were largely successful in having the High Court decision reversed. The Supreme Court took the view that the High Court judge should have given less priority to the abstract *ex post facto* scientific evidence and given more weight to the direct sensory evidence of locals and the opinion expressed by the specialist. Delivering the only judgment in the Supreme Court, Henchy J stated:[8]

> "[T]he scientific evidence ... even if accepted in full... only shows what *could* or *should* have happened in the way of damage by toxic emissions. In the light of what *did* happen in the way of toxic damage, I consider that the defendant's evidence could not be held to rebut the plaintiff's case. Theoretical or inductive evidence cannot be allowed to displace proven facts. It was proven as a matter of probability that John Hanrahan suffered ill-health as a result of toxic emissions from the factory... And there was a volume of uncontroverted evidence given by eyewitnesses that animals were seen and heard to be ill and in distress at a time when the observer was experiencing foul chemical smells or weeping eyes or irritated skin, which could have been caused only by the factory. It would be to allow scientific evidence to dethrone fact to dispose of this claim by saying, as was said in the judgment under appeal, that there was 'virtually no evidence in this case of injury to human beings or animals which had been scientifically linked to any chemicals emanating from the defendants factory.' "

On this basis, the Supreme Court was prepared to draw different inferences from the evidence and arrive at a different conclusion to that of the High Court judge in this case.

[7.11] Similarly, where the trial judge has drawn factual inferences from the agreed evidence and there are no questions concerning the candour or the plausibility of the witnesses who gave the evidence, the Supreme Court may be prepared to reverse the findings of the High Court judge.[9]

8. *Ibid*, at 644-5. Finlay CJ and Hederman J concurred with the judgment delivered by Henchy J.

9. See *Mullen v Quinnsworth Ltd (No 2)* [1991] ILRM 439; *Coleman v Clarke* [1991] ILRM 841; *Best v Wellcome Foundation Ltd* [1993] 3 IR 421.

[2] Appellate Jurisdiction in Civil Cases

Claim initiated in the District Court

[7.12] For claims heard at first instance in the District Court, both forms of appellate options are available. Either party may obtain a hearing *de novo* in the Circuit Court, and the decision of the Circuit Court is, in general, final and may not be further appealed. Alternatively, either party may appeal on a point of law to the High Court, in which case a further appeal on a point of law to the Supreme Court is also possible. We should also note that, in the context of a claim involving European Community law, an appeal to the Court of Justice may also arise, but we discuss that issue separately.[10]

(a) Hearing de novo in Circuit Court

[7.13] In general, an appeal lies to the Circuit Court from all decisions of the District Court in civil matters,[11] subject to quite limited exceptions.[12] Under the present statutory arrangements, therefore, virtually all decisions of the District Court in civil claims may be appealed for a *de novo* hearing in the Circuit Court.[13] However, it would seem that, provided some form of appeal mechanism remains open, such as an appeal on a point of law, it would be permissible to restrict the present generous arrangements for *de novo* appeals.[14] The decision of the Circuit Court judge on appeal from the District Court is 'final and conclusive and not appealable'.[15]

(b) Appeal on point of law by case stated to High Court

[7.14] The second form of appeal, an appeal on a point of law, lies from the District Court to the High Court. The form in which the appeal on a point of

---

10. On the appellate jurisdiction of the Court of Justice, including the likelihood of a case begun in the District Court being referred to the Court of Justice, see para **[7.54]**.
11. Courts of Justice Act 1924, s 84 as amended by the Courts of Justice Act 1936, s 57.
12. For example, the Extradition Act 1965, s 47(5).
13. Although the Courts of Justice Act 1924, s 84 does not expressly state that the appeal to the Circuit Court involves a *de novo* hearing of the case, s 83 of the 1924 Act (since replaced by the Courts (Supplemental Provisions) Act 1961, s 52) provided for an appeal on a point of law by case stated from the District Court to the High Court. This indicated an intention to provide for a different form of appeal in s 84. See Delany, *op cit*, at p 40.
14. In *Murphy v Bayliss*, Supreme Court, unrep, 22 July 1976 the Court held that, although the Extradition Act 1965, s 47(5) precluded a hearing *de novo* in the Circuit Court after a District Court hearing under the section, this did not prohibit an appeal on a point of law by way of case stated to the High Court. O'Higgins CJ commented that a provision which prevented some type of appeal would seem to be in conflict with Article 34.3.4° of the Constitution.
15. Courts of Justice Act 1924, s 84 as amended by the Courts of Justice Act 1936, s 57. The finality of the Circuit Court's decision on appeal may be subject to judicial review by the High Court under Article 34.3.1° of the Constitution: see *Tormey v Ireland* [1985] IR 289: para **[15.109]**.

law takes place is by means of a case stated. Such an appeal can be made either party while the case is still in progress in the District Court, referred to as a consultative case stated,[16] or else at the end of the District Court hearing, when the judge has made a final determination in the case.[17] Either party to the civil proceedings can request the judge of the District Court to refer any question of law to the High Court for determination in this way, and the point of law must be so referred unless the judge considers the request frivolous.[18] The refusal of a case stated may be subject to judicial review.[19]

[7.15] In form, a 'case stated' consists of a written document which includes the question or questions of law for determination by the High Court. A case stated will contain a recitation of the facts as found by the District Court judge and will end with a question being posed, which must allow of a 'Yes' or 'No' answer. The question or questions will be put in the following manner: 'On the basis of the foregoing findings of fact, was I correct in law in concluding that ... ?' The question is put in the first person because, in formal terms, it is put to the High Court by the judge of the District Court. However, in practice the content of the case stated document is prepared by agreement between the lawyers representing both parties and this document is then presented to the judge to be 'signed and stated'.

[7.16] The case stated is then transmitted to the High Court, where a hearing on the point or points of law raised will occur. At this hearing, there will be no oral evidence, there being only arguments by both parties concerning the points of law raised. The High Court judge will then give his or her decision on the points of law raised, in effect giving a 'Yes' or 'No' answer to each question posed in the case stated. On the basis of these answers, the case is returned to the District Court for a final determination in the matter, which must of course be in accordance with the view expressed by the High Court. Since the 'case stated' mechanism involves the remittal of the case from the High Court to the District Court, it may be said that the case remains in the District Court at all times, since the formal final order will be made by the judge of the District Court who sent the case stated to the High Court. In that respect, the case stated differs from the *de novo* hearing; where the Circuit Court makes a decision on appeal after a *de novo* hearing, the final court order is made in the Circuit Court and the case is not in any way returned to the District Court.

---

16. Courts (Supplemental Provisions) Act 1961, s 52 replacing the Courts of Justice Act 1924, s 83.
17. Summary Jurisdiction Act 1857, s 2 as extended by the Courts (Supplemental Provisions) Act 1961, s 51. In this instance, the application for the cases stated must be made within 14 days of the decision of the District Court.
18. See *Sports Arena Ltd v O'Reilly* [1987] IR 185.
19. See *The State (Turley) v Ó Floinn* [1968] IR 245.

(c) Further appeal on point of law to Supreme Court

[7.17] One important difference may be noted between the consultative case stated from the District Court and the case stated where there has been a final determination in the District Court. On a consultative case stated, the decision of the High Court can be appealed from the High Court to the Supreme Court, but only where the High Court judge grants leave (that is, permission) to appeal.[20] By contrast, on a case stated to the High Court after a final determination of the District Court, a further appeal lies to the Supreme Court without the need to seek leave to appeal from the High Court.[21] For this reason, the appeal after a final determination is more commonly used.[22]

[7.18] Figure 7.1 provides an outline of the appeal process from the District Court.

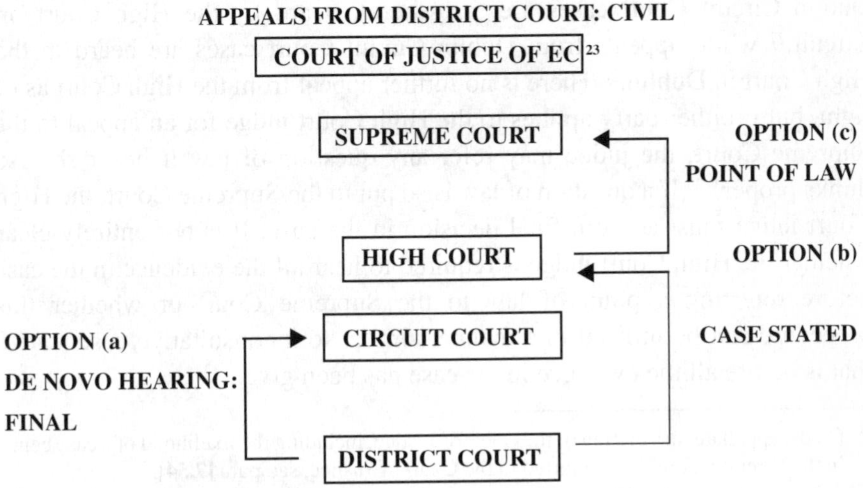

Figure 7.1

Claim initiated in the Circuit Court

[7.19] For claims heard at first instance in the Circuit Court, both forms of appellate option are available, as with claims begun in the District Court.

20. Courts (Supplemental Provisions) Act 1961, s 52(2). In *Minister for Justice v Wang Zhu Jie* [1993] 1 IR 426, this restriction was held to be within the limitations on the Supreme Court's appellate jurisdiction envisaged by Article 34.4.3° of the Constitution.
21. Summary Jurisdiction Act 1857, s 2 as extended by the Courts (Supplemental Provisions) Act 1961, s 52. See *Attorney General (Fahy) v Bruen* [1936] IR 750.
22. See Delany, *op cit*, p 180, citing Ryan and Magee, *The Irish Criminal Process* (Mercier, 1983), p 417.
23. See para **[7.52]**.

However, there are some differences in the detail. Either party to a Circuit Court action may obtain a hearing *de novo* in the High Court, and the decision of the High Court may be further appealed to the Supreme Court in some instances. Alternatively, either party in a Circuit Court action may appeal on a point of law to the Supreme Court. Again, we note here that, in the context of a claim involving European Community law, an appeal to the Court of Justice may also arise, but we discuss that issue separately.[24]

(a) Hearing de novo in High Court

[7.20] In general, an appeal lies to the High Court from all decisions of the Circuit Court in civil matters.[25] Under the present statutory arrangements, therefore, virtually all decisions of the Circuit Court in civil claims may be appealed for a *de novo* hearing in the High Court.[26] Appeals from non-Dublin Circuit Court cases are, in general, heard by the High Court on Circuit,[27] while appeals from Dublin Circuit Court cases are heard in the High Court in Dublin.[28] There is no further appeal from the High Court as of right, but if either party applies to the High Court judge for an appeal to the Supreme Court, the judge may refer any question of law if he or she 'so thinks proper'.[29] If a question of law is so put to the Supreme Court, the High Court judge must adjourn final decision in the case. It is not entirely clear whether the High Court judge is required to hear all the evidence in the case before referring a point of law to the Supreme Court or whether this procedure can be utilised in a manner similar to a consultative case stated, that is before all the evidence in the case has been given.[30]

---

24. On the appellate jurisdiction of the Court of Justice, including the likelihood of a case begun in the Circuit Court being referred to the Court of Justice, see para **[7.54]**.

25. Courts of Justice Act 1936, s 38 as carried forward by Courts (Supplemental Provisions) Act 1961, ss 22, 23 and 48 is the principal provision concerning appeals to the High Court from the Circuit Court. See also s 37 of the 1936 Act, which deals with appeals from Circuit Court actions in which no oral evidence is heard. In addition, s 31 of the 1936 Act deals with other instances, not falling within ss 37 or 38, where a decision of the Circuit Court is final.

26. Unlike the Courts of Justice Act 1924, s 84, which concerns appeals from the District Court to the Circuit Court (see para **[7.13]**), the Courts of Justice Act 1936, s 38 expressly states that the appeal from the Circuit Court to the High Court involves a rehearing of the action.

27. On the arrangements for the High Court on Circuit, see para **[4.51]**.

28. Courts of Justice Act 1936, s 38(1).

29. Courts of Justice Act 1936, s 38(3).

30. The majority decision of the Supreme Court in *Dolan v Corn Exchange* [1975] IR 315 suggests that all evidence must be heard by the High Court judge before the question of law is posed for the Supreme Court, thus precluding the High Court from making further findings of fact when the case is returned. However, this view is at variance with the later majority decision of the Supreme Court in *Doyle v Hearne* [1987] IR 601: see n 32.

(b) Appeal on point of law by case stated to Supreme Court

[7.21] The second form of appeal, on a point of law, lies from the Circuit Court to the Supreme Court. As with the appeal from the District Court to the High Court, the form the appeal takes is by case stated. If a question of law is so put to the Supreme Court, the Circuit Court judge must adjourn final decision in the case.[31] It is not clear, however, whether the Circuit Court judge is required to hear all the evidence in the case before referring a point of law to the Supreme Court or whether this procedure can be utilised in a manner similar to a consultative case stated, that is before all the evidence in the case has been given.[32] The form of the case stated is similar to that where the District Court refers a point of law to the High Court on case stated,[33] and as in that situation, where the Supreme Court gives its decision on the questions of law posed, the case is remitted to the Circuit Court for a final determination in accordance with the findings made by the Supreme Court.

[7.22] Figure 7.2 provides an outline of the appeal process from the Circuit Court.

31. Courts of Justice Act 1947, s 16.

32. We have already noted that, in relation to the similarly worded provisions of the Courts of Justice Act 1936, s 38(3), the majority decision of a three-judge Supreme Court in *Dolan v Corn Exchange* [1975] IR 315 suggests that all evidence must be heard by a High Court judge before a question of law is posed for the Supreme Court, thus precluding the High Court from making further findings of fact when the case is returned. A similar view on s 16 of the 1947 Act was expressed by another three-judge Supreme Court in *Corley v Gill* [1975] IR 313. However, a later 3-2 majority decision of a five-judge Supreme Court in *Doyle v Hearne* [1987] IR 601 held that the correct interpretation of s 47 was that a Circuit Court judge could adjourn final determination in a case at any time and was not required to wait until all evidence had been heard. Although there is a clear difference of opinion between the *Doyle* majority and the majorities in both *Dolan* and *Corley*, the majority in *Doyle* did not expressly overrule the previous Supreme Court decisions. See also Delany, *op cit*, pp 87-88 and 119-121.

33. See para **[7.15]**.

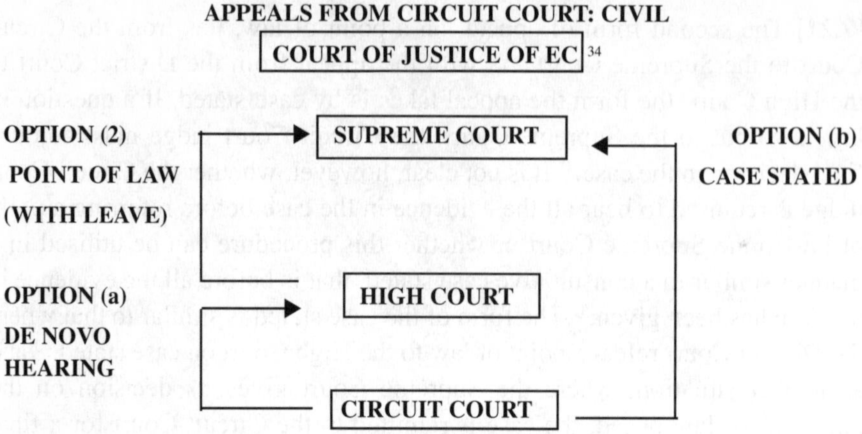

Figure 7.2

Claim initiated in the High Court

[7.23] For claims heard at first instance in the High Court, only one type of appeal is possible, namely an appeal on a point of law. This arises from the fact that the only court available to which an appeal may be made is the Supreme Court. Again, we note here that, in the context of a claim involving European Community law, an appeal to the Court of Justice may also arise, but we discuss that issue separately.[35]

(a) Appeals on point of law to Supreme Court

[7.24] The Supreme Court, being the 'Court of Final Appeal' under Article 34.4.1° of the Constitution, is not, in general a court that hears cases at first instance.[36] It is therefore confined to hearing points of law: there are no witness boxes in the Supreme Court.[37]

Article 34.4.3° and 4° provide:

> 3° The Supreme Court shall, with such exceptions and subject to such regulations as may be prescribed by law, have appellate

34. See para **[7.52]**.
35. On the appellate jurisdiction of the Court of Justice, including the likelihood of a case begun in the High Court being referred to the Court of Justice, see para **[7.54]**.
36. For the exceptional instances in which the Supreme Court is a court of first instance, see para **[5.63]**.
37. In exceptional circumstances, however, the Supreme Court may hear additional evidence, though even in such circumstances this would generally be in written form. On the principles applied by the Court, see *B v B* [1975] IR 54 (decided in 1970); *Dalton v Minister for Finance* [1989] IR 269; *Murphy v Minister for Defence* [1991] 2 IR 161.

> jurisdiction from all decisions of the High Court, and shall also have appellate jurisdiction from such decisions of other courts as may be prescribed by law.
>
> 4° No law shall be enacted excepting from the appellate jurisdiction of the Supreme Court cases which involve questions as to the validity of any law having regard to the provisions of this Constitution.'

It is clear from Article 34.4.4° that the Supreme Court always has jurisdiction to hear appeals from the High Court in constitutional cases. Article 34.4.3° also envisages a further substantial appellate jurisdiction 'from all decisions of the High Court', but this is subject to 'such exceptions and ... regulations as may be prescribed by law.' Although exceptions to the Supreme Court's jurisdiction can therefore be made, it would hardly be constitutional to enact any law that confined its jurisdiction to constitutional cases only. Indeed, the Supreme Court has made plain that any exception to its appellate jurisdiction must be provided for in clear statutory language.[38] At present, it can be said therefore that virtually all decisions initiated in the High Court may be appealed to the Supreme Court, with a number of limited exceptions.

(b) Liability and quantum

[7.25] Where a civil case involves a claim for damages, a typical appeal to the Supreme Court would involve the issue of liability (for example whether the defendant was in breach of a duty of care to the plaintiff in the circumstances which arose) and/or the issue of quantum (whether the amount of compensation awarded was correct). The appeal on liability is very like the appeals on points of law already discussed and the Supreme Court enjoys a wide discretion in relation to the legal issues involved, subject of course to the doctrine of precedent.[39] On the question of quantum, the Supreme Court's function in an appeal is limited to deciding whether the amount was within an acceptable range of damages; if so then the appeal will be dismissed even if the Supreme Court might, as a court of trial (looking at the matter *res integra*), have awarded less (or more).

[7.26] Where the Supreme Court allows the appeal on the liability question, it may order a re-trial of the action in the High Court, which would normally be presided over by a different High Court judge. In effect, therefore, a successful appeal to the Supreme Court results in a hearing *de novo* in the

38. See, eg, *The People (Attorney General) v Conmey* [1975] IR 341; *WJ Prendergast & Son Ltd v Carlow County Council* [1990] ILRM 749; *Minister for Justice v Wang Zhu Jie* [1993] 1 IR 426.

39. See Ch 12.

High Court.[40] Where the Supreme Court considers that the quantum of damages awarded in the High Court was excessive, it may, instead of ordering a re-trial on the issue, assess the correct level of damages itself. This is regarded as being part of its inherent jurisdiction under Article 34.4.3° of the Constitution.[41]

[7.27] Figure 7.3 provides an outline of the appeal process from the High Court.

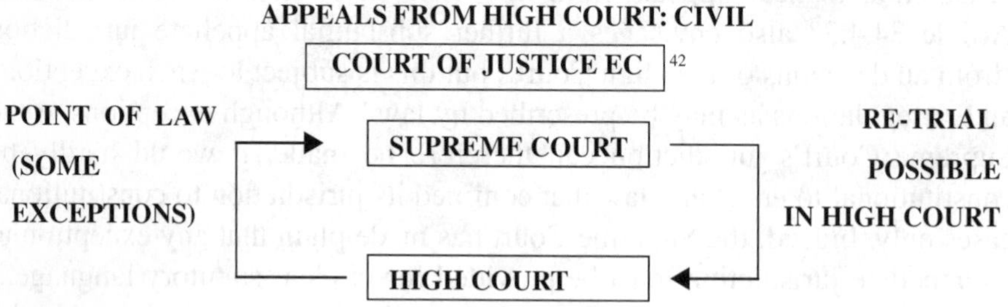

Figure 7.3

[3] Appellate Jurisdiction in Criminal Cases

Summary trials: District Court

[7.28] In respect of the criminal trials conducted summarily in the District Court, both forms of appellate options are available, subject to an important proviso. In general, a hearing *de novo* in the Circuit Court is available only in the event of a conviction in the District Court, and is thus generally only available to the defendant. As with civil cases, the decision of the Circuit Court is, in general, final and may not be further appealed. As to the appeal on a point of law to the High Court, this option is, in general open to both the prosecution and defence and if either appeals to the High Court, a further appeal on a point of law to the Supreme Court is also possible. As with civil

40. See, for example, *Dunne v National Maternity Hospital* [1989] IR 91. Where a re-hearing is ordered, the second trial of the action may take quite a different course. For example, in the second hearing in the *Dunne* case, new witnesses had come forward arising from the publicity attaching to the case, which was a claim in negligence against the defendant hospital. For an account of the re-hearing in this case, which did not proceed to final decision and was ultimately settled without admission of liability, see Kerrigan, *Nothing But the Truth* (Tomar Publishing, 1990).

41. See *Holohan v Donohoe* [1986] IR 45 and *Bakht v Medical Council* [1990] 1 IR 515. This approach is identical to that where the Supreme Court reviews findings of primary and secondary fact by a High Court judge: see paras **[7.09]-[7.11]**.

42. See para **[7.52]**.

cases, we note here that, in the context of a criminal matter involving European Community law, an appeal to the Court of Justice may also arise, but we discuss that issue separately.[43]

(a) Hearing de novo in Circuit Court

[7.29] As indicated, the general rule is that an appeal lies to the Circuit Court from any order made by the District Court in a criminal case, whether the order involves the payment of a fine or the imposition of a sentence of imprisonment, but that this appeal may only be brought 'by the person against whom the order shall have been made'.[44] In other words, the general rule is that only the defendant may bring such an appeal. There are some very limited exceptions to this general rule, by which, in effect the prosecution can appeal an acquittal in the District Court.[45] However, at present, such exceptions would not apply to the majority of criminal offences dealt with in the District Court, such as those under the Road Traffic Acts. Thus, in most cases an acquittal in the District Court cannot be appealed by the prosecution, though this restriction is alleviated by the right to appeal on a point of law by the case stated procedure. As in civil matters, the decision of the Circuit Court judge[46] on appeal by the defendant from the District Court in criminal cases is 'final and conclusive and not appealable'.[47]

---

43. On the appellate jurisdiction of the Court of Justice, including the likelihood of a criminal trial in the District Court requiring a reference to the Court of Justice, see para **[7.54]**.

44. Courts of Justice Act 1928, s 18, as amended by the Courts of Justice Act 1936, s 58.

45. These exceptional provisions, by which the prosecution can appeal an acquittal in the District Court, are found in some legislation dealing with 'regulatory' offences, such as fisheries or safety at work. Thus, the Fisheries (Consolidation) Act 1959, s 310 provides for an appeal by the prosecution against any District Court dismissal of a summons brought under the Act. In *Considine v Shannon Regional Fisheries Board* [1994] 1 ILRM 499, it was claimed that s 310 was invalid because it was in conflict with the requirement in Article 38.1 that criminal trials be 'in due course of law.' However, in the High Court, Costello J dismissed the claim, agreeing with the defendants' contention s 310 of the 1959 Act was valid under Article 34.3.4° of the Constitution, which provides that the appellate jurisdiction of the courts of local and limited may be 'determined by law.' Costello J relied to a large extent on the principles discussed by the Supreme Court in its majority decision in *The People (DPP) v O'Shea* [1983] IR 384 (on the status of *O'Shea* as a precedent, see para **[12.59]**). To the same effect as s 310 of the 1959 Act, see the Safety, Health and Welfare at Work Act 1989, s 52.

46. Note that the Circuit Court, when hearing an appeal from the District Court in criminal matters, comprises a Circuit Court judge alone. It is only where the Circuit Court exercises its first instance criminal jurisdiction that it comprises a judge and jury: see para **[5.80]**.

47. Courts of Justice Act 1928, s 18 as amended by the Courts of Justice Act 1936, s 58. The finality of the Circuit Court's decision on appeal may be subject to judicial review by the High Court under Article 34.3.1° of the Constitution: see *Tormey v Ireland* [1985] IR 289.

(b) Appeal on point of law by case stated to High Court

[7.30] As in civil cases, an appeal on a point of law by case stated lies to the High Court from decisions of the District Court in criminal matters and the relevant statutory provisions apply equally to criminal proceedings. Thus, in criminal cases the appeal can be made either while the criminal case is still in progress in the District Court, referred to as a consultative case stated,[48] or at the end of the District Court hearing, when the judge has made a final determination in the case.[49] Either the prosecution or defence can request the judge of the District Court to refer any question of law to the High Court for determination in this way. and the point of law must be so referred unless the judge considers the request frivolous.[50] The form of the case stated has been referred to earlier.[51]

(c) Further appeal on point of law to Supreme Court

[7.31] Again, as in civil cases, on a consultative case stated, the decision of the High Court can be appealed from the High Court to the Supreme Court, but only where the High Court judge grants leave (that is, permission) to appeal.[52] By contrast, on a case stated to the High Court after a final determination of the District Court in a criminal case, a further appeal lies to the Supreme Court without the need to seek leave to appeal from the High Court.[53] As stated in relation to civil cases, for this reason the appeal after a final determination is more commonly used.[54]

[7.32] Figure 7.4 provides an outline of the appeal process from the District Court in criminal matters.

---

48. Courts (Supplemental Provisions) Act 1961, s 52 replacing the Courts of Justice Act 1924, s 83.
49. Summary Jurisdiction Act 1857, s 2 as extended by the Courts (Supplemental Provisions) Act 1961, s 51. In this instance, the application for the cases stated must be made within 14 days of the decision of the District Court.
50. The 'frivolous' test does not apply where the appeal is sought under the 1857 Act by the prosecution, s 4 of the 1857 Act making a case stated mandatory in such a case: see *Sports Arena Ltd v O'Reilly* [1987] IR 185.
51. See para **[7.15]**.
52. Courts (Supplemental Provisions) Act 1961, s 52(2). In *Minister for Justice v Wang Zhu Jie* [1993] 1 IR 426, this restriction was held to be within the limitations on the Supreme Court's appellate jurisdiction envisaged by Article 34.4.3° of the Constitution.
53. Summary Jurisdiction Act 1857, s 2 as extended by the Courts (Supplemental Provisions) Act 1961, s 52. See *Attorney General (Fahy) v Bruen* [1936] IR 750.
54. See para **[7.14]**.

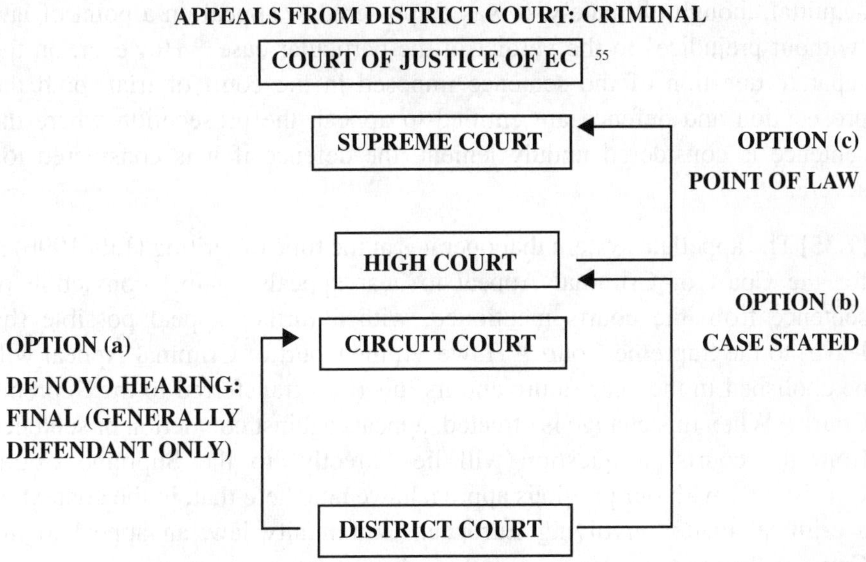

Figure 7.4

Trials on indictment

[7.33] Whereas we have seen that the appeal system from the District Court in civil and criminal matters is, broadly, similar, the appeal system concerning criminal trials on indictment involves a noticeable divergence from any arrangements in civil matters. We have seen that trials on indictment, which concern the most serious criminal offences, are conducted in the Circuit Court, the High Court (the Central Criminal Court) and (when they are in operation) special criminal courts.[56]

[7.34] Prior to 1924,[57] no mechanism for appeal by a convicted person against a guilty verdict of a jury in a criminal trial was possible. The only available mechanisms required either a reference by the trial judge of the conviction to an appeal court or the intervention of the prosecution.[58] With the establishment of a Court of Criminal Appeal in 1924[59], the convicted person was granted such a right of appeal against conviction, in essence an appeal on a point of law. Where the verdict of the trial court was a not guilty

55. See para **[7.52]**.

56. See paras **[5.70]** to **[5.96]**.

57. See generally Ryan and Magee, *The Irish Criminal Process* (Mercier, 1983), p 419.

58. A conviction could either be referred by the trial judge to the Court for Crown Cases Reserved under the Crown Cases Act 1848 or the prosecution could apply for a writ of error which, if granted, would result in a re-trial: see also para **[2.39]**.

59. Courts of Justice Act 1924, s 8.

verdict, the prosecution was not, however, empowered to appeal against the acquittal, though ultimately, it was empowered to appeal on a point of law 'without prejudice' to the verdict in the particular case.[60] However, on the separate question of the sentence imposed in the court of trial, both the prosecution and defence are entitled to appeal, the prosecution where the sentence is considered unduly lenient, the defence if it is considered too severe.

[7.35] The appellate system that operates at the time of writing (July 1996) is for the Court of Criminal Appeal to hear appeals against conviction or sentence from the courts mentioned, with a further appeal possible (by leave) to the Supreme Court.[61] However, the Court of Criminal Appeal will be abolished in the near future and its functions transferred to the Supreme Court.[62] When this change is effected, appeals against conviction or sentence from the courts in question will lie 'directly' to the Supreme Court. Consistently with our previous approach, we note here that, in the context of a criminal matter involving European Community law, an appeal to the Court of Justice may also arise, but we discuss that issue separately.[63]

Appellate arrangements prior to abolition of Court of Criminal Appeal

[7.36] The Court of Criminal Appeal established in 1961 pursuant to Article 34 of the Constitution[64] is a superior court of record.[65] The Court of Criminal Appeal is summoned by direction of the Chief Justice and comprises three judges, one Supreme Court judge (either the Chief Justice or another Supreme Court judge nominated by the Chief Justice) and two judges of the

---

60. See, however, para **[7.49]**.

61. We have seen (para **[7.21]**) that the Courts of Justice Act 1947, s 16 empowered the Circuit Court to refer any point of law before it to the Supreme Court. In *The People (Attorney General) v McGlynn* [1967] IR 232, it was held that, in the context of a trial on indictment, s 16 of the 1947 Act does not apply between the time the defendant is put in charge and when the jury delivers its verdict. The effect is that s 16 of the 1947 Act has little application in practice to trials on indictment.

62. Courts and Court Officers Act 1995, s 4. A Commencement Order (see para **[13.41]**) is required to bring s 4 of the 1995 Act into effect, and this will not occur until the backlog of civil appeals in the Supreme Court has been removed: see further para **[4.135]**. This seems likely to occur some time in 1997.

63. On the appellate jurisdiction of the Court of Justice, including the likelihood of a trial on indictment giving rise to an issue requiring a reference to the Court of Justice, see para **[7.54]**.

64. Courts (Establishment and Constitution) Act 1961, s 3(1) formally established the Court of Criminal Appeal, replacing the Court of Criminal Appeal established by the Courts of Justice Act 1924, s 8.

65. Courts (Supplemental Provisions) Act 1961, s 12, replacing the Courts of Justice Act 1924, s 30. On the concept of a court of record, see para **[4.41]**.

High Court (again, both nominated by the Chief Justice).[66] As already indicated, the Court is empowered to conduct appeals against conviction or sentence from trials in the Circuit Criminal Court,[67] the High Court (the Central Criminal Court)[68] and any special criminal court.[69] A further appeal lies to the Supreme Court, but only where the Court of Criminal Appeal, the Director of Public Prosecutions or the Attorney General certify that a point of law of exceptional public importance arises.[70] In an appeal against conviction, the Court of Criminal Appeal and, on further appeal, the Supreme Court, has three options: dismiss the appeal, quash the conviction and release the defendant or quash the conviction and order a re-trial.

---

66. Courts (Establishment and Constitution) Act 1961, s 3(2), replacing the Courts of Justice Act 1924, s 8.

67. Courts of Justice Act 1924, s 63, carried forward by the Courts (Supplemental Provisions) Act 1961, s 12. In *The State (Hunt) v Donovan* [1975] IR 39, the High Court and, on appeal, the Supreme Court held that s 63 only applied where the defendant had been tried on indictment in the Circuit Court. In that case, the prosecutor had pleaded guilty to an indictable offence in the District Court and, under the Criminal Procedure Act 1967, s 13(2)(b), had been sent forward for sentencing in the Circuit Court. He sought to appeal to the Court of Criminal Appeal against the sentence imposed in the Circuit Court, but it was held that s 63 did not apply to him as he had not been tried on indictment. The High Court and Supreme Court held that this restriction was not in conflict with the Constitution, noting that Article 34.3.4° allowed appeals from the Circuit Court to be determined by law. Nonetheless, the Criminal Procedure (Amendment) Act 1973, s 1 passed after the *Hunt* case, provides that an appeal against sentence may be made in the circumstances that arose in the *Hunt* case. When the Court of Criminal Appeal is abolished, such appeals will lie to the Supreme Court. For criticism of the *Hunt* decision, see Delany, *op cit*, pp 29-30.

68. Courts of Justice Act 1924, s 31 carried forward by the Courts (Supplemental Provisions) Act 1961, s 12. When the Court of Criminal Appeal is abolished, such appeals will lie to the Supreme Court.

69. Offences against the State Act 1939, s 44 carried forward by the Courts (Supplemental Provisions) Act 1961, s 12. When the Court of Criminal Appeal is abolished, such appeals will lie to the Supreme Court.

70. Courts of Justice Act 1924, s 29 provides that, where a convicted person has appealed unsuccessfully to the Court of Criminal Appeal, the Court itself, the Director of Public Prosecutions and the Attorney General are empowered to grant a certificate of leave to appeal to the Supreme Court where it is certified that 'a point of law of exceptional public importance' arises in the case and that it is desirable in the public interest that the opinion of the Supreme Court be given on that point. Examples of such cases included the *mens rea* required in order to convict a person of capital murder (*The People (DPP) v Murray* [1977] IR 360), the extension of time for applying for leave to appeal to the Court of Criminal Appeal (*The People (DPP) v Kelly* [1982] IR 90) and the admissibility of confessions obtained from a person while in Garda custody (*The People (DPP) v Kelly (No 2)* [1983] IR 1). Section 29 of the 1924 Act will be repealed by the Courts and Court Officers Act 1995 when the transfer of the jurisdiction of the Court of Criminal Appeal to the Supreme Court is effected under the 1995 Act.

[7.37] Figure 7.5 provides an outline of the appeal process from trials on indictment in place at the time of writing (July 1996).

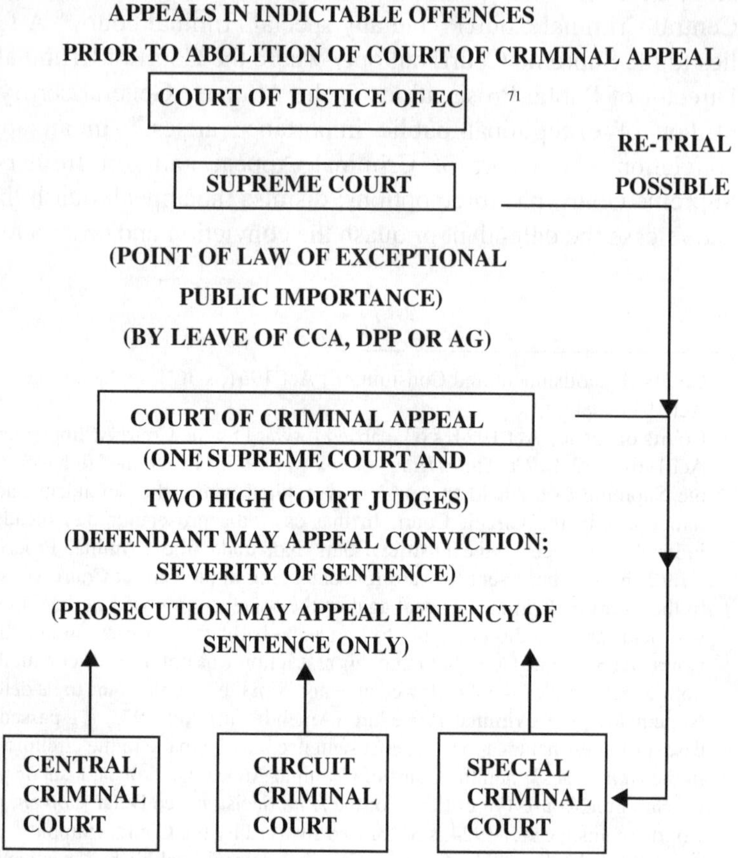

Figure 7.5

Appellate arrangements after abolition of the Court of Criminal Appeal

[7.38] When the functions of the Court of Criminal Appeal are transferred to the Supreme Court, the appellate arrangements will be simplified considerably. Appeals from trials on indictment will lie 'directly' to the Supreme Court, which will be conferred with all the powers of the Court of Criminal Appeal.[72] The Supreme Court, as successor to the Court of Criminal Appeal, will thus be empowered to dismiss an appeal against conviction, quash the conviction and release the defendant or quash the

71. See para **[7.52]**.

72. Courts and Court Officers Act 1995, s 4.

conviction and order a re-trial. It will also be empowered to hear appeals against sentence, whether from the prosecution or defence. The statutory provisions concerning an appeal from the Court of Criminal Appeal to the Supreme Court on a point of law of exceptional public importance will, of course, be repealed.[73]

[7.39] Figure 7.6 provides an outline of the appeal process from trials on indictment which will come into place when the Court of Criminal Appeal is abolished.

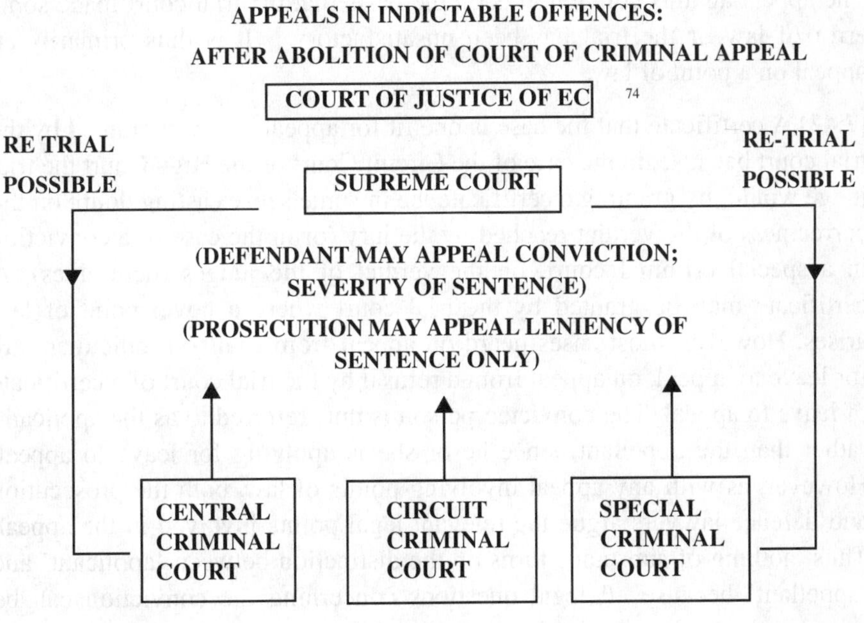

Figure 7.6

[7.40] We now turn to discuss in more detail the procedure in appeals from trials on indictment. The discussion is largely premised on the impending abolition of the Court of Criminal Appeal and the transfer of its jurisdiction to the Supreme Court.

---

73. Courts of Justice Act 1924, s 29 will be repealed by the Courts and Court Officers Act 1995 when the transfer of the jurisdiction of the Court of Criminal Appeal to the Supreme Court is effected under the 1995 Act.

74. See para **[7.52]**.

(a) Appeal against conviction

[7.41] A person convicted on indictment in the Circuit Court, High Court (Central Criminal Court) or a special criminal court may appeal that conviction to the Supreme Court, as successor to the Court of Criminal Appeal, either where the trial judge grants (or trial judges grant, in the case of a special criminal court) a certificate that the case is a fit case for appeal or the Supreme Court itself, as successor to the Court of Criminal Appeal, grants leave to appeal on appeal from a refusal by the trial judge or judges.[75] The appeal against conviction is on the basis that the trial court made some error of law or the trial has been unsatisfactory.[76] It is thus primarily an appeal on a point of law.

[7.42] A certificate that the case is one fit for appeal is rarely granted by the trial court because, in the case of the Circuit Court or the High Court the trial judge would, by granting a certificate, be in some sense casting doubt on the correctness of the verdict reached by the jury (or in the case of a conviction in a special criminal court, on the verdict of the judges themselves). A certificate may be granted by the trial court where a novel point of law arises. However, most cases heard on appeal from trials on indictment are for leave to appeal, on appeal from a refusal by the trial court of a certificate of leave to appeal. The convicted person is thus referred to as the applicant, rather than the appellant, since he or she is applying for leave to appeal. However, as with any appeal involving points of law, both the prosecution and defence lawyers argue the relevant legal points involved in the appeal. Thus, nothing of substance turns on the distinction between 'applicant' and 'appellant' because all legal questions concerning the conviction can be raised in the application for leave to appeal.[77]

[7.43] Applications for leave to appeal can be dismissed in a summary hearing where there appear to be no grounds on which to appeal,[78] but such summary dismissals are relatively rare and it is more usual for the application for leave to appeal to deal with any legal points in full. If, having heard the legal points raised, the Supreme Court, as successor to the Court of Criminal Appeal, decides that the conviction was wrong in law, it will 'allow the application for leave to appeal, treat the hearing of the application as the

75. Courts of Justice Act 1924, ss 31 and 63 and the Offences against the State Act 1939, s 44.
76. Courts of Justice Act 1924, ss 32 and 63 and the Offences against the State Act 1939, s 44.
77. The Supreme Court, as successor to the Court of Criminal Appeal is empowered to grant a legal aid certificate for the appeal in accordance with the Criminal Justice (Legal Aid) Act 1962 and also to admit a person to bail while his or her appeal is pending.
78. The power to dismiss summarily was introduced by the Criminal Procedure Act 1993.

appeal and allow the appeal.' It is also empowered, where it has allowed an appeal, either to order a re-trial or else to enter an acquittal of the defendant and order his or her release.[79]

(b) Appeal against sentence

[7.44] The second form of appeal which the Supreme Court, as successor to the Court of Criminal Appeal, hears is an appeal against sentence. In such cases the Court is asked to assess whether the sentence imposed by the trial court was within the range of sentences deemed appropriate to the particular crime and the particular convicted person[80]. Until 1993, only the convicted person could bring an appeal concerning sentence, an appeal against severity of sentence; but it is now possible for the prosecution to initiate an appeal on the leniency of the sentence.[81]

[7.45] Prior to 1993, where the appeal had been initiated by the defendant, it would seem that he or she had the choice of appealing: (a) against conviction and sentence, or (b) against conviction only or (c) against sentence only. Thus, where an appeal against conviction only was made and where this had been unsuccessful, the sentence given in the trial court would not be interfered with.[82] Where the convicted person appealed against the severity of sentence, and the appeal was unsuccessful (that is, where the trial court's sentence was upheld) it was possible for the sentence to be increased, though this was quite unusual. From the convicted person's point of view, of course, the purpose of such an appeal was to have the sentence reduced and that outcome was certainly more common than an increased sentence.

[7.46] However, as already indicated, it is now possible for the prosecution to initiate an appeal against the leniency of the sentence imposed in the trial court. Thus, the ability of the convicted person to appeal against conviction only, and leaving the sentence imposed in the trial court 'immune' from interference, has been affected to some extent by the right of the prosecution to appeal against leniency. As stated already, the principle to be applied in

---

79. Criminal Procedure Act 1993, s 3 replacing the Courts of Justice Act 1924, s 34 and the Courts of Justice Act 1928, s 5. Section 5 of the 1928 Act had conferred the power of re-trial, after it had been held in *Attorney General v Smith* [1927] IR 564 that s 34 of the 1924 Act did not allow this to be done. Section 3 of the 1993 Act has further extended the Court's powers on appeal, in particular with a view to reviewing new evidence where there is a suggestion of a miscarriage of justice: see further para **[7.47]**.

80. On sentencing principles generally, see O'Malley, 'Resisting the Temptation of Elegance: Sentencing Discretion Reaffirmed' (1994) 4 *Irish Criminal Law Journal* 1.

81. Criminal Justice Act 1993, s 2.

82. See *The People (Attorney General) v Earls* [1969] IR 414.

such an appeal is similar to that in an appeal by the convicted person, namely, whether the sentence imposed was within the range deemed appropriate to the offence and the individual circumstances of the defendant.

(c) Appeals concerning miscarriages of justice

[7.47] The Criminal Procedure Act 1993 introduced a statutory mechanism to review a conviction which it is claimed had resulted in a miscarriage of justice.[83] This was done against the background of well-publicised cases of miscarriages of justice, both in England and Ireland, many dating back to the 1970s. Prior to 1993, the appellate jurisdiction had limited the ability of appellate courts to engage in *de novo* fact-finding concerning the basis for a conviction under appeal. In an attempt to circumvent the limitations of the appellate system, some convicted persons had sought, in civil proceedings, to re-open issues determined in their criminal trial, but in those cases, the courts had held that the majority of these matters were *res judicata* and could not be re-examined.[84] The Criminal Procedure Act 1993 provides, in effect, for a full hearing in the Supreme Court, as successor to the Court of Criminal Appeal in connection with any conviction on indictment where the convicted person 'alleges that a new or newly-discovered fact shows that there has been a miscarriage of justice in relation to the conviction or that the sentence imposed is excessive.'[85]

[7.48] Section 2 of the 1993 Act provides that an application to the Supreme Court, as successor to the Court of Criminal Appeal, is made by the convicted person. By contrast with the position in the United Kingdom, therefore, the Court's jurisdiction is not conditional on a reference to it by the Minister for Justice.[86]

83. Criminal Procedure Act 1993, s 2.

84. See, for example, *Kelly v Ireland* [1986] ILRM 318; *Pringle v Ireland* [1994] 1 ILRM 467. On this case law, see generally, Byrne and Binchy, *Annual Review of Irish Law 1992*, pp 493-4.

85. Criminal Procedure Act 1993, s 2(1)(b). One of those persons who had been faced with the *res judicata* difficulty took advantage of the new procedure in the 1993 Act: *The People (DPP) v Pringle* [1995] 2 IR 547.

86. Under the review procedure in the United Kingdom, first introduced by the Criminal Appeal Act 1968, the British Home Secretary (in Northern Ireland, the Secretary of State for Northern Ireland) initially had the sole power to refer a case to the Court of Appeal. These powers were later conferred on an independent referrals body. Under the Criminal Procedure Act 1993, s 7, the Minister for Justice is empowered to establish a committee to inquire into miscarriages of justice.

(d) Appeal by prosecution without prejudice to verdict

[7.49] Section 34 of the Criminal Procedure Act 1967 empowers the Director of Public Prosecutions to appeal on a point of law to the Supreme Court arising out of a trial on indictment in which the accused person was found not guilty. This form of appeal is without prejudice to the outcome of the trial, so that even if the Supreme Court finds that there was an error of law in the trial, the person found not guilty cannot be re-tried. In effect, the procedure under s 34 of the 1967 Act can at most clarify the law for future cases.[87]

(f) Appeal against acquittals (abolished)

[7.50] As already indicated, the arrangements concerning appeals in respect of trials on indictment are restricted to appeals against convictions by the defendant, subject to the 'without prejudice' right of appeal for the prosecution. In the 1970s and 1980s, however, a series of cases established a controversial right of appeal against acquittals, limited to trials in the Central Criminal Court. In *The People (Attorney General) v Conmey*[88] the Supreme Court had held that, by virtue of Article 34.4.3° of the Constitution, a right of appeal to the Court existed in respect of all verdicts of the Central Criminal Court, the High Court. In *The People (DPP) v O'Shea*[89] the Supreme Court held that this right of appeal applied equally to the prosecution and the defence. Thus, in addition to acknowledging a right of appeal against conviction from the Central Criminal Court to the Supreme Court, the Court held that, where a person had been found not guilty in the Central Criminal Court, the prosecution could appeal the acquittal to the Supreme Court. In a later case, *The People (DPP) v Quilligan and O'Reilly*[90] the Supreme Court found that the acquittal of the two accused had been made on the basis of an error of law, and made an order allowing the appeal. However, the Court did not subsequently order a re-trial on the charges in question.[91] Since the Supreme Court had held that this jurisdiction arose

---

87. An example of such a reference is *The People v Rock* [1994] 1 ILRM 66.
88. [1975] IR 341. See the discussion of this case at para **[12.61]** in connection with its status as a precedent.
89. [1982] IR 384. See also the discussion of this case at para **[12.59]**.
90. [1987] IR 495.
91. In *The People (DPP) v Quilligan and O'Reilly (No 2)* [1989] IR 46, the Supreme Court, by a 3-2 decision, held that a re-trial should not be ordered in this case. Only two of the judges (Henchy and Griffin JJ) held that re-trials should never be ordered. The third judge in the majority, Hederman J, merely decided not to order a re-trial in the particular case: see para **[12.58]**. The defendants were later tried on other charges which had some connection with the original charges on which they were acquitted and, ultimately, the conviction of one of the defendants was upheld: see *The People (DPP) v Quilligan and O'Reilly (No 3)* [1993] 2 IR 305, discussed in Byrne and Binchy, *Annual Review of Irish Law 1992* (Round Hall Press, 1994), pp 234-9.

under Article 34.4.3° of the Constitution, it was permissible to remove the right of appeal by legislation. This was, indeed, effected by s 11 of the Criminal Procedure Act 1993,[92] so that the right of appeal against an acquittal is no longer available.[93]

[4] APPELLATE JURISDICTION OF COURTS FROM ADJUDICATIVE BODIES

[7.51] We note here that the District Court, the Circuit Court, the High Court and the Supreme Court have each been conferred with different appellate jurisdiction, both in the form of *de novo* hearings and appeals on points of law, from various adjudicative bodies, tribunals and Ministers where these exercise administrative or decision-making functions. We discuss a number of these elsewhere.[94] This appellate jurisdiction should be distinguished from the judicial review jurisdiction exercised exclusively by the High Court.[95]

[5] APPELLATE JURISDICTION OF THE COURT OF JUSTICE OF EC

[7.52] Finally, in this section of the chapter we examine certain aspects of the appellate jurisdiction of the Court of Justice of the European Communities, pursuant to Article 177 of the Treaty Establishing the European Community, the EC Treaty. We discuss elsewhere the jurisdiction of the Court of Justice under Article 177 of the EC Treaty to hear and determine points of European Community law on a reference to it by any court or tribunal of the Member States.[96] In essence, such a reference is similar to a case stated, in that a court or tribunal may refer a point of law to the Court of Justice, which gives a ruling on the point of law and remits the case to the court or tribunal of the Member State for final determination of

92. Section 11 of the 1993 Act was replaced by the Courts and Court Officers Act 1995, s 44, in order to take account of the abolition of the proposed Court of Criminal Appeal and the transfer of its jurisdiction to the Supreme Court.

93. The right of appeal against conviction from the Central Criminal Court to the Supreme Court will, of course, be preserved by the transfer of the jurisdiction of the Court of Criminal Appeal to the Supreme Court pursuant to the Courts and Court Officers Act 1995. While, of course, it might be possible for the right of appeal against acquittals to be reinstated at some time in the future, the decision in *The People (DPP) v O'Shea* was, and remains, controversial and it seems unlikely that appeals against acquittals in indictable matters will return. See generally Hogan and Whyte, *Kelly's The Irish Constitution*, 3rd ed (Butterworths, 1994) pp 505-10. As to appeals against acquittals in summary matters, see para **[7.29]**.

94. Chapter 8.

95. See generally para **[10.35]**.

96. On European Community law generally, see Ch 16.

the point of law in issue. What we examine here is the scope of the 'courts or tribunals' to which Article 177 refers and also the question whether there is an obligation or merely a discretion to refer questions of Community law to the Court of Justice.

[7.53] Before we consider these points, it should be reiterated that, since European Community law is part of domestic law, each court or tribunal envisaged by Article 177 of the EC Treaty is empowered to apply Community law, including the decisions of the Court of Justice, without the need for a reference to the Court. Put another way, all decisions of the Court of Justice on any area of Community law are binding precedents which must be followed in the domestic courts. The discussion of precedent in Chapter 12 should be read, therefore, with this is mind.

Courts and tribunals

[7.54] The courts envisaged by Article 177 of the EC Treaty are those established pursuant to Article 34 of the Constitution, and whose jurisdiction has been discussed in this Chapter. Thus, the Supreme Court, the Court of Criminal Appeal,[97] the High Court, the Circuit Court and the District Court and, where they are in operation, the special criminal courts are empowered by Article 177 of the EC Treaty to refer points of Community law for determination by the Court of Justice. All but the special criminal courts have exercised this power, but the majority of the cases referred to the Court of Justice are civil claims originating in the High Court.[98]

[7.55] As to the tribunals envisaged by Article 177 of the EC Treaty, this poses more difficulties, though a good starting point would be the case law of the courts in Ireland as to what constitutes a tribunal, person or body with adjudicative powers that must be exercised judicially.[99] Among the tribunals or bodies that would be included are the following:[100]

- the Labour Court
- the Employment Appeals Tribunal
- the Revenue Appeals Commissioners
- the Social Welfare Appeals Officers
- An Bord Uchtála (the Adoption Board)

97. The Courts and Court Officers Act 1995 envisages the abolition of the Court of Criminal Appeal: see para **[7.35]**.

98. See McMahon and Murphy, *European Community Law in Ireland* (Butterworths, 1989), p 225.

99. See para **[4.13]**.

100. See McMahon and Murphy, *op cit*, p 226. On adjudicative bodies generally, see Ch 8.

- An Bord Pleanála (the Planning Appeals Board)
- the Medical Council and other similar professional bodies established by statute.

Mandatory or discretionary references

(a) Mandatory references

[7.56] Article 177 of the EC Treaty provides:

> Where any such question [*that is, of Community law*] is raised in a case pending before a court or tribunal of a Member State, against whose decisions there is no judicial remedy under national law, that court or tribunal shall bring the matter before the Court of Justice.

[7.57] The mandatory tone of this part of Article 177 may be contrasted with the immediately preceding sentence, which provides:

> Where such a question [*that is, of European Community law*] is raised before any court or tribunal of a Member State, that court or tribunal may, if it considers that a decision on the question is necessary to enable it to give judgment, request the Court of Justice to give a ruling thereon.

It is thus clear that a court or tribunal 'against whose decisions there is no judicial remedy under national law' *must* refer a point of Community law to the Court of Justice, whereas any other court or tribunal *may* refer such a point if considered necessary. It has been made clear by the Court of Justice itself that the courts or tribunals under a mandatory obligation to refer include those whose decisions cannot be appealed, and not merely the final courts of appeal in the Member States. Thus, the Circuit Court on appeal *de novo* from the District Court and the High Court on appeal *de novo* from the Circuit Court may come within this mandatory provision, and the Supreme Court certainly does.[101]

(b) Discretionary references

[7.58] As to the courts or tribunals that fall within the discretionary category, the approach taken is that, where it is possible to avoid a reference and to decide a case on a basis other than Community law, that other basis should be used.[102] This is similar to the rule whereby the courts strive to avoid constitutional questions where a case can be decided on some other ground.[103] Once a Court or tribunal has made a decision to refer the case to

101. See McMahon and Murphy, *op cit*, p 227.
102. *Irish Creamery Milk Suppliers Association Ltd v Ireland* (1979) 3 JISEL 66.
103. See para **[15.75]**.

the Court of Justice, the reference must proceed ahead and not even the Supreme Court will interfere.[104] Finally, even where an Article 177 reference has been made, the courts may ultimately hold that the matter can be decided on issues other than Community law.[105]

104. *Campus Oil Ltd v Minister for Industry and Energy* [1983] IR 82.

105. *Doyle v An Taoiseach* [1986] ILRM 693. McMahon and Murphy, *op cit*, p 288 criticise the approach of the Supreme Court in *Doyle* where the Court declined to address the Community law issue, even after an Article 177 reference, and where the High Court, whose decision was appealed to the Supreme Court, had applied the Court's ruling in making its decision.

Chapter 8

The Government, Administrative Law and Adjudicative Bodies

[1] Introduction

[8.01] In previous chapters we discussed the administration of the judicial power of the State in the court system.[1] In this chapter, we outline the nature of the executive power of the State, which is performed by the Government, comprising the Taoiseach, or Prime Minister, and the other Government Ministers. We discuss elsewhere that much of the legislation enacted by the Oireachtas is initiated by the Government.[2] In this chapter, we focus on the establishment, largely by Government initiative, of many adjudicative or decision-making bodies, other than courts, to deal with particular problems. It is not possible to provide a complete listing of all such bodies, and this chapter contains a selection for illustrative purposes. We also note that the Government itself, through its Ministers, is involved in decision-making that resembles the function of judges in some respects. In effect, this chapter deals largely with what is termed administrative law.[3] This concerns the manner in which the activities of the Government and other adjudicative bodies are regulated and controlled. We also refer in this chapter to alternative mechanisms for controlling and regulating bodies, including the role of the Ombudsman in controlling the actions of Government and other State bodies, and the emergence of alternative dispute resolution (ADR).

[8.02] While administrative law encompasses the role of the executive branch of government in such control, it also includes the role of the courts. The courts may become involved by means of appeals from such bodies, whether by way of a *de novo* hearing or an appeal on a point of law. In addition, the High Court may be involved through the mechanism of judicial review, the modern successor to the prerogative writs of the medieval Anglo-Norman courts.[4] Judicial review also encompasses the power of the courts to declare invalid secondary or delegated legislation enacted by statutory bodies.[5]

1. Chapters 4 to 7.
2. See para **[13.28]**.
3. See Hogan & Morgan, *Administrative Law in Ireland*, 2nd ed (Sweet & Maxwell, 1991).
4. On judicial review, see Ch 10.
5. See paras **[13.58]**-**[13.60]**.

19th century development of the executive

[8.03] We have already noted that, during the 19th century, the essential elements of the system of government familiar today began to take shape, in particular the emergence of the separation of the three branches of government, legislative, executive and judicial.[6] The 19th century was also characterised by substantial law reform, including the overhauling of the administration of justice through the Judicature Acts 1873 and 1877, which replaced the complex web of courts that had developed since medieval times. Law reform also emerged to update the entire apparatus of State, from central to local government. To achieve these reforms, older institutions were reformed and many entirely new executive bodies were established. In the Irish context, the Land Commission is one example of such a body.[7]

[8.04] In effect, the 19th century saw a huge increase in the role and influence of the executive branch in the State, and this legacy continues to be felt in the latter part of the 20th century. In this chapter, therefore, we discuss to some extent how the executive branch of government, continues to control, at least indirectly, much of the apparatus of State.[8]

The constitutional setting

[8.05] The Constitution of Ireland 1937, Bunreacht na hÉireann, is not particularly informative on the role of the executive, though some basic points emerge. Article 28.2 provides:

> The executive power of the State shall, subject to the provisions of the Constitution, be exercised by or on the authority of the Government.

Article 28.1 states that the Government shall consist of not more than 15 members, usually referred to as Government Ministers. The Government is commonly referred to as the Cabinet, which reflects the name given to the executive prior to the establishment of the Irish Free State in 1922. Article 28.5 provides that the head of the Government, or Prime Minister, shall be called the Taoiseach. Article 28.6 requires the Taoiseach to nominate what amounts to a deputy Prime Minister, the Tánaiste, who is empowered to act for the Taoiseach during any 'temporary absence' or in event of the Taoiseach's permanent incapacity or death. Article 28.4.2° provides that the Government must meet and act collectively, while Article 28.4.2° states that the Government is also collectively responsible for the Departments of State

6. See para **[2.20]**.
7. See para **[2.42]**.
8. On the relevance of the political party system to this, see para **[13.28]**.

administered by the Ministers. However, the Constitution is silent on the specific functions of these Departments.

[8.06] Some clues as to the extent of the executive power are, however, provided. Article 28 states that, while the assent of Dáil Éireann is required to declare war, the Government is empowered to take 'whatever steps they consider necessary for the protection of the State' in the event of an actual invasion. This indicates at least that one major function of the Government is the preservation of the State from wartime invasion. In addition, Article 29.4 of the Constitution provides that the executive power of the State in connection with international relations shall also be exercised by the Government. We discuss the international treaty-making power of the Government elsewhere.[9] Article 28.4.3° specifies that the Government must prepare estimates of the receipts and expenditure of the State for each financial year and present them to Dáil Éireann for consideration. This emphasises that the Government is responsible for the overall financial planning of the State.

[8.07] Apart from these points, the Constitution is silent on specifics. However, it provides some description of the relationship between the Government and the Oireachtas, which comprises the two Houses of Parliament (Dáil Éireann and Seanad Éireann) and the President of Ireland, the head of State. Article 13.9 states that the majority of the powers of the President of Ireland are to be performed 'only on the advice of the Government.' This may be compared with the position of the monarch in Britain prior to the establishment of the Irish Free State in 1922,[10] and confirms the importance of the Government in connection, for example, with the appointment of judges.[11]

[8.08] On the relationship with the Houses of the Oireachtas, however, the Constitution does not adequately reflect reality. Article 13.1.1° provides that the Taoiseach is appointed by the President 'on the nomination of Dáil Éireann', while Article 28.4.1° states that the Government 'shall be responsible to Dáil Éireann'. Article 28.10 requires the Taoiseach (and the other members of the Government) to resign 'upon his ceasing to retain the support of a majority in Dáil Éireann.' In addition, Article 15.2.1° states that the 'sole and exclusive power of making laws for the State is hereby vested in the Oireachtas.' Taken at face value, these provisions indicate that the

9. See paras **[16.60]-[16.62]**.
10. See paras **[2.22]-[2.24]**.
11. See paras **[4.63]-[4.68]**.

Oireachtas has the power to 'hire and fire' the Government and has the exclusive power to pass laws.

The political party system

[8.09] However, to say that the Taoiseach must be elected by a vote in Dáil Éireann and that the Oireachtas must vote to pass all laws provides only a partial picture of reality. In particular, the Constitution makes no reference to the emergence of the highly-disciplined political party system that is a feature of politics.[12] In terms of the balance of power between the executive and legislative branches, this has been especially important in Britain and Ireland. The respective heads of the executive, the British Prime Minister and the Taoiseach, are also the leaders of political parties. They are elected by the parliamentary members of these parties who are elected at a General Election and who, in practice, vote *en bloc* on most issues, whether the election of the Taoiseach or the approval of legislation proposed by the Government. This voting pattern is 'enforced' by parliamentary managers referred to as whips.

[8.10] Thus, while it is true to say that the Taoiseach is elected by Dáil Éireann and that the Government require the Oireachtas to pass any laws they propose, in reality the Government has the majority of the effective power.[13] One indication of this is that the majority of Acts passed by the Oireachtas are initiated by the Government, rather than the ordinary members of the Oireachtas.[14] In recent years, members of the Oireachtas have called for a more effective input into Government decision-making, and there are some indications that the expansion of the powers and numbers of Oireachtas Committees in recent years has effected some shift from the almost complete dominance of the executive.[15] Nonetheless, the position remains that the Government retains control over a vast range of matters and that virtually all members of Dáil Éireann aspire to become members of the Government, that is, to 'get into power'.

---

12. See para **[13.28]**.

13. By contrast, in the United States of America, the head of the federal executive, the President, is elected by direct vote of the people. Members of Congress, the federal Parliament, play no part in the President's election, though they must approve the President's nominees as Secretaries of State, the equivalent of Ministers. The members of Congress are not as rigidly tied to party 'whips' as their counterparts in Britain and Ireland. In that sense, there is a clearer separation between the legislative and executive branches in the United States.

14. See para **[13.28]**.

15. See para **[13.16]**.

[2] The Organisation of the Government

[8.11] Having examined the provisions of the Constitution on the role of the executive, it remains to describe this more precisely. Article 28.12 provides that the organisation and distribution of business amongst Departments of State and the designation of members of the Government to be Ministers in charge of those Departments is to be regulated by law. This corresponds to the provisions of Article 36 on the regulation by law of the business of the courts.[16] The functions of Ministers are described in the Ministers and Secretaries Act 1924, as amended. The 1924 Act effected the transition from the pre-1922 arrangements for the executive as the Courts of Justice Act 1924 had done for the court system. By way of example of the allocation of business, s 1(iii) of the 1924 Act, which deals with the Department of Justice, provides:

> There shall be established ... (iii) The Department of Justice which shall comprise the administration and business generally of public services in connection with law, justice, public order and police, and all powers, duties and functions connected with the same... and shall include in particular the business, powers, duties and functions of the branches and officers of the public service specified in the Second Part of the Schedule to this Act, and of which Department the head shall be, and shall be styled, an t-Aire Dlí agus Cirt or (in English) the Minister for Justice.

The Second Part of the Schedule to the 1924 Act provides:

> Particular Branches of Administration Assigned to an Roinn Dlí agus Cirt (The Department of Justice)
>
> All Courts of Justice and the Offices thereof...
>
> Police.
>
> The General Prisons Board for Ireland and all Prisons.
>
> The Registrar of District Court Clerks.
>
> The Public Record Office.
>
> The Registry of Deeds.
>
> The Land Registry.
>
> The Commissioners of Charitable Donations and Bequests for Ireland.

Section 2(1) of the 1924 Act provides that each Minister:

> shall be a corporation sole under his style or name ... and may sue and ... be sued under his style or name ... and may acquire, hold and dispose of land

16. See para **[4.32]**.

for the purposes of the functions, powers or duties of the Department of State of which he is head ...

[8.12] The designation of the Minister as a 'corporation sole' indicates that the style or name 'Minister for Justice' has a separate legal identity from the individual who is the Minister at any given time, just as a limited liability company has a separate legal identity from the individuals who manage, or are shareholders in, that company.[17] The Ministers are assisted by deputy Ministers, called Ministers of State,[18] who are generally delegated responsibility for particular functions within the Department, but subject to the Minister's overall control.

[8.13] As the 1924 Act provides, Ministers are heads of the Departments of State with ultimate responsibility for its activities. However, the full-time staff of the Departments comprise the Civil Service, whose appointment is regulated by the Civil Service Commissioners Act 1956 and whose terms and conditions are regulated by the Civil Service Regulation Act 1956.[19] The day-to-day management of a Department's functions is in the hands of the Secretary of the Department. The Secretary is a permanent civil servant and thus remains within the Civil Service where there is a change of government. In fact, party political activity is prohibited for all high-ranking civil servants. In 1995, there were approximately 30,000 persons employed in the civil service.[20] This figure is confined to persons employed within Government Departments and does not include over 250,000 employed in the wider public service, including those employed in about 100 State bodies established by legislation (totalling 75,000),[21] those in the Garda Síochána (the police force), teachers, those employed in the health care sector and local authority staff, whose salaries are also ultimately paid by Government (whether central or local) out of State funds.

The Departments of State

[8.14] At the time of writing (July 1996), there are 16 Government Departments. As we have seen, Article 28.1 of the Constitution limits the total membership of the Government to 15, so that certain Ministers head more than one Department. We provide here merely a brief description of

---

17. See para **[1.25]**.
18. The Ministers and Secretaries (Amendment) Act 1977 introduced the title 'Minister of State', replacing the title 'Parliamentary Secretary', the title for deputy Ministers between 1924 and 1977.
19. See Hogan & Morgan, *op cit*, pp 75-102.
20. *Facts About Ireland* (Department of Foreign Affairs, 1995), p 46.
21. *Op cit*, p 50.

the Departments and their responsibilities, including those State bodies for which each has responsibility.

The *Department of the Taoiseach* has great influence over other Government Departments as provider of the secretariat to the Government. The Department therefore has some role in each of the other Departments of State. It also has specific responsibility for such additional matters as the Central Statistics Office and the National Archives.

The *Department of Finance* is responsible for the administration of the State's finances, including raising money for State purposes, the control of public expenditure and economic planning. It is also responsible for personnel matters within the Civil Service.

The *Department of Agriculture, Food and Forestry* has responsibility for the agriculture, food and forestry industries. This includes the implementation of European Community laws on the agriculture sector.[22]

The *Department of Arts, Culture and the Gaeltacht* has responsibility for arts and culture as well as the promotion of the Irish language. It is also responsible for the State broadcasting body Radio Telefís Éireann (RTE).

The *Department of Defence* has responsibility for the external security of the State, through the Defence Forces, the Irish army, air corps and naval service, which in 1995 comprised approximately 13,000 personnel. The reserve Defence Forces, including the civil defence, comprises a further 16,000 personnel.[23]

The *Department of Education* is responsible for the financing and general administration of the primary, secondary and third-level education services in the State.

The *Department of Enterprise and Employment* is responsible for the formulation of policy concerning industrial development, science and technology, employment (including training, work experience programmes, industrial relations and conditions of employment) and consumer protection.

The *Department of the Environment* is responsible for the co-ordination of local government administration, including housing, water, fire services and planning.

The *Department of Equality and Law Reform* is responsible for promoting equality of opportunity in the State and initiating a range of law reform measures in the equality and family law areas. The Department is also responsible for the civil legal aid regime.[24]

The *Department of Foreign Affairs* is responsible for the State's international relations, including signature and ratification of international

22. See Ch 16.

23. *Facts About Ireland, op cit*, p 58.

24. See para **[9.25]**.

agreements,[25] diplomatic representation abroad and the accreditation of foreign diplomats as well as foreign aid programmes.

The *Department of Health* is responsible for administering the health service provided by the State Health Boards and other hospitals and health services outside the State sector.

The *Department of Justice*, as we have seen, is responsible for the internal security of the State, though the Garda Síochána (the police force). In 1995, the total personnel in the Garda Síochána was approximately 10,500.[26] The Department is, of course, also responsible for the court service and the prison service.

The *Department of the Marine* is responsible for shipping the fishing industry and related marine industries.

The *Department of Social Welfare* is responsible for the administration of the social security system, including unemployment benefits.

The *Department of Tourism and Trade* is responsible for the promotion of tourism, though Bord Fáilte, the Irish Tourism Board, as well as certain trade-related matters.

The *Department of Transport, Energy and Communications* has a wide-ranging responsibility for many of the larger State bodies established by legislation since the establishment of the Irish Free State in 1922. These include bodies connected with road and rail transport (Coras Iompair Éireann), airport management (Aer Rianta) air transport (Aer Lingus), electricity generation, distribution and supply (Electricity Supply Board), natural gas distribution (Bord Gáis Éireann), the postal service (An Post) and telecommunications (Bord Telecom Éireann).

[8.15] We have referred already to the role of the Departments of State in the formulation of proposals for primary legislation (Acts of the Oireachtas), and we discuss this in more detail elsewhere as well as its role (and those of other agencies) in the implementation of primary legislation by secondary or delegated legislation.[27]

The overall influence of the Government

[8.16] It is clear, even from this brief description, that the Government has enormous influence in the State. Whether at central government or local government level,[28] its influence extends to the control of a great deal of

25. See para **[16.60]-[16.62]**.
26. *Facts About Ireland, op cit*, p 56.
27. See Ch 13.
28. On local government, see Keane, *The Law of Local Government in the Republic of Ireland* (Incorporated Law Society of Ireland, 1983) and Hogan & Morgan, *op cit*, pp 161-218, 739-41.

economic activity, including the establishment and overall control of the various State bodies; the stimulation of investment in industry; awarding of public works contracts, such as road building, by government Departments and local authorities; funding by Government Departments of social welfare programmes, the health service, the education service, the police service and the courts service; Ministerial licensing of numerous economic activities, from oil exploration to livestock marts; the establishment and continued funding of State agencies and inspectorates to regulate such disparate matters as public health, environmental safety and competition in the public and private sectors; and the involvement of the State indirectly in the control of professions, including the legal profession, through legislation and other executive influence.[29]

Recent reforms of the Government

[8.17] In recent years, there has been much debate internationally about the role of the State, in particular the executive, in the economy. These economic and political debates are largely outside the scope of this text. However, their impact is being felt within the legal system, through, for example, the proposal to create a semi-autonomous Court Service, thus separating day-to-day management of the courts from the Department of Justice, though continuing to be funded by the government.[30] This reflects an overall pattern of reform of the State sector, including the creation of similar semi-autonomous State bodies concerning public utilities, such as electricity generation, supply and distribution transport, the postal service and telecommunications. In some respects, the 'liberalisation' of these sectors is required by European Community law,[31] but the demands of international competitive market forces also weighs heavily. Ultimately, some bodies and other commercial undertakings formerly in public ownership have been, or are likely to be privatised, that is sold to private investors, including individuals as well as investment undertakings. Again, the debate about the scale of privatisation is outside the scope of this text, but should nonetheless be borne in mind.

[8.18] In parallel with these developments, the general organisation of the civil service is likely to be reformed in the future, with more responsibility and accountability being transferred to civil servants. Ultimately, this may

29. On the role of government in the legal profession, see discussion of the 1990 Fair Trade Commission Report in Ch 3.

30. See para **[4.129]** on the first *Report of the Working Group on a Courts Commission* (March 1996).

31. See Ch 16.

involve the dilution to some extent of the overall powers of Government and Ministers, but this is likely to be incremental.[32]

Policy and administration

[8.19] Not all functions of the Government or of the bodies referred to in this chapter are amenable to traditional forms of legal control, such as appeals to the courts or judicial review. A distinction may be drawn in this respect between policy and administration. Where the Government and the bodies it has created are engaged in policy making, judicial control is less likely. Thus, the balance to be struck between Government grant aid for investment by foreign companies and indigenous companies is a matter of policy which is more a matter for political debate than debate in courts. Similarly, where the Minister for Justice and officials in the Department propose a new approach to crime prevention, such a proposed policy is a matter for political debate rather than a matter to be challenged in court. By contrast, where government Ministers and the other bodies described here are engaged in an administrative decision which affects an individual, such a decision is amenable to judicial control and may become a matter for debate in court. The distinction between policy and administration is not clear-cut, since many policy matters may spill over into administration. Thus, if government policy on grant aid were to operate in an arbitrary manner, an affected party might be entitled to challenge this in the courts. Similarly, if the crime policy of government involved a breach of constitutional rights, this could also be challenged.[33] In this chapter, we focus primarily on those administrative decisions which are amenable to judicial control.

[3] Adjudicative Bodies and the Judicial Power

[8.20] We have already seen that the extensive powers conferred on various adjudicative bodies, including the State bodies, have been questioned on the ground that they were exercising elements of the judicial function reserved to the courts by Article 34.[34] A challenge to the powers of the Land Commission was rejected on the ground that they were essentially administrative, as opposed to judicial. Similar conclusions were reached concerning Bord na gCon, the Greyhound Board, in making an exclusion order against a greyhound trainer, and in the case of Bord na Móna, the Turf Development Board, when deciding whether to acquire land compulsorily. The powers of the Law Society of Ireland to remove solicitors from the Roll

32. See Hogan and Morgan, *op cit*, pp 63-7.

33. On the distinct nature of constitutional judicial review, see para **[15.28]**.

34. See para **[4.06]**-**[4.17]**.

of Solicitors and of Clerks of the District Court in issuing summonses in criminal matters were declared to be invalid, requiring amending legislation, while doubts about the validity of adoption orders made by An Bord Uchtála, the Adoption Board, precipitated an amendment to the Constitution. Assuming that the powers exercised by the bodies discussed in this Chapter are not liable to challenge under Article 34, they are nonetheless subject to judicial control.

The obligation to act judicially

[8.21] Although the bodies discussed in this chapter may not be exercising the judicial power, they must act judicially when engaged in an administrative action affecting an individual. The obligation to act judicially requires that they act *intra vires* (that is, within their powers)[35] and, subject to certain limitations,[36] comply with basic rules of natural justice or fair procedures.

[8.22] Although the rules of fair procedure are less formal than the rules of procedure and evidence of a court of law,[37] they require that a decision-making body be unbiased (*nemo judex in causa sua*) and that all sides involved have an opportunity to prepare their case and be treated in an even-handed manner, whether by oral hearing or by correspondence (*audi alteram partem*). Where such a body has been established under statute, it is sometimes provided that their decisions are subject to appeal to the courts, either by *de novo* hearing or on a point of law only. Where the statutory schemes do not provide for such appeals, they are subject to judicial review by the High Court.[38] Finally, where such bodies have been established outside a statutory framework, some may be amenable to judicial review, while the decisions of other non-statutory adjudicative may be challenged in the courts using private law remedies such as injunctions.[39]

Limits to judicial control

[8.23] Judicial control of adjudicative bodies, whether by judicial review or other private law remedies, has greatly increased in recent years. However,

35. The corollary is that they must not act *ultra vires*, that is outside their powers.

36. Although we will see that coroners' inquests are inquisitorial in nature (paras **[8.37]-[8.39]**), the basic principles of fair procedures must be observed.

37. See Ch 6.

38. See para **[10-35]**.

39. The judicial review procedure extends to decision-making bodies of a statutory or quasi-statutory nature, and this expresses the limit of administrative law, which is part of public law. Bodies exercising similar functions outside a statutory context are not amenable to judicial review but are subject to challenge using private law remedies, such as declarations and injunctions: see Ch 10.

recourse to the courts involves considerable expense and, although corporate bodies may be prepared to challenge adjudicative decisions in this way, such a route may be beyond the means of many individuals, particularly in light of the limitations to the State-funded civil legal aid scheme.[40] In addition, while the decisions of some adjudicative bodies may be appealed to the courts, in many instances judicial review is the only available remedy. In this respect, judicial review does not provide a comprehensive means of remedying faulty decision-making; it is limited to correcting *ultra vires* decisions and those which do not comply with fair procedures.

[8.24] In that context, there has been a growing trend towards the creation of alternative mechanisms by which legal disputes can be resolved outside the court system. Arbitration is a well-established alternative to litigation, which we consider later in this chapter.[41] However, arbitration may in some instances involve recourse to the courts and the relevant legislation expressly envisages this. Recourse to the courts, and to arbitration where appropriate, suffers from the additional problem that the adversarial procedure associated with both may be an inappropriate method of resolving a dispute.

The Ombudsman

[8.25] As part of the reform of the executive branch and the wider public sector, a more informal review mechanism has been adopted in this State. This borrows from the Scandinavian model of the Parliamentary Commissioner or Ombudsman. The Ombudsman Acts 1980 and 1984[42] provide that the Ombudsman, who is independent in the performance of his functions, may investigate any decision or failure to act which occurs 'in the performance of administrative functions' by most Government departments and a wide range of other State bodies specified in the Acts where such decision or failure to act 'may have adversely affected a person.'[43] The Ombudsman is empowered to investigate any such decision or failure to act where it was:

- (i) taken without proper authority,
- (ii) taken on irrelevant grounds,
- (iii) the result of negligence or carelessness,
- (iv) based on erroneous or incomplete information,

40. See Ch 9.
41. See paras **[8.31]-[8.36]**.
42. See Hogan & Morgan, *op cit*, pp 279-318.
43. Ombudsman Act 1980 s 4.

(v) improperly discriminatory,

(vi) based on an undesirable administrative practice, or

(viii) otherwise contrary to fair or sound administration.

While certain matters are excluded from the Ombudsman's remit,[44] the scope of the Office's powers are wide. The Ombudsman is empowered to investigate what has been termed maladministration or, put another way, to promote principles of good administration in the public service.

[8.26] In some respects, the role of the Ombudsman is similar to that of a judge.[45] However, a key distinction is that the Ombudsman Acts 1980 and 1984 provide that, while the Ombudsman may make 'findings' there is no power to make determinations that are binding on those to whom they are directed. Rather, it is provided that if the Ombudsman finds that a decision has adversely affected a person he may 'recommend ... that ... specified measures be taken to remedy, mitigate or alter' the adverse effect of the decision.[46] This regularly involves a recommendation to pay monetary compensation to the person adversely affected. If the response of the body to a 'finding' or recommendation is 'not satisfactory', the Ombudsman may make a formal report to this effect to both Houses of the Oireachtas. This may also be included in the annual report which the Ombudsman is required to make to both Houses of the Oireachtas. Thus, the ultimate sanction of the Ombudsman is not a fine or contempt of court, but the adverse publicity for a Government department or local authority if it became known that they had failed to take account any recommendation. It would seem that this 'sanction' has proved sufficiently persuasive in the vast majority of cases. Indeed, the present Ombudsman has suggested that the absence of a formal power to make binding determinations prevented the initiation of judicial review of the powers of the Office, especially in its early years.[47]

44. Section 5 of the 1980 Act excludes, eg, decisions in respect of which an appeal lies to the courts, decisions connected with national security, including the power of pardon and the administration of prisons. The Ombudsman's remit has been extended from time to time and it would appear that further extensions are likely in the future to monitor an Administrative Procedures Act, which would lay down specific principles of good administration, and to extend the remit to all public bodies in receipt of 50% or more of State funding: see *Annual Report of the Ombudsman 1995* (1996, Pn 2590), p 4.

45. The Ombudsman Act 1980 provides that the Ombudsman is appointed by the President, is to be paid the same salary as that of a High Court judge and may only be removed from office for stated misbehaviour or incapacity on resolutions passed by both Houses of the Oireachtas.

46. Ombudsman Act 1980, s 6(3).

47. *Annual Report of the Ombudsman 1995* (1996, Pn 2590), p 7.

[8.27] In recent years, the Ombudsman has dealt with about 3,000 complaints annually. In 1995,[48] about 25% concerned the refusal of social welfare payments by the Department of Social Welfare. Complaints against local authorities accounted for 22%, including housing allocation, planning enforcement and administration, access to information on the environment and service charges. Health boards accounted for 15%, with complaints concerning payment of supplementary welfare allowances far outstripping complaints concerning general hospital services such as hospital charges or waiting lists. Complaints against Bord Telecom Éireann comprised 12% of the total, the overwhelming majority involving telephone accounts. Others included complaints concerning the Department of Agriculture (for example, payments of farm grants), the Revenue Commissioners (for example, income tax), the Department of Education (for example, payment of higher education grants) and An Post (for example, postal delivery).

Other Ombudsmen

[8.28] The establishment of the office of Ombudsman has led to the creation of similar offices in a wide range of areas not covered by the Ombudsman Acts 1980 and 1984. Thus, the independent adjudicator provided for in the Solicitors (Amendment) Act 1994 performs a similar function for the solicitor's branch of the legal profession.[49]

[8.29] Similar offices have been established in recent years for the insurance industry and financial institutions. The Insurance Ombudsman of Ireland[50] and the Ombudsman for the Credit Institutions[51] provide an inexpensive method of resolving many disputes between consumers and the undertakings operating in the insurance and financial sectors. Although they operate on a non-statutory basis, their terms of reference have been modelled largely on those contained in the Ombudsman Acts 1980 and 1984 and they engage in considerable efforts to publicise their activities. Like the Ombudsman, both Offices publish Annual Reports of their activities, including case studies of their investigations. Likewise, the Advertising Standards Authority of Ireland has performed a similar watchdog and adjudicatory role for the advertising industry for many years.[52]

---

48. *Ibid*, pp 9, 32-6.
49. See para **[3.16]**.
50. The first and current (July 1996) incumbent is a barrister, Paulyn Marrinan Quinn.
51. The first and current (July 1996) incumbent is also a barrister, Brian Murphy.
52. See also the connection with statutory controls, discussed at para **[13.05]**.

Alternative dispute resolution (ADR) and small claims

[8.30] These developments may also be seen against the general background of alternative dispute resolution (ADR), which has emerged in recent years as an alternative to the more formal court system and arbitration routes.[53] The focus of ADR is on mediation and arriving at a satisfactory compromise between parties, particularly involving large-scale commercial disputes between companies.[54] Similar arrangements have been in place in the employment context for many years.[55] In marital breakdown disputes, solicitors have been obliged for a number of years to advise their clients of the options of reconciliation, mediation or a negotiated settlement as alternatives to litigation.[56] As to consumer complaints, the Insurance Ombudsman and the Ombudsman for the Credit Institutions provide a forum to resolve disputes in those sectors.[57] As to other consumer complaints, arising for example from retail transactions for the sale of goods, we have already seen that a Small Claims Court procedure has been initiated on a statutory basis, administered by Clerks of the District Court.[58] Although operated within the court structure, the small claims procedure was established with a view to ensuring informality in the resolution of such complaints. Indeed, proposals for reform of the Courts Service generally may also be seen against the background of the perceived inefficiency of current arrangements and the need to improve the competitiveness of the court system in relation to other comparable arrangements, such as ADR and arbitration.[59] We now turn to describe a selection of adjudicative bodies whose decisions are amenable to judicial control.

Arbitration

[8.31] As we have already noted, arbitration is a long-established form of dispute resolution, commonly used for commercial contract disputes, notably those arising from building contracts, insurance contracts and holiday contracts.[60] In addition, arbitration is regularly used to resolve

---

53. See the symposium 'Dispute Resolution: Civil Justice and its Alternatives' (1993) 56 MLR 277 *et seq*, which contains a series of contributions on this matter.
54. Such a service was launched in Ireland under the general auspices of the Irish Business and Employers Confederation (IBEC), a representative body of Irish employers: see 55 *Newsletter of the Confederation of Irish Industry*, No 11 (27 August 1991).
55. See para **[8.43]**.
56. Judicial Separation and Family Law Reform Act 1989, ss 5-8.
57. See, however Quinn, (1994) 12 ILT 18, an address by the Insurance Ombudsman which emphasises the inquisitorial nature of her role as opposed to the mediation involved in ADR.
58. See para **[5.35]**.
59. See para **[4.129]** on the *First Report of the Working Group on a Courts Commission* (March 1996).
60. See Forde, *Arbitration Law and Practice* (Round Hall Press, 1994).

disputes concerning compensation after the compulsory acquisition of land. Arbitration has also become increasingly significant against the background of commercial 'globalisation' since the 1980s. With the enormous increase in international trade, it is common for many companies to require that any disputes be referred to arbitration in a particular location whose procedures are known to them, such as London or Dublin, rather than be resolved in the courts of the State in which they are trading. Thus, arbitration has both a national and international aspect.

[8.32] The principal advantages of arbitration over litigation include: the choice of an expert adjudicator, whether an architect, engineer or lawyer as opposed to the imposition of a particular judge who may have no particular expertise in the area; procedural flexibility, subject to the essential rules of fair procedures; choice of location; enforcement of arbitral awards internationally; the possibility of a speedy decision; and confidentiality through a hearing in private.[61] The Arbitration Acts 1954 and 1980 set out much of the procedural and legal requirements concerning a reference to arbitration, the conduct of the arbitration itself and the role of the courts.

[8.33] As indicated, arbitration may arise automatically from the terms of a contract which includes an arbitration clause. These clauses are found increasingly in many commercial contracts. Section 5 of the Arbitration Act 1980 provides that where such an arbitration clause appears in a contract any attempt to bring court proceedings without referring the matter to arbitration must be stayed by a court where the other party to the contract applies for such a stay. Under the Arbitration Act 1954, the court had a discretion as to whether to grant a stay, but s 5 of the 1980 Act severely limited this discretion.[62]

[8.34] While the arbitration is held in private, the procedure is adversarial in nature and the arbitrator must act in an impartial manner, much like a judge in court. It is common for the rules of evidence, such as those governing hearsay, to be applied by arbitrators. In addition, the 1954 and 1980 Acts also lay down procedural requirements concerning the conduct of the arbitration and the arbitral award; these could be described as a detailed application of the rules of natural justice and fair procedures referred to at the outset of this chapter.

[8.35] The Arbitration Acts 1954 and 1980 also provide for mechanisms by which the courts may become involved in resolving difficult points of law. It is provided that the arbitrator may refer points of law to the High Court by way of consultative case stated and a further appeal lies to the Supreme

---

61. See Forde, *op cit*, pp 3-4. On delays in the court system and proposals for reform, particularly in the commercial area, see para **[4.137]**. Any reforms in the court system could not, of course, compete with the confidentiality of arbitration and ADR.

62. Forde, *op cit*, pp 23-8.

Court.[63] While the courts will provide such guidance as is requested, they are less likely to interfere with an arbitral award once it has been made. In line with courts in other jurisdictions, the courts have indicated that they are reluctant to interfere with the findings of an arbitrator. This is based on a policy of encouraging arbitration as an alternative to litigation and the view that excessive interference would undermine the entire basis of arbitration.[64]

[8.36] In addition to the 1954 and 1980 Acts, specific legislation may lay down particular arbitration schemes. These are common in the context of determining the level of compensation payable on the compulsory acquisition of land associated with planning, road construction and similar public civil engineering works. The most significant legislation in this respect remains the Acquisition of Land (Assessment of Compensation) Act 1919, which provides for the appointment of a property arbitrator where disputes concerning compulsory acquisition of land arises, for example by a local authority under a compulsory purchase order (CPO). The scheme in the 1919 Act has been extended to the exercise of similar powers under other legislation.[65] It has also been extended to claims for compensation arising from refusal of planning permission.[66] Under the 1919 Act, as amended, an appeal lies by way of case stated to the High Court. Although the 1919 Act would appear to preclude further appeal, it seems that a further appeal lies to the Supreme Court.[67]

Coroners' courts

[8.37] Perhaps the closest form of adjudicative bodies to the courts discussed in earlier chapters are the coroners' courts. Coroners have an extemely ancient common law pedigree as quasi-judicial offices, but their functions are now regulated by the Coroners Act 1962.[68] These conduct inquests, in public,[69] into any violent, suspicious or otherwise unexplained death. The

63. Arbitration Act 1954, s 35.

64. Forde, *op cit*, pp 115-6.

65. See, eg, Electricity Supply (Amendment) Act 1985, required by the decision in *Electricity Supply Board v Gormley* [1985] IR 129, which had found unconstitutional the Electricity Supply Act 1927, s 27 which contained no provision for compensation.

66. Local Government (Planning and Development) Act 1963, as amended.

67. See *Attorney General (Fahy) v Bruen* [1936] IR 750, Pye, 'Appeals to the Supreme Court in Planning Compensation Cases' (1987) 5 ILT 252 and McDermott & Woulfe, *Compulsory Purchase and Compensation: Law and Practice in Ireland* (Butterworths, 1992).

68. For criticisms of arrangements under the 1962 Act and the need for reform, see Cusack, 'The Coroner's Court' (1995) 1 *Medico-Legal Journal of Ireland* 82 (editorial).

69. Prior to the 1962 Act, the Coroners (Ireland) Act 1846 authorised a coroner to order that a dead body be brought to the nearest convenient tavern, public house or house licensed for the sale of intoxicating liquor and the owner of such premises was required to allow the body to be deposited there until the inquest had taken place. The 1846 Act, which replicated a similar statutory regime for the rest of the United Kingdom, was repealed by the 1962 Act, which requires a body be removed to a convenient mortuary or morgue pending the holding of the inquest in public.

inquests are presided over by medical practitioners, though many of these also possess legal training. The Coroners Act 1962 prescribes the procedure under which inquests must be held and the circumstances in which a coroner's jury must be summoned by the coroner.[70] Section 40 of the 1962 Act provides that a jury is required where the coroner is of opinion: that the deceased came by his or her death by murder, infanticide or manslaughter; that other statutory provisions require the holding of an inquest; that the death was caused by accident, poisoning or disease of a type notifiable to a Minister or government inspector; that the death occurred from the use of a vehicle in a public place; or it occurred in circumstances the continuance or recurrence of which would be prejudicial to the health and safety or the public.

[8.38] The coroner's court has some appearances of an ordinary court, in that it sits in public, it is presided over by a professional person, witnesses give their evidence under oath, and there is often a jury. In other respects, however, it differs markedly from an ordinary court, in that it is essentially an inquisitorial body rather than an adversarial one. In this respect, the coroner determines which witnesses are called and the sequence in which they give evidence and he or she also has wide discretion as to who may be represented at the inquest. In addition, the coroner and jury are severely limited by the 1962 Act as to the findings they may make. They are precluded by s 30 of the 1962 Act from giving a verdict which would involve the implication of either civil or criminal liability on the part of the deceased. Indeed, inquests are generally stayed pending the conclusion of any criminal proceedings.

[8.39] Where an inquest is opened and the Garda Síochána inform the coroner that criminal proceedings are contemplated, the inquest is then adjourned.[71] In that respect, it is confined to determining 'who, how, when and where', that is, to determine who the deceased person was, as well as how, when and where he or she died. In effect, the 1962 Act limits the coroner or inquest jury to the following types of verdicts: death from natural causes, death by reason of accident or misadventure; death by the deceased's own act[72] or an 'open verdict', where the other verdicts are inappropriate. In

70. The jury panel for coroners' courts are identical to those for courts operating under Article 34 of the Constitution and are governed by the Juries Act 1976: see para **[6.100]**. However, the procedure for selecting a coroners' jury is less formal. A coroners' jury may consist of six members, rather than the 12 associated with ordinary courts. In Britain and Northern Ireland, the jury ranges from seven to 11 in number.

71. The former procedure by which the inquest is adjourned indefinitely (*sine die*) is not permissible: *The State (Costello) v Bofin* [1980] ILRM 233.

72. Generally, the phrase 'when the balance of the mind was disturbed' is included in the verdict.

the United Kingdom, coroners' courts have been authorised by statute to make findings of suicide, but this is not permissible under the 1962 Act.[73] However, s 40 of the 1962 Act empowers a jury to make a finding of murder, manslaughter or infanticide, but this is confined to third party involvement in the death.[74]

Criminal injuries compensation

[8.40] We have already seen that the Malicious Injuries Acts 1981 and 1986, operated through the Circuit Court, provide a mechanism for compensating persons whose property has been damaged maliciously, such as in the course of a riot.[75]

[8.41] Different arrangements have been put in place to deal with compensation for personal injuries suffered in similar circumstances. In 1974, the Government published a non-statutory Scheme of Compensation for Injuries Inflicted Criminally, which established the Criminal Injuries Compensation Tribunal.[76] Similar schemes, though operating on a statutory basis, had been in place in Britain and Northern Ireland for many years.[77] The Tribunal determines the level of compensation payable to a person who has suffered injuries in the course of a criminal act such as an assault or a riot. While the 1974 Scheme is not statutory, the courts have held that its decisions are subject to judicial review.[78] Prior to 1986, the Tribunal was empowered to award general damages for the pain and suffering of any personal injuries suffered and any special damages such as loss of earnings.[79] However, in 1986 the relevant terms of the 1974 Scheme were amended, removing the power of the Tribunal to award general damages.[80] This was done primarily as a means of limiting the cost to the State of criminal injuries compensation, confining it to awards for loss of earnings.[81]

73. *The State (McKeown) v Scully* [1986] IR 524.
74. *Green v McLoughlin* [1991] 1 IR 309 (HC); Supreme Court, unrep, 26 January 1995.
75. See para **[5.49]**, discussing the Malicious Injuries Acts 1981 and 1986. Note also the proposal to abolish the scheme in the Malicious Injuries (Amendment) Bill 1996.
76. *Scheme of Compensation for Personal Injuries Criminally Inflicted* (1974, Prl 3658). The Scheme has been amended a number of times since 1974.
77. On the Northern Ireland scheme, see Dickson, *The Legal System of Northern Ireland*, 3rd ed (SLS Legal Publications, 1991).
78. See, eg, *The State (Hayes) v Criminal Injuries Compensation Tribunal* [1982] ILRM 210; *The State (Creedon) v Criminal Injuries Compensation Tribunal* [1989] ILRM 104.
79. On damages, see para **[10.06]**.
80. These changes should be linked to the limitations introduced to the malicious injuries statutory code by the Malicious Injuries (Amendment) Act 1986: see para **[5.49]**.
81. See *Gavin v Criminal Injuries Compensation Tribunal*, High Court, unrep, 9 February 1996.

BRAINSE CABRACH
CABRA BRANCH
TEL: 8691414

Employment

[8.42] Most States have established statutory bodies with extensive powers to deal with issues arising from the employment context. Some such bodies are empowered to investigate and mediate in industrial relations disputes with a view to a negotiated settlement where other means have failed. Others have been established to make determinations similar to a court of law, such as determining whether a dismissal was in breach of statutory requirements.

[8.43] In the first category, that is mediation and settlement, are the Labour Court and the Labour Relations Commission.[82] Neither body is a court exercising the judicial power under Article 34; rather their function is for the settlement of disputes which require the input of personnel who specialise in mediation between employers and employees. Both comprise representatives of employers, trade unions and other persons with expertise in the area of industrial relations. The Labour Relations Commission provides a conciliation service for individual disputes and also prepares codes of practice on industrial relations generally.[83] Where mediation in the Labour Relations Commission has failed, the Labour Court may investigate a dispute and is empowered to make decisions and issue recommendations to the parties. These are not always binding, but the parties may decide in advance of a Labour Court hearing that the Court's recommendations will be accepted and implemented by both sides. No appeal lies to the courts from decisions of the Labour Court, but they are subject to judicial review.[84]

[8.44] Attached to the Labour Court are Rights Commissioners and Equality Officers who may be used to assist in the settlement of disputes. They are also empowered to make determinations in certain matters, notably in relation to equal pay and other aspects of sexual discrimination at work, such as sexual harassment. Appeals from such determinations lie on a point of law to the High Court.[85]

[8.45] The Labour Court is also empowered to set minimum wages for certain low-pay sectors, through Joint Labour Committees (JLCs).[86] The Labour Court gives effect to the proposals of the JLCs in the form of statutory Orders, that is a form of delegated legislation. If, in making such an Order, the Labour Court fails to comply with the principles of fair

---

82. See Forde, *Industrial Relations Law* (Round Hall Press, 1991), pp 34-40.
83. These may be adopted by the Minister for Enterprise and Employment in statutory form: see para **[13.04]**.
84. Industrial Relations Act 1946, s 17. See, eg, *The State (Aer Lingus Teo) v Labour Court* [1987] ILRM 373; *Aer Lingus Teo v Labour Court* [1990] ILRM 485.
85. Forde, *Employment Law* (Round Hall Press, 1992).
86. Industrial Relations Act 1946, Part IV.

procedures referred to earlier the Order is liable to be declared invalid in the courts.[87]

[8.46] The Employment Appeals Tribunal hears and determines cases in which an employee claims that he or she has been unfairly dismissed by an employer within the meaning of the Unfair Dismissals Acts 1977 to 1994.[88] The Tribunal comprises three people, a solicitor or barrister who chairs the hearing, a representative of an employer's organisation and a representative of the trade union movement. The Tribunal's procedures are adversarial in nature, though the rules of evidence may not be applied as strictly as in a court. An appeal lies from the Employment Appeals Tribunal to the Circuit Court, which is empowered to conduct a full *de novo* re-hearing, and a further appeal and re-hearing may be had in the High Court.[89]

Inspectorates: national and local

[8.47] Various Acts have established inspectorates or other comparable bodies both at national and local level to enforce standards established by such legislation. At national level, legislation has established the National Authority for Occupational Safety and Health,[90] the Environmental Protection Agency,[91] the Irish Aviation Authority[92] and the National Standards Authority of Ireland.[93] At a more local level, larger local authorities are required to appoint fire officers to ensure compliance with fire safety legislation[94] and environmental health officers to enforce food safety legislation in retail outlets.[95] Similarly, inspectors may be appointed on an *ad hoc* basis to investigate the dealings of companies pursuant to the Companies Act 1990.

[8.48] In many instances, the statutory schemes establishing these agencies or inspectorates provide that an appeal lies to the courts in respect of decisions made by them. For example, s 20 of the Fire Services Act 1981 empowers a fire authority to serve a 'fire safety notice' on the owner of a potentially dangerous building, which the Act defines as a building likely to be a source of injury were a fire to occur in it. The notice can prohibit the use of the building to which it relates. Failure to observe the contents of the fire

87. See *Burke v Minister for Labour* [1979] IR 354, discussed at para **[13.76]**.
88. Forde, *op cit*.
89. See *McCabe v Lisney & Son Ltd* [1981] ILRM 289; *Flynn v Power* [1985] ILRM 36.
90. Safety, Health and Welfare at Work Act 1989.
91. Environmental Protection Agency Act 1992.
92. Irish Aviation Authority Act 1993.
93. National Standards Authority of Ireland Act 1996.
94. Fire Services Act 1981.
95. Health Act 1947.

safety notice is a criminal offence under s 4 of the 1981 Act and can be tried summarily in the District Court. In addition, s 20 of the 1981 Act provides that an owner on whom such a fire safety notice has been served may appeal to the District Court. On such appeal, the judge of the District Court can either confirm or annul the fire safety notice. A further appeal on a point of law lies to the High Court by case stated.[96]

[8.49] In addition to such statutory arrangements, the administrative decisions of such inspectorates and agencies,[97] as opposed to their policy decisions, are amenable to judicial review.

Intellectual property

[8.50] Under a series of Acts, the Controller of Patents, Designs and Trade Marks is empowered to make important determinations in the area of intellectual property law. Thus, the Patents Act 1992 empowers the Controller to decide to whether certain inventions are entitled to be registered as patents and thus attract the statutory protections available under the 1992 Act. Similarly, the Trade Marks Act 1996 empowers the Controller to determine whether certain symbols, drawings, marks and shapes connected with commercial products and services are entitled to the protection given under the 1996 Act.

[8.51] Section 96 of the Patents Act 1992 provides that an appeal lies to the High Court against most decisions of the Controller, such as refusal of a patent registration and that, on such appeal, the Court may exercise any power of the Controller. This amounts to a hearing *de novo*. Section 96(7) of the 1992 Act provides that a further appeal on a point of law lies to the Supreme Court. Slightly different arrangements apply under the Trade Marks Act 1996. As with the 1992 Act, s 79 of the 1996 Act provides that an appeal lies to the High Court from a determination by the Controller, and that, on such appeal, the Court may exercise any power of the Controller. However, s 79(3) of the 1996 Act provides that any further appeal to the Supreme Court on a point of law requires the leave of the High Court. Thus, there is no appeal to the Supreme Court as of right under the 1996 Act.

Ministers

[8.52] We have already referred to the policy functions of a Government Minister as political head of a Department of State, which are not a function subject to judicial control.[98] However, many administrative powers and

---

96. See *Transactus Investments Ltd v Dublin Corporation* [1985] IR 501. Similar functions are conferred on the District Court by the Safety, Health and Welfare at Work Act 1989.

97. See paras **[10.28]** and **[10.29]**.

98. See para **[8.19]**.

functions conferred on Ministers must be exercised judicially in accordance with the rules of fair procedures. Such functions include the important power to award licences for certain undertakings, ranging from oil exploration to livestock marts. The statutory schemes for the exercise of such powers may provide for an appeal to the courts. Thus, s 16 of the Abattoirs Act 1988 provides that an appeal lies to the Circuit Court from a refusal of an abattoir licence by the Minister for Agriculture. In the absence of such an arrangement, the powers are subject to judicial review and must be made in accordance with fair procedures.[99]

[8.53] Similarly, Ministers have increasingly been granted powers by the Oireachtas to promulgate secondary or delegated legislation. This generally involves laying down detailed statutory rules on matters covered in general terms in primary legislation.[100] The exercise of such delegated power must not be *ultra vires* the rule-making authority conferred by the Constitution or by the primary legislation or otherwise in breach of the principles of fair procedures.[101] The substantial law-making powers conferred on Ministers by the European Communities Act 1972 include the power to amend primary legislation, which would otherwise be unconstitutional.[102]

[8.54] In addition to such statutory powers, Ministers exercise comparable functions under a range of non-statutory schemes. The exercise of decision-making powers under non-statutory schemes is subject to judicial control, by means of private law remedies such as a claim for damages.[103]

Oireachtas Committees

[8.55] Until recently, the Oireachtas has rarely established committees with powers to compel attendance of witnesses in a manner akin to a court. By contrast, such Committees have become a feature of the Westminster Parliament in recent years and have been a feature of the Federal Congress of the United States for even longer. While such committees have occasionally proved controversial, they are also seen as part of the modernisation of Oireachtas procedures. Where such Oireachtas Committees have been established, the courts have made clear that the rules of fair procedures must be complied with and there must be no attempt to interfere with the judicial power reserved to the courts under Article 34 of the Constitution.[104] As part of the general reform of the Oireachtas and wider

99. See Hogan & Morgan, *op cit*, pp 409-502.
100. See para **[13.59]**.
101. See para **[13.65]**-**[13.76]**.
102. See para **[16.76]**.
103. *McKerring v Minister for Agriculture* [1989] ILRM 82.
104. *In re Haughey* [1971] IR 217.

public service, it is proposed to confer wide-ranging powers on virtually all Oireachtas Committees.[105]

Planning and development

[8.56] The Local Government (Planning and Development) Act 1976 established a planning appeals board, An Bord Pleanála, with power to hear appeals from either the granting or refusing of planning permission by a planning authority. The procedures which must be adopted in appealing to An Bord Pleanála are set out in the Local Government (Planning and Development) Regulations 1994.[106] Until 1994, an appeal on a point of law lay to the High Court from the decisions of An Bord Pleanála, but this was removed and its decisions may now be challenged only on judicial review.[107]

'Private' adjudicative bodies

[8.57] We have seen that, in the legal profession, disciplinary tribunals have important decision-making powers in respect of members of the profession which have an extremely important effect on that person's professional life.[108] Such tribunals are quite common within the professions, whether established by legislation[109] or otherwise.[110] In addition, such bodies are common within other non-statutory settings, such as schools[111] and sporting associations.[112] Where such bodies are established by statute, the courts may be directly involved, as in the case of the disciplinary bodies for solicitors. In other instances, the decisions of such bodies are subject to judicial control either by means of judicial review or other private law remedies.

---

105. The Committees of the Houses of the Oireachtas (Compellability, Privileges and Immunity of Witnesses) Bill 1995, if enacted, would greatly extend the powers of Oireachtas Committees. The powers contained in the Bill may be seen against the background of the perceived high costs entailed in establishing judicial tribunals of inquiry: see para **[8.65]**.

106. SI 86/1994. See generally Scannell, *Environmental and Planning Law in Ireland* (Round Hall Press, 1994) and O'Sullivan & Shepherd, *Irish Planning Law and Practice* (Butterworths).

107. Local Government (Planning and Development) Act 1963, s 82,, as amended by the Local Government (Planning and Development) Act 1992. See Scannell, *op cit*, p 257. For appeals in arbitration connected with refusal of planning permission, see para **[8.36]**.

108. See paras **[3.16]** and **[3.36]**.

109. See the Medical Practitioners Act 1978; Dentists Act 1985; Nurses Act 1985; Garda Síochána (Discipline) Regulations 1989.

110. See for barristers para **[3.36]**; for accountants, see the Charter of the Institute of Chartered Accountants in Ireland. The constitutional validity of the latter was upheld in *Geoghegan v Institute of Chartered Accountants in Ireland* [1995] 3 IR 86.

111. See *The State (Smullen) v Duffy* [1980] ILRM 46.

112. See *Clancy v Irish Rugby Football Union* [1995] 1 ILRM 193; McCutcheon, 'Judicial Scrutiny of Sports Administration' (1995) 14 ILT 171.

Public supply, works and services contracts

[8.58] Central and local government are responsible for the procurement of many major public supply, public works and public services contracts, including the provision of catering facilities, road building and the provision of professional services. Arising from European Community law requirements, the procurement procedures for such contracts must be open to bidding by undertakings from throughout the European Union. Where the appropriate procedures are not followed, an appeal lies to the High Court, which may quash any contract awarded in breach of Community law requirements.[113]

Rating and valuation

[8.59] The Valuation Tribunal was established by the Valuation Act 1988. It is empowered to hear applications in relation to the rateable valuation which has been placed on property by a local authority. The rateable valuation is the sum specified by a local authority as the basis for calculating the rates which the local authority may charge as a property tax on business premises in its functional area. The Tribunal succeeded to the jurisdiction formerly exercised by the Circuit Court in this respect. In light of that history, it is not surprising, perhaps, that the procedures in the Tribunal are similar to those in a courtroom and that in many instances counsel are retained to appear before the Tribunal. An appeal by way of case stated lies from a determination of the Tribunal to the High Court and a further appeal on a point of law lies to the Supreme Court.[114]

Revenue

[8.60] The Income Tax Act 1967, as amended, specifies a statutory scheme for the resolution of disputes concerning taxation. Initially, an assessment of tax is made by an Inspector of Taxes, a civil servant who is an officer of the Revenue Commissioners. If a taxpayer is dissatisfied with such an assessment, an appeal lies to the Appeal Commissioners, who are independent of the Revenue Commissioners,[115] and are empowered to conduct a full hearing concerning liability to tax, including any points of law that may arise. The procedure before the Appeal Commissioners is essentially adversarial, but the formal rules of evidence may not be applied as strictly as in a court. If either the Inspector of Taxes or the taxpayer is dissatisfied with the determination of the Appeals Commissioners, an appeal

113. European Communities (Review Procedures for the Award of Public Supply, Public Works and Public Services Contracts) Regulations 1994 (SI 309/94).

114. Valuation Act 1988, s 5.

115. Income Tax Act 1967, s 156.

by way of *de novo* hearing in the Circuit Court lies. A further appeal by way of case stated lies to the High Court and also to the Supreme Court. Alternatively, an appeal by case stated from the Appeals Commissioners lies to the High Court and this may be appealed by another case stated to the Supreme Court.[116]

[8.61] In addition, we may note that County Registrars and Sheriffs are empowered under the 1967 Act to seize a person's property where the person is in default in respect of tax which has been lawfully levied by an inspector of taxes.[117]

Social welfare

[8.62] The Social Welfare (Consolidation) Act 1993 provides that where an individual is refused a particular allowance or benefit under the social welfare legislation, an appeal may be made to an Appeals Officer of the Department of Social Welfare. Unlike the situation with respect to taxation matters, there is no direct appeal mechanism from an Appeals Officer to the court system. However, an aggrieved person may seek judicial review where, for example, it is alleged that the procedures adopted were unfair or that the Appeals Officer misapplied the law.[118]

Tribunals of inquiry

[8.63] Many of the statutory adjudicative bodies referred to in this chapter have a permanent status, in the sense that the legislation establishing them provide for an indefinite life span, subject to the power of the Oireachtas to repeal the legislation under which they were established. The Oireachtas also has power to establish by resolution tribunals of inquiry to investigate certain matters of public importance. In addition, the Oireachtas may resolve that such a tribunal be invested with the powers contained in the Tribunals of Inquiry (Evidence) Acts 1921 and 1979.[119] In recent years, such tribunals have been established to inquire into the circumstances surrounding an explosion on an oil tanker which resulted in substantial loss of life,[120] a St Valentine's Day disco fire resulting in almost 50 deaths,[121] the collapse of a

---

116. Income Tax Act 1967, ss 428-430.

117. See, eg, *Weekes v Revenue Commissioners* [1989] ILRM 165.

118. See, eg, *The State (Kershaw) v Eastern Health Board* [1985] ILRM 235. On reforms to the appeal mechanisms, see Cousins, *The Irish Social Welfare System: Law and Social Policy* (Round Hall Press, 1995) p 116.

119. Similar, though less extensive, powers are also contained in particular legislation, eg, Merchant Shipping Act 1894; Transport Act 1936; Safety, Health and Welfare at Work Act 1989; Environmental Protection Agency Act 1992.

120. *Report of the Tribunal of Inquiry into the Disaster at Whiddy Island, Bantry, Co Cork* (1979, Prl. 8911).

121. *Report of the Tribunal of Inquiry on the Fire at the Stardust, Artane, Dublin* (1982, Pl 853).

homicide prosecution in a particular case[122] and allegations relating to the beef industry in the State.[123] A tribunal of inquiry is typically also empowered to make recommendations with a view to preventing the future occurrence of the matter which gave rise to its establishment. This may include making recommendations for law reform.

[8.64] A tribunal thus established has powers similar to those of a court, including power to compel attendance of witnesses and of referral to the High Court where a person refuses to give evidence or is otherwise in contempt of the tribunal.[124] Indeed, in all instances where they have been established in recent years, they have been chaired by a High Court judge.[125] However, a tribunal operating under the 1921 and 1979 Acts is not exercising the judicial power reserved to the courts by Article 34 of the Constitution, it does not make determinations that pre-empt any pending or future civil or criminal proceedings and its essential role is one of 'fact finding'.[126] In that sense such a tribunal has an inquisitorial element, but bearing in mind that civil or criminal proceedings may emerge from its deliberations, the procedures adopted by them have tended to conform quite closely to those of a court, applying the rules of evidence as nearly as possible in the circumstances.[127]

[8.65] The adoption of court procedure includes according any interested party the right to be legally represented at the tribunal. Typically, this would involve a solicitor who would instruct junior and senior counsel. It has also become established practice for such parties to be awarded their costs of appearing before the tribunal, thus requiring the State to defray these costs. This has resulted in substantial costs being incurred by the State where such tribunals have been established.[128] In light of this, it may be that the role of such tribunals will be assumed in the future by Oireachtas Committees with investigative powers similar to those contained in the 1921 and 1979 Acts.[129] However, this remains a matter for future debate.

---

122. *Report of the Tribunal of Inquiry into 'the Kerry Babies case'* (1985, Pl 3514).
123. *Report of the Tribunal of Inquiry into the Beef Processing Industry* (1994, Pn 1007).
124. See *Kiberd v Mr Justice Hamilton* [1992] 2 IR 257.
125. 'Whiddy': Costello J; 'Stardust': Keane J; 'Kerry Babies': Lynch J; 'Beef Industry': Hamilton P.
126. See *Goodman International v Mr Justice Hamilton* [1992] 2 IR 542.
127. *Ibid.*
128. See further para **[3.43]**.
129. See para **[8.55]**.

Chapter 9

Access to Law

[1] Introduction

[9.01] In previous chapters, we described the jurisdiction of the courts and various adjudicative bodies who have decision-making powers concerning a variety of legal disputes. In this chapter, we describe the arrangements that have been put in place to ensure access to the courts. We begin by examining the constitutional background to the right of access to the courts. We then discuss the position of persons who represent themselves without engaging the services of lawyers, including the circumstances in which they may be assisted by lay persons in the presentation of their case. We then discuss the provision for access to legal aid and advice in both criminal and civil matters for those who wish to engage their own legal representation but without the means to do so. Finally, we discuss the extent to which court fees and other legal costs involved in litigation are compatible with the Constitution.

[2] The Constitutional Setting: Access to the Courts

[9.02] We have already seen that Article 34.1 requires that, in general, justice be administered in public.[1] This general principle emphasises that the courts should be accessible to all. The Constitution expressly confers a right of access to the courts in Article 40.4.2°, which is the modern version of the *habeas corpus* procedure by which a person has the right to have an inquiry into the validity of his or her imprisonment. The courts have also held that the right of access to the courts is an implicit or unenumerated personal constitutional right under Article 40.3.[2] On this basis, the courts have held unconstitutional the requirement that certain proceedings against State bodies required the permission or *fiat* of the Attorney General before they could be initiated.[3] It has also been held that the immunity of the Crown from suit which existed prior to the establishment of the Irish Free State was incompatible with the Constitution.[4] Similarly, the imposition of a two month limitation period for initiating civil proceedings, without any

1. See para **[4.19]**.
2. On unenumerated rights, see para **[15.50]**.
3. *Macauley v Minister for Posts and Telegraphs* [1966] IR 345.
4. *Byrne v Ireland* [1972] IR 241, discussed further at para **[15.43]**.

possibility of extending that time to take account of exceptional circumstances, has been held to be an unreasonable restriction on the right to litigate.[5]

[9.03] However, the courts have also held that access to the courts may be subject to some restrictions. For example, s 260 of the Mental Treatment Act 1945 requires a person to seek the leave of the High Court before negligence proceedings concerning committal to a psychiatric hospital can be initiated. It would seem that this pre-condition to proceedings, or partial curtailment of the right of access, is not unconstitutional.[6] Similarly, while unduly restrictive limitation periods may conflict with the Constitution, the courts have also emphasised that, at the other end of the scale, it would be contrary to the proper administration of justice in certain instances to allow an exceptionally old or 'stale' civil or criminal case to be litigated.[7] In addition, where a point has already been determined in the courts, a litigant may also be debarred from bringing further proceedings on the ground that the matter has already been litigated and that the issue is *res judicata*.[8] To raise the matter again would thus be an abuse of the processes of the court and also contrary to the proper administration of justice. The right of access to the courts is not, therefore, unrestricted, but may in some instances be limited or curtailed. We examine the current arrangements against that general background.

Parties representing themselves

[9.04] It is sometimes said that 'the man who represents himself has a fool for a client', but there have been many instances in which those involved in litigation, whether criminal or civil, have represented themselves with success. While we have seen that the procedures involved in litigation are complex,[9] some consumers of the court system have been confident enough to represent their own interests rather than engage the services of a solicitor or counsel. In such cases, the courts are generally more accommodating to the personal litigant (also referred to as the unrepresented litigant or the 'litigant *pro se*'), and the formal rules concerning pleadings or of criminal procedure are unlikely to be applied with the same rigour as would be the case where a claim is processed by a qualified lawyer. However, it appears

---

5. *Brady v Donegal County Council* [1989] ILRM 282, *per* Costello J in the High Court. On appeal, the Supreme Court not deal with this point.
6. *Murphy v Greene* [1990] 2 IR 566.
7. See para **[6.09]**.
8. For the controversy this gave rise to in 'miscarriage of justice' cases, see para **[7.47]**.
9. See Ch 6.

that a person representing himself does not have the right to a State-funded law library.[10]

[9.05] Where a convicted prisoner applies to the High Court pursuant to Article 40.4.2° of the Constitution seeking an inquiry into the validity of his imprisonment, the courts have emphasised their duty to investigate all possible grounds that might affect the legality of the detention and not merely those raised by the prisoner.[11] However, in line with the view that the right of access to the courts is not unrestricted, the courts may treat less favourably a series of applications under Article 40.4.2° where it appears that the prisoner is merely repeating grounds which have already been rejected in previous applications or court proceedings.[12]

[9.06] A similar general principle of latitude applies in other civil litigation conducted by personal litigants, subject to the principle that there must be some finality in litigation. The order made by a court to dismiss proceedings on the basis that they amount to an abuse of the processes of the courts is sometimes referred to as a 'Wunder Order', after a litigant of the 1960s and 1970s whose proceedings against the same defendant gave rise to at least ten decisions of the High Court and Supreme Court.[13]

[9.07] No official statistics exist on the percentage of civil and criminal matters conducted personally. It would appear, however, that in civil matters, personal litigants are relatively common in family proceedings. In criminal cases, personal representation is very unusual, owing perhaps to the long-standing availability of State-funded legal aid. However, there have been a number of cases in which personal litigants have successfully defended themselves in jury trials on indictment and in subsequent appeals.[14] A number of applications pursuant to Article 40.4.2° of the Constitution by convicted prisoners also appear to be made personally.

Proceedings involving minors and persons lacking competence

[9.08] There is wide-ranging provision made in law by which minors (those under 18 years) and adults who are not fully competent (by reason, for example, of mental disability) are assisted by others in civil and criminal matters. Thus, personal injuries actions involving a minor or an adult who is not fully competent may be initiated by a 'next friend', such as a parent.[15] In child care proceedings, a court may appoint a guardian *at litem*, that is a

10. See *MacGarbhith v Attorney General* [1991] 2 IR 412.
11. *The State (Smith) v Governor of Mountjoy Gaol* (1964) 102 ILTR 93.
12. *McGlinchey v Ireland* [1990] 2 IR 215.
13. See *Wunder v Hospitals Trust (1940) Ltd*, the judgments dating from 1 April 1966 to 10 June 1975: cited by McCarthy J in *Murphy v Greene* [1990] 2 IR 566.
14. See *The People (Attorney General) v Singer* (1961) 1 Frewen 214; *The People (DPP) v Marley* [1985] ILRM 17.
15. See, eg, *Dunne v National Maternity Hospital* [1989] IR 91; *Best v Wellcome Foundation Ltd* [1993] 3 IR 421.

person who represents the interests of the child separately from the views expressed by the child's parents or of a health board. The court may also join a child to any child care proceedings and appoint a solicitor on behalf of the child.[16] In criminal matters involving minors, the presence of the minor's guardian is generally required, both during police questioning and, later, in any court hearing.[17]

Parties assisted by lay persons: '*McKenzie* friends'

[9.09] A variant on a person representing himself or herself is where a litigant may be assisted by another lay person. In 1970, in *McKenzie v McKenzie*,[18] the English Court of Appeal re-affirmed the following statement made in 1831:

> "Any person, whether he be a professional man or not, may attend as a friend of either party, may take notes, may quietly make suggestions, and give advice; but no one can demand to take part in the proceedings as an advocate, contrary to the regulations of the court as settled by the discretion of the justices."[19]

The *McKenzie* case gave rise to the phrase 'McKenzie friend' to describe a person who may assist a personal litigant in court proceedings, whether civil or criminal. However, it should be stressed that a 'McKenzie friend' may not in general speak on behalf of the personal litigant, or indeed any other litigant.[20] This is also the case in respect of those giving advice to a complainant in a sexual assault case.[21] Similarly, in applications under Article 40.4.2° of the Constitution, the application may be initiated on behalf of the person alleged to be in unlawful custody by any person who has a *bona fide* interest in the question, but the initiator may not present the case in court.[22] There may, however, be exceptional circumstances where such third parties would be permitted to address the court.[23] In general, however, apart

16. Child Care Act 1991, ss 25, 26.
17. See *Travers v Ryan* [1985] ILRM 343; Children Act 1908, s 98.
18. [1971] P 33.
19. *Collier v Hicks* (1831) 2 B & Ad 663, at 669, quoted in Delany, *The Courts Act 1924-1991* (Round Hall Press, 1993), p 242.
20. *Battle v Irish Art Promotion Centre Ltd* [1968] IR 252.
21. See para **[9.31]**.
22. *Application of Woods* [1970] IR 154; *Cahill v Governor of Military Detention Barracks, Curragh Camp* [1980] ILRM 191.
23. See *B (PML) v J(PH)*, High Court, unrep, 5 May 1992, where Budd J cited with approval the decision of the New Zealand Court of Appeal in *In re GJ Mannix Ltd* [1984] 1 NZLR 309 to this effect, though in the particular circumstances of the case (a family case), he held that the case was not an 'exceptional' case requiring the 'friend' to address the court.

from the litigant, the right of audience in the courts, that is the right to address the courts, is reserved to solicitors and barristers.[24]

[3] Provision of State-Funded Legal Aid

[9.10] In light of these examples, it is clear that a personal litigant may present his or her case in court, may be facilitated by a 'friend' and will be given more latitude by the courts than a person with a legal qualification. In that sense, the maxim 'The law, like the Ritz Hotel, is open to all' can be said to be accurate. However, it remains the case that most consumers of the legal system would, if given the choice, opt to have their case, whether civil or criminal, prepared by a person with legal qualifications. This raises the question of who is to pay for the advice tendered by solicitors and barristers. This may not be a particularly grave issue for corporate litigants, such as companies, local authorities or Government Departments, since they may be prepared to regard litigation as an unavoidable but acceptable financial hazard.[25] However, the picture is different for individuals who are unlikely to become involved in litigation, particularly civil litigation, on more than one occasion.

[9.11] The question therefore is whether access to law is limited to those who can afford it. This is a fundamental issue, because while a law student may be familiar from textbooks with the rules and principles of the law, whether the law of negligence[26] or the requirement that a criminal charge be proved beyond reasonable doubt,[27] it remains to be seen whether such rules and principles are applied in practice. For many years it has been the tradition of the legal profession to engage in a certain percentage of work without charge, or at least without the expectation of payment; this is referred to as *pro bono* work.[28] However, while this remains a feature of legal practice in the State today, its origins lie in a sense of 19th century philanthropy. In a society where market forces may place pressure on such

24. See para **[3.22]**.
25. However, on the emergence of Alternative Dispute Resolution (ADR) arising from the perceived expense of litigation, see para **[8.30]**.
26. See para **[12.70]**.
27. See para **[6.16]**.
28. This would include cases in which litigants are engaged in a highly complex civil case which would not come within the 'no foal, no fee' arrangement (see para **[3.25]**). The solicitors and counsel may be engaged in such a case for many months, or years, without any expectation of payment, though if they are ultimately successful the losing party will be obliged to pay the costs incurred to the successful party. In the meantime, however, the (ultimately successful) litigant of limited means may have incurred substantial costs other than legal fees. See, eg, Kerrigan, *Nothing But the Truth* (Tomar, 1990), the account of *Dunne v National Maternity Hospital* [1989] IR 91.

traditions, it is difficult to avoid the conclusion that justice may not be fully served without State intervention.

[9.12] It has become accepted in most States that a person facing a serious criminal charge, but unable to pay for the services of professional legal advisers, should have such advice provided by the State. In civil claims, a similar conclusion has been reached, though this is a more recent phenomenon. In both instances, the test of whether a person should qualify for 'free legal aid' is whether justice could not be arrived at in its absence. Since legal aid has been provided with State assistance in criminal cases for many more years than in civil matters, we discuss criminal legal aid first.

[4] State-Assisted Criminal Legal Aid

Legal aid at trial

[9.13] Prior to 1962, a person accused of a criminal offence could only expect to be provided by the State with the assistance of a lawyer where the charge carried the death penalty. In all other cases the defendant was required to instruct a lawyer of his or her choice. Indeed, even in capital cases prior to 1962, it was not uncommon for the defendant to be represented by junior counsel while the prosecution was represented by senior and junior counsel.[29]

[9.14] The Criminal Justice (Legal Aid) Act 1962 fundamentally altered this picture. The 1962 Act introduced a system of legal aid applicable to all serious criminal cases. It provides that a defendant shall be granted legal aid where an application for legal aid is made by a defendant and it appears to a judge of the District Court (or the trial court) that (a) the defendant's means are insufficient to enable him or her to obtain legal aid from their own resources; and (b) by reason of 'the serious nature of the offence or of exceptional circumstances, it is essential in the interests of justice that the person should have legal aid in the preparation and conduct' and his or her defence and any necessary appeal against conviction. This two-fold test in the 1962 Act conferred a certain element of discretion on the judge making the determination, although the Act also provided that legal aid was mandatory on a charge of murder, which at the time carried the death penalty.[30]

29. See generally Greer, 'Legal Services and the Poor in Ireland' (1969) 4 *Ir Jur (ns)* 270.

30. The death penalty was restricted to a limited category of 'capital' murders in the Criminal Justice Act 1964 and was abolished by the Criminal Justice Act 1990.

[9.15] The decision of the Supreme Court in *The State (Healy) v Donoghue*[31] marked an important development in the operation of the 1962 Act. Here, the prosecutor, aged 18, had been charged with breaking and entering a building, to which he pleaded guilty in the District Court. He was virtually illiterate, having left school at 13. He did not apply for legal aid under the 1962 Act and he was not informed by the respondent judge of the terms of the 1962 Act. Shortly after his appearance on the breaking and entering charge, he was charged in the District Court with larceny, also before the respondent judge. On this charge, he applied for and was granted legal aid under the 1962 Act. The next appearance in court was on the breaking and entering charge, for which he was sentenced to three months detention by the respondent judge. Finally, he appeared before the respondent for sentence on the larceny charge, but by this time the solicitor assigned to him had withdrawn from the case due to a dispute in the legal profession about the operation of the scheme in the 1962 Act. The respondent judge, who refused an application by the prosecutor to have the case adjourned because of the withdrawal of the solicitor, sentenced him to six months detention on the larceny charge. The prosecutor then applied for judicial review of his convictions,[32] seeking to have them quashed on the basis that he had been deprived of a trial in due course law under Article 38.1 of the Constitution. In the High Court, Gannon J held that the larceny sentence should be quashed because the respondent judge had already made a determination under the 1962 Act that the prosecutor required legal representation. However, Gannon J would have allowed the breaking and entering sentence to stand since he did not consider that the 1962 Act or the Constitution required the judge to inform an accused person of his right to apply for legal aid. On appeal to the Supreme Court, it was held that both sentences were invalid. O'Higgins CJ stated:[33]

> "No one can be compelled to accept legal aid, and a person charged is entitled to waive his right in this respect and to defend himself ... However, if a person who is ignorant of his right fails to apply and on that account is not given legal aid then, in my view, his constitutional right is violated. For this reason it seems to me that when a person faces a possible prison sentence and has no lawyer, and cannot provide for one, he ought to be informed of his right to legal aid. If he person charged does not know of his right, he cannot exercise it; if he cannot exercise it, his right is violated."

31. [1976] IR 325.
32. On judicial review, see para **[10.35]**.
33. [1976] IR 325, 352.

This passage emphasises the need to inform an accused person of his or her right to legal representation and that, without this, any subsequent trial, even where a person has pleaded guilty, would violate constitutional requirements. Of course, O'Higgins CJ also noted that the right to a lawyer applied where there is the possibility of a sentence of imprisonment and that a person may also waive the right to be represented. On the question of waiver, the court should take account of the circumstances of the defendant, as in the *Healy* case, where the prosecutor's lack of education should have led the court to conclude that he would be unable to defend himself adequately. Indeed, Griffin J made the point that:[34]

> "Very few laymen, when charged in court where their liberty is in jeopardy, can present adequately their own cases, much less identify and argue legal questions."

Thus, notwithstanding the instances mentioned already where a person may choose to defend himself, the general principle to be applied is that, where a person runs the risk of being imprisoned, he should be informed of his right to legal aid and that, unless he is capable of conducting his own defence, he should be provided with legal representation.

[9.16] The Criminal Justice (Legal Aid) Act 1962 refers to legal assistance being 'assigned' by the court, rather than being chosen by the defendant. Those assigned are chosen from the panel of solicitors and barristers who inform the Law Society of Ireland and the Bar Council of Ireland of their willingness to act in cases covered by the 1962 Act. While the courts are entitled to refuse to assign a solicitor not on the panel or who has withdrawn from the panel,[35] in the majority of cases the solicitor nominated by a particular defendant will be assigned to represent him. Finally, we should note that the total cost of the scheme in 1995 was £7.988m, projected to rise to £9.322m in 1996.[36]

Attorney General's scheme in judicial review

[9.17] The Attorney General operates a non-statutory scheme that applies to applications for judicial review connected with criminal matters. The scheme, by which the Attorney General will meet the costs of legal representation in such cases where the High Court certifies that legal representation is required, was first announced in 1967 in the course of an application by a convicted prisoner under Article 40.4.2° of the

34. *Ibid*, 357.

35. *The State (Royle) v Kelly* [1974] IR 259.

36. *First Report of the Working Group on a Courts Commission* (Pn 2690, 1996), p 23. See further para **[4.129]**.

Constitution.[37] It has also been held that a person found guilty but insane in a criminal trial is entitled to legal aid to be represented at hearings before the Minister for Justice's Advisory Committee, which considers whether to release such a person from detention in hospital.[38]

Legal aid in police custody

[9.18] It has been argued in a number of cases that the right to legal aid should be extended to the pre-trial stage of the criminal process, where a person is in garda custody. The Irish courts have, however, been reluctant to do so. In *The People (DPP) v Healy*,[39] the Supreme Court held that, where a person makes a reasonable request for access to a solicitor during garda questioning, the gardaí must themselves make reasonable efforts to secure the attendance of a solicitor. By contrast with the decision in *The State (Healy) v Donoghue*, the courts have not stated that the gardaí must inform the person in custody of his right to request access to a solicitor.[40] Although the courts have not imposed this obligation as a matter of constitutional requirement, s 5 of the Criminal Justice Act 1984 imposes a statutory obligation on the gardaí to inform a person detained in custody of the right to consult a solicitor. It should be noted, however, that there is no formal provision made for payment of the solicitor by the State in such circumstances though, no doubt, any visit to a person in garda custody may be influential in the choice of solicitor if any criminal proceedings subsequently arise.

[5] State-Assisted Civil Legal Aid

[9.19] As already mentioned, the advent of State-assisted civil legal aid is a more recent phenomenon than its counterpart in criminal cases. Thus, in the United Kingdom, a limited form of criminal legal aid was first introduced in 1903, while civil legal aid was first introduced on a statutory basis in 1949.[41]

---

37. *Application of Woods* [1970] IR 154. See further Collins and O'Reilly, *Civil Proceedings and the State in Ireland* (Round Hall Press, 1990), p 53.
38. *Kirwan v Minister for Justice*, High Court, unrep, 29 July 1993.
39. [1990] 2 IR 73.
40. This may be contrasted with the position in the United States where, following the decision of the Supreme Court in *Miranda v Arizona* 384 US 436 (1964), the police are obliged to inform an arrested person of his right to legal counsel during police questioning. Failure to 'Mirandise' an arrested person renders inadmissible in evidence any statement or confession made during police questioning.
41. See Walker & Walker's *English Legal System*, 7th ed (Butterworths, 1994), p 234.

FLAC

[9.20] The tradition within the legal profession of engaging in *pro bono* work was considerably expanded by the establishment in 1969 of the Free Legal Advice Centres (FLAC). This was founded by law students who established law centres where members of the public could seek advice on a wide range of legal problems, including housing, social welfare and family law. The centres were staffed on a voluntary basis by law students, and practising lawyers made their services available free of charge to initiate and conduct court proceedings. The relevant court fees, which we refer to below, were met either by the client or from funds raised by FLAC. FLAC continues to provide legal services to the public, and it now operates in addition to the State-assisted scheme of civil legal aid and advice which it had campaigned for over many years.

Committee on Civil Legal Aid and the *Airey* case

[9.21] In *O'Shaughnessy v Attorney General*,[42] the High Court rejected an argument that the Criminal Justice (Legal Aid) Act 1962 was unconstitutional for failing to make provision for civil legal aid, and O'Keeffe P held that the methods by which the personal rights of a citizen were to be vindicated was exclusively a matter for the Oireachtas. This view would not be shared by many judges today, and indeed it is notable that the decision predated that in *The State (Healy) v Donoghue*.

[9.22] Arising from representations made by FLAC and other organisations, the then Government appointed a Committee on Civil Legal Aid and Advice to make recommendations for the introduction of a scheme of civil legal aid. The Committee reported in 1977, recommending that, in the medium term, a statutory scheme be established, with an interim non-statutory scheme to be put in place immediately.[43]

[9.23] In the meantime, proceedings had been initiated against the State alleging that the absence of a scheme was in breach of the European Convention on Human Rights and Fundamental Freedoms.[44] In *Airey v Ireland*,[45] the plaintiff had sought to initiate judicial separation proceedings in the High Court, but had apparently been unable to secure legal assistance to further process the matter. Ultimately, the European Court of Human Rights held that the State could be in breach of the right of access to the

42. High Court, unrep, 16 February 1971.
43. Committee on Civil Legal Aid and Advice: Report to Minister for Justice (Prl 6862, 1977). The Committee had been chaired by Pringle J, a High Court judge.
44. See generally Ch 16.
45. (1979) 2 EHRR 305.

courts under Article 6(1) of the Convention where the complexity of the legal issues involved in a case prevented effective access. The Court did not conclude that a State-assisted legal aid scheme was required for all litigants, and it pointed out that simplification of procedures was another mechanism for securing effective access. The requirement to secure effective access, the Court stated:[46]

> "may sometimes compel the State to provide for the assistance of a lawyer when such assistance proves indispensable for an effective access to court either because legal representation is rendered compulsory, as is done by the domestic law of certain contracting States for various types of litigation, or by reason of the complexity of the procedures or of the case."

Because of the complexity of the plaintiff's judicial separation case, the Court concluded that her rights under the Convention had been violated. This qualified, rather than absolute, right of access to the courts reflects the approach taken in *The State (Healy) v Donoghue*, which of course was decided after the High Court decision in *O'Shaughnessy v Attorney General*.

Non-statutory civil legal aid scheme

[9.24] In response to the *Airey* case, and of the recommendations of the Committee on Civil Legal Aid, the Government introduced a non-statutory scheme for civil legal aid in 1979,[47] which has been amended from time to time since then. Under the scheme, a Legal Aid Board was established to oversee its administration and a number of Law Centres were opened, staffed by solicitors, to provide legal advice and legal aid, including the initiation of court proceedings for those of limited means. The civil legal aid scheme was criticised for a number of years on the grounds that it was inadequately funded by the State. While the terms of the scheme appeared to be wide-ranging, the effect of the shortfall in funding was that it was confined, in reality, to family law cases and that even in this limited area substantial arrears in responding to need had developed.[48] Since the early 1990s, however, extra State funding has been obtained for the scheme, and it was ultimately accepted that the scheme be placed on a statutory footing. This was also influenced by the realisation that the 1979 scheme failed to meet an increasing number of international agreements which required the provision of civil legal aid.[49] In addition, the courts had indicated that the

46. *Ibid*, para 26.
47. Scheme of Civil Legal Aid and Advice (Prl 8543, 1979).
48. See Whyte, 'And Justice for Some' (1984) 6 DULJ (ns) 88; *The Closed Door; A Report on Civil Legal Aid Services in Ireland* (FLAC, 1987).
49. See Cousins, 'Access to the Courts' (1992) 14 DULJ (ns) 51.

failure to provide effective civil legal aid might, in some circumstances, breach the constitutional right of access to the courts.[50]

Civil Legal Aid Act 1995

[9.25] The Civil Legal Aid Act 1995 consolidated in statutory form the 1979 non-statutory scheme, as amended, and also took account of the international obligations on the State concerning civil legal aid.[51] The 1995 Act made provision for the replacement of the existing Legal Aid Board by the establishment of the Legal Aid Board as a separate legal entity, in effect a State body. The Board, consisting of a chairperson and 12 other members, is appointed by the Minister for Equality and Law Reform. Two members of the Board must be barristers, two must be solicitors and two must be members of the staff of the Board.[52] The principal functions of the Board are to provide, within its resources, legal aid and advice in civil cases to persons who satisfy the eligibility criteria of the 1995 Act, and to disseminate information concerning its services.[53] The Board must publish an Annual Report of its activities.[54]

[9.26] The Board has a chief executive, who is also a civil servant,[55] and is also empowered to appoint full-time staff to carry out its functions. These full-time staff are located in Law Centres.[56] A proportion of the staff are solicitors, who may be designated as civil servants, but the 1995 Act provides that this designation shall not occur unless staff representatives are consulted.[57] This preserves the position prior to the 1995 Act that administrative staff were designated as civil servants, but that solicitors were not; such solicitors thus enjoyed the full standing of solicitors under the Solicitors Acts 1954 to 1994.[58] In addition, the Board is empowered to establish a panel of solicitors and barristers in private practice who are

50. *S v Landy and Ors (Legal Aid Board)*, High Court, unrep, 10 February 1993, where Lardner J held that the mother of a child whom a health board wished to make a ward of court was entitled to legal aid to be represented in the proceedings.
51. Although at the time of writing (July 1996), the 1995 Act has yet to be brought into force, it is expected that this would occur in October 1996 and we accordingly outline the terms of the 1995 Act rather than the 1979 non-statutory scheme.
52. Civil Legal Aid Act 1995, s 4.
53. *Ibid*, s 5.
54. *Ibid*, s 9.
55. *Ibid*, s 10.
56. *Ibid*, s 30.
57. *Ibid*, s 11.
58. See para **[3.21]**.

willing to provide legal aid and advice under the Act.[59] These are similar to the panels for criminal legal aid.[60]

Staff and costs

[9.27] By 1995, the staff of the Legal Aid Board established under the 1979 non-statutory scheme comprised 75 solicitors (up from 39 in 1993), and 129 administrative staff (up from 60 in 1993) in 26 full-time Law Centres in the State (up from 16 in 1993). In 1992, the funding for the Board's activities was £2.7m, rising to £4.97m in 1994 and £6.2m in 1995.[61]

Legal advice and legal aid

[9.28] While the title of the 1995 Act refers to legal aid, it covers both legal advice and legal aid. Legal advice is defined in wide terms in s 25 to include any oral or written advice given to a person by a solicitor or barrister on the application of the law of the State.[62] Legal aid is defined in s 27 of the Act as representation by a solicitor or barrister in the categories of civil proceedings covered by s 28 of the Act as well as relevant preparatory work

Eligibility for legal aid and advice

[9.29] The 1995 Act sets out two basic tests of eligibility for legal aid: a 'merits' test and a 'means' test. For legal advice, the means test only applies. The merits test is laid down in s 24, which provides that a person shall not be granted legal aid unless, in the Board's opinion, a reasonably prudent person who could afford to engage such services would be likely to do so and where a solicitor or barrister would be likely to advise such a person to obtain such services at his or her own expense. The means test is contained in s 29, which provides that a person cannot receive legal aid or advice unless (a) he or she satisfies the requirements concerning financial eligibility specified in the Act and in any Regulations made under the Act; and (b) pays a contribution to the Board towards the cost of any legal aid or advice, the level of contribution to be laid down in Regulations made under the Act. The key financial eligibility question is the level of disposable income of the applicant (that is, gross income, less items such as income tax, mortgage repayments, rent, social insurance, health insurance contributions and other items to take account of, for example, dependent children) and, where applicable, disposable capital (excluding the value of any home). The Act

59. Section 30 of the 1995 Act.

60. See para **[9.16]**.

61. 455 Dáil Debates c 01 763 (29 June 1995).

62. Section 26(4) authorises the Board to grant advice concerning the law of another State if it deems this appropriate.

does not specify any particular sum as a ceiling above which a person is disqualified from receiving legal aid or advice from the Board; this is a matter for Regulations to be made under the Act.

[9.30] The qualifying disposable income figure is reviewed from time to time by reference to the consumer price index. In 1995, the disposable income limit was raised by 18.5% to £7,350. In 1995, the minimum contribution for legal advice was £4, plus an additional £19 where the applicant needs to take or defend court proceedings. The maximum contribution for legal aid in 1995 was £583.[63] Like criminal legal aid, civil legal aid and advice is means tested but, unlike criminal legal aid, involves payment of a contribution or fee. However, s 29(2) also provides that Regulations may give the Board the power to grant legal aid or advice without reference to the means of an applicant and may also empower the Board to waive any contribution.

Criteria for obtaining legal advice

[9.31] Section 26 of the 1995 Act empowers the Board to provide that legal advice if the applicant satisfies the means test in s 29 of the Act and any Regulations made under the Act. Section 26(2) confirms that legal advice may not deal with a criminal law matter, unless it concerns how legal aid can be obtained under by the Criminal Justice (Legal Aid) Act 1962. In addition, s 25(3) provides that a complainant in a sexual assault case is entitled to legal advice from the Legal Aid Board 'free of any contribution.' This provision continues the arrangement in place under the non-statutory scheme since 1991 whereby the Legal Aid Board provided legal advice to such complainants.[64]

[9.32] Legal advice may not be provided by the Board in respect of the excluded categories of civil matters referred to in s 28(9) of the Act.[65] Subject to that proviso, legal advice may be given in respect of virtually any legal matter. This includes advice to a person who has a case pending before a tribunal. As we will see, the 1995 Act prevents the Board from giving legal aid to such a person,[66] but it is not precluded from giving legal advice.

63. 455 Dáil Debates col 766.

64. Ministerial Policy Directive No 1 of 1991 (Pl 7936): *Iris Oifigiúil*, 22 March 1991. This was introduced after the enactment of the Criminal Law (Rape) (Amendment) Act 1990, and comprised the limited response to calls for a right of audience for an adviser to complainants. It was considered that a right of audience was incompatible with the adversarial nature of the criminal trial.

65. See para **[9.35]**.

66. See para **[9.34]**.

Criteria for obtaining legal aid

[9.33] Section 28(2) of the 1995 Act lays down the essential criteria under which the Board grants legal aid, by means of a legal aid certificate. Such a certificate must be granted if, in the Board's opinion:

(a) the applicant satisfies the financial eligibility criteria in s 29 of the Act;

(b) the applicant has as a matter of law reasonable grounds for instituting, defending or being a party to the proceedings for which legal aid is sought;

(c) the applicant is 'reasonably likely to be successful in the proceedings';

(d) the proceedings for which legal aid is sought are the most satisfactory means of achieving the result sought by the applicant; and

(e) having regard to all the circumstances (including the probable cost to the Board, measured against the likely benefit to the applicant), it is reasonable to grant the application.

Section 28(3) provides that factors (c) and (e) will not apply where the proceedings in question concern the welfare of a child, including custody or access. This was inserted to give effect to the decision of the Supreme Court in *MF v Legal Aid Board*,[67] in which the Court held that the test of reasonable likelihood of success in the equivalent of s 28(2) in the non-statutory scheme was appropriate only in disputes *inter partes*. In addition, s 28(5) provides that legal aid shall be provided by the Board where the State is obliged by international obligations to do so. In this respect, it refers expressly to international child abduction and custody cases[68] and those involving international enforcement of maintenance orders.[69]

Legal aid in courts and prescribed tribunals

[9.34] Section 27 of the 1995 Act provides that legal aid may be given in connection with any civil proceedings (save those excluded by s 28(9) of the Act) in any court, from the District Court to the Supreme Court. Proceedings brought to the European Court of Justice under Article 177 of the EC Treaty may also be legally aided. In general, the Board will grant legal aid in the lowest court having jurisdiction in the matter.[70] In addition, the Board may

67. [1993] ILRM 797.

68. Child Abduction and Enforcement of Custody Orders 1991.

69. Maintenance Act 1994.

70. Section 28(8) of the 1995 Act.

be authorised by Ministerial Order to provide legal aid for proceedings in any prescribed court or tribunal. During the passage of the Act, it was proposed that it apply immediately to hearings in the Employment Appeals Tribunal, but this was resisted on the grounds of excessive costs. However, a commitment was given that the required Ministerial Order would be made if the budgetary situation so allowed.[71]

Excluded matters

[9.35] Section 28(9) prohibits the Board from providing legal aid (and legal advice)[72] in the following categories of cases:

(a) defamation claims;

(b) disputes concerning rights and interests in or over land;[73]

(c) civil matters covered by the small claims procedure;[74]

(d) licensing;[75]

(d) conveyancing;

(e) election petitions;

(f) claims made in a representative, fiduciary or official capacity;

(g) claims brought by a person on behalf of a group of persons to establish a precedent on a particular point of law ('test cases');

(h) any other group or representative action.

These exclusions largely replicated the excluded categories in the non-statutory scheme, with the exception that it had originally been proposed to exclude claims concerning debt collection also. This exclusion was removed during the debate on the Act in the Oireachtas.[76] Another divergence from the non-statutory scheme is that the Minister for Equality and Law Reform is authorised by s 28(10), subject to the consent of the Minister for Finance, to remove by Order any of the excluded categories. As with the possible extension of the Act to claims before the Employment Appeals Tribunal, any removal of the excluded categories would depend on the general Government budgetary position.[77] In the meantime, test cases and defamation actions contemplated by those of limited means will continue to

71. Select Committee on Legislation and Security, L5, No 4, cols 269-72 (12 July 1995).

72. See para **[9.32]**.

73. Family law proceedings concerning land and landlord and tenant disputes concerning residential property are not excluded: s 28(9)(c) of the 1995 Act.

74. See para **[5.35]**.

75. Where hardship may arise, licensing disputes are not excluded: s 28(9)(c) of the 1995 Act.

76. 458 Dáil Debates cols 451-2 (15 November 1995).

77. 455 Dáil Debates col 770.

require the goodwill of members of the legal profession to proceed to court.[78]

[6] COURT FEES

[9.36] In addition to the cost of retaining a solicitor and barrister, another significant cost factor in civil litigation in particular is the requirement that fees be paid on all pleadings and other court documents. The precise rates of fees are set from time to time by amendments to the relevant rules of courts. In 1996, the fee on a High Court originating summons was £60, for setting down an action for trial it was £50, while the fee for filing a notice of appeal to the Supreme Court was £50. In the Circuit Court, the fee for issuing a Civil Bill was £25 in 1996. The annual sum raised by these fees in the period 1990 to 1994 averaged just over £9m.[79] Fees are not charged in family proceedings or in judicial review proceedings concerning criminal matters. While the fees may not appear excessive and constitute a low percentage of the full cost of going to court, they may represent a disincentive for those who are unable to avail of State-assisted civil legal aid and in proceedings to which the scheme does not apply.

[9.37] In 1972, the Committee on Court Practice and Procedure[80] recommended the abolition of all court fees on the ground that they might constitute an unreasonable bar to the right of access to the courts. Other recommendations in relation to how court fees could be reduced were also made. It is clear that not all fees have been abolished, though certain categories, such as family law proceedings, are now exempt. The issue of principle remains unresolved, though some judges continue to express doubts about the constitutional validity of court fees in certain cases.[81]

[7] LEGAL COSTS

[9.38] Another direct cost of litigation are the fees which must be paid to the lawyers involved in civil and criminal cases. We discuss elsewhere the general principles concerning costs in civil litigation in this jurisdiction, including the rule that 'costs follow the event'.[82] In those civil cases to which

78. For criticism of these exclusions, see Phelan, 'The Civil Legal Aid Bill 1995: A Critique' (1995) 13 ILT 109.

79. First Report of the Working Group on a Courts Commission (Pn 2690, 1996), pp 28-9: see para **[4.136]**.

80. *17th Interim Report of the Committee on Court Practice and Procedure: Court Fees* (Prl 2699, 1972).

81. See *MacGarbhith v Attorney General* [1991] 2 IR 412.

82. See para **[5.23]**.

the Civil Legal Aid Act 1995 applies, the State may also be required to bear the cost of the plaintiff's and/or defendant's legal representation.[83]

[9.39] In criminal cases covered by the Criminal Justice (Legal Aid) Act 1962, the costs of both the prosecution and defence are borne by the State. In criminal cases not covered by the 1962 Act, it is only in rare instances that a Court will award costs to either side. Where the prosecution is successful and the defendant is found guilty, the State is generally required to pay its own costs. The defendant will also have to pay his or her legal advisers' fees. In some cases where the defendant is acquitted, the trial judge has a discretion to award costs against the State.[84] In a summary prosecution in the District Court, rules of court provide that costs may never be awarded against a member of the Garda Síochána acting as prosecutor, and this special exemption has been held to be constitutionally valid.[85]

Small claims procedure and ADR

[9.40] We discuss elsewhere the introduction of a small claims procedure operated by Clerks of the District Court[86] and the emergence of Alternative Dispute Resolution (ADR)[87] as means of ensuring inexpensive access to justice.

83. See the Civil Legal Aid Act 1995, ss 33-36 on costs in successful and unsuccessful actions involving legally-aided persons.

84. See *The People (Attorney General) v Bell* [1969] IR 24.

85. See *Dillane v Ireland* [1980] ILRM 167.

86. See para **[5.35]**.

87. See para **[8.30]**.

Chapter 10

Remedies and Enforcement

[1] Introduction

[10.01] In this chapter we examine the different remedies and enforcement mechanisms deployed by the courts in civil and criminal matters. As to civil cases, we examine the basis on which the following remedies are awarded: damages (monetary compensation), injunctions and specific performance. We also outline the different enforcement mechanisms to ensure compliance with court orders in civil matters. As to criminal matters, we review the purposes of fines and imprisonment and examine alternative enforcement mechanisms such as community service orders and other enforcement mechanisms appropriate to 'regulatory' offences. We then examine contempt of court, a long-standing jurisdiction employed by the courts to ensure compliance with their orders in both civil and criminal matters. Finally, we examine judicial review, also available as a remedy in civil and criminal matters.

[2] Remedies in Civil Matters

[10.02] Before the courts will grant any remedy in a civil matter, the plaintiff must establish that some recognised legal wrong has been committed, for example, a breach of contract or a recognised tort such as negligence.[1] We do not consider here the necessary ingredients required by the law to establish that a remediable wrong has occurred.[2]

Damages

[10.03] An award of damages, that is monetary compensation, is the most common form of remedy sought in civil claims. The essential principle underlying an award of damages is that the sum awarded is to be a compensatory amount which places the injured person in the position he or she was, so far as money can do so, before the legal wrong was committed.

1. On the overlap between contract and other areas of liability see Phillips, 'The Concurrence of Remedies in Contract and Tort' (1977) 12 *Ir Jur (ns)* 234.
2. See, however, para **[12.70]** for discussion of the development of one area of law, negligence.

[10.04] This is a relatively straightforward matter in a negligence case concerning financial loss. Thus, in *Wall v Hegarty & Callanan*,[3] the plaintiff claimed that the defendants, solicitors, had negligently prepared his uncle's will, causing it to be declared invalid; that as a result he had lost an expected inheritance of £15,000; that the defendants' solicitors had owed him a duty of care in the preparation of the will; that they had failed in this duty, through their carelessness; and that they should therefore be required to compensate him in the sum of £15,000. The High Court agreed that the defendants owed the plaintiff a duty of care and were in breach of that duty. The plaintiff was awarded £15,000 damages having concluded that a loss had been sustained. In this instance, the damages award satisfies the principle that the plaintiff be restored to his position prior to the wrong, or *restitutio in integram*.

[10.05] This principle cannot, however, be applied in full in all cases. Where a person has received personal injuries, even the most skilled surgeon may not be capable of repairing the damage. In such a case, the award of damages reflects an attempt to compensate for the loss suffered. Similarly, in defamation cases, an award of damages is an attempt to compensate for the hurt and loss of reputation arising from the publication of a false statement.

[10.06] In a personal injuries claim, such as arises from a road traffic accident, damages are awarded under two headings, special damages and general damages. Special damages refers to pecuniary losses such as medical expenses or loss of earnings, including loss of earnings in the future after the trial of the action. The calculation of such future loss generally requires evidence from an actuary. General damages refers to non-pecuniary loss and this, in turn, is usually broken into three components: pain and suffering, loss of amenities and loss of expectation of life. The element of pain and suffering includes the immediate pain of the accident and continuing and future discomfort and pain such as the effects of future arthritis. Loss of amenities refers to the loss of the use of a limb; in this respect damages may be increased if the plaintiff is unable to participate in sports or other activities which he or she enjoyed prior to the accident. Loss of expectation of life refers to the damages awarded for any reduction in life expectancy. As we have already seen, in this jurisdiction, damages are awarded on the basis of a once-off lump sum award, rather than 'staged' or annual payments.[4]

3. [1980] ILRM 132: see para **[12.79]**.
4. See para **[5.08]**.

[10.07] While the general principle is that an award of damages is intended to compensate a person for actual loss, so far as money can do so, there are exceptional circumstances where exemplary or punitive damages may be awarded. These include circumstances where there has been a conscious and deliberate violation of rights or where the court is satisfied that the wrongdoer intended to make a profit over and above what would be awarded to the injured party. In this jurisdiction such exemplary damages are, usually, relatively modest.[5]

[10.08] Under s 22 of the Courts Act 1981 a court awarding damages of £150 or more may also order the payment of interest on all or part of that sum from the date of the cause of action to the date of the judgment.

Injunction

[10.09] The injunction was a remedy developed by the courts of equity[6] to prevent one party from acting in such a way as to interfere with the rights of another and to supplement the damages remedy available in the common law courts. Thus, a person who complains that another person has trespassed on his land may not be satisfied with the damages remedy. The trespasser may not, indeed, have any assets to meet the award of damages. The injunction is an order which simply states that the trespasser is to cease and desist from all acts of trespass.

[10.10] The injunction may also be used to prevent some future action which the applicant fears; this is referred to as a *quia timet* injunction. It may take the form of a mandatory injunction, by which the court orders a person to do something, for example, requiring a builder to use materials as agreed in the specifications of a building contract. Another form is the prohibitory injunction, by which a person is prohibited from doing something, as in the 'cease and desist' order used in the case of the trespasser.

[10.11] Once awarded after a full court hearing, an injunction has effect in perpetuity, that is for all time; this is referred to as a perpetual injunction. However, not all cases require a permanent injunction of this nature and, indeed, many situations are of such urgency that to wait for a full court hearing would render meaningless an application for a perpetual injunction. For example, where a person has left one company to become an employee of a rival company, it may very well be pointless for a lawyer to advise the first company that, in two years' time, when the case may come to court, the

5. Eg *Kennedy v Ireland* [1987] IR 587. See generally McMahon and Binchy, *Irish Law of Torts*, 2nd ed. (Butterworths, 1990).

6. See generally para **[2.08]** and Delany, *Equity and the Law of Trusts in Ireland* (Round Hall Sweet & Maxwell, 1996).

employee may be ordered by injunction not to pass on any trade secrets to the new employer. At that stage the secrets may have already been passed on and the first company may be out of business. In such circumstances, the injunction may be used as a holding order to 'freeze' the position of the parties until a full court hearing.[7]

[10.12] In the example given, the first company may apply to court, without notice to the rival company, for an interim injunction. The application without notice is referred to as an *ex parte* application, since only one party appears in court, contrary to the normal principle of the adversarial system that both parties should appear. The company applying for relief will outline to the court the background to the case; indicate that it intends to institute proceedings against its former employee and the rival company; present to the court the relevant initiating documents, which may include a claim for damages and/or a perpetual injunction, with a view to the court approving their issue without the normal notification requirements; and then apply for an interim injunction to preserve the *status quo* of the parties until the hearing of the intended action. Having heard the application, the judge may grant an interim injunction, in this case prohibiting the former employee from passing trade secrets to the rival company. Once this court order has been granted, it carries the full authority of the courts, and failure to obey its terms would constitute contempt of court.[8] However, since it is obtained on the basis of one party's presentation, an interim injunction has a limited life-span, generally 24 to 48 hours. In addition, the company obtaining the injunction must also undertake to serve the injunction on those affected by it; notify them when the next stage of the proceedings, an application for an interlocutory injunction, will take place; and undertake to the court to pay any damages to the affected parties in the event that the injunction should not have been granted in the first place.

[10.13] The next phase of the proceedings is the application for an interlocutory injunction, which takes place at the end of the 24 to 48 hour life of the interim injunction. At the interlocutory application, both parties are in court to present their case. However, the court does not make a final determination on the merits of the case, such as whether any restriction in

---

7. The injunction obtained to 'freeze' financial assets, where a bank is ordered not to reduce the assets in a specified bank account below a certain level pending the outcome of an action, is generally referred to as a Mareva injunction (after one of the first English cases in which it was discussed, *Mareva Compania Naviera SA v International Bulkcarriers SA* [1975] 2 Lloyd's Rep 509): see *Powerscourt Estates v Gallagher* [1984] ILRM 123. A similar type of remedy is the Anton Piller Order (also after one of the first English cases in which it was discussed, *Anton Piller KG v Manufacturing Processes Ltd* [1976] Ch 55), which allows one party to take documents and other items from a named premises; such orders are used, for example, in video piracy cases, but should be distinguished from discovery orders, discussed at para **[6.50]**.
8. See para **[10.32]**.

the employee's contract prohibiting him from joining another company is valid.[9] Rather, the court considers two factors; whether the applicant has made out a stateable legal case in connection with the claim it has instituted and whether the balance of convenience favours granting an injunction.[10]

[10.14] On the question of a stateable case, the court need only be satisfied that the applicant has some legal grounds on which to institute proceedings, but not necessarily that these will be successful.[11] The issue of the balance of convenience requires the court to consider, on the one hand, the position where an interlocutory injunction has been granted but the restriction on the former employee is found to be invalid at the final hearing and, on the other, where an interlocutory injunction is refused but at the final hearing the restriction is found to be valid. The balance of convenience generally favours the award of an interlocutory injunction in the example given. The courts will generally take the view that the consequences of refusing an injunction may be that the company seeking the injunction will have gone out of business before the case comes to hearing and that an award of damages is unlikely to be a sufficient remedy. By contrast, while the former employee may have his employment opportunities improperly restricted, this could be remedied by an award of damages. The court is also likely to be influenced by the requirement that, if an interlocutory injunction is granted, the employer must to continue the undertaking to pay any damages to the former employee and the rival company in the event that the restriction is ultimately found to be invalid.

Specific performance

[10.15] This is another equitable remedy developed to give a more effective remedy than damages in breach of contract cases. Specific performance is an order requiring the person in breach of contract to perform it according to the terms agreed. To obtain an order for specific performance, the court must be satisfied that damages would be an insufficient remedy and that there has been no undue delay or other matter which might disentitle the applicant to the remedy. In addition, there are certain types of contracts for which the remedy will not, usually, be granted. These include contracts of personal service, such as employment contracts. The remedy of specific performance is a particularly valuable remedy in connection with contracts for the sale of land.[12]

---

9. Such restrictions are referred to as covenants in restraint of trade: see generally Clark, *Contract Law in Ireland*, 3rd ed, (Sweet & Maxwell, 1991).

10. See *Campus Oil Ltd v Minister for Industry and Energy (No 2)* [1983] IR 88.

11. See *European Chemical Industries Ltd v Bell* [1981] ILRM 345.

12. See, eg, *Nestor v Murphy* [1979] IR 326, discussed at para **[14.28]** and generally Delany, *Equity and the Law of Trusts in Ireland* (Round Hall Sweet & Maxwell, 1996) and Farrell, *Irish Law of Specific Performance* (Butterworths, 1994).

Declaration

[10.16] Where a plaintiff does not seek any of the remedies discussed, such as damages, he or she may apply to court for a declaration. This was another remedy developed by the courts of equity with a view to determining the rights or status of a person. Thus, at the time when a person's rights might be dependent on a determination whether they were illegitimate,[13] the declaration was the appropriate remedy to seek. In this jurisdiction, the declaration is commonly used in constitutional claims, where for example the plaintiff seeks a declaration that a particular statutory provision is invalid on the ground that it is in conflict with a right contained in the Constitution of Ireland 1937, *Bunreacht na hÉireann*.[14]

[3] PROCEDURE FOR ENFORCEMENT OF COURT ORDERS

[10.17] A number of well-established procedures exist for the enforcement of monetary awards by courts and we discuss these briefly here. A key method is for the person in whose favour an award has been made, the judgment creditor, to seek a further court order authorising the property of the defaulter, including goods, to be seized and then sold. An order for *fieri facias* (commonly referred to as a *fi fa* order) may be issued by the High Court authorising a County Registrar (in Dublin, the County Sheriff) to cause to be made (*fieri facias*) a sufficient sum out of the defaulter's assets to discharge the debt. The *fi fa* order authorises the seizure of goods. Another enforcement method is the garnishee order, which assigns the judgment creditor any debt owed to the defaulter by a third party. A well-charging order may be obtained by a judgment creditor in order to 'attach' the court award to any real property, such as land, owned by the judgment debtor. The judgment debtor may also seek to have appointed a receiver by way of equitable execution to intercept any income and profits before they reach the defaulter. This would be used in large debt situations.[15] In contempt of court cases, which we discuss below, committal for contempt may be accompanied by an application for sequestration of assets. Sequestration authorises the sequestrators to take possession of all property and assets in the possession of the individual or organisation in contempt of

13. Many of the distinctions between the rights of a person born within marriage and one born outside marriage had been abolished prior to the abolition of the status of illegitimacy by the Status of Children Act 1987.

14. See Ch 15.

15. For attachment of earnings in family proceedings, see para **[10.20]**.

court and to manage that property and assets until the contempt has been purged.[16]

[10.18] One of the most difficult and controversial methods of enforcing a court order is an order for the possession and sale of land, particularly farm land. Such orders are obtained, for example, by a financial institution where there is default on a loan or mortgage and may well follow a well-charging order. As the folk memory of forced evictions remains vivid for many people, there have been occasions where land is placed for auction by court order but in which no bids have been made. In such circumstances, a bank attempting to recover a debt in relation to land may enter into an arrangement with the defaulting landowner under which the land is auctioned or otherwise sold without being categorised as a court sale.

[10.19] The Enforcement of Court Orders Acts 1926 and 1940, as amended by the Courts (No 2) Act 1986, empower the District Court to require a person in default of a court order to make payments in accordance with a schedule of payments arrived at by the court after an assessment of the defaulter's means. If the defaulter continues to default on such payments he or she may be attached for contempt of court[17] and lodged in prison for such failure. It may be noted, however, that no person may be sent to prison for inability to pay a debt, but only for wilful refusal to pay a debt within the person's means. There are, therefore, no longer any debtor's prisons in the original sense, which indeed, were one of the first purposes for which prisons were constructed. Nonetheless, a number of people continue to be imprisoned for wilful refusal to pay a debt, and this has been criticised by a United Nations Committee as an anachronism in the 20th century, which may result in the repeal of this legislation.[18]

[10.20] Other legislation intended to facilitate the enforcement of court awards has a more modern approach. In the context of awards of maintenance to spouses and children, the Family Law Act 1995 provides for improved mechanisms aimed at ensuring such awards are complied with; this includes attachment of earnings of defaulting spouses, by which the employer is required to pay a specified sum direct to the spouse and children in whose favour the maintenance order was made.

---

16. In *Larkins v National Union of Mineworkers* [1985] IR 671 an application was refused to appoint sequestrators to funds held in an Irish bank on behalf of the British NUM, who were in contempt of an order of the English High Court.

17. See para **[10.32]**.

18. See O'Flaherty, 'Implementation of the International Covenant on Civil and Political Rights' (1993) 11 ILT 225, 231.

Trans-national enforcememt

[10.21] A number of recent statutory provisions give effect to international agreements concerning enforcement in this jurisdiction of the orders of foreign courts. For example, the Enforcement of Judgments (European Communities) Acts 1988 and 1993 give effect to a 1968 Convention on the Enforcement of Judgments in Civil and Commercial Matters, the 'Brussels' Convention.[19] Such legislation is part of Private International Law, or the Conflict of Laws.[20]

[4] ENFORCEMENT IN CRIMINAL MATTERS

[10.22] Before the enforcement mechanisms referred to below arise for consideration, it must be established that a criminal offence has been committed. We do not consider here the necessary ingredients required by the law to establish that a criminal offence has been committed.

Fines and imprisonment

[10.23] We have already considered the principal enforcement mechanisms in criminal matters, namely fines and imprisonment, which characterise the punitive nature of criminal law.[21] While the sentence of imprisonment is a matter for the courts, the execution of the sentence is a matter for the executive branch. In this respect, the executive determines in most instances the actual length of time served by a person in prison. Legislation empowers the Minister for Justice to remit sentences of imprisonment, that is to reduce the sentence imposed in court.[22] In addition, the Minister is empowered to release prisoners from prison without affecting the sentence imposed by means of a form of parole known as temporary release.[23] It remains to consider the other enforcement mechanisms deployed in criminal matters.

Probation and binding to the peace

[10.24] The Probation of Offenders Act 1907 applies where a person has been charged in any court with an offence punishable by imprisonment. A probation order can take two forms: a conditional discharge and an absolute discharge.

---

19. See Byrne and Binchy, *Annual Review of Irish Law 1988*, pp 90-104.
20. See generally Binchy, *Irish Conflict of Laws* (Butterworths, 1988).
21. See paras **[6.03]-[6.05]**.
22. Criminal Justice Act 1951. See *Brennan v Minister for Justice* [1995] 1 IR 612, discussed at para **[4.13]**.
23. Criminal Justice Act 1960, s 2. For criticisms, see para **[5.13]**.

[10.25] The conditional discharge applies in any court where a person has been convicted of the offence, but the court considers that it is 'inexpedient', having regard to all the circumstances, to inflict any punishment other than a nominal punishment. Section 1 of the 1907 Act provides that the court may order a conditional discharge of the defendant, by which the defendant is required to enter into a recognisance, that is a bond or agreement, to be of good behaviour during a period not exceeding three years and, if in breach of probation during that period, to appear in court to be sentenced. The conditional discharge involves the supervision of the person by a probation officer, who is a civil servant within the Probation and Welfare Service of the Department of Justice. This jurisdiction may be compared with the power of the District Court under s 54 of the Courts (Supplemental Provisions) Act 1961 to bind a person to keep the peace, in succession to the former justices of the peace.[24] The absolute discharge applies only in the District Court. While the judge of the District Court will have concluded that the offence has been proved, an absolute discharge has the advantage for the person charged that no conviction is recorded or entered. Because of this aspect to an absolute discharge, probation orders are more frequently associated with the District Court.[25] The 1907 Act applies to corporate bodies as well as individuals and absolute discharges of companies are applied in 'regulatory' offences in the District Court.[26]

Community service

[10.26] The Criminal Justice (Community Service) Act 1983 introduced a regime common in many other States. The 1983 Act empowers any court, other than a special criminal court, to make a community service order in respect of any person over 16 years of age convicted of an offence for which a sentence of imprisonment might otherwise be imposed. The order obliges the convicted person to complete between 40 and 240 hours unpaid work

24. See para **[2.51]**. In *Gregory v Windle* [1994] 3 IR 613, it was held that the power was not in conflict with the Constitution of 1937.

25. Certain informal customs have built up around the absolute discharge mechanism. A person charged with an offence may offer in court to pay a sum of money to a named charity and the judge may then indicate that this would 'qualify' the person for an absolute discharge. This has occurred in some highly-publicised cases where a well-known personality of considerable means may offer to pay a large sum of money in return for an absolute discharge which, as indicated in the text, has the important effect that no conviction is recorded. In less-publicised but more frequent instances, the judge may ask for a contribution to the 'poor box', which in effect is an informal fund held by the Court for distribution to worthy causes.

26. See, eg, the account of summary prosecutions under the Safety, Health and Welfare at Work Act 1989 in the *Annual Report of the National Authority for Occupational Safety and Health 1994*.

under the supervision of a probation officer. The 1983 Act requires that such an order shall not be made unless the convicted person consents and the court is satisfied, having considered the convicted person's circumstances, that he or she is suitable to perform the work indicated in the community service order. The court must also explain to the convicted person that failure to perform the community service is itself an offence under the Act.

Compensation orders

[10.27] We have referred elsewhere to the jurisdiction to make compensation orders in criminal matters.[27]

Enforcement orders for 'regulatory' offences

[10.28] We have referred earlier to legislation creating what has been termed 'regulatory' criminal offences, such as environmental protection legislation and occupational safety legislation.[28] While such legislation creates offences and accompanying penalties, including fines and imprisonment, it also typically involves other enforcement mechanisms which do not fall neatly into the civil-criminal categorisation.

[10.29] By way of example, we may mention some enforcement powers conferred on inspectors of the National Authority for Occupational Safety and Health pursuant to the Safety, Health and Welfare at Work Act 1989. Section 36 of the 1989 Act empowers an inspector to issue an Improvement Notice where the inspector is of opinion that an undertaking is contravening or has contravened any relevant statutory provisions and may include directions as to how the employer can comply with the relevant statutory duties by a specified date. Section 37 of the 1989 Act empowers an inspector to issue a Prohibition Notice in relation to activities which the inspector is of opinion 'involve or ... are likely to involve a risk of serious personal injury to persons at any place of work.' The issuing of such a notice might require an immediate stoppage of work. Failure to comply with any such notice is itself an offence under the 1989 Act. In addition to the powers given to individual inspectors, the Authority itself may apply to the High Court under s 39 of the 1989 Act for a prohibition order in relation to certain activities. This can be obtained on an *ex parte* basis. The 1989 Act provides that failure to comply with such an order is an offence, and a defaulter may also be in contempt of court.

---

27. See para **[6.04]**.
28. See para **[6.11]**.

Trans-national enforcement

[10.30] As with enforcement of civil law on a trans-national basis, recent statutory provisions give effect to international agreements concerning enforcement of crimes committed on an international basis. These include the Genocide Act 1973[29] and the Criminal Justice Act 1994. The latter attempts to deal with the 'money laundering' elements of international drug trafficking.[30]

[5] CONTEMPT OF COURT

[10.31] Contempt of court concerns the manner in which the courts punish a person for any action that involves an interference with the administration of justice. In this jurisdiction, contempt of court remains regulated by common law principles developed by the courts over many centuries.[31]

Civil contempt and criminal contempt

[10.32] Two forms of contempt have developed: civil contempt and criminal contempt. Civil contempt consists of defiance of a court order, such as refusal to obey an injunction. Criminal contempt consists of any action intended to prejudice the due course of justice or which brings the administration of justice into disrepute. This includes contempt *in facie curiae*, that is in the face of the court, such as disrupting court proceedings; scandalising the courts, such as totally unfounded criticisms of the courts; breaching the *sub judice* rule, that is prejudicing pending court proceedings; subjecting a party to court proceedings to comment which ridicules that party, such as publishing scandalous material while their case in progress; and other interferences with the administration of justice, such as threatening a witness.

Procedure in civil contempt

[10.33] Where a civil contempt is alleged to have occurred it is a matter for the person who obtained the court order that has been disobeyed to bring this to the attention of the court in question. The court may then order that the contemnor, the person in contempt, be attached for contempt, that is,

---

29. See para **[5.85]**.

30. See also para **[6.66]**.

31. In the United Kingdom, contempt of court is regulated by the Contempt of Court Act 1981. The Law Reform Commission has made proposals for legislation in this area, in order to ensure that the law in the jurisdiction meets constitutional requirements as well as obligations arising from the European Convention on Human Rights (see para **[17.23]**): *Report on Contempt of Court* (LRC 47-1994). See generally, McGonagle, *A Textbook on Media Law* (Gill and Macmillan, 1996), pp 137-68.

brought before the Court. When the person comes before the Court he may inform the court that he is prepared to obey the Court order, and that is generally the end of the matter. Otherwise, the judge will order that the person be lodged in prison 'until he doth purge his contempt.' The effect of this is that the person must remain in prison until he or she is prepared to come before the Court to apologise and to undertake to obey the Court order in the future. Until that is done the person may not be released under any circumstances, except by order of the Court. It is a term of imprisonment unlike any other, therefore, with no time limit. It has been described as coercive, rather than having the punitive element of a sentence of imprisonment on foot of a conviction in criminal matters.[32] Sequestration of assets may also accompany the civil contempt procedure.[33]

Procedure in criminal contempt

[10.34] A prosecution for criminal contempt may be initiated by the Director of Public Prosecutions in the manner we described elsewhere.[34] However, reflecting its medieval origins, a prosecution may also be initiated by a judge, including the judge before whom an *in facie* contempt has occurred. Indeed, a judge may order a disruptive person to be arrested, initiate the prosecution, try the case without a jury and impose sentence. However, in light of the requirements of the Constitution, the Supreme Court has suggested that, in the absence of exceptional circumstances requiring the immediate protection of the administration of justice, the courts should be reluctant to initiate a prosecution without the intervention of the Director of Public Prosecutions and the procedural protections associated with a trial in due course of law pursuant to Article 38.1.[35]

[6] JUDICIAL REVIEW

[10.35] We have noted elsewhere that the medieval Anglo-Norman court of the King's Bench developed the prerogative writs as a means of ensuring that inferior courts and other adjudicative bodies complied with certain basic requirements of the common law.[36] In the aftermath of the foundation of the Irish Free State in 1922, these were transformed into the State Side orders and, in 1986, became orders for judicial review.[37] In keeping with their pre-

32. See *Keegan v de Burca* [1973] IR 223.
33. See para **[10.17]**.
34. See para **[6.65]**.
35. See *The State (DPP) v Walsh* [1981] IR 412.
36. See para **[2.32]**.
37. Rules of the Superior Courts 1986, Order 84 (SI 15/1986). The changes effected by the 1986 Rules were based largely on the Working Paper of the Law Reform Commission *Judicial Review of Administrative Action: The Problem of Remedies* (1979).

1922 origins, the jurisdiction in judicial review is vested in the High Court. While substantial procedural changes were effected in 1986, the original titles of the former prerogative and State Side orders remain in place.

[10.36] The Anglo-Norman courts had developed a number of prerogative writs. *Certiorari*, is used to quash the decision of a lower court or tribunal which has been found to have acted outside its powers. *Mandamus* is directed to a court or tribunal ordering it to fulfil a lawful obligation which it is not carrying out. An order of prohibition is directed at a court or tribunal preventing it from exercising its powers, either completely or until certain conditions have been met. *Habeas corpus* is the remedy which requires production of a person in court in order to determine whether the person is validly detained, for example in police custody or in prison. Of the four prerogative writs developed by the common law, only the *habeas corpus* remedy has been overtaken by the Constitution of Ireland 1937. Article 40.4.2° provides for a procedure for inquiring into the legality of a person's detention. For this reason, it is felt that the old writ of *habeas corpus* may be obsolete, though many judges continue to use the Latin phrase when referring to an application under Article 40.4.2°.[38]

[10.37] Judicial review should be distinguished from an appeal on a point of law from a lower court or tribunal. An appeal on a point of law concerns the issue involved in the lower court's decision, while judicial review is concerned with the authority of the lower court or tribunal to enter into an adjudication in the first place (its jurisdiction) or the procedures followed by it in the course of the adjudication. We consider elsewhere constitutional judicial review.[39]

[10.38] We have noted elsewhere that judicial review thus involves determining whether the court or tribunal acted *intra vires* (that is, within its powers) or *ultra vires* (that is, outside its powers and whether it complied with the basic rules of natural justice or fair procedures, in particular that it be unbiased (*nemo judex in causa sua*) and give all sides involved an opportunity to prepare their case and be given an even-handed hearing, whether an oral hearing or by correspondence (*audi alteram partem*).[40] An unusual example of *ultra vires* action quashed on judicial review was *The State (Walshe) v Murphy*,[41] in which the High Court held that the respondent, who had all the appearances of being a judge of the District Court, had not

38. See generally Hogan and Whyte, *Kelly's The Irish Constitution*, 3rd ed (Butterworths, 1994) p 898.

39. See para **[15.47]**.

40. See para **[8.22]**.

41. [1981] IR 275: see paras **[4.68]-[4.69]**.

met the formal qualification requirements to be appointed to that position in the first place and was thus not empowered to convict the prosecutor on a charge under the Road Traffic Acts.

Procedure in judicial review

[10.39] The application for judicial review is in two stages. The first stage involves an *ex parte* application to a High Court judge for leave to proceed, where the applicant sets out the grounds on which relief is being sought. This application is granted if the judge considers that the case discloses some ground for claiming relief, though no decision is made at this stage as to whether the applicant is likely to be ultimately successful. The applicant must then serve notice on the other party, called the respondent. The second stage is the application for judicial review itself, where the court determines whether, for example, an order of *certiorari* should issue. One of the major changes introduced in 1986 was that the Court may grant other remedies, such as an award of damages or a declaration on judicial review.[42]

42. See further Hogan & Morgan, *Administrative Law in Ireland*, 2nd ed (Sweet & Maxwell, 1991).

Chapter 11

Law Reform

[1] Introduction

[11.01] It is clear from earlier chapters that substantial reform has been effected in recent years in areas that directly concern the legal system. These include reform within both branches of the legal profession,[1] increases in the number of judges appointed to the courts,[2] changes in the jurisdiction of the different courts,[3] changes in court procedure,[4] reform of the appeals system[5] and significant changes to the State-assisted civil legal aid system.[6] In addition, substantial change in the management of the court system has also been recommended and is likely to be implemented in the future.[7] These changes have reflected reform within State institutions generally.[8] We have also noted that these procedural changes have been accompanied by changes in substantive law.[9] In this chapter, we outline the various mechanisms used to achieve such law reform.

[2] Judicial Decisions and Law Reform

[11.02] The process of judicial decision-making in this legal jurisdiction involves the application of existing legal principles, whether common law or statutory, to particular factual situations.[10] While this process does not constitute a formal element of law reform, its effect is similar. Thus, a decision of the High Court applying established common law principles of negligence in a new setting, such as the question of the liability of a solicitor to persons other than his client, establishes a precedent for subsequent similar cases.[11] The application in a new setting is equivalent to law reform. Similarly, a judicial interpretation of a statutory provision may lead to a

1. See Ch 3.
2. See Ch 4.
3. See Ch 5.
4. See para **[6.94]**.
5. See Ch 7.
6. See para **[9.25]**.
7. See para **[4.129]**.
8. See para **[8.17]**.
9. See paras **[5.07]-[5.16]**.
10. See generally Ch 12.
11. See *Wall v Hegarty & Callanan* [1980] ILRM 124, para **[12.79]**.

clearer understanding of what until then was unclear.[12] In some instances, the judicial clarification may require amending legislation to remedy a defect in the existing statutory provisions[13] or to remove an unwanted interpretation.[14] A decision of the courts that certain statutory provisions are in conflict with a provision of the Constitution may be followed by legislation to remedy the difficulty,[15] or it may require an amendment to the Constitution.[16]

[11.03] Such law reform, while significant, is largely reactive. However, many of the more significant reforms effected in recent years have been preceded by considered debate and discussion of the areas of law being reformed.

[3] Legislative and Constitutional Reform

[11.04] We discuss elsewhere the procedures followed in the Oireachtas for the enactment of primary legislation, including the use of *ad-hoc* Committees of Inquiry and the publication of Green Papers and White Papers prior to presentation of a Bill.[17] We also discuss elsewhere the increasing importance of secondary or delegated legislation.[18] In this chapter, we refer to other institutions which have contributed to law reform generally. Much of the impetus for reform began with the publication in 1961 of a Government White Paper on law reform.[19]

Committee on Court Practice and Procedure

[11.05] In 1962 the then Minister for Justice established a Committee on Court Practice and Procedure with a view to making recommendations

12. See, eg, *Nestor v Murphy* [1979] IR 326, para **[14.28]**.
13. Eg, the decision in *Rafferty v Crowley* [1984] ILRM 350 (para **[14.31]**), which the judge in the case accepted was an unsatisfactory result, led to the enactment of the Building Societies (Amendment) Act 1983 to remedy the problem highlighted by the decision. Similarly, *The State (Clarke) v Roche* [1986] IR 619 (para **[4.14]**) resulted in the passing within a matter of weeks of the Courts (No 3) Act 1986.
14. Many decisions of the courts on taxation legislation are followed by amending legislation to 'close tax loopholes.' Eg, the decision in *C McCann Ltd v Ó Cúlacháin* [1986] IR 196, the 'banana ripening' case, and other similar cases resulted in amendment to the statutory provisions concerning tax allowances for manufacturing.
15. Eg, the decision in *de Burca v Attorney General* [1976] IR 38 resulted in the enactment of the Juries Act 1976: see para **[6.100]**.
16. Eg, comments in *M v An Bord Uchtála* [1977] IR 287 resulted in a referendum which approved an amendment to Article 37 of the Constitution: see para **[4.16]**.
17. See paras **[13.30]-[13.32]**.
18. See paras **[13.58]-[13.80]**.
19. *Programme of Law Reform* (Pr 6379, 1962).

concerning reform in the administration of the courts. Between 1963 and 1978, the Committee published 20 Interim Reports concerning a wide range of topics.[20] Many of these Reports have been implemented, both by legislation[21] and other non-legislative changes in the administration of the courts.[22] The Committe is currently chaired by Blayney J, a judge of the Supreme Court.

Working Group on a Courts Commission

[11.06] We discussed elsewhere the establishment in 1995 of the Working Group on a Courts Commission.[23]

Fair Trade Commission

[11.07] We describe elsewhere the important reforms effected by the Fair Trade Commission's 1990 Report into Restrictive Practices in the Legal Profession.[24]

Report of the Constitution Review Group

[11.08] We refer elsewhere to the recommendations contained in the Report of the Constitution Review Group, published in 1996.[25]

Law Reform Commission

[11.09] The Law Reform Commission Act 1975 provided for the establishment of the Law Reform Commission, the first statutory body with a wide-ranging role to engage in research with a view to making considered recommendations on any area of law. The Law Reform Commission is not confined to a particular aspect of law reform, such as the courts structure. Indeed, the majority of its Working Papers, Consultation Papers and Reports have concerned virtually all aspects of the law.[26]

[11.10] Many of the Commission's recommendations have been implemented in legislation. This can be explained by the widespread

---

20. See O'Malley, *The Round Hall Guide to Sources of Law* (Round Hall Press, 1993) , p 210 for a complete list of the Committee's published reports. Three further reports of the Committee, submitted to the Minister for Justice between 1991 and 1994, have not been published at the time of writing (July 1996).
21. See para **[3.22]**.
22. See para **[4.48]**.
23. See para **[4.29]**.
24. See paras **[3.05]**-**[3.07]**.
25. See para **[15.139]**.
26. See O'Malley, *op cit*, pp 207-9 for a list of the Commission's publications to 1993. The Commission also publishes a complete list as an Appendix to each of its own publications.

discussion with interested parties, including Government and other State bodies, in which it engages prior to making final recommendations.[27]

[11.11] Each of the four Presidents of the Law Reform Commission to date have been senior members of the judiciary.[28] The Commission staff comprise full-time and part-time researchers and full-time administrative staff.

27. See the statement by the then President of the Law Reform Commission, Keane J, in (1987) 5 ILT 123. For criticisms of earlier failure to implement recommendations of the Commission, see Kerr, 'Is there Anybody Out There Listening?' (1983) 1 ILT 100.

28. Walsh J, the first President, was then senior ordinary judge of the Supreme Court. Keane J, the second President, was then a High Court judge (since appointed to the Supreme Court). O'Hanlon J was a senior judge of the High Court when appointed, though he withdrew as President a short time after his appointment: see para **[4.95]**. The current President, Hederman J, was the then senior ordinary judge of the Supreme Court until his retirement from the Bench in 1993.

Chapter 12

Precedent

[1] Introduction

[12.01] Appeals to precedent, that is the seeking of guidance for current practice from past events, are common in many organisational systems. Children pleading with their parents frequently claim parity with their perceived equals ('every other boy in my class will be allowed stay up to watch the football match'); in the world of commerce the case-study method provides exemplars to be imitated in decision-making and planning; and within bureaucracies the repetition of practices eventually establishes models of expected conduct. In this regard legal systems are little different with precedent being invoked to ensure the consistent application of the law.[1] In seeking consistency two objectives of justice are pursued. The first is that the law is applied equally, as similar cases are treated similarly. The second is that the law becomes certain and one can determine in advance the legal quality of a proposed course of action. Those who are subjected to a regime of regulation are entitled to fair notice of that which is required of them - a hallmark of authoritarianism is that one is uncertain of the laws which govern one's conduct. In this respect, if courts were allowed a discretion as to whether to follow an earlier case the perceived danger is that different courts would identify and apply different rules. That is not to say that judges would exhibit favouritism or bias, but the risk is that through the application of different judicial standards conflicting and contradictory rules might emerge. Thus, to ensure consistency the practice developed whereby courts followed earlier relevant decisions. This feature is shared by civil law and common law systems alike but in the case of common law systems precedent, encapsulated in the principle of *stare decisis* ('let the decision stand'), has a greater significance.[2] Since common law systems, unlike their civilian equivalents, lack the textual basis of an authoritative code their rules are to be found in the decisions of courts which are charged with the task of applying them. As a result judicial decisions are a source of law, loosely called 'case law', to which lawyers have recourse - they enjoy the force of

1. See generally Goldstein (ed) *Precedent in Law* (Clarendon Press, 1987); Cross & Harris, *Precedent in English Law* 4th ed (Clarendon Press, 1991); Stone, *Precedent and Law* (Butterworths, 1985).
2. See Cross & Harris, *op cit,* pp 10-15 comparing precedent in England and France.

law and are not simply examples to be imitated. The practice of following earlier cases has become so prevalent that its correctness is now beyond dispute and can be considered to be the principal rule of judicial decision-making in common law systems.[3]

[12.02] The operation of a system of precedent depends on a number of implicit conditions.[4] The first is that a hierarchy of courts exists which facilitates the ready evaluation of the force of any particular precedent. The second is that prior decisions are recorded in a reasonably accurate and reliable manner, thus providing the material which will govern future cases. A third condition is that the legal community accepts the binding force of precedent and is prepared to accept that propositions of law are validated by decided cases. Moreover, a system of precedent functions on the basis of a general acceptance that consistency, certainty and predictability are values worth pursuing and are to be preferred to competing values such as flexibility and the search for individual justice. The nature of a system of precedent is such that it restricts an adjudicator and denies him or her the discretion which other decision makers, such as government and legislators, might enjoy. The judge must decide a case on the basis of prior decisions even though a better, more just solution might be reached by ignoring those decisions. While a system of precedent might constrain a judge it also operates to legitimise his or her decisions and, it is hoped, preserve confidence in the judiciary. Decisions reached are not attributable to the preferences or whims of judges but to the preceding body of law which moulded them.

[12.03] When we speak of following cases it should be realised that the process is neither simple nor mechanical. On the contrary, it is complicated and involves the use of skills and techniques which are acquired through exposure to, and experience of, the methods and devices employed by courts. In one sense no two cases are similar, in that each case presents a unique set of circumstances which differentiates it from any other. The task of the courts is to identify cases which can be considered to be similar and to reach similar conclusions in those cases. To this extent the system is flexible in that courts are in essence required to place cases in conceptual categories from which the legal issues involved are analysed. But once two cases are placed in the same category, and thus deemed to be similar, the expectation

3. However, it must be noted that the application of precedent varies in different common law jurisdictions; see Tunc, 'The not so Common Law of England and the United States, or, Precedent in England and in the United States, a field study by an outsider' (1984) 47 MLR 150.

4. See Miers, 'Review of Stone, *Precedent and Law* (Butterworths, 1985)' (1986) 6 LS 331.

that earlier cases be followed strives to ensure consistency of application. In this respect the system of precedent establishes a methodology within which relevant legal principles are extracted from earlier decisions and are developed and expanded through their application in later cases.

[12.04] Although we have spoken so far of courts being expected to follow earlier decisions it should not be assumed that a court is required to follow every relevant decision which preceded it. A distinction is drawn between *binding authority* and *persuasive authority.* A court is required to follow the former, but in respect of the latter it enjoys a discretion as to whether or not it should adopt the decision. The principal rule which has emerged is that a court must follow the prior decisions of courts superior to it in the judicial hierarchy. This rule is so well established that it has rarely been questioned, in this jurisdiction at least. In addition, a court is generally expected to follow the earlier decisions of courts of co-ordinate, or equal, jurisdiction. The latter is not an inflexible rule and courts, on occasion, have expressed a freedom to depart from their own earlier decisions. On the other hand, a court is not bound by the decisions of an inferior court. Likewise, Irish courts are not bound by the decisions of foreign courts, as that would amount to a derogation from Irish sovereignty. However, the decisions of both inferior and foreign courts are of persuasive authority and so may be followed at the option of the court. The decisions of foreign courts are regularly cited in and adopted by Irish courts, especially where there is an absence of relevant Irish authority.

[12.05] When a court is said to be bound by an earlier decision it does not follow that everything which the earlier court said is binding. Judges do not adopt a uniform format when writing their judgments but a number of elements may be identified in each judgment. It will contain a recitation of the facts of the case coupled, if necessary, with comments on and an evaluation of the evidence which was adduced by the parties. A discussion and analysis of the relevant law will follow, and finally the law will be applied to the facts of the case. The part of the judgment which is binding is called the *ratio decidendi.* For present purposes it can be defined as being the reason for the decision; it consists of the relevant principle of law applied to the facts of the case.[5] Other statements of law which are contained in the case are called *obiter dicta.* They are not of direct relevance to the decision and, consequently, are not binding. They are, however, of persuasive authority and may be adopted at the option of the later court.

5. See further paras **[12.44]-[12.68]**.

[12.06] Several terms ought to be explained at this stage. When an appeal is successful the appellate court is said to have *reversed* the inferior court. The effect is that the decision of the lower court is replaced by that of the higher court and the party who initially lost the case now finds that he or she has won. However, once a decision becomes final and is no longer subject to the possibility of being appealed, the principle of *res judicata* applies and the parties to the case are bound by the decision and may not, in general, seek to have it re-opened. When an appellate court in a later case considers the earlier decision of a lower court to be erroneous it may *overrule* that decision. Its effect, however, is prospective only in that it does not affect the position of the parties to the earlier case. In other words by overruling a case a court states that it is not to be followed in the future. Courts do not often overrule decisions of courts of co-ordinate jurisdiction, preferring instead to *distinguish* them. A decision is said to be distinguished when a later court decides that, for one reason or another, it is not relevant to the case before it. A case might be distinguished because the later court discovers a material factual difference between the two cases or because different legal issues are involved. In essence, the subject matter of the two cases is perceived to differ and they are placed in separate conceptual categories. However, in practice, the effect of distinguishing a case can be equivalent to overruling it. By distinguishing it, a court can confine an earlier case to a very precise situation such that it becomes marginal and of limited importance. It will state that the decision was confined to its particular facts and is of no assistance in other cases. Moreover, if one court distinguishes a particular decision other courts might be more prepared to follow suit. In some cases a court might have reached a decision in ignorance of a relevant statutory provision or binding authority. In that event the decision is said to have been reached *per incuriam.* The consequence is that no valid proposition of law is established by the decision and a later court is not bound to follow it. Where it appears that a court decided a point without its being specifically argued or mentioned in the judgment it is said to have been decided *sub silentio* and, once again, a later court is not required to follow it. A difference of judicial opinion is evident on the question of a judge considering a point which was not specifically addressed in counsel's argument. In *G v An Bord Uchtála*[6] Walsh J spoke both of the right to life of the unborn and the constitutionality of certain decisions which were made by the Adoption Board. His brethren expressly reserved their opinions on those points as they had not been the subject of argument. In like fashion O'Higgins CJ and Griffin J did not join McCarthy J in commenting on the appropriate judicial evaluation of foreign cases in *Irish Shell Ltd v Elm Motors Ltd.*[7]

6. [1980] IR 32.
7. [1984] IR 511.

Law reports

[12.07] Access to reliable documents which accurately report judicial decisions is essential to the effective operation of a system of precedent. The most important decisions of earlier courts are published in collections known as law reports.[8] A report usually contains the judgment or judgments delivered, a synopsis of the arguments of counsel and a headnote, or abstract, which is prepared by the reporter, who by convention is a practising barrister. For this reason newspaper reports which are written by journalists, though illustrative, are not considered to be authoritative. Before being reproduced in the law reports the judgments are corrected by the judges who delivered them and it is the corrected text which is authoritative. The headnote is not part of the case, but is prepared principally for the purposes of reference; it allows the reader to know at a glance the contents of the case. It is important to realise that the headnote is not law, nor is it an authoritative interpretation of the decision. The two series of law reports which are currently published in Ireland are the 'Irish Reports', published by the Incorporated Council of Law Reporting for Ireland, and the 'Irish Law Reports Monthly', which are published commercially. The 'Irish Reports' enjoy a 'semi-official' status and are preferred to the 'Irish Law Reports Monthly' where a conflict arises between the two. Since March 1989 these have been supplemented by the 'Irish Times Law Reports' which are published each Monday in the *Irish Times.* Whilst the latter merely contain synopses of the judgments delivered they may be cited in court as they are reported by practising barristers. To these reports must be added a number of series which are no longer published, principal amongst them being the 'Irish Law Times Reports' and the 'Irish Jurist Reports'. As the number of reported cases in this country runs into thousands, if not tens of thousands, locating the appropriate case law can be a time-consuming and cumbersome exercise. To this end recourse is had to Digests of Cases, which contain abstracts of cases, and enable the reader to locate the relevant cases on a particular topic and allow him to trace the subsequent history of any given case.[9] Due to lack of resources, amongst other things, it was not possible to report all cases in this country, although matters have improved somewhat in

---

8. See O'Malley, *The Round Hall Guide to Sources of Law* (Round Hall Press, 1993); Grossman, *Legal Research* (Oxford University Press, 1994); Dane, Thomas & Cope, *How to Use a Law Library* 3rd ed (Sweet & Maxwell, 1996).

9. Murray & Dixon (eds) *The Irish Digest 1867-1893*; Maxwell (ed) *The Irish Digest 1894-1918*; Ryland (ed) *The Irish Digest 1919-1928*; Ryland (ed) *The Irish Digest 1929-1938*; Harrison (ed) *The Irish Digest 1939-1948*; Harrison (ed) *The Irish Digest 1949-1958*; Ryan (ed) *The Irish Digest 1959-1970*; De Blaghd (ed) *The Irish Digest 1971-1983*; Clancy & Ryan (eds) *The Irish Digest 1984-1988*; Clancy (ed) *The Irish Digest 1989-1993*; see also O'Malley *op cit* pp 24-29.

recent years.[10] Accordingly, the superior courts have adopted, and continue, the practice of circulating unreported judgments, which consist of the judicially corrected version of the judgment delivered in the case, to the principal law libraries in the country.[11] However, they do not contain the arguments of counsel nor are they accompanied by a headnote. The advantage of this practice is that it provides lawyers with the complete jurisprudence of the Irish superior courts and makes decisions available before they are eventually, if ever, reported. The judgments of the Court of Criminal Appeal have been collated and published commercially in three volumes which bear the title 'Frewen', the late registrar of that Court who compiled the first two volumes. The traditional paper-based sources have since the 1980s been supplemented by a legal database, ITELIS, which allows subscribers access to a wide range of legal materials. ITELIS contains all Irish reported cases since 1950 and a selection of unreported judgments since 1985 as well as an extensive selection of English, Commonwealth, American and European materials. In addition, CD-ROM services have been developed, the most recent innovation being Butterworths' 'Books on Screen' product which currently contains the All England Reports, but which it is expected will extend to Irish case law.

[2] *Stare Decisis* in the Irish Courts [12]

[12.08] As stated earlier the principle of *stare decisis* reflects the expectation that earlier cases be followed. Given the hierarchical structure of the court system there are two dimensions to the system of precedent. The first, which might be considered vertical, is that a lower court is bound by the decisions of higher courts. The second, which might be considered horizontal, concerns the extent to which courts are bound by the decisions of courts of co-ordinate jurisdiction. A general issue is whether a strict or liberal approach should be adopted in relation to precedent. A strict approach was

10. The regular publication since 1981 of the Irish Law Reports Monthly and the occasional publication of retrospective volumes of those Reports have contributed significantly to the recent improvement. Since January 1995 the Irish Current Law Monthly Digest contains headnotes of all Superior Court decisions.

11. Three indexes of unreported judgment have been compiled: Aston et al (eds) *Index to Unreported Judgments of the Irish Superior Courts 1966-1975* (Irish Association of Law Teachers, 1990); Aston & Doyle (eds) *Index to Irish Superior Court Written Judgments 1976-1982* (Irish Association of Law Teachers, 1984); Aston (ed) *Index to Irish Superior Court Written Judgments 1983-1989* (Bar Council, 1991). The indexes are commonly known as the *Green Index*, the *Red Index* and the *Blue Index* respectively.

12. See Dowrick, 'Precedent in Modern Irish Law' (1953) 69 LQR 25; Henchy, 'Precedent in the Irish Supreme Court' (1962) 25 MLR 544; Gavan Duffy, 'A Note on the Limitation of the Doctrine *Per Quod Servitium Amisit* and *Stare Decisis* in the Republic of Ireland' (1965) 14 ICLQ 1382.

favoured during the 19th century, and lasted well into the 20th, and was set out by the Lord Halsbury in *London Tramways Co v London County Council*:[13]

> "Of course I do not deny that cases of individual hardship may arise, and there may be a current of opinion in the profession that such and such a judgment was erroneous; but what is that occasional interference with what is perhaps abstract justice, as compared with the inconvenience - the disastrous inconvenience - of having each question subject to being re-argued and the dealings of mankind rendered doubtful by reason of different decisions, so that in truth and in fact there would be no real final Court of Appeal."

The difficulties associated with that approach are that it leads to the fossilisation of the law, it inhibits legal development and frustrates the possibility of doing justice in individual cases. On the other hand the concerns with a flexible approach are that it unsettles the law, results in an unwarranted degree of uncertainty and upsets legitimate expectations which are based on the earlier law. The resulting tension between the demands of certainty and the desire for adaptability form a recurring theme in considerations of the system of precedent.

Lower courts should follow the decisions of higher courts

[12.09] The principal rule is that an inferior court must follow the earlier decisions of superior courts. Thus, the High Court must follow the Supreme Court and the Circuit Court must follow both the High Court and Supreme Court. This rule is so well-settled that it has seldom been questioned by an Irish court. Thus, in *The State (Harkin) v O'Malley*[14] O'Higgins CJ observed that Gannon J, in the High Court, was bound to follow an earlier Supreme Court decision[15] which the Supreme Court then overruled on the grounds both that it was erroneously decided and was a *per incuriam* decision. And in *Carron v McMahon*[16] Finlay CJ noted that at the time of the decision under appeal the High Court was bound by *Russell v Fanning*,[17] a case which the Supreme Court itself then overruled in *Carron*. Unlike the position in which the House of Lords has found itself in the past - see, for instance, *Cassell & Co Ltd v Broome*[18] - the Supreme Court has rarely had to

13. [1898] AC 375, at 380. The law report incorrectly lists the appellant as 'London Street Tramways'; see Cross & Harris, *op cit* p 102.
14. [1978] IR 269.
15. *The People (Attorney General) v Doyle* (1964) 101 ILTR 136.
16. [1990] 1 IR 239, at 267.
17. [1988] IR 505.
18. [1972] AC 1027.

reprimand the High Court for failure to follow one of its decisions. The only recent case in which this has occurred is the decision in *McDonnell v Byrne Engineering Co Ltd*, of which only a newspaper report is available:[19]

> "The Supreme Court yesterday set aside an award of £100,205 and costs by a High Court jury to a nine-year-old Dublin boy, James McDonnell, Lower Gardiner Street Flats, who suffered a severe head injury on June 12th, 1973, when part of a mobile scaffolding tower collapsed on him at Railway Street, Dublin. The Court directed a new trial but did not award the costs of the appeal to the defendants in the action, who had appealed the amount as being excessive. The action had been taken on behalf of the boy by his mother, Mrs Elizabeth McDonnell. The defendants were Byrne Engineering Co Ltd, Jervis Lane, Dublin. The action had been heard before Mr Justice Murnaghan and a jury on November 15th and 16th last. Special damages had been agreed at £205 and the jury had assessed general damages at £100,000. Judgment for £100,205 and costs had been entered in favour of the boy. The jury had been asked only to assess general damages.
>
> The Chief Justice, Mr Justice O'Higgins, giving the judgment of the Supreme Court yesterday, said that the trial judge had been expressly asked to divide the question on damages, so that the jury would be asked to consider damages in relation to pain and suffering up to the trial, and to consider them separately for the future. The trial judge declined to do so. The matter was considered by the jury as one question. 'This question to the jury was not in accordance with the correct procedures nor in accordance with the appropriate legal principles,' said the Chief Justice. 'The jury verdict was a verdict which was subject to some incapacity.'
>
> It seemed to him, said Mr Justice O'Higgins, having regard to all the evidence and to the history of this young boy following the injury that the amount was excessive. He was expressing his own view and that of his colleagues that the verdict, in the circumstances, could not stand. The Court, he said, had come to the conclusion that it would not be appropriate to fix damages. Accordingly the plaintiff's claim should go back to the High Court for assessment in another trial.
>
> The Chief Justice said that under the Constitution, the Supreme Court was the final court of appeal. As such, it had the duty, when necessary, to declare what legal principles should apply to cases that were reviewed by the Court. Where necessary it had the duty to lay down guidelines for all courts and all judges as to the manner in which such cases were to be tried. It was equally the duty of all other courts and judges to follow directions as to law and procedures as given by the Supreme Court.
>
> The Chief Justice said that in relation to trial by jury in claims for damages for personal injury where future loss of earnings and pain and suffering

19. Irish Times, 4 October 1978.

were involved, the Supreme Court had, over the years, expressed certain views which were most recently stated in the Supreme Court decision of *Carroll v Clare County Council.*[20] In that judgment, he said, Mr Justice Kenny had stated that it was highly undesirable that a jury should be asked to award damages for the period up to the trial and for the future, under one heading, as one. He said it was essential that there should be separate questions in relation to this matter. The Chief Justice said that following this clear and concise statement it became the duty of all judges trying such cases to follow this directive. 'It is with real concern that this Court notes that despite being asked by counsel to leave the question on damages in accordance with the directions of this court, the trial judge, Mr Justice Murnaghan, expressly refused to do so. Not only did he refuse to do so, but he has indicated it is his intention to disregard this in other cases.' The Chief Justice continued: 'This Court will not permit this situation to continue and will insist that its directions be respected and obeyed.'

Unfortunately, said the Chief Justice, the only way this could be done was by means of its jurisdiction on appeal to review and set aside. 'This jurisdiction will be used,' he added. 'It should be made known that any verdict in damages arrived at as a result of procedures which this Court has condemned will, on that account alone, be in danger of being set aside.' This would be because of the views expressed by the Supreme Court … because the award would not have been obtained in accordance with due course of law.

In this case when counsel for the plaintiff, in accordance with what was stated in *Carroll v Clare County Council,* had asked that the question be left in the appropriate form, counsel for the defendants remained silent. 'Directions on law, directions in relation to procedures and directions in relation to their obedience must be the common concern of all litigants,' added the Chief Justice.

Mr Justice Griffin and Mr Justice Kenny were the other members of the Court."

[12.10] The situation might arise where a lower court is required to follow a decision of a higher court even though it is firmly believed to be erroneous and it is correctly anticipated that the decision will subsequently be overruled by the Supreme Court. For instance, the High Court and courts of trial are bound by decisions of the Court of Criminal Appeal. In *O'B v Patwell*[21] the Supreme Court noted that the High Court was bound to follow two decisions of the Court of Criminal Appeal[22] which it then proceeded to

20. [1975] IR 230.
21. [1994] 2 ILRM 465.
22. *The People (Attorney General) v Dermody* [1956] IR 307; *The People (Attorney General) v Coughlan* (1968) 1 Frewen 325.

overrule as having been incorrectly decided. In *The People (DPP) v Rock*[23] a Circuit Court judge followed a decision of the Court of Criminal Appeal[24] in preference to a conflicting decision of the High Court.[25] While it overruled the former decision the Supreme Court in *Rock* noted that the trial judge was bound to follow it:[26]

> "While ... the decision of the Court of Criminal Appeal should be overruled it represented, at the date of the Circuit Court hearing, in the hierarchy of courts, a decision of a court of final jurisdiction which the Court of Criminal Appeal is except where, in certain circumstances, the matter might be brought with the appropriate certificate by way of appeal to the Supreme Court ... In those circumstances, the learned trial judge was bound to follow the decision of the Court of Criminal Appeal if he considered that there was a conflict between it and a decision of the High Court."

The Supreme Court

[12.11] In the mid-1960s the Supreme Court departed from the strict rule of *stare decisis* which had been adopted in England and preferred a more relaxed approach. The first departure from the strict rule occurred in *The State (Quinn) v Ryan*[27] where the prosecutor challenged the constitutionality of s 29 of the Petty Sessions (Ireland) Act 1851. The validity of that provision had been upheld in two earlier Supreme Court decisions, *The State (Dowling) v Kingston (No 2)*[28] and *The State (Duggan) v Tapley.*[29] It was argued on behalf of the respondent that the Court was bound by those decisions. In holding the section to be unconstitutional, the Supreme Court declared its freedom to depart from a strict adherence to *stare decisis*. The new approach and the reasons which underlie it were explained by Walsh J:[30]

> "It has been urged upon this Court on behalf of the Attorney General and on behalf of the respondents that these sections have already been held to be not inconsistent with the Constitution of Saorstát Éireann in *The State (Dowling) v Kingston (No 2)* and not inconsistent with the provisions of the present Constitution in *The State (Duggan) v Tapley.* It has been further urged that these decisions are binding upon this Court. It is unnecessary in this case to explore the consequences of the fact that this Court is not the

23. [1994] 1 ILRM 66.
24. *The People (Attorney General) v Mills* (1955) 1 Frewen 153.
25. *The State (Foley) v Carroll* [1980] IR 150.
26. [1994] 1 ILRM 66, at 72.
27. [1965] IR 110.
28. [1937] IR 699.
29. [1952] IR 62.
30. [1965] IR 110, at 125-127.

Court which decided either of those cases; this Court was established in 1961. It is also unnecessary to express any final view upon the constitutionality of subjecting this Court (as distinct from all other Courts set up under the Constitution) to the rule of *stare decisis.* Neither is it necessary to discuss in detail the question of whether in the case of a Court of final appeal *stare decisis* can ever be anything more than judicial policy, albeit strong judicial policy. However, in view of the implications in the submissions advanced in this Court on behalf of the Attorney General and of the respondents it must be clearly stated, though one would have hoped it should not have been necesary to do so, that this Court is the creation of the Constitution and is not in any sense the successor in Ireland of the House of Lords. The jurisdiction formerly enjoyed by the House of Lords in Ireland is but part of the much wider jurisdiction which has been conferred upon this Court by the Constitution. I reject the submission that because upon the foundation of the State our Courts took over an English legal system and the common law that the Courts must be deemed to have adopted and should now adopt an approach to Constitutional questions conditioned by English judicial methods and English legal training which despite their undoubted excellence were not fashioned for interpreting written constitutions or reviewing the constitutionality of legislation. In this State one would have expected that if the approach of any Court of final appeal of another State was to have been held up as an example for this Court to follow it would more appropriately have been the Supreme Court of the United States rather than the House of Lords. In this context it is not out of place to recall that in delivering the judgment of the Supreme Court in *In the Matter of Tilson Infants*[31] Murnaghan J stated, at p 32: 'It is not a proper method of construing a new constitution of a modern state to make an approach in the light of legal survivals of an earlier law.'

So far as the provisions of the Constitution itself bear upon the place of *stare decisis* in constitutional cases the provisions of Article 34.3.3°, which is an amendment to the Constitution as enacted by the People, appear to me to clearly indicate that it is only in the case of a law or a provision of a law, the Bill for which had been referred to the Supreme Court by the President under Article 26 of the Constitution, that there is no longer jurisdiction in any Court to question the constitutional validity of that law or that provision of that law. It has been submitted on behalf of the Attorney General and the respondents that this amendment to the Constitution was designed only to meet a possible argument that because it was a Bill which *had been* approved by the Court that the law when enacted would be open to challenge again once it was signed by the President and that it was to be inferred from this provision that the Constitution impliedly imposed the rule of *stare decisis* in respect of constitutional cases. In my view this contention is quite unsustainable and it would be strange indeed if the

31. [1951] IR 1.

> Constitution in making such an express provision for Bills only would leave unexpressed but to be inferred a provision in similar terms applicable to Acts. To my mind the absence of such an express provision is an indication that the People in enacting this Constitution and the Oireachtas in amending it within the period limited by the transitory provisions of the Constitution, which have since expired, had no intention of creating by inference only a situation in which a decision of this Court upon the interpretation of the Constitution could be altered only by way of a national referendum for the purpose of amending the Constitution. Far from being daunted by this formidable but inescapable conclusion arising from their submissions counsel for the Attorney General and for the respondents urged that this was the position envisaged by the Constitution. Having regard to the express provision of the Constitution I have no hesitation in rejecting the submissions which lead to such a conclusion. This is not to say, however, that the Court would depart from an earlier decision for any but the most compelling reasons. The advantages of *stare decisis* are many and obvious so long as it is remembered that it is a policy and not a binding unalterable rule."

[12.12] A strict reading of *The State (Quinn) v Ryan* would confine the Court's relaxation of precedent to cases which involve the constitutionality of legislation. However, the wider application of the new approach was confirmed by the Court's decision in *Attorney General v Ryan's Car Hire Ltd*. Again the Court refused to follow two of its earlier decisions.[32] Kingsmill Moore J restated the Court's view on *stare decisis*:[33]

> "...the first question, then, is whether this Court is to accept and lay down the principle that it is to be bound irrevocably by an earlier decision, the so-called rule of '*stare decisis.*' The merits and demerits of this rule have been widely canvassed and there is no consensus of opinion among academic jurists or serving judges. The practice of Courts of ultimate resort varies, the United States Supreme Court and the ultimate Courts of most European countries and of Canada, South Africa and Australia holding themselves free, where they think requisite, to refuse to follow an earlier decision; while the House of Lords, somewhat uncomfortably, abides by the principle laid down by Lord Halsbury in *London Street Tramways Co v London County Council*,[34] that a decision of the House on a question of law is conclusive and binds it in all subsequent cases until (if ever) it is upset by legislative enactment. Not all the Law Lords have been content to be confined within the strait-jacket of an earlier case. Lord Denning has broken loose *(London Transport Executive v Betts (Valuation Officer)*;[35]

32. *Minister for Finance and Attorney General v O'Brien* [1949] IR 91; *Attorney General and Minister for Posts and Telegraphs v CIE* (1956) 90 ILTR 139.
33. [1965] IR 642, at 652-654.
34. [1898] AC 375.

Ostime v Australian Mutual Provident Society;[36] *Close v Steel Company of Wales*[37]). Lord Reid clearly strains at the bonds *(London Transport Executive v Betts (Valuation Officer)*;[38] *Midland Silicones Limited v Scruttons Limited*[39]). Lord Wright would like the House of Lords to have the same freedom as the United States Supreme Court: 8 Camb LJ 144. In *R v Taylor*[40] Lord Goddard, giving the judgment of a Court of Criminal Appeal, consisting of seven judges, refused to follow the decision of an earlier Court of Criminal Appeal where the subsequent Court unanimously considered the former decision to be wrong and where an accused person had been sentenced and imprisoned on the assumption that such earlier decision was correct. In *The State (Quinn) v Ryan*,[41] Mr. Justice Walsh in his judgment, to which the other members of the Court assented, refused to accept '*stare decisis*' as universally binding in constitutional cases, adding, at p 127: 'This is not to say, however, that the Court would depart from an earlier decision for any but the most compelling reasons. The advantages of *stare decisis* are many and obvious so long as it is remembered that it is a policy and not a binding, unalterable rule.'

This Court is a new court, set up by the Courts (Establishment and Constitution) Act 1961, pursuant to the Constitution and it is free to consider whether it should adopt the rule which prevails in the House of Lords or any of the less restrictive rules which have found favour in other jurisdictions. It seems clear that there can be no legal obligation on this Court to accept '*stare decisis*' as a rule binding upon it just because the House of Lords accepted it as a rule binding upon their Lordships' house. A decision which only purported to affect the House of Lords could not, by virtue of Article 73 of the Constitution of 1922, have been carried over into our law so as to bind the Supreme Court set up by that constitution; and if that Supreme Court in fact adopted the rule (as it would seem to have done in *Attorney General and Minister for Posts and Telegraphs v CIE*[42]) any such determination could only bind that Court and would not under Article 50 of our present Constitution be binding on the new Supreme Court created by Article 34.4, of our present Constitution and the Courts (Establishment and Constitution) Act 1961.

[Counsel] has properly drawn a distinction between the general principle of following precedent and the strict rule of *stare decisis*. The law which we have taken over is based on the following of precedents and there can be no

35. [1959] AC 213, at 247.
36. [1960] AC 459, at 489.
37. [1962] AC 367, at 388.
38. [1959] AC 213, at 232.
39. [1962] AC 466, at 475-477.
40. [1950] 2 KB 368.
41. [1965] IR 110.
42. (1956) 90 ILTR 139.

question of abandoning the principle of following precedent as the normal, indeed almost universal, procedure. To do so would be to introduce into our law an intolerable uncertainty. But where the Supreme Court is of the opinion that there is a compelling reason why it should not follow an earlier decision of its own, or of the Courts of ultimate jurisdiction which preceded it, where it appears to be clearly wrong, is it to be bound to perpetuate the error?

If it could safely be assumed that all members of a Supreme Court were perfectly endowed with wisdom and completely familiar with all branches of law, to treat their judgments as infallible would need but little justification. Judicial modesty has refrained from putting forward such a claim and to most jurists such a Court appears a Platonic rather than a practical ideal. Lord Halsbury in the *London Street Tramways Case* takes his stand on more pragmatic grounds: '... what is that occasional interference with what is perhaps abstract justice as compared with the inconvenience - the disastrous inconvenience - of having each question subject to being re-argued and the dealings of mankind rendered doubtful by reason of different decisions, so that in truth and in fact there would be no real final Court of Appeal.'

This argument from inconvenience would come more suitably from the mouth of an executive official than from that of a judge. The plea that 'it is expedient that one man should die for the multitude' must always be met uncompromisingly by a judge with the words, 'I find no fault in this just man,' and he must not falter in his determination. However desirable certainty, stability, and predictability of law may be, they cannot in my view justify a Court of ultimate resort in giving a judgment which they are convinced, for compelling reasons, is erroneous. Lord Halsbury himself was forced to make some modification. Faced with the hypothesis that a case might have been decided in ignorance of the existence of some relevant statutory provision or in reliance on some statutory provision which was subsequently discovered to have been repealed, he suggested that it would not be a binding authority because it was founded on a mistake of fact. The same reasoning would be applicable if the decision were given in ignorance of an earlier authority of compelling validity. Where a point has been entirely overlooked, or conceded without argument, the authority of a decision may be weakened to vanishing point. In my opinion the rigid rule of *stare decisis* must in a Court of ultimate resort give place to a more elastic formula. Where such a Court is clearly of opinion that an earlier decision was erroneous it should be at liberty to refuse to follow it, at all events in exceptional cases. What are exceptional cases? I have already given some examples of cases which I would consider exceptional, but I do not suggest that these close the category and I do not propose to attempt to make a complete enumeration. It is sufficient to consider whether the present case should fall within the exception."

[12.13] The judgments in those cases show that, while in general the Supreme Court will follow its own decisions, it reserves a freedom to depart from them where there are 'compelling reasons'. *Stare decisis* is now considered by the Court to be a policy, not an inflexible rule. It should be noted that when those cases were decided the House of Lords was considered to be strictly bound by its earlier decisions, a position which was relaxed two years later.[43] The circumstances in which the Court would be prepared to depart from an earlier decision are further outlined in *McNamara v Electricity Supply Board*.[44] In that case the Court, in holding that a trespasser is owed a duty of reasonable care by an occupier, declined to follow the older rule which was set out by the House of Lords in *Robert Addie and Sons (Collieries) Ltd v Dumbreck*.[45] That decision was adopted by the Supreme Court in *Donovan v Landy's Ltd*[46] which in turn was followed by the Court in *O'Leary v Wood Ltd*.[47] Despite this settled body of authority the Court it felt justified in departing from it. Walsh J declined to follow *Donovan v Landy's Ltd* on the grounds that it was wrongly decided.[48] Henchy J set out his reasons for not following *Donovan v Landy's Ltd*:[49]

> "The degree of certainty, continuity and predictability that judicial decisions should have, to enable people to arrange their conduct so as to avoid legal liability, would normally dictate that this Court should follow its own decisions in *O'Donovan v Landy's Ltd* and *O'Leary v Wood Ltd* which restated the law as laid down in *Addie's case*. But there are exceptional and compelling reasons for not doing so.
>
> Modern judicial decisions in jurisdictions in different parts of the common-law world show a widespread desire to escape from *Addie's case* on the ground of its unsuitability to modern social conditions and, perhaps more so, because a test of liability based on that case, whatever its original validity, runs counter to the principle that pervades the law of negligence since *Donoghue v Stevenson*[50] which is that a man is liable to damages if he has failed to take all reasonable steps to avoid injuring those whom he ought reasonably to have foreseen as likely to be injured by his conduct. In particular, the House of Lords (where the *Addie* test was originally laid down) has now ruled that *Addie's case* was wrongly decided and that an occupier is liable to a trespasser if, by the standards of common sense and

43. See *Practice Note* [1966] 1 WLR 1234; see generally Zander, *The Law Making Process* 4th ed (Butterworths, 1994) pp 191-199.
44. [1975] IR 1.
45. [1929] AC 358.
46. [1963] IR 441.
47. [1964] IR 269.
48. [1975] IR 1, at 15.
49. *Ibid*, at 23-24.
50. [1932] AC 562.

> common humanity, he could be said to be culpable in failing to take reasonable steps to avoid a danger to which the trespasser was likely to be exposed: see *Herrington v British Railways Board*[51]…
>
> In my opinion such a test correctly represents the law. Whether on the ground of juridical consistency, the social obligations of occupiers of property, or plain justice, I think is should be preferred to the principle of liability enunciated by *Addie's case* and last restated by this Court in *O'Leary v Wood*."

Griffin J agreed, stating:[52]

> "If, by reason of its rigidity or harshness, a rule is found to be unsatisfactory, it is undesirable that efforts to circumvent it should be made rather than that it should be reconsidered."

[12.14] In *McNamara* the Supreme Court refused to be unnecessarily constrained by precedent and was prepared to adapt the law in the light of changing social conditions and legal thinking. It is striking that the decisions which it declined to follow were themselves decided only a decade earlier. In other cases, however, the Court has acted more cautiously and has manifested a reluctance to interfere with precedent. That the desire to maintain 'judicial order and continuity' is strong is evident in Henchy J's judgment in *Mogul of Ireland Ltd v Tipperary (North Riding) County Council*:[53]

> "A decision of the full Supreme Court (be it the pre-1961 or the post-1961 Court), given in a fully-argued case and on a consideration of all the relevant materials, should not normally be overruled merely because a later Court inclines to a different conclusion. Of course, if possible, error should not be reinforced by repetition or affirmation, and the desirability of achieving certainty, stability, and predictability should yield to the demands of justice. However, a balance has to be struck between rigidity and vacillation, and to achieve that balance the later Court must, at the least, be *clearly* of opinion that the earlier decision was erroneous. In *Attorney General v Ryan's Car Hire Ltd* the judgment of the Court gave examples of what it called exceptional cases, the decisions in which might be overruled if a later Court thought them to be clearly wrong. While it was made clear that the examples given were not intended to close the category of exceptional cases, it is implicit from the use in that judgment of expressions such as 'convinced' and 'for compelling reasons' and 'clearly of opinion that the earlier decision was erroneous' that the mere fact that a

51. [1972] AC 877.

52. [1975] IR 1, at 32.

53. [1976] IR 260, at 272-273; see Ervine, 'The Supreme Court, *Stare Decisis* and the Malicious Injuries Code' (1975) 10 Ir Jur (ns) 93.

later Court, particularly a majority of the members of a later Court, might prefer a different conclusion is not in itself sufficient to justify overruling the earlier decision. Even if the later Court is clearly of opinion that the earlier decision was wrong, it may decide in the interests of justice not to overrule it if it has become inveterate and if, in a widespread or fundamental way, people have acted on the basis of its correctness to such an extent that greater harm would result from overruling it than from allowing it to stand. In such cases the maxim *communis error facit jus* applies…"

[12.15] The point was reiterated in *Hynes-O'Sullivan v O'Driscoll* when Henchy J stated his reasons for not overruling earlier decisions on qualified privilege as a defence to defamation:[54]

"… this Court is being asked to hold that the communication sent by the defendant to the IMA [Irish Medical Association] is protected by qualified privilege because, although the IMA in fact had no duty or interest in the matter, the defendant honestly and reasonably believed that it had. However, such a version of the law would run counter to two Supreme Court decisions: *Reilly v Gill*[55] and *Kirkwood Hackett v Tierney*.[56] While the point does not seem to have been specifically argued in those cases, it is clear from the observations made in the judgments that the court in each of those decisions was firmly of the opinion that an occasion of qualified privilege cannot exist unless the person making the communication has a duty or interest to make it and the person to whom it is made has a corresponding duty or interest to receive it. It would require exceptional circumstances before this Court should overrule such a clearly held and repeatedly expressed opinion …

Despite the obvious attractiveness of the suggested formulation of the law of qualified privilege, I am not prepared to support the overruling of *Reilly v Gill* and *Kirkwood Hackett v Tierney*, to the extent required by the defendant's submission …

Secondly, I consider that a previous decision of this Court, be it the court established by the Courts (Establishment and Constitution) Act 1961, or the court in its earlier form, should not be overruled unless the point at issue has been duly raised and adequately argued. The formulation now suggested was first advanced to this Court by counsel for the defendant when replying to the submissions of counsel for the plaintiff. The latter did not find it necessary to deal with this point, relying as he was on the law as stated in *Reilly v Gill* and *Kirkwood Hackett v Tierney*. The result is that we are being asked to overrule part of those decisions, on what has turned out to be an *ex parte* argument. I find that unsatisfactory, particularly having

54. [1989] ILRM 349, at 360-362.
55. (1951) 85 ILTR 165.
56. [1952] IR 185.

> regard to the possible but unknown ramifications of the suggested change in the law.
>
> Thirdly, I am of the opinion that the suggested radical change in the hitherto accepted law should more properly be effected by statute. The public policy which a new formulation of the law would represent should more properly be found by the Law Reform Commission or by those others who are in a position to take a broad perspective as distinct from what is discernible in the tunnelled vision imposed by the facts of a single case. That is particularly so in a case such as this, where the law as to qualified privilege must reflect a due balancing of the constitutional right to freedom of expression and the constitutional protection of every citizen's good name. The articulation of public policy on a matter such as this would seem to be primarily a matter for the Legislature.
>
> Finally and perhaps most crucially, the suggested restatement of the law should in my opinion not be made in this case because it is not necessary for the purpose of doing justice... If the law as to qualified privilege as stated in *Reilly v Gill* and *Kirkwood Hackett v Tierney* were to be overruled, it would be of no consequence for the purpose of this case. As was stated by this Court in *Mogul of Ireland v Tipperary (NR) County Council*[57] an overruling of a previous decision of this Court, whether it be the pre-1961 Act or the post-1961 Act court, should take place only when it is necessary for the purpose of doing justice. That requirement is absent in this case. Even if the court were to restate the law as requested, such restatement would be only *obiter* ...
>
> I respectfully adopt [the statement of law]... which was expressly approved by O'Byrne J in *Kirkwood Hackett v Tierney.* Since the judgment of O'Byrne J was the effective judgment of the court in that case, even if I disagreed with that version of the law I would not be free to refuse to follow it."

[12.16] In his dissenting judgment in *Doyle v Hearne* Griffin J cited Henchy J's judgment in *Mogul* and went on to indicate that '[s]o far as I have been able to ascertain, there is no case in which a previous decision of this Court was overruled by other than a unanimous decision of a court of five.'[58] However, the force of that observation is diluted by the fact that a divided Supreme Court overruled *Corley v Gill*,[59] an earlier decision of a three judge Supreme Court.[60]

57. [1976] IR 260.

58. [1987] IR 601, at 614.

59. [1975] IR 313.

60. See criticism of the decision in Hogan 'Precedent and Statutory Interpretation' (1989) 11 DULJ (ns) 196. Griffin J's remarks must be qualified. In *McNamara v Electricity Supply Board* [1975] IR 1 FitzGerald CJ did not join his colleagues in departing from the 'old' law on occupiers' liability; see para **[12.13]**; however, the judgment which appears in the law report is brief and was not approved by FitzGerald CJ before he died.

[12.17] The potentially conflicting concerns of maintaining 'judicial order and continuity' and ensuring consistency with developments in judicial thinking are evident in *The State (Lynch) v Cooney.* Commenting on the High Court's approach to the earlier decision *In re Offences against the State (Amendment) Bill, 1940*[61] Henchy J stated:[62]

> "…I would agree that the doctrine of *stare decisis* would have obliged the judge to follow it - even though the Supreme Court which gave that judgment was the Supreme Court which was empowered to function as such under the transitory provisions of the Constitution of Ireland, 1937, and was not the Supreme Court which was required by Article 34.1 of the Constitution to be established by law and which was eventually so established by the Courts (Establishment and Constitution) Act 1961. The maintenance of judicial order and continuity would support such a conclusion."

Further on, Henchy J considered the Supreme Court decision in *In re Ó Laighléis*[63] which he was prepared to overrule:[64]

> "What was merely *obiter* in [*In re Offences against the State (Amendment) Bill, 1940*] thus became part of the *ratio decidendi* in the *Ó Laighléis case*. The question, then, is whether that ruling should be still adhered to. In my opinion it should not. It should be overruled in the exercise of the power of this Court to do so as stated in *Attorney General v Ryan's Car Hire* and in *Mogul of Ireland v Tipperary (NR) County Council.*
>
> While it might be argued that the opinion of the then Supreme Court expressed in those decisions of 1939 [*recte* 1940] and 1957 was part of what was then current judicial thinking, that could not be said if the same opinion were expressed today. Decisions given in recent years in this and other jurisdictions show that the power of the Courts to subject the exercise of administrative powers to judicial review is nowadays seen as having a wider reach than that delimited by those decisions of 1939 [*recte* 1940] and 1957."

[12.18] In *Finucane v McMahon*[65] the concern of judicial consistency manifested itself in a somewhat unusual fashion. A majority of the Supreme Court refused to follow its earlier decision in *Russell v Fanning,*[66] believing it to have been wrongly decided. Finlay CJ and Griffin J thought that that

---

61. [1940] IR 470.
62. [1982] IR 337, at 376.
63. [1960] IR 93.
64. [1982] IR 337, at 380.
65. [1990] 1 IR 165.
66. [1988] IR 505.

decision was correct and acceded to the majority view reluctantly. Noting the view of the majority Finlay CJ stated:[67]

> "In these circumstances, having regard to the fundamental nature of the issues which arise in extradition cases, I am satisfied that it would be consistent with the jurisprudence of this Court that I should accept this view so that the basic principles underlying it may clearly represent the decision of this Court."

Griffin J was like-minded:[68]

> "Notwithstanding, and with due respect to [Walsh J's] views, as expressed in his judgment [in *Finucane* itself], I remain of the opinion that *Russell v Fanning* was correctly decided. But as I am aware that the principles stated and the conclusions reached by him are supported by [Hederman and McCarthy JJ], thus forming a majority of the Court, I do not propose to elaborate on my opinion. However, as this is a court of final appeal, although it may not be necessary to do so, I should like to say, having regard to the importance of precedent in our system of jurisprudence as providing a degree of certainty upon which members of the public are entitled to rely in the conduct of their affairs, the principles established in and the conclusions reached by the majority of the Court, are those which should now be applied in all cases in which the [point of law in question] is in issue."

[12.19] The stance adopted by Finlay CJ and Griffin J in acceding to the majority viewpoint was not required by the principle of *stare decisis*. They would, like all other judges, be bound by it in future cases, since it is the decision of the Supreme Court,[69] but they were entitled to deliver dissenting judgments in the instant case. In declining to do so, and thus ensuring that the Court was unanimous, their conduct was commendably statesmanlike. They ensured that an important point of law was resolved definitively, albeit not in the manner they would have preferred, and that it would not be open to question in later cases. Since the majority had refused to follow an earlier Supreme Court decision a dissent by two judges would potentially have weakened the authority with which the Court spoke. The existence of a strong dissent would have invited the overruling of that decision by a later Court, especially since it had ignored an earlier decision of the Court. Apart from leaving a particular point of law intolerably uncertain, that would invite judicial chaos, in that it would suggest that any particular majority of the

67. [1990] 1 IR 165, at 207.
68. *Ibid*, at 218.
69. See *Carron v McMahon* [1990] 1 IR 239, at 271 *per* Griffin J that the Supreme Court is now bound by *Finucane v McMahon*; see Humphreys, 'Reflections on the Role and Functioning of the Supreme Court' (1990) 12 DULJ (ns) 127.

Court would be entitled to overrule a differently constituted majority. If that approach became commonplace the system of precedent would be undermined to the point of collapse.

[12.20] It appears that the Court when composed of five judges will more readily reconsider the decision of a three judge Supreme Court. This point was alluded to by Henchy J in *Hamilton v Hamilton* where he considered a prior decision of a three judge Supreme Court to be law 'unless and until a different conclusion is reached by a full Court.'[70] This was amplified by McCarthy J in *Doyle v Hearne* where he commented on that suggestion:[71]

> "I do not take this expression of opinion as being one that invites reconsideration of and possible disagreement with any particular triumvirate of this Court, but it lends support to the view that decisions of this court constituted of less than its full complement may be reviewed."

While these observations are somewhat tentative they could assume a greater significance given the expansion of the Supreme Court and its authority to sit in two or more divisions at any given time.[72] It can be expected that the Court will sit in divisions thus increasing the number of three-judge decisions and intensifying the potential for the emergence of divergent judicial views.

The High Court

[12.21] There is comparatively scant judicial opinion on the question of *stare decisis* in the High Court. Some indications were provided, however, in the extra-judicial views of Black J in a lecture, 'The Doctrine of Precedent in Modern Irish Law' which he delivered in 1953.[73] While such opinions are valuable it would be mistaken to attribute great weight to them or to equate them with similar views delivered in a judicial capacity. Moreover, Black J opined that the Supreme Court would adopt the strict rule of *stare decisis* which then pertained in the House of Lords, a stance which, of course, was to be rejected some years later by the Supreme Court. In this respect he got it wrong which might be taken to detract from the force of his views. He also took the view that pre-1922 House of Lords decisions are binding in Ireland, a view which coincided with prevailing judicial opinion but which is no

70. [1982] IR 466, at 484.
71. [1987] IR 601, at 617.
72. Courts (Supplemental Provisions) Act, 1961, s 7(3) as amended by Courts and Court Officers Act, 1995, s 7; see para **[4.43]**.
73. The lecture is noted in Dowrick, 'Precedents in Modern Irish Law' (1953) 69 LQR 25.

longer sustainable.[74] Nevertheless with these caveats in mind Black J's views still merit some attention.

[12.22] The question of *stare decisis* in the High Court depends, in part, on the capacity in which that Court sits. It may sit as a Divisional Court consisting of two or more judges, as a single judge court of first instance in Dublin, as an appellate court hearing appeals from the Circuit Court or as the High Court on Circuit, hearing Circuit appeals and cases at first instance.

[12.23] The High Court rarely sits as a Divisional Court but the general view is that it is bound by it prior decisions in that capacity. This certainly was Black J's view which he based on the practice adopted by the English Court of Appeal.[75] Moreover, it is probable that a Divisional Court binds the High Court when it sits in its more usual single judge capacity, although there is no authoritative decision to that effect.[76] This conclusion is reached by analogy with the view that a five judge Supreme Court binds that Court when it consists of three judges.[77]

[12.24] Ordinarily the High Court, as a court of trial, is not considered to be absolutely bound by its earlier decisions. Nevertheless, Black J stated that his preference for following the decisions of a court of co-ordinate jurisdiction thus:[78]

> "If I were confronted with a decision of a court of co-ordinate jurisdiction, which appeared to me of merely doubtful soundness, I none the less applied the rule of comity and followed it, leaving it for an appellate court to settle the matter, and the longer the other decision had remained unchallenged, the more ready I was to follow it. But if I was presented with a decision of a court of co-ordinate jurisdiction, my dislike of which went beyond mere doubt, and amounted to a firm conviction that it was wrong, then I declined to follow it. Thus, in the important case of charities, *Re Nolan*[79] the late Mr Justice Gavan Duffy refused to follow a decision of Mr

74. See para **[12.33]**.

75. See Dowrick, *loc cit* at 26. The application of *stare decisis* in the English Court of Appeal is set out in *Young v Bristol Aeroplane Co Ltd* [1944] KB 718 where it held itself, in general, to be bound by its prior decisions. This approach was confirmed by the House of Lords in *Davis v Johnson* [1979] AC 317. There are certain exceptions to the strict rule: see Zander, *The Law-Making Process* 4th ed (Butterworths, 1994) pp 216-221; see also Pugsley, 'Precedent in the Court of Appeal' (1983) 2 CJQ 48.

76. See *Wavin Pipes Ltd v Hepworth Iron Co Ltd* [1982] 8 FSR 32, at para **[14.90]** where Costello J would have "felt constrained" to follow a rule of statutory interpretation which had been affirmed by a divisional court but for a conflicting decision of the Supreme Court.

77. See para **[12.20]**.

78. Dowrick, *loc cit* at 26-27.

79. [1939] IR 388.

Justice Barton in *Dwyer (deceased)*;[80] but later in *Re Clancy*[81] I refused to follow the last-mentioned decision of Mr Justice Gavan Duffy. My example was followed by Mr Justice Overend in *Re Morrissey*[82] and our view was eventually upheld by the Supreme Court in *Re Solomons*.[83]"

[12.25] Black J's commitment to *stare decisis* is evident in other High Court decisions where the matter was considered. In *Kearns v Manresa Estates Ltd*[84] Kenny J, in holding a 'name and arms' clause to be invalid, followed two earlier High Court decisions to the same effect.[85] In the course of his judgment he alluded to the fact that prior decisions are acted upon and in a sense create expectations of legal validity:

"There is another argument to which I attach considerable weight. Since the decisions in *re Montgomery decd* and *re de Vere decd*, titles to property included in the … estate and in other estates have been accepted on the basis that names and arms clauses are void for uncertainty in Ireland. A decision now that the clauses involved were valid would render those titles bad. Although I am not bound by decisions of other judges of the High Court, the usual practice is to follow them unless I am satisfied that they were wrongly decided."

[12.26] In *Irish Trust Bank Ltd v Central Bank of Ireland*[86] Parke J was reluctant to depart from an earlier High Court decision. He felt that unless an earlier decision could be clearly shown to have been wrongly decided a court of co-ordinate jurisdiction should follow it; the decision not to follow it should normally be made by an appellate court which enjoys the power to overrule it. Parke J was invited to overrule the prior decision of Gannon J in *Dunne v O'Neill*.[87] The matter was complicated by the fact that the Taxing Master, whose decision was the subject of review by Parke J, had refused to adopt *Dunne v O'Neill*. According to Parke J:[88]

"I think it might be said that the propriety of a Taxing Master reporting to a judge of the High Court that another judge of that Court was wrong in law is very much open to question. The situation would have been even more anomalous had this case, as it might very well have done, come on for hearing before Gannon J. Be that as it may I have no doubt that this portion

80. (1908) 46 ILTR 147.
81. [1943] IR 23.
82. [1944] IR 361.
83. [1949] IR 3.
84. High Court, unrep, 25 July 1975.
85. *In re Montgomery Decd* (1953) 89 ILTR 62; *In re de Vere Decd* [1961] IR 224.
86. [1976-7] ILRM 50.
87. [1974] IR 180.
88. [1976-7] ILRM 50, at 53-54.

of the Taxing Master's report provided a useful and well researched brief for counsel on behalf of the defendants.

[Counsel] on behalf of the defendants urged me that I should not follow or apply the principles quoted from the judgment of Gannon J. I fully accept that there are occasions in which the principle of *stare decisis* may be departed from but I consider that these are extremely rare. A Court may depart from a decision of a Court of equal jurisdiction if it appears that such a decision was given in a case in which either insufficient authority was cited or incorrect submissions advanced or in which the nature and wording of the judgment itself reveals that the judge disregarded or misunderstood an important element in the case or the arguments submitted to him or the authority cited or in some other way departed from the proper standard to be adopted in judicial determination. It is clear that none of these elements can be detected in *Dunne v O'Neill* or the judgment therein delivered. [Counsel] does not in fact contend any such thing but his argument rests solely on the fact that the decision is contrary to previous authorities and that I am therefore not obliged to follow it. Whatever may be the case in Courts of final appellate jurisdiction a Court of first instance should be very slow to act on such a proposition unless the arguments in favour of it were coercive. If a decision of a Court of first instance is to be challenged I consider that the appellate Court is the proper tribunal to declare the law unless the decision in question manifestly displays some one or more of the infirmities to which I have referred. The principle of *stare decisis* is one of great importance to our law and few things can be more harmful to the proper administration of justice, which requires that as far as possible lay men may be able to receive correct professional advice, than the continual existence of inconsistent decisions of Courts of equal jurisdiction. The present case affords an interesting example of what ought to be avoided. [Counsel for the plaintiffs] appeared for the applicants in *Dunne v O'Neill.* Not only are his arguments set out in detail in the judgment but they are adopted and made part of the *ratio decidendi* in a manner in which counsel is seldom gratified to experience. [He] appeared for the plaintiffs in the present case and it would be an ironic comment on the state of the law if counsel could find his arguments adopted and applied in one Court and yet be told in another Court of equal jurisdiction that they were fundamentally wrong and inconsistent with the authorities.

I find nothing to convince me that the judgment of Gannon J shows such disregard or inconsistency with previous authorities to justify me in departing from it. Although the report is scanty in information as to the authorities cited by counsel it is clear from a perusal of the judgment that almost all of the cases cited to me in argument and set out in the Taxing Master's report were considered by the learned judge. Indeed many of the passages relied upon by [counsel for the defendants] and cited in the Taxing Master's report are also cited and relied upon by the learned judge. I therefore take the view that the only grounds upon which I could properly

> be asked to descend from or fail to follow *Dunne v O'Neill* have not been established to my satisfaction.
>
> I would like, however, to make it clear that I have not formed my view merely as a reluctant adherent to the doctrine of *stare decisis*. My decision is not in the words of Bowen LJ 'a sacrifice made upon the altar of authority': *Montagu v Earl of Sandwich*.[89] I think that the argument on behalf of the defendants suffers from two disabilities."

[12.27] It should be noted that while Parke J was concerned with *stare decisis* in the High Court much of the language of his judgment was in more general terms, in that he referred to 'courts of first instance' and 'courts of equal jurisdiction' and did not confine his comments specifically to the High Court. In *Walsh v President of the Circuit Court and DPP*[90] Murphy J remarked that his decision to depart from an earlier High Court decision was reached with 'considerable hesitation'. Again he emphasised the desirability of maintaining the convention of following decisions of courts of co-ordinate jurisdiction but felt compelled by a Supreme Court decision to depart from the earlier High Court case.

[12.28] There is no definitive judicial pronouncement on the question of *stare decisis* when the High Court sits in an appellate capacity dealing with appeals from the Circuit Court or when it sits as the High Court on Circuit. Clearly it binds the Circuit Court in question and, on the basis of the judicial hierarchy, all other Circuit Courts. But whether it enjoys the same precedential force in courts of co-ordinate jurisdiction is uncertain. The authority of a Circuit Court, being a court of 'limited and local jurisdiction', is confined to its own circuit and by extension it might be argued that circuit matters determined in the High Court should be likewise circumscribed. On the other hand the High Court, unlike the Circuit Court, enjoys 'full original jurisdiction' and thus the authority of its decisions extends beyond that which is 'local and limited'. It would follow that its authority when it sits in these capacities is no different from that which it enjoys when it sits as a court of first instance in Dublin.

The Court of Criminal Appeal

[12.29] The Court of Criminal Appeal has also declared its freedom to depart from its earlier decisions. In *The People (Attorney General) v Moore*[91] the Court refused to follow its earlier decision in *The People (Attorney General) v O'Neill*.[92] The Court's views were outlined by Davitt P:

89. (1886) 32 Ch D 525, at 549.

90. [1989] ILRM 325.

91. [1964] Ir Jur Rep 6.

92. [1964] Ir Jur Rep 1.

> "There remains the question whether we are bound to accept and apply the principle enunciated in *O'Neill's case* even though we differ from it to the extent which we have indicated. We have not been referred to, nor are we aware of, any case in which the question whether this court is bound to follow its previous decisions has arisen. [Counsel], on behalf of the Attorney General, cited the case of *R v Norman*[93] in which the Court of Criminal Appeal in England expressly over-ruled its previous decision in *R v Stanley.*[94] In *Stanley's* case the Court consisted of the usual number of three judges; in *Norman's Case* there was a full court of thirteen, four of whom dissented. The constitution of the Court of Criminal Appeal in England is not dissimilar from ours; and its jurisdiction is much the same as ours except that they cannot direct a new trial where they reverse a conviction. An appeal lies from them to the House of Lords in the same circumstances as an appeal lies from us to the Supreme Court. This Court, as at present constituted, certainly claims no jurisdiction to *over-rule* the decision in *O'Neill's case.* We are, however, encouraged by the decision in *Norman's case* to take the course which we now propose to adopt. We are not unmindful of the principle of *stare decisis* and of the desirability of having uniformity in judicial decisions interpreting the law. We think, however, that the interests of justice will best be served by giving effect to our own opinions, even though they differ from some of those expressed in *O'Neill's case* ..."

[12.30] The Court upheld the conviction but certified two questions of law of exceptional public importance for the Supreme Court. However, the applicant abandoned his appeal to the Supreme Court thus depriving that Court of the opportunity to comment, *inter alia*, on the question of precedent in the Court of Criminal Appeal. The less strict approach of the English Court of Criminal Appeal was based on a concern for personal liberty; the Court would not uphold a conviction on the basis of a prior decision which it considered to be erroneous.[95] That approach is understandable, and it would require an unusual commitment to the maintenance of judicial continuity to uphold a conviction on the basis of a precedent which is considered to have been wrongly decided. However, in *Moore* the reverse occurred. The Court of Criminal Appeal upheld a conviction despite its earlier decision which would have warranted an acquittal. It might be argued that the libertarian concerns which infused the English decisions did not apply here and the Court's refusal to follow the earlier case could be considered to be questionable.

93. [1924] 2 KB 315.
94. [1920] 2 KB 235.
95. *R v Taylor* [1950] 2 KB 368.

[12.31] With the impending abolition of the Court of Criminal Appeal and the transfer of its functions to the Supreme Court[96] two issues arise. The first is whether the Supreme Court, when exercising its new criminal appellate jurisdiction, should adopt the approach suggested by *The People (Attorney General) v Moore,* if indeed that differs in any respect from the Court's current position in relation to *stare decisis*. The second concerns the status of existing Court of Criminal Appeal decisions and whether the Supreme Court ought to be bound by them. One view is that the Supreme Court ought to treat those decisions as it would its own and, thus, be bound by them unless there are 'compelling reasons' not to follow them. This would contribute to maintaining judicial continuity and an established body of authority would not be unsettled. Another view is that, given its position in the judicial hierarchy, the Supreme Court could not be bound by those decisions and is free to re-open any point which has not been decided by it as the court of final appeal. After all, had the transfer of jurisdiction not occurred, decisions of the Court of Criminal Appeal would not have bound the Supreme Court and were open to the possibility of being overruled by the Supreme Court, thus lacking the authority due to decisions of a court of ultimate resort.

Pre-1961 decisions

[12.32] Some questions have arisen as to the status of pre-1961 Irish decisions and pre-1922 decisions of the House of Lords. With respect to the former, although Article 34 of the Constitution deals with the courts, it was conceded in *The State (Killian) v Minister for Justice*[97] that the text of that Article envisaged their being established by statute. As noted earlier this was achieved by the Courts (Establishment and Constitution) Act 1961.[98] While the courts thus established are identical to the earlier courts, technically they are new courts and decisions of the pre-1961 courts are not decisions of those courts. That point was adverted to by Walsh J in *The State (Quinn) v Ryan* and was elaborated on by Kingsmill Moore J in *Attorney General v Ryan's Car Hire Ltd*[99] where he was of the view that a pre-1961 decision of the Supreme Court, to the effect that it should adopt a rigid practice of *stare decisis,* could not bind the 'new' Supreme Court. In contrast, Henchy J in *Mogul of Ireland v Tipperary (North Riding) County Council*[100] considered that neither pre- nor post-1961 decisions should be overruled unless they were clearly shown to be erroneous. He was unprepared to overrule a 1949

96. See para **[7.35]**.

97. [1954] IR 207.

98. See paras **[4.34]**-**[4.35]**.

99. [1965] IR 642.

100. [1976] IR 260.

decision of the Supreme Court which, had the matter been previously undecided, he would have decided the other way. And in *The State (Lynch) v Cooney*[101] the same judge expressed similar views regarding pre-1961 decisions.

Pre-1922 House of Lords decisions

[12.33] Prior to 1922 the House of Lords was the court of final appeal for Ireland and, accordingly, Irish courts were bound by its decisions. After 1922 the question was whether those decisions still bound the Irish courts. In *Exham v Beamish*[102] Gavan Duffy J suggested that only those decisions which had been accepted as being part of Irish law *before* 1922 were binding. On the other hand, Maguire CJ and Black J in *Boylan v Dublin Corporation*[103] and Murnaghan J in *Minister for Finance and Attorney General v O'Brien*[104] considered all pre-1922 decisions to be binding. In the light of the subsequent relaxation by the Supreme Court of the practice of *stare decisis* it can be presumed that those decisions are no longer to be considered to be binding. Indeed, it is interesting to note that in *Attorney General v Ryan's Car Hire Ltd*[105] the Supreme Court refused to follow its earlier decision in *Minister for Finance and Attorney General v O'Brien.* This issue was also touched on by McCarthy J in his judgment in *Irish Shell Ltd v Elm Motors Ltd.*[106] In a similar vein, Davitt P, in *Attorney General v Simpson,*[107] rejected the submission that an advice of the Privy Council in an Australian appeal, given before Irish appeals thereto were abolished, bound the Irish courts.

Decisions of inferior courts

[12.34] The decisions of inferior courts do not bind superior courts, but they are of persuasive authority. A superior court is free to ignore such decisions and enjoys the power to overrule them. The manner in which this freedom should be exercised has not been the subject of judicial consideration in Ireland but several tentative observations can be made. The first is that it can be presumed that a court enjoys at least the same measure of freedom in relation to inferior decisions as it does in respect of decisions of courts of co-ordinate jurisdiction. Second, as it is the court of final appeal the Supreme

101. [1982] IR 337.
102. [1939] IR 336.
103. [1949] IR 60.
104. [1949] IR 91.
105. [1965] IR 642.
106. [1984] IR 511; see para **[12.35]**.
107. [1959] IR 105, at 129.

Court is expected to provide authoritative rulings for all other courts to adopt and it must possess the corresponding freedom to overrule the prior decisions of inferior courts. Where there are conflicting decisions the Supreme Court inevitably is required to select the body of authority which it considers to be appropriate.[108] However, the tendency is not to unsettle an established line of authority and the Supreme Court usually overrules a case only where it considers it to be wrongly decided or no longer appropriate. Thus, in *Finlay v Murtagh* the Supreme Court overruled the earlier High Court decision *Somers v Erskine*[109] on the grounds that it was wrongly decided and was incompatible 'with modern developments in the law of torts'.[110] These grounds are similar to those which have been considered by Court to afford a compelling reason to overrule its own decisions and this suggests that the Court will be as scrupulous in its treatment of High Court decisions as it would be in the case of its own decisions.

Foreign decisions

[12.35] A court is not bound to follow the decisions of foreign courts. However, those decisions are of persuasive authority and may be followed at the option of the court. Decisions of other common law countries are frequently cited and adopted by Irish courts, particularly where there is no Irish authority governing the issue in question. Given the origin of the Irish legal system and the traditional links between the two systems it is not surprising to find that English decisions are the most commonly cited foreign decisions. But that is not to suggest that those decisions should be adopted uncritically by Irish Courts. In *Irish Shell Ltd v Elm Motors Ltd* McCarthy J criticised an observation by Costello J that English decisions should be followed unless they were shown to be erroneous:[111]

> "I do not necessarily agree or disagree with the analysis made by the learned trial judge but I deem it proper to comment on his observation that 'The High Court is not, bound to follow the decisions and judgments to which I have referred if there are compelling reasons for rejecting them'. I do not believe that the true inference from this observation is that, in the absence of compelling reasons for rejection, the High Court is bound to follow decisions and judgments of the House of Lords, the Court of Appeal in England, or the Judicial Committee of the British Privy Council, but lest any such view should be entertained, I would unequivocally deny the

108. See, eg, *UF (orse UC) v JC* [1991] 2 IR 330 where the Supreme Court had to choose between conflicting High Court decisions.

109. [1943] IR 348.

110. [1979] IR 249, at 255, 262.

111. [1984] IR 200, at 225-227.

existence of any such principle or the propriety of any such practice. Of the decisions of those courts decided prior to 1922, it is proper to say that they are part of the corpus of jurisprudence and law that was taken over on the foundation of Saorstát Eireann being the laws in force in Saorstát Eireann at the date of the coming into operation of the Constitution of the Irish Free State (Saorstát Eireann), subject to that Constitution and to the extent to which they were not inconsistent therewith. Similarly Article 50 of the Constitution provides:

> '1. Subject to this Constitution and to the extent to which they are not inconsistent therewith, the laws in force in Saorstát Eireann immediately prior to the date of the coming into operation of this Constitution shall continue to be of full force and effect until the same or any of them shall have been repealed or amended by enactment of the Oireachtas.
>
> 2. Laws enacted before, but expressed to come into force after, the coming into operation of this Constitution, shall, unless otherwise enacted by the Oireachtas come into force in accordance with the terms thereof.'

Article 50 was stated by Kingsmill Moore J in *The Educational Company of Ireland Ltd v Fitzpatrick (No. 2)*[112] as relating to 'statutes or law carried forward into our *corpus juris*' but that view has been questioned by Walsh J (with whom O'Higgins CJ agreed) in *Gaffney v Gaffney*[113] where he said at p 151 of the report: 'Contrary to what appears to have been the view of Kingsmill Moore J I do not think that Article 50 of the Constitution refers to any law other than statute law, and in my view the text of Article 50 makes that clear'. Walsh J may well have been echoing the observations of Gavan Duffy J in *Exham v Beamish*[114] where at pp 348-9 of the report he stated:

> 'As a matter of practice, we constantly refer to judgments in the English Courts and such judgments, as every lawyer will recognise, have often proved to be of great service to us; but let us be clear. In my opinion when Saorstát Eireann, and afterwards Eire, continued the laws in force, they did not make binding on their courts anything short of law. In my opinion, judicial decisions in Ireland before the Treaty, and English decisions which were followed here, are binding upon this Court only when they represent a law so well settled or pronounced by so weighty a juristic authority that they may fairly be regarded, in a system built up upon the principle of *stare decisis,* as having become established as part of the law of the land before the Treaty; and to bind, they must, of course, not be inconsistent with the

112. [1961] IR 323.
113. [1975] IR 133.
114. [1939] IR 336.

> Constitution. ... In my opinion, this Court cannot be fettered in the exercise of the judicial power by opinions of very different courts under the old regime, unless those opinions must reasonably be considered to have had the force of law in Ireland, so that they formed part of the code expressly retained. ... If, before the Treaty, a particular law was administered in a way so repugnant to the common sense of our citizens as to make the law look ridiculous, it is not in the public interest that we should repeat the mistake. Our new High Court must mould its own *cursus curiae;* in so doing I hold that it is free, indeed bound, to decline to treat any such absurdity in the machinery of administration as having been imposed on it as part of the law of the land; nothing is law here which is inconsistent with derivation from the People.'

Whilst observations of judges of the former Supreme Court in *Boylan v Dublin Corporation*[115] and *Minister for Finance v O'Brien*,[116] appear to support the view that decisions of the House of Lords upon law common to England and Ireland, given before the coming into operation of the Constitution of 1922, are a binding force in our courts, in my view the decision of this Court in *Attorney General v Ryan's Car Hire Ltd*[117] and *The State (Quinn) v Ryan*,[118] wherein the rigidity of the principle of *stare decisis* was denied, must now call into question the binding force of any such pre-1922 decision. Since 26 July 1966, the House of Lords has recognised that too rigid an adherence to precedent may lead to injustice of a particular case and also unduly restrict the proper development of the law. It stated its right, while treating former decisions of the House as normally binding, to depart from a previous decision when it appears right to do so: *Practice Note*.[119] Such a statement of principle by the House of Lords inevitably makes even weaker any case for following the decisions of that House whether they are in cases before or after the year 1922. There are many other jurisdictions like to our own where the *corpus juris* includes the common law such as the United Stated, Canada, Australia and New Zealand. These are nations where, in addition, there are written and, consequently, rigid Constitutions, unlike that of the United Kingdom. Whilst the judgments in cases decided in the English Courts at all levels will, on a great many occasions, provide convenient and, indeed, convincing statements of principle and attractive arguments in favour of such principles, they are no more than that and must be examined and questioned in the light of a jurisprudence whose fundamental law is radically different in its denial of a supremacy of parliament and its upholding of three co-equal organs of government, in the Legislature, the

115. [1949] IR 60.
116. [1949] IR 91.
117. [1965] IR 642.
118. [1965] IR 110.
119. [1966] 1 WLR 1234.

> Executive and the Judiciary. In no sense are our courts a continuation of or successors to the British courts. They derive their powers from a Constitution enacted by the people and would, in my view, find more appropriate guidance in the decisions of courts in other countries based upon a similar constitutional framework than in what, at times, appears to be an uncritical adherence to English precedent, which itself, appears difficult to reconcile from time to time…"

[12.36] In that case O'Higgins CJ and Griffin J declined to express an opinion on the points raised by McCarthy J. In *Tromso Sparebank v Beirne (No 2)* Costello J again stated that an Irish court should be reluctant to refuse to follow a firmly established principle in English law:[120]

> "I think the High Court should be slow to refuse to follow a principle established in English law since 1883. But if high legal authority *in England* questions the validity of the principle so that it appears it may well be changed either by judicial decision or by the legislature, then it seems to me that the Irish court is justified in not following it, should it consider it to be erroneous."

[12.37] In *M McC v J McC* Costello J declined to follow a series of English cases, but again emphasised the strong persuasive weight of English authority and implicit in his judgment is the view that such authority should be followed unless it is shown to be wrongly decided:[121]

> "I think I have liberty to give effect to this opinion even though it is contrary to the decisions of the English courts on the subject. These decisions are of persuasive weight and should not lightly be ignored. But the Irish courts are not bound by them and I think I am not required to follow decisions which I think misconstrued the effect of an earlier decision of the House of Lords which I would be prepared to follow."

[12.38] In recent years Irish courts have been willing to have recourse to decisions of jurisdictions other than England. In constitutional matters the courts pay special attention to decisions of courts in the United States, especially the federal Supreme Court, as the constitutions of both countries bear broad similarities and are rooted in similar legal philosophies. Recourse to decisions of the courts of the nearest common law jurisdiction, Northern Ireland, has been quite rare since 1922. The citation of decisions from other common law jurisdictions, such as Australia, Canada and New Zealand, has become more common in recent years. This trend seems likely to continue in

---

120. [1989] ILRM 257, at 261 (emphasis added). See also *In re United Bars Ltd and ors*, High Court, unrep, 3 June 1988 where Murphy J adhered to English precedent in the interests of certainty and predictability.

121. [1994] 1 IR 293, at 303.

the future, particularly in view of greater availability by electronic means of the case law of those countries. However, decisions of the English courts will still feature prominently for the foreseeable future. In this context, we might note the findings of a study conducted in 1983 by Professors Boyle and Greer which analysed the headnotes of reported cases between 1921 and 1975 (see Table 12.01).[122] The breakdown of the cases referred to in the headnotes of decisions of the courts in the Republic of Ireland was:

Origin of Decision	No.	%
English or Scottish Cases	1,058	50
Pre-1920 Irish Cases	356	17
Post-1920 Irish Cases	654	31
Post-1920 Northern Ireland Cases	23	1
Other	6	1

Table 12.01

[12.39] The equivalent data for decisions of the courts of Northern Ireland are outlined in Table 12.02:

Origin of Decision	No.	%
English or Scottish Cases	180	61
Pre-1920 Irish Cases	55	19
Post-1920 Irish Cases	9	3
Post-1920 Northern Ireland Cases	45	15
Other	8	3

Table 12.02

[12.40] For purposes of comparison we have compiled a different table in respect of decisions of the courts in the Republic of Ireland reported in 1995 (see Table 12.03).[123] These figures reveal the following breakdown of *cases referred to* in the course of the reported judgments:

122. Boyle and Greer, *The Legal Systems, North and South* (New Ireland Forum, 1983), p 46.

123. These figures are based on the cases cited judicially in the judgments reported in [1995] 1 IR, [1995] 1 ILRM and [1995] 2 ILRM. Decisions which were reported both in IR and ILRM were counted once only for the purpose of the table. The percentages have been rounded up and down for convenience.

Origin of Decision	No.	%
Post-1920 Irish Cases	336	56.5
English or Scottish Cases	197	33
Pre-1920 Irish Cases	18	3
Post-1920 Northern Ireland Cases	2	0.4
Court of Justice of European Communities	19	3.2
United States	14	2.4
Australia	7	1.2
Canada	1	0
New Zealand	1	0

Table 12.03

[12.41] If we take these figures as giving a broad (though not necessarily definitive) picture, it seems that in Ireland, post-1920 Irish decisions have overtaken English and Scottish precedents in terms of the number of references. This no doubt reflects the increase in judicial output in Ireland since 1975. However, it is also clear that English and Scottish decisions remain very important as sources of persuasive authority. Of the other common law jurisdictions listed, only two authorities from Northern Ireland were considered, while there were seven from Australia. One major change since the Boyle and Greer study is the increased importance of the decisions of the Court of Justice of the European Communities, a consequence of membership of the European Community. Finally, we may note that, in general, the courts in the Republic of Ireland seem reluctant to refer to authority from civil law systems.[124]

[12.42] Where the decisions of different jurisdictions lead to different conclusions an Irish court is not bound to prefer any particular line of authority and may choose to adopt one or other or neither.[125] McCarthy J in *Irish Shell Ltd v Elm Motors Ltd* anticipated that decisions from a variety of jurisdictions might be cited in and relied on by Irish Courts. However, in *The*

124. An exception is *Murphy v Attorney General* [1982] IR 241 where the High Court and Supreme Court referred to decisions of the Constitutional Courts of Germany and Italy. No doubt, a difficulty in translation may account for the absence of more references to such decisions. Whether an increased facility in languages will alter this pattern remains to be seen.

125. See, eg, *The People (Attorney General) v O'Dwyer* [1972] IR 416; *In re Keenan Brothers Ltd* [1985] IR 401.

MV 'Kapitan Labunets' Barr J expressed caution in regard to accepting foreign authority:[126]

> "...I apprehend that judges in this jurisdiction would have no difficulty in concurring with the view expressed by Lord Diplock on the subject of decisions of foreign courts in the course of his judgment in the House of Lords in *Fothergill v Monarch Airlines*[127] that 'the persuasive value of a particular court's decision must depend upon its reputation and its status, the extent to which its decisions are binding upon courts of co-ordinate and inferior jurisdiction in its own country and the coverage of the national law reporting system'."

Barr J's caution is particularly appropriate in relation to the citation of jurisprudence from civil law countries, where a system of binding precedent is unknown and prior decisions are primarily of illustrative value.

Secondary sources

[12.43] In some cases a court might be faced with an absence of authority, whether binding or persuasive. In those circumstances it might rely of the writings of jurists and often reference has been made to recognised textbooks and learned articles.[128] The traditional rule was that such materials could be cited only if the author was dead, an event which was considered to confer upon him an authoritative status which living authors lack. This rule has been relaxed and the courts now permit the citation of the works of living authors.[129] These sources are secondary in that they are not produced by a law-making agency and, unlike case law and legislation, they lack the force of law. Nevertheless such works can be of highly persuasive authority and often their reasoning is 'adopted' by courts. Moreover, in some cases a court might adopt a secondary source in preference to a persuasive precedent.[130]

---

126. [1995] 1 IR 164, at 168.
127. [1981] AC 251.
128. See, eg, *Kirby v Burke and Holloway* [1944] IR 207; *The People (DPP) v Lynch* [1982] IR 64; *Hynes Ltd v Independent Newspapers Ltd* [1980] IR 204; *Desmond v Brophy* [1985] IR 449.
129. See, eg, *Metropolitan Properties Ltd v O'Brien* [1995] 2 ILRM 383 citing Wylie, *Irish Conveyancing Law* (Butterworths, 1978); *Johnson and Kelly v Horace* [1993] ILRM 594 citing Wylie, *Irish Land Law* 2nd ed (Butterworths, 1986); *Iarnrod Eireann v Ireland* [1995] 2 ILRM 161 citing McMahon & Binchy, *Irish Law of Torts* 2nd ed (Butterworths, 1990); *Gleeson v Feehan* [1993] 2 IR 113 citing Brady, *Succession Law in Ireland* (Butterworths, 1989).
130. In *Kirby v Burke and Holloway* [1944] IR 207 Gavan Duffy J adopted the extra-judicial writings of Oliver Wendell Holmes in preference to the House of Lords decision in *Donoghue v Stevenson* [1932] AC 562.

[3] THE RATIO DECIDENDI AND OBITER DICTUM

[12.44] As has been already stated not every part of an earlier decision must be followed by a later court. In the course of a judgment it is probable that the judge will canvass and consider a number of propositions of law, some of which bear on the point in question and others of which are tangential thereto. The discussion of law in which the judge engages will typically set out reasons in support of accepting certain arguments and drawing a particular conclusion. In this respect the reasoning operates to justify the decision and to establish that it has been reached in accordance with the pre-existing law. Once it is decided a case becomes authority for a certain proposition of law and the part which is binding is called the *ratio decidendi*. Briefly stated it can be said to encapsulate a proposition of law for which the decision is authority. Black J stated that he would treat as part of the *ratio decidendi* 'any assertion of principle that its author believed and intended to be part of his *ratio decidendi*' and contrasted this with 'a principle which is not required for the decision or intended to be part of it.'[131] In *Considine v Shannon Regional Fisheries Board* Costello J stated:[132]

> "The doctrine of judicial precedent provides that a principle of law which is the basis for an actual decision of the Supreme Court must be followed by the lower courts. Like many general principles, the principle of judicial precedent can be easily stated but may be difficult to apply in practice. And undoubtedly there may be instances where the *ratio* of a case is not always easy to discover. Again, the principle is clear. The *ratio* of a case is discovered by determining what proposition of law justified the decision in the light of the material facts which the court decided."

[12.45] Cross and Harris offer the following explanation:[133]

> "The *ratio decidendi* of a case is any rule of law expressly or impliedly treated by the judge as a necessary step in reaching his conclusion, having regard to the line of reasoning adopted by him, or a necessary part of his direction to the jury."

[12.46] From the foregoing several points in relation to the *ratio decidendi* emerge - it is based on the facts of the case, it is a necessary part of the decision ('required' or 'the basis for') and it is treated as such by the court which decided the case.

[12.47] A proposition of law contained in the judgment which is not binding is termed *dictum* or *obiter dictum (dicta* and *obiter dicta* being the plural

---

131. Dowrick, *loc cit* at 27.
132. [1994] 1 ILRM 499, at 501. See further para **[12.59]**.
133. *Precedent in English Law* 4th ed (Clarendon Press, 1991), p 72.

forms respectively). The two expressions tend to be used interchangeably but, strictly speaking, there is a difference between them. When the point relates to a matter that was in issue in the case *dictum* is the expression used while *obiter dicta* refer to other, more tangential matters.[134] It is unusual for a court expressly to state the *ratio decidendi* of its decision, preferring instead to leave it concealed in its reasoning. This does not reflect a judicial predilection for obfuscation but rather a desire not to hinder or fetter future courts. A court is concerned with deciding the particular case before it and not potential future cases, which will be the task of later courts. Discovery of the *ratio decidendi,* therefore, is largely a matter of interpretation for later courts. It must be emphasised that when a court searches for the *ratio decidendi* of an earlier decision it is looking for the rule or principle which underlies the decision and for which the decision is authority. The task is essentially one of classifying statements of law as being *ratio decidendi* or *obiter dictum.*[135] In this context, it should be realised that judges infrequently employ the expression '*ratio decidendi*' and more often speak of the 'rule' or 'principle' which is contained in the earlier decision. In this respect the terms are largely synonymous and are used interchangeably. Given the nature of the exercise no precise formula for the extraction of the *ratio decidendi* has evolved, it being a matter of art rather than science. Despite that, several points can be made.

Ratio decidendi is based on the facts of the case

[12.48] Because courts decide actual cases, and not moot points, the *ratio decidendi* is based on the facts of the case rather than on any hypothetical set of circumstances. It is the rule which was applied as limited by those facts. A court's discussion of the case is normally confined to the actual facts and a decision, by its very nature, concerns those facts and no others. This is sometimes reflected in the observation that a case is authority only for that which it decides. Unfortunately this does not provide the simple solution which at first sight it might suggest. Every case can be read as presenting an individual set of facts which will never be repeated. Details such as the identity of the parties, the time and location of the event, and the event itself

---

134. See Zander, *The Law-Making Process* 4th ed (Butterworths, 1994), p 262. See also *The People (DPP) v Shaw* [1982] IR 1, at 47 *per* Griffin J "…I consider those *dicta* to have been *obiter.*"

135. Occasionally the distinction between the two is blurred; see eg *Elwyn (Cottons) Ltd v Master of the High Court* [1989] IR 14, at 16, *per* O'Hanlon J "I therefore adopt the decision of my learned colleague on this issue and the *ratio decidendi* underlying the said decision, although in the nature of *obiter dicta.*"; *Wall v Hegarty and Callanan* [1980] ILRM 124, at 127 *per* Barrington J "… the *dicta*, whether they were of the *ratio* or not, are clearly of high authority."

are unique to the particular case. However, to read cases in such a narrow manner would be so restrictive as to destroy the system of *stare decisis.* No two cases would be alike and, in consequence, no decision would be binding. But as it is authority for a particular proposition of law it is necessarily implicit that a case is capable of being applied beyond its own particular facts. It follows that courts are required to identify similarities and dissimilarities between cases and to adjudicate accordingly. Thus, if adequate reasons cannot be found to justify distinguishing the instant case from the earlier case the latter must be followed. In general, therefore, the individual details of a case do not limit its scope. For instance, the fact that the victorious plaintiff in the earlier case was injured by a car does not, of itself, preclude that case from being applied to a case which involves injury caused by a train. The function of the later court is to identify the categories into which the earlier court sought to place the particular individual facts. When the court decides that the earlier case is a relevant authority which must be followed it is placing the different sets of individual facts in the same category. To draw on the example already used, if the court in the case involving injury by the train decides that it is bound by the earlier case involving the car it, in effect, states that for the purposes of the rule there is no difference between a car and a train. In other words, the *ratio decidendi* of the earlier case allows recovery whether the injury is caused by a car or by a train. Thus, one must realise that facts can be stated at different levels of generality. It is in the identification of the appropriate level that the *ratio decidendi* is discovered. The agent of harm in the example under discussion can be described variously as a car, a motorised vehicle, a mechanical vehicle, a vehicle which might or might not be mechanical or a tangible thing. In equating, or indeed differentiating, cases the court selects a level of generality to apply to instant case. The irrelevance of certain factual differences will be obvious to all. For instance, injury caused by a Ford is not perceived to differ from injury caused by a Rolls Royce. However, different factors might enter into consideration when one asks whether injury caused by a car is to be equated with that caused by a runaway horse, a leakage of chemicals or the carelessness of a surgeon. The answer will depend on the level of generality which is selected. In searching for the appropriate level the later court is attempting to identify the rule which was invoked in the earlier decision. And that, in turn, requires the court to examine the earlier decision with a view to determining how it was reached.

Relevance of Reasoning and Arguments

[12.49] When it examines an earlier case the later court searches for indications in the judgment as to the rule which was invoked. The earlier court will usually have commented on the individual facts concerned and have defined the category which it had in mind. However, that in itself is not conclusive as the later court might ignore the stated category and redefine it. This is particularly so where the category has been drawn in especially broad, or especially narrow, terms. Thus, although the earlier court might have spoken of the agent of harm as being a tangible thing, the later court might decline to employ that level of generality, saying that the earlier case concerned a car or a vehicle and not tangible things in general. In so explaining the earlier decision the later court is, to an extent, refashioning the *ratio decidendi*. The earlier court will also have considered any relevant cases which preceded it. For instance, the court concerned with the injury caused by a car might have felt itself bound by, and followed, a precedent involving injury caused by a galloping horse. In that instance the category would have to include both galloping horses and cars and the appropriate level of generality is thereby defined, in part at least. The question which the later court will face is whether the new agent of harm, a train, fails into that category. In other words, it will be required to identify, for the purposes of the rule, the characteristics which are shared by galloping horses and cars and determine whether a train possesses those properties. Again, the later court will examine the earlier judgments in its attempt to ascertain the nexus between them. It might be that those cases indicate that galloping horses and cars are dangerous objects which are liable to cause serious personal injury and which should be kept under control. If that is the common characteristic identified by the court it is probable that a train, which also is a dangerous object, would come within the rule. But, by the same token, injury caused by a stationary horse might be distinguished as the latter does not possess the degree of danger shared by the other objects.

[12.50] This, of course, is to assume that the earlier courts will have commented on the categories which they had in mind. It is, however, not uncommon that a court will confine its discussion of the case to the particular facts. This, in part at least, is motivated by a desire to restrict consideration of the legal issues to the case in hand and a wish not to engage in speculation which is thought to be the more suitable subject of future litigation. In this respect, the later court is left to interpret the earlier court's silence. Thus, the later court might conclude that nothing has been said in the earlier case which prevents its application to the new case. That silence can be so construed was appreciated by McCarthy J in his judgment in *Ó Domhnaill v Merrick* where he expressed his disagreement with certain propositions which had been advanced in argument '... lest my silence on the topics might be considered to denote agreement ...'[136] Equally, a court

136. [1984] IR 151, at 167.

might rely on the silence of its predecessor to exclude the application of the precedent to the new case, saying that there is no indication in the earlier case which suggests that it should apply to the later.

[12.51] The earlier court's discussion of the relevant law might also indicate the rule which it had in mind. That court will have considered cases which preceded it and will have subjected them to the same form of analysis to which it will be subject in later cases. That analysis of earlier cases and the evaluation of their scope and effect will be taken into account by the later court in its efforts to discover the *ratio decidendi*. The earlier court will have expressed its reasons for choosing to follow, or not to follow, a preceding case, thereby stating a relationship between the two which indicates the rule which was applied. This is to state the rule in a somewhat oblique manner, but occasionally a court will state clearly the rule which it intends to apply. However, even where that occurs it does not dispose of the issue. The later court might not accept the stated rule as being the *ratio decidendi* of the earlier decision. The court might state that the purported rule was too broad for the particular decision and that a less expansive rule would have sufficed. Likewise, if the rule is expressed in narrow terms, which would suggest that the later case lies outside its scope, the court might conclude that the rule was so expressed as a particular application of a more general rule.

[12.52] It has been noted that the *ratio decidendi* of a case is based on its actual facts rather than on a hypothesis. A further characteristic is that a decision rests on the arguments which were advanced in the case. It is said that a point not argued is a point not decided.[137] For instance, a claim based on contract does not provide a binding rule in respect of tortious liability. The *ratio decidendi* of that case consists of some rule which forms part of the law of contract, not the law of torts. A further decision in a case on the same facts will be necessary to arrive at a binding rule which governs liability in tort. Once again, when this matter is being considered the later court will be required to examine the judgment in the earlier case in order to discover the basis on which the earlier case was decided. And in *Re Hetherington*[138] Browne-Wilkinson VC stated that a court is not bound by a proposition the correctness of which was assumed by the earlier court without its having been specifically considered. A related feature, which has already been observed, is a *per incuriam* decision.[139] That is one which has been made in ignorance of a relevant statute or binding authority and, in

137. See *The State (Quinn) v Ryan* [1965] IR 110, at 120, *per* Ó Dalaigh CJ.

138. [1990] Ch 1, at 10, citing *Baker v The Queen* [1975] AC 774; *Berns v Bethell* [1982] Ch 294, *Ashville Investments Ltd v Elmer Contractors Ltd* [1989] QB 488.

139. See para **[12.06]**.

consequence, is not itself binding. Although the earlier court will, in all probability, have thought that it was reaching a binding decision its ignorance of the earlier law deprives it of that quality. A relevant point has not been argued and, therefore, has not been decided.

[12.53] So far our consideration of this topic has proceeded on the assumption that a case consists of one judgment which advances one reason for the decision reached. Matters are more complicated where a judge advances several reasons in support of the decision or where a number of judgments are delivered. In respect of the former, it has been stated by Budd J in *Brendan Dunne Ltd v FitzPatrick*[140] that where a judge gives two reasons for the decision both are part of the *ratio decidendi*.[141] Thus, to return to our example of the injury caused by a car, were the court to hold the car owner liable on the grounds that a car is a dangerous object *and* that its situation on the highway increases the risk of injury to other users of the highway the *ratio decidendi* would include both those factors. This rule would incorporate injuries caused by cars and by runaway horses as both share the characteristics identified in the judgment. But it would exclude injury caused by trains as the latter do not pose additional threats to users of the highway.

Ratio Decidendi and Multiple Judgments

[12.54] Special considerations apply with regard to multi-judge courts, such as the Supreme Court and less frequently a Divisional Court of the High Court. It is a convention of the common law that each judge in a multi-judge court may (but not necessarily must) deliver a separate judgment indicating his or her reasons for the decision arrived at by the court. Thus, in a court of three or five judges such as the Supreme Court, it is possible for a decision to be arrived at by a majority of 3-2, with each judge expressing his or her views in quite different ways. Although as we shall see the delivery of separate judgments may give rise to some difficulties in determining the precise point established by the decision, the analysis of decisions of multi-judge courts is a key element in a law student's study. Analysis of the different reasons given by the judges in a Supreme Court decision help to develop the student's appreciation of the subtle distinctions inherent in the legal process. It is also important to appreciate that, while in a particular case, the judgment delivered by a judge who finds himself in a minority in the case is at best a consolation for the disappointed litigant, such dissenting

140. [1958] IR 29, at 45.

141. See *Considine v Shannon Regional Fisheries Board* [1994] 1 ILRM 499, at 501 *per* Costello J "It is, of course, clear that there may be more than one *ratio* in a decided case." See further para **[12.59]**.

judgments have, in many instances, proved highly influential in subsequent cases.[142] The practice of delivering separate, and dissenting, judgments was defended extra-judicially by the late McCarthy J, who had found himself in a minority in the Supreme Court on a number of occasions:[143]

> 'At the centre of the common law, the genius of its dynamism, is the interplay of judicial rationale - the multiple judgment system. Let it flourish. It has a proud history; it should continue to have a historical pride. It is for this reason that we write judgments - we may want to indulge in some semantic exercise; we may wish to polish our literary style; we may wish to temper the rigor of some decision; but most of all we wish to see the interpretation and growth of the law continue.'

Consistently with this view, McCarthy J criticised the restrictions imposed on the Supreme Court by Article 34.4.5° which requires the Court to deliver a single judgment where the constitutional validity of legislation enacted by the Oireachtas is in question, the 'one judgment rule'.[144] A similar restriction applies where the Court delivers judgment in a reference to it under Article 26.[145] The Supreme Court has held that Article 34.4.5° is confined to cases concerning the validity of post-1937 Acts only.[146] Thus separate judgments are delivered where a constitutional question arises concerning pre-1937 Acts,[147] where post 1937 secondary legislation is challenged[148] or where no statutory provision is at issue in a constitutional claim.[149] Supreme Court

142. Eg the dissenting judgment of Denning LJ (later Lord Denning MR) in *Candler v Crane, Christmas & Co* [1951] 2 KB 164 was largely adopted in *Hedley, Byrne & Co Ltd v Heller & Partners Ltd* [1964] AC 465: see further para **[12.75]**. Similarly, the dissenting speech of Lord Atkin in *Liversidge v Anderson* [1942] AC 206, in which he had criticised the views of the majority by comparing their attitude to interpretation of statutory language with that adopted by Humpty Dumpty in Lewis Carroll's *Alice Through the Looking Glass*. The speech was (much later) adopted as correctly setting out fundamental principles of administrative law: see *Anisminic Ltd v Foreign Compensation Tribunal* [1969] 2 AC 147.

143. Mr Justice McCarthy, 'Una Voce Poco Fa', in O'Reilly (ed), *Human Rights and Constitutional Law* (Essays in Honour of Brian Walsh) (Round Hall Press, 1992), p 162. McCarthy J's last judgment in *Attorney General v Hamilton* [1993] 2 IR 250, a dissenting judgment, has been compared with that of Lord Atkin in *Liversidge*: see obituary (1992) 14 DULJ (ns).

144. *Ibid*, 164-5.

145. See para **[5.65]**.

146. *The State (Sheerin) v Kennedy* [1966] IR 379. See generally, Hogan & Whyte, *Kelly's The Irish Constitution*, 3rd ed (Butterworths, 1994), pp 527-30.

147. Eg *McGee v Attorney General* [1974] IR 284 (para **[15.128]**); *Norris v Attorney General* [1984] IR 36 (para **[15.129]**).

148. Eg *Meagher v Minister for Agriculture and Food* [1994] 1 IR 329 (para **[16.76] - [16.87]**), in which the Court delivered a single judgment on the issue of the constitutional validity of the European Communities Act 1972, s 3, but delivered separate judgments on the validity of Regulations made pursuant to the power conferred by s 3.

judges are also free to deliver separate judgments in cases concerning judge-made rules, such as those concerning the duty of care in negligence,[150] or in cases concerning statutory interpretation.[151] Thus, in the majority of instances, each member of the Court may deliver a separate judgment. Where one judgment attracts the concurrence of the other members of the court or where a majority of the judgments delivered agree on the reasons for the decision few additional problems are created. The reasoning which attracts the unanimous, or at least majority, support of the court would form the basis of the *ratio decidendi.* However, where the court is unanimous but different reasons are advanced, none of which attracts the support of a majority, two possible approaches exist. One is that the *ratio* would consist of the sum of the reasons advanced. Thus, if two judges opt for Reason A and one each for Reasons B, C, and D the *ratio* of the case would consist of Reasons A, B, C, and D. While this approach might entail an element of desirable compromise the difficulty with it is that it results in the selection of the narrowest possible *ratio* which accommodates all the judgments delivered. This would come close to stating that the case is an authority only for that which it decides and it would lack a binding quality except in identical cases. With this in mind Professor Cross presented an alternative approach which he thought is probably closer to actual judicial practice.[152] He suggested that one should think of the case as comprising of a number of *rationes decidendi* and select that which can be said to attract the support of a majority. Therefore, if Reasons A and B are not mutually incompatible but are inconsistent with Reasons C and D the *ratio* would embrace A and B, thus attracting at least the partial support of three judges. But it should be recognised that this approach is of little avail in the, fortunately rare, case where five judges advance five separate and incompatible reasons. In that event, a later court is very much left to its own devices and can select any of the five different *rationes* or, indeed, a sixth of its own invention.

[12.55] As Professor Cross noted, dissenting judgments can be relevant when it comes to ascertaining the *ratio decidendi.* It is all too tempting to ignore those judgments in the, possibly mistaken, belief that they shed no light on the subject. Dissents can be relevant for several reasons. A dissent might be based on a different interpretation of the evidence or a different evaluation of legal issues which the case presents but nevertheless support the propositions of law advanced by the majority. Thus, the dissenting judgment of Walsh J in *The People (DPP) v Walsh*[153] was based largely on

149. Eg, *Attorney General v X* [1992] 1 IR 1 (para **[15.131]**).

150. See paras **[12.70]-[12.85]**.

151. See Ch 14.

152. 'The *Ratio Decidendi* and a Plurality of Speeches in the House of Lords' (1977) 93 LQR 378.

his evaluation of the evidence but his statement of the law is considered to be authoritative.[154] Moreover, in some cases the majority might agree on the result but for conflicting reasons and recourse must then be had to the dissenting judgments. This can be illustrated by an example where three reasons, A, B and C, are advanced in the judgments. The majority is composed of two judges who opt for reason A and one who opts for reason B but expressly disapproves of reason A. The dissenting judges advance reason C and also express their disapproval of reason A. The third judge of the majority also expresses his support of reason C but considers it inapplicable in the instant case (see Figure 12.01).

MAJORITY	2 judges accept Reason A 1 judge accepts Reason B, rejects Reason A, thinks Reason C valid but inapplicable
MINORITY	2 judges accept Reason C, reject Reason A

Figure 12.01

[12.56] In this event it is difficult to conclude that reason A is the *ratio* of the case as three judges, the two dissidents and one member of the majority, have expressed their disapproval of it. Nor can the *ratio* be said to be based on reason B as it enjoys the support of only one judge, namely the third majority judge. Thus, the available alternatives are that the *ratio* is based on reason C, which as a proposition of law was acceptable to three judges, or that the case possesses no discernible *ratio* and is merely authority for that which it decided. But the first alternative presents the difficulty of elevating the reasoning of a dissident minority into the *ratio* of the case and it would seem that we are left with the second.

[12.57] Another example which was considered by Professor Cross also concerns a case where there is a three-to-two majority. Two judges opt for Reason A, one for Reason B and the two dissidents opt for Reason C, but this time each of the judges in the majority expresses disapproval of Reason C (see Figure 12.02).

153. [1980] IR 294.

154. See *The People (DPP) v Kenny* [1990] 2 IR 110, at 131, *per* Finlay CJ "The judgment of Walsh J in that case was a dissenting judgment, but not by reason of the principles of law enunciated in it, but rather by reason of the view taken as to whether on the facts of the case the detention of the applicant was or was not unlawful."

MAJORITY	{ 2 judges accept Reason A, reject Reason C 1 judge accepts Reason B, rejects Reason C
MINORITY	{ 2 judges accept Reason C

Figure 12.02

[12.58] In these circumstances, Professor Cross suggested that reason A forms the *ratio decidendi* of the case. It cannot be Reason B as it is supported by only one judge and Reason C having been condemned by three judges could not be the *ratio* of the case. It could be said that Reason A is acceptable as being that which is least objectionable and formed part of the majority reasoning - in fact, it was supported by a 'majority of the majority'. To some extent, this issue is determined by later decisions, as can be illustrated by recent judicial practice in the Supreme Court and High Court concerning the decision in *The People (DPP) v O'Shea.*[155] In *O'Shea*, it was held by a 3-2 majority of the Supreme Court, comprising O'Higgins CJ, Walsh and Hederman JJ, with Finlay P and Henchy J dissenting, that the prosecution may appeal to the Supreme Court from an acquittal in the Central Criminal Court. In the course of the judgments two members of the majority, O'Higgins CJ and Walsh J, suggested that the Court could order a retrial in the event of a successful appeal (Reason A) while the remaining member of the majority, Hederman J, reserved his opinion on that question, merely holding that an appeal lay (Reason B). The two dissenting judges, Finlay P and Henchy J, held that the prosecution does not enjoy a right of appeal (Reason C). In *The People (DPP) v O'Shea (No 2)*[156] the Supreme Court, comprising the same judges, unanimously held that the DPP's appeal should be dismissed on the ground that the acquittal, which had been directed by the trial judge, had been justified as there was no sufficient evidence presented by the prosecution to justify putting the case to the jury. Thus, the question whether a re-trial could or should be ordered did not arise. However, on Professor Cross's analysis, part of the *ratio* of *O'Shea* is that the Supreme Court may order a retrial following a successful prosecution appeal.[157] Just over five years later, in *The People (DPP) v Quilligan and O'Reilly (No 2)*[158] the Court, again comprising five judges but

155. [1982] IR 384.

156. [1983] ILRM 592.

157. See also Hogan, 'Criminal Appeals - a New Departure' (1983) 5 DULJ (ns) 254, fn 2 considering another aspect of the *ratio decidendi*, namely the type of acquittals which are capable of being appealed, and applying Professor Cross's analysis.

158. [1989] IR 46. In *The People (DPP) v Quilligan and O'Reilly* [1986] IR 495, the Supreme Court had held that the acquittals in that case, again directed by the trial judge, had been based on an incorrect interpretation of the law. The trial judge had held that the defendants' arrests under s 30 of the Offences against the State Act 1939 were invalid since the crimes of which they were suspected did not involve a subversive element. The Supreme Court held that s 30 was sufficiently wide to include non-subversive crime.

with two changes in personnel, had to consider that very issue. Walsh and McCarthy JJ considered that *O'Shea* had dealt with the matter authoritatively in favour of the proposition that the Court had the power to order a retrial (Reason A). This is consistent with Professor Cross's analysis. By contrast Henchy J, with whom Griffin J agreed, observed that only two of the judges in *O'Shea* had supported that proposition and concluded that the point was still undecided, an approach which clearly rejects Professor Cross's analysis. Henchy and Griffin JJ concluded that the Court did not possess the power to order a retrial consequent to a successful prosecution appeal (Reason C). The fifth judge in *The People (DPP) v Quilligan and O'Reilly (No 2)*, Hederman J, again reserved his opinion on this issue, merely holding that a retrial should not be ordered in the case, but without further elaboration (Reason B). One of two alternative conclusions can be drawn from this. The first is that Henchy and Griffin JJ in *Quilligan and O'Reilly (No 2)* misinterpreted the *ratio* of *O'Shea* and, applying the analysis of Professor Cross, ought to have adopted the remarks of O'Higgins CJ and Walsh J, as was done by Walsh and McCarthy JJ in *Quilligan and O'Reilly (No 2)*. The other is that Professor Cross's analysis does not reflect the position in Ireland and that to acquire the status of *ratio* a proposition must secure the support of an outright majority of the judges who decided the case, not just a majority of the majority.

[12.59] In a more recent decision of the High Court, *Considine v Shannon Regional Fisheries Board*,[159] *O'Shea* was considered again. In *Considine*, Costello J rejected a constitutional challenge to the validity of s 310 of the Fisheries (Consolidation) Act 1959, which provides for an appeal against an acquittal in a summary prosecution under the Act. The Shannon Regional Fisheries Board had issued a summons against the plaintiff under the 1959 Act, alleging various breaches of the 1959 Act. The summons was dismissed in the District Court and the Board appealed to the Circuit Court under s 310. The plaintiff claimed that s 310 of the 1959 Act was invalid on the ground that it was in conflict with Article 38.1 of the Constitution, which provides that '[n]o person shall be tried on any criminal charge save in due course of law', and that a determination in the Circuit Court after an acquittal in the District Court would not be 'in due course of law.' In support of s 310, it was argued that Article 38.1 should be read in conjunction with Article 34.3.4° of the Constitution, which provides that '[t]he courts of first instance shall also include courts of local and limited jurisdiction with a right of appeal as determined by law' and that this contemplated the form of appeal in s 310 of the 1959 Act. It was also argued that one of the *rationes* of *O'Shea* was that Article 38.1 should not be interpreted as limiting the

159. [1994] 1 ILRM 499.

appellate jurisdiction of the courts, and that this was binding on Costello J as a High Court judge. Costello J accepted this latter argument. We have already noted that he referred in *Considine* to the difficulty of determining the *ratio* or *rationes* of a particular decision.[160] In relation to *O'Shea* itself, he noted two points which distinguished it from *Considine*. First, *O'Shea* had concerned Article 34.4.3°, which deals with the appellate jurisdiction of the Supreme Court, whereas Article 34.3.4°, which was at issue in *Considine*, concerns, for example, appeals to the Circuit Court from the District Court. Second, *O'Shea* dealt with the right of appeal from a verdict of a jury in a criminal trial in the Central Criminal Court, whereas *Considine* involved an appeal from a summary trial in the District Court. Despite these differences, he held that a number of legal principles laid down by the Supreme Court were binding on him. For present purposes, we refer only to the issue raised in *O'Shea* as to whether Article 34.4.3° was limited by Article 38.1. Costello J noted that O'Higgins CJ and Walsh J had expressly rejected this point, as indeed they had rejected the suggestion that Article 34.4.3° was limited by Article 38.5. Costello J also noted in *Considine* that the judgment of Hederman J, which he described as '[t]he third judgment making up the majority of the court', had not expressly dealt with this point, but Costello J commented 'by implication, he must have agreed with the conclusion of his colleagues.' In light of Hederman J's continued reservations on *O'Shea* as expressed in *Quilligan and O'Reilly (No 2)*, this comment seems difficult to justify. Nonetheless, Costello J concluded his judgment as follows:

> 'It seems to me that the decision of the Supreme Court is that Article 38.1 of the Constitution does not constitute an exception to the right of the appellate jurisdiction of the Supreme Court conferred by Article 34.4.3°. It is true that the Supreme Court was not dealing with Article 34.3.4° and was not dealing with an appeal from the District Court to the Circuit Court. However, it seems to me that the principle of law established by the Supreme Court's decision must apply with equal force to the provisions of that Article and I must therefore hold that in the light of the *O'Shea* case it has now been established that Article 38.1 would not prohibit an appeal under Article 34.3.4° from the District Court to the Circuit Court. Bound as I am by the principle established in the *O'Shea* case, I must therefore dismiss the plaintiff's claim.'

It is difficult to say definitively whether Costello J's judgment in *Considine* supports or rejects Professor Cross's analysis of the *ratio decidendi* in a multiple judgment case such as *O'Shea*. While Costello J accepted that the

160. See para **[12.44]**.

point at issue had been dealt with expressly only by O'Higgins CJ and Walsh J, he sought to add a third judge, Hederman J, to make a 'majority' of three. Ultimately, perhaps the most that can be said is that *O'Shea* - and any case like it - is authority only for that which it decided, but that this remains a matter for later courts to determine. In *Considine*, Costello J in effect held that *O'Shea* had determined at least four issues definitively: that an appeal against an acquittal in the Central Criminal Court lay to the Supreme Court, that Article 34.4.3° is not limited by Article 38.5, that Article 34.4.3° is not limited by Article 38.1 and, finally, that Article 34.3.4° is not limited by Article 38.1. The latter point was, of course, not addressed in *O'Shea* but Costello J nonetheless felt bound to come to that conclusion and to hold that s 310 of the Fisheries (Consolidation) Act 1959 was not invalid. To the extent that discussion of the *ratio decidendi* is descriptive, in that it attempts to focus on actual judicial practice, it would seem best to bear in mind Costello J's comment in *Considine* that 'the principle of precedent can be stated easily but may be difficult to apply in practice.'

[12.60] A final point about multi-judge decisions concerns the infrequent case where the court divides evenly. this can occur when one of the judges dies during the course of the hearing or must absent himself for some other unavoidable reason. Where an appellate court divides evenly the decision of the lower court stands. But the problem of determining the *ratio* in such an event remains. It would be tempting to select the reasoning of the judges who voted to dismiss the appeal as their judgments prevailed. But that would be to allow an external event, which inadvertently deprived the court of the ability to form a majority, shape the *ratio* of the decision. A solution which was proposed by Ó Dalaigh CJ in *Rexi Irish Mink Ltd v Dublin County Council*[161] is that in such a case the question of law is still undecided and the later court must determine which of the two views suggested should be adopted.

Significance of Obiter Dicta

[12.61] As we noted earlier, a statement of law which is not binding is called an *obiter dictum.* It consists of anything said by the earlier court which is not considered to be directly relevant or essential to the decision. However, although *obiter dicta* are not binding they do not lack significance as they are of persuasive authority. They may be adopted or followed at the option of the later court. The weight, or value, of an *obiter dictum* depends on a variety of factors, including the court in which it was delivered, the reputation of the judge who delivered it, how it has been dealt with in

161. [1972] IR 123, at 130

subsequent cases and its closeness to the instant case. It is not unusual for a statement which was *obiter* in one case to form the *ratio* of a subsequent case. In effect, the later court adopts the statement and bases its decision on it. Thus, in *The State (Raftis) v Leonard*[162] Murnaghan J followed two pre-1922 decisions, which he was otherwise reluctant to do, as they had been approved of, *obiter*, by the Supreme Court in *Walsh v Minister for Local Government*.[163] He did not feel free to adopt his own interpretation as the views of the Supreme Court should, in his opinion, be '...given the weight of an opinion of the Court and, as such, an acceptance that the law was as stated therein.'[164] On the other hand, it should be noted that the classification of a statement of law as being *obiter* can be contentious. In some cases a court's declaration that an earlier judicial opinion is *obiter* frees it from following what might otherwise be thought to be binding. This, in essence, is what occurred in *The People (DPP) v Shaw*[165] where Griffin J (in whose judgment three other judges concurred) argued that the remarks of Walsh J on the inadmissibility of unconstitutionally obtained evidence in *The People (Attorney General) v O'Brien*,[166] which had been followed in a number of cases, were in essence *obiter*. He stated that:[167]

> "... the test for the admissibility of such statements, in so far as it was propounded in *O'Brien's case*, was in terms which went beyond the issue presented to the Court in that case; it therefore lacks the authoritativeness that it would possess if it were a necessary element of the *ratio decidendi* of that decision."

And later he argued that:[168]

> "... the *ratio decidendi* of *O'Brien's case* goes no further than to lay down that where real evidence has been procured by illegal means, it falls within the discretion of the trial judge to decide whether public policy, based on a balancing of public interests, requires that such evidence be excluded. The specific and narrow issue involved in the case prevented its decision from being a vehicle in which to convey an authoritative and binding ruling on the test for the admission in evidence of oral, written, or other forms of statements tendered as confessions or admissions."

162. [1960] IR 381, at 419.
163. [1929] IR 377.
164. See also *The State (Lynch) v Cooney* [1982] IR 337, at 380 *per* Henchy J cited at para **[12.17]**.
165. [1982] IR 1.
166. [1965] IR 142.
167. [1982] IR 1, at 58.
168. *Ibid*, at 60.

In *The People (DPP) v Lynch*[169] a differently constituted Supreme Court took issue with these remarks. O'Higgins CJ disagreed with Griffin J's interpretation of the decision in *O'Brien*:[170]

> "I fear that I cannot agree with these views, either in relation to the ambit of the decision in *O'Brien's case* or in relation to the generality of the test which he suggests for the admission or exclusion of statements."

In the same case Walsh J in effect classified Griffin J's remarks as being themselves *obiter* when he observed that:[171]

> "It was not submitted in *Shaw's case*, nor was it the subject of any argument addressed to the Court, that *O'Brien's case* did not apply to statements or admissions made by an accused person."

In other words, a point not argued is a point not decided. The Supreme Court returned to this issue some years later. In *The People (DPP) v Healy* McCarthy J observed that Griffin J's remarks were 'not necessary for the decision in *Shaw*.'[172] Griffin J in turn re-iterated his earlier opinion:[173]

> "I have had the advantage of reading in advance the judgment which McCarthy J is about to deliver. In it he expresses the opinion that the examination of *The People (Attorney General) v O'Brien* in *The People (DPP) v Shaw*, and its reasoning, was not necessary for the decision in *Shaw's case*. I respectfully disagree. As in this case, the admissibility of the statements made by the defendant was directly in issue in *Shaw's case*. In the court of trial, the Court of Criminal Appeal, and in this Court the arguments advanced rested substantially on the principles enunciated by Kingsmill Moore J and Walsh J, who respectively delivered the leading majority and minority judgments in that case. It therefore became necessary for this Court to consider the extent to which the principles enunciated in the judgments in that case constituted a binding decision as to the tests to be applied in relation to the admissibility of statements made by the defendant. That was then my opinion and that of my colleagues who concurred in my judgment, and I see no reason to resile from what I said on the issue in *Shaw's case*. Further, although in this appeal substantial extracts from the judgments in *Shaw's case* were cited by counsel for both parties, at no time was there any argument or submission from counsel on either side that the examination of *O'Brien's case* or its reasoning was not necessary for the decision in that case."

169. [1982] IR 64.
170. *Ibid*, at 77.
171. *Ibid*, at 83.
172. [1990] 2 IR 73, at 90.
173. *Ibid*, at 85.

When the majority in *The People (DPP) v Kenny* took a different view to that enunciated in *Shaw* Griffin J remained unmoved:[174]

> "My judgment in *The People (DPP) v Shaw* had the support of Henchy J, Kenny J and Parke J. Having carefully considered all the arguments advanced in this case I can see no reason why I should resile from what I said in that case."

Another difference of opinion emerged between the judges in *Shaw*. Griffin J suggested that observations which were made in *The People (Attorney General) v Conmey*[175] to the effect that an appeal would lie from the Central Criminal Court directly to the Supreme Court were *obiter*.[176] Walsh J disagreed stating:[177]

> "I do not think that any judge would wish any statement which he might have made casually and as mere *obiter* to be treated as necessarily being an authority on the subject in question. However, when, as in *Conmey's case*, a fundamental issue is elaborately and substantially argued and the Court thinks it necessary for the purpose of the case to make an exhaustive and deliberate examination of the law and of the relevant constitutional provisions and, in the result, to state the law, the authority of such a statement of the law cannot be got rid of simply by claiming that it was not really necessary for the actual decision of the case ... Of course, some members of any court may from time to time be less than happy with some particular decision, but any such feeling cannot acceptably warrant either ignoring the decision so elaborately argued and decided or treating it as only 'a remark by the way'."

The different evaluations of *Conmey* were considered by Professor Casey:[178]

> "This judicial controversy is unusual, and does not appear to have any parallel in the earlier case-law of the Supreme Court. Further, the techniques employed are curious. It is perfectly understandable that the *Shaw* majority - three of whom did not sit in *Conmey's case* - should wish to reconsider that decision. And it can hardly be thought inappropriate that, even by way of *dictum,* they should serve advance notice of their desire to do so. But, with respect, it seems very odd to stigmatise the majority conclusion of *Conmey's case* as *obiter* ... only on the most restrictive view

174. [1990] 2 IR 110, at 137.
175. [1975] IR 341.
176. [1982] IR 1, at 47.
177. *Ibid*, at 44.
178. 'Criminal Appeals: the Confusion Persists' (1981) 16 Ir Jur (ns) 271, at 273-274; see by the same author 'Confusion in Criminal Appeals: the Legacy of Conmey' (1975) 10 Ir Jur (ns) 300.

could it be so considered; I might add that I know of no precedent in the common law world for the adoption of so restrictive an approach.

The desire to categorise the *Conmey* majority's conclusion as *obiter* is most interesting from the standpoint of judicial psychology. As is well known, the Supreme Court has power to overrule its own previous decisions (as well as those of its predecessors as final courts of appeal). And the present court has indicated that it is quite prepared to invoke this power in constitutional cases, as it has already done in others. But the court nonetheless seems to prefer to eschew overruling, and to rely instead on traditional, less direct methods to avoid following its earlier decisions. Thus in *State (Harkin) v O'Malley*[179] the court was at pains to show that *The People (Attorney General) v Doyle*[180] was not binding because (a) it was given without jurisdiction, and (b) it was a decision *per incuriam.*

It is doubtful, however, whether such an oblique approach is available in regard to *Conmey's case*. It can scarcely be categorised as a precedent *sub silentio,* since that term is employed only where a point appears to have been decided, though without argument or specific mention in the judgment(s). Nor can it properly be regarded as a decision *per incuriam;* this refers only to decisions given in ignorance of a statute or previous case in point. In *Morelle Ltd v Wakeling*[181] the English Court of Appeal declined to extend the *per incuriam* rule to cases in which the argument was not as full as it might have been. Now it is into this category, if any, that *Conmey's case* falls, since a number of relevant points do not appear to have been raised. Among these are: that 'no appeal against acquittal' was so familiar a principle in 1937 that the Constitution must be taken to have assumed its continuance in force; that for the Supreme Court to enter a conviction in an appeal against acquittal would deny the accused the jury trial required by Article 38.5; and that a Constitution which guarantees equal protection should not be construed so as to subject one class of acquitted defendants to a form of double jeopardy. These considerations would justify reconsidering *Conmey's case* and, perhaps, overruling it; but they cannot justify anything short of this."

[12.62] Implicit in the various remarks in *Shaw* and *Lynch* are different views of the *ratio decidendi*. Griffin J emphasised the role of the later court, in effect stating that it is for that court to determine what was necessary for the decision. On the other hand Walsh J highlighted the controlling role of the court which decided the case and its views of what was necessary for the decision. Correspondingly, there is a difference in their views on the freedom of a later court to treat a proposition of law as *obiter*. Nevertheless the cases demonstrate the emergence different bodies of judicial opinion on

179. [1978] IR 269.
180. (1964) 101 ILTR 136.
181. [1955] 2 QB 379.

the particular rules involved and the willingness of each 'side' to interpret earlier cases in a manner which denies authority to conflicting propositions of law. In this respect, a cynic could be led to the conclusion that the attribution of that status of *obiter dictum* to a proposition of law is little more than a device to evade the application of a statement of law which the court dislikes.[182]

Evolution of Principles

[12.63] So far we have been considering how the *ratio decidendi* of an earlier decision can be discovered and it is clear that a significant role is played by later courts. In this respect, the expression '*ratio decidendi*' can be understood in two senses and, indeed, some writers have suggested that it has two meanings. Professor Montrose wrote that:[183]

> "(1) The phrase sometimes signifies the rule of law propounded by the judge as the basis of his ultimate decision of the case. …(2) The phrase is sometimes used to mean the rule of law for which the case is of binding authority."

Professor Stone wrote of a distinction between:[184]

> "…that use of the term *ratio decidendi* which describes the process of reasoning by which decision was reached (the 'descriptive' *ratio decidendi*) and that which identifies and delimits *the* reasoning which a later court is bound to follow (the 'prescriptive' or 'binding' *ratio decidendi*) … This descriptive *ratio decidendi* may, of course, itself be sought at various levels; it may for instance be limited to the verbal behaviour of the judge, or it may seek to embrace the level of his total behaviour. Prescriptively used, on the other hand, the phrase *ratio decidendi* refers to a normative judgment requiring us to choose a particular *ratio decidendi* as legally required to be drawn from the prior case, that is, the binding *ratio decidendi*."

Professor Glanville Williams wrote:[185]

> "The phrase 'the *ratio decidendi* of a case' is slightly ambiguous. It may mean either (1) the rule that the judge who decided the case intended to lay down and apply to the facts, or (2) the rule that a later court concedes him to have had the power to lay down. The last sentence is rather clumsy, but what I mean is this. Courts do not accord to their predecessors an unlimited

---

182. The remarks attributed to Lord Asquith (1950) 1 JSPTL 359 seem apposite: "The rule is quite simple, if you agree with the other bloke you say it is part of the *ratio*; if you don't you say it is *obiter dictum*, with the implication that he is a congenital idiot."

183. 'The Ratio Decidendi of a Case' (1957) 20 MLR 587, at 588.

184. 'The Ratio of the Ratio Decidendi' (1959) 22 MLR 597, at 600-601 (reference omitted).

185. *Learning the Law* 11th ed (Stevens, 1982), p 75.

> power of laying down wide rules ... One circumstance that may induce a court to adopt [a] niggling attitude towards an earlier decision is the necessity of reconciling that decision with others. Or again, the court in the earlier case may have enunciated an unduly wide rule without considering all its possible consequences, some of which are unjust or inconvenient or otherwise objectionable. Yet another possibility is that the earlier decision is altogether unpalatable to the court in the later case, so that the latter court wishes to interpret it as narrowly as possible."

[12.64] Not all commentators agree with these observations[186] but nevertheless they do contain an essential truth, namely that the formulation of the *ratio decidendi* is the combined result of that which occurs in the court which decided the case and later courts. In a sense what is said by the court deciding the case is the raw material which is used by later courts to assemble the *ratio decidendi*. When a later court attempts to extract a binding proposition from an earlier case it examines the reasoning of the earlier court. The rule which is divined from the earlier case is the product of the reasoning in that case. As more cases are decided the rule becomes more detailed and, in effect, the courts are engaged in the process of adding flesh to what initially was a skeletal rule. Rules are not static but evolve through the course of litigation.

[12.65] Thus, the operation of the system of precedent does not result in the stagnation of rules. The process of adjudication as much involves the creation of law as its application. The system possesses a flexibility which requires later courts to make choices. The later court must select a binding proposition from a range of canvassed alternatives. As those choices are made rules are defined and redefined, their scope being expanded and contracted. This is not to say that later courts are presented with unrestricted choices or that the process results in a form of judicial anarchy. Whilst a case might present choices, the freedom of the later court is constrained within parameters set by the reasoning in the earlier case from which the relevant legal principle is extracted. If, in categorising that principle, the court makes unreasonable distinctions or is irrational in its analysis it runs the risk that its decision will in turn be ignored. For instance, were a court to disregard the earlier case on the grounds that it governed injuries caused by a Rolls Royce and not by other cars it would not be followed in later cases - we would all agree that the manufacture of the car which caused injury is immaterial to a rule which governs injuries caused by cars. By identifying similarities and placing cases in the same category the law develops through a process of reasoning by analogy, a point which was acknowledged by Costello J in *D v*

186. See, eg, Cross & Harris, *op cit* pp 72-74.

C.[187] Moreover, although courts, by interpreting cases, can revise rules they are not entitled to ignore precedents or, where binding, to overrule them. A court must accept the rule which has been determined in earlier cases and is permitted to define its scope in a manner which is reasonable and is not spurious or arbitrary. Developments in new cases must be consistent with earlier cases and the pattern which emerges is one of the law gently ebbing and flowing rather than of sudden tempestuous alterations which depend on the whims of particular judges.

[12.66] When we speak of the law evolving gradually it must be realised that its development does not follow a planned or predetermined course. In exercising choice courts select the directions in which the law should develop. The system of precedent operates to channel that development within certain constraints. The necessity to follow earlier cases ensures that new developments are accommodated within the pre-existing law. Thus, a court's reasoning is both retrospective and prospective. In the former sense the court attempts to justify a new decision as being consistent with the old law. It invokes earlier cases in support of its decision. In this context *stare decisis* operates as a standard by which to evaluate the legitimacy, or permissibility, of new decisions. A decision which is perceived as being unwarranted by preceding cases will itself be rejected in later cases. But at the same time, the court's reasoning is prospective in that it contains a set of options from which later courts will choose. And later courts will repeat the exercise when they come to consider the legal issues which are raised by the decision. Thus, as old questions are settled new ones are raised and the process continues unabated, surviving as the central feature of our legal system.

Precedent and legislation

[12.67] It is clear that the operation of the principle of *stare decisis* is sufficiently flexible to allow for the development of rules through the process of adjudication. The system operates in a manner which validates new developments which are capable of being considered to be warranted or authorised by the old law. Nevertheless, the potential for judicially-engineered change is limited and in many instances other law-making mechanisms, most notably legislation, must be employed to effect the change sought. The expansion of liability for negligence is probably the most significant common law development of the 20th century and might be attributed to judicial reaction to changing social and economic conditions. But the development which occurred was consistent, or could be construed

187. [1984] ILRM 173, at 189. See also *UF (orse UC) v JC* [1991] 2 IR 330, at 357 *per* Finlay CJ approving Costello J's reasoning and use of analogy.

as being consistent, with the pre-existing law of civil liability. Thus, for instance, the principle that liability should be based on fault was retained by the law and it would probably have been beyond the judicial capacity to have replaced it with a system of recovery based on social welfare principles. That latter development would have involved too fundamental a change from the old law to have been validly undertaken through the adjudicative system. Moreover, certain common law rules proved to be incapable of amendment or elimination by judicial action. The doctrine of 'common employment' relieved employers of vicarious liability when an employee was injured by the negligence of a fellow employee[188] - in other words a worker injured in those circumstances could not recover damages from his employer, a rule which was rightly condemned as being a 'nefarious judicial ploy'.[189] The doctrine was developed at common law, proved resistant to judicial change and was ultimately abandoned by legislation.[190] Likewise, at common law contributory negligence on the part of the plaintiff was an absolute defence to recovery. This rule was incorporated into Irish law[191] and while it was judicially modified[192] its eventual reform was effected by statute.[193] On the other hand, the rule which limited an occupier's duty of care to a trespasser was altered by the Supreme Court in *McNamara v Electricity Supply Board*;[194] that decision resulted in such an expansion of occupiers' liability that it was later curtailed by statute.[195]

[12.68] It is by no means clear why some common law rules resist judicial change while others are freely altered by the courts. It might have been thought that the old rules on common employment, contributory negligence and occupiers' liability enjoyed a similar degree of immutability yet, as we have seen, the last, but not the others, was altered by the courts. The explanation lies in a variety of factors which cumulatively facilitated judicial alteration in one case but not the others - developments in other neighbouring branches of the law, the willingness of courts to adapt in the light of changing social circumstances, the strictness of judicial adherence to

188. See McMahon & Binchy, *The Irish Law of Torts* 2nd ed (Butterworths, 1990) pp 314-315; the origin of the doctrine is attributed to an English decision *Priestly v Fowler* (1837) 3 M & W 1 and was adopted by the Irish courts; see, eg, *Waldron v Junior Army and Navy Stores* [1910] 2 IR 318; *Feeney v Pollexfen & Co Ltd* [1931] 589.

189. Fleming, *The Law of Torts* 8th ed (The Law Book Co, 1992) p 515.

190. Law Reform (Personal Injuries) Act 1958, s 1.

191. See, eg, *Butterly v Mayor of Drogheda* [1907] 2 IR 134.

192. See, eg, *Logan v O'Donnell* [1925] 2 IR 211; *McGlynn v Clark* [1945] IR 495.

193. Civil Liability Act 1961, s 34.

194. [1975] IR 1; see para **[12.13]**.

195. Occupiers' Liability Act 1995.

stare decisis and, indeed, the judicial values and preferences of the judges involved. It is hardly an accident of fate that the alteration of the law on occupiers' liability occurred after the Supreme Court had relaxed its rule on *stare decisis* and was occupied by 'activist' judges to whom a commitment to expanding the judicial role might be attributed. Nevertheless the precise dividing line between adjudication and legislation is difficult to draw and is no doubt mobile. What at one time is considered an appropriate subject for legislation might at another be thought suitable for reform by adjudication. However, it is not unusual for a court, in refusing to expand the law, to express the view that the relief sought is more appropriately achieved through legislation. In *UF(orse UC) v JC* Keane J, in the High Court, refused to expand the grounds of nullity of marriage stating:[196]

> "… if the judgments to which I have already referred correctly state the law, we have moved with remarkable abruptness to a position where a decree of nullity can now be granted in any case where the court concludes that a spouse because of an emotional disability or incapacity at the time of the marriage was unable to enter into and sustain a normal marital relationship. And all this, although the Oireachtas has studiously and for whatever reasons declined to implement in any way the report of the Attorney General on *The Law of Nullity in Ireland*[197] recommending that legislation should be introduced to deal with unfitness for marriage arising from mental disorder existing at the date of the solomnisation of the marriage and the report of the Law Reform Commission[198] recommending changes in the law, including a change relating to homosexuality which would enable the petitioner in this case to obtain relief. I am forced to the conclusion, which I reach with all respect to the High Court judges who have taken a different view, that to formulate new grounds for nullity in the manner suggested constitutes an impermissible assumption of the legislative function which Article 15.2.1° of the Constitution vests exclusively in the Oireachtas. I take that view mindful of the admonition of Fitzgerald CJ in *Maher v Attorney General*[199] at p 148 of the report that:
>
>> 'The usurpation by the judiciary of an exclusively legislative function is no less unconstitutional than the usurpation by the legislature of an exclusively judicial function.'

196. [1991] 2 IR 330, at 347-348; see also *Hynes-O'Sullivan v O'Driscoll* [1989] ILRM 349, *per* Henchy J cited at para **[12.15]**; *McNamara v Electricity Supply Board* [1975] IR 1, at 8 *per* FitzGerald CJ 'If the law concerning occupiers' liability is to change, it is not our function to change it; that would be the function of the legislature.'
197. Prl 5626, 1976.
198. *Report on Nullity in Marriage* LRC 9-1984.
199. [1973] IR 140.

> Or as McMahon J put it with characteristic terseness in *M (orse G) v M*[200] when declining to entertain a new ground of nullity (of a far more confined and specific nature):
>
> > 'For the courts to add new grounds would be to engage in legislation.'."

[12.69] In the event Keane J was overruled by the Supreme Court with Finlay CJ (for the majority) stating that their decision was 'a necessary and permissible development of the law of nullity'[201] What to one judge is 'impermissible legislation' is to another a 'permissible development'. This discloses the existence of different views of the cope of the judicial role and its potential for creativity or what is sometimes called 'judicial activism'. It cannot be said that one approach, be it 'conservative' or 'activist', is better or more correct than another and a view which prevails at any one time itself is susceptible to being replaced by a competing approach. What is obvious is that it cannot be denied that, regardless of the approach adopted by a court, the adjudicative process creates law. The theory, prevalent especially in the 19th century, that judges apply law and do not make law is no longer seriously advanced. The interpretation of a case, the effort to extract its *ratio decidendi* and the range of choice afforded to the court which is bound by it clearly demonstrate the creative potential which judges possess.

[4] Precedent in Action: An Example

[12.70] In order to put what has already been examined in context and to place it on a somewhat more understandable basis it is helpful to see how a particular rule has developed through a series of cases. The area which we have chosen is the law governing the liability in tort of professional persons, such as doctors, solicitors and accountants. This is an area which has occupied the attention of the Irish courts in recent years and will, no doubt, continue to do so for many years to come. But first, some background explanation is required.

[12.71] In 1932 the House of Lords, by a three-to-two majority, delivered a landmark decision in *Donoghue v Stevenson*[202] in which it was held that a consumer, who was injured as a result of eating a contaminated food product, could sue the manufacturer in negligence. The decision is significant in that it established that the existence of a contract between the plaintiff and defendant was not necessary in order to maintain an action in

200. [1986] ILRM 515.
201. [1991] 2 IR 330, at 357.
202. [1932] AC 562.

negligence. In the course of his speech Lord Atkin enunciated his now-famous neighbour principle:[203]

> "The rule that you are to love your neighbour becomes in law: You must not injure your neighbour and the lawyer's question: Who is my neighbour? receives a restricted reply. You must take reasonable care to avoid acts or omissions which you can reasonably foresee would be likely to injure your neighbour. Who then, in law, is my neighbour? The answer seems to be persons who are so closely and directly affected by my act that I ought reasonably to have them in contemplation as being so affected when I am directing my mind to the acts or omissions which are called into question."

[12.72] But despite the broad terms in which that principle was expressed Lord Atkin also formulated the somewhat narrower proposition that:[204]

> "…a manufacturer of products which he sells in such a form as to show that he intends them to reach the ultimate consumer in the form in which they left him, with no reasonable possibility of intermediate examination, and with the knowledge that the absence of reasonable care in the preparation or putting up of the products will result in an injury to the consumer's life or property, owes a duty to the consumer to take reasonable care."

[12.73] Some years later the Irish High Court had to consider the identical question in *Kirby v Burke and Holloway.*[205] A woman bought some jam which was subsequently eaten by members of her family, but not by her. The jam was contaminated and those who ate it became ill. They brought and action against the vendor and the manufacturer of the jam. The action against the vendor was dismissed, but damages were awarded against the manufacturer. An interesting feature of the decision is that although the plaintiffs cited *Donoghue v Stevenson* in support of their claim Gavan Duffy J did not adopt it but reverted to first principles:[206]

> "I have now to consider whether the law sustains the claim of the plaintiffs to make the manufacturer liable for the unpleasant consequences to them of eating his jam. The defendant manufactures a common article of food, jam, made from fruit of the particular season; he then distributes it for sale by retail grocers to members of the public; he intends it to be sold as food for human consumption and bought as food for human consumption. Before sending it out he pots the jam and places waxed paper over it, closes the pot

---

203. *Ibid*, at 580.
204. *Ibid*, at 599.
205. [1944] IR 207.
206. *Ibid*, at 213-215.

with a cover and packs it in a coloured cellophane wrapper, with the result that the jam, when sold over the counter, will be taken to be (as it is meant to be) in the condition in which it left the factory, and that the purchaser will have no reasonable opportunity to examine the contents for any visible defects; and a manufacturer must know, as a matter of ordinary experience, that a housewife, the probable purchaser, does not usually, on opening the pot at home, begin by scrutinising the contents for signs of corruption; why should she?

A particular pot of jam turns out to be unwholesome, when bought, and injurious to the consumers, and the question at once arises on what principle is the alleged liability of the maker, who intended no injury and made no contract with the consumers, to be determined? The inquiry involves the ascertainment of the foundation, upon the authorities, of liability for tort at common law.

In 1869, an Irish Court, following English decisions, held on demurrer that, in the absence of fraudulent misrepresentation, the law could give no redress against the manufacturers to a man (the purchaser's servant) injured by the explosion of a boiler in a steam engine, upon an allegation that the boiler was unsafe by reason of negligence in its construction: *Corry v Lucas*.[207] The confusion and conflict in later cases in England left the basis of liability in tort at common law so uncertain that at the time of the Treaty [ie of 1922] nobody could find in case law any sure guide to the actual legal position, and I have no Irish decision to guide me.

I am thus thrown back upon first principles in the endeavour to ascertain where the line is drawn at common law between conduct resulting in unintended hurt which entails liability for damage, and conduct resulting in unintended hurt which entails no liability.

In the quandary produced by the baffling inconsistencies among the pre-Treaty judicial pronouncements, I turn from the Courts to one of the outstanding juristic studies of the nineteenth century, *The Common Law* by Oliver Wendell Holmes, afterwards Mr Justice Holmes of the Supreme Court of the United States. The work was published in London in 1887. The law which I apply to this case is taken from his penetrating Lectures III and IV on torts and the theory of torts.

That master of the common law shows that the foundation of liability at common law for tort is blameworthiness as determined by the existing average standards of the community; a man fails at his peril to conform to those standards. Therefore, while loss from accident generally lies where it falls, a defendant cannot plead accident if, treated as a man of ordinary intelligence and foresight, he ought to have foreseen the danger which caused injury to his plaintiff.

Applying that norm to the facts, I have to inquire whether a man in the position of the defendant, making jam for the public to eat, is bound,

207. (1869) IR 3 CL 208.

according to the standards of conduct prevailing among us, to take specific precautions against the danger, to the hurt of customers, of infection to his jam from external causes before it finally leaves his factory; or, more exactly, though he may not have anticipated the precise injury that ensued to the plaintiffs from infection, was he bound, in conformity with those standards, to safeguard his jam from access by flies, as notoriously ubiquitous as they are notoriously dirty, during the interval between the moment when the jam is poured into a jam pot after boiling and the moment, three or four days later, when the jam pot is finally enveloped for sale and sent out? I answer this question, as I believe a jury of practical citizens would answer it, in the affirmative, because our public opinion undoubtedly requires of a jam manufacturer that he shall take care to keep flies out of his jam. Any novice would foresee that a fly might get in, given the chance, and I have already found as facts that the defendant failed to take adequate precautions and that the buyer was in no way at fault.

On the facts of the case now before me, there is no question of remoteness of damage. The test, as Holmes J puts it, is whether the result actually contemplated was near enough to the remoter result complained of to throw the peril of that result upon the actor. The plaintiffs are therefore entitled to succeed.

The much controverted 'Case of the Snail in the Bottle', while leaving subsidiary questions open, has settled the principle of liability on a similar issue finally against the manufacturer in Great Britain. But the House of Lords established that memorable conclusion only twelve years ago in *Donoghue v Stevenson*, by a majority of three Law Lords to two, 'a Celtic majority', as an unconvinced critic ruefully observed, against an English minority. Where lawyers so learned disagreed, an Irish judge could not assume, as I was invited to assume, as a matter of course, that the view which prevailed must of necessity be the true view of the common law in Ireland. One voice in the House of Lords would have turned the scale; and it is not arguable that blameworthiness according to the actual standards of our people depends upon the casting vote in a tribunal exercising no jurisdiction over them. Hence my recourse to the late Mr Justice Holmes. His classic analysis supports the principle of Lord Atkin and the majority. And to that principle I humbly subscribe."

[12.74] A certain nationalist fervour is discernible in that judgment, especially in the somewhat tongue-in-cheek remarks in the last paragraph. This might be attributed to a desire to develop an indigenous body of jurisprudence which is independent of that of the neighbouring island. In this regard, the reference to the uncertain state of English law on the matter in 1922 echoes the same judge's observations in *Exham v Beamish*[208] on the applicability of pre-1922 decisions in Ireland.[209] Despite Gavan Duffy J's

208. [1939] IR 336.

209. See para **[12.35]**.

refusal to adopt *Donoghue v Stevenson* Irish courts have subsequently accepted that it is applicable in Ireland.

[12.75] While *Donoghue v Stevenson* dealt with the relatively narrow issue of the liability of a manufacturer, Lord Atkin's neighbour principle has been adopted and developed by later courts, and it now applies to a wide range of categories beyond that of defective products. In general, courts have focused on that principle and used it as a guide in the development of the tort of negligence.[210] By using it as a guide the courts have tended to avoid categorising the neighbour principle as either *ratio* or *obiter.* Consideration of the development of the tort of negligence is beyond our scope and can be traced in any reputable textbook.[211] With regard to professional liability a crucial development was the decision of the House of Lords in *Hedley Byrne & Co Ltd v Heller and Partners Ltd*,[212] where it overruled the earlier Court of Appeal decision in *Candler v Crane, Christmas & Co*[213] and extended *Donoghue v Stevenson* to negligently performed professional services, where there was a contractual relationship or a relationship 'equivalent to contract' between the plaintiff and defendant. Liability would arise where the defendant was aware that the plaintiff relied on his or her skill and competence. In essence, the principle applies where the plaintiff is dependent on the defendant's expertise or specialist knowledge. The decision in *Hedley Byrne* was adopted by the Irish High Court in *Securities Trust Ltd v Hugh Moore & Alexander Ltd*.[214] In that case a shareholder in the defendant company held the shares on trust for the plaintiff company. The defendant company was unaware of this arrangement. The shareholder applied to the defendant company for a copy of their Memorandum and Articles of Association. The copy delivered contained an error, on the basis of which the plaintiff company bought shares in the defendant company at a price in excess of their market value. The investment was lost when the defendant company was wound up. The plaintiff company sued for damages for negligent misrepresentation. The matter was considered by Davitt P:[215]

---

210. See, eg, *Home Office v Dorset Yacht Co Ltd* [1970] AC 1004; *Anns v London Borough of Merton* [1978] AC *728*; *McNamara v Electricity Supply Board* [1975] IR 1; *Keane v Electricity Supply Board* [1981] IR 44.

211. See McMahon and Binchy, *The Irish Law of Torts* 2nd ed (Butterworths, 1989); Salmond and Heuston, *The Law of Torts* 20th ed (Sweet & Maxwell, 1992). Of the myriad of articles which *Donoghue v Stevenson* has generated we might, somewhat selectively, recommend Heuston, '*Donoghue v Stevenson* in Retrospect'(1957) 20 MLR 1; Smith and Burns, '*Donoghue v Stevenson* - the Not So Golden Anniversary' (1983) 46 MLR 147; Stapleton, 'The Gist of Negligence'(1988) 104 LQR 213 and 389; Dolding & Mullender, 'Tort Law, Incrementalism and the House of Lords' (1996) 47 NILQ 12.

212. [1964] AC 465.

213. [1951] 2 KB 164.

214. [1964] IR 417.

215. *Ibid*, at 420-422.

"In their statement of claim [the plaintiffs] aver that they applied for a copy of the Memorandum and Articles of Association through their agent, Mr Anderson, and were supplied with the one containing the printers' error. They claim that by reason of the negligent misrepresentation of the defendant Company they were induced to purchase the 850 Preference Shares at a price exceeding their market value and have thereby suffered damage. The substantial defences raised in the defendants' pleadings are: that the copy of the Memorandum and Articles supplied to Mr Anderson were not supplied to him as agent for the plaintiff Company; that the defendant Company owed no duty to the plaintiff Company to supply them with an accurate copy of the Memorandum and Articles; that there was no negligence on their part; and that the plaintiff Company did not suffer the alleged or any damage; or, alternatively, that the damages claimed are too remote.

The law to be applied in this case is not in controversy. It would appear that the proposition that innocent (ie non-fraudulent) misrepresentation cannot give rise to an action for damages is somewhat too broadly stated, and is based upon a misconception of what was decided by the House of Lords in *Derry v Peek*.[216] Such action may be based on negligent misrepresentation which is not fraudulent. This was pointed out in *Nocton v Lord Ashburton*,[217] particularly in the speech of Haldane LC. At p 948 he says:

> 'Although liability for negligence in word has in material respects been developed in our law differently from liability for negligence in act, it is none the less true that a man may come under a special duty to exercise care in giving information or advice. I should accordingly be sorry to be thought to lend countenance to the idea that recent decisions have been intended to stereotype the cases in which people can be held to have assumed such a special duty. Whether such a duty has been assumed must depend on the relationship of the parties, and it is at least certain that there are a good many cases in which that relationship may be properly treated as giving rise to a special duty of care in statement.'

It was apparently considered in some quarters that such a special duty could arise only from a contractual or fiduciary relationship. In *Robinson v National Bank of Ireland*[218] Haldane LC was at pains to dispel this idea. At p 157 he said:

> 'The whole of the doctrine as to fiduciary relationships, as to the duty of care arising from implied as well as express contracts, as to the duty of care arising from other special relationships which the Courts may find to exist in particular cases, still remains, and I should be very sorry if any word fell from me which would

216. (1889) 14 App Cas 337.
217. [1914] AC 932.
218. 1916 SC (HL) 150.

> suggest that the Courts are in any way hampered in recognising that the duty of care may be established when such cases really occur.'

The proposition that circumstances may create a relationship between two parties in which, if one seeks information from the other and is given it, that other is under a duty to take reasonable care to ensure that the information given is correct, has been accepted and applied in the case of *Hedley Byrne & Co Ltd v Heller and Partners Ltd*, recently decided by the House of Lords. Counsel for the defendant Company did not seek to dispute the proposition. He submitted, however, that the circumstances of this case created no such special relationship.

Section 18(1) of the Companies (Consolidation) Act 1908, provides:

> 'Every company shall send to every member, at his request, and on payment of one shilling or such less sum as the company may prescribe, a copy of the memorandum and of the articles (if any).'

At the time that Mr Anderson made his request to the secretary of the defendant Company for a copy of their Memorandum and Articles of Association he was a shareholder. The plaintiff Company had not then been registered as owner of any shares. He was a member of the defendant Company; his Company was not. The position was that he was entitled to receive a copy of the Memorandum and Articles; his Company was not. He was entitled to receive it personally *qua* member; he was not entitled to receive it *qua* agent of the plaintiff Company. In these circumstances I must, I think, conclude that the copy was requested and supplied, in accordance with the provisions of s 18(1), of the Act, by the defendant Company to Mr Anderson personally and not as agent for the plaintiff Company. It seems to me that there was no relationship between the parties in this case other than such as would exist between the defendant Company and any person (other than Mr Anderson) who might chance to read the copy supplied to him; or, indeed, between that Company and any member of the community at large, individual or corporate, who chanced to become aware of the last sentence in Article 155 of the defective reprint of the Memorandum and Articles. It can hardly be seriously contended that the defendant Company owed a duty to the world at large to take care to avoid mistakes and printers' errors in the reprint of their Articles. In my opinion, counsel is correct in his submission that in this case the defendant Company owed no duty to the plaintiff Company to take care to ensure that the copy of the Articles supplied to Mr Anderson was a correct copy. For these reasons there must, in my opinion, be judgment for the defendant Company."

Application to negligent solicitors

[12.76] The general principle has been applied to the case of a solicitor who neglected to initiate litigation within the statutory limitation period in *Finlay* *v Murtagh*.[219] The plaintiff engaged the defendant to act as his solicitor in proceedings which he sought to institute against a third party. The defendant neglected to bring the proceedings within the statutory limitation period and, consequently, it became time-barred. The issue in this case was whether the plaintiff could sue in tort for negligence or whether he was confined to suing for breach of contract. At the time, tort actions in the High Court were tried by jury whereas contract actions were tried by judge alone[220] and it might have been considered that the plaintiff's prospects would be enhanced by a jury trial. The Supreme Court (O'Higgins CJ, Henchy, Griffin, Parke and Kenny JJ) unanimously held that an action in tort would lie for the negligence of a solicitor. According to Henchy J:[221]

> "There has been no decision of this Court on the point at issue but we have been referred to three decisions of the High Court. In *McGrath v Kiely*[222] the client sued his solicitor for negligence and, alternatively, for breach of contract in failing to show due professional care in the preparation of an action for damages for personal injuries. The claim was pursued in court as one for breach of contract and no effort was made to pursue the claim in negligence. The parties agreed to treat the solicitor's default as a breach of contract. Therefore, that case throws no light on the present problem.
> The second case, *Liston v Munster and Leinster Bank*,[223] was an action by the personal representative of a customer of the bank against the bank for damages for negligence, for conversion, and for money had and received. The issue being whether the entire cause of action arose out of a contract, in which case notice of trial by a judge without a jury would be appropriate, or whether it lay partly in tort, in which case the notice of trial that had been served specifying trial by a judge with a jury would have been correct. In holding that the claim was partly for breach of contract and partly for conversion, O'Byrne J applied the following test which had been laid down by Greer LJ in *Jarvis v Moy, Davies, Smith, Vanderell & Co*[224] at p. 405 of the report:
>
> > 'The distinction in the modern view, for this purpose, between contract and tort may be put thus: where the breach of duty alleged arises out of a liability independently of the personal obligation undertaken by contract, it is tort, and it may be tort even though there may happen to be a contract between the parties, if the duty in fact arises independently of that contract.

219. [1979] IR 249.
220. Jury trial in High Court civil cases was subsequently abolished in most instances; see para **[4.50]**.
221. [1979] IR 249, at 254-258.
222. [1965] IR 497.
223. [1940] IR 77.
224. [1936] 1 KB 399.

> Breach of contract occurs where that which is complained of is a breach of duty arising out of the obligations undertaken by the contract.'

The third High Court case to which we were referred is *Somers v Erskine*.[225] There the question was whether an action commenced by a client against a solicitor for negligence, and sought to be continued against the solicitor's personal representative, had abated with the solicitor's death as an action in tort, or whether it survived his death as an action in contract. In an unreserved judgment Maguire P applied the same test as was applied by O'Byrne J in *Liston v Munster and Leinster Bank,* and held that the client's claim was essentially one in contract rather than in tort and that, therefore, the claim had survived the solicitor's death. In my opinion, the conclusion that an action by a client against a solicitor for damages for breach of his professional duty of care is necessarily and exclusively one in contract is incompatible with modern developments in the law of torts and should be overruled. In my view, the conclusion there reached does not follow from a correct application of the test laid down by Greer LJ in the *Jarvis Case.*

The claim made by the plaintiff in the *Jarvis Case* was one by a client against stockbrokers 'for damages for breach of contract arising out of the defendants' relationship with the plaintiff as stockbrokers and client.' Therefore, it is clear that the action was one for breach of contract, at least in form. But the particulars given in the writ show that the substance of the complaint was that the stockbrokers had departed from the specific instructions given by the client. Therefore, the cause of action arose from the breach of a particular binding provision created by the parties, and not from any general obligation of care arising from the relationship of stockbroker and client. The nub of the matter was that the stockbrokers had defaulted on a special personal obligation which was imposed by the contract. They could not have been made liable otherwise than in contract and the court held correctly that the claim was 'founded on contract' in the words of the statute which was being applied.

The test adumbrated by Greer LJ, which commended itself to O'Byrne J in *Liston v Munster and Leinster Bank* and to Maguire P in *Somers v Erskine,* correctly draws a distinction between a claim arising out of an obligation deriving from, and owing its existence to, a personal obligation undertaken pursuant to a contract (in which case it is an action in contract) and a claim arising out of a liability created independently of a contract and not deriving from any special obligation imposed by a contract (in which case an action lies in tort). The action in tort derives from an obligation which is imposed by the general law and is applicable to all persons in a certain relationship to each other. The action in contract is founded on the special law which was created by a contract and which was designed to fit the

225. [1943] IR 348.

particular relationship of that contract. As I understand it, therefore, the test propounded by Greer LJ does not support the conclusion reached by Maguire P that, because the contract of retainer implies a duty of professional care and skill and because a default in that duty has occurred, the cause of action lies exclusively in contract.

It has to be conceded that for over a hundred years there has been a divergence of judicial opinion as to whether a client who has engaged a solicitor to act for him, and who claims that the solicitor failed to show due professional care and skill, may sue in tort or whether he is confined to an action in contract. In *Somers v Erskine* (and in some English cases) it was held that the sole cause of action was the solicitor's failure to observe the implied term in the contract of retainer that he would show due professional skill and care. It is undeniable that the client is entitled to sue in contract for breach of that implied term. But it does not follow that the client, because there is privity of contract between him and the solicitor and because he may sue the solicitor for breach of the contract, is debarred from suing also for the tort of negligence. Since the decision of the House of Lords in *Hedley Byrne & Co Ltd v Heller & Partners Ltd* and the cases following in its wake, it is clear that, whether a contractual relationship exists or not, once the circumstances are such that a defendant undertakes to show professional care and skill towards a person who may be expected to rely on such care and skill and who does so rely, then if he has been damnified by such default that person may sue the defendant in the tort of negligence for failure to show such care and skill. For the purpose of such an action, the existence of a contract is merely an incident of the relationship. If, on the one side, there is a proximity of relationship creating a general duty and, on the other, a reliance on that duty, it matters not whether the parties are bound together in contract. For instance, if the defendant in the present case had not been retained for reward but had merely volunteered his services to the plaintiff, his liability in negligence would be the same as if he was to be paid for his services. The coincidence that the defendant's conduct amounts to a breach of contract cannot affect either the duty of care or the common-law liability for its breach, for it is the general relationship, and not any particular manifestation such as a contract, that gives rise to the tortious liability in such a case: see *per* Lord Devlin in the *Hedley Byrne Case* at p 530 of the report.

A comprehensive survey of the law governing the liability of a solicitor to his client in negligence is to be found in the judgment of Oliver J in *Midland Bank* v *Hett, Stubbs & Kemp*,[226] in which it was held that the solicitor's liability in tort exists independently of any liability in contract. That conclusion, which was reached at first instance and with which I agree, may be said to be reinforced by dicta in the judgments of the Court

[226] [1979] Ch 384.

of Appeal in *Batty v Metropolitan Realisations Ltd*[227] and *Photo Production Ltd v Securicor Ltd.*[228]

On a consideration of those cases and of the authorities mentioned in them, I am satisfied that the general duty of care created by the relationship of solicitor and client entitles the client to sue in negligence if he has suffered damage because of the solicitor's failure to show due professional care and skill, notwithstanding that the client could sue alternatively in contract for breach of the implied term in the contract of retainer that the solicitor will deal with the matter in hand with due professional care and skill. The solicitor's liability in tort under the general duty of care extends not only to a client for reward, but to any person for whom the solicitor undertakes to act professionally without reward, and also to those (such as beneficiaries under a will, persons entitled under an intestacy, or those entitled to benefits in circumstances such as a claim in respect of a fatal injury) with whom he has made no arrangement to act but who, as he knows or ought to know, will be relying on his professional care and skill. For the same default there should be the same cause of action. If others are entitled to sue in tort for the solicitor's want of care, so also should the client; that is so unless the solicitor's default arises not from a breach of the general duty of care arising from the relationship but from a breach of a particular and special term of the contract in respect of which the solicitor would not be liable if the contract had not contained such a term. Thus, if the client's instructions were that the solicitor was to issue proceedings within a specified time, or to close a sale by a particular date or, generally, to do or not to do some act, and the solicitor defaulted in that respect, any resulting right of action which the client might have would be in contract only unless the act or default complained of falls within the general duty of care owed by the solicitor.

The modern law of tort shows that the existence of a contractual relationship which impliedly deals with a particular act or omission is not, in itself, sufficient to rule out an action in tort in respect of that act or omission. For instance, in *Northern Bank Finance Corporation Ltd v Charlton*[229] it was unanimously held by this Court that a customer of a bank can sue the bank for the tort of deceit where the deceit arises from fraudulent misrepresentations made by the bank in the course of carrying out the contract between the bank and the customer. The existence of a contract, for the breach of which he could have sued, did not oust the customer's cause of action in tort.

Therefore, I conclude that where, as in the instant case, the client's complaint is that he has been damnified by the solicitor's default in his general duty of care, the client is entitled to sue in negligence as well as for

227. [1978] QB 554.
228. [1978] 1 WLR 856.
229. [1979] IR 149.

breach of contract. In the plaintiff's statement of claim, after reciting his accident and his retainer of the defendant as the solicitor to prosecute his claim for damages in respect of it, the plaintiff pleads that the defendant 'negligently failed to issue proceedings on behalf of the plaintiff in respect of the accident aforesaid within the time limited by the Statute of Limitations 1957.' That was intended to be, and is, a claim in negligence. Such being the case, by virtue of the provisions of s 94 of the Courts of Justice Act 1924, as amended, the plaintiff was entitled to service notice of a trial by a judge and jury."

[12.77] In his concurring judgment in *Finlay v Murtagh* Griffin J stated:[230]

"A solicitor holds himself out to the client who has retained him as being possessed of adequate skill, knowledge and learning for the purpose of carrying out all business that he undertakes on behalf of his client. Once he has been retained to pursue a claim for damages for personal injuries, it is the duty of the solicitor to prepare and prosecute the claim with due professional skill and care. Therefore, he is liable to the client in damages if loss and damage are caused to the client owing to the want of such skill and care on the part of the solicitor as he ought to have exercised.

[Counsel] for the defendant, contends that the duty owed by a solicitor to his client under his retainer is a duty which arises *solely* from the contract and excludes any general duty in tort; he submits that this action is one founded upon contract, in which event the plaintiff would not be entitled to have the action tried by a jury. [Counsel] for the plaintiff, submits that, apart from the duty which arises from contract, there is a general duty to exercise skill and care on the part of the solicitor, for breach of which he would be liable in tort if damage is suffered by the client as a result of the want of such skill and care. He submits that, as one claiming damages for negligence, this action is properly a claim in tort, in which case the plaintiff is entitled as of right to have the action tried before a judge and jury pursuant to s 94 of the Courts of Justice Act 1924, as amended.

There is abundant, if somewhat conflicting, authority on the question in England, and in argument we were referred also to two Irish cases in which the question arose.

In *Groom v Crocker*[231] the Court of Appeal in England had to consider whether the mutual rights and duties of a solicitor and his client were regulated by the contract of employment alone, and whether the solicitor was liable in tort. It was there held that the contract of employment regulated the relationship and that the solicitor was not liable in tort. In the course of his judgment, Sir Wilfred Greene MR said at p 205 of the report:

230. [1979] IR 249, at 259-263.
231. [1939] 1 KB 194.

> 'In my opinion, the cause of action is in contract and not in tort. The duty of the appellants was to conduct the case properly on behalf of the respondent as their client … The relationship of solicitor and client is a contractual one: *Davies v Lock*;[232] *Bean v Wade*.[233] It was by virtue of that relationship that the duty arose, and it had no existence apart from that relationship.'
>
> Scott LJ at p 222, having set out the duty of a solicitor, said that the tie between the solicitor and the client is contractual and that no action lies in tort for the breach of such duties. MacKinnon LJ put the position succinctly at p 229 where he said: 'I am clear that this is a claim for damages for breach of contract …'

After that unanimous decision of the Court of Appeal, it was generally accepted in England, at least until very recently, that the liability of a solicitor to his client was contractual only and that he could not be sued in tort either in the alternative or cumulatively. The case has been almost universally followed and applied there since it was decided; see, for example, *Bailey v Bullock*;[234] and Hodson and Parker LJJ at pp 477 and 481 respectively of the report of *Hall v Meyrick*;[235] *Cook v Swinfen*.[236] At p 510 of the report of *Clark v Kirby-Smith*[237] Plowman J said:

> 'A line of cases going back for nearly 150 years shows, I think, that the client's cause of action is in contract and not in tort: see, for example, *Howell v Young*[238] and *Groom v Crocker*'.

In *Heywood v Wellers*[239] James LJ said at p 461 of the report:

> 'It is well known and settled law that an action by a client against a solicitor alleging negligence in the conduct of the client's affairs is an action for breach of contract: *Groom v Crocker*.'

However, in that case Lord Denning did say at p 459 that *Groom v Crocker* might have to be reconsidered, and in *Esso Petroleum v Mardon*[240] at p 819 of the report he 'ventured to suggest' that that case, and cases which relied on it, are in conflict with other decisions of high authority which were not cited in them - decisions which show that, in the case of a professional man, the duty to use reasonable care arises not only in contract but is also imposed by the law apart from contract and is, therefore, actionable in tort; it is comparable to the duty of reasonable care which is owed by a master to his servant or *vice versa*; it can be put either in contract or in tort. In

232. (1844) 3 LT (OS) 125.
233. (1885) 2 TLR 157.
234. [1950] 2 All ER 1167.
235. [1957] 2 QB 455.
236. [1967] 1 WLR 457.
237. [1964] Ch 506.
238. (1826) 5 B & C 259.
239. [1976] QB 446.
240. [1976] QB 801.

Midland Bank v Hett, Stubbs & Kemp,[241] on which the plaintiff relied strongly, Oliver J, in a judgment in which he examined exhaustively all the leading cases on the subject of a solicitor's liability, held that a solicitor was liable in tort quite independently of any contractual liability.

In *Somers v Erskine*[242] the client sued his solicitor for damages for negligence in the discharge of his professional duty to the client. The solicitor died after the action was commenced and one of the issues which then arose was whether or not the cause of action had survived against his executrix. It was held by Maguire P that the action was in substance founded in contract and that, in considering whether an action is founded on contract or on tort, the court must look not merely at the form of the pleadings but at the substance of the action and decide whether it is founded on contract or tort. He adopted and applied the following passage from the judgment of Greer LJ in *Jarvis v Moy, Davies, Smith, Vanderell and Co*[243] (a claim against a stockbroker) at p 405 of the report:

> 'The distinction in the modern view, for this purpose, between contract and tort may be put thus: where the breach of duty alleged arises out of a liability independently of the personal obligation undertaken by contract, it is tort, and it may be tort even though there may happen to be a contract between the parties, if the duty in fact arises independently of that contract. Breach of contract occurs where that which is complained of is a breach of duty arising out of the obligations undertaken by the contract.'

That passage had been accepted and approved by O'Byrne J in *Liston v Munster and Leinster Bank*.[244] Applying that test, the learned President held that the substance of the client's claim was the breach of a duty arising out of an obligation created by contract, and said that he found it difficult to dissociate that duty from the contract. Counsel for the defendant in that case had urged that the duty which was alleged to have been broken was merely the ordinary common-law duty, the breach of which constituted negligence, ie, the duty to take reasonable care in the particular circumstances; but the President held that the duty arose out of a contractual obligation only.

I have had the advantage of reading in advance the judgment of Mr Justice Henchy and I agree with him that Maguire P did not correctly apply the test laid down by Greer LJ in the *Jarvis Case*. I agree with the analysis made by Mr Justice Henchy of the passage quoted from the judgment of Lord Justice Greer.

The only other Irish case cited in argument was *McGrath v Kiely*[245] in

241. [1979] Ch 384.
242. [1943] IR 348.
243. [1936] 1 KB 399.
244. [1940] IR 77.

which the client sued a surgeon and a solicitor, founding her claim for damages on both negligence and breach of contract. In the course of the hearing before Mr Justice Henchy it was conceded on behalf of the client that the liability sought to be imposed on each of the defendants arose *ex contractu,* so that the question of the liability of the defendants in tort was not argued and did not fall to be decided.

In *Somers v Erskine*,[246] the learned President was not prepared to accept that, in the case of a solicitor, there was a general duty to use reasonable care imposed by the law quite apart from contract. He took the view that because there was a contractual relationship between the solicitor and the client, and a liability in contract for breach of the duty owed to the client, there was no duty in tort. Counsel for the defendant had cited the passage in *Bevan on Negligence* (4th ed at p 1384) that states:

> 'A solicitor is liable for negligence both in contract and in tort. He is liable in contract where he fails to do some specific act to which he has bound himself. He is liable in tort where, having accepted a retainer, he fails in the performance of any duty which the relation of solicitor and client as defined by the retainer imposes on him.'

Authorities to support that proposition were not cited; if they had been cited, it is likely that the President would have come to a different conclusion. The law is concisely and clearly summed up in a few sentences in the well-known passage in the speech of Viscount Haldane LC in *Nocton v Ashburton*[247] at p 956 of the report:

> 'My Lords, the solicitor contracts with his client to be skilful and careful. For failure to perform his obligation he may be made liable at law in contract or even in tort, for negligence in breach of a duty imposed on him.'

See also what was said by Tindal CJ in *Boorman v Brown*[248] in the Court of Exchequer Chamber at p 525 of the report and by Lord Campbell in the House of Lords at p 44 of the report of the appeal. It is to be noted that these cases also were not cited in *Groom v Crocker*, or in the cases which followed it, and that the failure to do so led to the criticism of these cases by Lord Denning in *Esso Petroleum v Mardon.* In my opinion, the President was wrong in holding that the liability of the solicitor to the client was solely in contract. *Somers v Erskine* should not be followed.

Quite apart from the fact that *Somers v Erskine* was decided without the citation of relevant authorities and on an incorrect application of the test laid down by Greer LJ in the *Jarvis Case*, the decision is inconsistent with developments in the law of tort since the case was decided. It is now settled

245. [1965] IR 497.
246. [1943] IR 348.
247. [1914] AC 932.
248. (1842) 3 QB 511, (1844) 11 Cl & Fin 1.

law that whenever a person possessed of a special knowledge or skill undertakes, quite irrespective of contract, to apply that skill for the assistance of another person who relies on such skill, a duty of care will arise: see the speech of Lord Morris of Borth-y-Gest at p 502 of the report of *Hedley Byrne and Co Ltd v Heller & Partners Ltd*.[249] At p 538 of the report Lord Pearce said:

> 'In terms of proximity one might say that they are in particularly close proximity to those who, as they know, are relying on their skill and care although the proximity is not contractual.'

See also Lord Hodson at p 510 and Lord Devlin at p 530 of the report. Where damage has been suffered as a result of want of such skill and care, an action in tort lies against such person, and this applies whether a contractual relationship exists or not. This doctrine applies to such professional persons as solicitors, doctors, dentists, architects and accountants. Although in the *Hedley Byrne Case* the claim was in respect of a non-contractual relationship, the statements of the Law Lords were general statements of principle, and it is clear from their speeches that they did not in any way mean to limit the general principle and that their statements were not to be confined to voluntary or non-contractual situations.

Therefore, where a solicitor is retained by a client to carry out legal business (such as litigation) on his behalf, a general relationship is established, and 'Where there is a general relationship of this sort, it is unnecessary to do more than prove its existence and the duty follows' - *per* Lord Devlin at p 530 of the report of the *Hedley Byrne Case*. If, therefore, loss and damage is caused to a client owing to the want of such care and skill on the part of a solicitor as he ought to have exercised, there is liability in tort even though there would also be a liability in contract. Even if the relationship between the solicitor and the client was a non-contractual or voluntary one, the same liability in tort would follow.

In my opinion it is both reasonable and fair that, if the issues of fact are such that he would be entitled to succeed either in contract or in tort, the plaintiff should be entitled to pursue either or both remedies; there can be nothing wrong in permitting the plaintiff, who is the injured party, to elect or choose the remedy which to him appears to be that which will be most suitable and likely to attract the more favourable result.

In my judgment, the plaintiff in the instant case has a good cause of action in tort as well as in contract and is entitled to sue in respect of either or both remedies since he has suffered loss and damage as a result of the negligence of the defendant, as the plaintiff's solicitor, in failing to institute proceedings within the time limited by the Statute of Limitations 1957. Accordingly, the plaintiff is entitled as of right to have his action tried before a judge and jury…"

249. [1964] AC 465.

[12.78] The inclusion by Griffin J of doctors, dentists, architects and accountants[250] in his judgment in *Finlay v Murtagh* indicates the broad scope of the principle which the Court invoked. It was concerned with professional advisers generally not just solicitors. This point was reiterated by Griffin J in *Rohan Construction Ltd v Insurance Corporation of Ireland plc*:[251]

> "…I find it difficult to see how the fact that the same act amounted to both a tort and a breach of contract could enable the insurers to avoid liability under a Professional Indemnity Policy on the basis that it was a mixed claim- if that were the true legal position, such a policy would be of little avail to a professional man, such as a solicitor, accountant, architect, engineer, doctor, dentist etc, as the same act of negligence causing damage to the client is almost invariably a breach of contract also - see for example *Finlay v Murtagh*…"

Solicitor's duty to third parties

[12.79] *Finlay v Murtagh* was concerned with the duty owed by a solicitor to a paying client, but dicta in the case suggest that a duty would also be owed to non-paying clients and, possibly, others who are not clients but can be expected to rely on the solicitor's skill and expertise. This was an issue in *Wall v Hegarty and Callanan*[252] where the principle in *Finlay v Murtagh* was extended. The plaintiff was named as both executor and a beneficiary under a will which was prepared on behalf of the deceased by the defendants, a firm of solicitors. In the will the testator had left him a legacy of £15,000. The will was insufficiently attested and, on discovering the flaw, the next of kin challenged the validity of the will and accordingly he lost his legacy and incurred certain expenses as executor. The plaintiff had to concede that the will was invalid. He sued the defendants for negligence claiming, in essence, that the defendants owed him a duty to take care in its preparation, despite their not being in a solicitor-client relationship. The matter was decided in the High Court by Barrington J:[253]

> "At the hearing it was decided that I should defer the question of the quantification of the plaintiffs loss until I had first dealt with the substantial issue of whether a solicitor retained by a testator to draw up his will owes any duty to a legatee named in the will to ensure that the will and the legacy are valid.

250. See, eg, *Kelly v Haughey Boland & Co* [1989] ILRM 373 holding, on the basis of *Hedley Byrne*, that auditors owe a duty of care to third parties who they know or ought to know might wish to invest in the company, but dismissing the claim on the facts.

251. [1988] ILRM 373, at 379.

252. [1980] ILRM 124.

253. *Ibid*, at 126-130.

There is no doubt the he does owe a duty to a testator to show reasonable care and to exercise professional skills appropriate to a solicitor in ensuring that the testator's wishes are carried out. But if a legacy fails, the testator and his estate may suffer little or no damage. The legatee may suffer substantial damage but may have no right of action against the solicitor. The testator's estate may have a right of action against the solicitor in contract or in tort, but may be entitled only to nominal damages.

The plaintiff, in his statement of claim, pleads that a solicitor retained by a testator to prepare a will owes a duty to an executor and beneficiary named in the will to ensure that the testator's benevolent intentions in respect of the executor and beneficiary are not frustrated through lack of reasonable care on the part of the solicitor. At para 7 of the statement of claim, he pleads:

> 'The defendants and each of them as solicitors for William Wall, deceased, were obliged at all material times to conduct the affairs of the deceased in such manner as would ensure and protect the best interests of the plaintiff as the person named as his executor by the deceased and as a beneficiary under his said will and of all persons entitled to benefit from, or concerned with, the will of the deceased, which said duty the defendants failed to discharge.'

Traditionally, English law did not regard a solicitor as owing any such duty to a legatee named in a testator's will and, so far as I am aware, the law of Ireland was no different in this respect. A passage which appears on p 184 of the 1961 edition of Cordery's *Law Relating to Solicitors,* puts the matter as follows:

> 'Since the solicitor's duty to his client is based on the contract of retainer, he owes no duty of care to anyone other than his client, save where he is liable as an officer of the court.'

The chief authority relied on, in support of that proposition was *Robertson v Fleming*.[254] That was a decision of the House of Lords in a Scottish. case. It is arguable that the central question in that case was whether an issue which had been settled in the Second Division of the Court of Session properly raised the question of fact in dispute between the parties. But it is also arguable that this question of fact would have been irrelevant if a solicitor owed a duty, not only to his client, but also to the person for whose benefit his services had been retained. In any event, as Sir Robert Megarry has stated in the recent case of *Ross v Caunters*,[255] at p 304, the *dicta* whether they were of the *ratio* or not are clearly of high authority.

In that case, Lord Campbell LC rejected in the strongest possible terms, the suggestion that a solicitor retained by a testator might owe any duty to a

254. (1861) 4 Macq 167.
255. [1980] Ch 297.

legatee who was a stranger to him. In a passage which appears at p 177 of the report, he says:

> 'I never had any doubt of the unsoundness of the doctrine, unnecessarily (and I must say unwisely) contended for by the respondent's counsel, that A employing B, a professional lawyer, to do any acts for the benefit of C, A having to pay B, and there being no intercourse of any sort between B and C, - if through the gross negligence or ignorance of B in transacting the business, C loses the benefit intended for him by A, C may maintain an action against B, and recover damages for the loss sustained. If this were law, a disappointed legatee might sue the solicitor employed by a testator to make a will in favour of a stranger, whom the solicitor never saw or before heard of, if the will were void for not being properly signed and attested. I am clearly of opinion that this is not the law of Scotland, nor of England, and it can hardly be the law of any country where jurisprudence has been cultivated as a science.'

While Lord Campbell was in a minority in other aspects of the case, it would appear that a majority of his colleagues agreed with him on this point.

However, since *Robertson v Fleming* was decided, there have been two major advances in the law, material to the consideration of the present question. First was the development of negligence as an independent tort and the line of authority running from *Donoghue v Stevenson*[256] to *Hedley Byrne & Co Ltd v Heller & Partners Ltd.*[257] In particular was the famous passage in Lord Atkin's speech in *Donoghue v Stevenson*, where he stressed the duty to take reasonable care to avoid injuring one's neighbour, and went on to inquire:

> 'Who, then, in law is my neighbour? The answer seems to be - persons who are so closely and directly affected by my act that I ought reasonably to have them in contemplation as being so affected when I am directing my mind to the acts or omissions which are called into question.'

Lord Atkin went on to stress that the concept of 'neighbour' did not include merely persons in close physical proximity to the alleged tortfeasor; but also, all such persons as stood in such direct relationship with him, as to cause him to know that they would be directly affected by his careless act: see [1932] AC 562, at p 580.

The second important legal development which has taken place since *Robertson v Fleming,* is that it is now finally established, so far, at any rate, as the law of Ireland is concerned, that a solicitor owes two kinds of duties to his client. First, is his duty in contract to carry out the terms of his

256. [1932] AC 562.
257. [1964] AC 465.

retainer. Second is a duty in tort to show reasonable professional skill in attending to his client's affairs. It is clear that this duty in tort arises simply because he is purporting to act as a solicitor for his client and is independent of whether he is providing his professional services voluntarily or for reward: see the judgment of the Supreme Court in *Finlay v Murtagh*[258] and also the judgment of Oliver J in *Midland Bank v Hett, Stubbs & Kemp.*[259]

The Supreme Court in *Finlay v Murtagh* was merely dealing with a net point of law as to whether a solicitor owed a duty to a client in tort as well as in contract, but it is quite clear that the court, in holding that he did, derived the duty from the proximity principle outlined by Lord Atkin in *Donoghue v Stevenson.* For instance, the following passage appears in the judgment of Kenny J (at p 264):

> 'The professional person, however, owes the client a general duty, which does not arise from contract but from the 'proximity' principle *(Donoghue v Stevenson* and *Hedley Byrne & Co Ltd v Heller & Partners Ltd*) to exercise reasonable care and skill in the performance of the work entrusted to him. This duty arises from the obligation which springs from the situation that he knew or ought to have known that his failure to exercise care and skill would probably cause loss and damage. This failure to have or to exercise reasonable skill and care is tortious or delictual in origin.'

Indeed, Henchy, J, in a passage in his judgment, appears to anticipate the situation which has arisen in the present case. He says (at p 257):

> 'The solicitor's liability in tort under the general duty of care extends not only to a client for reward, but to any person for whom the solicitor undertakes to act professionally without reward, and also to those (such as beneficiaries under a will, persons entitled under an intestacy, or those entitled to benefits in circumstances such as a claim in respect of a fatal injury) with whom he has made no arrangement to act but who, as he knows or ought to know, will be relying on his professional care and skill. For the same default there should be the same cause of action. If others are entitled to sue in tort for the solicitor's want of care, so also should the client.'

Since the decision of the Supreme Court in *Finlay v Murtagh*, the specific question which arises in the present case arose for consideration in the English High Court in the case of *Ross v Caunters.*[260]

In that case, the testator instructed solicitors to draw up his will to include gifts of chattels and a share of his residuary estate to the plaintiff, who was his sister-in-law. The solicitors drew up the will naming the plaintiff as

258. [1979] IR 249.
259. [1979] Ch 384.
260. [1980] Ch 297.

legatee. The testator requested the solicitors to send the draft will to him at the plaintiff's home where he was staying, to be signed and attested. The solicitors sent the will to the testator with a covering letter giving instructions on executing it, but failed to warn him that under s 15 of the Wills Act 1837, attestation of the will by the beneficiary's spouse would invalidate the gift to the beneficiary. The plaintiff's husband attested the will which was then returned to the solicitors who failed to notice that he had attested it. In fact, prior to the execution of the will, the testator had, in correspondence, raised with his solicitors, the question 'Am I right in thinking that beneficiaries may not be witnesses?' The solicitors unfortunately did not answer this question which clearly provided them with an opportunity to warn the testator that the spouse of a beneficiary should not be a witness either.

The testator died two years after the execution of the will. Some time later, the solicitors wrote to the plaintiff informing her that the gifts to her under the will were void because her husband had attested it. The plaintiff brought an action against the solicitors claiming damages for negligence for the loss of the gifts under the will. Sir Robert Megarry VC, after an exhaustive analysis of the authorities, held that she was entitled to succeed.

In the present case, [counsel for] the plaintiff has relied strongly on *Ross v Caunters*. [Counsel for] the defendants has drawn the distinction that in *Ross v Caunters* there was a valid will - only the bequest was invalid - whereas in the present case there was no valid will. He has also stated that I should not, by following *Ross v Caunters*, extend the traditional boundaries of the law of negligence in this country. However, it appears to me that the decision of the English High Court in *Ross v Caunters* was already anticipated by the decision of our own Supreme Court in *Finlay v Murtagh* and, for my own part, I find the reasoning of Sir Robert Megarry in *Ross v Caunters* unanswerable.

I do not think that the fact that there was a valid will in *Ross v Caunters* and that there is not a valid will in the present case is a material distinction. The question is whether the testator's solicitor owes any duty at all to the named legatee. If he owes such a duty and if the legacy fails because of his failure to observe it, it is immaterial whether the gift fails because of a defect in the words granting the legacy or because of a defect in the will itself.

I fully accept the reasoning of Sir Robert Megarry that in a case such as the present, there is a close degree of proximity between the plaintiff and the defendant. If a solicitor is retained by a testator to draft a will, and one of the purposes of the will is to confer a benefit on a named legatee, the solicitor must know that if he fails in his professional duty properly to draft the will, there is considerable risk the legatee will suffer damage. To use Sir Robert's words, his contemplation of the plaintiff is 'actual, nominate and direct.'

Likewise, I accept Sir Robert's reasoning that there can be no conflict of public policy in holding that a solicitor has a duty to take care in drafting a will, not only to the testator but also to a named legatee in the will. There is no possible inconsistency between the duty to the testator and the duty to the legatee. Recognising a duty to a legatee tends to strengthen the chances that the testator's wishes will in fact be properly expressed in the will. The two duties march together.

The authorities are, as I said, analysed by Sir Robert Megarry with consummate ability in his judgment in *Ross v Caunters*, and it would be otiose for me to repeat here the exercise which he has carried out in his judgment. Suffice it to say that I am satisfied on the basis of the decision in *Finlay v Murtagh* that a solicitor does owe a duty to a legatee named in a draft will, to draft the will with such reasonable care and skill as to ensure that the wishes of the testator are not frustrated and the expectancy of the legatee defeated through lack of reasonable care and skill on the part of the solicitor.

If a solicitor owes any duty to a named legatee, then it is quite clear that the solicitor in the present case has failed to show the appropriate care and skill. It is unnecessary to labour the point. The case has been frankly met. No effort has been made to defend what was done, except to say that the defendants owed no duty to the plaintiff."

[12.80] In *Wall v Hegarty and Callanan* Barrington J went on to consider the question of the plaintiff's losses. He held that the lost bequest was not too remote and that the plaintiff could recover damages accordingly. In addition, the plaintiff was entitled to recover the probate costs he incurred as executor before being put on notice of the irregularity in the will:[261]

> "Even therefore, if the plaintiff's loss in getting involved in legal proceedings to prove the will did not flow directly from the original carelessness in drafting the will on the principle of *Donoghue v Stevenson,* it appears to me that the loss would still be recoverable because of the fact of the circumstances in which the will was sent to the plaintiff on the principles of the *Hedley Byrne case*."

Barrington J also held that the plaintiff should be entitled in principle, as executor, to recover the interest which would have been payable on the legacy although he sought to hear further argument on its particular application in the instant case.

Negligently Performed Property Transactions

[12.81] A significant proportion of a solicitor's business involves acting for clients in a variety of property transactions. Given the complexity of our land law it is inevitable that errors will occur and will be the subject of litigation by disappointed clients. *Desmond v Brophy*[262] is one such case

261. [1980] ILRM 124, at 130.
262. [1985] IR 449.

where the two plaintiffs independently retained the first defendant as solicitor to act for them in the purchase of two flats. They informed him of their concern that deposits paid by them would not pass to the builders until completion of the flats. Both believed that he would arrange matters so that the deposits would not pass to the builders until completion of the flats. The first defendant sent their deposit cheques to the builders' solicitors, intending that they hold them as stakeholder rather than as agent for the builders. He did not make this clear to the builders' solicitors who, in accordance with custom and their instructions, endorsed the cheque in favour of their clients. Before the contract was signed the builders went into liquidation and the plaintiffs lost their deposits. They sued the first defendant for negligence. The builders' solicitors were joined as defendants, by order of the Master of the High Court, and the plaintiffs made an alternative claim against them for the return of the deposits as monies had and received. The claim against the second defendants was dismissed. However Barrington J held the first defendant liable:[263]

> "For many years the Incorporated Law Society had been aware of the practice of builders demanding and receiving booking deposits and of the risks which purchasers who paid such booking deposits were running. The *Solicitors' Gazette* for January/February 1977 (Vol. 71, p. 17) contained an item under the heading 'Purchasers at risk on Deposits' where the problem was discussed. This item contained the following paragraph:
>
> > 'The purpose of this memorandum is to emphasise to solicitors the importance of putting on record to their clients the risks which they are taking. Clients in our experience are under the mistaken impression that once the monies are paid to a solicitor or through a solicitor they have the full protection as if their own solicitor was a stakeholder. It does, of course, seem quite unfair that the purchasers should be at risk in this way as while transactions like this might be a commercial risk to the builder, it could hardly be so described from the point of view of the purchasers.'
>
> A similar warning was issued by Mr Wylie at para 10.133 of his book on *Irish Conveyancing Law*.[264]
>
> Mr Brophy cannot be faulted for not being aware of these dangers. He discussed them with his clients and took what he considered to be proper steps to protect his clients against them. The question is whether these steps were reasonably adequate to protect his clients' interests…
>
> [Counsel] on behalf of [the builders' solicitors] referred to a passage in Wylie's *Irish Conveyancing Law* which appears on p 466 of the book at para 10.066. The passage reads as follows:

---

263. *Ibid*, at 452-457.

264. Professional Books, 1978.

> 'If the deposit is not paid to the vendor personally, the question arises as to what is the capacity of the third party who receives it. The general law recognises two basic capacities in such a case, namely, receipt as *agent* for the vendor and as *stakeholder*. The significance of the distinction is this. If the deposit is paid to the vendor's agent, eg, his auctioneer or solicitor acting in that capacity, the agent is liable to pay it to the vendor on demand. He must also account to the vendor for any interest earned or other profit made from the deposit. If the sale falls through, the purchaser can sue the vendor only, not the agent, for recovery. The advantage from the vendor's point of view is that he can demand the deposit immediately and use it, eg, in connection with some other transaction such as the purchase of a new house. It has been suggested that there are dangers in this from the purchaser's point of view in that, if the vendor suddenly goes bankrupt and the deposit has been spent by him, the purchaser may have difficulty in recovering it. On the other hand, it is settled that, if the deposit is paid to the vendor's agent, the purchaser has a lien on the vendor's land for its return, and in this respect the purchaser is better off than he would be if the deposit were paid to a stakeholder.'

This passage appears to reflect the law as stated by Mr Justice Kenny in his judgment in *Leemac Overseas Investment Ltd v Harvey*.[265] In a passage which appears at p 164 Mr Justice Kenny states:

> 'An auctioneer who receives a deposit as stakeholder has been said to be the agent for the vendor and the purchaser. *Harrington v Hoggart*[266] dealt with the issue whether a stakeholder was liable for the interest earned on the deposit, but in the course of his judgment Lord Tenterden said at p 586 of the report:
>
> > "A stakeholder does not receive the money for either party, he receives it for both; and until the event is known, it is his duty to keep it in his own hands".'

Similar language was used by Lord Justice Brown in *Ellis v Goulton*[267] at p 352 of the report:

> 'When a deposit is paid by a purchaser under a contract for the sale of land, the person who makes the payment may enter into an agreement with the vendor that the money shall be held by the recipient as agent for both vendor and purchaser. If this is done, the person who receives it becomes a stakeholder, liable, in certain events, to return the money to the person who paid it. In the absence of such agreement, the money is paid to a person who has not the character of stakeholder; and it follows that, when the

265. [1973] IR 160.
266. (1830) 1 B & Ad 577.
267. [1893] 1 QB 350.

> money reaches his hands, it is the same thing so far as the person who pays it is concerned as if it had reached the hands of the principal.'

At p 469 of his book Mr Wylie deals with deposits paid to solicitors and estate agents. In the case of a solicitor he puts the matter as follows:

> 'Again in the absence of a contrary agreement, a deposit paid to the vendor's solicitor is treated as paid to him as the vendor's agent rather than as a stakeholder.'

In the case of a deposit paid to an estate agent he puts the matter as follows:

> 'In the case of a sale by private treaty, it is usual that the "deposit" received by a house or estate agent will be a pre-contract deposit, and it would seem, in the light of recent authorities, that as a general principle this should not be regarded as being received as agent for the vendor, in the absence of express authority conferred by the latter. At most, therefore, the "agent" should be regarded as receiving such a deposit as a stakeholder.'

In *Sorrell v Finch*[268] it was held that, in the absence of special agreement, a pre-contract deposit paid by a prospective purchaser to an estate agent was not received by the estate agent with the implied or ostensible authority of the prospective vendor. In such circumstances the purchaser was at all times until contract the only person with any claim or right to the deposit monies and he could reclaim them on demand from the estate agent. [Counsel], on behalf of Mr. Brophy, relied on this case and also referred to *Burt v Claude Cousins & Co*[269] and to the notes on the decision in *Rayner v Paskell & Another* and *Regina v Pilkington* which are appended to the report of *Burt v Claude Cousins & Co* in Volume 2 of the Queen's Bench Reports for 1971 (see p 439). He also referred to *Barrington v Lee*.[270]

All of these were cases of deposits paid to estate agents and [counsel for Mr. Brophy] has attempted to apply the reasoning to preliminary deposits paid to solicitors in a pre-contract situation or on the basis that the deposit is paid 'subject to contract'. [He] relied, in particular, on the dissenting judgment of Lord Justice Denning in *Burt v Claude Cousins & Co*[271] which judgment was approved of by the House of Lords when they overruled *Burr v Claude Cousins & Co* in *Sorrell v Finch*.[272]

In his judgment in *Burt v Claude Cousins & Co* Lord Justice Denning distinguishes three situations in relation to a deposit. One is where a deposit is received 'as agent for the vendor', another is where a deposit is received 'as stakeholder' and a third is where nothing is said. It may be significant that in the first two cases Lord Justice Denning refers to 'an

268. [1977] AC 728.
269. [1971] 2 QB 426.
270. [1972] 1 QB 326.
271. [1971] 2 QB 426.
272. [1977] AC 728.

estate agent or a solicitor' but in the third case he refers only to an estate agent. Referring to the third case he says at p 615:

> 'If an estate agent, before any binding contract is made, asks for and receives a deposit, giving the receipt in his own name without more, the question arises: in what capacity does he receive it? As agent for the vendor? or as stakeholder? I cannot believe that he receives it as 'agent for the vendor', for, if that were so, the estate agent would be bound to pay it over to the vendor forthwith, and the vendor alone would be answerable for its return. That cannot be right. Seeing that no contract has been made, the vendor is not entitled to a penny piece. If the estate agent should pay it over to the vendor, he does wrong; and if the vendor goes bankrupt, the estate agent is answerable for it.'

It seems to me doubtful if this kind of reasoning can be applied to the case of a solicitor. But, more important, I do not think that the present case can be resolved by such general considerations. I think the same applies to evidence which the court received concerning the practice of some solicitors who act for builders and whose practice, in the absence of clear instructions, is guided by admirable considerations of what they consider to be fair as between their builder clients and prospective purchasers in relation to the payment of booking deposits. In the present case [the builders] had formulated a clear policy in relation to booking deposits and stage payments. These deposits and payments, whether received by the estate agent or the solicitor, were to go to the builder and the solicitor had no authority to accept these deposits except as agent for the builder. The fact that these deposits would go to the builder was explained by Mr. Lynch to [the plaintiffs] when they first showed interest in buying the flats.

[The plaintiffs] understood this and it was because they did not like it that they consulted Mr Brophy. Mr Brophy intended to bring about a situation where [the builders' solicitors] would hold the deposit and the first stage payment 'as stakeholders' and not as agents for the vendor. It would have been very easy for him to say, in his first letter, that the deposits were being paid to [the builders' solicitors] as stakeholders. Unfortunately, he did not do this.

In each case Mr Brophy's letter sending the cheque for the initial deposit was in similar terms. The question is whether this letter was sufficient to put [the builders' solicitors] on notice that the deposit was being paid to them as stakeholders and not in accordance with what they knew to be their instructions from their clients and their clients' general course of business. In my view it was not sufficient, in the circumstances of the case, to put them on notice that the deposit was being tendered on special terms. It is possible that an extremely careful solicitor would have written back to Mr. Brophy asking him precisely what he meant but I do not think it is reasonable, in the circumstances, to fault [the builders' solicitors] for not raising such a query. It appears to me that they correctly interpreted their own clients' instructions in paying the deposit over to them and that the letter was not sufficient to put them on notice that the deposit was being tendered on the basis that they were to be stakeholders.

When the first stage payment was made by Mr Brophy on the 11th January, 1980, he made clear that he was paying it on the same terms as those set out in his letter of the 5th November, 1979. Again I do not think the letter was sufficient to put [the builders' solicitors] on notice that the deposit was being paid to them as stakeholders.

It is always unfortunate when, as in the present case, the court has to decide which of two innocent persons must bear a loss. I do not think there was any lack of concern on the part of Mr Brophy for his clients' interests but unfortunately, in this case, it appears to me that he did not show reasonable professional skill in defending those interests and the clients as a result, are at a loss.

In the circumstances I hold that the plaintiffs are entitled to recover against Mr Brophy the loss which they have suffered."

[12.82] A solicitor's failure to take account of new legislation which affects his client's case has been held to amount to negligence,[273] as has a failure to advise a client of the financial implications involved in purchasing the freehold of a premises.[274] However, the mere fact that a solicitor made, what in retrospect transpires to be, a mistake does not render him or her liable. In *Park Hall School Ltd v Overend*[275] it was held that, given the uncertain state of the relevant law at the time, the defendant solicitors were not necessarily negligent when they made an erroneous assumption regarding the validity of a transaction in which their clients were involved. In *Fallon v Gannon*[276] the Supreme Court held that the duty of a solicitor in a case where counsel is briefed is to brief appropriate and competent counsel, to instruct counsel properly and to provide for the attendance of witnesses and other proofs. Moreover, the Court stated that a solicitor does not incur vicarious responsibility for the conduct of counsel, a matter of some significance given that negligence on the part of an advocate does not attract liability.[277]

273. *McMullen v Farrell* [1993] 1 IR 123.
274. *Kehoe v CJ Louth & Son* [1992] ILRM 282.
275. [1987] IR 1.
276. [1988] ILRM 193.
277. In *Rondel v Worsley* [1969] 1 AC 191 the House of Lords held on public policy grounds that liability would not attach for negligence of a barrister in the course of litigation; this was extended to solicitors who engage in advocacy; *Saif Ali v Sydney Mitchell & Co* [1980] AC 198; see McMahon & Binchy, *op cit* pp 278-280.

Developing the Standard of Care

[12.83] The standard of care which a professional person must exercise was considered by the Supreme Court in *O'Donovan v Cork County Council*.[278] In general, it is sufficient that the defendant adopted the approved practices of the profession provided, however, that those practices are not themselves defective. The matter was stated by Walsh J in the following terms:[279]

> "A medical practitioner cannot be held negligent if he follows general and approved practice in the situation in which he is faced: see *Daniels v Heskin*,[280] and the cases referred to therein.
>
> That proposition is not, however, without qualification. If there is a common practice which has inherent defects, which ought to be obvious to any person giving the matter due consideration, the fact that it has been shown to have been widely and generally adopted over a period of time does not make that practice any the less negligent. Neglect of duty does not cease by repetition to be neglect of duty."

[12.84] *Roche v Peilow*[281] provides an example of an approved professional practice which the Supreme Court considered to be inherently defective. The appellants engaged the respondent solicitors to act for them in the purchase of a new house from a building company. The latter had created an equitable charge in favour of a bank on the land on which the house was to be built. The charge was registered in the Companies Office but not in the Land Registry. When they came to investigate title the defendants made the usual Requisitions on the Title, but they did not make a search in the Companies Office. Only the latter search would have disclosed the existence of the charge. The building company went into liquidation, by which stage the appellants had paid £8,000 towards the purchase price. The liquidator was prepared to complete the contract, but the bank was unprepared to release the charge unless paid £6,000. The appellants sued the respondents alleging that they were negligent in that they failed to discover the existence of the charge in favour of the bank. The respondents denied that they were negligent as they had followed the approved practice of the profession. The Supreme Court (Walsh, Henchy, Griffin, Hederman and McCarthy JJ) held that the respondents were negligent. Walsh J explained the matter thus:[282]

> "The plaintiffs have alleged that the defendants were negligent and in breach of their contract with the [plaintiffs] for not discovering the

278. [1967] IR 173.
279. *Ibid*, at 193.
280. [1954] IR 73.
281. [1985] IR 232.
282. *Ibid*, at 249-252.

mortgage by making the appropriate searches in the Companies Office and of warning them of this additional risk. The plaintiffs had already paid the builders £8,000 on foot of their building contract when the builders went into liquidation. This followed a resolution of the shareholders of the building company on the 18th October, 1974 when it was resolved that the company be wound up. The lease had not yet been executed. The company was, through its liquidator, eventually compelled to grant a lease of the premises to the appellants but that, of course, was not valid as against the bank. The bank was and is willing to release the site upon payment to them of £6,000, but not otherwise. In default of such payment they are apparently prepared to recover the property from the appellants and, of course, with it would go the house which has now been built upon it.

The defendants, in answer to the claim in negligence, have stated that they acted in accordance with the common practice of solicitors in these matters, that is to say not to make all the necessary inquiries until the time for granting the lease had arrived. It appears that there is no general practice of pre-contract searches by solicitors in advising purchasers with regard to the purchase of houses provided by a system of a building contract to be followed by a lease. The question in this case is whether such a common practice has such inherent defects that they ought to be obvious to any person giving the matter due consideration.

It is clear from the evidence given by solicitors, including the defendants in this case, that this particular risk was well known to them and that they appreciated that in cases where money was being paid out during the course of a building contract if the site was not already secured it would be lost in the event of the insolvency or liquidation of the builder. In a case where no money was being paid out on foot of a building contract until completion then the risk would, to a very large extent, be diminished, even though in the event of loss of the site the purchaser might be very disappointed and might indeed suffer damage. While in a case such as the present one it could well be that the plaintiffs, even if they were made aware of the risk, might have elected to go on but the fact is that they were not made aware of it and so it is idle to speculate on what they might have done if they had become aware of it. In this transaction plaintiffs' position was fraught with very grave risks. The first one was that pointed out by their solicitors, namely, that by making periodic payments during the course of the building they were liable to lose it all if the builder went bankrupt or went into liquidation or, alternatively, they might be able to mitigate their loss by getting somebody else to complete the building. There was ample evidence that the plaintiffs were fully aware of this risk and accepted it. The second risk in their situation was the question of the site itself. They were not warned of this and the question is whether the defendants' failure to discover the mortgage and to pass the information on to the plaintiffs was negligence on the part of the defendants. In my view it was.

It is quite clear on the evidence in the case that this method of financing building was well known to solicitors and they also knew the risks inherent in it. In a case where the builder was a limited company, as well as making a search in the Land Registry it would also be clearly necessary to make a search in the Companies Office. It may well be that the general practice of solicitors not making these searches until the time has arrived for completion was based upon the experience that in most cases nothing goes wrong. However, that practice does not obviate the risk clearly inherent in such a practice. The whole object of a search is to discover these matters and no solicitor can permit his client to purchase lands or to commit himself irrevocably financially in the purchase or development of lands unless he has first of all ascertained whether or not the land is free from encumbrances. If it is not he must bring the fact to the notice of his client and allow the client, after proper advice to decide whether or not he should take the risk of accepting the transaction with the risk posed by the existence of the encumbrance.

In his judgment the learned President of the High Court cited a passage from the decision of this Court in *O'Donovan v Cork County Council*.[283] In my view the last paragraph of that passage governs this case. The learned President in deciding against the plaintiffs relied upon a passage in an English judgment, *Simmons v Pennington & Son*.[284] In that case the vendor had purchased shop premises in 1922. They were then being used as a shop and that user had continued ever since then. The premises, however, were subject to a restrictive covenant imposed by an indenture of 1870 under which their user was restricted to use for residential purposes. When the premises were put up for sale in 1951 the vendor in the conditions of sale stated:

> 'This property is sold subject the restrictive covenant as to user and other matters contained in a deed dated 29th September 1870 … as far as the same are still subsisting and capable of taking effect, and the purchaser shall in the conveyance to him covenant to observe the same in so far as aforesaid and to indemnify the vendor in respect thereof. A copy of the said restricted covenant may be inspected … and the purchaser whether he inspects the same or not shall be deemed to purchase with full notice thereof.'

The purchaser bought the premises at the auction and signed the contract of purchase. He made requisitions and one of them was the following:

> 'Is the property or any part thereof subject to any covenant or agreement restrictive of the user or enjoyment thereof or otherwise? If so has the same been duly observed or performed?'

The answer given to the vendor's solicitor to that was:

283. [1967] IR 173.
284. [1955] 1 WLR 183.

> 'Yes. See special condition No 7. There appeared to have been breaches of the covenant as to user but no notice of breach has been served.'

The purchaser's solicitors then wrote to the vendor's solicitors stating that the purchaser had not been informed before the sale that there was a restrictive covenant which restricted the use of the property to that of a private dwellinghouse and the purchaser was not prepared to complete and requested that the stakeholder should be instructed to return the deposit. This was refused and in the meantime the property, which was not insured by either party, was very badly damaged by fire. In the case which followed Denning LJ (as he then was) expressed the view that the answer to requisition No 14 was a fatal mistake in that it enabled the purchaser to get out of his bargain and that he was thus entitled to cancel the contract forthwith. He also held, however, that he was satisfied that the solicitors who gave the response were not negligent and expressed the view that the restrictions were in all probability obsolete but nevertheless the solicitors could not assert categorically that they were. The requisition to which the answer had been given was described as 'a stock requisition' but the answer given was, in the view of the learned judge, not a negligent answer. The Court of Appeal went on to hold that it was ill luck that the words which the solicitors used instead of protecting their client amounted to repudiation of the contract but that was not the solicitor's fault. It could not have been reasonably anticipated, the Court thought, that such a repudiation would flow from the answer to the requisition and that they had acted in accordance with the general practice of conveyancers. The Court went on to observe that no ill consequence had ever been known to flow from the answer. In the result, the Court held that the solicitor was not guilty of a breach of duty to his client. A number of observations may be made about that particular case. The first is that the conditions of sale were not particularly candid and the second is that it could scarcely be regarded as negligence to give a truthful answer to a requisition. It may well have been thought that a solicitor might not reasonably foresee that telling the truth in what was a stock answer to a stock question would fail to satisfy a purchaser. However, in my view, the case is totally different from the present case. The risk in the present case cannot be neutered by describing it as a stock risk. It is a very substantial and real risk. The fact that it was frequently undertaken does not in any way diminish the danger to which it gives rise. The consequences of the risk materialising could not be said to be unforeseeable as the evidence in this case indicates that it was a well known risk and the consequences were obvious if it should materialise. In my view, the decision in *Simmons v Pennington & Sons* is not applicable.

I have had the advantage of reading the judgments delivered by the then President of the High Court in *Taylor v Ryan*[285] and the judgment of Mr Justice Murphy in *Dermot C Kelly & anor v Finbarr J Crowley.*[286] The

285. High Court, unrep, 10 March 1983.

principles enunciated in those cases confirm, in my view, that the defendants were guilty of a failure in the duty they owed to the plaintiffs to the extent that they were negligent in law."

[12.85] Henchy J, concurring in *Roche v Peilow* stated:[287]

> "When the plaintiffs engaged the defendants to act as their solicitors in the purchase of a house, they were entitled to believe that their interests would be protected by the defendants with the degree of care to be expected from a reasonably careful and competent solicitor. That duty of care may be said to arise either as a matter of contract, by reason of an implied term to that effect in the contract of retainer, or alternatively, as an aspect of the tort of negligence arising out of the proximity of the relationship between solicitor and client: see *Finlay v Murtagh*.[288]
>
> In deciding whether the plaintiffs are entitled to succeed in their claim for damages for want of reasonable care on the part of the defendants, it is necessary to underline certain features of the house purchase in question. The house had yet to be built. The site of the house was one of a number of sites which were being developed by a building company. Those sites were contained in Folio 58474 of the Register of Freeholders for the County of Cork and the registered owner was the building company. The building company were to build a house on one of those sites for the plaintiffs for the sum of £9,450. That sum was to be paid in instalments payable at different stages of the building of the house, namely £1,000 as a booking deposit, £2,500 at first floor, £2,000 at roof-plate level, £2,500 at internal plastering and £1,450 on completion. In conjunction with that building agreement, the building company agreed to grant a 999 years lease of the house when it was completed.
>
> The plaintiffs instructed the defendants to act as their solicitors in connection with the transaction before they entered into any written contract with the building company. The contract to build the house was executed by the parties on the 19th February, 1973, and the agreement to grant the lease was executed on the same date. The plaintiffs' plea of negligence rests on the complaint that before they bound themselves contractually, the defendants as their solicitors should have made a search in the Companies Office to ascertain if a charge on the site had been registered by the building company under the Companies Act 1963. If such a search had been made it would have shown that the building company had given a charge to a bank, by deposit of title deeds, on the lands on Folio 58474 to secure all moneys due by the building company to the bank. Had that position been thus disclosed, the defendants would doubtless have informed the plaintiffs that the bank were equitable mortgagees and have

286. [1985] IR 212.

287. [1985] IR 232, at 252-255.

288. [1979] IR 249.

warned them of the perils involved in making stage payments to the building company, who had not the beneficial title and against whom there would be no effective redress in case of insolvency.

In ignorance of the bank's interest in the site, the plaintiffs executed the building agreement and the agreement for a lease. The defendants investigated the title in the normal way by serving requisitions on title. Neither the replies to the requisitions nor the certified copy of the folio disclosed the charge in favour of the bank. Only a search in the Companies Office would have brought to light that charge, and such a search was not made.

Meanwhile, the plaintiffs proceeded to make the stage payments required by the building contract. They had paid stage payments totalling £8,000 when the building company became insolvent and went into liquidation. While the liquidator was eventually prepared to grant the plaintiffs the lease contracted for, such a lease is valueless because the equitable estate is vested in the bank as a result of the charge, and the bank are not prepared to release the site from their charge unless they are paid £6,000.

The present claim by the plaintiffs against the defendants for damages for negligence and/or breach of contract rests on the contention that the financial loss incurred by them in connection with the attempted purchase of this house was caused by the defendants' failure to search for and discover the charge in favour of the bank. In particular they complain that before they were allowed by the defendants to enter into contractual relationship with the building company the defendants should have ascertained the bank's interest in the site and warned the plaintiffs of the financial risk involved in proceeding with the transaction when the building company had not an unencumbered title.

I have no doubt that the financial disaster that has befallen the plaintiffs may be said to result from the defendants' failure to discover and bring to their notice, before the contract, the existence of the bank's charge. The real question is whether that failure amounts to negligence by the defendants as solicitors.

The general duty owed by a solicitor to his client is to show him the degree of care to be expected in the circumstances from a reasonably careful and skilful solicitor. Usually the solicitor will be held to have discharged that duty if he follows a practice common among the members of his profession: see *Daniels v Heskin*[289] and the cases therein referred to. Conformity with the widely accepted practice of his colleagues will normally rebut an allegation of negligence against a professional man, for the degree of care which the law expects of him is no higher than that to be expected from an ordinary reasonable member of the profession or of the speciality in question. But there is an important exception to that rule of conduct. It was concisely put as follows by Walsh J in *O'Donovan v Cork County Council*:[290]

289. [1954] IR 73.

> 'If there is a common practice which has inherent defects, which ought to be obvious to any person giving the matter due consideration, the fact that it is shown to have been widely and generally adopted over a period of time does not make the practice any the less negligent. Neglect of duty does not cease by repetition to be neglect of duty.'

The reason for that exception or qualification is that the duty imposed by the law rests on the standard to be expected from a reasonably careful member of the profession, and a person cannot be said to be acting reasonably if he automatically and mindlessly follows the practice of others when by taking thought he would have realised that the practice in question was fraught with peril for his client and was readily avoidable or remediable. The professional man is, of course, not to be judged with the benefit of hindsight, but if it can be said that if at the time, on giving the matter due consideration, he would have realised that the impugned practice was in the circumstances incompatible with his client's interests, and if an alternative and safe course of conduct was reasonably open to him, he will be held to have been negligent.

I consider it to be beyond doubt that it was inimical to the plaintiffs' interests for the defendants to allow them to enter into contractual relations with the building company, and in particular to bind themselves to make stage payments, without first making a search in the Companies Office, which would have shown that the beneficial owner of the site was the bank. Because of the defendants' default in that respect, the plaintiffs were left open to disappointment and financial disaster if, as happened, the building company proved to be unable to discharge their indebtedness to the bank. As the evidence in the High Court showed, in not making that search the defendants were following a conveyancing practice common at the time among solicitors. However, adherence to that practice can avail as a defence only if it be shown that a reasonable solicitor, giving consideration at the time to the interests of the client, would have justifiably concluded that a search in the Companies Office was unnecessary or undesirable. Having regard to the fact that no undue delay, expense or difficulty was involved in making such a search, and bearing in mind that financial disaster of the kind actually sustained by the plaintiffs was reasonably foreseeable by the defendants as a risk for the plaintiffs, I consider that, notwithstanding that the defendants in not carrying out a search were conforming to a practice widespread at the time in the profession, they were nevertheless wanting in the duty of care owed by them to the plaintiffs. It is to avoid detectable pitfalls of the kind that beset the plaintiffs that prospective purchasers engage solicitors to act for them."

---

290. [1967] IR 173, at 193.

Chapter 13

Legislation

[1] Introduction

[13.01] The source of law which is known as 'legislation' consists of measures which are enacted or adopted by a legislative organ in a manner which is prescribed by a constitutional formula. In other words it is the product of a legislative or law-making process. In Ireland legislative authority is conferred on the Oireachtas by Article 15.2.1° of the Constitution which states that '[t]he sole and exclusive power of making laws for the State is hereby vested in the Oireachtas; no other legislative authority has power to make laws for the State.' Legislation falls into two categories. The first, *primary legislation*, consists of Acts of the Oireachtas, also called statutes,[1] which are enacted by the Oireachtas in a particular manner which is outlined later.[2] Acts of the Oireachtas are of three types; *Acts to amend the Constitution*; *public general Acts* which create law for the public at large; and *private Acts* which create law for particular individuals or groups of individuals, such as companies or local authorities. The second category, variously known as *secondary*, *subordinate* or *delegated* legislation, consists of measures enacted by a person or body to whom the Oireachtas has delegated legislative authority. In general, delegated legislation establishes detailed rules while the Act under which it is made contains general principles. Like primary legislation delegated legislation is a source of law and the two share many characteristics. The extent to which legislative power may be delegated, the relationship between primary and delegated legislation and the special features of delegated legislation will be considered below.[3] At this stage it is sufficient to observe that both species of legislation are regulatory measures which enjoy the force of law. It should be realised that they form part of a wider regulatory environment which is composed of a variety of mechanisms, both legal and non-legal, created by the acts either of public institutions or private individuals (see Figure 13.01). In this chapter we will also consider briefly other regulatory mechanisms

1. The term 'statute', which is now used synonymously with 'Act of the Oireachtas', originally referred to all the Acts passed in a particular parliamentary session; see *R v Bakewell* (1857) 7 E & B 848, *per* Lord Campbell CJ.
2. The legislative process is considered at paras **[13.08]-[13.26]**.
3. See paras **[13.58]-[13.80]**.

which have some of the appearances of legislation but which are not legislative in nature and lack the force of law.[4] These devices, which are sometimes called *quasi-legislation*, include codes of practice, administrative rules and circulars.

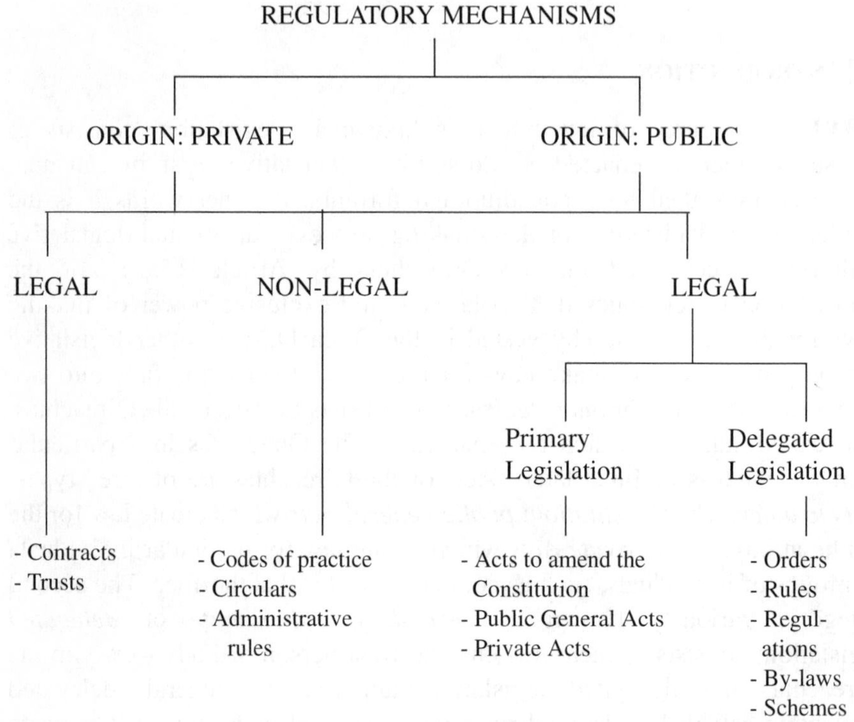

Figure 13.01

Comparison with other sources of law

[13.02] The process of legislating connotes the activity of deliberate law making. Unlike adjudication which is the concern of the judicial process its primary concern is with the creation of rules which will apply to future events, rather than with the resolution of individual disputes. In this respect, the process is prospective and abstract - it establishes standards to be adopted in sets of circumstances which have yet to occur. However, it should be realised that some legislative measures regulate past events, although this tends to be an exception to the general practice. Moreover, private Acts apply to individual sets of circumstances, a feature which is

4. See paras **[13.04]-[13.05]**.

shared by adjudication.[5] It is the regulatory nature of such instruments which allows them to be characterised as legislation. In contrast, adjudication is retrospective and concrete, being concerned with the resolution of past events according to pre-existing rules. Nevertheless, as we have seen in the preceding chapter, the adjudicative process does possess a creative dimension and, of course, the product of the adjudicative process is a source of law - the common law is often referred to as 'judge made' law. But the creative character of adjudication differs significantly from that of legislation. Common law rules emerge from their being identified from an existing body of law and applied by the adjudicator to the dispute which he or she is charged with resolving. The creative scope afforded to a judge is constrained by the pre-existing law and, in this respect, is incidental to the adjudicative function. On the other hand, legislators are not so constrained, being confined only by the constitutional or other formula which confers legislative capacity on them. Thus, despite their both being creative, the general distinction between legislation and adjudication is based on their respective functions, that of the former being law-making and that of the latter being law-application. Whatever their differences legislation and common law both enjoy the force of law.

[13.03] The private law of contract might also provide a regulatory mechanism of a different type. A contract is brought about by agreement of the parties rather than the act of a legislative body. The parties create the law which is to govern their relationship rather than having it imposed on them by an external agency. But that difference aside, contract shares the regulatory purpose of legislation. It seeks at the outset to establish the rules by which the parties are to be governed. Significant sectors of the economy now tend to be regulated through the mechanism of standard form contracts. The entitlements of those who engage, say, dry cleaners are governed primarily by such contracts, the contents of which are predominantly determined by the dry cleaning industry. The customer is typically presented with a 'take it or leave it' choice and, in practice, is not in a position to negotiate.[6] Like legislation, contractual regulation is legally enforceable and, in this sense, it enjoys the force of law. Nevertheless, despite these similarities contract is a very different phenomenon to legislation. Lying at the heart of contract law is the theory, realistic or otherwise, of contract as a

---

5. Parliamentary procedure in relation to the enactment of private acts shares some feature with litigation; see paras **[13.23]-[13.26]**.

6. It should be noted that legislation increasingly regulates contractual freedom especially in the area of consumer contracts; see Sale of Goods and Supply of Services Act 1980; European Communities (Unfair Terms in Consumer Contracts) Regulations 1995 (SI 27/ 1995).

bargain which is freely entered into by two equally situated parties. The law thereby created is the voluntary act of the parties. Legislation is the act of an agency external to those who are subjected to it.[7] Legislation might also be contrasted with the trust, a legal device which facilitates arrangements governing the ownership and management of property. Like contract, the trust is a creature of private law, it having been created by the act of a private party known as the settlor, and is legally enforceable. Although trusts and contracts are distinct legal instruments[8] they share a similar regulatory potential which is different in origin from legislation but which might be every bit as effective.

Quasi-Legislation

[13.04] In addition to those sources of law a range of regulatory instruments are promulgated by various Governmental agencies, in particular Government departments. Administrative rules, circulars, codes of practice[9] and the like are frequently issued by these agencies and seek to govern significant areas of Government business.[10] In some, but not all, circumstances their introduction is governed or provided for by statute.[11] To a large extent much of this administrative rule-making is routine in nature, setting out the administration's interpretation and implementation of various schemes and powers. Viewed thus, their purpose is to remove matters of detail from the text of statutes, in the main they are beneficial to the public and pose few legal difficulties. Often the statute expressly provides that the code of practice or administrative rule lacks legal status and does not impose legal liabilities. However, in some circumstances administrative rules seek to establish norms and standards which are expected to be adopted and their purpose, like that of legislation, is regulatory. Such rules are often used by Government as an alternative to, or surrogate for, legislation. For instance,

---

7. However, in some instances a court might be prepared to treat a contract as being equivalent to legislation; see *McCord v ESB* [1980] ILRM 153; see further para **[13.64]**.

8. See Delany, *Equity and the Law of Trusts in Ireland* (Round Hall Sweet & Maxwell, 1996) pp 50-53.

9. See Campbell, 'Codes of Practice as an Alternative to Legislation' [1985] Stat LR 127; Samuels 'Codes of Practice and Legislation' [1986] Stat LR 29.

10. See Hogan, 'The Legal Status of Administrative Rules and Circulars' (1987) 22 Ir Jur (ns) 194.

11. Eg Department of Labour, *Code of Practice: Dispute procedures, including procedures in essential services* (Department of Labour 1992) for which provision was made under the Industrial Relations Act 1990, s 42 and which was brought into effect by the Industrial Relations Act 1990 Code of Practice on Dispute Procedures (Declaration) Order 1992, (SI 1/1992); the *Rules of the Road* (The Stationery Office, 1992) are referred to in the Road Traffic Act 1961, s 3(4); the *Rules and Programme for Secondary Schools 1987/88 to 1994/95* (Pn 0983) are made under the Intermediate Education (Ireland) Acts 1878 to 1924.

national schools are governed not by legislation (in fact none exists) but by the *Rules for National Schools* which were made by the Minister for Education. Such rules mimic legislation and are formulated with the intention that they should be followed.[12] This form of law making has been termed 'quasi-legislation'[13] or 'ersatz legislation'.[14] While they lack the force of law the rules are capable of being enforced by a variety of informal mechanisms which include the conferring, or possible withholding, of discretionary entitlements and benefits, official pressure, appeals to the conscience or sense of national good and making compliance a condition of Government contracts and the like. The difficulty here is that such rules are enunciated without being subjected to parliamentary scrutiny and they operate beyond the legislative domain in a manner which is hardly compatible with the minimum demands of democracy. Moreover, in as much as they purport to confer rights and impose obligations additional legal difficulties are encountered. For example, corporal punishment in schools was abolished by means of a Ministerial circular.[15] It might be argued, with some force, that the abolition should have been effected by formal legislation, thus facilitating parliamentary scrutiny. And the circular does not, and cannot, alter the legal position of a pupil who is so punished - the common law defence of reasonable chastisement is still available to defeat both a criminal prosecution of, and (probably) a civil action against, an offending teacher.[16] Thus, while the teacher is administratively prohibited from so acting, and presumably is liable to discipline in the context of his or her employment, he or she commits no legal wrong in resorting to corporal punishment. A further difficulty is that there is no provision for the formal promulgation and publication of such rules and the possibility exists that those affected will be ignorant of their content.

[13.05] Regulatory schemes might also be created by private arrangements. Many industries, especially in the service sector, establish voluntary codes

12. See eg the Department of Education's *Procedures for Dealing with Allegations or Suspicions of Child Abuse* (M41/92) and *Guidelines on Countering Bullying Behaviour in Primary and Post-Primary Schools* (The Stationery Office, 1993).

13. Megarry, 'Administrative Quasi-legislation' (1944) LQR 125; see also Ganz, *Quasi-Legislation* (Sweet & Maxwell, 1987).

14. Ferguson, 'Legislation' in *Stair Memorial Encyclopedia of the Laws of Scotland* (1987) Vol 22 par 224.

15. In January 1982 the Minister for Education issued two circulars 9/82 and M5/82 which respectively abolished corporal punishment in primary and post-primary schools; see 333 *Dáil Debates* cols 1430-1431.

16. *Cleary v Booth* [1893] 1 QB 465; see Children Act 1908, s 37 preserving the right of a teacher to administer punishment; see also Law Reform Commission, *Report on Non-Fatal Offences Against the Person* (LRC 45-1994) pp 23-24.

of conduct to which members subscribe. In some cases, the regimes established by these measures are mirror images of equivalent statutory schemes. The advertising industry, for instance, is voluntarily regulated by the Advertising Standards Authority for Ireland. The Authority has created two codes of practice which it implements and which are universally followed by the industry.[17] In many respects the codes resemble legislation. The mandatory language in which they are drafted is similar to that of legislation; they provide for a complaints procedure, a system of adjudication by an independent committee and an enforcement mechanism. But despite their similarity to legislation the codes are, by their very nature, voluntary and compliance with them relies on the internal dynamics of the particular industry and the willingness of individuals to accept them as being binding. They might prove to be as effective, and indeed in some cases are more effective, than legislation enforced by a state agency but unlike legislation they lack the force of law and compliance cannot be coerced.

Characteristics of legislation

[13.06] Having distinguished legislation from other regulatory instruments the characteristics of legislation may now be considered. The principal characteristic of legislation is that it reduces rules to a written and fixed verbal form. A legislative rule is stated in an inflexible manner and no linguistic variations can be substituted. This contrasts with common law rules which, as has been seen, are unwritten and unfixed, in the sense that a variety of verbal formulae can, with equal accuracy, be employed to state them. A judge's articulation of a rule in the course of a decision is but an explanation or approximation of the rule. An example will demonstrate this characteristic of legislation. The prohibition on 'drug pushing', contained in s 15(1) of the Misuse of Drugs Act 1977, is stated thus:

> Any person who has in his possession, whether lawfully or not, a controlled drug for the purpose of selling or otherwise supplying it to another in contravention of regulations under section 5 of this Act shall be guilty of an offence.

The section cannot be stated in any other verbal form and an alternative statement of the rule can only amount to an explanation of it. It should, however, be noted that the rule stated in s 15(1) also contains an unwritten element. It is sufficient to note at this stage that the common law defences of insanity and infancy apply to the offence. Thus 'any person' does not

17. See *Code of Advertising Standards for Ireland* (4th ed) and *Code of Sales Promotion Practice* (2nd ed) (Advertising Standards Authority for Ireland,1995).

include lunatics or children under the age of seven. This theme will be returned to later.[18]

[13.07] A second characteristic of legislation is that rules tend to be stated in a precise rather than a general form. This is not a universal characteristic and some legislative rules are stated in general terms. However, that does not detract from the general observation. Several factors contribute to this characteristic. The subject matter of many, if not most, statutes is such that detailed provisions are required; this is especially true of statutes dealing with economic and social matters. For instance, a tax statute, to be workable, must specify precisely the details of the tax which is to be levied. To state the subject matter in general terms would result in a degree of vagueness and doubt which could undermine the purposes of the tax. Moreover, the desire for certainty in the law, whereby those who are affected by it are in a position to know exactly that which is required of them and to plan their activities accordingly, contributes to the relative precision of statutes. Related to this is an attempt by the legislature to provide for every eventuality which might arise or, in other words, to cover all conceivable loopholes. A further factor is an element of mistrust of the judiciary on the part of the legislature. If judges could be fully trusted, in the sense that their decisions would accord with the legislative preference, legislators could compose statutes in more general terms, secure in the knowledge that the courts would decide doubtful cases in the desired manner. On the other hand, some statutes are expressed in comparatively general terms, leaving their detailed operation to be supplied by judicial interpretation. This is achieved by the use of open-ended phrases such as 'in the opinion of the court' or 'reasonable'. However, some recent statutes contain non-exhaustive lists of factors to be taken into account when evaluating such open-ended concepts.[19] A point which should be made is that legal provisions which are contained in legislation need not necessarily be stated in precise terms, the law maker being free to employ general terms. The degree of precision employed will depend largely on the subject matter of the statute.

---

18. See paras **[14.25]**.

19. Eg Sale of Goods and Supply of Services Act 1980, sch, sets out factors to be considered when determining whether a contract term is 'fair and reasonable'; Occupiers Liability Act 1995, s 4(2) enumerates factors to be considered when determining whether an occupier acted with 'reckless disregard'.

[2] Legislative Process

[13.08] A description of the rules and procedures which are followed by a law-making body in the enactment of primary legislation explains the legislative process in a formal sense. This embraces the constitutional and other provisions which govern the legislative task and, in the main, we are concerned with the parliamentary stage. However, the formal process is surrounded by informal procedures, practices and influences which are every bit as vital to the enactment of legislation as the formal mechanisms. It should be noted that, in practice, informal factors contribute so significantly to the enactment of legislation that they can be considered to be controlling. These factors are, of course, not expressed in the formal rules but are necessarily understood to provide the context in which they operate. At this stage it is sufficient to observe that the determination of the legislative programme (that is, the selection of proposals for enactment) is governed by concerns which exist beyond the formal process but which are accommodated by it.[20] Likewise, while the Oireachtas debates proposals and enacts legislation, the formulation of policy and its translation into legal form occurs elsewhere. Most statutes are drafted not by the Oireachtas or any of its members but by parliamentary draftsmen, officials of the Attorney General's office who are employed for that purpose. Thus, while the Oireachtas formally enacts a statute, its text is usually the handiwork of the draftsman.[21] An appreciation of the interaction between the formal and informal is necessary for an understanding of the legislative process. The formal rules establish the mechanism through which proposals, which derive from a variety of sources, become law.

Formal process: constitutional arrangements

[13.09] In Ireland the legislative organ established by the Constitution is the Oireachtas, which consists of two Houses and the President. Legislation is passed by both Houses of the Oireachtas, Dáil Eireann and Seanad Eireann, and is signed into law by the President. The relationship between the two Houses is regulated by the Constitution which preserves the supremacy of the Dáil, which is the popularly elected House. While primary legislation other than a Money Bill may be initiated in either House, when the Act-to-be is known as a 'Bill', the Dáil enjoys the power to overrule the Seanad. Where the Seanad rejects or amends a Bill which has been passed by the Dáil, Article 23 provides that the Dáil may pass a resolution within 180 days which deems the Bill to have passed through both Houses.[22] Moreover, if a

20. See paras **[13.27]-[13.32]**.

21. See paras **[13.33]-[13.36]**.

22. Article 23.1.1°.

Bill which was initiated in and passed by the Seanad is amended by the Dáil it is deemed to have been initiated in the Dáil, thus requiring fresh consideration by the Seanad. Article 23 has been invoked on two occasions only but this should not be taken to suggest that the Dáil's supremacy is thereby diluted or undermined. Its possible invocation is a constraint within which the Seanad operates and its mere existence has proved to be sufficient to ensure that the Seanad does not challenge the primacy of the lower House. The relative weakness of the Seanad is amplified in two further provisions. The first, contained in Article 21, is that Money Bills[23] may be initiated in the Dáil only and sent to the Seanad for 'recommendations.' The Seanad has a 21 day period in which to make its recommendations which then may be accepted or rejected by the Dáil. Echoing the injunction of 'no taxation without representation' this provision, of course, ensures that financial matters fall within the exclusive preserve of the popularly elected House. The second provision, in Article 24 provides a procedure for the abridgement of time allowed to the Seanad to consider a particular bill. The rather cumbersome procedure which involves an interplay of the Government, the Dáil and the President is set out in Article 24.1:

> If and whenever on the passage by Dáil Eireann of any Bill, other than a Bill expressed to be a Bill containing a proposal to amend the Constitution, the Taoiseach certifies by messages in writing to the President and the Chairman of each House of the Oireachtas that, in the opinion of the Government, the Bill is urgent and immediately necessary in the preservation of the public peace and security, or by reason of the existence of a public emergency, domestic or international, the time for the consideration of such Bill by Seanad Eireann shall, if Dáil Eireann so resolves and if the President, after consultation with the Council of State, concurs, be abridged, to such period as shall be specified in the resolution.

In effect, once Article 24 is invoked the Bill is deemed to have passed through both Houses on the expiration of the specified time. The nature of the emergency envisaged by Article 24 is not specified and one commentator has suggested that it 'is wide enough to encompass a nuclear attack or, at the other extreme, an outbreak of smallpox in one town'.[24] A

23. Article 22.1.1°: 'A Money Bill means a Bill which contains only provisions dealing with all or any of the following matters, namely, the imposition, repeal, remission, alteration or regulation of taxation; the imposition for the payment of debt or other financial purposes of charges on public moneys or the variation or repeal of any such charges; supply; the appropriation, receipt, custody, issue or audit of accounts of public money; the raising or guarantee of any loan or the repayment thereof; matters subordinate and integral to these matters or any of them.'

24. Morgan, *Constitutional Law of Ireland* 2nd ed (Round Hall Press, 1990) p 95; see also Hogan & Whyte, *Kelly's The Irish Constitution* 3rd ed (Butterworths, 1994) p 194.

Bill thus passed remains in force for 90 days only unless within that time it is extended for a further period by resolutions of the both Houses. In practice, the Seanad has tended to facilitate the speedy passage of urgent legislation and Article 24 has not been invoked to date.

[13.10] On its being passed by both Houses of the Oireachtas a Bill is presented to the President to be signed into law. In the ordinary course of events the Bill is signed between five and seven days of its being passed.[25] The President may sign the Bill earlier than the fifth day at the request of the Government and with the concurrence of the Seanad.[26] An Article 24 Bill must be signed by the President on the day it is presented to him or her for signature.[27] A Bill becomes law, that is an Act of the Oireachtas, on the day it is signed by the President, who is required to promulgate it by the publication of a notice that it has become law in *Iris Oifigiúil* (the *Official Gazette*).[28] A different procedure is established in relation to Bills containing a proposal to amend the Constitution. Such proposals must be submitted to a national referendum[29] pending which, of course, it may not be signed by the President. On its being approved by the people it must be signed 'forthwith' and 'duly promulgated' by the President.[30] The importance of bringing the passing of a law to the attention of the public need hardly be emphasised and the process is important to maintaining the rule of law.[31] A copy of the text of the Act signed by the President is enrolled for record in the office of the Registrar of the Supreme Court.[32] This latter measure is not merely a matter of exaggerated protocol. It formalises the record and in the unlikely event of a dispute arising as to the text of an Act (as opposed to its interpretation) the text thus enrolled is conclusive evidence of its provisions.

25. Article 25.2.1°.
26. Article 25.2.2°. The provision, somewhat strangely, makes no reference to the Dáil in this regard. The Seanad passed motions for early signature to facilitate the speedy enactment of the Insurance (No 2) Act 1983 and the Offences Against the State (Amendment) Act 1985 both of which were required as 'emergency' measures; see 102 *Seanad Debates* cols 218-259 and 107 *Seanad Debates* cols 362-364, respectively.
27. Article 25.3°.
28. Article 25.4.2°.
29. Article 46.2.
30. Article 46.5.
31. Different provisions exist for publicising the enactment of delegated legislation; see para **[13.62]**. One criticism of quasi-legislation (administrative rules and codes of practice, etc) is that it lacks a mechanism of formal publication and thus the public is likely to be left in ignorance of its existence and application.
32. Article 25.4.5°.

Article 26

[13.11] In two circumstances the President may decline to sign a Bill. Under Article 26 he or she may, after consultation with the Council of State, refer a Bill to the Supreme Court for a decision on its constitutionality.[33] Pending the decision of the Supreme Court, the Bill may not be signed. If the Court upholds the constitutionality of the Bill the President is required then to sign it into law, after which its validity may no longer be questioned. If the Court decides that any provision of the Bill is repugnant to the Constitution the President must decline to sign it into law. The value of Article 26 is that it provides a mechanism by which an advance ruling on the constitutionality of proposed legislation might be obtained. This can be a matter of some importance where the constitutionality of a proposed law has been questioned or where it is constitutionally or politically desirable to clarify doubts in advance of its being implemented. While the power has been exercised a number of times by different Presidents it is better that it is used sparingly, given its associated difficulties.[34] Once a law has passed scrutiny under Article 26 its constitutionality may not be further questioned in legal proceedings.[35]

Article 27

[13.12] Article 27 establishes a procedure under which the President may decline to sign a Bill, deemed under Article 23 to have passed through both Houses of the Oireachtas, which contains a proposal of 'national importance' until the will of the People has be sought. The purpose of the procedure is to allow the People the opportunity to veto a legislative proposal, rather than seeking their affirmative support for the measure. On being presented with a petition, signed by a majority of the Seanad and not less than one third of the Dáil, the President may, after consulting the Council of State, decline to sign the Bill until the popular will has been ascertained in one of two ways. The first is that the Bill is submitted to a national referendum, thus directly canvassing the view of the People on the matter. The second is that the Bill is passed by a resolution of the Dáil after a dissolution and re-assembly of the Dáil, thus indirectly discerning popular sentiment on the measure. In that case a general election will have been held at which it can be assumed that the proposal in question will have featured

33. Article 26 is considered more fully at paras **[5.65]-[5.68]**.

34. These include the abstract nature of Article 26 proceedings, the fact that invalidity of a minor provision will defeat the entire Bill and the immunity from further challenge enjoyed by Bills which pass scrutiny; see Casey, *Constitutional Law in Ireland* 2nd ed (Sweet & Maxwell, 1992) pp 267-271.

35. Article 34.3.3°.

prominently in the campaign. Alternatively it might be a matter of such indifference to the electorate that it does not consider it worthwhile vetoing the proposal by returning opposition members in sufficient numbers to the new Dáil. Article 27 is designed to redress the imbalance between the Dáil and the Seanad by providing a mechanism where the Dáil has overruled the Seanad. Underlying it is an assumption that the Government is in a minority position in the Seanad, a position which does not often arise in practice. Moreover, the Dáil has rarely found it necessary formally to overrule the Seanad under the provisions of Article 23 and, hence, it is not surprising that Article 27 has yet to be invoked.

Formal process: parliamentary procedure

[13.13] The internal workings of the Oireachtas are governed by the *Standing Orders of Dáil Eireann relative to Public Business* (1995) and the *Standing Orders of Seanad Eireann relative to Public Business* (1979).[36] The Standing Orders regulate, *inter alia*, the manner in which legislation is introduced and processed through the House. Although most Bills may be initiated by any member of either House, in the overwhelming majority of cases they are initiated in the Dáil by the Government Minister who has responsibility for the subject matter in question. In recent years, however, the Government has initiated a number of Bills in the Seanad, a measure necessitated by the demands placed on Dáil time. To this end members of the Government enjoy the right to attend and be heard in both Houses.[37] The passage of a Bill through the House occurs in five stages in the initiating House.[38] When it passes through that House it is sent to the other House where the first stage is ignored.

[13.14] At the *first stage* the Minister responsible obtains the permission of the House to circulate the Bill. At this stage the House will know little or nothing of the proposal and thus is unlikely to oppose the measure. As an alternative to this somewhat formal device, the Standing Orders of each House allow for the introduction of a Bill by way of presentment, rather than requiring the prior consent of the House. This right is confined to Ministers, Ministers of State, private members who are supported by seven TDs or five Senators, and the leader of the Seanad.

36. Hereafter DSO and SSO respectively. Their enactment is provided for by Article 15.10 of the Constitution.

37. Article 28.8.

38. See *Morgan, op cit* pp 97-103; Coakley & Gallagher (eds) *Politics in the Republic of Ireland* 2nd ed (PSAI Press, 1993) p 131; McGowan Smyth, *The Houses of the Oireachtas* 4th ed (Institute of Public Administration, 1979) pp 41-47.

[13.15] At the *second stage* the general provisions of the Bill are debated. The general philosophy and principles of the Bill are debated, rather than its particular provisions. The sponsoring Minister introduces the Bill, outlines its principal provisions and presents the Government's case for its being enacted into law. The spokesmen for the other parties speak in response to the Minister and may either support or oppose the proposal. Other members, from both sides of the House, frequently contribute at this stage, the number and duration of contributions having been agreed in advance by the whips, the parties' business managers. At this stage the House may reject the Bill in its entirety and the opposition is presented with the opportunity to defeat the measure, if it can muster sufficient support in the House. This rarely occurs in the case of Government Bills.

[13.16] At the *third*, or *committee, stage* the details of the Bill are debated section by section. At this stage the general principles of the Bill have been accepted and debate proceeds on that basis. The desirability or wisdom of the Bill cannot now be questioned. The committee goes through the Bill section by section and amendments to its provisions, which are consistent with its general principles, can be taken. Usually the entire House sits as a committee in which case, of course, it is unable to deal with other matters thus limiting the volume of parliamentary business which can be transacted. As an alternative, the Bill could be sent to either a special or a select committee, which consists of a number of members chosen on the basis of party representation in the House as a whole. A select committee, unlike a special committee, enjoys the power to send for persons, papers and records, which was thought not to be of any great use in legislative debates.[39] In practice therefore, a special committee is likely to be considered to be the more appropriate forum. Two principal advantages may be associated with using committees at the third stage: they will typically consist of members with a special interest or expertise in the subject matter and their use frees up parliamentary time to deal with other business. In the past decade parliamentary reform has acquired a greater prominence on the political agenda. This has resulted in the establishment of a somewhat more effective committee system. As yet, it has been the exception to refer legislation, as opposed to other parliamentary business, to a committee although with the establishment of a Joint Committee on Legislation and Security greater use can be expected. A gradual change is evident as can be seen from the parliamentary history of the Courts and Court Officers Act 1995. Crucial amendments, including the appointment of an additional High Court judge

39. But see Brooke, 'Special Public Bill Committees' [1995] PL 351 discussing an experiment in the UK parliament where committees could hear evidence and discuss submissions.

and the qualification of solicitors for judicial appointment, were introduced on the basis of a unanimous view of the Committee. This is a welcome development and it is to be hoped that the committee system will be strengthened by the operation of more assertive committees which display a greater independence of party managers. On completion of its deliberations the committee, of whatever type, reports to the House.

[13.17] The *fourth* stage is the *report stage* and its purpose is to review the work which has been conducted at the committee stage. Amendments may be made if they arise out of the committee proceedings. In practice it is not unusual for the Minister to undertake to consider suggested amendments at the third stage and to table them at the report stage. In the meantime the Minister has presumably consulted his civil servants and other advisors on the matter and, where the amendment is moved by the Minister, the draftsman.

[13.18] The *fifth* or *final stage* completes the process. Usually it is taken immediately after the fourth stage and is primarily a formal matter. Only verbal amendments are permissible at this stage. After all stages are completed typographical errors can be changed by order of the Clerk of the Dáil or Seanad.[40]

Private members' bills

[13.19] A Bill which is not sponsored by a Minister, Minister of State, the Attorney General or the leader of the Seanad is known as a *private members' bill*. With some slight variations it undergoes the same legislative process as that for Government sponsored bills. Each party may have one such Bill before the House at a given time, the second stage is limited to six hours and the Bill is sent to a special or select committee rather than a committee of the whole House. Otherwise private members' Bills are treated no differently to Government Bills. However, given the Government's domination of the Oireachtas until recently, there was little prospect of a private members' Bill being enacted. There is no tradition of members of the Government parties introducing such legislation and Government parties have tended at the second stage to vote down a private members' Bill which is initiated by opposition members. Nevertheless, the initiation of a private members' Bill can serve to focus public and political attention on a particular topic and the device is sometimes resorted to with that purpose in mind rather than in the anticipation that it might be enacted. Moreover, in some instances the Government, despite voting against an opposition sponsored bill, might be

40. DSO 109; SSO 100.

forced into introducing its own legislation on the matter in question. And, of course, on rare occasions a private members' Bill might be successfully steered through the Oireachtas and become law. This has become somewhat more common in recent years. One important measure, the Judicial Separation and Family Law Reform Act 1989, was introduced as a private members' Bill sponsored by Alan Shatter TD, then an opposition backbencher. Its success was no doubt aided by the fact that at the time the Government was in a minority position in the Dáil and could not be assured of sufficient support to ensure its defeat. The Landlord and Tenant (Amendment) Act 1994 was also introduced as a private members' Bill, again sponsored by Deputy Shatter.

[13.20] A Bill which has not passed through both Houses before a general election lapses. However, after the election the House may pass a resolution which restores the Bill to the Order Paper and it commences in the re-convened House at the stage it had reached before the election. In this way the House has the option of restoring a Bill which was before it prior to the election and is likely to be invoked where the Bill was uncontroversial and enjoyed general cross-party support. This device allows the Oireachtas to keep 'alive' bills which would otherwise have terminated and it saves parliamentary time by avoiding the necessity of repeating the stages which had been successfully completed prior to the election.

[13.21] The five stage process outlined above is adopted in relation to public general Acts which, of course, count for the bulk of legislation. Somewhat different procedures are adopted in relation to consolidation legislation and private legislation.

Consolidation legislation

[13.22] A consolidation Act is one which re-enacts in one instrument all the statute law on a particular topic. Its purpose is not to alter the law but to collate it in one statute. An abbreviated procedure is adopted to facilitate the passage of such legislation. Three conditions must be satisfied for a proposal to be considered to be a consolidation measure: (i) it must declare in its long title that its purpose is to consolidate the law; (ii) the Attorney General must certify that this is the purpose of the legislation; (iii) notice of intention to introduce the Bill must be accompanied by a memorandum which sets out the legislation which is repealed by it and the sections of the Bill in which the law is reproduced. Once these conditions are met, the procedure which is followed differs in several respects from that which is adopted generally. Minimum time limits between the stages are specified. The only amendment permissible at the second stage is one which states a reason for challenging the Attorney General's certificate. In other words, the opposition is confined to questioning whether the Bill is in fact a consolidation measure. With the consent of both Houses the third stage is heard by the Oireachtas Joint Committee on Legislation. The only amendments which are permissible are those which remove ambiguity or bring the Bill into conformity with existing law. Once the Bill has passed through the initiating House it proceeds to the fourth stage in the other House.

Private legislation[41]

[13.23] Private Bills are subjected to a significantly different procedure which is partially judicial in character, reflecting the fact the such legislation principally affects individual rights and interests. Their origin lies in the medieval practice of petitioning the King for some special privilege or dispensation which he granted in the form of a statute.[42] Nowadays petitions are brought on the basis that the legislation is necessary to ameliorate an individual set of circumstances which is not adequately provided for by existing statute and common law. Until the end of the eighteenth century private legislation occupied a considerable portion of parliamentary time and during the nineteenth century was the preferred instrument to deal with, for instance, the provision of public utilities and transport. The eclectic range of matters which have been the subject of private legislation since the foundation of the State include public utilities,[43] harbours,[44] railways,[45] the Bank of Ireland,[46] the Methodist Church,[47] a sports field in Bagnalstown, Co Carlow,[48] the affairs of private institutions[49] and individual property settlements.[50] Another species of private legislation, known as a *Provisional Order Confirmation Bill*, is enacted to confirm provisional orders which

41. See generally Morgan, *op cit* pp 103-104; McGowan Smyth, *The Theory and Practice of the Irish Senate* (Institute of Public Administration, 1972) pp 70-80.
42. See McDonald, *Parliament at Work* (Methuen, 1989) pp 178-180.
43. Eg Sligo Lighting and Electric Power Act 1924.
44. Eg Dundalk Harbour and Port Act 1925; Limerick Harbour Act 1926; Cork Harbour Act 1933; Galway Harbour Act 1935.
45. Eg Dublin United Tramways (Lucan Electric Railway) Act 1927; Limerick Harbour Tramways Act 1931.
46. Bank of Ireland Act 1929; Bank of Ireland Act 1935.
47. Methodist Church in Ireland Act 1928.
48. Daniel McGrath Foundation Act 1945.
49. Eg Erasmus Smith Schools Act 1938; Convalescent Home Stillorgan (Charter Amendment) Act 1958; Royal College of Surgeons in Ireland (Charter Amendment) Act 1965; Institute of Chartered Accountants in Ireland (Charter Amendment) Act 1966; Royal College of Physicians of Ireland (Charter and Letters Patent Amendment) Act 1979.
50. Eg Poë Name and Arms (Compton Domvile Estates) Act 1936; The Altamont (Amendment of Deed of Trust) Act 1993.

have been made under statute by a Minister at the behest of a local authority or statutory body. Most commonly these measures have involved the extension of city boundaries[51] or matters relating to harbours.[52]

[13.24] Private Bills are introduced in the Seanad at the initiative of a promoter who appears before the House as a suitor. The process is governed by the *Standing Orders of the Dáil and the Seanad relative to Private Business* and is supervised by the Examiner of Private Bills, an official of the Oireachtas jointly appointed by the Ceann Comhairle and Cathaoirleach of the Seanad, to ensure compliance therewith. Notice of the Bill setting out its principal subject matter must be published in newspapers and a copy of the Bill must be deposited for inspection in the Private Bill Office of the Houses of the Oireachtas, the purpose being to bring the proposal to the attention of those who might in some way be affected by it. Those who believe that their interests are affected by the legislation may be admitted as adverse parties to contest the proposal. The parties are represented by a parliamentary agent and counsel. When the Examiner of Private Bills has reported compliance with Standing Orders or where they have been dispensed with by both Houses the Bill is deemed to have passed the first stage in the Seanad. The second stage reading in the Seanad is usually something of a formality since there is a general reluctance to reject a measure of this nature without a full consideration of its merits.

[13.25] After the second stage reading in the Seanad the Bill is referred for the third stage to a joint committee consisting of members of both Houses. At this stage the judicial character of the process is evident in the composition of the joint committee, the nature of the proceedings and the onus which is placed on the promoter to establish the necessity and justification for the measure. The joint committee consists of three members from each House and a Chairman, who may be a member of either House. Members must sign a declaration that they, and in the case of TDs their constituents, have no personal interest in the Bill; moreover, they must also declare that they will not vote on any issue without having attended and heard the relevant evidence. (In contrast, neither undertaking is expected in the case of public legislation.) The joint committee, being a select committee, has the power to call witnesses and hear evidence. It hears counsel for both the promoters and objectors and considers submissions put to it by relevant Government departments. In essence, the promoter is

51. Eg Local Government and Public Health Provisional Order Confirmation Act 1953 confirming City of Dublin (Extension of Boundaries) Order 1953.

52. Eg Pier and Harbour Provisional Order Confirmation Act 1932 confirming Limerick Harbour Order 1932.

required to establish a case for the proposed legislation with those opposed being given the opportunity to contest the case. The facts on which the promoter seeks the legislation and the reasons for it must be set out in the preamble to the Bill. When the preamble has been proved the parties withdraw and the committee continues to consider the Bill section by section in the normal manner. The committee reports back, with or without amendment, to both Houses. The fourth and fifth stages follow in the Seanad, after which it is sent for consideration to the Dáil where first three stages are waived.

[13.26] Resorting to private legislation as a means to remedy individual cases can prove to be both time-consuming and expensive. While this might prove to be irritating and cumbersome for corporate bodies it assumes a greater significance for individuals whose affairs have to be settled by this mechanism. The enactment of The Altamont (Amendment of Deed of Trust) Act 1993 was necessary to allow certain amendments to be made to a trust which was established in respect of Lord Altamont's properties. It was introduced as a Bill in 1990 and did not become law until 1993. In the interim the promoter, and no doubt his family, were left in a state of some uncertainty - anticipated dealings with his property would have to be postponed. The cost of private legislation is usually borne by the promoter and thus it is largely the preserve of the wealthy. Nevertheless, private legislation is the only mechanism by which certain legal instruments, such as deeds of trust and charters, may be altered and unless general legislation which provides an alternative mechanism is enacted recourse thereto will prove necessary.[53]

Informal process

[13.27] The preceding sections have concentrated on the formal rules and practices which govern the legislative process. They focused on the constitutional and legal parameters within which the process is constrained. However that only presents part of the picture and the process operates in the context of informal practices, conventions and understandings which are at least as important in shaping the enactment of legislation. The day-to-day operation of the legislature, the selection of legislative priorities and the adoption and implementation of a legislative programme are governed by factors which exist and function beyond the formal constitutional conventions. To this extent we find ourselves in the political realm and our inquiry takes into an area of overlap between law and political science.

53. In this regard see the remarks of Sen O'Toole 134 *Seanad Debates* col 1127.

Nevertheless, an understanding of the legislative process would be incomplete without alluding to these extra-legal factors.[54]

[13.28] The almost complete control exercised by the Government over the business of the Oireachtas has already been noted. The Government is usually assured of the support of a majority in the Dáil - either the Government parties enjoy an absolute majority or the Government has enlisted the support of a sufficient number of independent members to allow it to function. This, coupled with the Taoiseach's power to nominate 11 members to the Seanad (out of a total complement of 60), ensures that the Government will rarely be defeated on a vote in either House. The Government's numerical strength is reinforced by a relative lack of independence amongst backbenchers. The latter is the product of an amalgam of factors - a highly inflexible system of party discipline from which members rarely deviate, the political ambitions of members who aspire to promotion to Government in the future, a general unwillingness to 'rock the boat' and the direction of members' energies to other tasks, especially constituency work. In addition, the adversarial culture of our political system has tended to assign a confrontational role to the opposition. Politics is perceived as being concerned with the acquisition and exercise of power and the conventions by which it operates are almost pugilistic. On this view defeating the other side, or at least dealing it a body blow, is as important as influencing the enactment of legislation. It follows that active participation by the Oireachtas in formulating the legislative programme is almost non-existent and even the role it plays in scrutinising Government proposals is slight. Nowhere is the relative weakness of the Oireachtas more evident than in the paucity of private members' Bills which have been enacted. The enactment of the Judicial Separation and Family Law Reform Act 1989 was exceptional and owed its success to a combination of the tenacity of the sponsoring member and the fact that the Government, being in a minority position in the Dáil, was reluctant to take the political risk of opposing the measure outright. The previous private members' Bill to be successful was in 1965[55] and in the history of the State fewer than 20 such measures have been enacted. It is difficult to disagree with the observation that the Oireachtas has proved itself to be 'sadly ineffective'[56] in making laws. In the past few years gradual change is evident in the enactment of a private members' proposal, the Landlord and Tenant (Amendment) Act

---

54. See generally Chubb, *The Government and Politics of Ireland* 3rd ed (Longman, 1992) Chs 9-11; Coakley & Gallagher (eds) *Politics in the Republic of Ireland* 2nd ed (PSAI Press, 1993) Ch 7.

55. Protection of Animals (Amendment) Act 1965.

56. Chubb, *op cit* p 199.

1994, and the influence wielded by the Joint Committee on Legislation and Security in the passage of the Court and Court Officers Act 1995.[57] These efforts might prove to be a basis for the adoption of a more assertive legislative role by the Oireachtas and are to be welcomed but it remains to be seen whether they will be maintained in the future.

[13.29] Although the role the Oireachtas plays in formulating legislation is slight it would be a mistake to conclude that it exists merely to rubber stamp proposals which are presented to it by the Government. While the Government dominates the Oireachtas and dictates its business the relationship between the two is more subtle than might first appear. In practical political terms the requirement of presenting legislation before and steering it through the Oireachtas imposes a discipline on the Government. As a minimum it must ensure that a proposal secures the assent, or at least avoids the dissent, of its own supporters. This process, of course, does not occur on the floor of the House where it is exposed to the glare of publicity but in the privacy of the party meeting. Nevertheless, it acts as a negative check in the sense that a measure which is unacceptable will not be initiated. In this regard the Government's supporters are presented with the opportunity to filter or modify proposals before they are formally initiated in the Oireachtas. Once the Bill is initiated party ranks usually close but still the (admittedly slight) possibility exists that the Government will withdraw or amend a proposal in the light of opposition which it attracts. In that circumstance the Government's action might well be motivated by a concern to maintain its popularity with the electorate rather than by a fear of parliamentary defeat or a re-evaluation of the merits of the proposal. The significant point is that the Oireachtas becomes the forum in which the measure is brought to public attention and acts as a catalyst for wider debate. But even where a measure passes through the Oireachtas in the usual manner the debates on the Bill might later prove to be significant in interpreting the law.[58] The role of the Oireachtas is also significant in that its procedures formalise the process of law-making. This is not simply to engage in an arcane ritual or a piece of constitutional theatre. It both legitimates that which it produces and facilitates its recognition as law. Legislation is identified and assured the force of law by its having under-gone the process of enactment by the Oireachtas. In contrast, other instruments which seek to regulate, such as Ministerial circulars, lack that status and the accompanying force of law because they have not been subject to that process. In short, the

57. See paras **[13.16]** and **[13.19]**.
58. See paras **[14.88]-[14.95]**.

process of enactment by the Oireachtas, in accordance with the governing constitutional formula, distinguishes legal from non-legal measures.

Sources of and influences on legislation

[13.30] Apart from the annual enactment of a Finance Act and an Appropriation Act, giving effect to the budget and allocating Government expenditure respectively, the selection of measures to be included in the legislative programme is primarily a matter for the Government. It decides which proposals will be presented to the Oireachtas for enactment and the priority to be accorded to each. This is largely a matter of political choice but it will have been preceded by a complex policy making process which acts as a constraint within which the choice is exercised. Legislative proposals derive from a variety of sources which include the policies of the party in Government, bargaining between parties which make up a coalition Government, negotiation with the social partners and lobbying by a myriad of interest groups representing different sectors of society. The workings of the process and the manner in which the various participants interact and compete are primarily of interest to political scientists and students of policy making.[59] While the outcome of this process, legislation, is of interest to lawyers its operation is of less obvious interest. Nevertheless, events which precede and influence the enactment of a measure might prove to be important when it comes to the lawyer's task of statutory interpretation. In this regard a number of documents are relevant, in that they might assist in identifying the purpose of the legislation or the intent with which it was enacted.

[13.31] The relative weakness of the Oireachtas does not mean that the parliamentary debates on a measure are irrelevant and should be ignored. While the Government might be assured that a Bill will pass through the Oireachtas with relative ease the discipline of debate forces the Minister to justify the measure and to explain what it seeks to achieve. Thus, the legislative proceedings as reported in the *Dáil Debates* and *Seanad Debates* might merit scrutiny. In addition, many bills are published with an accompanying *explanatory memorandum* which briefly explains the reasons behind the proposal. Prior to initiating a Bill the Government might publish a *Green Paper* or *White Paper* on the subject. This follows the British practice of issuing such documents, which are consultative in nature, but the distinction between the two is unclear.[60] A green paper is somewhat more

59. See eg Chubb, *op cit* Ch 9; Coakley & Gallagher, *op cit* Ch 10.

60. See Sandford, 'Open Government: the Use of Green Papers' [1980] British Tax Review 351; Jordan, 'Grey Papers'(1977) 48 Political Quarterly 30.

discursive in that sets out various ideas and approaches without committing the Government to any particular course of action. A white paper tends to be more definitive in that it typically sets out a clear Governmental view on the matter.

[13.32] While the Government enjoys a near monopoly in selecting the contents of the legislative programme, particular proposals might owe their origin to the deliberations and activities of non-Governmental bodies. The Law Reform Commission[61] is charged with examining various areas of the law with a view to their reform. Its reports will typically set out the existing law, identify its deficiencies, examine alternative approaches, compare the law of other jurisdictions and make the recommendations it considers to be appropriate.[62] Indeed the Commission has adopted the practice of appending a draft Bill to its more recent reports. From time to time ad hoc committees are established to examine a particular topic and report to the Government, the Dáil or the Oireachtas. The composition of such bodies is usually representative of the various interests which are affected by the topic in question and their deliberations often result in recommendations for legislation.[63] An alternative is to nominate an individual, often a judge, to report on a topic again with a view to recommending improvements. In some instances the report of a Tribunal of Inquiry established under the Tribunals of Inquiry Acts 1921 and 1979 might contain recommendations for legislation. Legislation might also derive from the State's international obligations whether they be contained in a treaty[64] which are frequently accompanied by preparatory documents (*travaux préparatoires*) or result from a judicial decision which must be incorporated into domestic law.[65] In

61. See further paras **[11.09]-[11.11]**.

62. Eg The Statute of Limitations (Amendment) Act 1991 had its origin in the Commission's *Report on the Statute of Limitations: Claims in respect of latent personal injuries* (LRC 21-1987); the Larceny Act 1990 enacted some, but not all, of the recommendations of the *Report on Receiving Stolen Property* (LRC 23-1989).

63. Eg *Report of the Commission of Inquiry on Safety, Health and Welfare at Work* (Pl 1868) published in 1983 led to the enactment of the Safety, Health and Welfare at Work Act 1989. The provisions of the Criminal Justice (Public Order) Act 1994, ss 20-22 derive in the main from the recommendations in the *Report of the Committee on Public Safety and Crowd Control* (Pl 7107). On the other hand the recommendations in the *Report of the Committee to Enquire into Certain Aspects of Criminal Procedure* were only partially enacted in the Criminal Procedure Act 1993.

64. Eg Geneva Conventions Act 1962 giving effect to the conventions on prisoners of war etc; Genocide Act 1973, based on the UN Genocide Convention; Part II of the Extradition Act 1965, based on European Convention on Extradition.

65. In consequence of the decision of the European Court of Human Rights in *Norris v Ireland* (1988) 13 EHRR 186 male homosexual conduct was decriminalised by the Criminal Law (Sexual Offences) Act 1993.

recent years a large volume of legislation has resulted from obligations which have accrued from membership of the European Communities.[66] Much of the foregoing suggests that a desirable and welcome element of deliberation precedes legislation. In some cases, however, legislation is dictated by unanticipated events which require immediate attention. In the past security and economic matters have necessitated the speedy introduction of legislation and in some cases legislation has been enacted in less than 24 hours.[67] Judicial decisions can also prove to be the source of unforeseen difficulties which require legislative redress.[68]

Drafting of legislation[69]

[13.33] Given the Government's virtual monopoly over the legislative programme, individual proposals for legislation are formulated by the various Departments of State and are presented by the relevant Minister to the Government for approval. By this time the advice of the Attorney General will usually have been obtained. Once a proposal has secured Government approval and is scheduled on its legislative programme the Bill which is to be initiated in the Oireachtas must be drafted. That task is undertaken by the Office of the Parliamentary Draftsmen which is attached to that of the Attorney General. The Office employs a number of parliamentary draftsmen, barristers or solicitors of four years' standing who specialise in the art of legislative drafting. The protocol involved in securing the drafting of a measure is described succinctly by one parliamentary draftsman:[70]

> "The decision to introduce legislation is made on foot of a document known as a 'Memorandum for Government'. The Memorandum sets out in detail the background to the Bill and the view of the Ministers concerned

66. See further para **[16.154]**.

67. The Insurance (No 2) Act 1983 was enacted to deal with the impending collapse of a major insurance company. The Offences Against the State (Amendment) Act 1985 was enacted to provide the Government with the power to 'freeze' bank accounts which were suspected to contain terrorist funds. Both were passed in the space of a few hours; in both cases the opposition facilitated the enactment of the measure - see 345 *Dáil Debates* cols 189-190 and 356 *Dáil Debates* col 138 respectively. The Seanad did not impede the Bills' progress.

68. Eg the Solicitors (Amendment) Act 1960 which was enacted in consequence of *In Re Solicitors Act 1954* [1960] IR 239. The Building Societies (Amendment) Act 1983 was enacted to deal with an anomaly which resulted from the decision of the High Court in *Rafferty v Crowley* [1984] ILRM 350; in fact the trial judge had anticipated the likelihood of legislation and directed that a copy of his judgment be sent immediately to the relevant Minister.

69. See Donelan, 'The Role of the Parliamentary Draftsman in the Preparation of Legislation in Ireland' (1992) 14 DULJ 1.

70. *Ibid* at 3.

> with the bill. The Memorandum includes an outline draft of the Bill prepared by the civil servants in the department concerned with promoting the bill. This draft is known in Ireland as 'heads'."

Once a decision has been taken by the Government approving the 'heads' (with or without qualification), the Secretary of the Government sends the Attorney General a note of the decision. A letter requesting that the parliamentary draftsman be directed to draft legislation in accordance with the Memorandum and the 'heads' is sent by the Department concerned to the Attorney General. A draftsman is then nominated to draft the bill.

[13.34] In this manner the draftsman is instructed as to the contents and objectives of the proposed legislation and he or she, in effect, converts those instructions into a legally intelligible form. In the course of drafting the draftsman is likely to liaise with the civil servants who are involved in promoting the Bill as well as lawyers on the advisory side of the Attorney General's office. It is also possible that the Attorney General's advice will be sought on particular difficulties which were not foreseen when the measure was presented to Government.

[13.35] A cardinal feature of the drafting process is its centralised nature. Those who have been involved in the determination and development of the policy are not directly engaged in the drafting of the law which is to implement it although, as stated, liaison between them and the draftsman is likely to occur. Nevertheless, the point is that the drafting of the law is transferred from the Department which sponsors the legislation to the parliamentary draftsman. This might be justified on the basis that it brings uniformity to the process and ensures that laws are drafted in a standard format, style and language.[71] On this view it is better to employ a 'house style' than to have a different style for each sponsoring department. Moreover, it is argued that drafting is a specialist art, or indeed science, for which few possess the aptitude and which requires considerable experience to perfect. As one writer put it:[72]

> "What makes a good legislative draftsman is a good basic legal knowledge, a feeling for the proper use of the English language, a critical ability, lots of imagination and plenty of practice. Experience has shown that general legal ability by itself is not sufficient and that a competent lawyer without practical experience in legislative draftsmanship cannot perform the craft satisfactorily."

---

71. In some jurisdictions the matter is institutionalised through the adoption of formal guidelines for the draftsman.

72. Kolts, 'Observations on the Proposed New Approach to Legislative Drafting in Common Law Countries' [1980] Stat LR 144.

[13.36] The amount of experience which is believed to be necessary is uncertain with estimates varying from five to ten years. However, most legislative draftsmen will endorse the view that experience and practice at the task are essential to successful draftsmanship. On the other hand it might be argued that the assignment of the function of drafting to specialists is itself the source of many of the problems associated with the quality of legislation. In particular, it is said that it has resulted in legislation which is opaque, complex and overly elaborate where clarity and simplicity, would better serve the public.[73]

[3] LEGISLATIVE PRODUCT

The format of statutes

[13.37] The format of statutes is governed by a combination of constitutional and statutory provisions and conventional practices. Most Bills are introduced and passed in the English language, bilingual and Irish language Bills being rare exceptions. Article 25.4.4° requires that an official translation of laws be provided.[74] When published and made generally available Acts should appear in both languages with the respective texts printed side by side. In fact, matters are somewhat in arrears with the most recent bi-lingual volume of statutes being published in 1981.

[13.38] A statute has a *short title*, by which it is generally known and cited, and a *statutory number*.[75] For instance, the Misuse of Drugs Act 1977 is the short title, its statutory number being Number 12 of 1977. A statute also has a *long title* which appears at the head of the document in which it is contained. The long title of the Misuse of Drugs Act 1977 is:

> AN ACT TO PREVENT THE MISUSE OF CERTAIN DANGEROUS OR OTHERWISE HARMFUL DRUGS, TO ENABLE THE MINISTER FOR HEALTH TO MAKE FOR THAT PURPOSE CERTAIN REGULATIONS IN RELATION TO SUCH DRUGS, TO ENABLE THAT MINISTER TO PROVIDE THAT CERTAIN SUBSTANCES SHALL BE POISONS FOR THE PURPOSES OF THE PHARMACY ACTS, 1875 TO 1962, TO AMEND THE PHARMACOPOEIA ACT 1931, THE POISONS ACT 1961, THE PHARMACY ACT 1962, AND THE HEALTH ACTS 1947 TO 1970, TO REPEAL THE DANGEROUS DRUGS ACT 1934 AND SECTION 78 OF THE HEALTH ACT 1970 AND TO MAKE CERTAIN OTHER PROVISIONS IN RELATION TO THE FOREGOING. [*16th May 1977*]

---

73. See para **[13.54]**.
74. Article 25.4.4°: 'Where the President signs the text of a Bill in one only of the official languages, an official translation shall be issued in the other official language.' See para **[15.34]**.
75. See Interpretation Act 1937, s 7(1).

The long title states in very general terms the purpose and objectives of the statute. In the example given it can be seen that the object is to deal with dangerous and harmful drugs, to provide the Minister for Health with the power to make regulations on the matter and to amend various earlier statutes accordingly.

[13.39] In the past it was the practice to include a *preamble* which appeared after the long title, but before the main body of the Act. The preamble would typically recite the factual assumptions on which the legislation was based. The preamble to the Criminal Law (Ireland) Act 1828 reads:

> Whereas it is expedient, with a View to improve the Administration of Justice in Criminal Cases in Ireland, to define in what Circumstances Persons may be admitted to Bail in cases of Felony; and to make better Provision for taking Examinations, Informations, Bailments, and Recognizances, and returning the same to the proper Tribunals; and to relax in some Instances the technical Strictness of Criminal Proceedings, so as to ensure the Punishment of the Guilty without depriving the Accused of any just Means of Defence; and to abolish the Benefit of Clergy and some Matters of Form which impede the due Administration of Justice; and to make better Provision for the Punishment of Offenders in certain Cases.

[13.40] A number of Acts of the Oireachtas which were passed in 1922, 1923 and 1924 contain a preamble but the practice has been abandoned in the case of public Acts, as more extensive long titles tend to recite the statutory purpose.[76] Preambles are still included in private Acts. In that case the preamble recites the facts which the supporter of the Bill seeks to establish and which are found to be proved by the joint committee which conducts the third reading.[77] Preambles to private statutes can be lengthy and often exceed the actual text of the statute. For instance the Poë Name and Arms (Compton Domvile Estates) Act 1936, which contains two brief sections consisting of seven lines of text,[78] is preceded by a five page

76. See Thornton, *Legislative Drafting* 3rd ed (Butterworths, 1987) p 154. Preambles are commonplace in civil law jurisdictions and often precede European Community Directives. A recent measure which contains a preamble is the European Communities (Unfair Terms in Consumer Contracts) Regulations 1995 (SI 27/1995).

77. See para **[13.25]**.

78. The Act reads:

> '1. From and after the passing of this Act and thenceforward continuously the Name and Arms of the said Sir Hugo Compton Domvile Poë to be borne and used by him shall as regards the Name be Hugo Compton Domvile Poë Domvile and as regards the Arms be the Arms of Domvile quartered on the Arms of Poë.
>
> 2. This Act may be cited as the Poë Name and Arms (Compton Domvile Estates) Act 1936.'

preamble setting out the factual background which the sponsors were required to prove.

Dates of commencement

[13.41] The date which appears at the conclusion of the long title is that on which the Bill as passed by both Houses of the Oireachtas was signed into law by the President. Thus, the Misuse of Drugs Act 1977 became law on 16 May 1977. However, it should be noted that a statute might not come into effect until a later date, which is called the *date of commencement*. A statute which contains no provision concerning its commencement comes into force immediately.[79] For several reasons, however, it might be preferred to delay the commencement of a statute and one of a variety of devices might be employed in this regard. The commencement date might be stated expressly in the statute or the statute might give the Government or a particular Minister power to make an order bringing the Act into force at any time, or within a stated time, or not before a stated time. An increasingly common formula is to provide that the Act is to come into force a specified time (often one month) after its being passed.[80] On the other hand s 43(2) of the Misuse of Drugs Act 1977 deals with its commencement thus:

> Subsection 1 of this section and section 41(2) of this Act shall come into operation on the passing hereof and the other purposes and provisions shall come into operation on such day or days as may be fixed therefor by any order or orders of the Minister [for Health] either generally or with reference to any particular such purpose or provision and different days may be so fixed for different such purposes and different such provisions of this Act.

[13.42] Thus, with the exceptions of s 41(2) and s 43(1) which came into force immediately, the effective operation of the Act was delayed until the appropriate order was made by the Minister. Moreover, the Minister was given power to bring either the whole Act or selected parts thereof into operation at a later date. The Act was eventually brought into operation by the Misuse of Drugs Act 1977 (Commencement) Order 1979.[81] A variant on the formula used in the Misuse of Drugs Act 1977 is contained in s 2 of the Succession Act 1965 which deals with the commencement of that Act thus:

> This Act shall come into effect on such day, not earlier than the 1st day of July 1966, as the Minister [for Justice] by order appoints.

---

79. Article 25.4.1°.

80. Eg Criminal Justice (Public Order) Act 1994, s 1(3).

81. SI 28/1979.

[13.43] In this case the Minister was given power to bring the entire Act into force, but not before the specified date. That Act was brought into effect by the Succession Act 1965 (Commencement) Order 1966.[82] One reason for delegating the power to order the commencement of an Act to a Minister is to allow the necessary financial and administrative changes to be made before the legislation is brought into force. It should be noted that in both examples the respective Ministers were conferred with a power to bring the Act into force but were not expressly obliged to do so. In this context the decision of the Supreme Court in *The State (Sheehan) v The Government of Ireland*[83] is instructive. Section 60(1) of the Civil Liability Act 1961 makes local authorities liable for injuries suffered through their failure adequately to maintain public roads. However, s 60(7) provides that the section 'shall come into operation on such day, not earlier than the 1st day of April 1967, as may be fixed therefor by order made by the Government'. At the time of the proceedings no such order had been made and the prosecutor sought an order of mandamus directing the Government so to order. In rejecting his claim the Court noted that the wording of the section is enabling, or permissive, not mandatory. The only limit imposed was that the provision could not come into effect before the specified date and the Government's discretion is not otherwise fettered. The absence of limiting words such as 'as soon as convenient' or 'as soon as may be' confirmed the Court's view that the power is unlimited. The view of the majority was expressed by Henchy J:[84]

> "The uses of 'shall' and 'may', both in the sub-section and the section as a whole, point to the conclusion that the radical law-reform embodied in the section was intended not to come into effect before the 1st April 1967, and thereafter only on such day as *may* be fixed by an order made by the Government. Not, be it noted, on such date as *shall* be fixed by the Government. Limiting words such as 'as soon as may be' or 'as soon as convenient', which are to be found in comparable statutory provisions, are markedly absent. If the true reading of s 60, sub-s 7 were to the effect that the Government were bound to bring the section into operation, it would, of course, be unconstitutional for the Government to achieve by their prolonged inactivity the virtual repeal of the section.
>
> In my opinion, however, s 60, sub-s 7 by vesting the power of bringing the section into operation in the Government rather than in a particular Minister, and the wording used, connoting an enabling rather than a mandatory power or discretion, would seem to point to the parliamentary

82. SI 168/1966.

83. [1987] IR 550.

84. *Ibid* at 561 (emphasis in original).

> recognition of the fact that the important law-reform to be effected by the section was not to take effect unless and until the Government became satisfied that, in the light of factors such as the necessary deployment of financial and other resources, the postulated reform could be carried into effect. The discretion vested in the Government to bring the section into operation on a date after the 1st April 1967, was not limited in any way, as to time or otherwise."

[13.44] The question of the courts' power to direct a Minister to make an order for the commencement of a statutory provision arose again in *Rooney v Minister for Agriculture and Food.*[85] The plaintiff's cattle which were affected with bovine tuberculosis were slaughtered. He was offered compensation assessed on the basis of a non-statutory scheme which was administered by the defendant. At the time the relevant compensation provisions contained in the Diseases of Animals Act 1966 had not been brought into effect. The plaintiff argued that the defendant ought to have brought those provisions into effect rather than administer the non-statutory scheme which provided a less generous quantum of compensation. It was contended on the Minister's behalf that the non-statutory scheme provided a better safeguard of public funds and that it would be more expensive to implement the statutory scheme. O'Flaherty J spoke for a unanimous Supreme Court:[86]

> "I need only look at the provisions as regards the various steps that would have to be taken if s 20 and s 58 were in operation to realise that it would be vastly more expensive than the scheme which is at present in operation and no one has ever suggested that that, itself, ever represented anything but a huge cost to the exchequer …
>
> The court would be entitled to review such a decision [that is, not to implement the statutory scheme] and course of action (embodied in the scheme) if it were satisfied that the decision and course of conduct was *mala fides* - or, at the least, that it involved an abuse of power: see *Pine Valley Developments v Minister for the Environment.*[87] It may be that the court has no power to enjoin the Minister to make orders under s 20 (*cf The State (Sheehan) v Government of Ireland*)[88] in any circumstances but it certainly has no power to do so in the absence of proof of *mala fides* or abuse of power ... I hold that the Minister is not obliged to operate [the Act] since he has in place a reasonable scheme for providing a measure of assistance to herd-owners of diseased cattle. That it is not the ideal scheme that the plaintiff would wish to see in place is neither here nor there."

85. [1991] 2 IR 539.
86. *Ibid*, at 546.
87. [1987] IR 23.
88. [1987] IR 550.

[13.45] In *Rooney*, unlike *Sheehan*, what many would consider to be an acceptable policy reason, namely controlling public expenditure, was advanced for the non-implementation of the relevant provision. In this context it should be noted that in *Sheehan* Finlay CJ and Griffin J reserved their opinions on the question whether a court could direct the making of a commencement order where the implementation of the legislation would impose a burden on the public finances. *Rooney* differs somewhat in emphasis from *Sheehan* in that the court acknowledged the possibility that the implementation of a statute might be ordered by the courts. However, the circumstances in which judicial intervention might be successfully sought are exceedingly rare and a plaintiff would bear a great burden of proof. In practice, it is unlikely that unless express limits are imposed on the power to order the commencement of an Act the person or body so empowered would not be compelled to bring the statute into force. This, in effect, would allow a Minister to postpone indefinitely the implementation of Acts passed by the Oireachtas, subject only to the infrequently invoked device of parliamentary accountability. The commencement of both individual provisions, as evidenced in *Sheehan* and *Rooney*, and entire statutes has been delayed in this fashion. The Health (Mental Services) Act 1981 has yet to be brought into operation and as matters currently stand it is probable that it will be superseded by new legislation without its ever having been brought into effect.[89]

Internal organisation of statutes

[13.46] Provision is made for the internal organisation of statutes by the Interpretation Act 1937. Under s 6(2) an Act is divided into consecutively numbered *sections*, and a section may be further subdivided. In practice *sub-sections*, *paragraphs* and *sub-paragraphs* are the principal subdivisions employed. In general, a section deals with one point while sub-sections elaborate on or supplement the main point of the section. Section 6(3) of the same Act allows for the grouping of sections into consecutively numbered *parts* or *chapters*. Division into parts, each of which concerns a particular aspect, is common in Acts which deal with a large general subject and makes the Act less cumbersome. For instance, the Succession Act 1965 consists of twelve parts. In some cases an Act will contain one or more *schedules* which appear at the end of the document. A schedule, in effect, is an appendix which contains material which is too unwieldy to list in the main body of the Act. The Misuse of Drugs Act 1977 has one schedule which lists controlled drugs, of which there are in excess of 120. The Succession Act 1965 has two

89. See the 1995 White Paper *A New Mental Health Act* (Pn 1824).

schedules. The first sets out the rules as to the application of a deceased's assets and the second lists earlier legislation which is affected by the Act, whether repealed, amended or otherwise altered.

[13.47] Apart from its provisions an Act is usually accompanied by material which is inserted to assist the reader. An Act contains an arrangement of sections at the start. This states briefly the subject matter of each section and it operates as a list of contents. This brief listing is repeated in the margin beside the main body of the Act, section by section, and in that context is referred to as marginal notes. Marginal notes sometimes contain a reference to an earlier statute or common law rule which is affected by the section. For example, the marginal note to s 124 of the Succession Act 1965 reads, in part, 'New. Overrules *Rice v Begley* [1920] 1 IR 243'. By scanning the margin a user can quickly locate the provision sought. However, s 11(g) of the Interpretation Act 1937 provides that marginal notes are not part of the text of the statute and may not be considered in relation to its interpretation.[90]

The state of the statute book

[13.48] The immediate publication of legislation in an accessible form is, it might be thought, crucial to the rule of law. It is vital, from the perspective both of the Government and the individuals affected, that the provisions relevant to a particular issue are capable of being identified and obtained. To this end the promulgation of legislation formally announces its enactment and, therefore, its applicability. Nevertheless, the practical tack of locating the law still remains. The manner in which legislation is published and made available is important and, ideally, the law should be published in such a manner as to facilitate its being identified and located by members of the public. Unhappily, the state of the Irish statute book cannot be commended in this regard. Locating the law can prove to be a task which taxes even the most adroit of lawyers, not to speak of ordinary individuals.

[13.49] An initial problem faced by someone searching for the legislative provisions on a particular subject is that they are not necessarily to be found in one Act. In many cases the relevant provisions are contained in a number of statutes, sometimes supplemented by Ministerial orders or other species of delegated legislation. The problem is aggravated in this jurisdiction by the fact that Acts of a number of different parliaments stretching over a period in excess of 700 years are still in operation. The range of statutes currently in force embraces:

---

90. However, in *Rowe v Law* [1978] IR 55 O'Higgins CJ, dissenting, took the marginal note into consideration when interpreting the Succession Act 1965, s 90.

- Acts of the English Parliament (pre-1707);
- Acts of Parliaments sitting in Ireland (pre-1800);
- Acts of the British Parliament (1707-1800);
- Acts of the Parliament of Great Britain and Ireland (1801-1922);
- Acts of the Oireachtas of the Irish Free State (1922-1937);
- Acts of the Oireachtas (post-1937).

The British practice of publishing statutes in annual volumes has been adopted in Ireland since 1922, with Acts of the Oireachtas being published by the Stationery Office. Each volume of Acts of the Oireachtas begins with Acts to amend the Constitution and follows with the public general Acts arranged in the order of their enactment. Private legislation is published separately at the end of each volume. The volumes are not updated or revised. Thus, the Acts passed since 1922 are contained in more than 80 volumes, arranged chronologically rather than on a subject basis. Statutes which are later repealed, become spent or otherwise lose force are not excised. Likewise amended statutes are not revised and republished. Since 1922 no general revision of the statute book, along the lines of the British *Statutes Revised* or *Statutes in Force*,[91] has been published. As the number of operative statutes runs into thousands the difficulty of researching the applicable legislative provisions on a particular topic can be appreciated. Someone who seeks to rely on a provision must check to see whether, and to what extent, it has been affected by later legislation. The task of researching legislation is physically difficult and mentally demanding, and requires much time, resources and enthusiasm. It is somewhat lightened by having recourse to the *Index of Statutes*, published in 1996, which indexes Irish statutes enacted between 1922 and 1995. Likewise, the recent re-publication of Cullinan's 1885 revised edition of the pre-Union Irish Statutes[92] is of some benefit in that it is reasonably comprehensive, but unfortunately it is probably not entirely accurate.[93]

---

91. As to these measures see Miers & Page, *Legislation* 2nd ed (Sweet & Maxwell, 1990) pp 149-150.

92. *The Irish Statutes 1310-1800* originally published under the authority of the Irish Office at Westminster in 1885, re-published by Round Hall Press in 1995; Professor Osborough's introductory essay to the current volume outlines the history of the various efforts to revise the Irish statutes.

93. *Ibid.* It is probably impossible to be assured of the reliability of the records of older statutes given the haphazard arrangements for their publication in the medieval period; see further Grossman, *Legal Research: Historical Foundations of the Electronic Era* (Oxford University Press, 1994) Ch 3.

[13.50] Matters are further complicated by the fact that many pre-1922 statutes which have subsequently been repealed in Britain, but not in Ireland, are not published by the Stationery Office. This problem has been slightly alleviated in recent years by increased legislative activity in Ireland which has resulted in the enactment of statutes which supersede pre-1922 legislation. However, a number of important pre-1922 statutes, to one extent or another, remain in force and frequently their availability depends on the efforts of private publishers. In this way access to vital areas of the law is impeded and it is impossible to justify the failure to ensure the official publication of legislation which is currently in force in the State.[94]

Amendments

[13.51] Another source of difficulty is that the text of a provision might not actually be found in the statute of which it is part. Frequently statutes amend, alter or repeal earlier provisions. However, as noted above the text of those earlier provisions remains unaltered since statutes are not revised or reprinted to take account of subsequent changes. A relatively straightforward example is provided by the offence of robbery which is contained in s 23 of the Larceny Act 1916. That section was amended by s 5 of the Criminal Law (Jurisdiction) Act 1976 which reads:

> The Larceny Act 1916, is hereby amended by the substitution for section 23 of the following section:
>
> (1) A person is guilty of robbery if he steals, and immediately before or at the time of doing so, and in order to do so, he uses force on any person or puts or seeks to put any person in fear of being then and there subjected to force.
>
> (2) A person guilty of robbery, or of an assault with intent to rob, shall be liable on conviction on indictment to imprisonment for life.

But it is the old unaltered version of s 23 which appears in the Larceny Act 1916. Thus, to locate the offence prohibited by the 1916 Act one must consult the 1976 Act. That form of amendment, known as a *textual amendment*, involves the direct substitution of one form of words for another. The amendment is integrated into the existing law in much the same manner that a new part is put into an engine in place of the old. A *non-textual amendment* operates indirectly. It does not alter the text of the old law but consists of a discursive statement or narrative of the effect of the amendment on the old law. Examples include s 1(4) of the Infanticide Act 1949 which states:

---

94. See remarks of Sen Costello 124 *Seanad Debates* cols 929-931.

> Section 60 of the Offences Against the Person Act 1861 shall have effect as if the reference therein to the murder of any child included a reference to infanticide.

and s 8 of the Criminal Damage Act 1991 which provides:

> No rule of law ousting the jurisdiction of the District Court to try offences where a dispute as to title to property is involved shall preclude that court from trying offences under this Act.

[13.52] The supposed advantage of a non-textual amendment is that it should make sense when standing alone, although that is hardly the case in the example cited from the Infanticide Act 1949. The reader should be in a position to discern the effect of the amendment, a matter of convenience which is said to be important from a legislator's perspective. Non-textual amendments can be employed to effect in one measure a general amendment to a variety of provisions, a matter of some practical importance. Thus, s 8 of the Criminal Damage Act 1991 manages to amend each statutory provision which concerns the jurisdiction of the District Court to try offences - every such provision is now read subject to that provision. This alleviates the necessity of enacting a separate textual amendment of each relevant provision and in this way it saves time and avoids potential legislative oversight. In some cases non-textual amendments are unavoidable. General adaptations of the law are often a necessary consequence of constitutional change. Following independence it was necessary to adapt pre-1922 legislation, which would be carried over under Article 73 of the Constitution of the Irish Free State, to the circumstances of the new legal order. This was achieved by the Adaptation of Enactments Act 1922 which in fact was the first measure to be passed by the Oireachtas after the 1922 Constitution itself. It would have been difficult to the point of impossibility to effect the necessary amendments to each pre-1992 statute by the textual method. Likewise, following the 'decimalisation' of the currency it was necessary to convert all statutory references to 'old' money. This was achieved by s 9(1) of the Decimal Currency Act 1970 which provided a general formula for amending existing references to the now-outmoded shillings and pence.

[13.53] A consequence of over-reliance on the method of non-textual amendment is that a set of cross-references, interpretations and qualifications develops which adds to the complexity and lack of intelligibility of the statute book - it becomes exceedingly difficult to collect the text of legislation on a particular topic in a single instrument. For this reason the current view is that textual amendments are to be preferred for their relative simplicity.[95] For instance, s 1(4) of the Infanticide Act 1949 would have been as effective had it simply amended the text of s 60 of the

95. Thornton, *Legislative Drafting* 3rd ed (Butterworths, 1987) p 340; Miers & Page, *Legislation* 2nd ed (Sweet & Maxwell, 1990) pp 195-196.

Offences Against the Person Act 1861. A textual amendment would have provided:

> Section 60 of the Offences Against the Person Act 1861 is amended by the insertion of the words 'or infanticide' after the words 'murder of any child'.

This would have been a tidier method of amendment and would have facilitated the collation of the legislative text. As things stand at present s 60 is read as if the words 'or infanticide' are to be implied into the section but they do not form part of its text. Like its English counterpart, the Irish statute book contains a curious mixture of textual and non-textual amendments and the observation of one commentator applies here with equal force:[96]

> "The traditional United Kingdom style, therefore, produced a pottage comprising direct amendments, indirect amendments and provisions incorporating both techniques. The effect, at least to one not nurtured from his early years on English statutes, is confusing, particularly so as it rests on a stream of consistently invidious and inevitably inconsistent decisions as to which amendments should properly be effected by one method, which by the other, and which by both."

Statutory language

[13.54] The intelligibility of legislation might also be impeded by the manner in which it is drafted. A frequent criticism directed towards legislation is that it is drafted in obscure and complex language which lacks clarity and frustrates a proper understanding of its meaning. The expressed desire is for statutes to be drafted in 'plain English', in such a manner as to be capable of being readily understood by those who are affected by it.[97] In this regard the object is to ensure that statutes are reasonably intelligible to the general public. The English drafting style has been compared unfavourably with that which is adopted in various continental jurisdictions.[98] In particular, it is argued that the English style involved complex sentences and sections, prefers detail to statements of principle and is prone to qualification and subtraction. These criticisms might also be directed at the Irish drafting style, which is largely derived from its English counterpart, although in some instances Irish legislation has departed

96. Thornton, *op cit* p 339.

97. See Thomas, 'Plain English and the Law' [1985] Stat LR 139.

98. See eg Dale, *Legislative Drafting: a New Approach* (Butterworths, 1977); Dale, 'A London Particular' [1985] Stat LR 11; Clarence Smith, 'Legislative Drafting: English and Continental' [1980] Stat LR 14; Millet 'A Comparison of British and French Legislative Drafting (with particular reference to their respective Nationality Law)' [1986] Stat LR 130.

significantly from its progenitor.[99] Some criticisms of the supposed lack of intelligibility are overstated. In the first place there is probably no generally agreed criterion to be applied in this regard.[100] To say that legislation should be intelligible to the ultimate user or to those to whom it is directed begs the question. The community to whom statutes are directed is not itself homogeneous but is made up of various elements each of whose demands may differ in this respect. Nor is it obvious that a statute should of necessity be intelligible to an average member of the public. It has been correctly observed that '[a] legislative text is a legal text, not just a guide to effective action'.[101] It might therefore be urged, with some force, that the real consumers of legislation are the regulators, lawyers and other professionals whose activities are affected by it. The individual citizen's desire to be addressed in a simple, uncomplicated and straight-forward manner often has to yield to a competing goal of legal effectiveness. Other measures, such as explanatory leaflets and guides, can be adopted to achieve the goal of explaining the law to members of the public.[102] In the second place, it might be argued that copious detail in statutes is often unavoidable.[103] By its nature legislation tends to deal with complex and intricate subject matter, a phenomenon which is likely to continue as the regulatory function of the State is ever expanding. The necessary, or at least desirable, detail of legislation invites a degree of precision which tends to render it less simple. This stems partly from a wish to plan for an uncertain future and to anticipate every conceivable contingency. Moreover, since language is a relatively imprecise instrument elaboration, qualification and definition is inevitable in an effort to reduce possible ambiguity; and that, in itself adds to the complexity of legislation.

[13.55] A related complaint is that there is too much legislation. To question the quantity of legislation raises the much broader issue of the extent to which the State should be involved in the governance of society. This is principally a question of political philosophy rather than legal policy. But even then efforts to 'roll back the State' have often been accompanied by an

---

99. See Morris, 'The Road to Brussels - Two Routes Compared' [1988] Stat LR 33 contrasting the quite different Irish European Communities Act 1972 and the UK European Communities Act 1972.

100. See Miers, 'Legislation, Linguistic Adequacy and Public Policy' [1986] Stat LR 90.

101. *Ibid*, at 95.

102. For instance, the Department of Enterprise and Employment has published a number of leaflets outlining the principal provisions of a number of employment statutes. The Department of Social Welfare has published a similar booklet on social welfare entitlements.

103. See Wilson, 'The Complexity of Statutes' (1974) 37 MLR 497.

increased volume of legislation. The privatisation of functions which were previously assigned to the central agencies of state, or their delegation to semi-state bodies, is achieved by means of legislation. Thus, it has sometimes proved to be the case that to reduce the involvement of the State more, not less, legislation has been required. With these observations in mind the desire for simplicity while understandable is misplaced and fails to appreciate the context in which legislation is enacted and its purposes.

Tidying the statute book

[13.56] The untidy state of the statute book is notorious and a number of measures are adopted in an attempt to alleviate the problem. One is to enact statute law revision legislation which clears the statute book of its deadwood. Such legislation repeals those statutes which have become obsolete and are of no practical effect. However, it is usual expressly to provide that the revision does not affect any existing rules or principles. The most recent such effort in Ireland is the Statute Law Revision Act 1983. However, statute law revision is only a partial solution as old statutes which are still in operation are left untouched. A second method of alleviating the problem is to enact consolidating legislation.[104] A consolidating Act is one which re-enacts all the relevant provisions on a particular subject in one statute, making, at most, only minor amendments to the existing law. The special parliamentary procedure to expedite the enactment of such legislation[105] has been employed infrequently - the Fisheries (Consolidation) Act 1959, the Income Tax Act 1967, the Social Welfare (Consolidation) Act 1981 and the Social Welfare (Consolidation) Act 1993. Another measure is a codifying statute which enacts in one statute all the relevant provisions on a topic, often making major changes to the existing law. The general hostility in common law jurisdictions to codification has been reflected to some extent in Ireland but the Succession Act 1965 can be cited as an example of a codifying measure. These measures help to reduce the bulk and cumbersome nature of the statute book, but they are of limited assistance. Due to the time and effort involved in their drafting and preparation and competing demands on the parliamentary agenda such legislation tends to be infrequent.

Improving the quality of legislation

[13.57] A number of measures can be suggested which might lead to the improvement of the quality of legislation.[106] One is to modify the linguistic

---

104. See Lord Simon of Glaisdale & Webb, 'Consolidation and Statute Law Reform' [1975] PL 285.

105. See para **[13.22]**.

106. See generally *The Preparation of Legislation: report of a committee appointed by the Lord President of the Council* (Cmnd 6053) (the 'Renton Report') which considered the state of statute law in the UK and made various recommendations; many of its conclusions could usefully be adopted in Ireland.

style in which statutes are drafted. Although complexity is likely to remain as an inevitable feature of legislation, attention to the drafting style might make it somewhat more intelligible. Shorter sentences, better organisation and division of sections and less obscure language should go some way to securing this goal. A second measure is to scrutinise the quality of bills with greater vigour. Unlike the position in other countries[107] pre- and post-legislative scrutiny is virtually unknown in Ireland which is a matter of some concern given the weak role which is played by the Oireachtas in relation to the enactment of legislation. This might be achieved either by creating a special review body such as a 'Law Council'[108] or by expanding and strengthening the role of Oireachtas committees, especially the Joint Committee on Legislation and Security. A third measure is to alleviate the disorganised state of the statute book by enacting consolidating and statute law revision legislation, thus reducing the number of statutes which are in force. This, of course, would involve a commitment of financial and human resources (through, for instance, the recruitment of additional parliamentary draftsmen) which Governments are notoriously reluctant to approve. Moreover, it would require the allocation of time on the legislative programme, when other proposals might be considered by the Government to be more desirable or of greater political importance. Fourth, the manner in which legislation is published might be addressed. Legislative reform and statute law revision in itself does not reduce the actual physical bulk of the volumes of statutes which retain amended and repealed legislation. The user's requirement is to be provided with the up-to-date text of legislation, not to be presented with the opportunity to engage in a fascinating intellectual challenge of navigating through volume after volume of statutes. The publication of legislation in its current, as well as its historical, form is crucial and to this end the production on regular basis of a revised statute book should be undertaken. The publication on a commercial basis of the loose-leaf *Irish Current Law Statutes Annotated* improves matters somewhat, but since it dates from 1984 only much remains to be done. With the widespread familiarity with and use of information technology it is to be hoped that eventually the entire body of Irish statute law might be collated and made available electronically, as is happening in other jurisdictions.[109]

---

107. See eg Bennion, 'How They do Things in France' [1995] Stat LR 90; Iles, 'The Responsibilities of the New Zealand Legislative Advisory Committee' [1992] Stat LR 11.

108. The establishment of such a body in England, modelled on the French *Conseil d'Etat*, was proposed by Dale, *Legislative Drafting: a New Approach* (Butterworths, 1977); but see criticism in Kolts, 'Observations on the Proposed New Approach to Legislative Drafting in Common Law Countries' [1980] Stat LR 144.

109. See Hudson, 'The Scope of Computers' [1983] Stat LR 35; Campbell & McGurk, 'Revising Statutes with Computer Support' [1987] Stat LR 104; UK legislation is now available on the LEXIS database; see Harrison, 'The Statutes on LEXIS' [1982] Stat LR 51.

[4] DELEGATED LEGISLATION

[13.58] Delegated legislation consists of instruments enacted, not by a legislative organ, but by a subordinate body or official to which or to whom law-making power is delegated. Despite the apparently absolute terms in which Article 15.2.1° ('sole and exclusive') confers legislative power on the Oireachtas it is clear that, within certain limits, power may be delegated by it to subordinate bodies. It has been accepted by the courts that power may be delegated to supply the necessary detail to facilitate the implementation of the principles and policies which have been enacted by the Oireachtas. As long as the delegation satisfies this requirement it is not considered to usurp the legislative function, which remains the exclusive preserve of the Oireachtas. The delegate must be expressly conferred with legislative power by an Act of the Oireachtas since it does not possess an inherent law-making capacity. The exercise of delegated power is governed by the parent statute, which establishes the extent and scope of the delegation, the purposes for which the power may be exercised and the procedures, if any, to be followed in exercising the power.

[13.59] The exigencies of managing and regulating the modern state have resulted in an ever increasing volume of delegated legislation as opposed to primary legislation. In practice, power is delegated to a variety of bodies including Government Ministers, statutory boards, semi-state bodies and the like. By virtue of s 15 of the Interpretation Act 1937 such power includes a power to revoke or amend the instrument and to replace it with another. Several reasons exist for the use of delegated legislation rather than primary legislation. The first is that the constraints on parliamentary time would make it impossible for all necessary measures to be enacted as statutes. Accordingly, the Oireachtas is content to sketch the broad outline of the legislative scheme and to delegate its detailed implementation and application to the appropriate official or body. An indication of the balance between primary legislation and delegated legislation can be gleaned from a comparison of the number of public general Acts and statutory instruments which were enacted in recent years (see Table 13.01).

Year	Public General Acts	Statutory Instruments
1990	38	347
1991	32	374
1992	29	451
1993	40	422
1994	34	464

Table 13.01

[13.60] The growing importance of delegated legislation is clear from the ever-increasing number of statutory instruments which are enacted each year. Statutory instruments are supplemented by a variety of measures which are local or private in character and which are created by local authorities, statutory boards, semi-state bodies and the like. The figures in Table 13.01 are for statutory instruments only and do not take into account delegated legislation which is enacted in other forms and thus underestimate the quantity and importance of delegated legislation. Second, as the contents of delegated legislation tend to be of a technical or administrative nature it is often preferable that those who possess the appropriate expertise be given the law-making function. Thus, where a Minister is given power to make regulations he or she will be advised by the relevant experts in his or her department. This also facilitates consultation with relevant interest groups which might be affected by the measure. Moreover, in some instances power is delegated to a regulatory authority, an expert body or one on which various interests are represented. Examples are the power of the Law Society of Ireland to regulate the admission and training of apprentice solicitors;[110] the power of the Labour Court to make employment regulation orders on the basis of a proposal from a Joint Labour Committee (consisting of employers' and employees' representatives),[111] the power of Bord na gCon to regulate greyhound race tracks;[112] and the power of local authorities to make by-laws for the good government of their functional areas.[113] Third, delegated legislation facilitates flexible and timely responses to rapidly changing social and technical circumstances, which are not afforded by the constraints on parliamentary time.

[13.61] Much delegated legislation is enacted in the form of statutory instruments which affect the public at large. Statutory instruments are governed by the Statutory Instruments Act 1947, s 1(1) of which defines 'statutory instrument' as being an 'order, regulation, rule, scheme or by-law' which is made in pursuance of a statutory power. Differences exist between those categories of delegated legislation but they are not mutually exclusive. An *order* tends to be made in respect of a single exercise of a delegated power, such as a compulsory purchase order, a commencement order bringing a statute into effect and an order assigning functions to a particular official or body. *Rules* and *regulations* are clearly legislative in nature. Regulations tend to contain detailed provisions pertaining to the general

110. Solicitors Acts 1954 to 1994.
111. Industrial Relations Act 1990, s 48.
112. Greyhound Industry Act 1958, ss 13, 25 and 48.
113. Municipal Corporations Act 1840, ss 125-127; Local Government (Ireland) Act 1898, s 16.

matters which are contained in the parent statute. An example is the Safety, Health and Welfare at Work (Signs) Regulations 1995[114] which are made under the Safety, Health and Welfare at Work Act 1989. The term 'rule' is typically reserved for the instruments which govern court practice and procedure, such as the *Rules of the Superior Courts 1986*.[115] *By-laws* possess similar legislative characteristics to rules and regulations. In The *State (Harrington) v Wallace*[116] the Supreme Court adopted Lord Russell's definition of a by-law in *Kruse v Johnson* as being:[117]

> "an ordinance affecting the public, or some portion of the public, imposed by some authority clothed with statutory powers ordering something to be done or not to be done, and accompanied by some sanction or penalty for its non-observance."

[13.62] *Schemes* tend to be of an administrative nature and often consist of numerical material such as scales of fees and charges such as schemes of telephone charges, made by Bord Telecom under s 90 of the Postal and Telecommunications Act 1983. The Statutory Instruments Act 1947 provides for the printing and publishing of certain statutory instruments, their deposit in certain designated libraries and the publication of notice of their enactment in *Iris Oifigiúil*. The instruments affected are those which are enacted by one of a number of designated authorities[118] and which must either be laid before one of the Houses of the Oireachtas or affect the public generally or a section of the public and whose publication is *Iris Oifigiúil* is not otherwise required by statute. The Act establishes a systematic method of bringing the existence of statutory instruments to the public attention, a matter of obvious importance to the rule of law. In this respect the Act does for statutory instruments that which the publication provisions of the Constitution do for primary legislation.

[13.63] Like statutory instruments other forms of delegated legislation are legislative and depend for their validity on the parent statute. However, there is no established standard for their publication and a variety of arrangements are prescribed by different parent statutes. For instance, s 90 of the Postal and Telecommunications Act 1983 provides for the publication 'as soon as may be' of schemes of charges made by Bord Telecom. Nothing more

---

114. SI 132/1995.
115. SI 15/1986.
116. [1988] IR 290.
117. [1898] 2 QB 91, at 96.
118. The designated authorities are the President, the Government, a member of the Government, a Minister of State, a body exercising a Governmental or administrative function throughout the State and authorities having power to make rules of court; see Statutory Instruments Act 1947, s 2(1)(b).

definite is specified, the method of publication is not prescribed and the scheme need not be laid before the Dáil.

Contracts of adhesion

[13.64] In some instances the courts might be willing to treat contracts, especially those issued in standard form by public utilities which enjoy a monopoly, as being equivalent to delegated legislation. The words of Henchy J in *McCord v ESB* are apposite:[119]

> "… it is important to point out that the contract made between the plaintiff and the Board (incorporating the General Conditions Relating to Supply) is what is nowadays called a contract of adhesion: it is a standardised mass contract which must be entered into, on a take it or leave it basis, by the occupier of every premises in which electricity is to be used. The would-be consumer has no standing to ask that a single iota of the draft contract presented to him be changed before he signs it. He must lump it or leave it. But, because for reasons that are too obvious to enumerate, he cannot do without electricity, he is invariably forced by necessity into signing the contract, regardless of the fact that he may consider some of its terms arbitrary, or oppressive, or demonstrably unfair. He is compelled from a position of weakness and necessity vis-à-vis a monopolist supplier of a vital commodity, to enter into what falls into the classification of a contract and which, as such, according to the theory of the common law which was evolved in the *laissez-faire* atmosphere of the nineteenth century, is to be treated by the courts as if it had emerged by choice from the forces of the market place, at the behest of the parties who were at arm's length and had freedom of choice. The real facts show that such an approach is largely based on legal fictions. When a monopoly supplier of a vital public utility - which is what the Board is - forces on all its customers a common form of contract, reserving to itself sweeping powers, including the power to vary the document unilaterally as it may think fit, such an instrument has less affinity with a freely negotiated interpersonal contract than with a set of bye-laws or with any other form of autonomic legislation. As such its terms may have to be construed not simply as contractual elements but as components of a piece of delegated legislation, the validity of which will depend on whether it has kept within the express or implied confines of the statutory delegation and, even if it has, whether the delegation granted or assumed is now consistent with the provisions of the Constitution of 1937."

The significance of these observations is that they indicate a judicial willingness to subject contracts of adhesion to the same forms of judicial control as any formal instrument which implements a power of delegated legislation. Thus, it would appear that they will be subject to similar tests of

---

119. [1980] ILRM 153, at 161.

constitutional validity and compliance with the parent statute under which the public utility operates.

Delegated legislation and the Constitution

[13.65] Article 15.2.1° of the Constitution vests exclusive legislative power in the Oireachtas. On a literal reading of that provision any delegation of legislative power would seem to be invalid. However, the courts have recognised that delegated legislation is a feature of the legal environment and that it is not impermissible *per se* to delegate legislative power. The matter was alluded to by Hanna J in *Pigs Marketing Board v Donnelly*:[120]

> "It is axiomatic that powers conferred upon the Legislature to make laws cannot be delegated to any other body or authority. The Oireachtas is the only constitutional agency by which laws can be made. But the Legislature may, it has always been conceded, delegate to subordinate bodies or departments not only the making of administrative rules and regulations, but the power to exercise, within the principles laid down by the Legislature, the powers so delegated and the manner in which the statutory provisions shall be carried out. The functions of every Government are now so numerous and complex that of necessity a wider sphere has been recognised for subordinate agencies, such as boards and commissions. This has been specially so in this State in matters of industry and commerce. Such bodies are not law makers; they put into execution the law as made by the governing authority and strictly in pursuance therewith, so as to bring about, not their own views but the result directed by the Government."

[13.66] One might take issue with the assertion that subordinate bodies do not make law (although by 'law' Hanna J probably meant primary legislation) and there appears to be some confusion between the executive and legislative roles. Nevertheless, Hanna J's judgment anticipated the direction in which the law was to develop. He held the power of the Board to fix hypothetical prices under the Pigs and Bacon Act 1937 to be in accord with the Constitution:[121]

> "What is the legislative power which it is suggested the Pigs Marketing Board exercises? It is the fixing of the hypothetical price. It has been submitted that, while the Pigs Marketing Board has constitutional power to fix the appointed price because they are directed to consider certain matters in determining it, as there is no schedule of topics to be considered by the Pigs Marketing Board in fixing the hypothetical price, they are in the position of legislators in that respect. But I cannot accept this view of the duties of the Pigs Marketing Board in reference to the hypothetical price,

120. [1939] IR 413, at 421.
121. *Ibid*, at 421-422.

> for the Legislature has directed them to fix not any price, but the price which, in their opinion, would be the proper price under normal conditions. That is the statutory direction. It is a matter of such detail and upon which such expert knowledge is necessarily required, that the Legislature being unable to fix such a price itself, is entitled to say: 'We shall leave this to a body of experts in the trade who shall in the first place determine what the normal conditions in the trade would be apart from the abnormal conditions prescribed by the statute, and then form an opinion as to what the proper price in pounds, shillings and pence would be under such normal conditions.' The Pigs Marketing Board in doing so, is not making a new law; it is giving effect to the statutory provisions as to how they should determine that price.
>
> It would be futile to ask the Legislature to fix the normal price in pounds, shillings and pence, and in my view that duty has been properly placed upon the Pigs Marketing Board."

[13.67] The question, therefore, is one of identifying the extent to which delegation is constitutionally permissible and the test which has been adopted was established by the Supreme Court in *Cityview Press Ltd v An Chomhairle Oiliuna*:[122]

> "…that which is challenged as an unauthorised delegation of parliamentary power is more than a mere giving effect to principles and policies which are contained in the statute itself. If it be, then it is not authorised; for such would constitute a purported exercise of legislative power by an authority which is not permitted to do so under the Constitution. On the other hand, if it be within the permitted limits - if the law is laid down in the statute and details only are filled in or completed by the designated Minister or subordinate body - there is no unauthorised delegation of legislative power."

That test preserves a balance between the role of the Oireachtas as exclusive law-maker and its competence to delegate legislative power. The power to enact 'principles and policies' lies within the sole preserve of the Oireachtas and if the delegation purports to confer that power on a subordinate body or official it is invalid. A related matter is that it is impermissible to delegate power to enact regulations which conflict with other statutory provisions, even where the delegation *per se* satisfies the 'principles and policies' test. The concern in this respect is to deny the delegate the power to amend, either directly or indirectly, provisions which have been enacted by the Oireachtas, thus preserving its legislative exclusivity. It follows, of course, that the enactment of so-called 'Henry VIII clauses' which expressly authorise the delegate to amend an Act by secondary legislation would be

122. [1980] IR 381, at 399.

unconstitutional.[123] These factors must be considered in the light of other constitutional provisions and the presumption of constitutionality. With regard to the former, the Oireachtas may not confer a power to act in breach of the Constitution. Thus, in *East Donegal Co-Operative Livestock Mart Ltd v Attorney General*[124] the delegation of a power to exempt particular individuals from the operation of the parent statute was held to be invalid as it violated the constitutional guarantee of equality in Article 40.1. A consequence of the presumption of constitutionality[125] is that a post-1937 statute must where possible be interpreted in a manner which is consonant with the Constitution. In practice the courts have proved to be willing to avoid declaring a provision which delegates power to be unconstitutional and have tended to focus instead on the particular exercise of the delegated power. Thus, where a power is delegated in ambiguous terms the courts are prepared to construe it in as narrow a manner as is reasonably possible in order to preserve its constitutionality. In particular, a delegation of legislative power which appears to be too broad may be construed narrowly in order to preserve its constitutionality. This is demonstrated by the Supreme Court decision in *Cooke v Walsh*[126] where s 72 of the Health Act 1970 was interpreted sufficiently narrowly to exclude an unconstitutional delegation of legislative power.

[13.68] A distinction between a constitutionally impermissible delegation of power and an unconstitutional exercise of a valid power is evident in *Harvey v Minister for Social Welfare*.[127] There s 75 of the Social Welfare Act 1952 was held to be constitutional on the strength of the presumption of constitutionality, although the particular regulation made under that provision was held to be unconstitutional on the ground that it invaded the legislative domain. By virtue of s 75 the Minister was authorised to make regulations governing the case of a person who was in receipt of two or more stated social welfare payments and to disallow one payment. The power to cancel certain social welfare payments is, it was contended, legislative and thus confined to the Oireachtas. The Supreme Court invoked the presumption of constitutionality to save the provision:[128]

123. See Morgan, *Constitutional Law of Ireland* 2nd ed (Round Hall Press, 1990) p 108; but note the position regarding European Communities Act 1972, s 3 where Ministerial regulations may alter, amend or repeal other law, the constitutionality of which was upheld in *Meagher v Minister for Agriculture* [1994] 1 ILRM 1; see further paras **[16.76]-[16.87]**.

124. [1970] IR 317.

125. See further paras **[14.44]-[14.47]**.

126. [1984] IR 710.

127. [1990] 2 IR 232.

128. *Ibid*, at 240-241 (emphasis added).

"The impugned section having been enacted in 1952 is entitled to the presumption of constitutional validity which has been laid down by this Court, and in particular falls to be construed in accordance with the principles in the decision of this Court pronounced in *East Donegal Co-Operative Livestock Mart Ltd v Attorney General*[129]... it must be implied that the making of regulations by the Minister as is permitted or prescribed by s 75 of the Act of 1952 is intended by the Oireachtas to be conducted in accordance with the principles of constitutional justice and, therefore, that it is to be implied that the Minister shall not in exercising the power of making regulations pursuant to that section contravene the provisions of Article 15.2 of the Constitution. The Court is satisfied that the terms of s 75 of the Act of 1952 do not make it necessary or inevitable that a Minister for Social Welfare making regulations pursuant to the power therein created must invade the function of the Oireachtas in a manner which would constitute a breach of the provisions of Article 15.2 of the Constitution. The wide scope and unfettered discretion contained in the section can clearly be exercised by a Minister making regulations so as to ensure that what is done is *truly regulatory or administrative only* and does not constitute the making, repealing or amending of law in a manner which would be invalid having regard to the provisions of the Constitution."

[13.69] However, although s 75 was held to be valid the Court went on to hold that the impugned regulation - Social Welfare (Overlapping Benefits) Regulations 1953,[130] article 38[131] - was invalid on the grounds that it conflicted directly with a statutory provision, namely s 7 of the Social Welfare Act 1979 and the terms of the social welfare code generally. The view of a unanimous Supreme Court was expressed by Finlay CJ:[132]

"The … submission made on behalf of the applicant is that the provisions of Article 38 … are in direct contradiction to the provisions of s 7 of the Social Welfare Act 1979, and, as such, are an impermissible intervention by the Minister pursuant to the powers of making regulations vested in him by s 75 of the Act of 1952, in the legislative function and is, therefore, an unconstitutional exercise of that power which breaches Article 15.2 of the Constitution. I accept that this submission is correct. The very terms themselves of Article 38 [of the regulations] … make clear what its effect is and is intended to be, and that is that where a woman would, but for that article be entitled to two pensions she shall be entitled to one only. The situation which made her a person, at the time of the passing of those regulations, entitled to two pensions, was a situation created either by the

129. [1970] IR 317.
130. SI 14/1953.
131. Inserted by Social Welfare (Overlapping Benefits) (Amendment) Regulations 1979 (SI 118/1979), article 4.
132. [1990] 2 IR 232, at 244-245.

direct provisions of s 7 of the Act of 1979 or by the statutory provisions contained throughout the social welfare code prohibiting, for the purposes of the means test, the taking into consideration of the payment of social welfare pensions or allowances. If the effect of Article 38 is to be construed as terminating the widow's non-contributory pension, after pensionable age has been reached then it is in direct breach of s 7 and the expressed purpose of s 7. If, on the other hand, it is to be taken as abolishing the old age or blind (non-contributory) pension, then it is doing so by reason of the receipt of the social welfare pension or allowance and is in direct contradiction of the provisions which prevent that occurring. Quite clearly, for the Minister to exercise a power of regulation granted to him by these Acts so as to negative the expressed intention of the legislature is an unconstitutional use of the power vested in him."

[13.70] The apparently extensive delegation of power by s 1 of the Imposition of Duties Act 1957 is arguably unconstitutional. That section authorises the Government to make orders imposing, altering or terminating customs, excise and stamp duties. By virtue of s 2 of the Act such orders have 'statutory effect' but cease to have effect by the end of the following year unless they are confirmed by an Act of the Oireachtas. In effect, the Act permits the Government to impose or increase (or, less likely, reduce or abolish) a significant area of taxation without having recourse to the Oireachtas in the first place. The utility of such a mechanism to the Government is obvious - it allows for immediate changes in the rates of duty, thus facilitating revenue raising and it avoids the necessity of bringing the matter before the Oireachtas in the first place. The role of the Oireachtas, at best, is reduced to one of confirming such measures the following year in order to give them permanent effect. In the meantime, however, the order enjoys full force of law. The constitutionality of s 1 was touched on in *McDaid v Sheehy*[133] where the order in question had been confirmed by s 46 of the Finance Act 1976. In the High Court Blayney J took the view that s 1 involved an unconstitutional delegation of power on the grounds that it did not pass the 'principles and policies' test:[134]

"I have no doubt that the only conclusion possible is that such provisions [that is, of the 1957 Act] constitute an impermissible delegation of the legislative power of the Oireachtas. The question to be answered is: Are the powers contained in these provisions more than a mere giving effect to the principles and policies contained in the Act itself? In my opinion they clearly are. There are no principles and policies contained in the Act. Section 1 states baldly that 'the Government may by order' do a number of

133. [1991] 1 IR 1.

134. *Ibid*, at 9.

> things one of which is to impose a customs duty or an excise duty of such amount as they think proper on any particular description of goods imported into the State. In my opinion the power given to the Government here is the power to legislate. It is left to the Government to determine what imported goods are to have a customs or excise duty imposed on them and to determine the amount of such duty. And the Government is left totally free in exercising this power. It is far from a case of the Government filling in only the details. The fundamental question in regard to the imposition of customs or excise duties on imported goods is first, on what goods should a duty be imposed, and secondly, what should be the amount of the duty? The decision on both these matters is left to the Government. In my opinion, it was a proper subject for legislation and could not be delegated by the Oireachtas."

[13.71] Nevertheless, Blayney J went on to hold that the (initially invalid) order was saved by its statutory confirmation the following year as there was no doubt in his opinion but 'that the intention of the Oireachtas was that the order should be part of the law of the State.'[135] On appeal the Supreme Court declined to confirm Blayney J's holding that this delegation of legislative power was unconstitutional. It agreed that the order was saved by s 46 of the Finance Act 1976 and, thus, was valid at the time of the proceedings. Accordingly it concluded that it was unnecessary to consider the constitutionality of s 1 of the Imposition of Duties Act 1957 and observed that Blayney J's remarks in this respect were *obiter*. As a result s 1 is left in something of a constitutional limbo but most commentators consider that the delegation of power is impermissibly wide.[136]

Judicial scrutiny

[13.72] Constitutional questions aside, the validity of delegated legislation is tested within the framework of the parent statute. In this context, the courts examine the terms in which the power has been delegated, which is principally a matter of statutory interpretation. If the exercise of the power exceeds those terms it is said to be *ultra vires* and, therefore, the instrument is invalid. In many cases, however, the delegated power is conferred in broad open-ended terms and the question of validity is by no means self-evident. Thus, in *The State (Sheehan) v The Government of Ireland*[137] it was held that the absence of a qualification on the power to order the commencement of s 60 of the Civil Liability Act 1961 entitled the Government to defer its implementation.[138] But where a power is exercised

---

135. *Ibid*, at 11.

136. See Hogan, 'A Note on the Imposition of Duties Act 1957' (1985) 7 DULJ 134; Casey, *Constitutional Law in Ireland* 2nd ed (Sweet & Maxwell, 1992) p 182.

137. [1987] IR 550.

the courts examine the scope of the Act, the purpose of the power, consider whether the regulation is 'unreasonable' and, in some cases, review the procedure adopted in enacting the regulation. In a number of cases the courts have intervened and found delegated legislation to be deficient for various reasons. A somewhat strict approach was adopted in *Minister for Industry and Commerce v Hales*[139] where a regulation which purported to bring insurance agents engaged under *contracts for services* within the Holidays (Employees) Act 1961 was held to be *ultra vires* - the Act was interpreted as being confined to those engaged under *contracts of service* and did not extend to those engaged under *contracts for services*. In *Cooke v Walsh*[140] a regulation was impugned both on constitutional and statutory grounds. The regulation (Article 6 of the Health Services Regulations 1971[141]), which was enacted under s 72 of the Health Act 1970, purported to exclude a category of persons which was otherwise fully eligible for health care. By construing s 72 narrowly, the Supreme Court preserved the constitutionality of the delegation, but it went on to hold that the regulation exceeded the terms of the delegation as so construed. O'Higgins CJ spoke for the Court on both points:[142]

> "Section 72 of the Act, under which it is agreed this Regulation purports to have been made, is in the following terms:
>
> > '72-(1) The Minister may make regulations applicable to all Health Boards or to one or more than one Health Board regarding the manner in which and the extent to which the Board or Boards shall make available services under this Act and generally in relation to the administration of those services.
> >
> > (2) Regulations under this section may provide for any service under this Act being made available only to a particular class of the persons who have eligibility for that service.'
>
> The defendant has challenged the validity of the regulation. He mounts this challenge on two distinct grounds. In the first place he questions whether the regulation is properly made within the powers conferred on the Minister by s 72. Obviously, if he succeeds on this ground the regulation will be held to be *ultra vires* the Minister and on that account to be void. If, on the other hand, the regulation is held to be within the apparent authority conferred on the Minister by the section, then the court must consider

138. See para **[13.43]**.

139. [1967] IR 50.

140. [1984] IR 710.

141. SI 105/1971.

142. [1984] IR 710, at 727.

whether the section itself is valid having regard to the provisions of the Constitution. It is well settled that the consideration of any question involving the validity of a statute or a section thereof should, in appropriate circumstances, be postponed to the consideration of any other question, the resolution of which will determine the issue between the parties. It is, therefore, proper in this case that the question of *ultra vires,* apart from any question of constitutionality, should first be considered. In the consideration of such question, however, the validity of the section must be presumed and it must be interpreted in accordance with the existence of such a presumption. This means that if the section is capable of being interpreted in two ways, one of which would give a meaning which is consistent with what is permitted by the Constitution and the other of which would not, that meaning which is so consistent must be adopted.

The interpretation of the section is a prerequisite to a determination of whether what purports to be done by the regulation is, in fact, within the Minister's powers under the section. What then is permitted by s 72? The first subsection applies only to health boards and clearly relates to the manner in which these boards are to administer the health services provided for under the section. While it refers to the making of regulations 'regarding the manner in which and the extent to which the board or boards shall make available services', this must not be taken as meaning that such regulations may remove, reduce or otherwise alter obligations imposed on health boards by the Act. To attach such a meaning, unless compelled to do so by the words used would be to attribute to the Oireachtas, unnecessarily, an intention to delegate in the field of lawmaking in a manner 'which is neither contemplated nor permitted by the Constitution'. (See this Court's judgment in *Cityview Press v An Chomhairle Oiliuna*).[143] Accordingly, these words must be taken as applying only to standards, periods, places, personnel or such other factors which may indicate the nature and quality of the services which are to be made available. However, it is not so much on this subsection as on subs 2 that reliance was placed in justification of the regulation. I again quote this subsection:

> 'Regulations under this section may provide for any service under this Act being made available only to a particular class of the persons who have eligibility for that service.'

Here, again, it is necessary to seek a meaning for these words which absolve the National Parliament from any intention to delegate its exclusive power of making or changing the laws. Needless to say, if such a meaning is not possible then the invalidity of the subsection would be established. *Prima facie,* therefore, these words are to be interpreted in such a manner as to authorise only exclusions which the Act itself contemplates. Such exclusions may be possible in relation to particular

143. [1980] IR 381, at 399.

services for persons with limited eligibility. Those with such eligibility are classified under s 46 and the Minister, by subs 3, is given power to change or alter this classification. The obligation imposed on health boards is to provide, not all the services, but, such services as are specified, for persons with limited eligibility. While I do not find it necessary to come to a final decision in this regard it seems to me possible that regulations under the subsection could excuse a particular health board or health boards from the obligation to provide a particular service for a particular class of those with limited eligibility, while the obligation to provide that service for others with limited eligibility remained. I am, however, satisfied that the subsection is not to be interpreted as permitting by regulation the cancelling, repeal or alteration of anything laid down in the Act itself unless such is contemplated by the Act.

Having said this, I turn to what the Regulation purports to do. It, in effect, seeks to add new subsections to ss 52 and 56 of the Act which exclude, from the benefit of these sections and the statutory entitlement thereby afforded, a category of persons whose exclusion is in no way authorised or contemplated by the Act. Included in this category must, necessarily, be persons who by the Act are given full eligibility and full statutory entitlement to avail of the services provided for by the two sections without charge. This is, in reality, an attempt to amend the two sections by Ministerial regulation instead of by appropriate legislation. In my view, the National Parliament could not and did not intend to give such a power to the Minister for Health when it enacted s 2 of the Health Act 1970. Accordingly, in my view, the Regulation is *ultra vires* the Minister and is void."

Statutory purpose

[13.73] The exercise of delegated power must be confined to the purposes for which it is conferred. If regulations are purportedly made for another purpose they will be held to be *ultra vires*. In *Cassidy v Minister for Industry and Commerce*[144] the Supreme Court tested a Ministerial order, *inter alia*, in relation to the purpose which it sought to achieve. Under s 22A of the Prices Act 1958, as amended, the Minister enjoyed the power to regulate the maximum prices of certain commodities including alcohol. An offence was committed where a commodity was sold in excess of the maximum stipulated price. A voluntary arrangement was relied on by which publicans agreed to give the Minister notice of proposed price increases in order to allow him to consider their appropriateness. Publicans in Dundalk refused to abide by this informal price control mechanism. Accordingly, the Minister made orders which set maximum prices for the Dundalk area by which, *inter*

144. [1978] IR 297.

alia, the price of a half pint bottle of lager was set at 14p! The plaintiffs sought a declaration that the orders were invalid. The first ground of challenge was that the orders were made for a purpose which was not authorised by the Act, namely to compel publicans to abide by the voluntary scheme. The Supreme Court considered that point against the general background of price control by the State. It was satisfied that the Minister's purpose in making the orders was to control alcohol prices in Dundalk and thus the orders were valid. Their validity was unaffected by the 'secondary' purpose of enforcing the voluntary scheme. O'Higgins CJ and Griffin J concurred with Henchy J's judgment:[145]

> "Price control is looked on as an essential part of the strategy of the Government in the war against inflation. In practice, control of prices operates in two ways. The Minister for Industry and Commerce, the defendant, is charged with the duty of monitoring prices; he has worked out a voluntary and non-statutory arrangement whereby suppliers of goods and services agree that they will not increase their prices or charges without prior notice to him. Advance notice of a price increase enables him to have the increase vetted. If he finds it acceptable, he allows it to go through. If he finds it unjustified, he refuses to give it his approval. In the main, the Minister's veto is accepted as the determining factor in deciding whether or not there will be a price increase.
>
> Auxiliary to this voluntary method of price control, there is vested in the Minister by statute the power to compel prices to be held at specified levels. If, for example, a commodity is being sold, or is proposed to be sold, at an excessive price, the Minister is empowered to make a statutory instrument fixing the maximum price which may be charged for that commodity. An offence is committed if the commodity is then sold for more than the maximum price so fixed. This form of compulsory price control is allowed by the Prices Acts 1958 to 1972.
>
> In 1972 the associations representing licensed vintners were co-operating with the Minister in the voluntary control of the price of drink sold in public houses. In August 1972, it came to the notice of the Minister that this voluntary arrangement, or gentleman's agreement, was being broken in the town of Dundalk. Drink was being sold there at increased prices of which he had got no advance notice. By letter, and by sending a representative to Dundalk to make the case against the price increases, he sought to dissuade the publicans from persisting in charging the increased prices - but to no avail. Therefore, he turned to his statutory powers of price control. In exercise of those powers, he laid down by statutory instrument the maximum prices that could be charged for intoxicating liquor in the urban district of Dundalk. The relevant statutory instruments giving that

145. *Ibid*, at 306.

result are No 99 of 1973 and No 136 of 1973; the latter merely varies the maximum prices fixed by the former. Those maximum-price orders are expressly not applicable to premises registered under the Tourist Traffic Acts 1939 to 1970, (ie, hotels) and the maximum prices so fixed apply regardless of whether the drink is sold in a public bar or in a lounge bar … The trial judge disposed of the first of those grounds by finding as follows:

> 'There is no evidence to suggest that the Minister was under any misapprehension as to the basis upon which he could operate the informal price control which prevailed after 1968, or that he thought that there was any legal obligation on members of the licensed trade to notify intended price increases. I have no doubt that the Minister made the order because he considered that the price increases in the Dundalk area were excessive and with a view to promoting the objects of the Prices Acts 1958 to 72, by maintaining the stability of prices of intoxicating liquor in the Dundalk area.'

On a review of the correspondence and the oral evidence, I am satisfied that those findings were justified and could not be disturbed on appeal. The increases which the Dundalk publicans arrogated to themselves produced drink prices which were higher than those obtaining in any other provincial town and even higher than those obtaining in Dublin, where the overheads in the licensed trade are considered to be higher than elsewhere in the State. Those unwarranted increases evoked complaints from the public which the Minister could not ignore. The evidence is coercive of the conclusion that the Minister, in making these orders, was primarily concerned to restore the stability of prices that had existed in the retail drink trade before the unilateral decision of the Dundalk publicans to award themselves price increases. In other words, in making these orders the Minister was exercising his statutory powers so as to achieve the object set by the legislature.

However, I think that the Minister had a secondary purpose which is not covered by the judge's findings. It would seem from the correspondence and the oral evidence that the Minister, as well as wiping out the unwarranted price increases, hoped that the threat of making maximum-price orders would force the Dundalk publicans and their organisation to return to the system of voluntary price control. He was not authorised by statute to make maximum-price orders for such a purpose, but it seems to me clear from the evidence that this further purpose behind the making of the orders was very much a secondary or subordinate purpose. The evil which the Minister wished to eliminate by making the orders was the unwarranted increase in drink prices in the Dundalk area. Having regard to the scale of those increases, he would have been wanting in the exercise of his statutory powers if he had ignored them. It is true that in correspondence he complained of those increases as being 'unauthorised price increases' and as having been made 'without ... prior approval.' So they were. But for the Minister to label them as such is a far cry from proclaiming it to be his sole or primary intention to compel the Dundalk publicans to return to the system of voluntary price control. If price increases had been justifiable because of increased costs but had been made without prior notice to the Minister, there is nothing to suggest that he would have wiped them out by making maximum-price orders.

The evidence forces me to the conclusion that the primary and dominant purpose of the Minister in making these orders was to eliminate unwarranted price increases and that, while he also had as his aim the return of the publicans to the voluntary practice of not making price increases without giving him prior notice, that aim was merely subsidiary and consequential to the dominant and permitted aim. I would hold that the Minister did not act *ultra vires* in this respect. Where a power to legislate for a particular purpose is delegated and the power is exercised *bona fide* and primarily for that purpose, I consider that the exercise of the power is not vitiated if it is aimed also at the attainment of a subsidiary or consequential purpose which is not inconsistent with the permitted purpose. If the law were otherwise, many delegated powers would be unexercisable, for the permitted purpose frequently encompasses of necessity the attainment of other purposes. In my opinion the first ground of appeal fails.

Reasonableness

[13.74] Delegated legislation might also be rendered invalid by virtue of its being considered to be unreasonable. Although the exercise of a power might be for a purpose which is authorised by the parent Act the terms of the delegated legislation might be such as to lead to the conclusion that it is unreasonable. In this context a regulation is considered to be unreasonable if its terms are so arbitrary, oppressive or unjust that it could not be said to enjoy parliamentary authority. It is unlikely that the parent Act will expressly prohibit an unreasonable exercise of the delegated power and, in effect, the courts imply this requirement into the Act. The issue arose in *Cassidy v Minister for Industry and Commerce* where the Supreme Court held it to be unreasonable to set the same maximum price for alcohol sold in lounge bars and public bars. The Court's reasoning on this point was explained by Henchy J:[146]

"The second ground of appeal was dealt with by the trial judge as follows:

> 'In making the order, the Minister did not prescribe a separate scale of prices for lounge bars because he was advised, and took the view, that no satisfactory formula was available to distinguish a lounge bar from a public bar. There are no minimum levels of

146. [1978] IR 297, at 309.

> amenity, comfort, or service which can be regarded as essential to a lounge bar. I do not think that the plaintiffs' suggestion (that the matter should be left to the decision of District Justices who would be provided with suitable guidelines) is workable. In any event, the matter falls within the legislative discretion of the Minister to reconcile the exercise of property rights with the exigencies of the common good, and it is not reviewable by this Court unless the exercise of his discretion is obviously arbitrary or capricious which it clearly is not.'

The lounge bar is a well-recognised and widespread feature of the licensed trade in this country. A member of the public would probably recognise the term as meaning a secluded or segregated area, usually within or annexed to a public bar, where in consideration of prices somewhat higher than those charged in a public bar, patrons are provided with amenities such as seclusion, comfortable seating and tables and, varying from premises to premises, extras such as a carpeted floor, waiter service, television, service of food, and the like. Many licensees of public houses have concentrated on this aspect of the trade. Some licensees have spent large sums in equipping lounge bars and have committed themselves to the heavy running expenses in staffing them and supplying the services expected by those who patronise them. The proprietors have built up a valuable goodwill for their lounge bars - a goodwill that would obviously be devalued if, by reason of common maximum prices (which invariably become common minimum prices) the prices in lounge bars are reduced to those in public bars. While common maximum prices would put all public bars on an equal footing as regards gross profits on sales, it would bear hard on lounge bars where, in the absence of a maximum-price order, patrons are expected, and are willing, to pay 1p, 2p or 3p extra for each drink. It is not unlikely that common maximum prices would affect lounge bars by reducing employment in them, diminishing profits and lowering their capital values. Do the powers vested in the Minister allow property rights to be thus interfered with? Do the demands of statutory price control permit common maximum prices to be laid down so as to compel a licensee (as one of the plaintiffs stated in evidence would be his fate) to have to cease trading as a lounge bar?

It is clear from the evidence that the Minister considered the desirability of fixing separate maximum prices for lounge bars as distinct from public bars. He sought legal advice on the matter. The advice he got was that it was not practicable to frame a satisfactory definition of a lounge bar. I can well understand the difficulty of drafting a comprehensive definition which would specify the minimum physical requirements of a lounge bar, but I think it was a task not beyond the competence of a properly instructed draftsman. However, I am not satisfied that a definition was necessary to effect the desired result. Many of the commonest expressions in the licensing code are left without statutory definition eg, 'bar' and 'public bar.' It is left to the Courts to determine the true meaning and scope of such expressions. I see no reason why a similar approach could not have been adopted in regard to lounge bars. A scale of maximum prices could have been fixed for public bars and a separate scale of maximum surcharges could have been laid down for lounge bars, it being left to the Courts to determine whether a particular area of the licensed premises qualified for this purpose as a lounge bar.

If, on the other hand, it be the legislative policy that lounge bars should no longer exist as areas of licensed premises where prices higher than those in a public bar are charged, that policy should be implemented in a statute duly made in conformity with the Constitution. The change cannot be effected by Ministerial orders made under the Prices Acts. The purpose of such orders is 'to maintain stability of prices generally' (s 22A, sub-s 1, of the Prices Act 1958) and not to devalue or disrupt, unnecessarily or unfairly, property, trade or industry. The Minister has not been empowered by Parliament to do more than what is necessary to maintain the stability of prices generally.

The general rule of law is that where Parliament has by statute delegated a power of subordinate legislation, the power must be exercised within the limitations of that power as they are expressed or necessarily implied in the statutory delegation. Otherwise it will be held to have been invalidly exercised for being *ultra vires*. And it is a necessary implication in such a statutory delegation that the power to issue subordinate legislation should be exercised reasonably. Diplock LJ has stated in *Mixnam's Properties Ltd v Chertsey Urban District Council*:[147]

> 'Thus, the kind of unreasonableness which invalidates a by-law [*or, I would add, any other form of subordinate legislation*] is not the antonym of 'reasonableness' in the sense of which that expression is used in the common law, but such manifest arbitrariness, injustice or partiality that a court would say: 'Parliament never intended to give authority to make such rules; they are unreasonable and *ultra vires*.'

I consider that to be the correct test. Applied here it produces the conclusion that Parliament could not have intended that licensees of lounge bars would be treated so oppressively and unfairly by maximum-price orders. If the Minister had made a maximum-price order which forbade hotel owners to sell drink in their hotels at prices higher than those fixed for public bars, it would be generally accepted that such an order would be oppressive and unfair. The capital outlay and overhead expenses necessarily involved in the residential and other features of hotels are such that to force their drink prices down to those chargeable in a public bar would in many cases be ruinously unfair. Understandably, the Minister expressly excluded the application of the Dundalk maximum-price orders

147. [1964] 1 QB 214, at 237.

to hotels. To have done otherwise would have been unreasonable. But if the orders are construed as not distinguishing lounge bars in any way, and as forcing their prices down to those of public bars, they fail unreasonably to have regard to the fact that owners of lounge bars, like hoteliers, are entitled, because of capital outlay and overhead expenses, to separate treatment in the matter of drink prices, at least to the extent of not requiring them to sell at prices which may cause them serious economic hardship. For that reason the application of the orders to lounge bars is unjustifiable,

For another reason, these maximum-price orders are inapplicable to lounge bars. They apply, be it noted, only to sales of liquor in the urban district of Dundalk; we have been told that 17 such orders have been made for other localities throughout the State. In so far as these two impugned orders apply to public bars, their object and effect is, broadly speaking, to bring drink prices in Dundalk into line with drink prices elsewhere. The combination of the statutory price control, as effected by these orders, and the voluntary price control operating elsewhere results in a general standardisation of maximum prices for drink sold in public bars. Licensees of public bars, whether the bars are inside or outside the urban district of Dundalk, cannot generally point to unequal treatment in the matter of maximum prices; but there would be unequal treatment if the orders applied to lounge bars. Licensees of lounge bars would have their prices depressed to the level of the maximum prices fixed for public bars; that would be the result if the lounge bar happened to be situated in the urban district of Dundalk. If the lounge bar happened to be situated outside that urban district, the maximum-price orders would not apply so that, in such a lounge bar, prices in excess of the maximum prices in public bars might be charged. This would amount to unfair, unequal and arbitrary treatment. It would be plainly unjust and inequitable if, merely because his lounge bar is situated within the urban district, a licensee were compelled to charge no more than public-bar prices while his competitor, who might be trading only a short distance away, is not subject to such price control because his lounge bar happens to be outside the urban district. Discrimination of that kind would be justifiable only if it were based on some distinguishing economic factor; but there is none. The distinction would rest entirely on the haphazard circumstance of different locations.

Parliament cannot have intended that the Minister would exercise in such an arbitrary and unfair way the legislative powers of price control vested in him. That being so, it must be held that the orders would be *ultra vires* if they were to be applied to lounge bars…[i]f the Minister wishes to fix maximum prices for drinks sold in lounge bars, he may do so by exercising the powers vested in him by the Prices Acts but, to be valid, any maximum-prices orders so made should not be flawed by unfair and unjustifiable discrimination."

Bad faith

[13.75] Related to the question of unreasonableness is that of bad faith. It has been held that an otherwise valid exercise of delegated power will be deemed to be *ultra vires* if it is established that it was exercised in bad faith. This was confirmed by the Supreme Court in *Listowel Urban District Council v McDonagh* where Ó Dálaigh CJ (with the concurrence of Walsh and FitzGerald JJ) observed that there is a:[148]

> "… distinction between an *ultra vires* act done bona fide and an act, on the face of it regular, which will be held to be null and void if mala fides is discovered and brought before the court…a discretionary statutory power, if exercised in bad faith, can be condemned as invalid and…mala fides is a well-recognised ground of challenge…[t]he answer to the principal question put in the Case Stated, whether the court in deciding the appeal is entitled to enquire into 'whether or not the said opinion (ie of the Urban Council) was arrived at *bona fide*' will therefore be 'Yes'."

To assist in determining whether or not the power was exercised in bad faith the Court further held that it would be permissible to enquire into what transpired at the council meeting which passed the by-law, the views of the council members and council officials concerning the by-laws and the veracity of the opinions they expressed.

Compliance with procedures

[13.76] Procedural issues arose in *Burke v Minister for Labour*[149] where the Order in question was held to be invalid due to the failure of the designated rule making body to observe basic fairness in its enactment. Joint Labour Committees (JLCs) are empowered under the Industrial Relations Act 1946 to make recommendations to the Labour Court to fix minimum wages to be paid to certain categories of workers. Unless the Court refers the proposal back to the JLC it must either make an order in accordance with the proposals or refuse to make the order sought. An employer is obliged to pay the minimum rates set by the order, failure to comply with which is a criminal offence and the employer is also liable to pay arrears. A JLC considered a proposal to set a new minimum wage for workers in the hotel industry to give effect to an intervening national wage agreement. The proposal did not contain an adjustment in respect of the value of board and lodgings provided to workers. An amendment was tabled by the employers' representatives, which sought to have their submissions on that matter considered and adopted, but it was defeated by a vote at one of the JLC

---

148. [1968] IR 312, at 318-319.
149. [1979] IR 354.

meetings. At subsequent meetings it became clear that the JLC would not consider the submissions although no formal vote was taken. The Labour Court ultimately made an order which implemented the JLC's proposal. The Supreme Court held that the failure to consider the employers' submission amounted to a denial of basic fairness and rendered the order invalid. O'Higgins CJ, Griffin, Parke and Kenny JJ concurred in Henchy J's judgment:[150]

> "It will be seen, therefore, that the power to make a minimum-remuneration order is a delegated power of a most fundamental, permissive and far-reaching kind. By the above provisions of the Act of 1946 Parliament, without reserving to itself a power of supervision or a power of revocation or cancellation (which would apply if the order had to be laid on the table of either House before it could have statutory effect) has vested in a joint labour committee and the Labour Court the conjoint power to fix minimum rates of remuneration so that non-payment thereof will render employers liable to conviction and fine and (in the case of conviction) to being made compellable by court order to pay the amount fixed by the order of the Labour Court. Not alone is this power given irrevocably and without parliamentary, or even Ministerial, control, but once such an order is made (no matter how erroneous, ill-judged or unfair it may be) a joint labour committee is debarred from submitting proposals for revoking or amending it until it has been in force for at least six months. While the parent statute may be amended or repealed at any time, the order, whose authors are not even the direct delegates of Parliament, must stand irrevocably in force for well over six months.
>
> In the present case the order is not challenged on constitutional grounds. What is contended is that the manner of its making has tainted it with invalidity ...[having considered the facts Henchy J continued] ... Is an order so made valid? One of the main complaints of counsel for the plaintiffs is that the proposals for the order of 1978 should not have been forwarded by the Committee to the Labour Court for ratification until the employers' motion (that the proposals should take into account the cost to the employers of board and lodging) had been voted on. I do not consider that there is any real weight in this point. It is true that that motion was never put to a vote, but what was advocated by the motion was amply discussed at the meetings held on the 16th February, the 7th March, the 2nd May and the 11th May. It is manifest from the minutes of those meetings that a majority of the members repeatedly set their faces against the motion. The Act of 1946 empowers the Committee to adopt such procedure as is thought suitable for the discharge of their functions. It was well within the competence of the Committee to deem, as they impliedly did, that the employers' motion did not require a formal vote of rejection. The votes

150. *Ibid*, at 358-363.

taken were sufficient to show that the employers' motion, after full discussion, was held unworthy of support. It has not been suggested that, if the motion had been put to a vote, any other result would have been produced. So I reject the submission that the order of 1978 is invalid for want of a formal vote on that motion.

Whether the Committee were entitled to reject the motion (as they impliedly did) in such circumstances, where the order was made without any regard to the real cost to the employers of board and lodging supplied, is another matter. To appraise this point, it is necessary to bear in mind the nature and reach of the jurisdiction that was being exercised by the Committee.

As I have earlier observed, the delegated power that was vested in the Committee was of the most extensive nature. It enabled the Committee to formulate the proposals for an order fixing minimum rates of remuneration. All the Labour Court could do was to refer the proposals back to the Committee with observations. The Labour Court is given no power of initiation or amendment. It could but make or refuse to make the order. Essentially, therefore, the order-making body was the Committee. Apart from the skeletal provisions in the second schedule to the Act of 1946 as to its constitution, officers and proceedings, the Act of 1946 is silent as to how a committee are to carry out their functions in making orders.

Where Parliament has delegated functions of that nature, it is to be necessarily inferred as part of the legislative intention that the body which makes the orders will exercise its functions, not only with constitutional propriety and due regard to natural justice, but also within the framework of the terms and objects of the relevant Act and with basic fairness, reasonableness and good faith. The absoluteness of the delegation is susceptible of unjust and tyrannous abuse unless its operation is thus confined; so it is entirely proper to ascribe to the Oireachtas (being the Parliament of a State which is constitutionally bound to protect, by its laws, its citizens from unjust attack) an intention that the delegated functions must be exercised within those limitations.

Here the Committee undertook the task of making a statutory instrument fixing minimum rates of remuneration for certain workers in the hotel industry. The representatives of employers in the hotel industry, as members of the Committee, wished the Committee to give consideration, before such an order was made, to the actual cost to employers of board and lodging supplied to workers. That was an eminently reasonable proposal. It was not possible to assess a fair and reasonable figure for minimum remuneration until a fair and reasonable assessment was made of the gross value of cash remuneration plus board and lodging. By the self-denying restraint by which the Committee debarred themselves from looking at the data necessary to determine the true cost to the employer of board and lodging, the Committee left themselves open to the charge that the consequent minimum remuneration order may be unjust and unfair.

It is no answer to that charge to say that the Committee were following the practice adopted previously before such orders were made. Two wrongs do not make a right; but in this case there was the difference that the Committee were specifically and repeatedly asked to receive and have regard to evidence as to the cost of the benefits which the workers were getting in the form of board and lodging. Nor is it a good answer to say that, if the Committee had taken into account the true, rather than the estimated, cost of board and lodging, the figures fixed as minimum rates of remuneration would not have been materially affected. As the Committee did not hear such evidence, it is impossible to say what effect such evidence would have had on them. Even if such evidence would have made no difference, the Committee, by rejecting it unheard and unconsidered, left themselves open to the imputation of bias, unfairness and prejudice. Such accusations, if made, would be unmerited; the members of the Committee were, no doubt, all acting in good faith and to the best of their abilities.

However, the fact is that the Committee, in formulating the proposals for the order of 1978, were acting as an unelected body, functioning behind closed doors, to produce a statutory order fixing minimum rates of remuneration; and that order could not be varied for at least six months, and non-compliance with it could lead to criminal responsibility and civil compellability. Elementary fairness required that the employers as well as the employees, both of whom were represented on the Committee, should have been allowed to present and to see consideration given to material which was crucially relevant to the question of minimum rates of remuneration.

By failing to receive and consider that evidence, the Committee failed to keep within the confines of their statutory terms of reference as those must necessarily be inferred. In other words, the order of 1978 was made in excess of jurisdiction to that extent.

I would allow the plaintiffs' appeal and declare that the Employment Regulation Order (Hotels Joint Labour Committee) 1978, was and is void in so far as it purported to substitute new minimum rates of remuneration payable to hotel workers in receipt of board, or in receipt of board and lodging, and to revoke that part of the order of 1977 which dealt with minimum rates of remuneration payable to hotel workers in receipt of board, or in receipt of board and lodging."

Parliamentary scrutiny

[13.77] While the Oireachtas has no direct role in the enactment of delegated legislation, parliamentary control is achieved by a variety of mechanisms. In many cases the parent statute expressly retains the right of the Oireachtas, or one of its Houses, to annul, or less frequently to approve, the instruments made thereunder. Thus, the Act will provide that instruments be 'laid before' one or other or both Houses of the Oireachtas, who may within a stated time annul it. The 'laying before' procedure, which is governed by the Houses of the Oireachtas (Laying of Documents) Act 1966 and Standing Orders,[151] is largely symbolic but is nevertheless important in that it formalises the parliamentary role in relation to delegated legislation. However, given the fact the most delegated legislation is enacted by Ministers and that the Government in effect controls the Oireachtas it is highly unlikely that a particular measure will be annulled in this fashion. There is no parliamentary body which deals specifically with delegated legislation although scrutiny is facilitated by the existence of the Oireachtas Joint Committee on Legislation and Security within whose remit such matters would fall. Nevertheless, this state of affairs is indicative of the sense of priority which is attached to the issue. In the past scrutiny was achieved through the workings of the Seanad Select Committee on Statutory Instruments. That committee issued a number of reports over the years and identified problems with various instruments. Amongst the faults noted were overbroad provisions, delay in the publication or 'laying before' of instruments, lack of explanatory memoranda accompanying instruments, lack of citation of statutory authority under which instruments are enacted and poor drafting. The power of the Seanad Committee was simply to report to both Houses of the Oireachtas and the validity of the instruments complained of remained unaffected. Moreover, it was probably inevitable given the technical nature of its remit that its reports were rarely, if ever, debated in either House. However, as technical exercises the reports proved to be worthwhile and they were effective in that Government departments tended to take account of the observations and criticism which were made.

Domestic measures deriving from European Community law

[13.78] The large volume of European Community measures which are implemented into domestic law by means of statutory instrument is noted elsewhere.[152] A special regime of parliamentary scrutiny of such measures was envisaged from the outset. At first, s 4 of the European Communities Act 1972 provided that Ministerial regulations would lapse after six months unless confirmed by statute. This mechanism proved to be problematic for a number of reasons and only one such statute - the European Communities (Confirmation of Regulations) Act 1973 - was passed. Subsequently, the European Communities (Amendment) Act 1973 amended s 4 of the 1972 Act to provide an annulment mechanism rather than a confirmation procedure. The current position is that Ministerial regulations enjoy

151. DSO 143; SSO 122.

152. See para **[16.154]**.

permanent statutory effect unless they are annulled by a resolution of both Houses of the Oireachtas on the recommendation of the Joint Committee on European Affairs.[153] The Committee acts as a filter and the Oireachtas is confined to annulling regulations on its recommendation. The Committee established a sub-committee to monitor European Community law and its function in regard to legislation is twofold: it reviews domestic regulations which implement Community measures and it reports on draft European measures prior to their adoption at Community level. Previously this task was undertaken by the Oireachtas Joint Committee on the Secondary Legislation of the European Communities which produced numerous reports since its establishment in 1973.[154] That Committee was especially critical of the manner in which European Community measures were incorporated into national law on a number of grounds.[155] These included the manner of implementation, poor drafting, unusual or excessive use of power, the appropriateness of penalties, the failure to cite the authority for regulations and the lack of uniformity in language. In its 30th Report the First Joint Committee recommended that statutory instruments should be detailed and comprehensive so that the user is provided with all the necessary information in the one instrument.[156]

[13.79] The extensive powers to make regulations which are conferred on Ministers by s 3 of the European Communities Act 1972 were held to be constitutional in *Meagher v Minister for Agriculture.*[157] It is clear that the scope of delegated legislative power in respect of matters 'necessitated' by Community membership far exceeds that which would be permitted in domestic law. Dicta in *Meagher* envisaged that some measures might require implementation into national law by means of primary legislation, but most exercises of Ministerial regulatory power are in effect immunised. Thus, the Government enjoys a discretion as to whether to implement its Community obligations by primary or secondary legislation. In a number of cases where domestic law would be significantly affected by the Community measure primary legislation has been the chosen mechanism[158] - examples

153. European Communities Act 1972, s 4, most recently amended by European Communities (Amendment) Act 1995, s 1.

154. See 7th Report of the 6th Oireachtas Joint Committee on the Secondary Legislation of the European Communities.

155. See Robinson, 'Irish Parliamentary Scrutiny of European Community Legislation' (1979) 16 CMLRev 9.

156. Prl 5419, p 7.

157. [1994] 1 IR 329. See further para **[16.76]**.

158. See 2nd Report of 1st Oireachtas Joint Committee on the Secondary Legislation of the European Communities (Prl 3841) p 17 recommending that company law matters be implemented by primary rather than secondary legislation.

are the Central Bank Act 1989, the Liability for Defective Products Act 1991, the Animal Remedies Act 1993, the Package Holidays and Travel Trade Act 1995 and the Consumer Credit Act 1995. On the other hand, while regulations have tended to implement measures which are principally technical or administrative in nature, secondary legislation has also been resorted to in cases which have entailed significant alterations to domestic law. For instance, the European Communities (Unfair Terms in Consumer Contracts) Regulations 1995[159] implement Council Directive No 93/13/EEC on unfair terms in consumer contracts.[160] This measure, which has a major significance for the law governing consumer contracts, co-exists with the existing national legislation on the matter, in particular the Sale of Goods and Supply of Services Act 1980, and the two must be read side by side. The choice of delegated legislation to implement a measure of this magnitude might be criticised on several grounds.[161] One is that the diluted form of parliamentary scrutiny, which exists in the case of delegated legislation, is inappropriate for a measure which has such far-reaching consequences. Another is that it results in an important body of law being governed by two sets of measures which overlap and might potentially be in conflict. Moreover, the usual supremacy of primary legislation is inverted: the measures which are contained in the primary legislation (being domestic) are subordinate to those which are contained in secondary legislation (being European in origin). In contrast, Council Directives Nos 87/102/EEC and 90/80/EEC are implemented by the Consumer Credit Act 1995 which also made the appropriate alterations to existing domestic legislation and this, it might be argued, conforms to a better legislative policy.

[13.80] The implementation of European Community measures by non-legislative means (such as departmental circulars and administrative schemes)[162] has also attracted criticism.[163] Although such domestic measures are permitted by Community law the point is that parliamentary scrutiny is only possible when they are implemented in legislative form, be it primary or secondary.

159. SI 27/1995.

160. OJ 1993 No L95 pp 29-34.

161. See also Murphy, 'The Unfair Contract Terms Regulations 1995: A red card for the State' (1995) 13 ILT (ns) 156, questioning their constitutionality.

162. See observations on quasi-legislation at paras **[13.04]-[13.05]**.

163. See 11th Report of 1st Oireachtas Joint Committee on the Secondary Legislation of the European Communities (Prl 4669) p 5.

Chapter 14

Interpretation of Legislation

[1] INTRODUCTION

[14.01] In this chapter we examine the interpretation of legislation.[1] In the main we are concerned with the rules, principles, practices and techniques which are currently employed to determine the meaning of statutory provisions, which have aptly been called the 'conventions of interpretation'.[2] Some preliminary observations are warranted.

[14.02] We have noted that one of the characteristics of legislation is that it addresses its commands in a fixed verbal format.[3] It is that which, of course, falls to be interpreted. By its nature language is an imprecise instrument of communication. Interpretation is a necessary part of communication, not only in the case of difficult or doubtful linguistic constructions, but in every case where one wishes to understand that which is written or spoken by another. Words do not have settled, definite and uniform meanings - they are surrounded by uncertainty and doubt and usage adapts and evolves over time. For instance, does the term 'motor car' include a mechanically propelled three-wheeled vehicle or is that a 'motor tricycle'? Is a ruined castle a 'building'? Is a tomato 'vegetable' or 'fruit'? In most cases we experience few difficulties but it is worth reflecting for a moment on the variety of ways in which we attribute meaning to communicated statements. The expression 'feed the dog' is a much more complex statement than its terseness might suggest. We can take it that the person to whom those words are addressed understands whether the words contain a command or a request, knows which dog is to be fed, what food is to be provided, whether water is to be included, where the task is to be performed and the consequences in the event of his not complying with the direction. The context and manner in which the words are addressed, the relationship between the parties, the unstated assumptions which they make and their

1. See generally *Craies on Statute Law* 7th ed (Sweet & Maxwell, 1971); Maxwell, *The Interpretation of Statutes* 12th ed (Sweet & Maxwell, 1969); Bennion, *Statutory Interpretation* 2nd ed (Butterworths, 1992); Cross, *Statutory Interpretation* 3rd ed (Butterworths, 1995).
2. Miers & Page, *Legislation* 2nd ed (Sweet & Maxwell, 1990) p 160.
3. See para **[13.06]**.

shared beliefs and understandings are amongst the factors which contribute to the interpretative process. All this is to state the obvious but it helps to place the process of the interpretation of legislation in context.

[14.03] While much of the foregoing applies with equal force to the interpretation of legislation, problems become more pronounced. The meaning to be attributed to many, if not most, legislative provisions will prove to be uncontroversial either because it is sufficiently clear or because the community to which it is addressed attributes an agreed meaning to it. Nevertheless, problems of interpretation are apt to be exacerbated in the case of legislation for a variety of reasons. In the preceding chapter we noted the problems with the state of the statute book[4] and the intelligibility of legislation[5] and these factors have an obvious bearing on the difficulties encountered when interpreting legislation. The location of provisions in a number of disparate sources coupled with opaque drafting add to the complexity of legislation and hence accentuate the problems associated with its interpretation. Any of a number of difficulties might be encountered by interpreters. One is that of ascertaining which of a variety of provisions contained in different statutes applies to the particular case in hand. A second is that some provisions are drafted in awkward terms. This is compounded where the statute is drafted in archaic language or is the product of a number of draftsmen over the years. A striking example of a convoluted[6] provision is s 63(1) of the Settled Land Act 1882:

> Any land, or any estate or interest in land, which under or by virtue of any deed, will, or agreement, covenant to surrender, copy of court roll, Act of Parliament, or other instrument or any number of instruments, whether made or passed before or after, or partly before or partly after, the commencement of this Act, is subject to a trust or direction for sale of that land, estate or interest, and for the application or disposal of the money to arise from the sale, or the income of that money, or the income of the land until sale, or any part of that money or income, for the benefit of any person for his life, or any other limited period, or for the benefit of two or more persons concurrently for any limited period, and whether absolutely, or subject to a trust for accumulation of income for payment of debts or other purposes, or to any other restriction, shall be deemed to be settled land, and the instrument or instruments under which the trust arises shall be deemed to be a settlement; and the person for the time being beneficially entitled to the income of the land, estate, or interest aforesaid until sale, whether absolutely or subject as aforesaid, shall be deemed to be tenant for

4. See paras **[13.48]-[13.52]**.
5. See paras **[13.54]-[13.55]**.
6. See Wylie, *Irish Land Law* 2nd ed (Butterworths, 1986) p 432.

> life thereof, and the persons, if any, who are for the time being under the settlement trustees for sale of the settled land, or having power to consent to, or approval of, or control over the sale, or if under the settlement there are no such trustees, then the persons, if any, for the time being, who are by the settlement declared to be trustees thereof for the purposes of this Act are for purposes of this Act trustees of the settlement.

[14.04] Third, since statutes are drafted with a view to regulating future events the draftsman attempts to anticipate every possible contingency. This, in itself, adds to the complexity of legislation yet it is virtually inevitable that unforeseen cases will arise. In those circumstances the question to be determined is whether the provision should be interpreted to include or exclude the unforeseen event. Fourth, technical and social change frequently overtakes legislation. Provisions which were drafted in the last century can only with strained interpretation be applied to modern conditions.

The role of the courts

[14.05] While the task of interpreting a statute falls primarily on the courts it should be noted that a number of others bodies, agencies and individuals might be involved in the interpretation of the legislation. These include civil servants and administrative agencies charged with the function of implementing the legislation, tribunals involved in its application and lawyers and other specialists who advise clients affected by the legislation. To an extent these non-judicial bodies will lend to their interpretation a perspective and range of experience which is not necessarily shared by the courts.[7] For example, a lawyer or accountant who advises a client on a new revenue statute will examine it from the client's perspective and the interpretation canvassed will be coloured accordingly; the adviser in that case will seek to interpret the statute in a manner which minimises the client's liability. By the same token, a civil servant who has the function of collecting the new tax might wish to maximise the taxpayer's liability. Put simply, competing interests dictate the manner in which different participants approach the issue and this leads to competing interpretations. But although the interpretations suggested by different bodies might be influenced by their different perspectives, account must be taken of the likely interpretation which will be adopted by the courts. Interpretation by the courts differs from that by others in two respects. The first is that by their very nature the courts unlike other interpreters are impartial since they lack an interest in the outcome of the case. Second, interpretation by the courts enjoys the formal force of law. The courts are, therefore, the ultimate

7. Indeed one of the reasons for establishing tribunals is to bring a wider range of experience to the function of adjudication.

interpreters of legislation and their probable response to the statute operates as a parameter within which others will present competing interpretations. Because the courts have the last word on the subject, an interpretation by another agency will in part amount to a prediction of or attempt to anticipate their decision. The primacy of the courts' role in the interpretation of legislation was asserted by Barr J in *Shannon Regional Fisheries Board v An Bord Pleanála* where it was argued that a court ought not interfere with the interpretation of a tribunal unless it was shown to be irrational:[8]

> "I reject this proposition. Statutory interpretation is solely a matter for the courts and no other body has authority to usurp the power of the court in performing that function … [i]n the present case the meaning [of the provision] is not free from doubt and, therefore, it is a matter for the court to interpret the regulation."

[14.06] In practice, the bulk of legislation is implemented with little difficulty and without recourse to the courts. However, given the primacy of the courts as interpreters of legislation, it is necessary to focus on the manner in which they operate in this regard.

Intention of the legislature

[14.07] The stated objective of the courts is to discover 'the intention of the legislature'. In this respect, the exercise is one of unravelling the meaning which the Oireachtas expected the words to bear. However, to an extent the phrase is devoid of meaning. It is pointless to speak of the intention of a group of people in the sense that the group had a collective intent. One can hardly say that all the members of the Oireachtas intended the statute to bear one meaning to the exclusion of all other possibilities. The reality is that few members will, in all probability, have considered the meaning of the statute. Moreover, of those who did consider the matter it is conceivable that they had different intentions in mind and, indeed, the variety of intentions might not be recorded in a reliable form. The intention of the Minister who introduced the Bill, and who, therefore, was most closely associated with its drafting, cannot be ascribed to the Oireachtas - amendments to the Bill might have been made during its passage through the Oireachtas despite opposition from the Minister. By the same token, even were it known, the intention of the draftsman who was responsible for drafting the measure cannot be equated with that of the legislature. The draftsman is not the lawmaker nor does he or she act as agent for the lawmaker. As a concept 'the intention of the legislature' is nebulous and can best be regarded as a linguistic formula which reveals the nature of the exercise of legislative interpretation. It points

8. [1994] 3 IR 449, at 456.

to a constitutional arrangement based on the relationship between the legislature and the judiciary. It recognises that the function of legislating is given to the Oireachtas and that that function should not be undermined by the courts. The intention of the Oireachtas is expressed in legislation and the courts are required to give effect to that duly expressed intention. It conveys the idea that the principal constraint on statutory interpretation is that the courts are required to act in a manner which does not usurp the legislative function.

[14.08] The restrained role which this arrangement assigns to the courts is most evident in the view that a court is confined to interpreting the text of a provision. The primacy of the text was emphasised by Blayney J in *Howard v Commissioners of Public Works*[9] where he reiterated the fundamental proposition that the intention of the legislature is found in the words in which its expressed itself. It follows that a court may not add to the text even where this would lead to a more equitable result or one which better corresponds to the known or presumed legislative intention since that, it is said, would involve the court in law making.[10] The matter was explained by Barr J in *PJ v JJ*:[11]

> "A court is entitled to interpret legislation so as to resolve any ambiguity or obvious error therein. However, where the statute is clear in its terms, the court has no power to extend its provisions to make good what is perceived to be a significant omission. If the court took that course it would entail going beyond statutory interpretation and into the realm of law-making, a function which under the Constitution is reserved to the Oireachtas. Occasionally circumstances arise where the court is powerless to avoid injustice …"

[14.09] Thus, where an unanticipated event arises or where an obvious oversight on the part of the legislature is identified a court is powerless to supply the omission through interpretation. This arose in *McGrath v McDermott*[12] where the Supreme Court had to consider a 'loophole' in the Capital Gains Tax Act 1975. Taxpayers entered into a series of transactions which involved the purchase and disposal of shares in certain companies. The purpose of the transactions was to enable the taxpayers to become 'connected' with the companies so that they could claim allowable losses

9. [1994] 1 IR 101, at 151, citing *Craies on Statute Law* 7th ed (Sweet & Maxwell, 1971) and Maxwell, *The Interpretation of Statutes* 12th ed (Sweet & Maxwell, 1969).
10. See *H v H* [1978] IR 138; *Trustees of Kinsale Yacht Club v Commissioner of Valuation* [1994] 1 ILRM 457, at 464.
11. [1992] ILRM 273, at 276.
12. [1988] IR 258.

under the Act. While the transactions were not 'shams', their sole purpose was tax avoidance and no real losses were incurred by the taxpayers. It was argued that the transactions should be regarded as 'fiscal nullities' and should be disregarded for tax purposes. This argument had prevailed in similar cases before the US Supreme Court[13] and the House of Lords[14] but was rejected by the Supreme Court. Finlay CJ expressing the view of the majority advanced both constitutional and practical grounds for the restrained approach:[15]

> "It is, however, contended on behalf of the Revenue that this Court should introduce into the application of these statutory provisions a rule or principle which renders them inoperative unless the taxpayer can establish a real loss. It is with some hesitation conceded on their behalf that it is difficult to avoid the logical conclusion that a similar precondition would have to apply to the computation of a gain under the subsection. Such a principle, it is suggested, would be justified by the general undesirability and unfairness of tax avoidance and by the necessity for the courts to look on such schemes with disfavour…
>
> The function of the courts in interpreting a statute of the Oireachtas is, however, strictly confined to ascertaining the true meaning of each statutory provision, resorting in cases of doubt or ambiguity to a consideration of the purpose and intention of the legislature to be inferred from other provisions of the statute involved, or even of other statutes expressed to be construed with it. The courts have not got a function to add to or delete from express statutory provisions so as to achieve objectives which to the courts appear desirable. In rare and limited circumstances words or phrases may be implied into statutory provisions solely for the purpose of making them effective to achieve their expressly avowed objective. What is urged upon the Court by the Revenue in this case is no more and no less than the implication into the provisions of either s 12 or s 33 of the 1975 Act of a new subclause or subsection providing that a condition precedent to the computing of an allowable loss pursuant to the provisions of s 33(5) is the proof by the taxpayer of an actual loss, presumably at least coextensive with the artificial loss to be computed in accordance with the subsection…
>
> … for this Court to avoid the application of the provisions of the 1975 Act to these transactions could only constitute the invasion by the judiciary of the powers and functions of the legislature, in plain breach of the constitutional separation of powers.
>
> Such an approach appears to me to be entirely consistent with the decision of the former Supreme Court in *Revenue Commissioners v Doorley*[16] and with the decision of this Court in *Inspector of Taxes v Kiernan.*[17]

13. *Knetch v United States* 364 US 361 (1960).
14. *WT Ramsey Ltd v IRC* [1982] AC 300; *Furniss v Dawson* [1984] AC 474.
15. [1988] IR 258, at 275-277.
16. [1933] IR 750.
17. [1981] IR 117.

> Apart from the special constitutional rights vested in Dáil Éireann in regard to taxation legislation in their character as Money Bills, the acceptance by the Oireachtas of its special powers and duties in regard to tax legislation, with particular reference to the desirability of preventing the success of tax avoidance schemes, is exemplified (as was pointed out by counsel for the taxpayer) by the fact that since 1973 there have been 8 Finance Acts containing chapters especially headed with the words 'anti-avoidance' or similar words.
>
> Not only am I quite satisfied that it is outside the functions of the courts to condemn tax avoidance schemes which have not been prohibited by statute law, but I would consider it probable that such a role would be undesirable even if it were permissible. It is the Revenue Commissioners (whose advice is available to the Oireachtas in enacting taxation legislation) who have the practical expertise and experience to know the most likely types of avoidance to be anticipated and prohibited, and most importantly of all, the predictable consequences and side-effects of the terms of any prohibiting enactment."

[14.10] It is fair to assume that had the Oireachtas considered the point when it enacted the legislation, an anti-avoidance provision would have been inserted. Indeed, after the decision a provision to that effect was inserted in s 86 of the Finance Act 1989. Despite this, and its acceptance that tax avoidance schemes might result in unfair burdens to other taxpayers, the Court was unwilling to adopt an interpretation which had commended itself to courts in the US and England.

[14.11] The primacy of the text is further evident in *The State (Murphy) v Johnson*[18] where the Supreme Court declined to correct an obvious error in the text of the statute. The prosecutor had been charged with the offence of driving a vehicle with an unlawful concentration of alcohol in his body, contrary to s 49 of the Road Traffic Act 1961. At his trial in the District Court, a certificate of alcohol level provided by the Medical Bureau of Road Safety under s 23 of the Road Traffic (Amendment) Act 1978 was produced in evidence. Section 23 of the 1978 Act provided that this certificate was to be regarded as evidence of compliance by the Bureau with the requirements laid down in Part III of the 1978 Act 'or under Part III of the Act of 1968', the Road Traffic Act 1968. It was agreed that the reference to Part III of the 1968 Act was erroneous, since that Part dealt with driving licences, whereas a reference to Part V of the 1968 Act would have been more appropriate since it dealt with road traffic offences. The District Court judge held that, since this was an obvious error, he was entitled to read 'Part III of the 1968 Act' as meaning 'Part V of the 1968 Act' and he convicted the prosecutor.

18. [1983] IR 235.

The prosecutor relied on the error in s 23 of the 1978 Act in seeking to have his conviction under s 49 of the 1961 Act quashed on *certiorari*. He was successful, the Supreme Court holding that although the error in s 23 of the 1978 Act was obvious, it clearly and unambiguously referred to Part III of the 1968 Act and to read it as something other than this would be to amend the section, and this was not within the competence of the courts. Griffin J accepted that the courts proceed on the 'strong presumption' that the legislature does not make mistakes and that where possible statutory words 'must be construed so as to give a sensible meaning to them *ut res magis valeat quam pereat*.'[19] Nonetheless, in the instant case, he agreed that any attempt to substitute 'Part V of the Act of 1968' for 'Part III of the Act of 1968' would amount to amendment of s 23 of the 1978 Act rather than interpreting or construing it, and this was a function reserved solely to the Oireachtas.[20]

The traditional rules of interpretation

[14.12] In interpreting legislation the courts adopt a number of canons, or general rules, of interpretation. These are supplemented by a number of presumptions and maxims which exist in respect of linguistic usage and subject matter of the statute. The canons of interpretation are not rules in the sense that the courts are bound to apply any or all of them and are better regarded as general principles which guide the function of interpretation - they reflect different approaches which can legitimately be taken by the courts. But amongst those approaches that which was adopted was, ultimately, a matter of choice for the courts. Traditionally, the options open to the courts have been expressed in the form of three rules of interpretation: the *literal rule*, the *golden rule* and the *mischief rule*.

The literal rule

[14.13] The literal rule was thought of as being the primary canon of interpretation. Briefly stated, it required the court to attribute to a provision its literal meaning, which has been described variously as the ordinary, commonplace or grammatical sense in which the words are normally used. The literal rule reflected a growing acceptance by the courts of parliament's supremacy and a classic articulation was that of Tindal CJ in the *Sussex Peerage Case*:[21]

---

19. [1983] IR 235, at 240, citing *Maxwell on the Interpretation of Statutes* 12th ed (Sweet & Maxwell, 1969) p 230.
20. See also *The State (Rollinson) v Kelly* [1984] IR 248 where the Supreme Court also declined to 'correct' an error, though in that instance this conclusion was arrived at by a 3-2 decision.
21. (1844) 11 Cl & Fin 85, at 143.

> "The only rule of construction of Acts of Parliament is that they should be construed according to the intent of the Parliament which passed the Act. If the words of the statute are in themselves precise and unambiguous, then no more can be necessary than to expound those words in that natural and ordinary sense. The words themselves alone do, in such cases, best declare the intention of the lawgiver. But if any doubt arises from the terms employed by the legislature, it has always been held a safe means of collecting the intention, to call in aid the ground and cause of making the statute, and to have recourse to the preamble…"

[14.14] A more recent expression of the rule appears in the judgment of Budd J in *Rahill v Brady*:[22]

> "In the absence of some special technical or acquired meaning, the language of a statute should be construed according to its ordinary meaning and in accordance with the rules of grammar. While the literal construction generally has *prima facie* preference, there is also a further rule that in seeking the true construction of a section of an Act the whole Act must be looked at in order to see what the objects and intention of the legislature were; but the ordinary meaning of words should not be departed from unless adequate grounds can be found in the context in which the words are used to indicate that a literal interpretation would not give the real intention of the legislature."

[14.15] Underlying the literal rule was the view that the intention of the legislature is to be derived predominantly, if not exclusively, from the words in which it chose to express its commands. In this regard primacy was attached to the text of the legislation, and the rule was associated with the principle that a court may not add words to the text of an Act.[23] The connection between the two was outlined by Parke J in *H v H*:[24]

> "Such a construction would not be in conformity with one of the fundamental rules of interpretation ie that words may not be interpolated into a statute unless it is absolutely necessary to do so in order to render it intelligible or to prevent it from having an absurd or wholly unreasonable meaning or effect. No such necessity arises here. The words [of the provision] are clear and intelligible as they stand."

[14.16] It is clear, therefore, that if the provision was unambiguous on its face it was to be accorded its literal meaning even where this might have led to an undesirable or unjust result. The judicial role was to interpret that which the legislature had expressed, not to remedy its supposed defects.

---

22. [1971] IR 69, at 86.
23. See *McGrath v McDermott* [1988] IR 258; see para **[14.09]**.
24. [1978] IR 138, at 147.

Nevertheless, most formulations of the literal rule (as can be seen in the quotations above) accepted that a secondary or modified meaning might be adopted where the words are not clear and unambiguous. It is to the competing rules that we now turn our attention.

The golden rule

[14.17] A court was permitted to invoke the golden rule if the application of the literal rule would have led to an absurdity or inconsistency. In this case the provision would be attributed a modified or secondary meaning rather than that which was urged by the literal rule. An early articulation of the rule is that of Burton J in *Warburton v Loveland* where he stated:[25]

> "…I apprehend it is a rule in the construction of statutes, that, in the first instance, the grammatical sense of the words is to be adhered to. If that is contrary to, or inconsistent with any expressed intention, or any declared purpose of the statute; or if it would involve any absurdity, repugnance, or inconsistency in its different provisions, the grammatical sense must then be modified, extended, or abridged, so far as to avoid such inconvenience, but no farther."

Somewhat more complete is Budd J's treatment of the matter in *The People (Attorney General) v McGlynn*:[26]

> "What has been described as the golden rule in the construction of statutes is that the words of a statute must *prima facie* be given their ordinary meaning. That literal construction has, however, but *prima facie* preference. As Lord Shaw said in *Shannon Realties v St Michel (Ville de)*[27] at page 192 of the report:
>
> > '…where alternative constructions are equally open, that alternative is to be chosen which will be consistent with the smooth working of the system which the statute purports to be regulating; and that alternative is to be rejected which will introduce uncertainty, friction or confusion into the working of the system.'
>
> It might be that when regard is had to what the law was before the statute was enacted and to the defect in the law which the Oireachtas had the intention of remedying by the change in the law effected by the section, the conclusion would be reached that the real meaning of the words used was something different to their apparent literal meaning. Assuming for the

25. (1828) 1 Hud & B 623, at 648; see also *Grey v Pearson* (1857) HL Cas 61, at 106 *per* Lord Wensleydale adopting Burton J's formulation; *DPP v Flanagan* [1979] IR 265, at 277 *per* O'Higgins CJ.

26. [1967] IR 232, at 242.

27. [1924] AC 185.

> moment that an alternative construction of the section is open, the question is whether that alternative construction … is consistent with the smooth working of the system which the statute purports to regulate."

[14.18] When adopting the golden rule a court was not confined to examining the provision in isolation. The long title, the preamble and other provisions in the statute could be considered in an effort to discern the legislative intention. However, while the court could examine the statute 'as a whole' it was precluded from taking extrinsic materials or the parliamentary history of the provision into account.[28]

The mischief rule

[14.19] The other rule which competed with the literal rule was the mischief rule, which was the oldest of the three rules. It allowed a court to examine the pre-existing common law in order to determine the defect, or mischief, which the statute was designed to remedy. The statute was interpreted in a manner which was sufficient to deal with that defect. This rule was devised by the common law courts in the early 16th century and was outlined in *Heydon's case*:[29]

> "And it was resolved by them that for the sure and true interpretation of all statutes in general (be they penal or beneficial, restrictive or enlarging of the common law) four things are to be discerned and considered:
>
> 1st What was the common law before the making of the Act,
>
> 2nd What was the mischief and defect for which the common law did not provide,
>
> 3rd What remedy the Parliament hath resolved and appointed to cure the disease of the Commonwealth, and
>
> 4th The true reason of the remedy
>
> and then the office of all the judges is always to make such construction as shall suppress the mischief, and advance the remedy, and to suppress subtle inventions and evasions for the continuance of the mischief, and *pro privato commodo*, and to add force and life to the cure and the remedy, according to the true intent of the Act, *pro bono publico*."

[14.20] The mischief rule was devised by the common law courts at a time when they manifested a suspicion of statute law and sought to preserve the 'sanctity' of the common law; hence the concentration on the defect which the statute was designed to cure. An example of the application of the mischief rule is the decision in *Gorris v Scott*.[30] The plaintiff sought

---

28. See *Minister for Industry and Commerce v Hales* [1967] IR 50.
29. (1584) 3 Co Rep 7a, at 7b.
30. (1874) LR 9 Ex 125.

damages for the loss of his sheep which drowned having been washed overboard from the defendant's ship. The defendant was in breach of a statutory duty to equip the ship with pens and had they been provided the sheep would not have been lost. The action failed since the purpose of the duty (that is, the mischief towards which the statute was directed) was to prevent the spread of disease amongst animals during transportation, not to prevent their being lost overboard. At the time it was formulated, the mischief rule was the principal alternative to a literal interpretation and it was, to a large extent, overtaken by the golden rule.

[14.21] A certain degree of overlap existed between the three rules. The literal rule facilitated the taking into account of the context in which the words appeared. Like the mischief rule the golden rule sought to discover the legislative purpose although it tended to focus on the text of the legislation. The mischief rule was minimalist, in the sense that the provision was construed only as widely as was considered to be necessary to cure the defect in the common law. Whether, and to what extent, the principles of interpretation survive in those forms is open to question. But however they might be stated, two principal issues remain - how expansive the task of interpretation should be and whether account should be taken of the statutory context and purpose as opposed to reading the words in isolation.

[2] The Principal Approaches

[14.22] The canons of interpretation which are currently invoked by the courts can be stated in the form of two approaches, the literal approach and the schematic or teleological approach. Before considering those approaches some preliminary points should be noted. One is that interpretation is governed by the Interpretation Acts 1937 and 1993.[31] While the Acts do not establish general principles they contain a number of rules and definitions which are of general application, thus saving the need to specify these matters in each statute individually. The 1937 Act, which is the principal measure, provides for the interpretation of statutory powers and duties, the effect of repeals, the meaning of particular words and expressions as well as containing a schedule in which 37 frequently used words and phrases are defined. For instance, s 11(a) of the 1937 Act provides that words which import the singular should include the plural, and vice versa, unless a contrary intention appears;[32] s 11(b) provides that a word which imports the

31. See also Interpretation Acts 1889 and 1923 applying to pre-1938 statutes and statutory instruments. Certain other statutes also interpret words of general application in Acts passed later; eg Age of Majority Act 1985, s 2(2)(a) interpreting 'age of majority' and 'full age'.

32. See *The People (DPP) v Kelly (No 2)* [1983] IR 1.

masculine should be interpreted as including the feminine unless the contrary intention appears;[33] s 11(c) provides that the word 'person' includes corporate bodies unless the contrary intention appears.[34] Second, many statutes contain sections which define particular expressions used in the Act or which guide its interpretation. For example, s 1 of the Misuse of Drugs Act 1977 defines 25 words and phrases which appear in the Act. In this sense an interpretation section acts as a glossary of terms or mini-dictionary for the statute and its provisions are governing, a point which was acknowledged by Murnaghan J in *Mason v Levy*:[35]

> "Where a statute …defines its own terms and makes what has been called its own dictionary, a court should not depart from the definitions given by the statute and the meanings assigned to the words used in the statute."

[14.23] Accordingly, when faced with interpreting a provision a court will have first recourse to both the Interpretation Acts 1937 and 1993 and the interpretation section, if any, of the Act in which the provision in question appears.

The literal approach

[14.24] The literal approach is the modern articulation of the old literal rule which emerged in the 19th century as the preferred method of interpretation. It is still considered to be the primary principle of construction. Thus, in *Cork County Council v Whillock* O'Flaherty J stated:[36]

> "… it is clear to me that the first rule of construction requires that a literal construction must be applied. If there is nothing to modify, alter or qualify the language which the statute contains, it must be construed in the ordinary and natural meaning of the words and sentences."

While the literal approach requires a court to attribute the ordinary and natural meaning to the words, it is acknowledged that that meaning is to be derived from the context in which they appear. The authoritative statement of the literal approach is that of Henchy J in *Inspector of Taxes v Kiernan* where the Supreme Court was required to consider whether the expression 'cattle' in the Income Tax Act 1967 included pigs:[37]

33. See *Lonergan v Morrisey* (1947) 81 ILTR 130. The sole provision of the Interpretation (Amendment) Act 1993 contains the reverse proposition, namely that a word which imports the feminine should be construed as including the masculine, unless the contrary intention appears, in effect 'gender-proofing' statutes drafted since 1994.
34. See *Truloc Ltd v McMenamin* [1994] 1 ILRM 151; *DPP v Wexford Farmers' Club* [1994] 1 IR 546.
35. [1952] IR 40, at 47.
36. [1993] 1 IR 231, at 237.
37. [1981] IR 117, at 121-122.

"There is no doubt that, at certain stages of English usage and in certain statutory contexts, the word 'cattle' is wide enough in its express or implied significance to include pigs. That fact, however, does not lead us to a solution of the essential question before us. When the legislature used the word 'cattle' in the [Income Tax] Act of 1918 and again in the Act of 1967, without in either case giving it a definition, was it intended that the word should comprehend pigs? That the word has, or has been held to have, that breadth of meaning in other statutes is not to the point. A word or expression in a given statute must be given meaning and scope according to its immediate context, in line with the scheme and purpose of the particular statutory pattern as a whole, and to an extent that will truly effectuate the particular legislation or a particular definition therein. For example, s 1 of the Towns Improvement (Ireland) Act 1854, defines the word 'cattle' as including 'horse, mare, gelding, foal, colt, filly, bull, cow, heifer, ox, calf, ass, mule, ram, ewe, whether, lamb, goat, kid, or swine.' Unlike such an instance, the question posed here is whether the word 'cattle' includes pigs in a taxing Act when the word is left undefined.

Leaving aside any judicial decision on the point, I would approach the matter by the application of three basic rules of statutory interpretation. First, if the statutory provision is one directed to the public at large, rather than to a particular class who may be expected to use the word or expression in question in either a narrowed or an extended connotation, or as a term of art, then, in the absence of internal evidence suggesting the contrary, the word or expression should be given its ordinary or colloquial meaning. As Lord Esher MR put it in *Unwin v Hanson*[38] at p 119 of the report:

> 'If the Act is directed to dealing with matters affecting everybody generally, the words used have the meaning attached to them in the common and ordinary use of language. If the Act is one passed with reference to a particular trade, business, or transaction, and words are used which everybody conversant with that trade, business, or transaction, knows and understands to have a particular meaning in it, then the words are to be construed as having that particular meaning, though it may differ from the common or ordinary meaning of the words.'

The statutory provisions we are concerned with here are plainly addressed to the public generally, rather than to a selected section thereof who might be expected to use words in a specialised sense. Accordingly, the word 'cattle' should be given the meaning which an ordinary member of the public would intend it to have when using it ordinarily.

Secondly, if a word or expression is used in a statute creating a penal or taxation liability, and there is looseness or ambiguity attaching to it, the word should be construed strictly so as to prevent a fresh imposition of

38. [1891] 2 QB 115.

> liability from being created unfairly by the use of oblique or slack language: see Lord Esher MR in *Tuck & Sons v Preister*;[39] Lord Reid in *Director of Public Prosecutions v Ottewell*[40] and Lord Denning MR in *Farrell v Alexander*.[41] As used in the statutory provisions in question here, the word 'cattle' calls for such a strict construction.
>
> Thirdly, when the word which requires to be given its natural and ordinary meaning is a simple word which has a widespread and unambiguous currency, the judge construing it should draw primarily on his own experience of its use. Dictionaries or other literary sources should be looked at only when alternative meanings, regional usages or other obliquities are shown to cast doubt on the singularity of its ordinary meaning, or when there are grounds for suggesting that the meaning of the word has changed since the statute in question was passed. In regard to 'cattle', which is an ordinary and widely used word, one's experience is that in its modern usage the word, as it would fall from the lips of the man in the street, would be intended to mean and would be taken to mean no more than bovine animals. To the ordinary person, cattle, sheep and pigs are distinct forms of livestock."

[14.25] The principles outlined by Henchy J have received general judicial endorsement. Thus, in *Texaco (Ireland) Ltd v Murphy* McCarthy J adopting those principles stated:[42]

> "... the first rule of statutory construction remains that the words be given their ordinary literal meaning. True it is that one should seek to construe a statute as a whole, a principle perhaps less relevant to the construction of revenue legislation than, for instance, that with a social purpose ... the legal principle appears clearly to be that if the claim for allowance falls within the express wording of the permitting section, it must be upheld. Arguments based upon the application or otherwise of other sections, proximate or not, appear to me to be unsound in law."

The literal approach emphasises the ordinary use of language, which is to be attributed to statutory provisions in the first instance. It is significant that Henchy J noted that the context has a bearing on the interpretation of a provision. At one level this is to acknowledge that the meaning of language in ordinary communication is contextually derived. The remarks made earlier on the expression 'feed the dog' are apposite.[43] In relation to statutory interpretation the context facilitates the invocation of concepts which are unexpressed but are generally understood to apply. For example, a section in

---

39. (1887) 19 QBD 629, at 638.
40. [1970] AC 642, at 649.
41. [1975] 3 WLR 642, at 650-651
42. [1991] 2 IR 449, at 456-457.
43. See para **[14.02]**.

a penal statute which provides for the punishment of a 'person' who commits a defined act will not apply to underage persons or lunatics - the defences of infancy and insanity which were developed at common law will apply despite the statute's silence on the matter. In other words, the general principles of criminal capacity, which exclude children and the criminally insane from liability, form the context in which the word is to be understood. This states the obvious and it follows that a word or expression might bear different 'literal' meanings in different statutory contexts.

Technical meanings

[14.26] The literal approach has a special application in two instances, each of which draws on its particular context. The first is where the words in the statute are legal terms of art in which case they will bear that meaning rather than their ordinary meaning. This arose in *Minister for Industry and Commerce v Pim Brothers Ltd*[44] which concerned the interpretation of the Hire Purchase and Credit-Sale (Advertising) Order 1961 which applied to advertisements which offered goods for sale by way of hire purchase or credit-sale agreement. The defendants attached an advertisement to a coat which was displayed for sale in their premises. If the Order applied to the notice it was deficient in a number of respects. At issue was whether the display amounted to an 'offer'. In answering the question in the negative Davitt P, on a case stated to the High Court, opted for the legal rather than the ordinary sense of the words 'offer for sale':[45]

> "In one sense it could be described as an offer to sell. In popular terms the coat could properly be said to be on offer to the public. In the strictly legal sense, however, the advertisement was merely a statement of the cash price at which the defendants were prepared to sell the goods, with an indication that certain credit facilities, the exact nature of which were unspecified, would be available. This would not constitute an offer to sell which could be made a contract of sale by acceptance; *Harvey v Facey*[46]... If the expression 'offered or sale' ... is to be construed in the strict legal sense then the learned District Justice was clearly correct in his decision. In my opinion, it should be so construed."

[14.27] The second is where the statute is directed at a particular class rather than the public at large, in which case the words are assigned the meaning which would be understood by that class. This is what occurred in *Minister for Industry and Commerce v Hammond Lane Metal Co Ltd*[47] where the

44. [1966] IR 154.
45. *Ibid*, at 160.
46. [1893] AC 552.
47. [1947] Ir Jur Rep 59.

expression 'scrap lead' was assigned the meaning which it would bear in the scrap metal business, that being the class to which the relevant measure was directed. Judge Shannon, in the Circuit Court, expressed the matter thus:

> "The question for my determination is whether Article 3 of the Emergency Powers (Scrap Lead)(Maximum Prices) Order 1945, should be construed in its ordinary acceptation or its acceptation in the particular trade to which the Order was, in my opinion, intended primarily to apply. If I accept [counsel for the Minister's] submission I would hold the commodity in question to be 'scrap lead'. There is no doubt that it is 'scrap' and that it is in the main 'lead'. I think that the submission on behalf of the defendants is correct, and that I should look to the aims of the Order and consider the people to whom it was meant to apply. The Order was meant to apply to a particular trade and the control of certain sales in that trade. I must have regard to the meaning of words as accepted by that trade. The commodity in this sale was invoiced as 'battery lead'. There is a distinction in the trade between the meaning of 'scrap lead' and 'battery lead', and in view of that distinction I hold that the defendants did not sell 'scrap lead'."

The schematic or teleological approach

[14.28] Where the application of the literal approach leads to an 'absurdity' the courts have recourse to alternative approaches, which in the past, as we have seen, were articulated as the golden and mischief rules. Where the possibility of an absurdity arises a court may reject the literal interpretation and attribute to the words a secondary, modified meaning which they are capable of bearing. In adopting an alternative it may examine the provision in its wider statutory context and take into account the perceived defect of the pre-existing law. In recent years the courts have tended to avoid using the terms 'golden' and 'mischief' rules, preferring to invoke the scheme and purpose of the statute. An early instance of this is provided by *Frescati Estates Ltd v Walker*[48] where the Supreme Court was called on to interpret the word 'applicant' in relation to the planning permission provisions of the Local Government (Planning and Development) Act 1963. The defendant submitted that the word should bear its literal meaning, that is anyone who applies, while the plaintiffs argued that it should be interpreted in a modified sense to mean a person who applies with the consent of the owner (thus excluding the defendant). The Supreme Court accepted the plaintiffs' contention despite the Act being silent on the question of owners' consent. In the course of his judgment (in which his brethren concurred) Henchy J observed:[49]

48. [1975] IR 177.
49. *Ibid*, at 189-190 (emphasis added).

> "The fundamental rule that a statute must be construed so as to keep its operation within the ambit of the broad *purpose* of the Act rules out such an interpretation; otherwise it would be possible for persons, by means of frivolous or perverse applications, to cause the imposition of duties and liabilities which would be wholly unnecessary for the operation of the Act in the interests of the common good … I find nothing in the *scheme* of the Act that would allow interfering, if well-intentioned, outsiders to intrude into the rights of those with a legal interest …"

This hints at the emerging 'schematic or teleological' approach, the classic articulation of which is to be found in the judgment of Henchy J in *Nestor v Murphy*:[50]

> "The two defendants are a married couple. Their family home is in Lucan in the county of Dublin. It is held by them under a long lease and they are joint tenants of the leasehold interest. In July, 1978, they agreed to sell their interest to the plaintiff. They each signed a contract to sell to the plaintiff for £18,500. In form it is a binding and enforceable contract. However, they refuse to complete the sale. The reason they give is that the contract is void under s 3(1), of the Family Home (Protection) Act 1976, because the wife did not consent in writing to the sale before the contract was signed. That is the net point in this claim by the plaintiff for the specific performance of the contract.
>
> A surface, or literal, appraisal of s 3(1), might be thought to give support to the defendants' objection to the contract. That sub-section states: 'Where a spouse, without the prior consent in writing of the other spouse, purports to convey any interest in the family home to any person except the other spouse, then, subject to subs (2) and (3) and s 4, the purported conveyance shall be void.' Sub-sections 2 and 3 of s 3, and s 4, are not applicable to this case. By reason of the definition in s 1(1), the contract signed by the defendants is a 'conveyance'. Therefore, the argument runs, the provisions of s 3(1), make the contract void because a spouse (the husband), without the prior consent in writing of the other spouse, 'conveyed' an interest in the family home to the plaintiff.
>
> The flaw in this interpretation of s 3(1), is that it assumes that it was intended to apply when both spouses are parties to the 'conveyance.' That, however, is not so. The basic purpose of the sub-section is to protect the family home by giving a right of avoidance to the spouse who was not a party to the transaction. It ensures that protection by requiring, for the validity of the contract to dispose and of the actual disposition, that the non-disposing spouse should have given a prior consent in writing. The point and purpose of imposing the sanction of voidness is to enforce the right of the non-disposing spouse to veto the disposition by the other

50. [1979] IR 326, at 328-330.

spouse of an interest in the family home. The sub-section cannot have been intended by Parliament to apply when both spouses join in the 'conveyance'. In such event no protection is needed for one spouse against an unfair and unnotified alienation by the other of an interest in the family home. The provisions of s 3(1), are directed against unilateral alienation by one spouse. When both spouses join in the 'conveyance,' the evil at which the sub-section is directed does not exist.

To construe the sub-section in the way proposed on behalf of the defendants would lead to a pointless absurdity. As is conceded by counsel for the defendants, if their construction of s 3(1), is correct then either the husband or the wife could have the contract declared void because the other did not give a prior consent in writing. Such an avoidance of an otherwise enforceable obligation would not be required for the protection of the family home when both spouses have entered into a contract to sell it. Therefore, it would be outside the spirit and purpose of the Act.

In such circumstances we must adopt what has been called a schematic or teleological approach. This means that s 3(1), must be given a construction which does not overstep the limits of the operative range that must be ascribed to it, having regard to the legislative scheme as expressed in the Act of 1976 as a whole. Therefore, the words of s 3(1), must be given no wider meaning than is necessary to effectuate the right of avoidance given when the non-participating spouse has not consented in advance in writing to the alienation of any interest in the family home …

Because it is evident from the pattern and purpose of the Act of 1976 that the primary aim of s 3(1), is to enable a spouse who was not a party to a 'conveyance' of the family home, and did not give a prior consent in writing to it, to have it declared void, and because an extension of that right of avoidance to spouses who have entered into a joint 'conveyance' would not only be unnecessary for the attainment of that aim but would enable contracts to be unfairly or dishonestly repudiated by parties who entered into them freely, willingly and with full knowledge, I would hold that the spouse whose 'conveyance' is avoided by the provisions of s 3(1), is a spouse who has unilaterally (ie, without the other spouse joining) purported to 'convey' an interest in the family home without having obtained the prior consent in writing of the other spouse. It is only by thus confining the reach of the sub-section that its operation can be kept within what must have been the legislative intent."

[14.29] When this approach is invoked a court examines the general purpose and scheme of the statute. In ascertaining the statutory purpose the court may examine the long title to the Act its subject matter and the pre-existing law which it was designed to alter.[51] Once the statutory purpose is identified

51. See *Minister for Industry and Commerce v Hales* [1967] IR 50; *Charles McCann Ltd v Ó Culacháin* [1986] IR 196; *Weekes v Revenue Commissioners* [1989] ILRM 165.

the provision in question is interpreted in a manner which is consistent with it and which avoids the absurdity. In effect, the courts read words into the provision.

[14.30] The invocation of the schematic approach is premised on the court's having concluded that an absurdity would result from the literal interpretation. But there is no clear or concrete definition of what constitutes an absurdity. Various broadly synonymous expressions which are employed by the courts to justify the adoption of a non-literal meaning are little more definite. The schematic approach is adopted where the literal meaning is said to be repugnant, to render the statute unworkable or meaningless or to be grossly unreasonable. On the other hand, the mere fact that the literal meaning would lead to an unfair, unreasonable or inequitable result is insufficient to warrant its rejection. Something more is required and an absurdity is considered to arise where the literal interpretation leads to a conclusion which, it is thought, could not have been intended by the Oireachtas. It is this factor, the failure to give effect to assumed intention of the Oireachtas, which justifies the invocation of the schematic approach. Thus, whilst ordinarily the modification by the courts of statutory language is considered to be a usurpation of the legislative function, such modification is permissible where it is done to implement the 'true' or 'real' intention of the Oireachtas. Nevertheless, the identification of an absurdity leaves an element of discretion to the courts and, to this extent, they are in the position of exercising choice. What to one court is considered to be absurd might not be so viewed by another. In *Rafferty v Crowley* Murphy J refused to adopt the schematic approach and read an exception into the definition of 'prior mortgage' in s 80 of the Building Societies Act 1976 on the grounds that if the Oireachtas intended to create that exception it could easily have done so:[52]

> "Counsel on behalf of the vendor plaintiff has sought to adopt a schematic or teleological approach to the Act and in particular s 80 thereof. She says that the purpose of the Act, and in particular Pt VI thereof, is to ensure that advances made by building societies are fully and properly secured for the benefit of the society and its members. That being the intent of the Act - or so the argument goes - no purpose would be served and no benefit would be achieved by preventing or prohibiting a society from lending on the security of part of the lands comprised in and demised by a lease where the owner of that part (or his predecessor) had charged it with the payment of the rent apportioned to that part as such a charge does not reduce, in any way, the value of the leasehold interest. Again, it is pointed out that the

52. [1984] ILRM 350, at 352-353.

1976 Act expressly recognises the right of a building society to advance money on the security of leasehold property. Every person holding any part of lands demised by a lease is on risk for the payment of the entire of the rent thereby reserved. Accordingly, the mutual covenants and cross-charges benefit rather than prejudice the holders of any part of leasehold land and through him any person holding a mortgage or charge on such lands. Accordingly, there is nothing to be gained and no purpose served by interpreting the words 'a prior mortgage' in s 80 so as to include cross-charges of this nature.

Whilst I have every sympathy with the case made by the plaintiff and indeed I believe that it would be in the public interest generally to uphold this construction of s 80 of the 1976 Act I do not believe that the accepted canons of construction would permit me to support that view.

Reference was made to the decision of the Supreme Court in *Nestor v Murphy*[53] as an example of a case in which the schematic approach might be adopted. However, it appears clearly from the judgment of Henchy J, that the approach was justified so as to avoid 'a pointless absurdity'. Again, Henchy J pursued 'the pattern and purpose' of the legislation then under consideration where he was satisfied that by doing otherwise 'would not only be unnecessary for the attainment of that aim but would enable contracts to be unfairly or dishonestly repudiated by parties who entered into them freely, willingly and with full knowledge'. It would appear that the schematic approach is justified where - in the words of Lord Reid in *Luke v The Inland Revenue Commissioners*:[54]

> 'To apply the words literally is to defeat the obvious intention of the legislation and to produce a wholly unreasonable result.'

It is clear that by s 80 the legislature set its face against a building society making a loan on the security of a property which was subject to any prior mortgage. It would have been a relatively easy task to restrict the operation of the section to cases where the prior mortgage or charge exceeded specified amounts or perhaps a particular percentage of the value of the property in question. Alternatively, what could have been done was to exclude the various categories of prior charge as was done by s 32 of the United Kingdom Building Societies Act 1962. If that precedent did not commend itself to the draftsman he could have adopted the formula used in s 99 of the Companies Act 1963 which, having provided for the registration of (among other things) a charge on land wherever situate or any interest therein, goes on to provide:

> 'but not including a charge for any rent or other periodical sum issuing out of land.'

53. [1979] IR 326.

54. [1963] AC 557, at 577

> In fact it does not require reference to examples or precedents confidently to infer that the legislature in enacting s 80 in its existing form was conscious of that fact that it could have exempt from the scope of the prohibition certain prior mortgages or charges and deliberately chose not to do so. In these circumstances it seems to me that I am precluded from interpreting s 80 so as to achieve an effect - however desirable - not intended by the Oireachtas."

[14.31] It is obvious that Murphy J considered the plaintiff's suggestion to conform to better legal policy and realised the inconvenience of a literal interpretation of the Act. Indeed, given the far-reaching economic and social consequences which his decision entailed he directed that copies of his judgment be sent immediately to the Minister for the Environment and the Registrar of Friendly Societies. Nevertheless, he still felt constrained by his role as an interpreter to adopt the literal meaning. Within a short time of his judgment being delivered the Oireachtas passed the Building Societies (Amendment) Act 1983 to create the exception which had been omitted from the original Act, thus confirming Murphy J's view of the need for urgent legislative action. One conclusion to be drawn from this sequence of events is that in this case the schematic approach would have reflected the intention of the legislature since it acted almost immediately to 'correct' the decision. On the other hand, it might be said that the enactment of an amending statute merely amounts to a legislative recognition of oversight on its part and is not a reflection on the decision in *Rafferty v Crowley.*

Schematic interpretation of EC measures

[14.32] The schematic approach has been adopted with especial enthusiasm in cases where the provision in question is contained in an EC legal measure or a national measure which derives from the obligations of EC law. This is not to be unexpected since purposive interpretation is particularly associated with continental jurists and is often adopted in the interpretation of EC law. The connection was drawn by Murphy J in *Lawlor v Minister for Agriculture*[55] which concerned the interpretation of the European Communities (Milk Levy) Regulations 1985[56] which implemented Article 5(1) and (2) of Council Regulation No 1371/84/EEC into domestic law. In the course of his judgment upholding the validity of the regulations, Murphy J considered the schematic approach and its application to legislative measures which implement EC regulations:[57]

---

55. [1990] 1 IR 356.

56. SI 416/1985.

57. *Ibid,* at 374-376; see Murphy J's judgment to the same effect in *O'Brien v Ireland* [1991] 2 IR 387; see also *Greene v Minister for Agriculture* [1990] 2 IR 17.

"Attention was drawn to the appropriate canons of interpretation of EEC legislation. In particular reference was made to the second edition of HG Schermers, *Judicial Protection in the European Communities* (1979) at pp 15-23 and the comments to be found therein on the teleological and schematic approaches to interpretation. With respect, it seems to me that the principles of interpretation were most helpfully and authoritatively dealt with in the paper read by Professor Kutscher, the President of the Chamber at the Court of Justice in Luxembourg in 1976 on *Methods of Interpretation as seen by a Judge at the Court of Justice.* I may quote at some length a passage from page 1.36 of that paper as follows:

> 'It would be superfluous to point out once more what importance schematic interpretation has in the case law of the Court of Justice. Its application corresponds to the special features which characterise the legal system of the community. If this legal system takes the form of a broadly conceived plan and if it confines itself essentially to setting aims and directions as well as to establishing principles and programmes for individual sectors, and if in addition there is no legislature which fills in the framework drawn up by the treaties within a reasonable time…the judge is compelled to supplement the law on his own and to find the detailed rules without which he is unable to decide the case brought before him. The judge can succeed in this task only by having recourse to the scheme the guidelines and the principles which can be seen to underlie the broad plan and the programme for individual sectors. Without recourse to these guidelines and principles it is not even possible to give precise definition to the significance and scope of the general rules and concepts of which the treaties make such abundant use…It is plain that such a schematic interpretation which sees the rules of community law in their relationship with each other and with the scheme and principles of the plan, cannot escape a certain systemisation and therefore on occasion demand that solutions of a problem be inferred by deduction from general principles of law.'

It is interesting to note from his decision in *Buchanan & Co v Babco Ltd*[58] that Lord Denning MR was equally impressed by Judge Kutscher's paper and he explained the European method of interpretation in the following terms:

> 'They adopt a method which they call in English by strange words - at any rate they were strange to me - the schematic and teleological method of interpretation. It is not really so alarming as it sounds. All it means is that the judges do not go by the literal meaning of the words or by the grammatical structure of the sentence. They go by the design or purpose which lies behind it. When they come upon a situation which is to their minds within

58. [1977] QB 208, at 213.

> the spirit - but not the letter - of the legislation, they solve the problem by looking at the design and purpose of the legislature - at the effect which it was sought to achieve. They then interpret the legislation so as to produce the desired effect. This means that they fill in gaps, quite unashamedly, without hesitation. They ask simply: what is the sensible way of dealing with this situation so as to give effect to the presumed purpose of the legislation?'

It is proper to say, however that the House of Lords on appeal from the Court of Appeal in *Buchanan & Co. v Babco Ltd*[59] made it clear that they did not share Lord Denning's enthusiasm for the schematic or teleological approach nor did they find any justification for incorporating it in the English legal system.

It seems to me that in construing EEC regulations I am bound to apply the canons of interpretation so clearly adumbrated by Judge Kutscher in his paper and with regard to domestic legislation it does seem to me that similar principles must be applicable at least insofar as it concerns the application of Community regulations to this State. Moreover, it does seem to me that the teleological and schematic approach has for many years been adopted in this country - though not necessarily under the description - in the interpretation of the Constitution. The innumerable occasions in which the preamble to the Constitution has been invoked and in particular the desire therein expressed 'to promote the common good with due observance of prudence, justice and charity so that the dignity and freedom of the individual may be assured, true social order attained, the unity of our country restored and concord established with other nations' in seeking to 'fill the gaps' in the Constitution is itself an obvious example of the teleological approach. Indeed in somewhat more mundane circumstances arising in the interpretation of the Family Home (Protection) Act 1976 in *Nestor v Murphy*[60] Henchy J expressly decided that the court 'must adopt what has been called a schematic or teleological approach'."

[14.33] This was re-iterated more recently in *Bosphorus Hava v Minister for Transport*[61] where Murphy J considered the interpretation of Council Regulation 990/93/EEC, and of the domestic regulations[62] which were made on foot of it, by virtue of which aircraft owned by Serbian nationals were to be impounded. An aeroplane which was leased by the plaintiffs, a Turkish airline, from Yugoslav Airlines was seized in Dublin Airport. Murphy J outlined the principles of interpretation thus:[63]

59. [1978] AC 141.
60. [1979] IR 326.
61. [1994] 2 ILRM 551.
62. European Communities (Prohibition of Trade with the Federal Republic of Yugoslavia (Serbia and Montenegro)) Regulations 1993; SI 144/1993.
63. [1994] 2 ILRM 551, at 557-558.

"Counsel for each party is in agreement with the general principle that the regulations in question should be interpreted purposively. That is to say that the court should take a teleological or schematic approach to these regulations. Those rules of interpretation were referred to by me at some length in *Lawlor v Minister for Agriculture*[64] where I traced this rule of interpretation from the exciting paper read in 1976 by Professor Kutscher, then a judge of the Court of Justice in Luxembourg, and entitled *Methods of Interpretation as seen by a judge at the Court of Justice* through to the adoption and incorporation of the said principles in Irish domestic law by the Supreme Court in *Nestor v Murphy*[65] but their rejection by the House of Lords as part of the English legal system in *Buchanan (James) Ltd v Babco Forwarding Shipping (UK) Ltd.*[66] At any rate, there is no doubt that the schematic and teleological approach is a fundamental principle of interpretation to be applied to EC regulations and directives.

Occasionally, in both European and Irish law, difficulty is encountered in identifying the precise purpose or end which the legislation under consideration is intended to achieve. No such problem arises in the present case. The express purpose of the harsh commercial regime imposed by the regulations is to deter the Federal Republic from engaging in or continuing with activities which will lead to further unacceptable loss of human life and material damage. It is clear, beyond debate, that these regulations are intended to operate as a punishment, deterrent or sanction against the people or government of that troubled republic. Conversely, it is equally clear that the regulations are not intended to punish or penalise peoples or countries who have not in any way caused or contributed to these tragic events. Between these two propositions there may be some grey areas."

[14.34] Applying those principles, Murphy J concluded that it was not the purpose of the regulation to cause hardship to innocent parties unless that was necessary to effect the sanction imposed on Yugoslavia (or Serbia and Montenegro) and he ordered the release of the aeroplane.

[14.35] This schematic approach was also adopted, in somewhat different circumstances, in *Murphy v Bord Telecom Éireann.*[67] Article 119 of the EEC Treaty contains the principle of equality of pay for men and women engaged in equal work. The Anti-Discrimination (Pay) Act 1974 provides for equal pay where a man and a woman are engaged in 'like work', which includes work of equal value. The applicant did work which was of greater value than that performed by the male employee with whom she compared herself. Initially, it was held on the basis of the literal approach that that did not

64. [1990] 1 IR 356.
65. [1979] IR 326.
66. [1978] AC 141.
67. [1989] ILRM 53.

amount to 'like work'.[68] The matter was referred to the European Court of Justice which ruled, *inter alia*, that:[69]

> "... Article 119 of the EEC Treaty must be interpreted as covering the case where a worker who relies on that provision to obtain equal pay within the meaning thereof is engaged in work of higher value than that of a person with whom a comparison is to be made."

[14.36] The case was remitted to the High Court where Keane J employed the schematic approach to bring the 1974 Act within that ruling:[70]

> "In the present case, counsel seemed to agree that treating the national law as inapplicable meant that the relevant provisions of the Act of 1974 were of no effect and that the rights of the appellants under Article 119 could be protected only in proceedings in this Court. [Counsel] ... on behalf of the appellants submitted that the applicability of the national law could and should be preserved by giving a purposive interpretation to the relevant sections rather than the literal construction which would normally be demanded.
>
> In my view, it does not follow that, if the national law is inapplicable, the rights of the appellants under Article 119 can be protected only by proceedings in this Court. The Oireachtas has provided in the Act of 1974 a statutory machinery intended to give effect to the principle of equal pay for equal work and has entrusted the arbitral role between employers and employees in this area to the Labour Court. That tribunal in discharging its statutory function is as much bound to apply the law of the Community as is this court. Similarly, where national law and Community law conflict, it must give precedence to Community law. It is accordingly entirely appropriate in the light of the ruling of the Court of Justice of the EC in the present case to remit the matter to the Labour Court with a direction that the issues between the parties should be determined on the basis that the appellants and the male employee are employed in 'like work'. The statutory adjudication must, in other words, be arrived at by applying the relevant principle of Community law enunciated by the Court of Justice of the EC rather than the words of ss 2 and 3 of the Act of 1974 literally construed as our principles of statutory construction require. This seems to me entirely in, accordance with the judgments of the Court of Justice in *Simmenthal*[71] and in the present case.
>
> There are other considerations which indicate that remitting the case to the Labour Court with such a direction is the appropriate course. The Act of 1974 is presumed to be constitutional until the contrary is shown and it is a

68. See [1986] ILRM 483.
69. [1989] ILRM 53, at 56.
70. *Ibid*, at 59-62.
71. *Amministrazione della Finanze dello Stato v Simmenthal* [1978] ECR 629.

necessary corollary of that presumption that the Oireachtas is presumed not to legislate in a manner which is in breach of rights protected under Community law. Those rights already existed in our domestic law by virtue of s 2 of the European Communities Act 1972 when the Act of 1974 was passed by the Oireachtas. In the present case, in the light of the ruling of the Court of Justice of the EC, this court should seek if possible to adopt a teleological construction of the relevant sections of the Act of 1974, [that is] one which looks to the effect of the legislation rather than the actual words used by the legislature.

It should be pointed out, in this context, that [counsel] on behalf of the respondents did not press the court at the resumed hearing to adhere to the literal construction and reject the teleological construction relied on by [counsel for the appellants]. There were of course practical considerations which made this a sensible course for the respondents to adopt. If, however, a party in a case such as the present were to press for a literal construction of the Act which necessitated a finding that the Oireachtas had legislated in contravention of Community law and hence in a manner which appeared to violate the primacy given to Community law under the Constitution, I would have thought it desirable that the Attorney General should be joined in the proceedings before that issue was resolved. In the present case, however, that course is unnecessary since, having regard to the stance adopted by the parties, a teleological construction of the sections, if such is available, should be adopted.

Such a construction was urged upon me both at the original and the resumed hearing by [counsel] on behalf of the appellants. This requires reading into the wording of ss 2 and 3a proviso that, in cases where the work is of unequal value and the worker doing the work of greater value is in fact being paid less than the other worker, the work is to be treated as though it were of equal value, and reading s 3(c) as though the words 'at least' appeared before the words 'equal in value'. Such a construction necessarily involves a departure from the ordinary and natural meaning of the words 'equal in value'. In the light of the interpretation of Article 119 laid down by the Court of Justice of the EC, however, it is this approach, rather than the literal approach adopted in my earlier judgment, which must be adopted by the court.

In my earlier judgment, I indicated that this approach does not in the present case bring about a situation of equal pay for equal work, but rather one of equal pay for unequal work. It has not been contended on behalf of the appellants that the Act can be interpreted so as to enable their remuneration to be increased to a level which would reflect the superiority of their work over the work of the male employee. They have confined their claim to the raising of their remuneration to the level of the male employee. However, while this matter is not specifically addressed in the judgment of the court, I think it is implicit in their judgment that the principle enshrined in Article 119 is sufficiently respected by the national legislation if it ensures that workers of one sex engaged in work of superior value to that of work of the opposite sex are not paid a *lower* wage than the latter on grounds of sex.

I am satisfied, accordingly, that the teleological construction of the relevant sections in the present case ensures the primacy of Community law and the efficacy of Article 119, as interpreted by the Court of Justice of EC, in this State.

I should, however, add one rider. In my earlier judgment, I said that:[72]

> 'This teleological or schematic approach, which was adopted by the Supreme Court in *Nestor v Murphy*[73] is not appropriate in a case such as the present where the legislature could by the use of apt language have provided for a particular situation but has failed to do so, whether intentionally or by an oversight. For the same reason, it is not possible to pray in aid the provisions of the EEC Treaty or the council directive on equal pay in the absence of any ambiguity, patent or latent, in the language used by the legislature.'

This passage appears to me, on further consideration, to be misleading. While it is true that the language used by the Oireachtas, literally interpreted, yields a result which is at variance with the law of the Community, it does not follow, as this passage might have suggested, that the literal construction is the only construction available. On the contrary, in the light of the judgment of the Court of Justice of the EC, it is clear that it must give way in the present case to the teleological construction, for the reasons I have already given."

The approaches compared

[14.37] Few problems surround the terms in which the literal and schematic or teleological approaches are formulated.[74] It is when those approaches are to be applied that difficulties are encountered. It is clear the literal approach may be abandoned only where its adoption would lead to an absurdity, but the question which remains is how can that condition be identified. It is equally clear that judicial preference or a belief that a non-literal meaning would make for better policy or would improve the terms of the statute does not justify the conclusion that an absurdity arises. This is illustrated by *Rafferty v Crowley*[75] where the court was satisfied that the failure of the legislature to include an exemption for the case in question precluded its

72. [1986] ILRM 483, at 487.
73. [1979] IR 326.
74. Curiously while there is little doubt as to what it entails it is uncertain from the decisions whether the second approach should be called 'schematic *or* teleological' or 'schematic *and* teleological', both expressions being used.
75. [1984] ILRM 350.

being supplied by judicial interpretation - if the Oireachtas had wished there to be an exemption it would have written it into the statute. However, the very same reasoning could have been adopted by the Supreme Court in *Nestor v Murphy*[76] where it invoked the schematic approach and exempted certain conveyances from the prior written consent requirement of the Family Home (Protection) Act 1976 - if the Oireachtas wished to exempt those conveyances from the ambit of the Act it could easily have done so by inserting an express provision to that effect. This demonstrates the element of choice which is left to the courts and which could have resulted in both those cases having been decided in the opposite way. This is not to suggest that one or other decision was 'wrong'. Given the element choice both decisions can be said to be 'correct' in that they are based on generally accepted principles of interpretation. To this extent, the interpretation of legislation, despite its purpose being to give effect to the legislative expression of choice, possesses a creative dimension not unlike the position which pertains in respect of common law decision making. Ultimately the decision to prefer one approach to the other is a matter of choice which is based on the judicial perception of the legislative intention which motivated the statute.

[14.38] It should not be assumed that the literal and schematic approaches inevitably lead to different conclusions or that a provision is susceptible to being interpreted on the basis of one approach only. The nature of some statutes is such that different interpreters might adopt different approaches while directing their efforts to the same end, namely that of discovering the legislative intention. Moreover, the adoption of the different approaches might in some instances result in the same conclusion. These points are illustrated by a series of decisions on the interpretation of the phrase 'manufactured goods' in various revenue statutes - typically the provisions in question allowed for relief from tax for producers of manufactured goods. In *Charles McCann Ltd v Ó Culacháin*[77] the appellants imported unripened bananas into the State and subjected them to an artificial ripening process. They contended that the ripened bananas were manufactured goods within the meaning of s 54 of the Corporation Tax Act 1976. In the High Court Carroll J, applying *Inspector of Taxes v Kiernan*,[78] rejected the contention arguing that an ordinary person would not attribute the term 'manufacture' to the ripening process.[79] The Supreme Court, in overturning that decision,

76. [1979] IR 326.
77. [1986] IR 196.
78. [1981] IR 117.
79. See [1985] IR 298, at 305-306.

invoked the scheme and purpose of the statute. McCarthy J's judgment enjoyed the concurrence of Finlay CJ and Hederman J:[80]

> "At first sight, it might be thought that 'manufactured' is a simple word which has a widespread and unambiguous currency; closer examination, however, reveals the use of the word in many differing ways; in some instances the word implies virtual creation, in others alteration of appearance rather than make-up, of shape rather than substance. I doubt if true guidance can be obtained from the application of the third basic rule [in *Inspector of Taxes v Kiernan*]. The second [rule in *Kiernan*] is clearly to be applied and depends for its application upon there being ambiguity or doubt as to the meaning of the word, and certainly there is that. Since the decision of the High Court in this case Murphy J, in construing somewhat like legislation, the Finance Act, 1980, s 41(2) (as amended by the Finance Act, 1982, s 26 and Schedule 2 thereof) in *Cronin (Inspector of Taxes) v Strand Dairy Ltd*[81] having adverted to the judgment of Carroll J in the instant case, and that of Lord MacDermott LCJ in *McCausland v Ministry of Commerce*,[82] expressed his own view as follows:
>
> > 'It seems to me, therefore, that one must look at the goods alleged to have been manufactured and consider what they are; how they appear, what qualities they possess, what value attaches to them. One then looks at the process and seeks to identify to what extent that process conferred on the goods the characteristics which they are found to possess. It is obvious - as indeed Lord MacDermott pointed out (at p 43) that the question is to a large extent one of degree. Nobody would doubt that well made and fully finished furniture would constitute manufactured goods but it is unlikely that the ordinary man would accept that the trunk of a tree which had been felled and provided a convenient seat constituted a manufactured article.'
>
> I agree with the approach as so stated, subject to the qualification that one must also, in aid of construction of the particular word *as used in the statute,* look to the scheme and purpose as disclosed by the statute or the relevant part thereof. It is true that one may eventually put the question, as stated by Carroll J - whether an ordinary person would attribute the word 'manufacture' to the ripening process, not whether the ordinary person in the street would describe the bananas which have been subjected to the ripening process as 'manufactured goods', but one must ensure that the ordinary person, as so contemplated, is one adequately informed as to those matters identified in the judgment of Murphy J which I have cited. The scheme and purpose of the relevant part of the statute appear to me to be

80. [1986] IR 196, at 200-201.
81. High Court, unrep, 18 December 1985.
82. [1956] NI 36.

> the very context within which the word is used and the requirements of which must be examined in order to construe it. It is manifest that the purpose of Pt IV of the Act of 1976 was, by tax incentives, to encourage the creation of employment within the State and the promotion of exports - naturally outside the State - objectives of proper, social and economic kind which the State would be bound to encourage. Employment is created by labour intensive processes and exports by the creation of saleable goods. The operation described in the case stated clearly comes within both categories; in my judgment, it is then a matter of degree, itself a question of law, as to whether or not what the company has done to the raw material makes it goods within the definition in s 54. Applying that test, I am satisfied that the ripened bananas, having been subjected to the process as described, constitute a commercially different product and one within the definition."

[14.39] The interpretation of s 42(2) of the Finance Act 1980, which allowed relief for goods manufactured within the State in the course of a trade carried on by a company, was considered in *Ó Culacháin v Hunter Advertising Ltd*.[83] An advertising agency produced video tapes, photographic negatives and posters and sold them to its clients for use during their advertising campaigns. The company argued that the goods were their creation and that, for instance, blank film which is of minimal value is, through the editing process, converted into something of substantial value. Murphy J expressed his doubts as to whether an ordinary person would consider the respondents' activities to constitute a manufacturing process and continued:[84]

> "... it is not sufficient to have regard to the views of the ordinary person as to what constitutes a manufacturing process or manufactured goods. In addition one must postulate the judgment of an ordinary person who is adequately informed as to the relevant legal principles involved and in addition one must look to the scheme and purpose disclosed by the statute in question."

Thus echoing the decision in *McCann* he concluded that the purpose of the statute was to assist manufacturing industry not the services industries, into which latter category the respondents fell, and accordingly relief was denied.[85]

---

83. [1990] 2 IR 431.

84. *Ibid*, at 435. See also *Brosnan v Leeside Nurseries Ltd* [1994] 2 ILRM 459, at 464 *per* Murphy J '...I think that a *properly informed observer* asking himself the question whether or not these out of season dwarfed chrysanthemums were goods manufactured by the taxpayer, could only conclude that such was not the case.' (emphasis added).

85. See *Denis Coakley & Co Ltd v Commissioner of Valuation* [1991] 1 IR 402 (HC); [1996] 2 ILRM 90 (SC), in which the High Court had adopted *McCann* in relation to the interpretation of the Annual Revision of Rateable Property (Ireland) Amendment Act 1860, s 7.

[14.40] In *Irish Agricultural Machinery Ltd v Ó Culacháin*[86] the appellants assembled agricultural machines from component parts. They claimed relief under s 31 of the Finance Act 1975 on the grounds, *inter alia*, that their trading operations consisted wholly or mainly of the manufacture of goods. The Supreme Court adopted *McCann* in relation to the interpretation of 'manufacture' but without express reference to the scheme or purpose of the statute. Griffin J speaking for the Court stated:[87]

> "... it seems to me that an ordinary adequately informed person would attribute the word 'manufacture' to the process carried on by the appellant. All the machines have a utility, a quality and a value entirely distinct from the component parts which comprise the whole. Instead of a confusing array of innumerable components ... which would be of no use or value whatever to anyone engaged in agriculture, each of the machines is of immense utility and value, and it seems to me that the fact that they have been 'assembled' rather than fabricated begs the question. It does not necessarily follow that it cannot be described as manufacture."

[14.41] A difference in approach is evident in *Ó Laochdha v Johnson and Johnson (Ireland) Ltd.*[88] The respondents, who produced nappy liners and 'J cloths' by placing bales of fabric through sophisticated machines which rapidly cut, folded, and in the case of the 'J cloths' packaged, them. The employees required special training to operate the machinery and while the process did not alter the nature of the cloth it did enhance its financial value significantly. Carroll J held that the items in question amounted to manufactured goods under s 42 of the Finance Act 1980 but in doing so distinguished *McCann* and the earlier cases on the basis of the difference in the respective manufacturing processes:[89]

> "The present case differs from *Charles McCann Ltd v Ó Culacháin*[90] and *W Cronin (Inspector of Taxes) v Strand Dairies Ltd*[91] in that no change is effected in the raw material. The fabric in the J cloths and nappy liners is identical to the bulk fabric on the bale. The case differs from *Irish Agricultural Machinery Ltd v Ó Culacháin*[92] in that nothing is added so that there is no aggregation of component parts. The appellant [the inspector of taxes] therefore claims that all that has occurred is a sophisticated cutting, folding and packaging process where the quality of the bulk fabric has not

86. [1990] 1 IR 535.
87. *Ibid,* at 543.
88. [1991] 2 IR 287.
89. *Ibid,* at 289-290.
90. [1986] IR 196.
91. High Court, unrep, 18 December 1985.
92. [1990] 1 IR 535.

changed.

However the machinery which produces the two products is an expensive, sophisticated and fast machine. Looking at the end product one can immediately say that it is commercially different from the bales of fabric. The process adds more than 70% in value to the J cloths and 40% to the nappy liners according to the manufacturing costs set out in the case stated. It seems to me that the reduction in size and ease of handling combined with the inherent quality of the raw material has a utility, quality and worth which are due to, and cannot be dissociated from, the process carried out by the respondent. The fact that the process does not bring about any change in the raw material does not of itself prevent the process from being a manufacturing process. I can think of other products where the raw material is unchanged. A toothpick is part of a tree which has been cut and packaged but it has an intrinsic quality given to it by the process, namely size and convenience and being tailored to a purpose. Confetti is another. You can throw confetti where you could not throw bulk paper.

Even though the raw material is unchanged the quality of the end product is commercially enhanced by the process. I am quite sure that an ordinary person, even if he or she did not know how the actual process was carried out, would consider the process to be a manufacturing process."

[14.42] Given the ambiguity attaching to an expression such as 'manufactured goods' the abundance of decisions on its interpretation can hardly be a matter of surprise.[93] By the same token it is unobjectionable that the courts view the matter as being one of degree with the determination to be made based on the circumstances of particular cases. What is interesting is that in determining which side of the line any particular case falls a variety of methods of interpretation have been adopted in relation to the same provision. In *Charles McCann Ltd v Ó Culacháin*[94] the scheme and purpose of the statute was expressly referred and was influential in the ultimate resolution of the issue. Likewise in *Ó Culacháin v Hunter Advertising Ltd*,[95] although in that case the consideration of the scheme and purpose convinced the court that the goods were not 'manufactured'. In *Irish Agricultural Machinery Ltd v Ó Culacháin*[96] *McCann* was cited but the court also referred to the first principle in Henchy J's judgment in *Inspector of Taxes v Kiernan*.[97] This serves to confuse matters since while there are references both approaches the court was silent as to which, if either, it was adopting. All that can safely be said is that the court accepted the *McCann* definition

93. See *McNally v Ó Maoldomhnaigh* [1990] 2 IR 513 where the Finance Act 1971, s 22 was said to be ambiguous, thus allowing the object of the statute to be considered.
94. [1986] IR 196.
95. [1990] 2 IR 431.
96. [1990] 1 IR 535.
97. [1981] IR 117.

of 'manufactured goods' and the decision might well do little more than illustrate the application of *stare decisis* to statutory interpretation. In *Ó Laochdha v Johnson and Johnson (Ireland) Ltd*[98] Carroll J's concluding words ('an ordinary person ... would consider the process to be a manufacturing process') seem to amount to a return by her to her initial position in *McCann*. In that case she stated the criterion to be whether an ordinary person would consider the artificial ripening of bananas to be a manufacturing process, an approach which was overturned by the Supreme Court.[99]

[3] Aids To Interpretation

[14.43] The general approaches to interpretation which have been considered in the preceding section are supplemented by a variety of devices which are invoked in the course of interpretation. It should be noted that these devices, which are often expressed in the form of maxims and presumptions, do not supplant the general approaches but complement them. The devices in question include presumptions which derive from the nature of the legislation and what have been called 'linguistic canons of construction'[100] which exist in respect of statutory language. Like the general approaches they reflect judicial attitudes and practices adopted in the exercise of interpreting legislation and are invoked on the assumption that their application best identifies the intention of the legislature. In other words it is assumed that the Oireachtas intended the words to bear the meaning which the particular device would attribute to it. By the same token a draftsman will be aware of their existence and the courts' employment of them and it may be presumed he will take them into account when drafting legislation. Thus, if a particular object is sought to be achieved by legislation the draftsman might be directed towards a particular form of words to secure that objective.

Presumption of constitutionality

[14.44] It is presumed that all statutes enacted by the Oireachtas are constitutional until the contrary is established. This is based on an assumption that the Oireachtas intends to abide by the provisions of the Constitution. The presumption was outlined by the Supreme Court in *East Donegal Co-operative Livestock Mart Ltd v Attorney General*:[101]

98. [1991] 2 IR 287.
99. See para **[14.38]**.
100. Bennion, *Statute Law* 3rd ed (Longman, 1990) p 187.
101. [1970] IR 317, at 341.

"…an Act of the Oireachtas, or any provision thereof, will not be declared to be invalid where it is possible to construe it in accordance with the Constitution; and it is not only a question of preferring a constitutional construction to one which would be unconstitutional where they both may appear to be open but it also means that an interpretation favouring the validity of an Act should be given in cases of doubt. It must be added, of course, that interpretation or construction of an Act or any provision thereof in conformity with the Constitution cannot be pushed to the point where the interpretation would result in the substitution of the legislative provision by another provision with a different context, as that would be to usurp the functions of the Oireachtas. In seeking to reach an interpretation or construction in accordance with the Constitution, a statutory provision which is clear and unambiguous cannot be given an opposite meaning. At the same time, however, the presumption of constitutionality carries with it not only the presumption that the constitutional interpretation or construction is the one intended by the Oireachtas but also that the Oireachtas intended that proceedings, procedures, discretions and adjudications which are permitted, provided for, or prescribed by an Act of the Oireachtas are to be conducted in accordance with the principles of constitutional justice. In such a case any departure from those principles would be restrained and corrected by the Courts."

[14.45] It is also presumed that statutes passed by the Oireachtas of the Irish Free State accord with the Constitution under which they were enacted. A number of consequence flow from the presumption. One is that in cases where the validity of a statute is challenged it assigns the burden of proof to the party who alleges invalidity. Second, the presumption has a bearing on the interpretation of post-1937 statutes. Those statutes must, where possible, be interpreted in a manner which would render them constitutional, an approach that has been called the 'double construction' rule.[102] Thus, where a court is faced with two reasonable interpretations, one of which would result in the statute bearing a constitutional meaning, and the other of which would render the statute unconstitutional, the former must be adopted. In this respect, the presumption establishes a binding rule unlike the other principles of interpretation. On the other hand it is accepted that the presumption should not be invoked to save the validity of a statute where the effect would be amend or substitute the provision in question.[103] Third, it is also presumed that all powers and procedures created by the statute will be exercised in a manner which accords with the dictates of the Constitution. Thus, where a statute confers a power in open-ended terms it will be

102. Hogan & Whyte, *Kelly's The Irish Constitution* 3rd ed (Butterworths, 1994) pp 458-459.

103. *Dowling v Ireland* [1991] 2 IR 379.

construed as authorising only those exercises of the power which are compatible with the Constitution.[104]

[14.46] The presumption has determined the interpretation of a number of provisions. In *Quinn v Wren* the Supreme Court interpreted 'political offence' and 'offence connected with a political offence' in s 50 of the Extradition Act 1965 to exclude offences which were committed on behalf of the Irish National Liberation Army (INLA). In his judgment Finlay CJ invoked the presumption:[105]

> "The Act … having been passed since the coming into force of the Constitution, the first and fundamental rule which governs that interpretation is that it must be presumed that the Oireachtas intended an interpretation which will not offend any express or implied provision of the Constitution…
>
> The plaintiff states that he committed the offence charged for the purposes of the INLA, the aims and objectives of which are the establishment of a 32 county workers' republic by force of arms. The achievement of that objective necessarily and inevitably involves the destruction and setting aside of the Constitution by means expressly or impliedly prohibited by it: see Articles 15.6 and 39. To interpret the words 'political offence' contained in s 50 of the Act of 1965 so as to grant immunity or protection to a person charged with an offence directly intended to further that objective would be to give the section a patently unconstitutional construction. The Court cannot, it seems to me, interpret an Act of the Oireachtas as having an intention to grant immunity from extradition to a person charged with an offence, the admitted purpose of which is to further or facilitate the overthrow, by violence, of the Constitution and of the organs of State established thereby."

[14.47] The decision in that case is not beyond dispute[106] but, for present purposes, its interest lies in the fact that the presumption determined the interpretation which was adopted. Similarly, in *In re JH*[107] the Supreme Court construed s 3 of the Guardianship of Infants Act 1964 as involving a constitutional presumption, based on Article 42.1, that the best interests of a child are protected within the family unit unless there is compelling evidence to the contrary. Concerns of constitutionality arose in somewhat different circumstances in *National Union of Journalists v Sisk*.[108] There

104. See discussion of the constitutionality of exercise of powers of delegated legislation, paras **[13.65]-[13.71]**.

105. [1985] IR 322, at 337.

106. Its 'rather artificial reasoning' (*per* Hogan & Whyte, *Kelly's The Irish Constitution* 3rd ed (Butterworths, 1994) p 670) was endorsed in *Russell v Fanning* [1988] IR 505 but was subsequently departed from in *Finucane v McMahon* [1990] 1 IR 165.

107. [1985] IR 375.

108. [1992] ILRM 96.

ss 2, 3 and 4 of the Trade Union Act 1975, which governed the transfer of engagements, were interpreted in a fashion which facilitated the enjoyment of the freedom of association guaranteed by Article 40.6.1°(iii). In the absence of an express statutory limitation of the enjoyment of that right the Court refused to interpret it as containing an implied restriction. It should, however, be realised that the interpretation of a word need not necessarily be confined to the meaning which it bears in the Constitution, provided that a different meaning does not lead to the statute's being unconstitutional. Thus, in *Jordan v O'Brien*[109] the word 'family' in the Rent Restrictions Act 1946 was given a wider interpretation than that which in bears in Article 41 of the Constitution - the point is that the narrower meaning which the word bears in the Constitution was not necessary to ensure the validity of the Act.

Presumption of compatibility with EC law

[14.48] It is an accepted principle that EC secondary legislation, such as regulations and directives, should be interpreted in a manner which preserves its compatibility with the provisions of the Treaties.[110] In *Dowling v Ireland*[111] Murphy J recognised the similarity between that proposition and the presumption of constitutionality. In principle, it should follow from the applicability of EC law in, and its precedence over, domestic law that as a matter of domestic law a court should interpret legislation, be it EC or national, in a manner which is consistent with the Treaties. Moreover, the so-called doctrine of 'indirect effect' requires a court to interpret its domestic legislation in conformity with EC law, in so far as it has a discretion so to do.[112] Thus, cognizance should be taken of EC measures which are not directly effective when interpreting the national implementing legislation. Indeed, although the matter was not expressed in those terms, *Murphy v Bord Telecom Éireann*[113] illustrates the point where the demands of EC law overrode a literal reading of a domestic measure. The Anti-Discrimination (Pay) Act 1974 was interpreted in such a way as to preserve its validity under Article 119 of the Treaty of Rome.

---

109. [1960] IR 363.

110. *Blottner v Bestuur van de Niewe Algemene Bedrijfsvereniging* [1977] ECR 1141; *Statens Control v Larsen* [1978] ECR 1543; *Klench v Secretaire d'État à l'Agriculture et à la Viticulture* [1986] ECR 3477.

111. [1991] 2 IR 379.

112. *Von Colson and Kamann v Land Nordrhein-Westfalen* [1984] ECR 1891; see Hartley, *Foundations of European Community Law* 3rd ed (Oxford University Press, 1994) pp 222-225.

113. [1989] ILRM 53; see para **[14.36]**.

Presumption of compatibility with international law

[14.49] The nature of international law and its status is considered elsewhere.[114] While international law does not apply within the domestic legal system (unless it is specifically incorporated by a domestic legal measure) it can prove to be of assistance in statutory interpretation. In addition to having recourse to international legal instruments[115] there is a general presumption that the Oireachtas intended to abide by its international legal obligations when it enacted domestic legislation.[116] This principle was considered in *Ó Domhnaill v Merrick* where the extent of its operation was subject to different interpretations. In his majority judgment Henchy J stated:[117]

> "… one must assume that the statute was enacted (there being no indication in it of a contrary intention) subject to the postulate that it would be construed and applied in consonance with the State's obligations under international law, including any relevant treaty obligations. The relevance of that rule of statutory interpretation in this case lies in the fact that Article 6(1) of the Convention for the Protection of Human Rights and Fundamental Freedoms (1950) provides - 'In the determination of his civil rights and obligations or of any criminal charge against him, every one is entitled to a fair hearing *within a reasonable time* by an independent and impartial tribunal established by law.' I have supplied the emphasis.
>
> While the Convention is not part of the domestic law of the State, still, because the Statute of Limitations 1957, was passed after this State ratified the Convention in 1953, it is to be argued that the Statute, since it does not show any contrary intention, should be deemed to be in conformity with the convention and should be construed and applied accordingly."

However, in his dissenting judgment McCarthy J took a different approach. He agreed with the principle of interpretation in accordance with international law but was reluctant to invoke the Convention on the ground that it is had not been enacted into domestic law:[118]

---

114. See paras **[17.01]**.

115. See further para **[14.84]**.

116. The courts have also been prepared to construe common law rules in the light of international obligations; see *The State (DPP) v Walsh* [1981] IR 412; *Desmond v Glackin (No 2)* [1993] 3 IR 67: see para **[17.20]**.

117. [1984] IR 151, at 159.

118. *Ibid,* at 166. This argument is based in part on Article 29.6 of the Constitution which provides that '[n]o international agreement shall be part of the domestic law of the State save as may be determined by the Oireachtas'; see also *Croke v Smith and ors*, High Court, unrep, 31 July 1995, *per* Budd J at pp 34-35: '… while this Court can look to the European Convention and the United Nations principles as being influential guidelines with regard to matters of public policy … [where] there is a challenge to the constitutionality of [legislation] such Conventions may not be used as a touchstone with regard to constitutionality.'

> "I accept, as a general principle, that a statute must be construed, so far as possible, so as not to be inconsistent with the established rules of international law and that one should avoid a construction which will lead to a conflict between domestic and international law … but since the Convention is not part of the domestic law of the State (*In re Ó Laighléis*),[119] I cannot subscribe to the view that the Statute of Limitations … is to be limited by Article 6(1) of the Convention."

Presumption that all words bear a meaning

[14.50] It is assumed that the legislature intended that each word in a provision should contribute to its meaning. It is taken that the legislature did not intend words to be redundant and provisions are to be construed accordingly. The matter was alluded to by the Supreme Court in *Cork County Council v Whillock* where O'Flaherty J stated:[120]

> "… a construction which would leave without effect any part of the language of a statute will normally be rejected."

while Egan J explained the matter thus:[121]

> "There is abundant authority for the presumption that words are not used in a statute without a meaning and are not tautologous or superfluous, and so effect must be given, if possible, to all the words used, for the legislature must be deemed not to waste its words or say anything in vain."

Presumption that a statute should be given an 'updated' meaning

[14.51] Significant elements of the statute law which currently applies have been inherited from previous generations.[122] Frequent updating is not practicable with the result that legislation which was drafted in the language of earlier generations is to be applied to changed times. If the interpretation of such legislation were to be governed by the historical context in which it was enacted its adaptability to new circumstances would be appreciably retarded. The words of Lavery J in *The State (O'Connor) v Ó Caomhanaigh* are pertinent:[123]

> "Many statutes … were conditioned by the political, economic, religious and social sentiments of the time of their enactment or establishment but it is the provisions themselves which are to be looked at and examined - not the motives of those who enacted them."

---

119. [1960] IR 93. See further para **[17.17]**.
120. [1993] 1 IR 231, at 237.
121. *Ibid,* at 239.
122. See Hurst, 'The Problem of the Elderly Statute' (1983) 3 LS 21.
123. [1963] IR 112, at 118.

[14.52] Bennion has suggested that statutes should be given an 'updated' meaning, that is one which facilitates their being applied to new conditions.[124] This is based on the notion that an Act is 'always speaking' and that the legislature intended that the law be capable of applying to future circumstances. An interpreter should, accordingly, make allowances for changes in the law and in social and technological conditions. Thus, in *Attorney General v Edison Telephone Co*[125] the word 'telegraph' in the Telegraph Act 1863 was interpreted to include a telephone, despite the fact that that instrument had not been invented, nor it would appear to have been contemplated, in 1863.

[14.53] Broad but qualified support for the principle of 'updated' interpretation was expressed by Murphy J in *Keane v An Bord Pleanála*:[126]

> "I have no difficulty in accepting the desirability and, in general, the necessity for giving to legislation an 'updating construction'. Where terminology used in legislation is wide enough to capture a subsequent invention, there is no reason to exclude it from the ambit of the legislation. But a distinction must be made between giving an updated construction to the general scheme of the legislation and altering the meaning of particular words used therein."

[14.54] Murphy J appears to be less enthusiastic about updated construction than Bennion and would adopt that construction only if it could be shown to be within the general intent of the statute, as might be the case if wide terminology is employed. His explanation of the decision in *Edison Telephone* was that language in the Telegraph Act 1863 was sufficiently wide in that it 'anticipated every form of communication whether by signal or sound conveyed by means of electric currents of varying intensities along wires'.[127] In the instant case the question was whether an electronic navigation aid, known as the Loran-C system, was a 'lighthouse, buoy or beacon' within the meaning of s 638 of the Merchant Shipping Act 1894. In answering in the negative, Murphy J took account both of the general scheme of the legislation and the terms in which it was drafted:[128]

> "It is submitted on behalf of the respondents that the 'great object' of Part 11 of the 1894 Act was and remains to enable the Commissioners [of Irish

124. *Statute Law* 3rd ed (Longman, 1990) pp 181-186; see also Cross, *Statutory Interpretation* 3rd ed (Butterworths, 1995) p 51.

125. (1886) 6 QBD 244.

126. High Court, unrep, 4 October 1995, Supreme Court, unrep, 18 July 1996. The Supreme Court upheld the conclusions of Murphy J.

127. *Ibid,* at p 11.

128. *Ibid,* at pp 18-19.

> Lights], in the interests of the safety of mariners, to provide all necessary aids for navigation.
>
> I do not accept that it is possible to interpret this legislation or ascertain the statutory powers of the Commissioners of Irish Lights by reference to such a wide general principle. The history of the Commissioners was based on legislation conferring jurisdiction on the different bodies within particular geographical areas of the then United Kingdom. The powers given to the different Commissioners [in Britain and Ireland] in relation to navigation were defined by reference to precise equipment, that is to say, lighthouses, buoys and beacons and not by reference to navigational aids in general terms. The area of operations would appear to have been local rather than international and the means of signalling was identified, and as a result limited, to procedures which were visual or aural. What the authorities establish is that if a suitable formula had been used by the draftsman foreseeing scientific development or speculating in science fiction, it might have been possible to define a 'lighthouse' in the 1894 Act so as to include any structure or device emitting or radiating any wave motion, particle or source of energy which could be utilised to make contact with or provide warnings to vessels, vehicles or craft of any description and in any part of the world for the purpose of alerting them to potential danger or enabling them to fix their position. That course was not adopted … It does not seem to me that the general scheme of the Act or more particularly the range of the powers and duties expressly or implicitly conferred on the Commissioners or the particular words used in the 1894 Act would permit them to engage in the construction, maintenance or operation of a navigational aid system based on the transmission by and reception (on equipment which had not been invented) of a wave motion or impulse which had not then been identified."

[14.55] The more cautious approach which is evident in this decision is commendable. It is possible to anticipate social and technological change and legislation can be drafted in terms which embrace that anticipation. Where it is not so drafted it is reasonable to conclude that such change was not intended to come within the scope of the legislation and that the legislature reserved the matter for further legislation. The application of the updated construction technique to unanticipated change is more difficult to justify, since in this case it is not possible to impute an intention in that regard to the legislature or the draftsman. Moreover, it is precisely that change which raises the profound ethical, moral and social dilemmas which require express consideration by lawmakers.

Presumption against unclear changes in the law

[14.56] The effect of this presumption is that a change in the law must be achieved unambiguously, either by express terms or by a clear implication.

In the event of an ambiguity a court should decline to interpret the provision as changing the law. The presumption dates from the time when the bulk of the law consisted of common law rules and statute law played a comparatively unimportant role, in the main curing its defects or mischiefs.[129] Given the current importance of legislation as a source of law the presumption probably enjoys lesser significance than heretofore. Moreover, it overlaps with a number of other rules of interpretation (especially those urging strict construction) which insist that a desired statutory objective must be achieved clearly and unambiguously. Hence the presumption is unlikely to prove to be crucial in questions of interpretation. Nevertheless, a version of the presumption, that against implicit alteration of the law, was expressly endorsed by Henchy J in *Minister for Industry & Commerce v Hales*.[130] Applying the presumption he avoided an interpretation which would result in 'radical and far-reaching changes in the law of contract'.[131]

Presumption that penal statutes be construed strictly

[14.57] Based a concern to protect individual liberty, it is presumed that if the Oireachtas wishes to impose penal liability it will do so expressly in clear and unambiguous terms. The corollary is that penal statutes should be construed strictly, in a manner which leans against the creation or extension of penal liability by implication. One of the reasons advanced in *Frescati Estates Ltd v Walker*[132] for the interpretation which was adopted was that a literal reading of the provision would have led to the imposition of penal duties and liabilities on landowners. In *CW Shipping Co Ltd v Limerick Harbour Commissioners* a tug was held not to come within the licensing requirements of s 53(1) of the Harbours Act 1946 on the basis, *inter alia*, that:[133]

> "…a penal provision in a statute must be construed strictly, and this rule is a further constraint on giving to the terminology of [the section] the wide interpretation necessary if the use of tugs are to be brought within its ambit."

[14.58] Given its concern with individual liberty it is hardly surprising that the principle of strict construction is applicable in relation to statutes which confer police powers. In *The People (DPP) v Farrell*[134] it was stated that s 30

129. See Cross, *Statutory Interpretation* 3rd ed (Butterworths, 1995) pp 167-168.
130. [1967] IR 50, at 76.
131. *Ibid,* at 77; see also *DPP v McCreesh* [1992] 2 IR 239.
132. [1975] IR 177.
133. [1989] ILRM 416, at 424.
134. [1978] IR 13; see *in re Emergency Powers Bill 1976* [1977] IR 159, at 173, "[a] statutory provision of this nature which makes such inroads upon the liberty of the person must be strictly construed."

of the Offences Against the State Act 1939 must be strictly construed; the Court of Criminal Appeal refused to assume in the absence of evidence to that effect that the procedural requirements of that section had been complied with by the Gardaí. Likewise, road traffic legislation is to be construed strictly.[135] Extradition provisions are also to be construed strictly on the same basis that they constitute a 'penal statutory code involving penal sanctions on an individual'.[136] In some instances, however, legislation which imposes criminal sanctions, especially in the regulatory sphere, is subject to an 'intermediate' approach. Industrial legislation, such as the Factories Act 1955 and its successor the Safety, Health and Welfare at Work Act 1989, attracts an expansive interpretation in respect of some of its provisions while a stricter approach is taken in the interpretation of others.[137]

Presumption that revenue statutes be construed strictly

[14.59] This presumption, which is analogous to that requiring strict construction of penal provisions, is stated as the second proposition in Henchy J's judgment in *Inspector of Taxes v Kiernan*[138] and has received frequent judicial endorsement.[139] In his authoritative pronouncement on the matter in *Revenue Commissioners v Doorley*, Kennedy CJ equated the question of the imposition of tax with that of its exemption:[140]

> "The duty of the Court, as it appears to me, is to reject an *a priori* line of reasoning and to examine the text of the taxing Act in question and determine whether the tax in question is thereby imposed expressly and in clear and unambiguous terms, on the alleged subject of taxation, for no person or property is to be subjected to taxation unless brought within the letter of the taxing statute, ie within the letter of the statute as interpreted with the assistance of the ordinary canons of interpretation applicable to Acts of Parliament so far as they can be applied without violating the proper character of taxing Acts to which I have referred.
>
> I have been discussing taxing legislation from the point of view of the imposition of tax. Now the exemption from tax, with which we are immediately concerned, is governed by the same considerations. If it is clear that a tax is imposed by the Act under consideration, then exemption

135. See generally Pierse, *Road Traffic Law* 2nd ed (Butterworths, 1995).
136. *Aamand v Smithwick* [1995] 1 ILRM 61, at 67.
137. Compare *Franklin v Gramaphone Ltd* [1948] 1 KB 542, at 557 with *Harrison v National Coal Board* [1951] 1 All ER 1102, at 1107.
138. [1981] IR 117; see para **[14.24]**.
139. See eg *Kellystown Co v Hogan* [1985] ILRM 200; *Charles McCann Ltd v Ó Culacháin* [1986] IR 196; *Texaco (Ireland) Ltd v Murphy* [1991] 2 IR 449; *Trustees of Kinsale Yacht Club v Commissioner of Valuation* [1994] 1 ILRM 457. Of course, in many cases the literal approach will coincide with this presumption as *Inspector of Taxes v Kiernan* [1981] IR 117 demonstrates.
140. [1933] IR 750, at 765-766.

> from that tax must be given expressly and in clear and unambiguous terms, within the letter of the statute as interpreted with the assistance of the ordinary canons for the interpretation of statutes … [t]he Court is not, by greater indulgence in delimiting the area of exemptions, to enlarge their operation beyond what the statute, clearly and without doubt and in express terms, excepts for some good reason from the burden of a tax thereby imposed generally on that description of subject-matter. As the imposition of, so the exemption from, the tax must be brought within the letter of the taxing Act as interpreted by the established canons of construction so far as applicable."

Presumption against retrospective effect

[14.60] Article 15.5 of the Constitution provides that '[t]he Oireachtas shall not declare acts to be infringements of the law which were not so at the date of their commission'. This clearly prohibits the enactment of retrospective penal legislation and, probably, legislation which imposes a civil or revenue liability.[141] The philosophy underlying that provision is that it is inherently unjust to declare acts to be unlawful which were lawful at the time of their commission. Similar sentiments infuse the common law presumption that legislation does not operate retrospectively. The presumption was considered by the Supreme Court in *Hamilton v Hamilton* where O'Higgins CJ examined its history and underlying concern:[142]

> "This brings me to the subject of retrospectivity; it is necessary to state with some precision what I regard as such in a statute. Many statutes are passed to deal with events which are over and which necessarily have a retrospective effect. Examples of such statutes, often described as *ex post facto* statutes, are to be found in Acts of immunity or pardon. Other statutes having a retroactive effect are statutes dealing with the practice and procedure of the Courts and applying to causes of action arising before the operation of the statute. Such statutes do not and are not intended to impair or affect vested rights and are not within the type of statute with which, it seems to me, this case is concerned. For the purpose of stating what I mean by retrospectivity in a statute, I adopt a definition taken from *Craies on Statute Law*[143] which is, I am satisfied, based on sound authority. It is to the effect that a statute is to be deemed to be retrospective in effect when it 'takes away or impairs any vested right acquired under existing laws, or creates a new obligation, or imposes a new duty, or attaches a new disability in respect to transactions or considerations already past'…

141. See *Doyle v An Taoiseach* [1986] ILRM 693; *Magee v Culligan* [1992] 1 IR 223; *In re Hefferon Kearns Ltd (No 1)* [1993] 3 IR 177; see also Hogan & Whyte, *Kelly's The Irish Constitution* 3rd ed (Butterworths, 1994) pp 127-131.

142. [1982] IR 466, at 473-475.

143. 7th ed (Sweet & Maxwell, 1971) p 387.

Retrospective legislation, since it necessarily affects vested rights, has always been regarded as being prima facie unjust. In the early seventeenth century Coke sought to establish the principle that the common law could control such Acts and adjudge them void as being contrary to 'the natural law' or 'common right and reason' - see *Dr Bonham's Case*.[144] In this view he was supported by Lord Hobart in *Day v Savadge*[145] and by Lord Holt in *City of London v Wood*.[146] However, with the recognition by the English courts of the sovereignty of Parliament in the eighteenth century, this view was no longer maintained and Blackstone[147] was able to declare in his commentaries: 'If Parliament would positively enact a thing to be done which is unreasonable, there is no power in the ordinary forms of the Constitution that is vested with the authority to control it.' And further, that an Act of Parliament is 'the exercise of the highest authority that the Kingdom acknowledges on earth.'

It is, therefore, in the light of the existence of a sovereign parliament, entitled to legislate both retrospectively and prospectively, that the English courts have laid down the principles on which a statute should be examined for retrospectivity. The result is a rule of construction which leans against such retrospectivity and which, according to Maxwell, is based upon the presumption 'that the legislature does not intend what is unjust'[148]...

Having referred, perhaps unnecessarily, to the past and to the manner in which the courts (both in England and in Ireland) considered the question of retrospectivity in relation to the Acts of a sovereign parliament, I must now come to the present and to the examination of an Act of the Oireachtas for the same purpose. Our Oireachtas, or legislature, is subject to the Constitution - like all other organs of the State. Its powers are circumscribed by constitutional limitations. In considering and interpreting Acts of the Oireachtas we must assume, in the first instance, that what the legislature has done was not intended to contravene the Constitution...[O'Higgins CJ noted the effect of the presumption of constitutionality on interpretation and continued]...This approach to the interpretation and construction of Acts of the Oireachtas is required by the Constitution. While it may not replace the common-law rule, it certainly supersedes it once a question of the possible infringement of the Constitution arises."

In the same case Henchy J put the issue thus:[149]

144. (1610) 8 Co Rep 114(a).
145. (1614) Hob 85.
146. (1701) 12 Mod Rep 669.
147. 1 Comm 91.
148. See *Maxwell on The Interpretation of Statutes* 12 ed (Sweet & Maxwell, 1969) p 215.
149. [1982] IR 466, at 480-481.

"From a wide range of judicial decisions I find the relevant canon of interpretation at common law to be this. When an Act changes the substantive, as distinct from procedural, law then, regardless of whether the Act is otherwise prospective or retrospective in its operation, it is not to be deemed to affect proceedings brought under the pre-Act law and pending at the date of the coming into operation of the Act, unless the Act expressly or by necessary intendment provides to the contrary."

[14.61] It is clear from *Hamilton v Hamilton* that the presumption does not apply to every provision which operates retrospectively; its principal concern is with statutes which alter substantive law or which affect vested rights.[150] A difference in emphasis is evident in *Dublin County Council v Grealy* where Blayney J spoke of a presumption that a statute should apply prospectively and continued:[151]

"... the Act must express a clear and unambiguous intention to [operate retrospectively], or there must be some circumstances rendering it inevitable that the court should conclude that the Act is retrospective, or the change effected by the statute must be purely procedural."

[14.62] The constitutional dimension to the presumption was noted in *In re Hefferon Kearns Ltd (No 1)*[152] where Murphy J observed that an intention not to legislate retrospectively can be imputed to the Oireachtas given the 'particular obligations imposed upon it by the Constitution'.[153] In this manner he saw a harmony between the presumption and the relevant constitutional provisions. In that case the question was whether s 33 of the Companies (Amendment) Act 1990 which imposes civil liability for reckless trading applied to transactions which occurred prior to its enactment. Murphy J was satisfied that there was nothing in the Act to indicate an intention that it should apply retrospectively and concluded that:[154]

"... having regard to the common law principles and constitutional requirements...it is the absence of an intention indicated expressly or at any rate unambiguously implied that is decisive ..."

Moreover, he also concluded that retrospective application of the reckless trading provisions would violate Article 15.5. They made such conduct 'an

150. See also *O'H v O'H* [1990] 2 IR 558, holding the Judicial Separation and Family Law Reform Act 1989, s 29 not to apply to transactions completed prior to its enactment.
151. [1990] 1 IR 77, at 82.
152. [1993] 3 IR 177.
153. *Ibid,* at 184.
154. *Ibid,* at 186.

infringement of the law' which was not necessarily the case at the time the acts were committed.

[14.63] The presumption was rebutted in *Chestvale Properties Ltd v Glackin*[155] where Murphy J concluded that the provisions governing the appointment and functioning of inspectors under the Companies Act 1990 were intended to operate retrospectively. In particular, he held that an inspector was authorised to demand the production of documents which came into existence before the enactment of the Act despite the absence of express provision to that effect. The 1990 Act repealed the inspection provisions of earlier legislation and in their absence the only way an inspector could carry out his duties was if the 1990 powers were to operate retrospectively.

Presumption against extra-territorial effect

[14.64] It is accepted both in national[156] and international[157] law that the State may legislate with extra-territorial effect, that is with effect beyond its geographical boundaries. At the same time it is presumed that the operation of an Act is intended to be confined to the territory of the State unless a contrary intention is evident. This presumption was applied in *Chemical Bank v McCormack*[158] where the Bankers' Books Evidence Acts 1879 and 1959 were held not to apply to documents held by an Irish bank in its New York branch - the Acts lacked clear words indicating an intention to legislate extra-territorially.

Expressio unius est exclusio alterius

[14.65] This maxim, which can be broadly translated as meaning 'to express one thing is to exclude another', has been alluded to in several Irish cases. It was invoked by Henchy J in construing the Social Welfare (Insurance Appeals) Regulations 1952[159] in *Kiely v Minister for Social Welfare*:

> "The fact that Article 11(5) [of the Regulations] allows a written statement to be received in evidence in specified limited circumstances means that it cannot be received in other circumstances; *expressio unius est exclusio alterius*."

155. [1993] 3 IR 35.
156. *In re Criminal Law (Jurisdiction) Bill, 1975* [1977] IR 129; *McGimpsey v Ireland* [1990] 1 IR 110: see also para **[15.39]**.
157. *Lotus case* (1927) PCIJ Ser A No 10.
158. [1983] ILRM 350.
159. SI 376/1952.

The limits of the maxim are evident in *Inspector of Taxes v Arida Ltd*[160] which concerned the question whether the Circuit Court has jurisdiction to award costsin the event of a successful appeal from the Appeal Commissioners on an assessment of tax. Order 58, rule 1 of the Rules of the Circuit Court 1950[161] states that the question of costs lies within the discretion of the judge 'save as otherwise provided by statute'. Section 428(6) of the Income Tax Act 1967 allows the High Court to award costs on a case stated to it by the Appeal Commissioners. It was argued that that provision limited the general power to award costs - that on the basis of *expressio unius*, it should be inferred from the conferring of power the High Court that a Circuit Court judge has no such power. In rejecting that contention Murphy J expressed the view that an exception from the general law (in this case the power to award costs) should, if not expressly stated, be implied with clarity and he believed that this was not so in this case. He referred to an earlier decision *The State (Minister for Lands and Fisheries) v Judge Sealy*[162] which throws some light on matter. In some circumstances a statutory reference might amount to no more than a particular statement of a more general and widely accepted principle, in which case the particular statutory reference is superfluous and cannot be considered to be an expression of one thing to the exclusion of all others.

Ejusdem generis rule

[14.66] This rule is conveniently summarised by Carroll J in *Cronin v Lunham Brothers Ltd*:[163]

> "The *ejusdem generis* rule as applied to the interpretation of statutes means that where a general word follows particular and specific words of the same nature as itself, it takes its meaning from them and is presumed to be restricted to the same genus as those words. The rule applies to general words following words which are less general."

[14.67] Most commonly, the preceding limited words consist of a list of individual items establishing a particular genus followed by a general residual clause. That clause is typically inserted by the draftsman to ensure that items which might be inadvertently omitted from the preceding list are nonetheless included in the category. The effect of the rule is to apply a restricted meaning derived from the statutory context to words which would otherwise be unrestricted. For example, in the expression 'dogs, cats and

160. [1992] 2 IR 155.
161. SI 179/1950.
162. [1939] IR 21.
163. [1986] ILRM 415, at 417 (reference omitted).

other animals' the general words are to be interpreted in the light of the preceding specific items and thus an 'other animal' will be interpreted as falling into the same genus as, and to share the characteristics of, dogs and cats - it would be construed to mean domestic animals of some type and we can happily conclude that slugs, snails, crocodiles and snakes are not 'other animals'.

[14.68] The *ejusdem generis* rule has been invoked in a number of cases. In *The People (DPP) v Farrell*[164] it was applied to the interpretation of 'a Garda Síochána station, a prison or other convenient place' in s 30 of the Offences Against the State Act 1939 where a police car was held not to be a 'convenient place'. Applying the rule the Court of Criminal Appeal held that those general words must at least mean a convenient building of some type. In *Irish Commercial Society Ltd v Plunkett*[165] the expression 'other misconduct' in s 14(8) of the Industrial and Provident Societies (Amendment) Act 1978 was interpreted in the light of the immediately preceding words 'fraud' and 'misfeasance', thus limiting its meaning to misconduct which was of the same type as fraud and misfeasance. In *CW Shipping Co Ltd v Limerick Harbour Commissioners* O'Hanlon J applied the rule in considering whether a tug is a 'lighter, ferry-boat or other small boat' in s 53(1) of the Harbours Act 1953:[166]

> "I consider that the words 'or other small boat' should be construed as being *ejusdem generis* with the specific descriptive words which immediately precede them, and I do not regard a tug as being of the same genus as a lighter or a ferry-boat. It is a very specialised type of craft designed for carrying out towing (or occasionally pushing) of much larger vessels, and not for the carriage for hire of persons or goods."

[14.69] There are cases where the *ejusdem generis* rule will not apply. One is where the specific words do not create a genus to which the general words might be limited. In *Kielthy v Ascon Ltd*[167] it was held that the genus must be established by a number of specific categories and thus the enumeration of one specific category is insufficient to bring the rule into operation. Moreover, a listing of a number of specific items might not be capable of establishing a single genus as is evident in *Dublin Corporation v Dublin Cinemas Ltd* where the words in question were held to be 'too incongruous to constitute a genus'.[168] It is also established that the general words must

164. [1978] IR 13.
165. [1986] IR 258.
166. [1989] ILRM 416, at 424.
167. [1970] IR 122.
168. [1963] IR 103, at 109.

succeed the specific words and thus the rule will not apply where it precedes the enumeration of specifics. This point was noted by Griffin J in *Application of Quinn*:[169]

> "Where in a statute there are general words following particular and specific words, as a rule it is correct to say that the general words must be confined to things of the same kind as those specified; but the *ejusdem generis* rule is one to be applied with caution as it is a mere presumption which applies in the absence of any other indications of the legislature. Before the rule can apply the general words must *follow* specific words; in the present case the general words *precede* the specific words … [i]n my opinion, the general words … are not in any way limited by the words which subsequently appear in the sub-section …"

Apart from the particular point concerning general words which appear before specific words Griffin J's judgment discloses a degree of caution in the application of the rule.[170]

Noscitur a sociis

[14.70] The *ejusdem generis* rule can be considered to be a manifestation of a wider principle or practice by which meaning is attributed to a word by reference to the context in which it appears.[171] That practice is sometimes encapsulated in the Latin maxim *noscitur a sociis* (a thing is known by its associates). Henchy J's judgment in *Inspector of Taxes v Kiernan*[172] acknowledges the significance of context in general but in some cases the courts have specifically invoked the *noscitur a sociis* principle. Like the *ejusdem generis* rule it can be invoked to give a restricted meaning to otherwise general words. In *The People (Attorney General) v Kennedy*[173] it was held that an appeal by the Attorney General to the Supreme Court was not authorised by s 29 of the Courts of Justice Act 1924, despite the 'ordinary' meaning of the words in that provision. The appropriate mode of interpretation was explained by Black J:[174]

---

169. [1974] IR 19, at 30-31 (emphasis in original).

170. See also *O'Dwyer v Cafolla Ltd* (1950) 84 ILTR 44; *Attorney General v Leaf Ltd* [1982] ILRM 441 where the rule was not applied; see *contra O'Sullivan v Leitrim County Council* [1953] IR 71; *Kenny v Quinn* [1981] ILRM 385; *Irish Nationwide Building Society Ltd v Revenue Commissioners*, High Court, unrep, 2 October 1990 applying the presumption; see also *Point Exhibition Co Ltd v Revenue Commissioners* [1993] 2 IR 551, at 560 *per* Geoghegan J *obiter* doubting that a dance hall is an 'other place of public entertainment' in the Excise Act 1835, s 7 'having regard to the *ejusdem generis* rule of construction.'

171. See Cross, *Statutory Interpretation* 3rd ed (Butterworths, 1995) p 138; also Bennion, *Statute Law* 3rd ed (Longman, 1990) p 196.

172. [1981] IR 117.

173. [1946] IR 517; see also *Application of Quinn* [1974] IR 19, at 22.

174. *Ibid*, at 536.

"… we have an express grant of a right of appeal without any express limitation of parties, and it is said that as the words are clear, there can be no limitation. I am satisfied that to look at the provision in that way is to adopt an erroneous method of final approach.

A small section of a picture, if looked at close-up, may indicate something quite clearly; but when one stands back and examines the whole canvas, the close-up view of the small section is often found to have given a wholly wrong view of what it really represented.

If one could pick out a single word or phrase and, finding it perfectly clear in itself, refuse to check its apparent meaning in the light thrown upon it by the context or by other provisions, the result would be to render the principle of *ejusdem generis* and *noscitur a sociis* utterly meaningless; for this principle requires frequently that a word or phrase or even a whole provision which, standing alone, has a clear meaning must be given quite a different meaning when viewed in the light of its context."

[14.71] In *Dillon v Minister for Posts and Telegraphs*[175] the Supreme Court was required to consider whether the plaintiff, a candidate in a Dáil election, was entitled to avail of the free postage facilities provided to candidates by s 50 of the Prevention of Electoral Abuses Act 1923. The defendant contended, *inter alia*, that the plaintiff's election material was 'grossly offensive' under the provisions of Inland Postal Warrant, 1939[176] and thus could not be conveyed in the post. In rejecting that contention Henchy J invoked the principle:

"Assuming (without necessarily so holding) that that Act and those regulations have application to this case, one notes that Article 6 of the relevant regulations (The Inland Post Warrant 1939) prohibits the posting, conveyance, or delivery by post of 'any postal packet…having thereon, or on the cover thereof, any words, marks, or designs of an indecent, obscene or grossly offensive character'. Again assuming (without necessarily so deciding) that this brochure falls within the definition of 'postal packet' given in the 1908 Act, or within the more restricted definition of 'postal packet' given in the 1939 regulations, I would find it impossible to hold that the brochure is debarred from the benefit of free post because of the passage in it to which the Minister takes exception. That passage, and it is the only passage relied on for the purpose of this point, runs as follows:

> 'Today's politicians are dishonest because they are being political and must please the largest number of people.'

I am far from saying that even if the prohibition were simply against words of a grossly offensive character, I would have held that that sentence would

175. Supreme Court, unrep, 3 June 1981; see also *United States Tobacco International Inc v Minister for Health* [1990] 1 IR 394.

176. SR&O 202/1939.

offend against such a prohibition. And I venture to think that those who practise what is often dubbed the art of the possible would not feel grossly offended by such an expression of opinion which, denigratory and cynical though it might be thought by some, is no more than the small coinage of the currency of political controversy. Some of the most revered and successful politicians who have lived have failed, at least in the eyes of reputable historians, to align great political acumen and success with moral or intellectual honesty. A charge of dishonesty is one that rarely penetrates the epidermis of any seasoned politician.

But the embargo is not simply against words of a grossly offensive character. So I do not have to reject the Minister's objection on that ground. The embargo is against 'any words, marks or designs of an indecent, obscene or grossly offensive character'. That assemblage of words gives a limited and special meaning to the expression 'grossly offensive character'. As Stamp J said in *Bourne v Norwich Crematorium Ltd*:[177]

> 'English words derive colour from those which surround them. Sentences are not mere collections of words to be taken out of the sentence, defined separately by reference to the dictionary or decided cases, and then put back again into the sentence with the meaning which you have assigned to them as separate words...'

Applying the maxim *noscitur a sociis*, which means that a word or expression is known from its companions, the expression 'grossly offensive character' must be held to be infected in this context with something akin to the taint of indecency or obscenity. Much of what might be comprehended by the expression if it stood alone is excluded by its juxtaposition with the words 'indecent' and 'obscene'. This means that the Minister may not reject a passage as disqualified for free circulation through the post because it is apt to be thought displeasing or distasteful. To merit rejection it must be grossly offensive in the sense of being obnoxious or abhorrent in a way that brings it close to the realm of indecency or obscenity. The sentence objected to by the Minister, while many people would consider it to be denigratory of today's politicians, is far from being of a 'grossly offensive character' in the special sense in which that expression is used in the Act."

Generalia specialibus non derogant

[14.72] The proposition in this maxim is that a statute containing general subject matter is taken not to affect one which applies to a specific topic. Its effect is to prevent the unintentional repeal or qualification of a specific provision by a later one which is general in nature. The general provision may appear either in a subsequent enactment or later in the same

177. [1967] 2 All ER 576, at 578.

instrument.[178] In *McGonagle v McGonagle* O'Byrne J explained the maxim thus:[179]

> "It is a general rule of construction that a prior statute is held to be repealed, by implication, by a subsequent statute which is inconsistent with and repugnant to the prior statute. This rule, however, does not apply where, as in the present case, the prior statute is special and the subsequent statute general."

[14.73] In *DPP v Grey* the Supreme Court held that s 27 of the Excise Management Act 1827 (dealing with penalties for excise offences) was unaffected by s 8 of the Criminal Justice Act 1951 (which allows other offences to be taken into consideration when sentencing). Henchy J expressly invoked the maxim:[180]

> "There is therefore brought into application the rule of statutory interpretation that when Parliament has provided specifically by statute for a limited set of circumstances, there is a presumption that general words in a later statute are not to be taken as overriding the earlier specific provision, unless an intention to do so is clearly expressed."

McCarthy J, dissenting, took a different view:[181]

> "The Court has not been referred to any case in which this principle has been extended to the criminal law or the construction of a criminal statute which, of its nature, is subject to the canon of construction appropriate to a penal Act, in which the more lenient of two reasonable constructions must be given."

While McCarthy J does identify the not uncommon phenomenon of two rules leading to conflicting interpretations, his remarks on the application of the maxim to criminal cases should be qualified. In *McGonagle v McGonagle* the maxim was applied to a criminal evidence statute, to which the principle of strict construction might otherwise have applied. It would thus appear that there is nothing in principle to preclude its application to penal provisions. Nevertheless, the general application of the maxim to other statutes is beyond question.[182]

178. See *The People (DPP) v Kelly* [1982] IR 90, at 114; *Welch v Bowmaker (Ireland) Ltd* [1980] IR 251.

179. [1951] IR 123, at 127; see *The People (DPP) v T* (1988) 3 Frewen 141.

180. [1986] IR 317, at 327.

181. *Ibid,* at 330.

182. See *Duffy v Dublin Corporation* [1974] IR 33; *Short v Dublin County Council* [1982] ILRM 117; *The People (DPP) v Kelly* [1982] IR 90, at 114 *per* Henchy and Kenny JJ.

Can 'and' mean 'or'?

[14.74] An issue which sometimes arises is whether the word 'and' should be interpreted as bearing a disjunctive or conjunctive meaning, in other words whether 'and' should be interpreted as meaning 'or'. The issue arose in *Duggan v Dublin Corporation.* The applicant was the owner of a jewellery shop which had been raided by a three man gang. The gang committed extensive property damage inside the shop, struck the applicant on the arm with a baseball bat and stole a number of trays of rings and other items of jewellery. The gang escaped in a car driven by a fourth member. The jewellery stolen was valued at £10,650. The applicant claimed damages against the Corporation under s 6 of the Malicious Injuries Act 1981, which provides that a malicious injuries claim for stolen property can be made arising from a situation in which 'three or more persons …are tumultuously and riotously assembled together ...' The applicant's claim was dismissed in the Circuit Court, the judge deciding that, while the gang's actions amounted to 'riotous assembly' they did not constitute a 'tumultuous assembly'. On a case stated, the Supreme Court (Finlay CJ, McCarthy and O'Flaherty JJ), upheld that decision. The Court concluded that to construe the word 'and' in s 6 of the 1981 Act either in a disjunctive sense or as being 'mere surplusage' would be to amend the section, and such an interpretation was impermissible having regard in particular to s 5 of the Act (which dealt with claims for damage to property as opposed to stolen property), which had used the phrase 'unlawfully, riotously or tumultuously'. McCarthy J noted that counsel for the applicant:[183]

> "… has been unable to identify any case in which the word 'and' has been read as 'or', whereas there are a number in which the converse has been the case ... To me, in its ordinary sense, riotously differs from tumultuously in the measure of activity, noise, alarm and so on ... they are not mutually exclusive and, consequently, there is no requirement that the word 'and' is to be read as 'or'."

Repealed provisions

[14.75] In *The People (DPP) v Gilligan*,[184] the Court of Criminal Appeal considered the effect of a statutory provision which substituted a new section in existing law. In the instant case, the Court was concerned with s 3 of the Larceny Act 1990, which provides that the Larceny Act 1916 should be

---

183. [1991] ILRM 330, at 338; see *H v H* [1978] IR 138 and *Dillon v Minister for Posts and Telegraphs*, Supreme Court, unrep, 3 June 1981 where 'or' was interpreted as being conjunctive.

184. [1992] ILRM 769.

amended by the substitution for s 33 of the 1916 Act of the section set out in s 3 of the 1990 Act. The 1990 Act replaced the old offence of receiving stolen property with the new offence of handling stolen property. The applicant had been charged with receiving stolen property, contrary to s 33 of the 1916 Act as originally enacted. The offence was alleged to have taken place in January 1988. The 1990 Act had come into force in August 1990 and the applicant was put on trial in November 1990. It was argued that the applicant could not have been tried in November 1990 with the receiving offence since this had been abolished by the 1990 Act. The case turned on s 21(1)(e) of the Interpretation Act 1937, which provides that the 'repeal' of statutory provisions shall not affect pending civil or criminal proceedings. The applicant argued that s 3 of the 1990 Act had not repealed s 33 of the 1916 Act but had merely substituted a new section for the original s 33. The Court of Criminal Appeal (O'Flaherty, Keane and Barron JJ) rejected this argument. The Court concluded that since the 1990 Act had altered the legal meaning of the 1916 Act, this amounted to a repeal of s 33 of the 1916 Act. Thus, s 33 was regarded as still extant for the purposes of the charge against the defendant. The Court therefore dismissed the application on this ground. This view of s 21 of the Interpretation Act 1937 is important given the proliferation of the 'repeals by substitution' in the statute book.

Mandatory and directory provisions

[14.76] A statute might require a course of conduct to be adopted or an act to be performed yet its omission might not be of great significance. Such provisions might be considered to be directory (or discretionary)[185] rather than mandatory. The neglect of a directory provision does not affect the validity of other matters which are connected with it. The identification of a provision as being mandatory or directory is based on the intent of the legislation, with the provision being examined in relation to the overall statutory scheme. In general, the less important the provision the greater is the likelihood that it will be held to be directory. The test is set out in Henchy J's judgment in *The State (Elm Developments) v An Bord Pleanála*:[186]

> "Whether a provision in a statute or statutory instrument, which on the face of it is obligatory (for example, by the use of the word 'shall'), should be treated by the courts as truly mandatory or merely directory depends on the statutory scheme as a whole and the part played in that scheme by the

185. The term 'discretionary' was employed by the Supreme Court in *Bakht v The Medical Council* [1990] 1 IR 515, holding the requirement in the Medical Practitioners Act 1978, s 27(2)(d) to make qualification rules for non-EC trained medical practitioners to be mandatory.

186. [1981] ILRM 108, at 110.

> provision in question. If the requirement which has not been observed may fairly be said to be an integral and indispensable part of the statutory intendment, the courts will hold it to be truly mandatory, and will not excuse a departure from it. But if, on the other hand, what is apparently a requirement is in essence merely a direction which is not of the substance of the aim and scheme of the statute, non-compliance may be excused."

The Supreme Court held that the requirement, in Article 36 of the Local Government (Planning and Development) Regulations, 1977,[187] to include the grounds of appeal in a notice of appeal to An Bord Pleanála is directory. Henchy J explained:[188]

> "The decision of a planning authority to grant a development permission, while not necessarily final, will become final if an appeal is not lodged within the time fixed by the Act. Since an extension of that time is not provided for, the requirement as to time is mandatory, so that a departure from it cannot be excused. The requirement that the appeal be in writing is so obviously basic to the institution of an appeal that it too must be considered mandatory. So also must the requirement that the written appeal state the subject matter of the appeal, for the absence of such identification could lead to administrative confusion. The lodgment of a deposit of £10 with the appeal (perhaps not necessarily physically or contemporaneously with the appeal) would also seem to be an essential part of the statutory scheme, so as to discourage frivolous, delaying or otherwise, worthless appeals.
>
> The requirement that the appeal should state the grounds of appeal seems to me to rest on different considerations. Even when the appeal contains a full statement of the grounds of appeal, that statement is not conclusive as to the grounds that will be considered on the hearing of the appeal. That is because s 17 of the 1976 Act says this:
>
> > 'The Board in deciding a reference or appeal may take into account matters other than those raised by the parties to the reference or appeal if the matters either relate to the proper planning and development of the area of the relevant planning authority or are matters to which by virtue of s 24(2) of this Act the Board may have regard, provided that the matters are brought to the notice of those parties and they are accorded an opportunity of making observations thereon to the Board or, in the case of an oral hearing, the person conducting the hearing.'
>
> The effect of that provision is that the Board may always treat the grounds lodged with the appeal as merely interim or provisional grounds. Even if the objector in this case had lodged a set of grounds of appeal with his appeal, the Board would be entitled to entertain further or other grounds, at

187. SI 65/1977.

188. [1981] ILRM 108, at 111-112.

any stage up to the determination of the appeal, provided those further or other grounds relate to the proper planning and development of the area, or are matters to which by virtue of s 24(2) of the 1976 Act the Board may have regard, and provided the developer is given an opportunity of making observations thereon.

Because of that, the grounds of appeal required to be stated in the appeal are not to be equated with pleadings in court proceedings, or with a notice of appeal from one court to a superior court. They cannot circumscribe or identify the issues on which the appeal will be decided. The Board (or the person holding the oral hearing, if there is one) may go outside them. They cannot be treated with any confidence by the developer as indicative of the scope of the case he will have to meet on the hearing of the appeal. I deduce that the primary purpose of the requirement of stating grounds of appeal in a case such as this is to inform the Board as to the primary matters relied on, so that the procedure for the disposition of the appeal may be decided on. Whether that deduction be correct or not, I am satisfied that the grounds of appeal required are essentially informative. To hold that they must be given as part of, or contemporaneously with, the notice of appeal, would be to attribute a conclusiveness to them which the statute clearly shows they cannot have … [i]t would be unduly legalistic, and unfair, if laymen who may have no skill in such matters, but who may be vitally affected by the permission which they wish to appeal against, were to be shut out from appealing merely because their notice of appeal did not state their grounds of appeal, particularly when those grounds of appeal can never be anything more than an opening salvo in the appellate battle. In such circumstances, the requirement of stating the grounds of appeal is essentially informative and directory, and therefore not mandatory. When the appellant in this case furnished grounds of appeal, within a few weeks of his appeal, to the satisfaction of the Board, it did not lie in the mouth of the developer to say that he had been in any way wrong-footed or damnified, or that the spirit or purpose of the Acts and regulations had been breached. In seeking an order of prohibition against the Board, he is endeavouring to benefit from what is no more than a technical breach of a regulation, which breach has been put right by the appellant and has been therefore rightly overlooked by the Board in the interests of justice."

[14.77] The distinction between mandatory and directory provisions operates to prevent a party from relying on a minor breach of a statutory requirement to invalidate a procedure or administrative act.[189] In general, a comparatively unimportant provision in relation to the overall scheme will be held to be directory, thereby avoiding the unfortunate consequences which would otherwise attend its non-observance. On the other hand it is

189. See Hogan & Morgan, *Administrative Law* 2nd ed (Sweet & Maxwell, 1991) p 364; see also *Irish Refining plc v Commissioner of Valuation* [1990] 1 IR 568.

clear that a provision which is of greater importance should be held to be directory, breach of which will affect the validity that is dependent on it. However, the distinction between mandatory and directory provisions was blurred in *The State (D & D) v Groarke*.[190] There it was held that the obligation to specify the religious persuasion of a child in a fit person order, under s 23 of the Children Act 1908, is mandatory, on the basis that something connected with the welfare of a child was a 'very fundamental matter'.[191] While failure to obey that requirement would render the order 'incomplete' that alone would not affect the validity of the order by virtue of the 'intention and purpose of the statutory provisions … namely, the urgent protection the welfare of the child …'[192] In so ruling, the Court attached to the breach of a mandatory requirement the consequence (or, more accurately, non-consequence) which could be expected had it decided that the provision is directory.

[4] External Sources

[14.78] The rules and principles which we have examined in the preceding sections focus on the contents and context of the statute and as such a court which invokes them is concerned primarily with the internal materials of the statute. Traditionally, the courts refused to seek assistance in material which lies outside the statute, but in recent years that reluctance has abated and in some circumstances a court might find recourse to external materials to be of assistance.

Prior statutes

[14.79] The interpretation of an earlier statute might be applied to a later statute in either of two cases. The first is where the later statute expressly states that it should be construed with the earlier. This device is employed especially where a series of successive statutes on a particular subject form what in essence is an inchoate code. Thus, s 14(3) of the Larceny Act 1990 provides that it and the Larceny Act 1916 are to be 'construed together as one'. In a similar vein, s 1(3) of the Merchant Shipping Act 1992 provides:

> This Act shall be construed as one with the Merchant Shipping Acts 1894 to 1983 and may be cited together therewith as the Merchant Shipping Acts 1894 to 1992.

---

190. [1990] 1 IR 305.
191. *Ibid,* at 315.
192. *Ibid.*

In some cases a statute might provide for collective construction only in respect of certain of its provisions, as is evident in s 1(2) of the Child Abduction and Enforcement of Court Orders Act 1991:[193]

> The Courts (Supplemental Provisions) Acts, 1961 to 1988 and this Act, insofar as it affects the jurisdiction and procedure of any court in the State, shall be construed together as one.

The effect of such provisions is require that all provisions should be interpreted as if they were contained in the one statute. Accordingly the interpretation of the earlier statute will apply to the later unless there is some 'manifest discrepancy'.[194]

[14.80] Second, even in the absence of an express provision a statute might be construed in the light of a prior statute.[195] If words or expressions which have been used in the earlier legislation are repeated in a subsequent Act in a similar context they are liable to be given the meaning which was previously attributed to them. This is especially so where the words or expression have been judicially interpreted or have a clear and settled meaning.[196] This is based on an assumption that when it employed terms whose meaning was known or had been judicially determined, the Oireachtas intended to adopt that meaning. If it had sought to change the law it could be expected that different words would have been used. This proposition applies only where the statutes are *in pari materia*, that is their context is similar.[197] Henchy J explained the matter in *The State (Sheehan) v Government of Ireland* where he stated that:[198]

> "... in construing a particular statutory provision no provision of another statute may be used as an aid or a guide unless that other statutory provision is *in pari materia*, that is forming part of the same statutory context."

[14.81] Thus, in *Mogul of Ireland Ltd v Tipperary (North Riding) County Council*[199] s 1 of the Malicious Injuries (Ireland) Act 1853 was interpreted in

193. See also the more elaborate Worker Protection (Part-time Employees) Act 1991, s 8 providing for its being construed with a number of different series of statutes.

194. See *Canada Southern Ry Co v International Bridge Co* (1883) 3 App Cas 723, at 727.

195. However, there is a manifest reluctance to interpret a provision in the light of a subsequent amendment; see *Cronin v Cork and County Properties Ltd* [1986] IR 559; *Dublin County Council v Eighty Five Developments Ltd (No 1)* [1993] 2 IR 378.

196. See *Cronin v Youghal Carpets (Yarns) Ltd* [1985] IR 312.

197. The qualified nature of this proposition is evident in *Inspector of Taxes v Kiernan* [1981] IR 117 where the Supreme Court refused to adopt *Phillips (Inspector of Taxes) v Bourne* [1947] KB 533 on the interpretation of the word 'cattle' in a similar statute.

198. [1987] IR 550, at 562.

199. [1976] IR 260.

the light of s 135 of the Grand Jury (Ireland) Act 1836 as both formed part of the same legislative scheme. Likewise, the Redundancy Payments Act 1967 and the Minimum Notice and Terms of Employment Act 1973 have been construed as being *in pari materia*;[200] so too the phrase 'total income brought into charge' in the Corporation Tax Act 1976 was considered to be *in pari materia* with 'profits or gains brought into charge' in the Income Tax legislation.[201] On the other hand, the Finance Act 1975 and the Value Added Tax Act 1972 were held not to be *in pari materia*[202] nor were the Labourers Act 1936 and the Landlord and Tenant Act 1931.[203] In *Murphy v Dublin Corporation* the Supreme Court was invited to read together the Housing Act 1966 and the Local Government (Planning and Development) Act 1963 in order to achieve legislative harmony. The Court refused, holding that the Acts are not *in pari materia* since, in the words of Henchy J:[204]

> "… they lack a common subject matter or purpose. So it would be a breach of a fundamental rule of statutory interpretation to treat them as a statutory whole."

Legislative history

[14.82] The legislative process, which was outlined in the previous chapter,[205] is liable to result in the production of a variety of materials which might act as external assistance in the interpretation of a measure. The common law's traditional approach was to avoid examining the legislative history of a measure. This reluctance is evident in *Minister for Industry and Commerce v Hales*[206] where correspondence between the Minister who initiated the legislation and a citizen, which indicated the Minister's views on the meaning of the provision in question, was held to be inadmissible. Both in the terms of his judgment and the authorities cited, McLoughlin J was unequivocal in his rejection of such material:[207]

> "… the statute should be construed principally by the words of the statute itself which we should only modify or alter so far as it may be necessary to avoid some manifest absurdity or incongruity, [and] it would be departing very far from this canon of interpretation if we were to admit evidence of contemporaneous circumstances which would result in giving an

200. *Irish Leathers Ltd v Minister for Labour* [1986] IR 177.
201. *Cronin v Youghal Carpets (Yarns) Ltd* [1985] IR 312.
202. *Irish Agricultural Machinery Ltd v Ó Culacháin* [1990] 1 IR 535.
203. *Gough v Kinsella* (1971) 105 ILTR 116.
204. [1976] IR 143, at 149.
205. See paras **[13.08]-[13.36]**.
206. [1967] IR 50.
207. *Ibid,* at 68 (emphasis added).

interpretation to a section of the statute...which would be repugnant to the intentions of the legislature as indicated *by the Act in question*, construed as a whole."

[14.83] Nevertheless, in the past two decades the courts have gradually departed from this absolutist position and have examined the legislative history. In *Rowe v Law*[208] O'Higgins CJ, dissenting, considered the parliamentary history of s 90 of the Succession Act 1965 including various different drafts which had been mooted.[209] In *Finucane v McMahon*[210] Walsh J reviewed the political and historical background to extradition legislation when interpreting s 50 of the Extradition Act 1965. It is by now accepted that it is permissible to have recourse to the legislative history of a provision and to relevant external materials.

International treaties

[14.84] Where domestic legislation is based on an international treaty it is accepted that a court may examine the treaty and its associated preparatory materials (the so-called *travaux préparatoires*) as an aid to interpreting the domestic provision. This can be linked to the presumption of compatibility with international law[211] and it reinforces the assumption that the Oireachtas intended to abide by its international obligations. The propriety of looking at those materials was confirmed by the Supreme Court in *Bourke v Attorney General*[212] where it examined the *travaux préparatoires* of the European Convention on Extradition, on which s 50 of the Extradition Act 1965 was based. The wide range of materials which was evaluated by Ó Dálaigh CJ included the article of the European Convention on which s 50 was indirectly based, earlier drafts of that article, various working documents, the Belgian Extradition Law (of 1833) which was cited in those documents, the Norwegian Extradition Law (of 1908) and the German-Turkish Extradition Treaty of 1930. The force of this judgment might be thought to be somewhat diluted by Ó Dálaigh CJ's statement that he would have arrived at the same conclusion without reference to the *travaux préparatoires* but the propriety of having recourse to such materials is beyond question.[213]

208. [1978] IR 55.
209. See Power, 'Parliamentary History as an Aid to Statutory Interpretation' [1984] Stat LR 38.
210. [1990] 1 ILRM 505.
211. See para **[14.49]**.
212. [1972] IR 36.
213. See also *Aamand v Smithwick* [1995] 1 ILRM 61.

EC materials

[14.85] In the future, as more domestic legislation is based on EC law, it is likely that the interpretation which the EC measure attributes to the provision will be adopted in relation to its domestic counterpart. This is evident in the decision in *Deane v Voluntary Health Insurance Board*[214] where the Supreme Court considered whether the defendants were an 'undertaking' within the meaning of the Competition Act 1991. That Act defined 'undertaking' to mean a person or body 'engaged for gain in the production, supply or distribution of goods or the provision of a service'. The defendants provided health insurance on a non-profit making basis and it was contended that accordingly they were not 'engaged for gain'. The Supreme Court held that 'gain' was not confined to pecuniary gain or profit and that the defendants amounted to an 'undertaking'. While the Court appeared to have been satisfied that the term 'gain' was not ambiguous it was nevertheless prepared to adopt the interpretation of the EC measures on which the Competition Act 1991 is based. According to Finlay CJ:[215]

> "... it is stated that the purposes of the Act include the prohibition by analogy with Articles 85 and 86 of the Treaty establishing the EEC and in the interests of the common good the prevention, restriction or distortion of competition and the abuse of dominant positions in trade in the State. Articles 85 and 86 undoubtedly apply to a body corporate engaged in the supply of services even if it does not have as its object the making of commercial profits."

[14.86] The analogy between the domestic legislation and the equivalent Treaty provisions was expressed in the long title to the Competition Act 1991 thus facilitating the adoption of the EC interpretation of the measure. However, there is nothing in principle to preclude having recourse to the interpretation of EC measures where such a link exists, although it might not be explicitly stated.

Pre-parliamentary materials

[14.87] A significant number of 'official' materials fall into this category - Green and White Papers, reports of special commissions and tribunals of inquiry, Law Reform Commission reports, explanatory memoranda which accompany Bills. In *Maher v Attorney General*[216] the Supreme Court, in considering the constitutionality of s 44(2) of the Road Traffic Act 1968, examined a commission report on which the legislation in question was

214. [1992] 2 IR 319.
215. *Ibid*, at 331.
216. [1973] IR 140.

based. In *McLoughlin v Minister for the Public Service*[217] the explanatory memorandum which accompanied the Bill which eventually became the Act in question was examined and influenced the interpretation adopted by the Supreme Court. That material declared the purpose of the legislation and thus facilitated its interpretation accordingly. In the light of this decision it can be taken that, in general, pre-parliamentary materials may be employed as external assistance, at least where they are 'official' in origin. Those materials are accessible and are published in a reliable form, they contain the deliberations and/or conclusions of bodies which are established to consider legislative proposals and, having been submitted to public scrutiny, they form part of the informal legislative process.[218] As an indication of legislative intent or the purpose of legislation their usefulness is obvious. However, the same might not be said of other 'non-official' or 'private' documents which might be offered as evidence of legislative intent. For instance, private briefing documents, correspondence of the type in *Minister for Industry and Commerce v Hales*, documents submitted by interested parties in the course of lobbying and political party documents lack the qualities of 'official' documents and it is difficult to envisage circumstances which would justify their reception by a court of interpretation.

Parliamentary materials

[14.88] Parliamentary materials include the proceedings of both Houses of the Oireachtas, reported in the *Dáil Debates* and *Seanad Debates*, and reports of the various parliamentary committees. The traditional approach was that such materials could not be cited in court nor used as an aid to interpretation. This was based, in part, on constitutional considerations which are conveniently summarised by Miers:[219]

> "First, the primary constitutional duty of a judge is to give effect to the intention of Parliament as expressed in the words of the statute: the statute alone is the uniquely authoritative statement of that intention. Second, 'the rule of law as a constitutional principle requires that the citizen, before committing himself to any course of action, should be able to know in advance what are the legal consequences that will flow from it. Where those consequences are regulated by a statute, the source of that knowledge is what the statute says' … the citizen is entitled to rely on the words of the statute alone, or where it is judicially interpreted, on an interpretation based upon what he might reasonably understand by those words … as a

217. [1985] IR 631.
218. See paras **[13.27]**-**[13.36]**.
219. 'Taxing Perks and Interpreting Statutes: *Pepper v Hart*' (1993) 56 MLR 695, at 702 (references omitted).

constitutional ground rule the law which establishes … rights and duties should be what passes as law, and not what a representative of the executive thinks it is. Under the rule of law, ministerial glosses expressed during debate 'cannot affect the matter. Parliament … is sovereign only in respect of what it expresses by the words used in the legislation it has passed.' Thus the corollary of the proposition that what Parliament says (at least in the form of primary legislation) goes, is that it is only the judiciary, and no other person, who has the authority finally and compellingly to say what those laws mean."

[14.89] Another consideration was the belief that to open parliamentary debates in court was to subject Parliament's actions to judicial scrutiny, a course of action prohibited by the principle of Parliamentary privilege.[220]

[14.90] In as much as these concerns were based on a view of parliamentary supremacy they could only be of limited effect in Ireland, where judicial review of legislation, that is of Parliament's handiwork, is a central feature of the legal environment.[221] It was probably inevitable that an Irish court would depart from the English position and embrace the willingness of courts in other countries to consider parliamentary proceedings when interpreting legislation. This occurred in *Wavin Pipes Ltd v Hepworth Iron Co Ltd*[222] where Costello J held that a court could consider the parliamentary debates on the provision in question. He justified his departure from that approach on the strength of the Supreme Court decision in *Bourke v Attorney General*:

"… I should briefly here set out the reasons by which I have concluded that in certain circumstances a court is entitled to have regard to the parliamentary history of an Act to assist in its interpretation because to avoid overburdening an already long judgment I did not state them in my judgment in *Beecham Group Limited v Bristol Myers Company.*[223] The rules for the interpretation of statutes are judge-made. As long ago as 1769 it was established in England that 'the sense and meaning of an Act of Parliament must be collected from what it says when cast into law; and not from the history of changes it underwent in the House where it took its rise' (Willes J in *Millar v Taylor*,[224] quoted in Cross, *Statutory Interpretation* at p 134) and this rule has been applied ever since both in England and in this country. It should, however, be pointed out that this rule is not one followed in civil law jurisdictions, or in the United States of America, or in the

220. *Ibid,* at 703.
221. See Casey, 'Statutory Interpretation - a New Departure' (1981) 3 DULJ (ns) 110, at 114-115.
222. [1982] 8 FSR 32.
223. High Court, unrep, 13 March 1981.
224. (1769) 4 Burr 2303, at 2332.

European Court of Human Rights. I would have felt constrained to follow it, however, particularly as it has been re-affirmed by a divisional court in this country (see *Minister for Industry and Commerce v Hales*[225] in which the court refused to consider the legislative history of the Holiday (Employees) Act 1961) but for the decision of the Supreme Court in the *Bourke* case to which I have already referred.

There is no strict rule of construction which requires the court to examine only the words of the statute it is construing. In *McMahon v Attorney General*[226] the Supreme Court considered the Report of a Special Committee on electoral systems which preceded the Ballot Act 1872 on which provisions of the Electoral Act 1923 dealing with secrecy of the ballot were based. In *Maher v Attorney General*[227] the court found assistance in the interpretation of the Road Traffic Act 1968 in the Report of a Commission which had been established to consider the law relating to driving whilst under the influence of drink.

In the *Bourke* case the Supreme Court was called upon to interpret the phrase 'offence connected with a political offence' in s 50, Pt III, of the Extradition Act 1965. Part III of the Act dealt with the special arrangements for extradition between this country and the United Kingdom; Part II with extradition generally. The Act made it clear that Part II enacted as part of the municipal law of the State certain provisions of the Council of Europe Convention on Extradition signed on the 13 December 1957 and Part II contained a prohibition against extradition in respect of a political offence 'or an offence connected with a political offence' (s 11). In interpreting the phrase 'offence connected with a political offence' in Pt III of the Act the Supreme Court took the view that as s 11 and s 50 speak of the same thing, as the Convention could be examined to discover the meaning of s 11, the court was entitled to look at the Convention for the purpose of interpreting s 50. But the court not only examined the text of the Convention for the purpose of interpreting the meaning of the phrase 'offence connected with a political offence' used in s 50 of the Irish statute, it also examined the *travaux préparatoires* of the Convention. In the course of this examination it reached conclusions as to the meaning of the phrase and based these conclusions on the fact that the original draft of the Convention had been amended in the course of its consideration by the organs of the Council of Europe and on the reasons disclosed in the *travaux préparatoires* for such amendments.

In doing so the Supreme Court extended considerably the existing rules as to the use of treaties in the interpretation of statutes (*Salomon v Commissioners of Customs and Excise*;[228] *Post Office v Estuary Radio*

225. [1967] IR 50.
226. [1972] IR 69.
227. [1973] IR 140.
228. [1967] 2 QB 306.

> *Ltd*[229]). Parenthetically I think that it is relevant to note that not only had the House of Lords recently sanctioned the limited use of the *travaux préparatoires* of an international convention in the interpretation of a statute (see: *Fothergill v Monarch Airlines Ltd*[230]), but the Master of the Rolls, emboldened he said, by remarks of the Lord Chancellor in a debate in the House of Lords on 26 March of this year, has made use of the parliamentary history of the Employment Act 1980 for the purpose of interpreting some of its provisions (see: *Hadmor Productions Ltd v Hamilton*[231]). The arguments against the use by the courts of the parliamentary history of a statute for the purpose of its construction must apply with equal force to the history of the adoption of an international convention by an international organisation. And so, if the courts can properly look at the history of the adoption of an international convention for the purpose of ascertaining the meaning of the words used in it there would appear to be no reason in principle why in appropriate cases they should not be free when construing the words of a statute to obtain assistance from the history of its enactment by parliament. As I do not find persuasive the arguments against the use of the legislative history in the interpretation of statutes (which are helpfully brought together in the Report of the Law Commission and the Scottish Law Commission, 'The Interpretation of Statutes'), as I believe I am entitled to seek assistance from the legislative history in appropriate cases, as in the present the legislative history greatly assists in construing the meaning of 'available to the public' as used in the Patents Act, 1964, I have used it in support of the construction of the 1964 Act which I have already given …"

[14.91] In the instant case it was clear that an evaluation of the parliamentary history of the somewhat ambiguous provision would indicate the legislative intent of the Oireachtas. The interpretation urged by the defendants formed the basis of an opposition amendment which would have inserted express words into the section. That amendment was defeated and the fact of its rejection and the reasons given for its rejection indicated that the words should not be construed in the manner sought by the defendants.[232]

[14.92] It is uncertain from the terms of the judgment in *Wavin Pipes* when it is permissible to have recourse to the legislative proceedings on a provision, the only qualification being 'in appropriate cases'. In *FF v CF*,[233] which concerned the interpretation of s 2 of the Statute Law Revision (Pre-Union

229. [1968] 2 QB 740.
230. [1980] 3 WLR 209.
231. [1981] 3 WLR 139.
232. It might also be observed that Costello J was ideally situated to examine the history of the provisions, having at the time been the deputy who moved the unsuccessful amendment; see Hogan & Whyte, *Kelly's The Irish Constitution* 3rd ed (Butterworths, 1994) p 472-474.
233. [1987] ILRM 1.

Irish Statutes) Act 1962, Barr J referred to the second stage speech of the Minister for Justice and deduced the legislative intention from it. However, the conclusion was not especially controversial and the point was conceded by both parties. Subsequent decisions suggest that a cautious approach should be adopted and, in particular, that the legislative history should not be considered if the provision is clear and unambiguous. In *Wadda v Ireland*, concerning the interpretation of the Child Abduction and Enforcement of Court Orders Act 1991, Keane J stated:[234]

> "It was also submitted that I should have regard in construing the provisions of the Act … to statements made during the debates on the Bill in the Dáil by the minister responsible for introducing the measure. In this context, counsel relied on the decision of Costello J in *Wavin Pipes Ltd v Hepworth Iron Co Ltd* in which he held that the court could in defined circumstances have regard to its parliamentary history in order to ascertain the intention of the legislature in enacting a particular measure …
>
> The question does not arise, however, in the present case, for two reasons … [i]n the second place, there is no obscurity, ambiguity or potential absurdity in the relevant provisions which would justify the court having recourse to what was said in the Oireachtas in order to ascertain the legislative intention."

[14.93] Similar caution is evident in *Flynn and Village Crafts v Irish Nationwide Building Society Ltd*[235] where Lavan J cited Keane J's remarks and, being satisfied that the provisions in question were plain and unambiguous, refused to consult the *Dáil Debates*.

[14.94] The High Court cases decided after *Wavin Pipes* indicate a distinct lack of enthusiasm for consulting parliamentary materials, a position which may be contrasted with recent developments in England.[236] This together with the reiteration by the Supreme Court in *Howard v Commissioners of Public Works*[237] of the primacy of the text lead to the conclusion that such

234. [1994] ILRM 126, at 136-137; see also *CK v CK* [1993] ILRM 535.

235. High Court, unrep, 31 July 1995.

236. See *Pepper v Hart* [1993] 1 All ER 42 where the House of Lords has ruled that a court could consult *Hansard* (the House of Commons debates) in interpreting a statute. In a number of subsequent cases parliamentary materials have been used: *R v Warwickshire County Council, ex parte Johnson* [1993] 1 All ER 299; *Stubbings v Webb* [1993] 2 WLR 120; *Chief Adjudication Officer v Foster* [1993] 2 WLR 292. The decision in *Pepper v Hart* has resulted in an appreciable body of academic literature; see eg Bennion, 'Hansard - Help or Hindrance? A Draftsman's View of *Pepper v Hart*' [1993] Stat LR 149; Lyell, '*Pepper v Hart*: The Government Perspective' [1994] Stat LR 1; Lester, '*Pepper v Hart* Revisited' [1994] Stat LR 10; Jenkins, '*Pepper v Hart*: A Draftsman's Perspective' [1994] Stat LR 23.

237. [1994] 1 IR 101; see also *The People (DPP) v Quilligan* [1986] IR 496, at 511 *per* Walsh J "Whatever may have been in the minds of the members of the Oireachtas when the legislation was passed, in so far as their intention can be deduced, as it must be, *from the words of the statute*…" (emphasis added).

materials (and, indeed, other external materials) should be used sparingly, and should be consulted only as a last resort. There are several considerations to commend a restricted approach. If a statute is plain and unambiguous, or can be interpreted by using the established canons of interpretation, examining the parliamentary history of the measure will at best be unnecessary and at worst be a source of uncertainty. If parliamentary proceedings merely confirm the conclusion which the court would have independently reached consideration of them is redundant since that would add nothing, as was arguably the case in *FF v CF*.[238] On the other hand, where the parliamentary debates suggest a conclusion which is different from that which the ordinary canons of interpretation would suggest their being consulted makes uncertain that which would otherwise have a settled meaning. Thus, they are apt to become a source of confusion. Hence the importance of excluding consideration of parliamentary material where the provision is plain and unambiguous. The unanimous decision of the Supreme Court in *The People (DPP) v McDonagh*[239] in which the Court examined the history of s 2(1) of the Criminal Law (Rape) Act 1981, and the parliamentary history of the (British) Rape Act 1976 on which the 1981 Act was modelled, indicates that there are some instances where recourse to parliamentary materials is appropriate.

[14.95] Pragmatic considerations also apply. In some instances parliamentary materials might themselves reflect doubts as to the meaning of the proposal or at least not help to solve the problem. That aside, it is open to question whether it is reasonable or practical to expect a citizen (or more probably his legal advisers) as a matter of routine to consult these materials in order to ascertain the meaning of a statute. If the courts have frequent recourse to parliamentary materials the inevitable result would be that it would become standard practice to consult such materials. Lawyers are liable to feel compelled to consult parliamentary materials on a regular basis both to improve the service to their clients and to avoid the possibility of an action for negligence. This consideration has become especially important as the quantity of cases involving questions of statutory interpretation has increased significantly. In some, possibly many, instances access to parliamentary materials will prove to be problematic. This will be particularly so where the legal adviser does not enjoy access to a properly stocked library, a factor which is unlikely to be mitigated in the near future by the publication of parliamentary materials on CD-ROM or on-line format. But even where such access is enjoyed, as would be the case for most practising barristers who subscribe to the Law Library, it does not follow that it is reasonable to expect consultation of parliamentary materials,

238. [1987] ILRM 1.

239. Supreme Court, unrep, 11 July 1996. The only judgment was delivered by Costello P, who had delivered judgment in *Wavin Pipes*.

since that would extend the research time involved with the accompanying expense to clients. In addition, there is a fear that valuable court time will be wasted by needless reference to parliamentary materials. On the other hand, it might be said that these pragmatic concerns are over-estimated. The annotations in *Irish Current Law Statutes Annotated* regularly refer to the relevant portions of the parliamentary proceedings, thus providing a reasonably convenient point of reference in respect of post-1984 statutes. Moreover, a lawyer is expected to consult and read the relevant case law concerning the interpretation of the provision, a task which is not necessarily less onerous than that of consulting the relevant parliamentary materials. Of course, from the perspective of the authority they enjoy a distinction is to be drawn between case law, which has the force of law, and parliamentary materials which at most can provide guidance.

Dictionaries and reference works

[14.96] The third proposition in Henchy J's judgment in *Inspector of Taxes v Kiernan*[240] is that the ordinary meaning of a word should be derived primarily from the judge's own experience of its use. Dictionaries and other sources should be employed only when 'alternative meanings, regional usages or other obliquities are shown to cast doubt on the singularity of its ordinary meaning'[241] or where the meaning of the word might have changed since the enactment of the Act. This reluctance to resort to dictionaries was not shared by the Supreme Court in *Rahill v Brady* where reference was made to the *Shorter Oxford Dictionary.* Ó Dálaigh CJ took the view that:[242]

> "… reference to the better dictionaries does afford either by definition or illustration some guide to the use of a term in a statute … dictionaries are not to be taken as authoritative exponents of the meaning of words used in Acts of Parliament, it is nevertheless a well-known rule of courts of law that words should be taken in their ordinary sense and we are therefore sent for instruction to these books; per Lord Coleridge in *R v Peters*."[243]

Based on current practice this is a more accurate statement of the law, as dictionaries are frequently cited and used in statutory interpretation.[244]

---

240. [1981] IR 117.
241. *Ibid,* at 122.
242. [1971] IR 69, at 82.
243. (1886) 16 QBD 636, at 641.
244. See eg *Flynn v Denieffe* [1989] IR 722; *McGurrin v The Campion Publications Ltd*, High Court, unrep, 15 December 1993; *Trustees of Kinsale Yacht Club v Commissioner of Valuation* [1993] ILRM 393; *Carl Stuart Ltd v Biotrace Ltd* [1993] ILRM 633; *Shannon Regional Fisheries Board v An Bord Pleanála* [1994] 3 IR 449; *Keane v An Bord Pleanála*, High Court, unrep, 4 October 1995.

Chapter 15

The Constitution and its Interpretation

[1] Introduction

[15.01] In this chapter, we discuss the provisions of the Constitution of the Irish Free State 1922 and the Constitution of Ireland 1937, Bunreacht na hÉireann.[1] The 1937 Constitution provides, in effect, that it is superior to the sources of law described in previous chapters, namely common law and legislation. In particular, the High Court and Supreme Court are empowered to declare invalid any common law or legislative rule which is in conflict with the text of the 1937 Constitution. In this respect, we discuss the distinctive principles of constitutional interpretation and the development in recent years of significant case law concerning the fundamental rights which the Constitution recognises and supports.

[2] The 1922 Constitution

[15.02] We have described elsewhere the establishment of the Irish Free State on foot of the Anglo-Irish Treaty of December 1921[2] and the enactment of the Constitution of the Irish Free State in 1922.[3] From the perspective of Irish nationalists, the Treaty of 1921 was highly divisive, resulting in a split in the Sinn Féin Party, the approval of the Treaty by a narrow margin and a bitter Civil War in the Irish Free State that continued until 1923.[4]

---

1. The leading texts are: Casey, *Constitutional Law in Ireland*, 2nd ed (Sweet & Maxwell, 1992), Forde, *Constitutional Law of Ireland* (Mercier Press, 1987), Hogan & Whyte, *Kelly's The Irish Constitution*, 3rd ed (Butterworths, 1994) and Morgan, *Constitutional Law of Ireland* (Round Hall Press, 1990) (the latter focusing on the institutions of State only).
2. Although legal effect was not given to these Articles of Agreement until parallel legislation was enacted in the Irish Free State and at Westminster in 1922, they are commonly referred to as 'the Treaty' and we so describe them in the text for ease of reference.
3. See para **[2.55]**.
4. The majority within the Sinn Féin Party who accepted the terms of the Treaty, led by Arthur Griffith and Michael Collins, formed the Cumann na nGaedheal Party, later merging with other parties in 1933 to become Fine Gael (in the English language, the party of the Irish Nation). Many of those who voted against the Treaty, led by Eamon de Valera, fought in the Civil War until 1923, by which time the Cumann na nGaedheal Government (now led by William T Cosgrave, after the deaths of Collins and Griffith in 1922) had secured effective victory. In 1924, the preponderance of the anti-Treaty elements of Sinn Féin formed the Fianna Fáil Party (in the English language, the Soldiers of Destiny), and, led by deValera, abandoned their abstentionist policy, contested the 1927 General Election and took their seats in the Irish Free State's Dáil Éireann. By this time, those who continued to use the title Sinn Féin represented a very small proportion of the electorate in the Irish Free State, and further 'splits' within what remained of Sinn Féin were a feature of political life in succeeding decades. All governments in the Irish Free State and Ireland since 1922 have been led by either Fianna Fáil or Fine Gael. Since the 1970s, the majority have involved coalitions of different parties, including the Labour Party whose formation predated the 1921 Treaty. In the 1990s, the combined vote of Fianna Fáil and Fine Gael continues to exceed 65% of the total electorate in the Republic of Ireland, but to date (1996) they have never been involved in a coalition government together, preferring instead arrangements with other parties not involved in the 1921 'split'.

The British and Irish legal perspectives

[15.03] From a British legal perspective, the Irish Free State was the successor to Southern Ireland, and the Treaty and the 1922 Constitution merely required legislation to give effect with modifications to the arrangements envisaged by the Government of Ireland Act 1920.[5] Thus, from the British legal perspective, ultimate control remained at Westminster, subject to whatever powers were conferred by it on the Irish Free State and the other States beginning to form the British Commonwealth of Nations. Irish nationalists had never accepted the 1920 Act or the entity Southern Ireland. From an Irish perspective, the elections held in 1919, 1921 and 1922 were elections to a nationalist assembly, Dáil Éireann, even though they had utilised the electoral machinery of the Government of Ireland Acts 1914 and 1920. On this view, the First Dáil of 1919, acting on behalf of the Irish people, was the source of all lawful authority, the Second Dáil had approved the Treaty in 1921, and the Third Dáil, acting as a Constituent Assembly (a Constitution-making assembly) had approved the 1922 Constitution of the Irish Free State. While the distinction between the British and Irish legal perspective might appear technical, it became a factor in the replacement of the 1922 Constitution in 1937.[6] The essential elements of the Treaty became law as the Constitution of the Irish Free State, enacted as a Schedule to the last Act passed by the Third Dáil and the first Act passed by the Oireachtas of the Irish Free State, the Constitution of the Irish Free State (Saorstát Éireann) Act 1922.

Institutions of State and fundamental rights

[15.04] The 1922 Constitution may be divided into two component parts: an outline of the principal institutions of State and a description of certain fundamental rights of the citizens. Its text comprises a number of Articles, rather than the sections which characterise legislation.[7]

Separation of powers

[15.05] The 1922 Constitution described a tripartite division or separation of powers, namely the executive, the legislature and the judiciary. This

5. In the Westminster Parliament, the Irish Free State (Agreement) Act 1922 gave legal effect to the 1921 Articles of Agreement. After the enactment in Dublin of the 1922 Constitution, Westminster passed the Irish Free State Constitution Act 1922. The Irish Free State (Consequential Provisions) Act 1922, passed at the same time, modified the Government of Ireland Act 1920 to take account of the establishment of the Irish Free State, as successor, at least in the eyes of British law, to the entity Southern Ireland.

6. See para **[15.13]-[15.17]**.

7. See para **[13.46]**.

reflected developments in the political organisation of the State, particularly in the 19th century, described elsewhere.[8] It also contained a number of highly controversial elements which divided Irish nationalists. Critically, the Treaty and the 1922 Constitution in effect excluded from the Irish Free State the six administrative counties which at the end of 1921 had formed Northern Ireland.[9] Another limitation was that the Irish Free State remained within the British sphere of influence as a member of the British Commonwealth. There was a continued, albeit limited, British military presence in a number of ports of the Irish Free State (the 'Treaty ports').[10] However, the 1922 Constitution provided that the Irish Free State was not to be committed to active participation in any war without the consent of its legislature. On the organisation of the executive, there was a continued British political presence in the form of the Governor General, though this position was largely ceremonial. Real executive power lay with the Executive Council of the Irish Free State headed by the President of the Executive Council, in effect the Prime Minister of the Irish Free State. The Executive Council was to be elected from the legislative branch, which comprised the monarch (represented by the Governor General) and two Houses of the Oireachtas, Dáil Éireann (a directly elected Chamber of Deputies, elected by proportional representation) and the Senate (an indirectly elected Chamber whose membership was intended to include representatives of Southern Unionists). Members of the Oireachtas were required to swear an oath of fidelity to the British monarch. This requirement, together with the failure to achieve a 32-county Irish State, was a prime factor in the split within Sinn Féin in 1921 and the consequent Civil War.[11] As to the judicial branch, we have noted elsewhere that the 1922 Constitution provided for the establishment of a High Court, a Supreme Court and courts of local and limited jurisdiction.[12] An appeal to the Judicial Committee of the Privy Council was also included.

Fundamental rights

[15.06] The description of certain fundamental rights of citizens was influenced by the Bill of Rights and the Declaration of the Rights of Man

---

8. See para **[2.20]**.
9. See para **[2.45]**.
10. Control of the ports was ultimately transferred to Ireland by agreement in 1938, and the small remaining presence of British troops were then withdrawn.
11. After the ending of the Civil War in 1923, many of those who had voted against the 1921 'Treaty' ultimately took their seats in Dáil Éireann after the 1927 General Election, as members of the Fianna Fáil Party led by Eamon deValera. The oath of fidelity to the Crown was described at this stage as an 'empty formula'.
12. See para **[4.03]**

which had followed the 18th century revolutionary movements in the United States and France. They also reflected the dissatisfaction within Irish nationalism at the absence of legal protections for basic rights in the pre-1922 regime. Thus, Article 6 of the 1922 Constitution provided that no person could be deprived of liberty save in accordance with law and also guaranteed the right to *habeas corpus*, subject to an exception for the actions of the military forces of the Irish Free State during a state of war or armed rebellion.[13] Article 7 contained a protection against entry into a person's dwelling unless authorised by law. Article 8 concerned freedom of conscience and of religious belief, while Article 9 dealt with freedom of expression, freedom of assembly and freedom of association. Other important provisions included Article 43, which prohibited the Oireachtas of the Irish Free State from enacting any retrospective criminal laws, while Article 70 contained a right to a criminal trial 'in due course of law'.

Continuity of laws

[15.07] Article 73 provided for the continuity of pre-1922 laws as follows:

> Subject to this Constitution and to the extent to which they are not inconsistent therewith, the laws in force in the Irish Free State (Saorstát Éireann) at the date of the coming into operation of this Constitution shall continue to be of full force and effect until the same or any of them shall have been repealed or amended by enactment of the Oireachtas.

In *The State (Kennedy) v Little*,[14] O'Byrne J stated in the High Court that Article 73 indicated that it was 'intended to set up the new State with the least possible change in previously existing law.' The courts indicated that Article 73 extended not merely to pre-1922 statute law but also pre-1922 common law.[15] However, the courts concluded that pre-1922 court decisions were not binding on those established under the 1922 Constitution.[16] Nonetheless, the overall effect was that existing common law and statute law was carried over *in toto* into the Irish Free State subject to their being consistent with the Constitution itself.[17]

13. On *habeas corpus* generally, see para **[10.36]**. Note also the retrospective and implicit amendment of Article 6 by the Indemnity Act 1923, discussed in *R (Cooney) v Clinton* [1935] IR 245: see para **[15.10]**.
14. [1931] IR 39.
15. Eg, *The State (McCarthy) v Lennon* [1936] IR 485 (common law privilege against self-incrimination)
16. See para **[12.33]**.
17. See also Article 50 of the 1937 Constitution, para **[15.29]**.

Amendment of the 1922 Constitution

[15.08] The 1922 Constitution provided for two methods by which its text could be amended. Article 14 required that a Bill to amend the Constitution be passed by the Oireachtas and then submitted for approval by those on the electoral register in a referendum. However, Article 50 provided that, for eight years after the Constitution came into force, until December 1930, it could be amended by 'ordinary' legislation, that is by an Act of the Oireachtas, without the need for a referendum, though this was subject to the proviso that amendments must conform to the 1921 Treaty. No referendum to amend the 1922 Constitution was ever held, but its provisions were amended on several occasions between 1922 and 1936.[18]

[15.09] Article 50 was itself amended in 1929 to double the period during which ordinary legislation could be employed to amend the constitutional text, thus extending this power until December 1938.[19] In 1931, an amending Act inserted Article 2A into the Constitution.[20] This was an extremely lengthy provision, which empowered the Executive Council to establish special tribunals, staffed by military personnel, with extraordinary powers of detention, trial and sentence, including the use of the death penalty. The provisions of Article 2A effected the virtual abolition of the fundamental rights contained in the 1922 Constitution, including *habeas corpus* and the right to jury trial. After Fianna Fáil came to power in 1932, virtually all remaining traces of the 1921 Treaty were removed. In 1933, legislation was enacted to remove the oath of fidelity to the British monarch and also the requirement that amendments were limited by the terms of the 1921 Treaty.[21] Later that year, the right of appeal from the Supreme Court to the Privy Council was abolished.[22] In 1936, the Senate was abolished.[23] Later that year, King Edward VIII abdicated from the British throne, and legislation was required to confirm this in all Commonwealth States as well as to provide for the succession. The response of the Irish Free State was to

18. In total, 27 Acts expressly entitled Act to amend the 1922 Constitution were passed between 1923 and 1936. Other Acts appeared to amend the Constitution by implication, such as the Indemnity Act 1923 discussed in *R (Cooney) v Clinton* [1935] IR 245. In addition the Constitution (Removal of Oath) Act 1933, although not expressed to be an Act to amend the Constitution, involved the removal of the oath of fidelity to the British monarch as well as any reference to amendments being limited by the terms of the 1921 Treaty.
19. Constitution (Amendment No 16) Act 1929. In the event, the 1937 Constitution came into effect before this period expired.
20. Constitution (Amendment No 17) Act 1929.
21. Constitution (Removal of Oath) Act 1933.
22. Constitution (Amendment No 22) Act 1933.
23. Constitution (Amendment No 24) Act 1936.

remove from the 1922 Constitution any remaining references to the Crown and to abolish the office of Governor General.[24] Legislation was also enacted to provide that the Executive Council was conferred with the power to enter into international treaties and to appoint diplomatic representatives. Any former role exercised by the monarch in these areas would henceforth be done only 'when advised by the Executive Council so to do'.[25] By the end of 1936, therefore, the 1921 Treaty had been virtually removed completely.

Judicial responses to amendments

[15.10] The courts had initially been quite amenable to any amendments to the 1922 Constitution, though some important reservations later emerged. In 1924, the Court of Appeal of Southern Ireland[26] held in *R (Cooney) v Clinton*[27] that an Act could amend the 1922 Constitution by implication and retrospectively, subject to the proviso that it was within the terms of the 1921 Treaty. The Court dismissed a challenge to the validity of the Indemnity Act 1923, which retrospectively validated the decisions of military courts, established under Article 6 of the 1922 Constitution to try those on the Anti-Treaty side of the Civil War. The 1923 Act had been enacted in the immediate wake of the decision in *R (O'Brien) v Military Governor, North Dublin Union*,[28] in which the Court of Appeal had held that a state of war or armed rebellion within the meaning of Article 6 of the 1922 Constitution did not exist at that time, August 1923; the Civil War had ended in May 1923 for most anti-Treaty forces.[29]

[15.11] In 1928, the High Court held in *Attorney General v McBride*[30] that it was permissible for an Act, in this instance the Public Safety Act 1927,[31] to provide that its provisions were to prevail over any in the Constitution, without the need to specify which provisions of the 1922 Constitution were being 'amended'.

---

24. Constitution (Amendment No 27) Act 1936.
25. Executive Council (External Relations) Act 1936.
26. The Court of Appeal continued to operate until the establishment of the Supreme Court by the Courts of Justice Act 1924: see para **[4.41]**.
27. [1935] IR 245 (but decided in 1924).
28. [1924] 1 IR 32.
29. Although a state of widespread armed rebellion against the Free State no longer existed, sporadic violence continued, necessitating the continued operation of the military courts and their successors, the special tribunals established under Article 2A in 1931.
30. [1928] IR 451.
31. The Act was passed in response to the murder of the then Minister for Justice, Kevin O'Higgins, as he walked to Mass. The Act was the precursor to the provisions of Article 2A.

[15.12] In 1935, in *Moore v Attorney General*,[32] the Privy Council itself held that the abolition of the right of appeal to that court[33] was within the powers of the Oireachtas of the Irish Free State as a member of the British Commonwealth. This was based primarily on the greater freedom granted to Commonwealth States by the Statute of Westminster 1931, which had been enacted to give effect to an Imperial Conference of the Commonwealth Members. The Statute of Westminster 1931 provided that a Commonwealth State was empowered to enact legislation in conflict with an Act of the Westminster Parliament. In the case of the Irish Free State, this included the power to enact legislation in breach of the Treaty, which had been given legal effect in an Act of the Westminster Parliament, the Irish Free State (Agreement) Act 1922. From a British legal perspective, therefore, the Irish Free State had been freed from any constraints imposed by the 1921 Treaty.

[15.13] However, by this time the Irish Supreme Court had taken a different and, ironically, less liberal view of the powers of the Irish Free State. In *The State (Ryan) v Lennon*,[34] decided in December 1934, before the Privy Council decision in *Moore*, the Supreme Court held, by a majority,[35] that it was permissible to override the right to trial in due course of law in Article 72 of the 1922 Constitution through the establishment of the special tribunals pursuant to Article 2A.[36] The Court also accepted that the Oireachtas was empowered to extend the eight year time limit for amending the 1922 Constitution by ordinary legislation.[37] However, the Supreme Court judges unanimously agreed that the Oireachtas could not enact any legislation in conflict with the 1921 Treaty.

[15.14] This arose from the Irish perspective on the nature of the Third Dáil Éireann, acting in 1922 as a Constituent Assembly. Section 1 of the Constitution of the Irish Free State (Saorstát Éireann) Act 1922 had given

32. [1935] IR 472.
33. See para **[15.09]**.
34. [1935] IR 170.
35. Fitzgibbon and Murnaghan JJ; Kennedy CJ dissenting. Kennedy CJ, who had been the first Attorney General of the Irish Free State, a principal drafter of the 1922 Constitution and architect of the court system established by the Courts of Justice Act 1924, concluded that the establishment of the special tribunals conflicted not only with the 1921 Treaty but also with Natural Law, and on both grounds was invalid. While Fitzgibbon and Murnaghan JJ accepted that the Oireachtas was bound to adhere to the 1921 Treaty, they held that it did not prohibit the establishment of special tribunals. They rejected completely Kennedy CJ's view that legislation in conflict with Natural Law could be declared invalid. Kennedy CJ's views on the position of Natural Law were to re-emerge in the interpretation of the 1937 Constitution by a later generation of judges: see para **[15.113]**.
36. See para **[15.113]**.
37. Achieved by the Constitution (Amendment No 16) Act 1929.

legal force to the 1922 Constitution, which was scheduled to the 1922 Act. Section 2 gave legal effect to the 1921 Treaty, also scheduled to the 1922 Act. Section 2 provided that the Constitution was to be construed by reference to the Treaty and that:

> if any provision of the said Constitution or of any amendment thereof or of any law made thereunder is in any respect repugnant to any of the provisions of the Scheduled Treaty, it shall, to the extent only of such repugnancy, be absolutely void and inoperative.

Article 50 of the 1922 Constitution, which authorised amendments to the Constitution by ordinary legislation, echoed s 2 by providing that only amendments 'within the terms of the Scheduled Treaty' could be enacted. However, as already noted, in 1933, legislation was enacted to remove the oath of fidelity to the British monarch and also the requirement that amendments were limited by the terms of the 1921 Treaty.[38] This legislation had repealed s 2 of the 1922 Act and the words 'within the terms of the Scheduled Treaty' in Article 50.

[15.15] In *The State (Ryan) v Lennon*, the Supreme Court stated that the Oireachtas was simply not empowered to remove the restrictions which had been imposed in s 2 of the 1922 Act by the Oireachtas itself acting as a Constituent Assembly. From an Irish legal perspective, the Irish Free State drew its legitimacy from the Constitution-enacting vote of the Third Dáil in 1922, and s 2 of the 1922 Act had created a self-imposed straitjacket which the Oireachtas of the Irish Free State could not remove. While English law had moved on in the wake of the Statute of Westminster 1931, the Irish view was more restrictive.

[15.16] Since the Court in *Ryan* upheld the validity of the constitutional amendments directly in issue in the case, the views expressed on the deletion of s 2 of the 1922 Act could be described as *obiter* and thus not binding on any later court under the doctrine of precedent.[39] Nonetheless, they indicated a judicial attitude on the ability of the Oireachtas of the Irish Free State to depart from the 1921 Treaty.

[3] THE 1937 CONSTITUTION

[15.17] As already indicated, the 1921 Treaty and the 1922 Constitution had been substantially dismantled by the end of 1936. Quite apart from the comments in *The State (Ryan) v Lennon*, work had already begun on the

38. The Constitution (Removal of Oath) Act 1933: see para **[15.09]**.
39. See para **[12.47]**.

preparation of an entirely new Constitution to replace, not merely amend, the 1922 Constitution.[40] However, the *Ryan* case underlined the need to create a different root title for any new Constitution. In 1937, the Oireachtas of the Irish Free State, now comprising the Dáil alone, debated and approved the text of a new Constitution. Unlike in 1922, the Dáil did not enact the new Constitution, but referred it to a plebiscite or referendum of the electorate.[41] In July 1937, the draft Constitution was passed into law at the plebiscite and, in accordance with Article 62 of the Constitution itself, it came into effect on 27 December 1937 as the Constitution of Ireland 1937. The Irish language title for the 1937 Constitution is Bunreacht na hÉireann, which may be translated as the Basic Law of Ireland. Like the 1922 Constitution, its text comprises a number of Articles, rather than the sections which characterise legislation.[42]

Institutions of State and fundamental rights

[15.18] In some respects, the Constitution of Ireland 1937 reflects the amended text of the 1922 Constitution in 1936. Like its 1922 predecessor, the 1937 Constitution may be divided into two component parts: an outline of the principal institutions of State and a description of certain fundamental rights of the citizens. However, critical differences exist in the detailed provisions.

Rhetoric of the 1937 Constitution

[15.19] Many provisions of the 1937 Constitution reflect the concerns of its principal architect, Eamon deValera.[43] The text of the 1937 Constitution has been described as both 'law and manifesto', since it contains not only statements of basic legal principles but also general aspirations.[44] Articles 2 and 3, which assert that the 'national territory' of Ireland includes the entire island of Ireland, remain politically controversial in the 1990s.[45] Other

40. In 1932, Fianna Fáil formed a minority government with the support of the Labour Party. In the 1933 General Election, Fianna Fáil won an absolute majority in Dáil Éireann. Since its foundation in 1924, Fianna Fáil had been committed to the removal from the 1922 Constitution of any trace of the 1921 Treaty. This led to a policy of its replacement by an entirely new Constitution.
41. Provided for in the Plebiscite (Draft Constitution) Act 1937.
42. See para **[13.46]**.
43. See generally Keogh, 'The Constitutional Revolution: An Analysis of the Making of the Constitution', in Litton (ed), *The Constitution of Ireland 1937-1987* (Institute of Public Administration, 1987).
44. Kelly, 'The Constitution: Law and Manifesto', in Litton, *op cit*, p 208, citing the judgment of the Supreme Court in *In re the Criminal Law (Jurisdiction) Bill 1975* [1977] IR 129: see para **[15.39]**.
45. See para **[15.37]**.

provisions contain overtly religious statements. The first words of the Preamble recite that the Constitution is enacted by the people of Ireland 'In the Name of the Most Holy Trinity'. Article 41, which contains important guarantees of support for the Family in society, has been criticised for its statement that women should not be required 'to engage in labour to the neglect of their duties in the home' and also for its prohibition on divorce, which appeared to reflect the religious teachings of the Roman Catholic Church to the exclusion of other religious faiths and the views of those with no religious beliefs.[46] We discuss later the overall ethos of the Constitution and its impact on constitutional judicial review.[47]

Separation of powers

[15.20] The tripartite separation of powers seen in the 1922 Constitution is retained in the 1937 Constitution, though with major changes in the detail.

President of Ireland

[15.21] As might be expected, the 1937 Constitution contains no reference to the British Crown. The functions originally performed under the 1922 Constitution by the Governor General, such as the official promulgation of legislation, were, in effect, transferred by Articles 12 and 13 to the newly-established office of President of Ireland. While Article 12.1 provides that the President takes precedence over all other persons in the State, she is not formally designated as head of State.[48] The Presidency is not an office with executive powers, Article 13.9 providing that the majority of her functions, such as the appointment of judges, are performed on the advice of the Government.[49] An important exception is the power to refer Bills to the Supreme Court under Article 26.[50] Article 13.4 vests supreme command of the Defence Forces in the President, but Article 13.5 provides that the exercise of this power must be regulated by law; the Defence Act 1954 in effect vests actual command in the Minister for Defence. Thus, the President is titular commander-in-chief of the Defence Forces only. Provision is made in Article 12 for the direct election of the President, though where one candidate only is nominated no election is required. Article 31 established a Council of State to advise the President in the exercise of her powers, such

46. A reference in Article 44 to the 'special position' of the Roman Catholic Church was removed by referendum in 1972: see para **[15.72]**. On the origins of Article 44, see Keogh, *op cit*.

47. See paras **[15.111]-[15.138]**.

48. *The Report of the Constitution Review Group* (Pn 2632, 1996) (see para **[16.139]**) recommended such a change.

49. See para **[8.07]**.

50. See para **[5.65]**.

as whether to refer Bills to the Supreme Court under Article 26. In recent years, some suggestions have been made that the President's functions be expanded, though it seems unlikely that this will be acted on.[51]

Executive power

[15.22] As to the executive branch, the Executive Council of the Irish Free State was replaced by the Government of Ireland, comprising the Taoiseach, that is Prime Minister, and other Government Ministers. Unlike its predecessor, the Government is conferred with the sole and exclusive power to exercise executive authority, without reference to any other external power such as the British Crown[52] Another innovative element is that Article 30 of the 1937 Constitution describes in broad terms the role of the chief law officer of the State, the Attorney General.[53]

Comptroller and Auditor General

[15.23] The office of Comptroller and Auditor General is dealt with in Article 33, which replaced comparable provisions in Articles 62 and 63 of the 1922 Constitution. The function of this office is to ensure that any State income is raised in accordance with the relevant legislation (the comptroller function)and spent in accordance with the vote of the Oireachtas (the auditor function). The Comptroller is appointed by the President on the nomination of Dáil Éireann and holds office on the same basis as a member of the judiciary. The detailed functions of the Comptroller and Auditor General, which include examination of the spending of State bodies as well as Government Departments, are contained in the Comptroller and Auditor General Acts 1923 to 1993.

Legislative power

[15.24] Turning to the legislative branch, the 1937 Constitution provides that exclusive legislative power is vested in the Oireachtas, comprising the President and two Houses or Chambers, the directly-elected Dáil Éireann or Chamber of Deputies and the indirectly elected Seanad Éireann or Senate. In this respect, there is a broad similarity with the 1922 Constitution in its original form. In terms of legislative powers, the Dáil is vastly superior to the Seanad.[54]

51. See, eg, Mee 'The Changing Nature of the Presidency: The President and the Government should be Friends' (1996) 14 ILT 2, 30.
52. See para **[8.05]**.
53. See para **[3.54]**.
54. See para **[13.09]**.

Judicial power

[15.25] The provisions concerning the judicial branch, which we have described elsewhere in some detail,[55] are broadly similar to those in the 1922 Constitution, as amended.

'Entrenched' fundamental rights

[15.26] A significant feature of the 1937 Constitution is that it is, in effect, superior to any other source of law, including statute law. Like the original text of the 1922 Constitution, the 1937 Constitution prohibits the Oireachtas from enacting any law which is in conflict with the provisions of the Constitution, including the fundamental rights of citizens which we discuss later in this chapter.[56] Unlike the 1922 Constitution, this limitation on the Oireachtas cannot be overridden by ordinary legislation; a key feature of the 1937 Constitution is its 'entrenched' nature. Article 46 of the Constitution provides that, since 1941, its provisions may not be amended by ordinary legislation; amendments may only be effected by a referendum of the entire electorate.[57] Moreover, the High Court and Supreme Court are conferred with the power to declare invalid any law which conflicts with the constitutional text; this judicial power is referred to as constitutional judicial review.[58]

Restrictions on law-making authority of Oireachtas

[15.27] The 1937 Constitution places limits on the legislative authority of the Oireachtas. Article 15.2.1° appears to confer unlimited authority on the Oireachtas by providing:

> The sole and exclusive power of making laws for the State is hereby vested in the Oireachtas: no other legislative authority has power to make laws for the State.

However, this must be read in conjunction with Article 15.4, which provides:

> 1° The Oireachtas shall not enact any law which is in any respect repugnant to this Constitution or any provision thereof.
>
> 2° Every law enacted by the Oireachtas which is in any respect repugnant to this Constitution or to any provision thereof, shall, but to the extent only of such repugnancy, be invalid.

55. See paras **[4.24]-[4.35]**.
56. See para **[15.27]**.
57. See para **[15.68]**.
58. See para **[15.28]**.

Article 15.4 deals with laws enacted by the Oireachtas after 1937. For laws in place prior to this, Article 50.1 states:

> Subject to this Constitution and to the extent to which they are not inconsistent therewith, the laws in force in Saorstát Éireann immediately prior to the date of the coming into operation of this Constitution shall continue to be of full force and effect until the same or any of them shall have been repealed or amended by enactment of the Oireachtas.

This ensured continuity with laws enacted prior to the 1937 Constitution and echoes Article 73 of the 1922 Constitution.[59] However, Article 34 of the 1937 Constitution added an entirely new dimension to these provisions.

The basis for constitutional judicial review

[15.28] Article 34 of the 1937 Constitution expressly confers on the High Court and Supreme Court the power to determine whether any law is valid having regard to the Constitution.

Article 34.3.2° provides:

> Save as otherwise provided by this Article,[60] the jurisdiction of the High Court shall extend to the question of the validity of any law having regard to the provisions of this Constitution, and no such question shall be raised (whether by pleading, argument or otherwise) in any Court established under this or any other Article of this Constitution other than the High Court or the Supreme Court.

Article 34.4.3° and 4° provide:

> 3° The Supreme Court shall, with such exceptions and subject to such regulations as may be prescribed by law, have appellate jurisdiction from all decisions of the High Court...
>
> 4° No law shall be enacted excepting from the appellate jurisdiction of the Supreme Court cases which involve questions as to the validity of any law having regard to the provisions of this Constitution.

Thus, the High Court and, on appeal, the Supreme Court have exclusive jurisdiction to determine whether laws are valid or invalid on the ground that they are in conflict with any provision of the Constitution. The most significant provisions in this respect are those which recognise certain basic or fundamental rights, similar to those contained in the Constitution of the United States of America.

---

59. See para **[15.07]**.
60. This refers to the exclusive jurisdiction of the Supreme Court in referrals of Bills under Article 26: see para **[5.65]**.

Continuity of laws

[15.29] Like Article 73 of the 1922 Constitution,[61] Article 50 of the 1937 Constitution provided that the laws in the Irish Free State continued to have full force and effect unless they were inconsistent with the 1937 Constitution or were repealed by the Oireachtas established by the 1937 Constitution. While this carried forward pre-1922 laws as well as those of 1922 to 1937, the provisions of the 1937 Constitution concerning constitutional judicial review produced a different perspective on Article 50.[62]

English and Irish language text of Constitution and other legal documents

[15.30] Article 8.1 of the Constitution provides that the Irish language, Gaelige, is the national language and the first official language,[63] while Article 8.2 states that the English language is recognised as a second official language. In fact, the English language is the vernacular of 98% of the population of Ireland,[64] and the Irish language is the spoken and written language for a small number, mainly though not exclusively those living in certain western areas of Ireland, known as Gaeltacht areas.

Irish language text of Constitution prevails only in case of conflict

[15.31] The 1937 Constitution was enacted as a dual language text, in English and Irish.[65] Article 25.5.1° provides that the Taoiseach may, from time to time, supervise the preparation of the latest text of the Constitution, as amended, which must be in both languages. Article 25.5.2° provides that a copy of every such text, when authenticated by the signatures of the Taoiseach and the Chief Justice, must be signed by the President of Ireland and enrolled for record in the office of the Registrar of the Supreme Court. Article 25.4.3° specifies that such a copy 'shall, upon such enrolment, be conclusive evidence of this Constitution'. Thus, the texts in both languages have, in general, equal status.

[15.32] Article 25.5.4° provides that, 'in case of conflict between the texts of any copy of this Constitution ... the text in the national language shall

61. See para **[15.07]**.

62. See para **[15.43]**.

63. See generally Ó Máille, *The Status of the Irish Language - A Legal Perspective* (Bord na Gaeilge, 1990)

64. *Report of the Constitution Review Group* (Pn 2632, 1996), p 15.

65. The draft Constitution initially debated in the Oireachtas in 1937 was in the English language only, the Irish language text being published at a late stage, a point criticised at the time in view of the status being accorded the Irish text: see Hogan & Whyte, *op cit*, p 211.

prevail.' Thus, the Irish language version of the Constitution prevails, but only where a conflict arises. The courts have emphasised that, in general, they will seek to avoid any conflict between the English and Irish language texts when attempting to interpret a particular constitutional provision. In most instances, the English language version is referred to first and, only if there is some doubt as to its meaning, the Irish language version is used to clarify or elucidate the meaning of the English language text.[66]

Text of legislation and other official documents

[15.33] Article 8.3 of the 1937 Constitution states that provision may be made by law for the exclusive use of either of the official languages for official purposes. Such official purposes include the promulgation of legislation. In *Attorney General v Coyne and Wallace*,[67] the Supreme Court held that the effect of Article 8.3 was that legislation and other official documents could validly be published in either English or Irish alone and need not be published in both official languages, unless special provision is made requiring publication in a particular language of the two or in both. The vast majority of legislation is enacted in the English language only. In such instances, therefore, the English language text is the single definitive text.

[15.34] Article 25.4.3° provides that the President shall promulgate Acts of the Oireachtas in the language or languages in which they are passed by the Oireachtas.[68] Article 25.4.4° requires that, where legislation is enacted in one language version only, an 'official translation' must also be issued. Since most legislation is passed in the English language only, the vast majority of official translations are in the Irish language, and these versions have no legal significance. In the case of an Act passed in the Irish language only, the official translation into the English language has no legal significance. Apart from Acts to amend the Constitution, a very limited number of Acts have been enacted in both official languages, an example being the Republic of Ireland Act 1948.[69] Article 25.4.6° of the Constitution provides that, in case of conflict, the Irish text prevails in such instance.

[15.35] Official translations into Irish of Acts passed in English are, in general, published many years in arrears.[70] A similar picture emerges for

66. See Hogan & Whyte, *op cit*, pp 204-5.
67. (1967) 101 ILTR 17.
68. See para **[13.10]**.
69. See para **[15.41]**.
70. At the time of writing (July 1996), the latest year for which a bilingual version of the bound volumes of Acts of the Oireachtas has been published is the year 1982. Selected Acts are, however, published in bilingual form more speedily.

delegated or secondary legislation, including the various rules of court. In *Delap v Minister for Justice*,[71] the applicant sought an Irish version of the Rules of the Superior Courts 1986[72] in order to conduct High Court proceedings in Irish. Applying the decision of the Supreme Court in the *Coyne and Wallace* case, O'Hanlon J rejected the suggestion that the English version of the 1986 Rules lacked validity under Article 8 of the Constitution merely because no Irish version had, at that time (1990), been published. However, he accepted that, as an aspect of the constitutional right of access to the courts,[73] the applicant was entitled to conduct his proceedings in Irish, and on that ground held that he was entitled to have made available an Irish language text of the 1986 Rules within a reasonable period of time after they had been promulgated in English.

Right to self-determination

[15.36] Article 1 of the 1937 Constitution proclaims a clear declaration of independence and right to self-determination:

> The Irish nation hereby affirms its inalienable, indefeasible, and sovereign right to choose its own form of Government, to determine its relations with other nations, and to develop its life, political, economic and cultural, in accordance with its own genius and traditions.

This clear assertion was to be expected from a constitutional text seeking to mark out a new Basic Law (Bunreacht).

The national territory

[15.37] More controversial, however, are Articles 2 and 3. Article 2 contains an assertion that the national territory of Ireland 'consists of the whole island of Ireland, its islands and the territorial seas'. This claim is slightly modified by Article 3 which provides that '[p]ending the re-integration of the national territory' the laws enacted by the Parliament established by the 1937 Constitution 'shall have the like area and extent of application as the laws of Saorstát Éireann and the like extra-territorial effect'. This appears to limit the laws of Ireland to the 26 counties of the Irish Free State.[74] However, this modification is itself stated to be 'without prejudice to the right of the Parliament and the Government established by this Constitution to exercise jurisdiction over the whole' of the national territory.

---

71. The judgment was delivered in Irish sub nom. *Delap v an tAire Dlí agus Cirt*, High Court, unrep, 13 June 1990.
72. SI 15/1986: see para **[6.01]**.
73. See para **[9.02]**.
74. As provided for in the Government of Ireland Act 1920, as amended: see para **[2.45]**.

[15.38] Two issues thus arise concerning Articles 2 and 3: whether they involve political aspirations only or have a more binding legal significance; and whether the Oireachtas may enact laws applicable in the six counties of Northern Ireland. On the second point the courts are in agreement that the Oireachtas is prohibited from enacting legislation applicable in Northern Ireland, but quite different views have been expressed on the first point.

[15.39] In *In re the Criminal Law (Jurisdiction) Bill 1975*,[75] the Supreme Court indicated that Articles 2 and 3 belonged in the realm of political rhetoric. The Court stated:[76]

> "... the Constitution ... expresses not only legal norms but basic doctrines of social and political theory ... the Constitution contains more than legal rules: it reflects, in part, aspirations and aims and expresses the political theories on which the people acted when they enacted the Constitution.
>
> One of the theories held in 1937 by a substantial number of citizens was that a nation, as distinct from a State, had rights; that the Irish people living in what is now called the Republic of Ireland and in Northern Ireland together formed the Irish Nation; that a nation has a right to unity of territory in some form, be it as a unitary or federal state; and that the Government of Ireland Act 1920, though legally binding, was a violation of that natural right to unity which was superior to positive law.[77]
>
> This national claim to unity exists not in the legal but in the political order and is one of the rights which are envisaged in Article 2; it is expressly saved by Article 3 which states that the area to which the laws enacted by the parliament established by the Constitution apply."

This view of Articles 2 and 3 is, at first sight, plausible and certainly sensitive to those in Northern Ireland who do not share the 'Irish Nation' theory referred to by the Supreme Court. However, in *McGimpsey v Ireland*,[78] the Supreme Court rejected the view that Articles 2 and 3 involved political aspirations only. Finlay CJ stated that the correct interpretation of Articles 2 and 3 was as follows:[79]

1. The re-integration of the national territory is a constitutional imperative (*cf* Hederman J in *Russell v Fanning*).[80]
2. Article 2 of the Constitution consists of a declaration of the extent of the national territory as a claim of legal right.

75. [1977] IR 129.
76. *Ibid*, at 147. The judgment of the Court was delivered by O'Higgins CJ.
77. On natural law and positive law, see para **[15.113]**.
78. [1990] 1 IR 110.
79. *Ibid*, at 119. The other members of the Court concurred in this interpretation.
80. [1988] IR 505, at 537.

3. Article 3 of the Constitution prohibits, pending the re-integration of the national territory, the enactment of laws with any greater area or extent of application or extra-territorial effect than the laws of Saorstát Éireann and this prohibits the enactment of laws applicable in the counties of Northern Ireland.
4. The restriction imposed by Article 3 pending the re-integration of the national territory in no way derogated from the claim as a legal right to the entire national territory.

This interpretation of Articles 2 and 3 confirms that the territorial application of legislation enacted by the Oireachtas is limited to the 26 counties of Ireland. Moreover, in the *McGlinchey* case, the Supreme Court dismissed a challenge to the Anglo-Irish Agreement 1985, Article 1 of which provides that the United Kingdom and Irish governments:

(a) affirm that any change in the status of Northern Ireland would only come about with the consent of a majority of the people of Northern Ireland;
(b) recognise that the present wish of a majority of the people of Northern Ireland is for no change in the status of Northern Ireland...

The Supreme Court concluded that these provisions were not inconsistent with the constitutional imperative to seek the re-integration of the national territory, particularly since Article 29.2 committed the State to peaceful settlement of international disputes.[81]

[15.40] However, the view that re-integration of the national territory is a 'constitutional imperative' and that Article 3 is a 'claim of legal right' continues to attract considerably more publicity than this conclusion. Amendments to Articles 2 and 3 remain a key element in discussions concerning future political relationships on the island of Ireland and the relationships between the two jurisdictions in Ireland and the United Kingdom.[82]

Ireland and the Republic of Ireland

[15.41] Article 4 of the 1937 Constitution provides:

> The name of the State is Éire, or in the English language, Ireland.[83]

---

81. See generally para **[16.60]**.
82. On possible changes to Articles 2 and 3, see Hadden and Boyle, *The Anglo-Irish Agreement 1985 - A Commentary* (Sweet & Maxwell, 1989) (a reprint of an Annotation from Irish Current Law Statutes Annotated 1985).
83. The Irish language version reads: 'Éire is ainm don Stát, nó sa Sacs-Bhéarla, Ireland'.

The text of Article 4 has given rise to some difficulties concerning the name of the State,[84] but in the English language the correct name is 'Ireland'.[85]

Article 5 provides:

> Ireland is a sovereign, independent, democratic State.

While the Constitution created, to all intents and purposes, a republic,[86] there is no explicit reference to this in the constitutional text. By 1936, the sole remaining function of the British Crown concerned the accreditation of foreign diplomats, acting on the advice of the Executive Council of the Irish Free State.[87] Article 29.4.1° of the 1937 Constitution provides that the executive power of the State in connection with external relations shall be exercised by the Government. Thus, effective power rests with the Government. However, Article 29.4.2° provides that the Government is empowered (though not required) to continue the position as at 1936 by adopting any 'method of procedure used or adopted... by the members of any group or league of nations with which the State is or becomes associated for the purpose of international co-operation in matters of common concern.'[88] Between 1937 and 1948, Irish diplomats continued to be accredited in the name of the Crown acting on the advice of the Government. During this time, the State also continued its membership of the British Commonwealth, inherited from the Irish Free State. In 1948, the then Government announced its intention to withdraw from the Commonwealth. The Republic of Ireland Act 1948 gave effect to this decision. Section 2 of the 1948 Act provides:

> It is hereby declared that the description of the State shall be the Republic of Ireland.[89]

This 'description' of the State as the Republic of Ireland does not, of course, amend the name of the State, as contained in Article 4.
Section 3 of the 1948 Act provides that:

---

84. On the difficulties with the use of the word 'Éire' in the English language text, see paras **[2.71]** and **[15.42]**.

85. To simplify matters, the *Report of the Constitution Review Group* (Pn 2632, 1996) (see para **[15.139]**), p 11, recommended that the English language text of Article 4 be amended to read thus: 'The name of the State is Ireland,' with the Irish language text to read thus: 'Éire is ainm don Stát.

86. See the references to republican rhetoric in the judgment of Walsh J in *Byrne v Ireland* [1972] IR 241: para **[15.43]**.

87. See para **[15.09]**.

88. See para **[16.61]**.

89. The 1948 Act was enacted in both the English and Irish languages; in the Irish language text of s 2, 'Republic of Ireland' reads 'Poblacht na hÉireann.

> the President, on the authority and on the advice of the Government, may exercise the executive power or any executive function of the State in or in connection with its external relations.

While s 3 provided for the formal transfer from the British Crown to the President of the executive power in external relations,[90] it was and remains the Government who in practice exercise this power.

Sovereignty of the people and liability of the State

[15.42] The Preamble to the Constitution provides, in part:

> *We, the people of Éire ... Do hereby adopt, enact and give to ourselves this Constitution.*[91]

This enacting formula marks a clear break from the 1922 Constitution where, from an Irish legal perspective,[92] the Third Dáil enacted that Constitution as a Constituent Assembly. The 1937 Constitution ensured that the people of Ireland were the source of all legal authority. As with Articles 2 and 3 of the Constitution, this enacting formula is not simply a matter of political rhetoric but has important practical implications. Article 5 provides that 'Ireland is a sovereign, independent, democratic State' and Article 6.1 states:

> All powers of government, legislative, executive and judicial, derive, under God, from the people, whose right it is to designate the rulers of the State and, in final appeal, to decide all questions of national policy, according to the requirements of the common good.

The Constitution contains two practical instances of the sovereignty of the people: the power to elect their political representatives to Dáil Éireann in a general election intended to form the executive or Government; and the power to amend the Constitution itself.

[15.43] Another aspect of the sovereignty of the people emerged in *Byrne v Ireland.*[93] In that case, the plaintiff had suffered personal injuries when she fell into a trench which had been dug by employees of what was then the Department of Posts and Telegraphs. The evidence seemed to indicate that, in refilling the trench, these employees had been negligent and that this was the cause of the plaintiff's injuries. On this basis, the plaintiff appeared to have a simple task in claiming damages against the Minister for Posts and

---

90. The 1948 Act also repealed the Executive Authority (External Relations) Act 1936.

91. The English language version of the Preamble is in italics. The Irish language version was originally published in roman type, but later versions have appeared in italics.

92. See para **[15.15]**.

93. [1972] IR 241.

Telegraphs.[94] However, it was argued that, since those alleged to have been negligent were employees of the State, their actions were immune from any claim on the basis that the State had inherited the pre-1922 sovereign immunity from suit of the Crown and its servants. While this was accepted in the High Court, the Supreme Court held that any such immunity had not been carried over into Irish law under the 1937 Constitution. Thus the State was held vicariously liable for the injuries sustained by the plaintiff. The Court traced the historical development of the concept of sovereign immunity, and also explained how the Constitution created an entirely new legal order in the State. This explains, for example, the comment in the judgment of Walsh J that decisions of English courts might not be relevant to an understanding of the principles contained in the 1937 Constitution. Nonetheless, English precedent continues to play a significant role in the development of Irish law generally.[95] The following extract from the judgment of Walsh J represents the views of four of the five Supreme Court judges in *Byrne*.[96]

> "By the Constitution which was adopted and enacted by the People and came into force on the 29th December, 1937, the People created a State which is described in Article 5 of the Constitution as 'a sovereign, independent, democratic state' and under Article 4 the name of the State in the English language is 'Ireland'. If the State can be sued, then in my opinion it can be sued by its official name which is 'Ireland' in the English language.
>
> Article 6 of the Constitution provides that all powers of government - legislative, executive and judicial - 'derive, under God, from the people, whose right it is to designate the rulers of the State and, in final appeal, to decide all questions of national policy, according to the requirements of the common good'. Article 46 of the Constitution provides that every proposal for an amendment of the Constitution shall, upon having been passed or deemed to have been passed by both Houses of the Oireachtas, be submitted by referendum to the decision of the People, and Article 47 provides that every such proposal for an amendment shall be held to have been approved by the People if, upon having been so submitted, a majority of the votes cast at such referendum shall have been cast in favour of its enactment into law. The preamble to the Constitution is a preamble by the People formally adopting, enacting and giving themselves a Constitution.
>
> It appears to me abundantly clear from those provisions that the State is the creation of the People and is to be governed in accordance with the provisions of the Constitution which was enacted by the People and which

94. On negligence generally, see para **[12.70]**.

95. See para **[12.38]**.

96. The extract ends at p 575.

can be amended by the People only, and that in the last analysis the sovereign authority is the People. This is in contrast to the position in the United States of America where Chief Justice John Marshall initially established the basic premise that the United States was created by the States and the people of the States, and not by the people separated from the States. It is also in contrast to the position which prevailed in England and now in Great Britain that the King was the personification of the State and that, even with the development of a constitutional monarchy where the distinction between the King in his public and private capacities could be perceived, no legal acknowledgement of this distinction was made with the consequence that the King, or the Crown, was and remains the personification of the State in Great Britain.

Article 6 of our Constitution, having designated the powers of the government as being legislative, executive and judicial and having declared them to have been derived from the People, provided that these powers of government are exercisable only by or on the authority of the organs of State established by the Constitution. The question which now arises for decision is whether the judicial power of government which is exercised by the judiciary through the Courts is exercisable so as to bind the State itself, one of whose organs is the judiciary.

It has already been established that the State is a juristic person capable of holding property: see *Comyn v The Attorney General*[97] and *Commissioners of Public Works v Kavanagh*[98]. It was implicit in the judgments in those cases that the State could have been sued as such. Drummond's famous dictum that property has its duties as well as its rights is no less true in this context. Even in mediaeval England the petition of right was available for all proprietary actions in the wide sense of the term in that it lay not merely for the recovery of land but for claims for damages, for interference with proprietary rights, and also for the recovery of chattels. Not only in England but in many other countries in Europe the inviolability of property was acknowledged in law as a right superior even to that of sovereignty itself. The petition of right fell into disuse from the 15th century onwards until the 19th century during which time it was superseded by the real actions. In a very full investigation of the history of the petition of right, Lord Sommers in the *Bankers' Case*[99] was able to treat as precedents (for the competence of the petition of right in contract) cases in which the facts corresponded to those in modern suits in contract but which had been decided as proprietary actions. Therefore, the concept of proprietary actions lying against the State, even when the King was the personification of the State, is not a new one.

97. [1950] IR 142.
98. [1950] IR 142.
99. (1700) 14 St Tr 1.

The point which arises in the present case is whether a right of action lies against the State for a wrong and, in particular, whether the State is vicariously liable for the wrongs committed by its servants. The learned High Court judge, Mr Justice Murnaghan, who tried these issues came to the conclusion that the State is not so liable and he based his rejection of the submission on the statement in Article 5 of the Constitution that Ireland is 'a sovereign ... state'. He says that 'the simple statement that 'Ireland is a sovereign ... state' is completely inconsistent with the propositions that the State is subject to one of the organs of State, the judicial organ, and can be sued as such in its own courts'. This appears to me to assume that, even if the State is the sovereign authority and not simply the creation of the acknowledged sovereign authority, the People, the concept of being sued in court is necessarily inconsistent with the theory of sovereignty. In the first place I think that the learned trial judge misconstrued the intent of Article 5 if he construed it as a constitutional declaration that the State is above the law. Article 1 of the Constitution affirms that the Irish nation has the 'sovereign right to choose its own form of Government'. Our constitutional history, and in particular the events leading up to the enactment of the Constitution, indicate beyond doubt, to my mind, that the declaration as to sovereignty in Article 5 means that the State is not subject to any power of government save those designated by the People in the Constitution itself, and that the State is not amenable to any external authority for its conduct. To hold that the State is immune from suit for wrong because it is a sovereign state is to beg the question.

In several parts in the Constitution duties to make certain provisions for the benefit of the citizens are imposed on the State in terms which bestow rights upon the citizens and, unless some contrary provision appears in the Constitution, the Constitution must be deemed to have created a remedy for the enforcement of these rights. It follows that, where the right is one guaranteed by the State, it is against the State that the remedy must be sought if there has been a failure to discharge the constitutional obligation imposed. The Oireachtas cannot prevent or restrict the citizen from pursuing his remedy against the State in order to obtain or defend the very rights guaranteed by the Constitution in the form of obligations imposed upon the State; nor can the Oireachtas delegate to any organ of state the implementation of these rights so as to exonerate the State itself from its obligations under the Constitution. The State must act through its organs but it remains vicariously liable for the failures of these organs in the discharge of the obligations, save where expressly excluded by the Constitution. In support of this it is to be noted that an express immunity from suit is conferred on the President by Article 13, s 8, sub-s 1, and that a limited immunity from suit for members of the Oireachtas is contained in Article 15, s 13, and that restrictions upon suit in certain cases are necessarily inferred from the provisions of Article 27, s 3, of the Constitution.

It is also to be noted that Article 45 of the Constitution, which sets forth certain principles of social policy intended for the general guidance of the Oireachtas, contains an express provision that the application of those principles 'shall not be cognisable by any Court under any of the provisions of this Constitution'. This express exclusion from cognisance by the Courts of these particular provisions reinforces the view that the provisions of the Constitution obliging the State to act in a particular manner may be enforced in the Courts against the State as such. If, in particular cases, the State has already by law imposed on some organ of State or some servant of the State the duty to implement the right or protection guaranteed by the Constitution then, in cases of default, it may be sufficient and adequate in particular instances to bring proceedings against the person upon whom the duty has been so imposed; but that does not absolve the State, upon which the prime obligation has been imposed, from responsibility to carry out the duty imposed upon it. If under the Constitution the State cannot do any act or be guilty of an omission save through one or more of its organs or servants, it is nonetheless answerable because of the identification declared by the provisions of Article 6 the Constitution.

The suggestion advanced in this case that the State cannot be made amenable civil wrong stems from the English feudal concept that 'the King can do no wrong'. There is some authority for believing that this phrase originally meant precisely the contrary to what it now means, and that its original meaning was that the King must not, was not allowed to, and was not entitled to, do wrong. However, while for many centuries past there has been no doubt as to the meaning of the phrase 'the King can do no wrong', that is a concept which differs from the concept that he was immune from suit. A great variety of devices emerged for obtaining relief against the Crown; some of these took the form of suits against the officers or agents of the King personally where no consent was necessary, and some of them took the form of suits against the King himself where it was permitted by the grant of a petition of right rather than by suing by writ. The grant of a petition of right in such a case was based precisely on the proposition that the King had acted contrary to law. In the sphere of tort the petition of right did not normally lie outside real actions. Tortious immunity was a judge-made rule. It would appear to have been based on the view that it would be a logical anomaly for the King to issue or enforce a writ against himself. The theory was that the King, as the source of all justice, was incapable of committing a wrong. But the theory was reserved for torts which lay outside the sphere of interference with proprietary rights. There does not appear to be any record of how this doctrine fared in England during the years of the republic under the Cromwellian regime. The theory at least included the safeguard, frequently of little practical worth, that the servant of the Crown was personally liable for the wrongs committed by him in the performance of his service; this was based on the presumption that the officer who committed the wrongful act did so of his own accord and was thus liable for it because the King, who was incapable of committing a wrong, could not have authorised it.

By contrast, when the doctrine of sovereign immunity was imported into the United States, the doctrine was extended to cover the officers and agents of the State and over the course of years it could be availed of even by municipal authorities. The doctrine appears to have been imported into the common law in the United States as basic to the common law without, perhaps, a proper recognition of the nature of its origin, namely, that it rested upon the King being the personification of the State and, therefore, was applied only to a person. The fact that this English theory of sovereign immunity, originally personal to the King and with its roots deep in feudalism, came to be applied in the United States where feudalism had never been known has been described as one of the mysteries of legal evolution. It appears to have been taken for granted by the American courts in the early years of the United States - though not without some question, since Chief Justice Jay in *Chisholm v Georgia*[100] said: 'I wish the state of society was so far improved and the science of government advanced to such degree of perfection that the whole nation could in the peaceable course of law be compelled to do justice and be sued by individual citizens'. In later cases the United States courts defended the doctrine of immunity on the grounds that it was vital for the efficient working of government. Mr Justice Holmes sought to justify it in *Kawananakoa v Polyblank*[101] by saying that 'a sovereign is exempt from suit, not because of any formal conception or obsolete theory, but on the logical and practical ground that there can be no legal right as against the authority that makes the law on which the rights depends'. It had also been suggested that the immunity rested on a policy imposed by necessity. In *United States v Lee*[102] after full historical investigations the Supreme Court of the United States reached the conclusion:[103]

> 'that it has been adopted in our courts as a part of the general doctrine of publicists, that the supreme power in every State, wherever it may reside, shall not be compelled, by process of courts of its own creation, to defend itself from assaults in those courts.'

Other decisions based it on public policy. In England the enactment and operation of the Crown Proceedings Act 1947, and in the United States the Federal Torts Act 1945, would appear to have invalidated these rationalisations.

Under our own constitutional provisions it is the Oireachtas which makes the laws and it is the judiciary which administers them; there is no apparent

100. 2 Dall 419 (1793).

101. 205 US 349 at 353 (1907).

102. 106 US 196 (1882).

103. *Ibid*, at 206.

reason why the activities of either of these organs of state should compel the State itself to be above the law.

That the concept of state liability is not a juristic problem is also evident from the laws of several other countries. In France prior to the revolution the principle of *le Roi ne peut mal faire* prevailed as in the English legal theory upon the same basis of the King being the personification of the state. Since the revolutionary period the liability of the state gradually grew until finally, in the *Blanco* case of 1873, it was clearly established that the state was liable for the tortious act of its servant if it amounts to a *faute de service,* though the public servant involved may be personally liable for actions which are clearly outside the scope of his employment. In France these actions against the state for the tortious actions of its servants are heard in the administrative courts. In Germany the law developed in a somewhat similar way. Article 839 of the German Civil Code of 1896 and Article 34 of the Constitution of the Federal Republic of Germany make the state liable to a third party for the tortious activities of the state's servants in the exercise of their public functions, and these actions may be brought before the ordinary civil courts.

Many other countries in the world have imposed, to a greater or lesser extent, liability on the state for the tortious acts of public servants, and included in these are common-law countries in the British Commonwealth. Section 78 of the Constitution of the Commonwealth of Australia (appearing in s 9 of the Commonwealth of Australia Constitution Act 1900) provided that the legislature of Australia might make laws for conferring rights to proceed against the Commonwealth or a State in respect of matters within the limits of the judicial power. Part 9 of the Judiciary Act of 1903 permitted suits by and against the Commonwealth and the States; it gave a right to sue the Commonwealth both in contract and tort without a petition of right and laid down that:

in any suit in which the Commonwealth or a State is party the rights of parties shall as nearly as possible be the same and judgment may be given and costs awarded on either side as in a suit between subject and subject.

Under the Canadian Petition of Right Act the Crown can be sued in the Court of Exchequer and Separate Court on petition of right in contract and tort. Although a previous limitation in tort to 'public work' was abolished by the Exchequer Act 1938, a petition of right is still required. In New Zealand the Crown can now be sued in contract and tort under the Crown Proceedings Act 1950. Under the Crown Liability Act 1910, the former Union of South Africa could be sued without petition of right in contract and for torts arising 'out of any wrong committed by any servant of the Crown acting in his capacity within the scope of his authority as such servant'. In India a distinction has been drawn between acts of State and ordinary acts done under cover of municipal law. The latter case would include the negligence of the driver of a military vehicle in the ordinary use of that vehicle, as distinct from acts arising out of the exercise of a sovereign power like that of making war for which the State would not be liable: see *Union of India v Jasso*.[104]

In our own context it is to be noted that the Factories Act 1955, applies to factories belonging to or in the occupation of the State: see s 3, sub-s 9, and s 118 of the Act of 1955. Section 59 of the Civil Liability Act 1961 makes the Minister for Finance liable for the negligent use of a motor vehicle belonging to the State; that section replaced virtually identical provisions in s 116 of the Road Traffic Act 1961, which had replaced s 170 of the Road Traffic Act 1933. For an example of a similar statutory provision enacted by the Oireachtas of Saorstát Éireann, see s 6 of the Conditions of Employment Act 1936.

I have referred to these several different matters for the purpose of indicating that there is ample support for my view that immunity from suit for wrong is not a necessary ingredient of State sovereignty.

For many years in this country, like the American experience, the notion of sovereign immunity of the State seems to have been accepted as part of the common law, without full regard to its true origin in the common law. The confusion was increased by the fact that the King enjoyed some place under the Constitution of the Irish Free State 1922, and by the fact that in these years the law was practised and interpreted by persons who, quite naturally, had been mostly orientated by education and practice towards a system in which this concept of sovereign immunity of the Crown held sway ...

There is no basis, theoretical or otherwise, for a claim that the State can do no wrong or, in the particular context, that Saorstát Éireann could do no wrong; and there is no basis, in theory or otherwise, for a submission that the State cannot be made vicariously liable for a wrong committed by its officers, employees and servants in the course of the service of the State. Earlier in this judgment I have given my reasons for holding that immunity from suit is not a necessary ingredient of State sovereignty.

Several provisions of the Constitution of the Irish Free State imposed obligations upon the State and conferred rights on the citizens as against the State and a breach of these, or a failure to honour them, on the part of the State would clearly have been a wrong or a breach of obligation; it is of no consequence that the wrong or breach might not be within the recognised field of wrongs in the law of tort. In principle, a wrong which arises from the failure to honour an obligation must be capable of remedy, and a contrast between the citizen and the State in the pursuit of such a remedy is a justiciable controversy cognisable by the Courts, save where expressly excluded by a provision of the Constitution if it is in respect of obligations and rights created by the Constitution, or save where expressly excluded by law if it is simply in respect of rights or obligations created by law. To take one example, Article 10 of the Constitution of Saorstát

104. AIR 1962 Punj 315 (FB).

Éireann provided that all citizens of the Irish Free State 'have the right to free elementary education'. In my view, that was clearly enforceable against Saorstát Éireann if no provision had been made to implement that Article of its Constitution. There are several instances in the Constitution of Ireland also where the State undertakes obligations towards the citizens. It is not the case that these are justiciable only when some law is being passed which directly infringes these rights or when some law is passed to implement them. They are justiciable when there has been a failure on the part of the State to discharge the obligations or to perform the duties laid upon the State by the Constitution. It may well be that in particular cases it can be shown that some organ of the State already has adequate powers and in fact may have had imposed upon it the particular duty to carry out the obligations undertaken by the State, but that would not mean that the State was not vicariously liable for the non-performance of its various organs of their duties.

Even if one were to adopt the concept that the State can do no wrong because, as it acts by its organs, agents or employees, any wrong arising must be attributed to them rather than to the State itself, the doctrine of *respondeat superior* would still apply. That doctrine is not invalidated by showing that the principal cannot commit the particular tort. It rests not on the notion of the principal's wrong but on the duty of the principal to make good the damage done by his servants or agents in carrying on the principal's affairs. It may well be that in many cases the appropriate organ of State, or the officer or person, charged with the particular duty could be compelled by mandamus proceedings to carry out the duty imposed including, if necessary, an order to apply to the Oireachtas for the necessary finance: see *Conroy v Minister for Defence*.[105] However, that does not exonerate the State as the principal from the damage accruing from the failure to do so or from the damage accruing from the wrongful manner in which it was done.

Where the People by the Constitution create rights against the State or impose duties upon the State, a remedy to enforce these must be deemed to be also available. It is as much the duty of the State to render justice against itself in favour of citizens as it is to administer the same between private individuals. The investigation and the adjudication of such claims by their nature belong to the judicial power of government in the State, designated in Article 6 of the Constitution of Ireland, which is vested in the judges and the courts appointed and established under the Constitution in accordance with the provisions of the Constitution.

In my view, the whole tenor of our Constitution is to the effect that there is no power, institution, or person in the land free of the law save where such immunity is expressed, or provided for, in the Constitution itself. Article 13, s 8, sub-s 1 (relating to the President) and Article 15, ss 12 and 13

105. [1934] IR 342, at 679.

(relating to the Oireachtas) are examples of express immunities. For an example of a provision for the granting of immunity, see Article 29, s 3, by which diplomatic immunities may be granted. There is nothing in the Constitution envisaging the writing into it of a theory of immunity from suit of the State (a state set up by the People to be governed in accordance with the provisions of the Constitution) stemming from or based upon the immunity of a personal sovereign who was the keystone of a feudal edifice. English common-law practices, doctrines, or immunities cannot qualify or dilute the provisions of the Constitution: see *The State (Browne) v Feran.*[106] I think it is apposite to quote here the words of Murnaghan J. in *In re Tilson*:[107]

> 'The archaic law of England rapidly disintegrating under modern conditions need not be a guide for the fundamental principles of a modern state. It is not a proper method of construing a new constitution of a modern state to make an approach in the light of legal survivals of an earlier law.'

While the King had a limited place in the Constitution of Saorstát Éireann, he had no place in the present new republican form of constitution which was enacted in 1937 and came into force on the 29th December, 1937. The present Constitution provides at Article 28, s 2, that the executive power of the State shall, subject to the provisions of the Constitution, be exercised by or on the authority of the Government. Section 3 of that Article provides that war shall not be declared and that the State shall not participate in any war save with the assent of Dáil Éireann, except that in the case of actual invasion the section provides that the Government may take whatever steps it may consider necessary for the protection of the State and that the Dáil, if not sitting, shall be summoned to meet at the earliest practicable date. Article 29, s 4, reserves exclusively to the authority of the Government the exercise of the executive power of the State in connection with its external relations. By Article 15 the national parliament (to be known as the Oireachtas) consists of the President of Ireland, Dáil Éireann and Seanad Éireann. Article 34 expressly reserves the administration of justice to the judges and the courts to be appointed and established under the Constitution, subject to the provision in Article 37 for the exercise of limited functions and powers of a judicial nature by other persons or bodies duly authorised by law to exercise such functions in matters other than criminal matters. The defendants have placed reliance upon the provisions of Article 49 of the Constitution. Section 1 of that Article provides as follows:

> All powers, functions, rights and prerogatives whatsoever exercisable in or in respect of Saorstát Éireann immediately

106. [1967] IR 147.
107. [1951] IR 1, at 32.

> before the 11th day of December, 1936, whether in virtue of the Constitution then in force or otherwise, by the authority in which the executive power of Saorstát Éireann was then vested are hereby declared to belong to the people.

This is a reference to the Constitution (Amendment No 27) Act 1936, which provided in s 1 that several Articles of the Constitution of Saorstát Éireann set out in the schedule to that Act were amended. or otherwise dealt with, in the manner set out in the schedule. The Act came into force on the 11th December, 1936, and the effect of it was to remove from the Constitution of Saorstát Éireann all references to the King, the representative of the Crown, and the Governor General. In particular the effect of the changes, in so far as Article 51 of that Constitution was concerned, was to divest the King of the executive authority of Saorstát Éireann and to vest it in the Executive Council. At that date the King was Edward VIII who had abdicated from the throne of England on the 10 December. On the 12 December 1936, the Executive Authority (External Relations) Act 1936 came into force and it provided that the diplomatic representatives of Saorstát Éireann could be appointed on the authority of the Executive Council, and that every international agreement concluded on behalf of Saorstát Éireann should be concluded by or on the authority of the Executive Council. Section 3 of that Act provided that so long as the King recognised by Australia, Canada, Great Britain, New Zealand and South Africa as the symbol of their co-operation continued to act on behalf of those nations on the advice of their several governments for the purpose of the appointment of diplomatic and consular representatives and the conclusion of international agreements, and so long as Saorstát Éireann was associated with those nations, the King so recognised was thereby authorised to act on behalf of Saorstát Éireann for the like purposes as and when advised by the Executive Council to do so. The same section provided that, immediately upon the passing of that Act (12 December, 1936), King Edward VIII should cease to be King for the purpose of those activities and for all other, if any, purposes and that his successor for the time being would be his successor under the law of Saorstát Éireann. The joint effect of those two Acts was to remove the King entirely from the Constitution of Saorstát Éireann, to remove from him all powers and functions in relation to the executive or other authority of Saorstát Éireann or the exercise of any of the powers of government of Saorstát Éireann, and to authorise him to act on behalf of Saorstát Éireann only when so advised by the Executive Council to do so in respect of certain matters concerned only with external relations. It is to be noted that neither of these Acts made any reference whatsoever to the immunities or prerogatives of the King, if any, which existed in Saorstát Éireann on the 10th December, 1936; these Acts made no reference whatsoever to any question of succession to or transmission of these prerogatives or immunities, if any.

It is unnecessary to enquire what powers, functions, rights or prerogatives were exercisable by the King on the 10th December 1936, in or in respect of Saorstát Éireann as, for the reasons I have already given, they did not include a right of immunity from suit in the courts of Saorstát Éireann. Therefore, the provisions of Article 49, s 1, of the Constitution of Ireland which vested in and declared to belong to the People all the powers, functions, rights and prerogatives whatsoever exercisable in or in respect of Saorstát Éireann immediately before the 11th December 1936, whether in virtue of the Constitution of Saorstát Éireann or otherwise, did not carry over or set up an immunity from suit. It was quite within the competence of the People in enacting the Constitution of 1937 to provide for an immunity from suit which did not exist prior to the coming into operation of the Constitution, but no such provision was made. Section 2 of Article 49 provides that save to the extent to which provision is made by the Constitution or might thereafter be made by law for the exercise of any such power, function, right or prerogative by any of the organs established by the Constitution, the powers, functions, rights and prerogatives mentioned in s 1 shall not be exercised or be capable of being exercised in or in respect of the State, save only by or on the authority of the Government. Even assuming that such a common-law immunity from suit did exist so as to be capable of being carried over by Article 49 of the Constitution in accordance with the terms of the Article, it would become thereby the immunity of the People as distinct from the State. While the present action in its original form was an action brought against the People, the parties were changed so that it is now an action against the State and the Attorney General, and the original plea in the defence claiming the immunity of the People as the sovereign authority from such action must be read as a plea claiming such immunity on behalf of the State. In either its original form or in its present form the plea would, in my view, fail even if such immunity were vested in and belonged to the People, because there is rig evidence of any authority from the Government for the assertion of any such claim and, by virtue of s 2 of Article 49 of the Constitution, no such claim could be set up in respect of the State save only by or on the authority of the Government. It is to be noted that the same situation arose in *In re PC*[108] where Gavan Duffy J expressed the same view on the necessity for evidence of authority from the Government for the assertion of the claim of immunity."

[15.44] The effect of the *Byrne* case may be described in different ways. In one respect, it merely established that personal injuries cases involving the State should be treated no differently from personal injuries actions involving an individual and a company. However, the implications of the decision are more profound. In his judgment, Walsh J noted that in the

108. [1939] IR 305, at 311.

United Kingdom the Crown Proceedings Act 1947 regulates claims against the Crown, Ministries and Government Departments. Under s 40 of the 1947 Act, such claims may in general be brought only in respect of liability arising in the United Kingdom. After *Byrne*, no legislation was enacted to regulate the position of the State in civil proceedings so that the question of liability in respect of acts occurring outside the State is a matter for the Irish courts to determine.

[15.45] In *Ryan v Ireland*,[109] the plaintiff had been on active service with the Irish Army in Lebanon as part of a United Nations peacekeeping force when his post came under mortar attack from hostile forces. He instituted proceedings against the Department of Defence, claiming that there had been a failure to protect his position adequately against such attacks. The High Court and Supreme Court held that the Department owed a duty of care to the plaintiff while he was on active service and that, although the conditions in the Lebanon were not like those of a factory or other 'ordinary' place of work, they were in breach of that duty of care.[110] The *Ryan* case was thus dealt with solely on the basis of judge-made principles. A comparable claim in the United Kingdom might not proceed to court, arising from restrictions on claims against the British Ministry of Defence contained in the Crown Proceedings Act 1947, as amended by the Crown Proceedings (Armed Forces) Act 1987. In this respect, *Byrne v Ireland* introduced a dramatic change in the liability of the State in tort.

[15.46] In *Webb v Ireland*,[111] the High Court and Supreme Court affirmed the central conclusion in *Byrne* that Crown immunities or prerogatives did not survive the enactment of the 1937 Constitution. In the *Webb* case, the Court held that the prerogative concerning treasure trove had not been carried forward. However, the Court also held that in certain instances the Constitution substituted new versions of the old prerogatives and in the case of ancient treasures, the Court held that these became the property of the People of Ireland. *Webb* indicates, therefore, that the pre-1922 prerogatives may in some instances be transformed into 'constitutional' variants. It remains to be seen whether other aspects of the royal prerogative were carried over in a new form into Irish law,[112] such as the power to establish entities by Royal Charter, as was originally the case with the Honourable

109. [1989] IR 177.

110. For some criticism, see Byrne and Binchy, *Annual Review of Irish Law 1989* (Round Hall Press, 1990), pp 410-8.

111. [1988] IR 353.

112. See Kelly, 'Hidden Treasure and the Constitution' (1988) 10 DULJ (ns) 5; Morgan, 'Constitutional Interpretation: Three Cautionary Tales' (1988) 10 DULJ (ns) 24; Hogan & Whyte, *op cit*, 1134-7.

Society of the King's Inns,[113] or the power to grant letters patent to senior counsel.[114] The Executive Powers (Consequential Provisions) Act 1937, enacted after the 1937 Constitution had been approved by referendum but before it came into effect, empowers the Government to adapt any pre-1922 Charters and letters patent by substituting the Government for the Crown.[115]

[4] FUNDAMENTAL RIGHTS AND CONSTITUTIONAL JUDICIAL REVIEW

[15.47] We have noted that the 1937 Constitution may be divided into two components, those Articles which describe the institutions of State and those which describe the fundamental rights of persons. We turn now to discuss these fundamental rights provisions and the connected power of the courts to require the executive and legislature to comply with these provisions by means of constitutional judicial review.

Fundamental rights

[15.48] Many of the fundamental rights provisions are contained in Articles 40 to 44 of the 1937 Constitution, though other Articles also confer important rights. Among the rights explicitly recognised and supported by the Constitution are the following:

Retrospective criminal laws are prohibited: Article 15.5.

Sittings of the Oireachtas must, in general, be in public: Article 15.8.

The right to vote at Dáil elections is given equally to men and women: Article 16.1.2°.

Voting at Dáil elections must be by secret ballot: Article 16.1.4°.

Each Dáil constituency must contain a similar population base: Article 16.2.3°.

Courts must, in general, sit in public: Article 34.1.

Criminal trials must be held in due course of law: Article 38.1.[116]

Major criminal trials must be with a jury, subject to certain exceptions:[117] Article 38.5.

---

113. See para **[3.27]**.

114. See para **[3.45]**.

115. In *Geoghegan v Institute of Chartered Accountants in Ireland* [1995] 3 IR 86, the Royal Charter of the Institute of Chartered Accountants in Ireland, as amended in 1966 by an Act of the Oireachtas, was upheld as constitutionally valid.

116. See para **[4.33]**.

117. See para **[4.33]**.

> All citizens must be held equal before the law, but account may be taken of differences in capacity and of social function: Article 40.1.
>
> No titles of nobility may be conferred: Article 40.2.
>
> No person may be deprived of his or her liberty save in accordance with law: Article 40.4.
>
> The dwelling of every citizen is inviolable and may not be entered forcibly, save in accordance with law: Article 40.5.
>
> Liberty to express freely ones convictions and opinions, to assemble peacefully and without arms and to form associations and unions is guaranteed, subject to public order and morality: Article 40.6.
>
> The institution of the Family is recognised as the fundamental unit group of Society: Article 41.
>
> Parents have the right to educate their children, subject to limited rights of the State: Article 42.
>
> The right to own private property is recognised, but may be limited by the State: Article 43.
>
> Freedom of conscience and the free practice of religion are guaranteed, subject to public order and morality: Article 44.

Many of these provisions echo comparable Articles in the 1922 Constitution, but others, such as those on the Family, were new in the 1937 Constitution.

Rights subject to limitations

[15.49] It is notable that many rights are subject to certain limitations or qualifying words. In general, it may be said that few constitutional rights are absolute in nature; to some extent, the function of the courts in constitutional judicial review is to determine the precise meaning of the general limits placed on such rights.[118]

Unenumerated personal rights

[15.50] In addition to these rights, Article 40.3 has, since the 1960s, proved a source of an additional tranche of rights. In its original form,[119] Article 40.3 provided:

> 1° The State guarantees in its laws to respect, and, as far as practicable, by its laws to defend and vindicate the personal rights

[118] On the interpretative techniques used, see paras **[15.75]-[15.138]**.

[119] On its amendment, see para **[15.130]**.

of the citizen.

2° The State shall, in particular, by its laws protect as best it may from unjust attack and, in the case of injustice done, vindicate the life, person, good name and property rights of every citizen.

Between 1937 and 1963, it was not considered that Article 40.3 contained any additional list of constitutional rights beyond those already contained in the remainder of the constitutional text. This view was radically transformed by the decision in *Ryan v Attorney General*,[120] which marked a watershed in the development of constitutional judicial review. The plaintiff challenged the constitutionality of the Health (Fluoridation of Water Supplies) Act 1960. The Act had been introduced after the Government had appointed a Consultative Council comprising a representative group of experts to recommend proposals for the treatment of dental caries, particularly in children. Having consulted widely on the matter, the Council presented a lengthy Report to Government, in which it recommended that the addition of limited quantities of sodium fluoride in water supplies (up to 4 parts per million) would contribute substantially to the elimination of dental caries and that this would greatly outweigh any possible risk to public health, such as a possible risk to older persons of 'brittle bone' due to deposits of fluorine forming on the skeletal frame.

[15.51] On foot of this report, the 1960 Act empowered local authorities to add specified quantities of sodium fluoride to public water supplies in the State. Although the Consultative Council's Report had been based on the most recently-available scientific data concerning safe levels of fluoride in water, the addition of fluoride to public water supplies was surrounded with some controversy, including the question whether the improvement in children's teeth was justified by the risks for older persons and also the general question of whether such a mass public health measure should be 'imposed' by legislation. Indeed, in the 1990s, fluoride in public water supplies is not a universal rule.[121]

[15.52] As to the constitutional issues raised, the plaintiff in *Ryan* claimed that the 1960 Act infringed a number of her constitutional rights, including her right to bodily integrity. Her counsel defined this as the right to be free from any process imposed by the State which might be harmful to her life or health. The plaintiff faced considerable difficulty in asserting that the 1960 Act on this ground, since there is no mention of the right to bodily integrity in the text of the Constitution. Nonetheless, her counsel argued that such a

120. [1965] IR 294.

121. In the United Kingdom, while fluoride is added to many public water supplies, this is not the case in all local authorities, including those in Northern Ireland.

right was implicit in Article 40.3. Crucially, this argument was accepted by the High Court and, on appeal, by the Supreme Court. The plaintiff was ultimately unsuccessful in her challenge to the 1960 Act, since the High Court and Supreme Court held that it was not been established that the 1960 Act was in fact harmful to the plaintiff's health and, in any event, she could filter any fluoride out of her own personal water supply without great expense. The courts also stated that they would be reluctant to interfere with legislation that involved finely-balanced judgments on social policy, unless it was clearly established that there was a breach of a constitutional right. This cautious approach to constitutional judicial review has been echoed many times since the *Ryan* case. Nonetheless, the decision in *Ryan* that Article 40.3 contains a guarantee to protect an unspecified list of rights in addition to those expressly referred to in the constitutional text has been of great importance in the development of Irish constitutional law.[122]

[15.53] These unspecified personal rights are referred to as unenumerated rights, since there is no complete list of the rights guaranteed under the general terms of Article 40.3.[123]

[15.54] Since the *Ryan* case, the following rights have been recognised as unspecified personal rights:[124]

- the right to bodily integrity: *Ryan v Attorney General*;
- the right not to be tortured or ill-treated: *The State (C) v Frawley*;[125]
- the right to travel within the State: *Ryan v Attorney General*;
- the right to travel outside the State: *The State (M) v Attorney General*;[126]
- the right to communicate: *Attorney General v Paperlink Ltd*;[127]
- the right to marry: *Ryan v Attorney General*;
- the right to marital privacy: *McGee v Attorney General*;[128]
- the right to individual privacy: *Kennedy v Ireland*;[129]

122. See further paras **[15.126]-[15.134]**.

123. In *McGee v Attorney General* [1974] IR 284, Henchy J stated that any attempt to compile a full list of such rights would be 'difficult, if not impossible.

124. See *Report of the Constitution Review Group* (Pn 2632, 1996), p 246.

125. [1976] IR 365.

126. [1979] IR 73.

127. [1984] ILRM 343.

128. [1974] IR 284: see para **[15.128]**.

129. [1987] IR 587.

the right to procreate: *Murray v Ireland*;[130]

the rights of an unmarried mother concerning her child: *G v An Bord Uchtála*;[131]

the rights of a child: *In re the Adoption (No 2) Bill 1987*;[132]

the right to independent domicile and to maintenance: *CM v TM (No 2)*;[133]

the right of access to the courts: *Macauley v Minister for Posts and Telegraphs*;[134]

the right to legal representation in certain criminal cases: *The State (Healy) v Donoghue*;[135]

the right to fair procedures: *In re Haughey*;[136]

the right to earn a livelihood: *Murphy v Stewart*.[137]

It is clear that the unspecified personal rights guaranteed protection by Article 40.3 cover a wide range of matters. However, like many of the rights expressly stated in the constitutional text, they are not absolute, but are to some extent limited by the requirement that the State must respect and defend them 'as far as practicable.' Thus, in the *Ryan* case, while the courts accepted that the right to bodily integrity was guaranteed protection by Article 40.3, they also concluded that it had not been established that the State had failed to protect it 'as far as practicable' in the Health (Fluoridation of Water Supplies) Act 1960.

Example of declaration of invalidity

[15.55] A common method by which constitutional cases are brought before the courts is for a person to issue a High Court plenary summons seeking a declaration that a specified statutory provision is not valid on the ground that it is conflict with a provision, or provisions, of the Constitution.[138] However, constitutional points may also arise by way of 'ordinary' judicial review, that is, through an application for *certiorari* seeking to quash a District Court decision.[139] A combination of both may also be involved.[140]

130. [1985] IR 532 (HC); [1991] ILRM 465 (SC).
131. [1980] IR 32.
132. [1989] IR 656.
133. [1991] ILRM 268.
134. [1966] IR 345: see also para **[9.02]**.
135. [1976] IR 325: see also para **[9.15]**.
136. [1971] IR 217.
137. [1973] IR 97.
138. Eg, *Norris v Attorney General* [1984] IR 36: see para **[15.129]**.
139. Eg, *The State (Healy) v Donoghue* [1976] IR 326: see para **[9.15]**.
140. See Collins and O'Reilly, *Civil Proceedings and the State in Ireland* (Round Hall Press, 1989), p 137.

[15.56] In *King v Attorney General*,[141] the plaintiff had been convicted in the District Court of certain offences under s 4 of the Vagrancy Act 1824, as amended. s 4 of the 1824 Act was commonly referred to as the 'sus' law. It created a large number of offences, broadly associated with persons suspected of being in public places with a view to committing criminal offences. For example, it created the offence of being in possession of implements, such as a crowbar, with the intention of breaking into a house or other building. It also created more wide-ranging offences, including the quintessential vagrancy offences of being a 'person wandering abroad ... not having any visible means of subsistence, and not giving a good account of himself', that is being poor in public,[142] and 'wandering abroad and endeavouring by the exposure of wounds or deformities to obtain or gather alms', that is begging in public.[143]

[15.57] As amended, s 4 of the 1824 Act also created the offence of being a 'suspected person or reputed thief' who was 'loitering about or in' public places with the intention of committing a felony. s 15 of the Prevention of Crimes Act 1871 provided that, to convict a person as a 'suspected person,' it was not necessary to establish any act tending to show a criminal intent and a conviction could be based on the person's 'known character'. The courts had held that 'known character' could include past convictions; thus a person could be convicted under s 4 merely on the ground that a judge considered that he or she intended to commit a felony because he or she had a previous conviction under s 4.

[15.58] The plaintiff in the *King* case had been convicted in the District Court under s 4 of the 1824 Act on a number of charges, including the following: that, being a suspected person, he had been loitering on a public road between 8.30 pm and 9.30 pm on a particular date with intent to commit a felony, namely to housebreak and steal; and that, on the same date, and the same time and place he had in his possession housebreaking implements, namely two screwdrivers, a tyre lever, hacksaw, haversack, shifting spanner and a candle, with intent to commit a felony, namely to steal. He sought a declaration that the relevant parts of s 4 of the 1824 Act concerning 'loitering with intent' were invalid on the ground that they were

141. [1981] IR 233.

142. This provision was repealed by the Housing Act 1988 which now regulates homelessness.

143. The provisions of s 4 concerning possession of housebreaking implements and on public begging remain in place (1996). Those concerning 'wandering abroad' which were declared invalid in the *King* case have been replaced by provisions in the Criminal Justice (Public Order) Act 1994 requiring persons to 'move on' when instructed by a Garda to do so.

in conflict with various provisions of the Constitution and he also sought orders of *certiorari* quashing the convictions.

[15.59] The High Court and Supreme Court held that the 'loitering with intent' offence did not comply with a number of constitutional provisions. It was in conflict with the right to a trial in due course of law in Article 38.1, particularly because evidence of past convictions could be used to convict a person and no evidence of an act involving criminal intent, or *mens rea*, was required. s 4 was in conflict with the right to be held equal before the law in Article 40.1, since a person could be convicted of something which was lawful for another person to do, such as to 'walk slowly, dawdle or stop altogether in a public street'.[144] The courts also considered that s 4 failed to meet the requirements of Article 40.4, that a person may only be deprived of liberty in accordance with law. The courts considered that Article 40.4 requires that a person should only be convicted of an offence if it is established beyond reasonable doubt that he has broken a clearly stated rule, whereas the language of s 4 was so vague and unclear that it conferred an arbitrary and overbroad power to charge and convict a person. In these circumstances, the High Court, and the Supreme Court granted a declaration that the 'loitering with intent' elements of s 4 were invalid and also quashed the convictions on *certiorari*.[145]

Effect of declaration of invalidity

[15.60] Where a declaration of invalidity concerning a statutory provision is granted, this amounts to a 'judicial death certificate'.[146] If the statutory provision in question is not replaced,[147] it is no longer a law capable of being enforced, despite having being enacted by the Oireachtas or other pre-1937 legislative authority. The courts thus have a negative power to declare a law invalid, but do not have the power to declare what might be enacted to replace the invalid law.

144. [1981] IR 233 at 242-3, *per* McWilliam J (High Court).

145. See the text of the orders made, [1981] IR 233 at 244. Where the courts consider a non-statutory rule of law, as in *Byrne v Ireland* [1972] IR 241, there is no statutory provision to be declared invalid. In such circumstances, the High Court or Supreme Court grants a declaration concerning the person's rights without anything more.

146. *Murphy v Attorney General* [1982] IR 241 at 307, *per* Henchy J.

147. In many instances, a replacement may not be deemed either necessary or constitutionally permissible. Thus, the 'loitering with intent' provisions of the Vagrancy Act 1824, s 4 declared invalid in *King v Attorney General* [1981] IR 233 (see para **[15.59]**) were not replaced by any broadly comparable provision. Rather, the Criminal Justice (Public Order) Act 1994, s 8 requires a person in a public place to 'move on' when so requested by a Garda.

[15.61] However, the reasons given for declaring legislation invalid may, in effect, point the way for the Oireachtas where a replacement law is required. Thus, in *de Burca v Attorney General*,[148] the Supreme Court found the Juries Act 1927 unconstitutional on the grounds that it effectively excluded women and persons of little property from sitting on juries and this amounted to invalid discrimination under Article 40.1. The legislative response, the Juries Act 1976, provides that jurors be drawn primarily from the electoral roll, thus removing the discriminatory aspects of the 1927 Act found invalid in the *de Burca* case.

[15.62] The courts have also occasionally provided more positive indications of what legislative provisions might be required to fill the gap created by a finding of unconstitutionality.[149] Indeed, even where it is found that legislation is not invalid, the courts may nonetheless indicate that there is a strong case for amending the law, but that this is a matter for the Oireachtas.[150]

[15.63] Not all 'successful' constitutional cases involve declarations of invalidity. Thus, in *The State (Healy) v Donoghue*[151] the Supreme Court identified the need to interpret the Criminal Justice (Legal Aid) Act 1962 in a manner that coincided with the constitutional dimension of the right to legal representation identified in the case, but no textual alterations to the 1962 Act were required.

Effect in cases involving common law rule

[15.64] Where a constitutional action involves a challenge to a common law rule rather than legislation, a 'successful' action has a different impact. In *Byrne v Ireland*,[152] the plaintiff successfully established that the supposed immunity of the State from suit had not been carried forward by Article 50 of the 1937 Constitution. We have seen that, since *Byrne*, no legislation has been enacted to regulate proceedings against the State, and are dealt with simply by reference to the principles in *Byrne*.[153] By contrast with constitutional cases involving legislation, where a successful claim may

148. [1976] IR 38.

149. See the comments of the Supreme Court in *Blake v Attorney General* [1982] IR 117 at 141-2. See also the Supreme Court's jurisdiction under Article 26: para **[5.65]**.

150. See the comments of Henchy J in *Cahill v Sutton* [1980] IR 269 at 288: see para **[15.77]**. See also his comments in *Norris v Attorney General* [1984] IR 36 at 78-9. A similar approach is evident where the courts are forced to an unsatisfactory interpretation of legislation: see *Rafferty v Crowley* [1984] ILRM 350, discussed at para **[14.31]**.

151. [1976] IR 325: see para **[9.15]**.

152. [1972] IR 241.

153. See paras **[15.44]-[15.46]**.

involve a 'judicial death certificate', *Byrne* involved the creation of constitutional judge-made principles regulating this area in a positive manner.[154]

Retrospective or prospective effect of invalidity

[15.65] In *Murphy v Attorney General*,[155] the question arose as to whether a declaration of invalidity has full retrospective effect or applies prospectively only, from the date of the decision of the court. The plaintiffs were a married couple and were both earning salaries as teachers. They were taxed under ss 192 to 196 of the Income Tax Act 1967, which provided for an 'aggregation' of the incomes of married couples; that is, where husband and wife were both earning, their incomes were added together, counted as one income and taxed on that basis. Under ss 192 to 196 of the 1967 Act, a married couple could opt for separate taxation of their incomes, but in such a case they would not be given two tax free allowances and their total income tax would be same as if their incomes were aggregated. The plaintiffs pointed out that, if they had remained unmarried but had decided to cohabit, they could be taxed separately, would be entitled to a tax free allowance each and their total tax bill would be less than that of a married couple.

[15.66] They sought declarations that the aggregation system in the 1967 Act failed to comply with the guarantee by the State in Article 41 to protect the Family. The High Court and Supreme Court accepted this argument and declared invalid ss 192 to 196 of the 1967 Act. The question then arose as to whether that decision had retrospective effect to the date when the 1967 Act was enacted; and, if so, whether the State was required to refund all tax collected from married couples between 1967 and 1980 (when the decision in *Murphy* was given), or at least the excess they paid over and above what unmarried couples would have paid. Ultimately, while the Supreme Court concluded that the declaration of invalidity was retrospective, it also held that only persons who had already initiated proceedings could seek compensation arising from the unconstitutionally collected taxes. This, in effect, restricted the retrospective benefit of the decision to the plaintiffs in the *Murphy* case.[156] The Finance Act 1980, enacted in the wake of the *Murphy* case, inserted 'new' ss 192 to 196 into the Income Tax Act 1967, introducing double income tax allowances for married couples, whether only one or both spouses have an income. To that extent, of course, all married

154. See also *McKinley v Minister for Defence* [1992] 2 IR 333.

155. [1982] IR 241.

156. See generally, Hogan & Whyte, *op cit*, 480-87. For a different retrospection problem, see para **[4.110]** n 279.

couples benefited, at least prospectively, from the *Murphy* case. Indeed, by introducing measures applicable to married couples with one income only, the *Murphy* case produced tangible benefits for a wider category of persons than those envisaged by the outcome in the case.

Representative actions

[15.67] Moreover, the restriction of the benefit of a 'test' case such as *Murphy* to a small group of persons can be avoided by the institution of a representative action, in which a large group or class of persons may be represented by one or more persons who actually conduct the litigation.[157] This form of 'class action' has become more common in recent years.[158]

Amendments to 1937 Constitution

[15.68] Article 51 of the 1937 Constitution authorised amendments by ordinary legislation for a three year period after the entry into office of the first President of Ireland, that is until 25 June 1941. Thereafter, a referendum of the entire electorate has been required. Unlike the comparable provision in Article 50 of the 1922 Constitution, Article 51 was hedged around with a number of restrictions which prevented its extension beyond 1941. Prior to 1941, two Acts were enacted amending the text of the 1937 Constitution by means of ordinary legislation.

[15.69] The First Amendment of the Constitution Act 1939 was enacted immediately after the invasion of Poland by Germany at the beginning of World War II and it extended the provisions of Article 28.3.3° of the Constitution to include a state of emergency where no actual invasion of the State had occurred. Article 28.3.3° provides, in effect, that legislation enacted under its terms is exempt from challenge for being in conflict with the Constitution. The extension of Article 28.3.3° in 1939 facilitated the establishment of military tribunals comparable to those provided for under Article 2A of the 1922 Constitution and the conferral of extraordinary powers on Ministers for the duration of World War II.

[15.70] The Second Amendment of the Constitution Act 1941 was enacted just before the expiry of the three year limitation period for amendment by 'ordinary' legislation. By contrast with the First Amendment, this contained over 20 amendments to 16 Articles. Some were of a technical or drafting type, but others involved substantive change. Among these were changes to

---

157. See Collins and O'Reilly, *Civil Proceedings and the State in Ireland* (Round Hall Press, 1990), p 125.

158. Eg, *Duff and Ors v Minister for Agriculture (No 2)*, High Court, unrep, 10 July 1992; *Tate v Minister for Social Welfare* [1995] 1 IR 418 (para **[16.143]**); *Abrahamson and Ors v Law Society of Ireland*, High Court, unrep, 23 July 1996 (para **[3.14]**).

Article 24.2 concerning Bills deemed to have been passed by both Houses of the Oireachtas;[159] Article 25.4 concerning the signature of Bills by the President;[160] the requirement that one judgment only be delivered by the Supreme Court in judgments given under Articles 26 and 34 on the constitutionality of Bills or post-1937 Acts;[161] an immunity from further constitutional challenge of any Bill approved by the Supreme Court on a reference to it under Article 26;[162] a further extension of Article 28.3.3°; clarification that the High Court only had original jurisdiction in cases seeking to challenge the constitutional validity of legislation;[163] and empowering the High Court to state a case to the Supreme Court after an inquiry under Article 40.4.2°.[164]

[15.71] Between 1959 and 1995, referenda have been held to consider 16 amendments to the Constitution. Each has involved a separate vote to approve an amendment to a constitutional provision, though some referenda have been combined with a General Election and up to three separate constitutional amendments have been voted on in a single referendum held on the same date. Of the 16 proposed constitutional amendments, 12 have been approved and four rejected. A number of recent referenda have provoked substantial and sometimes heated debate, particularly those concerning the right to life of the unborn and the referenda proposing the introduction of divorce.

[15.72] The Third Amendment of the Constitution Act 1972 amended Article 29.4 to facilitate membership of the European Communities.[165] The Fourth Amendment of the Constitution Act 1972 amended Article 16, reducing the voting age from 21 to 18. The Fifth Amendment of the Constitution Act 1972 amended Article 44, removing a reference to the 'special position' of the Roman Catholic church. The Sixth Amendment of the Constitution Act 1979 amended Article 37 to ensure the validity of adoption orders.[166] The Seventh Amendment of the Constitution Act 1979 amended Article 18 to facilitate election of some members of Seanad Éireann by graduates of certain third-level institutions other than those already referred to in Article 18.[167] The Eighth Amendment of the Constitution Act 1983 added Article 40.3.3° to the Constitution concerning

159. See para **[13.09]**.
160. See para **[13.10]**.
161. See para **[12.54]**.
162. See para **[5.68]**.
163. See para **[15.28]**.
164. See para **[10.36]**.
165. See para **[16.63]**.
166. See para **[4.16]**.
167. Over 17 years later (1996), no legislation had been enacted to give effect to this amendment.

the right to life of the unborn and the equal right to life of the mother.[168] The Ninth Amendment of the Constitution Act 1984 further amended Article 16, facilitating voting by non-citizens in general elections.[169] The Tenth Amendment of the Constitution Act 1987 further amended Article 29.4 to facilitate ratification of the Single European Act, while the Eleventh Amendment of the Constitution Act 1992 also amended Article 29.4 to facilitate ratification of the Treaty on European Union.[170] The Thirteenth Amendment of the Constitution Act 1992 and the Fourteenth Amendment of the Constitution Act 1992 amended Article 40.3.3° on the right to life of the unborn.[171] The Fifteenth Amendment of the Constitution Act 1996 amended Article 41 to facilitate the enactment of divorce legislation.[172]

[15.73] Of the four rejected proposals to amend the Constitution, two concerned attempts, in 1959 and 1968, to replace the proportional representation system in elections to Dáil Éireann.[173] In 1986, a proposal to remove the ban on divorce in Article 41 was rejected. Another referendum on this topic in 1995 was narrowly approved and later upheld after a referendum petition to the courts.[174] In 1992, we have noted that two amendments to Article 40.3.3° were approved; a further proposal was rejected.[175]

[15.74] At the time of writing (July 1996), it is expected that a proposal to amend the Constitution to widen the circumstances in which bail be refused will be held towards the end of 1996.[176] Independently, significant amendments to the constitutional text have been recommended in the Report of the Constitution Review Group.[177]

Rules of self-restraint in constitutional judicial review

[15.75] In an attempt to ensure that the courts do not overstep the boundaries between the judicial power and the other two branches of government, the executive and the legislature, some 'rules of self-restraint' have been developed.[178] These include the requirement that only justiciable matters

168. See para **[15.130]**.
169. See now the Electoral Act 1992.
170. On both, see para **[16.67]**.
171. See para **[15.133]**.
172. See para **[15.112]**.
173. See Hogan & Whyte, *Kelly's The Irish Constitution*, 3rd ed (Butterworths, 1994), p 166.
174. See para **[15.91]**.
175. See para **[15.133]**.
176. See para **[15.83]**.
177. *Report of the Constitution Review Group* (Pn 2632, 1996): see para **[15.139]**.
178. See Hogan & Whyte, *op cit*, p 449.

may be litigated, rather than political controversies;[179] that constitutional issues will be avoided where a case may be decided on a narrower ground, for example, that Ministerial Regulations were *ultra vires* an Act;[180] that a litigant must establish personal standing or *locus standi* to raise a constitutional point;[181] that a presumption of constitutionality is applicable to post-1937 legislation;[182] and that the least amount of legislative text is declared invalid or severed, thus leaving intact as much legislative text as is possible.[183]

Locus standi

[15.76] It is a fundamental requirement of public law litigation, of which constitutional cases form part, that the person initiating the claim establish that he or she has an identifiable personal interest in the point at issue. This is referred to as locus standi or standing. In *Byrne v Ireland*,[184] the plaintiff's locus standi or standing was clear: the reliance by the defendants on the supposed immunity from suit of the State was a direct bar to her claim against the Department of Posts and Telegraphs. However, in a number of instances, constitutional actions have failed because the plaintiff has been unable to establish any direct or personal connection with the operation of the legal rule being challenged.

[15.77] The leading case on *locus standi* in constitutional cases is *Cahill v Sutton*.[185] In that case, the plaintiff had initiated an action against the defendant, a doctor, in respect of certain medical treatment she had received. Her action was initiated four years after she became aware of the facts she alleged were the basis for her claim. Her claim was based on an alleged breach of contract, and s 11(2)(b) of the Statute of Limitations 1957[186] specified that such claims must be initiated within three years from the date of the events or facts on which the claim is based. The plaintiff was thus statute-barred and, apparently, precluded from initiating her claim. However, she then raised a constitutional point, claiming that s 11(2)(b) of the 1957 Statute was invalid because it failed to contain any saver allowing an extension of time for a person who did not become aware of the facts on which a claim would be based until after the expiration of the specified time

179. See para **[15.97]**.
180. See para **[14.44]**.
181. See para **[15.76]**.
182. See para **[14.44]**.
183. *Maher v Attorney General* [1973] IR 140; *Desmond v Glackin (No 2)* [1993] 3 IR 67.
184. [1972] IR 241: see para **[15.43]**.
185. [1980] IR 269.
186. See generally para **[6.07]**.

limit and, on that basis, was in breach of Article 40.3 for failing to uphold the right of access to the courts.[187] Although the absence of such a saver, to deal with cases of 'latent' injury, was a justifiable criticism of s 11(2)(b), the question in *Cahill* was whether the plaintiff should be allowed to raise this point when she did not fall into this category of person: after all, she had known of the facts well within the three year time limit in s 11(2)(b). In those circumstances, the Supreme Court refused to allow her raise the constitutional point. Henchy J explained this in the following passage:[188]

> "At all material times she [the plaintiff] was aware of all the facts necessary for the making of a claim against Dr Sutton. Her present claim is founded on breach of contract. Within weeks of the commencement of her treatment in 1968 she knew of the facts which, according to her, constituted a breach of contract, and of their prejudicial effect on her. Yet she did not bring her action within the three-year period. It is clear - indeed, it is admitted - that the plaintiff would still be shut out from suing after the three-year period of limitation even if the suggested saving provision had been included in the Act of 1957.
>
> That being the legal predicament in which the plaintiff finds herself, the argument formulated on her behalf is not that she is unjustly debarred from suing because of the alleged statutory defect but that a person to whom the suggested saving provision would apply if it had been enacted could claim successfully in the High Court a declaration that s 11, sub-s 2(b), is unconstitutional because the suggested saving provision is not attached to it. Therefore, the plaintiff is seeking to be allowed to conjure up, invoke and champion the putative constitutional rights of a hypothetical third party, so that the provisions of s 11, sub-s 2(b), may be declared unconstitutional on the basis of that constitutional *jus tertii* - thus allowing the plaintiff to march through the resulting gap in the statute. The question which the Court has to consider is whether such an indirect and hypothetical assertion of constitutional rights gives the plaintiff the standing necessary for the successful invocation of the judicial power to strike down a statutory provision on the ground of unconstitutionality.
>
> Little or no help on this question is to be found in the decisions of the Courts in the early years following on the enactment of the Constitution in 1937, for it does not appear that the issue of standing was dealt with as an issue in any constitutional case before 1969. In that year the High Court had to decide in *East Donegal Co-Operative v The Attorney General*[189] whether the plaintiffs (who were three co-operative societies and four individuals) had the necessary standing to question the constitutionality of certain provisions of the Livestock Marts Act 1967. The plaintiffs

---

187. See para **[9.02]**.
188. This extract ends at p 596.
189. [1970] IR 317.

contended that the Act of 1967 gave excessive and arbitrary powers to the Minister for Agriculture and Fisheries in regard to the granting and the revocation of licences to operate livestock marts. In the High Court O'Keeffe P held that the three plaintiffs who were co-operative societies operating livestock marts, and the four individual plaintiffs (each of whom was a shareholder in a livestock mart), had the necessary standing to question the constitutionality of the statutory provisions in issue because, although none of the plaintiffs had yet been actually affected adversely by the challenged sections, those sections (assuming that they gave to the Minister the powers suggested) constituted a threat to the existence of the marts in which the plaintiffs had an interest. Understandably, that ruling was affirmed when the case came on appeal to this Court. The nub of the ruling in both courts derives from the direct threat posed by the questioned sections to the property rights of each of the plaintiffs. As the judgment of this Court put it:[190]

> 'In the present case all the plaintiffs are engaged in the type of business which is directly affected, and subject to control, by the provisions of the Act and it is the opinion of this Court that they have, therefore, a right to maintain these proceedings.'

Therefore, that decision does not provide any direct authority on the point in question in this case, for the plaintiffs in that case were deemed to have the necessary standing because they were asserting their own rights as the basis of their constitutional challenge, whereas in this case the plaintiff's challenge requires her to rely not on a violation of her own constitutional rights but on the notional complaint of a hypothetical third party that his constitutional rights have not been upheld. In so far as the judgment of this Court in the *East Donegal Co-Operative Case* contains observations on the law applicable to a situation such as that, they must be deemed to be *obiter dicta*.

The general approach to the question of standing that has been adopted in other jurisdictions was described as follows in the judgment of this Court in the *East Donegal Co-Operative Case*:[191]

> 'With regard to the *locus standi* of the plaintiffs the question raised has been determined in different ways in countries which have constitutional provisions similar to our own. It is unnecessary here to go into this matter in detail beyond stating that at one end of the spectrum of opinions on this topic one finds the contention that there exists a right of action akin to the *actio popularis* which will entitle any person, whether he is directly affected by the Act or not, to maintain proceedings and challenge the validity of any Act passed by the parliament of the country of which he is a citizen or to whose laws he is subject by residing in

190. *Ibid*, 339.

191. *Ibid*, 338.

> that country. At the other end of the spectrum is the contention that no one can maintain such an action unless he can show that not merely do the provisions of the Act in question apply to activities in which he is currently engaged but that their application has actually affected his activities adversely. The Court rejects the latter contention and does not find it necessary in the circumstances of this case to express any view upon the former.'

It should be observed that the contrast drawn in that passage is between two widely divergent opinions or contentions and not between two opposing judicial attitudes taken up in other countries. In point of fact, in no comparable jurisdiction to which the Court's attention has been directed does either of those two polarised opinions or contentions seem to have received authoritative judicial acceptance. On the contrary, in other jurisdictions the widely accepted practice of courts which are invested with comparable powers of reviewing legislation in the light of constitutional provisions is to require the person who challenges a particular legislative provision to show either that he has been personally affected injuriously by it or that he is in imminent danger of becoming the victim of it. This general rule means that the challenger must adduce circumstances showing that the impugned provision is operating, or is poised to operate, in such a way as to deprive him personally of the benefit of a particular constitutional right. In that way each challenge is assessed judicially in the light of the application of the impugned provision to the challenger's own circumstances.

This general, but not absolute, rule of judicial self-restraint has much to commend it. It ensures that normally the controversy will rest on facts which are referable primarily and specifically to the challenger, thus giving concreteness and first-hand reality to what might otherwise be an abstract or hypothetical legal argument. The resulting decision of the court will be either the allowance or the rejection of the challenge in so far as it is based on the facts adduced. If the challenge succeeds, the impugned provision will be struck down. If it fails, it does not follow that a similar challenge raised later on a different set of facts will fail: see *Ryan v The Attorney General*.[192] In that way the flexibility and reach of the particular constitutional provision invoked are fully preserved and given necessary application.

While a cogent theoretical argument might be made for allowing any citizen, regardless of personal interest or injury, to bring proceedings to have a particular statutory provision declared unconstitutional, there are countervailing considerations which make such an approach generally undesirable and not in the public interest. To allow one litigant to present and argue what is essentially another person's case would not be conducive

---

192. [1965] IR 294, at 353.

to the administration of justice as a general rule. Without concrete personal circumstances pointing to a wrong suffered or threatened, a case tends to lack the force and urgency of reality. There is also the risk that the person whose case has been put forward unsuccessfully by another may be left with the grievance that his claim was wrongly or inadequately presented.

It is true that a Bill that has passed through Parliament but has not been signed by the President of Ireland may be refereed by him to this Court under Article 26 of the Constitution for a decision as to the constitutionality of one or more of its provisions. It is also true that in those circumstances the Court has not the benefit of a case presented by an aggrieved litigant on the basis of his personal situation, so the Court may have to decide the issue *in vacuo* by reference to abstract or projected considerations. However, that is a special and limited jurisdiction which has been specially vested in this Court by Article 26, and its existence or nature cannot be taken as inhibiting the High Court or the Supreme Court from exercising the general jurisdiction to review legislation in the manner that will most effectively give force to constitutionally guaranteed rights within the general constitutional framework. Indeed, the existence of that jurisdiction may indicate an intention on the part of the framers of the Constitution that the power of the President of Ireland to obtain such a binding advisory opinion from the Supreme Court as to the constitutionality of newly made and questionable legislation should fill the vacuum that might exist until a duly qualified litigant comes forward to challenge the constitutionality of the statutory provision in question.

There is also the hazard that, if the Courts were to accord citizens unrestricted access, regardless of qualification, for the purpose of getting legislative provisions invalidated on constitutional grounds, this important jurisdiction would be subject to abuse. For the litigious person, the crank, the obstructionist, the meddlesome, the perverse, the officious man of straw and many others, the temptation to litigate the constitutionality of a law, rather than to observe it, would prove irresistible on occasion.

In particular, the working interrelation that must be presumed to exist between Parliament and the Judiciary in the democratic scheme of things postulated by the Constitution would not be served if no threshold qualification were ever required for an attack in the Courts on the manner in which the Legislature has exercised its law-making powers. Without such a qualification, the Courts might be thought to encourage those who have opposed a particular Bill on its way through Parliament to ignore or devalue its elevation into an Act of Parliament by continuing their opposition to it by means of an action to have it invalidated on constitutional grounds. It would be contrary to the spirit of the Constitution if the Courts were to allow those who were opposed to a proposed legislative measure, inside or outside Parliament, to have an unrestricted and unqualified right to move from the political arena to the High Court once a Bill had become an Act. It would not accord with the smooth working of the organs of State established by the Constitution if the enactments of the National Parliament were liable to be thwarted or delayed in their operation by litigation which could be brought at the whim of every or any citizen, whether or not he had a personal interest in the outcome.

The Constitution has given Parliament the sole and exclusive power of making laws. The Courts normally accord those laws the presumption of having been made with due observance of constitutional requirements. If a citizen comes forward in court with a claim that a particular law has been enacted in disregard of a constitutional requirement, he has little reason to complain if in the normal course of things he is required, as a condition of invoking the court's jurisdiction to strike down the law for having been unconstitutionally made (with all the dire consequences that may on occasion result from the vacuum created by such a decision), to show that the impact of the impugned law on his personal situation discloses an injury or prejudice which he has either suffered or is in imminent danger of suffering.

This rule, however, being but a rule of practice must, like all such rules, be subject to expansion, exception or qualification when the justice of the case so requires. Since the paramount consideration in the exercise of the jurisdiction of the Courts to review legislation in the light of the Constitution is to ensure that persons entitled to the benefit of a constitutional right will not be prejudiced through being wrongfully deprived of it, there will be cases where the want of the normal *locus standi* on the part of the person questioning the constitutionality of the statute may be overlooked if, in the circumstances of the case, there is a transcendent need to assert against the statute the constitutional provision that has been invoked. For example, while the challenger may lack the personal standing normally required, those prejudicially affected by the impugned statute may not be in a position to assert adequately, or in time, their constitutional rights. In such a case the court might decide to ignore the want of normal personal standing on the part of the litigant before it. Likewise, the absence of a prejudice or injury peculiar to the challenger might be overlooked, in the discretion of the court, if the impugned provision is directed at or operable against a grouping which includes the challenger, or with whom the challenger may be said to have a common interest - particularly in cases where, because of the nature of the subject matter, it is difficult to segregate those affected from those not affected by the challenged provision.

However, those examples of possible exceptions to the rule should not be taken as indicating where the limits of the rule are to be drawn. It is undesirable to go further than to say that the stated rule of personal standing may be waived or relaxed if, in the particular circumstances of a case, the court finds that there are weighty countervailing considerations justifying a departure from the rule.

As to the instant case, it is reduced to a question whether there are such countervailing considerations. The plaintiff's complaint that s 11, sub-s 2(b) of the Statute of Limitations 1957 is invalid on constitutional grounds is based on the fact that there is not attached to it a saver for those whose claims might become statute barred despite non-culpable ignorance of crucial facts: but the plaintiffs predicament is that her action would be statute barred even if s 11, sub-s 2(b) of the Act of 1957 had been so qualified. So she cannot be heard to say that the alleged unconstitutionality has wrought her personally any actual or threatened prejudice. Therefore, she is wanting in personal *locus standi.* Her counsel is driven to grounding her allegation of unconstitutionality on the actual prejudice that would be suffered by a hypothetical person whose action would be statute barred under s 11, sub-s 2(b), despite his non-culpable ignorance of crucial facts.

The primary rule as to standing in constitutional matters is that the person challenging the constitutionality of the statute, or some other person for whom he is deemed by the court to be entitled to speak, must be able to assert that, because of the alleged unconstitutionality, his or that other person's interests have been adversely affected, or stand in real or imminent danger of being adversely affected, by the operation of the statute.

On that test, the plaintiff must be held to be disentitled to raise the allegation of unconstitutionality on which she relies. Even if the Act of 1957 contained the saving clause whose absence is said to amount to an unconstitutionality, she would still be barred by the statute from suing. So the alleged unconstitutionality cannot affect her adversely, nor can it affect anybody whose alter ego or surrogate she could be said to be. As to such other persons, although the statute was passed in 1957, the plaintiff is unable to instance any person who has been precluded from suing for damages because of the absence from the statute of the saving clause for which she contends. Therefore, her case has the insubstantiality of a pure hypothesis. While it is true that she herself would benefit, in a tangential or oblique way, from a declaration of unconstitutionality, in that the consequential statutory vacuum would enable her to sue, that is an immaterial consideration in view of her failure to meet the threshold qualification of being in a position to argue personally, or vicariously, a live issue of prejudice in the sense indicated.

Were the Courts to accede to the plaintiff's plea that she should be accorded standing merely because she would indirectly and consequentially benefit from a declaration of unconstitutionality, countless statutory provisions would become open to challenge at the instance of litigants who, in order to acquire standing to sue, would only have to show that some such consequential benefit would accrue to them from a declaration of unconstitutionality - notwithstanding that the statutory provision may never have affected adversely any particular person's interests, or be in any real or imminent danger of doing so. It would be contrary to precedent, constitutional propriety and the common good for the High Court, or this Court, to proclaim itself an open house for the reception of such claims.

> The plaintiff's lack of standing to raise the constitutional point is aggravated and compounded by her inordinate and inexcusable delay in initiating and prosecuting her claim. Dr Sutton died in 1980 and his personal representatives have now become defendants in this action. At this remove it would be virtually impossible for the personal representatives to defend this claim on the merits, now that Dr Sutton has died almost 12 years after the alleged acts of negligence took place.
>
> Apart from the fact that no case has been made out for overlooking the plaintiff's unexplained delay both in instituting and in prosecuting her claim in due time, there is no pressing constitutional need to entertain the claim that s 11, sub-s 2(b) of the Act of 1957 is invalid for the reason alleged. In the 23 years since that Act was passed, it does not appear that any would-be plaintiff has come forward claiming that s 11, sub-s 2(b) has unconstitutionally precluded him from suing. If the Court were now, on hypothetical grounds, to declare s 11, sub-s 2(b) to be invalid, it would not only allow the plaintiff to proceed with her belated claim at a time when the possibility of a fair trial has passed but it would also allow all other claims of a like nature to be revived and instituted pending a statutory replacement for s 11, sub-s 2(b), save to the extent that such claims might be barred by provisions other than those contained in that sub-section. Of course, the Courts will not be deterred by arguments of inconvenience from declaring a statutory provision invalid on constitutional grounds, provided the proceedings are properly constituted and the circumstances warrant the making of such an order.
>
> However, the plaintiff's inability to overcome the fact that she would still be statute barred even if Parliament had not left what is claimed to be an unfair lacuna in the statute, being compounded by inordinate, unexplained and inexcusable delay and by her failure to identify any real need (either in the public interest generally or in the live interest of any specific person) to strike down s 11, sub-s 2(b) of the Act of 1957, must be held to leave her disqualified from proceeding with her claim".

General **locus standi** *principle*

[15.78] The judgment of Henchy J in *Cahill* indicates that, in general, only a person with a personal interest in the point at issue will be regarded as having sufficient standing or *locus standi* to initiate a constitutional claim. Among the reasons given was that, with the exception of references to the Supreme Court under Article 26 of the Constitution,[193] the courts generally deal with cases based on concrete sets of facts rather than considering points of law in a vacuum. This is supported by the distinction in the doctrine of precedent between the binding nature of the *ratio decidendi* of a case and the non-binding nature of *obiter dicta*.[194] Indeed, Henchy J referred to certain

193. See para **[5.68]**.

comments in the *East Donegal Co-operative* case as being *obiter.*[195] This general approach in *Cahill* has been followed in subsequent cases. Thus, in *King v Attorney General,*[196] the plaintiff was restricted to challenging only those parts of s 4 of the Vagrancy Act 1824 in respect of which he had been convicted, notwithstanding some doubts cast on s 4 as a whole.

[15.79] In exceptional circumstances, as Henchy J noted, the normal *locus standi* requirement will be waived in order to ensure the protection of constitutional rights. Thus, the courts have relaxed the requirement in cases involving the rights of the unborn, since an unborn person clearly cannot sue.[197] He also referred to cases where an executive or legislative action affects 'a grouping which includes the challenger, or with whom the challenger may be said to have a common interest.' This relaxation of the rule has been applied in the case of a challenge to the Single European Act[198] and the Anglo-Irish Agreement 1985.[199]

The growth of constitutional judicial review

[15.80] A second justification for the *locus standi* rule referred to by Henchy J in *Cahill* was the risk of abuse, whereby 'the crank, the obstructionist ... the officious man of straw' might be tempted to litigate the constitutionality of a

194. See para **[12.47]**.
195. See para **[15.77]**.
196. [1981] IR 233: see para **[15.59]**.
197. See *Society for the Protection of Unborn Children Ltd v Coogan* [1989] IR 734.
198. *Crotty v An Taoiseach* [1987] IR 713.
199. *McGimpsey v Ireland* [1990] 1 IR 110. In this case, the plaintiffs, both members of the Ulster Unionist Party, challenged the validity of the 1985 Agreement on the ground that it was in conflict with Articles 2 and 3 of the Constitution. In the High Court, the defendants argued that the plaintiffs lacked *locus standi* to invoke Article 2 because, as members of a unionist party, they did not believe that the national territory consists of the whole island of Ireland and were only invoking Article 2 as a 'tactical manoeuvre' to have the 1985 Agreement declared invalid. This was rejected by Barrington J in the High Court on the basis that the plaintiffs were deeply concerned about the present state of Northern Ireland and of all Ireland; were opposed to any form of sectarianism; had participated in peace movements seeking to accommodate the various traditions living on the island of Ireland; and sincerely believed that the 1985 Agreement had aggravated the problems on the island rather than solving them. In those circumstances, he concluded 'it would be inappropriate... to refuse to listen to their complaints.' He also indicated that, as the plaintiffs had been born in Ireland, they were Irish citizens, although no evidence to that effect had been introduced. In the Supreme Court, these conclusions was not challenged by the defendants, and the Court proceeded to deal with the case. However Finlay CJ expressed considerable doubt as to whether the plaintiffs had established that they were Irish citizens and, if so, whether a citizen would have *locus standi* to challenge an executive or legislative act 'for the specific and sole purpose of achieving an objective directly contrary to the purpose of the constitutional provision invoked'. For exceptional relaxation, see *Iarnród Éireann v Ireland*, Supreme Court, unrep, 16 July 1996.

law. In the context of the appropriate relationship between the legislative and judicial branches, he considered that the absence of a *locus standi* rule might be interpreted as encouraging those who had opposed legislation during its debate in the Oireachtas to continue their opposition to the legislation by a constitutional action, that is, 'to move from the political arena to the High Court'.

[15.81] Despite this and the other 'rules of self-restraint',[200] cases involving politically-charged matters have been debated with increasing frequency in the courts. There has been a significant growth in constitutional litigation, particularly since the 1960s; indeed this reflects a growth in litigation generally.[201] It has been suggested that the emergence of constitutional judicial review in the 1960s is characteristic of the emergence of Irish society generally from the economic and intellectual isolationism associated with earlier decades, the introduction of television and general awareness of civil rights movements, particularly in the United States and Northern Ireland.[202] While no official statistics are available on the growth, Table 15.01 lists the number of Irish cases cited in successive editions of Professor John Kelly's textbooks on Irish constitutional law between 1967 and 1994.[203]

Irish cases cited in *Kelly*, 1967-1994

Year	Irish cases
1967	130
1980	480
1984	650
1987	850
1994	1,100

Table 15.01

[15.82] Table 15.01 indicates that, between 1922 and 1967, there were in the region of 130 decisions of the Irish courts (primarily of the High Court and Supreme Court) worthy of comment in a text dealing with Irish constitutional law. By 1980, almost 350 more cases were referred to, and

200. See para **[15.75]**.

201. See para **[4.127]**.

202. Casey, 'Changing the Constitution: Amendment and Judicial Review', in Farrell (ed), *de Valera's Constitution and Ours* (Gill and Macmillan, 1987), p 156. See also the comments of Walsh J, para **[4.73]**, n 194.

203. Sources for material in Table 15.1: table of cases in Kelly, *Fundamental Rights in the Irish Law and Constitution*, 2nd ed (Allen Figgis, 1967); Kelly, *The Irish Constitution*, 2nd ed (Jurist, 1984), xxx, and Supplement (1987), iii; table of Irish cases in Hogan & Whyte, *op cit*.

between 1980 and 1984 another 270 decisions of note required discussion. In the ten years between 1984 and 1994, the total number of cases almost doubled, growing from 650 to 1,100. It is hardly surprising that commentators have referred to an 'explosion of constitutional litigation'.[204] This is not merely a question of volume but also of the range of important matters dealt with. The following sample of cases may help illustrate this.

The Constitution and the legal system

[15.83] Constitutional litigation has involved issues of direct importance to the legal system. In 1963, in *The People (Attorney General) v O'Brien*,[205] the Supreme Court held that evidence obtained in conscious and deliberate violation of constitutional rights was automatically inadmissible in court. In 1966, in *The People (Attorney General) v O'Callaghan*,[206] the Supreme Court held that the right to a trial in due course of law in Article 38.1 and the right to liberty under Article 40.4 required that bail could only be refused in very limited circumstances. The limitations thus imposed on the Oireachtas have led, in recent years, for calls to amend the Constitution in order to reverse the effect of the *O'Callaghan* case.[207] In 1975, in *de Burca v Attorney General*,[208] the Supreme Court declared invalid the Juries Act 1927 for its discriminatory exclusion, contrary to Article 40.1, of women and those of little property from sitting on juries. Many decisions of the courts have also defined the meaning of the judicial function within Article 34, thus determining whether certain persons and bodies are empowered to exercise powers conferred on them by statute.[209] Similarly, constitutional provisions have been central to many decisions determining the extent of the original jurisdiction of the courts[210] and the appellate jurisdiction of the Supreme Court.[211]

The legislative power

[15.84] Many constitutional cases have required consideration of the limits to the legislative power in areas with a political dimension. In 1961, in *O'Donovan v Attorney General*,[212] the High Court held invalid the Electoral Act 1959 for failing to respect the proportionality rule for Dáil

---

204. Hogan & Whyte, *op cit*, xciii.
205. [1965] IR 142.
206. [1966] IR 501.
207. At the time of writing (July 1996), a referendum to restrict the right to bail is expected in November 1996.
208. [1976] IR 38: see para **[6.100]**.
209. See para **[4.13]**.
210. See para **[5.52]**.
211. See para **[7.24]**.
212. [1961] IR 114.

constituencies in Article 16.2. The decision of the Supreme Court in 1964 in *Ryan v Attorney General*,[213] established that the legislature was restricted not only by the rights expressly stated in the constitutional text but also by the unspecified personal rights in Article 40.3. In 1971, the Supreme Court held in *McMahon v Attorney General*[214] that various provisions of the Electoral Act 1963 had failed to respect the requirement of a secret ballot in Article 16.1.4°. In 1976, in *In re the Emergency Powers Bill 1976*,[215] a reference to the Supreme Court under Article 26, the Court imposed procedural limitations on what became the Emergency Powers Act 1976, which had been enacted on foot of a declaration of emergency by the Oireachtas under Article 28.3.3°. The political fallout from the Article 26 reference led to the resignation of the then President.[216] In 1980, in *Cityview Press Ltd v An Chomhairle Oiliúna*,[217] the Court upheld the validity of wide-ranging delegation of powers by the Oireachtas to Ministers and other bodies to promulgate secondary legislation, subject to certain restrictions.

[15.85] Earlier in 1980, in *Murphy v Attorney General*,[218] the Supreme Court declared invalid ss 192 to 196 of the Income Tax Act 1967 concerning the taxation of married couples for being in breach of Article 41. The decision indicated that one of the central features of the legislature's powers, tax collection, was subject to constitutional judicial review. Another major aspect of taxation policy, the collection of rates on agricultural land under the Valuation (Ireland) Act 1852, was declared invalid by the Supreme Court in 1984 in *Brennan v Attorney General*[219] for being in breach of the property rights in Article 43. Both these issues had previously been the subject of unsuccessful political campaigns to amend the statutory provisions in question. Notwithstanding the views of Henchy J in *Cahill v Sutton*, therefore, *Murphy* and *Brennan* both involved a 'move from the political arena to the High Court'. In 1981, in *Blake v Attorney General*,[220] the Supreme Court declared invalid the Rent Restrictions Acts 1946 and 1960, which had placed artificial limits on the rent chargeable by landlords in certain private rented dwellings.[221] It should be noted that not all such constitutional challenges are successful,[222] but the rate of increase in

213. [1965] IR 294: see para **[15.126]**.
214. [1972] IR 69.
215. [1977] IR 159.
216. President Cearbhall Ó Dálaigh had previously been Chief Justice and the first Irish judge of the Court of Justice of the European Communities.
217. [1980] IR 381: see para **[13.67]**.
218. [1982] IR 241: see para **[15.65]**.
219. [1983] ILRM 449 (HC); [1984] ILRM 355 (SC).
220. [1982] IR 117.
221. This necessitated the enactment of the Housing (Private Rented Dwellings) Act 1982, by which the State in effect subsidises those unable to afford the market rents now payable in such dwellings.

constitutional litigation in the 1980s and 1990s reflects a greater tendency to challenge legislative measures.

The executive power

[15.86] In 1971, in *Byrne v Ireland*,[223] the Supreme Court held that the State could be sued, thus sweeping away the former immunity from suit based on the royal prerogative. On Christmas Eve 1986, in *Crotty v An Taoiseach*,[224] the High Court granted the plaintiff an interim injunction preventing the Government from depositing the instrument of ratification of the Single European Act. The Supreme Court ultimately held in Crotty that certain provisions of the Single European Act were in conflict with the Constitution as it then stood, necessitating the holding of a referendum to amend the Constitution. While the judgments delivered in Crotty were based on legal reasoning, they caused considerable political embarrassment to the then Government. In 1993, in *Meagher v Minister for Agriculture and Food*,[225] the Supreme Court delivered a more welcome judgment, at least for the executive, upholding the constitutionality of the wide power given to Ministers under s 3 of the European Communities Act 1972, authorising them to amend primary legislation by means of secondary or delegated legislation where this was done to implement European Community laws.

[15.87] In the politically-sensitive area of relations between the State and the United Kingdom, the courts dealt with numerous extradition cases in the 1980s and 1990s. Whether extradition was refused or granted in such cases, the courts were inevitably involved in some element of controversy.[226] In a connected area in 1990, the Supreme Court in *McGimpsey v Ireland*[227] considered Articles 2 and 3 of the Constitution and upheld the validity of the Anglo-Irish Agreement 1985.

Sexual privacy and the right to life

[15.88] A long sequence of constitutional cases has concerned various aspects of sexuality and the right of privacy, sometimes referred to as the right to be let alone or the right to choose. In 1973, in *McGee v Attorney General*,[228] the Supreme Court, by a 4-1 majority, declared invalid s 17 of

222. *Madigan v Attorney General* [1986] ILRM 136 (unsuccessful challenge to residential property tax in Finance Act 1984); *Browne v Attorney General* [1991] 2 IR 58 (unsuccessful challenge to 'benefit in kind' tax on cars in Finance Act 1982).

223. [1972] IR 241: see para **[15.43]**.

224. [1987] IR 713: see further para **[16.63]**.

225. [1994] 1 IR 329: see para **[16.76]**.

226. See generally Forde, *Extradition Law in Ireland*, 2nd ed (Round Hall Press, 1995).

227. [1988] IR 567 (HC); [1990] 1 IR 110 (SC): see para **[15.39]**.

228. [1974] IR 284: see para **[15.128]**.

the Criminal Law Amendment Act 1935, which had prohibited the importation into the State of most forms of contraception, including spermicidal jelly, on the ground that it conflicted with the plaintiff's right to marital privacy under Articles 40.3 and 41. The decision caused political concern at the time,[229] and it not until 1979 that legislation was enacted to regularise the statutory position.[230] In 1983, in *Norris v Attorney General*,[231] the Supreme Court rejected, by a 3-2 majority, a challenge to ss 60 and 61 of the Offences against the Person Act 1861 which made buggery a criminal offence in all cases, including those where the act occurred between consenting adults. The plaintiff had claimed that ss 60 and 61 of the 1861 Act were in conflict with his right to privacy as a homosexual male. While this case was unsuccessful, it was part of a wider campaign to replace ss 60 and 61 with legislation which would remove consensual sexual acts involving male homosexuals, from the realm of the criminal law.[232]

[15.89] In light of the acceptance by the courts of the right of privacy, concern was expressed that the right to choose methods of contraception could be extended to the right to choose the termination of a pregnancy, in effect a right to abortion. This led to a series of constitutional referenda and litigation in the 1980s and 1990s concerning abortion and the right to life of the unborn. These included the 1992 case *Attorney General v X*,[233] in which the Supreme Court held that Article 40.3.3° of the Constitution permitted abortions where the right to life of the mother was in immediate danger. In 1995, the Supreme Court delivered two decisions involving the right to life. In *In re the Regulation of Information (Services Outside the State for the Termination of Pregnancies) Bill 1995*,[234] the Court found that the Bill in

229. See McMahon, 'The Law Relating to Contraception in Ireland', in Clarke (ed), *Morality and the Law* (Mercier, 1982).

230. Health (Family Planning) Act 1979. The Act required that spermicidal jellies and condoms could lawfully only be obtained on the prescription of a doctor for '*bona fide* family planning purposes'. The then Minister for Health described this as 'an Irish solution to an Irish problem'. The Health (Family Planning) (Amendment) Act 1985, also highly contentious at the time, removed the prescription requirement. The Health (Family Planning) (Amendment) Act 1992 and the Health (Family Planning) (Amendment) Act 1993 removed virtually all restrictions on the sale of condoms (and femidoms). Indeed, by 1993, in the context of the use of condoms in AIDS-awareness campaigns, there was little political opposition to treating condoms as instruments of public health.

231. [1984] IR 36.

232. The Criminal Law (Sexual Offences) Act 1993 repealed ss 60 and 61 of the 1861 Act, replacing them with provisions concerning sexual offences with persons under the age of 18 and those otherwise incapable of giving informed consent. The 1993 Act was enacted in the wake of the decision of the European Court of Human Rights in *Norris v Ireland* (1988) 13 EHRR 186: see para **[17.11]**.

233. [1992] 1 IR 1: see para **[15.131]**.

question, which authorised giving information to pregnant women on abortion services abroad, was not repugnant to the Constitution.[235] In another 'right to life/right to die' case, *In re a Ward of Court*,[236] the Court authorised the withdrawal of nourishment from a woman in a near-permanent vegetative state (near-PVS) who had been on life support for over 20 years. All these decisions have been subjected to considerable public discussion and have fuelled media interest in the judiciary.

Marital breakdown and divorce

[15.90] Two important decisions in 1995 concerned marital breakdown. In *TF v Ireland*,[237] the Supreme Court rejected claims that the Judicial Separation and Family Law Reform Act 1989 was in conflict with Article 41 of the Constitution. This was crucial to whether the, then proposed, Government-backed referendum to remove the ban on divorce in Article 41 and to replace it with a provision authorising legislation on divorce would proceed, as the 1989 Act was known to be the model for any proposed divorce legislation. Just one week before the divorce referendum took place, the Court held in *McKenna v An Taoiseach*[238] that Dáil Éireann and the Government had acted in excess of their respective legislative and executive powers, in the case of Dáil Éireann by authorising the spending of money in support of the changes proposed to Article 41 in the divorce referendum, and, in the case of the Government, actually spending that money.

[15.91] The *McKenna* case produced further litigation in 1996 in the wake of the narrow approval in the 1995 referendum of the removal of the ban on divorce. In *Hanafin v Minister for the Environment*,[239] the Supreme Court dismissed a referendum petition under the Referendum Act 1994 in which it had been argued that the unconstitutional spending by the Government in support of the divorce referendum had invalidated the referendum result. This decision to uphold the referendum result, while primarily a matter of legal interpretation of the 1994 Act, also removed the final obstacle to the introduction in the Oireachtas of the detailed legislation concerning divorce associated with the 1995 divorce referendum.

234. [1995] 1 IR 1: see para **[15.134]**.

235. The Bill was enacted as the Regulation of Information (Services Outside the State for the Termination of Pregnancies) Act 1995.

236. [1995] 2 ILRM 401. The case was known as the 'right to die' case: see para **[15.136]**.

237. [1995] 1 IR 321.

238. [1995] 2 IR 10.

239. [1996] 2 ILRM 141.

Criticisms of and limits to constitutional judicial review

[15.92] These decisions indicate the increasing importance of constitutional judicial review. By the 1970s, the courts had begun to develop this jurisdiction to such an extent that the then Taoiseach commented that 'it would be a brave man who would predict, these days, what was or was not contrary to the Constitution'.[240] This has raised questions as to whether such a power is consistent with a democratic State.

[15.93] The simplest form of objection is that it is fundamentally undemocratic for 'unelected judges' to declare invalid laws enacted by the elected representatives of the people. This argument finds some support in writings on United States constitutional law, where constitutional judicial review is regarded as highly politicised.[241] However, the 1937 Constitution expressly provides for constitutional judicial review, whereas this power was implied by the United States courts from the text of the United States Constitution.[242]

[15.94] However, the development by the Irish courts of the concept of unspecified or implied personal rights under Article 40.3 raises issues comparable to those made in the United States context. The question thus arises whether constitutional judicial review means 'government by judges' and whether it can be said that 'We are under a Constitution, but the Constitution is what the judges say it is.'[243]

[15.95] The most recent comprehensive analysis of the 1937 Constitution has described constitutional judicial review as 'conspicuously successful.'[244] This may have been influenced by the feeling that, for many years, the judiciary had been 'forced' to deal with matters which, for whatever reason, the Oireachtas had simply ignored and that the results of their judicial efforts were largely 'beneficial, rational, progressive and fair'.[245]

[15.96] More recently, the executive and the Oireachtas have become noticeably active in law reform generally.[246] The Constitution itself and the principles established by the courts in constitutional cases impose a

---

240. Quoted in Hogan & Whyte, *op cit*, xci.
241. See generally, Hogan, 'Unenumerated Personal Rights: *Ryan's* Case Re-Evaluated' (1990-1992) 25-27 Ir Jur (ns) 95.
242. In particular the judgment of Marshall CJ in *Marbury v Madison*, 1 Cranch 137 (1803). This was alluded to by Walsh J in *Byrne v Ireland* [1972] IR 241: see para **[15.43]**.
243. Hughes J, a judge of the United States Supreme Court, speaking in 1907, quoted by Hogan, 'Constitutional Interpretation', in Litton, *op cit*, p 173.
244. *Report of the Constitution Review Group* (Pn 2632, 1996), p 159.
245. Professor John Kelly, Preface to Hogan & Whyte, *op cit*, xcii.
246. See paras **[5.07]**-**[5.13]**.

limitation on certain executive and legislative measures, but it must also be borne in mind that the judicial function is limited to those cases initiated in the courts and by the 'rules of self-restraint' which the courts themselves have adopted.

[15.97] In a characteristic flourish, Professor John Kelly had commented, in 1967, that, in any event:[247]

> "If they [the people] allow villains into Government, a piece of paper will not protect them from the consequences, nor must they expect a few learned men in wigs and gowns to save the fools from the knaves they have elected."

More recently the relative position of constitutional judicial review was summarised by a leading commentator thus:[248]

> "Though the courts play a significant role under the Constitution they are far from being the ultimate policy-makers in our society. There are obvious limits on their powers, especially since so many policy choices involve public expenditure priorities. The courts have no power to decree a new social welfare or health service scheme, a more progressive taxation system, or a new policy for full employment. Such policy choices remain the prerogative of the Government and Oireachtas. The electorate, of course, retains the ultimate policy choice of whether to keep judicial review or abolish it. It is noteworthy that no government - no matter how irritated by a particular decision - had proposed its abolition. This suggests that judicial review, as it has now developed, has come to be accepted - indeed to be prized - as a valuable constitutional safeguard."

The reality that the judiciary do not control national budgets or plan national policies places constitutional judicial review in context. Indeed, as part of the 'rules of restraint', the courts have emphasised a number of times that they do not wish to become involved in such policy choices. Thus, in *O'Reilly v Limerick Corporation*,[249] Costello J rejected the plaintiff's contention that he had a constitutional right to be provided with a serviced halting site. He referred to the distinction between commutative justice and distributive justice first adopted by the pre-Christian Greek philosopher Aristotle. Commutative justice refers to the obligations arising from dealings or transactions involving individuals and the State, which Costello J considered was the ambit of the judicial function. Distributive justice, by

247. Kelly, *Fundamental Rights in the Irish Law and Constitution*, 2nd ed (Allen Figgis, 1967), p 73.

248. Casey, 'Changing the Constitution: Amendment and Judicial Review', in Farrell (ed), *de Valera's Constitution and Ours* (Gill and Macmillan, 1987), pp 160-1.

249. [1989] ILRM 181.

contrast, refers to the relationship between the individual and the State concerning the distribution and allocation of State resources, which Costello J considered was a matter outside the judicial function. If he held in the plaintiff's favour, he noted that this:

> "would be the imposition by the Court of its view that there had been an unfair distribution of national resources. To arrive at such a conclusion, it would have to make an assessment of the validity of the many competing claims on those resources, the correct priority to be given to them and the financial implications of the plaintiff's claim."

Costello J declined to engage in this process. This provides some general guide as to the limits of the judicial power; however, the distinction between commutative and distributive justice is no easier to draw than the distinction between justiciable matters and political controversies.[250] The examples given above of constitutional litigation indicate that the courts, on occasion, have been concerned, at least indirectly with policy-related matters.

[5] PRINCIPLES OF CONSTITUTIONAL INTERPRETATION

[15.98] Having outlined the general development of constitutional judicial review since the 1960s, it remains to discuss the principles of interpretation developed by the courts in the elucidation of constitutional principles. In general terms, developments have to some extent mirrored those in the interpretation of legislation.[251] Thus, in some cases, the courts have applied a literal or grammatical rule of interpretation to the Constitution while in others they have developed an historical approach. More recently, a purposive or harmonious approach would appear to have emerged as the dominant approach to constitutional interpretation.

[15.99] The text of some constitutional provisions renders it impossible to make a simple comparison between legislation and the Constitution. This arises in particular from references in some Articles to natural law and natural rights. This necessitated the development of particular rules of constitutional interpretation in order to reflect this intellectual influence.[252] While the influence of natural law may now be less strong, it would appear that it remains in some instances as an important interpretative aid alongside the harmonious approach to interpretation.

---

250. See para **[4.17]**.
251. See para **[14.28]**.
252. See para **[15.113]**.

The literal or grammatical approach

[15.100] In a number of cases, a literal approach to the constitutional text has been applied by the courts. This approach may be compared with the approach taken in the interpretation of legislation. The literal approach, whether used in a statutory or constitutional context, can be supported on the basis that the courts remain faithful to the text of the material being examined and are thus not open to the criticism that they have substituted their own personal or subjective judgment for a more objective determination. Nonetheless, as with statutory interpretation,[253] a literal approach to the constitutional text can prove problematic.

[15.101] A literal approach to Article 34.4.3°, which concerns the appellate jurisdiction of the Supreme Court, has proved controversial in some instances. Article 34.4.3° provides: 'The Supreme Court shall, with such exceptions and subject to such regulations as may be prescribed by law, have appellate jurisdiction from all decisions of the High Court ... ' While this provision has not, in general, proved difficult to interpret,[254] the Supreme Court held, in *The People (DPP) v O'Shea*,[255] that the Court's appellate jurisdiction extended to appeals against acquittals in the Central Criminal Court.

[15.102] The decision in *O'Shea* was by a majority of 3-2. The majority, O'Higgins CJ, Walsh and Hederman JJ, relied primarily on a literal interpretation of Article 34.4.3°. This was criticised by the two minority judges, Finlay P and Henchy J, on two grounds. First, it failed to have regard to the historical principles of double jeopardy and *autrefois acquit* which regarded an acquittal as a final verdict and that these principles were consistent with various other constitutional provisions such as the right to a trial in due course of law under Article 38. Second, the minority suggested that a literal approach to one constitutional provision was inappropriate and that it must be seen in the light of the Constitution as whole. At a narrow level, the minority considered that a literal interpretation of Article 34.4.3° failed to recognise that various determinations of the High Court were not amenable to appeal, such as the quasi-administrative allocation of judicial duties by the President of the High Court.[256] However, Henchy J also articulated a more general objection to the literal approach:

---

253. See para **[14.28]**.
254. See para **[7.24]**.
255. [1982] IR 384: see para **[7.50]**. See paras **[12.58]** and **[12.59]** on the status of *O'Shea* as a precedent.
256. See para **[4.49]**.

> "Any single constitutional right or power is but a component in an ensemble of interconnected and interacting provisions which must be brought into play as part of a larger composition, and which must be given such an integrated interpretation as will fit it harmoniously into the general constitutional order and modulation. It may be said of a constitution more than of any other legal instrument, that 'the letter killeth, but the spirit giveth life'. No single constitutional provision (particularly one designed to safeguard personal liberty or the social order) may be isolated and construed with undeviating literalness."

This passage anticipates our discussion below of the purposive or harmonious approach to constitutional interpretation. Henchy J seemed to link this approach with that in statutory interpretation because he immediately went on to quote with approval the following comments of Black J in *The People (Attorney General) v Kennedy*,[257] a case involving statutory interpretation:[258]

> "A small section of a picture, if looked at close-up, may indicate something quite clearly; but when one stands back and views the whole canvas, the close-up view of the small section is often found to have given a wholly wrong view of what it really represented. If one could pick out a single word or phrase and, finding it perfectly clear in itself, refuse to check its apparent meaning in the light thrown upon it by the context or by other provisions, the result would be to render the principle of *ejusdem generis* and *noscitur a sociis* utterly meaningless; for this principle requires frequently that a word or phrase or even a whole provision which, standing alone, has a clear meaning must be given a quite different meaning when viewed in the light of its context."

Although Henchy J was in a minority in the *O'Shea* case, these comments on the limitations of the literal approach to interpretation, whether in a statutory or constitutional setting, carry great weight.[259]

---

257. [1946] I R 517, at 536.

258. In *Kennedy*, the Supreme Court had considered the Courts of Justice Act 1924, s 29, which gave jurisdiction to the Court to hear an appeal from the Court of Criminal Appeal. Section 29 provided that such appeal lay where a certificate that the case involved points of law of exceptional public importance was granted by the Court of Criminal Appeal or the Attorney General (or now also the Director of Public Prosecutions). The defendant's conviction had been quashed on appeal to the Court of Criminal Appeal and the Attorney General then sought to bring an appeal to the Supreme Court under s 29. The Court concluded that, notwithstanding a literal reading of s 29 by which an appeal seemed to lie, the correct meaning was that no appeal lay from the decision by the Court of Criminal Appeal quashing a conviction. s 29 of the 1924 Act will be repealed when the jurisdiction of the Court of Criminal Appeal is transferred to the Supreme Court under the Courts and Court Officers Act 1995: see para **[7.35]**.

259. On the abolition of appeals against acquittals, see para **[7.50]**.

[15.103] A variation on the literal approach was used in *Ryan v Attorney General*,[260] in which the High Court and Supreme Court held that Article 40.3 contained a guarantee to protect an unspecified number of personal rights. In the High Court, Kenny J conducted a literal or grammatical analysis of Article 40.3.1° and 2°, which provide:

> 1° The State guarantees in its laws to respect, and, as far as practicable, by its laws to defend and vindicate the personal rights of the citizen.
>
> 2° The State shall, in particular, by its laws protect as best it may from unjust attack and, in the case of injustice done, vindicate the life, person, good name and property rights of every citizen.'

Commenting on these, Kenny J stated:

> "The words 'in particular' show that sub-s 2° is a detailed statement of something which is already contained in sub-s 1° which is the general guarantee. But sub-s 2° refers to rights in connection with life and good name and there are no rights in connection with these two matters specified in Article 40. It follows, I think, that the general guarantee in sub-s 1° must extend to rights not specified in Article 40."

While the grammatical analysis involved here was described as 'logically faultless', it has been criticised for introducing an element of uncertainty which is repugnant to the concept of the rule of law itself.[261] Despite this criticism, the courts have continued to develop the unspecified unenumerated rights under Article 40.3, though the grammatical approach of Kenny J in *Ryan* has been replaced by the purposive or harmonious approach.[262]

Historical approach and 'original understanding'

[15.104] In The *People (DPP) v O'Shea*,[263] Finlay P and Henchy J criticised the majority's conclusion that appeals to the Supreme Court lay from acquittals in the Central Criminal Court on the ground that this ignored the common law's historical double jeopardy rule. Similar references to well-established principles of law or the state of the law in 1937 when the Constitution was passed are to be found in other cases.[264] Indeed, this echoes an approach of the United States Supreme Court by which it seeks to find an

260. [1965] IR 294: see para **[15.126]**.

261. Kelly, *Fundamental Rights in the Irish Law and Constitution*, 2nd ed (Allen Figgis, 1967), p 42. See also Hogan, 'Unenumerated Personal Rights: *Ryan's* Case Re-Evaluated' (1990-1992) 25-27 Ir Jur (ns) 95.

262. See para **[15.108]**.

263. [1982] IR 384: see para **[15.102]**.

264. See Hogan & Whyte, *op cit*, pp cix-cxvii.

'original understanding' of the text of the Constitution, based on the views of those who drafted its text in 1787.[265] This approach has been associated in recent years with commentators and judges who disapprove of the judicial activism and liberalism of the United States Supreme Court in the 1960s.[266] While references to the historical state of the law in 1937 are likely to continue, they are unlikely to prove decisive in many instances.

[15.105] The approach of the courts to the interpretation of legislation is instructive in this context; while in some instances an original or historical meaning may be required to interpret some statutory language, in others the language may develop a somewhat different meaning over time.[267] Similarly, the courts have developed common law principles, such as the duty of care in negligence, to accommodate new situations.[268] It should come as no surprise that in constitutional interpretation a similar pragmatic approach is evident.

[15.106] In the High Court judgment in *McGee v Attorney General*,[269] O'Keeffe P rejected the plaintiff's claim that s 17 of the Criminal Law Amendment Act 1935, which prohibited the importation of contraceptive items, including spermicidal jelly, conflicted with the plaintiff's right to marital privacy by preventing her and her husband from using such items. O'Keeffe P rejected the idea that the right to marital privacy existed at all, since this would suppose that those who voted to enact the 1937 Constitution had, in effect, also voted to create a right of marital privacy and to repeal s 17 of the 1935 Act. O'Keeffe P doubted that this was the intention of the people in 1937. This, arguably defensible, historical analysis of the state of public opinion in 1937 was rejected by the Supreme Court who declared s 17 of the 1935 Act invalid. In this respect, Walsh J commented that 'no interpretation of the Constitution is intended to be final for all time.' This approach has been adopted in a number of subsequent cases.

[15.107] Thus, between 1937 and 1975, juries were composed almost exclusively of men; nonetheless, in *de Burca v Attorney General*,[270] the Supreme Court found the consequent exclusion of women to be discrimination prohibited by Article 40.1 of the Constitution. Similarly, between 1937 and 1984 legislation required unanimous jury verdicts in

---

265. Such texts include Hamilton's, *The Federalist Papers*.

266. Eg, Judge Robert Bork's, *The Tempting of America: The Political Seduction of the Law* (1990).

267. See para **[14.51]**.

268. See para **[12.65]**.

269. [1974] IR 284.

270. [1976] IR 38: see para. **[6.100]**.

criminal trials; in *O'Callaghan v Attorney General*,[271] the Supreme Court held that the introduction of majority verdicts by the Criminal Justice Act 1984 was not in conflict with the Constitution. It would seem from these cases that there is no 'original understanding' of the Irish Constitution.[272]

Purposive or harmonious approach

[15.108] We have seen that, in The *People v O'Shea*,[273] Henchy J stated that the courts should avoid examining a constitutional provision in isolation and should ensure that each provision is given an 'integrated interpretation as will fit it harmoniously into the general constitutional order'. This harmonious approach requires the courts to interpret a provision in a way that is consistent with the 'general scheme' of the Constitution. In that respect the harmonious approach is also a purposive approach and it seeks to avoid any internal inconsistency in the Constitution.

[15.109] This approach was applied by the Supreme Court in *Tormey v Attorney General*.[274] The plaintiff had been returned for trial to the Circuit Criminal Court, but wished to be tried in the High Court, the Central Criminal Court. Prior to 1981, he was entitled to elect for trial in the Central Criminal Court, but that right had been removed by s 31 of the Courts Act 1981. The issue raised was whether this was consistent with Article 34.3.1°, which provides that 'the High Court [is] invested with full original jurisdiction in and power to determine all matters and questions, whether of fact or law, civil or criminal'. The High Court and, on appeal, the Supreme Court, rejected the plaintiffs claim. The Supreme Court held that Article 34.3.1° should not be given a literal meaning. Using the harmonious approach, the Court pointed out that the High Court retained an original jurisdiction under Article 34.3.1° through its power to order judicial review of trials in the Circuit Criminal Court or through its power to make declaratory orders.[275] Delivering the judgment of the Court, Henchy J stated:

> "It is to be pointed out at the outset that the terms in which original jurisdiction is vested in the High Court by Article 34, s 3, sub-s 1 cannot be read literally. To do so would produce absurdity and bring Article 34, s 3, sub-s 1 into conflict with other constitutional provisions. At first view it might be thought that there is given to the High Court jurisdiction to determine 'all matters and questions', but that cannot be so, for in the

271. [1993] 2 IR 17: see para **[6.111]**.
272. See also Whyte, 'Constitutional Adjudication, Ideology and Access to the Courts', in Whelan (ed), *Law and Liberty in Ireland* (Oak Tree Press, 1993).
273. [1982] IR 384: see para **[15.102]**.
274. [1985] IR 289: see para **[5.82]**.
275. See paras **[10.16]** and **[10.35]**.

> nature of things there are matters and questions which are not amenable to determination by any court. They are not justiciable. Consequently, 'all matters and questions' must be read as confined to 'all justiciable matters and questions'. But even 'all justiciable matters and questions' expresses too widely the jurisdiction conferred by Article 34, s 3, sub-s 1, for other constitutional provisions show that an original jurisdiction in certain justiciable matters and questions shall, or may, be exercised by other courts, tribunals, persons or bodies. For example, it is implicit in Article 26 that no court other than the Supreme Court shall have jurisdiction to rule on the constitutionality of a Bill referred by the President under that Article; Article 34, s 3, sub-s 3 debars the High Court from considering the constitutionality of a statutory provision declared constitutional by the Supreme Court in a reference under Article 26; and Article 34, s 4, sub-s 6 provides more generally that the High Court cannot entertain any question which has been determined by the Supreme Court. Furthermore, an original jurisdiction may be exercised by courts of summary jurisdiction to try minor offences (Article 38, s 2), by special courts to try offences of the kind specified in Article 38, s 3, sub-s 1, by military tribunals to try offences against military law (Article 38, s 4, sub-s 1), and by persons or bodies exercising limited functions and powers of a judicial nature in matters other than criminal matters, duly committed to them under Article 37. The jurisdiction to try thus vested by the Constitution in courts, tribunals, persons or bodies other than the High Court must be taken to be capable of being exercised, at least in certain instances, to the exclusion of the High Court, for the allocation of jurisdiction would otherwise be overlapping and unworkable."

Henchy J states that a literal approach would produce 'absurdity' and that this should be avoided. This is reminiscent of the golden and teleological rules of statutory interpretation.[276] The harmonious approach goes further, ensuring that the Constitution is internally consistent and is not contradictory. The harmonious approach was summed up in *Tormey* thus:

> "As indicated earlier in this judgment, Article 34, s 3, sub-s 1, despite its unqualified and unambiguous terms, cannot be given an entirely literal construction. The rule of literal interpretation, which is generally applied in the absence of ambiguity or absurdity in the text, must here give way to the more fundamental rule of constitutional interpretation that the Constitution must be read as a whole and that its several provisions must not be looked at in isolation, but be treated as interlocking parts of the general constitutional scheme. This means that where two constructions of a provision are open in the light of the Constitution as a whole, despite the apparent unambiguity of the provision itself, the Court should adopt the

276. See para **[14.28]**.

construction which will achieve the smooth and harmonious operation of the Constitution. A judicial attitude of strict construction should be avoided when it would allow the imperfection or inadequacy of the words used to defeat or pervert any of the fundamental purposes of the Constitution. It follows from such a global approach that, save where the Constitution itself otherwise provides, all its provisions should be given due weight and effect and not be subordinated one to the other. Thus, where there are two provisions in apparent conflict with one another, there should be adopted, if possible, an interpretation which will give due and harmonious effect to both provisions. The true purpose and range of a Constitution would not be achieved if it were treated as no more than the sum of its parts."

In summary, the harmonious approach means that the Constitution cannot contradict itself; where there appears to be a conflict, the harmonious approach requires the courts to interpret provisions in a manner that ensures internal consistency. In *Tormey*, this was achieved by concluding that, although the High Court does not hear all cases at first instance, it retains a 'full' jurisdiction under Article 34.3.1° through its judicial review and declaratory powers. The harmonious approach has been applied in a number of cases in recent years, and it would appear that it has now been accepted as the dominant canon of interpretation.[277]

European influence on harmonious approach

[15.110] The harmonious approach is virtually identical to the approach adopted by the Court of Justice of the European Communities in its interpretation of the Treaties which form the basis for European Community law.[278] Seen in conjunction with the emergence in recent years of the teleological approach to the interpretation of legislation,[279] it is evident that European Community law has had an important influence on Irish interpretative techniques. The courts have also given a cautious indication that, in limited circumstances, international conventions to which Ireland is a party, such as the European Convention on Human Rights, might have a persuasive authority.[280]

Natural law and constitutional interpretation

[15.111] We have already referred to the Constitution as 'manifesto', a mixture of law and political aspiration, as in the case of Articles 2 and 3.[281]

277. Eg, *Attorney General v X* [1992] 1 IR 1; *In re the Regulation of Information (Services Outside the State for the Termination of Pregnancies) Bill 1995* [1995] 1 IR 1: see paras **[15.131]-[15.135]**.

278. See para **[16.54]**.

279. See para **[14.20]**.

280. *Desmond v Glackin (No 2)* [1993] 3 IR 67, *per* O'Hanlon J: para **[17.20]**.

281. See para **[15.37]**.

Some Articles also allude to concepts which require further explanation. For example, Article 41, which deals with the family, reads thus:

> 1.1° The State recognises the Family as the natural primary and fundamental unit group of Society, and as a moral institution possessing inalienable and imprescriptible rights, antecedent and superior to all positive law.
>
> 2° The State, therefore, guarantees to protect the Family in its constitution and authority, as the necessary basis of social order and as indispensable to the welfare of the Nation and the State.
>
> 2.1° In particular, the State recognises that, by her life within the home, woman gives to the State a support without which the common good cannot be achieved.
>
> 2° The State shall, therefore, endeavour to ensure that mothers shall not be obliged by economic necessity to engage in labour to the neglect of their duties in the home.
>
> 3.1° The State pledges itself to guard with special care the institution of Marriage, on which the Family is founded, and to protect it against attack.
>
> 2° A Court designated by law may grant a dissolution of marriage where, but only where, it is satisfied that:
>
> i. at the date of the institution of the proceedings, the spouses have lived apart from one another for a period of, or periods amounting to, at least four years during the previous five years,
>
> ii. there is no reasonable prospect of a reconciliation between the spouses,
>
> iii. such provision as the Court considers proper having regard to the circumstances exists, or will be made for the spouses, any children of either of them and any other person prescribed by law, and
>
> iv any further conditions prescribed by law are complied with.
>
> 3° No person whose marriage has been dissolved under the civil law of any other State but is a subsisting valid marriage under the law for the time being in force within the jurisdiction of the Government and Parliament established by this Constitution shall be capable of contracting a valid marriage within that jurisdiction during the lifetime of the other party to the marriage so dissolved.'

[15.112] Article 41 encapsulates many of the difficulties inherent in the interpretation of the Constitution. Thus, from the literal and historical approach, Article 41.2 may appear to reflect the view that 'a woman's place is in the home'. This interpretation has been rejected as incorrect,[282] but in any event it appears dated and has been criticised for failing to reflect the increase from 5.6% to 32.4% in the proportion of married women who work outside the home, the absence of any reference to those who care for elderly relatives in the home and the failure to refer to any role for husbands and fathers.[283] Article 41.3 presents another problem for the historical approach. Prior to 1996, Article 41.3.1°, by which that the State pledges itself to guard with special care the institution of marriage, was followed by a ban on divorce in Article 41.3.2°. This ban was replaced in 1996 by the 'new' Article 41.3.2° quoted above, which permits divorce in certain circumstances.[284] The creation of a divorce jurisdiction must of necessity involve a re-appraisal of the pledge to guard the family in Article 41.3.1°. In addition, pre-1996 decisions concerning annulment of marriages which had emphasised that the Constitution supports marriage as an institution involving a lifelong commitment would also require re-assessment.[285] These problems of interpretation can be resolved, however, by the rules of interpretation already referred to, which require that Article 41 is interpreted in accordance with changes in its own text, in the light of changes in society and also by avoiding any interpretation that would produce an internal contradiction.

The language of Article 41.1, moreover, gives rise to more difficult interpretative problems.

Natural law and positive law

[15.113] Article 41.1 refers to the family as 'a moral institution possessing inalienable and imprescriptible rights, antecedent and superior to all positive law.' This is an allusion to the concept or theory of natural law that individuals are endowed with certain rights by virtue of their human personality and that these are superior to positive law, that is the law of human institutions, such as a legislature. These rights, called natural rights, are inalienable in the sense that they may not, in general, be given away by

---

282. Mr Justice Walsh, 'The Constitution and Constitutional Rights', in Litton (ed), *The Constitution of Ireland, 1937-1987* (Institute of Public Administration, 1987).

283. The *Report of the Constitution Review Group* (Pn 2632, 1996), pp 333-4, recommended that Article 41.2 might be revised to read: 'The State recognises that home and family life gives to society a support without which the common good cannot be achieved. The State shall endeavour to support persons caring for others within the home.'

284. The original text of Article 41.3.2°, prohibiting divorce, was: 'No law shall be enacted providing for the grant of a dissolution of marriage.' This was replaced by the text of Article 41.3.2° in the main body after its terms had been approved in the 1995 divorce referendum and which became the Fifteenth Amendment of the Constitution Act 1996.

285. Eg, *N(K) v K* [1985] IR 733.

the individual, are imprescriptible in that they may not, in general, be taken away by the State and are antecedent to positive law in that they pre-date positive law, that is, exist in some pre-existing state. The concept of natural law and natural rights originated with the pre-Christian Greek philosophers such as Aristotle.[286] However, it has long been associated with Christian philosophers, beginning in medieval times with St Thomas Aquinas, and its inclusion in the 1937 Constitution has been attributed largely to the Christian, and in particular Roman Catholic, influence on the drafters of the 1937 text.

[15.114] In general terms, the natural law theory begins with the assumption that some natural authority confers rights on human beings. For the pre-Christian Greek philosophers, the ultimate authority was a metaphysical or absolute state of nature. For Christian philosophers, the ultimate authority is, of course, a metaphysical divine being, God.

[15.115] All natural law philosophers have in common the concept that the moral validity of any laws enacted by human institutions, that is positive law, is dependent on its compliance with the basic principles of natural law and natural rights. Thus, natural law is a 'higher law' and superior to positive law, a concept expressly referred to in Article 41.1. Natural law philosophers are thus engaged in a discussion about the moral standing of laws enacted by human institutions.

[15.116] One of the consequences of such 'moral disagreement' over the content of laws is that a law which does not comply with natural law is morally wrong or bad and that, in general, one would be entitled to disregard such a law. In the 16th and 17th Centuries, this concept gave rise to the suggestions by some English judges, such as Lord Coke, that legislation enacted in conflict with natural law, or the law of God, could be declared invalid by the courts. However, this suggestion was not acted on and later judges and writers on English law ultimately accepted the view that the English legislature was entirely free to enact any form of legislation and the courts were obliged to give effect to it.[287] In the modern English era, therefore moral disagreement over the content of laws is a matter for political debate rather than judicial decision. It is also manifested in the political concept of 'civil disobedience' whereby individuals refuse to comply fully with the application of a law, though accepting that this may involve criminal prosecution and imprisonment. The political campaigns of

---

286. On the Aristotelian concepts of commutative and distributive justice, see para **[15.97]**.

287. See generally para **[2.09]**.

Mahatma Ghandi in India in the 1930s and of Martin Luther King in the United States of America in the 1960s are examples of this.

[15.117] Among the rights regarded as part of natural law theory are the right to life, which is referred to in Article 40.3 of the 1937 Constitution, and to equality before the law, referred to in Article 40.1. A difficulty with the natural law theory is that the precise scope of natural rights may either be difficult to discern or the views of philosophers may change over time. Thus, in ancient Greece, the concept of equality was effectively reserved for citizens of Athens; other persons were excluded from the political process and the concept of slavery was also 'accommodated' within the general equality guarantee. Some philosophers have criticised the natural law tradition for its lack of specificity. In addition, the long association of the natural law theory with Christian philosophy, and in particular the Roman Catholic church, has resulted in a negative response from philosophers who espouse a secular approach to the content of law.

Natural law and utilitarianism

[15.118] The theory of utilitarianism has long been associated with the 19th century writings of the English philosophers Jeremy Bentham and John Stuart Mill. Utilitarianism developed in part by way of opposition to what was seen as the vagueness of the natural law theory and its insistence that a 'higher' law determined whether positive law was valid. Utilitarians begin by rejecting the concept that law can include a 'higher' law. They are also associated with rejecting the notion of individual rights or natural rights.

[15.119] For utilitarians therefore, English law comprises the common law and statute law and there is no question of such laws being declared invalid for being in conflict with a 'higher' law as Lord Coke had suggested. Nonetheless, Bentham's theory requires that positive law conform with the principle of utility, which requires that laws meet the 'happiness' (or needs) of the community as a whole. This is sometimes inaccurately summarised as a crude assertion of 'majority rule', but Bentham acknowledged that the interests of the community may sometimes best be served by laws which respect the needs of a minority in the community even though this might marginally diminish the 'happiness' of the majority. Thus utilitarianism may be used in support of laws which respect minority interests. In that respect, it is not necessarily opposed in practice to a theory of rights.[288] Many important legal reforms of the 19th century have been attributed to utilitarianism, such as the reform of the court system and rationalisation of legal procedures.[289]

---

288. Kelly, 'The Constitution: Law and Manfesto', in Litton (ed), *op cit*, p 216.

289. See para **[2.21]**.

[15.120] Indeed, John Stuart Mill, a utilitarian, may be regarded as a founder of the 'liberal' movement, in particular the concept that the law should not concern itself with matters of private morality unless these conflicted with the common good of society. Thus, where a person engaged in an activity in private, Mill had argued that this ought not necessarily be regulated by law even if the majority in society found such activity morally wrong. In the 20th century, this principle has been adopted in a number of States as the basis for much law reform. It has been resisted by many supporters of the natural law theory, particularly in areas concerning sexual freedom. This may be attributed in part to the fact that many who support natural law theory do so from a theological or religious standpoint.

[15.121] Thus, in many States, moral disagreement over the content of laws has focused on what is sometimes referred to as the 'liberal agenda'. In Ireland, this has included calls for legislation removing access to contraceptive devices, legislation providing for divorce (which required a prior amendment of the Constitution); decriminalisation of homosexual sexual acts; the right to choose (that is, the right of women to control their fertility through access to abortion); and, to a lesser extent, the right to die in dignity (described by its opponents as a euphemism for euthanasia). Many of these calls have been resisted by those who support the natural law theory on the ground that such matters are contrary to natural law or are 'unnatural' and are not matters of rights or liberty but merely of 'licence'.

[15.122] Thus, the natural law theory, while supporting the concept of rights, has been portrayed by some as 'conservative' and inimical to individual liberty, while utilitarianism has been portrayed as 'liberal' and progressive even though it does not necessarily use the language of rights.

[15.123] In the second half of the 20th century, there has been a resurgence of interest in natural law and utilitarianism. While natural law and utilitarianism remain quite different theories, both are moral theories in that they subject positive laws to a test of whether they are morally good or bad. In addition, it may be said that, in recent years, many of those who have developed the natural law theory cannot always be categorised as 'conservative'.[290]

---

290. In the late 1950s and early 1960s in Britain, Lord Devlin, a distinguished Law Lord, and Professor HLA Hart, a distinguished academic with some sympathy for the natural law theory, delivered a series of lectures and articles on the topic of law and morality in the context of proposals for law reform in areas such as divorce, homosexuality and abortion: see Devlin, *The Enforcement of Morals* (Oxford, 1961) and Hart, *Law, Liberty and Morality* (Oxford, 1963). From the 1970s, this debate was taken up by leading academics such as Professor Ronald Dworkin. For an Irish perspective on this and related developments in jurisprudence, see Quinn, Ingram and Livingtone (eds), *Justice and Legal Theory in Ireland* (Oak Tree Press, 1995). See also Clarke (ed), *Morality and the Law* (Mercier, 1982), a collection of essays which anticipated many of the developments in the late 1980s and early 1990s.

The Constitution, natural law and utilitarianism

[15.124] The 1937 Constitution clearly rejects the basic premise of utilitarianism that individual rights do not exist. However, the Constitution also reflects some elements of utilitarianism by subjecting the exercise of rights to the requirements of the common good, as in the case of property rights under Article 43. Nonetheless, the dominant influence, as indicated by Article 41, is that individuals have rights which are anterior and superior to positive law.

[15.125] A crucial question in this respect is whether the Constitution, by invoking natural law principles, established natural law as a 'higher' law by which the Constitution itself is bound. This has two implications. First, it has been argued that the courts must interpret the Constitution consistently with natural law. Second, and more profoundly, it has been suggested that the Constitution may not be amended in a manner that would be in conflict with natural law. This argument, which has been associated with those who oppose many elements of the 'liberal agenda', arose with particular vigour in the immediate aftermath of the decision of the Supreme Court in *Attorney General v X*,[291] in which the Court held that Article 40.3.3° permitted abortions where the right to life of the mother was in immediate danger.[292] To place this debate in context, it is necessary to refer back to earlier decisions of the courts on Article 40.3

Ryan v Attorney General

[15.126] In *Ryan v Attorney General*,[293] Kenny J had stated that, in addition to discerning a list of unenumerated rights from a grammatical analysis of Article 40.3, such rights were also implicit in the 'Christian and democratic nature of the State' as indicated by the overall text of the 1937 Constitution. He instanced the right to marry as a personal right implicit in the Christian nature of the State, while the right to travel freely within the State was mentioned as a right implicit in the democratic nature of the State.[294] In concluding that the right to bodily integrity was also a right guaranteed protection under Article 40.3, Kenny J cited with approval a reference to the right in a Papal Encyclical written by Pope John XIII, *Pacem In Terris*. This Encyclical was written by a Pope who was regarded as a reforming and

291. [1992] 1 IR 1: see para **[15.131]**.
292. Eg, Mr Justice O'Hanlon's 'Natural Rights and the Irish Constitution' (1993) 11 ILT 8 (see also para **[4.95]**). See also the essays in Quinn and Ors (ed), *Justice and Legal Theory in Ireland* (Oak Tree Press, 1993).
293. [1965] IR 294: see para **[15.50]**.
294. See also *King v Attorney General* [1981] IR 233 on the right to 'dawdle': see para **[15.59]**.

'liberal' influence within the Roman Catholic Church, evidenced in particular by the establishment of the Second Vatican Council during his reign. Nonetheless, the impression might have been created that 'Christian' equalled 'Roman Catholic' as far as the 'Christian and democratic' nature of the State was concerned.

[15.127] Thus, the general question arose as to whether any existing, or more significantly, any proposed law, that was in conflict with the 'Christian' nature of the Constitution would be declared invalid. This question came to the fore in the late 1960s and early 1970s when law reform generally had begun to feature in the Oireachtas.[295] In the late 1960s, Private Members Bills seeking to legalise the importation of contraceptive devices, a criminal offence under s 17 of the Criminal Law Amendment Act 1935, were introduced by Senator Mary Robinson,[296] but were overwhelmingly defeated. The issue was shortly to become a matter for the courts.[297]

McGee v Attorney General

[15.128] After *Ryan v Attorney General*, the next major decision concerning Article 40.3 was in 1973, *McGee v Attorney General*.[298] The plaintiff, a married woman, had been advised by her doctor that to have any more children would seriously endanger her life.[299] Together with her husband, she took the decision to use a form of contraception to avoid further pregnancy. Her doctor advised a particular method which required her to import spermicidal jelly into the State. This was impounded by the Revenue Commissioners pursuant to the powers conferred by s 17 of the Criminal Law Amendment Act 1935, which made the importation of such material a criminal offence. The plaintiff sought a declaration that s 17 was in conflict with her right to privacy.[300] By a 4-1 majority, the Supreme Court accepted that s 17 of the 1935 Act was in conflict with the plaintiff's right to marital privacy under Articles 40.3 and 41. In his judgment in *McGee*, Walsh J alluded to the principles of natural law in concluding that s 17 of the 1935 Act had breached the plaintiff's rights under Articles 40.3 and 41.

295. See para **[11.04]**.

296. Elected President of Ireland in 1990.

297. Thus involving, in one sense, the transfer from the Oireachtas to the Four Courts referred to by Henchy J in *Cahill v Sutton* [1980] IR 269: see para **[15.77]**.

298. [1974] IR 284.

299. See the dramatic summary of the facts by Henchy J: p 625.

300. Her senior counsel was Seán MacBride SC, her junior counsel Mary Robinson.

Walsh J:

"... Articles 40, 41, 42 and 44 of the Constitution all fall within that section of the Constitution which is titled "Fundamental Rights". Articles 41, 42 and 43 emphatically reject the theory that there are no rights without laws, no rights contrary to the law and no rights anterior to the law.[301] They indicate that justice is placed above the law and acknowledge that natural rights, or human rights, are not created by law but that the Constitution confirms their existence and gives them protection. The individual has natural and human rights over which the State has no authority; and the family, as the natural primary and fundamental unit group of society, has rights as such which the State cannot control. However, at the same time it is true, as the Constitution acknowledges and claims, that the State is the guardian of the common good and that the individual, as a member of society, and the family, as a unit of society, have duties and obligations to consider and respect the common good of that society. It is important to recall that under the Constitution the State's powers of government are exercised in their respective spheres by the legislative, executive and judicial organs established under the Constitution. I agree with the view expressed by O'Byrne J in *Buckley and Others (Sinn Fein) v The Attorney General*[302] that the power of the State to act for the protection of the common good or to decide what are the exigencies of the common good is not one which is peculiarly reserved for the legislative organ of government, in that the decision of the legislative organ is not absolute and is subject to and capable of being reviewed by the Courts. In concrete terms that means that the legislature is not free to encroach unjustifiably upon the fundamental rights of individuals or of the family in the name of the common good, or by act or omission to abandon or to neglect the common good or the protection or enforcement of the rights of individual citizens.

Turning to the particular submission made on behalf of the plaintiff, I shall deal first with the submission made in relation to the provisions of Article 41 of the Constitution which deals with the family. On the particular facts of this case, I think this is the most important submission because the plaintiff's claim is based upon her status as a married woman and is made in relation to the conduct of her sexual life with her husband within that marriage. For the purpose of this Article I am of opinion that the state of the plaintiffs health is immaterial to the consideration of the right she claims are infringed in relation to Article 41. In this Article the State, while recognising the family as the natural primary and fundamental unit group of society and as a moral institution possessing inalienable and imprescriptible rights antecedent and superior to all positive law, guarantees to protect the family in its constitution and authority as the

301. That is, the Constitution rejects the utilitarian theory - eds.

302. [1950] IR 67 at 83.

necessary basis of social order and as indispensable to the welfare of the nation and the State. The Article recognises the special position of woman, meaning the wife, within that unit; the Article also offers special protection for mothers in that they shall not be obliged by economic necessity to engage in labour to the neglect of their duties in the home. The Article also recognises the institution of marriage as the foundation of the family and undertakes to protect it against attack. By this and the following Article, the State recognises the parents as the natural guardians of the children of the family and as those in whom the authority of the family is vested and those who shall have the right to determine how the family life shall be conducted, having due regard to the rights of the children not merely as members of that family but as individuals.

It is a matter exclusively for the husband and wife to decide how many children they wish to have; it would be quite outside the competence of the State to dictate or prescribe the number of children which they might have or should have. In my view, the husband and wife have a correlative right to agree to have no children. This is not to say that the State, when the common good requires it, may not actively encourage married couples either to have larger families or smaller families. If it is a question of having smaller families then, whether it be a decision of the husband and wife or the intervention of the State, the means employed to achieve this objective would have to be examined. What may be permissible to the husband and wife is not necessarily permissible to the State. For example, the husband and wife may mutually agree to practice either total or partial abstinence in their sexual relations. If the State were to attempt to intervene to compel such abstinence, it would be an intolerable and unjustifiable intrusion into the privacy of the matrimonial bedroom. On the other hand, any action on the part of either the husband and wife or of the State to limit family sizes by endangering or destroying human life must necessarily not only be an offence against the common good but also against the guaranteed personal rights of the human life in question.

The sexual life of a husband and wife is of necessity and by its nature an area of particular privacy. If the husband and wife decide to limit their family or to avoid having children by use of contraceptives, it is a matter peculiarly within the joint decision of the husband and wife and one into which the State cannot intrude unless its intrusion can be justified by the exigencies of the common good. The question of whether the use of contraceptives by married couples within their marriage is or is not contrary to the moral code or codes to which they profess to subscribe, or is or is not regarded by them as being against their conscience, could not justify State intervention. Similarly the fact that the use of contraceptives may offend against the moral code of the majority of the citizens of the State would not *per se* justify an intervention by the State to prohibit their use within marriage. The private morality of its citizens does not justify intervention by the State into the activities of those citizens unless and until the common good requires it. Counsel for the Attorney General did not seek to argue that the State would have any right to seek to prevent the use of contraceptives within marriage. He did argue, however, that it did not follow from this that the State was under any obligation to make contraceptives available to married couples. Counsel for the [Revenue Commissioners] put the matter somewhat further by stating that, if she had a right to use contraceptives within the privacy of her marriage, it was a matter for the plaintiff to prove from whence the right sprang. In effect he was saying that, if she was appealing to a right anterior to positive law, the burden was on her to show the source of that right. At first sight this may appear to be a reasonable and logical proposition. However, it does appear to ignore a fundamental point, namely, that the rights of a married couple to decide how many children, if any, they will have are matters outside the reach of positive law where the means employed to implement such decisions do not impinge upon the common good or destroy or endanger human life. It is undoubtedly true that among those persons who are subject to a particular moral code no one has a right to be in breach of that moral code. But when this is a code governing private morality and where the breach of it is not one which injures the common good then it is not the State's business to intervene. It is outside the authority of the State to endeavour to intrude into the privacy of the husband and wife relationship for the sake of imposing a code of private morality upon that husband and wife which they do not desire.

In my view, Article 41 of the Constitution guarantees the husband and wife against any such invasion of their privacy by the State. It follows that the use of contraceptives by them within that marital privacy is equally guaranteed against such invasion and, as such, assumes the status of a right so guaranteed by the Constitution. If this right cannot be directly invaded by the State it follows that it cannot be frustrated by the State taking measures to ensure that the exercise of that right is rendered impossible. I do not exclude the possibility of the State being justified where the public good requires it (as, for example, in the case of a dangerous fall in population threatening the life or the essential welfare of the State) in taking such steps to ensure that in general, even if married couples could not be compelled to have children, they could at least be hindered in their endeavours to avoid having them where the common good required the maintenance or increase of the population. That, however, is not the present case and there is no evidence whatever in the case to justify State intervention on that ground. Similarly it is not impossible to envisage a situation where the availability of contraceptives to married people for use within marriage could be demonstrated to have led to or would probably lead to such an adverse effect on public morality so subversive of the common good as to justify State intervention by restricting or prohibiting the availability of contraceptives for use within marriage or at all. In such a case it would have to be demonstrated that all the other resources of the

State had proved or were likely to prove incapable to avoid this subversion of the common good while contraceptives remained available for use within marriage.

In my opinion, s 17 of the Act of 1935, in so far as it unreasonably restricts the availability of contraceptives for use within marriage, is inconsistent with the provisions of Article 41 of the Constitution for being an unjustified invasion of the privacy of husband and wife in their sexual relations with one another. The fundamental restriction is contained in the provisions of sub-s 3 of s 17 of the Act of 1935 which lists contraceptives among the prohibited articles which may not be imported for any purposes whatsoever. On the present state of facts, I am of opinion that this provision is inconsistent with the Constitution and is no longer in force.

For the reasons I gave earlier in this judgment, the prohibition of the importation of contraceptives could be justified on several grounds provided the effect was not to make contraceptives unavailable. For example, the law might very well prohibit for health reasons the importation of some if not all contraceptives from sources outside the country if, for example, there is a risk of infection from their use. No such reason has been offered in the present case and in any such instance, for the reasons already given, the law could not take other steps to see that contraceptives were not otherwise available for use in marriage.

As this particular case arose primarily out of the ban on importation, I think that, in so far as Article 41 is concerned, the declaration sought should only go in respect of sub-s 3 of s 17 of the Act of 1935. That does not necessarily mean that the provisions as to sale in sub-s 1 of s 17 cannot be impugned. If, in the result, notwithstanding the deletion of sub-s 3, the prohibition on sale had the effect of leaving a position where contraceptives were not reasonably available for use within marriage, then that particular prohibition must also fall. However, for the moment I do not think it is necessary to make any declaration in respect of that.

So far I have considered the plaintiffs case only in relation to Article 41 of the Constitution; and I have done so on the basis that she is a married woman but without referring to her state of health. I now turn to the claim made under Article 40 of the Constitution. So far as this particular Article is concerned, and the submissions made thereunder, the state of health of the plaintiff is relevant. If, for the reasons I have already given, a prohibition on the availability of contraceptives for use in marriage generally could be justified on the grounds of the exigencies of the common good, the provisions of s 1 of Article 40 (in particular, the proviso thereto) would justify and would permit the State to discriminate between some married persons and others in the sense that, where conception could more than ordinarily endanger the life of a particular person or persons or particular classes of persons within the married state, the law could have regard to this difference of physical capacity and make special exemptions in favour of such persons. I think that such an exemption could also be justified under the provisions of s 3 of Article 40 on the grounds that one of the personal rights of a woman in the plaintiff's state of health would be a right to be assisted in her efforts to avoid putting her life in jeopardy. I am of opinion also that not only has the State the right to do so but, by virtue of the terms of the proviso to s I and the terms of s 3 of Article 40, the State has the positive obligation to ensure by its laws as far as is possible (and in the use of the word 'possible' I am relying on the Irish text of the Constitution) that there would be made available to a married woman in the condition of health of the plaintiff the means whereby a conception which was likely to put her life in jeopardy might be avoided when it is a risk over and above the ordinary risks inherent in pregnancy. It would, in the nature of things, be much more difficult to justify a refusal to do this on the grounds of the common good than in the case of married couples generally. ... Both in its preamble and in Article 6 the Constitution acknowledges God as the ultimate source of all authority. The natural or human rights to which I have referred earlier in this judgment are part of what is generally called the natural law. There are many to argue that natural law may be regarded only as an ethical concept and as such is a re-affirmation of the ethical content of law in its ideal of justice. The natural law as a theological concept is the law of God promulgated by reason and is the ultimate governor of all the laws of men. In view of the acknowledgement of Christianity in the preamble and in view of the reference to God in Article 6 of the Constitution, it must be accepted that the Constitution intended the natural human rights I have mentioned as being in the latter category rather than simply an acknowledgement of the ethical content of law in its ideal of justice. What exactly natural law is and what precisely it imports is a question which has exercised the minds of theologians for many centuries and on which they are not yet fully agreed. While the Constitution speaks of certain rights being imprescriptible or inalienable, or being antecedent and superior to all Positive law, it does not specify them. Echoing the words of O'Byrne J in *Buckley and Others (Sinn Féin) v The Attorney General*,[303] I do not feel it necessary to enter upon an inquiry as to their extent or, indeed, as to their nature. It is sufficient for the court to examine and to search for the rights which may be discoverable in the particular case before the court in which these rights are invoked.

In a pluralist society such as ours, the Courts cannot as a matter of constitutional law be asked to choose between the differing views, where they exist, of experts on the interpretation by the different religious denominations of either the nature or extent of these natural rights as they are to be found in the natural law. The same considerations apply also to the question of ascertaining the nature and extent of the duties which flow from natural law; the Constitution speaks of one of them when it refers to the inalienable duty of parents to provide according to their means for the

303. [1950] IR 67, at 82.

religious, moral, intellectual, physical and social education of their children: see s 1 of Article 42. In this country it falls finally upon the judges to interpret the Constitution and in doing so to determine, where necessary, the rights which are superior or antecedent to positive law or which are imprescriptible or inalienable. In the performance of this difficult duty there are certain guidelines laid down in the Constitution for the judge. The very structure and content of the Articles dealing with fundamental rights clearly indicate that justice is not subordinate to the law. In particular, the terms of s 3 of Article 40 expressly subordinate the law to justice. Both Aristotle and the Christian philosophers have regarded justice as the highest human virtue. The virtue of prudence was also esteemed by Aristotle as by the philosophers of the Christian world. But the great additional virtue introduced by Christianity was that of charity - not the charity which consists of giving to the deserving, for that is justice, but the charity which is also called mercy. According to the preamble, the people gave themselves the Constitution to promote the common good with due observance of prudence, justice and charity so that the dignity and freedom of the individual might be assured. The judges must, therefore, as best they can from their training and their experience interpret these rights in accordance with their ideas of prudence, justice and charity. It is but natural that from time to time the prevailing ideas of these virtues may be conditioned by the passage of time; no interpretation of the Constitution is intended to be final for all time. It is given in the light of prevailing ideas and concepts. The development of the constitutional law of the United States of America is ample proof of this. There is a constitution which, while not professing to be governed by the precepts of Christianity, also in the Ninth Amendment recognises the existence of rights other than those referred to expressly in it and its amendments. The views of the United States Supreme Court, as reflected in the decisions interpreting that constitution and in the development of their constitutional law, also appear firmly to reject legal positivism as a jurisprudential guide.

Three United States Supreme Court decisions were relied upon in argument by the plaintiff: *Poe v Ullman*;[304] *Griswold v Connecticut*;[305] and *Eisenstadt v Baird*.[306] My reason for not referring to them is not because I did not find them helpful or relevant, which indeed they were, but because I found it unnecessary to rely upon any of the dicta in those cases to support the views which I have expressed in this judgment.

Lastly, I wish to emphasise that I have given no consideration whatsoever to the question of the constitutionality or otherwise of laws which would withhold or restrict the availability of contraceptives for use outside of

304. 367 US 497 (1961).
305. 381 US 479 (1965).
306. 405 US 438 (1972).

marriage; nothing in this judgment is intended to offer any opinion on that matter.

For the reasons I have given, I would grant the plaintiff a declaration that sub-s 3 of s 17 of the Criminal Law Amendment Act, 1935, is not, and was not at any time material to these proceedings, of full force and effect as part of the laws of the State."

By contrast, Henchy J eschewed any reference to natural law but took an approach consistent with the later emergence of the harmonious approach in concluding that the plaintiff's rights under Article 40.3 had been violated.

Henchy J:

"The essential facts of this case may be summarised as follows. The plaintiff, who is aged 29, lives in the restricted quarters of a mobile home with her husband, who is a fisherman earning about £20 per week, and their four children who were born in December 1968, in January 1970 and (the twins) in November 1970. Her medical history shows that during each pregnancy she suffered from toxaemia; that during her second pregnancy she developed a serious cerebral thrombosis from which she nearly died, and which left her temporarily paralysed on one side; and that during her last pregnancy she suffered from toxaemia which was complicated by hypertension. She has been advised by her doctor that if she becomes pregnant again there will be a very great risk that she will suffer a further cerebral thrombosis, which is an illness that apparently has a mortality rate as high as 26% in married women of her age and which would be apt to cause her a disabling paralysis if it did not prove fatal.

Confronted with that dire prospect, she has had to decide between sexual abstinence and the use of a contraceptive - no question apparently having arisen as to a surgical intervention. With the agreement of her husband, and having due regard to her obligations to her husband, her children and herself, she decided in favour of contraception. Because of her medical history of vascular thrombosis and hypertension, her doctor advised against an oral contraceptive and recommended instead an intra-uterine device which was to be used with a contraceptive jelly. The doctor fitted the device and gave her a small supply of the contraceptive jelly. This jelly is not made in this State, so she had to order a further supply from England. When the packet containing it was sent to her by post, it was intercepted and seized by the Customs authorities because, being a 'contraceptive' as defined by sub-s 4 of s 17 of the Criminal Law Amendment Act 1935, its importation is prohibited by s 42 of the Customs Consolidation Act 1876, as applied by sub-s 3 of s 17 of the Act of 1935.

In the present proceedings the plaintiff has challenged the constitutional validity of s 17 of the Act of 1935 and has claimed that it was not carried over by Article 50 of the Constitution because it is inconsistent with certain provisions in Articles 40, 41, 42, 44 and 45 of the Constitution. The primary contention is that it trenches on her rights under sub-s 1 of s 3 of Article 40 which provides that: 'The State guarantees in its laws to respect, and, as far as practicable, by its laws to defend and vindicate the personal rights of the citizen'.

The Act of 1935, as its long title shows, is not aimed at population control but at the suppression of vice and the amendment of the law relating to sexual offences. Section 17 follows immediately on a section directed against the practice of prostitution in public and immediately precedes a section making criminal certain acts which offend modesty or cause scandal or injure the morals of the community. The section creates a criminal prohibition in an area in which the legislature has thought fit to intervene in the interests of public morality. What it seeks to do, by means of the sanction of the criminal law, is to put an end, as far as it was possible to do so by legislation, to *the use* of contraceptives in the State. It does not in terms make the use of contraceptives a crime, but the totality of the prohibition aims at nothing less. Presumably because contraceptives are of differing kinds and vary in the ways, internal and external, they can be used, and because of the difficulty of proving their use in the intimacy of the sexual act, the section strikes at their availability. Sub-section 1 of s 17 of the Act of 1935 makes it an offence to sell, or expose, offer, advertise, or keep for sale or to import to attempt to import for sale any contraceptives. In effect, this makes it legally impossible to sell or buy a contraceptive in the State. Had the prohibition stopped there, it would have left the loophole that contraceptives could be imported otherwise than for sale. That loophole, however, is sealed by sub-s 3, of s 17 which makes contraceptives prohibited articles under the customs code so that their importation for any purpose, if effected with the intention of evading the prohibition, is an offence: see s 186 of the Customs Consolidation Act, 1876; *Frailey v Charlton*[307]; *Attorney General v Deignan*.[308]

Because contraceptives are not manufactured in this State, the effect of s 17 of the Act of 1935 as a whole is that, except for contraceptives that have been imported without the intention of evading the prohibition of importation, it is not legally possible to obtain a contraceptive in this State. It is doubtful if the legislature could have taken more effective steps by means of the criminal law to put an end to their use in the State.

It is the totality and absoluteness of the prohibition effected by s 17 of the Act of 1935 that counsel for the plaintiff impugn as infringing what they say are her constitutionally guaranteed rights as a citizen. As has been held in a number of cases, the unspecified personal rights guaranteed by sub-s 1 of s 3 of Article 40 are not confined to those specified in sub-s 2 of that section. It is for the Courts to decide in a particular case whether the right relied on comes within the constitutional guarantee. To do so, it must be

307. [1920] 1 KB 147.
308. [1946] IR 542.

shown that it is a right that inheres in the citizen in question by virtue of his human personality. The lack of precision in this test is reduced when sub-s 1 of s 3 of Article 40 is read (as it must be) in the light of the Constitution as a whole and, in particular, in the light of what the Constitution, expressly or by necessary implication, deems to be fundamental to the personal standing of the individual in question in the context of the social order envisaged by the Constitution. The infinite variety in the relationships between the citizen and his fellows and between the citizen and the State makes an exhaustive enumeration of the guaranteed rights difficult, if not impossible.

The dominant feature of the plaintiffs dilemma is that she is a young married woman who is living, with a slender income, in the cramped quarters of a mobile home with her husband and four infant children, and that she is faced with a considerable risk of death or crippling paralysis if she becomes pregnant. The net question is whether it is constitutionally permissible in the circumstances for the law to deny her access to the contraceptive method chosen for her by her doctor and which she and her husband wish to adopt. In other words, is the prohibition effected by s 17 of the Act of 1935 an interference with the rights which the State guarantees in its laws to respect, as stated in sub-s 1 of s 3 of Article 40?

The answer lies primarily in the fact that the plaintiff is a wife and a mother. It is the informed and conscientious wish of the plaintiff and her husband to maintain full marital relations without incurring the risk of a pregnancy that may very well result in her death or in a crippling paralysis. Section 17 of the Act of 1935 frustrates that wish. It goes further; it brings the implementation of the wish within the range of the criminal law. Its effect, therefore, is to condemn the plaintiff and her husband to a way of life which, at best, will be fraught with worry, tension and uncertainty that cannot but adversely affect their lives and, at worst, will result in an unwanted pregnancy causing death or serious illness with the obvious tragic consequences to the lives of her husband and young children. And this in the context of a Constitution which in its preamble proclaims as one of its aims the dignity and freedom of the individual; which in sub-s 2 of s 3 of Article 40 casts on the State a duty to protect as best it may from unjust attack and, in the case of injustice done, to vindicate the life and person of every citizen; which in Article 41, after recognising the family as the natural primary and fundamental unit group of society, and as a moral institution possessing inalienable and imprescriptible rights antecedent and superior to all positive law, guarantees to protect it in its constitution and authority as the necessary basis of social order and as indispensable to the welfare of the nation and the State; and which, also in Article 41, pledges the State to guard with special care. the institution of marriage, on which the family is founded, and to protect it against attack.

Section 17, in my judgment, so far from respecting the plaintiffs personal rights, violates them. If she observes this prohibition (which in practice she can scarcely avoid doing and which in law she is bound under penalty of fine and imprisonment to do), she will endanger the security and happiness of her marriage, she will imperil her health to the point of hazarding her life, and she will subject her family to the risk of distress and disruption. These are intrusions which she is entitled to say are incompatible with the safety of her life, the preservation of her health, her responsibility to her conscience, and the security and well-being of her marriage and family. If she fails to obey the prohibition in s 17, the law, by prosecuting her, will reach into the privacy of her marital life in seeking to prove her guilt.

In *Griswold v Connecticut*[309] the American Supreme Court held that a Connecticut statute which forbade the use of contraceptives was unconstitutional because it violated a constitutional right of marital privacy which, while unexpressed in the American Constitution, was held to be within the penumbra of the specific guarantees of the Bill of Rights. In a judgment concurring in the opinion of the court, Goldberg J. said:[310]

> 'The State, at most, argues that there is some rational relation between this statute and what is admittedly a legitimate subject of state concern - the discouraging of extra-marital relations. It says that preventing the use of birth-control devices by married persons helps prevent the indulgence by some in such extra-marital relations. The rationality of this justification is dubious, particularly in light of the admitted widespread availability to all persons in the State of Connecticut, unmarried as well as married, of birth-control devices for the prevention of disease, as distinguished from the prevention of conception, see *Tileston v Ullman*.[311] But, in any event, it is clear that the state interest in safeguarding marital fidelity can be served by a more discriminately tailored statute, which does not, like the present one, sweep unnecessarily broadly, reaching far beyond the evil sought to be dealt with and intruding upon the privacy of all married couples.'

Goldberg J cites with approval[312] the words of Harlan J in *Poe v Ullman*:[313]

> '... the intimacy of husband and wife is necessarily an essential and accepted feature of the institution of marriage, an institution which the State not only must allow, but which always and in every age it has fostered and protected. It is one thing when the State exerts its power either to forbid extra-marital sexuality altogether, or to say who may marry, but it is quite another when, having acknowledged a marriage and the intimacies inherent in it,

309. 381 US 479 (1965).
310. *Ibid*, 498.
311. 129 Conn 84, 26A, 2d 582.
312. 381 US 479 at 499.
313. 367 US 497 at 533 (1961).

> it undertakes to regulate by means of the criminal law the details of that intimacy.'

It has been argued that *Griswold's Case* is distinguishable because the statute in question there forbade the use of contraceptives, whereas s 17 of the Act of 1935 only forbids their sale or importation. This submission was accepted in the High Court. However, I consider that the distinction sought to be drawn is one of form rather than substance. The purpose of the statute in both cases is the same: it is to apply the sanction of the criminal law in order to prevent the use of contraceptives. What the American Supreme Court found in *Griswold's Case to* be constitutionally objectionable was that the sweep of the statute was so wide that proof of an offence would involve physical intrusion into the intimacy of the marriage relationship, which the court held to be an area of constitutionally protected privacy. If the plaintiff were prosecuted for an offence arising under or by virtue of s 17 of the Act of 1935, while there might not be the same degree of physical intrusion, there would necessarily be a violation of intimate aspects of her marital life which, in deference to her standing as a wife and mother, ought not to be brought out and condemned as criminal under a glare of publicity in a courtroom. Furthermore, if she were found guilty of such an offence, in order to have the penalty mitigated to fit the circumstances of her case, she would have to disclose particulars of her marital dilemma which she ought not to have to reveal.

In my opinion, s 17 of the Act of 1935 violates the guarantee in sub-s 1 of s 3 of Article 40 by the State to protect the plaintiff's personal rights by its laws; it does so not only by violating her personal right to privacy in regard to her marital relations but, in a wider way by frustrating and making criminal any efforts by her to effectuate the decision of her husband and herself, made responsibly, conscientiously and on medical advice to avail themselves of a particular contraceptive method so as to ensure her life and health as well as the integrity, security and well-being of her marriage and her family. Because of the clear unconstitutionality of the section in this respect, I do not find it necessary to deal with the submissions made in support of the claim that the section violates other provisions of the Constitution.

What stands between the plaintiff and the exercise of any constitutional right claimed by her in this case is sub-s 3 of s 17 of the Act of 1935. With that subsection out of the way, her cause of complaint would disappear because what she wishes to do (to import the required contraceptive by post) would then be legal as the importation, not being for sale, would not be forbidden by sub-section 1. Since s 17 without sub-s 3 can stand as a self-contained entity, independently operable and representing the legislative intent, sub-s 3 is capable of being severed and declared unconstitutional. Therefore, I would allow the appeal to the extent of declaring that sub-s 3 of s 17 of the Act of 1935 is without validity as being inconsistent with the Constitution. In the particular circumstances of this

> case, I do not find it necessary to make any adjudication on the constitutionality of the remaining part of the section."

The different approaches of Walsh and Henchy JJ in *McGee* resulted in a similar conclusion, namely that the prohibition of the importation of contraceptives was in conflict with the plaintiff's right to marital privacy. In referring to the natural law,[314] Walsh J noted that the courts were not bound by the theological views expressed by one particular faith in determining whether the natural rights of a person under the Constitution had been violated, thus indicating that the content of natural law under the 1937 Constitution was not linked to a particular theological teaching. As Henchy J later pointed out in *Norris v Attorney General*,[315] this use of the natural law theory by Walsh J resulted in a finding that was, in fact, prohibited by the theological teachings of the Roman Catholic Church, which clearly prohibit the use of contraceptive devices in any circumstances as a means of birth control.[316] However, the differences between the natural law and harmonious approaches were to appear in the *Norris* case.

Norris v Attorney General

[15.129] In 1983, in *Norris v Attorney General*,[317] the Supreme Court rejected, by a 3-2 majority, a challenge to ss 60 and 61 of the Offences against the Person Act 1861 which made buggery a criminal offence in all cases, including those where the act occurred between consenting adults. The plaintiff had claimed that ss 60 and 61 of the 1861 Act were in conflict with his right of privacy as a homosexual male. O'Higgins CJ (with whom Finlay P and Griffin J concurred) pointed out that buggery had been condemned as gravely sinful by St Paul and all Christian churches and that this should inform the Court's interpretation of Article 40.3 of the Constitution.

O'Higgins CJ (Finlay P and Griffin J concurring):

> "... I now turn to what I have described as the core of the plaintiff's case. This is the claim that the impugned legislation constitutes an unwarranted

314. He did not expressly refer to the views on natural law of Kennedy CJ in *The State (Ryan) v Lennon* [1935] IR 170: see para **[15.13]**.

315. [1984] IR 36: see para **[15.129]**.

316. The Roman Catholic Church did not regard the contraceptive pill as being in the same category as intra-uterine devices (IUDs) or condoms. Use of the pill was not regarded as automatically morally wrong since it could be taken to regulate the menstrual cycle rather than as a contraceptive device; if used for the former purpose, the user was not in breach of Roman Catholic teaching even if its use also had the effect of preventing conception. This approach is part of the broader concept of 'double effect'.

317. [1984] IR 36.

interference with his private life and thereby infringes his right to privacy. This claim is based on the philosophical view, attributed to John Stuart Mill, that the law should not concern itself in the realm of private morality except to the extent necessary for the protection of the public order and the guarding of citizens against injury or exploitation. It is a view which received significant endorsement in the report of the Wolfenden Committee on Homosexual Offences and Prostitution. That committee's report, furnished to the British Parliament in 1957, contained the following statement in support of its recommendation for limited decriminalisation:

> 'There remains one additional counter argument which we believe to be decisive, namely, the importance which society and the law ought to give to individual freedom of choice in action in matters of private morality. Unless a deliberate attempt is to be made by society, acting through the agency of the law, to equate the sphere of crime with that of sin, there must remain a realm of private morality and immorality, which is, in brief and crude terms not the law's business. To say this is not to condone or encourage private immorality.'

The Wolfenden Committee had been established by the Scottish Home Office and, although it recommended (in effect) the removal of criminal sanctions from homosexual conduct when carried out in private between adult responsible males, the British Parliament was very slow to accept that recommendation and to act upon it. It was not until the Sexual Offences Act 1967 (which was introduced as a private member's bill) that the law was changed in England and Wales; in Scotland the change was not made until the passing of the Criminal Justice (Scotland) Act 1980. In relation to Northern Ireland, the British Parliament declined to act until compelled to do so as a result of the recent decision of the European Court of Human Rights in *Dudgeon v United Kingdom*.[318] The caution shown by successive British Governments and Parliaments is understandable because what was proposed was a significant reversal of legislative policy in an area in which deep religious and moral beliefs were involved.

From the earliest days, organised religion regarded homosexual conduct, such as sodomy and associated acts, with a deep revulsion as being contrary to the order of nature, a perversion of the biological functions of the sexual organs and an affront both to society and to God. With the advent of Christianity this view found clear expression in the teachings of St. Paul, and has been repeated over the centuries by the doctors and leaders of the Church in every land in which the Gospel of Christ has been preached. Today, as appears from the evidence given in this case, this strict view is beginning to be questioned by individual Christian theologians but, nevertheless, as the learned trial judge said in his judgment, it remains the teaching of all Christian Churches that homosexual acts are wrong.

318. (1981) 4 EHRR 149.

In England, buggery was first treated as a crime by the statute 25 Hen VIII c 6, having been previously dealt with only in the ecclesiastical courts. In Ireland, it first received statutory condemnation in the statute of the Irish Parliament 10 Chas 1, sess 2, c 20. Subject to statutory changes as to punishment, it continued to be prohibited and punished as a crime in accordance with the provisions of the Act of 1861 which were complemented by the later provisions of the Act of 1885 [the Criminal Law Amendment Act 1885]. While those statutory provisions have now been repealed in the entire of the United Kingdom, the question in this case is whether they ceased to operate in Ireland at the time of the enactment of the Constitution in 1937.

In the course of the trial of this action in the High Court, reference was made to the Wolfenden Report, to the Kinsey Survey on homosexual behaviour conducted in the United States and to a similar survey conducted in Sweden. No such survey has been conducted in Ireland, but the trial judge, on the evidence he heard, was prepared to conclude that there is probably a large number of people in this country with homosexual tendencies. Of these, however, only a small number are exclusively homosexual in the sense that their orientation is congenital and irreversible. It is this small group (of those with homosexual tendencies) who must look to the others for the kind of relationship, stable or promiscuous, which they seek and desire. It follows that the efforts and activities of the congenital homosexual must tend towards involving the homosexually orientated in more and more deviant sexual acts to such an extent that such involvement may become habitual. The evidence in this case and the text-books provided as part thereof indicate how sad, lonely and harrowing the life of a person, who is or has become exclusively homosexual, is likely to be. Professor West in his work, *Homosexuality Re-Examined,* states at p 318:

> 'Exclusive homosexuality forces a person into a minority group; cuts off all prospect of fulfilment through a family life with children and hampers participation in mainstream social activities which are mostly geared to the needs of heterosexual couples.'

He goes on to talk of those, whose life centres on short-term liaisons, as facing loneliness and frustration as they lose their sexual attractiveness with advancing age. Other authors, also referred to, indicate the instability of male homosexual relations, the high incidence of suicide attempts, and the depressive reactions which frequently occur when a relationship ends (Harrison; Reid, Barrett & Hewer). These are some of the consequences which, experience has indicated, tend to follow on a lifestyle which is exclusively homosexual.

Apart from these sad consequences of exclusive homosexuality, unfortunately there are other problems thereby created which constitute a threat to public health. Professor West in his work already mentioned, which was published in a revised form in England over ten years after the decriminalisation of homosexual conduct, says at p 228: 'Far from being immune from venereal infection, as many used to like to believe, male homosexuals run a particularly high risk of acquiring sexually transmitted diseases'. The author goes on to show that in the post-decriminalisation decade in Britain many forms of venereal disease (syphilis, gonorrhoea, urethritis and intestinal infection) have shown an alarming increase in males, and that this is attributable directly to the increase in homosexual activity and conduct. In relation to syphilis, the author gives this serious warning:

> 'A promiscuous homosexual with such a reservoir of infection can transmit the disease, in all innocence, to a whole sequence of victims before the carrier is discovered. The diagnosis at this stage is not always obvious, even when suspected, since blood tests for this infection do not usually become positive until some weeks after the primary chancre has appeared.'

He might well have added that, in the case of the novice or the new entrant into homosexual activity, reticence or shame might well delay further the tracing and discovery of the carrier.

Apart from these known consequences of fairly widespread homosexual behaviour and conduct, one other matter of particular importance should be noted. This is the effect of homosexual activity on marriage. It has to be accepted that, for the small percentage of males who are congenitally and irreversibly homosexual, marriage is not open or possible. They must seek such partnerships as they can amongst those whose orientation disposes them to homosexual overtures. But for those so disposed or orientated, but not yet committed, what effect will the acceptance of such overtures be likely to have on marriage? Again, precise information in relation to Ireland is not available. One can only look to what the Wolfenden Committee said in its report (para 55) before the changes in the law occurred in the United Kingdom:

> 'The second contention, that homosexual behaviour between males has a damaging effect on family life, may well be true. Indeed we have had evidence that it often is: cases in which homosexual behaviour on the part of the husband has broken up a marriage are by no means rare, and there are also cases in which a man in whom the homosexual component is relatively weak, nevertheless, derives such satisfaction from homosexual outlets that he does not enter upon a marriage which might have been successfully and happily consummated. We deplore this damage to what we regard as the basic unit of society.'

That view was based on the limited experience available to the Committee prior to any changes in the law. It indicates, however that homosexual activity and its encouragement may not be consistent with respect and regard for marriage as an institution. I would not think it unreasonable to conclude that an open and general increase in homosexual activity in any society must have serious consequences of a harmful nature so far as marriage is concerned.

I have been speaking of homosexuality and of its possible consequences in accordance with what, in my view, can be gathered from the evidence in this case. What I have said can be summarised as follows:

(1) Homosexuality has always been condemned in Christian teaching as being morally wrong. It has equally been regarded by society for many centuries as an offence against nature and a very serious crime.

(2) Exclusive homosexuality, whether the condition be congenital or acquired, can result in great distress and unhappiness for the individual and can lead to depression, despair and suicide.

(3) The homosexually orientated can be importuned into a homosexual lifestyle which can become habitual.

(4) Male homosexual conduct has resulted, in other countries, in the spread of all forms of venereal disease and this has now become a significant public-health problem in England.

(5) Homosexual conduct can be inimical to marriage and is *per se* harmful to it as an institution.

In the United Kingdom the decisive factor in bringing about decriminalisation of homosexuality was the acceptance of the view advocated by the Wolfenden Committee, and repeated in this case by the plaintiff, that homosexuality was concerned only with private morality and that the law has no business in entering into that field. Whether such a view can be accepted in Ireland depends not on what was done by a sovereign parliament in the United Kingdom but on what our Constitution ordains and requires.

The preamble to the Constitution proudly asserts the existence of God in the Most Holy Trinity and recites that the people of Ireland humbly acknowledge their obligation to 'our Divine Lord, Jesus Christ'. It cannot be doubted that the people so asserting and acknowledging their obligations to our Divine Lord Jesus Christ, were proclaiming a deep religious conviction and faith and an intention to adopt a Constitution consistent with that conviction and faith and with Christian beliefs. Yet it is suggested that, in the very act of so doing, the people rendered inoperative laws which had existed for hundreds of years prohibiting unnatural sexual conduct which Christian teaching held to be gravely sinful. It would require very clear and express provisions in the Constitution itself to convince me that such took place. When one considers that the conduct in question had been condemned consistently in the name of Christ for almost two thousand years and, at the time of the enactment of the Constitution, was prohibited as criminal by the laws in force in England, Wales, Scotland and Northern Ireland, the suggestion becomes more incomprehensible and difficult of acceptance.

But the plaintiff says that the continued operation of such laws was inconsistent with a right of privacy which he enjoys. Here, in so far as the law and the State are concerned, he asserts a 'no go area' in the field of private morality. I do not accept this view either as a general philosophical proposition concerning the purpose of law or as having particular reference to a right of privacy under our Constitution. I regard the State as having an interest in the general moral well-being of the community and as being entitled, where it is practicable to do so, to discourage conduct which is morally wrong and harmful to a way of life and to values which the State wishes to protect.

A right of privacy or, as it has been put, a right 'to be let alone' can never be absolute. There are many acts done in private which the State is entitled to condemn, whether such be done by an individual on his own or with another. The law has always condemned abortion, incest, suicide attempts, suicide pacts, euthanasia or mercy killing. These are prohibited simply because they are morally wrong and regardless of the fact, which may exist in some instances, that no harm or injury to others is involved. With homosexual conduct, the matter is not so simple or clear. Such conduct is, of course, morally wrong, and has been so regarded by mankind through the centuries. It cannot be said of it, however, as the plaintiff seeks to say, that no harm is done if it is conducted in private by consenting males. Very serious harm may in fact be involved. Such conduct, although carried on with full consent, may lead a mildly homosexually orientated person into a way of life from which he may never recover. As already indicated, known consequences are frustration, loneliness and even suicide. In addition, it is clearly established that an increase in the practice of homosexuality amongst males increases the incidence of all forms of venereal disease, including the incapacitating and often fatal disease of syphilis. Surely in the light of such possible consequences, no one could regard with equanimity the freeing of such conduct from all legal restraints with the certain result that it would increase and its known devotees multiply. These, however, are not the only considerations.

There is the effect of homosexuality on marriage. As long ago as 1957 the Wolfenden Committee acknowledged, in relation to Great Britain, the serious harm such conduct caused to marriage not only in turning men away from it as a partnership in life but also in breaking up existing marriages. That was the conclusion reached as to the state of facts before the criminal sanctions were removed. One can only suspect that, with the removal of such sanctions and with the encouragement thereby given to homosexual conduct, considerably more harm must have been caused in Great Britain to marriage as an institution. In Ireland, in this respect, the State has a particular duty. Article 41, s 3, sub-s 1, of the Constitution provides: 'The State pledges itself to guard with special care the institution of Marriage, on which the Family is founded, and to protect it against attack'. Surely, a law which prohibits acts and conduct by male citizens of a

> kind known to be particularly harmful to the institution of marriage cannot be regarded as inconsistent with a Constitution containing such a provision. On the ground of the Christian nature of our State and on the grounds that the deliberate practice of homosexuality is morally wrong, that it is damaging to the health both of individuals and the public and, finally, that it is potentially harmful to the institution of marriage, I can find no inconsistency with the Constitution in the laws which make such conduct criminal. It follows, in my view, that no right of privacy, as claimed by the plaintiff, can prevail against the operation of such criminal sanctions."

By contrast, Henchy and McCarthy JJ pointed out that positive law in Ireland did not criminalise all the seven deadly sins and that it was inappropriate to use natural law in the manner suggested by O'Higgins CJ.

Henchy J (dissenting):

> "Before entering on the precise question of unconstitutionality on which this appeal turns, I should like to point out that we are not called upon in this case to express an opinion upon whether the law on this topic should be as it is or upon what the purpose of the law should be. Such considerations are for moral philosophers, legal theorists, lawmakers and the like. In a case such as the present, where the legal materials we are considering are written instruments (ie, statutory provisions on the one hand and overriding constitutional provisions on the other) and are not amenable to the judicial development or extension which would be the case in regard to unwritten or case law, we must take those legal materials as we find them. The judicial function in a case such as this is to lay the impugned statutory provisions down beside the invoked constitutional provisions and if, in the light of the established or admitted facts, a comparison between the two sets of provisions shows a repugnancy, the statutory provisions must be struck down either wholly or in part - if the test of severability laid down [in] *Maher v The Attorney General*[319] is applicable.
>
> ... The main ground on which it is submitted that the impugned statutory provisions are unconstitutional is that they violate an essential component of the plaintiff's right of privacy. That a right of privacy inheres in each citizen by virtue of his human personality, and that such a right is constitutionally guaranteed as one of the unspecified personal rights comprehended by Article 40, s 3, are propositions that are well attested by previous decisions of this Court. What requires to be decided - and this seems to me to be the essence of this case - is whether that right of privacy, construed in the context of the Constitution as a whole and given its true evaluation or standing in the hierarchy of constitutional priorities, excludes as constitutionally inconsistent the impugned statutory provisions.

---

319. [1973] IR 140, at 147.

Having regard to the purposive Christian ethos of the Constitution, particularly as set out in the preamble ('to promote the common good, with due observance of Prudence, Justice and Charity, so that the dignity and freedom of the individual may be assured, true social order attained, the unity of our country restored, and concord established with other nations'), to the denomination of the State as 'sovereign, independent, democratic' in Article 5, and to the recognition, expressly or by necessary implication, of particular personal rights, such recognition being frequently hedged in by overriding requirements such as 'public order and morality' or 'the authority of the State' or 'the exigencies of the common good', there is necessarily given to the citizen, within the required social, political and moral framework, such a range of personal freedoms or immunities as are necessary to ensure his dignity and freedom as an individual in the type of society envisaged. The essence of those rights is that they inhere in the individual personality of the citizen in his capacity as a vital human component of the social, political and moral order posited by the Constitution.

Amongst those basic personal rights is a complex of rights which vary in nature, purpose and range (each necessarily being a facet of the citizen's core of individuality within the constitutional order) and which may be compendiously referred to as the right of privacy. An express recognition of such a right is the guarantee in Article 16, sub-s 4, that voting in elections for Dáil Éireann shall be by secret ballot. A constitutional right to marital privacy was recognised and implemented by this Court in *McGee v The Attorney General*;[320] the right there claimed and recognised being, in effect, the right of a married woman to use contraceptives, which is something which at present is declared to be morally wrong according to the official teaching of the Church to which about 95% of the citizens belong. There are many other aspects of the right of privacy, some yet to be given judicial recognition. It is unnecessary for the purpose of this case to explore them. It is sufficient to say that they would all appear to fall within a secluded area of activity or non-activity which may be claimed as necessary for the expression of an individual personality, for purposes not always necessarily moral or commendable, but meriting recognition in circumstances which do not engender considerations such as State security, public order or morality, or other essential components of the common good.

Put in specific terms, the central issue in this case is whether the plaintiff's claim to be entitled to engage in homosexual acts in private must give way to the right and duty of the State to uphold considerations of public order and morality. In my opinion the legal test by which that issue should be determined is this: where, as in this case, a pre-Constitution legislature has condemned as criminal all homosexual acts between males (ranging from

320. [1974] IR 284.

acts of gross indecency, the commission of which does not require even physical contact, to acts of sodomy) and thereby blights and thwarts in a variety of ways the life of a person who is by nature incapable of giving expression to his sexuality except by homosexual acts, and who wishes to be entitled to do so consensually in private, the onus lies on the Attorney General, representing the State, if he is to defeat the individual's claim, to show that to allow him that degree of privacy would be inconsistent with the maintenance of public order and morality.

In my judgment the Attorney General has signally failed to discharge that onus. In the High Court, ten witnesses were called, all on behalf of the plaintiff. Although homosexual acts in private between consenting adults have largely ceased to be criminal in England and Wales since 1967; although in most European countries for many years the legal position has been no less liberal; although a similar degree of decriminalisation has been in force for varying periods in different jurisdictions throughout the world, including some 20 or so States in the United States of America; and although there have been many studies by experts of the social, religious and other effects of such decriminalisation; not a single witness was called by the Attorney General to rebut the plaintiff's case that the degree of decriminalisation sought by him posed no real threat to public order or morality. On the contrary, the consensus of the evidence given was that the beneficial effects, both in terms of individual fulfilment of personality and of the social, political and religious mores of the community, that would flow from a relaxation of the impugned provisions would outweigh any possible ill-effects on society as a whole.

... It is an indisputable fact that the evidence of all ten witnesses condemned, in one degree or another, and for a variety of reasons, the impugned sections for being repugnant to the essential human needs of compulsive or obligatory homosexuals and as not being required by - indeed, as being inconsistent with - public order and morality or any of the other attributes comprehended by the constitutional concept of the common good.

In response to this massive and virtually unanimous volume of evidence, given almost entirely by experts in sociology, theology and psychiatry, the Attorney General adduced no oral evidence whatsoever. If the matters pleaded by him in his defence were susceptible of proof, at least to the extent of disproving or casting doubt on the conclusions expressed by the plaintiff and his witnesses, it would have been well within the resources and competence of the State to adduce such evidence. But the hearing in the High Court is notable for the total absence of controverting evidence. True, efforts were made in cross-examination to get witnesses to accept contrary opinions that were said to have been expressed in the writings or pronouncements of other experts or authorities. But a close study of the evidence shows that the largely unanimous conclusions expressed on oath were essentially as I have summarised them and that they stood uncontroverted at the end of the hearing of the evidence.

What choice, then, was open to the trial judge? In my opinion, since this was an oral hearing, on oath, carried out under our adversary system (which is based on the determination, from sworn testimony, according to the required onus and level of proof of the relevant issues), where the outcome of the case depended on a judicial conclusion from the actual or potential effect on our society of specified statutory provisions or of their alternatives, when the conclusions expressed overwhelmingly supported the plaintiff's case, the trial judge was bound in law to reject the Attorney General's defence and to uphold, at least in part, the plaintiff's case. The decision of this court in *Northern Bank Finance v Charlton*[321] shows that, if the judge had found the factual conclusions in accordance with the plaintiff's uncontroverted evidence, his findings could not be overturned on an appeal to this Court.

In the course of his judgment the judge said that what he had to decide was:

> '... whether there are grounds on which the legislature, under current social conditions and having regard to the prevailing ideas and concepts of morality and the current knowledge of matters affecting public health etc., could now reasonably come to the conclusion that the acts declared unlawful are such as ought to be prohibited for the attainment of the true social order mentioned in the preamble, the implementation of the principles of social policy directed by Article 45 and the preservation of the public order and morality mentioned in Article 40 of the Constitution.'

Assuming that to be a correct statement of the foundation on which the case fell to be decided, it was not open to the judge to disregard the consensus of the sworn testimony before him and, in the absence of any sworn evidence to the contrary, and relying presumably on suggestions made in the course of cross-examination and on his own intuition, to reach the conclusion that the impugned provisions, if now enacted would, regardless of their impact on the plaintiff and on those in like case, be constitutionally justifiable.

The question whether the constitutional provisions he relied on gave the necessary justification depended on a complex of expert evidential considerations - social, moral, medical and others - and, since the unrebutted consensus of the evidence was against the existence of such justification, the judge was debarred from holding otherwise. The position would be quite different if the Attorney General had chosen to present evidence to the contrary. But he decided not to, although it appears from the cross-examination that such evidence was available. As was made clear by the decision of this Court in *Ryan v The Attorney General*,[322] where a constitutional challenge depends on expert opinion about the actual or

321. [1979] IR 149.
322. [1965] IR 294.

potential effect of questioned statutory provisions, the constitutional point must be ruled on the basis of the facts or opinions as admitted to be correct or as duly found by the judge from the evidence given. Where the evidence given is entirely to one effect, it cannot be rejected.

The learned judge (who dealt with this difficult case with commendable thoroughness), in substituting his own conclusions on the personal and societal effects of the questioned provisions, seems to have laid undue stress on the fact that the prohibited acts, especially sodomy, are contrary to the standards of morality advocated by the Christian Churches in this State. With respect, I do not think that should be treated as a guiding consideration. What are known as the seven deadly sins are anathematised as immoral by all the Christian Churches, and it would have to be conceded that they are capable, in different degrees and in certain contexts, of undermining vital aspects of the common good. Yet it would be neither constitutionally permissible nor otherwise desirable to seek by criminal sanctions to legislate their commission out of existence in all possible circumstances. To do so would upset the necessary balance which the Constitution posits between the common good and the dignity and freedom of the individual. What is deemed necessary to his dignity and freedom by one may be abhorred by another as an exercise in immorality. The pluralism necessary for the preservation of constitutional requirements in the Christian, democratic State envisaged by the Constitution means that the sanctions of the criminal law may be attached to immoral acts only when the common good requires their proscription as crimes. As the most eminent theologians have conceded, the removal of the sanction of the criminal law from an immoral act does not necessarily imply an approval or condonation of that act. Here the consensus of the evidence was that the sweep of the criminal prohibition contained in the questioned provisions goes beyond the requirements of the common good; indeed, in the opinion of most of the witnesses it is inimical to the common good. Consequently, a finding of unconstitutionality was inescapable on the evidence.

Having given careful consideration to all the evidence, I find that the essence of the unconstitutionality claimed lies not in the prohibition, as a crime, of homosexual acts between consenting adult males but primarily in making that prohibition apply without qualification to consenting adult males who are exclusively and obligatorily homosexual. The combined effect of the questioned sections is to condemn such persons, who are destined by nature to be incapable of giving interpersonal outlet to their sexuality otherwise than by means of homosexual acts, to make the stark and (for them) inhumane choice between opting for total unequivocal sexual continence (because guilt for gross indecency may result from equivocal acts) and yielding to their primal sexual urges and thereby either committing a serious crime or leaving themselves open to objectionable and harmful intrusion by those who would wish to prevent such acts, or to intolerance, harassment, blackmail and other forms of cruelty at the hands of those who would batten on the revulsion that such acts elicit in most heterosexuals.

One way or the other, the impugned provisions seem doomed to extinction. Whether they be struck down by this Court for being unconstitutional or whether they be deemed invalid elsewhere in accordance with the decision in *Dudgeon v United Kingdom*[323] (for being in contravention of the European Convention for the Protection of Human Rights and Fundamental Freedoms) they will require to be replaced with appropriate statutory provisions. It would not be constitutional to decriminalise all homosexual acts, any more than it would be constitutional to decriminalise all heterosexual acts. Public order and morality, the protection of the young, of the weak-willed, of those who may readily be subject to undue influence, and of others who should be deemed to be in need of protection; the maintenance inviolate of the family as the natural primary and fundamental unit of society; the upholding of the institution of marriage; the requirements of public health; these and other aspects of the common good require that homosexual acts be made criminal in many circumstances. The true and justifiable gravamen of the complaint against the sections under review is that they are in constitutional error for overreach or overbreadth. They lack necessary discrimination and precision as to when and how they are to apply.

The opinion expressed by some of the witnesses in the High Court that homosexual acts in private should be decriminalised must not be taken literally. Indeed it is likely that most, if not all, of the witnesses who gave that opinion would wish, on mature consideration, to qualify it. Even the liberalising Sexual Offences Act 1967, which was passed in England in consequence of the Wolfenden Report, makes extensive exceptions (e.g., in respect of members of the armed services, in respect of acts committed on merchant ships, and because of limitations imposed by the nature of the statutory definitions) to the immunity from prosecution granted. Similar restricting limitations have been inserted in the Homosexual Offences (Northern Ireland) Order 1982, which was enacted for the purpose of removing the incongruity in that jurisdiction between the now-impugned statutory provisions and the European Convention, as found in the *Dudgeon* decision.

I make reference to these matters to indicate that, despite my finding of unconstitutionality in the impugned sections on the ground that by their overreach and lack of precision and of due discrimination, they trench on an area of personal intimacy and seclusion which requires to be treated as inviolate for the expression of those primal urges, functions and aspirations which are integral to the human condition of certain kinds of homosexuals; save in circumstances when the common good requires otherwise, the Constitution leaves a wide range of choice to the Oireachtas in framing a

323. (1981) 3 EHRR 149.

law in place of the questioned provisions. Not only will the Oireachtas be empowered to make homosexual acts criminal but, for the purpose of upholding the requirements of the common good in its full constitutional connotation, it will be necessary for such legislation to hedge in such immunity from criminal sanctions as it may think fit to confer (on acts of a homosexual nature in private between consenting adults) with appropriate definitions of adulthood, consent and privacy and with such exceptions relating to prostitution, immoral exploitation, publicity, drug abuse, commercialisation, family relationships and such other matters or areas of exception as the Oireachtas may justifiably consider necessary for the preservation of public order and decency."

[15.130] The majority in the *Norris* case clearly took a 'conservative' natural law approach to the interpretative issue posed and O'Higgins CJ appeared critical of the view of John Stuart Mill, as adopted by the Wolfenden Committee in 1957, that there were certain matters which were not the law's business. The reference to St Paul by O'Higgins CJ is reminiscent of Kenny J's allusion to the Papal Encyclical in *Ryan v Attorney General*,[324] but, arguably, it seemed to be more conservative than that of Walsh J in the *McGee* case. Although Walsh J was not a member of the Supreme Court in *Norris*,[325] he agreed with the essential conclusion that, while the right of privacy under natural law prohibited the State from interfering with the right of married couples to use contraceptives, the State was entitled to prevent homosexual men from engaging in consensual sexual acts.[326] Thus, Walsh J's natural law approach was not as extensive as the purposive and harmonious approach favoured by Henchy J in *Norris*, which appeared to involve a more secular interpretation of the Constitution. Despite the emphasis by the majority in *Norris* on a 'conservative' view of

324. [1965] IR 294: see para **[15.126]**.

325. He was, at the time, President of the Law Reform Commission and thus the 'sixth judge' of the Supreme Court: see para **[4.41]**.

326. See his dissenting judgment as a judge of the European Court of Human Rights in *Norris v Ireland* (1988) 13 EHRR 186, a successful claim by the plaintiff in *Norris v Attorney General* that the State was in breach of the European Convention on Human Rights in continuing to maintain ss 60 and 61 of the 1861 Act on the statute books. This confirmed its earlier decision in *Dudgeon v United Kingdom* (1981) 4 EHRR 149 (referred to by both O'Higgins CJ and Henchy J in *Norris v Attorney General*), in which it had also held that ss 60 and 61 of the 1861 Act were in breach of the Convention. In his judgment, Walsh J reviewed in some detail the views expressed by Mill, Devlin and Hart (see para **[15.123]**) on the role of the law in areas of personal morality. He concluded that the State was entitled to take a different view on homosexual sexual acts from that of other States, and on the basis of this 'margin of appreciation' should not have been found in breach of the Convention. In the wake of the majority decision, the Criminal Law (Sexual Offences) Act 1993 repealed ss 60 and 61 of the 1861 Act and replaced them with provisions which no longer make buggery between consenting adults a criminal offence.

natural law, the earlier acceptance by the Supreme Court in *McGee* of the right of privacy led to concern that the right to choose methods of contraception could be extended to the right to choose the termination of a pregnancy, that is, a right to abortion,[327] even though this had been expressly disavowed by some of the judges in *McGee* and by others in later cases.[328] The campaign to ensure that abortion would not be introduced by a constitutional 'test case' on the right to privacy culminated in the insertion of Article 40.3.3° into the Constitution, which provides:

> The State acknowledges the right to life of the unborn and, with due regard to the equal right to life of the mother, guarantees in its laws to respect, and, as far as practicable, by its laws to defend and vindicate that right.

Those supporting its wording intended that it would prohibit abortion, while also preserving existing arrangements to protect the life of the mother. These included surgical interventions in ectopic pregnancies, that is where the foetus is outside the womb and is not viable but where the mother's life may be at risk unless the foetus is removed. However, the intention to ensure that such interventions would not be prohibited produced a wording that some commentators, including the then Attorney General, considered could be open to the interpretation that abortion was being made lawful in some limited circumstances.[329] The insertion of Article 40.3.3° was followed by a series of cases which prohibited the distribution of information concerning abortion services abroad, including the addresses of abortion clinics in Britain.[330]

---

327. Abortion, the procuring of a miscarriage, is a criminal offence under the Offences Against the Person Act 1861, ss 58 and 59, the sections immediately preceding those which made buggery a criminal offence and which were discussed in *Norris v Attorney General* [1984] IR 36.

328. Eg, Walsh J in *G v An Bord Uchtála* [1980] IR 32. In the *Norris* case, McCarthy J (who was one of the two judges in the minority of the view that ss 60 and 61 of the 1861 Act were inconsistent with the Constitution) stated, *obiter*, that he would not declare invalid ss 58 and 59 of the 1861 Act if the issue were to arise. He was aware at the time (1983) that the campaign to insert Article 40.3.3° was nearing fruition. Despite this comment from a judge who would have been regarded as the most 'liberal' on the Supreme Court at that time, those who feared that the right to privacy would lead, at some time, to a 'test' case on abortion pointed out that this had happened in the United States Supreme Court in 1972 in *Roe v Wade*, 410 US 113 (1972), a year before the decision in *McGee v Attorney General*. See generally Hogan & Whyte, *op cit*, pp 790-810 on the connection between *McGee* and the abortion referenda and litigation between 1983 and 1993.

329. See generally Hesketh, *The Second Partitioning of Ireland?* (Bramsda, 1990).

330. Eg, *Attorney General (Society for the Protection of Unborn Children Ltd) v Open Door Counselling Ltd* [1988] IR 593; *Society for the Protection of Unborn Children Ltd v Coogan* [1989] IR 734.

Attorney General v X

[15.131] In 1992, in *Attorney General v X*,[331] the High Court granted the Attorney General an injunction prohibiting the defendant, a 14-year-old girl who had become pregnant having been raped, from leaving the State with a view to obtaining an abortion. The girl had stated that she would commit suicide if she was required to bring the pregnancy to full term. In the High Court, Article 40.3.3° was interpreted to mean that abortion was prohibited in such circumstances. However, on appeal, the Supreme Court held, by a 4-1 majority, that Article 40.3.3° permitted abortions where, as here, the right to life of the mother was in immediate danger. The majority reached this conclusion by a textual analysis of Article 40.3.3° and accepted that it should adopt the harmonious approach to the constitutional text. The Court accepted that, in certain circumstances, there could be a conflict between 'the right to life of the unborn' and 'the equal right to life of the mother'; that where such conflict of rights could not be avoided, the Constitution required that its provisions be interpreted harmoniously and that the rights thereby guaranteed should be interpreted in concert in accordance with the concepts of prudence, justice and charity. Finlay CJ stated:

> "I accept the submission made on behalf of the Attorney General, that the doctrine of the harmonious interpretation of the Constitution involves in this case a consideration of the constitutional rights and obligations of the mother of the unborn child and the interrelation of those rights and obligations with the rights and obligations of other people and, of course, with the right to life of the unborn child as well.
>
> Such a harmonious interpretation of the Constitution carried out in accordance with concepts of prudence, justice and charity, as they have been explained in the judgment of Walsh J in *McGee v Attorney General*[332] leads me to the conclusion that in vindicating and defending as far as practicable the right of the unborn to life but at the same time giving due regard to the right of the mother to life, the court must, amongst the matters to be so regarded, concern itself with the position of the mother within a family group, with persons on whom she is dependent, with, in other instances, persons who are dependent upon her and her interaction with other citizens and members of society in the areas in which her activities occur. Having regard to that conclusion, I am satisfied that the test proposed on behalf of the Attorney General that the life of the unborn could only be terminated if it were established that an inevitable or immediate risk to the life of the mother existed, for the avoidance of which a

331. [1992] 1 IR 1.

332. [1974] IR 284: see para **[15.128]**.

> termination of the pregnancy was necessary, insufficiently vindicates the mother's right to life.
>
> I, therefore, conclude that the proper test to be applied is that if it is established as a matter of probability that there is a real and substantial risk to the life, as distinct from the health, of the mother, which can only be avoided by the termination of her pregnancy, such termination is permissible, having regard to the true interpretation of Article 40.3.3° of the Constitution."

The acceptance by the Supreme Court of the harmonious approach and the submission by counsel for the Attorney General in the *X* case that Article 40.3.3° authorised abortion in limited circumstances appeared to confirm the views expressed in 1983 that the text might authorise abortion in certain circumstances, but it was sharply criticised for appearing to disregard the apparent intention of those who voted for the insertion of Article 40.3.3° into the Constitution less than ten years before.[333]

[15.132] It was in the context of this conclusion that the debate then arose in 1992 as to whether the courts were obliged to interpret the Constitution in the light of the natural law, that is whether natural law took priority over the text of the Constitution.

[15.133] In response to the *X* case, three further proposed amendments to Article 40.3.3° were put to a referendum in late 1992. The first of these concerned the 'substantive' issue of abortion, and proposed to insert an additional clause into Article 40.3.3° authorising abortion where the life of the mother was at risk, though excluding the risk of suicide.[334] This was rejected in the referendum, but two further clauses were approved, and these provide that Article 40.3.3° 'shall not limit freedom to travel between the State and another state and 'shall not limit freedom to obtain or make available, in the State, subject to such conditions as may be laid down by law, information relating to services lawfully available in another state.'

Regulation of Information Bill 1995 case

[15.134] The latter clause concerning information resulted in the Oireachtas passing the Regulation of Information (Services Outside the State for the Termination of Pregnancies) Bill 1995. In *In re the Regulation of Information (Services Outside the State for the Termination of Pregnancies)*

333. This was noted by the dissenting judge, Hederman J. See also the extensive critique in Byrne and Binchy, *Annual Review of Irish Law 1992* (Round Hall Press, 1994), pp 159-85.

334. The proposed clause was: 'It shall be unlawful to terminate the life of the unborn unless such termination is necessary to save the life, as distinct from the health, of the mother where there is an illness or disorder of the mother giving rise to a real and substantial risk to her life, not being a risk of self-destruction.'

Bill 1995,[335] the Court found that the Bill was not repugnant to the Constitution.[336] In the course of argument in the case, it was suggested that the 1995 Bill was repugnant to the Constitution since it was in conflict with natural law. The judgment of the Court, delivered by Hamilton CJ, stated:

> "These arguments raise the question of the role of the natural law in the development of constitutional jurisprudence with regard to the identification 'of the personal rights of the citizen' referred to in Article 40.3.1° of the Constitution and the guarantee therein set forth on the part of the State to respect, and as far as practicable, by its laws to defend and vindicate such rights.
>
> It is fundamental to this argument that, what is described as `the natural law' is the fundamental law of this State and as such is antecedent and superior to all positive law, including the Constitution and that it is impermissible for the people to exercise the power of amendment of the Constitution by way of variation, addition or repeal, as permitted by Article 46 of the Constitution unless such amendment is compatible with the natural law and existing provisions of the Constitution and if they purport to do so, such amendment would have no effect.
>
> The court does not accept this argument."

[15.135] For the first time, the Supreme Court was required to consider whether natural law was superior to the Constitution. The Court rejected this argument, and concluded that the Constitution was the supreme law in the State. Having reviewed various provisions of the Constitution limiting the powers of the executive and legislative branches and the case law on Article 40.3, the Court commented:

> "From a consideration of all the cases which recognised the existence of a personal right which was not specifically enumerated in the Constitution, it is manifest that the court in each such case had satisfied itself that such personal right was one which could be reasonably implied from and was guaranteed by the provisions of the Constitution, interpreted in accordance with its ideas of prudence, justice and charity. The courts, as they were and are bound to, recognised the Constitution as the fundamental law of the State to which the organs of the State were subject and at no stage recognised the provisions of the natural law as superior to the Constitution.
>
> The people were entitled to amend the Constitution in accordance with the provisions of Article 46 of the Constitution and the Constitution as so amended by the fourteenth amendment is the fundamental and supreme law of the State representing as it does the will of the people."

---

335. [1995] 1 IR 1.

336. The Bill was enacted as the Regulation of Information (Services Outside the State for the Termination of Pregnancies) Act 1995.

While the decision of the Court establishes that natural law cannot take priority over the text of the Constitution, it nonetheless remains that the Constitution invokes 'higher law' principles which require elucidation in order to interpret its meaning. Thus, it would seem wrong to conclude that the *Regulation of Information Bill 1995* case signalled the 'death of natural law'.[337] This can be supported by referring to one other decision of the Court.

Ward of Court case

[15.136] Just over two months after its decision in the *Regulation of Information Bill* case, the Supreme Court was faced with another difficult issue. In *In re a Ward of Court*,[338] the family of a woman who had suffered irreversible brain damage during surgery in April 1972, and who had subsequently been made a ward of court,[339] applied for an order that all artificial nutrition and hydration of her should cease. The woman was described as being in a near-persistent or permanent vegetative state (near-PVS); she appeared to have minimal cognitive capacity but seemed to recognise her family and the nursing staff who cared for her and reacted to strangers by showing distress. Her heart and lungs functioned normally, but she was unable to speak, was spastic, could not swallow, was incontinent and bedridden. She received nutrition through a gastronomy tube, which had been inserted under general anaesthetic into her stomach. It appeared that her condition was unlikely to improve. The institution in which she received medical treatment and care refused her family's request to remove the gastronomy tube. The issue raised for the Court was whether, after 22 years in this condition, it was permissible to order that the nutrition and hydration provided by the gastronomy tube be removed. This in turn raised the question of the extent of the right to life of the woman and whether any circumstances existed in which the courts could, in effect, decide not to prolong life.

[15.137] In approaching the case, the Court agreed with the distinction drawn by Taylor LJ (later Lord Taylor LCJ) in *In re J (A Minor)*[340] between terminating life, which he had stated was unlawful, and not prolonging life, which might be permissible in certain circumstances. Having quoted the distinction drawn by Taylor LJ, Hamilton CJ stated:

337. See Twomey, 'The death of the Natural Law?' (1995) 13 ILT 270.
338. [1995] 2 ILRM 401.
339. On the wardship jurisdiction, see para **[5.61]**.
340. [1991] Fam 33.

> "Having regard to the provisions of Article 40.3.2° of the Constitution, this statement of the law applies with even greater force in this jurisdiction. Even in the case of the most horrendous disability, any course of action or treatment aimed at terminating life or accelerating death is unlawful."

The Court went on to consider whether the order sought by the woman's family was permissible. By a majority of 4 to 1, the Court accepted that it was. Hamilton CJ referred to the decision of the Court in the *X* case and its use of the harmonious approach of constitutional interpretation where, as in that case, the right to life of the unborn and the right to life of the mother appeared to conflict. Hamilton CJ commented:

> "I am satisfied that in this case, if there was an interaction of constitutional rights which I was not capable of harmonising, the right to life would take precedence over any other rights. The nature of the right to life and its importance imposes a strong presumption in favour of taking all steps capable of preserving it save in exceptional circumstances. The problem is to define such circumstances. The definition of such circumstances must, of necessity, involve a determination of the right to life acknowledged by the Constitution."

He referred to the judgment of Walsh J in *G v An Bord Uchtála*,[341] in which he had stated that the right to life involved certain ancillary rights. In the context of the woman in the *Ward of Court* case, Hamilton CJ continued:

> "These rights include the right to live life in its fullest content, to enjoy the support and comfort of her family, to social contact with her peers, to education, to the practice of her religion, to work, to marry and have children, to privacy, to bodily integrity and to self-determination. These rights are not, however, unqualified: they may be subject to the constitutional rights of others and to the requirements of the common good. They, however, spring from the right to life which is recognised by the Constitution.
>
> As the process of dying is part, and an ultimate inevitable consequence, of life, the right to life necessarily implies the right to have nature take its course and to die a natural death and, unless the individual concerned so wishes, not to have life artificially maintained by the provision of nourishment by abnormal artificial means, which have no curative effect and which are intended merely to prolong life.
>
> This right, as so defined, does not include the right to have life terminated or death accelerated and is confined to the natural process of dying. No person has the right to terminate his or her life or to accelerate or have accelerated his or her death.

341. [1980] IR 32: see para **[15.130]**.

> In this case, the [woman's] ... life is being artificially maintained by the provision of life sustaining nourishment through a gastronomy tube inserted in her body. Such treatment is in no way, nor intended to be, curative and she will continue to be in the condition in which she now is, and has been for over twenty years, if she continues to be provided with nourishment in this manner."

Hamilton CJ thus accepted that, in limited circumstances, the right to life included the right to die, to 'let nature take its course'. He concluded that the particular circumstances of this case involved such exceptional circumstances. He stated: 'The true cause of the [woman's] death will not be the withdrawal of [the] nourishment but the injuries which she sustained on 26 April 1972 [during her surgery]'.

[15.138] Although the judgment of Hamilton CJ in the *Ward of Court* case would appear to support the overriding importance of the harmonious approach to the exclusion of any natural law or religious component, this may be an inaccurate view. Indeed, in the *Ward of Court* case, Hamilton CJ referred to the right of the woman to the practice of her religion, that the woman's family had approached the case from a religious viewpoint seeking to ensure that her religious faith would be upheld and had introduced evidence from moral theologians who had advised the family that withdrawal of the gastronomy tube was not contrary to their religious beliefs. Moreover, in a judgment concurring in the decision that the gastronomy tube be withdrawn, Denham J quoted with approval the comment of Walsh J in *Quinn's Supermarket Ltd v Attorney General*,[342] that the Constitution 'reflects a firm conviction that we are a religious people.' She commented:

> "This foundation is an aid in interpreting the law and the Constitution. In regard specifically to the right to life, it enables the interpretation to be inclusive of a spiritual or religious component. This approach is signalled in the first words of Article 40.3.1° where the unqualified 'respect' for life is stated. In respecting a person's death, we are also respecting their life - giving to it sanctity. That concept of sanctity is an inclusive view which recognises that in our society persons, whether members of a religion, or not, are all under the Constitution protected by respect for human life. A view that life must be preserved at all costs does not sanctify life. A person, and/or her family, who have a view as to the intrinsic sanctity of the life in question are, in fact, encompassed in the constitutional mandate to protect life for the common good; what is being protected (and not denied or ignored or overruled) is the sanctity of that person's life. To care for the dying, to love and cherish them, and to free them from suffering rather than

342. [1972] IR 1.

simply to postpone death, is to have fundamental respect for the sanctity of life and its end."

Thus, while the harmonious interpretation may be said to represent the most significant canon of interpretation of the Constitution, the religious or spiritual or natural law component remains as a significant aid to its interpretation. The judgment of Denham J in the *Ward of Court* case thus indicates that it would be inaccurate to describe contemporary constitutional interpretation as comprising an exclusively secular approach; thus a 'liberal' version of natural law may be relevant in some instances.[343]

[6] REPORT OF CONSTITUTION REVIEW GROUP

[15.139] In 1995,[344] a Constitution Review Group was established with a general remit to review the terms of the 1937 Constitution 'to establish those areas where constitutional change may be desirable or necessary, with a view to assisting the all-Party Committee on the Constitution, to be established by the Oireachtas.' The Group was precluded from examining Articles 2 and 3, divorce, the right to bail, cabinet confidentiality and votes for emigrants, which were the subject of separate consideration.[345] The Group published its final report, running to over 700 pages, in May 1996.[346] Aside from those matters on which it was prevented by its terms of references form commenting, the Report is a comprehensive analysis of the 1937 Constitution and contains wide-ranging proposals for the amendment of the Constitution. It is not proposed to summarise the content of the Report. We mention some recommendations by way of illustration only.

[15.140] The Group recommended reform of the 1937 Constitution rather than its replacement. Indeed, the essential distribution of powers between the three arms of government, executive, legislative and judicial, would remain intact if the Group's recommendations were enacted by the people.

343. On the complex medical ethical and legislative issues arising from the *Ward of Court* case, which was widely reported in the media as the 'right to die' case, see Tomkin and Hanafin, 'Medical Treatment at Life's End: The Need for Legislation' (1995) 1 *Medico-Legal Journal of Ireland* 3.

344. A Committee on the Constitution had previously been established in the 1960s: *Report of the Committee on the Constitution* (Pr 9817, 1967). One of the few recommendations of this Committee actually implemented was the deletion by the Fifth Amendment of the Constitution Act 1972 of the reference to the 'special position' of the Roman Catholic church.

345. A referendum on divorce was held in 1995, resulting in the removal of the ban on divorce in Article 41: see para **[15.91]**. At the time of writing (July 1996), a referendum on bail is anticipated: see para **[15.83]**.

346. *Report of the Constitution Review Group* (Pn 2632, 1996).

However, the Report recommended a full review of the role and functions of the Senate.[347] It also proposed a specific reference be included concerning membership of the United Nations.[348] As to the courts, the Group recommended the retention of the existing integrated court system and did not recommend, for example, the establishment of a Constitutional Court.[349] Nor did it recommend change to Article 34 concerning the delineation of the judicial power.[350] In connection with fundamental rights, a number of significant changes were proposed. Thus, the Group recommended that Article 40.3 be amended to provide a comprehensive list of fundamental rights to take account of those identified to date as well as those contained in the European Convention on Human Rights and Fundamental Freedoms and the United Nations International Covenant on Civil and Political Rights.[351] At the time of writing (July 1996), the Group's Report has been referred to an Oireachtas Committee on the Constitution. It remains to be seen whether the Group's Report will be implemented.

347. *Ibid*, pp 65-71.
348. *Ibid*, p 113.
349. *Ibid*, pp 143-4.
350. *Ibid*, pp 146-57.
351. *Ibid*, pp 245-64. See also para **[17.25]**.

Chapter 16

European Community Law and the European Union

[1] INTRODUCTION

[16.01] On 1 January 1973, Ireland became a Member State of what was then the European Communities. This involved the amendment of Article 29 of the 1937 Constitution to enable the State ratify a Treaty of Accession to three international organisations or Communities, the European Coal and Steel Community (ECSC), the European Atomic Energy Community (EAEC or Euratom) and the European Economic Community (EEC). Each Community had been established by three separate Treaties signed by six States in the 1950s; the effect of the referendum was that these three Treaties were incorporated into Irish law. The three original Treaties were later amended, notably by the Single European Act 1986, and the Treaty on European Union 1992.

[16.02] As we will see, one of the effects of the Treaty on European Union was that the Treaty Establishing the European Economic Community, the most significant of the three Treaties, was re-named the Treaty Establishing the European Community. We will refer in this chapter to this Treaty as the EC Treaty. Another effect of the Treaty on European Union was to establish an entity called the European Union. By 1995, there were 15 Member States of the European Union.

[16.03] This chapter deals primarily with the legal effects of the State's membership of the European Union.[1] Membership required the State to subscribe to a new legal system or order, thus creating a new source of law in Ireland, European Community law. One of the most significant aspects of this new source of law is that it derives from an institutional structure that operates outside the State, by contrast with the sources of law discussed in previous chapters.

1. The leading text describing the impact of European Community law in Ireland is McMahon and Murphy, *European Community Law in Ireland* (Butterworths, 1989). For an overview of the impact prior to the Treaty on European Union, see McCutcheon, 'The Legal System', in Keatinge (ed) *Ireland and EC Membership Evaluated* (London, 1991), pp 209-229.

Financial and economic context

[16.04] There are a number of reasons why Ireland joined the European Communities in 1973, and we will refer to one just three only. Since the establishment of the Irish Free State in 1922, the United Kingdom (and in particular England) remained a major trading partner for the State. When, in the 1960s, the United Kingdom began negotiations to join the European Communities it was necessary from a strategic point of view for Ireland to do likewise. In addition, it was considered that membership would open up new markets for Irish companies and thus lessen dependency on the British market in the long term. The European Communities had also already established policies which it was considered would benefit certain sectors, in particular those in agriculture and associated industries. With the emergence of globalisation of trade in the 1980s and 1990s, membership continued to be of increased significance.

[16.05] In an international trading context, the European Union has become a single trading entity consisting of 15 Member States, with a combined population of over 370 million people. By 1994, its combined Gross Domestic Product (GDP) was worth ECU 6,190 billion, compared with a GDP for the United States of America of ECU 6,245 billion and for Japan of ECU 2,408 billion. The Federal Republic of Germany accounted for almost 30% of the total GDP of the European Union; indeed 80% of its total GDP is accounted for by four Member States, Germany, France, Italy and the United Kingdom.[2]

[16.06] The European Union is financed from two sources: customs duties imposed on goods imported into the Union and other contributions from the 15 Member States themselves. In 1994, this combined income came to a total of over £54 billion. About 30% of this annual income was contributed by Germany, France being the next major contributor with 19% of the total, followed by Italy at 14.6% and the United Kingdom at 11.6%. This income is then re-distributed among the Member States under the various laws and policies adopted by the Community and Union. By far the biggest single item of this redistribution or spending comes under the heading of support for agriculture, which in 1994 accounted for more than £25 billion, or just under 50% of the total European Union budget.

[16.07] As for the contribution made by Ireland in 1994, this came to £543 million, about 1% of the total income of the European Union. However, Ireland's receipts from the European Union budget in 1994 came to £1.95

---

2. Source: Eurostat, *Statistics in Focus: Economy and Finance*, 1996, No 1 (published by the Commission of the European Communities).

billion, or just under 4% of the total budget. It may be noted that the total budget of the State for 1994 was almost £10 billion, so that the income from the European Union represented nearly 20% of total Government income in 1994.

[16.08] It is clear that, in financial terms, Ireland is a net beneficiary of European Union membership. Of course, membership is not simply a one-way street in this respect, and it involves certain responsibilities as well as entitlements. For example, the State is required to allow virtually unrestricted access to the Irish market for goods and services from other Member States and may not enact any protectionist laws to shield industry in Ireland from foreign competition. The political arguments about the benefits and losses arising from membership have been debated in the years prior to and since 1973. In general terms, it may be said that the arguments for membership have been supported by a majority of the State's population, though this is not to say that Ireland contains no 'Euro-sceptics'.

[2] Origins of the European Communities

[16.09] The history of the European Union begins with the aftermath of World War II. The widespread devastation throughout Europe in 1945, whether in terms of the effect of the Holocaust, the virtual economic ruin of the Allied and Axis States or the breakdown of the pre-war monarchies, brought home the need for complete restructuring of European, and world, institutions. The establishment of the United Nations Organisation in 1945[3] can be seen as the first move in the direction of establishing a new world order. In Europe, it was recognised that institutional change was necessary to avoid future wars on the European mainland. A number of 'grand ideas' for closer co-operation between all the Allied powers were presented, some leading to the creation of enduring organisations, others remaining as ideas and little more.

Military co-operation: NATO and WEU

[16.10] On the military front, the establishment of the North Atlantic Treaty Organisation (NATO) brought military co-operation between the United States and the major European Allied States, acting as a counterpoint in the Cold War to the Warsaw Pact alliance of the States of Central and Eastern Europe. The European Allies also formed an organisation called the Western European Union (WEU), with slightly less overt Cold War connotations of military co-operation and mutual defence.

3. See generally on international law para **[17.01]**.

Human rights protection: Council of Europe

[16.11] In terms of human rights protection, the Convention for the Protection of Human Rights and Fundamental Freedoms, signed in 1950 by the States of the Council of Europe, established a basis for the protection of those basic rights that had been so clearly negated in World War II. A novel feature of the Convention, in the context of the early 1950s, was that it established a Commission on Human Rights with power to hear complaints from individuals concerning human rights violations. Before the 1950 Convention, such international agreements tended to confer rights only on States to lodge complaints against other States. The Convention also established a Court of Human Rights to operate as decision-maker on whether the Convention itself had been violated.[4]

Economic co-operation

[16.12] On the economic front, the end of World War II presented two major problems. First, the need to rebuild the economies of Europe and, second, the prevention of future wars based on economic aggression. The general need for the States of Europe to co-operate to achieve these aims was recognised, and continues to be recognised in the late 1990s, but putting detailed reality on that idea was more difficult. What later became the enormously influential trading bloc the European Union began in 1952 in modest circumstances.

[3] THE THREE EUROPEAN COMMUNITIES

1. The European Coal and Steel Community

[16.13] The European Coal and Steel Community (ECSC), was established by a Treaty signed in Paris in April 1951 by the six original Member States, France, Germany, Italy, Belgium, the Netherlands and Luxembourg. This Treaty became known as the 'Treaty of Paris'. The ECSC Treaty, which came into effect in July 1952, aimed at ensuring the peaceful and co-operative development of the coal and steel industries of the six Member States, especially those of France, Germany and Italy. These were the industries that had formed the basis both for the industrial development of those States but to some extent also the two World Wars of the 20th century. The ECSC Treaty provided that the coal and steel industry in the six Member States would be developed and co-ordinated on an agreed basis by a full-time ECSC High Authority acting in conjunction with a Council of Ministers representing the governments of the Member States. It also

4. See further para **[17.08]**.

established an Assembly to represent the peoples of the Member States and a Court of Justice to ensure the observance of the legal rules that were to be agreed by the ECSC institutions.

[16.14] The ECSC was to prove a success and the institutional framework it established became the model for two further Treaties and Communities established in 1957 by the same six Member States. The other two Communities, the European Atomic Energy Community (EAEC or Euratom) and the European Economic Community (EEC), were established by two Treaties signed on the same day in Rome in March 1957. Although there are, therefore, two 'Treaties of Rome', the title 'Treaty of Rome' is usually taken to refer to the Treaty establishing the EEC.

2. The European Atomic Energy Community

[16.15] The EAEC or Euratom Treaty, which came into force in January 1958, followed the pattern of the ECSC Treaty in that it was confined to a relatively narrow sector of economic activity, in this instance the development of the civil nuclear energy industry (the military side of the industry being excluded).

3. The European Economic Community

[16.16] The EC Treaty, which also came into force in January 1958, followed the pattern of the other two Treaties in terms of the institutional structures it established: a Commission (the equivalent of the ECSC High Authority) sharing decision-making powers with a Council representing Ministers from the governments of the Member States. An Assembly and Court of Justice were also established. Legislative mechanisms for the enforcement of Community rules were also included in the Treaty. In that context, the Commission and the Court of Justice were the focus of procedures for the enforcement of the legal obligations created by the Treaty. It is also important to note that the Treaty differed from the other two Treaties in that, as we shall see, it appeared to cover virtually all aspects of economic activity, hence the emphasis of this chapter on the EC Treaty.

The aims of the European Community

[16.17] The EC Treaty is a lengthy document, comprising over 200 Articles, and it deals with the organisation of virtually all commercial and economic activity, including agriculture, manufacturing and services, whether in the public sector or private sector. The overall aim of the Treaty is to ensure that the Member States create a single trading entity, within which any obstacles to free trade would be eliminated.

Ever Closer Union

[16.18] The first words of the Preamble to the EC Treaty, provide that the original six signatory Member States were:

> DETERMINED to lay the foundations of an ever closer union among the peoples of Europe.

It must be said that, even after the amendments made by subsequent Treaties, these words remain in place, indicating that the 'ever closer union' remains an objective rather than a concrete achievement. Indeed, an enduring debate since the 1950s has been the extent to which what is now the European Union should be confined to economic co-operation or should extend to closer political co-operation and union. While some States would wish to see the European Union restricted to economic co-operation, the history of events since the 1950s indicates a gradual, if piecemeal, movement in the direction of closer political integration or union. However, this remains a controversial issue of political debate and is essentially outside the scope of this text.[5]

Common Market

[16.19] In 1957, Article 2 of the EC Treaty specified that:

> The Community shall have as its task, by establishing a common market, to promote throughout the Community a harmonious development of economic activities.

The phrase 'Common Market' came to encompass the three European Communities. The fact that the phrase 'common market' appears in the EC Treaty indicates it is the most important of the three Treaties. However, as with the idea of 'an ever closer union', it must be said that, the idea of a 'common market' has not been fully achieved, though considerable progress has been made since 1957.

Transitional period to common market

[16.20] In 1957, Article 7 of the EC Treaty had stated:

> The common market shall be progressively established during a transitional period of twelve years.

This transitional period, which Article 7 divided into three stages of four years each, would end in January 1970 when the common market should have been fully in place. The target date proved impossible to meet, for

5. There is an enormous literature on the political development of the European Community and Union. For a discussion, see Keatinge (ed), *op cit*.

reasons which included an insistence that the legal measures needed to achieve the common market be arrived at by unanimous agreement of the Member States.[6]

Internal market: 1992

[16.21] The Single European Act 1986 inserted a new Article 7a into the EC Treaty, setting a further 'target date' of 1992 for achieving an updated version of the 'common market', the 'Internal Market'. Even 1992 proved somewhat ambitious, though certainly the vast bulk of what constitutes a single market had been put in place or was at an advanced stage by the end of 1992.

Community activities

[16.22] In 1957, Article 3 of the EC Treaty contained some of the specific activities of the Community in order to achieve the task established in Article 2. Among these activities were:

> the elimination, as between Member States, of customs duties and quantitative restrictions on the import and export of goods, and of all other measures having equivalent effect;
>
> ... the abolition ... of obstacles to the free movement of goods, persons, services and capital;
>
> ... the approximation of the laws of Member States to the extent required for the functioning of the common market.

The Four Freedoms and the Internal Market

[16.23] As well as the phrase 'common market', the idea of 'The Four Freedoms'(from the reference in Article 3 to free movement of goods, persons, services and capital) became another phrase that was used to sum up the objectives of the European Community. It is notable that the 'Four Freedoms' appeared again in the amendments made to the EC Treaty by the Single European Act 1986. In setting the end of 1992 as the date for achieving an 'Internal Market', Article 7a of the EC Treaty (inserted by the Single European Act) stated:

> The internal market shall comprise an area without internal frontiers in which the free movement of goods, persons, services and capital is ensured in accordance with the provisions of this Treaty.

As we have seen, Article 3 also indicated that the intention of the original Member States was to eliminate customs duties and other restrictions on the import and export of goods so that free trade could occur. This would

6. See the discussion of the Luxembourg Accords, para **[16.35]**.

involve the dismantling of many existing national laws of a protectionist nature. Article 3 also recognised that, to do this, the laws of the Member States would require 'approximation' to the extent required for the functioning of the common market. The word 'approximation' indicated that there were differences between the laws of the Member States in a number of areas and that these would need to be ironed out to achieve a true 'common market' for 'The Four Freedoms'.

Subsidiarity and the Community

[16.24] A further refinement of the activities of the European Community, the principle of subsidiarity, was added in 1992 by the Treaty on European Union. This added a new Article 3b to the EC Treaty. Article 3b specifies:

> In areas which do not fall within its exclusive competence the Community shall have due regard to the principle of subsidiarity ...

The principle of subsidiarity requires the Community to take into account that certain areas of economic activity might best be regulated by each Member State through its own national laws. In essence, subsidiarity requires the Community to refrain from taking action in some areas, thus allowing some continued diversity or differences between the laws of the Member States. The concept of subsidiarity is one familiar to States that operate a federal system, such as the Federal Republic of Germany or the United States of America. In such systems, the central or federal government and federal Parliament develop policy and legislate on certain 'core' issues, leaving other local issues to dealt with by the individual units that make up the federation.

Subsidiarity and federalism

[16.25] It should be noted, however, that, while subsidiarity is mentioned in the Treaty on European Union, it would be quite inaccurate to describe the European Union as having created a federal structure. Indeed, while some Member States might wish to see a federal union of the Member States, other Member States would regard this as unacceptable. In this respect, the use of subsidiarity in the Treaty on European Union is seen primarily as a 'brake' on excessive interference by the Community in certain sensitive issues of national concern. To that extent, it reflects continuing tension about the future direction of the European Community and Union, with some Member States willing to engage in further integration, including further political integration, while others would wish to see the Community and Union being restricted primarily to trade and economic issues.

Detailed activities of the Community

[16.26] The EC Treaty contains much more than merely a statement of general objectives. It goes on to deal with some detailed aspects of the activities of the Community. In 1957, these included:

- the gradual establishment during the 'transitional period' of a Customs Union between the Member States, effectively banning custom duties on imports and exports between the Member States (Articles 9 to 17)
- the gradual establishment of a Common Customs Tariff to lay down a common set of customs duties for imports and exports from and to 'third countries', that is trade with non-Member States (Articles 18 to 29)
- the gradual elimination of quantitative restrictions (quotas) on imports and all measures having equivalent effect between Member States (Articles 30 to 37)
- the gradual establishment of a Common Agricultural Policy (CAP), by which the Member States would have an agreed strategy for the development of this sector (Articles 38 to 47)
- the gradual securing of the right of establishment, that is, the freedom of movement of workers and of services, including the right of self-employed persons to pursue their careers and of service organisations to set up in any Member State (Articles 48 to 66)
- the progressive abolition of restrictions on movement of capital (Articles 67 to 73)
- the gradual establishment of a Common Transport Policy, which, like the CAP, would require the Member States to agree a common strategy for the development of transport and its infrastructure(Articles 74 to 84)
- the development of general rules concerning competition between undertakings, including restrictions on price fixing, the abuse by an undertaking of a dominant position within the common market and limits on State aid to undertakings (Articles 85 to 92)
- provision for the 'approximation of the laws of the Member States' in order to achieve the objectives of the common market (Article 100)

- the development of a Community social policy, including improvement of working conditions for workers and the principle of equal pay for men and women (Articles 118 and 119)
- the institutional arrangements for the Community, including the Council, the Commission, the European Assembly (now called the European Parliament), the Court of Justice and the Court of Auditors (Articles 137 to 188)[7]
- legislative mechanisms for the detailed implementation of the general aims of the Treaty (Article 189)[8]
- financial provisions, including the adoption of the Budget (Articles 199 to 209)
- the conferral of legal personality on the Community (Article 210)
- the conclusion of the Treaty for an unlimited period (Article 240).

This partial listing of the provisions of the EC Treaty indicate the ambitious scope of the original six Member States of the Community. It is hardly surprising that all these objectives were not met in the 12 year transitional period initially set in 1957. It should also indicate how, in some respects, the Treaty resembles a constitution, setting out general principles and also the institutional framework for the Community.

Obstacles to the aims of the EC Treaty

[16.27] In 1957, there were many obstacles to achieving a 'common market' for 'The Four Freedoms' and the other aims and objectives of the European Economic Community. It may be helpful to itemise these to indicate the task faced by the original Member States.

Obstacles to free movement of goods

[16.28] In relation to free movement of goods, many Member States' laws imposed quotas ('quantitative restrictions') on the amount of goods of various types that they would permit into their State. Other obstacles to free trade were the high import duties or tariffs imposed by Member States. Many such quotas, duties and tariffs were intended to protect native companies from outside competition. More restrictions came in the form of laws that imposed specific national standards to which imported goods (from televisions to major pieces of industrial machinery) would be required to comply before they could be brought into the Member State. Many of these restrictions have been removed since 1957, largely through the process

7. See para **[16.88]**.
8. See para **[16.129]**.

of 'approximating' the laws of the Member States. In relation to quotas, duties and tariffs, the Member States have established the Customs Union and the Common Customs Tariff (CCT) envisaged by the EC Treaty. In relation to standards, many national standards have been replaced by 'harmonised' Community standards so that goods manufactured in one Member State can be sold in any other Member State if they meet technical criteria laid down in the 'harmonised' Community law.

Obstacles to free movement of persons

[16.29] In connection with free movement of persons, there was the need to deal with the fact that most Member States again imposed restrictions on the number of foreign workers they would allow to enter their workforce. Other problems included the non-recognition of qualifications of foreign workers, including such diverse examples as hairdressers, veterinary surgeons, dentists or lawyers. Many of these 'right of establishment' issues have since been dealt with.[9] But, once these initial problems were overcome, others arose in this area of 'social policy', such as, for example, ensuring equal social security and pension rights for workers who have worked in different Member States.

Obstacles to free movement of services

[16.30] As to free movement of services, once again many Member States in the 1950s imposed severe restrictions on the establishment and operation of services. For example, the provision of water, electricity, transport (especially rail and air transport), postal and telecommunication services were operated by State bodies who held a virtual monopoly of such services. In the 1950s, very few States saw privatisation or the de-regulation of such services as either desirable or realistic. In the private sector, services such as insurance and banking were again subject to restrictions that, in effect, prevented foreign companies competing with local companies. And, in relation to non-recognition of qualifications, there was an overlap with the freedom of workers. Again, many though not all of these areas have been subject to 'approximation' laws intended to create a 'level playing pitch', another common phrase associated with this area.

Obstacles to free movement of capital

[16.31] In relation to the free movement of capital, most States also operated restrictions, by means of exchange control laws, on the extent to which money could be invested in projects outside the State. This was not just a question of limiting the amount people could bring with them on foreign

---

9. See para **[3.80]** for the arrangements concerning lawyers.

holidays, but extended to restricting the use of large sums for foreign speculation or investment in foreign industrial projects.

Other obstacles to the four freedoms

[16.32] Other obstacles to trade covered all aspects of 'The Four Freedoms'. For example, many States operated different forms of entities for conducting business. What in Britain or Ireland would be described as a limited liability company might find an equivalent in France or Italy, but the legal consequences of forming the equivalent in France might be very different. Another major area of difficulty was the abuse by undertakings (whether in the public sector or the private sector) of powerful monopoly positions to prevent others from competing in the same area of trade. As we have seen, the EC Treaty also contains provisions to prevent certain anti-competitive activities. Again, a large effort at Community level was required to remove these obstacles to free trade.

[4] DEVELOPMENT OF THE EUROPEAN COMMUNITY AND UNION

[16.33] As has been noted already, a number of changes to the original three Treaties, in particular the EC Treaty, have been made since the 1950s. The effect of these is that the scope of the original Treaties has been considerably expanded, though the focus still remains on achieving a 'common' or 'internal' market where economic-related activities are to the forefront. Future developments may involve further expansion both of activities and membership.

'Merger Treaty'

[16.34] In institutional terms, the first significant move was what is commonly called the 'Merger Treaty' of April 1965, which established a common set of institutions for the three Communities. Until the Merger Treaty, there had been separate Commissions and Councils for the three Communities, with a single Assembly and Court of Justice. From the time the Merger Treaty came into effect in July 1967, the three Communities have been subject to a single Commission, Council, Assembly, now called the European Parliament, and Court of Justice.

'Luxembourg Compromise'

[16.35] At about the same time, there was unease in some Member States, in particular in France, that vital national interests would be threatened if, as was scheduled under the third stage of the 'transitional period' in the EC Treaty, certain decisions could be made by majority voting rather than unanimous agreement. Under a series of arrangements in 1966 known as the

Luxembourg Accords (or the 'Luxembourg Compromise'), it was agreed that any Member State could, in effect, block a proposed Community law where it was deemed by that Member State to conflict with a 'vital national interest'. This procedure became known as the 'veto'. Although no amendment to the EC Treaty was made to incorporate these arrangements, they became part of the understanding between the Member States in the late 1960s and into the 1970s when Ireland became a Member State. The effect of the Luxembourg Accords was that relatively little progress was made in the 1970s in achieving the original aims of the EC Treaty. It became clear to the Member States in the 1980s that the unanimity requirement could lead to the economic collapse of the Communities in the face of growing global competition.

Single European Act

[16.36] Ultimately, the Single European Act, which was signed in February 1986 and came into force in July 1987, re-affirmed and also extended the provisions contained in the original EC Treaty that many 'approximating' laws could be made on the basis of a form of majority voting known as qualified voting majority (QVM). It also set the end of 1992 as the target date for achieving what became known as the 'Internal Market' or the 'Single Market'. The Single European Act also extended the scope of the EC Treaty to include areas such as political and monetary co-operation, research and technological development and environmental policy. In addition, the Single European Act involved a recognition of the fact that the Member States had, informally, been engaged in co-operation concerning the wider political aspects of the Community. For many years, the Member States had acknowledged that, internationally, the Community needed to 'speak with one voice' and to agree a common trade and foreign policy where this was possible. The Single European Act provided formal political mechanisms for this European Political Co-operation (EPC) to be developed, though outside the legal enforcement mechanisms (such as through the Court of Justice) specified in the Community Treaties. To this extent, the Single European Act acknowledged that certain aspects of the European Community and Union have more of a political than a legal importance.[10]

Treaty on European Union

[16.37] Further extensions to the original Treaties, and in particular the EC Treaty, were agreed in the Treaty on European Union, which was signed in

---

10. Note, however, that while elements of the European Union may operate primarily in the political sphere, this may still involve legal consequences in Irish law: see *Crotty v An Taoiseach* [1987] ILRM 400, para **[16.66]**.

the city of Maastricht in February 1992, hence the more common 'the Maastricht Treaty'. The Treaty on European Union, which came into effect in October 1993, deals with certain aspects of economic and monetary union, such as the possible establishment of a European Central Bank (ECB) and the creation of a common or single currency for all Member States. In addition, some important new areas of competence, particularly concerning sustainable (environmentally-friendly) development were inserted into the existing Treaties.

[16.38] A further indication of the expanding activities of the European Union were provisions in the Treaty on European Union concerning closer co-operation in defence and foreign policy matters. These were influenced by the collapse in 1989 and 1990 of the Soviet-dominated Communist governments in the States of Central and Eastern Europe. In that respect, the Treaty on European Union represents part of the response of the States of Western Europe to these major political changes.

[16.39] As with the Single European Act, the most significant amendments made by the Treaty on European Union were again made to the EC Treaty, including the provisions that concerned monetary union. These amendments were so numerous and extensive that the full title of the EEC Treaty was changed from 'Treaty Establishing the European Economic Community' to 'Treaty Establishing the European Community'. This is now usually shortened to 'EC Treaty'. This meant that, after the TEU came into effect in 1993, the EEC became the EC. This change re-affirmed that the vast bulk of what comprises European Community law emerges from what is now the EC Treaty.

[16.40] To indicate the wide scope of the Treaty on European Union, it amended the text of Article 2 of the EC Treaty to include the following as part of the overall task of the European Community:

- economic and monetary union,
- balanced development,
- sustainable and non-inflationary growth respecting the environment,
- a high degree of convergence of economic performance,
- a high level of employment and of social protection,
- the raising of the standard of living and quality of life and
- economic and social cohesion and solidarity among Member States.

These additional headings indicate the further expanding nature of the Community and Union.

[5] European Community Law and the European Union

[16.41] The Treaty on European Union also established another entity called the European Union (EU). The European Union could be described as a 'holding company' for the three Communities, the ECSC, the EAEC and the EC. Echoing the 1957 Preamble to the EC Treaty, Article A of the Treaty on European Union states that the creation of the Union 'marks a new stage in the process of creating an ever closer union among the peoples of Europe.' Article A goes on to state:

> The Union shall be founded on the European Communities, supplemented by the policies and forms of co-operation established by this Treaty.

The European Union is therefore not an entirely new entity, but is very much based on the existing Treaties of the Communities. Thus, in this chapter, the phrase 'European Union' describes the organisations created by the three original Treaties, as amended in particular by the Single European Act and the Treaty on European Union; indeed, since the Treaty on European Union came into force in 1993, it has become common for media commentators to refer simply to the 'European Union' rather than the 'European Community'.

The 'acquis communautaire'

[16.42] However, from the perspective of enforceable rules of law, the European Union is dependent on the existing Communities. Thus, Article B of the Treaty on European Union states that the Union shall 'maintain in full the 'acquis communautaire' and build on it. The phrase 'acquis communautaire' refers to the legal principles established by the three original Treaties, as amended by the Single European Act and the Treaty on European Union in particular. Thus, the phrase 'European Community law' is used in this chapter to indicate those rules which form one of the essential characteristics of the European Union.

Policies and co-operation in the European Union

[16.43] In relation to the policies referred to in Article A, the Treaty on European Union added to the existing provisions on foreign policy co-operation first introduced in the Single European Act and introduced new procedures concerning what was re-named Common Foreign and Security Policy (CFSP). As to the co-operation referred to in Article A, it introduced the first reference in a Treaty to co-operation on judicial and home affairs

(JHA). This includes co-operation between the Justice Ministers of the European Community and Union concerning, for example, immigration and drug-related activity. In this respect, the TEU in fact formalised for the first time existing co-operation between the Justice Ministers on such matters.

The Three Pillars

[16.44] In attempting to describe the nature of the European Union, the Member States who negotiated the Treaty on European Union made a comparison between the Treaty and a Greek temple supported by what became known as 'The Three Pillars'. In this analogy, the TEU is based on the following Three Pillars:

1. The Treaties establishing the ECSC, the EAEC and (especially) the EC;
2. Common Foreign and Security Policy (CFSP); and
3. Co-operation on Judicial and Home Affairs (JHA).

In terms of the political development of the European, each of these Three Pillars carries equal weight.

[16.45] However, it is important to bear in mind that, from a legal perspective, the first of these three pillars carries most weight. This is because the amendments made by to the existing Treaties, and in particular the EC Treaty, are legally enforceable under the mechanisms established by the Treaties. By contrast, in relation to the areas covered by the two other pillars, CFSP and JHA, not all the Member States who negotiated the TEU were willing to commit themselves to legally enforceable policies and co-operation in those areas. For that reason, the TEU provides that CFSP and JHA do not come under the enforcement mechanisms established by the Treaties. For the present, therefore, these 'Two Pillars' of the European Union remain matters for 'voluntary' co-operation between the Member States, guided by but not legally bound by the 'acquis communautaire'.

[16.46] The changes made to the original Treaties by the Single European Act and the Treaty on European Union underline the dynamic nature of the European Union. These changes must be taken into account when assessing the nature of the Union itself. Like with the Constitution of Ireland, the assessment may vary in the light of prevailing ideas and concepts.[11]

11. See para **[15.128]**.

Increased Membership

From Six to Fifteen

[16.47] Other changes in the European Union have arisen from the accession of new Member States. In 1973, Ireland, the United Kingdom and Denmark joined the six original Member States. Greece joined in 1981, with Spain and Portugal following in 1986. The most recent accessions were of Austria, Finland and Sweden in 1995. The original 'Communities of the Six' had become, by 1995, a 'Union of Fifteen'.

European Economic Area

[16.48] It seems likely that, by the year 2000, further States will become Member States. These may include what remains of the States of the European Economic Area (EEA), an entity that formerly included Austria, Finland and Sweden, who became full Member States of the European Community and Union in 1995. The largest Member State of the EEA is now Norway, whose citizens have rejected membership of the European in two referenda, in 1972 and 1994.[12] The Member States of the EEA in effect operate a free trade area with the Member States of the European Union, but of course are not full Member States.

Central and Eastern Europe and Mediterranean States

[16.49] Future Member States of the European Union might include some of the States of Central and Eastern Europe, such as the Czech Republic, Slovakia, Poland and Hungary (the 'Visegrad States'), Slovenia, Estonia,

---

12. In 1992, the then Member States signed the Agreement on the European Economic Area, the EEA Agreement, as adjusted by the 1993 Protocol to that Agreement. The EEA Agreement was signed between the Member States and the then seven States of the European Free Trade Association (EFTA), Austria, Finland, Iceland, Liechtenstein, Norway, Sweden and Switzerland. The effect of the EEA Agreement was that, within the EEA, which consists of the Member States of the European Community and Union and those of EFTA (apart from Switzerland, which ultimately decided in a referendum not to join the EEA), many of the core elements of European Community law apply as they do in the Member States of the Union. For example, much of the law on the 'Four Freedoms' of persons, services, capital and goods as well as those on competition, social policy, the environment, education, research and development were, in effect, extended to the EEA. As already noted in the text, three EFTA States, Austria, Finland, and Sweden, became full Member States of the European Union in 1995, thus superseding the provisions of the EEA that dealt with them. This has considerably limited the geographical scope of the EEA, though it remains of considerable importance in terms of the relationship between the Union and the remaining EEA States, Norway, Iceland and Liechtenstein. For an excellent analysis of the background to and effect of the EEA Agreement, see Anthony Whelan's Annotation to the European Communities (Amendment) Act 1993 for *Irish Current Law Statutes Annotated.*

Latvia and Lithuania as well as Mediterranean States such as Turkey, Cyprus and Malta. The European Union has entered into Association Agreements with these States; these are regarded as stepping stones to membership, involving a special relationship without involving the full rights or duties of membership.[13]

1996 Intergovernmental Conference

[16.50] Regardless of any such 'widening' of the European Union, Article N of the Treaty on European Union required the Member States to convene an Inter-Governmental Conference (IGC) in 1996 to consider further amendments to the Treaties. At the time of writing (July 1996), this IGC had yet to make final recommendations, but further changes to the Treaties may be expected in 1997 or 1998, resulting in further 'deepening' of the 'ever closer union' already established by the European Union. For this State, a key issue may be whether such changes will involve any alteration to the State's policy of military neutrality, which has allowed the State participate in United Nations peace-keeping operations but not any NATO-sponsored military actions.

The moving train

[16.51] Whether looked at from the perspective of the existing Member States or from that of the States wishing to become Member States in the future, the European Union is very much 'a moving train'.[14] We must now examine the precise legal nature of the rules created by this moving train that Ireland joined in 1973.

[6] THE NATURE OF EUROPEAN COMMUNITY LAW

[16.52] As we have already seen, the European Communities had been established in the 1950s by means of Treaties signed on behalf of the six original Member States. The Treaties established the Court of Justice of the European Communities, and Article 164 of the EC Treaty states that:

> The Court of Justice shall ensure that, in the interpretation and application of this Treaty, the law is observed.

In two of the earliest cases decided by the Court of Justice, it made clear that 'the law' created by the EC Treaty in particular was of a different nature to any other form of international agreement.

---

13. Similar Association Agreements exist with a number of African, Caribbean and Pacific States (ACP States) who will remain outside the European Union.

14. See McMahon and Murphy, *op cit*, p 11.

The Van Gend en Loos *case*

[16.53] In *Van Gend en Loos v Nederlandse Belastingenadministratie*[15] the Court of Justice was required to consider whether the EC Treaty had created legal rights for companies such as Van Gend en Loos and whether such legal rights could be enforced in national courts. The Court answered these questions in the affirmative, and in the process held that the EC Treaty had 'direct effect'. In other words, the Court held that the EC Treaty was also part of the domestic laws of the Member States.

[16.54] The Court of Justice held that, in analysing the provisions of the EC Treaty, it should consider 'the general scheme and wording of those provisions'. This is similar to the harmonious approach later adopted by the Irish courts in the interpretation of the 1937 Constitution.[16] The Court then referred to the Preamble to the EC Treaty, noting that it referred not only to the Member States but also to the 'peoples of Europe'.[17] It also pointed out that the powers exercised by the Community institutions would affect not only the Member States but also their citizens. In addition, the Court referred to Article 177 of the EC Treaty, which confers jurisdiction on it to give rulings concerning the interpretation of the Treaty and of the validity of an act of the Community institutions '[w]here such a question is raised before any court or tribunal of a Member State'. In the Court's view, Article 177 thus acknowledged that an issue of Community law could be dealt with in national courts. In a passage that has been quoted many times, the Court continued:[18]

> "The conclusion to be drawn from this is that the [European Economic] Community constitutes a new legal order of international law, for the benefit of which the States have limited their sovereign rights, albeit within limited fields, and the subjects of which comprise not only Member States but also their nationals. Independently of the legislation of Member States, Community law therefore not only imposes obligations on individuals but is also intended to confer upon them rights which become part of their legal heritage. These rights arise not only where they are expressly granted by the Treaty, but also by reason of obligations which the Treaty imposes in a clearly defined way upon individuals as well as upon Member States and upon the institutions of the Community."

15. [1963] ECR 1.
16. See para **[15.109]**.
17. See para **[16.18]**.
18. [1963] ECR 1 at 12.

The Court of Justice did not conclude that all Treaty provisions were legally enforceable in this way. In fact, a three-part test was established in this respect:

1. the provision in question must be clear and precise;
2. it must be unconditional; and
3. it must be such that no further action is required by the Community institutions or the Member States or, if the provision requires the Member States to amend their laws, it leaves no discretion to the Member States about the content of those amendments.

In *Van Gend en Loos*, the Government of the Netherlands had, in 1960, re-classified a particular chemical substance being imported by Van Gend en Loos in such a way that it attracted a higher import duty than had applied on 1 January 1958, when the EEC Treaty had come into effect. Article 12 of the EC Treaty states:

> Member States shall refrain from introducing between themselves any new customs duties on imports or exports or any charges having equivalent effect, and from increasing those which they already apply in their trade with each other.

The plaintiff company, Van Gend en Loos, argued that Article 12 prohibited the re-classification of the chemical substance as it had the effect of increasing the import duty. The Court of Justice agreed, concluding that Article 12 had 'direct effect' in Dutch law, preventing the State from imposing the higher duty on the plaintiff company and allowing the plaintiff to raise that point in the Dutch national courts.

The **Costa** *case*

[16.55] Just over one year later, in *Costa v ENEL*,[19] the Court of Justice expanded on the general approach it laid down in *Van Gend en Loos*. In *Costa*, the plaintiff objected to the Italian law which had nationalised the Italian electricity industry to the extent of refusing to pay his electricity bill. When he was sued for non-payment in the Italian courts, his defence was that the Italian law was contrary to a number of provisions of Community law, including Articles 92 to 94 of the EC Treaty concerning State aids to industry. The Italian court referred the question whether Community law could be raised in such circumstances. The Court answered emphatically in the affirmative:

19. [1964] ECR 585, at 593.

> "By contrast with ordinary international treaties, the EEC Treaty has created its own legal system, which, on the entry into force of the Treaty, became an integral part of the legal system of the Member States and which their courts are bound to apply.
>
> By creating a Community of unlimited duration, having its own institutions, its own personality, its own legal capacity and capacity of representation on the international plane and, more particularly, real powers stemming from a limitation of sovereignty or a transfer of powers from the States to the Community, the Member States have limited their sovereign powers, albeit within limited fields, and have thus created a body of law which binds both their nationals and themselves ...
>
> It follows from these observations that the law stemming from the Treaty, an independent source of law, could not, because of its special and original nature, be overridden by domestic legal provisions, however framed, without being deprived of its character as Community law and without the legal basis of the Community itself being called into question."

Although Costa's challenge to the Italian law was ultimately unsuccessful,[20] this passage has been quoted many times in subsequent cases.

[16.56] *Van Gend en Loos* and *Costa* remain the key decisions that describe what has been called the supremacy of Community law over national law. However, one further point of particular importance for Ireland was added by the decision of the Court of Justice in *Internationale Handelsgesellschaft v Einfuhr-und Vorratsstelle für Getreide und Futtermittel*.[21]

The Internationale Handelsgesellschaft *case*

[16.57] In *Internationale Handelsgesellschaft*, the plaintiff company had obtained an export licence for maize under a European Community Regulation, one of the detailed legal instruments provided for in the Treaties aimed at achieving the 'common market'.[22] To obtain the licence, it was required by the Community Regulation to deposit a sum of money with the relevant German licensing authority as a guarantee that it would comply with the terms and conditions laid down in the licence, in particular that it would export the quantity of maize to which the company had committed itself by a given time. The company failed to export the quantity of grain within the time limit to which it had committed itself, and it was then notified, again in accordance with the Community Regulation, that its

20. By the early 1990s, however, ENEL, the Italian equivalent of the Electricity Supply Board, was being prepared for privatisation, in line with many similar State bodies in the Member States of the European Union.
21. [1970] ECR 1125.
22. On the making of a Community Regulation, see para **[16.131]**.

deposit would be forfeited. The company then instituted proceedings claiming that the forfeiture provisions of the Community Regulation were in conflict with its fundamental rights under certain provisions of the German Basic Law, the German equivalent of the Constitution of Ireland. These fundamental rights were described as the principles of freedom of action and disposition, of economic liberty and of proportionality. Echoing the language of the *Van Gend en Loos* and *Costa* cases, the Court of Justice rejected the plaintiff company's argument, stating:[23]

> "Recourse to the legal rules or concepts of national law in order to judge the validity of measures adopted by the institutions of the Community would have an adverse effect on the uniformity and efficiency of Community law. The validity of such measures can only be judged in the light of Community law. In fact, the law stemming from the Treaty, an independent source of law, cannot because of its very nature be overridden by rules of national law, however framed, without being deprived of its character as Community law and without the legal basis of the Community itself being called in question. Therefore, the validity of a Community measure or its effect within a Member State cannot be affected by allegations that it runs counter to either fundamental rights as formulated by the constitution of that State or the principles of a national constitutional structure."

The Court went on to state that, while the fundamental rights provisions of the German Basic Law could not take priority over Community law, similar though not necessarily identical fundamental rights were part of the *corpus* of Community law. The Court stated[24]:

> "However, an examination should be made as to whether or not any analogous guarantee [*that is, analogous to those in the German Basic Law*] inherent in Community law has been disregarded. In fact, respect for fundamental rights forms an integral part of the general principles of law protected by the Court of Justice. The protection of such rights, whilst inspired by the constitutional traditions common to the Member States, must be ensured within the framework of the structure and objectives of the Community. It must therefore be ascertained ... whether the system of deposits has infringed rights of a fundamental nature, respect for which must be ensured in the Community legal order."

As with the general approach of the Court in *Van Gend en Loos* and *Costa*, the decision in *Internationale Handelsgesellschaft* can be compared with developments in constitutional interpretation in Ireland. The concept of fundamental rights as being 'inherent' in Community law is similar to the

---

23. [1970] ECR 1125, at 1134.
24. *Ibid.*

jurisprudence concerning the unenumerated personal rights under Article 40.3 of the Constitution.[25]

[16.58] The views of the Court of Justice in these three leading cases can be summed up as follows:

- by contrast with ordinary international treaties, the Treaties establishing the European Communities had created a new Community legal order or system;
- by signing the Treaties, the Member States had permanently limited their sovereign powers and transferred them to the new Community legal order, even if only in relation to the subjects covered by the Treaties;
- the new Community legal order had became an integral part of the legal systems of the Member States and their courts were required to apply its rules;
- the new Community legal order could be relied on in the national courts by the citizens of the Member States;
- the law stemming from the Treaty could not be overridden by any domestic law of a Member State, including the national constitutions of the Member States, since this would call into question the legal basis of the Community; and
- although Community law took priority over even fundamental rights provisions in national constitutions, respect for fundamental rights formed an integral part of Community law, inspired by the constitutional traditions common to the Member States.

The clear effect of these three decisions was that, in the event of a conflict, the new Community legal order took priority over national legal rules, even those contained in national constitutions.

[16.59] When the Government of Ireland entered into negotiations with a view to joining the European Communities, it was clear that certain provisions of the Constitution, which we will now discuss, were in direct conflict with the views of the Court of Justice in these cases. In order to join the new Community legal order, it was therefore necessary to amend the Constitution so that Community law would take priority over Irish law, including the 'basic law' (*Bunreacht*) contained in the 1937 Constitution.

25. See para **[15.50]**.

The Constitution and international agreements

[16.60] We have already seen that the 1937 Constitution of 1937 describes and places limits on the powers of the main institutions of State. Article 6 of the Constitution specifies that the executive, legislative and judicial powers of government can only be exercised by the organs of State established by the Constitution. This Article makes clear that no international organisation can exercise these powers. Article 15.2 provides that the Oireachtas has exclusive law-making powers, while Article 34 requires that justice be administered only in courts established by the Constitution and that the Supreme Court is the final court of appeal.[26]

[16.61] These provisions are underlined by Article 29 of the Constitution, which deals with the international relations of the State. Article 29.4.1° specifies :

> The executive power of the State in ... connection with its external relations shall ... be exercised by or on the authority of the Government.

In other words, external relations, or what would now be described as international relations or foreign affairs, are a matter for the Taoiseach and the other government Ministers appointed under Article 28 of the Constitution. Many aspects of international relations are dealt with by way of Treaties or other agreements between States. Article 29.4.2° also provides that, for this purpose, the Government may adopt any 'method of procedure used or adopted ... by the members of any group or league of nations with which the State is or becomes associated for the purpose of international co-operation in matters of common concern.'[27]

The legal effect of international agreements: dualist approach

[16.62] Article 29.4 makes clear that the Government is responsible for conducting the State's international relations. However, equally important is the effect of any international agreement adopted by the Government on behalf of the State. Article 29.3 deals with this point and provides:

> Ireland accepts the generally recognised principles of international law as its rule of conduct in its relations with other States.

This provision acknowledges that the Government should conduct relations with other States on the basis of generally recognised principles of international law.[28] One of the principles of international law accepted by

---

26. See para **[15.28]**.
27. On the history of this provision, see para **[15.43]**.
28. It may be queried whether there is an agreed list of generally accepted principles of international law. However, in *Crotty v An Taoiseach* [1987] ILRM 713 the High Court and Supreme Court referred to the Vienna Convention on the Interpretation of Treaties of 1963 as containing some significant generally accepted principles of international law. See further para **[17.19]**.

most States is that agreements between States do not generally form part of the national, or domestic, law of those States unless they are specifically enacted into law by the Parliaments of the States in question. This requirement to have two legal events (the signing of an international agreement followed by separate implementing national legislation, in turn leading back to ratification of the agreement) before the agreement becomes part of national law, is known as the dualist approach to international law. Article 29.6 of the Constitution adopts the dualist approach by providing:

> No international agreement shall be part of the domestic law of the State save as may be determined by the Oireachtas.

This preserves the role of the Oireachtas under Article 15.2 as the exclusive law-making body for the State. While Article 29.4 empowers the Government to enter into international agreements, Article 29.6 ensures that only the Oireachtas can incorporate such agreements into Irish law. International agreements do not therefore have any legal force in the domestic law of Ireland unless they have been incorporated into law by means of an Act of the Oireachtas. As we note elsewhere, this dualist approach has been confirmed a number of times by the courts in Ireland.[29]

Adapting the Constitution to the Community legal order

[16.63] It was clear that the provisions of the Constitution, and in particular Article 29, were in direct conflict with the primacy of Community law, as described by the Court of Justice in *Van Gend en Loos*, *Costa*, and *Internationale Handelsgesellschaft*. In order to comply with the requirements of the Community legal order, the following subsection, Article 29.4.3°, was added to Article 29.4 after a referendum in 1972 had approved the proposed amendment to the Constitution:

> 3° The State may become a member of the European Coal and Steel Community (established by Treaty signed at Paris on the 18th day of April, 1951), the European Economic Community (established by Treaty signed at Rome on the 25th day of March, 1957) and the European Atomic Energy Community (established by Treaty signed at Rome on the 25th day of March, 1957). No provision of this Constitution invalidates laws enacted, acts done or measures adopted by the State necessitated by the obligations of membership of the Communities or prevents laws enacted, acts done or measures adopted by the Communities, or institutions thereof, from having the force of law in the State.

In the wake of the Single European Act, a further constitutional amendment was required in 1987, though only after the Supreme Court had held in

29. See para **[17.17]**.

Crotty v An Taoiseach[30] that this was so. In December 1986, the Oireachtas had enacted the European Communities (Amendment) Act 1986 to give effect in Irish law to the relevant provisions of the Single European Act. However, before the Government had deposited the formal instruments of ratification with the Italian Government, as required by the Single European Act, the High Court granted to the plaintiff in *Crotty* an interlocutory injunction prohibiting the Government from depositing the instrument of ratification. The injunction could hardly have been granted in more dramatic circumstances; Barrington J heard legal argument in his home on Christmas Eve 1986 and delivered judgment after only a short adjournment to consider the matter.

[16.64] In 1987, a Divisional High Court (Hamilton P, Barrington and Carroll JJ) upheld the validity of the 1986 Act on the ground that it came within the scope of Article 29.4.3°. The High Court held that, in connection with Title III of the Single European Act, which concerned European Political Co-Operation (EPC),[31] it had no function since EPC had been kept outside the scope of enforceable Community law and had thus not been incorporated into Irish law by the 1986 Act.

[16.65] On appeal, the Supreme Court in *Crotty* accepted that the 'licence' contained in the first sentence of Article 29.4.3° authorising the State to join the Communities contained an acknowledgement that it had joined a 'moving train'. Delivering the judgment of the Supreme Court, Finlay CJ stated that Article 29.4.3° was:

> an authorisation given to the State not only to join the Communities as they stood in 1973, but also to join in amendments of the Treaties so long as such amendments do not alter the essential scope or objectives of the Communities.

The Court thus considered whether the amendments to the existing Treaties, including the extension of the aims of the Communities to include protection of the environment, the introduction of qualified voting majority (QVM) in the Community institutions,[32] or the establishment of a Court of First Instance attached to the Court of Justice[33] involved an alteration to the scope or objectives of the Communities. The Court concluded that they did not, noting that the Communities which the State joined in 1973 constituted 'a developing organism'. The Court thus agreed with the High Court in

30. [1987] IR 713.
31. See para **[16.36]**.
32. See para **[16.36]**.
33. See para **[16.123]**.

upholding the validity of the 1986 Act which had incorporated these provisions into Irish law. This aspect of the case acknowledges that not every change to the Treaties requires a constitutional amendment.

[16.66] However, the Court held, by a 3-2 majority (Walsh, Henchy and Hederman JJ; Finlay CJ and Griffin JJ dissenting) that the provisions of Title III were unconstitutional. The majority concluded that the commitment by the State in Title III to endeavour to agree a common foreign policy with other Member States restricted its freedom to formulate an independent foreign policy, and this was inconsistent with the sovereignty of the State under Article 5 of the Constitution. This conclusion necessitated a referendum to amend the Constitution.[34]

[16.67] The amendment simply added the Single European Act to the list of Treaties referred to in Article 29.4.3° so that it read as follows:

> 3° The State may become a member of the European Coal and Steel Community (established by Treaty signed at Paris on the 18th day of April, 1951), the European Economic Community (established by Treaty signed at Rome on the 25th day of March, 1957) and the European Atomic Energy Community (established by Treaty signed at Rome on the 25th day of March, 1957). The State may ratify the Single European Act (signed on behalf of the Member States of the Communities at Luxembourg on the 17th day of February, 1986, and at the Hague on the 28th day of February, 1986). No provision of this Constitution invalidates laws enacted, acts done or measures adopted by the State necessitated by the obligations of membership of the Communities or prevents laws enacted, acts done or measures adopted by the Communities, or institutions thereof, from having the force of law in the State.

Most recently, in 1992, ratification of the Treaty on European Union (and an Agreement on Patents of 1989)[35] required further amendments to Article 29.4. A certain amount of re-positioning of the relevant provisions of the Constitution resulted from this so that they currently read as follows:

> 3° The State may become a member of the European Coal and Steel Community (established by Treaty signed at Paris on the 18th day

34. See McCutcheon, 'The Irish Supreme Court, European Political Co-operation and the Single European Act' (1988) LIEI 93, replying to some of the criticisms of the majority decision in *Crotty*.

35. The amendment effected by Article 29.4.6° was required because the 1989 Patents Agreement involved the creation of a Court whose decisions would be legally binding in the national laws of the Member States. Its decisions would thus supersede those of the courts established by the Constitution, including the High Court and Supreme Court. This is now provided for in the Patents Act 1992. See further Byrne and Binchy, *Annual Review of Irish Law 1992* (Round Hall Press, 1994), pp 42-6.

of April, 1951), the European Economic Community (established by Treaty signed at Rome on the 25th day of March, 1957) and the European Atomic Energy Community (established by Treaty signed at Rome on the 25th day of March, 1957). The State may ratify the Single European Act (signed on behalf of the Member States of the Communities at Luxembourg on the 17th day of February, 1986, and at the Hague on the 28th day of February, 1986).

4° The State may ratify the Treaty on European Union signed at Maastricht on the 7th day of February, 1992, and may become a member of that Union.

5° No provision of this Constitution invalidates laws enacted, acts done or measures adopted by the State which are necessitated by the obligations of membership of the European Union or of the Communities, or prevents laws enacted, acts done or measures adopted by the European Union or by the Communities or by institutions thereof, or by bodies competent under the Treaties establishing the Communities, from having the force of law in the State.

6° The State may ratify the Agreement Relating to Community Patents drawn between the Member States of the Communities and done at Luxembourg on the 15th day of December, 1989.

[16.68] What is now Article 29.4.5° of the Constitution allowed the State to comply with the terms of *Van Gend en Loos*, *Costa* and *Internationale Handelsgesellschaft*. Article 29.4.5° has two major effects:

1. nothing in the Constitution can prevent laws enacted, acts done or measures adopted by the European Union or by the Communities, or by institutions of the European Union or of the Communities, from having the force of law in the State; and
2. nothing in the Constitution can invalidate laws enacted, acts done or measures adopted by the State where these were necessitated by membership of the European Union or of the Communities.

The principal area of doubt on the meaning of what is now Article 29.4.5° was the scope of that was 'necessitated' by membership of the European Community and Union. This gave rise to a number of cases in the courts in Ireland.[36] However, it is clear that Article 29.4.5° permits all laws enacted by the institutions of the European Community and Union to have priority over laws enacted by the institutions established by the Constitution itself, notably laws enacted by the Oireachtas. In keeping with the decisions of the Court of Justice, from the date that Ireland became a member of the Communities, 1 January 1973, Community law took priority over the

36. See *Meagher v Minister for Agriculture and Food* [1994] 1 IR 329, para **[16.76]**.

Constitution, at least in those areas covered by the Treaties establishing the Communities.

[16.69] In summary, therefore, the effect of Article 29.4.5° is that European Community law is part of the domestic law of Ireland and, where there is a conflict between Community law and any provisions of the Constitution (or any other domestic laws), Community law takes priority. In *Doyle v An Taoiseach*,[37] it was commented that Community law 'has the paramount force and effect of constitutional provisions'. In effect, Article 29.4.5° has created a set of 'European constitutional provisions' that take priority over Irish constitutional provisions.

Incorporating the Treaties and Community acts

[16.70] In addition to the amendments made to Article 29.4 of the Constitution, the incorporation of Community law into the law of Ireland was completed by the European Communities Act 1972. This short, but highly important, Act has been the vehicle for the implementation in the law of the State of many of the detailed laws that have emerged from the European Union.

Definition of The Treaties

[16.71] Section 1 of the 1972 Act contains the definition of 'the Treaties governing the European Communities.' This definition has been amended a number of times since 1972 to incorporate amending Treaties to the three original Treaties of the ECSC, the EAEC and the EC Treaty, notably the Accession Treaties for new Member States as well as the Single European Act and the Treaty on European Union. The most recent definition of 'the Treaties governing the European Communities' is contained in the European Communities (Amendment) Act 1994.

[16.72] It should be noted that these definitions, while they include amendments to the three original Treaties, do not include those provisions of the Single European Act and Treaty on European Union that fall outside the jurisdiction of the Court of Justice, in particular the provisions in the Single European Act concerning European Political Co-operation (EPC) and those in the Treaty on European Union concerning Common Foreign and Security Policy (CFSP) and co-operation on Judicial and Home Affairs (JHA).[38] Thus, these' Two Pillars' of the European Union do not form part of the domestic law of the State.

37. [1986] ILRM 693.

38. See para **[16.43]**.

Binding effect of Treaties and Community acts

[16.73] Section 2 of the 1972 Act states:

> From the 1st day of January, 1973, the treaties governing the European Communities and the existing and future acts adopted by the institutions of those Communities shall be binding on the State and shall be part of the domestic law thereof under the conditions laid down in those treaties.

In some respects, it might be said that s 2 of the 1972 Act merely repeats in another form what is already contained in Article 29.4.5° of the Constitution. Nonetheless, it does provide an explicit statement that the Treaties and the acts of the Community institutions are part of the domestic law of the State. This includes confirmation that decisions of the Court of Justice concerning Community law are binding on all courts in Ireland, including the Supreme Court. It also confirms in Irish law the enforcement procedures provided for by the Treaties, including references by Irish courts and other tribunals of points of Community law to the Court of Justice under Article 177 of the EC Treaty.

Incorporation of Community acts by Ministerial Regulations

[16.74] This explicit incorporation of Community law is also relevant to ss 3 and 4 of the 1972 Act, which deal with the precise way in which the detailed rules of Community law could be incorporated into Irish law. Section 3 provides:

> (1) A Minister ... may make Regulations for enabling section 2 of this Act to have full effect.
>
> (2) Regulations under this section may contain such incidental, supplementary and consequential provisions as appear to the Minister making the Regulations to be necessary for the purposes of the Regulations (including provisions repealing, amending or applying, with or without modification, other law, exclusive of this Act).
>
> (3) Regulations under this section shall not create an indictable offence.

Section 4 of the 1972 Act, as originally enacted in 1972, provided that Ministerial Regulations under s 3 would have statutory effect but would cease to do so unless confirmed by Act of the Oireachtas passed within six months of their making. The European Communities (Confirmation of Regulations) Act 1973 was the only Act made under this original version of s 4 of the 1972 Act. This was because, later in 1973, the European Communities (Amendment) Act 1973 amended s 4 of the 1972 Act so that it provided that Regulations under the 1972 Act 'shall have statutory effect' unless annulled by resolutions passed by both Houses of the Oireachtas on the basis of a report from what is now the Joint Committee on European Affairs.[39] Since 1973, no such annulling resolutions have been passed by the Houses of the Oireachtas so that, in practice, Regulations made under s 3 of the 1972 Act have had full statutory effect.

[16.75] The effect of ss 3 and 4 of the 1972 Act is to empower a Minister to make Regulations in order to implement in domestic law any act of the Community institutions, where such Community act required effect to be given to them in this way. The scope of s 3, particularly when read in conjunction with the amended form of s 4, was criticised, *inter alia,* on the ground that it conferred a power to amend an Act of the Oireachtas, primary legislation, by means of Regulations, secondary legislation.[40]

The Meagher *case*

[16.76] Despite these criticisms, the validity of s 3 of the 1972 Act was, in large measure, upheld by the 1993 decision of the Supreme Court in *Meagher v Minister for Agriculture and Food*.[41] In *Meagher*, the applicant unsuccessfully challenged the validity of the European Communities (Control of Oestrogenic, Androgenic, Gestagenic and Thyrostatic Substances) Regulations 1988[42] and the European Communities (Control of Veterinary Medicinal Products and their Residues) Regulations 1990.[43] These Regulations had implemented a number of Community Directives[44] aimed at prohibiting the use of certain hormone growth promoters in farm animals, including clembuterol (commonly known as 'angel dust').

[16.77] The 1988 Regulations provided that search warrants could be issued to authorised officers of the Department of Agriculture and Food and to members of the Garda Síochána to enter lands and other premises with a view to taking samples from animals to ascertain if growth promoters prohibited under the Regulations were being used. Pursuant to a warrant issued under the 1988 Regulations, officers entered the applicant's farm and took relevant samples. The applicant was later served with 20 summonses alleging offences under the 1988 and 1990 Regulations. The applicant initiated judicial review proceedings in which he claimed that the 1988 and

39. The reference to the Joint Committee on European Affairs, a Joint Committee of the Houses of the Oireachtas, was inserted by the European Communities (Amendment) Act 1995.

40. See McCutcheon, *op cit*; Hogan and Morgan, *Administrative Law in Ireland*, 2nd ed (Sweet & Maxwell, 1991) pp 17-19; but see *contra* Curtin, 'Some Reflections on European Community Law in Ireland' (1989) 11 DULJ (ns) 207.

41. [1994] 1 IR 329.

42. SI 218/1988.

43. SI 171/1990.

44. See para **[16.136]**.

1990 Regulations were *ultra vires* the 1972 Act and also that s 3 of the 1972 Act was invalid.

[16.78] Both the 1988 and 1990 Regulations provided that, notwithstanding the six month time limit for initiating summary criminal prosecutions in s 10 of the Petty Sessions (Ireland) Act 1851,[45] prosecutions under the 1988 and 1990 Regulations could be initiated within two years from the date of the alleged offence. This, in effect, amounted to an amendment of s 10 of the 1851 Act by Ministerial Regulations.

[16.79] The applicant contended that the general power in s 3 of the 1972 Act to implement Community acts by Ministerial Regulations was not 'necessitated' by membership of the Communities under Article 29.4 of the Constitution and was thus in conflict with the exclusive law-making power of the Oireachtas. It was clear that, if s 3 was not 'saved' by Article 29.4.5°, it was in conflict with the limited power of delegation granted to the Oireachtas by Article 15 of the Constitution[46] and that the only appropriate legislative mechanism would have been an Act of the Oireachtas implementing the Directives, which could have provided for the required extension to the time limit in the 1851 Act.

[16.80] The Minister contended that the power in s 3 of the 1972 Act was 'necessitated' by membership of the Community and was thus immune from challenge. The Minister referred to Article 189 of the EC Treaty which provides that, while a Directive is binding on each Member State 'it shall leave to the national authorities the choice of form and methods.'[47] The Minister therefore argued that under Community and Irish law the amendment of the 1851 Act by the 1988 Regulations was valid since it was open to the national authorities to choose how to give effect to the Directives. The Minister also argued that the particular use of the s 3 power in this instance was justified and that the two year time limit was required in order to ensure effective implementation of the Directives since complex sampling and testing of animals to detect the presence of the prohibited substances was required and this required a time period greater than six months.

[16.81] In the High Court, Johnson J rejected the Minister's argument on the immunity of s 3. He concluded that, under Article 189 of the EC Treaty the Minister was obliged to consider the appropriate method by which to implement the Directives in question. He did not consider that Article

45. See para **[6.08]**.

46. *Cityview Press Ltd v An Chomhairle Oiliúna* [1980] IR 381: see para **[13.67]**.

47. See para **[16.136]**.

29.4.5° conferred an absolute discretion in this respect but that, in certain cases, an Act would be the appropriate choice for the implementation of Directives. Since s 3 of the 1972 Act conferred what appeared to be an unfettered discretion, Johnson J held it was invalid.[48] The decision of Johnson J was ultimately overturned by the Supreme Court, this breathing life back into the many pre-1993 Regulations made under s 3 of the 1972 Act, over 400 in total, which had effected changes to primary legislation.

[16.82] In the course of delivering the judgment of the Court, Finlay CJ stated:

> The Court is satisfied that, having regard to the number of Community laws, acts done and measures adopted which either have to be facilitated in their direct application to the law of the State or have to be implemented by appropriate action into the law of the State, the obligation of membership would necessitate facilitating of these activities in some instances at least, and possibly in a great majority of instances, by the making of ministerial Regulations rather than legislation of the Oireachtas.
>
> The Court is accordingly satisfied that the power to make Regulations in the form in which it is contained in s 3(2) of the Act of 1972 is necessitated by the obligations of membership by the State of the Communities, and now of the Union, and is therefore by virtue of Article 29.4.3°, 4° and 5° immune from constitutional challenge.

The Court in *Meagher* accepted that there might be particular instances where the making of Regulations under s 3 of the 1972 Act would not be 'necessitated' under Article 29.4.5° and that an Act of the Oireachtas would therefore be required. However, the Court held that the presumption of constitutionality[49] made it inappropriate to consider this question as a hypothetical matter and that, therefore, each exercise of the s 3 power should

---

48. In the wake of the High Court decision, two Acts were passed to reverse its effects. In the immediate context of the case, the Animal Remedies Act 1993 now provides the statutory basis for control of growth promoters in animals. At the wider level of the many Regulations which had effected changes to primary legislation, s 5(1) of the European Communities (Amendment) provided that all pre-1993 Regulations were 'hereby confirmed' from the date on which they purported to come into operation. However, in view of the then pending Supreme Court appeal, s 5(2) provided that this was subject to its being in accordance with the Constitution. Since the Supreme Court ultimately upheld the validity of s 3 of the 1972 Act, the confirmation in the 1993 Act 1993 became moot. However, s 5(4) of the 1993 Act remains important as it provided for a blanket extension of the time limit for initiating prosecutions to two years in respect of all Regulations made under s 3 of the 1972 Act, including those which had originally provided, for example, a 12 month time limit. Such a blanket extension may be open to question.

49. See para **[14.44]**.

be considered on its own merits. Turning to the use of the use of the power in this case, the judges delivered separate judgments.

[16.83] Blayney J examined the Directives on which the Regulations were based as well as the nature of Community law. He accepted that a fundamental prerequisite of membership was the supremacy of Community law over domestic law. He cited in this context the decision of the Court of Justice in *Francovich v Italian Republic*.[50] He noted that Directive 85/358/EEC, one of the Directives implemented by the 1988 Regulations, was mandatory and required Member States to make arrangements for taking official and random on-the-spot samples on farms in order to detect prohibited substances in farm animals; this justified the authorisation of searches under the 1988 Regulations.

[16.84] On the question of criminal offences, Blayney J noted that the applicant accepted that the 1985 Directive required the creation of offences for breaches of the principles contained in the Directive. On the time limit for prosecutions, the uncontroverted evidence was that, in view of the complexities involved in taking and analysing samples from a farm, it was necessary to extend the six month time limit in s 10(4) of the Petty Sessions Act 1851. Blayney J held that this supported the view that the extension was required in order to ensure that, in accordance with Article 189 of the EC Treaty, effective sanctions were in place to ensure that the Directive was implemented. Since the State was obliged to implement the 1985 Directive, Blayney J uphold the validity of the 1988 Regulations because they correctly implemented the requirements of the Directive; the fact that the Regulations had also amended an Act was irrelevant.

[16.85] In a concurring judgment, Denham J rejected the argument that an Act of the Oireachtas was required where a Directive lays down a set of rules and principles that must be implemented by the Member States. She stated:

> ... The role of the Oireachtas in such a situation would be sterile. To require the Oireachtas to legislate would be artificial. It would be able solely to have a debate as to what has already been decided, which debate would act as a source of information. Such a sterile debate would take up Dáil and Senate time and act only as a window on Community Directives for the members of the Oireachtas and the nation. That is not a role envisaged for the Oireachtas in the Constitution.

Denham J thus underlined the extent to which law-making authority has been transferred from the Oireachtas to European Community and Union

50. [1991] ECR 1-5357: see para **[16.141]**.

institutions. While her comments only apply where a Directive lays down mandatory rules and principles, most Directives come into this category. *Meagher* thus involves a considerable extension of its decision in *Cityview Press Ltd v An Chomhairle Oiliúna*,[51] at least where implementation of Community law is concerned.

[16.86] In *Meagher*, the Court accepted that the s 3 power had been validly exercised, particularly because the Directives in question left no discretion to the Member States as to whether the rules contained in them would be implemented. Since the rules in the Directives were mandatory, they were 'directly applicable' and were legally enforceable in the State irrespective of any domestic implementing legislation. On that basis, the method legislative method chosen by the Minister was not open to challenge and the 1988 and 1990 Regulations were upheld.

[16.87] The Supreme Court's interpretation of Article 29.4.5° in *Meagher* has been criticised by some commentators.[52] While it was welcomed in Government circles on the ground that it did not invalidate the hundreds of Regulations made by many different Ministers under s 3 of the 1972 Act, it also upheld the situation where primary legislation may be amended by secondary legislation. Although there is some visibility in the implementation of Directives by Ministerial Regulations, these are not as visible as Acts of the Oireachtas. The volume of European Community acts implemented by Ministerial Regulations has grown substantially in recent years,[53] and since many of these involve amendments to primary legislation, this has further complicated the state of the statute book in Ireland.[54]

[7] Institutions of the European Community and European Union

[16.88] Having examined the scope and nature of the Treaties concerning the European Community and European Union Treaties, we turn to examine the law-making procedure contained in the EC Treaty in particular. As already indicated, the EC Treaty remains the most important Treaty of those signed in the 1950s by the six original Member States. In what follows, we discuss the functions of the main institutions of the European Community and Union provided for in the EC Treaty. It will become clear that the functions of the

51. [1980] IR 381: see para **[13.67]**.
52. Eg, Hogan, 'The implementation of European Union Law in Ireland: the Meagher case and the democratic deficit' (1994) 3 IJEL 190.
53. See para **[16.154]**.
54. See para **[13.49]** on the different sources of primary legislation in Ireland.

various institutions have evolved considerably over the years and that their powers have been altered in many ways by the Single European Act and the Treaty on European Union.

[16.89] Article 4 of the EC Treaty provides that the tasks entrusted to the Community shall be carried out by the following institutions:

- a Commission,
- a Council,
- a European Parliament,
- a Court of Justice and
- a Court of Auditors.

The institutions of the European Community and Union resemble in some respects those of Member States, in that they were conferred with executive, legislative and judicial powers. However, any comparison between the Community institutions and those of the Member States breaks down when the detailed powers are examined. Executive powers were conferred by the Treaties, but these are shared between a full-time Community institution, the Commission, and ministerial representatives of the Governments of the Member States, the Council. The major decision-making powers were given to the Council while the Commission was given the main power to initiate proposals to implement the aims of the Treaties.

[16.90] Some legislative powers have been conferred by the Treaties on the European Parliament, and this has increased under the Single European Act and Treaty on European Union, but the main law-making powers remain with the Commission and Council of Ministers. The Treaties also created a Court of Justice, and (as we have already seen) the Court has the power to issue authoritative rulings on Community law. The Court is also a key component of the enforcement mechanisms provided for in the EC Treaty and we will discuss enforcement in the context of the Court's jurisdiction. Finally, the Court of Auditors performs functions for which parallels are found in all Member States, namely ensuring that funds have been properly spent by Community institutions. What follows is a description of the powers and functions of the main institutions of the European Community and Union.

The Commission

Embryonic government and guardian of Treaty

[16.91] The Commission of the European Communities (whose working title has not been changed even after the Treaty on European Union) has been described as an embryonic Government of the Community. Throughout the EC Treaty, the Commission is given the power to initiate measures to implement the aims of the Treaty provisions. Many Articles of the Treaty refer to the Council acting on a proposal from the Commission. Although, as we will see, the EC Treaty confers final decision-making powers in most areas on the Council, the Council cannot act without an initial proposal from the Commission. This has the effect of empowering the Commission to set the agenda for large areas of action in the Community and Union. In addition, the Council has, over the years, delegated many day-to-day tasks to the Commission, thus reinforcing the Commission's powers. We will also see, in the context of the jurisdiction of the Court of Justice, that the Commission is empowered by Article 169 of the EC Treaty to bring proceedings to the Court where there has been a failure by Member States to implement Treaty obligations.[55] In this respect, the Commission is rightly referred to as the 'guardian' of the Treaty.

[16.92] In practice, the Commission and Council (and, increasingly, the Parliament) are involved in a power-sharing arrangement. The Commission remains, as yet, a Government in embryonic form unless and until the Council agrees otherwise. In fact, over the years, the Council has delegated a number of functions to the Commission and this has increased the day-to-day powers of the Commission.

Commission as collegiate body

[16.93] Article 157 of the EC Treaty provides that the Commission is a collegiate body consisting, at present, of 20 members, usually called Commissioners. The Commissioners are nominated by the governments of the 15 Member States on a full-time basis for a period of five years, the most recently-appointed Commission beginning its term in January 1995. Article 157 provides that the Commission must include at least one national of each of the Member States. Given that there are currently 15 Member States, this indicates that all 15 are entitled to nominate a Commissioner each. By an agreed practice, the other five Commissioners are nominated by the five largest Member States, France, Germany, Italy, Spain and the United Kingdom, who thus have two nominees each. The main headquarters of the Commission is in Brussels, with some sections located in Luxembourg.

The President, Commissioners and portfolios

[16.94] The head of the Commission is called the President, who might be described as the Prime Minister of this embryonic Government. The

55. See para **[16.114]**.

President is initially chosen by the Governments of the Member States but must also be approved by the European Parliament. The President then allocates each Commissioner a particular area of responsibility, again similar to a Government Minister, and the Commissioner then takes charge of the equivalent of a Government Department. The Commissioner appointed by the Government of Ireland for the period 1995 to 2000, Pádraig Flynn, was allocated responsibility for Employment and Social Affairs. He would therefore be commonly referred to as the Commissioner for Employment and Social Affairs.

Directorates General

[16.95] The Departments in the Commission are called Directorates General (DGs); of which there are 23 in all. These DGs also contain the full-time officials of the Commission, in other words the permanent civil service of the European Community and Union. In all, there are about 15,000 officials (the so-called 'Eurocrats'). Each Directorate General (DG) is headed by a Director General, who is the equivalent of the Secretary of a Government Department. Thus the officials in the fifth Directorate General (DG V), which deals with Employment, Industrial Relations and Social Affairs, are the civil servants with whom Commissioner Flynn and Commissioner Martin Bangemann, the Commissioner for Industrial Relations, deal.

Initiation power

[16.96] The effect of the various EC Treaty provisions conferring the power of initiation on the Commission is that it is involved in the initiation of virtually all Community proposals designed to implement the aims of the Community and Union as set out in the Treaties. The Commission will forward such proposals to the governments of the Member States for final decision by the Council of Ministers. The Commission must also forward proposals to the Parliament, whose powers and functions we discuss below. Having heard initial comments from these other institutions the Commission may, and, in some instances, must, then reformulate the proposals. This process can take some time, depending on the political sensitivities involved in the proposal in question. While the Commission's functions include the initiation of policies and the drafting of proposals to achieve the objectives of the Treaties, the final decisions on most areas rests with the Council of Ministers. However, as we will see, in many areas the Council has 'delegated back' to the Commission the day-to-day implementation of Council functions.

Role of Advisory Committees

[16.97] In addition to forwarding proposals to the Member States and to the other Community institutions, the Commission is assisted in its functions by a large number of advisory and specialist committees representative of government, employers, the farming community and other workers. These include the Economic and Social Committee (ECOSOC), established under Article 193 of the EC Treaty, which must be consulted by the Council and the Commission. Numerous other advisory committees, comprising national experts in particular areas, have also been established under the Treaties and these are consulted where proposals are initiated by the Commission within their areas of expertise.

Policing Community policies

[16.98] We have already mentioned that the Commission is empowered to initiate proceedings in the Court of Justice against Member States who fail to implement their Treaty obligations. Another area in which the Commission has been given important powers by the EC Treaty is to enforce or 'police' the implementation of Community policies. For example, in relation to competition policy, this includes the power to impose fines on individuals or companies for breaches of Community rules on competition. This has become particularly important in recent years as the Community has developed more detailed rules in this area. Thus, in addition to its executive functions under the Treaty, the Commission exercises a judicial function which would otherwise be associated with a court only.[56]

The Council

Decision-making body representing Governments

[16.99] In the wake of the Treaty on European Union, the Council decided that its name should be altered from 'Council of the European Communities' to 'Council of the European Union'. As already indicated, the Council is the main decision-making body of the European Community and Union, though we have seen that this is dependent to a large extent on proposals being initiated by the Commission. Article 146 of the EC Treaty provides that the Council shall consist of a representative of each Member State at ministerial level, authorised to take decisions on behalf of the Government of that Member State. The Council of Ministers therefore currently consists of 15 Ministers from the governments of the 15 Member States. Each area of Community and Union activity has its own separate Council. For example, the Council of Agriculture Ministers consists of the 15 Agriculture Ministers

---

56. See generally McMahon and Murphy, *op cit*, pp 435-8.

from the Member States. This Council deals with the biggest area of expenditure of the Community and Union, the Common Agricultural Policy. The Council of Finance Ministers (ECOFIN) deals with customs and other taxation issues.

European Council and Foreign Ministers Councils

[16.100] In addition to Council meetings involving Ministers responsible for particular areas of Community policy, two other 'unofficial' Councils began meeting in the late 1960s. The first of these consisted of meetings between the Heads of State and heads of Government of the Member States. These 'Summit' meetings became known as the 'European Council'. In addition, meetings between the Foreign Ministers of the Member States emerged to co-ordinate responses to the 'foreign policy' of the Community. Neither of these meetings were formally recognised until they were included in the Single European Act in 1986.[57]

Delegation of powers to Commission

[16.101] Article 145 of the EC Treaty authorises the Council to confer powers on the Commission to implement rules laid down by the Council. Such delegated powers are in addition to those conferred on the Commission by the EC Treaty itself, in particular the power of initiation. Over the years, many aspects of the Council's day-to-day functions have been delegated to the Commission. This is hardly surprising, as the Ministers who make up the Council must also carry out ministerial functions at national level whereas the Commission is a full-time Community institution.

COREPER

[16.102] The various Councils of Ministers meet on a regular basis and the agenda for such meetings are prepared by the Committee of Permanent Representatives (COREPER), who in effect are the ambassadors of the Member States to the Community and Union. The existence of COREPER allows for permanent liaison between the Ministers and the Commission so that there is no lack of continuity between Council meetings. The function of COREPER is to ensure that, where possible, agreement over matters of concern can be dealt with before Council meetings

57. It was the inclusion of provisions on a common foreign policy in the Single European Act that led the Supreme Court in *Crotty v An Taoiseach* [1987] IR 713 to hold that certain aspects of the SEA went beyond the original terms of Article 29.4.3° of the Constitution, thus requiring a further amendment to ratify the SEA: see para **[16.66]**.

Rotating Presidency

[16.103] Under Article 146 of the EC Treaty, the Presidency of the Council currently rotates between all 15 Member States on an agreed cycle. Under this arrangement, the Presidency of the Council of Ministers was conferred on Ireland for the period July to December 1996. While the Presidency does not involve any additional decision-making powers, the Member State in question is involved in advance preparation of agendas for Council meetings and in ensuring that Council meetings are as successful as possible. This agenda-setting power confers considerable informal power on the Member State holding the Presidency of the Council, particularly in the context of summit meetings and meetings at foreign ministerial level.

Unanimity and Majority Voting

[16.104] Article 148 of the EC Treaty provides that, 'save as otherwise provided in this Treaty, the Council shall act by a majority of its members'. While many provisions of the Treaty require unanimity, the Luxembourg Accords of 1966 in effect required unanimity in all cases, contrary to Article 148.[58] This anomaly was not dealt with until the amendments effected to the EC Treaty by the Single European Act and the Treaty on European Union. As a result, certain decisions continue to require unanimity but other specified matters may be decided by qualified voting majority (QVM). Under this arrangement, the vote of each Minister from the 15 Member States is given a specific weighting, as specified in Article 148 of the EC Treaty. The effect has been that many decisions have been agreed at a much quicker pace since the QVM procedure was introduced under the Single European Act. Whereas a single Member State could 'veto' a proposal under the Luxembourg Accords, the QVM procedure has had the effect that such a Member State will know that, if the issue came to a vote, the proposal could be voted through in any event. For this reason, although relatively few decisions at Council meetings involve a vote, the QVM procedure has had a significant impact.

[16.105] It should, however, be borne in mind that certain decisions at Council level still require unanimity. Thus, any changes in the Treaties themselves require a unanimous decision of the Council; Article N of the Treaty on European Union (replacing Article 236 of the EC Treaty) requires that any such amendments be reached by 'common accord'. Similarly, any changes in the decision-making procedures, such as extension of the QVM arrangement must be unanimous. Decisions in certain politically-sensitive

58. See para **[16.35]**.

areas such as agricultural policy continue to require unanimity, thus continuing the possibility of a 'veto' in Council by a single Member State in order to prevent a decision being made. However, in practice, as with QVM, the actual use of the 'veto' is quite rare, and compromise decisions are in many instances the outcome.

The European Parliament

Directly elected representatives

[16.106] Article 137 of the EC Treaty specifies that the European Parliament shall consist of representatives of the peoples of the Member States. Until 1979, however, the members of the European Parliament were not elected by the peoples of the Member States but nominated by the national Parliaments. This explains in part why the European Parliament (originally referred to as the European Assembly) was initially conferred with quite limited functions. Since 1979, elections have been by direct vote of the people of the Member States, members (MEPs) being elected for a fixed five year term.

[16.107] The total membership of the European Parliament is 626, divided between the 15 Member States. The number allocated to each Member State is not in direct proportion to the Member State's population. Although the larger Member States are allocated a large number of MEPs, the smaller States are given more per head of population. For example, Germany, with a population of over 80 million people, is allocated 99 MEPs. The United Kingdom, whose population is just under 60 million, is allocated 87 MEPs. Ireland, with a population of 3.5 million, is allocated 15 MEPs. Luxembourg, with a population of about 400,000, is allocated 6 MEPs.

Initially limited powers

[16.108] The powers initially conferred on the Parliament by the EC Treaty were confined primarily to two matters: to approve (or disapprove) the proposed members of the Commission and to pass (or refuse to pass) the annual budget for the Community. The power to approve the Commission members was limited to voting en bloc for or against the entire Commission, and objection could not be taken to a particular Commissioner. This considerably limited the impact of this power as it would be embarrassing to refuse to approve the entire list of Commissioners. In relation to the Community's annual budget, the Parliament's power of veto has proved quite important, as on occasion it has held back its implementation until certain requirements were met.

Consultative legislative function

[16.109] As is already clear, the European Parliament is not the main law-making body in the European Community, and so it is quite unlike most national Parliaments. In terms of law-making, the Parliament was, initially, a consultative body, with some powers of influence but with no power to amend legislative proposals from the Commission. For many years, MEPs have called for additional legislative powers to be conferred on the Parliament. The case for additional powers was strengthened when a procedure for direct elections was agreed in the 1970s.

Co-operation procedure

[16.110] Under the Single European Act, the Parliament was given a much increased role, in what is called the Co-Operation Procedure. Under this procedure, which applies to many proposed Community laws, proposals from the Commission are sent to the Parliament for its views, and the Commission usually takes into account the Parliament's comments before sending amended proposals for final decision by the Council of Ministers. In certain situations, only a unanimous decision of the Council can block a Parliament objection, so this has created a great deal of legislative influence for the Parliament.[59]

Co-decision procedure

[16.111] Under the Treaty on European Union, the Parliament is now also empowered to enact certain legislation jointly with the Commission or Council under what is called the Co-Decision Procedure. Where this procedure applies, both the Council and Parliament will be named in the legislative title. The reverse side of this procedure is that, if the Parliament votes against a legislative proposal from the Commission in the areas covered by co-decision, this can in certain instances have the effect of blocking, or vetoing, the proposal. Where the Parliament indicates its rejection of a Commission or Council proposal, procedures for attempting to resolve objections from the Parliament must be made through a Conciliation Committee. If the Conciliation Committee fails to resolve a problem, the proposed law cannot be passed, even by a unanimous vote of the Council of Ministers. It should be borne in mind, however, that both the Co-Operation and Co-Decision Procedures do not apply to all aspects of the European Community and Union, and that certain areas require only that the Commission and Council consult with the Parliament.

---

59. See further para **[16.139]**.

The Court of Justice

[16.112] As we have already seen,[60] Article 164 of the EC Treaty states that:

> The Court of Justice shall ensure that, in the interpretation and application of this Treaty, the law is observed.

Binding effect of decisions

[16.113] In the wake of *Costa*, *Van Gend en Loos* and *Internationale Handelsgesellschaft*,[61] the Court has established that its decisions on the interpretation of Community law are binding on all courts in the Member States, including the Supreme Court in Ireland. It should be noted, however, that the binding nature of Community law only applies to the areas of law with which the European Community and Union is concerned. There are certain areas of the laws of the Member States that remain unaffected by European Community law, such as areas of criminal law and family law as well as most aspects of national court procedure. As to the precise mechanisms by which the Court exercises its jurisdiction under the EC Treaty, this can arise in three main ways.

Failure to fulfil Treaty obligations

[16.114] Article 169 of the EC Treaty empowers the Commission to initiate proceedings in the Court of Justice against a Member State if it considers that 'a Member State has failed to fulfil an obligation under this Treaty'. The most common form of such proceedings is that the Commission alleges that a Member State has failed to implement in national law a Community Directive.[62] Originally, Article 171 of the EC Treaty provided that the Court of Justice could only make a 'finding' that the Member State had failed to fulfil its obligations. Since the Treaty on European Union, Article 171 now authorises the Court to impose a fine on a Member State that fails to comply with a decision of the Court that it has failed to fulfil its Treaty obligations. It should also be noted that Article 170 provides that a Member State may also initiate similar proceedings against another Member State for failure to implement a Treaty obligation. Such proceedings are quite rare, and this reflects the fact that the Commission is seen as the primary 'guardian' of the Treaty.

---

60. See para **[16.52]**.
61. See paras **[16.53]-[16.59]**.
62. See para **[16.136]**.

Actions for annulment

[16.115] Article 173 of the EC Treaty empowers the Court to review the legality of any acts, other than recommendations and opinions, adopted by the Commission, the Council and the Parliament. Article 173 goes on:

> It shall for this purpose have jurisdiction in actions brought by a Member State, the Council or the Commission on grounds of lack of competence, infringement of an essential procedural requirement, infringement of this Treaty or of any rule of law relating to its application, or misuse of powers.

Article 174 of the EC Treaty provides that, if the action under Article 173 is well founded, 'the Court of Justice shall declare the act concerned to be void'. Thus, actions under Article 173 are generally referred to as actions for annulment. Article 175 of the EC Treaty provides for a complementary form of action, the action for failure to act, where a Community institution has failed to carry out its functions. The jurisdiction of the Court of Justice under Articles 173 and 174 may be compared with the process of judicial review in Irish public law, where decisions, including legislative acts, may be declared invalid for being *ultra vires*, whether on the basis that Ministerial Regulations are unauthorised by the Act under which they were made or where any legislative act is challenged for being in conflict with the Constitution.[63]

Article 173 action and Article 177 reference

[16.116] The third basis for the Court's jurisdiction arises from proceedings brought before it by natural or legal persons. In this respect, Article 173 of the EC Treaty also provides that any natural or legal person may, under the same conditions as already described for Member States and Community institutions, institute proceedings against a decision addressed to that person or against any other Community act that 'is of direct and individual concern' to the person. Again, this is comparable to the requirement of *locus standi* in Irish public law.[64] However, even more significant is Article 177 of the EC Treaty, which provides a direct link between the Court of Justice and the national courts and tribunals of the Member States. Article 177 of the EC Treaty provides:

> Where such a question [*that is, interpretation of the Treaty or the validity or interpretation of acts of the Community institutions*] is raised before any court or tribunal of a Member State, that court or tribunal may, if it

63. See paras **[13.72]** and **[15.55]**.
64. See para **[15.76]**.

considers it necessary to enable it to give judgment, request the Court of Justice to give a ruling thereon.

Article 177 and case stated

[16.117] The vast majority of cases that come before the Court of Justice involve references under Article 177 of the EC Treaty and thus originate in the Member States. In the case of Ireland, the majority originate in civil proceedings initiated in the High Court.[65] Thus, in a series of such references in the 1980s and 1990s, the Court held that the State had, in effect, failed to fulfil its obligations to implement a 1979 Directive on equality in social welfare.[66] Any court or tribunal may refer any point of Community law arising in the case to the Court of Justice under Article 177 for what it describes as a 'preliminary' ruling. This procedure is similar to the case stated appeal on a point of law, in that, having dealt with the point of Community law, the case will be returned by the Court of Justice to the court or tribunal which will then dispose of the case in accordance with the Court of Justice's preliminary ruling.[67] The decisions of the Court, while preliminary in that sense, involve definitive determinations on the application and scope of Community law. Many of the Court's most significant decisions, including those in *Costa*, *Van Gend en Loos* and *Internationale Handelsgesellschaft*, involved references from domestic courts or tribunals under Article 177.

Damages for failure to implement Treaty obligations

[16.118] We should also mention at this stage one further refinement of the Court's jurisprudence on the effect of Community law in the national laws of the Member States. We have seen that, under Article 169 of the EC Treaty, the Commission may initiate proceedings against the Member State before the Court of Justice, which may lead to the imposition of a fine. However, the Court of Justice has also been required, in Article 177 proceedings, to consider the effect on individuals and other legal persons in such a Member State of the failure to implement Treaty obligations, such as the failure to implement a Community Directive. In this context, we draw attention to our later discussion of the decision of the Court in *Francovich v*

---

65. See para **[7.54]**.
66. See para **[16.143]**.
67. On the case stated procedure, see para **[7.15]**. On the issue of whether, and to what extent, Irish courts are obliged to refer points of Community law to the Court of Justice, see paras **[7.56]-[7.58]**.

Italy,[68] where the Court held that individuals may claim damages from the defaulting State for such failures.

Administrative arrangements

[16.119] Article 165 of the EC Treaty provides that the Court (which still carries the name Court of Justice of the European Communities, even after the Treaty on European Union) currently consists of 15 judges. While the precise method of appointment of the judges is not specified, the position is that each Member State is entitled to nominate one member or judge of the Court. The current member of the Court nominated by the Irish government is Judge John Murray, who was Attorney General at the time he was nominated. Article 167 of the EC Treaty provides that half of the judges are required to retire every three years, thus making the term of appointment of a judge six years. Article 167 also provides that judges thus retiring are eligible for re-appointment. In practice, many of the judges remain on the Court, by means of the re-appointment mechanism, until the retirement age laid down for senior judges of the State from which they were nominated (in the case of Judge Murray, this is 72 years of age). Article 167 also provides that the Court is to be presided over by a President of the Court, who is elected by the judges of the Court for a three-year term, and to which the President may be re-elected.

[16.120] The Court is empowered to form chambers, each consisting of three or five judges, and the Court can decide many cases as a chamber in accordance with its own Rules of Procedure.[69] However, the Court must sit in plenary session, that is, as a Court of 15 judges, where a Member State or Community institution so requests. The judges are assisted by legal research référendaires, who may prepare draft judgments and engage in related research.

Advocates-General

[16.121] Article 166 of the EC Treaty provides that the Court of Justice shall be assisted by Advocates-General, currently totalling seven in all. Equivalents of these Advocates-General are a feature of many of the Civil Law legal systems of the Member States, but are found only by way of exception in common law jurisdictions.[70] Article 166 provides that an Advocate-General is required to make 'reasoned submissions' on cases brought before the Court. These reasoned submissions typically consist of a

68. [1991] ECR I-5357: see para **[16.141]**.

69. See the position in the Irish Supreme Court in the wake of the Courts and Court Officers Act 1995, para **[4.43]**.

70. Eg, the guardian *ad litem* in wardship proceedings: see para **[5.61]**.

summary of the factual circumstances of the case, the legal issues arising, an analysis of previous decisions of the Court and a recommendation to the Court on how it should decide the case. In the vast majority of cases, the Court will, in fact, decide the case in accordance with the Advocate-General's reasoned submission.

[16.122] The limited number of positions of Advocates-General are rotated amongst the larger and smaller Member States on an agreed system. The effect of this system for a small Member State such as Ireland was that it did not become 'eligible' to nominate an Advocate-General until 1995, over 22 years after acceding to the European Communities. The person nominated as Advocate-General by the Government of Ireland was Mr Nial Fennelly, SC.[71]

Court of First Instance

[16.123] Article 168a of the EC Treaty (inserted by the Single European Act) provides for a Court of First Instance (CFI), with power to determine certain issues of Community law, subject to a right of appeal on points of law only to the Court of Justice. The Court of First Instance was proposed because, by the 1980s, the Court of Justice had become unable to cope with the number of cases coming before it. The Court of First Instance came into being in 1989.[72] Reflecting the composition of the Court of Justice, the Court of First Instance consists of 15 judges, thus enabling each Member State to nominate a judge. The first judge of the Court of First Instance nominated by the Government of Ireland was Barrington J, who had been a judge of the High Court before his appointment to the Court of First Instance and who was appointed to the Supreme Court in 1995.[73] In his place the Government nominated Mr John Cooke, SC. Unlike the Court of Justice, the Court of First Instance is not assisted by Advocates-General, but a judge of the Court itself may be selected to act as Advocate-General for a particular case.

[16.124] The categories of cases which the Court of First Instance may hear are determined from time to time by the Council under Article 168a of the EC Treaty on the basis of a request of the Court of Justice and after consultation with the Commission and Parliament. However, Article 168a also specifies that the Court of First Instance cannot be given jurisdiction to hear and determine questions referred for a preliminary ruling under Article 177 of the EC Treaty. At present, the Court of First Instance has jurisdiction, for example, in relation to disputes brought by officials of the Commission

71. See Fennelly, 'Reflections of an Irish Advocate General' (1996) 5 IJEL 5.

72. On foot of Council Decision 88/591/ECSC, EEC, Euratom.

73. See para **[4.67]**.

and other institutions of the Community and Union (referred to as staff cases) and also in relation to appeals from certain competition decisions of the Commission.

The Court of Auditors

[16.125] Article 188a of the EC Treaty (formerly Article 206 of the EEC Treaty) provides that the Court of Auditors shall carry out the audit of the European Community and Union. The Court of Auditors is not a Court in the same sense as the Court of Justice, and its functions are broadly similar to those performed by the Comptroller and Auditor General under the Constitution of Ireland.[74] It is thus responsible for ensuring that the Community budget is properly spent by the other Community and Union institutions and by any body established under the Treaties. It is also required by Article 188c of the EC Treaty to assist the Parliament and Council in exercising their powers of control over the implementation of the budget. The Court of Auditors consists of 15 members, each Member State being entitled to nominate a member. The present member of the Court of Auditors nominated by the Government of Ireland is Mr Barry Desmond, formerly a Minister for Health and later an MEP. The term of office of a member of the Court of Auditors is six years, though members are eligible for re-appointment.

[8] The Form of European Community and Union Laws

[16.126] As we have already seen, the Court of Justice has established the supremacy of European Community law over national laws. The form of that *corpus* of European Community and Union laws is ultimately based on the Treaties establishing the Communities and the legal instruments that the Community and Union institutions are authorised to make under the Treaties.

The Treaties

[16.127] We have already seen that, as well as setting out the institutional structure for the European Community and Union, the text of the Treaties establishing the three European Communities, as amended since the 1950s, lay down detailed arrangements and timetables concerning the establishment of the 'common market' and 'internal market'. Like the 1937 Constitution,[75] some of these provisions could be described as aspirational and lack the mandatory element typical of legally enforceable rules. However, other

74. See para **[15.23]**.
75. See para **[15.19]**.

provisions of the EC Treaty in particular have all the hallmarks of a legally enforceable rule, as the Court of Justice first made clear in *Van Gend en Loos*, where Article 12 of the EC Treaty was found to have 'direct effects' in national law.[76]

[16.128] Similarly, Article 119 of the EC Treaty provides:

> Each Member State shall ... ensure ... the application of the principle that men and women should receive equal pay for equal work.

For the purpose of this Article, 'pay' means the ordinary basic or minimum wage or salary and any other consideration, whether in cash or in kind, which the worker receives, directly or indirectly, in respect of employment from his employer.

> Equal pay without discrimination based on sex means:
>
> (a) that pay for the same work at piece rates shall be calculated on the basis of the same unit of measurement;
>
> (b) that pay for work at rate times shall be the same for the same job.'

Article 119 has formed the basis for many cases on equal pay that have been considered both by the Court of Justice and by courts in the Member States.[77]

[16.129] However, more significantly, Article 189 of the EC Treaty also empowers the institutions of the European Community and Union to approve legally binding instruments in order to implement the general principles contained in the Treaties. There are three types of legally binding instruments provided for in Article 189: Regulations, Directives and Decisions. We should also mention Recommendations and Opinions, which though not legally binding are of some importance nonetheless.

[16.130] All these instruments are proposed initially by the Commission (with the Parliament now involved in some joint initiatives arising from the changes to the EC Treaty effected by the Treaty on European Union), but the final decision usually rests with the Council. However, the Council can also agree to delegate certain law-making powers to the Commission.

Regulations

[16.131] Article 189 of the EC Treaty states:

> A Regulation shall have general application. It shall be binding in its entirety and directly applicable in all Member States.

---

76. See para **[16.54]**.

77. See McMahon and Murphy, *op cit*, pp 492-503 and *Murphy v Bord Telecom Éireann* [1989] ILRM 53, para **[14.35]**.

Article 189 does not provide much information on the precise form of a Regulation. In essence, it is law in the sense that it will set out certain legally enforceable rules. However, an Article 189 Regulation is not to be confused with statutory Regulations, the domestic secondary or delegated legislation made under an Act of the Oireachtas, whether Regulations made under the European Communities Act 1972 or any other Act.[78] In accordance with the decisions of the Court of Justice in *Van Gend en Loos*, *Costa* and *Internationale Handelsgesellschaft*,[79] once a Regulation is made under the powers conferred by the EC Treaty, it automatically becomes law in all 15 Member States of the Community and Union. Like the legally enforceable provisions of the Treaties, a Regulation made under Article 189 is a clear instance of the 'direct effects' of Community law, since the Oireachtas has no formal function whatever in its enactment and the Regulation thus by-passes the normal law-making procedure under the 1937 Constitution.

[16.132] As we will see, a Regulation differs from a Directive in that it has legal force in the Member States without the need for any further domestic legislative act. All necessary legislative acts have taken place once the procedures provided for in the EC Treaty have been completed. By contrast, a Directive generally requires some form of 'domestic' law to implement its terms. This means that, in relation to a Regulation, there will usually be no Irish law to 'implement' it, because there is simply no need. The Regulation is already law once it is made.

[16.133] Each Regulation is given an official number. The full text of a Regulation is published in the L (Legislative) Series of the Official Journal of the European Communities (OJEC), which is the official daily gazette of all important European Community and Union laws and other important information.[80] In recent years, well in excess of 3,000 Regulations have been made *each year* and then published in the Official Journal, and this provides some indication of the level of legislative activity at European level. By way of contrast, about 30 Acts and in the region of 400 Statutory Instruments are promulgated each year in Ireland.[81]

---

78. On domestic delegated or secondary legislation, see para **[13.58]**.
79. See paras **[16.55]-[16.58]**.
80. The Official Journal is published in two series. The 'L' (Legislation) Series contains the text of Regulations, Directives and Decisions. The 'C' (Information and Notices) Series contains other significant pieces of information, including proposals for the more important proposed Regulations and Directives. The Journal is published in a number of different official languages of the Community and Union. The English language version is published with a pink edge to each page, while, for example, the version in French is published with a blue edge to each page.
81. See para **[13.59]**.

[16.134] A Regulation is generally employed as the appropriate legislative vehicle where the topic covered does not overlap with any existing national laws. For example, the detailed provisions of the Common Agricultural Policy (CAP), such as intervention prices, milk quotas and so forth are dealt with by means of Regulations. In connection with the CAP, Regulations concerning intervention prices are made by the Council. However, as already indicated, the Council delegates day-to-day aspects of Community policy, including the CAP, to the Commission. Such delegation will include the power to make Regulations concerning the implementation of the CAP, such as the detailed administrative arrangements for payment of subsidies. Indeed, such Commission Regulations form a large part of the 3,000 annual entries for Regulations in the L Series of the Official Journal.

[16.135] An example of a Regulation is Council Regulation (EEC) No 2455/92 of 23 July 1992 on the export and import of certain dangerous chemicals, OJ No L 251, 29.8.1992, p 13. This 1992 Council Regulation lays down detailed rules concerning the export from and import into the Community of certain chemicals listed in the Regulation itself. The notation 'OJ No L 251, 29.8.1992, p 13' indicates that it was published in Issue No 251 of the L Series of the Official Journal for 1992, published on 29 August 1992, and that it can be found on p 13 of that issue. Like any domestic legislative document, such as an Act of the Oireachtas, the 1992 Regulation is open to amendment. This occurred in 1994, by means of Council Regulation (EC) No 3135/94 of 15 December 1994, OJ No L 332, 22.12.1994, p 1. Note the change from '(EEC)' to '(EC)' between 1992 and 1994: this arises from the changes effected by the Treaty on European Union.

Directives

[16.136] Article 189 of the EC Treaty states:

> A Directive shall be binding, as to the result to be achieved, upon each Member State to which it is addressed, but shall leave to the national authorities the choice of form and methods.

A Directive is the legal mechanism employed where existing national laws are in place and there is a need to approximate or harmonise them in order to fulfil the general aims of the Treaties. By contrast with a Regulation, therefore, a Directive is not 'directly applicable' immediately. Instead, it will set out the basic rules which must be implemented by all the Member States on a particular topic. The Member States are then left to decide how best to implement the requirements of a Directive so that it fits into the existing law of the State in question. Apart from this difference, Directives resemble Regulations in terms of setting down legislative rules in a format that is similar to domestic legislation. Generally, a Directive sets a time limit within which a Member State must implement its requirements. This can range from a number of months to a number of years, though a period of two to three years is common.

[16.137] As with a Regulation, a Directive is given an official number. The full text of a Directive is also published in the Official Journal of the European Communities. The number of Directives agreed each year is relatively small by comparison with the number of Regulations. As we will see, the total number of Directives Ireland was required to implement between the time it became a Member State in 1973 to the end of 1993 was 1,148.[82] Despite the fact that this would not represent half the number of Regulations made *each year*, Directives have tended to have a higher profile as Community legislation since, in practice, they generally require the enactment of domestic legislation to implement them. In addition, Directives also tend to require the amendment of existing domestic legislation. Although this should increase their visibility, we have already noted the problems arising from the implementation of Directives by domestic delegated or secondary legislation.[83] As with a Regulation, any significant Directive must be made by the Council. However, the Commission is also empowered by various Council Directives to make Directives involving minor adjustments or updating of Council Directives: these are usually known as Directives involving Adaptations to Technical Progress (ATPs).

[16.138] An example of a Directive is Council Directive No 93/13/EEC of 5 April 1993 on unfair terms in consumer contracts, OJ No L 95, 21.4.1993, p 29, which was implemented by the European Communities (Unfair Terms in Consumer Contracts) Regulations 1995.[84]

Co-Operation procedure

[16.139] It may be helpful to describe the sequence of events involved in agreeing a Directive. The example we take is of a Directive agreed under the Co-Operation Procedure in Article 189c of the EC Treaty, first introduced by the Single European Act. The main procedures involved are as follows:

1. The Commission circulates a tentative Proposed Directive to relevant Government Departments and other State agencies in Member States and to any relevant Community Advisory Committee.

---

82. See para **[16.149]**.
83. See para **[16.87]**.
84. SI 27/1995. For criticism of the 1995 Regulations, see Murphy 'The Unfair Contract Terms Regulations 1995: A red card for the State' (1995) 13 ILT 156.

2. The Advisory Committee gives an Opinion on the Proposed Directive.
3. The Commission adopts and publishes a Proposed Directive, taking account of any Advisory Committee's Opinion, and forwards the Proposal to the Council, the Parliament and the Economic and Social Committee (ECOSOC).
4. The Council passes the Proposal to a Working Group, whose activities are co-ordinated by the Committee of Permanent Representatives (COREPER).
5. The Parliament refers the Proposal to the appropriate Committee.
6. The Economic and Social Committee gives an Opinion on the Proposed Directive.
7. The Parliament gives an Opinion on the Proposed Directive, having considered the report of the relevant Committee, and publishes suggested Amendments to the Proposed Directive.
8. The Commission takes a view on Parliament's Opinion and publishes an amended Proposed Directive, which may or may not include all of Parliament's suggested amendments.
9. The Council adopts a Common Position on the Proposed Directive (if necessary by Qualified Voting Majority(QVM), the Common Position being, in effect, an agreed text of the Proposed Directive, which may or may not be the same as the amended Proposal from the Commission.
10. If, within three months of the Common Position, the Parliament amends the Common Position, the Commission must within a further month review the Parliament's amendments and may revise its proposal, in which case the Council, within a further three months:
    (a) may adopt the Commission's revised proposal (if necessary by QVM); or
    (b) may adopt the Parliament's amendments that were not approved by the Commission or otherwise amend the Commission's revised proposal (in which cases the Council would be required to vote unanimously); or
    (c) may fail to act, in which case the Commission proposal lapses.

11. If, however, but also within three months of the Common Position, the Parliament either approves the Common Position or takes no position on it, then the Council adopts the Directive.

Failure to implement Directive

[16.140] As already mentioned, a Directive specifies a date requiring Member States to implement its terms. In many cases, however, Member States do not comply with the deadline set. A further problem arises in connection with incomplete implementation of a Directive or other Community law requirements. In either case, the Commission may initiate proceedings against the Member State under Article 169 of the EC Treaty.[85] However, the late implementation of Directives has also been discussed in a number of cases by the Court of Justice where individual citizens claim their rights have been affected by the failure of a Member State to fulfil Treaty obligations. In this respect, the Court has confirmed the approach in *Van Gend en Loos* and *Costa* that Community law, whether in the form of the Treaties or of Directives, can have 'direct effects' in domestic law.

Francovich *case*

[16.141] In *Francovich v Italian Republic*,[86] the Court reiterated that 'direct effect' arises where a Directive is clear and unconditional and is intended to create individuals rights, leaving no discretion to Member States except in the form of implementing means. In *Francovich*, the Court considered its well-established jurisprudence in the rather novel context of the impact on individuals of the failure of the Italian State to implement in Italian law Directive 80/987/EEC of 20 October 1980 on the protection of employees in the event of an insolvency, OJ No L 283, 28.10.1980, p 23. The 1980 Directive required Member States to put in place specific measures by 23 October 1983 to guarantee, for example, payment of salary arrears to employees whose employers have become insolvent. This had not been done. The plaintiffs were Italians whose employer had become insolvent and at the time they were owed substantial salary arrears. The liquidator informed them that they were unlikely to receive any payment for salary arrears. The plaintiffs then brought proceedings against the Italian State claiming the amounts that would have been due to them.

[16.142] The Court of Justice concluded that a Member State might be required to make good any damage suffered by individuals as a result of

---

85. See para **[16.114]**.
86. [1991] ECR I-5357.

infringements of Community law attributable to the Member State. The Court stated such State liability would arise of three conditions are met:

> the result required by the Directive must involve the granting of rights to private individuals
>
> the contents of these rights must be identified by reference to the provisions of the Directive
>
> there must be cause and effect relationship (or causative link) between the breach of the Member State's obligation and the damage suffered by the persons concerned.

The Court of Justice concluded that, if these conditions are met, a private individual has a right to claim compensation arising directly from Community law. The Court held that the exact procedures by which such a claim would be processed was a matter for national law. Although the decision in the *Francovich* case was in some respects new, it could also be seen as a development of the 'direct effect' approach of earlier cases.[87] It also indicates that the Court's role in the development of Community jurisprudence is not confined to the early decisions of the 1960s.

[16.143] The effect of *Francovich* emerged dramatically in Ireland arising from the failure to implement Directive 79/7/EEC on equal treatment for men and women in social security by the 1984 deadline specified in the 1979 Directive. The Social Welfare Act 1984 formally implemented the 1979 Directive, but the 1984 Act did not come into effect until 1986, a delay justified at the time on the cost involved. A series of claims was initiated by a number of married women in the High Court, who claimed damages arising from the failure to implement the 1979 Directive. In effect, these were claims to be paid the relevant social welfare benefit due in the period between 1984, when the Directive should have been implemented, and 1986, when it was. The State defended the proceedings to the full, and numerous references under Article 177 of the EC Treaty were made to the Court of Justice.[88] The Court of Justice concluded that the 1979 Directive came within the test laid down in *Francovich* and held that full payment to the women involved. Ultimately, in a representative action or final 'test case' on behalf of the women affected, *Tate v Minister for Social Welfare*,[89] the High

87. See generally Collins, 'Community Law as a source of rights and remedies in the Irish legal order' (1994) 2 IJEL 173. *Francovich* was cited with approval in *Meagher v Minister for Agriculture and Food* [1994] 1 IR 329: see para **[16.83]**.

88. *McDermott and Cotter v Minister for Social Welfare* [1987] ECR 1453; *Cotter and McDermott v Minister for Social Welfare* [1991] ECR I-1155; *Emmott v Minister for Social Welfare* [1991] ECR I-4269.

89. [1995] 1 IR 419.

Court concluded that the State was fully liable. The Government finally announced in 1995 that up to £265m in arrears would be paid to the 70,000 married women affected.[90] The need to pay such a large amount brings home the necessity in some instances to implement Directives within agreed time limits.[91]

Decisions

[16.144] Article 189 of the EC Treaty states:

> A Decision shall be binding in its entirety upon those to whom it is addressed.

This indicates that, by contrast with a Regulation or Directive, a Decision usually has limited scope and does not always apply to all Member States. However, it is legally binding on those concerned with it. The text of Decisions are also published in the Official Journal of the European Communities. For example, when the Irish Government proposed in 1993 to provide £175m to the Irish State airline Aer Lingus as part of the rescue plan for the airline, approval from the European Commission was required in view of its responsibility to ensure that this did not breach Community laws regulating competition. The eventual approval of the Commission came in the form of Commission Decision 94/118/EC of 21 December 1993, OJ No L 54, 25.2.94, p 30. If the cash injection had been rejected by the Commission, this would also have been in the form of a Decision.[92]

[16.145] Where the Commission finds that there is a breach of Community competition policy, it is also empowered to conduct investigations of any such breach and if it finds a company or Member State in breach of Community law, it can also take a Decision declaring the activity illegal. Such a Decision would be similar to a court judgment and could even include the imposition of a fine: some Decisions made by the Commission have involved fines of tens of millions of pounds.

Recommendations and Opinions

[16.146] Article 189 of the EC Treaty also specifies that Recommendations can be made or Opinions delivered. Article 189 states:

---

90. See Cousins, 'Equal Treatment in Social Welfare: The final round?' (1995) 4 IJEL 195, p 203.

91. In the British context, the *Factortame* case gave rise to a similar obligation to pay compensation arising from a failure to implement correctly a Directive concerning access to British fishing waters: see *Brasserie du Pêcheur SA v Federal Republic of Germany/Reg v Secretary of State for Transport, ex p Factortame Ltd* [1996] 2 WLR 506, discussed in Flynn, 'State Liability in Damages for Failure to Observe EC Law' (1996) 14 ILT 170.

92. See the Decision establishing the Court of First Instance: para **[16.123]**.

Recommendations and Opinions shall have no binding force.

Obviously, Recommendations and Opinions need not be implemented in national laws even when made or delivered by the Council or Commission. However, they may have some important effects notwithstanding. Thus, in the context of child care facilities for women in paid employment, the 1992 Council Recommendation of 31 March 1992 on child care, 92/241/EEC, OJ No L 123, 8.5.1992, p 16, may form the basis for discussion at national level in the Member States on the provision of child care facilities to ensure equal participation by women in the workforce. Although not legally binding, the Recommendation may be a persuasive authority.

[9] IMPLEMENTATION OF EUROPEAN COMMUNITY LAW IN IRELAND

Self-executing Treaties and Regulations

[16.147] We have already described how the combination of Article 29.4.5° of the Constitution and the European Communities Act 1972 has given effect in general terms to the Treaties of the European Community and Union. As to the detailed legislative acts of the institutions adopted under Article 189 of the EC Treaty, Community Regulations are largely self-executing, are 'directly applicable' and in general do not require domestic implementing measures. As we have already noted, the vast bulk of legislative activity at Community level involves the enactment of Regulations and, since no domestic implementing measures are required, the effect of these Community Regulations on Irish law is largely 'invisible'. In this respect, many aspects of what might be described as the 'Irish-European Law of Agriculture' is to be found in the annual volumes of the Official Journal of the European Communities rather than in the annual volumes of the Acts of the Oireachtas or the annual volumes of Irish Statutory Instruments.

Community Regulations requiring domestic enforcement procedures

[16.148] There are some exceptions to the general rule that Community Regulations do not require implementing domestic legislation. For example, the European Communities (Rules on Competition) Regulations 1993[93] were made under s 3 of the European Communities Act 1972 to facilitate the full implementation of Council Regulation No 17/62 and Council Regulation (EEC) No 4064/89 to enable investigations concerning anti-competitive practices to be carried out by the European Commission under Articles 85

93. SI 124/1993.

and 86 of the EC Treaty and the 1962 and 1989 Council Regulations. While it is true that the Council Regulations are in most respects self-executing, the 1993 Irish Regulations enable designated officers of the Department of Enterprise and Employment to assist European Commission officials carry out their functions, and in this context confer powers of entry and inspection on Departmental officers. The 1993 Regulations specify that it is an offence to obstruct any investigations being carried out and a maximum penalty of £1,000 and/or imprisonment of 12 months are specified. This 'domestic' element to the 'directly applicable' Community laws was enacted to ensure the effective implementation of those Community provisions.

Community Directives requiring domestic enforcement procedures

[16.149] The principal need for domestic implementing measures arises from the requirement to implement or 'transpose' Directives in accordance with Article 189 of the EC Treaty. At the end of 1993, there were 1,148 Directives which Ireland was due to have implemented in domestic law, of which 1,019 (or 88.7% of the total) had in fact been implemented.[94] It is clear from this total that the implementation of Community Directives over the years has required an enormous amount of domestic legislative activity in Ireland. Not only has Community membership required the amendment and updating of existing law, but it has also created entirely new areas of legal regulation where domestic law made no provision before.

Areas affected by implementing domestic legislation

[16.150] It is virtually impossible to provide a comprehensive list of the wide range of areas of law affected by the implementation of Directives, even if one were to leave aside the creation of entirely new subjects of legal regulation arising from the directly applicable provisions of Community law. However, the areas involved include the following:

- agriculture and fisheries
- chemical safety, including pharmaceuticals and pesticides
- coal and steel industries
- company law, including disclosure of financial information and insolvency
- competition, including State aids to industry, public procurement and competition between private undertakings
- contract law, in particular consumer protection

94. See Eleventh Annual Report by the Commission to the European Parliament on monitoring the application of Community law - 1993, OJ No C 154, 6.6.1994, p 1, at p 7.

- customs duties
- educational qualifications (recognition and the right of establishment)
- employment and labour law, including equal access to employment, equal pay, maternity leave, employment protection and movement of migrant workers
- environmental protection
- exchange control and capital movements
- financial services, including banking and other credit provision
- food safety
- insurance
- intellectual property, including copyright, patents and trade marks
- international enforcement of civil judgments
- international relations
- manufacturing standards for products
- nuclear/radiological safety
- occupational pensions
- social security equality
- taxation, especially indirect taxation such as VAT
- telecommunications and other media
- transport.

Areas not affected by Community law

[16.151] Hardly any area of domestic law has *not* been affected by Community law. Areas such as criminal law and family law might be mentioned as being largely unaffected by European Community and Union membership. However, even these areas have been affected to some extent. At a simple level, virtually all domestic implementing provisions involve the creation of criminal offences, albeit of a summary nature where the Regulations are made under s 3 of the European Communities Act 1972.[95] In relation to family law, many areas of domestic family law remain untouched by the Treaties, though some elements of employment law have an indirect impact, for instance in relation equality of access to employment and to child care facilities.[96] Even an area as contentious in the Irish context as abortion

95. See para **[16.74]**.

96. See the Recommendation on Child Care at para **[16.146]**.

has been the subject of litigation in the Court of Justice and in the negotiation of the Treaty on European Union.[97]

Implementation by Acts and Ministerial Regulations

[16.152] Article 189 specifies that the form and method of implementation of Directives is a matter for each Member State to decide. We have seen that, in Ireland, the European Communities Act 1972 empowers a government Minister to implement Directives by means of Regulations made under s 3 of the 1972 Act. Not all of these Directives have been implemented by means of Regulations made under s 3 of the European Communities Act 1972, though the majority have been implemented in this way, with a minority being implemented by means of Acts of the Oireachtas or by means of Regulations made under other Acts. Nor has the same form used consistently for the same topics areas. For example, in the area of company law, a number of Directives were implemented by means of Companies Acts, amending the principal Act in this area, the Companies Act 1963. The Companies (Amendment) Act 1977, the Companies (Amendment) Act 1983 and some provisions of the Companies Act 1990 implemented a number of Directives in this way. But other Directives in this area were implemented by the European Communities (Companies) Regulations 1973, the European Communities (Companies: Group Accounts) Regulations 1992 and the European Communities (Accounts) Regulations 1993, these three sets of Regulations being made under s 3 of the 1972 Act. This poses some difficulties for those attempting to assemble a complete list of the relevant legislative provisions on company law.[98]

[16.153] In relation to Directives, some have been implemented by means of Regulations made under the 1972 Act, others under relevant Acts where these exist. Thus, a number of Directives in the area of safety and health at work have been implemented through Regulations made under the Safety, Health and Welfare at Work Act 1989; the Safety, Health and Welfare at Work (General Application) Regulations 1993 implemented seven Directives in the area of safety and health at work. On the environmental front, Regulations under the Air Pollution Act 1987 and the Environmental Protection Agency Act 1992 also implement Directives.

97. See Byrne and Binchy, *Annual Review of Irish Law 1992* (Round Hall Press, 1994), p 208.

98. In the area of company law, there are happily some excellent collections of the legislative materials: see McCann, *The Companies Acts 1963-1990* (Butterworths, 1993) which, despite its title, includes the relevant Regulations implementing Directives in this area, including those made in 1993.

Volume of implementing legislation

[16.154] To indicate the scale of the domestic legislative activity involved, Table 16.1 notes the number of Acts of the Oireachtas and Statutory Instruments in 1993 and 1994 which involved implementation of Community law obligations.[99]

Year	Total No of Acts	Acts with EC element
1993 1994	40 34	6 7
Year	**Total No of SIs**	**SIs with EC element**
1993 1994	422 464	73 116

Volume of Legislation Implementing EC Obligations
Table 16.1

[16.155] While the number of Acts involved represents quite a large proportion of the total number enacted in 1993 and 1994, the proportion of statutory instruments represents over 20% of the total for the two years; indeed the 116 statutory instruments in 1994 represents exactly 25% of the total for the year. In many instances, these statutory instruments involved the repeal and revocation of existing statutory provisions on the topics they covered, including primary legislation, while in others entirely new domestic legislative provisions were involved. Were it not for the effective constitutional immunity granted to such statutory instruments,[100] they would otherwise have required primary legislation.

Indirect legislative effects of Community law

[16.156] We may also note the indirect effect of Community law on domestic legislative activity. For example, the Competition Acts 1991 and 1996 contain legal provisions which are based on Articles 85 and 86 of the EC Treaty. The 1991 Act was not 'necessitated' by membership, but the rules contained in it owe their form and substance to Articles 85 and 86.

---

99. Source: European Community chapters in Byrne and Binchy, *Annual Review of Irish Law 1993* (Round Hall Sweet & Maxwell, 1996) and Byrne and Binchy, *Annual Review of Irish Law 1994* (Round Hall Sweet & Maxwell, 1996).

100. See para **[16.82]**.

Effects on interpretive approaches

[16.157] We have already discussed the *Francovich* case in connection with the effects of late implementation of a Directive.[101] A connected issue arises where a Treaty provision or Directive is not fully implemented in domestic law or is implemented in language that contains some ambiguity. Again, the concept of 'direct effect' is relevant here. In this respect, an Irish court will refer back to the text of the relevant Directive or Treaty provision. In a case of ambiguity, the text of the Directive takes priority over any implementing domestic law. An example of this is found in *Murphy v Bord Telecom Éireann*.[102] In that case, the statutory words contained in the Anti-Discrimination (Pay) Act 1974 were interpreted by reference to Article 119 of the EC Treaty concerning equal pay on which the 1974 Act was based. The decision in this case also illustrates the influence in Irish law of the teleological approach to statutory interpretation that is a feature of Civil Law systems.[103] Similarly, the harmonious approach to constitutional interpretation was largely influenced by the similar approach adopted by the Court of Justice to interpretation of the EC Treaty.[104]

101. See para **[16.141]**.
102. [1989] ILRM 53: see para **[14.35]**.
103. See also *Tate v Minister for Social Welfare* [1995] 1 IR 419: para **[16.143]**.
104. See para **[16.54]**.

Chapter 17

International Law

[1] Introduction

[17.01] In this chapter, we discuss public international law,[1] also referred to simply as international law or the law of nations. Exercising its treaty-making power under Article 29.4 of the 1937 Constitution,[2] the Government has ratified on behalf of the State a number of international treaties and other agreements with many States. These include the Treaties associated with the European Community and European Union. As we have seen, these Treaties differ from other international agreements in that they have 'direct effect' in Irish law, that is they constituted a new source of Irish law on the State's accession to membership of the European Communities in 1973.[3] The general rule for international agreements is contained in Article 29.6 of the Constitution, which provides that no international agreement may form part of the domestic law of the State save as may be determined by the Oireachtas. In effect, an international agreement has no formal standing in domestic Irish law unless incorporated into domestic law, usually by an Act of the Oireachtas. In this chapter, we discuss the impact in Irish law of a number of international treaties concluded by the Government, other than those involving the European Community and European Union.

[2] Membership of International Organisations

[17.02] The State is party to many international organisations. Since 1955, the State has been a member of the United Nations Organisation (UNO) and was a founder member of the Council of Europe in 1949. Both organisations are primarily committed to human rights protection. Organisations associated with the United Nations and of which Ireland is also a member include the International Maritime Organisation (IMO), the International Labour Organisation (ILO) and the World Health Organisation (WHO).

1. As to private international law, see Binchy, *Irish Conflict of Laws* (Butterworths, 1989).
2. See para **[16.61]**.
3. See para **[16.63]**.

[17.03] In light of the State's policy of military neutrality,[4] it has not sought membership of the North Atlantic Treaty Organisation (NATO).[5] In recent years, the State has taken observer status in the Western European Union (WEU).[6]

[17.04] International organisations play an increasingly important role in trade; the State is a member of the World Trade Organisation (WTO), established in 1994 as successor to the organisation called the General Agreement on Tariffs and Trade (GATT). The GATT was influential in the early 1990s in the removal of many international barriers to trade;[7] in that respect, it played a complementary role to that of the European Community.[8] The State is also a member of the Organisation for Economic Co-operation and Development (OECD), the International Bank for Reconstruction and Development (IBRD) (also known as the World Bank) and the European Bank for Reconstruction and Development (EBRD) (which was founded in the aftermath of the collapse in 1989 and 1990 of the Communist regimes of Central and Eastern Europe and the end of the Cold War with a view to assisting those States in transforming to market economies). The State is also a member of the Organisation for Security and Co-operation in Europe (OSCE), the successor to the Conference for Security and Co-operation in Europe (CSCE), which has emerged in the aftermath of the Cold War as a major influence in seeking to establish agreed principles on security, arms control, human rights and co-operation on economic, social and cultural matters in Europe.

The Council of Europe

[17.05] The State was in 1949 became a founder member of the Council of Europe. We have singled out this organisation for further discussion as the consequences of membership have featured in a range of litigation in the Irish courts and also taking account of its increasing association with the European Union.

[17.06] The Council of Europe was one of the first institutions established after World War II in an attempt to prevent the mass violation of human rights which had occurred during the war. Its first major initiative was the

4. See para **[16.50]**.
5. See para **[16.10]**.
6. See para **[16.10]**.
7. The last Director-General of GATT, former Attorney General and European Communities Commissioner Peter Sutherland SC, was centrally involved in facilitating the finalising of the so-called Uruguay Round of GATT, which removed many international barriers to trade and also provided for the establishment of the WTO as successor to GATT.
8. See para **[16.28]**.

drafting of the Convention for the Protection of Human Rights and Fundamental Freedoms 1950.[9] The State ratified the Convention in 1953.

Convention on Human Rights and Fundamental Freedoms

[17.07] The Convention has proved to be a model for many other international human rights Conventions. The Convention, as amended and expanded by later Protocols, contains provisions guaranteeing the following rights:[10]

- the right to life (Article 2)
- freedom from torture or inhuman or degrading treatment or punishment (Article 3)
- freedom from slavery and forced or compulsory labour (Article 4)
- the right to liberty and security of person (Article 5)
- the right to a fair and public hearing within a reasonable time by an independent and impartial tribunal established by law (Article 6)
- freedom from retrospective criminal and penal legislation (Article 7)
- the right to respect for private and family life, home and correspondence (Article 8)
- the right to freedom of thought, conscience and religion (Article 9)
- the right to freedom of expression (Article 10)
- the right to freedom of assembly and of association with others (Article 11)
- the right to marry and found a family (Article 12)
- the right to an effective remedy before a national authority (Article 13)
- the right to peaceful enjoyment of possessions (First Protocol, Article 1)
- the right to education (First Protocol, Article 2)
- the right to free elections at reasonable intervals by secret ballot (First Protocol, Article 3)

9. The late Sean MacBride SC, one time Minister for External Affairs and leading member of the Irish Bar, Nobel and Lenin Peace Laureate, was closely involved in the drafting of the Convention.

10. See Collins and O'Reilly, *Civil Proceedings and the State in Ireland* (Round Hall Press, 1989), pp 218-20.

- freedom from deprivation of liberty due to inability to fulfil a contractual obligation (Fourth Protocol, Article 1)
- the right of a national of a Contracting State to choose a place of residence in that State and to move within and beyond the territory of that State (Fourth Protocol, Article 2)
- the right of a national of a Contracting State to enter the territory of that State and freedom from expulsion from that State (Fourth Protocol, Article 3)
- freedom of aliens from collective expulsion from a Contracting State (Fourth Protocol, Article 4)
- freedom from the death penalty in peacetime (Sixth Protocol, Article 1)
- the right not to be expelled from the territory of a Contracting State save in compliance with the law and fair procedures (Seventh Protocol, Article 1)
- the right of appeal against conviction or sentence in a criminal matter (Seventh Protocol, Article 2)
- the right to receive compensation owing to a miscarriage of justice (Seventh Protocol, Article 3)
- freedom from double jeopardy in criminal matters (Seventh Protocol, Article 4)
- the right of spouses to equal treatment in family law proceedings (Seventh Protocol, Article 5).

As with the rights and guarantees in the 1937 Constitution,[11] many of these rights are subject to certain restrictions. While many of the rights contained in the Convention also mirror those contained in the 1937 Constitution, other Articles, in particular those concerning torture and forced or compulsory labour, reflect the intention to prevent in the future the atrocities of the Holocaust and concentration camps of World War II.

Enforcement mechanisms

[17.08] A central part of the Convention was the establishment of mechanisms for its enforcement. This may be done by way of complaint, either by an individual citizen or a member State, to the European Commission of Human Rights, situated in Strasbourg, France.[12] If a

11. See para **[15.49]**.
12. This is an entirely different body from the Commission of the European Communities: para **[16.91]**.

complaint of breach of the Convention is deemed to be well-founded the Commission may bring the matter to the European Court of Human Rights, which was not established until 1959. The decision of the Court is a final determination of the matter.

[17.09] In addition to the Commission and Court, the Council of Europe operates through a Parliamentary Assembly and Committee of Ministers which also have important consultative and decision-making powers. The Committee of Ministers has an arbitration role in all disputes under the Convention by which it seeks to arrive at a 'friendly settlement'. Only if this is not possible is the matter referred to the Court of Human Rights. After a decision is made by the Court, it is transmitted to the Committee of Ministers which is responsible for ensuring enforcement of the judgment.[13]

[17.10] Other features of the Convention are representative of similar international agreements. As already indicated, in the absence of legislation incorporating the Convention into Irish law, the Convention is not enforceable as such in an Irish court. In addition, Member States of the Council of Europe are not obliged to accept the jurisdiction of the Commission or Court but Ireland has accepted jurisdiction. Finally, a Member State may, where necessary in the interests of the State, enter into derogations from provisions in the Convention. While these aspects clearly distinguish the Council of Europe and the Convention for the Protection of Human Rights and Fundamental Freedoms from the European Community, it should be noted that the enforcement mechanism provided for in the Convention was a new departure in 1950. The role of the European Court of Human Rights has proved to be very significant, particularly since the 1970s when its workload began to increase dramatically.[14]

Influence on Irish law

[17.11] The first individual case to be brought before the Court was *Lawless v Ireland*.[15] In a case initiated by the Irish Government against the Government of the United Kingdom, *Ireland v United Kingdom*,[16] the Court found that police procedures in Northern Ireland in the early 1970s constituted inhuman and degrading treatment contrary to the Convention. In *Airey v Ireland*,[17] Ireland was found to be in breach of the Convention in

13. The procedure is described in detail in Collins and O'Reilly, *op cit*, pp 223-42.
14. See Collins and O'Reilly, *op cit*, p 224; O'Boyle, 'The Reconstruction of the Strasbourg Human Rights System' (1992) 14 DULJ (ns) 41.
15. (1961) 1 EHRR 25: see para **[17.17]**.
16. (1978) 2 EHRR 25.
17. (1979) 2 EHRR 305.

failing to provide Mrs Airey with access to legal aid in her separation proceedings in the Irish courts, which eventually led to the introduction of a civil legal scheme.[18] The decision in *Norris v Ireland*[19] eventually resulted in the enactment of the Criminal Law (Sexual Offences) Act 1993.[20] The decision in *Keegan v Ireland*[21] has resulted in the publication of the Adoption (No 2) Bill 1996, which will introduce a right of consultation for the natural father in adoptions.

Other Council of Europe Conventions

[17.12] In addition to the Convention on Human Rights and Fundamental Freedoms, a number of other Conventions have been signed since 1950 under the auspices of the Council. These include the European Social Charter (1961), the European Convention on Social Security (1972), the European Convention on the Legal Status of Migrant Workers (1977) and the Convention for the Protection of Individuals With Regard to the Automatic Processing of Data (1982). The latter Convention was implemented in Irish law by the Data Protection Act 1988.

Membership

[17.13] Each of the 15 Member States of the European Union is also Member States of the Council of Europe. This was no doubt influential in the development of a human rights element in the decisions of the Court of Justice of the European Communities.[22]

[17.14] Since the fall of the Communist regimes in Central and Eastern Europe in 1989 and 1990, membership of the Council of Europe has expanded considerably. While this might be considered to be a welcome development, it has created further strains on the existing administrative and decision-making structures within the Council of Europe. Major reforms in the arrangements, including the appointment of full-time judges to the European Court of Human Rights, are due to be implemented in the near future.[23]

Creation of obligations between States, not individuals

[17.15] The treaties and agreements considered in this chapter create important obligations between the States involved, but they do not confer

18. See para **[9.23]**.
19. (1988) 13 EHRR 136.
20. See para **[17.17]**.
21. Judgment of 26 May 1994.
22. See para **[16.57]**.
23. See O'Boyle, *op cit*, p 41.

any legal rights on the individual citizens of those States. Thus, an Irish court is precluded from giving legal force to international treaties in that it must refuse to regard its provisions as part of domestic law unless incorporated into domestic law by the Oireachtas.

[17.16] This application of the dualist theory of international law has been expressed on a number of occasions in the Irish courts in connection with the Convention on Human Rights and Fundamental Freedoms 1950 of the Council of Europe.[24] The Convention has not been incorporated into Irish law, but its provisions have been invoked on a number of occasions in support of arguments challenging the constitutionality of domestic legislation. In all these cases, the courts have affirmed that, since the Convention is not part of Irish law, its provisions cannot be relied on directly.

[17.17] In *In re Ó Laighléis*,[25] the applicant had been interned under the Offences against the State (Amendment) Act 1940. The 1940 Act was immune from constitutional challenge, as its provisions had been upheld by the Supreme Court in 1940 on a reference to it under Article 26.[26] Undaunted, the applicant sought an inquiry into the legality of his detention under Article 40.4.2° and asserted that the internment power was in conflict with the right to liberty in Article 5 of the Convention and the right to a fair trial in Article 6. The Supreme Court, in a judgment delivered by Maguire CJ, rejected the suggestion that the Convention was in any respect relevant to the validity of the 1940 Act:[27]

> "The Court cannot accept the idea that the primacy of domestic legislation is displaced by the State becoming a party to the Convention ... The insuperable obstacle to importing the provisions of the Convention ... into the domestic law of Ireland - if they be at variance with that law is, however, the terms of the Constitution of Ireland. By Article 15, s 2, sub-s 1 of the Constitution it is provided that 'the sole and exclusive power of making laws for the State is hereby vested in Oireachtas: no other legislative authority has power to make laws for the State'. Moreover, Article 29, the Article dealing with international relations, provides at s 6 that 'no international agreement shall be part of the domestic law of the State save as may be determined by the Oireachtas'.
>
> The Oireachtas has not determined that the Convention of Human Rights and Fundamental Freedoms is to be part of the domestic law of the State,

24. See para **[17.07]**.
25. [1960] IR 93.
26. *In re the Offences against the State (Amendment) Bill 1940* [1940] IR 470.
27. [1960] IR 93, at 125.

> and accordingly this Court cannot give effect to the Convention if it be contrary to domestic law or purports to grant rights or impose obligations additional to those of domestic law.
>
> No argument can prevail against the express command of section 6 of Article 29 of the Constitution before judges whose declared duty it is to uphold the Constitution and the laws.
>
> The Court accordingly cannot accept the idea that the primacy of domestic legislation is displaced by the State becoming a party to the Convention for the Protection of Human Rights and Fundamental Freedoms. Nor can the Court accede to the view that in the domestic forum the Executive is in any way estopped from relying on the domestic law. It may be that such estoppel might operate as between the High Contracting Parties to the Convention, or in the court contemplated by Section IV of the Convention [*that is, the European Court of Human Rights*] if it comes into existence,[28] but it cannot operate in a domestic Court administering domestic law. Nor can the Court accept the contention that the Act of 1940 is to be construed in the light of, and so as to produce conformity with, a Convention entered into ten years afterwards."

This passage encapsulates the dualist approach to international law that international law forms no part of ordinary domestic law. The decision in *ó Laighléis* has been followed on a number of occasions. Its most formal application was, perhaps, in *Norris v Attorney General.*[29] In 1977, the plaintiff had instituted proceedings challenging the constitutional validity of ss 61 and 62 of the Offences against the Person Act 1861. The challenge was dismissed in the High Court in 1980. In 1981 the European Court of Human Rights held in *Dudgeon v United Kingdom*[30] that these sections, which were at that time still in force in Northern Ireland, were in conflict with the right of privacy in Article 8 of the Convention on Human Rights. When *Norris* came before the Supreme Court, *Dudgeon* was, not surprisingly, referred to by counsel for the plaintiff in addition to the arguments concerning the alleged invalidity of ss 60 and 61. In 1983, the Supreme Court held, by a 3-2 majority, that ss 61 and 62 of the 1861 Act were not unconstitutional. In the course of his judgment for the majority in *Norris*, O'Higgins CJ pointed out that the ruling in *Dudgeon* case was not relevant to a decision on the constitutional validity of ss 60 and 61 of the 1861 Act and he expressly followed the *Ó Laighléis* case in this respect. He summarised the submissions of counsel and his response thus:

---

28. See para **[17.08]**. The applicant subsequently initiated an individual application under the Convention, which culminated in the first, albeit unsuccessful, decision of the Court, *Lawless v Ireland* (1961) 1 EHRR 25.

29. [1984] IR 36: see para **[15.129]**.

30. (1981) 4 EHRR 149.

"Mrs Robinson [counsel for the plaintiff] has argued that this decision by the European Court of Human Rights should be regarded by this Court as something more than a persuasive precedent and should be followed. She contends that, since Ireland confirmed and ratified the Convention, there arises a presumption that the Constitution is compatible with the Convention and that, in considering a question as to inconsistency under Article 50 of the Constitution, regard should be had to whether the laws being considered are consistent with the Convention itself. While I appreciate the clarity of her submission, I must reject it. In my view, acceptance of Mrs Robinson's submission would be contrary to the provisions of the Constitution itself and would accord to the Government the power, by an executive act, to change both the Constitution and the law. The Convention is an international agreement to which Ireland is a subscribing party. As such, however, it does not and cannot form part of our domestic law, nor affect in any way questions which arise thereunder. This is made quite clear by Article 29, s 6 of the Constitution which declares: 'No international agreement shall be part of the domestic law of the State save as may be determined by the Oireachtas'... Neither the Convention on Human Rights nor the decision of the European Court in *Dudgeon v United Kingdom* is in any way relevant to the question which we have to consider in this case."

This was undoubtedly a correct statement of the law, though as Henchy J, one of the dissenting judges pointed out, ss 60 and 61 seemed to be 'doomed to extinction' in view of the *Dudgeon* ruling. This appeared to be confirmed, though not until over five years later, when the Court of Human Rights ruled that ss 61 and 62 of the 1861, as they operated in Ireland, were in conflict with Article 8 of the Convention: *Norris v Ireland*.[31] A further five years passed before effect was give to this decision in the Criminal Law (Sexual Offences) Act 1993, 16 years after the plaintiff had instituted his proceedings in the Irish courts.

Decisions of international courts not binding

[17.18] From the point of the doctrine of precedent, *Norris* makes clear that decisions of the Court of Human Rights or of any other court exercising jurisdiction under an international treaty are not binding on Irish courts. In *E v E*,[32] O'Hanlon J affirmed this in relation to a decision in which the State had been a party. In the *E* case, the defendant's legal representatives, having appeared on his behalf in lengthy family proceedings without payment, withdrew from the case. The defendant then applied unsuccessfully for civil legal aid to the Legal Aid Board under the non-statutory Scheme of Legal

31. (1988) 13 EHRR 186.
32. [1982] ILRM 497.

Aid introduced in the wake of the decision of the Court of Human Rights in *Airey v Ireland*.[33] He then served notice on the Attorney General of his intention to seek an indemnity from the State in respect of any legal costs incurred by him in the family proceedings, claiming in effect that the refusal of legal aid to him indicated that the Scheme was failing to meet the requirements of effective access to the courts specified by the Court in *Airey*. The defendant's case was complicated by the fact that an internal appeal under the Legal Aid Scheme was still pending and O'Hanlon J considered that this debarred him from raising any question concerning the validity of the Scheme; in any event, he considered that, under the means test then applicable, the defendant was indeed entitled to legal aid. However, on the issue whether the decision in *Airey*, in which the State had been defendant, was legally binding, O'Hanlon J answered clearly in the negative. He noted that counsel for the defendant had sought to distinguish *Ó Laighléis* on the basis that a decision of the Court of Human Rights 'bound the State for the future and could be given effect to in later proceedings brought against the State in the domestic courts.' O'Hanlon J commented:[34]

> "I am unable to accept that this contention is correct. It appears to me that the defendant... is claiming that the State ... did not go far enough in complying with the requirement of the European Convention, as interpreted by the Court of Human Rights in the *Airey* case, and that as a result [he] ... is in danger of finding himself without any legal representation in continuing proceedings of a nature and complexity comparable to those which obtained in the *Airey* case. As this contention is strongly disputed by the Attorney General, it appears to me to be a dispute which should properly be determined by the procedure provided for in the European Convention, involving a reference of the matter to the European Commission [of Human Rights] initially, with the possibility of a later determination by the Court of Human Rights."

The view that matters involving the Convention must be pursued through the machinery provided under its terms, rather than through the national courts, is entirely consistent with the dualist approach to international law. The judgment in *E* also anticipated the long process of litigation that was involved in *Norris*.

Presumption of conformity with international law

[17.19] While *Ó Laighléis*, *E* and *Norris* continue to represent an accurate statement of the law, the courts have occasionally referred to the Convention and other international Conventions as aids to the interpretation of Irish law.

33. (1979) 2 EHRR 305: see para **[9.23]**.
34. [1982] ILRM 497, 499-500.

Thus, in order to elucidate the provisions of Article 29.3 by which the State accepts the 'generally recognised principles of international law', in *Crotty v An Taoiseach*[35] Barrington J referred to the Vienna Convention on the Law of Treaties 1969 as reflecting the relevant principles concerning the ratification of treaties even though the State had not ratified the Treaty.

[17.20] Similarly, case law of international courts may prove influential, notwithstanding the views expressed in *Ó Laighléis*. Thus, in *Desmond v Glackin (No 2)*,[36] a case alleging contempt of court against a Government Minister, O'Hanlon J appeared favourably disposed towards a decision of the Court of Human Rights. The issue arose in judicial proceedings in which the applicant, a stockbroker, had raised a number of constitutional issues concerning the powers of the first respondent, who had been appointed as an inspector under the Companies Act 1990. The appointment had been made by the second respondent, the Minister for Industry and Commerce, to investigate the sale of a valuable site, in which the first applicant had been involved as financial adviser. The sale had been the subject of considerable public debate prior to the appointment of the first respondent as inspector.[37]

[17.21] On an *ex parte* application to the High Court, the applicants had obtained leave to seek judicial review of the inspector's appointment[38] and also mandatory interim relief prohibiting him from questioning the first applicant further on his involvement in the transactions leading to the sale of the site in question. The affidavit grounding the application alleged that the respondents had obtained certain information from the Central Bank in breach of the Central Bank Acts 1942 to 1989 and the interim relief included an injunction prohibiting the use of any such information.

[17.22] The second respondent, the Minister for Industry and Commerce, gave an extensive live radio interview to Radio Telefís Éireann in which he stated that he had been 'amazed' by the application for interim relief, agreed in response to a question posed that the effect of the injunction was that the High Court had facilitated the blocking of the inspector's investigation under the 1990 Act. He also criticised the High Court for accepting the averment in the applicants' grounding affidavit that he (the Minister) had acted in breach of the Central Bank Acts. The applicants unsuccessfully applied to have the Minister attached for contempt of court. Although

---

35. [1987] IR 713: see para **[16.63]**.
36. [1993] 3 IR 67. See also para **[14.49]** on the presumption of compatibility of legislation with international law.
37. See Byrne and Binchy, *Annual Review of Irish Law 1992* (Round Hall Press, 1994), pp 67-83, 239-42.
38. See para **[10.35]**.

O'Hanlon J considered that the Minister had been ill-advised to give a response on a live radio broadcast, he accepted that the matter was of ongoing public interest and involved an 'exceptional situation' which, having regard to the provisions protecting freedom of expression in Article 40 of the Constitution, should not be punished as contempt.

[17.23] O'Hanlon J had been referred to the decision of the Court of Human Rights in *Times Newspapers Ltd v United Kingdom*.[39] This arose from the publication by the *Sunday Times* of a series of articles in the late 1960s which had been highly critical of the manufacturers of Thalidomide, a drug which had been developed to relieve the effects of morning sickness in pregnant women. Although Thalidomide did relieve these effects, it also produced many adverse side effects in the children born to such women. The articles had been published at a time when numerous claims for damages arising from the use of Thalidomide were pending in the English courts against the manufacturers. In *Attorney General v Times Newspapers Ltd*,[40] the House of Lords had held that the newspaper was in contempt of court for having published material likely to prejudice the outcome of these cases. In *Times Newspapers Ltd v United Kingdom*,[41] the European Court of Human Rights held that this aspect of British contempt law was in breach of the guarantee of freedom of expression in Article 10 of the European Convention. In *Desmond*, O'Hanlon J quoted extensively from the speeches in the House of Lords and the judgments in the Court of Human Rights in the *Times Newspapers* cases. He commented:

> "The very exhaustive examination of the law of contempt of court by the House of Lords in the *Times Newspapers* case is a persuasive authority of considerable importance. I am of opinion that the decision of the Court of Human Rights in relation to the same case is also of significance when considering whether the stringent rules adopted by the Law Lords should be accepted as a correct statement of the law of contempt of court as applied in this jurisdiction."

He noted that, in Ireland, the law of contempt must be considered against the background of the Constitution. While Article 40 guaranteed freedom of expression, it was also stipulated that organs of public opinion should not be used to undermine 'public order or morality or the authority of the State.' He considered that this was comparable to the limitation on freedom of expression in Article 10(2) of the European Convention to the extent 'necessary ... for maintaining the authority and impartiality of the judiciary.'

---

39. (1979) 2 EHRR 245.
40. [1974] AC 273.
41. (1979) 2 EHRR 245. Arising from this decision, the Westminster Parliament enacted the Contempt of Court Act 1981. On proposed legislation in Ireland, see para **[10.31]**.

In the *Times Newspapers* case, the Court of Human Rights held that it was not necessary to maintain the authority of the judiciary for the *Sunday Times* to have been found contempt of court. O'Hanlon J stated:

> "As Ireland has ratified the Convention and is a party to it, and as the law of contempt of court is based (as was stated by Lord Reid [in *Attorney General v Times Newspapers Ltd*]) on public policy, I think it is legitimate to assume that our public policy is in accord with the Convention or at least that the provisions of the Convention can be considered when determining issues of public policy. The Convention itself is not a code of legal principles which are enforceable in the domestic courts, as was made clear in *In re Ó Laighléis*,[42] but this does not prevent the judgment of the European Court from having a persuasive effect when considering the common law regarding contempt of court in the light of the constitutional guarantees of freedom of expression contained in our Constitution of 1937. Henchy J expressed the view in *The State (Director of Public Prosecutions) v Walsh*[43] that there was a presumption that our law of contempt is in conformity with the Convention, particularly Articles 5 and 10(2)."

This passage would appear to indicate that, at least in some instances, the Convention and the decisions of the Court of Human Rights may be used as 'persuasive authority'. Ultimately, however, O'Hanlon J did not expressly rely on the decision of the Court of Human Rights. In concluding that no contempt had occurred, he concluded:

> "I consider the case falls well within the scope of the 'exceptional situations' referred to by both Lord Reid and Lord Simon of Glaisdale in the *Times Newspapers* case where 'the law strikes [the balance] in favour of freedom of discussion'. I also apply the *dictum* of Lord Morris in the same case when he said, 'If in doubt whether the conduct complained of amounts to 'contempt' the complainant will fail.'"

Thus, while O'Hanlon J appeared to favour the outcome in the Court of Human Rights in the *Times Newspapers* case, he was able to decide *Desmond* on the basis of the principles expressed in (though not necessarily the outcome in) the House of Lords. In that respect, the influence of the Convention remained in the background. This cautious attitude to importation of the Convention and similar human rights instruments is consistent with the approach of the Court of Justice of the European Communities.[44]

---

42. [1960] IR 93.
43. [1981] IR 412 at 440.
44. See para **[16.57]**.

Enforcement mechanisms at international level

[17.24] It is clear that, save in exceptional instances, the international organisations and agreements to which the State is party do not operate in the sphere of domestic law enforcement. The conduct of international relations is primarily a matter for the Government, subject of course to the limits imposed by the Constitution.[45] Similarly, the enforcement of agreements and treaties to which the State is party operates primarily at the level of international diplomatic relations. In practical terms, once a State is party to an international organisation or agreement, the enforcement mechanisms are quite different from those which would apply where breach of a rule of domestic law is involved.

[17.25] However, it is increasingly the case that compliance or non-compliance with international obligations is subject to public scrutiny and examination. Thus, the United Nations International Covenant on Civil and Political Rights 1968 (ICCPR) provides that those States who ratify its terms are subject to review by the Human Rights Committee established under its terms. The Human Rights Committee comprises an independent body of lawyers and other experts in the field of human rights protection. While the Committee is not a court as understood by Article 34 of the 1937 Constitution, it sits in public when reviewing the implementation by a State of the ICCPR. In 1989, the State ratified the ICCPR and in 1993, the Human Rights Committee held public hearings which considered the State's report on its implementation. The hearings also heard submissions from interested parties, including non-governmental organisations (NGOs) involved in monitoring human rights.[46]

Bilateral Treaties

[17.26] In addition to the power to sign and ratify Treaties concerning international organisations, the Government may enter into bilateral arrangements with other States. These include Treaties between the State and another State concerning the avoidance of double taxation where Irish nationals work in the other States and *vice versa*. Similarly, extradition Treaties between the State and another State are entered into on the basis of mutual arrangements. Finally, we also note in this context the Anglo-Irish Agreement 1985, entered into between the State and the United Kingdom.[47]

45. See para **[16.63]**.

46. For an account of the hearings and their outcome, see O'Flaherty, 'Implementation of the International Covenant on Civil and Political Rights - Ireland before the Human Rights Committee' (1993) 11 ILT 225. See also para **[15.140]**.

47. See para **[15.39]**.

BRAINSE CABRACH
CABRA BRANCH
TEL: 8691414

Index

abuse of process, 6.09
access to law
(*see also* **legal aid and advice, litigants**)
constitutional right, 9.02
court fees, 9.36
legal costs, 3.43, 9.38
small claims, 5.35
accountants and law, 3.86
accusatorial system
(*see* **criminal procedure**)
ACLET, 3.72
actio popularis
(*see* **constitution**)
Act of Union, 2.18
adjudicative bodies, 8.20
administration and courts
(*see* **court officers**)
administration of justice
(*see* **courts**)
administrative law
(*see* **government, natural justice**)
Admiralty, Court of, 2.39
ADR, 5.12, 5.35, 8.30
adversarial nature
(*see* **court procedure**)
Advertising Standards Authority of Ireland, 5.12, 13.05
Advisory Committee on Legal Education and Training (ACLET), 3.72
American revolution, 2.20, 15.43
anecdotes of law, 3.49
Anglo-Irish Agreement (1985), 15.39
Anglo-Irish Treaty (1921), 2.55
Anglo- Norman Invasion, 2.03
Anton Piller Order, 10.11
appeal commissioners, 8.60
appeals
(*see* **Appellate Jurisdiction of Courts**)
appeals officer (social welfare), 8.62
Appellate Jurisdiction of Courts
(*see also* **Circuit Court, Court Of Criminal Appeal, Court Of Justice Of European Communities, District Court, High Court, Supreme Court**)
acquittal, appeal against (indictment), 7.50
acquittal, appeal against (summary), 7.29
case stated 7.15
de novo hearing, 7.04
function of court on (*de novo*), 7.04
function of court on (point of law), 7.05-7.11
judicial review, distinguished from appeal, 10.37
miscarriage of justice, 7.47
point of law, appeal on, 7.05
primary findings of fact, 7.07
secondary findings of fact, 7.08
transcript, use of, 7.06
arbitration, 8.31
advantages over litigation, 8.32
adversarial procedure, 8.34
appeals from, 8.35
courts, appeals to, 8.35
stay of court proceedings, 8.33
architects and law, 3.85
arrestable offence, 6.61
Assize courts
(*see* **inferior courts**)
Attorney General, 3.54
appointment, 3.55
Bar and, 3.56
constitutional challenges, role in, 3.59

Director of Public Prosecutions and, 3.58
extradition, 3.58, 4.75
fiat (former), 9.02
government legal adviser, 3.55
judicial review, legal aid scheme, 9.17
judicial vacancies, 3.60
Parliamentary Draftsman's Office, 3.57, 13.33
prosecution of offences, 3.58, 3.63
public interest, 3.59
relator actions, 3.59

audi alteram partem
(*see* **natural justice**)

bail
(*see* **criminal procedure)**

Bankruptcy and Insolvency, Court of, 2.39

Bar, the
(*see* **barristers**)

barristers
admission and education, 3.29
advocacy, 3.48
anecdotes, 3.49
Attorney General, 3.56
Bar, The, 3.27
cab rank rule, 3.40
Code of Conduct, 3.37
devil, 3.34
discipline, 3.36
fees, 3.43
functions of, 3.46
increased numbers, 3.28
instructions, 3.40
judiciary and, 4.66
junior counsel, 3.44
King's Inns, Honourable Society of, 3.29
Law Library, 3.32
law reporting and, 12.07
master, 3.34
mode of dress, 3.50
pro bono work, 9.11
senior counsel, 3.44
solicitor, instructions from, 3.40
statutory regulation, 3.47, 5.24
tyro, 3.34
two senior rule, 3.47, 5.24
wigs, 3.50-3.52

binding authority
(*see* precedent)

binding to the peace, 2.51 10.25

book of evidence
(*see* **criminal procedure**)

Bord Pleanála (planning board), 8.56

brehon law
Anglo-Norman Invasion, 2.02
Brehons, 2.02
common law, predominance over, 2.16
Dáil Éireann courts and, 2.61
fishery rights, 2.16
gavelkind, 2.16
Irish law tracts, 2.02
tanistry, 2.16

Bunreacht na hÉireann
(*see* **Constitution of Ireland**)

cabinet
(*see* **government**)

canon law, 1.17

case stated, 7.15

Central Criminal Court
(*see* **High Court**)

certiorari, 10.36

Chancery
(*see* **equity**)

Chief State Solicitor, 3.26
Children's Court
(*see* **District Court**)
Circuit Court
adjudicative tribunals and, 7.51
appellate jurisdiction (civil), 7.13
appellate jurisdiction (criminal), 7.29
Circuit Family Court, 5.44
circuits, 4.53
civil bill, 2.66, 6.52
consent jurisdiction (civil), 5.40
county courts (former) and, 2.66, 5.38
county registrar, 4.123
court of record, 4.52
defence (civil), 6.52
District Court, President of, 4.52
establishment, 4.52
European Court of Justice and, 7.54
exclusive jurisdiction (civil), 5.44
ex officio member, 4.52
first instance jurisdiction (civil), 5.30-5.37
first instance jurisdiction (criminal), 5.71-5.79
geographical limit to jurisdiction, 4.53
inferior court, 4.30
Irish language areas, 4.53
jury abolished in civil cases, 4.52
jury court in criminal cases, 4.52, 5.80
local and limited jurisdiction, 4.30, 4.53
mode of address, 4.61
number of judges, 4.52
original jurisdiction
(*see* **first instance jurisdiction**)
pleadings, 6.52
President of, 4.52
regional organisation, 4.53
style or title of judges, 4.52
temporary judges, 4.52
transfer in criminal cases, 5.82, 15.109
Civil Court of Appeal, former proposal for, 4.44
civil law, distinguished from criminal law, 6.02
civil law systems
common law, distinguished from, 1.06
inquisitorial nature (criminal), 6.66
legislation and, 13.40, 13.54
precedent and, 12.01
civil legal aid
(*see* **legal aid and advice**)
civil procedure
(*see also* **court procedure**)
abuse of process, 6.07
balance of probabilities, 6.16
burden of proof, 6.16
compensation and, 6.03
compromise or settlement, 6.54
counterclaim, 6.45
defendant, 6.12
discovery of documents, 6.50
interrogatories, 6.51
parallel criminal proceedings, 6.10
parties, 6.12
plaintiff ,6.12
pleadings
Circuit Court, 6.52
District Court, 6.53
function of, 6.21
High Court, 6.26-6.51
res judicata, 7.47

rules of court, 6.01
settlement or compromise, 6.54
statute of limitations, 6.07
time limits, 6.07
Collegiate Court
(*see* **Supreme Court**)
commentaries, 1.18
Committee on Civil Legal Aid and Advice, 9.22
Committee on Court Practice And Procedure
establishment, 11.05
reports of, 11.05
Committees of Oireachtas, 8.55 13.16
common informer, 6.63
common law
(*see also* **precedent, sources of law**)
chancery, courts of, and, 1.08, 2.07
civil law system
contrast with, 1.07
separation from, 2.06
Constitution and, 15.64
English common law, 1.06, 2.04-2.09
equity and, 1.08, 2.07
Irish law and, 2.11-2.19
judge-made law, 2.10
legislation, distinguished from, 1.11
parliament and, 2.09
system of law, as, 1.06
Common Market
(*see* **European Community Law**)
Common Pleas, Court of, 2.39
community service, 10.26
company
(*see* **legal personality**)
compensation, 6.03
compensation order, 6.04
Conference for Security and Co-Operation in Europe (CSCE), 17.04
conflict of laws, 10.21 17.01
Constitution of Ireland (1937)
(*see also* **Constitution of Irish Free State (1922)**)
abortion, 15.130-15.135
actio popularis, 15.77
administration of justice
(*see* **judge**)
amendments to, 15.68- 15.74
American influence, 15.43, 15.81, 15.128, 15.130
appeal against acquittal 7.50, 12.58, 15.102
Aquinas, St Thomas 15.113
Aristotle, 15.113
armed service and, 15.45
articles (generally), 15.17
avoidance of constitutional issues, 14.44, 15.75
bodily integrity, 15.52
buggery, 15.129
changing meaning of, 15.104-15.107
Christianity and, 15.113- 15.115
common good, 15.128, 15.129
Comptroller and Auditor General, 15.23
conflict between English and Irish language texts of, 15.31
Constitution Review Group, Report of (1996,) 15.139-15.140
constitutional judicial review
conferral of power of, 15.28

criticisms of, 15.93
growth of, 15.80
limits to, 15.97
continuity of laws, 15.29
contraceptives, 15.128
courts and
(*see* **courts**)
Crown prerogatives and, 15.43-15.46
divorce and, 15.73, 15.90-15.91, 15.112
English language text of, 15.30
English law, 15.129
entrenched rights, 15.26
equality, 15.48
establishment of courts
(*see* **courts**)
European Community law and
(*see* **that title**)
European Convention on Human Rights and
(*see* **Council Of Europe**)
euthanasia and, 15.136- 15.138
executive power and, 15.86-15.87
fair procedure,s 15.48
family and, 15.111-15.112
flouridation of water and, 15.50-15.52
French Revolution and, 15.43
fundamental rights (generally), 15.48-15.54
government, branches of, 15.20
Greek philosophy and, 15.113
habeas corpus and, 10.36
harmonious approach, 15.109, 15.131
Hart-Devlin debate, 15.123
historical approach, 15.104-15.106
homosexuality, 15.129
human rights (generally), 15.48-15.54
immunity of law on Article, 26 decision, 15.68
immunity of State from suit, 15.43-15.46
implied rights: *see* personal rights
inquiry into legality of detention, 10.36
interpretation (generally), 15.98-15.125
invalidity of laws, declaration of
common law rule and 15.64
effect of 15.60
example of 15.55-15.59
filling gaps, whether permissible 15.62
judicial death certificate and 15.60
prospective effects, 15.65
retrospective effects, 15.65
Ireland and Republic of Ireland, 15.41
Irish Free State, of
(*see* **Constitution of Irish Free State**)
Irish language text of, 15.31-15.32
Judaeo-Christian thought and, 15.128
jus tertii, 15.77
justiciable controversies, 15.75, 15.97
legal aid and
(*see* **legal aid and advice**)
legal system and 15.83
legislation, comparison with rules of interpretation, 15.98-15.110
legislature, restrictions on, 15.27 15.84
limitations on rights, 15.49
literal interpretation, 15.100-15.102

locus standi, 15.76-15.79
marital breakdown and, 15.90-15.91
Mill, John Stuart, 15.120
moral code and, 15.128
national territory and, 15.37
natural justice and, 15.54
natural law and, 15.111-15.138
Northern Ireland and, 15.38-15.39
Oireachtas and
(*see* **that title**)
overbreadth, 15.59
Papal Encyclical, 15.126
People, and, 15.42-15.43
personal rights, 15.50-15.54
political controversies, 15.76, 15.97
preamble, 15.42
prerogatives and, 15.43-15.46
presumption of constitutionality, 14.44, 15.75
President and, 15.21
privacy, 15.128-15.130
property, 15.85
prospective effect of declaration of invalidity of law, 15.65
remedy for enforcement of rights, 15.43
representative actions, 15.67
Republic of Ireland and Ireland, 15.41
retrospection and declaration of invalidity of law, 15.65
rhetoric of, 15.19
'right to die', 15.136-15.138
right to life of unborn, 15.130-15.135
rights (generally), 15.48-15.54
self-determination and, 15.36
self-restraint, judicial rules of, 15.75
separation of powers, 15.20-15.28
severability, 15.75
sexual privacy and, 15.88-15.89
sovereignty of State, 15.43
state of opinion at enactment of, 15.104-15.107
structure, 15.17, 15.18
successor to Constitution of Irish Free State, 15.18
Supreme Court, reference to, 5.65
treasure trove, 15.46
unenumerated rights
(*see* **personal rights**)
United States influence, 15.43, 15.81, 15.128, 15.130
Utilitarianism and, 15.118-15.125
Wolfenden Committee, 15.129

Constitution of Irish Free State (1922)
amendments to, 15.08-15.09
Anglo-Irish Treaty (1921) and, 15.02
British and Irish perspectives on, 15.03
continuity of laws, 15.07
fundamental rights in, 15.06
judicial responses to amendments, 15.10-15.16
institutions of State and, 15.04
separation of powers and, 15.05
succeeded by Constitution of Ireland (1937), 15.17

Constitutional monarchy (Britain), 2.24

Constitution Review Group, Report of (1996), 15.139-15.140

contempt of court
attachment, 10.33
civil contempt, 10.32
criminal contempt, 10.32

prosecution (criminal), 10.34
sequestration of assets, 10.33

contingency fees, 3.25

Continuing Legal Education (CLE), 3.76

contract law, 1.26 13.64

contracts of adhesion, 13.64

Controller of Patents, Designs and Trade Marks, 8.50

Coroners Court, 8.37
criminal proceedings and, 8.39
inquests, 8.37
inquisitorial nature of, 8.38
jury in, 8.37
restrictions on, 8.39
verdicts of, 8.39

costs
'follow the event', 5.23
legally aided cases, in, 9.38-9.39
taxation of ,5.26
two senior rule, 3.47, 5.24

Council of Europe
history of, 17.06
Commission of Human Rights, 17.08
Committee of Ministers, 17.09
connection with European Community, 17.10
Convention on Human Rights and Fundamental Freedoms, 17.07
Court of Human Rights, 17.08
domestic law and, 17.11
Parliamentary Assembly, 17.09

county courts, 2.53

County Registrar, 4.123
seizure power of, 8.61

court administration
(*see* **courts, court officers**)

court fees, 9.36

Court of Appeal (Civil)
English 2.75
former proposal for 4.44

Court of Appeal of Ireland (former), 2.47

Court of Appeal of Southern Ireland (former), 2.59

Court of Criminal Appeal
abolition of, 4.44, 7.35
appeals from, 7.36
appellate jurisdiction, 7.35
composition, 7.36
establishment, 7.36
leave to appeal, 7.36
not bound by own decisions (*see* **precedent**)
of Irish Free State, 2.68
re-trial, 7.36
transfer of jurisdiction to Supreme Court, 7.35

Court of Justice of the European Communities
actions for annulment and 16.115
administrative arrangements
advocate-general, 16.121
appointment of judges, 16.119
chambers, sitting in, 16.120
Court of First Instance, 16.123
number of judges, 16.119
référendaires, 16.119
retirement of judges, 16.119
appellate jurisdiction, 7.52
courts and tribunals, from, 7.54
case stated, comparison with, 16.117
discretionary references, 7.57
mandatory references, 7.56
binding effect of decisions of, 16.113
damages for failure to implement obligations, 16.118

failure to fulfil treaty obligation, and 16.114
interpretation of EC law and, 16.52-16.59
judge of, qualified for appointment to Irish courts, 4.67
references to, 16.116
court of record, meaning, 4.41
court officers
administrative arrangements, 4.115
county registrar, 4.123, 8.61
District Court clerk, 4.123
Examiner, 4.117
High Court Central Office, 4.119
increased powers of, 4.118, 4.123
Master of the High Court, 4.118
Official Assignee in Bankruptcy, 4.117
registrar, 4.120
sheriff, 8.61
sittings of courts, 4.124
small claims, 5.35
Taxing Master, 4.121 5.26
vacations, 4.124
court procedure
(*see also* **civil procedure, criminal procedure**)
adversarial nature of, 6.80
accusatorial criminal procedure, 6.96
affidavits, 6.84
compensation and punishment, 6.03
costs, 5.26-5.28
evidence, rules of, 6.86
hearsay, 6.89
oath, 6.81
opinion, 6.93
judge and jury, 6.99
judicial review, on, 10.39
Legal Diary, 6.46
limitation periods, 6.07
oath, 6.81
public and private law, 6.02
testimony
oral, 6.83
written, 6.84
time limits, 6.07
witnesses, sequence of, 6.95
courts
(*see also* **judges**)
adjudicative bodies, appeals from, 8.30-8.65
administration of justice, meaning, 4.1-4.18
administration of justice, private, in, 4.20-4.22
administration of justice, public, in, 4.19-4.23
appeals
(*see* **7.01-7.58**)
Circuit Court
(*see* **that title**)
Constitution
(*see* **that title**)
Court of Criminal Appea
(*see* **that title**)
Court of Justice of European Communities
(*see* **that title**)
Court officers
(*see* **that title**)
Court terms, 4.124
Courts Service, 4.138
delays, 4.135
District Court
(*see* **that title**)
efficiency and quality, 4.130
establishment of (1924), 2.64-2.70 4.03
establishment of (1961), 4.34-4.37

European Court of Human Rights
(*see* **Council of Europe**)
fees, 9.36
financing of, 4.136
first instance courts, 5.03, 5.04
'former' courts, 4.37, 12.17
'famous trials', books concerning, 4.98
High Court
(*see* **that title**)
inferior courts, 4.30
Irish Free State, in, 2.64-270, 4.03
Ireland, in, 4.34-4.37
judges
(*see* **that title**)
jurisdiction
(*see* **Circuit Court, Court of Criminal Appeal, Court of Justice of European Communities, District Court, High Court, Supreme Court**)
jury
(*see* **that title**)
justiciable controversies, 4.17
limited judicial functions, 4.10
local and limited jurisdiction, courts of, 4.30
management of, 4.125
Ombudsman, distinguished from, 8.26
political controversies, 4.17
public sittings, 4.19-4.23
record, court of, 4.41
reforms, proposals for, 4.125
regulation of business by law, 4.32
sittings of courts, 4.124
Special Criminal Court
(*see* **that title**)
superior courts, 4.41
Supreme Court
(*see* **that title**)
television in court, 4.23
terms, 4.124
tribunal of inquiry distinguished from, 8.64
Working Group on Courts Commission, 4.126
workload of, 4.127

courts service
Northern Ireland, 4.129
proposal for, 4.138

Criminal Injuries Compensation Tribunal, 8.41

criminal law
binding to the peace, 10.24
civil law and, 6.03
community service, 10.26
contempt of court, 10.32 10.34
criminal procedure
(*see* **that title**)
felony
(*see* **criminal procedure**)
fine, 10.23
function of, 1.25, 6.03
imprisonment
executive branch and, 10.23
imposition by courts, 10.23
parole, 10.23
temporary release, 10.23
misdemeanour
(*see* **criminal procedure**)
presumption of innocence, 6.98
probation, 10.24
punishment and, 6.03
'regulatory' offences, 10.28
enforcement mechanisms, 10.29
trans-national enforcement, 10.30

criminal legal aid
(*see* **legal aid and advice**)

criminal procedure
(*see also* **court procedure, criminal law**)
accusatorial nature, 6.96
acquittal, appeal against (indictment), 7.50
acquittal, appeal against (summons), 7.29
adversarial nature, 6.80
appeals
(*see* **Appellate Jurisdiction of Courts**)
arraignment, 6.77
arrestable offence, 6.61
bail, 6.73
beyond a reasonable doubt, 6.16
bill of indictment (former), 2.51
book of evidence, 6.72
burden of proof, 6.16
compensation orders, 6.04
Constitution and, 4.33
contempt of court, 10.34
coroners courts and, 8.39
corporate bodies and, 1.31
Director of Public Prosecutions (*see* **that title**)
District Court clerk, function of, 4.14
felony, 6.59
Garda Síochána, function of, 6.62, 6.66
guilty plea, 6.78
indictable offences triable summarily, 5.75, 6.71
indictment (sample), 6.75
inquests and, 8.39
inquisitorial system, contrast, 6.66
jury and, 4.50, 6.99
misdemeanour, 6.59
non-jury courts, 5.87
not guilty plea, 6.78
parallel civil proceedings, 6.10
particulars of offence, 6.76
plea bargaining, 6.78
preliminary examination, 6.72
presumption of innocence, 6.97
proof by formal admission, 6.94
proof by formal statement, 6.94
statement of offence, 6.76
summons, 6.64
summary trial, 5.71
title of parties, 6.12

Crown Cases Reserved, Court for, 2.39

Dáil Éireann
(*see* **Oireachtas and Parliament**)

Dáil Éireann Courts
abolition, 2.62
Brehon law and, 2.61
establishment, 2.60

damages
compensatory purpose, 10.03
constitutional case, 10.07
exemplary damages, 10.07
general damages, 10.06
interest on award of, 10.08
judicial review, and, 10.39
personal injuries claim, in, 10.06
punitive damages, 10.07
restitutio in integram, 10.04
special damages, 10.06

defendant
civil action, in 6.12
criminal prosecution, in 6.12

Departments of State
(*see* **government**)

***de novo* hearing**
(*see* **Appellate Jurisdiction of Courts**)

Dickens, Charles
Bleak House, 4.92 6.13
law reform and, 2.21
Director of Public Prosecutions
Attorney General and, 3.63
contempt of court and 10.34
creation of office, 3.61
functions, 3.61
independence, 3.62
panel of barristers and, 3.64
prosecute, discretion to, 6.69
removal of, 3.62
disciplinary tribunals, 8.57
discovery of documents
(*see* **civil procedure**)
distinguishing
(*see* **precedent**)
District Court
appellate jurisdiction, 7.51
civil process, 6.53
Children's Court, 5.77
consent jurisdiction (civil), 5.31
court of record 4.54
criminal legal aid and, 9.13-9.16
District Justice (obsolete), 4.54
districts, 4.55
enforcement order, 10.19
establishment, 4.54
European Court of Justice and, 7.52
first instance jurisdiction (civil), 5.30-5.37
first instance jurisdiction (criminal), 5.71-5.79
indictable offences and, 5.75
inferior court, 4.30
Irish language and, 4.55
judge of District Court (title), 4.54
jury, absence of, 4.54
local and limited jurisdiction, 4.30
minor offences and, 5.72
mode of address, 4.62
number of judges, 4.54
original jurisdiction
(*see* **first instance jurisdiction**)
petty sessions (former) and, 2.65, 4.30
pleadings, limited nature of, 6.53
preliminary examination, 6.72
President of, 4.55
regional organisation, 4.55
temporary judges, 4.54
divisions of the law, 1.24
EAEC, 16.15
economic analysis of law, 1.20
EC, 16.39
ECSC, 16.13
EEC, 16.16
Employment Appeals Tribunal, 8.46
enforcement mechanisms
(*see* **remedies and enforcement**)
enforcement order, 10.19
engineers and law, 3.85
English court system
Assize Courts (former), 2.74
County Courts, 2.53
Court of Appeal, 2.75
Crown Court, 2.74
High Court, divisions of ,
Chancery Division, 2.74
Family Division, 2.74
Queen's Bench Division, 2.74
House of Lords, 2.75
Court of Appeal, appeal with leave to, 2.75
High Court, 'leap frog appeal' from, 2.75

Magistrates Courts, jurisdiction of, 2.52
English law
(*see* **constitution, legislation, sources of law, precedent**)
equity
Chancery, Court of, 1.08, 2.07
common law and, 2.08
flexibility and, 2.07
injunction and, 10.09
Lord Chancellor, 2.08
specific performance and, 10.15
EU, 16.41
Euratom, 16.15
European Atomic Energy Community (Euratom), 16.15
European Coal and Steel Community (ECSC), 16.13
European Commission of Human Rights
(*see* **Council of Europe**)
European Communities
(*see also* **European Community Law, European Union**)
accession by State to treaties of, 16.01
activities of, 16.22, 16.26
aims of, 16.17
obstacles to, 16.27-16.32
Commission of European Communities
advisory committees, 16.97
collegiate body, 16.92
Commissioners, 16.94
directorates-general, 16.95
ECOSOC, 16.97
embryonic government, 16.91
guardian of treaties, 16.91
initiation power, 16.96
policing community policies, 16.98
President of, 16.94
Common Market
aim to achieve, 16.19
transitional period to, 16.20
internal market and, 16.21
Constitution and
(*see* **European Community Law**)
Council of European Union
decision-making body, 16.99
Commission, delegation of powers to, 16.101
COREPER 16.102
European Council, 16.100
Finance Ministers Council (ECOFIN), 16.99
Foreign Ministers Council, 16.100
governments, representing, 16.99
majority and unanimity voting, 16.104
rotating presidency, 16.103
'Summit', 16.100
unanimity and majority voting, 16.104
Council of Europe, connection with, 16.11
Court of Auditors
function, comptroller and auditor, as, 16.125
membership 15.125
Court of Justice
(*see* **Court of Justice of the European Communities**)
development of
'Merger Treaty', 16.34
'Luxembourg compromise', 16.35

Single European Act, 16.36
Treaty on European Union, 16.37
EAEC, 16.15
ECSC, 16.13
EEC, 16.16
EEC becomes EC, 16.39
Euratom, 16.15
European Parliament
consultative powers, 16.109
co-decision procedure, 16.111
co-operation procedure, 16.110
directly elected, 16.106
initially limited, 16.108
membership, 16.107
'ever closer union,' 16.18
federalism and, 16.25
four freedoms, 16.23
free movement of capital, obstacles to, 16.31
free movement of goods, obstacles to, 16.28
free movement of persons, obstacles to, 16.29
free movement of services, obstacles to, 16.31
other obstacles, 16.32
institutions of, 16.88-16.125
legislative procedures
consultative procedure, 16.109
co-decision procedure, 16.111
co-operation procedure, 16.110 16.139
Maastricht Treaty, 16.37
origins, 16.09-16.12
Single European Act, 16.36
subsidiarity and, 16.24
treaties of 16.13-16.16 16.34-16.40

European Community Law
acquis communautaire, 16.42
Constitution of Ireland
amendment of, 16.63
international agreements and, 16.60-16.62
Patents Convention and, 16.67
priority of European law and, 16.68
Single European Act and 16.63-**6.67**
Treaty on European Union and, 16.67
decisions
binding on address*see*, 16.144
competition policy and, 16.145
publication of, 16.144
direct effects of ,16.54
directives
binding as to result, 16.136
co-operation procedure, enactment of, by, 16.139
damages for failure to implement, 16.142
directly applicable, after time limit, 16.141
domestic legislation required to implement, 16.149
example of, 16.138
failure to implement, effect of, 16.140-16.143
incomplete implementation, effect of, 16.157
national legislation required to implement, 16.137
number of, 16.137
publication of, 16.137
regulation, contrasted with, 16.132
domestic law
areas affected by, 16.150
areas not affected by, 16.151
effect on statute book 16.87

implementation in, by secondary legislation, 16.152
indirect legislative effects, 16.156
interpretive techniques, effect on, 16.157
volume of implementing legislation, 16.154
European Union and, 16.41
foreign lawyers, recognition of qualifications, 3.80-3.81
forms of ,16.126-16.146
incorporation into Irish law
amendment of primary legislation by Regulations, 16.76-16.87
binding effects of treaties, 16.73
treaties defined, 16.71
Ministerial regulations, use of, 16.74-16.87
moving train, 16.51 16.65
nature of
different from other international law, 16.54
directly applicable in national courts, 16.55
fundamental rights and, 16.57
new legal order, 16.54
part of domestic law of member states, 16.55
permanent limitation of sovereignty, 16.54
supremacy over domestic law, 16.57
official journal, 16.133
opinions
no binding force 16.146
recommendations
no binding force 16.146
regulations
community policies and, 16.134
direct effect of, 16.131
directive, contrasted with, 16.132
domestic legislation unnecessary (generally), 16.132
domestic legislation required 16.148
example of, 16.135
number of, 16.133
publication of, 16.133
self-executing, 16.147
treaties of communities, direct effects of, 16.127

European Convention on Human Rights
(*see* **Council of Europe**)

European Court of Human Rights
(*see* **Europe**)

European Court of Justice
(*see* **Court of Justice of European Communities**)

European Economic Community (EEC), 16.16

Council of European Union
based on acquis communautaire, 16.42
federalism and, 16.25
financial and economic context, 16.04
founded on European Communitie,s 16.41
'holding company' for European Communities, 16.41
inter-governmental conference (1996), 16.50
membership, 16.47-16.49
policies and co-operation in 16.43
subsidiarity, 16.25
'Three Pillars', 16.44
treaty on European Union, 16.37

evidence
(*see* **court procedure)**
Exchequer, Court of, 2.39
executive
(*see* **government**)

Fair Trade Commission
report on legal profession 3.05
Family Court
(*see* **Circuit Court)**
family law, 1.27
mediation and reconciliation, 8.30
famous trials, 4.98
fees, court, 9.36
fees, lawyers, 3.43
felony, 6.59
***Fiat* of Attorney General (former)**, 9.02
fire officers, 8.47
FLAC, 9.20
foreign qualifications
recognition 3.78-3.79
European Community 3.80-3.81
Four Courts, 2.31, 4.43, 4.51
Free Legal Advice Centres (FLAC), 9.20
French revolution, 2.20

Garda Síochána, 8.14
arrest and detention, 6.66
common informer, 6.63
investigating magistrates, contrasted with, 6.66
prosecution on indictment, in, 6.61
summary prosecution, in, 6.62
Gatt, 17.04
General Agreement On Tariffs And Trade (Gatt), 17.04
Predecessor Of World Trade Organisation (Wto), 17.04
Removal Of Trade Barriers, 17.04
Government
Administration And Policy, 8.19
Constitutional Monarchy (Uk), 2.24
Constitution Of Ireland And, 8.05-8.08
Departments Of State,
Listing Of 8.14
Organisation Of 8.11
Increased Role, 8.03
Judicial Review Of, 8.19
Ministers,
Adjudicative Functions, 8.52-8.54
Corporations Sole, 8.11
Courts, Appeals To, 8.52-8.54
Political Head Of Department, 8.11
19th Century Developments, 2.20
Ombudsman
(*see* **that title)**
Policy And Administration, 8.19
Political Party System, 8.09, 13.28
Reform Of, 8.17-8.18
Relationship With Oireachtas, 8.10, 13.28
Government Commissions And Committees
Garda Custody, On, 13.32
Public Safety And Crowd Control, On, 13.32
Safety, Health And Welfare At Work, On, 13.32
Government Minister
(*see* **government)**

Grattan's Parliament, 2.17

habeas corpus, 10.36
High Court
adjudicative bodies, appeals from, 7.51
appellate jurisdiction (civil), 7.14, 7.20
appellate jurisdiction (criminal), 7.30
binding effects of decisions (*see* **precedent**)
Central Criminal Court, 5.84
Chief Justice and, 4.49
Circuit, on, 4.51
Commercial Court (proposed), 4.137
concurrent jurisdiction, 5.43
constitutional judicial review, 4.27, 5.56, 15.28
court of record, 4.49
Divisional Court, 4.50
Divisions
former, 2.47
informal, 4.50
proposed, 4.137
ex officio members, 4.49
first instance jurisdiction (civil), 5.51-5.61
first instance jurisdiction (criminal), 5.85
full original jurisdiction, 4.29, 15.109
inherent jurisdiction, 4.29
Irish Free State, in, 2.67
Judicature Acts, 2.32
judicial review, 5.57, 10.35
jury in, 4.50
Master of, 4.118
modes of address, 4.59-4.60
number of judges, 4.49
original jurisdiction (*see* **first instance jurisdiction**)
President of, 4.49
President of Circuit Court, 4.49
registrars of, 4.120
reserved offences (criminal), 5.85
style or title of judges of, 4.49
superior court of record, 4.49
Supreme Court judges in, 4.49
taxing master, 4.121
Home Rule, 2.43
House of Lords, 2.38
human rights
(*see* **Constitution, Council of Europe**)

ILO, 17.02
In camera, 4.19
Indictment
(*see* **criminal procedure**)
inferior courts
(*see also* **superior courts**)
assize courts, 2.49
Circuit Court, 4.30
District Court, 4.30
justice of the peace, 2.50
nisi prius, 2.49
petty sessions, 2.51
quarter sessions, 2.50
injunction
Anton Piller order, compared with, 10.11
equitable remedy, 10.09
interim, 10.12
interlocutory, 10.13
balance of convenience, 10.13
stateable case, 10.13
mandatory, 10.10
Mareva injunction, 10.11
perpetual, 10.11

prohibitory, 10.10
undertaking as to damages, 10.12

inquests, 8.37

inquisitorial procedure
(*see also* **civil law, court procedure**)
civil law systems
(*see* **that title**)
coroners court, in, 8.38
criminal procedure, reforms, in, 6.66
wardship jurisdiction, in, 5.61

inspectorates, 8.47
enforcement powers of, 10.29

Institute of Professional Legal Studies (Northern Ireland), 3.73

Institutions of State
19th century developments, 2.20
legislature
(*see* **legislation**)
separation of powers, 2.20 15.20-15.28

Insurance Ombudsman of Ireland, 8.29

intellectual influences on law
(*see also* **sources of law**)
Aristotle, 1.23 15.97
economic analysis of law, 1.20
English law, 2.62, 12.38, 15.129
gender studies, 1.23
Judaeo-Christian teaching, 15.128
jurisprudence, 1.19
Marxism, 1.23
natural law, 1.21, 15.113-15.119
periodical literature, 1.18
religious faith, 1.22 15.113-15.119
Roman Catholic church, 1.21, 15.128
textbooks, 1.18
utilitarianism, 1.20

intellectual property, 8.50

International Covenant on Civil and Political Rights (ICCPR), 15.140, 17.25

International Labour Organisation (ILO), 17.02

international law
bilateral treaties, 17.26
Council of Europe
(*see* **that title**)
customary principles of, 17.19
domestic law and, 16.61, 17.15
enforcement mechanisms, 17.24-17.25
European Community law
(*see* **that title**)
implementation required in domestic law, 16.61, 17.15
international courts, decisions of, 17.18
membership of organisations, 17.02
nations, law of, 17.01
presumption of conformity with, 17.19

International Maritime Organisation (IMO), 17.02

interpretation of Constitution
(*see* **Constitution**)

interpretation of legislation
absurdity, avoidance of
(*see* **golden, schematic, teleological**)
aids to 14.43-14.77
(*see* **presumptions**)
'and' equals 'or', 14.74
archaic language, 14.03
canons of, 14.12
class of persons, addressed to, 14.26

commission, use of report of, 14.87
contextual rule
(*see* **golden, schematic, teleological**)
corporate bodies and, 14.22
courts, role of (general), 14.05
criminal penalties, creating, 14.57
dictionaries, 14.96
directory and mandatory provisions, 14.76-14.75
ejusdem generis, 14.66-14.69
European Community law and, 14.32-14.36, 14.85
explanatory memorandum 14.87
expressio unius est exclusio alterius, 14.65
external sources, 14.78-14.96
feminine and masculine, 14.22
generalia specialibus non derogant, 14.72-14.73
golden rule of, 14.17-14.18
in pari materia, 14.80-14.81
intention of legislature, 14.07-14.09
Interpretation Acts, 14.22
legislative history, 14.82
drafts of legislation, 14.83
EC materials, 14.85
international treaties 14.84
parliamentary materials 14.88
pre-parliamentary materials 14.87
literal rule 14.13-14.16, 14.24-14.25
compared with schematic/ teleological approach 14.37-14.42
'loophole', 14.09
mandatory and directory provisions, 14.76-14.75
marginal notes, 13.47
masculine and feminine, 14.22
mischief rule of, 14.19-14.21
noscitur a sociis, 14.70-14.71
'or' equals 'and', 14.74
ordinary meaning: *see* literal rule
parliamentary debates, use of, 14.88
penal statutes, 14.58-14.58
'person', corporate bodies and, 14.22
plural and singular, 14.22
presumptions
all words bear a meaning, that, 14.50
constitutionality, of, 14.44-14.47
EC law, compatibility with, 14.48
extra-territorial effect, against, 14.64
international law, compatibility with, 14.49
penal statute to be construed strictly, that, 14.57-14.58
retrospective effect, against, 14.60-14.63
revenue statute to be construed strictly, that, 14.59
unclear changes in law, against, 14.56
updated meaning, of, 14.51-14.55
prior statutes, 14.79
reference works, 14.96
repealed provisions, 14.75
report of commission, use of, 14.87
revenue statutes, 14.59
schematic approach, 14.28-14.36
compared with literal approach, 14.37-14.42

singular and plural, 14.22
technical meanings, 14.26-14.27
teleological approach, 14.28-14.36
compared with literal approach, 14.37-14.42
text, primacy of, 14.11
traditional rules of, 14.12
travaux préparatoires, 14.84
typographical errors, 14.11

Ireland
Irish Free State, successor to, 15.17
Republic of Ireland, description of State, 15.41
State, name of, 15.41

Irish Aviation Authority, 8.47

Irish Court of Appeal, 2.47

Irish Free State
(*see also* **Constitution of Irish Free State, Constitution of Ireland**)
Anglo-Irish Treaty (1921), 2.55 15.02
British Commonwealth and, 15.41
British Crown and, 15.09
Constitution of
(*see* **Constitution of Irish Free State**)
court system, 2.64 4.03
replacement of, 4.04
Ireland as successor of, 15.17
Privy Council and, 15.09

Irish language
Circuit Court judges and, 4.53
Constitution and, 15.30-15.35
District Court judges and, 4.55
text of official documents, 15.33

Irish legal history
Act of Union, 2.18
Anglo-Norman Invasion, 2.03
Brehon law and
(see **that title**)
common law influence, 1.06
English law and, 2.03
initial reception of, 2.11
Poyning's law, 2.11-2.14
Tudor settlement, 2.15
Government of Ireland Act 1920, 2.45
Grattan's Parliament, 2.17
Home rule, 2.43
Ireland, establishment of, 2.71
Irish Free State, establishment of 2.55
land reform, 2.41
penal laws, 2.16

Joint Labour Committees, 8.45 13.76

judicial power
(*see* **courts**)

Judge of the District Court (style or title), 4.54

judges
(*see also* **Circuit Court, Court Of Criminal Appeal, Court Of Justice Of European Communities, District Court, High Court, Supreme Court**)
appointment and qualifications
age profile, 4.87
barristers, 4.66
class background, 4.74
formal qualifications, 4.64-4.69
government, role of, 4.70-4.72
ideology, 4.73
Judicial Appointments Advisory Board, 4.75-4.86
political allegiances, 4.70
solicitors, 4.66
training and education, 4.88
women, 4.72

barristers and, 4.66
biographies of, 4.94
constitutional judicial review, 15.28
criticism of, 4.93
immunity from suit, 4.106
independence of, 4.89
interviews with, 4.93-4.95
judicial function, meaning of, 4.12
Judicial Studies Institute, 4.88
jury, and
(*see* **jury**)
justiciable matters, 4.17
law-making function, 2.10
pensions, 4.112
political allegiances, 4.73
political controversies, 4.17
precedence between, 4.39
promotion, 4.87
public controversy and, 4.92 4.95
qualifications: *see* appointment
removal of, 4.91
remuneration of, 4.100
retirement, 4.109
training and education, 4.88
vacation of office, 4.108

Judicial function
(*see* **judge**)

judicial review, constitutional
(*see* **Constitution**)

judicial review
appeal on point of law distinguished, 10.37
certiorari, 10.36
damages, may be awarded on, 10.39
habeas corpus, 10.36
High Court, exclusive jurisdiction, 10.35
inquiry into lawfulness of detention, 10.36
legal aid, 9.17
mandamus, 10.36
prerogative writs and, 10.35
procedure, 10.39
prohibition, 10.36
State side orders (former), 10.35

judiciary
(*see* **judge**)

junior counsel
(*see* **barristers**)

jurisdiction of courts
(*see also* **courts**)
changes to, 5.17
decrease in value of money, 5.20
increase in workload and, 4.127

jurisprudence, 1.19

jury
Circuit Court, in, abolition of, 4.52
civil claims, in, 4.50
composition 6.100-6.101
Constitution and, 6.100
coroners court, 8.37
criminal cases, in, 4.52
directed verdicts, 6.107
final arbiter, 6.110
grand jury (former), 2.51
inquests, 8.37
judge, role of, 6.106-6.107
legal directions, 6.106
majority verdicts, 6.111
personal injuries actions, in High Court, abolition of, 4.50
petty jury (former), 2.51
representative nature of, 6.100
scope of decision-making, 6.110
selection process, 6.102
verdict, 6.107

Justice, administration of
(*see* **courts**)

Justice of the District Court (obsolete style or title), 4.54
justice of the peace
(*see also* **inferior courts**)
binding over to keep the peace, 2.50
District Court as successor to, 2.65

King's Bench, Court of, 2.36
King's Inns, 3.29

Labour Court, 8.43
Labour Relations Commission, 8.43
LA Law, 1.01
Landed Estates Court, 2.34
land, sale of, 10.18
law and laws, 1.04
law clerks (solicitors), 3.83
law clerks (research), 4.48
law officers
(*see* **Attorney General, Director Of Public Prosecutions**)
law reform
Committee on Court Practice and Procedure, 11.05
Constitution Review Group, 11.08
court decisions, 11.02
Fair Trade Commission, 11.07
generally, 11.01
Law Reform Commission
establishment, 11.09
presidents, of 11.10
reports of, 11.09, 13.32
working paper on judicial review, 10.35
Working Group on Courts Commission, 10.06
law reporting
(*see* **precedent**)
lawyers
(*see* **barristers, solicitors**)
legal aid and advice
(*see also* **access to law**)
access to courts, 9.02
civil legal aid and advice
Airey case, 9.23
committee on civil legal aid and advice, 9.22
cost, 9.27
courts, in, 9.34
criteria for grant of, 9.31
European Community matters, 9.34
excluded matters, 9.35
FLAC, 9.20
legal advice, definition, 9.28
legal aid, definition, 9.28
Legal Aid Board, 9.25
merits test, 9.29
non-statutory scheme, 9.24
recovery of costs, 9.39
scope (general), 9.34
statutory scheme, 9.25
tribunals, 9.34
criminal legal aid and advice
assignment, 9.16
constitutional aspect, 9.15
cost, 9.16
means test, 9.14
murder, in, 9.14
pre-1962, 9.13
recovery of costs, 9.39
seriousness test, 9.14
European Convention on Human Rights and, 9.23
FLAC, 9.20
Garda custody, in, 9.18
judicial review, in, 9.17

law books, State funding of, 9.04
Legal Aid Board
(*see* **legal aid and advice**)
legal education
Advisory Committee on Legal Education and Training (ACLET), 3.74
Continuing Legal Education (CLE), 3.76
Judicial Studies Institute, 4.88
King's Inns, Honourable Society of, 3.29
Law Society of Ireland, 3.10
universities and, 3.65
vocational training, 3.72
legal executives, 3.84
legal theory, 1.19
legal personality
corporations and, 1.30
limited liability company, 1.31
natural persons, 1.30
legal profession
(*see also* **barrister, judge, solicitor, universities**)
fusion (proposal), 3.08
separate branches, 3.02
legal representation
(*see also* **barristers, legal aid and advice, solicitors**)
fees, 3.25 3.43
pro bono work, 9.35
tribunal of inquiry, 3.43 8.65
legal system, meaning, 1.02-1.03
legislation
(*see also* **interpretation of legislation**, **Oireachtas, Parliament**)
Acts
delegated legislation, distinguished from, 13.01
primary legislation, 13.01
statute, synonymous with, 13.01
administrative schemes, 13.04, 13.80
amendments, non-textual 13.51-13.53
bills
become Acts, 13.10
consolidation, 13.22
private, 13.23
private members', 13.19
public bills, 13.09-13.18
restoration of, 13.20
characteristics of, 13.06
codification, 13.56
commencement
date signed by President, 13.41
delay of, reasons for, 13.41
failure to order, 13.43-13.45
order for, 13.42
common law, distinguished from, 13.02
consolidation of, 13.56
contract, distinguished from, 13.03 13.64
delegated legislation
bad faith, 13.75
bye-laws, 13.61
Constitution and, 13.65-13.71
contracts of adhesion, contrasted with, 13.64
EC obligations, implementation by, 13.78 16.76 16.154
growth of, 13.59
Oireachtas, scrutiny by, 13.77
order, 13.61
procedures, compliance with, 13.76
reasonableness of, 13.74
regulations, 13.61

rules, 13.61
schemes, 13.62
statutory instruments, 13.60
ultra vires rule, 13.72-13.73
departmental circulars, 13.04, 13.80
de-regulation and, 13.55
drafting of
centralised nature, 13.35
heads of bill, 13.33
intelligibility of, 13.54 13.57
parliamentary draftsman's office, 13.33
style of, 13.54 13.57
enactment, process of
Committees of Oireachtas, role of, 13.16
constitutional provisions, 13.09
Dáil Éireann, powers of, 13.09, 13.29
Government, role of, 13.13 13.28
Iris Oifigiúil, publication in, 13.10
President, role of, 13.10
reference to People, 13.12
reference to Supreme Court, 5.65 13.11
Seanad Éireann, powers of, 13.09
stages of debate in Oireachtas, 13.14
standing orders of Oireachtas, 13.13
English language, in, 13.37 15.34
'ersatz legislation', 13.04 13.80
European Community law, effect of, 13.78, 16.76, 16.154
explanatory memorandum, 13.31
format of
chapters of ,13.46
long title, 13.38
marginal notes, 13.47
parts of, 13.46
preamble, private acts, 13.40
preamble, public acts (former), 13.39
schedules to, 13.46
sections of, 13.46
short title, 13.38
statutory number, 13.38
Green Paper and, 13.31
influences on, 13.30
intelligibility of, 13.54 13.57
Irish language, in, 13.37 15.34
legislation, meaning of, 13.01
official translations, 13.37 15.34
parliaments, applicable to Ireland, 13.49
Parliamentary draftsman, 3.57
'plain' English and, 13.54 13.57
primary legislation
Acts of Oireachtas, 13.01
delegated legislation, distinguished from, 13.01
statutes, 13.01
President of Ireland and, 5.65 13.10
quality of, 13.57
quasi-legislation, 13.04 13.80
secondary legislation
(*see* **delegated legislation**)
self-regulation 13.05
sources of 13.30
court decisions 13.32
EC membership 13.32 16.154
government commissions 13.32
international obligations 13.32
law reform commission 11.09 13.32
tribunal of inquiry 13.32
urgent need 13.32

state of statute book, 13.48
amendments to previous Acts, 13.51
annual volumes, 13.48
codification, 13.56
consolidation, 13.56
EC obligations and, 13.78 16.76 16.154
index to statutes (1922-1995), 13.48
index to statute (pre-1800), 13.48
parliaments, applicable to Ireland, 13.48
pre-1922 legislation subsequently repealed in Britain, 13.50
statute, synonymous with Act, 13.01
voluntary codes, 13.05
White Paper and, 13.31
legislature
(*see* **legislation, Oireachtas, Parliament**)
limitation of actions, 6.07-6.08
limited judicial functions, 4.07-4.16
litigation
(*see* **alternative dispute resolution, arbitration, court procedure, litigants**)
litigants
assumed names, 4.22
competence, persons lacking, 9.08
McKenzie friends, 9.09
minors, 9.08
next friend, 9.08
personal litigants, 9.04
pseudonyms, 4.22
representative actions, 15.67
representing self, 9.04
Local Government, 8.16
environmental health officers, 8.47
fire officers, 8.48
locus standi
(*see* **Constitution**)
Lord Chancellor, 2.26 4.131
Lord Lieutenant, 2.23

***McKenzie* friend, 9.09**
***Magill* (current affairs magazine)**, 4.95
Magistrates Court, 2.52
management of courts
(*see* **courts**)
mandamus, 10.36
***Mareva* injunction**, 10.11
Marxism and law, 1.23
Matrimonial Causes and Matters, Court of, 2.39
media, in court, 4.19-4.23
mediation, family proceedings, in, 8.30
Military courts and tribunals, 5.87
minister
(*see* **government**)
minors, litigants, as, 9.08
miscarriage of justice, 7.47
misdemeanour, 6.59

National Authority for Occupational Safety and Health, 8.47
inspectors, powers of, 10.29
National Parliament
(*see* **Oireachtas, Parliament**)
National Standards Authority of Ireland, 8.47

natural justice
audi alteram partem, 4.92, 8.22, 10.38
nemo judex in causa sua, 4.92, 8.22, 10.38
natural law
(*see* **Constitution**)
natural rights
(*see* **Constitution**)
negligence
(*see* **precedent, torts**)
nisi prius, 2.49, 4.51
non-jury criminal court
(*see* **Special Criminal Court**)
North Atlantic Treaty Organisation (NATO), 16.10, 17.03
Northern Ireland
(*see also* **Northern Ireland Court System)**
Anglo-Irish Agreement (1985) and, 15.39
composition of, 2.45
Constitution of Ireland and, 15.38
Council of Legal Education for Northern Ireland, 3.73
direct rule, 2.72
establishment of, 2.54
Institute of Professional Legal Studies, 3.73
Parliament of, 2.54, 2.72
Northern Ireland Court System
Assize Courts (former), 2.74
County Courts, 2.53
Court of Appeal, 2.75
Crown Court, 2.74
High Court, divisions of
Chancery Division, 2.74
Family Division, 2.74
Queen's Bench Division, 2.74
House of Lords, 2.75
Court of Appeal, appeal with leave to, 2.75
Magistrates Courts, jurisdiction of, 2.52
oaths
juror, 6.104 6.105
witness, 6.83
obiter dicta
(*see* **precedent**)
obiter dictum
(*see* **precedent**)
OECD, 17.04
Oireachtas
(*see also* **legislation, parliament)**
chambers of, 13.24
Committees of, 8.55 13.16
Constitution and, 13.09 15.27
Dáil Éireann, 13.24
delegation of legislative function
(*see* **legislation)**
European Community law
(*see* **that title**)
executive and, 8.08 13.28
legislative authority, 13.09 15.27
President and, 13.10 13.24
Seanad Éireann, 13.09
tribunals of inquiry and, 8.63
Ombudsman
judicial power, compared, 8.26
jurisdiction of, 8.25
parliamentary commissioner, 8.25
'private' Ombudsmen, 8.28
Ombudsman for Credit Institutions, 8.28
Open File **(TV series)**, 4.95
order for sale of land, 10.18
Organisation for Economic Co-Operation and Development (OECD), 17.04

Organisation for Security and Co-Operation in Europe (OSCE), 17.04
original jurisdiction of courts
(*see* **Circuit Court, District Court, High Court, Special Criminal Court, Supreme Court**)
origins of law
(*see* **sources of law**)
OSCE, 17.04
overruling
(*see* **precedent**)

Pale, The, 2.14
Palles, Christopher, (Chief Baron) Foreword, 4.94
para-legals, 3.84
Parliament
(*see also* **legislation, Oireachtas**)
common law and, 2.09
Grattan's Parliament, 2.17
pre-1922 parliaments, 13.49
parliamentary draftsman
(*see* **legislation**)
penal laws, 2.16
per incuriam
(*see* **precedent**)
periodicals, use of
(*see* **sources of law**)
personal injuries actions
abolition of High Court juries and, 4.50
court procedure and, 5.08
persuasive authority
(*see* **precedent**)
petty jury, 2.51
petty sessions
(*see also* **inferior courts**)
Justice of the Peace and, 2.50
Resident Magistrate and, 2.52
plaintiff, 6.12
Planning Board, 8.56
plea
(*see* **criminal procedure**)
plea bargaining
(*see* **criminal procedure**)
pleadings
(*see* **civil procedure**)
point of law, appeal on
(*see* **Appellate Jurisdiction of Courts**)
police
(*see* **Garda Síochána**)
political party system
government influence, 8.09 13.28
Poyning's law, 2.11-2.14
precedent
binding authority, 12.04
civil law systems and, 12.01 12.42
Commonwealth decisions, 12.38
Court of Criminal Appeal
abolition of, 12.31
not bound by own decisions, 12.29
Court of Justice of European Communities, 12.41 16.113
digests, 12.07
dissenting judgments, 12.54
distinguishing, 12.06
divided court, 12.60
English decisions, 12.35-12.41
European Court of Human Rights, 17.17
establishment of new courts (1961), 12.32
evolution of principles, 12.63-12.66
foreign decisions, 12.35-12.42

hierarchy of courts and, 12.02
High Court
  not bound by own decisions, 12.21-12.28
House of Lords decisions, 12.33
inferior courts, 12.34
law reports, 12.07
legislation and, 12.67-12.69
lower courts bound by higher courts, 12.09
multiple judgments, 12.54-12.60
negligence and, 12.70-12.85
obiter dicta
  (*see* ***obiter dictum***)
obiter dictum, 12.05 12.61-12.66
overruling, 12.06
per incuriam, 12.06
persuasive authority, 12.04
pre-1922 decisions, 12.3
pre-1961 decisions, 12.32
Privy Council decisions, 12.33
ratio decidendi, 12.05 12.44-12.66
rationes decidendi
(*see* ***ratio decidendi***)
res judicata, 12.06
reversing, 12.06
secondary sources, 12.43
several reasons for decision, 12.54-12.60
stare decisis, 12.01 12.08-12.42
sub silentio, 12.06
Supreme Court
  decisions binding on all other courts, 12.09
  multiple judgments in, 12.54-12.60
  overruling own decisions, 12.11-12.20
technology and, 12.07
textbooks, 12.43
United States decisions, 12.38
unreported judgments, 12.07
preliminary examination, 6.72
prerogative writs, 10.35
prerogatives: *see* constitution
President of Ireland
  Council of State and, 15.21
  defence forces, supreme command of, titular, 15.21
  Government and, 8.07 15.21
  head of State, as, 15.21
  judicial appointments and, 4.63
  monarch, comparison with, 8.07
  Oireachtas and, 13.10
  powers of, extension, 15.21
  reference of Bills to Supreme Court, 5.65 15.21
private, administration of justice in, 4.19-4.23
private international law, 10.21, 17.01
private prosecution, 6.63, 6.67
privy council, 2.59, 12.33, 15.09
probate, court of, 2.39
probation, 10.24
***pro bono* work**, 9.11
procedure
  (*see* **court procedure**)
professions
  adjudicative bodies, 8.57
  law and, 3.85-3.87
prohibition, 10.36
prosecution, 6.12
pseudonyms, litigants, use of, 4.22
public, administration of justice, in, 4.19
Quarter Sessions, 2.51
Queen's Bench Division, 2.36

rating, 8.59
ratio decidendi
(*see* **precedent**)
rationes decidendi
(*see* **precedent**)
recognition of foreign qualifications, 3.78
remedies and enforcement
binding to the peace, 2.51 10.24
community service, 10.26
compensation orders, 6.04 10.27
contempt of court
(*see* **that title**)
damages
(*see* **that title**)
declaration, 10.16
enforcement orders 10.19
family proceedings, in, 10.20
fieri facias, 10.17
fines, 10.23
imprisonment, 10.23
injunction
(*see* **that title**)
judicial review
(*see* **that title**)
parole, 5.13 10.23
probation, 10.24
regulatory offences, in, 10.29
remittal of fines and sentences, 4.13 10.23
specific performance
sale of land, order for, 10.18
temporary release, 5.13 10.23
trans-national enforcement
civil, 10.21
criminal, 10.30
resident magistrates, 2.52
revenue
Appeal Commissioners, 8.60
courts, appeals to, 8.60
reversing
(*see* **precedent**)
rights
(*see* **constitution**)
Rights Commissioners, 8.44
royal prerogative
Constitution and, 15.43-15.46
Curia Regis, 2.03
executive, development of, 2.24
King's Council, 2.03
Parliamentary power and, 2.22
senior counsel and, 3.45
rule of law, 1.33
Rumpole of the Bailey, 1.01

safety at work, government commission on, 13.32
sale of land, order for, 10.18
Saorstát Éireann
(*see* **Irish Free State**)
scholarly writing, 1.18
senior counsel
(*see* **barristers**)
separation of powers
(*see* **Constitution**)
settling or compromise
(*see* **civil procedure**)
sheriffs 8.61
Single European Act
(*see* **European Community Law**)
small claims, 5.35
social welfare, appeals officer, 8.62
solicitors
admission and education, 3.12
advertising, 3.24
barristers, instructions to, 3.21

Chief State Solicitor, 3.26
compensation fund, 3.17
contentious business, 3.21
conveyancing, 3.19
discipline, 3.16
exemptions from examinations, 3.14
firms and incorporated practices, 3.18
Incorporated Law Society (*see* **law society**)
increasing numbers, 3.11
judicial appointments, 3.23
Law Society, 3.10
'no foal, no fee' litigation 3.25
pro bono work, 9.11
rights of audience, 3.22
state solicitors, 3.26

sources of law
academic writing, 1.18
canon law, 1.17
commentaries, 1.18
common law, 1.10
Constitution, 1.12
European Community law, 1.13
ideational sources, 1.01
intellectual influences, 1.19
international law, 1.16
judge-made law, 1.10
legislation, 1.11
scholarly writing, 1.18
statute law, 1.11

Special Criminal Court
Constitution and, 5.87
composition, 5.95
establishment, 5.94
non-jury, 5.86
non-scheduled offences, 5.92
scheduled offences, 5.91

specific performance, 10.15

stare decisis
(*see* **precedent**)

State Side Orders (former), 10.35

State solicitors, 3.26

Statute of Limitations
abuse of process, 6.09
civil matters, in, 6.07
criminal matters, in, 6.08

statute law
(*see* **legislation**)

statutory interpretation
(*see* **interpretation of legislation**)

sub silentio
(*see* **precedent**)

superior courts, 2.30, 4.41, 4.49

Supreme Court
appellate jurisdiction (civil), 7.17, 7.21, 7.24-7.26
appellate jurisdiction (criminal), 7.31, 7.35, 7.38-7.50
acquittal, appeal against, 7.50
case conferences, 4.47
Chief Justice, 4.41, 4.49, 5.69
collegiate court, 4.45-4.47, 12.54
Court of Appeal of Southern Ireland, successor to (1924), 2.69
Court of Criminal Appeal, successor to, 7.35
court of record, 4.41
divisions, sitting in, 4.43
establishment (1924), 2.69
establishment (1961), 4.41
European Court of Justice and, 7.52
ex officio member, 4.41
final appeal, court of, 4.26
first instance jurisdiction 5.63-5.68
High Court judges in 4.41
Law Reform Commission and 4.41

modes of address 4.59-4.60
number of judges 4.41
'one judgment' rule 12.54
original jurisdiction: *see* first instance jurisdiction
overruling own decisions (*see* **precedent**)
President of High Court, 4.41
research assistants, 4.48
separate judgments, 4.46 12.54
simultaneous sittings in divisions, 4.43
superior court of record, 4.41
Supreme Court of Justice (Irish Free State), successor to (1961), 4.41
television cameras in, 4.23
transfer of jurisdiction of Court of Criminal Appeal to, 7.35
Taoiseach, An, 8.05

technology and law
precedent and, 12.07
legislation and, 13.57
television and law
Constitution and, 15.81
LA Law, 1.01
television cameras in court, 4.23
tribunal of inquiry
contempt of, 8.64
cost of, 3.43 8.65
court, distinguished from, 8.64
evidence, rules of, 8.64
legal representation at, 8.65
powers of, 8.64
Oireachtas, appointment by, 8.63
Tudor settlement, 2.15
'Two senior' rule, 3.47 5.24
United Kingdom
Act of Union, 2.17
Anglo-Norman Invasion, 2.03
Home Rule, 2.43
Poyning's law, 12.11
universities, legal profession and, 3.65
UNO, 17.02, 17.25
United Nations Organisation (UNO), 17.02, 17.25
utilitarianism, 1.20-1.22, 15.118-15.119
vacations, 4.124
valuation tribunal, 8.59
Western European Union (WEU), 16.10 17.03
women and law, 1.23 4.72
World Health Organisation (WHO), 17.02
World Trade Organisation (Wto)
removal of trade barriers, 17.04
successor to GATT, 17.04